D1327814

21 DEC 2001

14 MAY 2002

31 MAY 2002

12 NOV 2002

10 JAN 2003

21 MAR 2003

THE HANDBOOK OF
GROUP
COMMUNICATION
THEORY
&
RESEARCH

EDITORIAL REVIEW BOARD

THE HANDBOOK OF
GROUP
COMMUNICATION
THEORY
&
RESEARCH

Editor
LAWRENCE R. FREY

Associate Editors
DENNIS S. GOURAN
MARSHALL SCOTT POOLE

SAGE Publications
International Educational and Professional Publisher
Thousand Oaks   London   New Delhi

For information:

SAGE Publications, Inc.
2455 Teller Road
Thousand Oaks, California 91320
E-mail: order@sagepub.com

SAGE Publications Ltd.
6 Bonhill Street
London EC2A 4PU
United Kingdom

SAGE Publications India Pvt. Ltd.
M-32 Market
Greater Kailash I
New Delhi 110 048 India

Printed in the United States of America

Library of Congress Cataloging-in-Publication Data

Main entry under title:

The handbook of group communication theory and research / editor
Lawrence R. Frey ; associate editors Dennis S. Gouran and Marshall
Scott Poole.
  p. cm.
  Includes indexes.
  ISBN 0-7619-1027-1 (alk. paper)
  1. Communication in small groups. I. Frey, Lawrence R. II.
Gouran, Dennis S., 1941- III. Poole, Marshall Scott, 1951-
  HM133 .H354 1999
  302.3'4—dc21   98-58134

This book is printed on acid-free paper.

99 00 01 02 03 04 05 7 6 5 4 3 2 1

Acquisition Editor: Margaret H. Seawell
Editorial Assistant: Renée Piernot
Production Editor: Astrid Virding
Editorial Assistant: Nevair Kabakian
Typesetter: Christina M. Hill
Cover Designer: Candice Harman

Contents

PART VI: Group Communication Contexts and Applications

Introduction

LAWRENCE R. FREY
The University of Memphis

The importance of small groups has never been more clear: From the day we are born with the help of a "birthing group" to the day we are mourned by a group of family and friends, small groups are woven into the fabric of our individual lives, while at the collective level, from the classroom to the courtroom, they are the stitches that hold together the communal cloth. The small group is, thus, one of the most important social configurations.

The significance of the small group is particularly apropos and compelling in the "postmodern era," in which the decentered and saturated self (Gergen, 1991) no longer has a sense of place (Meyrowitz, 1985). In a fragmented world, the small group, being the generative site at which individuals and collectives (such as organizations and institutions) are made and remade, should be, as Poole (1998) claims, *the* fundamental unit of analysis for the study of microlevel social processes.

Scholars from many different disciplines have, of course, long recognized the importance of small groups. The body of scholarship in some fields has accumulated to the point

where handbooks and other edited texts that synthesize theory and research on groups have appeared on a regular basis over the past five decades (e.g., 1950s: Cartwright & Zander, 1953; 1960s: Cartwright & Zander, 1960, 1968; 1970s: Hare, 1976; Ofshe, 1973; Shaw, 1971, 1976; 1980s: Shaw, 1981; and 1990s: Hare, Blumberg, Davies, & Kent, 1994).

What is different at this point in time is that the turn to discourse that characterizes the social sciences and humanities in general is also readily apparent in the study of groups. Scholars from many other disciplines have started to recognize the constitutive and functional nature of communication in groups, that communication is both the functional means by which groups accomplish whatever their goals may be and, even more important, that groups themselves are best regarded as emerging from or constituted in communication.

Answers to many of the perplexing questions about group interaction, therefore, can be found in the group communication scholarship. Although many answers appear in journal articles and some scholarly texts that focus on particular issues (such as Hirokawa and Poole's, 1996, excellent text on communication and group decision making), as well as in numerous textbooks that help practitioners who work with groups and group members alike, there has not been a central resource available that attempts to document and synthesize the work done in the group communication field. This text is designed to fill that gap.

The ability to write this text today is a direct result of where the field has been yesterday. As has been documented elsewhere (see Frey, 1996) and in this volume (see the chapter by Gouran; also see the chapter by Poole), as the relatively "new kid on the block," the group communication field certainly has experienced its fair share of growing pains. The study of group communication has progressed from its early emphasis on pedagogy toward the beginning of the 20th century; to the "grand old days" of the mid-century, when psychological and sociological theories and research programs reigned supreme; to the "decade of discontent" during the 1970s, when scholars experienced an "epistemic crisis concerning the criteria appropriate for apprehending the proverbial elephant" (Frey, 1996, p. 27); to the infusion of substantive group communication theories in the 1980s; to the present decade of reconstruction and multiculturalism, which present new philosophical, conceptual, theoretical, methodological, technological, and cultural opportunities in the study of group communication.

Although substantial problems have been experienced along the way, the developmental process has resulted in a mature field. The creation of a separate Group Communication Division in the National Communication Association is merely one of the many signs that the field has come of age. Gouran (1994), Poole (1994, 1998), Propp and Kreps (1994), and many others argue that the field has never been stronger and more vibrant in terms of the number of people studying group communication and the quality of the theory and research they produce. The high quality of this

work is due, in part, to scholars' recognition that the study of group communication must encompass a broad spectrum of relevant issues: verbal, nonverbal, written, and electronic forms of communication; task and relational communicative activities; and concern for all levels of group communication, from individual group members, to dyads and subgroups within groups, to the group as a collective unit, to connections between groups and their environments, including other groups. There are also new paradigms and methodologies that are being adopted and adapted by those who study group communication, as many of the chapters in this volume demonstrate. There also have been many useful developments in more traditional research methods, such as laboratory experiments, that address problems in earlier applications.

The many roads traveled by those who have contributed to the study of group communication, as well as their convergence at this moment in time, have produced the need for this *Handbook of Group Communication Theory and Research*. Although no text should ever claim to be a definitive telling of a discipline's story, this text weaves together a narrative of some of the most important stories that need to be told about the field of group communication. Similar to other handbooks, the goals of this text are at least twofold. First, the authors were given the task of summarizing and synthesizing theory and research in the subarea of the group communication field for which they were responsible. In many cases, these summaries themselves constitute new and original theoretical and conceptual frameworks for making sense of the material reviewed. Second, the authors were asked to set appropriate agendas for future theory and research in the subarea being examined. It was not sufficient to merely describe the territory or status quo; the authors also had to suggest new maps and roads. In this way, each chapter and the entire set of chapters serve as crossroads, both in the sense of being sites where various roads pursued in each subarea meet and in terms of documenting a crucial point in time when important choices for the future must be made.

ORGANIZATION OF THE HANDBOOK

Organizing an entire field is never an easy task and is always a potentially contested matter. The organization of this text represents the interface of a deductive process of an a priori determination of some important sections and chapters that seemed necessary to include and an inductive process that resulted from an open call for chapter proposals. As a result of this process, the text is divided into six broad areas of scholarship about group communication: (a) foundations of group communication theory and research, (b) individuals and group communication, (c) task and relational group communication, (d) group communication processes, (e) group communication facilitation, and (f) group communication contexts and applications. The sections and chapters are previewed below.

Part I: Foundations of Group Communication Theory and Research

The field of group communication is now approximately a half century old. In that time, it has developed from an infant to a mature discipline characterized by a variety of conceptual/theoretical positions and methodological practices. Part I provides foundational grounding by examining historical, theoretical, and methodological issues and perspectives that presently characterize the study of group communication, as well as offering agendas for the future. The purpose of reviewing foundational material is not only to re-member and understand the past but also to "re-member" and move forward (see Frey, 1996).

In Chapter 1, Dennis S. Gouran traces the development of the study of communication in groups within the communication field from the 1950s to the present. After noting the pedagogical origins of this emergent area of study, early work in the 1940s, and precur-

sors in social psychology and sociology disciplines, the chapter progresses through five successive decades of scholarly activity. The 1950s are characterized as a time when social-scientific inquiry began to take hold. The 1960s are portrayed as exhibiting a developing focus on interaction in groups. Continuing with the focus on interaction, the 1970s are marked by the exploration of how communication in groups develops and how the characteristics of utterances relate to the outcomes that groups achieve. The 1980s are viewed as a period of substantial activity aimed at the development of theories of communication in groups and research agendas designed to test them. Finally, the 1990s showed increased attention to the refinement of theories generated in the previous decade, the formulation of new theories and theoretical perspectives, a new emphasis on the study of natural groups, and diversification in the types of issues and concepts addressed. The chapter ends with a discussion of neglected areas of research and some suggestions concerning how the study of communication in groups can continue to advance.

Chapter 2, by Marshall Scott Poole, offers a critical review and analysis of significant contributions, challenges, and problems characterizing contemporary theoretical perspectives that guide the study of group communication. Poole begins by exploring the nature of theory, distinguishing some characteristics that can be used to evaluate theories, and considering some important conceptual questions that frame theories about group communication. He then reviews theoretical contributions concerning group communication using a three-part typology: (a) general theories that explain group communication in general, (b) focused theories that seek to understand specific group communication phenomena, and (c) agenda-setting statements that shape group communication theories by suggesting particular issues and frames of reference that should be considered. Given that the other chapters in this volume explore relevant focused theories, Poole concentrates on explicating general theories (specifically,

Functional, Symbolic Convergence, and Structuration Theory) and agenda-setting perspectives. With regard to the latter, he reviews the tradition of critique that has driven much of the scholarship in the group communication field and then focuses on five major agenda-setting perspectives: the Interact System Model, the Socio-Egocentric Model, the Bona Fide Groups Perspective, Natural Groups and the Naturalistic Paradigm, and the Feminist Perspective. He ends the chapter by suggesting some directions for future group communication theory development that call attention to some promising theories and perspectives that might be reintroduced into the field and by posing some questions that require answers from theory and research.

Chapter 3, by Edward A. Mabry, explores a conceptual and linguistic root metaphor that has been perhaps the driving force in group communication theory, research, pedagogy, and practice: the systems metaphor. As Mabry points out, conceiving of entities and their component parts as a "system" (e.g., family system, ecosystem, and solar system) has become a pervasive pattern of thinking in contemporary scholarship in general, as well as in common parlance, and nowhere is that better illustrated than in the study of small groups. After providing an overview of heuristic and pedagogical applications of the systems metaphor by those who study and teach about small groups, Mabry discusses the philosophical and scientific grounding of systems theories, reviewing four dominant models (organic, mechanical, equilibrium, and adaptive), as well as three important elements employed in systemic approaches to the study of groups (structure, purpose, and change). He then examines the impact the systems metaphor has had on the study of group communication and explains how group communication can be conceptualized as a systemic process and some theoretical frameworks in group communication (specifically, Field Theory, Social Exchange Theory, Developmental Theory, and Adaptive Systems Theory) that are tied to systems thinking. He concludes the chapter by explicating possible directions for future theoretical and methodological applications of systems thinking in the study of group communication.

Chapter 4, by Marshall Scott Poole, Joann Keyton, and Lawrence R. Frey, addresses four key characteristics of group communication that ultimately affect decisions about methodological practices: the complexity of group interaction, the fluidity and permeability of group boundaries and borders, the need for a behavioral focus, and the systemic nature of groups. Specifically, these characteristics create four challenges for group communication researchers that revolve around decisions concerning the level of analysis to be employed, ways to account for shifting group boundaries and group membership, observation and coding of group interaction, and measurement of group outcomes. The chapter describes these challenges and offers some methods, as well as research examples, that address them. The authors argue that each of these challenges should be addressed as group communication scholars identify their research goals; design research studies, including the conceptualization and operationalization of relevant variables; and analyze the data obtained.

Part II: Individuals and Group Communication

In a short, provocative piece titled "Humans Would Do Better Without Groups," Buys (1978) argued that because of the many problems caused by groups, people would do better without them. In a humorous response titled "Groups Would Do Better Without Humans," Anderson (1978) suggested that, in fact, groups would do better without people because "humans seldom work at maximum ability levels, seldom communicate with any degree of logic and are constantly in need of socio-emotional satisfaction for their simpering insecurities about affection, esteem, love, etc." (p. 557).

Individuals and groups are, of course, inherently connected; the nucleus or core of any group is its individual members (see Frey, 1997). Any meaningful discussion of group communication, therefore, must begin with an examination of individual group members. Arrow and McGrath (1993) explain the genesis of the word *member:*

> Small groups operate within a physical, technological, temporal, and social environment. The boundary of a small group forms a "membrane" across which resources and products move in and out of the group. And the most fundamental resource of any group is the people who form the group—its *members*. The word *member* comes from the same Latin root—*membrum*—as membrane and referred at first chiefly to the various parts of a body (members) that are enclosed within the boundary of the skin, the *membrana* (*Webster's Ninth,* 1985). Extending the concept to the group level, *members* came to mean the distinguishable parts—the people—within the group's boundary. (p. 337)

Part II explores the dynamic relationship between individuals and groups. Beth Bonniwell Haslett and Jenn Ruebush begin in Chapter 5, this volume by examining, from a Systems Perspective, the effects of individual differences on group communication processes and outcomes, seeking to answer the question, "What differences do individual differences make?" They first focus on some important individual differences that research shows makes a difference, including cognitive style, sex/gender, and communicative predispositions (such as communication apprehension) and skills (such as conflict management). Because of the significant trend toward diversity in contemporary organizations, and elsewhere in society, they then examine in some detail the effects of cultural diversity and group composition on group communication processes and outcomes. Although they focus on organizational work groups in particular, much of what they discuss is equally relevant for other types of groups. They conclude with some suggested directions for future research that, if pursued, should help to further understanding of the conditions under which the promised benefits of group diversity accrue. As their chapter shows, group communication

theory and research are critical for understanding and effectively managing cultural diversity in groups.

Chapter 6, by Carolyn M. Anderson, Bruce L. Riddle, and Matthew M. Martin, continues the theme of individuals and groups by exploring the socialization processes that occur as people join, adapt to, and exit from groups. They view group socialization as an inherently communicative process, concerned with the symbolic practices of social influence that help newcomers and established members, or all members of a new group, to create and re-create a unique group. Group socialization, therefore, is viewed not as a one-way process in which groups instill beliefs, values, attitudes, and practices into members, but as a reciprocal process of social influence in which groups affect individuals, and vice versa. Moreover, group socialization processes carry over in the sense that individuals' experiences in one group affect how they adapt and communicate in other groups to which they belong or will belong. To illuminate these processes, Anderson and colleagues first highlight relevant models of group socialization by integrating contributions from diverse disciplines. They then advance two original, theoretically-grounded phase models of group socialization, one from the individual group member's perspective and one from the group's perspective, that clarify how communication influences essential characteristics associated with socialization in groups, and then provide frameworks for reviewing research about group socialization and for setting the agenda for those who seek to study this crucial process.

Part III: Task and Relational Group Communication

Scholars generally agree that there are two main dimensions of group life: task and social. These two dimensions are clearly interrelated; in fact, Bales (1950, 1953) and many other scholars since have argued that the primary issue facing work-oriented groups is the need to maintain a balance, or equilibrium, between task and social (maintenance or socioemotional) demands. Unfortunately, scholars too often have depicted the task and social dimensions as being in competition with each other, which resulted in the privileging of the former and downplaying of the latter, as reflected, for example, in the sheer number of studies devoted to each dimension, with studies of task-group communication and decision making far outweighing studies of relational communication in groups. Part III seeks to remedy this gap by examining, in separate chapters, what is known from a communication perspective about each dimension of group life. The chapters as a set provide an overview of what extant research shows, as well as what remains to be known, about engaging in both high-quality task and high-quality relational communication processes in groups.

Chapter 7, by Randy Y. Hirokawa and Abran J. Salazar, examines the task dimension of group life, specifically, task-group communication and decision-making performance. There is a wealth of empirical information concerning what leads to high-quality group decision making/problem solving, and much of this has focused on the contribution of group members' communicative behavior. To organize and synthesize this literature, Hirokawa and Salazar first examine three conceptual perspectives that position communication in different ways relative to group decision making: (a) the Mediational Perspective, which views communication as a conduit through which the "true" determinants of group decision making (such as members' effort) are able to exert influence; (b) the Functional Perspective, which views the performance of communication serving particular functions (such as the identification of available choices) as being critical to high-quality group decision making; and (c) the Constitutive Perspective, which views group decision making as a developmental process emerging from and constituted in communication. They then employ these conceptual perspectives to explicate, and later to assess, research examining the relationship between communication and a variety of group decision-making performance outcomes (focusing most on accuracy and quality), and then propose some specific directions for future research that can lead to building integrative, as well as more comprehensive, theories and models of task-group communication and decision-making performance.

Chapter 8, by Joann Keyton, reviews seminal and representative research on relational messages, processes, and outcomes in interacting groups. To date, there has been no attempt to organize or summarize this literature. Keyton reviews research by communication scholars as well as the work of scholars from other disciplines who address relational issues in groups. This research reflects attention to a wide variety of groups, ranging from task-oriented groups (e.g., organizational teams) to relationship-oriented groups (e.g., support groups). Thus, the phrase "relational communication" in the context of groups is used to refer to the affective or expressive verbal and nonverbal messages that create the social fabric of a group by promoting relationships between and among members. Although few lines of clear, systematic research on relational communication in groups exist, much of the task-oriented literature provides insights into relational issues within groups, and Keyton explicates these studies within an organizing framework. Following this review, research on relatively new topics that affect relational life in groups is discussed. The chapter ends with an evaluative summary of the extant literature and an agenda for future research on relational communication in groups.

Part IV: Group Communication Processes

Many factors affect groups, including the nature of the task, members' personalities and abilities, and environmental factors that impinge, to name a few. From a communication perspective, however, communication processes lie at the heart of groups: "Communication is the lifeblood that flows through the veins of groups" (Frey, 1994, p. x). Communication is, thus, the medium through which groups are both created and sustained and through which other factors exert their influence.

There are, of course, numerous communication processes that characterize groups. Part IV examines five important, and certainly interrelated, communication processes in groups: information processing, nonverbal communication, influence processes, communication and leadership, and communication and group creativity. Information processing, influence processes, and communication and leadership have received extensive coverage in the literature; nonverbal communication and communication and group creativity represent important, but understudied, topics of interest.

In Chapter 9, Kathleen M. Propp examines collective information processing in groups. As she notes, all groups, regardless of their purpose, share the common need to acquire and process information. Focusing specifically on information in task groups, Propp believes that the often-reported superiority, as well as the sometimes noted inferiority, of group compared to individual decision making/ problem solving is often attributable to how information is collectively processed in groups. Propp first establishes the significance of information in the performance of group tasks and draws an important distinction between knowledge that group members hold individually versus the communication of that knowledge as information. Next, she explores what research shows about the role of communication in the subprocesses constituting collective information processing: information search, information storage and retrieval, and weighting and use of information. She then introduces an original, four-phase distillation model of collective information processing to illuminate how a group develops a final information base from which a decision will be made, as mediated by characteristics of the knowledge/information, group, and task environment. The model helps one to summarize, organize, and link disparate research findings reported across many disciplines on information use in groups. She then provides an in-depth exploration of noncommunica-

tive factors that have an impact on the model and concludes with suggestions for future research on collective information processing.

In Chapter 10, Sandra M. Ketrow examines the important, but understudied, topic of nonverbal communication in groups. As she points out, group communication theory, research, and practice have a long history of studying verbal communicative behavior, but nonverbal aspects, which carry significant weight in determining the meaning of messages, have received substantially less attention. Ketrow seeks to remedy the neglect by examining what is known and needs to be known about the nature and effects of nonverbal communication in groups. She begins by explaining the significance, as well as omission, of nonverbal cues within the group context, and provides parameters for their study, with a particular focus on the communicative functions served by nonverbal cues. She then discusses relevant research conducted on nonverbal communication in the group context, as well as some literature that potentially may be generalized from other contexts (such as dyads) to groups, and focuses on visual (including kinesic behavior and physical appearance cues and artifacts), place, contact, time, and auditory codes. She concludes the chapter by arguing for the importance of studying nonverbal communication in groups, identifying four functional areas that deserve consideration (the role of nonverbal behavior in relational communication, emotional communication, identity management and impression formation, and interaction management in groups), and discussing some important methodological challenges that confront those who seek to map and understand this territory.

Chapter 11, by Renée A. Meyers and Dale E. Brashers, examines influence processes in group interaction. They start by identifying four boundary conditions, based on past research, for the chapter: a focus on decision-making groups, verbal influence processes, three source production sites of influence (individual, subgroup, and group/intergroup), and the instrumental purpose of social influence as inducing or persuading another to comply with one's suggestions, proposals, or recommendations. They use these defining features to frame and organize a review of the relevant literature and advance an original organizing grid that permits categorization of research primarily with regard to its message level and message source production site. The interface of valence, argument, and conflict communication strategies with the three source production sites mentioned yields nine cells into which prominent theories, models, and research programs are classified and reviewed. Meyers and Brashers end the chapter by exploring directions for future research on group influence processes, both examining some recent developments in existing research programs and speculating on some new and potentially profitable directions for research on argumentation and conflict communication in groups.

In Chapter 12, Charles Pavitt theorizes about the relationship between group communication and leadership, probably the process-outcome relationship most studied in the group context after communication and decision making. Pavitt finds that, although there is a wealth of theory and research on group leadership, communication- and noncommunication-based approaches have not been differentiated sufficiently. He believes the problem has been a lack of attention to the explanatory forms that communication-based theories of any phenomenon, including group leadership, can take. His goal in this chapter, therefore, is to explicate and apply appropriate explanatory forms for theorizing about the relationship between communication and group leadership. He focuses, in particular, on two forms: functional and input-process-output models. He first explains the nature of these communication-based explanatory models and then examines theory and research related to the functional approach to group leadership and that related to the emergent, charismatic, and mediational approaches that represent input-process-output models. Pavitt ends his discussion by suggesting how four classic, noncommunication-based, orga-

nizational leadership theories—Contingency Theory, the Normative Model, Situational Theory, and Path-Goal Theory—might be transformed into communication-based approaches, while cautioning about the danger of integrating causal and functional theorizing in communication-based explanations of group leadership.

Chapter 13, by Susan Jarboe, concludes the examination of group communication processes by focusing on the relationship between group communication and creativity processes. This area of study emerged largely during the 1990s and is of interest to scholars and professionals alike who wish to enhance the creative potential of individuals, groups, and organizations. Given that many of today's creativity endeavors occur in group settings, Jarboe addresses and assesses what we know about creativity and group communication processes. She begins by examining the way creativity is conceptualized and defined in three contexts: within individuals, groups, and organizations. The discussion of creativity in groups, in particular, focuses on models of creative group problem solving and decision making, communicative strategies for encouraging creative group thinking, and group-level barriers that undermine creating thinking. She then explores disciplinary links between group communication and creativity and seeks to set the agenda by suggesting potential profitable lines of inquiry and identifying important methodological issues in need of attention. Jarboe ends the chapter by challenging scholars to remove some of the roadblocks and barriers that appear to prevent the study of creativity from becoming a central concern of group communication scholarship.

Part V: Group Communication Facilitation

As anyone who has ever worked in a group is only too aware, groups sometimes do not yield the benefits believed to accrue from them vis-à-vis working as individuals, such as increased productivity and higher quality decision making. Indeed, there is a genre of jokes about the inefficiency of groups (e.g., "Committees are groups that keep minutes and waste hours"). To achieve the benefits possible from group work, groups often need help and guidance in meeting the goals they set—that is, they need *facilitation*. Group facilitation can be defined as "any meeting technique, procedure, or practice that makes it easier for groups to interact and/or accomplish their goals" (Frey, 1995, p. 4), where meeting procedures are "sets of rules or guidelines which specify how a group should organize its process to achieve a particular goal" (Poole, 1991, p. 55). Many of these procedures are directed toward structuring group communication processes; thus, Part V examines group communication facilitation.

Chapter 14, by Beatrice G. Schultz, provides an introductory overview of group communication facilitation that reviews some of the history, theories, research studies, and practical strategies for observing, evaluating, and changing group communicative behavior. Specifically, she examines the dual processes of diagnosis—how specifically chosen individuals (facilitators, consultants, and/or group members) can observe and evaluate important group components, such as interactional patterns and decision-making outcomes—and intervention—how these individuals can provide group members with feedback and suggest potential remedies for altering problematic group communicative behavior. Contrasting "explanatory theories" for improving group interaction derived from theory and research with "practical theories" that offer specific recommendations for doing so derived from the experiential knowledge gained from trainers, consultants, and group members through diagnosis and intervention, Schultz shows how group communication facilitation pivots on a dialectic between theory and practice. She concludes the review by positing means for surmounting the typical obstacles group members face and offering suggestions for future research.

Chapter 15, by Sunwolf and David R. Seibold, examines the impact of formal discussion/decision-making/problem-solving facilitation techniques—"process procedures"—on individual group members, group processes, and task outcomes. After considering limitations of group discussions that are not guided by process procedures, they propose an original, synthetic model, the Function Impact Model, that serves as a conceptual and functional framework for reviewing and synthesizing 56 process procedures and 33 relevant research studies conducted across numerous disciplines that span more than a 50-year time period. The model portrays facilitation procedures as serving one of four separate, yet interrelated, group process functions within a group: providing structure (structuring), facilitating analysis (analyzing), encouraging creativity (creating), or managing conflict and developing agreement (agreeing). The Function Impact Model views these four functions of process procedures as being affected by member, group, and task characteristics during the group communication process. Sunwolf and Seibold conclude the chapter by examining limitations of extant research on process procedures and offering suggestions for enhancing the vitality of this research.

Chapter 16, by Craig R. Scott, examines the facilitative influence of new communication technologies on group communication. The use of advanced electronic and digital technologies—especially those supporting communication and collaboration—is having substantial effects on the ways groups work in contemporary organizations. Scholarly interest in technology and group/teamwork issues has given rise to a new interdisciplinary field: computer-supported collaborative work. Scott reviews and synthesizes recent research on a wide variety of group communication technologies (GCTs) used to facilitate group interaction. He first proposes a synthesis of existing systems-based models, called the Meeting-Process Model, that focuses on relationships among four sets of inputs (context, group/member characteristics, task characteristics, and technology), meeting processes, four sets of outcomes (task/decision performance, meeting efficiency, member satisfaction, and communication), and feedback. After defining key terms, he uses the model to review recent GCT research related to the four outcomes conducted in two contexts: laboratory research groups and organizational work teams. For each outcome, he compares findings contrasting GCTs with face-to-face group interaction, as well as findings regarding variations in the features of a single technology. At the end of the chapter, he advances some claims that can be made on the basis of the research reviewed, compares the findings across the two contexts studied as well as to previous reviews of literature in this area, and suggests directions for future work on the facilitative impact of communication technologies on groups.

Part VI: Group Communication Contexts and Applications

This introduction started with the notion that groups are woven into the fabric of people's lives, but it probably is more accurate to say that people are woven into the fabric of group life. Familial, educational, recreational, social, occupational, health, spiritual, commercial, and political/civic groups are merely some of the groups into which humans are woven over the course of their life span. These and other groups "help define who we are and what we want to be, how we live and relate to others, and, as companies move increasingly toward using teams in the workplace, how successful we will be professionally" (Frey & Barge, 1997, p. xi).

Many group communication contexts and applications could be examined; Part VI highlights four considered to be important for understanding group communication: family groups, groups in the formal educational setting, social support groups, and organizational work groups. Virtually everyone participates in a few, if not all, of these types of groups, and, to some extent, they reflect different periods of time over the course of people's life span, from our earliest group of the family to the organizational work groups in

which we participate for a significant portion of our lives.

In Chapter 17, Thomas J. Socha examines what is clearly the most important first group of people's lives—the family—and the one from which we undoubtedly learn much about how to interact in other groups. Unfortunately, as Socha shows, the family typically has not been studied as a group per se, either by group communication or family communication scholars. Consequently, what is known about communication processes in families remains largely disconnected from what is known about communication processes in groups in general. Socha's agenda is to reopen the dialogue between those who study communication in groups and in families. After articulating some reasons for reaffirming the connections between these scholars, he reviews early sociological and psychological research applying group interaction observational methods (such as Bales's, 1950, Interaction Process Analysis) to the family. He then explores conceptual and theoretical approaches to studying communication in families, as well as a variety of measurement instruments designed to understand family interactions. Emerging from these discussions are potential insights about families that are applicable to other types of groups, and vice versa. Socha concludes by calling for an integrative, life-span developmental approach to the study of group communication that regards the family as people's first group.

Chapter 18, by Terre H. Allen and Timothy G. Plax, continues the life-span developmental thread of this section by exploring group communication in the formal educational context. Unfortunately, despite the significance of group communication within the classroom and the wealth of research in the field of education on the effects on a variety of outcomes of group instruction—especially comparisons among individualistic, competitive, and cooperative (small group) learning—group communication scholars have virtually ignored this context/application. Allen and Plax seek to enlighten group communication scholars about this important domain by reviewing, synthesizing, and evaluating the extant research. After providing a historical overview, as well as establishing definitional parameters, of groups in the formal educational context, they examine, from comparative philosophical and theoretical perspectives, types of grouping procedures used within the classroom that differ fundamentally in terms of the communication patterns engendered, with a particular emphasis on cooperative and collaborative learning groups. They then explore research on cognitive and affective outcomes derived from studies of cooperative learning groups at the lower-elementary, upper-elementary, high school, and college levels, as well as some limited research on collaborative learning groups. They conclude the chapter by identifying some limitations of the current literature and suggesting some profitable directions for future group communication research.

Chapter 19, by Rebecca J. Welch Cline, explores communication in social support groups. With 8 to 10 million adults in the United States participating in at least a half-million support groups (Wuthnow, 1994), the social support/self-help group has become one of the most important group forms in contemporary society relative to health. Cline first offers some reasons for the growth of these groups and then explores several defining features of them, including the health benefits of social support. She then focuses on support group communication processes at three levels: (a) the macro-level—the effects of group ideology (specifically, internal versus external locus of control or attributions of responsibility) on group communication processes; (b) middle-ground concepts—the role of climate and leadership in shaping communicative behavior in these groups; and (c) the micro-level—communicative behavior in which support group members engage. Attempting to sort fact from fiction, Cline reviews and synthesizes available empirical research about the value of participating in these groups with respect to affective and cognitive, communication and relational, and health behavioral outcomes. She identifies several important

limitations in the extant literature that must be confronted, such as the absence of theory and the presence of threats to validity. She concludes the chapter by setting some agendas for future research on social support groups, including a sharpened focus on both the group as a unit and group communication processes.

In Chapter 20, Howard H. Greenbaum and Jim L. Query, Jr. explore what is known about communication processes in what is a fundamental feature of contemporary organizations—the work group. From designing organizational programs to their implementation, oversight, and evaluation, the work group has become the primary means by which the business of organizations is accomplished. A considerable body of literature about such groups has accumulated; unfortunately, there is a lack of unifying theoretical frameworks available to facilitate synthesis of these research studies. Greenbaum and Query respond to this need by using a systems-based, conceptual framework developed previously by Greenbaum and colleagues—the Group Variables Classification Systems (GVCS)—to classify, organize, and synthesize research findings on communication in natural organizational work groups. The GVCS categorizes the independent, dependent, and moderating variables of any particular study with regard to four system stages (Input, Process, Output, and Feedback), four variable types (Task, Member, Structure, and Environment), and the variable-class relationships formed by the matrix of system stages and variable types. The categorization of 55 recent studies about communication in natural organizational work groups, culled from more than 300 published in almost 90 journals, allows Greenbaum and Query to advance key claims about the strengths and weaknesses of the extant literature and to propose directions for future research on communication in natural organizational work groups.

CLOSING COMMENTS

There is a story in Greek mythology of the Athenian hero Thesus, who must confront the

Minotaur, a creature that is half man and half bull and resides in a labyrinth beneath Crete and to whom seven Athenian youths and maidens are sacrificed annually as a tribute. The danger Thesus faces, quite aside from the task of killing the Minotaur and ending the reign of terror, is becoming lost in the labyrinth and, thereby, being unable to return to his beloved Athens. To prevent this from occurring, Ariadne, the daughter of Crete's King Minos, who is also in love with Thesus, gives him a ball of thread to help him find his way back. After completing the task, Thesus is able to retrace his steps by following the string he has unraveled. The mass of literature that has accumulated in the field of group communication constitutes something of a cognitive labyrinth through which, unassisted, one may have considerable difficulty and frustration finding his or her way. The chapters in this volume can be viewed in certain senses as a kind of thread that the contributors are providing to assist those interested in mastering the knowledge the field has produced to find their way through and to complete their journey with a feeling of accomplishment and greater sense of appreciation for having undertaken the journey.

Weaving this thread has been no easy task. The choices about which topics and chapters to include, how to organize the text, and how the chapters should be written posed enormous conceptual and practical problems. In keeping with the theme of this text, I believed that these difficulties were best managed as a group communication process, and I established appropriate group processes and procedures. I have been extremely fortunate to have worked in a small group with Dennis S. Gouran and Marshall Scott Poole as the Associate Editors. One could not ask for two scholars more experienced and respected in the field of group communication, in particular, and the communication discipline, in general; more diligent and helpful in bringing this text to fruition; and more gracious and kind in their demeanor and style. I have worked with many groups in my professional life, but none so effective and pleasurable as this one in demonstrating how the task and social dimensions of group life can, in fact, complement each other so well. Moreover, this small group was interdependent with a much larger group of almost 50 individuals who served as the editorial review board for both the initial selection of chapter proposals from the open call issued and the provision of feedback about the various drafts submitted. This editorial review board was composed not only of scholars in the field of group communication but also of leading scholars from many other fields of the communication discipline. We are indebted to these individuals who gave so willingly of their time and energy to help make this a high-quality text. We also want to thank Margaret Seawell, editor at Sage Publications, for her support of this text from its very inception, and the team at Sage who produced it. Most important are the 25 authors with whom Dennis, Scott, the reviewers, and I had the pleasure to work. We thank them for their commitment to this project, giving it top priority despite many other responsibilities and obligations, taking the substantial time necessary to write high-quality chapters, and putting up with our intense and seemingly unending editorial feedback. It sometimes is the case that people cannot practice what they preach, but these various groups of people clearly demonstrated their ability to engage in group communication *praxis.*

The group communication processes employed have resulted in a group outcome, a text about group communication, that no one of us could have written alone. There is a popular saying from Systems Theory that a "group is more than the sum of its parts." I hope this text will be viewed as more than the sum of its chapters; that it not only constitutes a review and synthesis of what we currently know about group communication theory and research but also helps to establish new conceptual perspectives, theories, and research agendas for future group communication scholars to pursue. We will have to wait until the second edition of the text to see whether and how that potential has been realized.

REFERENCES

Anderson, L. R. (1978). Groups would do better without humans. *Personality and Social Psychology Bulletin, 4,* 557-558.

Arrow, H., & McGrath, J. E. (1993). Membership matters: How member change and continuity affect small group structure, process, and performance. *Small Group Research, 24,* 334-361.

Bales, R. F. (1950). *Interaction process analysis: A method for the study of small groups.* Cambridge, MA: Addison-Wesley.

Bales, R. F. (1953). The equilibrium problem in small groups. In T. Parsons, R. F. Bales, & E. A. Shils (Eds.), *Working papers in the theory of action* (pp. 111-161). Glencoe, IL: Free Press.

Buys, C. (1978). Humans would do better without groups. *Personality and Social Psychology Bulletin, 4,* 123-135.

Cartwright, D., & Zander, A. (Eds.). (1953). *Group dynamics: Research and theory.* Evanston, IL: Row, Peterson.

Cartwright, D., & Zander, A. (Eds.). (1960). *Group dynamics: Research and theory* (2nd ed.). Evanston, IL: Row, Peterson.

Cartwright, D., & Zander, A. (Eds.). (1968). *Group dynamics: Research and theory* (3rd ed.). New York: Harper & Row.

Frey, L. R. (1994). The call of the field: Studying communication in natural groups. In L. R. Frey (Ed.), *Group communication in context: Studies of natural groups* (pp. ix-xiv). Hillsdale, NJ: Lawrence Erlbaum.

Frey, L. R. (1995). Applied communication research on group facilitation in natural settings. In L. R. Frey (Ed.), *Innovations in group facilitation: Applications in natural settings* (pp. 1-23). Cresskill, NJ: Hampton.

Frey, L. R. (1996). Remembering and "re-membering": A history of theory and research on communication and group decision making. In R. Y. Hirokawa & M. S. Poole (Eds.), *Communication and group decision making* (2nd ed., pp. 19-51). Thousand Oaks, CA: Sage.

Frey, L. R. (1997). Individuals in groups. In L. R. Frey & J. K. Barge (Eds.), *Managing group life: Communicating in decision-making groups* (pp. 52-79). Boston: Houghton Mifflin.

Frey, L. R., & Barge, J. K. (1997). Introduction. In L. R. Frey & J. K. Barge (Eds.), *Managing group life: Communicating in decision-making groups* (pp. xi-xx). Boston: Houghton Mifflin.

Gergen, K. (1991). *The saturated self: Dilemmas of identity in contemporary life.* New York: Basic Books.

Gouran, D. S. (1994). The future of small group communication research: Revitalization or continued good health? *Communication Studies, 45,* 29-39.

Hare, A. P. (1976). *Handbook of small group research* (2nd ed.). New York: Free Press.

Hare, A. P., Blumberg, H. M., Davies, M. F., & Kent, M. V. (1994). *Small group research: A handbook.* Norwood, NJ: Ablex.

Hirokawa, R. Y., & Poole, M. S. (Eds.). (1996). *Communication and group decision making* (2nd ed.). Thousand Oaks, CA: Sage.

Meyrowitz, J. (1985). *No sense of place: The impact of electronic media on social behavior.* Oxford, UK: Oxford University Press.

Ofshe, R. J. (Ed.). (1973). *Interpersonal behavior in groups.* Englewood Cliffs, NJ: Prentice Hall.

Poole, M. S. (1991). Procedures for managing meetings: Social and technological innovation. In R. A. Swanson & B. O. Knapp (Eds.), *Innovative meeting management* (pp. 53-109). Austin, TX: 3M Meeting Management Institute.

Poole, M. S. (1994). Breaking the isolation of small group communication studies. *Communication Studies, 45,* 20-28.

Poole, M. S. (1998). The small group should be *the* fundamental unit of communication research. In J. S. Trent (Ed.), *Communication: Views from the helm for the 21st century* (pp. 94-97). Boston: Allyn & Bacon.

Propp, K. M., & Kreps, G. L. (1994). A rose by any other name: The vitality of group communication research. *Communication Studies, 45,* 7-19.

Shaw, M. E. (1971). *Group dynamics: The psychology of small group behavior.* New York: McGraw-Hill.

Shaw, M. E. (1976). *Group dynamics: The psychology of small group behavior* (2nd ed.). New York: McGraw-Hill.

Shaw, M. E. (1981). *Group dynamics: The psychology of small group behavior* (3rd ed.). New York: McGraw-Hill.

Wuthnow, R. (1994). *Sharing the journey: Support groups and America's new quest for community.* New York: Free Press.

PART I

Foundations of Group Communication Theory and Research

1

Communication in Groups

The Emergence and Evolution of a Field of Study

DENNIS S. GOURAN
The Pennsylvania State University

Participation in groups is an inescapable fact of life that has attracted considerable scholarly interest in a variety of disciplines. In the field of Communication, this interest developed almost immediately with the creation of the National Association of Academic Teachers of Public Speaking in 1914. Early interest, however, focused on the training of students in speech classes to become better contributors to the decision-making and problem-solving groups in which they might find themselves in the public arena. It was not until the second half of the 20th century that interest in communication in groups began to result in original scholarly inquiries (theoretical speculation and empirical research) aimed at enlarging understanding of the ways in which communication is related to other aspects of groups, such as the characteristics of members and the outcomes they achieve across different social contexts. Once scholarly inquiry took hold, however, it began to increase decade by decade in almost geometric progression.

The purpose of this chapter is to trace the emergence and evolution of the study of groups as it has developed in the discipline of Communication during the 20th century. In short, the chapter attempts to take the reader through the labyrinth of theory and research relating to communication in groups that has developed in the field of Communication and uses highlights from the historical record to mark the way.

As a topic of research interest, communication in groups, for all practical purposes, has a history of just more than 50 years. Although there was a smattering of research in the late 1930s and 1940s dealing with such topics as the effects of group discussion on college students' social attitudes (Robinson, 1941), the relationship of discussion to group divergence in judgment (Simpson, 1939), and gender (defined then solely as biological sex) differences in group discussion (Timmons, 1941), the only research of any lasting significance during the 1940s was Alma Johnson's (1943) development and application of an instrument designed to measure reflective thinking ability based on Dewey's (1910) earlier identified steps (in this volume, see the chapters by Hirokawa and Salazar and by Propp). The instrument was an outgrowth of Johnson's (1939,

1940) interest in communication pedagogy. Such efforts notwithstanding, a community of research-oriented scholars did not begin to develop until the 1950s.

Despite the noted starting point, the origins of this research subfield can be traced to occurrences earlier in the century, both in the field of Communication in general and in cognate disciplines. In addition to exploring these precursors and some of the more substantial external influences on the establishment of a research presence in the study of communication in groups, this chapter illuminates major trends in each of the decades from 1950 through the 1990s. Each decade appears to have had its own character, but the scholarship it subsumes, nevertheless, added to the continuity and relatively orderly advancement of inquiry and knowledge of the nature, functions, and consequences of communication in groups.

The history of communication research, as related to groups, in its early stages reveals comparatively little direct concern with interaction among members other than as a vehicle by which they could engage collectively in the completion of tasks. By the 1990s, however, communicative content had taken on overriding importance in the research agendas of communication scholars studying groups. The story of how this occurred is the primary thrust of this chapter. Additionally, the final section of the chapter projects possibilities and presents speculations concerning where future research on communication on groups may go and the types of topics and issues it might most profitably address.

The chapter does not provide a comprehensive overview of all the work that has been done by communication scholars interested in the study of group processes, even though the volume of material covered is fairly large. A number of such reviews have been published fairly recently at various points and cover different periods of time (e.g., Cohen, 1994; Cragan & Wright, 1980, 1990; Frey, 1996; Gouran, 1985, 1994a; Gouran & Fisher, 1984; Poole, 1994). In addition, most of the chapters in this volume, to some extent, have

a historical character, and contributors review pertinent scholarship as it pertains to the particular topics they address. Nor does this chapter examine much of the considerable body of inquiry, theory, and research generated in cognate disciplines. Again, where appropriate, other contributors deal with such matters. The principal concern here is to illuminate the issues of interest over time and the major trends in scholarship in the field of Communication from decade to decade.

PEDAGOGICAL ORIGINS

To understand how communication in groups developed as a research interest, it is helpful to have some awareness and appreciation of the concerns that scholars and educators in Communication had in groups prior to the 1950s. Early attention was pedagogical in nature and related largely to the public arena; for this period, one could even think of Group Communication as a subspecialty of the larger area of Public Address. In this respect, it is noteworthy that the lead article in the very first issue of the *Quarterly Journal of Speech* (then the *Quarterly Journal of Public Speaking*) dealt with the group forum as a pedagogical tool for improving participation in public life (see Lyman, 1915). Group discussion was seen as an instrument of democracy, a view introduced by Alfred Sheffield in 1922 and subsequently promulgated and articulated more fully by A. Craig Baird in 1928 with the publication of the text *Public Discussion and Debate*. That view continued well into the 1950s, with public meetings thought of as a means by which people could collectively arrive at decisions and engage in other forms of cooperative activity aimed at solving mutually shared problems. Instruction in this specialized type of group communicative activity began in the early 1920s and still persists today.

Central to developments in the teaching of discussion was the influential book *How We Think*, published originally in 1910 by the eminent philosopher John Dewey. In addition to Baird and Sheffield, prominent figures applying Dewey's notions prior to or concurrent with Alma Johnson's (1943) previously mentioned development of an instrument for measuring reflective thinking ability and her experiment examining its effects on the problem-solving effectiveness of groups were Robert Allison (1939), J. Jeffrey Auer (1939), Douglas Ehninger (1943), Halbert Gulley (1942), James McBurney and Kenneth Hance (1939), and Joseph O'Brien (1939).

As those teaching public discussion (or about it) became more sophisticated in their thinking and acquired more experiences in working with and studying classroom groups, they increasingly were given to making claims of the type that called for verification. For instance, McBurney and Hance (1939) offered suggestions for how to minimize the negative influence of various types of disruptive group members, such as those who pontificate, express cynicism, or exhibit high levels of egocentrism. Interest also began to grow concerning how the performance of groups might be improved. Merely participating and following set procedures were seen as insufficient; educators contended that knowing how to do so effectively was the key to successful group performance. Although probably not intentionally, those who developed an interest in and concerns about such matters were laying a foundation for the research agendas that came into existence in the 1950s.

DEVELOPMENTS IN COGNATE DISCIPLINES

As the pedagogical interest in groups grew among teachers and students of discussion and group process as a form of public address, research related to the small group was also developing in Sociology and Social Psychology. This interest was stimulated by the work of Kurt Lewin during the 1930s and 1940s. Lewin attempted to advance a science of group dynamics modeled, in part, on theories in Physics and highly reflective of the *Systems Perspective,* that is, the view that entities have elements and properties linked to one another in such a way that changes in the properties of one element predictably alter the relationships of such properties to the properties of other elements (Bergmann, 1957; see Mabry's review of the Systems Perspective as applied to group communication in Chapter 3 of this volume). The Systems Perspective is reductionistic in its assumption concerning the value of microscopic forms of analysis in revealing the more global aspects of complex processes (see Wilson, 1998).

Lewin, his students, and their successors were able to show not only that empirical questions concerning how particular variables relate to other variables within an overall group system could be answered, but also that the answers were frequently both illuminating on theoretical grounds and practical in their implications for how group members might be of assistance to one another in performing collective tasks. This early work emerging from a Systems Perspective laid a foundation for research dealing with communication in groups beginning in the 1960s, lasting well into the 1990s, and, I suspect, continuing into the next millennium.

Lewin's pioneering work in the study of leadership styles with colleagues Ronald Lippitt and Ralph White (Lewin, Lippitt, & White, 1939; Lippitt & White, 1943) complemented the interest among communication scholars in discussion as a tool of democracy. An escapee from Nazi Germany, Lewin was concerned with showing the ill effects of autocratic rule and the potential benefits of more democratic forms of performing group tasks. Lewin and his associates' research on the topic generally supported his trust in democratic forms of governance, which was compatible with the earlier-mentioned pedagogical tradition in the emergent subfield of Group Communication. Perhaps more important than the specific findings, however, was the fact that his inquiries established that *a science of group process* was possible. In short, Lewin produced evidence that changes in particular variables characteristic of groups (for instance, leadership style) were systematically related to changes in other variables (for instance, group members' satisfaction and motivation). The work culminated in what acquired the label *Field Theory* (see Lewin, 1936, 1951) and was at the base of much of the research on small groups conducted in Social Psychology throughout the 1940s and 1950s. In the discipline of Communication, Field Theory served as a stimulus for scholars to begin looking at communication as a dynamic process and was a direct precursor of later theorizing from the functional perspective explained later in this chapter. In fact, it was due largely to Lewin that the term *group dynamics* came into existence.

Lewin was also important for his establishment of the National Training Laboratory (NTL) in Bethel, Maine, in the late 1940s. The NTL was devoted to the study of experiential group processes and had much to do with the sensitivity training/encounter group movement in the United States during the 1960s and 1970s (see Schultz, Chapter 14, this volume). For scholars in Communication, however, it may have had more to do with intensifying interest in the interpersonal aspects of group process and in making clear that socioemotional, or maintenance, needs of members can exert a powerful influence on group performance. The NTL also had an impact on making talk during group meetings a primary focus of attention.

Later work by the prominent sociologist Robert Freed Bales and others, moreover, made it even more apparent that interaction was something more than the conduit for exchanging messages that people interested in groups initially believed it to be. Instead, it could reveal much about such matters as relationships among members (see Keyton, Chapter 8, this volume), sources and patterns of influence (see Meyers and Brashers, Chapter 11, this volume), and reasons for differences in the quality of the performance of groups (see Hirokawa and Salazar, Chapter 7, this volume), among other processes and outcomes. Especially influential was Bales's (1950) publication of the text *Interaction Process Analysis: A Method for the Study of Small Groups* and studies that grew from it (e.g., Bales & Strodtbeck, 1951; Bales, Strodtbeck, Mills, & Roseborough, 1951). IPA, as it was

called, provided a means for coding both the task and relational content of verbal and nonverbal transactions occurring during group meetings (in this volume, see the chapters by Keyton, Pavitt, and Socha). This work also provided a further basis for the view that groups constitute systems and that communication within them exhibits systemlike regularities, especially in respect to stages of development of both groups and their members' interactions. Applications of IPA led to Bales's (1970; Bales & Cohen, 1979) later development of an even more elaborate method for identifying and understanding relationships among members of groups called SYMLOG (System for the Multiple Level Observation of Groups), a methodology that would subsequently prove to have considerable longevity and impact on studies of groups (see Keyton, 1997, this volume).

Another influence was the effort by Raymond B. Cattell (1948, 1951a, 1951b) to develop a comprehensive theory of group process in respect to an analogue to personality, which he referred to as "syntality." *Syntality* represents the composite set of attributes of the members of a group and has an important bearing on the ways in which they function. Of most relevance to the present discussion was Cattell's notion that the effective synergy of a group—the amount of collective energy that can be devoted to the completion of a task—is the residual when the amount of synergy devoted to a group's maintenance needs is subtracted from the total synergy. The significance of this view, which continued to be of scholarly interest into the 1990s (see Salazar, 1995), was to call attention to the need to consider the social dimensions of group process, as well as the means (for instance, coordination of effort) by which group members attempt to fulfill the requirements of their tasks. Ivan Steiner (1972, 1974) later articulated a similar notion in a formula positing that a group's actual productivity is the difference between its potential productivity and losses attributable to process, by which he meant behavior in excess of "the pattern demanded by the task" (p. 9; see Hirokawa and

Salazar, Chapter 7, this volume). Both Cattell and Steiner's formulations stressed the importance of relational factors, but in a negative way, that is, as deterrents to group productivity. As relational factors began to emerge as a focus in later studies of communication in groups, however, they increasingly were viewed as having not only negative consequences but also many positive ones as well (see Keyton, this volume).

Such developments in cognate disciplines as those mentioned above—along with the arrival of questions that began to exceed the boundaries of pedagogy among teachers of group discussion and writers of instructional materials and that required testing—helped in important ways to set the stage for the kind of sustained research activity that began to appear in the 1950s among communication scholars. Advances in cognate disciplines, as do pedagogical concerns, continue to this day to influence inquiry concerned with communication in groups.

THE EMERGENCE OF RESEARCH: THE 1950s

The decade 1950-1959, although not exactly a watershed marked by a large amount of research dealing with groups, was, nevertheless, an important historical juncture. During this period, some scholars began to conduct empirical studies related to questions that had arisen in response to pedagogically-based claims concerning the sources of individual and group decision-making effectiveness. Of particular interest were such topics as critical thinking ability, the use of meeting agendas that presumably made it more likely that group members would employ critical thinking ability, and ways in which members' personality characteristics related to the performance of groups. These topics reflected continuing concern with helping people to take on more meaningful roles in those aspects of group life in which they might become involved and, hence, were consistent with the earlier pedagogical tradition and its emphasis on discussion as a tool of democracy.

The decade opened with reservations concerning the legitimacy of group communication as an area of study. Earnest Brandenburg (1950) questioned whether or not group discussion was merely a form of propaganda because it could be used to influence social judgments in some of the same ways those of questionable ethical bent exhibited in other forms of public discourse, in which they drew on devices identified by the Columbia University-based Institute for Propaganda Analysis, such as glittering generalities, name-calling, and bandwagon appeals (see Jowett & O'Donnell, 1986). Robert Gunderson (1950) raised the prospect that group dynamics was merely some sort of hoax designed to leave unsuspecting participants with a sense of false hope for improving their ability to solve problems. Despite these criticisms, serious scholarship concerning groups began to take hold. R. Victor Harnack (1951), for instance, conducted a study of the effects of competition and cooperation in small groups and found that cooperatively-oriented groups tended to perform better. Harnack (1955) followed with a study demonstrating that training in the formulation and recognition of group goals tended to increase intragroup cooperation.

In addition to the kind of work that Harnack was doing, by mid-decade, scholars were investigating a variety of other issues and topics. Black (1955) looked at the rhetorical causes of breakdown in group discussion, and Crowell, Katcher, and Miyamoto (1955) considered how self-concept in respect to communication skill affected individuals' performance in group discussion. Occurring at the same time was research by Barnlund (1955) on the effects of leadership training on participation in decision-making groups, an investigation by Wischmeier (1955) of the relative effectiveness of group-centered and leader-centered approaches to leadership of group discussions, and work by Grissinger (1955) on the comparative influence of panel discussions versus formal debate on audience members' attitudes. Also of interest was the development of methodological procedures and instruments for research purposes, such as

Matthews and Bendig's (1955) measure of group discussion outcomes—essentially an index of members' agreement on decision proposals—and Dickens's (1955) formula for assessing the spread or evenness of participation in group discussion.

As the decade progressed, so did interest in the nature and effects of group members' personal characteristics. Scheidel, Crowell, and Shepherd (1958), for example, were concerned with ways in which members' personality attributes, such as motives, aggression, and achievement needs, affect their group discussion behavior. Utterback and Fotheringham (1958) focused more specifically on the role of motivation (defined as interest in a discussion task) as a source of influence on such group and individual outcomes as shift of opinion, consensus, and quality of judgment.

Keltner (1957) returned to the theme of cooperation established in Harnack's research and introduced the term *groupthink* into the literature on group process. Unlike Janis (1972, 1982), who subsequently popularized the term to reference a problematic aspect of group process, in which cohesiveness and leaders' preferences diminish the exercise of critical thinking of group members (see Keyton, chapter 8, this volume), Keltner used the expression in a positive sense to refer to a form of cooperative thinking. Brilhart (1960) reinforced Keltner's notions concerning "group thinking" as a constructive form of discussion activity in a case study of two discussion groups which showed that the one characterized by a high level of "promotively interdependent thinking" performed much more effectively than the other. Bane (1958) and Crowell (1958) offered further support to the value of cooperative thinking in groups in inquiries dealing, respectively, with the assessment of training in group discussion and group-centered versus problem-centered discussion.

What the sorts of inquiries mentioned above began to suggest, in addition to reinforcing concerns about factors that inhibit and promote member participation and how best to involve participants in group decision-making and problem-solving discussions, was that events in groups are not idiosyncratic but, rather, have some degree of regularity and, with appropriate understanding of the type acquired through scientific study, may even be predictable well beyond chance occurrence. Such awareness was consistent with the Systems Perspective underlying Lewin's development of Field Theory. The realization established by the Systems Perspective, and as originally enunciated by Lewin, that there are factors that influence interaction in groups and affect its consequences, carried over into the decade of the 1960s (and beyond), but with a somewhat different cast and much sharper focus. In particular, the studies mentioned contributed to the view that characteristics of members and groups have an important bearing on their performance. Mastery of discussion methods alone was insufficient to ensure that groups, especially task-oriented ones, would function effectively. These inquiries further demonstrated that the kinds of questions that began to emerge as a result of the field's early emphasis on discussion pedagogy and training for participation in problem-solving and decision-making groups were amenable to systematic inquiry, as practiced elsewhere in the social sciences.

A DEVELOPING FOCUS ON INTERACTION: THE 1960s

With the 1960s came research activity that centered on communication in groups as both *functional* (the ways in which utterances aid in the satisfaction of task requirements and, hence, affect the outcomes a group achieves) and *developmental* (how utterances reflect the influence of prior interactions and shape the characteristics of subsequent interaction), although these particular terms were not in evidence. Studies from these two perspectives, of course, were not the only ones being conducted. Some studies concentrated on global aspects of interaction, such as Giffin and Ehrlich's (1963) investigation of the effects of participating in group discussion under different conditions of leadership on attitudes toward a change in company policy. Others were concerned with the impact of group structural properties, as in the case of Harnack's (1963) study of the effects of an organized minority on a discussion group. Goldberg (1960) inquired into the effects of sharing evaluative feedback from fellow group members and an external evaluator concerning participants' performance on their subsequent discussion behavior, and Lerea and Goldberg (1961) considered how socialization, defined as the "tendency to enter into or withdraw from social contact with others" (p. 60), affects group behavior. Finally, Stone (1969) was interested in primacy and recency (that is, what is heard early as opposed to later) effects as determinants of jurors' decisions. Despite such cases, most studies showed evidence of the influence of the two theoretical perspectives mentioned (see Poole, Chapter 2, this volume, for a much more extensive discussion of the origins and development of the developmental and functional perspectives).

The functional perspective represented continuation of the earlier-developed interest in how such variables as members' abilities and styles of behavior—including communicative behavior—as well as groups' satisfaction of task requirements relate to the outcomes that members and groups achieve. This perspective also reflected a relatively linear view of task-related communication as progressing from a starting point, such as the delineation of a problem, to a destination, such as adopting a solution, in a straightforward fashion along a clearly defined path. The perspective also carried certain presumptions about the most effective manner in which decision-making and problem-solving groups undertake tasks, namely, in the sequence associated with Dewey's (1910) method of reflective thinking, or at least adaptations of it, such as the *standard agenda,* which laid out five general steps that problem-solving groups are advised to follow: definition of the problem, analysis of the problem, proposing possible solutions, testing solutions

against criteria, and selecting or construction a final solution (see Phillips, 1966).

Among those adopting a more-or-less functional perspective were scholars concerned with reflective thinking ability and its relationship to the outcomes that groups achieve. Notable for this focus were studies by Pyron and Sharp (1963), Pyron (1964), and Sharp and Milliken (1964), all of which uncovered partial support for the view that those who tend to exhibit the patterns of thought originally identified by Dewey, or have the capabilities he identified, not only contribute to better outcomes in group problem-solving and decision-making discussions but also exert more influence than other group members while enhancing their own standing among them.

Concurrent with studies of reflective thinking ability were others dealing with agendas based on the steps in reflective thinking compared to alternative models, such as a single-point agenda. Characteristic of this line of inquiry were investigations by Brilhart and Jochem (1964), Bayless (1967), and Larson (1969). None of these studies established clear superiority of the reflective thinking approach or agendas based on it; however, this research tended to be deficient in tracking the extent to which participants in the studies actually conformed to the process procedures they were asked to employ. Nor was there much effort to determine the quality of thought exercised by group members. This body of research, thus, failed to establish that a particular sequence of activity and a pattern of thought are not necessarily correspondent, a concern that would become more of an issue in the 1990s (see Gouran & Hirokawa, 1996; see also Sunwolf & Seibold, Chapter 15, this volume, regarding research on group process procedures).

Despite deficiencies in the line of work, the research mentioned above kept alive a concern with the communication/outcome relationship—specifically, the ways in which communication serves to assist a group in satisfying the requirements of tasks (see Harnack, 1968; in this volume, see Chapter 2 by Poole and Chapter 7 by Hirokawa and Salazar). From it would subsequently emerge the development of a general theory (see discussion below). The work also revealed a continuing commitment to understanding the dynamics of group processes so that participants could become more effective contributors, make better decisions, and develop workable solutions to collectively shared problems.

At the same time as some scholars were pursuing members' reflective thinking ability and their use of methods of group performance based on it, others were beginning to become less concerned with outcomes and more intrigued with the dynamics of group interaction—especially, how it unfolds and the extent to which types of exchanges in which members engage might be predictable. For these scholars, interaction sequences were objects of considerable research attention. This attention was consistent with Lewin's view that outcomes, such as unanimous or high-quality decisions, were merely regions or locations in the "life-spaces" of groups and that focusing on how interaction facilitated movement to these regions was key to understanding the successes and failures of groups.

The developmental, or process, view, as it became known, gained impetus with the publication of two studies by Thomas Scheidel and Laura Crowell (1964, 1966), in which they attempted to determine the predictability and redundancy of interaction sequences in groups and found that discussion does not unfold in linear fashion as suggested in earlier phase development research, such as that reported by Bales and Strodtbeck (1951). Bales and Strodtbeck uncovered evidence of a recurrent chronological pattern of interaction in problem-solving groups, which they characterized as orientation, evaluation, and control. What Scheidel and Crowell determined, instead, is that interaction is processual in nature and has systemlike properties. In short, it is governed by a set of internal relationships among the elements composing and characterizing a group and, at the same time, is influenced by other elements in the external environment (see Mabry, Chapter 3, this volume).

Even though their purpose was not to make utterances and their characteristics the foci of attention, Scheidel and Crowell had that effect, and others began to consider in greater depth how interaction in groups develops and otherwise evolves, as well as how it comes to define the relationships among group members. Berg (1967), for instance, did a descriptive analysis of themes in task-oriented group discussions and found that, in some respects, they reflect the emerging culture of a group. Geier (1967) investigated the characteristics of utterances that relate to the emergence of leadership in groups. Gouran (1969) attempted to distinguish consensus from nonconsensus groups in terms of attributes of discussion content, but in so doing found that the extent to which discussion statements exhibit particular attributes is topic dependent. For the three topics he used, only one communication variable (statements giving orientation) consistently distinguished groups reaching consensus from nonconsensus groups. Finally, Leathers (1969) traced ways in which particular characteristics of discussion statements serve to disrupt the group decision-making process. These and the pioneering studies by Scheidel and Crowell did much to set the stage for the formally acknowledged developmental perspective on group process as it was to emerge and take shape in the 1970s and 1980s.

Contributing to the emergence of the developmental perspective was work in other disciplines, such as Bruce Tuckman's (1965) identification of stages of development in therapeutic groups (see Keyton, Chapter 8, this volume). Also contributing were implications concerning the predictability of communication in groups drawn from Information Theory and the Mathematical Theory of Communication (see Pierce, 1961), both of which are grounded in the Systems Perspective. Still further contributing to a greater concentration on the ways in which interaction in groups unfolds was a general recommendation advanced by conferees at a national meeting in New Orleans sponsored by the (then) Speech Association of America (now the National Communication Association) urging the discipline as a whole to pay considerably more attention to messages, their interconnections, and the ways in which they link those who produce them. The concern underlying the recommendation had been brewing for some time and became a major point of emphasis during the conference (see Kibler & Barker, 1968).

Because of the focus on the characteristics of interaction that developed in the 1960s, coding schemes focusing on utterance-level content were developed and applied in such studies as those by Scheidel and Crowell (1964, 1966), Gouran (1969), and Leathers (1969). These schemes, or classification systems, were study specific, however, and lacked general applicability, at least in the sense that they were not designed to apply cross-situationally to group interaction. In addition, they did not appear to be firmly grounded in any specific theories. It was not until subsequent decades that more generally applicable and theoretically grounded instruments for the coding of group interaction began to emerge.

By the end of the decade, it was clear that scholarship related to the study of communication in groups, whether from a functional or a developmental perspective, would henceforth devote unprecedented attention to what members say to one another, how the content of speech acts affects relationships among members, and what, in particular, such acts have to do with the outcomes that groups achieve. Responsible in some measure for this sharpening of a communication focus were the individuals mentioned above, but the most substantial and systematic efforts were yet to come.

EXPLORATION: THE 1970s

Whereas the 1960s saw the beginnings of a more narrow emphasis on messages to the study of communication in groups, the sharpening focus had the almost paradoxical effect of broadening the issues and range of questions about interaction that scholars chose to address. The result was a proliferation of inquiry but no consensus concerning what needed to be known. Hence, communication researchers went off in many directions; nevertheless, they retained the centrality of messages in groups as a primary interest. One might, therefore, think of the 1970s as a period of exploration, in which scholars working in the area began describing communication more fully and identifying specific variables they thought might influence communication in groups, as well as ways in which group communication influences other variables. How the characteristics of messages affect consensus, how deviance and pressures for uniformity in groups are manifested in communicative behavior, how group members become acculturated through communication, and what distinguishes various types of leaders and leadership emergence, communicatively speaking, were among the wide-ranging topics that researchers of the time explored.

Despite the diversification of topics, issues, and contexts of investigation, many studies of the 1970s had in common their grounding in a Systems Perspective, in that they were concerned with the ways in which both the flow and characteristics of interaction are interrelated. This perspective pervaded influential textbooks of the period, including ones by Fisher (1974) and Tubbs (1978). Scholars during this decade also remained concerned (as they had been in the 1950s and 1960s) with finding bases for improvement in the performance of groups and their members, but not necessarily in respect to addressing social and political issues. Being skilled in group decision making and problem solving within professional arenas, such as organizations, appeared to be at least as important, if not more so.

The 1970s began with considerable criticism of the extant research on group communication (see, for example, Bormann, 1970; Fisher, 1971; Gouran, 1970b; Larson, 1971; Mortensen, 1970), which, to some extent, has carried over to the present. In fact, David Seibold (1994) fairly recently criticized the

Group Communication field for a preoccupation with reflection and self-examination at the expense of "just doing" research. His observation seems to be a bit unfair in the light of the rather substantial amount of research activity reported in this chapter and elsewhere throughout the volume; however, Seibold may well be justified in his concern that an area of scholarly activity that attracts as much self-criticism as has the study of communication in groups suggests a lack of the right sort of scholarly progress, or at least a need to devote more attention to theory and empirical research.

Of concern to critics in the early 1970s were restrictive approaches to scholarship following models and methods of research developed first in the natural sciences and then applied to social sciences, a lack of sufficient attention to communicative acts, and the virtual absence of formal communication-based theory to guide the selection of research questions and the design of studies. These criticisms, however, appeared to focus not so much on inquiry by scholars in Communication as they did on studies of groups in general, the bulk of which had been conducted in Social Psychology and Sociology. Joseph McGrath and Irwin Altman (1966) had earlier made similar observations concerning group research within these and other disciplines. Given the small volume of research about groups that actually had been conducted by communication scholars prior to this point in time, the criticisms being raised within this field, to some degree, were misplaced.

The initial impact of the sorts of criticisms noted appeared to lie in serving as a stimulus for inquiry, as scholars increased their efforts to study a variety of issues relevant to group communication. Also contributing to the expansion of interest in groups, in general, were two important books published outside the communication field. One was Marvin Shaw's (1971) *Group Dynamics: The Psychology of Small Group Behavior,* and the other was Irving Janis's (1972) *Victims of Groupthink: A Psychological Study of Foreign-Policy Decisions and Fiascoes.*

Although Shaw intended his volume as a textbook, it was clearly one of the most comprehensive surveys of research on groups then in existence. More important from a communication perspective, Shaw's accent was largely on interaction in groups, and he introduced readers to studies showing that literally hundreds of factors demonstrably influence it and, in turn, are influenced by it. Janis focused more on decision making in groups but dealt with a large number of different variables that affect, or are affected by, the ways in which members of groups communicate with one another, including leadership, such group characteristics as cohesiveness, the various roles that participants enact, and the influence of external constraints. Because his work also examined some real-life group fiascoes, such as President Kennedy and his National Security Council's decision that led to the disastrous Bay of Pigs invasion, Janis also did much to establish the value of case studies of natural groups as a means of understanding group inputs, processes, and outcomes.

For whatever reasons, the 1970s witnessed a substantial increase in studies of groups, especially the communicative aspects of them. John Cragan and David Wright (1980) provide a reasonably complete summary of them. Mention here of some of the different types of topics and issues addressed, however, will give the reader a good flavor of the period.

During the 1970s, a number of scholars began to show an interest in the communicative aspects of group leadership (e.g., Baird, 1977; Bormann, Pratt, & Putnam, 1978; Gouran, 1970a; Knutson & Holdridge, 1975; Lumsden, 1974; Sargent & Miller, 1971; Schultz, 1974, 1978; Yerby, 1975; see Pavitt, Chapter 12, this volume, regarding the group communication-leadership relationship); however, the studies varied considerably with regard to the issues addressed. Bormann et al. (1978), for instance, looked at males' responses to females' dominance (as manifested in their communicative behavior) in groups, whereas Sargent and Miller (1971) attempted to determine those aspects of communicative behavior that distinguish various styles of leadership, and Schultz (1974, 1978) was concerned with types of communicative behavior that predict leadership emergence. Other scholars were concerned with the influence of specific communication variables on outcomes—notably, consensus and group member satisfaction, and, to a lesser extent, group decision-making effectiveness (e.g., Bell, 1974, 1979; Bradley, 1978; Courtright, 1978; Gouran, 1973a; Gouran, Brown, & Henry, 1978; Jurma, 1979; Kline, 1970, 1972; Knutson, 1972; Leathers, 1972; Marr, 1974). Still others attempted to understand the processual nature of communication in groups as an unfolding, predictable sequence of activity (e.g., Ellis, 1979; Ellis & Fisher, 1975; Fisher, 1970a, 1970b; Gouran & Baird, 1972; Jablin, Seibold, & Sorenson, 1977; Leathers, 1971; Mabry, 1975a, 1975b, 1975c; Stech, 1970), while also considering some of the measurement problems associated with conducting such research (Gouran & Whitehead, 1971). Arthur Bochner (1974), in particular, identified many measurement problems that constituted threats to the validity of published research, such as the lack of similarity in group tasks and questionable levels of reliability in the content coding of communicative acts, not to mention ways of estimating it. Bochner led others to show greater sensitivity to important aspects of research design, especially with regard to the analysis of group interaction and the interpretation of pertinent data.

Most of the studies cited above were quantitative, laboratory investigations of zero-history groups that continued the "variable-analytic" tradition of studying the effects of one variable on another (or, at least, the interrelationships among a highly limited number of independent and dependent variables) against which one critic (Bormann, 1970) had inveighed strongly. The decade, however, was not without departures from this tradition. Beginning to emerge were case studies of natural groups that focused on explaining such phenomena as group development, such as Chesebro, Cragan, and McCullough's (1973) investigation of a consciousness-raising group; failures in decision making, including Gouran's

(1976) examination of the communicative behavior of President Nixon and his inner circle in the Watergate affair; and leadership, for example, Wood's (1977) identification of adaptive communicative behavior by two leaders in a university administration group. Also emerging were more sophisticated, elaborate, and generally applicable coding schemes for the classification of group interaction, such as those developed and utilized by Ellis and Fisher (1975), Fisher (1970a), Leathers (1971), Mabry (1975b), and Stech (1970).

Changes in methodological procedures were not the only ones in evidence. Responses to criticisms concerning the lack of theory also began to surface. Dennis Gouran (1973b), for example, developed a metatheoretical perspective showing possible connections among contexts of group interaction, functions of communicative behavior, and group outcomes. This work helped to provide grounding for the later development of the Functional Theory perspective on group process. B. Aubrey Fisher and Leonard Hawes (1971) generated a grounded model of interactional sequences in groups—the Interact Systems Model—that proved to be useful in uncovering the level of predictability one can expect in various types of group discussions, but especially in task-oriented groups (in this volume, see Chapters 2 [Poole], 3 [Mabry], and 12 [Pavitt]). Their work laid important foundations for subsequent fleshing out of the developmental perspective.

The impact of these efforts and others, however, was not immediate. For the most part, scholars continued to formulate and conduct research projects on the basis of largely idiosyncratic considerations, albeit that the studies exhibited a general influence of the Systems Perspective. Still, when all is said and done, growth in the sheer amount of inquiry was the most striking and important achievement during this decade. It awakened others interested in the study of communication in groups to the substantial possibilities open to them and, in addition, called attention to necessary safeguards in conducting inquiries in traditional ways and to some alternative methodologies available for doing research.

Despite the achievements of the 1970s, a problem with the splurge of interest was that it complicated efforts to synthesize knowledge and to develop theories into which disparate information could be integrated. The idiosyncratic approach to group communication research continued throughout much of the decade, notwithstanding the fact that several critics, as mentioned above, had expressed dismay in the early 1970s over the lack of theory and integratability of extant research findings. Their voices did not go unheeded in the long term, however, and by the 1980s, these concerns were addressed in the explosion of theories about communication in groups.

ADVANCEMENT IN THEORIES: THE 1980s

The 1980s saw sustained interest in the study of communication in groups and a volume of research activity that exceeded even the dramatic increase in the 1970s over that which characterized earlier decades. Cragan and Wright (1990) noted seven lines of research, including criticism of the field, for the period and summarized nearly 90 studies dealing with various aspects of groups published in communication journals. Three of these they characterized as representing "traditional" lines: leadership, pedagogy, and discussion. Although not new, three others—communication variables affecting group outcomes, the process of communication in groups, and communication variables studied in natural and laboratory group settings—reflected less of the earlier pedagogical concern with how better to prepare individuals for participation in groups and more of a concern with understanding how groups function.

Many different topics were studied by scholars, including deviance and conformity (Alderton, 1980; Andrews, 1985; Bradley, 1980; Gouran & Andrews, 1984; Gouran, Ketrow, Spear, & Metzger, 1984), conflict (Baxter, 1982; Wall, Galanes, & Love, 1987; Wall & Nolan, 1987), account analysis (Geist & Chandler, 1984; Tompkins & Cheney, 1983), choice shifts (Alderton, 1982; Alderton & Frey, 1983; Boster & Hale, 1989; Boster & Mayer, 1984; Boster, Mayer, Hunter, & Hale, 1980; Cline & Cline, 1980; Kellermann & Jarboe, 1987; Mayer, 1985; also see the extensive review by Seibold & Meyers, 1986, on social influence in groups), consensus (DeStephen, 1983a, 1983b; DeStephen & Hirokawa, 1988; Sigman, 1984), leadership (Alderton & Jurma, 1980; Barge, 1989; Bunyi & Andrews, 1985; Owen, 1986; Schultz, 1980, 1982; Smith & Powell, 1988; Sorenson & Savage, 1989; Spillman, Spillman, & Reinking, 1981), group discussion procedures (Burleson, Levine, & Samter, 1984; Jarboe, 1988; Putnam, 1982; see Sunwolf & Seibold, Chapter 15, this volume), quality circles (Stohl, 1986, 1987; Stohl & Jennings, 1988), and argument (Canary, Brossmann, & Seibold, 1987; Frey, 1989; Schultz, 1982, 1986; Schultz & Anderson, 1984; Seibold, Canary, & Ratledge, 1983; Seibold, McPhee, Poole, Tanita, & Canary, 1981; see the critical assessment by Alderton & Frey, 1986).

Many of the studies cited either were exploratory in nature or drew on theory in cognate disciplines. Moreover, as was the case in the 1970s, even when they dealt with the same general topic, they did not consistently address common sets of issues or concerns. Alderton and Jurma (1980), for instance, were interested in the relationship of leaders' task-related communication as mediated by biological sex to group members' satisfaction, whereas Spillman et al. (1981) were concerned with how communication contributes to leadership emergence as a function of both biological sex and psychological gender orientation. Similarly, whereas Seibold and colleagues (1981) focused on describing how arguments in decision-making group discussions develop, Schultz (1982, 1986) attempted to determine how argumentativeness as a behavioral trait affects group members' perceptions of emergent leadership.

Although not identified as a line of research by Cragan and Wright (1990), the measurement of the characteristics of interaction continued to receive attention. Among those advancing the measurement of interaction by developing new coding schemes were Hirokawa (1982b, 1983a), Poole (1981, 1983b), Poole and Folger (1981), Poole and Roth (1989a, 1989b), Putnam (1983), and Seibold et al. (1981). These coding schemes also showed better theoretical grounding, especially in respect to being guided by Functional, Developmental, and Structuration Theory.

Most important, emergent programs of research began to reflect substantive theoretical developments. There had been enough individuals doing programmatic research in the 1970s and early 1980s that the cumulative effects of their efforts, however exploratory, permitted the formulation of theories, or, at least, general theoretical perspectives. Four that emerged, underwent periodic revision and refinement, became increasingly formal in structure, and seemed to exert considerable continuing influence on inquiry into communication in groups well into the late 1990s were Functional Theory, Developmental Theory, Structuration Theory, and Symbolic Convergence Theory. A fifth, Socio-Egocentric Theory, also came into existence during the 1980s; however, it served more as a challenge to presumptions of the first four, which are the primary focus of this section of the chapter (see also Poole's coverage of these and other theories of group communication in Chapter 2 of this volume).

The first two theories had their origins in research that occurred in the 1960s and 1970s focusing on particular characteristics of group interaction and their consequences. Those associated with Functional Theory tended to be concerned with explaining how interaction affects group outcomes—especially the quality of decisions and effectiveness of solutions to problems. Those linked to Developmental Theory were more interested in how group interaction unfolds and shapes itself over time. Structuration Theory, originally developed by the prominent social theorist Anthony Giddens (1976, 1979), was appropriated for the study of communication in groups and shared some concerns addressed by Developmental Theory. It differed, however, in its inclusion of internal factors (rules and resources) that shape and are shaped by patterns of group interaction, as well as its identification of structures as the generative mechanisms underlying interaction in groups. Symbolic Convergence Theory reflected a broader interest in processes of meaning construction that originate at the dyadic and group level and culminate—and even influence occurrences—at the organizational, institutional, and societal levels. Socio-Egocentric Theory emerged as a result of questions concerning how one can know that what participants in groups say has impact and posits conditions under which the presumption that it does not applies—specifically, the content of all utterances is vacuous and the exclusive function of utterances is to regulate turn-taking.

Functional Theory received considerable impetus in a study by Hirokawa (1980), who identified communication-based reasons for differences in the performance of effective and ineffective decision-making groups, especially those related to the communicative accomplishment of specified task requirements. The basic features of the theory were subsequently articulated in greater detail by Gouran and Hirokawa (1983), Gouran (1985, 1988), and Hirokawa and Scheerhorn (1986). The basic premise of this theory is that groups have a greater likelihood of reaching appropriate and high-quality, or otherwise effective, decisions under circumstances in which communication serves to ensure that essential task requirements are satisfied (see Hirokawa & Salazar, Chapter 7, this volume). These requirements, for the most part, represent adaptations of the Dewey (1910) model of reflective thinking discussed previously.

As Functional Theory was evolving during the 1980s, it generated a great deal of research, most of which was conducted by Hirokawa and his associates (see, for example, Hirokawa, 1982a, 1982b, 1983a, 1983b, 1985, 1987, 1988; Hirokawa, Ice, & Cook,

1988; Hirokawa & Pace, 1983). The evidence from these studies provided support for the theory, albeit not consistently. Part of the problem was that how well communication serves such functions, as opposed to having only a surface-level appearance of serving them (i.e., merely being correlated with them as opposed to explaining them), unfortunately did not receive sufficient attention. The theory did, however, prove to have rather considerable utility in accounting for failures of decision-making groups in case studies of natural groups, such as the one conducted by Gouran (1984) on the Watergate affair and two others dealing with the space shuttle *Challenger* disaster (Gouran, Hirokawa, & Martz, 1986; Hirokawa, Gouran, & Martz, 1988).

Developmental Theory arose, in part, as a continuation of interest in earlier research on developmental stages of group interaction, in which a major presumption had been that communication in groups unfolds in some kind of identifiable linear progression (see, for example, Bales & Strodtbeck, 1951; Bennis & Shepard, 1956; Fisher, 1970a, 1970b; Tuckman, 1965)—a view that was still in evidence in some research in the 1980s (e.g., Bell, 1982), although one that was called into question by Scheidel and Crowell's (1964, 1966) previously cited research. Influenced in part by Scheidel and Crowell's work, Poole (1981, 1983a, 1983b, 1983c) challenged this assumption in a series of investigations that compared linear and multiple sequence models—which entail the view that group interaction progresses in many different fashions—and produced substantial evidence that the latter types are more accurate representations of the reality of group interaction (in this volume, see Chapter 2, by Poole; Chapter 3, by Mabry; and Chapter 6, by Anderson, Riddle, and Martin).

This research was paralleled by efforts by Poole and his associates (see, for example, Poole & Doelger, 1986; Poole, McPhee, & Seibold, 1982; Poole & Roth, 1989a, 1989b; Poole, Seibold, & McPhee, 1985, 1986; see also Poole, Chapter 2, this volume) to ground research findings about group development in

Structuration Theory. This line of research received added support from work not directly emanating from Structuration Theory, for example, Fisher and Stutman's (1987) investigation of critical events in group decision-making discussions and Hirokawa's (1985) comparison of group decisional outcomes as a function of imposed discussion formats.

As applied to groups and as mentioned above, Structuration Theory offers an evolutionary view of interaction in which underlying "structures" (defined as combinations of rules and resources that group members have available to them) affect the surface behavior of group members (that is, their communicative behavior), which, in turn, results in alterations of structures. Poole, Seibold, and McPhee (1996) characterize "structuration" as *the process by which systems are produced and reproduced through members' use of rules and resources*" (p. 117), where a "system" is a "social entity . . . pursuing various practices that give rise to observable patterns of relations" (p. 117). A major contribution of Structuration Theory, as it emerged in the 1980s, then, was to illuminate ways in which interaction in groups constrains and is constrained by the rules and resources that contribute to the uniqueness and similarities of the members' working together, including how they coordinate activity, as well as how they produce and exchange messages.

Symbolic Convergence Theory, the last of the four major theories developed during this period to explain the influence of communication in groups, emerged from work that Ernest Bormann and his students were doing at the University of Minnesota in the 1960s and 1970s and which Bormann (1990) has explained in the text *Small Group Communication: Theory and Practice*. The theory received more formal articulation in the mid-1980s (see Bormann, 1985, 1986; see also Bormann, 1996).

The theory, as applied to groups, posits that members, especially at points in time in which they are releasing tension, tend to remove themselves from the here and now through the mechanism of "fantasy themes"; for example, they make jokes, project themselves and others into imaginary situations, tell stories, and otherwise engage in acts of imagination. Of the many such themes introduced, most have no longevity. In some instances, however, the themes and comments in which they are embedded elicit further related comments or embellishments and activate a process in which members begin to construct scenarios (some having villains and heroes) that provide the basis for an emergent group identity, complete with common values, beliefs, and rituals. Like Developmental and Structuration Theory, then, Symbolic Convergence Theory is concerned with the contingent aspects of group interaction. It has a more specific focus of interest, however, in those aspects of communication that come to define the culture of a group, how its members see themselves as a group, their vision of the future, and what they may do over time as a result of the type of identity and culture they create.

Symbolic Convergence Theory was at the base of a number of case studies of natural groups in the 1980s (see, for example, Cragan & Shields, 1981; Ford, 1989; Koester, 1982; Kroll, 1983; Olson, 1986). In most instances, the focus was on tracing the emergence of fantasy themes; these studies showed far less attention to the precise development of group cultures. An exception was a study by Eyo (1985), who was able to relate fantasy types to team and organizational goals—in particular, he found that achievement fantasies were better adapted to goals involving productivity and quality than were mastery fantasies. Nevertheless, the research cited and later research (e.g., Ball, 1994; Lesch, 1994) have proved useful in illustrating various aspects of the dynamics of groups as identity and culture develop and change.

Although Symbolic Convergence Theory did not stimulate as great a volume of research as the other theories mentioned, it did prove useful as an analytical tool and in helping scholars to interpret the outcomes of other studies not growing directly from the theory. Gouran (1986), for instance, related Symbolic Convergence Theory to the processes by which members of groups come to make collectively shared inferences that subsequently can affect the decisions they reach, which was consistent with earlier research he had done on group members' responses to unwarranted inferences advanced in discussions (see Gouran, 1983).

Although it is perhaps most clearly evident in the cases of Developmental Theory and Structuration Theory, all four of the theories just reviewed show the general influence of the Systems Perspective. Each assumes that the elements and attributes that characterize groups are interrelated, at least to some degree, in such ways that alterations in the elements or their properties have some type of demonstrable impact either on the properties of the other elements or on their relationships to one another. With Functional Theory, for instance, researchers presume that acts that serve particular functions will have different consequences from ones that do not. In Symbolic Convergence Theory, one fantasy that chains out along particular lines will not have the same impact on the emergent culture of a group as will another one that chains out along other lines. Despite the influence of the Systems Perspective, however, Functional Theory and Symbolic Convergence Theory fell short in comparison to Developmental Theory and Structuration Theory. Developmental Theory posited predictable sequences of communicative activity. Structuration Theory, as advanced by Poole and associates, moreover, had the added virtue of more careful articulation of the generative mechanisms that drive group "systems," specifically, the underlying structures.

A final theory that developed in the decade was introduced by Dean Hewes (1986). Hewes (1979) had earlier written a substantial critique of the traditional ways in which interaction was analyzed in the communication discipline and also questioned many of the assumptions about influence that group communication scholars had been making, for instance, that what a group member says at any given moment is partially, if not completely, determined by an immediately preceding comment or, perhaps and more important, that groups reach decisions different from the ones they would have reached in the absence of interaction. Hewes remained unconvinced throughout the first half of the 1980s that, despite their claims to the contrary, group scholars had actually demonstrated that communication makes a difference in respect to task-related outcomes. At least, he could not find evidence of sound warrants for the view that it does; hence, he developed what he referred to as the Socio-Egocentric Model of Group Decision-Making. The model predicts group decisions on the basis of prediscussion preferences of group members. Disconfirmation of the predictions presumably would constitute evidence of communicative influence, or, at least, particular sorts of disconfirmations could be taken as evidence of such influence.

The model, which Hewes (1996) subsequently revised, has received few specific tests of its predictions. It has, nevertheless, served—and continues to serve—as an important reminder to those who presume that communication automatically makes a difference in respect to the outcomes that groups achieve of the necessity for accumulating baseline data, particular departures from which would make more convincing the argument that communication has the sorts of consequences that both theorists and researchers have been prone to attribute to it.

In a kind of theoretical turnabout, it is noteworthy that Tschan (1995) has challenged the presumption that communication does not make a difference and has produced evidence showing the circumstances under which it does; however, his focus was on group productivity, as assessed in the performance of a mechanical assembly task, not decision making as such. More direct evidence has been presented by Hoffman and Kleinmann (1994), who discerned in a comparison of the Group Valence Model and the Valence Distribution Model (both of which have to do with the number of positive and negative statements group members express toward decision proposals; see Meyers & Brashers, Chapter 11, this volume) that communication does exert an influence on group decisional outcomes and that such outcomes cannot be accounted for adequately by prediscussion distributions of choice preferences of members of decision-making groups.

DIVERSIFICATION, APPLICATION, AND A GROWING CONCERN WITH CONTEXT: THE 1990s

The 1990s were a time of not only sustained but also growing activity among scholars interested in the study of communication in groups. This activity exhibited the dialectic of both stability and change. Stability was evidenced in continued efforts to develop and refine the theories that had emerged in the 1980s and to expand the research base related to them; the persistence of interest in topics, such as leadership and argumentation, that had received substantial attention in earlier periods; an abiding concern for improvement in the performance of groups and their members; and the lingering influence of the Systems Perspective, along with the quantitative methods of investigation to which it lent itself.

Change was evidenced in attention to topics and issues that had not been investigated previously, or, at least, not in any depth or with much frequency. Among the changes occurring was a reduction in the amount of inquiry devoted to group decision making and problem solving. This shift in focus ostensibly was the result of the sort of previously explained criticisms being advanced, as well as research by Scheerhorn, Geist, and Teboul (1994) showing that decision making was not even the communicative act engaged in the most by decision-making groups (information dissemination was). Questions also were raised concerning the appropriateness of rational models for explaining group decision making (see Beach, 1997; Canary, Brossmann, Brossmann, & Weger, 1995; and Zey, 1992, who prefers to characterize models of the type developed in Communication as "reasoned-choice" models). These questions reflected some of the earlier thinking of Nobel Laureate Herbert A. Simon (1978), who had questioned even the possibility of completely rational choice, as did Cohen, March, and Olsen (1972). Other changes included an increased appreciation for the diversity of existing types of groups; a concern with natural and, especially, bona fide groups, as well as naturalistic modes of inquiry; the emergence of more case studies of natural groups; and a substantial growth of interest in communication technology as related to group processes. In the latter case, a good deal of the work dealt with decision-making groups, but early on, outcomes received limited attention in favor of focusing on the description of interaction among members of groups using technology. The period also exhibited significant growth in book-length treatments of particular topics in group communication. The work that contributed to the stability and change of the present period is partially chronicled below.

As mentioned above, those associated with developments in theory during the 1980s continued to refine their thinking in the light of new evidence, critiques, and the issues raised by them. Functional Theory (see, for example, Gouran, 1991, 1994a; Gouran & Hirokawa, 1996; Gouran, Hirokawa, Julian, & Leatham, 1993; Gouran, Hirokawa, McGee, & Miller, 1994; Hirokawa, 1990, 1994; Pavitt, 1994; Salazar, Hirokawa, Propp, Julian, & Leatham, 1994) and Structuration Theory (e.g., Gouran, 1990; Holmes, 1992; Meyers & Seibold, 1990; Poole & Baldwin, 1996; Poole & Holmes, 1995; Poole et al., 1996) received increased attention in research and reached a greater level of conceptual specificity in respect to their propositional structures and the factors considered to be relevant to group decisional processes. Measurement of group interaction in research emanating from the Functional and Structurational perspectives also continued to show strong theoretical grounding (see, for example, Poole & DeSanctis, 1992; Poole, Holmes, Watson, & DeSanctis, 1993; Salazar et al., 1994).

Developmental Theory ceased to be concerned primarily with phase development, expanded its scope, and became the generic label for a family of theories and models concerned with patterns of interaction. Poole and Baldwin (1996) characterize these as phase, critical event, continuous, and social construction models (in this volume, see Chapters 2 [Poole] and 3 [Mabry]).

Both Symbolic Convergence Theory (see Bormann, 1996) and Socio-Egocentric Theory (see Hewes, 1996) also underwent revision. In the case of Symbolic Convergence Theory, the major advance was in its extension as an overarching framework for understanding the symbolic communities associated with more specific—what Bormann refers to as "special"—theories of communication in groups. The theory, moreover, was enriched by continued case studies, for example, Cragan and Shields's (1992) application of it to corporate strategic planning. Such developments were prompted, in part, by the sort of reviews and critiques of theory and research offered by Cragan and Wright (1990), Poole (1990), and Sykes (1990) at the beginning of the decade. These scholars, among other things, had noted fragmentation—specifically, the absence of a clearly focused set of questions—in scholarship, as well as a need for more concern with theory development and clearer accent on the ways in which both endogenous and exogenous variables influence interaction. Changes in Socio-Egocentric Theory lay more in the conceptual refinement of the arguments originally advanced in support of it and in its extension to "open tasks," that is, ones that have no determinate solutions.

Newly emergent in the 1990s was the Bona Fide Groups theoretical perspective. Originated by Linda Putnam and Cynthia Stohl (1990) and encouraged by such scholars as Frey (1994c), a strong proponent of the Naturalistic Paradigm explained below, this perspective sets groups within larger organizational, institutional, and social contexts and considers ways in which multiple roles and role boundaries (both their rigidity and fluidity), as well as shifting borders and group membership, influence the behavior of group members. The recognition of the interdependence of groups with their immediate context and the surrounding environment, as articulated by Putnam and Stohl, added important elements to scholars' understanding of communication in groups and affected the development of the theories previously discussed. Scholars working with Structuration Theory acknowledged the influence of exogenous influences on group processes (see Poole, 1996). Gouran and Hirokawa (1996) expanded Functional Theory to include consideration of the external constraints that act on the members of decision-making and problem-solving groups. Neither Developmental nor Functional Theory, however, dealt with such influences in as specific a way as the Bona Fide Groups Perspective. This perspective continued to evolve throughout the 1990s (see Putnam, 1994; Putnam & Stohl, 1994, 1996) and was a major stimulus to the significantly increased attention to natural groups that occurred, such as that shown by Sunwolf and Seibold (1998) in an investigation of the structuration of rules in jury decision making involving participants identified by processes actually used in juror selection.

Related to the Bona Fide Groups Perspective, but different in important respects, was another newly emergent perspective—at least, as applied to the study of communication in groups. This new perspective was the Naturalistic Paradigm mentioned above. Its first major proponent, Lawrence Frey (1994c), drew on work by Lincoln and Guba (1985) to challenge the historically dominant positivistic tradition in research concerned with communication in groups (e.g., variable-analytic research and laboratory studies of zero-history groups), along with its objectivist underpinnings, and then proceeded to characterize scholarly inquiry conducted from the Naturalistic perspective along several dimensions. These dimensions and specific positions include: research setting (in situ), ontological and epistemological lens (intersubjectivist), type of group (bona fide), research foci (e.g., creating and sustaining group identity, socializing new members, providing social support, developing high-quality interpersonal relationships, and making changes in group pro-

cesses, in addition to making decisions and solving problems), methodological procedures (phenomenologically oriented case studies employing qualitative methods, such as participant observation and in-depth interviews), and researchers' relationships with members of natural groups (viewed as a partnership and as a tool for social action, and based on sustained interactions). This paradigm set the stage for many subsequent studies in the 1990s.

A number of topics that attracted attention in the 1970s and 1980s remained on the research agendas of group communication scholars in the 1990s, in terms of both original studies and attempts to synthesize the literature. Among these were argument and social influence (Garlick & Mongeau, 1993; Gebhardt & Meyers, 1995; Meyers & Brashers, 1998; Seibold, Meyers, & Sunwolf, 1996), cohesiveness (Keyton & Springston, 1990), conflict (Jarboe & Witteman, 1996; Nicotera, 1994, 1997; Pace, 1990), decision quality and effectiveness (Graham, Papa, & McPherson, 1997; Mayer, Sonoda, & Gudykunst, 1997), deviance (Thameling & Andrews, 1992), gender (Andrews, 1992; Diliberto, 1992; Meyers & Brashers, 1994; Propp, 1995), leadership and superior/subordinate relationships (Barge, Schlueter, & Duncan, 1990; Jurma & Wright, 1990; Ketrow, 1991; Kolb, 1997; Pavitt & Sackaroff, 1990), phase development (Keyton, 1993), decision-making and problem-solving procedures (Hollingshead, 1998; Jarboe, 1996; Keyton, 1995; Lee, 1998; Pavitt, 1993b; Young, 1992), roles and role emergence (Salazar, 1996; Schultz, Ketrow, & Urban, 1995), group member satisfaction (Anderson & Martin, 1995; Keyton, 1991; Witteman, 1991), status effects on influence (Wittenbaum, 1998), and synergy and cooperative behavior (Sabourin & Geist, 1990; Salazar, 1995). Scholars also continued to discuss, critique, develop, and, in some cases, apply research methods for studying group communication (for example, Bormann, Bormann, & Harty, 1995; Cragan & Shields, 1995; Frey, 1994a, 1994c, 1995a; Jarboe, 1991; Keyton, 1995,

1997; Kreps, 1995). New to the literature was a concern with communication in children's groups (Keyton, 1994; Socha & Socha, 1994) and women's groups (Meyers & Brashers, 1994; Wyatt, 1993), and with listening as a factor in perceptions of leadership (Bechler & Johnson, 1995; Johnson & Bechler, 1997, 1998).

Although the potential importance of computer technology as an instrument of communication and support in groups had been recognized in the discipline of Management Information Systems since the early 1980s, this topic did not take much hold in communication scholarship until the 1990s. Once it did, however, it became a major object of attention (see Scott, Chapter 16, this volume). The two matters of greatest interest were electronic communication (computer-mediated communication, to be more specific) and group decision support systems (GDSSs), which combine "communication, computer, and decision technologies to facilitate decision making and related activities of work groups" (Poole, DeSanctis, Kirsch, & Jackson, 1995, p. 300). Studies to date have been both numerous and sophisticated (see, for example, Contractor & Seibold, 1993; Ferris, 1995; Poole & DeSanctis, 1990, 1992; Poole & Holmes, 1995; Poole et al., 1993; Sambamurthy, Poole, & Kelly, 1993; Walther, 1992, 1994; Walther, Anderson, & Park, 1994; Walther & Burgoon, 1992; Wheeler, Mennecke, & Scudder, 1993). Lacking in this body of scholarship has been sufficient attention to what may be the unique effects of technology on communication in groups and the outcomes they achieve; however, progress in that direction is beginning. Ferris's (1995) research on comparative modalities, for example, points to media preferences as a factor that may account for how group members relate to and use computer technology and, hence, to the outcomes they individually and collectively achieve.

Spurred by continuing critiques of the artificiality of laboratory groups and controlled environments, as well as limitations imposed by the type of tasks (researcher-created, objec-tive-answer tasks) typically studied by scholars interested in communication in groups (see, for example, critiques by Frey, 1994b; Propp & Kreps, 1994; Putnam, 1994; Putnam & Stohl, 1990, 1996; Scheerhorn et al., 1994; Stohl, 1995), the 1990s saw an increase in the volume of case studies of natural groups, even for understanding traditional interest in the relationship between communication and group decision making, in addition to a host of other topics, the value of which Gouran (1994b) discussed in an epilogue to Frey's (1994b) edited collection of original studies of natural groups. Case studies of the period were more wide ranging than those of the 1970s and 1980s, especially in respect to the types of groups investigated, the processes studied, and the methodologies employed. They covered such conventional topics as communication and group decision making related to involvement in Vietnam in the Kennedy Administration (Ball, 1990, 1994), but, increasingly, they explored new types of groups and topics, including the uses of parliamentary procedure in a community group (Weitzel & Geist, 1998), as well as the use of power and social influence in a city council (Barge & Keyton, 1994), gang communication (Conquergood, 1994), the communicative activities of a search committee for a university provost (Eisenberg, Murphy, & Andrews, 1998), and communication difficulties stemming from role definition/coordination problems in health-care teams (Berteotti & Seibold, 1994). Adelman and Frey (1997) even published a widely reviewed, award-winning book detailing the group communicative practices that help create and sustain community in a residential facility (Bonaventure House) for people living with AIDS. Methodologies within this body of research included participant observation by the researchers, interviewing of group members, members' self-reports collected via questionnaires, and textual analysis. In general, these studies had a strong ethnographic flavor.

By the 1990s, scholarship dealing with communication in groups had reached the point that those associated with the discipline were having substantial impact on the study of groups, even across other disciplines as a whole. Gouran and Shaw (1990), for instance, showed strong connections between work in Social Psychology and what communication scholars interested in groups were establishing, such as the communicative characteristics of leadership style and the ways in which communication serves to ensure that the requirements of group tasks are satisfied. Earlier reviews and syntheses, even those in Communication, had predominantly favored scholarship in disciplines other than Communication. One sees this influence, for instance, in the contrast between reviews of research related to gender and group processes published by J. E. Baird (1976) and Shimanoff and Jenkins (1996). The former drew almost exclusively on research published in Psychology, whereas the latter included a great deal of communication scholarship. Further evidence of the growing volume and significance of the efforts of group communication scholars was the dedication to the area of the Fall 1990 and Spring 1994 issues of *Communication Studies,* edited by Sykes and Frey, respectively, as well as the November, 1994, issue of *Small Group Research,* edited by Keyton and featuring contributions by Frey (1994c), Hirokawa (1994), and Pavitt (1994). One overview of such work was published in Japanese (see Gouran & Nishida, 1996).

Group communication scholarship also reached a point by the mid-1990s where scholars were beginning to publish more entire books on focused topics. This is not to suggest that there were no such books in the 1980s. Phillips and Wood (1984), for instance, published an edited collection of original essays on the subject of group consensus. Hirokawa and Poole (1986) also had published the first edition of the text *Communication and Group Decision-Making.* Of course, the decade had its share of textbooks drawing on relevant theory and the research literature. As in the case of other published surveys and syntheses during the 1980s, however, scholarship from other disciplines served as the principal source of resource material.

In addition to the case study by Adelman and Frey (1997) mentioned earlier, Barge (1994) and Northouse (1997) both published full-length treatments of leadership from a communication perspective. It was possible for Frey and Barge (1997), moreover, to produce an integrated edited textbook on decision-making groups from a predominantly communication perspective. Beyond an edited collection of case studies (Frey, 1994b) involving natural groups, Frey (1995b) also edited and published a collection of original research studies that applied new innovations in the facilitation of communication to natural groups and is currently working on a second edition of the 1994b collection that will feature case studies of communication processes in bona fide groups (Frey, in press). Miller and McKinney (1993) had earlier brought out an edited collection of original essays and studies related exclusively to communication in government commissions, such as the Warren Commission's investigation of the assassination of President Kennedy, the 1970 and 1985 presidential commissions on pornography that were to determine its effects and propose legislative means for dealing with them, and the Rogers Commission's inquiry into the causes of the *Challenger* disaster. Hirokawa and Poole (1996) published a second edition of their edited collection of essays on communication and group decision making; for the most part, the contributions were all new or were substantially different from those in the original 1986 edition. In each of these works, the amount of material by communication scholars referenced was substantially greater than was possible in earlier published collections, including the 1996 seventh edition of Cathcart, Samovar, and Henman's edited book titled *Small Group Communication: Theory & Practice,* a staple in the field, but one that nonetheless in earlier editions had a heavy concentration of previously published, as opposed to original, essays from scholars outside the field of Communication or communication scholars not based in group communication.

The 1990s, then, were a time when the study of group communication not only flourished but also advanced in many important ways. Previously emergent theories received substantive attention and underwent refinement and change; the Bona Fide Groups Perspective and the Naturalistic Paradigm came into their own and exerted a powerful influence on the types of groups and topics examined, as well as the types of inquiries used to examine them; new areas of inquiry opened; case studies expanded; studies of natural groups, with the attendant application of naturalistic research methods (for example, qualitative methods), appeared with increasing frequency; and scholarship, in general, was developed to the point where specialized treatments of various topics of interest from a predominantly communication perspective could be undertaken. Perhaps the most important development was that as the end of the decade drew near, communication scholars interested in groups had established a presence within the general field of Group Studies that they had not enjoyed previously.

DIRECTIONS: 2000 AND BEYOND

The future is always difficult to predict, let alone to influence. On the other hand, one can suggest some needs that it would be good for scholars interested in the study of communication in groups to address. Most of the specific suggestions for further research within particular areas covered in this volume are offered by the contributors. Other suggestions have been articulated in the recently published volume by Trent (1998), in which both Gouran (1998) and Poole (1998) address future needs in some detail. Some more general directions that emerge from the overview provided herein may be worth mentioning, however.

Given the sustained attention to Functional, Developmental, Structuration, Symbolic Convergence, and Socio-Egocentric Theory over the decades of the 1980s and 1990s, continued investigation of the implica-tions and predictions derived from these theories would be helpful in ensuring reasonable continuity in the progression of research and inquiry into the 21st century. Especially in need of greater research are Socio-Egocentric Theory and, to a lesser extent, perhaps, Symbolic Convergence Theory. At least to date, these two theories have not generated research in the same volume as Functional, Developmental, and Structuration Theory. In particular, the gauntlet thrown down by Socio-Egocentric Theory concerning whether communication makes a difference needs to be addressed.

Actually, Joseph Bonito and Andrea Hollingshead (1997), in their review of participation in groups, have brought together a considerable amount of scholarship suggesting that communication in groups is influential and have identified numerous respects in which it appears to be. Helpful to placing this scholarship in proper perspective is Charles Pavitt's (1993a) discussion of five different senses (no influence, influence through preference display, influence through information, influence through preference display and information, and influence through interaction) in which the matter of the impact of communication in groups has been and can be addressed.

Hewes (1996) has provided an excellent model, which poses the theoretical equivalent of a null hypothesis, that can be used to develop more meaningful tests of the extent to which communication in groups is influential. In combination with the species of influence noted by Pavitt and the variables Bonito and Hollingshead identified as relating to communication and the relationship of communicative behavior, in turn, to outcomes groups experience or achieve, the bases for fruitful research agendas exist and should be pursued. These and other such agendas are also implicit in the work that has emerged from the other four major theories previously reviewed, as well as in the more recent additions of the Bona Fide Groups Perspective and the Naturalistic Paradigm.

Among the topics in need of sustained inquiry is the effects of technology on group processes and outcomes. We have the capacity for people in groups to communicate with one another in a variety of new ways and in contexts involving their physical dispersement. Scholars have been looking into the potential of various technologies to affect the performance of groups but have only scratched the surface. Given the rapid developments in technology, this should be an area of high priority.

Another need is to begin looking at the longer-range impact of communication in groups, not only on members, but also on others who may be affected. We know little about the persisting effects of communication in groups on either members or others, particularly in respect to the ways in which it affects people's subsequent attitudes toward groups (such as the development of "group-hate"; see Frey, 1999; Keyton, Harmon, & Frey, 1996; Sorensen, 1981), motivations to participate in them, and future behavior, despite the fact that we have reason to believe, from the Bona Fide Groups Perspective, that prior group experiences bear some relationship to these matters.

Given that prior group experiences affect people, it is also important to do a better job of determining the effects of antecedents on group processes of interest. Antecedent variables—such as members' communicative predispositions (see Keyton & Frey, in press), interest in the task, attitudes toward the issues being discussed, and past successes and failures of groups in which participants have been members—continue to be an object of neglect, even though, as in the case of long-range effects of communication, there are good reasons for believing that these sources of influence affect what group members think and, hence, both what they say and how they say it in interactions with one another. In making messages in groups the central focus, we inadvertently may have eliminated consideration of some important factors that are instrumental in their formation, transmission, reception, and interpretation. Gouran (1994a, 1998) has

discussed this issue, but a research agenda has not as yet fully emerged.

A particularly important antecedent variable is the cultural background of group members. Too much of the research that has accumulated to date has been conducted within a narrow cultural framework, in which those studied have been largely white males from the middle class (see Wyatt, 1993, in press). With the rise of internationalism in business and politics, groups will increasingly have members of diverse cultural composition; thus, we need to know more about how cultural differences affect group interaction and outcomes.

That there is good reason to pursue research on cultural differences is suggested in a recent study of decision-making styles of representatives of five different countries by Yi (1997). Yi discovered that some differences one might expect from Hofstede's (1980; see also Hofstede & Bond, 1984) four dimensions of culture (individualism-collectivism, masculinity-femininity, power distance, and uncertainty avoidance), as well as discussions, such as the one by Cathcart and Cathcart (1996), of differences in patterns of behavior between cultural groups, do surface, but others do not. In some instances, intracultural differences were greater than cross-cultural differences. For those interested in cross-culturally oriented research, Lustig and Cassotta (1996) have laid out an agenda based on Hofstede's work in the areas of group leadership, conformity, and discussion processes that could keep researchers engaged for a substantial length of time. Haslett and Ruebush (Chapter 5, this volume) also offer specific directions for future research on the impact of culture and, more generally, diversity on communication in groups.

It would also be helpful if scholars were to continue exploring the types of variables in which they have been interested over the periods covered in this review. They would be well advised, however, to do so in the context of multivariate inquiries. If research has revealed anything, it is that communication processes, as they unfold in groups, are complex, with a high degree of interrelatedness among factors both internal and external to them. Richer understandings will emerge only when scholars show greater concern for such interconnections and states of interconnectedness. To date, Poole and his associates in their studies of structuration processes in groups have made possibly the most significant contributions to this end (for a summary and synthesis of the research supporting this generalization, see Poole et al., 1996). Other scholars would do well to follow the example set.

An especially inviting area for future research is group process procedures, such as those designed to facilitate group discussion, decision making, and problem solving. Procedures are integral to group interaction. Most of the research to date, however, has been published in disciplines other than Communication (see Jarboe, 1996), and it has not been particularly concerned with the connections to communicative behavior (for an exception, see the previously cited case studies on facilitating group communication in Frey, 1995b). We need to learn more about the ways in which communication constrains and is constrained by process procedures. That may, in the long run, help scholars to eliminate some of the anomalies associated with communication-outcome relationships. To this end, the agenda that Susan Jarboe (1996) has articulated presents an excellent starting point, as do the critical reviews of literature and suggestions for future research stemming from the Function Impact Model proposed by Sunwolf and Seibold (Chapter 15, this volume).

Scholars could and should venture even farther than they already have into the realm of natural and bona fide groups. Educational groups engaged in cooperative learning, for instance, offer a potentially fruitful area of research (see Allen & Plax, Chapter 18, this volume). Additionally, in spite of all the major trials that have been in the news recently, it is remarkable how little our field has contributed to a knowledge of legal process and jury decision making. One sees a conspicuous absence of references to research on these topics

by communication scholars in such reviews as those published by Abbott, Hall, and Linville (1993) and Krivoshey (1994). We should be doing more with this area of study.

The same applies to the political and legislative realms. With the easy accessibility to government committee hearings, scholars should be taking advantage of this resource to learn more about external sources of influence on group deliberative processes, particularly in respect to problem analysis and solution generation. In the light of major achievements in medicine and related delivery systems, which often come about as a result of team efforts, it also would be of value to learn more about health- and health-care related group decision making, as well as its ethical ramifications. Finally, it is also surprising that communication scholars interested in groups and group processes have almost completely neglected cults as an area of study, with one exception being Lesch's (1994) study of a coven of witches. Historically, attention to cults has been the province of the Sociology of Religion (see, for example, Collins, 1991; Lewis, 1996; Saliba, 1996). Given the role that communication (especially that of charismatic leaders; see Pavitt, Chapter 12, this volume) plays in shaping cult members' unquestioned commitment and loyalty, however, there is much potentially to be learned. Access, admittedly, poses a problem for inquiry, but this does not appear to be insurmountable.

These are but a few of the possibilities for research—and there are many more articulated throughout this volume—that will not only sustain group communication as an area of scholarly inquiry well into the 21st century but also could be consequential for what occurs in people's social and professional lives. The work that has accumulated to date and that has been typified in this necessarily abbreviated review provides an excellent foundation from which to launch the types of initiatives mentioned. The field is, thus, well positioned to move in these directions. What remains is for those interested to take the necessary steps.

REFERENCES

Abbott, W. F., Hall, F., & Linville, E. (1993). *Jury research: A review and bibliography*. Philadelphia: American Law Institute American Bar Association Committee on Continuing Professional Education.

Adelman, M. B., & Frey, L. R. (1997). *The fragile community: Living together with AIDS*. Mahwah, NJ: Lawrence Erlbaum.

Alderton, S. (1980). Attributions of responsibility for socially deviant behavior in decision-making discussions as a function of situation and locus of control of attributor. *Central States Speech Journal, 31*, 117-127.

Alderton, S. M. (1982). Locus of control-based argumentation as a predictor of group polarization. *Communication Quarterly, 30*, 381-387.

Alderton, S. M., & Frey, L. R. (1983). Effects of reactions to arguments on group outcome: The case of group polarization. *Central States Speech Journal, 34*, 88-95.

Alderton, S. M., & Frey, L. R. (1986). Argumentation in small group decision-making. In R. Y. Hirokawa & M. S. Poole (Eds.), *Communication and group decision-making* (pp. 157-173). Beverly Hill, CA: Sage.

Alderton, S. M., & Jurma, W. E. (1980). Genderless/gender-related task leader communication and group satisfaction: A test of two hypotheses. *Southern Speech Communication Journal, 46*, 48-60.

Allison, R. (1939). Changing concepts in the meaning and values of group discussion. *Quarterly Journal of Speech, 25*, 117-120.

Anderson, C. M., & Martin, M. M. (1995). The effects of communication motives, interaction involvement, and loneliness on satisfaction: A model of small groups. *Small Group Research, 26*, 118-137.

Andrews, P. H. (1985). Ego-involvement, self-monitoring, and conformity in small groups: A communication analysis. *Central States Speech Journal, 36*, 51-61.

Andrews, P. H. (1992). Sex and gender differences in group communication: Impact on the facilitation process. *Small Group Research, 23*, 74-94.

Auer, J. J. (1939). Tools of social inquiry: Argumentation, discussion and debate. *Quarterly Journal of Speech, 25*, 533-539.

Baird, A. C. (1928). *Public discussion and debate*. Boston: Ginn.

Baird, J. E., Jr. (1976). Sex differences in group communication: A review of relevant research. *Quarterly Journal of Speech, 62*, 179-192.

Baird, J. E., Jr. (1977). Some nonverbal elements of leadership emergence. *Southern Speech Communication Journal, 42*, 352-361.

Bales, R. F. (1950). *Interaction process analysis: A method for the study of small groups*. Cambridge, MA: Addison-Wesley.

Bales, R. F. (1970). *Personality and interpersonal behavior*. New York: Holt, Rinehart & Winston.

Bales, R. F., & Cohen, S. P. (with Williamson, S. A.). (1979). *SYMLOG: A system for the multiple level observation of groups*. New York: Free Press.

Bales, R. F., & Strodtbeck, F. L. (1951). Phases in group problem solving. *Journal of Abnormal and Social Psychology, 46*, 485-495.

Bales, R. F., Strodtbeck, F. L., Mills, T. M., & Roseborough, M. E. (1951). Channels of communication in small groups. *American Sociological Review, 16*, 461-468.

Ball, M. A. (1990). A case study of the Kennedy administration's decision-making concerning the Diem coup of November, 1963. *Western Journal of Speech Communication, 54*, 557-574.

Ball, M. A. (1994). Vacillating about Vietnam: Secrecy, duplicity, and confusion in the communication of President Kennedy and his advisors. In L. R. Frey (Ed.), *Group communication in context: Studies of natural groups* (pp. 181-198). Hillsdale, NJ: Lawrence Erlbaum.

Bane, C. L. (1958). Evaluation of training in discussion. *Western Speech, 22*, 148-153.

Barge, J. K. (1989). Leadership as medium: A leaderless group discussion model. *Communication Quarterly, 37*, 237-247.

Barge, J. K. (1994). *Leadership: Communication skills for organizations and groups*. New York: St. Martin's.

Barge, J. K., & Keyton, J. (1994). Contextualizing power and social influence in groups. In L. R. Frey (Ed.), *Group communication in context: Studies of natural groups* (pp. 85-105). Hillsdale, NJ: Lawrence Erlbaum.

Barge, J. K., Schlueter, D. W., & Duncan, G. (1990). Task structure as a moderator of task and relational skills. *Communication Studies, 41*, 1-18.

Barnlund, D. C. (1955). Experiments in leadership training for decision-making discussion groups. *Speech Monographs, 22*, 1-14.

Baxter, L. A. (1982). Conflict management: An episodic approach. *Small Group Behavior, 13*, 23-42.

Bayless, O. L. (1967). An alternate pattern for problem-solving discussion. *Journal of Communication, 17*, 188-197.

Beach, L. R. (1997). *The psychology of decision making: People in organizations*. Thousand Oaks, CA: Sage.

Bechler, C., & Johnson, S. D. (1995). Leadership and listening: A study of member perceptions. *Small Group Research, 26*, 77-85.

Bell, M. A. (1974). The effects of substantive and affective conflict in problem-solving groups. *Speech Monographs, 41*, 19-23.

Bell, M. A. (1979). The effects of substantive and affective verbal conflict on the quality of decisions of small problem-solving groups. *Central States Speech Journal, 30*, 75-82.

Bell, M. A. (1982). Phases in group problem-solving. *Small Group Behavior, 13*, 475-495.

Bennis, W. G., & Shepard, H. A. (1956). A theory of group development. *Human Relations, 9*, 415-437.

Berg, D. M. (1967). A descriptive analysis of the distribution and duration of themes discussed by small task-oriented groups. *Speech Monographs, 34*, 172-175.

Bergmann, G. (1957). *Philosophy of science*. Madison: University of Wisconsin Press.

Berteotti, C. R., & Seibold, D. R. (1994). Coordination and role-definition problems in health-care teams: A hospice case study. In L. R. Frey (Ed.), *Group communication in context: Studies of natural groups* (pp. 107-131). Hillsdale, NJ: Lawrence Erlbaum.

Black, E. B. (1955). A consideration of the rhetorical causes of breakdown in discussion. *Speech Monographs, 22,* 15-19.

Bochner, A. P. (1974). Special reports: Task and instrumentation variables as factors jeopardizing the validity of published group communication research, 1970-1971. *Speech Monographs, 41,* 169-178.

Bonito, J. A., & Hollingshead, A. B. (1997). Participation in small groups. In B. R. Burleson (Ed.), *Communication yearbook 20* (pp. 227-261). Thousand Oaks, CA: Sage.

Bormann, E. G. (1970). The paradox and promise of small group research. *Speech Monographs, 37,* 211-217.

Bormann, E. G. (1985). Symbolic convergence theory: A communication formulation. *Journal of Communication, 35*(4), 128-138.

Bormann, E. G. (1986). Symbolic convergence theory and communication in group decision-making. In R. Y. Hirokawa & M. S. Poole (Eds.), *Communication and group decision-making* (pp. 219-236). Beverly Hills, CA: Sage.

Bormann, E. G. (1990). *Small group communication: Theory and practice* (3rd ed.). New York: Harper & Row.

Bormann, E. G. (1996). Symbolic convergence theory and communication in group decision making. In R. Y. Hirokawa & M. S. Poole (Eds.), *Communication and group decision making* (2nd ed., pp. 81-113). Thousand Oaks, CA: Sage.

Bormann, E. G., Bormann, E., & Harty, K. C. (1995). Using symbolic convergence theory and focus group interviews to develop communication designed to stop teenage use of tobacco. In L. R. Frey (Ed.), *Innovations in group facilitation: Applications in natural settings* (pp. 200-232). Cresskill, NJ: Hampton.

Bormann, E. G., Pratt, J., & Putnam, L. L. (1978). Power, authority, and sex: Male response to female leadership. *Communication Monographs, 45,* 119-155.

Boster, F. J., & Hale, J. L. (1989). Response scale ambiguity as a moderator of choice shift. *Communication Research, 16,* 532-551.

Boster, F. J., & Mayer, M. (1984). Choice shifts: Argument qualities or social comparisons. In R. N. Bostrom (Ed.), *Communication yearbook 8* (pp. 93-410). Beverly Hills, CA: Sage.

Boster, F. J., Mayer, M. E., Hunter, J. E., & Hale, G. E. (1980). Expanding the persuasive arguments explanation of the polarity shift: A linear discrepancy model. In D. Nimmo (Ed.), *Communication yearbook 4* (pp. 165-176). New Brunswick, NJ: Transaction Books.

Bradley, P. H. (1978). Power, status, and upward communication in small decision-making groups. *Communication Monographs, 45,* 33-43.

Bradley, P. H. (1980). Sex, competence, and opinion deviation: An expectation states approach. *Communication Monographs, 47,* 101-110.

Brandenburg, E. (1950). Public discussion as a "propaganda" technique. *Central States Speech Journal, 1,* 29-32.

Brilhart, J. K. (1960). Fostering group thinking. *Today's Speech, 8*(2), 9-11, 19.

Brilhart, J. K., & Jochem, L. M. (1964). Effects of different patterns on outcomes of problem-solving discussion. *Journal of Applied Psychology, 48,* 175-179.

Bunyi, J. M., & Andrews, P. H. (1985). Gender and leadership emergence: An experimental study. *Southern Speech Communication Journal, 50,* 246-260.

Burleson, B. R., Levine, B. J., & Samter, W. (1984). Decision-making procedure and decision quality. *Human Communication Research, 10,* 557-574.

Canary, D. J., Brossmann, B. G., & Seibold, D. R. (1987). Argument structures in decision-making groups. *Southern Speech Communication Journal, 53,* 18-37.

Canary, D. J., Brossmann, J. E., Brossmann, B. G., & Weger, H., Jr. (1995). Toward a theory of minimally rational argument: Analyses of episode-specific effects of argument structures. *Communication Monographs, 62,* 182-212.

Cathcart, R., & Cathcart, D. (1996). Group lifetimes: Japanese and American versions. In R. S. Cathcart, L. A. Samovar, & L. D. Henman (Eds.), *Small group communication: Theory & practice* (7th ed., pp. 345-355). Madison, WI: Brown & Benchmark.

Cathcart, R. S., Samovar, L. A., & Henman, L. D. (Eds.). (1996). *Small group communication: Theory & practice* (7th ed.). Madison, WI: Brown & Benchmark.

Cattell, R. B. (1948). Concepts and methods in the measurement of group syntality. *Psychological Monographs, 55,* 48-63.

Cattell, R. B. (1951a). Determining syntality dimension as a basis for morale and leadership measurement. In H. Guetzkow (Ed.), *Groups, leadership and men* (pp. 16-27). Pittsburgh, PA: Carnegie Press.

Cattell, R. B. (1951b). New concepts for measuring leadership, in terms of group syntality. *Human Relations, 4,* 161-184.

Chesebro, J. W., Cragan, J. F., & McCullough, P. (1973). The small group technique of the radical revolutionary: A synthetic study of consciousness raising. *Speech Monographs, 40,* 136-146.

Cline, R. J., & Cline, T. R. (1980). A structural analysis of risky-shift and cautious-shift discussions: The diffusion of responsibility theory. *Communication Quarterly, 28,* 26-36.

Cohen, H. (1994). *The history of Speech Communication: The emergence of a discipline, 1914–1945.* Annandale, VA: Speech Communication Association.

Cohen, M. D., March, J. G., & Olsen, P. J. (1972). A garbage can model of organizational choice. *Administrative Science Quarterly, 17,* 1-25.

Collins, J. J. (1991). *The cult experience: An overview of cults, their traditions, and why people join them.* Springfield, IL: Charles C Thomas.

Conquergood, D. (1994). Homeboys and hoods: Gang communication and cultural space. In L. R. Frey (Ed.), *Group communication in context: Studies of natural groups* (pp. 23-55). Hillsdale, NJ: Lawrence Erlbaum.

Contractor, N. S., & Seibold, D. R. (1993). Theoretical frameworks for the structuring of processes in group decision support systems: Adaptive structuration theory and self-organizing systems theory. *Human Communication Research, 19,* 528-563.

Courtright, J. A. (1978). A laboratory investigation of groupthink. *Communication Monographs, 45,* 229-246.

Cragan, J. F., & Shields, D. C. (1981). *Applied communication research: A dramatistic approach.* Prospect Heights, IL: Waveland.

Cragan, J. F., & Shields, D. C. (1992). The use of symbolic convergence theory in corporate strategic planning: A case study. *Journal of Applied Communication Research, 20,* 199-218.

Cragan, J. F., & Shields, D. C. (1995). Using SCT-based focus group interviews to do applied communication research. In L. R. Frey (Ed.), *Innovations in group facilitation: Applications in natural settings* (pp. 233-256). Cresskill, NJ: Hampton.

Cragan, J. F., & Wright, D. W. (1980). Small group communication of the 1970's: A synthesis and critique of the field. *Central States Speech Journal, 31,* 197-213.

Cragan, J. F., & Wright, D. W. (1990). Small group communication of the 1980s: A synthesis and critique of the field. *Communication Studies, 41,* 212-236.

Crowell, L. (1958). Group- or problem-centered discussion? *Western Speech, 22,* 134-137.

Crowell, L., Katcher, A., & Miyamoto, S. F. (1955). Self-concepts of communication skill and performance in small group discussions. *Speech Monographs, 22,* 20-27.

DeStephen, R. S. (1983a). Group interaction differences between high and low consensus groups. *Western Journal of Speech Communication, 47,* 340-363.

DeStephen, R. S. (1983b). High and low consensus groups: A content and relational interaction analysis. *Small Group Behavior, 14,* 143-162.

DeStephen, R. S., & Hirokawa, R. Y. (1988). Small group consensus: Stability of group support of the decision, task process, and group relationships. *Small Group Behavior, 19,* 227-239.

Dewey, J. (1910). *How we think.* Boston: D. C. Heath.

Dickens, M. (1955). A statistical formula to quantify the "spread of participation" in group discussion. *Speech Monographs, 22,* 28-30.

Diliberto, J. A. (1992). A communication study of possible relationships between psychological sex type and decision-making effectiveness. *Small Group Research, 23,* 379-407.

Ehninger, D. (1943). A logic of discussion method. *Quarterly Journal of Speech, 29,* 163-167.

Eisenberg, E. M., Murphy, A., & Andrews, L. (1998). Openness and decision making in the search for a university provost. *Communication Monographs, 65,* 1-23.

Ellis, D. G. (1979). Relational control in two group systems. *Communication Monographs, 46,* 153-166.

Ellis, D. G., & Fisher, B. A. (1975). Phases of conflict in small group development: A Markov analysis. *Human Communication Research, 1,* 195-212.

Eyo, B. (1985). *Quality circles, involvement teams, and participative management in modern business culture: Study of rhetorical visions of line unit managers, employees, and facilitators.* Unpublished doctoral dissertation, University of Minnesota, Minneapolis.

Ferris, S. T. (1995). *An investigation of a role of computer-mediated communication as a media choice in the facilitation of task performance in small groups.* Unpublished doctoral dissertation, The Pennsylvania State University, University Park.

Fisher, B. A. (1970a). Decision emergence: Phases in group decision-making. *Speech Monographs, 37,* 53-66.

Fisher, B. A. (1970b). The process of decision modification in small discussion groups. *Journal of Communication, 20,* 51-64.

Fisher, B. A. (1971). Communication research and the task-oriented group. *Journal of Communication, 21,* 136-149.

Fisher, B. A. (1974). *Small group decision making: Communication and the group process.* New York: McGraw-Hill.

Fisher, B. A., & Hawes, L. C. (1971). An interact system model: Generating a grounded theory of small groups. *Quarterly Journal of Speech, 57,* 444-453.

Fisher, B. A., & Stutman, R. K. (1987). An assessment of group trajectories: Analyzing developmental breakpoints. *Communication Quarterly, 35,* 105-124.

Ford, L. A. (1989). Fetching good out of evil in AA: A Bormannean fantasy theme analysis of *The Big Book* of Alcoholics Anonymous. *Communication Quarterly, 37,* 1-15.

Frey, L. R. (1989). Exploring the input-throughput-output relationship in small groups: Communicative predispositions, argumentation and leadership. *World Communication, 18,* 43-70.

Frey, L. R. (1994a). Call and response: The challenge of conducting research on communication in natural groups. In L. R. Frey (Ed.), *Group communication in context: Studies of natural groups* (pp. 293-304). Hillsdale, NJ: Lawrence Erlbaum.

Frey, L. R. (Ed.). (1994b). *Group communication in context: Studies of natural groups.* Hillsdale, NJ: Lawrence Erlbaum.

Frey, L. R. (1994c). The naturalistic paradigm: Studying small groups in the postmodern era. *Small Group Research, 25,* 551-577.

Frey, L. R. (1995a). Applied communication research on group facilitation in natural settings. In L. R. Frey (Ed.), *Innovations in group facilitation: Applications in natural settings* (pp. 1-23). Cresskill, NJ: Hampton.

Frey, L. R. (Ed.). (1995b). *Innovations in group facilitation: Applications in natural settings.* Cresskill, NJ: Hampton.

Frey, L. R. (1996). Remembering and "re-membering": A history of theory and research on communication and group decision making. In R. Y. Hirokawa & M. S. Poole (Eds.), *Communication and group decision making* (2nd ed., pp. 19-51). Thousand Oaks, CA: Sage.

Frey, L. R. (1999). Teaching small group communication. In A. L. Vangelisti, J. A. Daly, & G. W. Friedrich (Eds.), *Teaching communication: Theory, research, and methods* (2nd ed., pp. 99-113). Mahwah, NJ: Lawrence Erlbaum.

Frey, L. R. (Ed.). (in press). *Communication in context: Studies of bona fide groups* (2nd ed.). Mahwah, NJ: Lawrence Erlbaum.

Frey, L. R., & Barge, J. K. (Eds.). (1997). *Managing group life: Communicating in decision-making groups.* Boston: Houghton Mifflin.

Garlick, R., & Mongeau, P. A. (1993). Argument quality and group member status as determinants of attitudinal minority influence. *Western Journal of Communication, 57,* 289-308.

Gebhardt, L. J., & Meyers, R. A. (1995). Examining consistency from a communication perspective. *Small Group Research, 26,* 147-168.

Geier, J. G. (1967). A trait approach to the study of leadership in small groups. *Journal of Communication, 17,* 316-323.

Geist, P., & Chandler, T. (1984). Account analysis of influence in group decision-making. *Communication Monographs, 51,* 67-78.

Giddens, A. (1976). *New rules of sociological method: A positive critique of interpretive sociologies.* New York: Basic Books.

Giddens, A. (1979). *Central problems in social theory: Action, structure, and contradiction in social analysis.* London: Macmillan.

Giffin, K., & Ehrlich, L. (1963). The attitudinal effects of a group discussion on a proposed change in company policy. *Speech Monographs, 30,* 377-379.

Goldberg, A. (1960). An experimental study of the effects of evaluation upon group behavior. *Quarterly Journal of Speech, 46,* 274-283.

Gouran, D. S. (1969). Variables related to consensus in group discussions of questions of policy. *Speech Monographs, 36,* 387-391.

Gouran, D. S. (1970a). Conceptual and methodological approaches to the study of leadership. *Central States Speech Journal, 21,* 217-223.

Gouran, D. S. (1970b). Response to "The paradox and promise of small group research." *Speech Monographs, 37,* 218-219.

Gouran, D. S. (1973a). Correlates of member satisfaction in group decision-making discussions. *Central States Speech Journal, 24,* 91-96.

Gouran, D. S. (1973b). Group communication: Perspectives and priorities for future research. *Quarterly Journal of Speech, 59,* 22-29.

Gouran, D. S. (1976). The Watergate coverup: Its dynamics and its implications. *Communication Monographs, 43,* 176-186.

Gouran, D. S. (1983). Communicative influences on inferential judgments in decision-making groups: A descriptive analysis. In D. Zarefsky, M. O. Sillars, & J. Rhodes (Eds.), *Communication in transition: Pro-*

ceedings of the Third Summer Conference on Argumentation (pp. 667-684). Annandale, VA: Speech Communication Association.

Gouran, D. S. (1984). Communicative influences on decisions related to the Watergate coverup: The failure of collective judgment. *Central States Speech Journal, 35,* 260-268.

Gouran, D. S. (1985). The paradigm of unfulfilled promise: A critical examination of the history of research on small groups in Speech Communication. In T. W. Benson (Ed.), *Speech Communication in the twentieth century* (pp. 90-108, 386-392). Carbondale: Southern Illinois University Press.

Gouran, D. S. (1986). Inferential errors, interaction, and group decision-making. In R. Y. Hirokawa & M. S. Poole (Eds.), *Communication and group decision-making* (pp. 93-111). Beverly Hills, CA: Sage.

Gouran, D. S. (1988). Group decision making: An approach to integrative research. In C. H. Tardy (Ed.), *A handbook for the study of human communication: Methods and instruments for observing, measuring, and assessing communication processes* (pp. 247-267). Norwood, NJ: Ablex.

Gouran, D. S. (1990). Exploiting the predictive potential of structuration theory. In J. A. Anderson (Ed.), *Communication yearbook 13* (pp. 313-322). Newbury Park, CA: Sage.

Gouran, D. S. (1991). Rational approaches to decision-making and problem-solving discussion. *Quarterly Journal of Speech, 77,* 343-358.

Gouran, D. S. (1994a). The future of small group communication research: Revitalization or continued good health? *Communication Studies, 45,* 29-39.

Gouran, D. S. (1994b). On the value of case studies of decision-making and problem-solving groups. In L. R. Frey (Ed.), *Group communication in context: Studies of natural groups* (pp. 305-315). Hillsdale, NJ: Lawrence Erlbaum.

Gouran, D. S. (1998). The signs of cognitive, affiliative, and egocentric constraints in patterns of interaction in decision-making and problem-solving groups and their potential effects on outcomes. In J. S. Trent (Ed.), *Communication: Views from the helm for the 21st century* (pp. 98-102). Boston: Allyn & Bacon.

Gouran, D. S., & Andrews, P. H. (1984). Determinants of punitive responses to socially proscribed behavior: Seriousness, attribution of responsibility, and status of the offender. *Small Group Behavior, 15,* 525-543.

Gouran, D. S., & Baird, J. E., Jr. (1972). An analysis of distributional and sequential structure in problem-solving and informal group discussions. *Speech Monographs, 39,* 16-22.

Gouran, D. S., Brown, C. R., & Henry, D. R. (1978). Behavioral correlates of perceptions of quality in decision-making discussions. *Communication Monographs, 45,* 51-63.

Gouran, D. S., & Fisher, B. A. (1984). The functions of human communication in the formation, maintenance, and performance of small groups. In C. C. Arnold & J. W. Bowers (Eds.), *Handbook of rhetorical and communication theory* (pp. 622-658). Boston: Allyn & Bacon.

Gouran, D. S., & Hirokawa, R. Y. (1983). The role of communication in decision-making groups: A functional perspective. In M. S. Mander (Ed.), *Communications in transition: Issues and debate in current research* (pp. 168-185). New York: Praeger.

Gouran, D. S., & Hirokawa, R. Y. (1996). Functional theory and communication in decision-making and problem-solving groups: An expanded view. In R. Y. Hirokawa & M. S. Poole (Eds.), *Communication and group decision making* (2nd ed., pp. 55-80). Thousand Oaks, CA: Sage.

Gouran, D. S., Hirokawa, R. Y., Julian, K. M., & Leatham, G. B. (1993). The evolution and current status of the functional perspective on communication in decision-making and problem-solving groups. In S. A. Deetz (Ed.), *Communication yearbook 16* (pp. 573-600). Newbury Park, CA: Sage.

Gouran, D. S., Hirokawa, R. Y., & Martz, A. E. (1986). A critical analysis of factors related to decisional processes involved in the *Challenger* disaster. *Central States Speech Journal, 37,* 119-135.

Gouran, D. S., Hirokawa, R. Y., McGee, M. C., & Miller, L. L. (1994). Communication in groups: Research trends and theoretical perspectives. In F. L. Casmir (Ed.), *Building communication theories: A sociocultural approach* (pp. 241-268). Hillsdale, NJ: Lawrence Erlbaum.

Gouran, D. S., Ketrow, S. M., Spear, S., & Metzger, J. (1984). Social deviance and occupational status: Group assessment of penalties. *Small Group Behavior, 15,* 63-86.

Gouran, D. S., & Nishida, T. (Eds.). (1996). *Communication and culture.* Tokyo: Hassaku-sha.

Gouran, D. S., & Shaw, M. E. (1990). Group dynamics. In G. L. Dahnke & G. W. Clatterbuck (Eds.), *Human communication: Theory and research* (pp. 123-155). Belmont, CA: Wadsworth.

Gouran, D. S., & Whitehead, J. L., Jr. (1971). An investigation of ratings of discussion statements by participants and observers. *Central States Speech Journal, 22,* 263-268.

Graham, E. E., Papa, M. J., & McPherson, M. B. (1997). An applied test of the functional communication perspective of small group decision-making. *Southern Communication Journal, 62,* 269-279.

Grissinger, J. A. (1955). The comparative influence on audience opinion of panel discussion and formal debate. *Speech Monographs, 22,* 60-67.

Gulley, H. (1942). Debate versus discussion. *Quarterly Journal of Speech, 28,* 305-307.

Gunderson, R. G. (1950). Group dynamics—hope or hoax? *Quarterly Journal of Speech, 36,* 34-38.

Harnack, R. V. (1951). Competition and cooperation. *Central States Speech Journal, 3,* 15-20.

Harnack, R. V. (1955). An experimental study of the effects of training in the recognition and formulation of goals upon intra-group cooperation. *Speech Monographs, 22,* 31-38.

Harnack, R. V. (1963). A study of the effects of an organized minority upon a discussion group. *Journal of Communication, 13,* 12-24.

Harnack, R. V. (1968). John Dewey and discussion. *Western Speech, 32,* 137-149.

Hewes, D. E. (1979). The sequential analysis of social interaction. *Quarterly Journal of Speech, 45,* 56-73.

Hewes, D. E. (1986). A socio-egocentric model of group decision-making. In R. Y. Hirokawa & M. S. Poole (Eds.), *Communication and group decision-making* (pp. 265-291). Beverly Hills, CA: Sage.

Hewes, D. E. (1996). Small group communication may not influence decision making: An amplification of socio-egocentric theory. In R. Y. Hirokawa & M. S. Poole (Eds.), *Communication and group decision making* (2nd ed., pp. 179-212). Thousand Oaks, CA: Sage.

Hirokawa, R. Y. (1980). A comparative analysis of communication patterns within effective and ineffective decision-making groups. *Communication Monographs, 47,* 312-321.

Hirokawa, R. Y. (1982a). Consensus group decision-making, quality of decision, and group satisfaction: An attempt to sort "fact" from "fiction." *Central States Speech Journal, 33,* 407-415.

Hirokawa, R. Y. (1982b). Group communication and problem-solving effectiveness: A critical review of inconsistent findings. *Communication Quarterly, 30,* 134-141.

Hirokawa, R. Y. (1983a). Group communication and problem-solving effectiveness: An investigation of group phases. *Human Communication Research, 9,* 291-305.

Hirokawa, R. Y. (1983b). Group communication and problem-solving effectiveness II: An exploratory investigation of procedural functions. *Western Journal of Speech Communication, 47,* 59-74.

Hirokawa, R. Y. (1985). Discussion procedures and decision-making performance: A test of a functional perspective. *Human Communication Research, 12,* 203-224.

Hirokawa, R. Y. (1987). Why informed groups make faulty decisions: An investigation of possible interaction-based explanations. *Small Group Behavior, 18,* 3-29.

Hirokawa, R. Y. (1988). Group communication and decision-making performance: A continued test of the functional perspective. *Human Communication Research, 14,* 487-515.

Hirokawa, R. Y. (1990). The role of communication in group decision-making efficacy: A task-contingency perspective. *Small Group Research, 21,* 190-204.

Hirokawa, R. Y. (1994). Functional approaches to the study of group discussion: Even good notions have their problems. *Small Group Research, 25,* 542-550.

Hirokawa, R. Y., Gouran, D. S., & Martz, A. E. (1988). Understanding the sources of faulty group decision-making: A lesson from the *Challenger* disaster. *Small Group Behavior, 19,* 411-433.

Hirokawa, R. Y., Ice, R., & Cook, J. (1988). Preference for procedural order, discussion structure, and group decision performance. *Communication Quarterly, 36,* 217-226.

Hirokawa, R. Y., & Pace, R. (1983). A descriptive investigation of the possible communication-based reasons for effective and ineffective group decision-making. *Communication Monographs, 50,* 363-379.

Hirokawa, R. Y., & Poole, M. S. (Eds.). (1986). *Communication and group decision-making.* Beverly Hills, CA: Sage.

Hirokawa, R. Y., & Poole, M. W. (Eds.). (1996). *Communication and group decision making* (2nd ed.). Thousand Oaks, CA: Sage.

Hirokawa, R. Y., & Scheerhorn, D. R. (1986). Communication in faulty group decision-making. In R. Y. Hirokawa & M. S. Poole (Eds.), *Communication and group decision-making* (pp. 63-80). Beverly Hills, CA: Sage.

Hoffman, L. R., & Kleinman, G. B. (1994). Individual and group in group problem solving: The valence model redressed. *Human Communication Research, 21,* 36-59.

Hofstede, G. (1980). *Culture's consequences: International differences in work-related values.* Beverly Hills, CA: Sage.

Hofstede, G., & Bond, M. H. (1984). Hofstede's cultural dimensions: An independent validation using Rokeach's value survey. *Journal of Cross-Cultural Psychology, 15,* 417-433.

Hollingshead, A. B. (1998). Group and individual training: The impact of practice on performance. *Small Group Research, 29,* 254-280.

Holmes, M. E. (1992). Phase structures in negotiation. In L. L. Putnam & M. E. Roloff (Eds.), *Communication and negotiation* (pp. 83-107). Newbury Park, CA: Sage.

Jablin, F. M., Seibold, D. R., & Sorenson, R. L. (1977). Potential inhibitory effects of group participation on brainstorming performance. *Central States Speech Journal, 28,* 113-121.

Janis, I. L. (1972). *Victims of groupthink: A psychological study of foreign-policy decisions and fiascoes.* Boston: Houghton Mifflin.

Janis, I. L. (1982). *Groupthink: Psychological studies of policy decisions and fiascoes* (2nd ed.). Boston: Houghton Mifflin.

Jarboe, S. C. (1988). A comparison of input-output, process-output, and input-process-output models of small group problem-solving effectiveness. *Communication Monographs, 55,* 121-142.

Jarboe, S. (1991). Two multivariate methods for analyzing small group interaction: A data base comparison. *Small Group Research, 22,* 515-547.

Jarboe, S. (1996). Procedures for enhancing group decision making. In R. Y. Hirokawa & M. S. Poole (Eds.), *Communication and group decision making* (2nd ed., pp. 345-383). Thousand Oaks, CA: Sage.

Jarboe, S. C., & Witteman, H. R. (1996). Intra-group conflict management in task-oriented groups: The influence of problem source and problem analysis. *Small Group Research, 27,* 316-338.

Johnson, A. (1939). Teaching the fundamentals of speech through group discussion. *Quarterly Journal of Speech, 25,* 440-447.

Johnson, A. (1940). Discussion: A technique of applying scientific method to social problems. *Southern Speech Journal, 6,* 26-28.

Johnson, A. (1943). An experimental study in the analysis and measurement of reflective thinking. *Speech Monographs, 10,* 83-96.

Johnson, S. D., & Bechler, C. (1997). Leadership and listening: Perceptions and behavior. *Speech Communication Annual, 11,* 57-70.

Johnson, S. D., & Bechler, C. (1998). Examining the relationship between listening effectiveness and leadership emergence: Perceptions, behaviors, and recall. *Small Group Research, 29,* 452-471.

Jowett, G. S., & O'Donnell, V. (1986). *Persuasion and propaganda.* Beverly Hills, CA: Sage.

Jurma, W. E. (1979). Effects of leader structuring style and task-orientation characteristics of group members. *Communication Monographs, 46,* 282-285.

Jurma, W. E., & Wright, B. C. (1990). Follower reactions to male and female leaders who maintain or lose reward power. *Small Group Research, 21,* 97-112.

Kellermann, K., & Jarboe, S. (1987). Conservatism in judgment: Is the risky shift-ee really risky, really? In M. L. McLaughlin (Ed.), *Communication yearbook 10* (pp. 259-282). Newbury Park, CA: Sage.

Keltner, J. W. (1957). Groupthink and individual thinking. *Today's Speech, 5*(2), 5-6.

Ketrow, S. M. (1991). Communication role specializations and perceptions of leadership. *Small Group Research, 22,* 492-515.

Keyton, J. (1991). Evaluating individual group member satisfaction as a situational variable. *Small Group Research, 22,* 200-219.

Keyton, J. (1993). Group termination: Completing the study of group development. *Small Group Research, 24,* 84-100.

Keyton, J. (1994). Going forward in group communication research may mean going back: Studying the groups of children. *Communication Studies, 45,* 40-51.

Keyton, J. (1995). Using SYMLOG as a self-analytical group facilitation technique. In L. R. Frey (Ed.), *Innovations in group facilitation: Applications in natural settings* (pp. 148-174). Cresskill, NJ: Hampton.

Keyton, J. (1997). Coding communication in decision-making groups. In L. R. Frey & J. K. Barge (Eds.), *Managing group life: Communicating in decision-making groups* (pp. 234-269). Boston: Houghton Mifflin.

Keyton, J., & Frey, L. R. (in press). The effects of predispositions on group communication. In L. R. Frey (Ed.), *New directions in group communication.* Thousand Oaks, CA: Sage.

Keyton, J., Harmon, N., & Frey, L. R. (1996, November). *Grouphate: Implications for teaching group communication.* Paper presented at the meeting of the Speech Communication Association, San Diego, CA.

Keyton, J., & Springston, J. (1990). Redefining cohesiveness in groups. *Small Group Research, 21,* 234-254.

Kibler, R. J., & Barker, L. L. (Eds.). (1968). *Conceptual frontiers in Speech Communication*. New York: Speech Association of America.

Kline, J. A. (1970). Indices of opinionated and orienting statements in problem-solving discussions. *Speech Monographs, 37*, 282-286.

Kline, J. A. (1972). Orientation and group consensus. *Central States Speech Journal, 23*, 44-47.

Knutson, T. J. (1972). An experimental study of the effects of orientation behavior on small group consensus. *Speech Monographs, 39*, 159-165.

Knutson, T. J., & Holdridge, W. E. (1975). Orientation behavior, leadership, and consensus: A possible functional relationship. *Speech Monographs, 42*, 107-114.

Koester, J. (1982). The Machiavellian princess: Rhetorical dramas for women managers. *Communication Quarterly, 30*, 165-172.

Kolb, J. A. (1997). Are we still stereotyping leadership? A look at gender and other predictors of leader emergence. *Small Group Research, 28*, 370-393.

Kreps, G. L. (1995). Using focus group discussions to promote organizational reflexivity: Two applied communication field studies. In L. R. Frey (Ed.), *Innovations in group facilitation: Applications in natural settings* (pp. 177-199). Cresskill, NJ: Hampton.

Krivoshey, R. M. (Ed.). (1994). *Readings in trial advocacy and the social sciences: Vol. 1. Juries: Formation and behavior*. New York: Garland.

Kroll, B. S. (1983). From small group to public view: Mainstreaming the women's movement. *Communication Quarterly, 31*, 139-147.

Larson, C. E. (1969). Forms of analysis and small group problem-solving. *Speech Monographs, 36*, 452-455.

Larson, C. E. (1971). Speech Communication research on small groups. *Speech Teacher, 20*, 89-107.

Leathers, D. G. (1969). Process disruption and measurement in small group communication. *Quarterly Journal of Speech, 55*, 287-300.

Leathers, D. G. (1971). The feedback rating instrument: A new means of evaluating discussion. *Central States Speech Journal, 22*, 32-42.

Leathers, D. G. (1972). Quality of group communication as a determinant of group product. *Speech Monographs, 39*, 166-173.

Lee, J. (1998). Maintenance communication in superior-subordinate relationships: An exploratory investigation of group social context and the "Pelz Effect." *Southern Communication Journal, 63*, 144-159.

Lerea, L., & Goldberg, A. (1961). Research notes: The effects of socialization upon group behavior. *Speech Monographs, 28*, 60-64.

Lesch, C. L. (1994). Observing theory in practice: Sustaining consciousness in a coven. In L. R. Frey (Ed.), *Group communication in context: Studies of natural groups* (pp. 57-82). Hillsdale, NJ: Lawrence Erlbaum.

Lewin, K. (1936). *Principles of topological psychology* (F. Heider & G. M. Heider, Trans.). New York: McGraw-Hill.

Lewin, K. (1951). *Field theory in social science: Selected theoretical papers* (D. Cartwright, Ed.). New York: Harper & Row.

Lewin, K., Lippitt, R., & White, R. K. (1939). Patterns of aggressive behavior in experimentally created "social climates." *Journal of Social Psychology, 10*, 271-299.

Lewis, I. M. (1996). *Religion in context: Cults and charisma*. New York: Cambridge University Press.

Lincoln, Y. S., & Guba, E. G. (1985). *Naturalistic inquiry*. Beverly Hills, CA: Sage.

Lippitt, R., & White, R. K. (1943). The "social climate" of children's groups. In R. G. Barker, J. Kounin, & H. Wright (Eds.), *Child behavior and development: A course of representative studies* (pp. 485-508). New York: McGraw-Hill.

Lumsden, G. (1974). An experimental study of the effect of verbal agreement on leadership maintenance in problem-solving discussion. *Central States Speech Journal, 25*, 270-276.

Lustig, M. W., & Cassotta, L. L. (1996). Comparing group communication across cultures: Leadership, conformity, and discussion processes. In R. S. Cathcart, L. A. Samovar, & L. D. Henman (Eds.), *Small group communication: Theory & practice* (7th ed., pp. 316-326). Madison, WI: Brown & Benchmark.

Lyman, R. L. (1915). The forum as an educative agency. *Quarterly Journal of Public Speaking, 1*, 1-8.

Mabry, E. A. (1975a). Exploratory analysis of a developmental model for task-oriented small groups. *Human Communication Research, 2*, 66-74.

Mabry, E. A. (1975b). An instrument for assessing content themes in group interaction. *Speech Monographs, 42*, 291-297.

Mabry, E. A. (1975c). Sequential structure of interaction in encounter groups. *Human Communication Research, 1*, 302-307.

Marr, T. J. (1974). Conciliation and verbal responses as functions of orientation and threat in group interaction. *Speech Monographs, 41*, 6-18.

Matthews, J., & Bendig, A. W. (1955). The index of agreement: A possible criterion for measuring the outcome of group discussion. *Speech Monographs, 22*, 39-42.

Mayer, M. E. (1985). Explaining choice shift: An effects coded model. *Communication Monographs, 52*, 92-101.

Mayer, M. E., Sonoda, K. T., & Gudykunst, W. B. (1997). The effect of time pressure and type of information on decision quality. *Southern Communication Journal, 62*, 280-292.

McBurney, J. H., & Hance, K. G. (1939). *The principles and methods of discussion*. New York: Harper & Brothers.

McGrath, J. E., & Altman, I. (1966). *Small group research: A synthesis and critique of the field*. New York: Holt, Rinehart & Winston.

Meyers, R. A., & Brashers, D. E. (1994). Expanding the boundaries of small group communication research: Exploring a feminist perspective. *Communication Studies, 45*, 68-85.

Meyers, R. A., & Brashers, D. E. (1998). Argument in group decision making: Explicating a process model and investigating the argument-outcome link. *Communication Monographs, 65*, 261-281.

Meyers, R. A., & Seibold, D. R. (1990). Perspectives on group argument: A critical review of persuasive arguments theory and an alternative structurational view. In J. A. Anderson (Ed.), *Communication yearbook 13* (pp. 268-302). Newbury Park, CA: Sage.

Miller, C. M., & McKinney, B. C. (Eds.). (1993). *Government commission communication*. Westport, CT: Praeger.

Mortensen, C. D. (1970). The status of small group research. *Quarterly Journal of Speech, 56,* 304-309.

Nicotera, A. M. (1994). The use of multiple approaches to conflict: A study of sequences. *Human Communication Research, 20,* 592-621.

Nicotera, A. M. (1997). Managing conflict in communication in groups. In L. R. Frey & J. K. Barge (Eds.), *Managing group life: Communicating in decision-making groups* (pp. 104-130). Boston: Houghton Mifflin.

Northouse, P. G. (Ed.). (1997). *Leadership: Theory and practice*. Thousand Oaks, CA: Sage.

O'Brien, J. F. (1939). A definition and classification of the forms of discussion. *Quarterly Journal of Speech, 25,* 236-243.

Olson, C. (1986). *A case study of credentialing in small groups*. Unpublished doctoral dissertation, University of Minnesota, Minneapolis.

Owen, W. F. (1986). Rhetorical themes of emergent female leaders. *Small Group Behavior, 17,* 475-486.

Pace, R. C. (1990). Personalized and depersonalized conflict in small group discussions: An examination of differentiation. *Small Group Research, 21,* 79-96.

Pavitt, C. (1993a). Does communication matter in social influence during small group discussion? Five positions. *Communication Studies, 44,* 216-227.

Pavitt, C. (1993b). What little we know about formal group discussion procedures: A review of relevant research. *Small Group Research, 24,* 217-235.

Pavitt, C. (1994). Theoretical commitments presupposed by functional approaches to group discussion. *Small Group Research, 25,* 520-541.

Pavitt, C., & Sackaroff, P. (1990). Implicit theories of leadership and judgments of leadership among group members. *Small Group Research, 21,* 374-392.

Phillips, G. M. (1966). *Communication and the small group*. Indianapolis: Bobbs-Merrill.

Phillips, G. M., & Wood, J. T. (Eds.). (1984). *Emergent issues in human decision making*. Carbondale: Southern Illinois University Press.

Pierce, J. R. (1961). *Symbols, signals, and noise: The nature and process of communication*. New York: Harper Torchbooks.

Poole, M. S. (1981). Decision development in small groups I: A comparison of two models. *Communication Monographs, 48,* 1-24.

Poole, M. S. (1983a). Decision development in small groups II: A study of multiple sequences in decision-making. *Communication Monographs, 50,* 206-232.

Poole, M. S. (1983b). Decision development in small groups, III: A multiple sequence model of decision development. *Communication Monographs, 50,* 321-341.

Poole, M. S. (1983c). Structural paradigms and the study of group communication. In M. S. Mander (Ed.), *Communications in transition: Issues and debates in current research* (pp. 186-205). New York: Praeger.

Poole, M. S. (1990). Do we have any theories of group communication? *Communication Studies, 41,* 237-247.

Poole, M. S. (1994). Breaking the isolation of small group communication studies. *Communication Studies, 45,* 20-28.

Poole, M. S. (1996). Group communication and the structuring process. In R. S. Cathcart, L. A. Samovar, & L. D. Henman (Eds.), *Small group communication: Theory & practice* (7th ed., pp. 85-96). Madison, WI: Brown & Benchmark.

Poole, M. S. (1998). The small group should be *the* fundamental unit of communication research. In J. S. Trent (Ed.), *Communication: Views from the helm for the 21st century* (pp. 94-97). Boston: Allyn & Bacon.

Poole, M. S., & Baldwin, C. L. (1996). Developmental processes in group decision making. In R. Y. Hirokawa & M. S. Poole (Eds.), *Communication and group decision making* (2nd ed., pp. 215-241). Thousand Oaks, CA: Sage.

Poole, M. S., & DeSanctis, G. (1990). Understanding the use of group decision support systems: The theory of adaptive structuration. In J. Fulk & C. Steinfield (Eds.), *Organizations and communication technology* (pp. 173-195). Newbury Park, CA: Sage.

Poole, M. S., & DeSanctis, G. (1992). Microlevel structuration in computer-supported group decision making. *Human Communication Research, 19,* 5-49.

Poole, M. S., DeSanctis, G., Kirsch, L., & Jackson, M. (1995). Group discussion support systems as facilitators of quality team efforts. In L. R. Frey (Ed.), *Innovations in group facilitation: Applications in natural settings* (pp. 299-321). Cresskill, NJ: Hampton.

Poole, M. S., & Doelger, J. A. (1986). Developmental processes in group decision-making. In R. Y. Hirokawa & M. S. Poole (Eds.), *Communication and group decision-making* (pp. 35-61). Beverly Hills, CA: Sage.

Poole, M. S., & Folger, J. P. (1981). A new method of establishing the representational validity of interaction coding schemes: Do we see what they see? *Human Communication Research, 8,* 26-42.

Poole, M. S., & Holmes, M. E. (1995). Decision development in computer-assisted group decision making. *Human Communication Research, 22,* 90-127.

Poole, M. S., Holmes, M. E., Watson, R., & DeSanctis, G. (1993). Group decision support systems and group communication: A comparison of decision-making processes in computer-supported and nonsupported groups. *Communication Research, 20,* 176-213.

Poole, M. S., McPhee, R. D., & Seibold, D. R. (1982). A comparison of normative and interactional explanations of group decision-making: Social decision schemes versus valence distributions. *Communication Monographs, 49,* 1-19.

Poole, M. S., & Roth, J. (1989a). Decision development in small groups IV: A topology of group decision paths. *Human Communication Research, 15,* 323-356.

Poole, M. S., & Roth, J. (1989b). Decision development in groups V: Test of a contingency model. *Human Communication Research, 15,* 549-589.

Poole, M. S., Seibold, D. R., & McPhee, R. D. (1985). Group decision-making as a structurational process. *Quarterly Journal of Speech, 71,* 74-102.

Poole, M. S., Seibold, D. R., & McPhee, R. D. (1986). A structurational approach to theory-building in group decision-making research. In R. Y. Hirokawa & M. S. Poole (Eds.), *Communication and group decision-making* (pp. 237-264). Beverly Hills, CA: Sage.

Poole, M. S., Seibold, D. R., & McPhee, R. D. (1996). The structuration of group decisions. In R. Y. Hirokawa & M. S. Poole (Eds.), *Communication and group decision making* (2nd ed., pp. 114-146). Thousand Oaks, CA: Sage.

Propp, K. M. (1995). An experimental examination of biological sex as a status cue in decision-making groups and its influence on information use. *Small Group Research, 26,* 451-474.

Propp, K. M., & Kreps, G. L. (1994). A rose by any other name: The vitality of group communication research. *Communication Studies, 45,* 7-19.

Putnam, L. L. (1982). Procedural messages and small group work climates: A lag sequential analysis. In M. Burgoon (Ed.), *Communication yearbook 5* (pp. 331-350). New Brunswick, NJ: Transaction Books.

Putnam, L. L. (1983). Small group work climates: A lag-sequential analysis of group interaction. *Small Group Behavior, 14,* 465-494.

Putnam, L. L. (1994). Revitalizing small group communication: Lessons learned from a bona fide group perspective. *Communication Studies, 45,* 97-102.

Putnam, L. L., & Stohl, C. (1990). Bona fide groups: A reconceptualization of groups in context. *Communication Studies, 41,* 248-265.

Putnam, L. L., & Stohl, C. (1994). Group communication in context: Implications for the study of bona fide groups. In L. R. Frey (Ed.), *Group communication in context: Studies of natural groups* (pp. 284-292). Hillsdale, NJ: Lawrence Erlbaum.

Putnam, L. L., & Stohl, C. (1996). Bona fide groups: An alternative perspective for communication and small group decision making. In R. Y. Hirokawa & M. S. Poole (Eds.), *Communication and group decision making* (2nd ed., pp. 147-178). Thousand Oaks, CA: Sage.

Pyron, H. C. (1964). An experimental study of the role of reflective thinking in business and professional conferences and discussions. *Speech Monographs, 31,* 157-161.

Pyron, H. C., & Sharp, H., Jr. (1963). A quantitative study of reflective thinking and performance in problem-solving discussion. *Journal of Communication, 13,* 46-53.

Robinson, K. F. (1941). An experimental study of the effects of group discussion upon the social attitudes of college students. *Speech Monographs, 8,* 34-57.

Sabourin, T. C., & Geist, P. (1990). Collaborative production of proposals in group decision making. *Small Group Research, 21,* 404-427.

Salazar, A. J. (1995). Understanding the synergistic effects of communication in small groups: Making the most out of group member abilities. *Small Group Research, 26,* 169-199.

Salazar, A. J. (1996). An analysis of the development and evolution of roles in the small group. *Small Group Research, 27,* 475-503.

Salazar, A. J., Hirokawa, R. Y., Propp, K. M., Julian, K. M., & Leatham, G. B. (1994). In search of true causes: Examination of the effect of group potential and group interaction on decision performance. *Human Communication Research, 20,* 529-559.

Saliba, J. A. (1996). *Understanding new religious movements.* Grand Rapids, MI: W. B. Eerdmans.

Sambamurthy, V., Poole, M. S., & Kelly, J. (1993). The effects of variations in GDSS capabilities on decision-making processes in groups. *Small Group Research, 24,* 523-546.

Sargent, J. F., & Miller, G. R. (1971). Some differences in communicative behaviors of autocratic and democratic leaders. *Journal of Communication, 21,* 233-252.

Scheerhorn, D., Geist, P., & Teboul, JC. B. (1994). Beyond decision making in decision-making groups: Implications for the study of group communication. In L. R. Frey (Ed.), *Group communication in context: Studies of natural groups* (pp. 247-262). Hillsdale, NJ: Lawrence Erlbaum.

Scheidel, T. M., & Crowell, L. (1964). Idea development in small discussion groups. *Quarterly Journal of Speech, 50,* 140-145.

Scheidel, T. M., & Crowell, L. (1966). Feedback in group communication. *Quarterly Journal of Speech, 52,* 273-278.

Scheidel, T. M., Crowell, L., & Shepherd, J. R. (1958). Personality and discussion behavior: A study of possible relationships. *Speech Monographs, 25,* 261-267.

Schultz, B. (1974). Characteristics of emergent leaders of continuing problem-solving groups. *Journal of Psychology, 88,* 167-173.

Schultz, B. (1978). Predicting emergent leaders: An exploratory study of the salience of communicative functions. *Small Group Research, 9,* 109-114.

Schultz, B. (1980). Communication correlates of perceived leaders. *Small Group Behavior, 11,* 175-191.

Schultz, B. (1982). Argumentativeness: Its effect in group decision-making and its role in leadership perception. *Communication Quarterly, 30,* 368-375.

Schultz, B. (1986). Communicative correlates of perceived leaders in the small group. *Small Group Behavior, 17,* 51-65.

Schultz, B., & Anderson, J. (1984). Training in the management of conflict: A communication theory perspective. *Small Group Behavior, 15,* 333-348.

Schultz, B., Ketrow, S. M., & Urban, D. M. (1995). An examination of functional role behavior and its consequences of individuals in group settings. *Small Group Research, 26,* 521-541.

Seibold, D. R. (1994). More reflection or more research? To (re)vitalize small group communication research, let's "just do it." *Communication Studies, 45,* 103-110.

Seibold, D. R., Canary, D. J., & Ratledge, N. T. (1983, November). *Argument and group decision-making: Interim report on a structurational research program.* Paper presented at the meeting of the Speech Communication Association, Washington, DC.

Seibold, D. R., McPhee, R. D., Poole, M. S., Tanita, N. E., & Canary, D. J. (1981). Argument, group influence, and decision outcomes. In G. Ziegelmueller & J. Rhodes (Eds.), *Dimensions of argument: Proceedings of the Second Summer Speech Communication Association/American Forensics Association Conference on Argumentation* (pp 663-692). Annandale, VA: Speech Communication Association.

Seibold, D. R., & Meyers, R. A. (1986). Communication and influence in group decision-making. In R. Y. Hirokawa & M. S. Poole (Eds.), *Communication and group decision-making* (pp. 133-155). Beverly Hills, CA: Sage.

Seibold, D. R., Meyers, R. A., & Sunwolf (1996). Communication and influence in group decision making. In R. Y. Hirokawa & M. S. Poole (Eds.), *Communication and group decision making* (2nd ed., pp. 242-268). Thousand Oaks, CA: Sage.

Sharp, H., Jr., & Milliken, J. (1964). The reflective thinking ability and the product of problem-solving discussion. *Speech Monographs, 31,* 124-127.

Shaw, M. E. (1971). *Group dynamics: The psychology of small group behavior.* New York: McGraw-Hill.

Sheffield, A. D. (1922). *Joining in public discussion.* New York: George H. Doran.

Shimanoff, S. B., & Jenkins, M. M. (1996). Leadership and gender: Challenging assumptions and recognizing resources. In R. S. Cathcart, L. A. Samovar, & L. D. Henman (Eds.), *Small group communication: Theory & practice* (7th ed., pp. 327-344). Madison, WI: Brown & Benchmark.

Sigman, S. J. (1984). Talk and interaction strategy in a task-oriented group. *Small Group Behavior, 15,* 33-50.

Simon, H. A. (1978). Rationality as a process and as product of thought. *American Economic Review, 68,* 1-16.

Simpson, R. H. (1939). The effect of discussion on intragroup divergences of judgment. *Quarterly Journal of Speech, 25,* 546-552.

Smith, C. M., & Powell, L. (1988). The use of disparaging humor by group leaders. *Southern Speech Communication Journal, 53,* 279-292.

Socha, T. J., & Socha, D. M. (1994). Children's task group communication: Did we learn it all in kindergarten? In L. R. Frey (Ed.), *Group communication in context: Studies of natural groups* (pp. 227-246). Hillsdale, NJ: Lawrence Erlbaum.

Sorensen, S. M. (1981, May). *Group-hate: A negative reaction to group work.* Paper presented at the meeting of the International Communication Association, Minneapolis, MN.

Sorenson, R. L., & Savage, G. T. (1989). Signaling participation through relational communication: A test of the leader interpersonal influence model. *Group and Organizational Studies, 14,* 325-354.

Spillman, B., Spillman, R., & Reinking, K. (1981). Leadership emergence: Dynamic analysis of the effects of sex and androgyny. *Small Group Behavior, 12,* 139-157.

Stech, E. L. (1970). An analysis of interaction structure in the discussion of a ranking task. *Speech Monographs, 37,* 249-256.

Steiner, I. D. (1972). *Group process and productivity.* New York: Academic Press.

Steiner, I. D. (1974). *Task-performing groups.* Morristown, NJ: General Learning Press.

Stohl, C. (1986). Quality circles and changing patterns of communication. In M. L. McLaughlin (Ed.), *Communication yearbook 9* (pp. 511-531). Beverly Hills, CA: Sage.

Stohl, C. (1987). Bridging the parallel organization: A study of quality circle effectiveness. In M. L. McLaughlin (Ed.), *Communication yearbook 10* (pp. 416-429). Beverly Hills, CA: Sage.

Stohl, C. (1995). Facilitating bona fide groups: Practice and paradox. In L. R. Frey (Ed.), *Innovations in group facilitation: Applications in natural settings* (pp. 325-332). Cresskill, NJ: Hampton.

Stohl, C., & Jennings, K. (1988). Volunteerism and voice in quality circles. *Western Journal of Speech Communication, 52,* 238-251.

Stone, V. A. (1969). A primacy effect in decision-making by jurors. *Journal of Communication, 19,* 239-247.

Sunwolf, & Seibold, D. R. (1998). Jurors' intuitive rules for deliberation: A structurational approach to communication in jury decision making. *Communication Monographs, 65,* 282-307.

Sykes, R. E. (1990). Imagine what we might study if we really studied small groups from a speech perspective. *Communication Studies, 41,* 200-211.

Thameling, C. L., & Andrews, P. H. (1992). Majority responses to opinion deviates: A communicative analysis. *Small Group Research, 23,* 475-502.

Timmons, W. M. (1941). Sex differences in discussion. *Speech Monographs, 8,* 68-75.

Tompkins, P. K., & Cheney, G. (1983). The uses of account analysis: A study of organizational decision-making and identification. In L. L. Putnam & M. E. Pacanowsky (Eds.), *Communication and organizations: An interpretive approach* (pp. 123-146). Beverly Hills, CA: Sage.

Trent, J. S. (Ed.). (1998). *Communication: Views from the helm for the 21st century.* Boston: Allyn & Bacon.

Tschan, F. (1995). Communication enhances small group performance if it conforms to task requirements: The concept of ideal communication cycles. *Basic and Applied Social Psychology, 17,* 371-393.

Tubbs, S. L. (1978). *A systems approach to small group interaction.* Reading, MA: Addison-Wesley.

Tuckman, B. W. (1965). Developmental sequences in small groups. *Psychological Bulletin, 63,* 384-399.

Utterback, W. E., & Fotheringham, W. C. (1958). Experimental studies of motivated group discussion. *Speech Monographs, 25,* 268-277.

Wall, V. D., Galanes, G. J., & Love, S. G. (1987). Small task-oriented groups: Conflict, conflict management, satisfaction, and decision quality. *Small Group Behavior, 18,* 31-55.

Wall, V. D., & Nolan, L. L. (1987). Small group conflict: A look at equity, satisfaction, and styles of conflict management. *Small Group Behavior, 18,* 188-211.

Walther, J. B. (1992). Interpersonal effects in computer-mediated interaction: A relational perspective. *Communication Research, 19,* 52-90.

Walther, J. B. (1994). Anticipated on-going interaction versus channel effects on relational communication in computer-mediated interaction. *Human Communication Research, 20,* 473-501.

Walther, J. B., Anderson, J. F., & Park, D. W. (1994). Interpersonal effects in computer-mediated interaction: A meta-analysis of social and antisocial communication. *Communication Research, 21,* 460-487.

Walther, J. B., & Burgoon, J. K. (1992). Relational communication in computer-mediated interaction. *Human Communication Research, 19,* 50-88.

Weitzel, A., & Geist, P. (1998). Parliamentary procedure in a community group and vigilant decision making. *Communication Monographs, 65,* 244-259.

Wheeler, B. C., Mennecke, B. R., & Scudder, J. N. (1993). Restrictive group support systems as a source of process structure for high and low procedural order groups. *Small Group Research, 24,* 504-522.

Wilson, E. O. (1998). *Consilience: The unity of knowledge.* New York: Alfred A. Knopf.

Wischmeier, R. R. (1955). Group and leader-centered leadership: An experimental study. *Speech Monographs, 22,* 43-48.

Witteman, H. (1991). Group member satisfaction: A conflict-related account. *Small Group Research, 22,* 24-58.

Wittenbaum, G. M. (1998). Information sampling in decision-making groups: The impact of members' task-relevant status. *Small Group Research, 29,* 57-84.

Wood, J. T. (1977). Leading in purposive discussions: A study of adaptive behavior. *Communication Monographs, 44,* 152-165.

Wyatt, N. (1993). Organizing and relating: Feminist critique of small group communication. In S. P. Brown & N. Wyatt (Eds.), *Transforming visions: Feminist critiques in communication studies* (pp. 51-86). Cresskill, NJ: Hampton.

Wyatt, N. (in press). Voice and empowerment in group contexts: A radical feminist analysis of group communication. In L. R. Frey (Ed.), *New directions in group communication.* Thousand Oaks, CA: Sage.

Yerby, J. (1975). Attitude, task, and sex composition as variables affecting female leadership in small problem-solving groups. *Speech Monographs, 42,* 160-168.

Yi, J. S. (1997). *Cross-cultural differences in decision-making styles: A study of college students in five countries.* Unpublished doctoral dissertation, The Pennsylvania State University, University Park.

Young, K. S. (1992). *The use of a procedural model of problem solving by students in a group discussion class when called upon to make a binding decision.* Unpublished doctoral dissertation, The Pennsylvania State University, University Park.

Zey, M. (Ed.). (1992). *Decision making: Alternatives to rational choice models.* Newbury Park, CA: Sage.

2

Group Communication Theory

MARSHALL SCOTT POOLE
Texas A&M University

Group communication scholars have been preoccupied with theory for at least 25 years. This attention was stimulated by critical evaluations of the area by Bormann (1970, 1980), Gouran (1970, 1985), Mortensen (1970), and Cragan and Wright (1980), all of whom concluded that group communication research was producing piles of isolated facts that did not tie together, primarily because of the lack of central organizing frameworks. Scholars responded by developing theories, and in their influential review of group communication research of the 1980s, Cragan and Wright (1990) concluded that scholars had begun to fill the theoretical vacuum noted in previous critiques. They expressed a concern, however, that, although there had been a healthy burst of theory development in the Group Communication field, actual research had pursued many diverse paths with relatively few studies building on these theories.

This chapter reassesses this conclusion at the end of the 1990s by reviewing theoretical developments in the study of group communication. Several good summaries of current theory and research have appeared over the past 20 years, notably those of Cragan and Wright (1980, 1990), Frey (1996), and Gouran

(1985, also Chapter 1, this volume). This chapter offers a critical analysis of the various theoretical trends that have emerged in group communication scholarship since 1965. It is not meant to be a history, nor does it attempt to summarize theories in detail. Rather, its goal is to highlight significant contributions, challenges, and problems faced by prevailing theories, while pointing to promising directions for future theory development.

THEORY IN THE STUDY OF GROUP COMMUNICATION

It is difficult to define "theory." The term has been used to refer to "grand ideas" and formulations that are designed to account for the whole range of human phenomena; "theories of the middle range," which are general in that they apply to a broad range of cases, yet are limited to a particular area of human existence (such as small groups); "mini-theories" that attempt to account for a specific phenomenon, such as "group polarization"; and simple explanations offered for findings from one or more studies, such as "the Pelz effect." Theoretical ideas concerning group communication can be grouped into three

37

sets: (a) *general theories,* which draw on grand theories, are middle-range theories that can be applied to explain and/or understand group communication in general; (b) *focused theories,* which often draw on general theories, concentrate on specific phenomena of group communication, such as influence, leadership, or temporal development; and (c) *agenda-setting statements,* which do not comprise theories in their own right but, rather, serve to shape how group communication theories develop by suggesting particular issues or problems they should address or frames of reference they should adopt. All three classes of theoretical thinking are crucial to the successful development of group communication scholarship, and all three appear in this chapter. I devote more space, however, to general theories and agenda-setting statements because the other chapters in this volume cover many of the extant focused theories in considerable detail.

What makes a good theory? In an earlier essay, I (Poole, 1990) ventured that theories should be evaluated on the basis of two sets of criteria. The first set has been worked out largely by philosophers of science (see Diesing, 1991) and is familiar to most scholars: Theories should be general and parsimonious; they also should help to explain, understand, and sometimes to predict things. Depending on whether the theorist aspires to build traditional social-scientific theory, interpretive theory, critical theory, practical theory (see Craig, 1989, 1995; Craig & Tracy, 1995), or process theory (see Mohr, 1982; Poole, Van de Ven, Dooley, & Holmes, in press), to name a few, exactly what constitutes effective explanation and understanding varies. The second set of criteria has been explicated by sociologists and historians of science (see Diesing, 1991) and is concerned with the development of research communities: Theories should capture the imagination, solve troubling puzzles, and address concerns meaningful to both academia and the larger society.

Fulfilling this extensive list of prerequisites is a tall order. No group communication theory has been uniformly successful in satisfying these requirements, but this could be said of almost all social-scientific theories. One reason why it is so difficult to satisfy them is that the requirements are, to some extent, antagonistic. For example, to develop a well-defined parsimonious theory, it may be necessary to employ specialized terminology or models that render the theory inaccessible to much of the academic community. On the other hand, an evocative metaphor may enlist a large number of followers who subsequently break into camps as the metaphor is developed into more specific theoretical forms. On the whole, however, the tensions created by trying to satisfy conflicting criteria serve to keep inquiry vibrant and healthy. Shifting concerns from one to another criterion over time ensures well-rounded and useful theories. Indeed, theories probably die out when they can no longer sustain these dynamic tensions.

Dissecting theories one after another in terms of this lengthy list of criteria would be exhausting—not to mention tedious—for the reader. Moreover, for the criteria related to building research communities, as well as for prediction and some types of explanation, some of the theories considered in this chapter do not have sufficient history to permit a measured judgment. The discussion, thus, touches on relevant criteria as the need arises but leaves many judgments to the reader.

An important consideration running through several of these desiderata is the nature of the questions theorists and researchers pose. It is useful to think of theorizing as a question-answering and problem-solving activity, along the lines laid out by the Pragmatist philosophers (see Diesing, 1991). One good way to situate and compare group communication theories, then, is to consider the questions they *attempt* to answer and those they *could* answer if properly extended.

QUESTIONS ABOUT GROUPS

Reviewing the literature on groups, in general, and group communication, in particular, reveals a number of recurrent questions. One set of questions concern the *genesis of groups* and is captured by the more general question,

How do groups form and differentiate themselves from their environment? One way of framing this question is in terms of boundary establishment and maintenance, a perspective derived from Systems Theory (see Mabry, Chapter 3, this volume). An insightful discussion of this issue appears in Campbell's (1958) essay on the "entitativity" of groups. A different framing is to inquire into the social construction of groups, that is, how they come to have identity distinct from other social entities and what they mean to their members (Bormann, 1969; Putnam & Stohl, 1990). Both framings are intimately related to the problem of defining what is a group. As indicated by the numerous lengthy discussions of the defining characteristics of groups (Shaw, 1981) and the various types of groups (Argote & McGrath, 1993; Hackman, 1990; Shaw, 1981), there is no simple answer.

The role of group cohesiveness—the attraction a group holds for its members—is also relevant to the emergence and maintenance of groups (see Keyton, Chapter 8, this volume). Group formation and maintenance, moreover, have also been construed as critical outcomes of group activity, as reflected in McGrath's (1991) stipulation of "group well-being" as one of three key outcomes of group processes, along with production and member support.

Groups are born of individuals, so a second set of questions arises around the issue of the *individual-group relationship*. From an instrumental standpoint, this has been framed in terms of questions about group composition (see Haslett & Ruebush, Chapter 5, this volume): How do different types of individuals "fit together" in groups? and What is the impact of composition on group processes and outcomes? A different instrumental framing centers on the question, How are individuals socialized into groups? One perspective views socialization as the processes by which groups instill their beliefs, values, and practices into individuals. A more contemporary perspective regards socialization as a negotiation between individuals and groups (see Anderson, Riddle, & Martin, Chapter 6, this volume).

Another question in this set is concerned with the balance between individuals and groups: Do individuals give up their identities and meld with groups, or do they preserve their individual motivations, beliefs, values, and practices, even when these run counter to the majority? This is not an either-or choice, and it is interesting to explore how individuals and groups navigate back and forth on this continuum, as well as how they cope with conflicts between group and individual needs. This leads directly to the question, How are the needs of individual members satisfied by groups? Satisfaction of member needs ultimately is linked to the preservation of the group, which is why McGrath (1991) made member support the second of his three key outcomes of group activity. Although individuals bring their "selves" to groups, however, belonging to a group confers identity in its own right, and some research has centered on how groups confer identity and how individuals identify with groups. A related question stems from the fact that individuals rarely belong to only one group at a time: How do multiple memberships affect both the individual, a particular group, and its members?

Groups are going concerns in which members make significant parts of their lives. A key process that gives significance to social life, as many have noted, is *differentiation* of people into different roles, statuses, or types. This raises a third set of issues connected to the question, How are members differentiated in groups? One way in which members deal with their relationships with fellow members is to adopt or accept differentiated roles that give them a sense of place in a group. The social process of differentiation—which different research traditions have treated as status negotiation, division of labor, and leadership emergence—is an important puzzle. At the group level, differentiation of individual roles creates organizational complexity, which confers the potential advantage of group adaptability but also potential problems of conflict and lack of understanding resulting from different perspectives. A key issue is how groups manage differentiation so that it does not threaten their integration. One way of doing this is to develop role structures, and much attention has been devoted to defining and categorizing the many functional roles that emerge and develop in groups. Perhaps the most intriguing role in groups is that of leader (see Pavitt, Chapter 12, this volume). Puzzles about leadership that have stimulated theory and research include the following: What is the nature of leadership? How is leadership enacted in interaction? and What makes leaders effective in groups? Finally, groups are subject to outside pressures that influence processes of internal differentiation. The impact of external forces on internal distinctions is a puzzle that has attracted considerable attention from theorists in recent years.

One important source and consequence of differentiation is power. Answers to questions surrounding power and influence in groups attempt to illuminate how individual members figure in group activities. One perspective on this issue regards power as a result of distinctive resources held by members. This perspective attempts to identify these bases, how members build them, and how they can be used to influence group processes and outcomes. Another perspective treats power as a capacity of a group as a whole and focuses on how it can be harnessed and increased. A related topic with more emphasis on communication is the study of influence in groups (see Meyers & Brashers, Chapter 11, this volume). Influence strategies, minority influence, and the role of argumentation in groups represent three important foci for this research. A very different framing of power issues is created by the study of democracy in groups (e.g., Gastil, 1993a, 1993b). Indeed, the roots of group communication scholarship and practice are anchored in a concern with cultivating democratic discussion (see Frey, 1996; Gouran, Chapter 1, this volume).

A fourth set of questions concerns *how groups act and interact*. A central question has been, How do groups make decisions? This has been the predominant—some would say overly dominant—area of activity in group communication theory, research, and peda-

gogy. One way to frame this question is to ask what groups *should* do to make good decisions. This perspective attempts to identify requisites for effective group decision making, that is, the communicative functions that must be fulfilled for high-quality decision making. A different framing is not so concerned with outcomes, focusing simply on describing and explaining what groups do when they make decisions. Some studies from this perspective have attempted to examine the effects of input variables, such as task and decision-making procedure, on decision-making processes. Others have opted to study group decision-making interaction directly, in terms of the distributive structure of communication in a decision-making session, its sequential structure, or the phases through which groups pass as they make decisions.

The emphasis on group decision making has drawn attention away from other forms of group action in which groups actually *do* things in addition to just talking and choosing. A set of issues stems from the question, What role does communication play in helping groups act effectively? From an instrumental point of view, one concern is how communication contributes to the coordination of members' actions. Although the subject of some inquiry in the fields of Sociology, Psychology, and Management Science, this issue has received remarkably little attention from group communication scholars. How communication processes may differ in different types of groups—teams, crews, and coacting groups, for example—is also of interest (Argote & McGrath, 1993).

As groups make decisions and act, they interact with people, groups, organizations, and other systems external to the group. An important question, then, is this: How do groups relate to their *environments?* Boundary spanning inherently is of interest to group communication scholars, but most studies of this phenomenon have been conducted by management researchers (e.g., Ancona, 1987, 1990; Ancona & Caldwell, 1992). Of interest are the communicative strategies for boundary spanning and factors that shape their effectiveness. Of equal interest, but also underresearched, are relationships among two or more groups. Organizational communication researchers have used network analysis to explore this question, but it has received little attention in group communication research. Another interesting avenue would be to explore contingency factors in group environments that influence group effectiveness. Considering the question of the relationship of groups to their environments brings us full circle to the first question considered in this section, which pertains to how groups establish and maintain boundaries.

Another set of questions centers on social entities that are a fundamental part of human existence—*primary groups.* Primary groups are ones to which members have an "organic" relationship, as this term was used by Durkheim (1933/1964). They include families (see Socha, Chapter 17, this volume) and key reference groups, such as peer groups and close friendship groups (for classic studies, see Homans, 1950; Whyte, 1943). We have not explored in sufficient depth how communication operates in primary groups and the nature of its impact on members and on such groups themselves. In addition, we know little about how communication and other processes in primary groups differ from those in other groups. There is also a dearth of knowledge concerning the long-term effects of membership in primary groups on people's participation in groups later in their lives (see Socha, 1997). These are important, but understudied, topics.

The last two sets of questions relate to the recapitulation of individual-level processes in groups. We typically think of individuals as the entities who feel and think, but some theorists have attempted to extend these processes into the group context. The thinking aspect of human experience is reflected in an upsurge of interest in *group cognition.* The central question is, How does communication contribute to group cognition? Many researchers argue that phenomena analogous to individual cognitive processes, such as memory, attention, and reasoning, can be discerned in

social interaction. Some researchers make the more extreme claim that some cognitive processes, such as remembering and reconstructing, are inherently socially based. The "group mind" hypothesis, which holds that social collectives think much as individuals do, has been brusquely dismissed for decades, but it is once more being entertained in more sophisticated forms (see, for example, Weick & Roberts, 1993). Communication is part and parcel of any account of socially mediated cognition, but group communication theory and research have remained strangely silent on these issues.

The complement to the cognitive question is, How does communication contribute to the *emotional life* of groups? Anger, humor, fear, boredom, and other emotional states are shaped by the group contexts in which they are enacted. Processes as diverse as contagion and complementarity have been advanced to explain how groups contribute to emotional states of their members. Group communication theory and research have paid remarkably little attention, however, to emotions in groups (see Keyton, Chapter 8, this volume). Indeed, whether groups, as entities, can enjoy emotional states or climates is still an open issue.

This constellation of driving questions covers considerable ground and will, no doubt, continue to grow as group communication theory and research expand. Indeed, the questions on cognition and emotion would not have been on a list compiled 5 years ago. The questions are also interconnected in the sense that asking one question either raises or implies answers for others. For instance, if we view individuals as being socialized into groups, then this implies that socialization is one technique for group boundary maintenance. The cascade of answers as we move from one question to others is evident in many chapters of this volume.

It is now time to turn from questions to some of the answers advanced thus far in group communication theory. These questions are implicitly part of all that follows, because to understand group communication theories is to consider the questions they pose. One key to grasping the direction of the group communication field as a whole is to consider what questions it has and has not addressed. Some of the questions just advanced have received considerable attention, but others have been underemphasized and some have been largely ignored. Although it is important to enlarge and detail answers to familiar questions, it is equally important to extend the reach of our theories by encompassing additional questions. As this review indicates, general theories are best equipped to expand their coverage of questions and issues. Focused theories have a more limited range, but they can provide very useful answers to the particular questions they are designed to address. Agenda-setting positions, though they do not answer questions themselves, serve the important function of expanding the questions research considers as well as reinterpreting existing questions.

GENERAL THEORIES OF GROUP COMMUNICATION

General theories apply to a wide range of group communication phenomena; however, it is not unusual for such theories to be developed in the context of research on specific communication phenomena—such as group decision making—or in answer to particular questions—such as how groups form and maintain themselves. One consequence of this is that other scholars often incorrectly assume that these theories are devoted solely to that specific context or question. In determining whether a theory is general or focused, it is necessary to look at its potential, rather than actual, field of application. To the extent that a theory can illuminate more contexts and questions than those to which it was initially applied, it is general. Each of the three theories discussed in this section is general, in the sense that it can illuminate a broad range of questions about group communication and applies to numerous group contexts.

Functional Theory

Function, a term with a long history in the social sciences, refers to the *effect* or *consequence* a given behavior or structure has for a group system (Skidmore, 1979). Theories concerned with group functions assume that the important effects are those that enable a group to address a particular problem or to achieve its goals (in this volume, see Chapters 1 [Gouran] and 7 [Hirokawa and Salazar]). Such theories require that the theorist define requisite needs, goals, problems, and challenges that groups must satisfy or overcome to be effective and to maintain their well-being. Communicative behaviors are analyzed to determine which functions they serve in terms of these requisites. The result of functional theory and research is an understanding of how communication contributes to group effectiveness.

As Pavitt (1994; see also Chapter 12, this volume) argues in a penetrating article on functional theories in group communication, functional explanations must satisfy the following formula developed by Wright (1971): The function of X is Z if and only if

1. Z is a consequence of X's being there, and
2. X is there because it does Z (p. 532).

Pavitt uses the example of the "coordinating function" from Benne and Sheats's (1948) functional theory of group roles to illustrate the formula. To establish that the coordinating function contributes to successful task performance in a group, researchers must establish that

1. successful task performance is a consequence of coordinating being performed during a group discussion, and
2. coordinating is performed during group discussion because it leads to successful task performance (Pavitt, 1994, p. 533).

Both claims must be supported by specific generative mechanisms that indicate (a) how coordination leads to successful task performance and (b) how communicative acts performing the coordinating function come about during discussion. In any theory assuming that group members consciously plan and monitor their actions (i.e., most theories of group communication), it is also important to establish that members know about the connection between coordination and task performance, at least at the level of tacit knowledge.

One of the earliest and most subtle functional theories of groups is Bales's (1953) Equilibrium Theory. Bales posited that effective groups must meet both task and socioemotional needs, which involves maintaining a balance between task and socioemotional activity (in this volume, see Chapters 3 [Mabry] and 8 [Keyton]). Bales and Strodtbeck (1951) defined a sequence of problems that groups had to solve to carry out problem-solving tasks—orientation, evaluation, and control—and posited a set of acts that addressed these problems. In addressing each problem, socioemotional issues arise as a consequence of disagreements among members and the tension that builds up because of a focus on work rather than intragroup relationships. This socioemotional energy has to be bled off, which may be accomplished through positive activities, such as joking and congratulating members for good ideas, and through negative activities, such as the expression of frustration or even aggression against other members. If socioemotional issues are not addressed from time to time, the mounting tension may otherwise inhibit the group's ability to make progress in its work. Hence, Bales (1953) posited that groups face an equilibrium problem that leads them to tack back and forth between concern with task and concern with socioemotional issues, with mixtures of these activities during transition periods. Bales's (1950) influential coding system, Interaction Process Analysis (IPA), was designed to capture the activities that served these functions (in this volume, see Chapters 8 [Keyton], 12 [Pavitt], and 17 [Socha]).

The distinction between task and socioemotional behavior remains a fundamental as-

sumption of group communication research; however, the details of Bales's theory and the notion of the equilibrium problem are not very conspicuous in group communication research. This is unfortunate, because the theory goes well beyond the task/socioemotional distinction.

One important extension of Equilibrium Theory was research on the functional differentiation of roles in groups, which showed that distinct task and socioemotional roles tend to emerge in groups. Concomitant with this work, a number of scholars were compiling lists of roles in groups, some with more than 50 functional roles (e.g., Benne & Sheats, 1948; Carter, Haythorn, Meirowitz, & Lanzetta, 1951). This tendency to attach functions to persons also found its way into leadership theory in the various functional representations of leadership (e.g., Bass, 1990; Bowers & Seashore, 1966; Yukl, 1989; see Pavitt, Chapter 12, this volume).

One of the most influential group communication theories is Gouran and Hirokawa's (1983, 1986, 1996) Functional Theory of group decision making (see also Gouran, Hirokawa, Julian, & Leatham, 1993; in this volume, see Gouran [Chapter 1] and Hirokawa & Salazar [Chapter 7]). This theory draws on Bales's (1953) Equilibrium Theory, Janis's (1982) theory of decision-making errors, and Dewey's (1910) reflective thinking model (see Propp, Chapter 9, this volume). It posits that in effective decision-making groups, communication serves both promotive functions that facilitate sound reasoning and critical thinking and counteractive functions that prevent a group from making errors. Gouran and colleagues (Gouran & Hirokawa, 1996; Gouran et al., 1993) posit that communication enables group members to pool information, identify and remedy individual errors, and make persuasive arguments (in this volume, see Propp [Chapter 9] regarding collective information processing and Meyers and Brashers [Chapter 11] on influence processes in groups). If group activities are in the service of adequate problem analysis, clear and realistic goal setting, and critical and realistic evaluation of information and options, a group should be more likely to make an effective decision.

Functional Theory has evolved through two decades of empirical research and has a solid evidentiary base. Gouran, Hirokawa, and colleagues have assimilated these empirical findings into the theory, which has become increasingly sophisticated over the years. Recently, Gouran and Hirokawa (1996) have moved to broaden the theory to respond to cognitive, affiliative, and egocentric constraints acting on decision-making groups.

Functional Theory has several notable strengths. It is closely tied to the traditional interest of group communication scholars and educators in promoting rational decision making and critical, reflective discussion (see Gouran, Chapter 1, this volume). Functional Theory directly addresses what communication *does* in groups, emphasizing "the bottom line"—decision-making effectiveness. Scholars operating from this theory have also attempted to include in their research not only artificial tasks but also studies of the consequences of actual group decisions, both epochal (e.g., the *Challenger* launch decision; see Gouran, Hirokawa, & Martz, 1986; Hirokawa, Gouran, & Martz, 1988) and everyday (e.g., organizational work teams; see Propp & Nelson, 1996).

Critics of Functional Theory argue that assessing outcomes is by no means straightforward (see Billingsley, 1993; Gouran et al., 1993; Poole, 1990; Stohl & Holmes, 1993). Valid criteria for judging the effectiveness of "real-world" decisions are difficult to define and often conflict. Moreover, what might appear to be a sound decision in the short run is often problematic in the long term, and vice versa. Other critics argue that the almost exclusive focus on rational decision making in the theory is too narrow and that the role of precedent, intragroup relationships, environmental constraints, and politics should be taken into account. Stohl and Holmes (1993) suggest additional communicative functions based on these considerations.

There is also difficulty in delimiting a set of requisite critical functions, even for the limited case of group decision making (see Gouran et al., 1993). Functional studies have revealed that different functions are critical in different experimental situations. Gouran and Hirokawa (1996) have also posited that the appropriate set of critical functions will differ over time. For example, functions critical when a group is defining a problem at the outset are likely to be different from those important to finalizing a solution. Furthermore, functions may be interchangeable, in that they may be sufficient, but not necessary, for effectiveness; as a result, those functions that are carried out may often compensate for those that are not fulfilled. These circumstances pose challenges to the determinacy of Functional Theory.

One option is to add complexity to functional theories, as Bales and Cohen (1979) did in extending Bales's earlier theory in their Systematic Multiple Level Field Theory. They also developed an associated observational system for the analysis of groups, SYMLOG (see Keyton, 1995, 1997, Chapter 8, this volume). Systematic Multiple Level Field Theory conceptualizes a group's relational field on the basis of a three-dimensional perceptual space that depicts how group members see themselves and other members: dominant/submissive (up/down), friendly/unfriendly (positive/negative), and instrumentally controlled/emotionally expressive (forward/backward). Bales conceived of each group member as located in this space and asserted that the functions of communication and other activity in a group determined members' location, as well as any changes in their position. The space is not, however, simply an observer's construct. Bales believed that group behavior operates on several levels of meaning and that to understand a member's position in a group, it is necessary to "alternate" between different perceptual spaces—those of the member, other members, and observers. Bales and Cohen devoted a considerable amount of attention to how this is to be achieved in explicating SYMLOG.

Bales and Cohen combined Field Theory, research on the perception of social behavior, and Bales's own successive developments of Equilibrium Theory in proposing Systematic Multiple Level Field Theory. The advantage of this formulation is that it transcends the more limited problem-solving focus of Equilibrium Theory and offers a general theory of group dynamics. By positing multiple functional implications of members' behavior, the theory overcomes the difficulties that arise when researchers try to identify critical functions or key consequences of behavior. One shortcoming, however, is that the theory moves theoretical focus away from commonsense, immediately observable functions, such as evaluative statements, toward the underlying implications of functions, such as their expression of positivity or dominance. Moreover, with its multiple levels of perception and analysis, SYMLOG is extremely complicated to apply. It is far from clear how to resolve conflicts and contradictions among different perspectives, although Bales and Cohen provide some suggestions.

Systematic Multiple Level Field Theory and its observational system, SYMLOG, have received relatively little attention from group communication scholars (see Cegala, Wall, & Rippey, 1987; Keyton, 1995, 1997, also Chapter 8, this volume). In view of the importance of Bales's earlier work in grounding group communication research, the theory and SYMLOG merit more attention from group communication scholars.

McGrath's (1991) Time, Interaction, and Performance (TIP) Theory, one of the most elaborate functional theories, accords communication a major role. McGrath distinguishes three classes of functions in groups: (a) *production functions* contribute to the system in which a group is embedded; (b) *member support functions* contribute to individual members, meeting their needs and keeping them motivated; and (c) *group well-being functions* help a group remain an intact and continuing social system. Purposeful action in groups involves four modes of activity, each of which has important communicative ele-

ments: goal choice, means choice, policy choice, and goal-attainment activities. Each of these modes has different consequences for the three classes of functions.

TIP Theory posits that members and a group as a whole have limited time and energy; therefore, they must allocate their efforts to a limited set of modes and functions. People simultaneously are members of multiple groups and, consequently, are faced with trade-offs in the amount of energy they can devote to a group at any given time. Moreover, there may be conflicts among functions and modes of achieving them within a group. As a result, group interaction is characterized by shifting patterns of activities devoted to different functions at different times. An effective group addresses those functions that are most critical at a given point in time and, harking back to Bales, maintains a balance among the three functions and four modes.

TIP Theory is the most comprehensive functional theory of groups to date. It has the advantage of considering a broad range of functions not confined to task-related matters. Neither is it an overly rational approach. The theory also incorporates the realistic assumptions that group members have divided loyalties and competing priorities and that groups, as well as their members, have finite amounts of time and energy. This assumption enables TIP Theory to model the group as an "economy," in which different tasks, functions, and activities compete for members' attention. The result is a model with the capacity to match the varied patterns of behavior exhibited by groups and their members in a variety of contexts.

All the functional theories discussed in this section are general, in that they can cover many contexts and questions. Although Gouran and Hirokawa's Functional Theory has not been applied to other aspects of group communication, it could be extended readily to group phenomena other than decision making once relevant, meaningful outcomes are defined.

Functional theories are valuable because they focus attention squarely on observable interactions and their consequences for groups.

Their concern with group outcomes ensures that researchers attend to "differences that make a difference." This focus has been very valuable in research on communication and group decision making, which has fairly well defined (though hard to measure) outcome constructs. The concern with outcomes, however, also poses key problems for Functional Theory. As noted, valid measurement of outcomes is difficult, especially for "real-world" groups. Moreover, as goals and desired outcomes of groups change, critical functions change, too. It is important, therefore, for functional theories to incorporate the dynamics of group development and the need to balance disparate functions, as TIP Theory has done.

It is also important to guard against the tendency noted by Giddens (1977) for functional theories to reify the systems and functions they posit. A type of circular reasoning is sometimes applied: A system needs to have a particular function met to survive or to be effective, so if the system is surviving or effective, it must be the result of behavior that serves that function; conversely, if a system is decaying or ineffective, the function must not be satisfied. If function and system are set up to presuppose one another, then there is no way of falsifying their relationship. Functional Theory, as articulated by Gouran and Hirokawa, has addressed this issue head on by insisting on independent measurement of functions (usually via direct observational coding of interaction) and group outcomes (usually by independent judges who evaluate only the product/decision and not the group interaction).

Giddens also warns against the conservatism inherent in functional thinking. There is a tendency to assume that if something serves an essential function, then it must be good and should be retained. Dysfunctions or paradoxes involved in functional activities and structures should also be explored, however, and the possibility that they might be healthy should be considered (see Barge & Frey, 1997; Smith & Berg, 1987). Action is rarely uniform in its consequences, as sociologists have ob-

served in studies of the unintended consequences of social systems (see, for example, Skidmore, 1979). Analyses of functions should focus not only on their beneficial consequences but on their negative consequences as well. For example, critical thinking is widely regarded as desirable, but taken to an extreme, it may paralyze a group and, thereby, render it unable to respond quickly to threats.

Another challenge is the tendency for functional analyses to be "self-sealing." Once a convincing set of functions has been articulated, the easiest course is to explain everything in a group system in terms of these functions and to assimilate all group activities to this limited set. Thus, other aspects of behavior are disregarded in favor of those that can be understood within the functional framework.

Finally, Pavitt (1994) argued that most functionally oriented theories of group communication are deficient in terms of the evidence they provide, suggesting that the current body of studies related to Functional Theory needs to be supplemented. Specifically, although most functional theories attempt to establish that functions promote group outcomes, current theories do not establish microlevel generative mechanisms that indicate how functions come to be performed in groups. A complete functional explanation would have to satisfy all the criteria outlined above, which sets an important agenda for functional theories of group communication.

Symbolic Convergence Theory

A series of in-depth studies of learning groups led Bormann (1969, 1972; see also Bormann, 1986, 1996; Bormann, Cragan, & Shields, 1994) to formulate Symbolic Convergence Theory (SCT). The central concern of SCT is how groups and larger collectives create a common consciousness with shared emotions, motives, and meanings that bind members into a coherent unit (in this volume, see Chapters 1 [Gouran], 7 [Hirokawa and Salazar], and 8 [Keyton]).

Symbolic convergence begins with the sharing of group fantasies, a phenomenon noted by Bales (1970). Bormann defines a *fantasy* as any message that does not refer to the immediate "here and now" of a group; it may, for example, be a joke, a symbolic allusion, or an imagined future. If this dramatization is picked up and elaborated on by other group members, members come to share similar interpretations and emotions and to develop common experiences. In this process, called *fantasy chaining,* the group may identify laudable and condemnable actions and people, spin out a common plot, and reinterpret the group's past, especially notable successes and failures. If this *fantasy theme* is repeated, elaborated, and woven together with other similar themes, it may become a *fantasy type,* a recurrent stock dramatization on which group members can call. Fantasy types provide characteristic interpretations for group members and may fit their experiences into an archetypal interpretation, such as the battle between good and evil.

As fantasy types develop further, they may come to constitute a *rhetorical vision* for a group that indicates its place in the world and projects its future. For example, if members collectively see their group as a band of pioneers blazing a trail in the wilderness, this implies a certain attitude toward outsiders and some of the actions the group may conceivably take (e.g., "circling the wagons" in response to a threat). The group may eventually develop a *saga,* an interpretation of its history that dramatizes particular events and socializes newcomers and confidants to its common meanings (see Anderson et al., Chapter 6, this volume, regarding group socialization).

Through this process, members converge around a symbolic representation of their group that then guides and motivates their actions, and, as such, is a channeling influence. For example, with regard to group decision making, Bormann (1986, 1996) indicates that *symbolic convergence* shapes group decision making by creating a sense of common identity and shared motivations among members, fostering creativity through the sharing of fan-

tasies, influencing assumptions and premises that govern group decisions, and suggesting both realistic and unrealistic ways of coping with problems and situations. Group members may even share fantasies about the decision-making process and how it should or will go.

Symbolic Convergence Theory does not posit deterministic relationships concerning the influence of various variables on symbolic convergence or the effects of symbolic convergence on other group processes and outcomes. Instead, it indicates how the grounds for group identity and collective action are constituted. Hence, the theory "does not provide [for] prediction and control . . . but it does allow for understanding after the event and for anticipating possible developments" (Bormann, 1996, p. 112).

Symbolic Convergence Theory is an artful blend of social-scientific and humanistic approaches; it affords some of the explanatory power of the former while retaining aspects of the interpretive sensitivity of the latter. Indeed, both quantitative and interpretive methods have been used to analyze symbolic convergence processes in group (see Bormann et al., 1994). The theory also has the advantage of clearly linking groups to larger collectives. Group fantasy chaining is the starting point for the creation and spread of rhetorical visions that foster social movements and unify publics. Thus, unlike many theories of group communication, SCT does not stop at the boundaries of a group; rather, it enables researchers to grasp clearly how a group is nested in and affected by larger social units, such as organizations and social movements. Moreover, unlike many functional theories, SCT does not rest solely on rational foundations; indeed, its stated goal is to explore the relationship between the irrational and the rational (Bormann et al., 1994).

Because SCT is cast at the conjunction of the social-scientific and humanistic worlds, it has encountered the criticism that it does not fulfill the goals of social science. For example, SCT has been criticized because it does not permit precise prediction or strong explanation. It also has been criticized because it does not specify what causes fantasies to chain out, nor does it make specific predictions regarding the outcomes of fantasy chaining. Perhaps these problems are inevitable; linked as it is to human choice and to the uncertainties of collective action, proponents of SCT accept these limitations.

Other critics have charged that SCT produces formulaic analyses that uncover little new knowledge (e.g., Hart, 1986; Leff, 1980). Although these charges have, for the most part, been leveled at the applications of SCT in rhetorical studies, they apply as well to social-scientific group communication research. Bormann et al. (1994), however, counter that the insights derived from applications of SCT depend heavily on a researcher's skills. A researcher who does not conduct searching, careful analysis and engage in creative application of the theory will render a formulaic, pedestrian study. Of course, this could occur with *any* theory. Especially important in applications of SCT are ensuring that identified fantasy types and rhetorical visions reflect the perspective of the participants, determining an overall pattern that lends coherence to the symbolic construction, and tracing its functions and consequences for participants. Studies by Bormann and his colleagues illustrate several approaches, both qualitative and quantitative, that meet these criteria.

One avenue not often considered by SCT scholars is the possibility that rhetorical visions and sagas may have more than one layer of meaning. For example, one might consider the ideological functions of some rhetorical visions that conceal actual conditions of disadvantage or dominance with a meaningful story that appears to give groups control over their own destiny. Stohl and Coombs (1988) suggest that quality circles—a group method that involves employees engaging in a discussion about how to improve their organization (see Schultz, Chapter 14, this volume)—which management sometimes uses to promulgate a narrative of participation, are subject to this type of control. One perspective

that would facilitate this type of in-depth analysis is Psychoanalytic Theory, which emphasizes the multiply layered nature of fantasy and other imagery. Bormann et al. (1994) go to lengths to distance SCT from Freudian theory, but psychoanalysis provides a potentially powerful lens for understanding deeper aspects of rhetorical visions and why they motivate groups.

Symbolic Convergence Theory has been pursued largely by group communication scholars, but its nuanced and well-developed view of fantasy and symbolism, and their role in groups and organizations, has much to offer scholars in other fields who study groups. Moreover, SCT has an increasingly strong research base to support its claims. The future, it is hoped, portends increased influence of this theory in other disciplines.

Structuration Theory

Structuration Theory, first applied to the group context in an agenda-setting essay by Poole, Seibold, and McPhee (1985) and then examined in two research programs on group decision making (see Poole, Seibold, & McPhee, 1996), addresses the issue of how group activities are constituted through members' actions (in this volume, see Chapters 1 [Gouran], 3 [Mabry], and 7 [Hirokawa and Salazar]). Scholars working from this theory explore the processes by which the production and reproduction of groups occur and the factors that influence these processes.

Structuration Theory rests on a distinction between *system,* the observable pattern of relations in a group, and *structure,* the rules and resources members use to generate and sustain the group system. Giddens (1984) characterizes structures as "recipes" for acting that comprise a configuration of rules and the material and social resources used to bring about the action. Structuration Theory construes the observable group system as a set of practices constituted by members' structuring behavior. The key items of interest are not surface-level behaviors or functions but, rather, the structures and structuring processes that support them. For example, a conflict management episode in a group discussion would be viewed as part of the group system that should be explored by asking such questions as, What rules and resources enable and guide conflict management?, How are generalized, socially shared versions of these conflict management rules and resources appropriated by the group?, and How does the particular manner of appropriation influence the process of conflict management, for good or ill? Also relevant is the question, Does group interaction give rise to other structuring processes that counteract or undermine the management of conflict in this group? For example, a particularly effective rhetorician might contribute good ideas for resolving a conflict but also use his or her skill to dominate the group, turning it toward his or her preferred, but suboptimal, alternatives. In this case, the structuring of control through argument would undermine effective conflict resolution. Structurational research, therefore, involves the search for a hidden order of structures and structuring processes underlying the observable group system.

The central concept in the theory is *structuration,* which refers to the processes by which systems are produced and reproduced through members' use of rules and resources. This definition rests on several key assumptions and distinctions. First, not only is a system produced and reproduced through structuration, but so too are the structures. Structures are *dualities:* They are both the medium and the outcome of action. They are the medium of action because group members draw on structures to interact. They are its outcome because rules and resources exist only by virtue of being used in practices; whenever a structure is employed, the activity reproduces it by invoking and confirming it as a meaningful basis for action. For instance, when a group takes a vote, it is employing the rules behind voting to act, but more than this, it is reminding members that these rules exist, working out a way of using the rules, and perhaps creating a special version of them. In short, by voting, the group is producing and reproduc-

ing the rules for present and future use. Hence, structures have a virtual existence; they exist in a continuous process of structuration. Consequently, a voting procedure does not, for all practical purposes, exist for a group if the group never employs it or never makes it a regular part of its procedures.

Structuration Theory attempts to shift the focus from systems or structures to structuration, which emphasizes the dynamic interrelationship of system and structure in interaction. Neither stability nor change is taken as the "basic state" of a group; each is explained in terms of the same model of continuous production and reproduction. In this view, neither the description of systems alone nor the enumeration of structures and their relationships is the central object of inquiry; the study of structuration focuses directly on group interaction processes.

Structures sometimes are created "from scratch," but more often than not, groups appropriate them from existing institutional structures. Majority voting schemes, for example, are used throughout democratic societies and are embodied in formal, written rules of many committees (e.g., Robert's Rules of Order), so it is not surprising that people carry this structure with them from one group to another. The *appropriation* process, by which structural features are adapted to specific groups and circumstances, and which may lead to structural innovation and change, is an important focus of research in Structuration Theory.

Two classes of factors influence structuration. The first class is concerned with action in groups and its relation to social institutions. It includes (a) *characteristics of the group and its situation,* such as the group's tasks, group composition, historical precedents, structures appropriated from relevant institutions, and structures created by the group; (b) *members' degree of insight* into the structures they use and the group system as a whole; (c) *differential distributions of resources,* which create power and status distinctions; and (d) the *unintended consequences of action* that arise as a result of the complexity of group systems and their environments.

The second set of influences on structuration are the dynamics through which different structural features mediate and interact with each other. Two types of structural dynamics can be distinguished. First, one structure *mediates* another when its production and reproduction involve the reproduction of the other. For example, the capitalist economic metaphor, in which choices are based on rationalistic cost-benefit calculations (see Lakoff & Johnson, 1980), often mediates the use of decision rules in groups (Thibaut & Kelley, 1959). The second dynamic, *contradiction,* occurs when "the operation of one structural principle in the production of a societal system presumes that of another which tends to undermine it" (Giddens, 1979, p. 141). For example, numerous investigators have reflected on the contradiction between the social, collegial nature of group action and members' individualistic striving for control and personal position in groups. Mediations and contradictions involve many complicated relationships and influences, which Poole et al. (1985) describe in more detail.

Structuration Theory has been applied in the study of argumentation in groups by Seibold, Meyers, and their colleagues (see Meyers & Seibold, 1990; Poole et al., 1985; Seibold & Meyers, 1986), in the study of computerized group support technologies by Poole, DeSanctis, and colleagues (summarized in Poole et al., 1996; see also Scott, Chapter 16, this volume, on communication technologies and group communication), and to juries by Keough and Lake (1993) and Sunwolf and Seibold (1998). Each application of Structuration Theory must be adapted to the particular case, which results in situated theories of structuration, such as DeSanctis and Poole's (1994; Poole & DeSanctis, 1990) Adaptive Structuration Theory, a theory that focuses on the use of technology in task-oriented groups. Research using Structuration Theory has explored the role of group interaction in structuration, different schemes for identifying structures and structuring moves, factors that influence structuration, and structural dynamics (see Poole et al., 1996, for a summary).

The strength of Structuration Theory is that it acknowledges the role of action in constituting groups, group interaction, and their products. With its focus on structuring processes and modes of appropriation, the theory can account for variations in group practices and explain variance unaccounted for in theories that concentrate strictly on regularities in group communication. Structuration Theory also explores and attempts to mediate several tensions in group communication research, notably those between action and structure, micro- and macrolevels of analysis, and a group and its environment. A further strength of the theory is its wide scope for application: Structuration Theory is a general theory that can be applied to any group phenomenon (or, for that matter, any social phenomenon), including development of group culture, norms, and interpersonal relationships in groups, as well as particular group contexts, such as families (see Socha, Chapter 17, this volume) and social support/self-help groups (see Cline, Chapter 19, this volume). It is not confined to the domain of group decision making, as has sometimes been supposed.

Several criticisms have been lodged against Structuration Theory. Gouran (1990, 1994) has encouraged researchers to specify the antecedent conditions that make some structures more likely to come into play and influence outcomes. Without such specification, Gouran (1990) argues, "the principal value of the structurational perspective may be reduced to providing post hoc explanations of specific instances of decision-making activity" (p. 318). Gouran's suggestion points to an area that needs more attention in structurational research; however, the claim that Structuration Theory does not allow for prediction is somewhat overstated. Although current versions of the theory do not enable the prediction of the content or pattern of structuring processes, they do allow for prediction at a higher level of analysis that centers on properties of the structuration process itself. For example, Poole and DeSanctis (1990) defined a specific type of structuring process, the stabilizing appropriation, and showed that it could predict effectiveness of conflict management in computer-supported groups (Poole, Holmes, & DeSanctis, 1991).

Structuration itself is, by definition, an elusive phenomenon, and this poses a great challenge to researchers. A key problem is how to get at a duality that continuously and instantaneously produces and reproduces itself and, in the bargain, involves both macrolevel social institutions and microlevel behavior. The best option is to conduct a series of studies, each of which gets at one or more aspects of the larger process. A problem with this research strategy, however, is maintaining continuity and consistency across a long series of studies. Ten years after it was begun, the Adaptive Structurational research program is still in progress (see Poole et al., 1996, for an account of studies and findings from this program).

The nature of structures themselves also presents challenges to researchers. For one thing, an extremely large number of structures might possibly come into play in any given group. One route is to select a priori a set of structures on which to focus, such as those provided by a group decision support system. This carries the danger that researchers may inadvertently ignore other structuring processes that have a much stronger impact. Moreover, some structures are easier to study than others. Structures embodied in material artifacts, such as rule books and group decision support systems, are relatively easy to investigate because they are prespecified and members often refer to or use the artifact as they draw on the structure. Other structures, however, such as the configuration of roles and positions, enjoy a more evanescent existence and persist only in the fabric of a group's activities and customs. It is harder to access such structures because most clues to their existence and operation come from members' behavior. The problem is that a number of alternative structures might account for the same behavior. Without more evidence, the researcher faces indeterminacy.

In a probing analysis, Seyfarth (1998) suggested that structures should not be considered intersubjective constructs, but, rather, products of individual cognitive schemata. He advanced a model of structuration as the convergence of individual cognitive schemata, rather than as a group-level phenomenon. This view of structuration has the advantage of being consistent with current conceptualizations of group memory and information processing (see Propp, Chapter 9, this volume). Seyfarth's ambitious study, however, provided mixed evidence for this interpretation of structuration.

Another thorny problem is the issue of how structures persist in groups over time. The linkage from the synchronous mutual entailment of system and structure to their diachronous production and reproduction over time is fraught with problems of logic (see Poole, 1983). Some theorists, such as Archer (1982), suggest that action and structure should be seen as forming a cycle of alternating influences, rather than as operating simultaneously, as suggested by structurational analyses that draw on Giddens's work. Archer's view makes it easier to conduct research, because one only has to focus on either action or structure. It is difficult, however, to demarcate when action or structure, respectively, are dominant, and analysis of the substantial transitional periods between the action and structure phases, when both action and structure operate, is difficult to conceptualize within Archer's framework.

Another challenge for structurational research is avoiding self-fulfilling, circular analyses. Structuration is reflected in all aspects of social life, and its very ubiquity makes it easy to read into any case. It is quite easy to reinterpret almost any ongoing process in structurational terms, but the veracity of this potentially facile interpretation is difficult to evaluate. Some analysts simply use structurational vocabulary and concepts to dress up relatively shallow observations. One remedy for this potential problem is systematic study of a number of cases for comparative purposes. Finding variation in structuration processes and continually testing discoveries and hypotheses across multiple cases enhance the grounding of structurational studies.

Structuration Theory is, in the final analysis, "intrinsically incomplete if not linked to a conception of social science as critical theory" (Giddens, 1984, p. 287). Although Structuration Theory is intended to make group members more cognizant of the unrecognized forces that drive them, there has not been much critical inquiry using the theory in group communication research. Poole et al. (1985) used critical concepts extensively, yet relatively little subsequent scholarship has taken a critical perspective. Wyatt (1993) developed this point in her critical analysis of structurational theories in group communication. She argued that the theories are grounded in sexist principles because they rely heavily on Giddens's Structuration Theory, which, according to Wyatt, is based on exclusionary, male-oriented interpretations and, therefore, is incapable of facilitating feminist analysis. Wyatt, however, has misinterpreted Giddens in several respects; for example, she claims that Giddens defines power as domination, whereas he actually defines it as a capacity in which differential distributions of resources lead to domination structures (see Giddens, 1979). This definition is similar in most respects to the alternative Wyatt offers. Her basic point, however—that feminist values should be used to explicate structuration—is valid: Structuration Theory is a general theory that invites extensions informed by different perspectives, such as feminism and social democracy.

Despite the validity of the particular point noted, the application of Structuration Theory to group communication is not susceptible to the same criticisms Wyatt lodges against Giddens, because it does not slavishly adhere to Giddens's theory. Structurational theories of decision development and adaptive structuration also draw on such theorists as Barthes (1974), as well as develop their own constructs, such as "spirit of technology" (the general goals and attitudes a technology promotes; DeSanctis & Poole, 1994). They also rely on a much more microlevel conceptuali-

zation of action than Giddens offers. Wyatt's critique of Structuration Theory in group communication scholarship, therefore, misses the mark, although her insistence that the theory should be imbued with positive values is a worthy one. This aspect of the structurational perspective needs further development.

Finally, it is worth considering whether the gain in explanatory power in some cases is sufficient to justify the use of a structurational approach. From a social-scientific point of view, structuration contributes to variance explained in group processes and outcomes only to the extent that groups are free to adapt and alter structures. In cases when institutions are so sedimented that the groups embedded within them have little freedom to alter available structural features or when exogenous variables are so powerfully constraining that group behavior is virtually determined, the use of structurational concepts will add little explanatory power (see Poole & Roth, 1989, for an example of such a case). In such instances, it may be better to employ Occam's razor and develop simpler causal theories. Of course, the degree of constraint itself can be regarded as a valuable parameter in Structuration Theory.

FOCUSED THEORIES OF GROUP COMMUNICATION

The three general theories of group communication discussed above have promoted useful advances, but much of the theory-building activity in the area has emerged from study of particular group phenomena. A number of these focused theories are based on theories developed in other disciplines, or other areas of the communication field, to explain communication processes in groups. Many such theories are discussed in other chapters of this volume. The focal point of some of the theories discussed (presented in the order they appear in the remainder of this volume), as well as a few specific ones, include theories of:

- Group development, such as phase and multiple sequence models (Mabry, Chapter 3; Anderson et al., Chapter 6; Keyton, Chapter 8; see also Poole & Baldwin, 1996)

- Individual group member differences, such as Status Characteristics Theory and theories of in-group/out-group, cultural difference, and group composition (Haslett & Ruebush, Chapter 5)
- Group socialization, such as Uncertainty Reduction Theory and the original Group Socialization Model proposed (Anderson et al., Chapter 6)
- The task dimension of group life, such as the Mediational Perspective of group decision making (Hirokawa & Salazar, Chapter 7)
- The relational dimension of group life, such as Interaction Theory, Fundamental Interpersonal Relations Orientation (FIRO), and Groupthink (Keyton, Chapter 8)
- Information processing in groups, such as the original Distillation Model of collective information processing (Propp, Chapter 9)
- Nonverbal behavior in groups, such as functional theories of nonverbal cues (Ketrow, Chapter 10)
- Influence processes in groups, such as Social Comparison Theory, Persuasive Arguments Theory, and the Group Valence Model, as well as theories of majority/minority influence, bargaining, negotiation, and conflict communication (Meyers & Brashers, Chapter 11)
- Group leadership, such as trait, style, emergent, and contingency approaches, as well as systemic input-process-output models (Pavitt, Chapter 12)
- Creativity processes in groups, such as cognitive theories of divergent versus convergent production and models of individual creative thinking (Jarboe, Chapter 13)
- Group diagnosis and intervention, such as T-Group Theory, Tavistock training, and theories of communication as counteractive influence (Schultz, Chapter 14)

- Group process procedures, such as the original Function Impact Model proposed (Sunwolf & Seibold, Chapter 15)
- Groups' use of communication technologies, such as Adaptive Structuration Theory and the synthesized Meeting-Process Model proposed (Scott, Chapter 16)
- Family communication, such as the application of the Structural-Functional Perspective and Rules Theory, as well as the dialectical and life-span developmental approaches (Socha, Chapter 17)
- Group communication in the educational context, such as theories of cooperative versus collaborative learning and motivational theories (Allen & Plax, Chapter 18)
- Support/self-help group communication, such as internal versus external locus of control theories (Cline, Chapter 19)
- Organizational work groups, such as the Group Variables Classification System (Greenbaum & Query, Chapter 20)

Two observations can be made about these and other focused theories of group communication. First, they are remarkably diverse. They are grounded in a wide range of specific assumptions and lead in quite different directions. Focused theories also vary greatly in terms of their level of development. Some are spelled out clearly, whereas others remain at the metaphorical level. This makes comparative assessment and integration, which require fairly complete theoretical specification, difficult at best.

One of the great challenges and opportunities for future scholarship, then, is the integration of different focused theories. For example, it is important to begin sorting out the numerous theories of influence processes in groups, as Meyers and Brashers have done in this volume (Chapter 11). As their chapter demonstrates, trying to put the different theories into a coherent framework points out some similarities between seemingly disparate focused theories, illuminates a number of gaps in the literature, and suggests new directions for theory, research, and practice.

Second, some focused theories are more closely tied to general theories than are others. For example, the contingency model of group decision development (Poole & Roth, 1989), which identifies relationships between input variables (such as task complexity) and decision paths, has been articulated in the framework of Structuration Theory. A number of focused theories, such as the valence theories of influence (McPhee, Poole, & Seibold, 1981; Poole, McPhee, & Seibold, 1982; see Meyers & Brashers, Chapter 11, this volume), however, have rather ambiguous links to more general theoretical frameworks. Buried within many focused theories are hidden assumptions and unarticulated links to more general theoretical structures. Attempts to work out these connections have the potential to lead to improved specification of these focused theories and further refinement of the general theories to which they are tied, as well as to the potential articulation of novel theoretical frameworks.

AGENDA-SETTING PERSPECTIVES

Group communication scholarship has been blessed with a number of essays that critique previous theory and research and argue for course corrections and new directions. For the most part, group communication scholars have been responsive to these agenda-setting arguments, which do not build theory themselves but call for and shape theoretical development.

A Tradition of Critique

For the past 20 years, group communication theory and research have been driven by critiques. Influential criticisms were lodged in the early 1970s by Bochner (1974), Bormann (1970), Gouran (1970), and Mortensen (1970); in the early 1980s by Bormann (1980), Cragan and Wright (1980), and Gouran (1985); and in the early 1990s by Poole (1990), Putnam and Stohl (1990), and Sykes (1990). These cri-

tiques have been widely cited and have directly motivated much theory building and research in the field (see Frey, 1996; Gouran, Chapter 1, this volume). They have served to keep group communication scholarship vital and growing. Critiques pose problems and puzzles that have the potential to stimulate path-breaking theory and research. They keep scholars from becoming complacent by suggesting novel directions and by letting newcomers know that there is a place for them in the solution of current problems. Perhaps most important, critique is a basic epistemological tool of science, including the social sciences. Popper (1959) argued that advances in scientific knowledge stem not from positive support for theories but, rather, from efforts to rule out competing explanations and objections. In short, science advances through debate and divergence, not through acquiescence and convergence on one point of view. The best way to advance knowledge, it follows, is to foment a constant stream of criticism and response.

Despite the value of critiques, problems may arise when they become the defining moments of a research field. Good critiques suggest positive actions to be taken, but these are often based on opposition to or negation of current practices. A field that takes its directions from critique is, in a certain sense, moving away from its past. This is especially problematic if the critique is powerful enough to discredit the past for many, as did Bormann's (1970) argument against studying zero-history groups in laboratory settings. It is harder to build on previous research if it is unclear what parts are worth preserving. For example, are *all* results from previous laboratory research on zero-history groups suspect, or are some salvageable? If so, which ones? The answers to these questions are often left ambiguous by the critique.

In its disjunction with the past, critique creates a vacuum: We have a sense of what the field is not and should not be, and perhaps what it should be, but our view of what it is and has been is slanted by the critique. This makes it more problematic to define the center of the field and threatens to turn research into redress rather than (re)construction. Centering efforts on reacting to critiques may prevent scholars from realizing the positive aspects of the field and, thereby, hinder development of research traditions. In attempting to create something novel to redress old problems, it is easy to create idiosyncratic research lines that do not proliferate. The extant body of research then becomes a bunch of little islands—none of them large enough to support a thriving community.

It is important to attend to the direction and take advantage of the momentum imparted by critique, but also to avoid its attendant difficulties. It appears that group communication theory, in particular, and group communication research, more generally, is learning to do this.

At least five major agenda-setting perspectives have been articulated over the past 20 years: the Interact System Model, the Socio-Egocentric Model, the Bona Fide Groups Perspective, Natural Groups and the Naturalistic Paradigm, and the Feminist Perspective. This section discusses each in turn and attempts to evaluate its place in group communication inquiry.

The Interact System Model

The upsurge of interest in group communication in the 1970s was strongly motivated by the work of B. Aubrey Fisher. Fisher's agenda is outlined by the Interact System Model (Fisher & Hawes, 1971; in this volume, see Chapters 3 [Mabry], 8 [Keyton], and 12 [Pavitt]). The rationale behind the Interact System Model was to build a grounded theory of communication by discovering patterns of communicative behavior in groups. The theory distinguished two system models: the Interact System Model (ISM) and the Human System Model (HSM) (see Pavitt, Chapter 12, this volume). The fundamental unit of analysis for the ISM was the *interact*, a contiguous pair of acts representing an act-response linkage. Fisher and Hawes believed that the nature of group communication could be uncovered

through analysis of interact patterns to discover common act-response pairs, phases built from interacts, and cycles of phases. These patterns could then be related to the HSM, which represented the structural relationships among group members in terms of power, status, and liking. These insights could then be built into emergent theories of communication and its impact on groups. This strategy was meant to ensure that the resulting theories would be closely tied to communication itself, rather than to theories and insights borrowed from other disciplines.

By focusing research on group communication patterns, the ISM spawned an upsurge of interest in modeling interaction and in the analysis of group discourse. It also struck a chord among many scholars in suggesting that theories should be built from the ground up, not posited deductively and abstractly, as were Bales's theory and Dewey's reflective thinking model. The grounded theory approach influenced much subsequent research and has enjoyed a renaissance in the recent agenda-setting perspectives on bona fide groups and naturalistic inquiry (see below).

One significant problem with this approach to theory building, however, was that a very large number of theories could be advanced to account for a given set of group interaction patterns. In themselves, data give scholars little guidance as to how to specify theories or how to select among competing explanations or accounts. Hence, although it stimulated a good deal of research, the Interact System Model did not stimulate much theory construction by group communication scholars.

Hewes (1979) also criticized the ISM for omitting the individual from the analysis of group patterns. Research using the ISM analyzed patterns of communicative behavior without identifying individual members, under the assumption that the entire system should be the focus rather than individuals. In attempting to move away from psychologically focused group research toward process-focused research, the ISM segregated individual explanatory factors in the HSM. Hewes argued that this segregation prevented the influence of individual differences among group members and their unique communicative activity from contributing to the explanation of group behavior. Hewes averred that human action, the constituent of group interaction, ultimately must be explained at its level of generation—that is, in human cognitive and motivational processes. This argument, extended in Hewes's Socio-Egocentric Model, established a critical nexus for thought about group communication from 1980 to the present.

The Socio-Egocentric Model

The premise that communication has important impacts in groups is taken for granted by most group communication scholars. Hewes (1986, 1996), however, argues that, on the basis of existing research, we have no unambiguous evidence that communication has an effect on group outcomes. This issue is a fundamental one, because at stake is the ability of communication-based explanations to add value to explanations based on psychological or contextual variables that are independent of group interaction. Hewes argues that establishing that communication makes a difference depends on showing that members influence one another through communication and that this influence process explains outcomes (see also Pavitt's [Chapter 12, this volume] discussion of Hewes's position). Hewes (1996) defines influence as

the odds (**Prob**) of event X (overt behavior, action, or covert mental activity) originating with person B at some time t + n given that person A originated Y (overt behavior, etc.) at some earlier time t, does not equal the odds that B would originate X despite A's earlier behavior. (p. 181)

In short, influence can be said to occur when one group member's behavior can be shown to be contingent on another member's behavior.

To establish that group communication has an impact, Hewes argues, it is necessary to compare the explanatory power of communication-based explanations to a baseline model that does not include communicative influence. Accordingly, he advanced the Socio-Egocentric Model (S-E Model), which assumes that each group member generates messages only in response to input variables and to his or her own previous behavior. In the S-E Model, a member's behavior is not contingent on any other member's behavior; the group is simply a collection of people who act individualistically. The S-E Model, thus, serves as a baseline to indicate the degree to which group behavior and outcomes can be explained by a model that does not assume any communicative influence. The degree to which communication serves as a significant explanation for group behavior and outcomes can be assessed by comparing this baseline model to models that include various types of communicative influence. If there is a significant difference in prediction or variance explained, then that difference indicates the size of the "communication effect." Hewes (1996) makes a convincing case that very little group communication research has even addressed the issue of whether communication makes a difference, and he finds flaws in the few studies that have done so. Moreover, Hewes, Planalp, and Streibel (1980) report a study suggesting that the S-E Model performs better than models based on communicative influence, as defined above.

The S-E Model has a wide variety of potential applications in group research that range from decision making to conflict management to provision of social support. As long as group activity is conceptualized and measured at the individual level and there are sufficient observations to estimate conditional probabilities of act-to-act influence, a baseline model equivalent to a zero-order Markov model can be constructed and contrasted with models that assume the influence of communicative processes. If evidence of communicative influence is found, then hypotheses regarding its ability to account for outcomes can be contrasted with the baseline model's predictive power. In a tightly reasoned and informative analysis, Pavitt (1993) distinguished several definitions of influence in groups based on individual-level contributions, and thereby provided a useful supplement to the S-E Model.

Hewes performed a valuable service by casting down this gauntlet. It is important to test foundational assumptions in any area, and he has challenged one, if not *the,* most important, assumptions of group communication scholarship. His analysis sets a tough standard for group communication researchers to satisfy, but, as he has done in other essays, Hewes gladly dons the garb of "methodological Puritanism."

Like all Puritanisms, Hewes asserts its universality; however, the definition of influence employed by the S-E Model adopts act-to-act contingencies as the basic unit of analysis and centers on individual-to-individual influence, which places limits on the applicability of the model. First, consider the assumption that group communication is best conceptualized as individual-to-individual influence. Although such influence certainly is important, there is no way to demonstrate that it is *the* best indicator that communication has had an impact. An alternative perspective would be to set the criterion for communication as *convergence of members around a common viewpoint* conditional on preceding communicative acts. Meaningful influence then could be said to occur when members' beliefs or attitudes move toward (or away from) a common central attitudinal or belief point as a result of a previous member's remark. Like the S-E Model, this definition retains an emphasis on influence, but unlike that model, this definition connects the assessment of communicative impacts to a group property, rather than reducing it to individual-to-individual action.

Alternative definitions of communicative impact may be based on grounds very different from individual influence. For instance, one might argue that communication has an impact when researchers can identify a structure, such as a rhetorical vision, (a) whose construction is extended over a long space of time in varied interactions and (b) whose ef-

fect can be discerned by comparing its narrative structure with the subsequent course of group actions over its remaining life span. In this case, impact would be measured not in terms of the individual causal efficacy of the narrative structure but by identifying a pattern that could be used to interpret the group's past and to project its future. It would be a stretch to read this diffuse and unevenly operating case back into a conditional probability model of influence, yet a good case could be made for communicative impact in this instance.

The assumption that influence is best gauged based on act-to-act dependencies also introduces significant limitations on the research process. To obtain accurate estimates of act-to-act relationships based on conditional probabilities, there must be recurrent patterns of interaction that generate a large sample of act-to-act and person-to-person pairs. Hence, influence can be determined only for those act and person pairs that occur with some regularity in a group. This immediately rules out consideration of cases in which a single act has profound effects on a group. It ignores critical incidents that fundamentally alter a group's direction and whose reverberations are felt long afterward, such as a sharp conflict that creates enmities between two key members of a group. One way to save the appearances is to argue that the effects of critical incidents will show up in changed patterns of commonly occurring acts, but this carries the undesirable consequence of requiring indirect measurement of the primary phenomenon.

O'Keefe, Delia, and O'Keefe (1980) also criticized the stochastic modeling that underlies Hewes's definition of influence on the grounds that act-to-act connections in interaction are variable because norms external to the interaction stream govern interactants' behavior. Following such norms means that, in some cases, an act influences the next act, but, in other cases, it influences the fourth act following it, in other cases the seventh, and so forth, in an irregular fashion. For instance, a question demands an answer, but not necessarily in the next or third or even fourth act following the question. In such cases, calculating the communicative impact of an act to compare to the baseline would be problematic because there is no consistent conditional relationship. Although conditional relationships may exist, their variability and inconsistency make it impractical to use quantitative methods to identify them. The group context multiplies this difficulty above and beyond dyadic cases, as group members often compete for the floor and interrupt chains of discussion, rendering ascertaining linkages between acts problematic. One limitation of O'Keefe and colleagues' argument, however, is that it is based on pragmatics rather than principle. In principle, Hewes's definition is still valid because there *are* conditional relationships— they just cannot be easily detected or measured with conventional techniques.

A final criticism of the act-to-act contingency assumption rests on the fact that this definition of influence hinges on *changes* in behavior. The magnitude of the conditional probability is a function of coordinated changes in interactors' behavior, such that when one person changes his or her behavior, then the second person will change his or her behavior in response, but otherwise the interactors persist in their current behavioral states. One thing that might dampen this relationship is a time delay in the responses of members to changes in another's behavior. Hewes et al. (1980) advanced a more complex model that specifically tracks these changes and allows for the timing of responses to others, but the model has quite stringent data requirements in that it requires measuring lengths of time between acts. A model based on coordinated changes, however, cannot deal very well with the case in which one person decides to stand his or her ground in the face of influence attempts by the other. Consider the case in which person 1 is trying to influence person 2 to vote for a particular proposal, and researchers code the valence each expresses for the proposal. Suppose that person 2 is enraged by person 1's attempts to influence him or her and sticks to his or her position ever more strongly in response to person 1's varied influence attempts, each of which carry different

amounts of positive valence toward the proposal. The conditional probability definition would not indicate influence in this case because person 2's valence cannot be predicted using the valence of person 1's acts. Certainly, however, person 1's behavior is influencing person 2; it is just not influencing it in a way that causes person 2 to be swayed toward person 1's position.

The debate over the S-E Model is still evolving. Whatever its outcome, Hewes's challenge has forced scholars of group communication to reconsider and problematize a cherished assumption.

Bona Fide Groups

One of the implicit presuppositions that has often guided group scholarship, both in communication and in other disciplines, is the assumption "that a group has a fixed location, an existence apart from its environment, and a boundary formed by static borders" (Putnam & Stohl, 1996, p. 149). Putnam and Stohl (1990, 1994, 1996) challenged this presupposition by advancing the "bona fide group" as an ideal type that can be used to frame group communication theory and research. Bona fide groups exhibit characteristics not acknowledged by much previous theory and research: permeable and fluid boundaries, shifting borders, and interdependence with context. Putnam and Stohl contend that these are critical defining features of "real-life" groups and that the concerns they pose imply a novel research agenda. Taking the bona fide group as a reference point encourages scholars to focus on largely unexplored matters, such as the impacts on internal group processes of membership in multiple groups, permeability of group boundaries, group identity management processes, intergroup communication, and negotiation of jurisdiction and autonomy between groups and their external systems.

The Bona Fide Groups Perspective issues an explicit call to redirect group communication theory and research toward a focus on the place of groups within organizations, communities, and other systemic structures. It posits that agencies external to a group have a much more powerful role in group life than most current theory acknowledges, and it challenges researchers to consider explicitly the group's relation to "outsiders." This perspective has been welcomed in recent scholarship (Frey, 1994c, in press) because it moves beyond the bounded, well-defined group that implicitly has served as an ideal type for most contemporary theories of group communication. These theories pay so much attention to what happens within a group that they neglect the real and very interesting problems posed by a group's interaction with its environment and the contextual constraints that impinge on and affect groups. The Bona Fide Groups Perspective places this environmental interaction firmly in the foreground.

To capitalize on the promise of this perspective, however, it is important to avoid a radical switch from an overly internal to an overly external focus. March and Olsen's (1976) work on major decisions in organizations is a good example of what can happen when such a radical shift occurs. Their analysis showed how what seemed at first sight to be an internally driven group decision was shaped by organizational dynamics, shifting group composition, and chance factors. Their effort to debunk rational theories of group decision making, however, led them to neglect the important role of cohesive teams in many organizations (see Larson & LaFasto, 1989). It is as much an error to neglect internal group processes as it is to neglect external influences on groups.

Natural Groups and the Naturalistic Paradigm

Frey (1994a, 1994c, 1996) has advocated the study of a wide variety of groups in their natural settings as one corrective for the overemphasis in past group communication research on laboratory studies of zero-history, decision-making groups solving artificial problems. In his view, group communication theory and research do not reflect the wide variety of purposes served by groups nor the broad array of activities in which groups engage. For instance, a study of several natural task groups by Scheerhorn, Geist, and Teboul (1994) suggests that the majority of a group's interaction has nothing to do with decision making but focuses, instead, on information sharing and other functions (see also Mintzberg, 1983; Monge, McSwen, & Wyer, 1989, for studies that show similar results). This suggests that the emphasis on decision making in much group communication research may lead to the neglect of many important group dynamics.

To develop a fuller understanding of natural groups, Frey argues, researchers should consider adopting the Naturalistic Paradigm, as articulated by Lincoln and Guba (1985). This paradigm is based on the assumptions that

1. Realities are multiple, constructed, and holistic.
2. Knower and known are interactive and inseparable.
3. Only time- and context-bound working hypotheses (idiographic statements) are possible.
4. All entities are in a state of mutual simultaneous shaping, so that it is impossible to distinguish causes from effects.
5. Inquiry is inherently value-bound. (Frey, 1994c, pp. 554-555)

To implement the Naturalistic Paradigm in group communication research, Frey advocates the study of groups *in situ,* a focus on bona fide groups (as defined by Putnam & Stohl, 1990, 1994, 1996), and the application of the naturalistic research methodology outlined by Lincoln and Guba (1985). An appropriate scholarly product of research, Frey argues, is a case study that is idiographically interpreted and, when applied to other group contexts, is done so tentatively. Moreover, researchers should strive to be partners with research participants in a sustained, longitudinal research process; research should benefit and empower participants through a social-action research program.

Implementing the Naturalistic Paradigm encourages researchers to study a wide range of groups in addition to task groups, including "families, support groups, children's groups, church groups, deviant or fringe groups," and a variety of processes in addition to decision making, including "how group members create and sustain group identity, socialize new members, provide social support, develop high-quality interpersonal relationships, and make changes in group process" (Frey, 1994c, p. 557). Focusing on natural groups from the vantage point of the Naturalistic Paradigm, Frey argues, would expand the pool of groups and concepts studied and, consequently, increase theoretical diversity in group communication scholarship.

Coupled with the Bona Fide Groups Perspective, the Naturalistic Paradigm has stimulated a new surge of research on group communication. Since registering this challenge, Frey (1994b, 1995) has edited two volumes of studies on a wide variety of groups in context, many of which follow approaches consistent with the Naturalistic Paradigm. Another contribution of the Naturalistic Paradigm is its call for a new research paradigm in group communication studies. Lincoln and Guba's (1985) work represents an important attempt to develop coherent philosophical and theoretical foundations for qualitative research, and it offers a very useful perspective for group communication scholars.

Seibold (1994), however, registered two qualifications concerning the use of the naturalistic approach in the study of group communication. First, he notes that concentrating on the *most common* group activities, such as sharing information, does not guarantee that theory and research are tapping into the *most important* group activities. Decision making, Seibold maintains, is embedded in almost all other significant group activities. To the extent this counterargument is valid, the emphasis on decision making in group communication theory and research that Frey (1996) documents and laments may not be as misplaced as he implies.

Second, Seibold points to difficulties and ambiguities in defining what is a natural group

or team. The usual procedure in field research is to take at face value the groups studied; that is, if a set of people calls itself a group and/or is called a group by others or by some embedding organization, and/or interacts frequently, it is treated as a group. Seibold reminds us, however, of the problematic nature of any criteria used to define groups, whether formulated on the basis of members' perceptions, perceptions of others, or artifactual evidence, such as minutes or organizational charts. Indeed, the Bona Fide Groups Perspective registers exactly this argument in its emphasis on the fluid nature of group boundaries and shifting borders. If this is the case, then the "natural" groups that naturalistic researchers define and study are also arbitrary constructions of the researcher, just as are laboratory groups.

A central challenge, therefore, for naturalistic group communication researchers is to minimize the imposition of their constructions on natural groups. This extends not only to delimiting what is the group under study, but also to the conclusions researchers draw. Proponents of the Naturalistic Paradigm understand this concern and, consequently, stress the need for the co-construction of understanding by the researcher and research participants, a useful and empowering move. It is important to remember that the researcher has more power in the academic side of this process than the participant by virtue of her or his position as the final gatekeeper for the published work. There is a potential conflict between the desire of the researcher to draw conclusions that will catch the attention of other scholars (these often must be framed in general, definitive terms) and the charge of the Naturalistic Paradigm that the researcher remain tentative in applying conclusions to other cases and even to the case at hand after the study ends (because the group studied may evolve in directions that change it fundamentally).

For example, in his account of an excellent study by Adelman and Frey (1994) applying the Naturalistic Paradigm to investigate communication and community building in a residential facility for people with AIDS, Frey

(1994c) draws the conclusion that "community living is best understood as a precarious balance between dialectical tensions" (p. 571). This statement has a universalizing tone and quality that seems out of character with the premises of the Naturalistic Paradigm. Although drawing conclusions of this type is a natural and understandable goal of scholarship, it may come into conflict with the need to recognize multiple realities and to remain tentative when making generalizations. Balancing the need to understand participants in lived context with the necessity to take knowledge away and report it to others (thus freezing what is known and alienating it from its context) is an exceptionally difficult undertaking, and I know of no fully satisfactory procedure for doing so.

Feminist Perspectives

In a pointed critique, Wyatt (1993) reminds us that a great deal of past research on groups has been stimulated by military and corporate funding. As a result, she contends, group research has focused primarily on task groups and has been concerned with increasing group effectiveness. These tendencies have distorted the research agenda, resulting in selective attention to only a few sides of multifaceted group processes and to interest in a restricted range of groups. Despite the fact that little group communication research has relied on funded support, insofar as it has been influenced by research in other fields, group communication research is subject to the same distorting influences. For example, the general model of discourse adopted by most group communication scholars has been the rationally driven, disputational approach that Wyatt characterizes as a "white, middle-class, male" model. She makes a persuasive argument that other models of group discourse should be considered, especially "the oral discourse patterns and collaborative strategies for sharing experience used most often by women" (p. 79).

Heeding this call, Meyers and Brashers (1994) offer a constructive prescription for a Feminist Perspective in group communication theory and research. They propose that two values important in feminist thinking—connection and cooperation—can be used to guide theory-building and research efforts. They argue, for instance, that rather than thinking of group decision making as a process governed by influence and persuasion, it might be better thought of as a communal process of collaborative emergence. By moving away from a focus on task-oriented, decision-making groups and reorienting our thinking around cooperation and connection, group communication theorizing may reveal different types of groups to study and different processes to explain. Meyers and Brashers work out, in some detail, useful and interesting exemplars of new topics for such theory and research.

The Feminist Perspective calls for a "transvaluation of values" underlying the study of group communication, as well as advocates different assumptions about the nature of group communication and the methods used to study it. This move has great potential to bring greater enlightenment to theory and research, as well as to pedagogy and other applied practices. Theorizing is a value-driven undertaking, and it is easy to forget that theories entail value judgments that are part and parcel of statements about phenomena. Challenges from feminist and other viewpoints serve as useful "wake-up calls" for lines of work grown complacent from too much time spent in well-worn tracks. Challenges that label other perspectives "sexist," however—as Wyatt did in describing Structuration Theory—are less helpful because they encourage the same sort of stereotyping that feminists condemn.

It is also important that such efforts go beyond being merely "calls" for new directions. Feminist and other value systems need to be put into action in theory and research, as Edelsky (1981) did in her study of cooperatively shared floor in group discourse (see Wyatt, 1993, for accounts of this and other examples of feminist research in group communication). Once bodies of scholarship have been produced and integrated, these perspectives can be contrasted with and critiqued from other points of view, perhaps even from the instrumental point of view against which they react.

FUTURE DIRECTIONS FOR GROUP COMMUNICATION THEORY

The preceding section shows the riches contained in recent discourse about, around, and against group communication theories. It stakes important challenges and directions for those who wish to contribute to future theory and research. With such a strong base, group communication theory is in a good position for the future. This section first glosses some promising resources available for further theory development and then proposes some issues that seem to require answers from group communication theory.

Old (and Not-So-Old) Resources for Theory Building

Curiously, some of the best opportunities for the advancement of group communication theory may come from revisiting classic sources that are often embedded deep within seemingly new formulations. For example, Social Exchange Theory is a commonly unacknowledged source in group communication research. As Roloff (1981) showed, this theory has important implications for communication theory in general (see also Deutsch & Krauss, 1965; Homans, 1961), and the classic works of Thibaut and Kelley (1959; Kelley & Thibaut, 1978) elaborate exchange theories in the group context. These theories are worth revisiting because they articulate an explanation for microlevel interaction and address the issue of how micro- and macrolevel patterns of interaction relate. Joining newer developments in Game Theory to the classical social exchange models has the potential to greatly expand the reach of Social Exchange Theory within the group context by employing more realistic models that include multiple actors with different motivations.

Homans (1950) presented one of the most important and well-developed theories of group behavior in his text *The Human Group*. With its careful and in-depth analysis of previous case studies of groups, this volume offers an intriguing theory of group interaction that has great relevance for group communication scholarship. The model posits that a group must balance activity in its external system, which deals with production and the group's environment, with activity in the internal system, which deals with relations among members and development of the group. It is worth noting that Homans construes "production" broadly to mean anything a group does that contributes to or changes its environment; thus, for example, the external system of streetcorner gangs consists of their interaction with other people in the neighborhood and the good or bad feelings this produces. This deceptively simple scheme provides an excellent framework for explaining and understanding complex group processes, as illustrated in Homans's detailed and insightful discussion of five cases. Homans's theory has the potential to support integration of internally focused theories, such as Symbolic Convergence Theory, and externally focused theories, such as the Bona Fide Groups Perspective.

Most histories of group communication theory list Field Theory as one of the key intellectual sources of the field (see, for example, Frey, 1996; in this volume, see Chapters 1 [Gouran] and 3 [Mabry]). Much can be gained by revisiting the original writings of Lewin (1948, 1951, 1953), as well as those of the Michigan School of group dynamics (e.g., Cartwright & Zander, 1968). These scholars developed such concepts as group cohesiveness, climate, and conflict management styles, and were among the first to highlight group interaction in their research. Although these concepts continue to play a major role in group communication theory and research, the theory that undergirds them is not mentioned very much. Field Theory has the potential to integrate findings in such areas as group development and leadership by focusing attention on how these processes build the group field and advance the group as a whole through its field.

Although group communication scholarship has been fortunate to have developed three general theories, there is always room for more. Understanding is best advanced by multiple perspectives engaged in debate and competing for attention. Properly updated and reinvigorated, these three classic frameworks—Social Exchange Theory, Homans's theory, and Field Theory—could each provide the basis for a general theory that adds another voice to the conversation about group communication processes.

More recent directions also hold promise for expanding group communication theory. Since the early work of Hawes and Foley (1973) and especially Hewes (1975, 1980), the potential of formal models of group communication has been evident (for general discussions of formal modeling, see Berger, Cohen, Snell, & Zelditch, 1962; Coleman, 1960, 1964; Leik & Meeker, 1975). Stochastic modeling of communication sequences has played an important role in group communication research and continues to offer powerful tools for the analyst (see Poole et al., in press). Another type of modeling focused on nonlinear systems also holds great promise. Contractor and Seibold (1993; Contractor, 1994) have argued that the nonlinear Self-Organizing Systems Theory (SOST) offers a promising framework for the study of evolution and change in groups (see Mabry, Chapter 3, this volume). SOST attempts to model how groups autonomously develop and sustain structures that create islands of coherence in a larger interaction system, such as an organization, and how, in turn, these self-organizing processes influence other group processes and outcomes. The potential of this and other nonlinear systems theories for group and organizational communication theory has been explored in a recent volume edited by Barnett and Thayer (1997).

A different type of formal theory was offered by MacKenzie (1976) in his text *A Theory of Group Structures*. MacKenzie attempted to develop dynamic models of group structures, such as division of labor and influence, and to relate the dynamics of such structures to group work processes. This rich and complex framework explicitly tackles the question of defining structures and their relationships, an issue raised by Structuration Theory.

Recent trends in cognitive science have spawned the development of *information-processing models* of groups. Reviews by Hinsz, Tindale, and Vollrath (1997) and Propp (Chapter 9, this volume) suggest that the application of the information-processing metaphor to groups reveals aspects of groups not considered in previous group communication theories. Such phenomena as group memory, parallel processing, and collective attention are highlighted by this perspective.

Future Directions

In 1990, I registered what I then perceived to be several shortcomings of group communication theorizing. Following the traditions of group communication scholarship, my arguments were developed in a critical manner, with less charity than I now believe those theories deserved. This section suggests some more positive directions for the development of group communication theories.

It is important for those proposing or extending group communication theory to frame problems and puzzles so that they are significant to scholars inside and outside the field, as well as to the general public (Poole, 1990). Functional Theory has been most successful in this respect, with its emphasis on group effectiveness. Appealing to the general public probably rests more than anything on showing the "real-world" significance of group communication. This suggests the utility of an emphasis on outcomes and other issues that resonate with everyday concerns, such as healthy family communication (see Socha, Chapter 17, this volume) and the role of group communicative practices in education (see Allen & Plax, Chapter 18, this volume).

Reconsidering the list of questions cata-logued in the first part of this chapter reveals some areas that have received relatively little attention and that might pose intriguing prob-lems that would provoke wider interest in group communication. Issues that have en-joyed less attention than they deserve include the relationship of individuals to groups, how communication figures in collective group ac-tion, how groups relate to their environments, the influence of communication in primary groups (the exception in this case being family communication research), and the communi-cation of emotion in groups. The fine set of studies in Frey's (1994b, 1995, in press) edited volumes suggests that theory building fol-lowed by practical application will follow in at least some of these areas.

A shortcoming of group communication scholarship is that it has contributed sur-prisingly little to mainstream communication theory, certainly much less than have inter-personal and mass communication scholar-ship. This is due, in part, to the fact that individuals, either interacting with one an-other or projecting themselves through mass media, have been the favored unit of analysis of the large majority of contemporary social scientists in the United States. Groups and organizations have been construed as contexts for communication rather than as fundamen-tal units in and of themselves.

It is important to establish group concepts as part of basic communication theory. One way to do this is to press the argument that the multiperson exchange common in group com-munication is a fundamental unit of commu-nication (Poole, 1998). Warriner (1956) made an early and convincing argument that groups are just as "real" as individuals. Lewin, Asch, and other pioneers of social-psychological ap-proaches took the primacy of the group as fundamental; only later did the individual replace the group as the primary unit of analy-sis, and it has been argued that this occurred as much because of the methodological con-venience of controlled laboratory research as for theoretical reasons (Steiner, 1974). Much interesting social interaction in such processes

as persuasion, socialization, and support oc-curs in group contexts. Dyadic situations, in which message exchanges among individuals are relatively orderly and meanings are fairly easy to untangle, are ill-suited to represent group interaction and certainly do not exhaust its interesting possibilities (see Keyton, Chap-ter 8, this volume, on the problem of mak-ing claims about relational communication in groups on the basis of research conducted on dyads). In the face of these considerations, it is not clear why individuals rather than groups should be regarded *prima facie* as the primary unit of social analysis.

The primacy of the individual is likely at-tributable to the fact that individuals, bounded by skin, seem whole and unitary, whereas groups do not. What better fundamental unit than the neat, unitary individual in which to cast theories? As Laing (1969) and others have observed, however, the individual self is often divided and fragmented, just as a group often comprises individualistic members, each seek-ing his or her own ends. Both "group" and "individual" are constructions, and each is whole in some cases and fragmentary in oth-ers. Like an individual, a group may maintain a strong entitativity, or it may be noncohesive and fragmentary. The interesting question in this case is, What processes enable a group to create and maintain entitativity?

In the short run, to establish the importance of their field to mainstream Communication Studies, it will be necessary for group commu-nication scholars to show how the basic foci of communication research—such as mes-sages, persuasion, relationships, and iden-tity—are influenced by group processes. Re-gardless of the shifts that have been occurring in the communication discipline, these four concepts still receive the lion's share of atten-tion. To move into the spotlight, one must move toward center stage. Unless group com-munication scholars do so, it will be much more difficult to gain acceptance of traditional group concepts, such as collective decision making and cohesiveness, as well as more re-cently emphasized concepts, such as cooperation and connection, as part of the discipline's canon.

Another important direction for group communication theorists is to expand linkages to other fields. Although communication is of critical importance, it is not the only important occurrence in groups. Linking communication theory to the concerns of group scholars in other fields would facilitate the development of more encompassing and ambitious theories. These theories are also likely to be more interesting because they would have to appeal to a larger audience (see Poole, 1994). Studies of computerized group decision support systems by group communication scholars in collaboration with management and psychology scholars provide an exemplar of this type of work (see Scott, Chapter 16, this volume).

Two other ways to give a boost to group communication theory are to enhance its variety and to attempt integration. These moves may seem to contradict each other, but both are critical avenues in the development of vibrant theory and research. Theorizing is charged by imagination, and there is nothing that sparks the imagination better than variety (Weick, 1989). Calls for studying groups other than traditional decision-making groups (e.g., Frey, 1994a, 1994c, 1996; Propp & Kreps, 1994), for example, are useful because they introduce variety into the field. Different types of groups direct emphasis toward different concepts and puzzles. Variety of this sort suggests new ideas, as well as new perspectives on old ideas.

Running in the opposite direction (but not canceling) the push toward variety must be the impulse toward integration. It is curious how few integrations of the focused group communication theories have been attempted in recent years. Both Hirokawa and McLeod's (1993) interesting melding of Functional and Structurational Theory, as well as Hirokawa and Salazar's (1997) integration of Mediational, Functional, Symbolic Convergence, and Structuration Theory, illustrate the potential of such efforts. Attempts at integration introduce new ideas and focus attention on new phenomena, because they identify gaps in seemingly adequate theories. Another type of integration that would be useful involves pulling together specific theories under the umbrella of a more general theory. Both kinds of integration are in short supply at present, and that is unfortunate because they would contribute to theoretical thinking about group communication. There are other types of integration as well. In a stimulating discussion, Barge (1994) considers how changing the language games implicit in group communication theories to resonate with those of organizational members might promote linkages between different theories and appeal to a wider audience. Poole and Van de Ven (1989) consider four ways in which theories that appear contradictory or in opposition can be mediated: by acknowledging and unpacking their oppositions, by articulating their operation in a temporal matrix, by showing how they operate together in a spatial matrix, and by developing a new construct that cuts through the opposition or paradox.

CONCLUSION

Scholarship can be likened to a conversation. Each scholar tries to tie into developing strands and make a contribution to the discussion. The conversation among group communication scholars has been proceeding apace with regard to theory construction, research studies, pedagogical practices, and practical applications. It is time to expand that conversation to a wider circle both within and outside the field of Communication.

REFERENCES

Adelman, M. B., & Frey, L. R. (1994). The pilgrim must embark: Creating and sustaining community in a residential facility for people with AIDS. In L. R. Frey (Ed.), *Group communication in context: Studies of natural groups* (pp. 3-22). Hillsdale, NJ: Lawrence Erlbaum.

Ancona, D. G. (1987). Groups in organizations: Extending lab models. In C. Hendrick (Ed.), *Group processes and intergroup processes* (pp. 207-231). Beverly Hills, CA: Sage.

Ancona, D. G. (1990). Outward bound: Strategies for team survival in the organization. *Academy of Management Journal, 33,* 334-365.

Ancona, D. G., & Caldwell, D. F. (1992). Bridging the boundary: External process and performance in organizational teams. *Administrative Science Quarterly, 37,* 634-665.

Archer, M. (1982). Morphogenesis versus structuration: On connecting structure and action. *British Journal of Sociology, 23,* 455-483.

Argote, L., & McGrath, J. E. (1993). Group processes in organizations: Continuity and change. In C. L. Cooper & I. T. Robertson (Eds.), *International review of industrial and organizational psychology* (Vol. 6, pp. 333-389). New York: John Wiley and Sons.

Bales, R. F. (1950). *Interaction process analysis: A method for the study of small groups.* Cambridge, MA: Addison-Wesley.

Bales, R. F. (1953). The equilibrium problem in small groups. In T. Parsons, E. A. Shils, & R. F. Bales (Eds.), *Working papers in the theory of action* (pp. 111-161). Glencoe, IL: Free Press.

Bales, R. F. (1970). *Personality and interpersonal behavior.* New York: Holt, Rinehart & Winston.

Bales, R. F., & Cohen, S. P. (with Williamson, S. A.). (1979). *SYMLOG: A system for multiple level observation of groups.* New York: Free Press.

Bales, R. F., & Strodtbeck, F. L. (1951). Phases in group problem solving. *Journal of Abnormal and Social Psychology, 46,* 485-495.

Barge, J. K. (1994). On interlinking language games: New opportunities for group communication research. *Communication Studies, 45,* 52-67.

Barge, J. K., & Frey, L. R. (1997). Life in a task group. In L. R. Frey & J. K. Barge (Eds.), *Managing group life: Communication in decision-making groups* (pp. 29-79). Boston: Houghton Mifflin.

Barnett, G., & Thayer, L. (1997). *Organization-communication: Emerging perspectives V. The renaissance in systems thinking.* Norwood, NJ: Ablex.

Barthes, R. (1974). *S/Z: An essay.* New York: Wang and Hill.

Bass, B. M. (1990). *Bass & Stogdill's handbook of leadership: Theory, research, and managerial applications* (3rd ed.). New York: Free Press.

Benne, K. D., & Sheats, P. (1948). Functional roles of group members. *Journal of Social Issues, 4,* 41-49.

Berger, J., Cohen, B. P., Snell, J. L., & Zelditch, M., Jr. (1962). *Types of formalization in small-group research.* Boston: Houghton Mifflin.

Billingsley, J. M. (1993). An evaluation of the functional perspective in small group communication. In S. A. Deetz (Ed.), *Communication yearbook 16* (pp. 601-614). Newbury Park, CA: Sage.

Bochner, A. P. (1974). Special reports: Task and instrumentation variables as factors jeopardizing the validity of published group communication research, 1970-1971. *Speech Monographs, 41,* 169-178.

Bormann, E. G. (1969). *Discussion and group methods: Theory and practice.* New York: Harper & Row.

Bormann, E. G. (1970). The paradox and promise of small group research. *Speech Monographs, 37,* 211-217.

Bormann, E. G. (1972). Fantasy and rhetorical vision: The rhetorical criticism of social reality. *Quarterly Journal of Speech, 58,* 396-407.

Bormann, E. G. (1980). The paradox and promise of small group research revisited. *Central States Speech Journal, 31,* 214-220.

Bormann, E. G. (1986). Symbolic convergence theory and communication in group decision-making. In R. Y. Hirokawa & M. S. Poole (Eds.), *Communication and group decision-making* (pp. 219-236). Beverly Hills, CA: Sage.

Bormann, E. G. (1996). Symbolic convergence theory and communication in group decision making. In R. Y. Hirokawa & M. S. Poole (Eds.), *Communication and group decision making* (2nd ed., pp. 81-113). Thousand Oaks, CA: Sage.

Bormann, E. G., Cragan, J. F., & Shields, D. C. (1994). In defense of symbolic convergence theory: A look at the theory and its criticisms after two decades. *Communication Theory, 4,* 259-294.

Bowers, D. G., & Seashore, S. (1966). Predicting organizational effectiveness with a four-factor theory of leadership. *Administrative Science Quarterly, 11,* 238-263.

Campbell, D. T. (1958). Common fate, similarity, and other indices of the status of aggregates of person as social entities. *Behavioral Science, 3,* 14-25.

Carter, L., Haythorn, W., Meirowitz, B., & Lanzetta, J. (1951). The relations of categorizations and ratings in the observation of group behavior. *Human Relations, 4,* 239-254.

Cartwright, D., & Zander, A. (Eds.). (1968). *Group dynamics: Research and theory* (3rd ed.). New York: Harper & Row.

Cegala, D. J., Wall, V. D., & Rippey, G. (1987). An investigation of interaction involvement and the dimensions of SYMLOG: Perceived communication behaviors of persons in task-oriented groups. *Communication Studies, 38,* 81-93.

Coleman, J. S. (1960). The mathematical study of small groups. In H. Solomon (Ed.), *Mathematical thinking in the measurement of behavior: Small groups, utility, factor analysis* (pp. 5-146). Glencoe, IL: Free Press.

Coleman, J. S. (1964). *Introduction to mathematical sociology.* Glencoe, IL: Free Press.

Contractor, N. S. (1994). Self-organizing systems perspective in the study of organizational communication. In B. Kovacic (Ed.), *New approaches to organizational communication* (pp. 39-66). Albany: State University of New York Press.

Contractor, N. S., & Seibold, D. R. (1993). Theoretical frameworks for the study of structuring processes in group decision support systems: Adaptive structuration theory and self-organizing systems theory. *Human Communication Research, 19,* 528-563.

Cragan, J. F., & Wright, D. W. (1980). Small group communication research of the 1970's: A synthesis and critique. *Central States Speech Journal, 31,* 197-213.

Cragan, J. F., & Wright, D. W. (1990). Small group communication research of the 1980s: A synthesis and critique. *Communication Studies, 41,* 212-236.

Craig, R. T. (1989). Communication as a practical discipline. In B. Dervin, L. Grossberg, B. J. O'Keefe, & E. Wartella (Eds.), *Rethinking communication: Vol. 1. Paradigm issues* (pp. 97-122). Newbury Park, CA: Sage.

Craig, R. T. (1995). Applied communication research in a practical discipline. In K. N. Cissna (Ed.), *Applied communication in the 21st century* (pp. 147-155). Mahwah, NJ: Lawrence Erlbaum.

Craig, R. T., & Tracy, K. (1995). Grounded practical theory: The case of intellectual discussion. *Communication Theory, 3,* 248-272.

Diesing, P. (1991). *How does social science work? Reflections on practice.* Pittsburgh, PA: University of Pittsburgh Press.

DeSanctis, G., & Poole, M. S. (1994). Capturing the complexity in advanced technology use: Adaptive structuration theory. *Organization Science, 5,* 121-147.

Deutsch, M., & Krauss, R. M. (1965). *Theories in social psychology.* New York: Basic Books.

Dewey, J. (1910). *How we think.* Boston: D. C. Heath.

Durkheim, E. (1964). *The division of labor in society* (G. Simpson, Trans.). New York: Free Press. (Original work published 1933)

Edelsky, C. (1981). Who's got the floor? *Language in Society, 10,* 383-421.

Fisher, B. A., & Hawes, L. C. (1971). An interact system model: Generating a grounded theory of small groups. *Quarterly Journal of Speech, 57,* 444-453.

Frey, L. R. (1994a). The call of the field: Studying communication in natural groups. In L. R. Frey (Ed.), *Group communication in context: Studies of natural groups* (pp. ix-xiv). Hillsdale, NJ: Lawrence Erlbaum.

Frey, L. R. (Ed.). (1994b). *Group communication in context: Studies of natural groups.* Hillsdale, NJ: Lawrence Erlbaum.

Frey, L. R. (1994c). The naturalistic paradigm: Studying small groups in the postmodern era. *Small Group Research, 25,* 551-577.

Frey, L. R. (Ed.). (1995). *Innovations in group facilitation: Applications in natural settings.* Cresskill, NJ: Hampton.

Frey, L. R. (1996). Remembering and "re-membering": A history of theory and research on communication and group decision making. In R. Y. Hirokawa & M. S. Poole (Eds.), *Communication and group decision making* (2nd ed., pp. 19-51). Thousand Oaks, CA: Sage.

Frey, L. R. (Ed.). (in press). *Group communication in context: Studies of bona fide groups* (2nd ed.). Mahwah, NJ: Lawrence Erlbaum.

Gastil, J. (1993a). *Democracy in small groups: Participation, decision-making, and communication.* Philadelphia: New Society.

Gastil, J. (1993b). Identifying obstacles to small group democracy. *Small Group Research, 24,* 5-27.

Giddens, A. (1977). Functionalism: *Après la lutte.* In A. Giddens, *Studies in social and political theory* (pp. 96-128). New York: Basic Books.

Giddens, A. (1979). *Central problems in social theory: Action, structure, and contradiction in social analysis.* Berkeley: University of California Press.

Giddens, A. (1984). *The constitution of society: Outline of the theory of structuration.* Berkeley: University of California Press.

Gouran, D. S. (1970). Response to "The paradox and promise of small group research." *Speech Monographs, 37,* 217-218.

Gouran, D. S. (1985). The paradigm of unfulfilled promise: A critical examination of the history of research on small groups in Speech Communication. In T. W. Benson (Ed.), *Speech Communication in the twentieth century* (pp. 90-108, 386-392). Carbondale: Southern Illinois University Press.

Gouran, D. S. (1990). Exploiting the predictive potential of structuration theory. In J. A. Anderson (Ed.), *Communication yearbook 13* (pp. 313-322). Newbury Park, CA: Sage.

Gouran, D. S. (1994). The future of group communication research: Revitalization or continued good health? *Communication Studies, 45,* 29-39.

Gouran, D. S., & Hirokawa, R. Y. (1983). The role of communication in decision-making groups: A functional perspective. In M. S. Mander (Ed.), *Communications in transition: Issues and debate in current research* (pp. 168-185). New York: Praeger.

Gouran, D. S., & Hirokawa, R. Y. (1986). Counteractive functions of communication in effective group decision-making. In R. Y. Hirokawa & M. S. Poole (Eds.), *Communication and group decision-making* (pp. 81-92). Beverly Hills, CA: Sage.

Gouran, D. S., & Hirokawa, R. Y. (1996). Functional theory and communication in decision-making and problem-solving groups: An expanded view. In R. Y. Hirokawa & M. S. Poole (Eds.), *Communication and group decision making* (2nd ed., pp. 55-80). Thousand Oaks, CA: Sage.

Gouran, D. S., Hirokawa, R. Y., Julian, K., & Leatham, G. B. (1993). The evolution and current status of the functional perspective on communication in decision-making and problem-solving groups. In S. A. Deetz (Ed.), *Communication yearbook 16* (pp. 573-600). Newbury Park, CA: Sage.

Gouran, D. S., Hirokawa, R. Y., & Martz, A. E. (1986). A critical analysis of factors related to decisional processes involved in the *Challenger* disaster. *Central States Speech Journal, 37,* 119-135.

Hackman, J. R. (Ed.). (1990). *Groups that work (and those that don't): Creating conditions for effective teamwork.* San Francisco: Jossey-Bass.

Hart, R. P. (1986). Contemporary scholarship in public address: A research editorial. *Western Journal of Speech Communication, 50,* 283-295.

Hawes, L. C., & Foley, J. M. (1973). A Markov analysis of interview communication. *Speech Monographs, 40,* 208-219.

Hewes, D. E. (1975). Finite stochastic modeling of communication processes: An introduction and some basic readings. *Human Communication Research, 1,* 271-283.

Hewes, D. E. (1979, November). *Discourse can't "behave": Structure, structure, where is the structure?* Paper presented at the meeting of the Speech Communication Association, San Antonio, TX.

Hewes, D. E. (1980). Stochastic modeling of communication processes. In P. R. Monge & J. N. Capella (Eds.), *Multivariate techniques in human communication research* (pp. 393-427). New York: Academic Press.

Hewes, D. E. (1986). A socio-egocentric model of group decision-making. In R. Y. Hirokawa & M. S. Poole (Eds.), *Communication and group decision-making* (pp. 265-312). Beverly Hills, CA: Sage.

Hewes, D. E. (1996). Small group communication may not influence decision making: An amplification of socio-egocentric theory. In R. Y. Hirokawa & M. S. Poole (Eds.), *Communication and group decision making* (2nd ed., pp. 179-213). Thousand Oaks, CA: Sage.

Hewes, D. E., Planalp, S. K., & Streibel, M. (1980). Analyzing social interaction: Some excruciating models and exhilarating results. In D. Nimmo (Ed.), *Communication yearbook 4* (pp. 123-144). New Brunswick, NJ: Transaction Books.

Hinsz, V. B., Tindale, R. S., & Vollrath, D. A. (1997). The emerging conceptualization of groups as information processors. *Psychological Bulletin, 121,* 43-64.

Hirokawa, R. Y., Gouran, D. S., & Martz, A. E. (1988). Understanding the sources of faulty group decision making: A lesson from the *Challenger* disaster. *Small Group Behavior, 19,* 411-433.

Hirokawa, R. Y., & McLeod, P. L. (1993, November). *Communication, decision development, and decision quality in small groups: An integration of two approaches.* Paper presented at the meeting of the Speech Communication Association, Miami Beach, FL.

Hirokawa, R. Y., & Salazar, A. J. (1997). An integrated approach to communication and group decision making. In L. R. Frey & J. K. Barge (Eds.), *Managing group life: Communicating in decision-making groups* (pp. 156-181). Boston: Houghton Mifflin.

Homans, G. C. (1950). *The human group.* New York: Harcourt, Brace & World.

Homans, G. C. (1961). *Social behavior: Its elementary forms.* New York: Harcourt, Brace & World.

Janis, I. L. (1982). *Groupthink: Psychological studies of policy decisions and fiascoes* (2nd ed.). Boston: Houghton Mifflin.

Kelley, H. H., & Thibaut, J. (1978). *Interpersonal relations: A theory of interdependence.* New York: Wiley.

Keough, C. M., & Lake, R. (1993). Values as structuring properties of contract negotiations. In C. Conrad (Ed.), *The ethical nexus* (pp. 171-191). Norwood, NJ: Ablex.

Keyton, J. (1995). Using SYMLOG as a self-analytical group technique. In L. R. Frey (Ed.), *Innovations in group facilitation: Applications in natural settings* (pp. 148-174). Cresskill, NJ: Hampton.

Keyton, J. (1997). Coding communication in decision-making groups. In L. R. Frey & J. K. Barge (Eds.), *Managing group life: Communicating in decision-making groups* (pp. 236-269). Boston: Houghton Mifflin.

Laing, R. D. (1969). *The divided self.* New York: Pantheon.

Lakoff, G., & Johnson, M. (1980). *Metaphors we live by.* Chicago: University of Chicago Press.

Larson, C. E., & LaFasto, F. M. J. (1989). *Teamwork: What must go right/What can go wrong.* Newbury Park, CA: Sage.

Leff, M. C. (1980). Interpretation and the act of rhetorical criticism. *Western Journal of Speech Communication, 44,* 337-349.

Leik, R. K., & Meeker, B. F. (1975). *Mathematical sociology.* Englewood Cliffs, NJ: Prentice Hall.

Lewin, K. (1948). *Resolving social conflicts.* New York: Harper.

Lewin, K. (1951). *Field theory in social science: Selected theoretical papers* (D. Cartwright, Ed.). New York: Harper & Row.

Lewin, K. (1953). Studies in group decision. In D. Cartwright & A. Zander (Eds.), *Group dynamics: Research and theory* (pp. 285-301). Evanston, IL: Row, Peterson.

Lincoln, Y. S., & Guba, E. G. (1985). *Naturalistic inquiry.* Beverly Hills, CA: Sage.

MacKenzie, K. (1976). *A theory of group structures* (2 vols.). New York: Gordon & Breach.

March, J. G., & Olsen, J. P. (1976). *Ambiguity and choice in organizations.* Bergen, Norway: Universitetsforlaget.

McGrath, J. E. (1991). Time, interaction, and performance (TIP): A theory of groups. *Small Group Research, 22,* 147-174.

McPhee, R. D., Poole, M. S., & Seibold, D. R. (1981). The valence model unveiled: Critique and alternative formulation. In M. Burgoon (Ed.), *Communication yearbook 5* (pp. 259-278). New Brunswick, NJ: Transaction Books.

Meyers, R. A., & Brashers, D. E. (1994). Expanding the boundaries of small group communication research: Exploring a feminist perspective. *Communication Studies, 45,* 68-85.

Meyers, R. A., & Seibold, D. R. (1990). Perspectives on group argument: A critical review of persuasive arguments theory and an alternative structurational view. In J. A. Anderson (Ed.), *Communication yearbook 13* (pp. 268-302). Newbury Park, CA: Sage.

Mintzberg, H. (1983). *The nature of managerial work.* New York: Harper & Row.

Mohr, L. B. (1982). *Explaining organizational behavior: The limits and possibilities of theory and research.* San Francisco: Jossey-Bass.

Monge, P. R., McSwen, C., & Wyer, C. (1989). *Profile of meetings in corporate America.* Austin, TX: 3M Meeting Management Institute.

Mortensen, C. D. (1970). The status of small group research. *Quarterly Journal of Speech, 56,* 304-309.

O'Keefe, B. J., Delia, J. G., & O'Keefe, D. J. (1980). Interaction analysis and the analysis of interaction organization. *Studies of Symbolic Interaction, 3,* 25-57.

Pavitt, C. (1993). Does communication matter in social influence during small group discussions? Five positions. *Communication Studies, 44,* 216-226.

Pavitt, C. (1994). Theoretical commitments presupposed by functional approaches to group discussion. *Small Group Research, 25,* 520-541.

Poole, M. S. (1983). Decision development in small groups, III: A multiple sequence theory of group decision development. *Communication Monographs, 50,* 321-341.

Poole, M. S. (1990). Do we have any theories of group communication? *Communication Studies, 41,* 237-247.

Poole, M. S. (1994). Breaking the isolation of small group communication studies. *Communication Studies, 45,* 20-29.

Poole, M. S. (1998). The small group should be *the* fundamental unit of communication research. In J. S. Trent (Ed.), *Communication: Views from the helm in the 21st century* (pp. 94-97). Boston: Allyn & Bacon.

Poole, M. S., & Baldwin, C. L. (1996). Developmental processes in group decision making. In R. Y. Hirokawa & M. S. Poole (Eds.), *Communication and group decision making* (2nd ed., pp. 215-241). Thousand Oaks, CA: Sage.

Poole, M. S., & DeSanctis, G. (1990). Understanding the use of group decision support systems: The theory of adaptive structuration. In J. Fulk & C. Steinfield (Eds.), *Organizations and communication technology* (pp. 175-195). Newbury Park, CA: Sage.

Poole, M. S., Holmes, M., & DeSanctis, G. (1991). Conflict management in a computer-supported meeting environment. *Management Science, 37,* 926-953.

Poole, M. S., McPhee, R. D., & Seibold, D. R. (1982). A comparison of normative and interactional explanations of group decision-making: Social decision schemes versus valence distributions. *Communication Monographs, 49,* 1-19.

Poole, M. S., & Roth, J. (1989). Decision development in small groups IV: A typology of decision paths. *Human Communication Research, 15,* 323-356.

Poole, M. S., Seibold, D. R., & McPhee, R. D. (1985). Group decision-making as a structurational process. *Quarterly Journal of Speech, 71,* 74-102.

Poole, M. S., Seibold, D. R., & McPhee, R. D. (1996). The structuration of group decisions. In R. Y. Hirokawa & M. S. Poole (Eds.), *Communication and group decision making* (2nd ed., pp. 114-146). Thousand Oaks, CA: Sage.

Poole, M. S., & Van de Ven, A. H. (1989). Using paradox to develop organizational and management theories. *Academy of Management Review, 14,* 562-579.

Poole, M. S., Van de Ven, A. H., Dooley, K., & Holmes, M. (in press). *Theory and methods for the study of organizational change and development processes.* New York: Oxford University Press.

Popper, K. (1959). *The logic of scientific discovery.* New York: Basic Books.

Propp, K. M., & Kreps, G. L. (1994). A rose by any other name: The vitality of group communication research. *Communication Studies, 45,* 7-19.

Propp, K. M., & Nelson, D. (1996). Problem-solving performance in naturalistic groups: A test of the ecological validity of the functional perspective. *Communication Studies, 47,* 35-45.

Putnam, L. L., & Stohl, C. (1990). Bona fide groups: A reconceptualization of groups in context. *Communication Studies, 41,* 248-265.

Putnam, L. L., & Stohl, C. (1994). Group communication in context: Implications for the study of bona fide groups. In L. R. Frey (Ed.), *Group communication in context: Studies of natural groups* (pp. 284-292). Hillsdale, NJ: Lawrence Erlbaum.

Putnam, L. L., & Stohl, C. (1996). Bona fide groups: An alternative perspective for communication and small group decision making. In R. Y. Hirokawa & M. S. Poole (Eds.), *Communication and group decision making* (2nd ed., pp. 147-178). Thousand Oaks, CA: Sage.

Roloff, M. E. (1981). *Interpersonal communication: The exchange approach.* Beverly Hills, CA: Sage.

Scheerhorn, D., Geist, P., & Teboul, JC. B. (1994). Beyond decision making in decision-making groups: Implications for the study of group communication. In L. R. Frey (Ed.), *Group communication in context: Studies of natural groups* (pp. 247-262). Hillsdale, NJ: Lawrence Erlbaum.

Seibold, D. R. (1994). More reflection or more research? To (re)vitalize small group communication research, let's "just do it." *Communication Studies, 45,* 103-110.

Seibold, D. R., & Meyers, R. A. (1986). Communication and influence in group decision-making. In R. Y. Hirokawa & M. S. Poole (Eds.), *Communication and group decision-making* (pp. 133-155). Beverly Hills, CA: Sage.

Seyfarth, B. (1998). *Are reasons structures?: A cognitive-structurational approach toward explaining small group processes.* Unpublished doctoral dissertation, University of Minnesota–Twin Cities.

Shaw, M. E. (1981). *Group dynamics: The psychology of small group behavior* (3rd ed.) New York: McGraw-Hill.

Skidmore, W. (1979). *Theoretical thinking in sociology* (2nd ed.). Cambridge, UK: Cambridge University Press.

Smith, K. K., & Berg, D. N. (1987). *Paradoxes of group life: Understanding conflict, paralysis, and movement in group dynamics.* San Francisco: Jossey-Bass.

Socha, T. J. (1997). Group communication across the life span. In L. R. Frey & J. K. Barge (Eds.), *Managing group life: Communicating in decision-making groups* (pp. 3-28). Boston: Houghton Mifflin.

Steiner, I. D. (1974). Whatever happened to the group in social psychology? *Journal of Experimental Social Psychology, 10,* 94-108.

Stohl, C., & Coombs, C. (1988). Cooperation or cooptation: An analysis of quality circle training manuals. *Management Communication Quarterly, 2,* 63-89.

Stohl, C., & Holmes, M. E. (1993). A functional perspective for bona fide groups. In S. A. Deetz (Ed.), *Com-

munication yearbook 16 (pp. 601-614). Newbury Park, CA: Sage.

Sunwolf, & Seibold, D. R. (1998). Jurors' intuitive rules for deliberation: A structurational approach to communication in jury decision making. *Communication Monographs, 65,* 282-307.

Sykes, R. E. (1990). Imagining what we might study if we really studied small groups from a speech perspective. *Communication Studies, 41,* 200-211.

Thibaut, J. W., & Kelley, H. H. (1959). *The social psychology of groups.* New York: John Wiley.

Warriner, C. K. (1956). Groups are real: A reaffirmation. *American Sociological Review, 21,* 349-354.

Weick, K. (1989). Theory construction as disciplined imagination. *Academy of Management Review, 14,* 516-531.

Weick, K., & Roberts, K. (1993). Collective mind in organizations: Heedful interrelating on flight decks. *Administrative Science Quarterly, 38,* 357-381.

Whyte, W. F. (1943). *Street corner society.* Chicago: University of Chicago Press.

Wright, G. H. von. (1971). *Explanation and understanding.* Ithaca, NY: Cornell University Press.

Wyatt, N. (1993). Organizing and relating: Feminist critique of small group communication. In S. P. Brown & N. Wyatt (Eds.), *Transforming visions: Feminist critiques in communication studies* (pp. 51-86). Cresskill, NJ: Hampton.

Yukl, G. A. (1989). *Leadership in organizations* (2nd ed.). Englewood Cliffs, NJ: Prentice Hall.

3

The Systems Metaphor in Group Communication

EDWARD A. MABRY
University of Wisconsin–Milwaukee

THE SYSTEMS METAPHOR AND ITS APPLICATION TO GROUP COMMUNICATION

One of the most dominant, and probably the most taken-for-granted, constructs applied to the study of communication in small groups is *systemness*. This is understandable, for the systems construct also dominates specialized languages used in expressing most forms of physical, mental, and social experience. Virtually every major component of daily life embraces the systems construct; for example, the solar system, ecosystem, political system, management system, family system, and the autoimmune system. In fact, von Bertalanffy (1968), the architect of modern Systems Theory, viewed it as a "new philosophy of nature" (p. xxi) and hoped it would lead to an intellectual unification of the sciences.

Viewing the systems construct, like other theoretical constructs, as a metaphor is constructive (Morgan, 1986). The term *metaphor* is not being used in the literary sense. Instead, after Osborne and Ehninger (1962), the systems metaphor is a *linguistic* metaphor, that is, a metaphor connecting literal and figurative relationships to amplify representational

meaning. Like Krippendorff's (1989) assessment of how scientific discourse functions as an intellectual frame of reference, the systems construct also functions as an *epistemological* metaphor—a language tool (tool set) that aids paradigmatic representation.

Dachler (1984) noted that a variety of metaphoric systems analogies (e.g., mechanistic or organismic) are used effectively for explaining social collectives such as organizations, institutions, or society. More appealing, however, is the invocative metaphoric quality of the construct. If the systems construct is itself a metaphor, we must assume that it functions intellectually as a *root metaphor* that references a knowledge paradigm. Whether intentional or not, that is how systems theorists have positioned its value in scientific discourse (e.g., Buckley, 1967; von Bertalanffy, 1968; Wiener, 1948).

Heuristic Applications of the Systems Metaphor to Groups

Marking the foundation point for a body of thinking is a risky undertaking. Clearly, publication of Bales's (1950) text, *Interaction Process Analysis: A Method for the Study of*

71

Small Groups, was a watershed event influencing the conceptualization of groups as social systems throughout the second half of the 20th century. Bales (1950) posited a method for observing groups—Interaction Process Analysis (IPA; in this volume, see Chapters 8 [Keyton], 12 [Pavitt], and 17 [Socha])—extrapolated from, and isomorphic with, his theory of groups as dynamic, equilibrium-seeking social systems. The groups-as-social-systems analogy subsequently evolved into a dominant theoretical paradigm in social-scientific thinking about human groups (in this volume, see chapters 1 [Gouran] and 2 [Poole]).

A core assumption of systems theorizing is that *communication* is the observable phenomenon binding together constituent components of systemic entities (Buckley, 1967; Monge, 1973). Thus, group members (or sets of groups) are joined together as a social system through their communication. The importance of this position is that it simultaneously instantiates theorized qualities of systemness with an imperative to focus on communication as a necessary operational frame of reference for studying groups. Readers of this volume will clearly see evidence of how this stance is embraced across a broad array of theoretical issues, methodological practices, and group communication processes and contexts.

Pedagogical Applications of the Systems Metaphor

At the time Bales's (1950) seminal work was published, the discipline of Speech predominantly focused on groups as public contexts of rational discussion and argument (cf. McBurney & Hance, 1950). Within a decade, textbooks on group discussion (e.g., Gulley, 1960; Harnack & Fest, 1964) typically included chapters about using Bales's IPA method to observe and analyze group communication processes and variations on his dynamic equilibrium model of group development to explain group decision-making processes.

Shifting attention from issues of reasoning and oral style used in public deliberations to explaining how content patterns of communication constitute systemic processes influencing group integration and performance reflected a paradigmatic change of thought about group communication. This change of perspective, however, was evolutionary. Frey (1996), for example, characterized the study of group communication and decision making during the period 1970-1980 as a "Decade of Discontent." According to Gouran (Chapter 1, this volume), research in group communication was in transition during this period as scholars moved from individual-centered to group-centered theoretical models and methodologies focusing on behavioral versus cognitive measures of communication. During this transition period, group communication textbooks became more explicit in either grounding core concepts in systems terms or actually framing their subject matter as the study of groups-as-systems (e.g., Fisher, 1974; Mabry & Barnes, 1980; Tubbs, 1978).

More recently, praxiological approaches to communication are being advanced that more clearly connect communicating with systemic development. Bormann's (1990) expanded application of Symbolic Convergence Theory to group decision making reflects this trend (in this volume, see Chapters 1 [Gouran], 2 [Poole], and 7 [Hirokawa & Salazar]). From this theoretical perspective, effective group membership is viewed as members participating in the construction of shared meanings about themselves and group practices and outcomes. Bormann (1996) forcefully argued that symbolic convergence leading to shared consciousness among group members is a fundamental property of groups as communication systems. The dialectical perspective, as applied to groups, advanced by Barge (1994) and Frey and Barge (1997), also capitalizes on the communication-system duality. Dialectical theory stresses the role of communication in managing (at individual and group levels) competing influences for shaping group actions. Awareness of how communicative behavior privileges the selection of one choice over another in the face of dialectical tensions is a key element in strategically applying communicative practices to group functions, such as leading, procedure setting, and resolving conflicts.

Chapter Overview

The preceding remarks are intended to form a frame of reference for the chapter. What follows is a discussion of issues divided into three parts. The first part examines the philosophical and scientific grounding of systems theories. The second part concentrates on the impact systems metaphors have on studying group communication. The final part looks at directions that future applications of systems thinking can take and provides concluding observations about the groups-as-systems metaphor.

THE SYSTEMS METAPHOR: EVOLUTION AND IMPLICATIONS

The Symbolic Representation of Organized Complexity

There is little doubt that the concept of systems as a linguistic metaphor provides its greatest value in establishing an intellectual (and empirical) mechanism for understanding how individuals perceptually experience (as participants and observers) sensations of *entities.* In many instances, the individual is part of the entity, yet it is doubtful that systems metaphors would exist if people's experiences with families, workplaces, and social institutions were easily expressed in the ordinary exercise of social perception. That, however, is not the case. Our awareness of social order, a prerequisite of rational action, is often impaired because what we strain to understand is a hodgepodge of only loosely coupled or fragmented experiences. Using White's (1992) metaphor, social experience is a "mess." Appropriating language frameworks, like systemness, is one rhetorical device for imposing a sense of orderliness on an otherwise chaotic social landscape. It helps us to reinstate self-

control over the disempowering sensation of living in the mess. In short, if the systems metaphor did not exist, we would have to create it or another symbolic tool with similar instrumental properties.

Systems theorists also point to another (somewhat similar) reason for the paradigm's development. The growth of knowledge about biological, physical, and social phenomena over the first half of the 20th century became problematic: Once seemingly disparate aggregates of information were moving toward convergent applications. The concept of *information,* in fact, is a good example. Developed originally in mathematical statistics for applications in the study of electrical engineering, it quickly found its way into biological and social-scientific theories and research. These applications required new mental models capable of integrating findings from molar and molecular theories cutting across the spectrum of scientific investigation (see Buckley, 1967; von Bertalanffy, 1968).

At this point, it is necessary to provide a sense of grounding and scope underlying the systems metaphor. This is accomplished by briefly sketching four dominant models that have framed systems theorizing: organic, mechanical, equilibrium, and adaptive (or cybernetic) models.

Organic Systems

Analogizing physical or social order to living things seems as old as human reflective experience. Buckley (1967) traced organic analogies of social organization to sociologist Herbert Spencer. This class of models was framed by the assumption that social entities were manifestly related and integrated by mutual dependencies among their identifiable parts. Thus, a society, social institution, or group functions like an organic whole because its constitutive parts exist to satisfy mutual needs. Changes in one part affect the entire system; therefore, damage to or growth of one part putatively damages or leads to growth in the entire system.

The weakness of this metaphor was its lack of external validity. Clearly, neither organisms (especially complex animals, such as primates and humans) nor social entities evidence holistic mutual dependence. Change in group leadership is a good example (see Pavitt, Chapter 12, this volume, on group communication and leadership). Leaders are often analogized as the "heart" of a group, yet groups can and do lose leaders—metaphorically, have their "heart cut out"—and persevere. Similarly, a family does not cease to be a "family" even when parents separate or die (see Socha, Chapter 17, this volume, on communication in family groups). These types of group systems undergo changes (e.g., members assume new roles, goals are redefined, and old procedures for reaching goals are dropped in favor of new ones). Empirical contradictions to this metaphor, thus, forced its abandonment.

Mechanistic Systems

The view that human social activity could be explained by principles derived by physics and mechanics dates to at least the 17th century and generally is referred to as *social physics* or *social mechanics* (Buckley, 1967). Early uses of mechanistic metaphoric allusions tended to make overly general references to energy transformation, inertial motion, and, presumably, counterbalancing force fields. The dubious empirical validity of the knowledge on which these theories were based, however, undermined their credibility.

Despite this demise, conceptual elements in Italian economist Vilfredo Pareto's *rational mechanics* analogy clearly had a significant impact on such sociological theorists as Homans (1950) and Parsons (1951)—the latter an early collaborator of Bales—whose work has shaped the study of groups as social systems. Pareto's work contributed to structural-functionalist social theories suggesting concepts such as *interdependence* and systemic *equilibrium,* reflected primarily in equilibrium models of systems (Buckley, 1967).

Equilibrium Models

A primary contribution to modern social systems theorizing was Pareto's allusion to what is now conceived to mean *social equilibrium* (Parsons, 1951). Human collectivities, like societies (or small groups), were thought to model an integrated assembly of elements held together in an equilibrated state (a state of balance) as a function of their mutual interrelatedness and interdependence. Mechanical models, however, assumed that equilibrium was achieved through some sort of social energy or inertial leverage. The force exerted among the parts was attributable to operational proximity or functionality, as one finds in the follow-through of a mill turned by wind or a gyroscope.

Modern equilibrated systems theories, in contrast, substitute symbolic action (including communication) and its relevant consequences (e.g., formation and transmission of beliefs, values, and norms) that are attributable to human interaction. Equilibrated systems are marked by countervailing pressures, or tensions, emerging from social stress. Stressors include such actions as seeking or resisting power, conflicts over procedures or analyses of issues, task demands, and role ambiguities or contradictions. Clearly, the groups-as-equilibrated-systems analogy is the foundation for many areas of group communication research, including the relationship of group communication to cohesion, consensus, decision making, goal achievement, leadership, and performance effectiveness.

Adaptive Models

The clearest weakness in the preceding systems analogies is that systemic structure, components and the relationships among them, were assumed to direct system activities (or functions). How social action is motivated—internally or externally—could not be explained apart from how the holistic system was structured.

This vestige of mechanistic reasoning is not compelling in the light of examples that systems learn, reactively change their internal structure, and proactively modify their environments. The first significant integration of adaptive processes into the systems metaphor came with Wiener's (1948) discussion of *feedback* as a core construct in his outline of *cybernetic* systems.

According to Rosenblueth, Wiener, and Bigelow (1943), feedback is a class of purposive behavior that can take either a positive or a negative form. *Positive feedback* reflects system outputs containing properties similar to original inputs that reenter the system as new inputs. *Negative feedback* is referential in that new inputs are formed as discrepancies between outputs and system goals are detected, and these new, negative inputs trigger changes in the system's performance that constrain its movement away from the reference point goal producing the negative inputs. For example, a group that covers agenda items before the end of a meeting's allotted time can use the excess time to create and work on new tasks (positive feedback). Conversely, a group may sense that prolonged discussion of one or more items has placed finishing the agenda in the allotted time at risk and establishes time limits on the consideration of other items as a means to complete all of its work on time (negative feedback).

As Buckley (1967) noted, although *feedback* is a mechanistic principle, the concept has proved its utility in explaining how a system can change and adapt to circumstances outside itself. More significantly, the delineation of feedback as a core construct in defining *information* (identifying positive and negative valences of feedback, as well as their empirical derivations, as analogous phenomena) in the context of Information Theory (Cherry, 1966) clearly frames the importance of adaptive activity as a constituent of human communication.

Adaptation is a significant precept in contemporary systems thinking. The manner in which a system achieves adaptability is a key factor in describing different types of systemic activity. Homeostatic systems react to predetermined routines for sensing and adjusting to information; nonredundant patterning may imply too much or too little of *x,* and the system adapts by changing one or more ongoing functions. More complex systems are not limited to this sort of preprogrammed scripting. Complex systems adapt by collecting and analyzing information and selecting responses from available options. These issues are addressed in greater detail below.

Types of Metaphors: Systems as Forms of Theory Generation

The language for explaining systems thinking provides a powerful set of constructs for studying groups. The elements of particular significance are systemic structure, purpose, and change.

Systemic Structure

Boundaries and the part-whole relationship. Fisher (1974) believed that arguments over when groups become groups were futile; however, he did think that distinguishing "groups" from a "collection of individuals" was an instructive exercise in helping to understand group functioning. Thus, Fisher, like many other scholars studying groups, validated the need to identify what Campbell (1958) viewed as the *entitativity* of a group, or the point at which individuals become group members by forming a sense of inclusion and mutual recognition.

In systems language, the integrity of a system (group) is the *boundary* formed by the way(s) system components (people) are interrelated. This is another way of instantiating the *part-whole relationship.* According to Ashby (1956), the organization of a system is predicated on the point of view of its observers. Observers are responsible for attributing what constitutes a *part* and whether that part is interrelated to other parts. Thus, we can talk about "John's cohesive group" as a discrete whole, or about "John, Mary, Harry, and Marie functioning cohesively as *John's group*." In addition, "John's group" can be one of many groups in an organization, but its members are always part of "John's group" even though they may be members of other groups.

Networks as system infrastructure. Rapoport and Horvath (1968) viewed *networks* as the topography of system organization. There is widespread agreement among systems theorists that "network" is a fundamental construct in explaining systems. There seems to be less agreement, however, on the importance of delineating the content of network activity.

General Systems Theory (GST), the most broadly conceived area of systems thinking, emphasizes the integrity of network patterns in facilitating system organization. Within this theory, networks, as a concept derived from social mechanics, typically are explained as the interchange connections, or *channels,* formed among system components. Message content carried over network channels is treated as less important than how well the entire network functions in providing the structural integrity needed for unifying various parts of the system. This seems somewhat shortsighted in that what the network conveys should be related to how successfully a particular network configuration can perform.

Systemic Purpose

Purpose and goals. Systems can be divided into two categories based on the interplay between system processes and goals: *goal oriented* and *goal directed.* Goal-directed systems are feedback-controlled systems and will be discussed in a separate section.

Goal orientation is a familiar construct in the study of group communication. What a group strives to achieve—its purpose or *goal*—is a meaningful reference point for describing and predicting its communication. A *task*-oriented group is expected to hew toward behavior consonant with received work, for instance, analyzing information, identifying member skills, and deciding on courses of action (see Hirokawa and Salazar, Chapter 7, this volume), whereas a *support* group emphasizes such behaviors as helpfulness, constructive confrontation, and personal validation (see Cline, Chapter 19, this volume).

Goal orientation also affords group members a way of monitoring the appropriateness of their actions. Goals are self-referential, normative, and indicative of homeostatic processes. Hence, a task group has strayed from its preferred path when members engage in too much social interaction, whereas members of a support group will probably seek to refocus the group on supportive communication after a prolonged period of destructive conflict.

Feedback and learning. Goal-directed feedback is a unique attribute of complex adaptive systems (Buckley, 1967). This distinction is predicated on how goals are generated. In adaptive systems, information processing related to receiving feedback has the effect of creating a systemic goal; the system responds by selecting a trajectory of action.

Scheidel (1986) noted that typical systems models of groups treat feedback temporally as though it were just another message in the unfolding course of group deliberation. Scheidel argued, however, that feedback could take one of two primary forms. Comments might focus on *divergent* thinking, which involves generating and analyzing ideas, or on *convergent* thinking, which involves narrowing information and selecting ideas. Knowing the content of goal-directed feedback messages, therefore, provides the grounds for understanding a group's goal path, even when a goal is ambiguous or in a preformative stage of development.

Systemic Change

Adaptive systems change according to their abilities for acquiring, processing, and reacting to feedback. A precondition of this ability is their openness. *Openness* refers to the permeability of a system's boundaries, that is, how capable it is of interacting with its environment.

Systems cannot adapt if they are unable to engage in these activities. In relatively *closed* systems, where there is limited interaction with the outside environment, the interaction that takes place leads to disorderliness in system organization, a state labeled *entropy.* Such systems lack a repertoire of responses compatible with information they receive and are either too rigid or not sophisticated enough to create new response options. Ineffectual capabilities for responding to contextual circumstances is disaccretive for systems. Janis's (1982) explication of *groupthink,* the tendency for group members to act uncritically rather than risk conflicts that might disturb group cohesiveness (see Keyton, Chapter 8, this volume), is compatible with the notion of entropy experienced in a closed, decision-making group context.

Adaptive systems possess sufficient openness for engaging in constructive exchanges with their environments. Two constructs associated with the effects of such interactions are *morphostasis* and *morphogenesis.* Except for their origin, these constructs bear intriguing similarities to Scheidel's (1986) view of divergent and convergent thinking.

Selective constraints and morphostasis. The term *morphostasis* refers to system-environment interaction that stimulates a system to repeat a course of action or continue along a particular goal path. A system is constrained insofar as it pursues a goal in ways that prevent it from deviating from past or current experience. The parallel with homeostatic functioning is not coincidental. Environmental information that functions as negative feedback to stimulate initiating or maintaining an activity coincides with cybernetic *stasis.* For example, groups that rely on (or internally generate) information indicating the likelihood of predictable consequences resulting from a known or tried course of action are more likely to embrace that path of activity (Guzzo, 1986; Knutson & Kowitz, 1977).

Selective elaboration and morphogenesis. Adaptive systems are characterized by their ability to engage in *negentropic* innovation or restructuring of system activities to accommodate environmental feedback. Negentropy is a result of positive feedback. Negative feedback produces stability by reinforcing the continuation of behavioral processes and the infrastructure supporting them (e.g., group norms and procedure). Positive feedback functions as a resource for stimulating changes in behaviors and system structures that make them possible. This process is referred to as structural *elaboration* because the system's infrastructure is used as the basis for adding new mechanisms for supporting innovative activities or modification to align it with changes in the ordering or frequency of occurrence of existing activities (Buckley, 1967).

According to Maruyama (1968), negentropic processes create change through learning and growth by stimulating deviations from existing goal paths. In open systems, this happens because the system has resources (e.g., processing capability and structural flexibility) for crafting responses that help it to assimilate with the environment or establish greater self-control by changing its relationship to the environment (Ellis, Werbel, & Fisher, 1978). The term *morphogenesis,* thus, denotes the ability of a system to modify its goals, behavioral processes, and structure through interaction with its environment.

How amenable group communication theory and research are to embracing a morphogenetic systems metaphor is not clear. Recent reviews and assessments of group communication literature (e.g., Frey, 1994a, 1994b, 1994c, 1995, 1996; Hirokawa & Poole, 1996) reflect a growing use of the morphogenetic systems metaphor. Applications of Adaptive Systems Theory to group communication study are evident in Self-Organizing, Structuration, and Self-Referential systems theories examined in the next section.

STUDYING GROUPS AS COMMUNICATION SYSTEMS

The purpose of this section is to examine how the systems metaphor has been integrated into the study of communication in groups. As the earlier discussion of heuristic and pedagogical applications demonstrated, the systems metaphor is now a significant paradigm that shapes the view of those who study and teach groups from a communication perspective. Two issues frame the present discussion: (a) conceptualizing group communication as a systemic process, and (b) positioning some theoretical frameworks in group communication that are tied to systems thinking. These issues are not addressed through an exhaustive summary of the relevant literature; other contributors to this volume are charged with that responsibility. Instead, this analysis identifies exemplars (evidence of trends and particular pieces of work) to demonstrate how the systems metaphor has influenced and is influencing the domain of study.

Group Communication Process and Systemic Functions

Explanations of group communication tend to treat systemic processes and group communication processes as synonyms. The danger in this is that distinctions between communicative action and communication consequences can be obscured. Hewes (1996) underscored this point with his assertion that few studies of group communication causally link observable communication process variables, such as procedural sequences or confirming/disconfirming messages, to outcomes such as group decision quality or leadership emergence. According to Keltner (1995), conceptualizing communication as a process and studying it processually are two different things. Moreover, there is little agreement among scholars using the systems metaphor on the constituents of systemic processes, save for the presence of communication and the processing of information (Buckley, 1967).

Hewes's (1996) work also reflects this ambiguity, as he views *process* as patterns of interaction, including such variables as turn-taking and networks, that systems theorists typically treat as part of a system's infrastructure.

One approach to conceptually clarifying distinctions between systemic and communication processes involves using a view of communication processes that is grounded in the systems metaphor. Although the construct of *process* is complex and controversial, Hawes's (1973) seminal work on conceptualizing communication process is informative. Hawes advanced three defining postulates of communication process: (a) spatio-temporal structuring of behavior (*concatenaity*), (b) construction of meaning based on the interdependence of message content and relationship of interactants (*simultaneity*), and (c) validation of meaning through patterned use of symbols needed for reconstructing meaning (*functionality*). The sections below examine applications of a communication-as-process orientation to understanding the dynamics of group-systems.

Group Coordination and Integration

Group communication scholars typically have conceptualized integrative consequences of communication in structural terms (cf. Mabry & Barnes, 1980). Gouran and Baird (1972), for example, distinguished between distributional and sequential communication structures. *Distributional structure* is the array of messages across identifiable content classifications (e.g., problem analysis, asking for information, agreement, and disagreement). *Sequential structure* indicates the *ordering* of observed messages (e.g., a question followed by an opinion versus, say, a question followed by a factual statement). Hawes (1973) postulated the *interact*, a two-message chain of interaction, as the minimal unit of communication process. Another form of structure is *temporal* structure (Mabry & Barnes, 1980). Temporality involves the distribution of communicative acts and act sequences across time, as in the identification of phasic cycles used in constructing theories of group development (in this volume, see Chapters 1 [Gouran], 2 [Poole], and 6 [Anderson, Riddle, & Martin]). A final type of communication structure is, of course, *network* connectivity. Thus, four types of communication structures contribute to group coordination and integration: distributional, sequential, temporal, and connective.

Structural coordination and integration is only one incarnation of a systems metaphor in group communication research. Another example is Fisher's (1985, 1986) equating of group leadership to an information-processing model based on Ashby's (1956) "law of requisite variety." The *law of requisite variety* represents a theorem in cybernetics asserting that the action opportunities of a system are mutually constrained by the joint freedom of action associated with each system component. Fisher reasoned that group leadership was an annealing process transforming entropy into negentropy. Effective leadership is behavior that best satisfies group information-processing needs dictated by what other group members cannot supply on their own. Accordingly, leaders are those members distinguishable not by traits, skills, or styles, but by their behavioral diversity within and across meetings (see Pavitt, Chapter 12, this volume).

Fisher's theory suffers somewhat by an oversimplification of Ashby's work. The case of requisite variety cited by Fisher is a special case in which all systemic regulators of entropy (in this case, possible group leaders) are equally constrained. Fisher, however, overlooked Ashby's (1956) principle of *amplification,* which asserts that regulators may be unequally powerful and, thus, produce differing quantities of negentropy. Parallels in groups would be instances where members are differentially skilled (or observant) and, consequently, provide more (or less) salient information-processing activity. The overarching conclusion concerning the application of requisite variety is clear: Group-systems act in accordance with the amount and relative strength of action choices revealed through the interaction of group members.

Group Regulation and Stabilization

Systemic activity is controlled by constraining attributes of system components (e.g., group members' abilities or preferences) and through feedback. Feedback provides information regarding necessary or opportune adaptations to external or internal states. External feedback can bring good or bad news: Good news might be a bonus for exemplary team effort; bad news might come in the form of group work products being rejected because of poor quality. External feedback is *normative,* in that it provides information about group (or individual) departures from expected performance (Mabry & Barnes, 1980).

Feedback is always about something. Germane to the study of groups as systems is the importance of feedback to group tasks and task procedures (Haslett & Ogilvie, 1992). Tasks are both constitutive and normative for groups (Hackman, 1969; Poole, 1985). Tasks are *constitutive* in that they provide a frame of reference that group members use for interpreting expectations and procedures; however, tasks are collective interpretations, or *representations,* of how group members think they are supposed to act and, in this way, are normative.

Task representations index how a task is defined (what actions should or should not be taken) and procedures members should use for completing it (see Jarboe, 1996). Task feedback can originate either externally or internally. *External feedback* focuses on confirming or disconfirming *group*-level task representations. External feedback is more likely to result in groups' redefining goals or performance expectations or changing procedural processes to improve performance efficiency or quality. *Internal feedback* focuses on confirmatory or disconfirmatory action related to *individual* interpretations about task-performance expectations or procedural processes. Thus, internal feedback is more likely to be targeted at changing members' attitudes about the amount of effort a task requires or reallocating effort to new task priorities. In these ways, feedback continuously orients the system in relationship to its goals. The interplay between message structures (e.g., distributional or connective) and feedback provides a type of routinization that lends predictability and stability to dynamic systems.

Group Learning and Motivation

Feedback processes like those examined above are an integral part of systemic learning and motivation. The resolution of entropy, for example, is the basis of information acquisition. Adaptive morphogenic systems models, such as those portrayed in Self-Organizing and Structurational systems theories, focus on explaining how group-systems acquire new information and patterns of activity. In self-organizing systems, openness provides the capability of accepting environmental inputs from which the system acquires information. This enables autocatalytic processes to emerge. *Autocatalysis* exists when the outcomes of one process, such as information processing, stimulate another structure-elaborating process, such as realizing, or *learning,* that one method of analyzing information works better on some tasks than others. Autocatalysis facilitates sharing of experience or information among the system's members and provides the communicative bases for motivation.

Self-motivation is developed less clearly in systems thinking. Adaptive structuration theories implicitly locate motivation in the interdependence between a group's task context and its members' behavioral choices of task appropriations. Drawing on an implicit cybernetic model, Salazar (1996) hypothesized that ambiguous group contexts stimulate the acquisition of information, which, in turn, stimulates group learning and group performance (see Propp, Chapter 9, this volume, regarding collective information processing in groups). In this way, entropy causes the system to engage in negentropic, information-seeking activities, even when those activities require the system to redefine its goals or restructure its internal relationships.

Group Innovation and Change

The issue of systemic change is less straightforward than it might appear. Communication research on group change typically approaches the phenomenon from the study of Developmental Theory (in this volume, see Chapters 1 [Gouran], 2 [Poole], and 6 [Anderson et al.]). Systemic change, however, has been modeled in various ways in previous literature, most notably in the calculation of feedback effects in cybernetic theories (see Hewes, 1996; VanLear, 1996). It is this underlying appeal to the systems metaphor in the conceptualization of these models that deserves attention.

The contrast between morphostatic and morphogenic models is instructive with regard to understanding group innovation and change. Morphostatic systems are characterized by homeostatic processes, in that change is predetermined by structural constraints. Buckley (1967) viewed this type of change as ritualistic in the sense that a thermostat will turn on or off a furnace (or air conditioner) only at preset temperatures, just as a group will begin a meeting only when its designated leader arrives, regardless of how capable members would be in conducting the meeting without the leader.

Synergies among members also influence group adaptation and change. Members' skills or preferences for behaving, shaped by ego development or beliefs, affect their communication. Therefore, group members' exposure to information about, or practiced adeptness at, making qualitatively good decisions affects the quality of group decision-making interaction (Hirokawa, Erbert, & Hurst, 1996).

Preferences for structuring work also influence group interaction and outcomes. Putnam (1979) showed that groups evidenced less conflict and were more productive when members shared similar needs for structure in processing task information. Procedural instructions and task-type inputs (such as difficulty or solution complexity) also have causal effects on communication and task performance (Jarboe, 1988, 1996; Mabry & Attridge, 1990).

Depending on whether they are precipitated by external or internal conditions, innovation and change have varying implications for a group. External feedback and effects of information-seeking interactions with the environment locate the origins of innovation or change outside the group; however, synergies that follow from requisite variety, or restructuring caused by adapting to external information, are internally-located events. In either instance, the nature of these systemic changes seems to be different from the sorts of dynamic changes observed at microstructural levels of a system (VanLear, 1996).

Theoretical Orientations

Group communication theory is deeply rooted in theoretical orientations advanced by many social-scientific domains of study. The diversity of these orientations often obscures an overarching commonality: Most theories of group behavior at some level embrace one or more metaphors of systemness as a conceptual frame of reference. Four theoretical perspectives grounded in defining attributes of the systems metaphor deserve attention: Field Theory, Social Exchange Theory, Developmental Theory, and Adaptive Systems Theory.

Field Theory

Field Theory focuses on explaining the interdependencies of the part-whole relationship. Lewin (1951) noted that Field Theory functioned more like a methodological template for extrapolating theory from experience than a theory of experience per se; von Bertalanffy (1968) advanced a similar position regarding GST.

The crux of the theory as it applies to groups is that groupness (wholeness) is an overarching goal. Achieving *groupness* depends on how successful members are at

(a) managing and dissipating tensions created by simultaneously attempting to achieve individual and group goals, and (b) moving toward goals in the face of barriers in the group's external environment or members' countervailing efforts at satisfying their own needs. The level of groupness that a group succeeds in achieving is another way of expressing its entitativity as a system.

Field Theory has provided a rich body of information about groups and group communication. Kurt Lewin, a seminal and well-known theorist, is also widely credited with fostering the rise of the *group dynamics* movement (see Gouran, Chapter 1, this volume). Conceptual threads of Field Theory can be found in studies of group cohesion, composition effects, conflict, leadership, and performance effectiveness. Areas of group communication study in which Field Theory is particularly influential include functional theories of decision making (cf. Gouran & Hirokawa, 1996; in this volume, see Chapters 1 [Gouran], 2 [Poole], and 7 [Hirokawa & Salazar]), effects of group members' attributes on group process and performance (see Haslett & Ruebush, Chapter 5, this volume), relationships between tasks and group performance (Poole, 1985; see Hirokawa & Salazar, Chapter 7, this volume), and procedural processes and practices augmenting group effectiveness (Jarboe, 1996; see Sunwolf & Seibold, Chapter 15, this volume).

Social Exchange Theory

The construct of *social exchange* found its way into studies of group communication through the work of Homans (1961) and Thibaut and Kelley (1959). The kernel idea of social exchange is straightforward: People are motivated to interact because they anticipate obtaining something of value, at the least possible cost to themselves, through their interactions with others—a perspective fostered by contemporary views of rational behavior in the field of economics. According to Homans (1961), the symbolic *content* of interaction, which he called *sentiments,* conveys attributional information about the individuals engaged in the interaction. Genuine interaction takes place when rewards and punishments are attached to sentiments (or other group behavior) by interactants that can be affected by them.

Thibaut and Kelley (1959) posited that individuals seek to meet minimum expectations for obtaining something of value from their participation (called *comparison levels*); they will leave a situation if their expectations cannot be met. When their participation is obligatory, individuals interact in ways that maximize the most valuable rewards they perceive are available while minimizing potential costs of participation (called the *comparison level for alternatives*).

Kelley and Thibaut (1969) noted that in situations like group problem solving, participants are *interdependent* because they must rely on one another to help produce valued outcomes. This reliance involves different forms of group performance that are not always distributed equally across group members: (a) exchanging information or influence, (b) exercising coordination or control, and (c) receiving positive and negative rewards for group actions in proportion to individuals' contributions.

The mechanism of social exchange is often cited by scholars in their consideration of what motivates people to communicate and in theories explaining the structure of communication processes. For example, the former is evident in studies of group conflict. Putnam (1986) noted that most research on group conflict is based either on Social Exchange Theory or Game Theory (a variation on cybernetic systems models that focuses on relationships between information processing and choices in decision making).

An application of social exchange to the conceptualization and measurement of communicative action and process structure in groups is evident in Fisher and Hawes's (1971) Interact Systems Model of groups (in this volume, see Chapters 2 [Poole], 8 [Keyton], and 12 [Pavitt]). Using the *interact* (contiguous paired sequences of messages) as the basic

empirical unit of communicative behavior, Fisher and Hawes operationalized group-systems in terms of three hierarchically embedded levels of microstructural organization in group interaction. The first, and most locally grounded, level of group communication process involves *patterns* of message choices and message sequences, such as question-answer or opinion-disagreement. The second level of system organization involves *interact phases* composed of clusters of redundant patterns of interacts. Finally, there are *cycles* of interact phases associated with group task performance. Similarly, Hewes's (1986) proposition that interlocking messages created through mutual attention among group members, empirically similar to interacts, should be taken as the minimal unit of communication for predicting group communication effects is clearly rooted in the logic of social exchange (although he did not discuss that connection).

Developmental Theory

The core constructs of morphostasis and morphogenesis are most evident in group development research and studies of how groups are *situated* in context. The latter issue, addressed primarily with respect to organizational groups (see Greenbaum & Query, Chapter 20, this volume, for research on communication in organizational work groups), also bears directly on the systemic processes underlying group openness and is discussed below. This section reviews the conceptual connections between theories of group development and the morphological structure of dynamic systems.

Theories of group development are identifiable according to their morphological assumptions. Morphostatic theories are often labeled *equilibrium* theories of group development. The prototypical equilibrium model was advanced by Bales and Strodtbeck (1951), who theorized that groups must manage internal tensions arising from conflicts between *task* and *social-emotional* issues as members strive to produce outcomes (e.g., decisions and solutions to problems) (in this volume, see

Chapters 2 [Poole], 7 [Hirokawa & Salazar], 8 [Keyton], and 12 [Pavitt]).

According to Bales and Strodtbeck, the dynamics of these tension states produce three distinguishable *phases* of group communicative activity. The first phase, *orientation,* is marked by high amounts of informational messages and forms the anchor period for rates of asking for and giving messages of opinion and suggestion, as well as positive and negative reactions. The second phase of *evaluation* is characterized by a significant decline in informational behavior and a plateau in opinionation, accompanied by elevations in suggestion behavior and positive and negative reactions. The final phase of *control* is marked by a continued sharp decline in informational behavior, a slight decline in opinionation, a deceleration in the increase of suggestion behavior and negative reactions, and a continued increase in positive reactions. Bales (1953) interpreted phases as reflecting a cyclical pattern of equilibrium in homeostatic group systems.

Morphogenic theories of group development reflect a variety of approaches to explaining how systems manifest elaborating, rather than homeostatic, patterns of development. Poole and Baldwin's (1996) typology of group development models includes phase, critical event, continuous, and social construction models. A brief assessment of the implications of these theories with respect to the systems metaphor follows.

Phase models. Like Bales and Strodtbeck's (1951) homeostatic model, phase models assume there is a cyclical pattern of dynamic activity characterizing a system. Phase models typically are divided into two categories: unitary sequence and multiple sequence models.

Unitary sequence models define a specific number and order of phases that groups enact. For example, using interact units, Fisher (1970) tested a four-phase model of decision development: orientation, conflict, emergence, and reinforcement. Mabry (1975), using themes denoting systemic functions, tested a model of phasic progression in task activity:

latency, adaptation, integration, and goal attainment.

Poole (1981) criticized these and other unitary models as insufficiently generalizable. He proposed that the phases and phase sequences groups enact are contingent on task and situational factors. His research revealed that although groups emulate some of the same phases, the exact composition, number, and ordering of phases evolves more particularistically. He argued for the use of *multiple sequence models,* with multiple sequences being caused by such variables as task characteristics, group composition, and the level conflict evoked by task issues (see Poole & Baldwin, 1996).

Critical event models. This class of models of group development incorporates assumptions closely related to the cybernetic concept of *punctuated equilibrium* (Eldredge & Gould, 1977). Gersick (1988), for example, argued that the majority of a group's time is characterized by periods during which members are absorbed in discussions and conflicts about issues related to goals and procedures that emulate equilibrated states. Group movement toward completing the task is stimulated by internal or external pressures, or *triggering mechanisms,* to meet performance expectations that the current equilibrium is perceived as blocking. Thus, equilibrium states are destabilized, or "punctuated," by critical events, and the system reconstitutes its stability by either focusing on new issues presumably closer to its expected outcomes (e.g., the group moves from gathering information to considering decision alternatives) or completing the task (e.g., the group makes a decision). The level of system openness, in terms of the amount of external feedback it processes, and the level of systemic integration, in terms of the amount of internal feedback exchanged among system components (e.g., group members), contribute to the causal circumstances and rate at which these destabilizing punctuation periods take place and, thus, influence group-system development.

Continuous and social construction models. Poole and Baldwin (1996) noted similarities in these models, as both have been informed by Poole's multiple sequence model of development (see Poole, Chapter 2, this volume). *Continuous models* are characterized by what Scheidel and Crowell (1964) discerned as a "spiral" of interaction that moves group decision-making processes toward a final decision based on the sequencing of internal feedback in a group. As Scheidel (1986) noted, convergent feedback facilitates moving a group toward closure on a decision, whereas divergent feedback expands the basis of issues a group must embrace. The sequencing of these feedback trajectories creates the spiral-like inflections in group interaction. The content of these inflections can vary so widely, and include so many redundancies, that it is unlikely that one could validly project that the inflected cycles will adhere to a phase-like coherence.

Poole's (1983a, 1983b) initial expansion of the continuous model of group development incorporated the concept of *breakpoints* (or punctuated equilibrium) to clarify how group interaction moved between inflection points. This Social Construction Model formed the basis of Poole and Doelger's (1986) explanation of how conversational structure functions as a resource underlying the emergence of group phases. Subsequently, Poole and De-Sanctis (1992) applied Adaptive Structuration Theory to explain how communicative practices within a group provide organized coherence that members use in the assignment of meaning to group action (i.e., how the group "appropriates" structure through its activities). Social construction models are related most closely to the principles of selective constraint and elaboration. Group interaction unfolds recursively as it is guided by conversational trajectories. The consequences of structurational appropriations parallel those of requisite variety. Development is shaped by contingencies affecting how a group perceives its goals and how it connects those goals to available resources (either material or social).

Adaptive Systems Theory

This section concentrates on applications of the systems metaphor that are tied most closely to the adaptive systems models discussed above. The choice is not arbitrary; adaptive systems models have provided the grounding for many studies in group communication.

Structuration Theory. Poole, Seibold, and McPhee (1996) define the construct of *structuration* as a "process by which systems are produced and reproduced through members' use of rules and resources" (p. 117). Coined originally by Giddens (1984), in his discussion of social institutions, structuration is a rich metaphor for alluding to complex, mutually causal social processes that has demonstrated the capacity to frame explanations across a relatively wide range of group communication issues.

Adaptive structuration, a variation on the conceptualization of structuration, has proved to be especially valuable for grounding theory in the study of a particular type of group communication context—computer-mediated group decision support systems (GDSSs; see Scott, Chapter 16, this volume; DeSanctis & Poole, 1994; Poole & DeSanctis, 1990, 1992). Poole and DeSanctis's (1992) theoretical goal was to account for the acquisition and enactment of structure—or *appropriation*—in the interactions of groups (with particular attention to groups using GDSSs). This is accomplished by distinguishing between the ethos (or "spirit") of a technological affordance and its instrumental use. The analysis yields a multilevel, multidimensional scheme to account for the appropriation moves that members of GDSSs employ while using the technology. Research indicates that technological design restrictiveness reduces control appropriations and that groups using the technology in ways consistent with how it was designed (*faithful* appropriations) are more productive than groups engaging in unintended appropriations (*ironic* appropriations).

Self-Organizing Systems Theory. One application of an adaptive cybernetic systems model to group communication is Contractor's (1994; Contractor & Grant, 1996; Contractor & Seibold, 1993; Contractor & Whitbred, 1997) delineation of Self-Organizing Systems Theory (SOST). To qualify as a self-organized system, a group must meet four systemic conditions.

First, two or more members have to share a mutual causal relationship, whereby their actions affect one another. Second, one or more members must experience autocatalysis as a consequence of group membership; that is, the nature of an individual's subsequent behavior is altered through the causal effects of system processes. Third, the group's interaction with its environment must emulate a negentropic process, whereby energy (or information) is imported for the purpose of reducing entropy and exported with concomitant entropy-producing consequences on the environmental context (e.g., an encompassing organizational unit in which the group is embedded). Fourth, one or more group members must be accessibly open to uncontrolled (i.e., random) influences in the external environment.

Contractor and Whitbred (1997) have mathematically expressed the *generative mechanisms* (the underlying empirical requisites) for modeling phases of group development based on Poole's work with continuous models. Although Contractor's work is limited to tests of SOST using simulation techniques, he has demonstrated the viability of applying the theory to group contexts, such as technologically mediated GDSSs.

The principle of self-organization can be extended to even more complex theoretical schemes. Recent discussions of the application of Chaos Theory to organizational and group communication is one example (see, for example, Poole, 1997; Tutzauer, 1997).

The concept of *chaos* alludes to the presence of nonlinear dynamic processes that dictate a system's ability to establish and maintain equilibrium. A stable equilibrium exists when feedback or other events shift a system's trajectory of action but the system can restore itself to that trajectory or a similar one. This might happen, for instance, if a group changed conversational topics regarding a task issue—for example, in response to a member entering the meeting late—and then returned to a closely related topic a few minutes later. An unstable, or chaotic, condition would arise if the group was unable to reestablish its conversational focus and continued talking about various nontask themes without ever returning to the previously discussed task theme.

The applicability of Chaos Theory to group communication research seems apparent; however, knowledge gained by using it might not meet certain tests of empirical adequacy. Tutzauer (1997) notes that chaotic conditions may not be reproducible because mathematical algorithms for modeling chaotic states are sensitive to the initial conditions producing chaos: They require an exact replication of those initial conditions. This would necessitate the extraordinary condition of using matched groups that begin their meetings in exactly the same way.

Self-Referential (Autopoietic) Systems Theory. The theory of autopoiesis, or self-referential systems, is grounded in theoretical biology (see Maturana, 1988; Maturana & Varela, 1980; Varela, 1984). Maturana, in attempting to conceptualize the holistic nature of biological systemic activity, observed the unique, logically binding duality resulting from contrasting the Greek concepts of *praxis* (action) and *poiesis* (creative production) and coined the term *autopoiesis* to express the essence of that dynamic process sustaining autonomous organization in living systems (Maturana & Varela, 1980). Autopoiesis implies a phenomenon in living systems in which the integrity of the system's structural components (e.g., cells, tissues, and organs) is constituted in their inherent interaction, thus creating interdependent closure with respect to system boundaries, organization, and identity.

True autopoietic systems are the products of composite-unity: The coherence of a system's parts constitutes its identity as an organized whole (Mingers, 1995). As a result of their unique holistic interdependence, autopoietic systems are capable of self-cognition, self-consciousness, and, therefore, self-referenced learning and adaptation.

Biological entities (including humans) and other living systems are autopoietic systems. Aggregates of living systems, such as groups, however, are *not* inherently autopoietic; they are *heteropoietic* to the extent that their self-producing activities are artifacts of embeddedness in other systems. Although the position is controversial, because neither Maturana nor Varela has made the position clear (Mingers, 1995), social systems could emulate autopoietic systems because of their unique reliance on communication (Luhmann, 1992). This would occur as interaction became mutually structuring and permitted the system to perform holistically. General Systems theorists view this as achieving a state of entitativity. Thus, when individuals become *structurally coupled,* such as perceiving group membership as synonymous with their task enactments, they could be engaging in autopoiesis.

Compared to other social systems theorizing, the most counterintuitive notion in Self-Referential Systems Theory is that autopoietic systems are *not* conceived as open or goal-directed systems (see Luhmann, 1986; Mingers, 1995). This makes sense at the level of biological systems, where life tasks are all-consuming. In biological systems, tasks are life imperatives. In social systems, tasks evolve from a sense of purpose and are indexical in the sense that they frame symbolic meanings and punctuate spatio-temporal awareness. A second departure from other systems metaphors is that Self-Referential Systems Theory views system-environment interaction as a proactive product of its constant need for environmental scanning, rather than the capability to act whenever environmental forces become too intrusive. An autopoietic system, therefore, is self-actualized and selects what it needs (or wants) against a background of what it perceives that an environmental context can provide.

CAPITALIZING ON THE POWER OF THE SYSTEMS METAPHOR

The purpose of this section is to assess the potential of the systems metaphor for further shaping the group communication research agenda. The section focuses on emerging theoretical and methodological orientations that expand on viewing groups as systemic entities.

The Situated Group: Systemic Embeddedness and Identity

Putnam and Stohl (1990, 1996) advanced the construct of the bona fide group as a metaphor for understanding the social contexts of natural groups (as contrasted with artifactual groups often used in laboratory research) (in this volume, see Chapters 1 [Gouran] and 2 [Poole]). Bona fide groups have permeable boundaries, shifting borders, and interdependencies with environmental agents (e.g., individuals, groups, and organizations). A bona fide group is capable of maintaining groupness even though its members have multiple and often competing roles in other groups, and its membership may vary for reasons not fully under the group's control.

The capacity for maintaining a dynamic identity given these characteristics is viewed as a primary attribute of groupness (Putnam & Stohl, 1996). From this perspective, group decisions, for example, will be triangulated between individual members' and the group's internal and external interaction and the group's unique interaction about its decision options. A similar process of structuring group interaction may underpin both group membership and members' role appropriations.

The work of Putnam and Stohl (1990, 1996) underscores how the systems metaphor can refocus research designs and research agendas. By paying greater attention to communication in natural groups (versus artificial groups studied in naturalistic contexts), the Bona Fide Groups Perspective helps to set the agenda while clarifying the task.

Methodologies suited to this task, however, are less clear. Analyses of situated discourse that treat groups as discourse systems offers one option (see Boden, 1994; Geist & Chandler, 1984; Lazega, 1992; Psathas, 1995). Identity-framing discourse moves, such as defining the resource power of members' knowledge claims, or boundary-framing moves, such as using alignment talk based on legitimized organizational positions as a tactic in differentiating oneself or the group from others, are informative. These procedures create theoretically relevant and methodologically diverse opportunities for studying group communication as *praxis*. Application of communication ethnography proposed by Frey (1994c) offers another alternative with a rich heritage in social-scientific research (in this volume, see Chapters 1 [Gouran], 2 [Poole], and 4 [Poole, Keyton, & Frey]).

Groups as Discourse Communities

Approaching groups as communities of discourse, a variety of issues not always conceived in homologous terms can be reconceptualized. Hewes's (1996) Socio-Egocentric Theory of group communication, which hypothesizes that turn-taking and other conversational structuring tactics are less important for group performance than themes tied to task information, is ripe for methodological reframing. This hypothesis could be juxtaposed to data from conversational-analytic assessments; for example, how locutionary structure contributes to recognizing unproductive requests, relationships between turn management and cohesive discourse that make group interaction less effortful in productive versus unproductive groups, or identifying the periodicity of discursive procedural talk (e.g., alignment talk and accounting practices) within such task process themes as problem identification and analysis or solution selection.

There is some evidence, albeit indirect, bearing on these issues. Poole and DeSanctis (1992), using textual analysis, showed that discursive appropriations in GDSS groups varied according to whether group behavior was constrained more by technological procedures or by socially constructed norms. Courtright, Fairhurst, and Rogers (1989), using a variety of methods (including ones modeled after conversational analysis), compared superior-subordinate communication in "organic" (i.e., self-managed) and "mechanistic" (e.g., traditionally managed) organizational management systems. They found that both *grammatical* forms (e.g., assertions, questions, and talkovers) and *response* forms (e.g., support, nonsupport, and extension) differentiated workplace communication in the two management systems. These studies provide useful exemplars of how microsocial data can be employed to support propositions derived from complex systems theories.

Reconnecting Communication as Meaning, Process, and Structure

The systems metaphor permits communication scholars wide latitude in conceptualizing core constructs, such as *process* and *structure*. Identifying discursive practices is one example. Noting the distributive or sequential qualities of interaction is another, quite different, perspective. Monge and Kalman (1996) make a convincing case for viewing communication structure and process interdependently as the convergence of *sequentiality, simultaneity,* and *synchronicity*. These concepts are quite familiar in the context of the systems metaphor.

Less clear is the role of message content (particularly meaning) in discerning how to apply the groups-as-systems metaphor. Approaches to studying group communication content are theoretically and methodologically diverse (see Poole et al., Chapter 4, this volume). Researchers often define systemic patterns through the content definitions of process structures, as has been the case in studies of group development. More general theoretical stances, such as Functional Theory, link communication content to group consequences (in this volume, see Chapters 1 [Gouran], 2 [Poole], and 7 [Hirokawa & Salazar]).

The power of the systems paradigm lies in transcending such middle-range theorizing (i.e., theorizing not immediately connectable to lawlike empirical generalizations). Recent efforts, such as Putnam and Stohl's (1996) case exemplar of structurational processes in bona fide groups and applications of Functional Theory to *in situ* group decision making (e.g., Gouran & Hirokawa, 1996; Hirokawa et al., 1996), are promising. Additional work that includes dynamic connectivity among members as a definition of system states, or the relative impact of externally versus internally generated negentropic stimuli on mapping goal paths, would be consistent with this direction.

Less understood is whether communication is the nexus between process and structure, as Hawes's (1973) conceptualization implies, or whether process and structure create autopoiesis and, thereby, render meaning as a symbolic objectification of the subjective experience of systemness. This question has important theoretical and methodological implications. Theoretically, Hawes's position implies that communication creates systemness. In contrast, Autopoietic Theory implies that communication emulates systemness, which nullifies the issue of logical precedence. Methodologically, if communication and systemness are coproduced, operationalizing communication instantiates systemness; however, if communication and systemness are consubstantial, they become separately problematized—their interdependency notwithstanding. Thus, defining one would not simultaneously define the other.

Luhmann's (1986) proposition that communication is the mode of social system reproduction provides some clarification for these issues. He argued that autopoietic reproduction is a "communicative synthesis of information, utterance, and understanding" (p. 175). Understanding autopoietic systemness, therefore, requires explaining a system's separate cocreation of "communicative synthesis" and "information, utterance, and understanding."

Empirically interpreting constructs like synthesis is challenging because such constructs suffer from fuzzy explication. More attention to the tasks of elaborating and paradigmatically reconceptualizing the systems metaphor in group communication should help to define the research agenda for the 21st century.

REFERENCES

Ashby, W. R. (1956). *An introduction to cybernetics.* London: Chapman and Hall.

Bales, R. F. (1950). *Interaction process analysis: A method for the study of small groups.* Cambridge, MA: Addison-Wesley.

Bales, R. F. (1953). The equilibrium problem in small groups. In T. Parsons, R. F. Bales, & E. A. Shils (Eds.), *Working papers in the theory of action* (pp. 111-161). Glencoe, IL: Free Press.

Bales, R. F., & Strodtbeck, F. L. (1951). Phases in group problem solving. *Journal of Abnormal and Social Psychology, 46,* 485-495.

Barge, J. K. (1994). *Leadership: Communication skills for organizations and groups.* New York: St. Martin's.

Boden, D. (1994). *The business of talk: Organizations in action.* Cambridge, MA: Polity.

Bormann, E. G. (1990). *Small group communication: Theory and practice* (3rd ed.). New York: HarperCollins.

Bormann, E. G. (1996). Symbolic convergence theory and communication in group decision making. In R. Y. Hirokawa & M. S. Poole (Eds.), *Communication and group decision making* (2nd ed., pp. 81-113). Thousand Oaks, CA: Sage.

Buckley, W. (1967). *Sociology and modern systems theory.* Englewood Cliffs, NJ: Prentice Hall.

Campbell, D. T. (1958). Common fate, similarity, and other indices of the status of aggregates of persons as social entities. *Behavioral Science, 3,* 14-25.

Cherry, C. (1966). *On human communication: A review, a survey, and a criticism* (2nd ed.). Cambridge, MA: MIT Press.

Contractor, N. S. (1994). Self-organizing systems perspective in the study of organizational communication. In B. Kovacic (Ed.), *New approaches to organizational communication* (pp. 39-66). Albany: State University of New York Press.

Contractor, N. S., & Grant, S. J. (1996). The emergence of shared interpretations in organizations: A self-organizing systems perspective. In J. H. Watt & C. A. VanLear (Eds.), *Dynamic patterns in communication processes* (pp. 215-230). Thousand Oaks, CA: Sage.

Contractor, N. S., & Seibold, D. R. (1993). Theoretical frameworks for the study of structuring processes in group decision support systems: Adaptive structuration theory and self-organizing systems theory. *Human Communication Research, 19,* 528-563.

Contractor, N. S., & Whitbred, R. C. (1997). Decision development in work groups: A comparison of contingency and self-organizing systems perspectives. In

G. A. Barnett & L. Thayer (Eds.), *Organization—communication: Emerging perspectives V. The renaissance in systems thinking* (pp. 83-104). Greenwich, CT: Ablex.

Courtright, J. A., Fairhurst, G. T., & Rogers, L. E. (1989). Interaction patterns in organic and mechanistic systems. *Academy of Management Journal, 32,* 773-802.

Dachler, P. (1984). Some explanatory boundaries of organismic analogies for the understanding of social systems. In H. Ulrich & G.J.B. Probst (Eds.), *Self-organization and management of social systems: Insights, promises, doubts, and questions* (pp. 132-147). Berlin: Springer-Verlag.

DeSanctis, G., & Poole, M. S. (1994). Capturing the complexity in advanced technology use: Adaptive structuration theory. *Organization Science, 5,* 121-147.

Eldredge, N., & Gould, S. J. (1977). Punctuated equilibria: The tempo and mode of evolution reconsidered. *Paleobiology, 3,* 115-151.

Ellis, D. G., Werbel, W. S., & Fisher, B. A. (1978). Toward a systemic organization of groups. *Small Group Behavior, 9,* 451-469.

Fisher, B. A. (1970). Decision emergence: Phases in group decision-making. *Speech Monographs, 37,* 53-66.

Fisher, B. A. (1974). *Small group decision making.* New York: McGraw-Hill.

Fisher, B. A. (1985). Leadership as medium: Treating complexity in group communication research. *Small Group Behavior, 16,* 167-196.

Fisher, B. A. (1986). Leadership: When does the difference make a difference? In R. Y. Hirokawa & M. S. Poole (Eds.), *Communication and group decision-making* (pp. 197-218). Beverly Hills, CA: Sage.

Fisher, B. A., & Hawes, L. C. (1971). An interact system model: Generating a grounded theory of small groups. *Quarterly Journal of Speech, 57,* 444-453.

Frey, L. R. (Ed.). (1994a). *Group communication in context: Studies of natural groups.* Hillsdale, NJ: Lawrence Erlbaum.

Frey, L. R. (1994b). Introduction: Revitalizing the study of small group communication. *Communication Studies, 45,* 1-6.

Frey, L. R. (1994c). The naturalistic paradigm: Studying small groups in the postmodern era. *Small Group Research, 25,* 551-577.

Frey, L. R. (Ed.). (1995). *Innovations in group facilitation: Applications in natural settings.* Cresskill, NJ: Hampton.

Frey, L. R. (1996). Remembering and "re-remembering": A history of theory and research on communication and group decision making. In R. Y. Hirokawa & M. S. Poole (Eds.), *Communication and group decision making* (2nd ed., pp. 19-51). Thousand Oaks, CA: Sage.

Frey, L. R., & Barge, J. K. (Eds.). (1997). *Managing group life: Communicating in decision-making groups.* Boston: Houghton Mifflin.

Geist, P., & Chandler, T. (1984). Account analysis of influence in group decision-making. *Communication Monographs, 51,* 67-78.

Gersick, C. J. G. (1988). Time and transitions in work teams: Toward a new model of group development. *Academy of Management Journal, 31,* 9-41.

Giddens, A. (1984). *The constitution of society: Outline of a theory of structuration.* Berkeley: University of California Press.

Gouran D. S., & Baird, J. E., Jr. (1972). An analysis of distributional and sequential structure in problem-solving and informal group discussions. *Speech Monographs, 39,* 16-22.

Gouran, D. S., & Hirokawa, R. Y. (1996). Functional theory and communication in decision-making and problem-solving groups: An expanded view. In R. Y. Hirokawa & M. S. Poole (Eds.), *Communication and group decision making* (2nd ed., pp. 55-80). Thousand Oaks, CA: Sage.

Gulley, H. E. (1960). *Discussion, conference, and group process.* New York: Holt.

Guzzo, R. A. (1986). Group decision making and group effectiveness in organizations. In P. S. Goodman & Associates (Eds.), *Designing effective work groups* (pp. 34-71). San Francisco: Jossey-Bass.

Hackman, J. R. (1969). Toward understanding the role of tasks in behavioural research. *Acta Psychologica, 31,* 97-128.

Harnack, R. V., & Fest, T. B. (1964). *Group discussion: Theory and technique.* New York: Appleton-Century-Crofts.

Haslett, B., & Ogilvie, J. R. (1992). Feedback processes in task groups. In R. S. Cathcart & L. A. Samovar (Eds.), *Small group communication: A reader* (6th ed., pp. 342-356). Dubuque, IA: William C. Brown.

Hawes, L. C. (1973). Elements of a model of communication process. *Quarterly Journal of Speech, 59,* 11-29.

Hewes, D. E. (1996). Small group communication may not influence decision making: An amplification of socio-egocentric theory. In R. Y. Hirokawa & M. S. Poole (Eds.), *Communication and group decision making* (2nd ed., pp. 179-212). Thousand Oaks, CA: Sage.

Hirokawa, R. Y., Erbert, L., & Hurst, A. (1996). Communication and group decision-making effectiveness. In R. Y. Hirokawa & M. S. Poole (Eds.), *Communication and group decision making* (2nd ed., pp. 269-300). Thousand Oaks, CA: Sage.

Hirokawa, R. Y. & Poole, M. S. (Eds.). (1996). *Communication and group decision making* (2nd ed.). Thousand Oaks, CA: Sage.

Homans, G. C. (1950). *The human group.* New York: Harcourt, Brace & World.

Homans, G. C. (1961). *Social behavior: Its elementary forms.* New York: Harcourt, Brace & World.

Janis, I. L. (1982). *Groupthink: Psychological studies of policy decisions and fiascoes* (2nd ed.). Boston: Houghton Mifflin.

Jarboe, S. (1988). A comparison of input-output, process-output, and input-process-output models of small group problem-solving effectiveness. *Communication Monographs, 55,* 121-142.

Jarboe, S. (1996). Procedures for enhancing group decision making. In R. Y. Hirokawa & M. S. Poole (Eds.),

Communication and group decision making (2nd ed., pp. 345-383). Thousand Oaks, CA: Sage.

Kelley, H. H., & Thibaut, J. W. (1969). Group problem solving. In G. Lindzey & E. Aronson (Eds.), *The handbook of social psychology: Vol. 4. Group psychology and phenomena of interaction* (2nd ed., pp. 1-101). Reading, MA: Addison-Wesley.

Keltner, S. (1995). Message feedback in work groups. In L. R. Frey (Ed.), *Innovations in group facilitation: Applications in natural settings* (pp. 119-147). Cresskill, NJ: Hampton.

Knutson, T. J., & Kowitz, A. C. (1977). Effects of information type and levels of orientation on consensus-achievement in substantive and affective conflict. *Central States Speech Journal, 28*, 54-63.

Krippendorff, K. (1989). On the ethics of constructing communication. In B. Dervin, L. Grossberg, B. J. O'Keefe, & E. Wartella (Eds.), *Rethinking communication: Vol. 1. Paradigm issues* (pp. 66-96). Newbury Park, CA: Sage.

Lazega, E. (1992). *Micropolitics of knowledge: Communication indirect control in workgroups.* New York: Aldine de Gruyter.

Lewin, K. (1951). *Field theory in social science: Selected theoretical papers* (D. Cartwright, Ed.). New York: Harper.

Luhmann, N. (1986). The autopoiesis of social systems. In F. Geyer & J. Van Der Zouwen (Eds.), *Sociocybernetic paradoxes: Observation, control and evolution in self-steering systems* (pp. 172-192). Beverly Hills, CA: Sage.

Luhmann, N. (1992). What is communication? *Communication Theory, 2*, 251-258.

Mabry, E. A. (1975). Exploratory analysis of a developmental model for task-oriented small groups. *Human Communication Research, 2*, 66-74.

Mabry, E. A., & Attridge, M. D. (1990). Small group interaction and outcome correlates for structured and unstructured tasks. *Small Group Research, 21*, 315-332.

Mabry, E. A., & Barnes, R. E. (1980). *The dynamics of small group communication.* Englewood Cliffs, NJ: Prentice-Hall.

Maruyama, M. (1968). The second cybernetics: Deviation-amplifying mutual causal processes. In W. Buckley (Ed.), *Modern systems research for the behavioral scientist: A sourcebook* (pp. 304-316). Chicago: Aldine.

Maturana, H. (1988). Reality: The search for objectivity or the quest for an interesting argument. *Irish Journal of Psychology, 9*, 25-82.

Maturana, H., & Varela, F. J. (1980). *Autopoiesis and cognition: The realization of the living.* Dordrecht, The Netherlands: D. Reidel.

McBurney, J. H., & Hance, K. G. (1950). *Discussion in human affairs.* New York: Harper.

Mingers, J. (1995). *Self-producing systems: Implications and applications of autopoiesis.* New York: Plenum.

Monge, P. R. (1973). Theory construction in the study of communication: The system paradigm. *Journal of Communication, 23*, 5-16.

Monge, P. R., & Kalman, M. E. (1996). Sequentiality, simultaneity, and synchronicity in human communication. In J. H. Watt & C. A. VanLear (Eds.), *Dynamic patterns in communication processes* (pp. 71-92). Thousand Oaks, CA: Sage.

Morgan, G. (1986). *Images of organization.* Newbury Park, CA: Sage.

Osborne, M. M., & Ehninger, D. (1962). The metaphor in public address. *Speech Monographs, 29*, 223-234.

Parsons, T. (1951). *The social system.* Glencoe, IL: Free Press.

Poole, M. S. (1981). Decision development in small groups I: A comparison of two models. *Communication Monographs, 48*, 1-24.

Poole, M. S. (1983a). Decision development in small groups II: A study of multiple sequences in decision making. *Communication Monographs, 50*, 206-232.

Poole, M. S. (1983b). Decision development in small groups, III: A multiple sequence theory of group decision development. *Communication Monographs, 50*, 321-341.

Poole, M. S. (1985). Task and interaction sequences: A theory of coherence in group decision-making interaction. In R. L. Street & J. N. Cappella (Eds.), *Sequence and pattern in communicative behavior* (pp. 206-224). London: Edward Arnold.

Poole, M. S. (1997). A turn of the wheel: The case for renewal of systems inquiry in organizational communication research. In G. A. Barnett & L. Thayer (Eds.), *Organization—communication: Emerging perspectives V. The renaissance in systems thinking* (pp. 47-63). Greenwich, CT: Ablex.

Poole, M. S., & Baldwin, C. L. (1996). Developmental processes in group decision making. In R. Y. Hirokawa & M. S. Poole (Eds.), *Communication and group decision making* (2nd ed., pp. 215-241). Thousand Oaks, CA: Sage.

Poole, M. S., & DeSanctis, G. (1990). Understanding the use of group decision support systems: The theory of adaptive structuration. In J. Fulk & C. Steinfield (Eds.), *Organizations and communication technology* (pp. 175-195). Newbury Park, CA: Sage.

Poole, M. S., & DeSanctis, G. (1992). Microlevel structuration in computer-supported group decision making. *Human Communication Research, 19*, 5-49.

Poole, M. S., & Doelger, J. A. (1986). Developmental processes in group decision-making. In R. Y. Hirokawa & M. S. Poole (Eds.), *Communication and group decision-making* (pp. 35-61). Beverly Hills, CA: Sage.

Poole, M. S., Seibold, D. R., & McPhee, R. D. (1996). The structuration of group decisions. In R. Y. Hirokawa & M. S. Poole (Eds.), *Communication and group decision making* (2nd ed., pp. 114-146). Thousand Oaks, CA: Sage.

Psathas, G. (1995). *Conversational analysis: The study of talk-in-interaction.* Thousand Oaks, CA: Sage.

Putnam, L. L. (1979). Preference for procedural order in task-oriented small groups. *Communication Monographs, 46*, 193-218.

Putnam, L. L. (1986). Conflict and group decision-making. In R. Y. Hirokawa & M. S. Poole (Eds.), *Communication and group decision-making* (pp. 175-196). Beverly Hills, CA: Sage.

Putnam, L. L., & Stohl, C. (1990). Bona fide groups: A reconceptualization of groups in context. *Communication Studies, 41,* 248-265.

Putnam, L. L., & Stohl, C. (1996). Bona fide groups: An alternative perspective for communication and small group decision making. In R. Y. Hirokawa & M. S. Poole (Eds.), *Communication and group decision making* (2nd ed., pp. 147-178). Thousand Oaks, CA: Sage.

Rapoport, A., & Horvath, W. J. (1968). Thoughts on organization theory. In W. Buckley (Ed.), *Modern systems research for the behavioral scientist: A sourcebook* (pp. 71-75). Chicago: Aldine.

Rosenblueth, A., Wiener, N., & Bigelow, J. (1943). Behavior, purpose, and teleology. *Philosophy of Science, 10,* 18-24.

Salazar, A. J. (1996). Ambiguity and communication effects on small group decision-making performance. *Human Communication Research, 23,* 155-192.

Scheidel, T. M. (1986). Divergent and convergent thinking in group decision-making. In R. Y. Hirokawa & M. S. Poole (Eds.), *Communication and group decision-making* (pp. 114-146). Beverly Hills, CA: Sage.

Scheidel, T. M., & Crowell, L. (1964). Idea development in small discussion groups. *Quarterly Journal of Speech, 50,* 140-145.

Thibaut, J. W., & Kelley, H. H. (1959). *The social psychology of groups.* New York: John Wiley.

Tubbs, S. L. (1978). *A systems approach to small group interaction.* Reading, MA: Addison-Wesley.

Tutzauer, F. (1997). Chaos and organization. In G. A. Barnett & L. Thayer (Eds.), *Organization—communication: Emerging perspectives V. The renaissance in systems thinking* (pp. 213-227). Greenwich, CT: Ablex.

VanLear, C. A. (1996). Communication process approaches and models: Patterns, cycles, and dynamic coordination. In J. H. Watts & C. A. VanLear (Eds.), *Dynamic patterns in communication processes* (pp. 35-70). Thousand Oaks, CA: Sage.

Varela, F. (1984). Two principles for self-organization. In H. Ulrich & G.J.B. Probst (Eds.), *Self-organization and management of social systems: Insights, promises, doubts, and questions* (pp. 25-32). Berlin: Springer-Verlag.

von Bertalanffy, L. (1968). *General system theory: Foundations, development, applications.* New York: George Braziller.

White, H. C. (1992). *Identity and control: A structural theory of social action.* Princeton, NJ: Princeton University Press.

Wiener, N. (1948). *Cybernetics: Or control and communication in the animal and the machine.* New York: John Wiley.

4

Group Communication Methodology

Issues and Considerations

MARSHALL SCOTT POOLE
Texas A&M University

JOANN KEYTON
The University of Memphis

LAWRENCE R. FREY
The University of Memphis

Each specific research context poses its own particular challenges for the social scientist, and the group context is no exception. Until recently, reviews of the group context in Communication (e.g., Cragan & Wright, 1980, 1990; Propp & Kreps, 1994) and related disciplines, such as Psychology (Bettenhausen, 1991; Cohen & Bailey, 1997; Levine & Moreland, 1990; McGrath, 1997), focused almost exclusively on what is studied rather than on how research is conducted. McGrath's (1984) review has recently been joined by excellent general reviews of group methods by Weingart (1997), Kashy and Kenny (in press), and McGrath and Altermatt (in press), as well as some more narrowly focused reviews of particular methods, such as Frey's (1994b) review of naturalistic methods in group research, and critical reviews of particular methods that have been used in group research (e.g., Frey, 1994b, 1996).

This chapter addresses issues specific to conducting research on group communication. Communication research, with its focus on group interaction processes and their systemic relationship to input and outcome variables, faces a unique constellation of problems. We organize this discussion of group communication methodology around four key characteristics of groups that pose challenges to researchers. We first introduce these challenges in general terms and then discuss issues these challenges raise for conducting communication research in specific group contexts and methods for addressing them.

CHALLENGES FOR GROUP COMMUNICATION RESEARCHERS

A group is a complex entity, composed, on one level, of individuals who contribute in varying degrees to it, but, on another level and in line with Systems Theory (see Mabry, Chapter 3, this volume), as an entity that can be more, and sometimes less, than the sum of its parts. This sets up a level-of-analysis issue, best captured by the question, "Should a group be treated as an entity, or should the focus be on the individual group members?" Of course, different research questions direct attention to different levels. Studies of group performance, for example, generally treat a group as an entity in making the overall group outcome produced the primary concern. Studies of group members' attitudes, in contrast, direct attention to individuals. Some research questions also address the individual member–group entity relationship, such as studies of how group members' predispositions influence group communication processes and performance (see Haslett & Ruebush, Chapter 5, this volume).

Another levels-of-analysis question centers on how group members' individual characteristics interact to create group-level constructs or effects. For example, diversity in groups, or group heterogeneity, has received much attention recently (see Haslett & Ruebush, Chapter 5, this volume), but relatively little attention has been directed toward understanding how individual differences among members combine to affect group processes and products. For example, is it the combined or average level of group members' experience with a task that makes a difference in group performance, or does having a couple of experienced members suffice? As another example, should the proportion of argumentative individuals in a group be used as the operative factor in determining the likelihood of intragroup conflicts and impasses, or does having one argumentative member create a threshold past which adding others does not significantly increase the probability of conflict or impasse?

A related levels-of-analysis issue results from the fact that members of groups create complex relationships at several levels, which leads to the nonindependence of individual-level data. Most statistical tests for analyzing quantitative data rest on the assumption of independence of observations, an inherently untenable assumption if the interlocking behavior in a group system causes dependencies among members' attitudes and behaviors. Moreover, the degree of dependency in data varies widely. Some members influence each other strongly, whereas others are isolated from the group and exert little influence, and still others are somewhere in between.

A second key characteristic of groups that poses a challenge for communication researchers concerns the fluidity and permeability of group boundaries and borders (see Putnam & Stohl, 1990, 1994, 1996). The boundaries and borders of groups often change, in part, because their membership changes over time. New members sometimes join, and/or established members may leave (see Anderson, Riddle, & Martin, Chapter 6, this volume), which may produce significant changes in group inputs, processes, and outcomes (see Sinclair-James & Stohl, 1997), and consultants or other guests sit in on a group from time to time and temporarily become part of that system. Tracking the influence of such membership variation over time is challenging. Group boundaries and borders also change because groups have varying degrees of interdependence with other individuals, groups, and larger structures (e.g., organizations and institutions) from their various environments. At some points, a group may be insulated from outside influences; at other points, it may open itself up to those influences and may even temporarily merge with other groups or temporarily dissolve itself while its members work with other groups or units. These group boundary and border issues are not particularly salient in laboratory research, where researchers construct short-term groups that are isolated from most external influences, except those imposed by the researcher. Boundary and border issues do pose significant challenges, however, to those studying groups in their natural contexts, including whether and under what conditions a researcher can gain access to the desired groups and whether the researcher should be considered part of those groups.

Third, in one way or another, studying group communication means studying behavior. A behavioral focus on what people say to one another (either verbally or nonverbally) is key to distinguishing research about groups that is communication-based from research that adopts a social-psychological perspective (see Levine & Moreland, 1990). One way to do this is to use observers to code group interaction. The advantage of this procedure is that actual communicative behavior is the unit of analysis. This procedure, however, poses serious challenges, some of which apply to studies of dyadic interaction. There is, for example, a potential gap between observers' coding of group members' communicative behavior and the meaning of that behavior to those members. As one illustration, we know there is an important difference between members' compliance with a group norm (performing a normative behavior) and their internalization of that norm (believing in its value). The group context also produces some unique problems for observing and coding communicative behavior because of the sheer number of people involved. It is difficult to know, for instance, what constitutes the beginning and end of a speech act. Should separate speech acts, interacts, or more complex combinations be coded? Moreover, even recording and transcribing group interaction can be problematic because of multiple members talking simultaneously and the often fast-paced nature of group interaction. Adding to this difficulty is the fact that established groups often make conversational links to previous discussions for which the researcher may have no referent.

Another way of studying group communicative behavior is to ask members about the behavior through the use of questionnaires and interviews. This procedure has the advantage of tapping into members' cognitions and attitudes about their communicative behavior (such as whether they feel comfortable voicing objections to a group norm), and, in the case of in-depth interviewing and open-ended questionnaires, obtaining the symbols that members naturally use to describe their behav-

ior. One disadvantage of this procedure, of course, is that what members say may not accurately reflect their actual behavior.

The systemic nature of groups, the fourth key characteristic, can create confusion regarding the designation or status of group constructs and variables. The same construct—group cohesiveness, for example (see Keyton, Chapter 8, this volume)—may be regarded as an input variable that proceeds and influences group processes, a process variable that tracks how members feel about their group, or a desirable outcome variable that results from group inputs and processes. Of course, cohesiveness could be all three simultaneously: a preoperative input variable, a developmental process, and a reconstituted outcome. This multiple conceptualization of group cohesiveness, as well as numerous other variables, is attributable to the cyclical and recursive nature of group systems. Researchers, therefore, are confronted by numerous possibilities when conceptualizing and operationalizing variables.

A related issue concerns the length of time that variables should be studied. Most research studies, especially laboratory studies but even many field studies, rely on single observations of a group meeting (see Frey, 1994b). Such designs have the advantage of producing neat and clean data, but they fail to capture the types of systemic changes that occur over time. One suggestion is to conduct longitudinal designs, but it is difficult to know in many cases when to begin and when to end, not to mention the time-consuming nature of such research and the often "excruciating" analysis of the resulting data (see Hewes, Planalp, & Streibel, 1980).

Outcomes, in particular, deserve attention, because their assessment is not a straightforward matter. For one thing, a multitude of group outcomes potentially could be studied. Outcomes can be classified according to group performance factors (e.g., productivity measures, such as decision quality, time to produce decisions, utility of decisions, decision accuracy, and degree of consensus; see Hirokawa & Salazar, Chapter 7, this volume), but individual performance factors are also created in groups (e.g., members' contribution to a group's output, their learning or personal development, and the number of speaking turns they take). Moreover, from a Systems Perspective, outcomes occur over the life of a group, not just at the point of a group's termination. There also are socioemotional and relational factors at the individual and group level, respectively (see Keyton, Chapter 8, this volume). Individual socioemotional outcomes include members' satisfaction, feelings of attraction to their group, confidence in the group's decisions, and perceptions of equity. Relational outcomes at the group level include the development of power relationships, norms, and level and type of conflict, as well as communication climate. In any group situation, multiple outcomes are likely to be obtained simultaneously, and some serve positive ends, whereas others simultaneously constitute harm. For example, settling a conflict among members quickly may help a group achieve its goal of reaching consensus but destroy the group's norm of respecting and addressing differences of opinions. Short-term and long-term outcomes may also be dialectical. A decision that seems to be acceptable immediately after a group meeting may, in the long run, turn out to be a disaster. Placating a member may be helpful for achieving cohesiveness in the short term but be unfortunate over the long term because it hinders reaching high-quality group decisions. There are also differences in criteria for judging the degree to which outcomes are satisfactory. Criteria for rational choice have often been used to evaluate decision-making outcomes, but these have been criticized for ignoring other aspects of choice making (Zey, 1992). In some cases, there are no accepted criteria for judging group decisions and other outcomes. Thus, the systemic nature of groups creates multiple levels of outcomes at multiple points in time.

Researchers should consider these four key characteristics of groups—the complexity of group interaction, fluidity of group boundaries, need for a behavioral focus, and the systemic nature of groups—as they identify their research goals; design research studies, including the conceptualization and operationalization of variables; and analyze the data obtained. Often, the primary issue that needs to be addressed in the research process is the level of analysis chosen for group communication research.

LEVEL-OF-ANALYSIS ISSUES

The *unit of analysis,* or unit of observation, is the researcher's determination of the level of what or who is to be studied (Babbie, 1995). Group communication researchers can choose to examine individuals' generalized group experiences, individuals in a particular group, a particular group as a whole unit, and/or relationships among groups. In each case, as described below, the research is concerned with a different level of analysis.

Individual Group Member Level of Analysis

One choice is to focus on the general way in which *individuals* communicate in groups. Putnam's (1979) research on people's preference for procedural order in groups is a good example. This study details criterion and construct validity issues confronted in developing the Preference for Procedural Order Scale, which measures, on the basis of data collected from more than 1,500 research participants, individuals' desire for order in groups.

Researchers may also focus on *individuals in a particular group.* For example, Berteotti and Seibold (1994) used survey procedures to analyze problematic issues surrounding health care teams. The researchers collected via questionnaires data about individual members' perceptions of their duties and roles within the health care team, quality of their working relationships with other team members, and the level of information received from various members. This research is an example of the unit of analysis emphasizing the "attributes, skills, and psychological and behavioral processes of team members" (Guzzo, 1995, p. 6).

Although both of these context levels focus on individuals, the distinction between the two is not trivial. The primary theoretical assumption that drives most group research is that individuals are members of a group who interact in a face-to-face (or its technological equivalent) setting. A second assumption is that regardless of a group's goal or activity, members perceive that some degree of interdependence is required to accomplish the goal or fulfill the activity. It is these two assumptions that distinguish group research from research about collections of people (e.g., a study of the interactions of a particular political action group deciding on whom the members will support in the next election versus a study of a group of Republicans).

A variation on studying individuals in groups is to examine the communicative behavior of specific individual members or dyads, most often leader-subordinate pairs. Evaluation of this specific dyadic pairing was so common during the 1970s that Cragan and Wright (1980) labeled it as a traditional line of group communication research. A recent advance in the study of focal individuals in groups has been the development of methods for simulating the communication of all members except the focal individual(s) in a group (see Galletta, Flor, Scott, & Tinaikar, 1995; Garfield, Satzinger, Taylor, & Dennis, 1997; Satzinger, Garfield, & Nagasundarum, 1996). One method involves having members interact through computer-mediated communication; the group simulator looks and acts like regular groupware. Participants type comments into the system, just as they normally would; instead of exchanging those comments with others, however, the simulator presents individuals with comments that appear to be from other group members but, in fact, are drawn from a script written by the experimenter. This offers the possibility of controlling the inputs to focal individuals so that the impacts of different interaction styles can be studied.

These points illuminate the concern of group membership; that is, whether people are being asked to respond about their group experiences in general, or are reporting their experiences in a specific group. Because group members, by definition, are interdependent, the communicative behavior of one affects the others. Thus, studying the first contextual level—individuals who communicate in groups—yields information about people who interact in group settings, such as what communicative strategies they might use. As Hoyle and Crawford (1994) argue, "Individual level data that refer to group phenomena are relevant for investigations of research questions ranging from how groups function to how membership in a group affects the personal life of group members" (p. 465). It is at the second level, individuals in a particular group, that researchers explore how members of a specific group interact to accomplish their goal or task.

Group Level of Analysis

At the group level of analysis, researchers typically study group processes or outcomes. This unit of analysis focuses on the *group as an entity,* which emphasizes "patterns of intragroup interaction as members exchange information or coordinate their physical efforts as they work" (Guzzo, 1995, p. 6). For example, Mabry and Attridge (1990) examined both group processes (coding group interaction using Bales's, 1950a, 1950b, Interaction Process Analysis, IPA; in this volume, see Chapters 8 [Keyton], 12 [Pavitt], and 17 [Socha]) and group outcomes (products from case studies evaluated by trained observers). This approach differs considerably from the individual level of analysis, in that group members are analyzed as a collective unit. The focus, therefore, is on what a group does, not on the members' characteristics (e.g., beliefs and personalities) and their messages.

To satisfy the challenge of working at this level of analysis, Spillman, Bezdek, and Spillman (1979) created a unique method for obtaining and assessing group-level data about consensus decisions following group discussions. On the basis of mathematical procedures associated with the Theory of Fuzzy

Sets, members rate their preference for each topic or idea as compared to every other topic or idea generated by the group. Analysis of this matrix allows groups to determine their distance from consensus and demonstrates that members do not necessarily choose one alternative while rejecting all others. Although data are generated at the level of the individual group member, results are calculated and analyzed at the group level.

Cline (1994) provides yet another example of the group unit of analysis. In analyzing the Watergate transcripts, she looked for evidence that an illusion of unanimity allowed groupthink (Janis, 1972, 1982) to develop. Although the transcripts were records of the interactions of only some of the key figures in the cover-up and the utterance was the unit of analysis, Cline successfully used the transcribed interaction as evidence to conclude that the group suffered from an illusion of unanimity.

Intergroup Level of Analysis

As a final approach, researchers can study the *communicative behavior that occurs between or among groups* within interdependent or dependent fields. For example, Ancona and Caldwell (1992) studied boundary spanning between groups and other groups or individuals. Extending group research to its outer contextual limits, another unit of analysis would assess the effects of the context or environment and perhaps emphasize time pressure or the role of organizational systems. For example, in a longitudinal study of a city council's debate, Barge and Keyton (1994) found that power issues that surfaced among members were attributable to the representative power of the elected officials' constituencies and/or the power given the mayor by virtue of the city's constitution. The debate would not have existed if council members and the mayor had displaced their interaction from these particular environmental influences. Carbaugh (1985, 1986) has formulated a theoretical approach for studying cultural communication within groups embedded

within organizations. This level of analysis in general, however, has received less attention than the others (Guzzo, 1995).

Managing Level-of-Analysis Issues

Group communication researchers must cope with several challenges and dilemmas posed by the level-of-analysis issue. Guzzo (1995) criticized the tendency to use aggregates of individuals, rather than groups, in much of the extant research. He argued that when researchers are interested in making inferences back to teams, rather than individuals, it is important that the unit of analysis be more than just a collection of individuals assembled for the purposes of research. It often is difficult, however, to identify populations of naturally occurring teams sufficiently large enough to satisfy traditional canons of quantitative research design. It also is difficult to find equivalent groups/teams for establishing the kind of control groups that are desired in such research. For both reasons, quantitative analysis in studies of teams often lack statistical power. In response, Guzzo noted, researchers return to the laboratory to conduct research on artificial groups and tasks. Although they solve some of the problems of internal validity (e.g., through random assignment), however, laboratory simulation groups potentially lack both certain types of internal validity (e.g., a shared history of working together) and external validity (see Bormann, 1970, 1980; Cragan & Wright, 1980; Frey, 1994a, 1994b; Putnam & Stohl, 1990).

Another challenge is maintaining consistency in units of analysis. Measurements that relate to differing units of analysis should be included in the same study only if the relationships between levels have been specified. One common practice is to aggregate individual-level measures to represent a group, as when members' individual ratings of satisfaction with their group are combined to represent the group's level of satisfaction. There are, however, team-level constructs that have no individual-level analogues, such as the degree to which a team has distributed expertise.

Similarly, constructs like trust and power are connected to a group, but individual members may exhibit a good deal of variation in them (Ilgen, Major, Hollenbeck, & Sego, 1995). In such cases, it is not appropriate simply to assign each member of the team the same value on a group-level variable and then analyze the data at the individual level. This creates dependencies among observations, a violation of the assumptions underlying most statistical tests (see Kashy & Kenny, in press; see also the discussion below of a different type of nonindependence problem).

One measure that should be taken when considering individual members' responses is the degree of *group convergence*—the amount of agreement among members' responses on constructs measured at the individual level. Using simple averages without testing for differences potentially ignores intragroup disagreement and divergent viewpoints. The intraclass correlation coefficient can be calculated and tested for significance to determine the degree of dependency resulting from group variables in the data for a given construct (Shrout & Fleiss, 1979). A significant intraclass correlation suggests that the construct should be construed at the group level; a nonsignificant coefficient suggests that it should be conceptualized at the individual level.

Within-and-between analysis (WABA) is designed explicitly to assess whether the group or individual level of analysis is appropriate for a construct (Dansereau, Alutto, & Yammarino, 1984; Dansereau & Markham, 1987). Yammarino and Markham (1992) succinctly summarized the three steps in WABA analysis:

First, each variable in a study is assessed to determine whether the variable varies primarily (a) between groups, (suggesting within-group homogeneity), (b) within groups (suggesting within-group heterogeneity), or both between and within groups (suggesting individual differences rather than within-group homogeneity or heterogeneity). Second, relationships among variables in a study are assessed to determine whether the correlations between variables is primarily a function of (a) between-group covariance, (b) within-group covariance, or (c) within and between-group covariances (suggesting individual differences). Third, the results of the first two steps are assessed for consistency and combined to draw the best overall conclusion from the data. (p. 169)

Software for conducting WABA analyses has been developed by Dansereau et al. (1986). This technique has been applied to group leadership (Yammarino, 1990), time spent communicating by group members (Yammarino & Naughton, 1988), and the expression of affect in groups (Yammarino & Markham, 1992), among other constructs.

The degree of convergence may also be used as a construct in its own right. The standard deviation of group members' scores (see, for example, Pinto, Pinto, & Prescott, 1993) or the Gini coefficient (Alker, 1965), both of which index the degree of variability in group members' responses, can be used as group-level indices. Another approach is that of Wekselberg, Goggin, and Collings (1997), who used the intraclass correlation coefficient to create a group measure of congruence of attitudes and agreement on group goals.

In some cases, cross-level analysis must be employed to relate data collected at one level of analysis to constructs at another level of analysis. Mossholder and Bedeian (1983) note that cross-level inference "occurs when relations among variables at one level are inferred from analyses performed at a different level" (p. 547). There are many legitimate uses of cross-level inference in group communication research, but two problems related to such inferences must be considered. First, there is the "fallacy of the wrong level," that is, "making direct translation of properties or relations from one level to another" (Galtung, 1967, p. 45). Researchers may confuse data collected at one of the individual levels with interpretations at the group level, especially when individual-response data are used in aggregate form to represent a higher-level construct. This occurs, for example, when individual group members respond to a satisfaction questionnaire and their aggregated scores are used to stand for the satisfaction level of the group as a whole. The question arises, however, as to whether a group per se can be satisfied. Such affective constructs as satisfaction are more properly construed at the level of the individuals who possess them; this construct, thus, more properly should be referred to as "average member satisfaction."

A second problem in cross-level inference is the ecological fallacy of imputing to members properties of the group as a whole (see Babbie, 1995). For example, simply because a group demonstrates a high average cohesiveness score from a questionnaire does not mean that all members are attracted to the group. Glick (1985) details many of the cross-level inference problems that plague research on climate in organizations. His warnings and suggestions about mixing units of theory, observation, and analysis are also pertinent to group communication researchers.

The various techniques for multilevel analysis take a different approach to the level-of-analysis issue by assessing the influence of group and individual factors simultaneously. The questions asked in multilevel analysis are whether and to what extent higher-level constructs affect relationships among variables at lower levels of abstraction. For example, a researcher might be interested in the impact of a technology, such as a Group Decision Support System (GDSS; see Scott, Chapter 16, this volume, regarding communication technology and group communication), on group members' satisfaction. A multilevel analysis would attempt to sort out the degree to which technology influenced members' satisfaction and the degree to which their satisfaction level varied as a function of the group in which they participated. Depending on the nature of group interaction, members might reinforce each others' reactions to the GDSS, and, thereby, create a group-level effect that varied. As a result, different groups would be expected to exhibit different levels of satisfaction and different reactions to the technology, regardless of the condition to which they were assigned. The effects of other higher-level

variables, such as organizational unit or culture, could also be incorporated into a multilevel analysis.

To conduct a multilevel analysis, the effects resulting from the independent variables are estimated using individual-level data. Tests then are conducted to determine whether there is a group effect that influences the magnitude of individual-level effects. Basically, group effects are assumed to moderate the impact of the independent variables on individuals' scores. In analysis of variance, this is done by nesting the higher-level variable within the factors (see Kashy & Kenny, in press; Mossholder & Bedeian, 1983). If the nested groups factor is significant, then group-level effects should be included in the model. Variance can be partitioned to determine the relative strength of group and individual effects (this is also the basis for calculating an intraclass correlation coefficient). In multilevel regression analysis, the level 1 regression model is first estimated using the independent variables and the individual-level variables. The level 2 model uses the higher-level variable (e.g., group) to predict the slope and coefficients of the level 1 model estimated for each group. The extent to which the higher-level variable can explain variation in the form of the regression equation for level 1 indicates whether group-level constructs are appropriate.

Specialized procedures and statistical packages have been developed for fitting multilevel models, including hierarchical linear modeling (HLM; Bryk & Raudenbush, 1992) and VARCL (Longford, 1989). It is also possible, however, to conduct multilevel analyses using standard statistical packages, such as BMDP, SAS, LISREL, and EQS (see Kashy & Kenny, in press; Muthen, 1994). One caution in using these methods is that the number of variables and the precision of estimation of regression coefficients for each group are limited by group size. Analyses can be performed for smaller groups (five or six members), but the regression coefficient estimates will be worse than for larger groups (eight or more members). Bryk and Raudenbush (1992) recommend five as a minimum size for regression analysis, and many of their groups (in most cases, school classes) have 20 or more members each. These cautions are not as much a cause for concern in analysis-of-variance (ANOVA) designs because the independent variables take on a limited range of values.

A final method that deals with the issue of level of analysis is the Social Relations Model (Kashy & Kenny, in press; Kenny & LaVoie, 1984). In some cases, an intermediate dyadic level must be interposed between the individual and group levels. This is the case when relationships among group members are considered because such relationships often form in dyads (see Keyton, Chapter 8, this volume, regarding the relational dimension of group life). For example, members' perceptions of other members' levels of positive emotional expression in a group discussion depend, in part, on their prior interactions with one another, as well as the mean level of emotionality in the group and their own tendencies in interpreting others' emotions. If member A has experienced high levels of positive emotional expression in his or her previous interactions with member B, and if member B is rather withdrawn in the discussion, A may rate B lower than he or she would have otherwise, in the light of expectations that B would behave positively "in most instances."

Kenny and his colleagues designed the Social Relations Model to sort out the effects of dyads and groups. The most common design for this type of analysis is to have each member rate or interact with every other member in the group in a round-robin fashion. These data can then be analyzed for individual, dyadic, and group effects on ratings or interactions. Although round-robin ratings are fairly easy to obtain, round-robin interactions are more difficult to arrange and may not be feasible for many projects. The Social Relations Model, nevertheless, offers another tool for sorting out levels effects.

An obvious difficulty in group communication research is maintaining a stable and consistent conceptualization of the construct of interest and its operationalization. The de-

gree of fit between the conceptualization and operationalization affects the clarity, informativeness, and, hence, interpretation and utility of the data (Miller & Boster, 1989). The various methods for framing and conducting research at and across different levels of analysis can aid researchers in "keeping things straight."

A corollary of multiple levels in groups is dependencies in data gathered at the individual level. It is important that researchers employing individual-level measures test for the independence of data by means of the intraclass correlation coefficient and ANOVA tests mentioned above. If the data are nonindependent, then one option is to aggregate across the group, which has the unfortunate consequence of eliminating individual-level scores. Another option is to employ individual measures but use nesting or multilevel analysis to control for group effects.

This section has highlighted the difficulties inherent in attempting to identify the effects of a particular level of analysis—be it individual, group, or organizational—when levels are often strongly interdependent. Just as levels interpenetrate and shade into one another, so, too, do a group and its environment. Defining and delineating group boundaries, examined in the next section, is an undertaking fraught with ambiguity.

FLUIDITY AND PERMEABILITY OF GROUP BOUNDARIES

Much has been said about the need to study "bona fide" groups (see Putnam & Stohl, 1990, 1994, 1996; in this volume, see Chapters 1 [Gouran] and 2 [Poole]). A primary characteristic of such groups is the fluidity and permeability of their boundaries. There are at least two sources of this fluidity/permeability: (a) changes in membership and (b) shifting patterns of connectivity to other groups, whereby, at some times, a given group stands on its own and, at other times, it combines into a larger collective with another group. Typical laboratory studies prevent fluidity/permeability from surfacing by composing clearly defined and bounded groups from scratch. Many field studies also control for it by measuring groups at only one point in time. Both strategies, in effect, amount to ignoring this issue. The only way in which the complexity of fluidity and permeability can be addressed is to study groups in their natural environments over the course of time.

To take the fluidity and permeability of group boundaries into account requires longitudinal research designs, but longitudinal research is not sufficient. Researchers must also explicitly include boundary shifts as part of the ongoing process of research. Longitudinal studies of group communication have rarely included, as central priorities, group boundaries, membership shifts, or groups' connections to other groups. If boundary fluidity/permeability is to be taken seriously, shifts in membership and intergroup linkages must be taken into account in group communication theory and research. This requires that certain issues be addressed, such as how individuals' behavior contributes to groups, how individuals become members and take on different roles in groups, individuals' "careers" in groups, how groups deal with leave-taking by departing members and the arrival of new members (see Anderson et al., Chapter 6, this volume), and what forces give a group a stable sense of identity over time, even as its membership changes. Moreland and Levine (1982) are among the few studying group behavior who have considered these and related issues.

Studies by Insko and colleagues (1982) and Jacobs and Campbell (1961) suggest how the impact of membership changes could be investigated in the laboratory. These studies involved the creation of laboratory groups observed through numerous "generations"; a generation was created by withdrawing and replacing members one by one until the groups had undergone complete turnover. This design has been used primarily to study the evolution of norms and traditions but could be applied for other purposes as well. Indeed, if researchers wish to conduct laboratory studies that takes the natural environments of groups into account, this should be considered one of the basic designs. It has the advantage of controlling many competing explanations and allowing for the manipulation of other variables and, thereby, providing a basis for causal inference. This design, however, also has disadvantages, including substantial research costs, research participant mortality, and lack of apparent ecological validity in other respects.

Field studies can take advantage of natural variation in boundary fluidity/permeability; the major challenge is how to assess and incorporate it into theories. Teams or groups in the field often are treated as intact social systems, and changes in membership or mergers and linkages with other teams are either discounted or regarded as something the original intact group does as a unit. Instead, it would be useful to interrogate the "entitativity" of groups, that is, to acknowledge that the basic entities being studied may undergo substantive changes that sometimes leave them intact, sometimes leave them as changed but still recognizable units, and sometimes eliminate the original unit through merger or dissolution.

Several field studies provide models for this type of research. With regard to membership changes, March and Olsen (1976) focused on shifting membership as a key factor influencing the development of ideas and decision-making outcomes. Their book-length study is a model of long-term inquiry in organizational settings. A set of studies that employed a systematic data-gathering and analytic procedure to track events related to boundary fluidity is also reported in Van de Ven, Venkataraman, Polley, and Garud (1989). A good exemplar in the communication field is the sustained work by Adelman and Frey (1994, 1997; Frey, Adelman, & Query, 1996; Frey, Query, Flint, & Adelman, 1998) on communication and community building in a residential facility for people with AIDS. This work is based on a 9-year ethnographic program of research that included participant observation; in-depth interviewing of residents, staff, and volunteers; and questionnaires administered at four different times over a 2-year period. The unique nature of the facility, in which the average length of stay at the time was 7 months (with most memberships terminating because of death), provided the researchers with opportunities to study the effects of continual and significant membership changes on the ability of collective communicative practices to help create and sustain community in this highly fragile context.

With regard to interactions between groups and their environment (including other groups), Geist and Chandler (1984) studied how groups constructed images of, and negotiated their own jurisdictions with, other teams. One of the most sustained efforts of this type is the research on gang communication by Conquergood (1991, 1992, 1994; Conquergood & Siegel, 1990). On the basis of years of participant observation, Conquergood examined, among other things, the symbolic boundary that is constructed between the People and Folks Nations, the two supergang confederations to which all gangs belong. He showed how local gang branches are embedded within these gang nations and energized by the organizational resources they provide, and how the fundamental external boundary that must be negotiated by local members is the hostility-charged border between these nation states.

Recent advances in methodology promise tools for handling the study of membership changes and intergroup linkages. Communication Network Theory and network analytic techniques (see Monge & Contractor, in press) typically have been applied to the study of entire organizations, but group communication researchers who wish to take a group's natural situation into account could employ them to identify boundary-related constructs. Network analysis provides researchers with the opportunity to assess the degree to which individuals belong to single or multiple groups and the overlap in activity among different groups. The potential of this approach is suggested by the informal network analysis that Homans (1950) developed in his case study of the Bank Wiring Room, which showed how group members' status and influence were affected by the cliques to which they belonged and by how those cliques were connected to one another via shared members. Another set of methods that promises to help track boundary fluidity and permeability in the study of group and organizational processes is detailed in Poole, Van de Ven, Dooley, and Holmes (in press). These methods are designed to test theories explaining how event sequences unfold in groups and organizations, and they are appropriate for tracing over time the impact of membership shifts and overlaps.

A particularly effective approach for studying group boundaries is ethnography, as demonstrated in the studies by Adelman and Frey and by Conquergood mentioned above. Sustained participant observation, coupled with in-depth interviews of group members, provides researchers with the ability to study the fluidity and permeability of group boundaries, shifting group borders, and the interdependence of groups with their environments. Some specific techniques associated with, and additional examples of, ethnographic group communication research are detailed in Frey (1994a) and Dollar and Merrigan (in press).

CODING GROUP COMMUNICATION

The study of group communication often involves some form of observing and analyzing actual group interaction. Interaction may be observed as it occurs live, recorded on audiotape or videotape, and/or transcribed in written form. Although the acquisition of group interaction data may sometimes be intrusive (e.g., when group members are aware that they are being observed), coding and analysis generally proceed after group interaction has occurred; thus, the analysis of group interaction is relatively unobtrusive compared to some other research techniques.

The observation and analysis of group interaction (like other forms of interaction, such as dyadic) generally can be classified into two streams: qualitative and quantitative. Qualitative analysis, which includes ethnographic observations of group discourse and conversation analysis, among other techniques, is the less-utilized of the two in terms of its application to the study of group communication (for discussions of qualitative discourse-analytic methods in interpersonal and group communication research, see Poole, Folger, & Hewes, 1987; Tracy, 1991). There are, however, some notable studies that interested readers should consult. For example, the ethnographic study of an AIDS support group by Cawyer and Smith-Dupre' (1995) validated four functions of supportive messages. Lesch (1994) documented the communicative strategies employed by members of a witches' coven to sustain shared consciousness, as well as to weather the storms of a change in the coven's membership. Murphy (1998) studied airline flight attendants' resistance to organizational policies and practices by analyzing hidden transcripts—interactions, stories, myths, and rituals in which employees participated beyond the direct observation of organizational power holders. Poole, DeSanctis, Kirsch, and Jackson (1995) identified differences in interactional processes among four quality teams using a group decision support system. In each case, the researchers employed inductive qualitative communication coding schemes that were developed while and/or after the data were collected.

The more typical observational procedure in group communication research is to employ *interaction analysis,* quantitative observational schemes that allegedly enable one to "classify objectively the communicative behaviors (or actions) of group members in accordance with a set of carefully defined, preestablished categories" (Hirokawa, 1988b, p. 231). In this procedure, trained observers identify segments of group interaction as codable units and then classify these units within the categories of a predetermined observational scheme. Such schemes provide information used to determine the interactive structure of a group, the distributional structure of interaction, and/or the sequential structure among the categorized units (see Hirokawa, 1988b).

Interaction analysis has its share of critics. Bochner (1978), for example, argued that the technique oversimplifies the complex nature of human communication by reducing it to fixed categories and freezing processes into codes. Hawes (1978) questioned the theoretical foundation of interaction analysis because it violates the constructive nature of communication, whereas O'Keefe, Delia, and O'Keefe (1980) complained that it does not uncover important structural features of group interaction. Despite such criticisms, interaction analysis remains perhaps the most important tool in group communication research; hence, we focus on it, in particular, here.

Several reviews of interaction analysis have appeared that discuss many of the methods and procedures used in communication and psychology research, as well as research in other disciplines; readers are referred to them for specific methods (see, for example, Folger, Hewes, & Poole, 1984; Hirokawa, 1988b; McGrath & Altermatt, in press; Meyers, Seibold, & Brashers, 1991; Poole et al., 1987; Trujillo, 1986; Weingart, 1997). Here, we concentrate on several important issues relevant to using quantitative coding schemes in group communication research. Specifically, we focus on the choices researchers make when designing group interaction-analytic schemes, for these choices define the purpose and scope of a coding scheme and impose implicit limitations on its applicability.

One important choice that designers of coding schemes make is the *unit of analysis.* The most common unit of analysis is the message (generally defined as an utterance or idea unit), but other useful units include topics, words, and timed segments (see Folger et al., 1984; Frey, Botan, Friedman, & Kreps, 1991, 1992; Frey, Botan, & Kreps, in press). Although the message generally is the most intuitively obvious unit of analysis for communication researchers, other units may be more appropriate for describing various aspects of group interaction. For example, to encode a characteristic of group interaction as a whole, such as the conflict management style employed, a unit of analysis spanning several messages or turns may be more useful than a single message unit. In contrast, to code language intensity, the best unit of analysis is the individual word; looking words up in a "dictionary" of intensifiers probably is more reliable than attempting to judge the intensity of complex phrases. At the most general level, Hirokawa (1988a) utilized the entire group discussion as the unit of analysis. He had coders rate entire discussions regarding the degree to which they served certain critical functions (see Poole et al., 1987, regarding global ratings of interaction).

A second choice designers make is the *particular aspects of group communication* that constitute the focus of coding. The most common foci in group communication coding systems are the communicative functions that a message serves in group interaction, such as "gives information," "positive reinforcement," and "altercasting." Functional coding schemes, such as IPA, concentrate on the purpose of a message independent of the content of discussion (hence, the term "process analysis" in IPA), and the resulting flexibility seems to be one strength of such coding schemes.

This flexibility and generality come at some expense. McGrath (1997), in critiquing the IPA, argued that "IPA data were not very useful to anyone interested in studying any particular content question. . . . Hence, it was of little use to anyone working from any other theoretical formulation" (pp. 9-10; see Socha's review of research, Chapter 17, this volume, which reaches a similar conclusion about using IPA to study family communication). Embedded in McGrath's comment are two issues. First, all functional schemes are grounded in some theory. IPA, for example, is grounded in Bales's (1953) Equilibrium Theory of group problem-solving functions (in this volume, see Chapters 2 [Poole], 3 [Mabry], and 12 [Pavitt]). As another example, compliance-gaining coding schemes are grounded in a specific notion of interpersonal influence that has not been formally stated as a theory but draws on Social Exchange Theory. Hence, no matter how universal or general a functional coding scheme may be, and no matter how neutral its categories may seem, it always represents a particular perspective. Needless to say, such coding schemes may not be useful in many cases, particularly

when the theory or perspective underlying a study is inconsistent with the theory that grounds the functional scheme. For example, one could not use IPA to study compliance-gaining strategies in groups. Moreover, because functional coding schemes aspire to some degree of generality, they often are not able to take the specific context into account. This is reflected in the fact that special coding rules have to be developed to apply functional coding schemes in particular studies. For example, because legal opinions often are used as information in jury deliberations, researchers might have to write additional rules to specify what counts as "information giving" and "opinion giving" when applying IPA; if the system were applied literally, both types of communicative acts would be coded as giving opinions.

The need to formulate such rules underscores the fact that functional coding schemes do not take into account the content of group discussion. When understanding the group interaction depends on grasping content, coding systems based on principles other than functions must be developed. For example, Poole, McPhee, and Seibold (1982) coded the valence of comments in group problem-solving discussions, with valence defined as the degree of support for specific topics. Wheelan et al. (1994) coded both the functional purpose and content themes of communicative acts during group discussions. They first used the Group Development Observation System (Verdi & Wheelan, 1992; Wheelan & Verdi, 1992) to code group communication into one of seven functional categories based on the psychoanalytic work of Bion (1961), Stock and Thelen (1958) and Thelen (1954): dependency, counterdependency, flight, fight, pairing, counterpairing, and work statements (in this volume, see chapters 8 [Keyton] and 14 [Schultz]). They then coded the content themes that emerged during group discussion: "A theme was said to exist if at least two individuals engaged in a sustained discussion of a topic over time" (Wheelan et al., 1994, p. 161). The latter type of coding was grounded in the participants' communication specific to the purpose of the groups—in this case, small groups that were part of a Group Relations Conference. As a result, Wheelan and colleagues were able to discern which topics were accepted by group participants and identified how the members' functional comments created patterns of group development.

A third choice facing designers of group interaction analytic schemes is the *level of observer inference* that coders must make. Coding schemes draw on coders' knowledge of language and social context when they are given the latitude to assign codings according to their own judgment. There are variations in the degree to which coders are allowed to exercise this knowledge in making judgments. At one end of the scale are mechanical devices and computer software that greatly constrain human judgment. For example, content analytic programs based on dictionaries automatically classify sentences. A less stringent alternative specifies a choice tree that presents a complete set of classifications and a series of simple binary questions that "lead" coders to the proper classification (e.g., Anderson, 1983). The most common method emphasizes utility and pragmatic impact, as opposed to logical completeness. Coding system designers compile as complete a list of categories as possible, write enough rules to enable coders to recognize and distinguish the categories, and rely on coders' native knowledge and skills for the rest. This strategy is advantageous for coding complex meanings for which it is difficult, if not impossible, to develop complete a priori classification rules. Reliance on coders' judgment, however, makes the procedure harder to control and may result in inconsistent classifications if the observational categories are not sufficiently developed and defined.

A fourth choice revolves around whether *coding categories are to be univocal or multivalent.* Many traditional sources recommend that coding categories be mutually exclusive and exhaustive (see, for example, Berelson, 1952; Budd, Thorp, & Donohew, 1967; Holsti, 1969; Kaid & Wadsworth, 1989;

Krippendorff, 1980; Stempel, 1989; Weber, 1990). Assigning a single code to each act (mutual exclusivity) may be problematic if more than one meaningful function is served by an act. In view of the fact that messages typically have multiple layers of meaning and that more than one consequence can be taken from any occurrence, multifunctional coding may be preferred for many applications (see Hewes, 1979).

A particularly interesting method for interaction analysis that allows for multifunctionality and multiple levels is the System for the Multiple Level Observation of Groups (SYMLOG), developed by Bales and Cohen (1979) as an extension of IPA (see Keyton, 1995, 1997; Keyton & Wall, 1989; in this volume, see Chapters 2 [Poole] and 8 [Keyton]). Theoretically more complex than IPA, SYMLOG is also more flexible (McGrath, 1984) in allowing researchers to capture group communication processes at both the individual member and group levels, as well as from both members' and observers' perspectives. Research studies by Keyton (1995), Keyton and Springston (1990), and Wall and Galanes (1986) demonstrate how SYMLOG can be used in the study of group communication. For example, Keyton (1995) used the multiple perspectives available in SYMLOG to examine the communication of a group of physicians by acquiring both physicians' individual ratings of themselves and ratings of the physicians by the critical care and intensive care nursing staffs. Thus, both participants' and observers' viewpoints were represented. In addition, ratings at both the individual and averaged group levels were used to provide feedback to the group. The flexibility provided by SYMLOG's multifunctionality and multiple perspectives created a rich system of feedback that proved compelling to the physicians.

Weighing against the enhanced sensitivity of multifunctional coding is an increase in the difficulty of attaining intercoder reliability when multiple functions may be attributed to ambiguous acts. There is the danger of "overcoding" in such cases; that is, reading more functions into an act than it serves, merely because multifunctionality is possible.

A final choice that designers make involves the *type of meaning* the group interaction analytic scheme is intended to capture. Although finer distinctions are possible, Poole et al. (1987) distinguished observer-privileged meanings from subject-privileged meanings. *Observer-privileged meanings* are those that are accessible to outside observers, whereas *subject-privileged meanings* are those understandings that insiders and participants would have of the same incidents. Clearly, a coding scheme designed to capture subject-privileged meaning is harder to design than an observer-privileged system. Poole and colleagues describe procedures and methods for the validation of coding systems designed to acquire both observer- and subject-privileged meanings (see also Folger et al., 1984).

Common to many coding schemes is the external role of coders. IPA, for example, explicitly specifies coders' role as being that of the generalized other, in asking observers to attempt to put themselves in the shoes of the person toward whom that coder is oriented (Bales, 1950a). Most coding schemes, however, require the researcher to adopt a more "objectivist" stance by employing "blind" coders who know neither the purpose of the study nor the groups being observed. This procedure helps to minimize biases introduced by previous experience with the group studied and by the desire to fulfill expectations about research questions or hypotheses. Such coders, however, may miss much of "the action" because they are not as familiar with the particular system of meaning in the groups under study as a group member or as a "vested" observer would be. When coders are privy to a group's naturally occurring system, as were the nurses in Keyton's (1995) study, their coding judgments are valuable sources of insight into the meaning of events to group members, and they often have important information about the history of the group that they utilize in making classifications. These same experiences, however, may also introduce bias unless coders are quite careful and reflective.

To test the premise that external observers can make valid assessments of naturally occurring groups, Kacen and Rozovski (1998) designed a field study to make direct comparisons among group members, as well as between both direct and indirect observers. Heart patients in support groups were the target participants, and social work students served as direct and indirect observers (the latter watched a videotape of the groups' interactions). Kacen and Rozovski found that, with the exception of one self-revelation variable, all three groups evaluated similarly over a 10-week period of time the progress and outcomes of the groups. They concluded that group processes may be evaluated adequately by observers external to a group and pointed out that these findings strengthen the argument of being able to observe process-outcome relationships.

In summary, coding is not, as some might assume, a straightforward process of assigning messages to categories. The design of coding schemes involves a complex set of choices, and these choices determine what claims the resulting data can support.

ADDRESSING GROUP OUTCOMES

Researchers studying groups probably will always be interested in identifying and measuring outcomes. Doing so is important not only for scholars interested in the effects of various inputs and processes on outcomes, but also for practitioners who work with groups and group members. The study of group outcomes raises the issue of level of analysis, but it also raises the issues of group complexity and systemic properties.

Outcomes, especially those at the group level, frequently are evaluated in terms of only one source of data, either from external observers or from group members. Both types of data, however, have shortcomings. External evaluators are likely to evaluate outcomes differently—often more negatively—than are the group members who produced them, because they are not aware of the special problems and exigencies that entered into the group's work. At the same time, group members' responses are also likely to contain bias, either because they want to make their group look good or because they are too close to the work to make measured, accurate evaluations.

One way to overcome these shortcomings is to measure several different types and levels of outcomes to produce a triangulated view. For example, in studying group communication and decision making, researchers could ask group members to evaluate their own performance (such as the perceived quality of their decisions). Additionally, researchers could ask observers to identify the quality of group members' individual contributions, and subject matter experts could evaluate the utility of the group's decision. Moreover, in the most complete design, researchers would evaluate both short-term and long-term outcomes. Continuing with the example, researchers could use individuals' attraction to the group as a midpoint individual-process measure, along with quantity and quality of positive socioemotional talk as a longer-term measure of process. Thus, a composite view of group outcome would exist at multiple levels of both process and content. In such an approach, no one point of view (short or long term, individual or group level, or process or content) would be omniscient. Such an approach would allow researchers to address the complexity of group interaction, because outcomes are more typically simultaneous and competing than they are singular and representative of the group as a whole.

When the outcomes in question relate to group performance or quality of a product, a special problem may result. Some evidence suggests that group members and observers who have viewed the group's interaction make performance judgments more on the basis of whether the group activities fit the types of interactions they think effective groups should have than on careful evaluation of the product. Gladstein (1984) found that sales teams' evaluations of their performance were related to their perceptions of such

things as openness of communication and strong leadership, but they were unrelated to the actual sales figures for each team; moreover, sales figures were not determined by the process variables of openness and leadership. This suggests that members' evaluations were made on the basis on how they thought their team should have done if the members had engaged in such behaviors as open communication and strong leadership rather than on real productivity. A later study by Martell and Guzzo (1991) revealed that performance ratings were confounded with raters' implicit theories of group effectiveness.

The results of these studies can be taken in two ways. The most obvious conclusion is that outcomes should be evaluated independently by observers/judges who have no knowledge of how the groups being judged interacted. It is also possible, however, that members and close observers are aware of problems and difficulties that keep groups from performing to their potential and that they take these into account in making evaluations. It may well be the case that these "corrected" outcome measures, which allow for confounding factors, such as the difficulty of the task the group faced, are as valid as so-called "objective" measures of outcomes. For example, it would be difficult to call inferior the performance of a sales team that turns in annual revenues of only $20,000 but has succeeded in breaking into a lucrative, previously closed market when comparing that performance to that of a team with $300,000 in annual revenues garnered in a safe and assured, but declining, market. Multiple perspectives may well be the best way to obtain valid evaluations of even group performance and quality outcomes.

These points suggest the need for multidimensional measures of group outcomes. McGrath (1991) has explicitly argued for this approach and advances three distinct classes of group outcomes: performance, group well-being, and members' need satisfaction. Reagan and Rohrbaugh (1990) advanced a scheme for evaluating groups that defines four different perspectives on outcomes that a group might address: (a) consensual perspective, which emphasizes pattern maintenance and tension management; (b) rational perspective, which emphasizes goal attainment; (c) political perspective, which emphasizes adaptation and adjustment; and (d) empirical perspective, which emphasizes integration of information and members' viewpoints. They posited that groups must engage in trade-offs among these competing values, and they developed an instrument for assessing in groups the degree of emphasis placed on each perspective.

CONCLUSION

This chapter has identified four key issues specific to designing and conducting research on group communication. In emphasizing these, we do not mean to turn attention away from the more general, context-free advice on research design that is contained in the many excellent texts on social-scientific methodology. It is important, however, to acknowledge that the small group, in general, and group communication, in particular, are special contexts that simultaneously present unique challenges and opportunities for investigators. Attention to the special problems of the group context will help to increase both the internal and external validity of group communication research. Those embarking on the study of group communication are venturing into a unique territory where much still remains uncharted; for such an adventure, it is always helpful to have both traditionally valid and reliable equipment as well as special tools designed to meet the demands of the situation.

REFERENCES

Adelman, M. B., & Frey, L. R. (1994). The pilgrim must embark: Creating and sustaining community in a residential facility for people with AIDS. In L. R. Frey (Ed.), *Group communication in context: Studies of natural groups* (pp. 3-22). Hillsdale, NJ: Lawrence Erlbaum.
Adelman, M. B., & Frey, L. R. (1997). *The fragile community: Living together with AIDS.* Mahwah, NJ: Lawrence Erlbaum.
Alker, H. (1965). *Mathematics and politics.* New York: Macmillan.

Ancona, D. G., & Caldwell, D. F. (1992). Bridging the boundary: External activity and performance in organizational teams. *Administrative Science Quarterly, 37,* 634-665.
Anderson, P. A. (1983). Decision making by objection and the Cuban missile crisis. *Administrative Science Quarterly, 28,* 201-222.
Babbie, E. (1995). *The practice of social research* (7th ed.). Belmont, CA: Wadsworth.
Bales, R. F. (1950a). *Interaction process analysis: A method for the study of small groups.* Cambridge, MA: Addison-Wesley.
Bales, R. F. (1950b). A set of categories for the analysis of small group interaction. *American Sociological Review, 15,* 257-263.
Bales, R. F. (1953). The equilibrium problem in small groups. In T. C. Parsons, R. F. Bales, & E. A. Shils, *Working papers in the theory of action* (pp. 111-161). Glencoe, IL: Free Press.
Bales, R. F., & Cohen, S. P. (with Williamson, S. A.). (1979). *SYMLOG: A system for the multiple level observation of groups.* New York: Free Press.
Barge, J. K., & Keyton, J. (1994). Contextualizing power and social influence in groups. In L. R. Frey (Ed.), *Group communication in context: Studies of natural groups* (pp. 85-105). Hillsdale, NJ: Lawrence Erlbaum.
Berelson, B. (1952). *Content analysis in communications research.* New York: Free Press.
Berteotti, C. R., & Seibold, D. R. (1994). Coordination and role-definition problems in health-care teams: A hospice case study. In L. R. Frey (Ed.), *Group communication in context: Studies of natural groups* (pp. 107-131). Hillsdale, NJ: Lawrence Erlbaum.
Bettenhausen, K. L. (1991). Five years of groups research: What we have learned and what needs to be addressed. *Journal of Management, 17,* 345-381.
Bion, W. R. (1961). *Experiences in groups, and other papers.* New York: Basic Books.
Bochner, A. P. (1978). On taking ourselves seriously: An analysis of some persistent problems and promising directions in interpersonal research. *Human Communication Research, 4,* 179-191.
Bormann, E. G. (1970). The paradox and promise of small group research. *Speech Monographs, 37,* 211-217.
Bormann, E. G. (1980). The paradox and promise of small group research revisited. *Central States Speech Journal, 31,* 214-220.
Bryk, A. S., & Raudenbush, S. W. (1992). *Hierarchical linear models.* Newbury Park, CA: Sage.
Budd, R. W., Thorp, R. K., & Donohew, L. (1967). *Content analysis of communication.* New York: Macmillan.
Carbaugh, D. (1985). Cultural communication and organizing. In W. B. Gudykunst, L. P. Stewart, & S. Ting-Toomey (Eds.), *Communication, culture, and organizational processes* (pp. 31-47). Beverly Hills, CA: Sage.
Carbaugh, D. (1986). Some thoughts on organizing as cultural communication. In L. Thayer (Ed.), *Organi-*

zational communication: Emerging perspectives: Vol. 1. Organization (pp. 85-101). Norwood, NJ: Ablex.

Cawyer, C. S., & Smith-Dupre', A. (1995). Communicating social support: Identifying supportive episodes in an HIV/AIDS support group. Communication Quarterly, 43, 243-258.

Cline, R.J.W. (1994). Groupthink and the Watergate cover-up: The illusion of unanimity. In L. R. Frey (Ed.), Group communication in context: Studies of natural groups (pp. 119-223). Hillsdale, NJ: Lawrence Erlbaum.

Cohen, S. G., & Bailey, D. E. (1997). What makes teams work: Group effectiveness research from the shop floor to the executive suite. Journal of Management, 3, 239-290.

Conquergood, D. (1991). "For the nation!" How street gangs problematize patriotism. In R. Troester (Ed.), Peacemaking through communication (pp. 8-21). Annandale, VA: Speech Communication Association.

Conquergood, D. (1992). Life in Big Red: Struggles and accommodations in a Chicago polyethnic tenement. In L. Lamphere (Ed.), Structuring diversity: Ethnographic perspectives on the new immigration (pp. 95-144). Chicago: University of Chicago Press.

Conquergood, D. (1994). Homeboys and hoods: Gangs and cultural space. In L. R. Frey (Ed.), Group communication in context: Studies of natural groups (pp. 23-55). Hillsdale, NJ: Lawrence Erlbaum.

Conquergood, D. (Producer), & Siegel, T. (Producer & Director). (1990). The heart broken in half [Videotape]. Chicago: Siegel Productions.

Cragan, J. F., & Wright, D. W. (1980). Small group communication research of the 1970's: A synthesis and critique. Central States Speech Journal, 31, 197-213.

Cragan, J. F., & Wright, D. W. (1990). Small group communication research of the 1980s: A synthesis and critique. Communication Studies, 41, 212-236.

Dansereau, F., Alutto, J. A., & Yammarino, F. J. (1984). Theory testing in organizational behavior: The varient approach. Englewood Cliffs, NJ: Prentice Hall.

Dansereau, F., Chandrasekaran, G., Dumas, M., Coleman, D., Ehrlich, S., & Bagchi, D. (1986). Data inquiry that tests entity and correlational/causal theories. Williamsville, NY: Institute for Theory Testing.

Dansereau, F., & Markham, S. E. (1987). Levels of analysis in personnel and human resources management. In K. Rowland & G. Ferris (Eds.), Research in personnel and human resources management (pp. 1-50). Greenwich, CT: JAI.

Dollar, N. J., & Merrigan, G. (in press). Ethnographic practices in group communication. In L. R. Frey (Ed.), New directions in group communication. Thousand Oaks, CA: Sage.

Folger, J. P., Hewes, D. E., & Poole, M. S. (1984). Coding social interaction. In B. Dervin & M. Voight (Eds.), Progress in the communication sciences (Vol. 4, pp. 115-161). Norwood, NJ: Ablex.

Frey, L. R. (1994a). The call of the field: Studying communication in natural groups. In L. R. Frey (Ed.),

Group communication in context: Studies of natural groups (pp. ix-xiv). Hillsdale, NJ: Lawrence Erlbaum.

Frey, L. R. (1994b). The naturalistic paradigm: Studying small groups in the postmodern era. Small Group Research, 25, 551-577.

Frey, L. R. (1996). Remembering and "re-membering": A history of theory and research on communication and group decision making. In R. Y. Hirokawa & M. S. Poole (Eds.), Communication and group decision making (2nd ed., pp. 19-51). Thousand Oaks, CA: Sage.

Frey, L. R., Adelman, M. B., & Query, J. L., Jr. (1996). Communication practices in the social construction of health in an AIDS residence. Journal of Health Psychology, 1, 383-397.

Frey, L. R., Botan, C. H., Friedman, P. G., & Kreps, G. L. (1991). Investigating communication: An introduction to research methods. Englewood Cliffs, NJ: Prentice Hall.

Frey, L. R., Botan, C. H., Friedman, P. G., & Kreps, G. L. (1992). Interpreting communication research: A case study approach. Englewood Cliffs, NJ: Prentice Hall.

Frey, L. R., Botan, C. H., & Kreps, G. L. (in press). Investigating communication: An introduction to research methods (2nd ed.). Boston: Allyn & Bacon.

Frey, L. R., Query, J. L., Jr., Flint, L. J., & Adelman, M. B. (1998). Living together with AIDS: Social support processes in a residential facility. In V. J. Derlega & A. P. Barbee (Eds.), HIV & social interaction (pp. 129-146). Thousand Oaks, CA: Sage.

Galletta, D. F., Flor, P. R., Scott, W. L., & Tinaikar, R. (1995, August). Mindstorms: Using software that simulates group processes for efficient study of certain GDSS variables. Paper presented at the meeting of the Association of Information Systems, Pittsburgh, PA.

Galtung, J. (1967). Theory and methods of social research. New York: Columbia University Press.

Garfield, M., Satzinger, J., Taylor, N., & Dennis, A. R. (1997, August). The creative road: The effects of feedback and technique. Paper presented at the meeting of the Association of Information Systems, Indianapolis, IN.

Geist, P., & Chandler, T. (1984). An account analysis of influence in group decision making. Communication Monographs, 51, 67-78.

Gladstein, D. (1984). Groups in context: A model of task group effectiveness. Administrative Science Quarterly, 29, 499-517.

Glick, W. H. (1985). Conceptualizing and measuring organizational and psychological climate: Pitfalls in multilevel research. Academy of Management Review, 11, 601-616.

Guzzo, R. A. (1995). Introduction: At the intersection of team effectiveness and decision making. In R. A. Guzzo & E. Salas (Eds.), Team effectiveness and decision making in organizations (pp. 1-8). San Francisco: Jossey-Bass.

Hawes, L. C. (1978). The reflexivity of communication research. Western Journal of Speech Communication, 42, 12-20.

Hewes, D. E. (1979). The sequential analysis of social interaction. Quarterly Journal of Speech, 65, 56-73.

Hewes, D. E., Planalp, S. K., & Streibel, M. (1980). Analyzing social interaction: Some excruciating models and exhilarating results. In D. Nimmo (Ed.), *Communication yearbook 4* (pp. 123-144). New Brunswick, NJ: Transaction Books.

Hirokawa, R. Y. (1988a). Group communication and decision making performance: A continued test of the functional perspective. *Human Communication Research, 14,* 487-515.

Hirokawa, R. Y. (1988b). Group communication research: Considerations for the use of interaction analysis. In C. H. Tardy (Ed.), *A handbook for the study of human communication: Methods and instruments for observing, measuring, and assessing communication processes* (pp. 229-245). Norwood, NJ: Ablex.

Holsti, O. (1969). *Content analysis for the social sciences and humanities.* Reading, MA: Addison-Wesley.

Homans, G. (1950). *The human group.* New York: Harcourt, Brace & World.

Hoyle, R. H., & Crawford, A. M. (1994). Use of individual-level data to investigate group phenomena: Issues and strategies. *Small Group Research, 25,* 464-485.

Ilgen, D. R., Major, D. A., Hollenbeck, J. R., & Sego, D. J. (1995). Raising an individual decision-making model to the team level: A new research model and paradigm. In R. A. Guzzo & E. Salas (Eds.), *Team effectiveness and decision making in organizations* (pp. 113-148). San Francisco: Jossey-Bass.

Insko, C. A., Gilmore, R., Moehle, D., Lipsitz, A., Drenan, S., & Thibaut, J. W. (1982). Seniority in generational transition in laboratory groups: The effects of social familiarity and task experience. *Journal of Experimental Social Psychology, 18,* 557-580.

Jacobs, R. C., & Campbell, D. T. (1961). The perpetuation of an arbitrary tradition through several generations of a laboratory microculture. *Journal of Abnormal and Social Psychology, 62,* 649-658.

Janis, I. L. (1972). *Victims of groupthink: A psychological study of foreign-policy decisions and fiascoes.* Boston: Houghton Mifflin.

Janis, I. L. (1982). *Groupthink: Psychological studies of policy decisions and fiascoes* (2nd ed.). Boston: Houghton Mifflin.

Kacen, L., & Rozovski, U. (1998). Assessing group processes: A comparison among group participants', direct observers', and indirect observers' assessment. *Small Group Research, 29,* 179-197.

Kaid, L. L., & Wadsworth, A. J. (1989). Content analysis. In P. Emmert & L. L. Barker (Eds.), *Measurement of communication behavior* (pp. 197-217). White Plains, NY: Longman.

Kashy, D. A., & Kenny, D. A. (in press). The analysis of data from dyads and groups. In H. T. Reis & C. M. Judd (Eds.), *Handbook of research methods in social psychology.* Cambridge, UK: Cambridge University Press.

Kenny, D. A., & LaVoie, L. (1984). The social relations model. In L. Berkowitz (Ed.), *Advances in experimental social psychology* (Vol. 18, pp. 142-182). Orlando, FL: Academic Press.

Keyton, J. (1995). Using SYMLOG as a self-analytical group facilitation technique. In L. R. Frey (Ed.), *Innovations in group facilitation: Applications in natural settings* (pp. 148-174). Cresskill, NJ: Hampton.

Keyton, J. (1997). Coding communication in decision-making groups. In L. R. Frey & J. K. Barge (Eds.), *Managing group life: Communicating in decision-making groups* (pp. 234-269). Boston: Houghton Mifflin.

Keyton, J., & Springston, J. (1990). Redefining cohesiveness in groups. *Small Group Research, 21,* 234-254.

Keyton, J., & Wall, V. D. (1989). SYMLOG: Theory and method for measuring group and organizational communication. *Management Communication Quarterly, 2,* 544-567.

Krippendorff, K. (1980). *Content analysis: An introduction to its methodology.* White Plains, NY: Longman.

Lesch, C. L. (1994). Observing theory in practice: Sustaining consciousness in a coven. In L. R. Frey (Ed.), *Group communication in context: Studies of natural groups* (pp. 57-82). Hillsdale, NJ: Lawrence Erlbaum.

Levine, J. M., & Moreland, R. L. (1990). Progress in small group research. In M. R. Rosenzweig & L. W. Porter (Eds.), *Annual review of psychology* (Vol. 41, pp. 585-634). Palo Alto, CA: Annual Reviews.

Longford, N. T. (1989). Fisher scoring algorithm for variance component analysis of data with multilevel structure. In R. D. Bock (Ed.), *Multilevel analysis of educational data* (pp. 297-310). New York: Academic Press.

Mabry, E. A., & Attridge, M. D. (1990). Small group interaction and outcome correlates for structured and unstructured tasks. *Small Group Research, 21,* 315-332.

March, J. G., & Olsen, J. P. (1976). *Ambiguity and choice in organizations.* Bergen, Norway: Universitetsforlaget.

Martell, R. F., & Guzzo, R. A. (1991). The dynamics of implicit theories of group: When and how do they operate? *Organizational Behavior and Human Decision Processes, 50,* 51-74.

McGrath, J. E. (1984). *Groups: Interaction and performance.* Englewood Cliffs, NJ: Prentice Hall.

McGrath, J. E. (1991). Time, interaction, and performance (TIP): A theory of groups. *Small Group Research, 22,* 147-174.

McGrath, J. E. (1997). Small group research, that once and future field: An interpretation of the past with an eye to the future. *Group Dynamics: Theory, Research, and Practice, 1,* 7-27.

McGrath, J. E., & Altermatt, T. W. (in press). Observation and analysis of group interaction over time. In H. T. Reis & C. M. Judd (Eds.), *Handbook of research methods in social psychology.* Cambridge, UK: Cambridge University Press.

Meyers, R. E., Seibold, D. R., & Brashers, D. (1991). Argument in initial group decision-making discussions: Refinement of a coding scheme and a descriptive quantitative analyses. *Western Journal of Speech Communication, 55,* 47-68.

Miller, G. R., & Boster, F. J. (1989). Data analysis in communication research. In P. Emmert & L. L. Barker

(Eds.), *Measurement of communication behavior* (pp. 18-39). New York: Longman.

Monge, P. R., & Contractor, N. S. (in press). Emergence of communication networks. In F. M. Jablin & L. L. Putnam (Eds.), *Handbook of organizational communication* (2nd ed.). Thousand Oaks, CA: Sage.

Moreland, R. L., & Levine, J. M. (1982). Socialization in small groups: Temporal changes in individual-group relations. In L. Berkowitz (Ed.), *Advances in experimental social psychology* (Vol. 15, pp. 137-192). New York: Academic Press.

Mossholder, K. W., & Bedeian, A. G. (1983). Cross-level inference and organizational research: Perspectives on interpretation and application. *Academy of Management Review, 8,* 547-558.

Murphy, A. G. (1998). Hidden transcripts of flight attendant resistance. *Management Communication Quarterly, 11,* 499-535.

Muthen, B. (1994). Multilevel covariance structure analysis. *Sociological Methods and Research, 22,* 376-398.

O'Keefe, B. J., Delia, J. G., & O'Keefe, D. J. (1980). Interaction analysis and the analysis of interaction organization. *Studies of Symbolic Interaction, 3,* 25-57.

Pinto, M. B., Pinto, J. K., & Prescott, J. E. (1993). Antecedents and consequences of project team cross-functional cooperation. *Management Science, 39,* 1281-1297.

Poole, M. S., DeSanctis, G., Kirsch, L., & Jackson, M. (1995). Group decision support systems as facilitators of quality team efforts. In L. R. Frey (Ed.), *Innovations in group facilitation techniques: Applications in natural settings* (pp. 299-322). Cresskill, NJ: Hampton.

Poole, M. S., Folger, J. P., & Hewes, D. E. (1987). Analyzing interpersonal interaction. In M. E. Roloff & G. R. Miller (Eds.), *Interpersonal processes: New directions in communication research* (pp. 220-256). Newbury Park, CA: Sage.

Poole, M. S., McPhee, R. D., & Seibold, D. R. (1982). A comparison of normative and interactional explanations of group decision-making: Social decision schemes versus valence distributions. *Communication Monographs, 49,* 1-19.

Poole, M. S., Van de Ven, A. H., Dooley, K., & Holmes, M. (in press). *Theory and methods for the study of organizational change and development processes.* New York: Oxford University Press.

Propp, K. M., & Kreps, G. L. (1994). A rose by any other name: The vitality of group communication research. *Communication Studies, 45,* 7-19.

Putnam, L. L. (1979). Preference for procedural order in task-oriented small groups. *Communication Monographs, 46,* 193-218.

Putnam, L. L., & Stohl, C. (1990). Bona fide groups: A reconceptualization of groups in context. *Communication Studies, 41,* 248-265.

Putnam, L. L., & Stohl, C. (1994). Group communication in context: Implications for the study of bona fide groups. In L. R. Frey (Ed.), *Group communication in context: Studies of natural groups* (pp. 284-292). Hillsdale, NJ: Lawrence Erlbaum.

Putnam, L. L., & Stohl, C. (1996). Bona fide groups: An alternative perspective for communication and small group decision making. In R. Y. Hirokawa & M. S. Poole (Eds.), *Communication and group decision making* (2nd ed., pp. 147-178). Thousand Oaks, CA: Sage.

Reagan, P., & Rohrbaugh, J. (1990). Group decision process effectiveness: A competing values approach. *Group and Organization Studies, 15,* 20-43.

Satzinger, J., Garfield, M., & Nagasundarum, M. (1996, August). *The effects of group memory on groupware idea generation.* Paper presented at the meeting of the Association of Information Systems, Phoenix, AZ.

Shrout, P. E., & Fleiss, J. L. (1979). Intraclass correlations: Uses in assessing rater reliability. *Psychological Bulletin, 86,* 420-428.

Sinclair-James, L., & Stohl, C. (1997). Group endings and new beginnings. In L. R. Frey & J. K. Barge (Eds.), *Managing group life: Communicating in decision-making groups* (pp. 308-334). Boston: Houghton Mifflin.

Spillman, B., Bezdek, J., & Spillman, R. (1979). Development of an instrument for the dynamic measurement of consensus. *Communication Monographs, 46,* 1-12.

Stempel, G. H., III. (1989). Content analysis. In G. H. Stempel III & B. H. Wesley (Eds.), *Research methods in mass communication* (2nd ed., pp. 124-129). Englewood Cliffs, NJ: Prentice Hall.

Stock, D., & Thelen, H. A. (1958). *Individual behavior and group achievement.* New York: New York University Press.

Thelen, H. A. (1954). *Dynamics of groups at work.* Chicago: University of Chicago Press.

Tracy, K. (1991). Discourse. In B. M. Montgomery & S. Duck (Eds.), *Studying interpersonal interaction* (pp. 179-197). New York: Guilford.

Trujillo, N. (1986). Toward a taxonomy of small group interaction-coding systems. *Small Group Behavior, 17,* 371-394.

Van de Ven, A. H., Venkataraman, S., Polley, D., & Garud, R. (1989). Process of new business creation in different organizational settings. In A. H. Van de Ven, H. Angle, & M. S. Poole (Eds.), *Research on the management of innovation* (pp. 221-298). New York: Harper & Row.

Verdi, A. F., & Wheelan, S. (1992). Developmental patterns in same-sex and mixed-sex groups. *Small Group Research, 23,* 356-378.

Wall, V. D., Jr., & Galanes, G. J. (1986). The SYMLOG dimensions and small group conflict. *Central States Speech Journal, 37,* 61-78.

Weber, R. P. (1990). *Basic content analysis* (2nd ed.). Newbury Park, CA: Sage.

Weingart, L. R. (1997). How did they do that? The ways and means of studying group process. *Research in Organizational Behavior, 19,* 198-239.

Wekselberg, V., Goggin, W. C., & Collings, T. J. (1997). A multifaceted concept of group maturity and its measurement and relationship to group performance. *Small Group Research, 28,* 3-28.

Wheelan, S. A., McKeage, R. L., Verdi, A. F., Abraham, M., Krasick, C., & Johnston, F. (1994). Communication and developmental patterns in a system of interacting groups. In L. R. Frey (Ed.), *Group communication in context: Studies of natural groups* (pp. 153-180). Hillsdale, NJ: Lawrence Erlbaum.

Wheelan, S., & Verdi, A. F. (1992). Differences in male and female patterns of communication in groups: A methodological artifact? *Sex Roles, 27*(1/2), 1-15.

Yammarino, F. J. (1990). Individual- and group-directed leader behavior descriptions. *Educational and Psychological Measurement, 50,* 739-759.

Yammarino, F. J., & Markham, S. E. (1992). On the application of within and between analysis: Are absence and affect really group-based phenomena? *Journal of Applied Psychology, 77,* 168-176.

Yammarino, F. J., & Naughton, T. J. (1988). Time spent communicating: A multiple levels of analysis approach. *Human Relations, 41,* 655-676.

Zey, M. (Ed.). (1992). *Decision making: Alternatives to rational choice models.* Newbury Park, CA: Sage.

PART II

Individuals and
Group Communication

5

What Differences Do Individual Differences in Groups Make?

The Effects of Individuals, Culture, and Group Composition

BETH BONNIWELL HASLETT
JENN RUEBUSH
University of Delaware

The dynamic relationship between individuals and the groups in which they participate is a key component of human social development. Although each person is a unique, independent individual, simultaneously she or he is a member of many groups that affect her or him in important ways. Initially, individuals are members of families; later, they participate in classroom and peer groups and, subsequently, in a wide variety of groups, such as work and social groups. Individuals' contributions significantly influence groups and, conversely, groups influence individual members. As many scholars note, groups help meet individuals' personal, interpersonal, and task needs; groups also provide the concerted social action necessary to support human life and individual achievement. Relationships between individuals and groups, however, also produce a set of dialectical tensions that need to be managed, such as the tension between individuals' desire for auton-

omy and their dependence on groups, their desire to cooperate and their desire to compete, and their desire to influence/control coupled with their desire to be influenced/controlled (see Barge & Frey, 1997; Smith & Berg, 1987).

In this chapter, we explore how groups and individuals influence each other. Within the context of a Systems Perspective (see Mabry, Chapter 3, this volume), we focus on the role of individuals in groups and look at individual differences and their impact on group processes and outcomes. In particular, we concentrate on some important factors, including sex/gender, culture, and group composition, that add significant diversity to work groups. Current trends and realities, such as that 75% of new, entry-level workers are minorities and/or women (Boyett & Conn, 1992), highlight the increasingly diverse workforce in the United States. Because of the reliance on work groups in contemporary organizations (see

Greenbaum & Query, Chapter 20, this volume), it is necessary to understand the nature and effects of individual differences and group composition if group communication and productivity are to be enhanced. Although we are particularly concerned in this chapter with the effects of these variables in work groups, much of what is outlined here can be applied usefully to groups in general.

FOCUSING ON INDIVIDUALS IN GROUPS

The interface between an individual and a group is complex. People gain a sense of identity from group memberships as well as contributing their unique skills to these groups. Individuals identify with those groups that are an important part of their self-concepts and/or when the groups' collective interests are seen as valuable.

Through interaction with others, individuals create and sustain reality. As Hardin and Higgins (1996) note, an experience "survives as a reliable, valid, and predictable state of the world to the extent that it is socially verified" (p. 29). Salient individuals and reference groups help people develop shared realities. Most individuals simultaneously belong to many groups, but some groups have greater salience than others. Moreover, the relevance of membership in a specific group may fluctuate over time. Within groups, the most active members tend to adopt the perspective of the group more readily (Abrams, Wetherall, Cochrane, Hogg, & Turner, 1990; Burnstein, 1982). Through such processes, salient group memberships play an important role in developing individuals' self-concepts and shared social realities (Socha, 1997).

Another important element in understanding the relationship between individuals and groups is the dynamic tension that frequently occurs between them. Some scholars suggest that individuals and groups are inherently in competition because their interests and needs often conflict. According to Ridgeway (1993), however, in work groups, members' competitive interests can be redirected toward co-operative needs required for task management. Task competence becomes legitimized as the source of status in such groups, and individuals compete with each other in terms of their task competence. As Ridgeway notes, "The competence-based status hierarchy that emerges harnesses members' competitive interests in self-maximization to their cooperative interests in task success" (p. 115). Thus, cooperative and competitive desires may complement one another in task groups.

Following this brief overview of the mutual influence and dialectical tensions between individuals and groups, we next examine the issue of individual differences and their impact on group processes and performance. A Systems Perspective provides the organizing frame of reference for this discussion. Individual differences and group composition are treated as input variables (variables that exist prior to group interaction) and include such social characteristics as group members' sex/gender and cultural background. We consider the impact of these inputs on group processes, or throughput variables, such as members' interaction styles and participation rates, and on group outcomes, such as productivity (see Table 5.1 for an overview of input variables and their influence on group processes and outcomes). Moreover, because cultural differences provide the overarching context in which cognitive abilities and communicative skills develop, we emphasize them and their impact on group processes and performance. We conclude with directions for future research on individual differences and group composition.

THE IMPACT OF INDIVIDUAL DIFFERENCES ON GROUPS

Numerous individual difference variables affect group interaction and outcomes. Within groups, members may vary significantly in terms of their backgrounds, personalities, motivations, commitments, perceptions, and communicative predispositions and abilities. For example, Hare and Davies (1994) conclude that, within groups, "Age, sex, social class, ethnic group, and personality variables

Table 5.1 A Systems Approach to Individual-Level and Group-Level Differences in Work Groups

Inputs	Throughputs (Group Processes)	Outcomes
Individual-level differences Person perception processes: individuating vs. categorical	Participation rates	In-group vs. out-group judgments Identification with group Commitment to group
Cognitive style: Myers Briggs Type Inventory preferences	Presenting information Listening behaviors Alternatives considered Short-term vs. long-term thinking Problem formulation	Processing time Numbers of ideas Quality of decision making
Sex/gender Physical	Perceived status Conflict styles Task/socioemotional behavior Leadership Communication style Nonverbal behavior Contribution of ideas Language use Persuasive strategies Different communication goals	Member satisfaction Member performance Group climate
Psychological	Level of dominance Degree of consideration Initiation	
Communication skills: communication apprehension	Participation rates Interaction style Conflict style Response to conflict Seating preferences Tolerance of ambiguity Generation of ideas	Attribution of failure Quality of decision making Member satisfaction Perceptions of group contribution Perceived member credibility Perceived member effectiveness Perceived member likability Perceived social attractiveness Leadership emergence Perceived member status
Conflict management: conflict style	Interaction patterns Type of strategy used Sequence of conflict strategies	Quality of decision making

(Continued)

Table 5.1   *(Continued)*

Inputs	*Throughputs (Group Processes)*	*Outcomes*
Culture 　Glenn's model	Interaction behavior Reasoning processes Analysis of information Conflict management Social relationships Turn-taking	Solution/decision complexity Group cohesiveness
Hofstede's model	Status relationships Aggressiveness Tolerance for uncertainty Individualism vs. collectivism Leadership patterns Participation level Group norms Pressure for conformity Conflict management Task/social concern Competitive vs. cooperative 　tactics Decision-making processes	Member satisfaction
Group-level differences 　Ting-Toomey's dimensions	Conflict management Reasoning processes Emotional expressiveness Nonverbal behaviors	
Group composition: sex and racioethnic	Shared leadership Boundary spanning/monitoring 　of environment Guard activities Conflict management Interaction behaviors Participation rates Contributions to decision 　making Conformity processes Availability of information Process difficulties Social influence processes Alternative views presented Amount of conflict	Member satisfaction with group 　processes and outcomes Group cohesiveness Quantity and quality of ideas 　produced Creativity of solutions Team effectiveness Intergroup relations Member commitment to group Minority members' sense of 　social isolation Leadership emergence Attitude changes in prejudice 　and stereotyping Understanding among members Evaluation of members Appropriate and flexible 　responses Quality of decision making Feasibility of ideas Hiring practices

are all associated with different patterns of individual interaction" (p. 193). Although a full review of individual difference variables is well beyond the scope of this chapter, we discuss those that are most relevant to working in diverse task groups. In particular, individuals' person perception processes, cognitive style, and demographic characteristics, such as sex/gender and culture, are important sources of diversity that influence group processes and outcomes.

Person Perception Processes

Person perception involves forming impressions of others and is usually differentiated on a continuum from *individuating processes* (driven by personal attributes, such as intelligence and self-confidence) to *category-based processes* (driven by attributes of the category in which a perceived individual is placed, such as being female or African American) (Fiske & Neuberg, 1990). Individuating processes can be based on cues others emit or on seeing another's perspective through role taking (Chandler, 1977). Whereas individuation (specification) requires time and repeated experience, categorization is often nonconscious, automatic, and used to process information and make judgments rapidly and efficiently (Dovidio & Gaertner, 1993; Haslett, Geis, & Carter, 1992).

Categorical judgments frequently result in dividing people into *in-groups* (homogeneous or similar to self) and *out-groups* (heterogeneous or dissimilar to self). Group members perceive in-group and out-group members very differently. As Bento (1997) explains:

Outgroups are perceived as more homogeneous than ingroups; outgroup members are seen as more similar to each other, more interchangeable, and more different from the ingroup; members of the ingroup are more similar to the self. These phenomena occur even when the categorization is arbitrary or has no social meaning . . . and become more pronounced when the categorization is meaningful (e.g., when it reflects commonly used categories such as race and gender). (p. 98)

Cognitions and attitudes toward out-group members, consequently, are less positive than those directly toward in-group members (Dovidio, Gaertner, Anastasio, & Sanitioso, 1992; see also Meyers & Brashers, chapter 11, this volume). In both in-group and out-group cases, cognitions tend to be accepted as factual by those holding them (Bento, 1997).

Cognitive theories alone are insufficient to explain perceived homogeneity because motivations also influence perception. McGarty, Haslam, Hutchinson, and Turner (1994) suggest that categorizing self and others reflects both social motivation and cognitive variables:

Social cognition and the social context are interdependent. There is an interplay between how we view other people and what we think, in that the way we interact with other people, and the impact they have on us, varies as a consequence of the group memberships we perceive them to have. (p. 270)

Depending on an individual's need at a given time, in-groups may seem to be more or less homogeneous than out-groups. Furthermore, an individual may perceive herself or himself as more or less homogeneous with members of a given group.

Thus, individuals have consistent ways of perceiving others; however, interaction can lead to new understandings and changes in the ways people are perceived. In the context of a group, members' motivation and commitment to the group are important determinants of person perception processes. These perception processes, in turn, influence individuals' and groups' interactional processes and outcomes. For example, committed members are likely to identify more strongly with a group and demonstrate higher rates of participation in the group.

Cognitive Style

Cognitive style reflects ways in which people tend to process information. Although there are many different measures of cognitive style, the Myers Briggs Type Inventory (MBTI) is one of the most widely used and tested instruments. Based on the work of psychologist Carl Jung, the MBTI measures individuals' preferences in, among other things, information gathering, information processing, and decision making (Myers, 1987).

The MBTI consists of four dimensions. *Extraversion/introversion* references how individuals gather information and differentiates individuals on the basis of whether they gather energy and information from external sources and interaction with others (extraversion) or internally, through thinking and introspection (introversion). The *intuition/sensing* dimension reflects how individuals process information. Intuitive thinkers, in processing information, reason globally, think in patterns, are future oriented, and creatively visualize numerous possibilities. In contrast, sensers focus on their five senses and direct experiences, are present oriented, and emphasize facts, details, and practicality. *Thinking/ feeling* characterizes how people evaluate information and make decisions. Thinkers make decisions primarily on the basis of analysis, logic, and principles, whereas feelers focus most on human values and needs and sympathize with others. This does not mean that thinkers ignore human needs nor that feelers ignore analysis; this dimension indicates what factors an individual is likely to give most priority to in making decisions. Finally, *judging/perceiving* refers to how people use information and decision-making processes to organize their activities. Judgers tend to be structured, organized, decisive, and in control, whereas perceivers tend to be unstructured, unorganized, spontaneous, and flexible.

Preferences on these four dimensions combine to form 16 distinct cognitive patterns or types that represent ways in which individuals gather information, process it, and subsequently make decisions. According to Myers (1987), one can develop skills in the cognitive styles that are not preferred; for example, a thinker can become more aware of human needs and values in making decisions. The preferred cognitive tendencies, however, tend to be what people rely on and are most comfortable using in their daily tasks, including group work.

According to Corlett and Yeakley (1995), MBTI preferences lead to difficulties in listening and interacting between those who have different preferred cognitive styles. Sensers listen and assess at a practical level, whereas intuitives try to understand the underlying assumptions and possibilities raised. Those with a thinking cognitive style analyze and organize while listening and, thus, focus on message structure, claims, and logic. In contrast, those with a feeling cognitive style look for the values inherent in a message and evaluate the source of the message on that basis.

Each cognitive style also prefers a different way of presenting information to others. Sensers present facts and details, intuitives provide possibilities and potentials, thinkers articulate the logic and rationale underlying an issue, and feelers emphasizes values and needs. Cognitive style, therefore, influences the ways in which people both listen to and communicate with others.

Research shows that cognitive style has important effects in the group context. Volkema and Gorman (1998), for example, examined the effects of group composition, based on cognitive styles, on decision-making processes (problem formulation and ideation) and outcomes (quality of the decision and time needed to make it). Two types of four-person groups were created: a single-temperament group (composed of all sensing-judging individuals, a common managerial cognitive style) and a multitemperament composition (a balance of the four MBTI temperaments). Cognitive-based group composition appeared to influence problem formulation, as multitemperament groups developed and used explicit governing objectives (discussions and decisions on objectives) in formulating the problem, whereas single-temperament groups did not. Multitemperament groups also outperformed single-temperament groups (speedier decisions and higher quality decisions). Volkema and Gorman concluded that "multitemperament groups can make significant contributions to the number and types of objectives developed during the problem formulation stage, positively impacting performance" (p. 117). In addition, Stager (1967) found that groups composed of high conceptual members (intuitives) considered multiple options and long-term thinking in their decisions.

These findings suggest that to maximize the quality of group performance, organizational leaders may want to have a balance of cognitive types represented in work groups. Lawrence (1982) suggests a Z-model of decision making in teams. In this model, individuals high on the sensing dimension are relied on in the information-gathering phase, where their attention to detail and facts are invaluable. In generating possible solutions, the ability of intuitive thinkers to visualize alternatives creatively is very useful. In evaluating various alternatives, judgers are helpful in weighing benefits and feelers are helpful in weighing the human costs. All cognitive styles are valued for their contributions to the quality and feasibility of a group's decision. Thus, a balance of cognitive styles is believed to contribute to high-quality group decision making because the strengths and weaknesses of one cognitive style balance those of other cognitive styles.

Sex/Gender

Another salient source of individual differences is sex/gender. Every culture marks physiological sex differences in terms of distinct expectations, roles, duties, and behaviors associated with being female or male. Such markings are also often attributed on the basis of psychological gender differences (e.g., amount of masculinity or femininity).

Sex/gender differences influence group interaction because, according to Status Characteristics Theory (Berger, Wagner, & Zelditch, 1985), diffuse external status characteristics, such as those associated with sex/gender and age, transfer to group settings (see Ketrow, Chapter 10, this volume, regarding these and other nonverbal cues as status characteristics in groups). The theory suggests that higher status group members tend to partici-

pate more, challenge ideas more, and have more influence on group outcomes than lower status members (see Propp, Chapter 9, this volume, on the effects of status characteristics on collective information processing in groups).

Without knowledge of, or experiences with, fellow group members, people form expectations and make judgments about others on the basis of external characteristics, such as sex/gender and ethnicity (Martin & Shanahan, 1983). With respect to sex, all the social expectations appear to be in one direction, with women being viewed as supportive, agentive, indirect, and possessing lower social status and power than men (Haslett et al., 1992). This lower social status has been associated with women as a group being underpaid, undervalued, and subject to systemic bias, which have resulted in lack of opportunities for advancement (see Dunn, 1996; Haslett et al., 1992; Higginbotham & Romero, 1997; Martin, 1991).

General social status also influences perceptions of members' power and status in groups. According to Ridgeway and Berger (1986), individuals possess referential beliefs that certain social categories of people (e.g., males) occupy more valued positions and have greater status in society than others (e.g., females). These expectations transfer to group settings, such that individuals representing higher status categories are expected to have higher status within groups (Ridgeway, 1989). More diffuse competence is also associated with membership in higher status categories; thus, group members "anticipate greater task competence from higher- rather than lower-valued categories of the characteristic" (Ridgeway, 1993, p. 122). Ridgeway (1993), for example, found that dominance behavior elicited more compliance when it was enacted by those having high external status (e.g., membership in a highly valued category, like being male). A study by Smith-Lovin, Skvoretz, and Hudson (1986) demonstrated that groups' status structures were differentiated primarily along sex lines, with males having higher status and participation rates, and then differentiated further across same-sex group members.

Sex/gender differences have been well documented with regard to communicative behavior. Women appear to use communication for connection and collaboration with others; men use it to emphasize independence and competition (Tannen, 1990). A study by Offerman and Schrier (1985) revealed that female undergraduates' self-reported communication strategies focused on connection and minimized status differences, whereas men stressed strategies that acknowledged status differences. With regard to psychological gender, a study by Seibert and Gruenfeld (1992) found that those scoring high on masculinity demonstrated higher levels of initiation and dominance behavior, whereas higher scores for femininity were associated with higher levels of consideration and greater degrees of submissive behavior. Because role expectations attributed on the basis of psychological gender tend to reflect sex-role expectations, the results from studies exploring sex and those focusing on gender are very similar.

Some sex differences in conflict styles also have been documented. Rahim (1983) found that female managers were higher on compromise, collaboration, and avoidance and lower on accommodation than their male counterparts. Ruble and Schneer (1994) observed that women were more likely to compromise and men more likely to compete in task-oriented settings. Men's and women's conflict style may be influenced, however, by their hierarchical position within organizations. Chusmir and Mills (1989) detected no differences between men and women in their preferred conflict style when organizational position was held constant: Both preferred collaboration and compromise most and accommodation and competition least. There is also evidence that men and women use similar strategies to accomplish different purposes. For example, although both men and women exhibit cooperative behavior, women report doing so for altruistic reasons, whereas men describe doing so for self-centered reasons (Stockard, Van de Kragt, & Dodge, 1988).

Keashly (1994) noted that although preferred conflict strategies may not be different for women and men, the use of similar strategies may be perceived differently because "sex-role expectations appear to influence behavior and perceptions of behavior in particular circumstances" (p. 185). Perceptions of conflict behavior, as well as many other behaviors, are influenced by "the gender of the perceived, the gender of the target, and features of the dyadic relationship such as commitment, status and role" (p. 183). For example, although men and women used equally controlling negotiation tactics in a study by Burrell, Donohue, and Allen (1988), men were perceived as more controlling than women.

In the context of group interaction, an early review by Baird (1976) revealed sex differences in group communication consistent with traditional sex-role expectations. That is, men were more task oriented, aggressive, and competitive, and were more likely to assume leadership in task-oriented group contexts. In contrast, women were more cooperative and sensitive to nonverbal cues (see Ketrow, Chapter 10, this volume, on nonverbal sex differences in group communication), as well as less likely to emerge as leaders. More recent studies have documented some changes in males' and females' behavior in groups. Aries (1982) discovered that women dominated verbally in mixed-sex groups, although their interactional styles and nonverbal behaviors, as well as those of the men, remained sex-role stereotypic. Specifically, males initiated task-oriented interaction, whereas females tended to react by agreeing or disagreeing with the task comments. Moreover, group composition did not influence the rate of socioemotional or task behaviors for men or women. When the content of group discussions was examined, sex differences along traditional lines surfaced, with women being more expressive and men more instrumental in their remarks. Aries concluded that women help promote a group climate in which members feel that they are heard and responded to in a respectful manner. Women's interactions in groups, thus, tend to be social and indirect, whereas men's communication tends to be more task oriented and direct (Kramarae, 1990).

Other research shows that, in mixed-sex groups, women demonstrate lower rates of participation, are less satisfied, and perform at a lower level than men when males are the majority (Johnson & Schulman, 1989; Rozell & Vaught, 1988). Tannen (1990) suggests that women are less likely to offer ideas in mixed-sex groups and that men often become frustrated by women's indirectness and relationally-oriented remarks.

Sex differences in language use in groups also have been investigated. Generally, research has found that men interrupt others more than women do and that women are interrupted more than men (Tannen, 1990; Zimmerman & West, 1975). A study by Grob, Meyers, and Schuh (1997), however, observed that men were interrupted significantly more than women and that men used significantly more disclaimers (e.g., a comment that weakens the statement that follows, such as "I don't know if this is accurate, but. . . ."). Smith-Lovin and Brody (1989) note that the difference in interruption behaviors is not

> the result of a sex difference in frequency of interruption, or even a simple dominance effect. Instead, it is produced because men discriminate in their interruption attempts, disrupting the speech of women far more frequently than that of men, while women do not discriminate, interrupting women and men equally often. (p. 432)

A series of investigations has also looked at sex differences with respect to persuadability. Eagly's meta-analysis (1978) revealed that sex differences, although small, appear to be a result of the immediate context, as well as sex-role expectations and behaviors. Eagly and Carli (1981) noted that when people were being observed by an influencing agent, women were more likely to be persuaded than men by group pressure. When attempting to persuade others, women reported using more personal and negotiation strategies; men re-ported using more reward/coercion and indirect strategies, such as indirect requests (Offerman & Schrier, 1985). Eagly (1983) contends that status inequity in natural contexts and expectations about males' and females' social interaction in laboratory settings account for sex differences discovered in studies of social influence.

Finally, some researchers have suggested that new technologies, such as group decision support systems (GDSSs), can begin to equalize the contribution rates of men and women in groups (Gopal, Miranda, Robichaux, & Bostrom, 1997; see Scott, Chapter 16, this volume, regarding the effects of new technologies on group communication). Although females generally express more computer anxiety and communication apprehension than men, they also view such support systems more favorably (Gopal et al., 1997). Gopal and colleagues suggest that GDSSs might facilitate group diversity and high rates of participation among all group members because such systems eliminate knowledge of status characteristics, such as sex/gender or minority status, that may otherwise limit members' participation.

Communication Skills

Communication skills are at a premium in work groups: To solve problems and to build and maintain harmonious relationships in groups, effective communication among members is crucial. Ideas must be expressed and subsequently evaluated for high-quality group decisions to emerge; if members cannot articulate their ideas clearly and persuasively, then their group decisions will be affected adversely. Good listening skills also are required if ideas are to be understood as intended and not misperceived. Thus, in multiple ways, good communication skills are a necessity in groups. In what follows, we look more specifically at the research on the effects of group members' communication skills, especially those dealing with communication apprehension and conflict resolution.

Communication Apprehension

To share ideas and influence others, individuals must communicate. For those who are reticent and fearful of speaking, communication is more difficult. *Communication apprehension* reflects both discomfort about speaking in public and low self-perceived competency in speaking (Rosenfeld, Grant, & McCroskey, 1995), and it extends across multiple communication contexts (e.g., public speaking, meetings, groups, and dyads) (McCroskey & Beatty, 1984; see also Anderson, Riddle, & Martin, Chapter 6, this volume). In fact, self-perceived communication competence and communication apprehension appear to be inversely related, such that the higher the individuals' apprehension, the more they judge themselves as being incompetent communicators (Rubin, Rubin, & Jordan, 1997). A meta-analysis of studies of communication apprehension by Allen and Bourhis (1996) revealed a "consistent negative relationship between the level of communication apprehension and communication skills ($r = -.22$). . . . This relationship indicates that as a person becomes more apprehensive both the quantity and quality of communication behavior diminishes [sic]" (p. 214).

Numerous studies have investigated how people's communication apprehension affects their communicative behaviors in groups. For example, reticent individuals have been found to interact less frequently in groups than more outgoing individuals (Burgoon, 1977; Daly, 1974). Members with high levels of communication apprehension were shown to be more dissatisfied with group communication than members with lower levels of apprehension (Anderson & Martin, 1994). McCroskey and Richmond (1992) found that individuals who were high on group communication apprehension talked much less, chose less visible seating, tended to make irrelevant comments, and avoided disagreement.

Research also shows that communication apprehension affects group members' interaction in brainstorming groups (a process procedure in which members generate as many ideas as possible and criticism is ruled out; see Sunwolf & Seibold, Chapter 15, this volume). Comadena (1984) found that brainstorming group participants who contributed more ideas had less communication apprehension, perceived the task as more attractive, and displayed more tolerance for ambiguity than individuals producing fewer ideas. In another study, both apprehensive and nonapprehensive individuals were satisfied with their group's performance on a brainstorming task, but low apprehensives perceived more status differences across group members (Jablin, Sorenson, & Seibold, 1978).

In general, reticent group members are evaluated negatively as communicators by other group members. Studies demonstrate that such individuals, in contrast to non-reticent members, are viewed as less credible and less effective, and their contributions are judged to be less relevant (McCroskey & Richmond, 1976). In contrast, McCroskey, Hamilton, and Weiner (1974) found that group members who are more willing to communicate were judged as both more credible and likable. In addition, those who scored higher in communication apprehension were rated, by others and themselves, as lower in emergent group leadership and in social and task attraction (Hawkins & Stewart, 1991).

Shy people also exhibit many of the characteristics displayed by apprehensive communicators. For example, Bradshaw and Stasson (1998) discovered that shy participants in groups perceived their own contributions as less important and were less satisfied with their group than non-shy group members. Shy participants also reported holding back more ideas than non-shy participants and attributed failure to the group itself rather than to individual members.

Conflict Management

Conflict appears to be inevitable in task groups because of the challenges inherent in getting individuals to work together and make decisions. Conflict potentially influences group processes and outcomes in positive or negative ways. The impact of conflict on group decision making, for example, can be positive because debate about ideas may lead to more creative, high-quality decisions. Nicotera (1997) points out that conflict can promote group cohesiveness, help maintain a balance of power, facilitate positive changes and healthy growth by individuals and groups, contribute to obtaining group goals, and lead to creative problem solving. Intense or unresolved conflict, however, may paralyze groups by inhibiting discussion and, in other respects, interfering with members' ability to make decisions. The management of group conflict appears to be a function of members' personal style and cultural background, as well as the group norms that develop.

Differences in how individuals approach conflict have been well established. K. W. Thomas and Kilman (1986) identified two underlying dimensions of conflict: *assertiveness* (concern for self) and *cooperativeness* (concern for others). On the basis of these two dimensions, they identified five conflict management styles: *avoiding* (low on assertiveness and cooperation), *competing* (assertive but not cooperative), *accommodating* (unassertive and cooperative), *collaborating* (assertive and cooperative), and *compromising* (moderate assertiveness and cooperativeness). Avoiding is a strategy of withdrawal that is based on the belief that conflict is so detrimental that it cannot even be managed. Competing privileges self-interests over others' interests, whereas accommodating satisfies others' needs but sacrifices self-interests. Both collaboration and compromise incorporate both parties' needs; collaboration aims at mutual gain, whereas compromise entails some gain and loss for each party. Although people use more than one conflict management style, especially over the course of a lengthy conflict episode (see Folger, Poole, & Stutman, 1997), they tend to develop a preferred style.

Other ways of conceptualizing conflict management styles include assessing types of conflict behavior; however, the same behavior may be classified as different management styles. Folger et al. (1997) point out that, for example, a threat is a competitive approach to conflict management but could also be viewed as an avoidance style if the threat prevents someone from raising an issue. According to these scholars, it is most useful to view conflict styles as behavioral orientations toward conflict that reflect a "general expectation about how the conflict should be approached, an attitude about how best to deal with the other party" (p. 187). Regardless of how one views conflict styles, Folger et al. (1997) argue that the concept itself is fundamentally inadequate because it focuses on individuals rather than interactants.

Some scholars, however, have looked at how conflict styles influence group processes. For example, Jones and White (1985) found that groups whose members favored problem solving were more effective at task completion than groups whose members favored accommodation. In addition, conflict styles fostering open identification and expression of conflict tended to enhance the quality of solutions groups developed (Wall, Galanes, & Love, 1987).

Social conflict may also emerge from persistent and annoying behavior by some group members (e.g., a group member continues to raise issues already settled). Mikolic, Parker, and Pruitt (1997) observed the following sequence of communicative strategies used by both groups and individuals to stop such annoying behavior: First, requests to stop it are made, followed by impatient demands, complaints, angry statements, threats, harassment, and, finally, abuse. Groups appeared to use more escalation and problem-solving strategies than did individuals. In addition, women used more escalation tactics than did men, partially because of anger over being treated unfairly.

As has been shown, individual differences in communicative traits and skills influence group processes and outcomes. In particular, such skills influence who will participate and whether or not that participation is valued. Conflict management skills, as well as other communicative skills, clearly are necessary for dealing with the problems faced when working in groups. Both individuals' cognitive and communicative skills, however, are affected by cultural characteristics. We now turn to a consideration of cultural effects in groups.

THE EFFECTS OF CULTURE ON GROUP PROCESSES AND OUTCOMES

Culture, broadly defined, may be viewed as the shared ways, passed on from generation to generation, of living and the basic assumptions that guide a group's attitudes, beliefs, and values. As Ferdman (1995) argues, however, although culture refers to shared belief systems among group members, it is enacted by individuals. To bridge the gap between the collective group and the individual, he developed the concept of *cultural identity* to reflect the multifaceted aspects of personal identity. As Ferdman explains:

> Individual members of a particular group will vary in the extent to which they perceive specific attributes [of the group] as central to their cultural identity and in the value they give these attributes. In addition, they will vary in the degree to which they see themselves as having these attributes. (p. 52)

Another concept that is relevant to explaining cultural effect is *cultural diversity,* which Cox (1993) defines as "the representation, in one social system, of people with distinctly different group affiliations of cultural significance" (p. 6). Both cultural identity and cultural diversity emphasize within-group variation in socially meaningful categories, like national culture, rather than focusing on between-group boundaries as culturally distinct, such as noting cultural differences between North Americans and Australians.

Generally, *diversity* as a concept incorporates both within-group differences and differences across national cultures. As the world becomes more interconnected, groups must deal with the interactional complexities presented by cross-cultural communication, as well as diversity within a culture, such as differences between African Americans and

Asian Americans. The following discussion explores the impact of both senses of culture (within and across cultures) on group processes and outcomes.

Cultural Differences

Glenn (1981) and Hofstede (1980) have conceptualized broad dimensions on which cultures differ. Glenn's work focuses on differences in thinking patterns, whereas Hofstede emphasizes relational differences across cultures. Both scholars developed their conceptualizations from extensive cross-cultural experience and research studies.

Glenn's Model

Glenn contends that cultures generally are characterized by either associative or abstractive thought processes. *Associative thinking* is based on experiences and shared personal relationships; *abstractive thinking* organizes and analyzes thought impersonally and objectively. Associative thinking cultures, such as those in Latin American countries, focus on the particular and, therefore, value personal knowledge and experience (the subjective). In contrast, abstractive thinking cultures, such as the United States, focus on general principles and relationships among events; consequently, they value intersubjective (shared) and objective (externally verified) knowledge. Thus, individuals from each cultural orientation tend to weigh information differently and validate their conclusions on the basis of different criteria.

In a study of United Nations documents, Glenn discovered that associative-thinking countries emphasized specific details and relationships in events, whereas abstractive-thinking countries focused on universal principles and underlying rationales involved when making decisions. Thus, different cultures have different frameworks for interpreting events. Interpretive differences also develop because different cultures emphasize or prioritize events and actions differently. For successful cross-cultural understanding to occur,

Glenn believes that cultural differences in thought patterns must be taken into account. For example, participants in mixed-cultural groups that include representatives from both abstractive- and associative-thinking cultures may tend to misunderstand one another's positions and reasoning. A failure to recognize this can have any number of adverse consequences. For example, reaching agreement on a solution may be more problematic because the thought processes and weighting of different aspects of information will diverge across members of abstractive and associative thinking cultures.

Hofstede's Model

In contrast to Glenn, Hofstede (1980) concentrates on cultural differences in social relationships. Drawing on data gathered from more than 40 countries, Hofstede uncovered four basic dimensions along which people of differing cultural backgrounds vary: individualism-collectivism, masculinity-femininity, power distance, and uncertainty avoidance. *Individualism-collectivism* reflects the degree to which the individual versus the group is valued in a culture. *Masculinity-femininity* reflects the degree of aggressiveness/dominance (masculinity) or submissiveness (femininity) that characterizes cultures. *Power distance* represents the type of authority relationships that are culturally valued. High power-distance cultures value strong, hierarchical, and distant authority relationships, whereas cultures low on power distance value reduced status differentiation and more informal relationships. *Uncertainty avoidance* (high versus low) reflects the degree to which cultural members are comfortable with ambiguity and uncertainty. Hofstede's research established that national cultures could be distinguished from one another on these dimensions. The United States, for example, is a highly individualistic culture with a high tolerance for uncertainty. In contrast, Japan is a highly collectivist and high power-distance culture that values strong, hierarchical status relationships.

Hofstede found strong correlations between power distance and uncertainty avoidance in his sample of countries and argued that four possible cultural types reflect different implicit organizational structures. Large power distance coupled with weak uncertainty avoidance reflect cultures with a *family* model of organization (e.g., India), whereas a linkage of large power distance and high uncertainty avoidance reflects a *pyramid-type* organization (e.g., Japan). Low power distance coupled with weak uncertainty avoidance represent cultures with a *market-type* organization (e.g., Scandinavia), whereas a linkage of low power distance with high uncertainty avoidance reflects a *machine-type* organization (e.g., Germany). In addition, Hofstede noted that the combination of masculinity and weak uncertainty avoidance in a culture was related to members' high levels of need for achievement; thus, these dimensions appear to influence people's motivation as well.

Hofstede's cultural dimensions have obvious implications for affecting group processes and outcomes. Power distance preferences, for example, should influence group members' preferred leadership styles (e.g., authoritarian versus democratic styles; see Pavitt, Chapter 12, this volume). Tolerance for ambiguity may affect group decision-making processes and outcomes, with those preferring less ambiguity seeking more simple, direct solutions. As noted earlier, masculinity and femininity preferences influence group members' interactional styles, motivation, and general level of participation. Finally, individualism-collectivism values may partially determine such processes as the development of group norms and pressure for conformity and such outcomes as group cohesiveness and members' identification with a group.

Culture and Conflict

As our understanding of the characteristics of different cultures increases, we are also learning more about culture as a factor that influences conflict management. Conflict management style affects what is at issue, as well as how those involved manage it. In cross-cultural contexts, including culturally diverse groups, the likelihood of conflict is heightened because of the important cultural differences previously discussed and, more specifically, cultural differences with respect to managing conflict.

Ting-Toomey (1985) outlined some cultural influences on how people understand and manage conflict. *Cultural cognitive constraints* direct one's thinking in particular ways, *cultural emotional constraints* provide guidelines for what emotional expressions are appropriate in public, and *cultural behavioral constraints* govern the behaviors appropriate within particular sociocultural contexts. Cultures also vary in the degree to which they require social conformity by members. For example, diverse, heterogeneous cultures, such as the United States, have a *low cultural demand/low cultural constraint* (LCC) system. In contrast, relatively homogeneous cultures, like Japan, reflect a *high cultural demand/high cultural constraint* (HCC) system. As Ting-Toomey explains:

> In a normative heterogeneous system, in which individual opinions and differences are highly treasured and tolerated, a certain degree of conflict is probably viewed as productive and functional. In a normative homogeneous system, in which group harmony and consultative decision-making are highly valued, interpersonal antagonisms and public tensions are probably scorned and suppressed. (p. 74)

Thus, cultural background partially determines what conflict is permissible and how it should be handled.

According to Ting-Toomey, members of LCC cultures rely on verbally explicit codes when stating their ideas, whereas members of HCC cultures rely on the implicitly shared social and cultural knowledge of the context. She notes that LCC cultural members clearly separate the person from the conflict issue; for HCC cultural members, the issue and the individual raising it are inseparable. A direct style focused on solutions would more likely be used by LCC cultural members, whereas HCC cultural members would likely use an indirect style focused on the relationships among participants. For example, Chua and Gudykunst (1987) observed that North Americans and Western Europeans (members of HCC cultures) use more direct styles than Asians and East Indians (members of LCC cultures). Finally, Ting-Toomey hypothesizes that LCC cultural members use rational, factual analysis, whereas HCC cultural members use intuitive-affective reasoning. These contrasts between LCC and HCC cultures parallel Glenn's contrasts between associative- and abstractive-thinking cultures.

The individualism-collectivism (I-C) dimension of culture has been used to distinguish cultural differences relative to conflict management. An important mediating individual-level factor of I-C is *self-construal,* or one's view of one's self. Oetzel (1998a) has explored the impact of individuals' self-construal on their communicative behavior, including conflict management, in small homogeneous and heterogeneous groups of European Americans and Japanese. For both homogeneous and heterogeneous groups, *independent self-construal* (reflecting the individualistic end of the I-C continuum) was significantly and positively related to the number of speaking turns individuals took and their use of competitive tactics, whereas *interdependent self-construal* (reflecting the collectivist end of the I-C continuum) was related to use of cooperative tactics. Self-construal was not related, however, to whether group members initiated conflict. Oetzel suggests that this may reflect culturally patterned norms concerning conflict or the limited number of conflicts experienced in the group meetings observed. European Americans did take more turns, used more competitive tactics, and initiated more conflicts than did their Japanese counterparts in heterogeneous groups; they also used more competitive tactics in homogeneous groups. Oetzel concluded that cultural I-C has both a direct and an indirect effect for turn-taking and conflict tactics and a direct effect for initiating conflicts.

Group communication processes also vary according to the heterogeneity of group composition, as well as members' self-construal and I-C. Oetzel (1998b) discovered that heterogeneous groups had more unequal turn-taking among members and used a majority decision-making method more than homogeneous groups. In addition, homogeneous Japanese groups used more cooperative and less competitive conflict tactics than European American homogeneous groups; Japanese groups also experienced fewer conflicts. Groups having members with high independent self-construal used more competitive tactics, and groups with varying levels of individual self-construal had unequal turn-taking. Oetzel also noted that groups composed of members from individualistic cultures were more competitive than groups composed of members from collectivistic cultures. Members of collectivistic groups had fewer conflicts than members of individualistic groups, but they did not necessarily avoid conflict. As previously suggested, heterogeneous groups experienced more conflict because of a clash in culturally preferred ways of interacting, including dealing with conflict.

As we have shown thus far, cognitive, communicative, and cultural differences influence group processes and outcomes in many ways. These differences can have positive consequences, such as improved group communication and decision making, or negative consequences, such as increased conflict and lowered group cohesion. More effective management of group processes and outcomes undoubtedly will evolve as the effects of these differences are understood more fully. Understanding these effects, however, is complicated by the issue of diversity among group members. Diversity is a catch-all term that describes groups in which there may be multiple differences among members—for variables such as sex/gender and culture—that can potentially influence group interaction and outcomes. We look next at studies of diversity in groups and shift our focus from individual differences to aspects of group composition, with a particular focus on racioethnic diversity.

THE EFFECTS OF GROUP COMPOSITION ON GROUP PROCESSES AND OUTCOMES

D. C. Thomas, Ravlin, and Wallace (1996) provide a conceptual analysis of the effects of diversity on groups. They suggest that cultural diversity influences groups through (a) *relative cultural difference*—the degree to which group members are culturally discrepant from one another, (b) *cultural composition*—the cultural heterogeneity of a group, and (c) *sociocultural norms*—the influence of general cultural values on group functions and structures.

To test these potential influences, Thomas and colleagues had culturally diverse groups analyze five case studies as part of a course at a Japanese university. The sample consisted of 46 males and 5 females, representing 16 different nationalities, who had significant work experience. The course instructor established five culturally homogeneous groups (all Japanese) and eight culturally heterogeneous groups. Demographic information about group members was gathered and psychological constructs relevant to group processes were measured prior to the task-group meetings. Relative cultural distance was measured by Kogut and Singh's (1988) index of national cultural distance. Group processes were assessed with respect to the amount and type of conflict experienced, leadership developed, and boundary-spanning activity engaged in (i.e., contact with other groups). Group outcome measures included members' perceived role ambiguity, commitment to the group and its decisions, group cohesiveness, and satisfaction, including satisfaction with group processes.

The results revealed a significant relationship between group members' relative cultural distance and their relative psychological distance (as measured by tolerance for ambiguity, action orientation, individualism, locus of control, structural preference, and national identity). Second, relative cultural distance was negatively related to members' satisfaction and judgment of group cohesiveness. That is, the more people perceived themselves as being different from the other group members, the less they were satisfied with their group membership and with the cohesiveness of the group. Third, group heterogeneity was negatively related to group cohesiveness, shared leadership, boundary-spanning activities, and guard activities (monitoring information shared with other groups). A positive relationship was found, however, between the degree of cultural heterogeneity in groups and the quality of group decision making and generation of ideas.

To test the effects of national culture on group processes, the investigators compared the homogeneous Japanese groups with the Japanese members in heterogeneous groups. Japanese members of homogeneous groups had more positive evaluations of their group's processes and outcomes than did their counterparts in heterogeneous groups. Thus, expectations derived from their own culture may have been more influential than group norms for Japanese participants.

Conflict, Diversity, and Group Outcomes

More conflict typically results from diversity in groups, and this can have both positive and negative effects. Tjosvold (1992) suggests that conflict based on cognitive resources—differences in members' knowledge, skills, attitudes, and orientations to problems—allows groups to achieve creative and high-quality solutions. Conflict stemming from individuals' social categories—sex/gender and race, for example—however, may make teamwork more difficult because of members' differences in interactional style and lack of commitment to and identification with the group, and lower participation by some members (Ibarra, 1992). Some research suggests that with time and intervention strategies (e.g., feedback and education; regarding group fa-

cilitation and intervention, in this volume, see Chapters 14 [Schultz] and 15 [Sunwolf & Seibold]), process costs can be lowered. Process costs will also vary as a function of the impact of diversity on a group's task; not all tasks are influenced by diversity. For example, routine tasks that involve little interaction with others may not be influenced by group diversity.

Although interaction may be more complex in heterogeneous groups, positive results often occur. For example, Marcus-Newhall, Miller, Holtz, and Brewer (1993) demonstrated that intergroup biases are lessened when subgroups include members who represent different social categories (e.g., racioethnicity and sex/gender). Northcraft, Polzer, Neale, and Kramer (1995) suggest that heterogeneous groups can negotiate differences in members' perspectives and achieve an integrated resolution that benefits group performance and cohesiveness. Education about diversity issues and appreciation of diverse members should contribute to the effectiveness of cross-cultural teams. As Northcraft et al. observe, "A good organization makes multiple identity allegiance possible; a great organization makes multiple identity allegiance valuable" (p. 88).

Differential Rates of Participation Among Group Members

As organizations and groups experience growing diversity, the effective use of everyone's talents becomes more complex. Thus, more attention is being directed at group process and outcome issues, especially those involving member participation and satisfaction and group cohesion. Kirchmeyer and Cohen (1992), for example, reported that minority group members (based on race/ethnicity and/or gender) contributed less to decision making than did majority group members. In many groups, a minority member was the lowest contributor (see also Ketrow's review of this literature, Chapter 10, this volume). Minority members were also less committed to their group; however, groups that engaged in effective conflict management, such as discussing differences of opinion openly, achieved more balanced contributions from minority and majority group members.

Kirchmeyer (1993) explored the reasons for the lower rates of group participation by minority members. In particular, she assessed whether or not communicative competence, group attachment, orientations (masculinity/femininity), and motives differed between minority and nonminority members of diverse groups, and, if so, what these factors contributed to group decision making. Low communicative competence, low masculinity, and high femininity were associated with minority status and low contributions to the group. For minority members, however, a strong desire to work well with others resulted in more participation and more contributions to group decision making.

Of the variables studied, communicative competence was the one that differentiated most between minority and nonminority group members, with minorities reporting that they had less ability to communicate interpersonally. Communicative competence, masculinity, and competition needs were also positively correlated with one another. Group attachment was only slightly related to communicative competence and need for relationships. Kirchmeyer also found that minority status was associated with low participation rates, independent of any effects of the personal variables measured. That is, minority status directly limited members' contributions to groups.

Low contribution rates among minority group members, however, were still largely unexplained; for example, sex-role orientation explained only 17% of the variance and minority status an additional 9%. Some research suggests that minority group members may have less desire to contribute because they often feel excluded and tend not to identify with heterogeneous groups (Cianni & Romberger, 1991) and because they are assigned a lower status position (Asante & Davis, 1985; Haslett et al., 1992).

Research has documented that cultural heterogeneity influences the functioning and effectiveness of groups. In addition, relative cultural distance among group members influences their relationship to the group and their evaluation of the group's effectiveness. Within heterogeneous, multicultural groups, members' national cultural norms appear to provide the basis for behavioral norms that may not be consistent with a given group's norms and, thus, contribute to increased conflict and misunderstanding among group members.

Critical Mass and Group Composition

One of the issues to consider when discussing diversity is the number of group members from underrepresented social groups. Phrased somewhat differently, the question is whether diversity effects require a critical mass of members from underrepresented social groups, such as 40% of a group's membership, or whether such effects hold when there is only one or a few minority individuals. Moscovici (1985), for example, argues that minority influence is a matter of behavioral style, not the number of minority members in a particular group. He suggests that the major quality of minority style and influence is consistency. Consistency or tenacious commitment to a particular view often impresses others and compels them to evaluate that perspective; subsequent examination of the perspective may lead to conversion. Minority influence, therefore, is similar to conversion, whereas majority influence involves gaining compliance. Thus, Moscovici's analysis is distinct from analyses of minority influence based on power and dependency in relation to a majority (see Meyers & Brashers, Chapter 11, this volume, on social influence processes in groups, in general, and majority/minority influence, in particular).

Other scholars, however, have found that diversity in terms of numerical proportions of diverse populations constituting a group makes a difference. Kanter (1977) studied groups with skewed numbers of women (15% or less) in a manufacturing organization and found that majority group members (males) had heightened awareness of their differences from the minority group, exaggerated those differences, and expressed heightened identification with the majority group. Wolman and Frank (1975) observed that as minority group membership increased, minority members' sense of social isolation decreased.

Minority status may have different effects depending on whether it is based on gender or racial underrepresentation. An interesting study by Craig and Rand (1998) examined the effects of solo status in four-person, same-sex groups that contained either a racial solo or a target of the same race (solo groups were either three Whites and one Black or three Blacks and one White). No significant sex differences across the groups emerged; however, significant racial effects were revealed, with Black solos judged more positively and selected as leaders more frequently than White targets across all groups. The researchers suggest that the Black groups' judgments might reflect in-group bias, whereas the White groups' judgments may reflect overcompensation resulting from members' effort to try to appear nonbiased.

Tolbert, Andrews, and Simons (1995) explored two potential effects of increased numbers of minority members in groups. One possible effect, as the social contact hypothesis suggests, is that as the number of minority members increases, majority group members have more contact with them, and this greater social contact should lead to decreased prejudice and stereotyping. This effect should occur provided that other conditions exist, such as recognized common goals. In contrast, the competition hypothesis suggests that as the number of minority group members increases, more social differentiation is experienced by group members. As different groups compete for scare social and material resources, discrimination and conflict increase. Tolbert et al.'s study supported the competition hypothesis: With increasing numbers of female faculty, additional women were less likely to be hired. Tsui, Egan, and O'Reilly (1992) also found that as more women were represented

in an organization, their male coworkers expressed lowered commitment to the organization and spoke of leaving. Tolbert et al. (1995), however, point out that such minority status may be mitigated by the hierarchical placement of group members and whether the minority characteristic is ascribed (e.g., race) or achieved (e.g., education).

Larkey (1996) focused on how communication processes are affected by cultural diversity. She defined diversity among group members in two distinct ways: as a function of differences in worldviews and as a function of identity differences (i.e., in contrast to other group memberships they hold). Minority status, for Larkey, refers to being a member of a particular racioethnic or gender minority; such minority groups are underrepresented in positions of power and influence, even though they may be a numerical majority.

Larkey suggests that work group interactions are influenced by the surrounding organizational context. Organizations may be either *monolithic* (generally homogeneous with little integration of minority group members), *plural* (some minority members present, largely in lower level positions, with some policies in place to encourage more hiring), or *multicultural* (integration of minorities throughout the organization, with expressions of diverse ways of thinking and working encouraged). Organizations may reflect a mix of two or three types, although one type tends to predominate.

Work groups reflect the type of organization in which they are situated, with monolithic organizations reinforcing categorical perceptions (e.g., in-group versus out-group judgments) and multicultural organizations encouraging judgments based on individuation (appreciation of individual differences). In Larkey's studies, categorical perceptions fostered interaction that excluded people who were perceived as different, enhanced negative evaluations, led to misunderstanding, and encouraged conformity in ideas. Perceptions that valued differences, in contrast, led to interactions that included all group members, encouraged varied viewpoints, and developed more understanding among members.

Diversity in group composition, as this review demonstrates, has been explored from a number of different perspectives, including demographic, communicative, cognitive, and cultural influences. The diversity effects examined above focused primarily on conflict and other group processes. In the next section, we look primarily at the effects of group diversity on outcomes, such as creativity and quality of decision making.

Diversity, Creativity, and Group Decision Making

One of the potential benefits of diversity is that different perspectives can be brought to bear on a problem or issue. Different frames of reference introduced by group members during their discussions can increase creative insights into complex issues (Souder, 1987; see Jarboe, Chapter 13, this volume, regarding group communication and creativity processes). High levels of creativity and performance are associated with organizations that encourage expression of diverse viewpoints and seek members with diverse backgrounds (Goddard, 1985; Moenaert & Souder, 1990). More monitoring of the environment and new sources of information result from greater diversity among group members' networks (Lipnac & Stamps, 1993). The variety of information discussed broadens people's views and enhances their ability to evaluate information (Rohrbaugh, 1979; see Propp, Chapter 9, this volume). This enhances a group's ability to respond appropriately and flexibly. In quickly changing environments, Cox and Blake (1991) suggest, a diverse workforce is able to monitor, identify, and respond more quickly to environmental disturbances.

Cultural heterogeneity appears to have an overall positive effect on group performance. D. C. Thomas et al. (1996) note that the presence of more varied perspectives in heterogeneous groups typically leads to better solutions. Being exposed to different viewpoints also may suggest alternative ways of viewing

problems and, thereby, contribute to improved group performance. The findings obtained from an experiment by D. C. Thomas and colleagues indicate that process costs may be mitigated by time and increasing familiarity among heterogeneous group members. In short, the interactional complexities associated with diversity become easier to deal with over time. It is interesting how personal comments from group members in this study indicate a valuing of diverse points of view. Thomas and colleagues also note, however, that the effects of cultural heterogeneity may depend on the nature of the task. Although cultural heterogeneity improves idea generation and decision making, it may not affect other group tasks, such as performing routine, repetitive tasks.

In their review of the literature on diversity in groups, McLeod, Lobel, and Cox (1996) conclude that "both laboratory and field studies have shown that heterogeneity among group members with respect to age, tenure, education, and functional area is related to group and organizational creativity, adaptability, and innovation" (p. 251). In addition, groups that maintain heterogeneity over time by replacing those who leave with the same or different type of diversity also appear to be more innovative than groups with no membership changes (King & Anderson, 1990; Pelz & Andrews, 1966).

Other positive outcomes accrue from cultural diversity in groups. For example, Cox and Blake (1991) suggested that ethnically diverse employees provide different insights that help companies market products more effectively. McLeod et al. (1996) explored the impact of ethnic diversity on the production of high-quality ideas on a task relevant to ethnic diversity (a brainstorming task called "The Tourist Problem"). Two judges, both experts in the travel industry, evaluated the ideas from homogeneous (all-Anglo) and heterogeneous groups (composed of three or four members who were Asian Americans, African American, and Hispanic Americans). Heterogeneous groups generated significantly more effective and more feasible ideas, although members of homogeneous groups reported marginally higher levels of interpersonal attraction. Based on these findings, McLeod et al. suggest that for "simple tasks, with low communication requirements, groups may be able to realize the benefits of diversity sooner and with relatively little effort, whereas for complex tasks, direct process interventions and more time would be needed" (p. 258).

In an exploration of group processes and performance over time, Watson, Kuman, and Michaelsen (1993) discovered that although homogeneous groups scored higher on group process and performance measures initially, at the end of the study (17 weeks), heterogeneous groups scored equally well. This may indicate that early process difficulties (e.g., more difficulty in agreeing on what is important and ability to work together) for heterogeneous groups were resolved. As expected, heterogeneous groups produced more perspectives on problems and generated more alternative solutions. One factor that may have influenced these results, however, was that process and performance feedback was given to the groups, although both homogeneous and heterogeneous groups received the feedback at regular intervals, so presumably both would benefit. Such feedback may be an important aid in facilitating group functioning and performance and, if so, would tend to reinforce McLeod et al.'s (1996) suggestion that direct intervention may facilitate the work of heterogeneous groups.

DIRECTIONS FOR FUTURE RESEARCH

As this chapter demonstrates, many individual differences influence group processes and outcomes. One area for future research is to examine more of the specific circumstances under which individual differences affect group processes and outcomes. Salazar (1997) notes that some communication processes may affect other types of group processes and outcomes, whereas others may not, and the same is true for individual differences. Not all such differences necessarily influence groups;

some may have an influence within one type of circumstance, such as a particular type of group composition, but not within another type.

One specific circumstance that deserves more consideration is the cultural context in which group interaction occurs. As this review shows, researchers have specified some of the cultural, cognitive, and communicative expectations that individuals bring to groups and their effects on them. Oetzel (1998b), for example, suggests testing different types of homogeneous and heterogeneous groups, such as those in non-Euro-American cultures. Our understanding of homogeneity and heterogeneity has been limited by the lack of representation across cultures and contexts.

Because group interaction often occurs within a particular organizational milieu and task environment, it is essential that research be conducted on bona fide groups, those that have permeable boundaries and are interdependent with their contexts (Putnam & Stohl, 1990, 1996; Stohl & Putnam, 1994; in this volume, see Chapters 1 [Gouran] and 2 [Poole]). Group members' attitudes toward organizational life, cultural practices, and societal beliefs about diversity provide relevant larger contexts for group interaction. Groups also change over time, as well as expand and contract their boundaries. Because groups and the cultures in which they are embedded change continuously, research studies should also analyze how culturally diverse groups evolve.

Another potential direction for future research is the context in which groups operate, or the issue of framing. As Barge and Keyton (1994) explain, framing is the power to define an interactional context. As their analysis of the Waco City Council revealed, the way in which the interactional context was defined helped determine who acquired and used power during group discussions. The larger issue is that of framing group discussion in ways that allow group members to develop a common context and become an effective unit. The context outside the group, incorporated in group members' sources of power and information, appears to influence members' specific communicative acts. People undoubtedly will frame issues in very distinct ways as a result of individual differences (such as sex/gender), culture, and group composition. Thus, these factors appear to be important avenues for further research.

Perspectives on group processes and outcomes also need to be expanded through the use of different analytic frameworks. For example, Meyers and Brashers (1994) suggest that two feminist values, those of connection and cooperation, should be introduced as alternative foci to the usual emphasis on influence and competition in theory and research about groups. As we reframe our implicit group values, different group processes may emerge, as well as different outcomes and interactional patterns, especially in culturally diverse groups.

CONCLUSION

Group communication scholars clearly need to focus on understanding the conditions under which the benefits of group diversity accrue, because diversity is here to stay. As noted earlier, the United States is becoming a more diverse society, and the workplace is also becoming more diversified as a result of demographic changes and global world markets. Communication processes should be a critical component, if not the centerpiece, of research efforts devoted to understanding the nature and effects of diversity. Effective communication can enhance the flow of ideas and reduce process costs and, consequently, lead to high-quality group performance and member relations. The study of communication among diverse group members will also have important pragmatic application by helping to reduce some of the detrimental in-group/out-group conflicts that result when group members fail to realize that their common interests lie in high-quality task performance and in member relations that benefit all.

REFERENCES

Abrams, D., Wetherall, M., Cochrane, S., Hogg, M. A., & Turner, J. C. (1990). Knowing what to think by knowing who you are: Self-categorization and the nature of norm formation, conformity and group polarization. *British Journal of Social Psychology, 29,* 97-119.

Allen, M., & Bourhis, J. (1996). The relationship of communication apprehension to communication behavior: A meta-analysis. *Communication Quarterly, 44,* 214-226.

Anderson, C. M., & Martin, M. M. (1994, November). *How argumentativeness, verbal aggressiveness, and communication apprehension affect members' perceptions of cohesion, consensus, and satisfaction in small groups.* Paper presented at the meeting of the Speech Communication Association, New Orleans, LA.

Aries, E. J. (1982). Verbal and nonverbal behavior in single-sex and mixed-sex groups: Are traditional sex roles changing? *Psychological Reports, 51,* 127-134.

Asante, M., & Davis, A. (1985). Black and white communication. *Journal of Black Studies, 17,* 77-93.

Baird, J. E., Jr. (1976). Sex differences in group communication: A review of relevant research. *Quarterly Journal of Speech, 62,* 179-192.

Barge, J. K., & Frey, L. R. (1997). Life in a task group. In L. R. Frey & J. K. Barge (Eds.), *Managing group life: Communicating in decision-making groups* (pp. 29-51). Boston: Houghton Mifflin.

Barge, J. K., & Keyton, J. (1994). Contextualizing power and social influence in groups. In L. R. Frey (Ed.), *Group communication in context: Studies of natural groups* (pp. 85-106). Hillsdale, NJ: Lawrence Erlbaum.

Bento, R. F. (1997). When good intentions are not enough: Unintentional subtle discrimination against Latinas in the workplace. In N. V. Benokraitis (Ed.), *Subtle sexism* (pp. 95-116). Thousand Oaks, CA: Sage.

Berger, J., Wagner, D. G., & Zelditch, M., Jr. (1985). Introduction: Expectation states theory: Review and assessment. In J. Berger & M. Zelditch (Eds.), *Status, rewards, and influence* (pp. 1-72). San Francisco: Jossey-Bass.

Boyett, J. H., & Conn, H. P. (1992). *Workplace 2000: The revolution reshaping American business.* New York: Dutton.

Bradshaw, S. D., & Stasson, M. F. (1998). Attributions of shy and not-shy group members for collective group performance. *Small Group Research, 29,* 283-307.

Burgoon, J. K. (1977). Unwillingness to communicate as a predictor of small group discussion behaviors and evaluation. *Central States Speech Journal, 28,* 122-133.

Burnstein, E. (1982). Persuasion as argument processing. In H. Brandstätter, J. H. Davis, & G. Stocker-Kreichaguer (Eds.), *Group decision making* (pp. 103-124). New York: Academic Press.

Burrell, N. A., Donohue, W. A., & Allen, M. (1988). Gender-based perceptual biases in mediation. *Communication Research, 15*, 447-469.

Chandler, M. (1977). Social cognition: A selective review of current research. In W. F. Overton & J. Gallager (Eds.), *Knowledge and development* (pp. 202-237). New York: Plenum.

Chua, E. C., & Gudykunst, W. B. (1987). Conflict resolution in low- and high-context cultures. *Communication Research Reports, 4*, 2-37.

Chusmir, L. H., & Mills, J. (1989). Gender difference in conflict resolution style of managers: At home and at work. *Sex Roles, 20*, 149-163.

Cianni, M., & Romberger, B. (1991). Belonging in the corporation: Oral histories of male and female white, black and hispanic managers. *Proceedings of the Academy of Management, 51*, 358-362.

Comadena, M. E. (1984). Brainstorming groups: Ambiguity tolerance, communication apprehension, task attraction, and individual productivity. *Small Group Behavior, 15*, 251-264.

Corlett, E., & Yeakley, F. (1995, August). *Materials from Creative Approaches Unlimited.* Presented at the Myers-Briggs Type Inventory Qualifying Workshop, Reston, VA.

Cox, T., Jr. (1993). *Cultural diversity in organizations: Theory, research, and practice.* San Francisco: Berrett-Koehler.

Cox, T., Jr., & Blake, S. (1991). Managing cultural diversity: Implications for organizational competitiveness. *Academy of Management Executive, 5*, 45-56.

Craig, K. M., & Rand, K. A. (1998). The perceptually "privileged" group member: Consequences of solo status for African Americans and Whites in task groups. *Small Group Research, 29*, 339-358.

Daly, J. A. (1974). *The effects of differential durations of time on interpersonal judgments based on vocal activity.* Unpublished master's thesis, West Virginia University, Morgantown.

Dovidio, J. F., & Gaertner, S. L. (1993). Stereotypes and evaluative intergroup bias. In D. M. Mackie & D. L. Hamilton (Eds.), *Affect, cognition, and stereotyping: Interactive processes in group perception* (pp. 167-193). San Diego: Academic Press.

Dovidio, J. F., Gaertner, S. L., Anastasio, P., & Sanitioso, R. (1992). Cognitive and motivational bases of bias: Implications of aversive racism for attitudes towards Hispanics. In S. B. Knouse, P. Rosenfeld, & A. Culbertson (Eds.), *Hispanics in the workplace* (pp. 73-106). Newbury Park, CA: Sage.

Dunn, D. (1996). *Workplace/women's place.* Los Angeles, CA: Roxbury.

Eagly, A. H. (1978). Sex differences in influenceability. *Psychological Bulletin, 85*, 86-116.

Eagly, A. H. (1983). Gender and social influence: A social psychological analysis. *American Psychologist, 38*, 971-981.

Eagly, A. H., & Carli, L. (1981). Sex of researchers and sex-typed communications as determinants of sex differences in influenceability: A meta-analysis of social influence studies. *Psychological Bulletin, 90*, 1-20.

Ferdman, B. M. (1995). Cultural identity and diversity in organizations. In M. M. Chemers, S. Oskamp, & M. A. Costanzo (Eds.), *Diversity in organizations: New perspectives for a changing workplace* (pp. 37-61). Thousand Oaks, CA: Sage.

Fiske, S. T., & Neuberg, S. T. (1990). A continuum of impression formation, from category-based to individuating processes: Influences of information and motivation on attention and interpretation. In M. P. Zanna (Ed.), *Advances in experimental social psychology* (Vol. 23, pp. 1-74). Orlando, FL: Academic Press.

Folger, J. P., Poole, M. S., & Stutman, R. K. (1997). *Working through conflict: Strategies for relationships, groups, and organizations* (3rd ed.). New York: HarperCollins.

Glenn, E. (with Glenn, C. G.). (1981). *Man and mankind: Conflict and communication between cultures.* Norwood, NJ: Ablex.

Goddard, R. W. (1985). Bringing new ideas to light. *Management World, 14*, 8-11.

Gopal, A., Miranda, S. M., Robichaux, B. P., & Bostrom, R. P. (1997). Leveraging diversity with information technology: Gender, attitude, and intervening influences in the use of group support systems. *Small Group Research, 28*, 29-71.

Grob, L., Meyers, R., & Schuh, R. (1997). Powerful/powerless language use in group interactions: Sex differences or similarities? *Communication Quarterly, 45*, 282-303.

Hardin, C. D., & Higgins, E. T. (1996). Shared reality: How social verification makes the subjective objective. In R. M. Sorrentino & E. T. Higgins (Eds.), *Handbook of motivation and cognition: The interpersonal context* (Vol. 3, pp. 28-84). New York: Guilford.

Hare, A. P., & Davies, M. F. (1994). Social interaction. In A. P. Hare, H. Blumberg, M. Davies, & M. V. Kent (Eds.), *Small group research: A handbook* (pp. 164-193). Norwood, NJ: Ablex.

Haslett, B. J., Geis, F. L., & Carter, M. R. (1992). *The organizational woman: Power and paradox.* Norwood, NJ: Ablex.

Hawkins, K. T., & Stewart, R. A. (1991). Effects of communication apprehension on perceptions of leadership and intragroup attraction in small task-oriented groups. *Southern Communication Journal, 57*, 1-10.

Higginbotham, E., & Romero, M. (1997). *Women and work: Exploring race, ethnicity, and class.* Thousand Oaks, CA: Sage.

Hofstede, G. (1980). *Culture's consequences: International differences in work-related values.* Beverly Hills, CA: Sage.

Ibarra, H. (1992). Homophily and differential returns: Sex differences in network structure and access in an advertising firm. *Administrative Science Quarterly, 37*, 422-447.

Jablin, F. M., Sorenson, R. L., & Seibold, D. R. (1978). Interpersonal perception and group brainstorming performance. *Communication Quarterly, 26*, 36-44.

Johnson, R. A., & Schulman, G. I. (1989). Gender-role composition and role entrapment in decision-making groups. *Gender & Society, 3*, 355-372.

Jones, R. E., & White, C. S. (1985). Relationships among personality, conflict resolution styles, and task effectiveness. *Group and Organization Studies, 10,* 152-167.

Kanter, R. M. (1977). *Men and women of the corporation.* New York: Basic Books.

Keashly, L. (1994). Gender and conflict: What does psychological research tell us? In A. Taylor & J. B. Miller (Eds.), *Conflict and gender* (pp. 167-190). Cresskill, NJ: Hampton

King, N., & Anderson, N. (1990). Innovation in working groups. In M. A. West & J. F. Farr (Eds.), *Innovation and creativity at work: Psychological and organizational strategies* (pp. 110-135). Chichester, UK: Wiley.

Kirchmeyer, C. (1993). Multicultural task groups: An account of the low contribution level of minorities. *Small Group Research, 24,* 127-143.

Kirchmeyer, C., & Cohen, A. (1992). Multicultural groups: Their performance and reactions with constructive conflict. *Group & Organizational Management, 17,* 153-170.

Kogut, B., & Singh, H. (1988). The effect of national culture on the choice of entry mode. *Journal of International Business Studies, 19,* 411-432.

Kramarae, C. (1990). Changing the complexion of gender in language research. In H. Giles & W. P. Robinson (Eds.), *Handbook of language and social psychology* (pp. 345-361). New York: Wiley.

Larkey, L. K. (1996). Toward a theory of communicative interactions in culturally diverse work groups. *Academy of Management Review, 21,* 463-491.

Lawrence, G. (1982). *People types and tiger stripes.* Gainesville, FL: CHART.

Lipnac, J., & Stamps, J. (1993). *The teamnet factor: Bringing the power of boundary crossing into the heart of your business.* Essex Junction, VT: Oliver Wright.

Marcus-Newhall, A., Miller, N., Holtz, R., & Brewer, M. B. (1993). Cross-cutting category membership in role assignment: A means of reducing intergroup bias. *British Journal of Social Psychology, 32,* 125-145.

Martin, P. Y. (1991). Gender, interaction, and inequality in organizations. In C. L. Ridgeway (Ed.), *Gender, interaction, and inequality* (pp. 208-231). New York: Springer-Verlag.

Martin P. Y., &. Shanahan, K. (1983). Transcending the effects of sex composition in small groups. *Social Work in Groups, 6,* 19-32.

McCroskey, J. C., & Beatty, M. J. (1984). Communication apprehension and accumulated communication anxiety state experiences: A research note. *Communication Monographs, 51,* 79-84.

McCroskey, J. C., Hamilton, P. R., & Weiner, A. N. (1974). The effect of interaction behavior on source credibility, homophily, and interpersonal attraction. *Human Communication Research, 1,* 42-52.

McCroskey, J. C., & Richmond, V. P. (1976). The effects of communication apprehension on the perceptions of peers. *Journal of the Western Speech Communication Association, 40,* 14-21.

McCroskey, J. C., & Richmond, V. P. (1992). Communication apprehension and small group communication. In R. S. Cathcart & L. A. Samovar (Eds.), *Small group communication: A reader* (6th ed., pp. 361-374). Dubuque, IA: Wm. C. Brown.

McGarty, C., Haslam, S. A., Hutchinson, K. J., & Turner, J. C. (1994). The effects of salient group membership on persuasion. *Small Group Research, 25,* 267-293.

McLeod, P. L., Lobel, S. A., & Cox, T. H., Jr. (1996). Ethnic diversity and creativity in small groups. *Small Group Research, 27,* 248-264.

Meyers, R. A., & Brashers, D. E. (1994). Expanding the boundaries of small group communication research: Exploring a feminist perspective. *Communication Studies, 45,* 68-85.

Mikolic, J. M., Parker, J. C., & Pruitt, D. G. (1997). Escalation in response to persistent annoyance: Groups versus individuals and gender effects. *Journal of Personality and Social Psychology, 72,* 151-163.

Moenaert, R., & Souder, W. (1990). An information transfer model for integrating marketing and R&D personnel in new product development projects. *Journal of Product Innovation Management, 7,* 91-107.

Moscovici, S. (1985). Innovation and minority influence. In S. Moscovici, G. Mugny, & E. Van Avermaet (Eds.), *Perspectives on minority influence* (pp. 1-24). Cambridge, UK: Cambridge University Press.

Myers, I. (1987). *Introduction to type.* Palo Alto, CA: Consulting Psychologists Press.

Nicotera, A. M. (1997). Managing conflict communication in groups. In L. R. Frey & J. K. Barge (Eds.), *Managing group life: Communicating in decision-making groups* (pp. 104-130). Boston: Houghton Mifflin.

Northcraft, G. B., Polzer, J. T., Neale, M. A., & Kramer, R. M. (1995). Diversity, social identity, and performance: Emergent social dynamics in cross-functional teams. In S. E. Jackson & M. Ruderman (Eds.), *Diversity in work teams: Research paradigms for a changing workplace* (pp. 69-96). Washington, DC: American Psychological Association.

Oetzel, J. (1998a). Culturally homogeneous and heterogeneous groups: Explaining communication processes through individualism-collectivism and self-construal. *International Journal of Intercultural Relations, 22,* 135-161.

Oetzel, J. (1998b). Explaining individual communication processes in homogeneous and heterogeneous groups through individualism-collectivism and self-construal. *Human Communication Research, 25,* 202-224.

Offerman, L. R., & Schrier, P. E. (1985). Social influence strategies: The impact of sex, role, and attitudes toward power. *Personality and Social Psychology Bulletin, 11,* 286-300.

Pelz, D. C., & Andrews, F. M. (1966). *Scientists in organizations: Productive climates for research and development.* New York: Wiley.

Putnam, L. L., & Stohl, C. (1990). Bona fide groups: A reconceptualization of groups in context. *Communication Studies, 41,* 248-265.

Putnam, L. L., & Stohl, C. (1996). Bona fide groups: An alternative perspective for communication and small group decision making. In R. Y. Hirokawa & M. S. Poole (Eds.), *Communication and group decision making* (2nd ed., pp. 147-178). Thousand Oaks, CA: Sage.

Rahim, M. A. (1983). A measure of styles of handling interpersonal conflict. *Academy of Management Journal, 26,* 368-376.

Ridgeway, C. L. (1989). Understanding legitimation in informal status orders. In J. Berger, M. Zelditch, Jr., & B. Anderson (Eds.), *Sociological theories in progress: New formulations* (pp. 131-159). Newbury Park, CA: Sage.

Ridgeway, C. L. (1993). Legitimacy, status, and dominance behavior in groups. In S. Worchel & J. A. Simpson (Eds.), *Conflict between people and groups: Causes, processes, and resolutions* (pp. 110-127). Chicago: Nelson-Hall.

Ridgeway, C. L., & Berger, J. (1986). Expectations, legitimation, and dominance behavior in task groups. *American Sociological Review, 51,* 603-617.

Rohrbaugh, J. (1979). Improving the quality of group judgment: Social judgment analysis and the Delphi technique. *Organizational Behavior and Human Performance, 24,* 73-92.

Rosenfeld, L. B., Grant, C. H., & McCroskey, J. C. (1995). Communication apprehension and self-perceived communication competence of academically gifted students. *Communication Education, 44,* 79-87.

Rozell, E., & Vaught, R. (1988). The interaction effects of women in groups: A review of the literature and implications. *Arkansas Business and Economic Review, 21,* 1-15.

Rubin, R. B., Rubin, A. M., & Jordan, F. F. (1997). Effects of instruction on communication apprehension and communication competence. *Communication Education, 46,* 104-115.

Ruble, T., & Schneer, J. (1994). Gender differences in conflict-handling styles: Less than meets the eye? In A. Taylor & J. B. Miller (Eds.), *Conflict and gender* (pp. 155-166). Cresskill, NJ: Hampton.

Salazar, A. J. (1997). Communication effects on small group decision-making: Homogeneity and task as moderator for the communication-performance relationship. *Western Journal of Communication, 61,* 35-65.

Seibert, S., & Gruenfeld, L. (1992). Masculinity, femininity, and behavior in groups. *Small Group Research, 23,* 95-112.

Smith, K. K., & Berg, D. N. (1987). *Paradoxes of group life: Understanding conflict, paralysis, and movement in group dynamic.* San Francisco: Jossey-Bass.

Smith-Lovin, L., & Brody, C. (1989). Interruptions in group discussions: The effects of gender and group composition. *American Sociological Review, 54,* 424-435.

Smith-Lovin, L., Skvoretz, J. K., & Hudson, C. (1986). Status and participation in six-person groups: A test of Skvoretz's comparative status model. *Social Forces, 64,* 992-1005.

Socha, T. J. (1997). Group communication across the life span. In L. R. Frey & J. K. Barge (Eds.), *Managing group life: Communicating in decision-making groups* (pp. 3-28). Boston: Houghton Mifflin.

Souder, W. (1987). *Managing new product innovation.* Lexington, MA: Lexington Press.

Stager, P. (1967). Conceptual level as a composition variable in small-group decision making. *Journal of Personality and Social Psychology, 5,* 152-161.

Stockard, J., Van de Kragt, A. J., & Dodge, P. J. (1988). Gender roles and behavior in social dilemmas: Are there sex differences in cooperation and its justification? *Social Psychology Quarterly, 51,* 154-163.

Stohl, C., & Putnam, L. L. (1994). Group communication in context: Implications for the study of bona fide groups. In L. R. Frey (Ed.), *Group communication in context: Studies of natural groups* (pp. 284-292). Hillsdale, NJ: Lawrence Erlbaum.

Tannen, D. (1990). *You just don't understand: Women and men in conversation.* New York: William Morrow.

Thomas, D. C., Ravlin, E. C., & Wallace, A. W. (1996). Effect of cultural diversity in work groups. In P. Bamber, M. Erez, & S. Bacharach (Eds.), *Research in the sociology of organizations* (Vol. 14, pp. 1-33). Greenwich, CT: JAI.

Thomas, K. W., & Kilman, R. H. (1986). *Thomas-Kilman conflict mode instrument.* Tuxedo, NY: Xicom.

Ting-Toomey, S. (1985). Toward a theory of conflict and culture. In W. B. Gudykunst, L. P. Stewart, & S. Ting-Toomey (Eds.), *Communication, culture, and organizational processes* (pp. 71-87). Beverly Hills, CA: Sage.

Tjosvold, D. (1992). *The conflict-positive organization: Stimulate diversity and create unity.* Reading, MA: Addison-Wesley.

Tolbert, P. S., Andrews, A. O., & Simons, T. (1995). The effects of group proportions on group dynamics. In S. E. Jackson & M. Ruderman (Eds.), *Diversity in work teams: Research paradigms for a changing workplace* (pp. 131-160). Washington, DC: American Psychological Association.

Tsui, A. S., Egan, T. D., & O'Reilly, C., III. (1992). Being different: Relational demography and organizational attachment. *Administrative Science Quarterly, 37,* 549-579.

Volkema, R. J., & Gorman, R. H. (1998). The influence of cognitive-based group composition on decision-making process and outcome. *Journal of Management Studies, 35,* 105-122.

Wall, V. D., Galanes, G. J., & Love, S. B. (1987). Small, task-oriented groups, conflict, conflict management, satisfaction, and decision quality. *Small Group Behavior, 18,* 31-55.

Watson, W. E., Kuman, K., & Michaelsen, L. K. (1993). Cultural diversity's impact on interaction process and performance: Comparing homogeneous and diverse task groups. *Academy of Management Journal, 36,* 590-603.

Wolman, C., & Frank, H. (1975). The solo woman in a professional peer group. *American Journal of Orthopsychiatry, 45,* 164-171.

Zimmerman, D., & West, C. (1975). Sex roles, interruptions and silence in conversations. In B. Thorne & N. Henley (Eds.), *Language and sex: difference and dominance* (pp. 105-129). Rowley, MA: Newbury.

6

Socialization Processes in Groups

CAROLYN M. ANDERSON
The University of Akron

BRUCE L. RIDDLE
Kent State University

MATTHEW M. MARTIN
West Virginia University

Becoming socialized into a new group is not the relatively straightforward process of being taught, learning, accepting, or leaving that might come to mind when thinking about it. It is the active process of coming to terms with the old and the new.

—Pepper (1995, p. 123)

Although researchers have studied numerous aspects of small groups, surprisingly few scholars have addressed socialization processes. Considering the social nature of culture in the United States that continually draws us into groups, it seems safe to conclude that a clear understanding of the process of joining and adapting to groups is an area of communication research well worth addressing. In this chapter, we advance the idea that socialization processes affect the communication among group members and various other group dynamics. Additionally, socialization processes experienced by individuals in one group affect how they adapt and communicate in other groups to which they belong or will belong. Moreover, positive socialization of members creates stronger commitments to confront and balance the multiple issues and tensions involved in participating in group activities. Thus, valid reasons exist for turning attention to understanding socialization processes in groups.

The discussions in this chapter focus on two communication phase models of socialization in groups. The models illustrate socialization processes for both individual members and groups by focusing on the life span of a single group to demonstrate the effects of socialization on the task (see Hirokawa & Salazar,

Chapter 7, this volume) and relational (see Keyton, Chapter 8, this volume) dimensions of group life. Furthermore, they clarify how communication over the course of socialization processes creates and sustains such group processes as establishing norms, rules, and roles. The models address both individuals who belong to multiple groups, including decision-making, social, and self-help (see Cline, Chapter 19, this volume) groups and the group as an entity. For individual members, the model illustrates that communication processes and outcomes of one group experience affect the "library of experiences" that people build. In their library, individuals store information about their group experiences that influence how they communicate and react in simultaneous and subsequent groups. The treatment of socialization processes also applies both to individuals who voluntarily join new or existing groups and to those who are assigned to groups. For the group, the model illustrates socialization processes over the life span of a single group experience. The model also reflects the fluid nature of socialization processes in that groups may move quickly through the phases of group life or regress to a previous phase. Given that socialization is a two-way process of groups influencing individuals and vice versa, a dual perspective of the individual and the group is essential in developing a comprehensive understanding of socialization processes in groups (see Jablin, 1987).

The models advanced in this chapter provide frameworks both for reviewing research on socialization in groups and for setting the agenda for those who seek to study it. From an applied perspective, group members can also potentially benefit from understanding the powerful impact that socialization processes have on members, intragroup and intergroup relationships, group tasks, and group outcomes. The contention is that a clearer understanding of socialization processes helps explain whether individuals develop an affinity or a distaste for working in groups and developing relationships with group members.

The chapter has three sections and concluding remarks. The first section provides definitions of socialization and highlights relevant models by integrating contributions from diverse disciplines. The integration of cross-disciplinary research is a necessary step in building more complete models of socialization and other group processes (see Gouran, 1994; McGrath & Gruenfeld, 1993). In the second section, a theoretical framework is discussed that provides the grounding for the communication-based models of group socialization advanced in this chapter. The model for individual members is introduced, and the discussion clarifies how communication influences essential characteristics associated with socialization processes. Following this discussion, a model for groups is introduced. In explicating the models, propositions are advanced that provide a foundation for understanding socialization processes. The third section presents an agenda for theory and research on socialization in groups. Concluding remarks denote the benefits of group socialization research.

DEFINITION OF GROUP SOCIALIZATION

As a generic term, *socialization* refers to the process by which newcomers become part of a group's patterns of activities (see Stryker & Statham, 1985). Some definitions suggest that socialization occurs when group members create shared meaning about roles and rules through interaction (Mead, 1956), or when they acquire certain knowledge and skills that make them competent members of a group (see Dion, 1985). Although these and other definitions focus on individuals, Moreland and Levine's (1982) influential work focuses attention not just on how individuals adapt and change in groups, but also on the changes occurring in groups. To reflect this position, Moreland and Levine define socialization as the reciprocal process of members and groups coming together to satisfy needs and accomplish goals.

The preponderance of communication research on socialization has been in the organizational context, and most of this literature has traditionally conceptualized socialization as a one-way process that places responsibility on newcomers to understand and interpret the organizations they join (Jablin, 1982, 1984). Within this context, socialization has been viewed as a process of newcomers' adjusting and adapting to organizational life by "learning the ropes" (Harris & Cronen, 1979). Ideas commonly held are that newcomers should learn the values, norms, and required behaviors (Van Maanen, 1976); acquire the knowledge and skills necessary to assume appropriate roles (Caplow, 1964; Van Maanen & Schein, 1979); and be indoctrinated about what is important (Schein, 1968). The task of newcomers is to fit into the organization by transforming themselves from naive, nonperforming members into contributing members (Comer, 1991; Hess, 1993). This transformational process is often seen as a "meltdown" of individuals into members who identify with and are committed to their organization (Katz & Kahn, 1978).

Although such one-sided definitions or explanations give insight into what is expected of newcomers when they enter groups, they address only half of the socialization process, for they do not account for how groups are affected by newcomers. Jablin (1985) has suggested that just as organizations attempt to socialize newcomers, newcomers also affect organizations. Certainly, the "newness" brought by newcomers has the potential to influence an organization's or group's structure, culture, and communication patterns. Thus, more contemporary descriptions of socialization have added this important, two-way interactional dimension to the concept. Interactive and cultural approaches to the study of socialization, therefore, place equal importance on changes to the social unit as on the changes affecting new members. Newcomers are viewed as active participants in the socialization process versus simply responding to or absorbing an existing culture. Pepper (1995) suggests that "socialization is about cultural reproduction" (p. 135), by which he means that newcomers and the groups they enter negotiate to find a good mutual fit by creating a unique group culture (e.g., values, norms, and communicative practices).

Including the notion of group systemic change in definitions of socialization raises other important issues. For example, although some groups, such as understaffed community groups, often readily welcome new members and the changes they engender (Cini, Moreland, & Levine, 1993), other types of groups, such as those found in business organizations, may not readily welcome newcomers or the changes they bring. The introduction of newcomers can threaten the stability of established group relationships and, thereby, force members to reevaluate them (Moreland & Levine, 1989). Rothwell (1998) notes that groups may not want to change established performance patterns, see the value of adding new members to an already effective group, or be open to new ideas. Newcomers' survival in such groups often depends on playing the role of "newcomer" (e.g., avoiding disagreements and talking little). When newcomers meet these expectations, they usually do not have an immediate and notable impact on groups (Jablin, 1984).

Another condition that has not been fully addressed in definitions of socialization is that of newly formed groups, in which all members must simultaneously find their place within a group and socialize one another. Members of new groups negotiate their fit by drawing on their library of previous group experiences as guides when establishing norms, rules, and roles.

In the light of existing definitions and explanations of socialization and the discussion above, a communication-based definition applicable to socialization processes in the group context should reflect a two-way process of social influence (changing others' ideas and opinions through communication; see Meyers & Brashers, Chapter 11, this volume) and change taking place both in individuals and in groups. Furthermore, various types of groups, whether task or social, existing or newly formed, need to be covered by the definition. Thus, the following definition of group socialization is offered: *Socialization in groups is a reciprocal process of social influence and change in which both newcomers and/or established members and the group adjust and adapt to one another through verbal and nonverbal communication as they create and recreate a unique culture and group structures, engage in relevant processes and activities, and pursue individual and group goals.*

The definition suggests a specific focus on communicative behaviors, social influence and change, and the creation of group structures, processes, and outcomes. As will be explained below, communication patterns among newcomers and established members, or members in newly formed groups, help members and groups to reduce uncertainty about tasks and intragroup relationships. Effective group socialization requires that members communicate openly with one another, accept newcomers and new ideas, and be willing, if not eager, to facilitate continuous change (improvement). Furthermore, effective socialization in groups means that both individual and group goals (both task and relational) are achieved, and that individual and group levels of satisfaction and comfort remain sufficiently positive throughout the group's life span. Last, the definition implies that socialization is an ongoing process that continues at both individual and group levels until the member leaves or the group disbands.

DISCIPLINARY MODELS OF GROUP AND ORGANIZATIONAL SOCIALIZATION

Scholars from many disciplines have studied the experiences of newcomers to groups; among them are anthropologists (Van Gennep, 1908/1960), community and organizational psychologists (Etzioni, 1961; Schein, 1968), social psychologists (Moreland & Levine, 1982, 1984), and sociologists (Ebaugh, 1988; Simmel, 1950). Depending on the theoretical perspective adopted, aspects of the group socialization process have been viewed differently. For example, social psychologists and sociologists have developed Social Exchange Theory to suggest that individuals join groups for rewards that membership brings (e.g., friendships) but become dissatisfied or leave when costs (e.g., task load) outweigh rewards. Furthermore, the social exchange approach explains the development of members' commitment to a group during the socialization process. According to Moreland, Levine, and Cini (1993), newcomers judge the value of membership, which, in turn, influences how committed they will be to the group.

One exemplary model of group socialization influenced by Social Exchange Theory is that of Moreland and Levine (1982, 1984, 1988). Their model illustrates how social influence and behavioral control affect the socialization process over time as individual members strive to fulfill personal needs and goals, and as the group as a whole tries to influence members to conform behaviorally and become committed to the group's goals. In Moreland and Levine's model, newcomers and established members of the group they join investigate the potential rewards and costs of newcomer membership, evaluate strength of commitment to each other, and negotiate newcomers' and established members' role positions. The model also addresses marginal members, those who are on the fringes of a group and may need to be resocialized, as well as members who choose to leave. Moreland and Levine suggest that evaluation (i.e., reward/cost determination), member-group commitment, and role transitions are continuous and recursive psychological processes inherent in socialization. Analyzed from a social exchange perspective, when the benefits from group membership are low, members' commitment weakens and forces them and the group as a whole to redefine members' behavioral expectations, intragroup relationships, and continued membership. McGrath and Gruenfeld (1993) consider Moreland and Levine's model especially noteworthy for focusing on how group socialization develops and changes over time, considerations that were missing from earlier models proposed by Lacoursiere (1980), Tuckman (1965), and Tuckman and Jensen (1977) (see Keyton, Chapter 8, this volume).

Another influence on theorizing about socialization emerges from a Symbolic Interaction Perspective, especially as applied to the organizational context. Models by Jones (1983) and Reichers (1987), for example, suggest that newcomers come to know an organization through interactions with insiders. These interactions socially construct for newcomers the meaning of the organization and their place within it. In Jones's (1983) model, newcomers take an active role in pursuing goals and role-performance outcomes by relying on past experiences and self-evaluations of the effectiveness of previous behaviors. The model also considers ways in which individual differences (e.g., self-efficacy expectations) and attributional processes (e.g., the gap between newcomers' perceptions and those of established members) mediate how newcomers make sense of groups, adjust to them, and contribute to group outcomes. The Reichers (1987) model also considers the rate at which newcomers negotiate adjustments to organizations. This rate depends on their active and interactive behaviors, such as asking questions and inviting coworkers to lunch.

Finally, organizational communication scholars have introduced models of socialization framed within a cultural paradigm that emphasizes the mechanisms through which newcomers come to know and accept an organization's and group's goals, values, problems, and practices. Lester's (1987) model, for example, explains ways in which newcomers reduce uncertainty about role performances and evaluate chances for success or failure. Newcomers learn organizational beliefs, norms, and values through such communicative behaviors as rituals (e.g., office parties) and feedback from established members. Hess's (1993) model describes the need for personalization of socialization processes and addresses outcomes (e.g., group effectiveness) that result from successful assimilation of newcomers. The central premise is that newcomers experience normlessness and aliena-

tion when socialization practices consist mainly of task information and do not address their personal needs to assimilate and identify with the group's culture.

THEORETICAL FRAMEWORK FOR PROPOSED MODELS OF GROUP SOCIALIZATION

Structuration, Functional, and Symbolic Convergence theories provide solid foundations for constructing communication models of group processes (see Poole, 1990), and these theories helped shape the ideas advanced in this chapter about socialization processes in groups. Because these theories are discussed elsewhere in this volume (see Chapters 1 [Gouran], 2 [Poole], and 7 [Hirokawa & Salazar]), the discussion here concerns the value of phase models and the role of Uncertainty Reduction Theory in group communication research, for they have both influenced thinking about how communication and socialization processes relate to each other.

Phase Models

Phase models are particularly useful because they focus on ways in which communication in groups follows patterns and develops in stages or phases. *Phases* are defined as "qualitatively different subperiods within a total continuous period of interaction" (Bales & Strodtbeck, 1951, p. 485). Assumptions of most phase models are that each phase has distinct characteristics, some characteristics cut across phases, and groups may remain in one phase indefinitely (see Cissna, 1984; Gouran & Fisher, 1984).

The phase approach has been useful for understanding various aspects of group communication. For example, unitary phase models, such as Bales and Strodtbeck's (1951) three-phase model of orientation, evaluation, and control, have inspired more complex models, such as the multiple sequence model (see Poole & Baldwin, 1996), that describe multiple and recursive changes in communicative behaviors in decision-making groups (in this volume, see Chapters 2 [Poole] and 3 [Mabry]).

Historically, phase models have proven convenient for discussions of linear stages of socialization processes in organizations. Van Maanen's (1976) representative model, for example, describes three linear phases of socializing new organizational members: anticipatory (e.g., newcomers form expectations), encounter (learnings from day-to-day experiences), and metamorphosis (e.g., their acceptance of the organization's culture). Exemplar work by Jablin (1982, 1984, 1985) has described and examined more fully characteristics of each phase to explain the effects of newcomers' expectations and communication experiences during socialization. One flaw in these linear models is their suggestion that newcomers progress directly toward metamorphosis when, in fact, they can regress to prior phases or never become fully assimilated (Hess, 1993).

In this chapter, a phase approach frames the communication-based models of group socialization advanced, with the understanding that the progression of socialization processes can be nonlinear. Each phase presents a convenient way to address, from both an individual member and a group perspective, essential characteristics that explain how communication serves to shape socialization activities associated with participating in group tasks and developing intragroup relationships.

Uncertainty Reduction Theory

Berger (1975, 1979) and Berger and Calabrese (1975) formulated Uncertainty Reduction Theory (URT) on the basis of Heider's (1958) belief in the "natural" human tendency to make sense of the world. The central premise of URT is that uncertainty about self, others, and how to behave motivates an individual to seek information. Although URT was developed as an interpersonal communication theory (see Berger, 1987), the basic template has been applied in theory and research on socialization in organizational communica-

tion contexts (e.g., Falcione & Wilson, 1988; Kramer, 1994; Lester, 1987; Mignerey, Rubin, & Gorden, 1995; Riddle, 1994; Teboul, 1997).

In describing URT, Berger and Calabrese (1975) created axioms and deduced theorems for three phases of relational development: entry (characterized by learning rules and norms), personal (clarifying issues, such as values), and exit (dissolving relationships). Berger (1975) and Clatterbuck (1979) explained that, in initial interactions, uncertainty reduction consists of proactive communicative behaviors (e.g., seeking information) and retroactive attributions (e.g., explaining past actions). By observing and engaging in communication, individuals acquire information that helps to reduce uncertainty about past and current behaviors and to predict future behaviors. The greater the amount of information acquired, the more uncertainty is reduced and the more accurate predictions are likely to be.

Uncertainty Reduction Theory has also been applied to explaining socialization processes in organizations. Falcione and Wilson's (1988) descriptive model of socialization processes, for example, traces how patterns of communication between newcomers and established members contribute to reducing newcomers' uncertainty about jobs and organizations by providing the information necessary for making predictions about meeting personal goals, developing appropriate roles, and achieving organizational outcomes.

Given URT's application to interpersonal and organizational contexts, and that the group context shares some of the properties of these contexts, the theory should offer insight into group socialization processes. As Kramer (1994) notes, some level of uncertainty is experienced by individuals in every group experience. Thus applied, URT should explain how new and established members communicate to reduce uncertainty about their own behavior, group processes, intragroup member relationships, and group task performance.

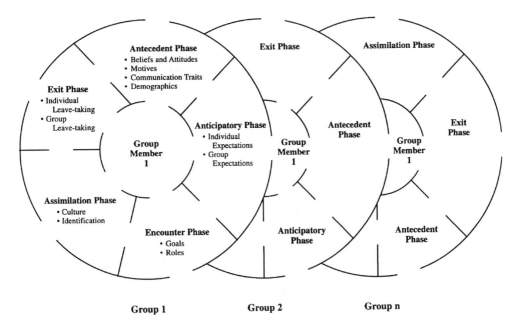

Figure 6.1. Group Socialization Model: Individual Members
NOTE: The model illustrates that in a group, individual members move through temporally and developmentally distinct socialization phases in a nonlinear cycle. Simultaneously, individuals belong to other groups that are likely to be in different phases of socialization processes.

COMMUNICATION MODELS OF GROUP SOCIALIZATION

Two models are introduced that integrate research on communication, socialization, and groups within the theoretical frameworks, definition of socialization, assumptions about the process, and chapter objectives advanced above. The model for individual members is a microlevel model that provides a conceptual framework for explaining how communication helps members and a group adapt and adjust in creating and shaping a unique culture. The model illustrates how distinct phases and essential characteristics appropriate to group processes provide foundations for understanding communication during socialization processes, while retaining the fluid nature of the initial and continuous socialization of members. Furthermore, socialization processes influence and affect individuals and groups not only in solo but also in multiple group experiences, because individuals hold membership in more than one group at any given time and past group experiences influence future group experiences. Because individuals are changed by group communication, as are groups, a perspective that addresses how individuals and groups change is essential to understanding socialization. Following discussion of the socialization model for individual members, a corollary model is briefly discussed that places emphasis on socialization processes for groups.

Group Socialization Model: Individual Members

The model describing individual members' experience of being socialized into groups addresses five phases: antecedent, anticipatory, encounter, assimilation, and exit (see Figure 6.1). These phases categorize the progression of the socialization process with respect to communicative practices and activities, with each phase distinguished by specific characteristics that influence the socialization process for individuals. The model encompasses several group experiences and suggests that individuals simultaneously belong to multiple groups; hence, the illustration is of multiple wheels. Furthermore, the wheels suggest that individuals are located in time and space in different phases of socialization in the multiple groups to which they belong.

In conceptualizing the model for individual members, assumptions were made concerning the socialization maturation process. Individuals bring to groups personal characteristics and a library of experiences of being in groups, adapt to groups and members through communicative behaviors that help reduce uncertainty, change roles on the basis of the development of group processes, and, as a result, make changes in their library of experiences that, then, influence their socialization in simultaneous and subsequent groups. Several assumptions also underlie the maturation process for groups. Some groups are newly formed; others add new members. As groups move through socialization phases, they may adapt or change when newcomers enter, accept or reject members, move through the processes at varying rates, and find it necessary to revisit phases of the process to resocialize less committed members.

Each phase in the model contains important characteristics that influence the socialization process, yet the characteristics can and often do permeate other phases (see Barge & Frey, 1997; Hess, 1993). These characteristics are neither exhaustive nor necessarily original; they have been recast by employing characteristics known to influence socialization processes in groups and organizations. The following discussion of each phase references relevant research and describes how communication influences socialization.

Antecedent Phase

Individuals bring beliefs and attitudes, motives, personality, and other types of antecedent factors (e.g., knowledge) to group experiences (see Bond & Shiu, 1997; Bonito & Hollingshead, 1997; Gouran, 1994; Haslett & Ruebush, Chapter 5, this volume). These antecedent factors influence people's susceptibility, readiness, and acceptability of socialization. They also influence how people approach group work, accept group goals, participate in group tasks, and build intragroup relationships. In effect, antecedent factors affect individual and group processes and outcomes (Mignerey et al., 1995; Smith & Berg, 1987). Antecedent factors also affect the illusions new members have about groups (Polzer, Kramer, & Neale, 1997) and judgments established members make about the acceptability of newcomers (Moreland, 1985). Even though some groups have an established culture into which newcomers are socialized, whereas other groups may be new or relatively new and must develop a culture, both types of groups are influenced by what individuals bring with them (Jones, 1983). In essence, the convergence of antecedent factors characterizes a group's unique and variable composition and has serious implications for group socialization. The antecedent factors selected for purposes of the discussion here are beliefs and attitudes, motives, communication traits, and demographics.

Beliefs and attitudes. Individuals bring to groups their beliefs and attitudes about groups, such as those about group work and the type of relationships they wish to form with other members. They enter new groups with salient beliefs about the activities and interactions that should take place, established from previous groups to which they belonged (Scheerhorn & Geist, 1997). As Moreland (1985) explains, individuals' adjustment to new groups is influenced by prior group experiences and existing social networks.

Beliefs and attitudes toward groups are related to personality and prior group experiences. For example, individuals with high needs for autonomy and control may enter groups with negative attitudes toward participatory decision making and, thus, hinder socialization processes by engaging in non-cooperative behaviors. Individuals with many positive group experiences probably approach new groups with more optimism than people whose group experiences have been primarily negative and may, therefore, hate groups. "Grouphate" describes the negative view that some people have of working in groups (Sorensen, 1981; see Keyton, Chapter 8, this volume), which can influence their active participation in group socialization and group work activities (see Keyton, Harmon, & Frey, 1996). Sinclair-James and Stohl (1997) claim that negative feelings about groups and members can carry over to subsequent group situations.

Motives. Motives for joining groups can influence people's approach to groups and group work. Schutz (1966) identified the needs of inclusion, control, and affection that motivate individuals to join groups (see Keyton, Chapter 8, this volume). He saw group members as differing in needs to associate with others (inclusion), direct behaviors or be directed by others (control), and express positive feelings in their relationships (affection). Extending Schutz's ideas, Rubin and Martin (1998) argue that a needs perspective of motives suggests *things lacking,* whereas a broadened view from a communication lens suggests that motives explain *reasons why* individuals communicate.

Motives for communicating with others are relatively general and consistent dispositions to communicate (Atkinson, 1965) that influence contextually who speaks to whom and what they talk about (Rubin & Martin, 1998). For example, Rubin, Perse, and Barbato (1988) identified such motives as escape and relaxation as reasons why individuals interact interpersonally. Research on people's motives in groups, in general, suggests that when members interact to meet needs of inclusion and affection, and not to meet needs of control and escape, they experience greater satisfaction and perceive their groups as being more cohesive (Anderson & Martin, 1995; Martin & Anderson, 1998). As applied to group socialization, members who communicate more for

inclusion and affection may work harder and more effectively at becoming socialized than those who are low on these needs. Additionally, those who communicate for control needs are more goal oriented in their communicative behaviors. Members who communicate for control reported after a group situation that they communicated more in group interactions compared to members with less pronounced control tendencies (Martin & Anderson, 1998). Following this reasoning, individuals with a high need for control might take a more active role in socializing others into groups. Highly motivated people, then, may be more receptive and help promote group socialization.

Communication traits. Participation in groups is influenced by members' personality and communication traits. The effects of various personality traits in groups are documented elsewhere (see Bonito & Hollingshead, 1997; Davies, 1994); hence, the focus here is on communication traits. *Communication traits* are defined as a subset of personality traits that explain individuals' consistencies and differences in message-sending and message-receiving behaviors (see Infante & Rancer, 1996). The discussion here is of communication apprehension, argumentativeness, and verbal aggressiveness, because these traits have proven salient in interpersonal and organizational research and should also prove relevant to group socialization.

Communication apprehension describes one's level of comfort in communicating in a variety of situations, including the context of groups (McCroskey, 1977). The presence of this trait in group members creates barriers to socialization processes both for members and for groups, because socialization processes are more difficult for people who are deficient in social/communication skills (Driskell, Hogan, & Salas, 1987). For example, in groups, highly apprehensive individuals talk less, avoid conflicts, are perceived more negatively, and are less liked by members than individuals who are not apprehensive about communicating (McCroskey, Hamilton, & Weiner, 1974;

McCroskey & Richmond, 1990, 1992; see Haslett & Ruebush, Chapter 5, this volume). Highly apprehensive people also attend fewer meetings and report less group cohesiveness (Anderson & Martin, 1995; Hawkins & Stewart, 1991). These types of communicative behaviors and perceptions would make it more difficult for members of new groups to socialize with one other or for members in established groups to help newcomers adapt, and vice versa. Communication apprehension, however, tends to diminish with additional group experiences (Keyton et al., 1996).

Argumentativeness involves making and refuting arguments (Infante & Rancer, 1982; Rancer, 1998), whereas *verbal aggressiveness* involves attacking the self-concept of another (Infante & Wigley, 1986; Wigley, 1998). Research on these traits has shown that members who are argumentative and not verbally aggressive express greater satisfaction with communication and perceive their groups as reaching higher levels of consensus and cohesion than members who are not argumentative but are verbally aggressive (Anderson & Martin, 1999). Argumentative members also make contributions that are more active, rational, and thorough than their low-argumentative counterparts (see Infante & Rancer, 1996). Because research suggests that verbally aggressive individuals alienate others (see Wigley, 1998), it seems safe to assume that group socialization processes would be affected by the inclusion of such members, regardless of whether they are new or established members (although this, too, may make a difference). In effect, then, members who are argumentative and/or verbally aggressive in groups could affect socialization processes in positive and negative ways, respectively.

Demographics. Some demographic influences in groups are discussed by Haslett and Ruebush (Chapter 5, this volume). Their relevance for socialization is clear in terms of the effects and stereotypes they engender in newcomers and established group members. Among other considerations, Davies (1994) reported that numerous studies show that race and gender influence how group members talk to one another. For example, Cohen (1982, 1984) found that when groups subdivide along racial distinctions, such as all Whites or all Blacks in a subgroup, stereotypes about race were reinforced, thus weakening group cohesion. As members seek to reduce uncertainty about a group and other members, such group practices may prevent assimilation of all members into the group's culture by leaving some members feeling like outsiders (Hess, 1993). Gender biases could also affect group socialization. Historically, men are identified more often as task leaders, whereas women are identified more often as relational leaders of groups (see Gouran & Fisher, 1984). Thus, women may be expected to provide supportive communication and feedback to newcomers, whereas men may be expected to provide functional information and feedback about task and role performance. Men also often have difficulty with women as task leaders, and both men and women report less affinity for having women as leaders (Bradley, 1980; Yerby, 1975), biases that could influence newcomers' openness to socialization processes in groups with female leaders.

Anticipatory Phase

For individuals and groups, the anticipatory phase describes the pre-affiliation expectations that group members form about each other. Mobley, Griffeth, Hand, and Meglino (1979) consider these expectations a part of the process of socialization because that process is affected by what both individuals and groups anticipate will happen. The more individuals and groups are accurate in their expectations about what will happen and the less inflated their communication expectations (e.g., about the supportive communication to be received), the more likely it is that socialization will succeed (Van Maanen, 1976, 1977). The following discussion examines individual and group expectations relative to the anticipatory phase of group socialization.

Individual expectations. Anticipatory socialization has been studied with respect to expectations that new employees have in choosing and entering organizations (Jablin, 1985). Newcomers often learn what they can about an organization prior to joining and use this information to form judgments about how they will fit in (Van Maanen, 1976). These judgments are influenced, in part, by "the way they have learned to deal with new situations" (Jones, 1983, p. 465). Additional influences on newcomers' expectations come from friends, peers, family members, the media, and other agents serving as sources of information (Jablin, 1985). Jablin (1987) even traces vocational socialization to childhood and suggests that young family members watch, listen, and question parents about their workplaces, and that these early experiences are used to frame their approaches to entering the world of work. Similarly, according to Ebaugh (1988), individuals learn how to interact in groups, in part, from modeling interactions in their family (see Socha, Chapter 17, this volume) and early group experiences in schools (see Allen & Plax, Chapter 18, this volume).

Based on the findings of organizational socialization research, group researchers and those who facilitate groups can expect that new members will be trying to work through the transition from previous group experiences (Zahrly & Tosi, 1989). These experiences affect how they form expectations about the types of relationships they want with other members and the types of role behaviors in which they will engage (Hess, 1993; Jablin, 1982). Newcomers tend to worry about failure (Lester, 1987), lack confidence in their ability to assimilate into new groups (Colby, Hopf, & Ayres, 1993; Jones, 1983, 1986), and experience frustration from an absence of information, conflicting information, or too much information (Van Maanen, 1976, 1977).

Feldman (1976) notes that newcomers attempt to estimate whether their needs for individual identity and personal control will be satisfied and that successful adjustment is jeopardized when their predictions about

these conditions are not confirmed after entry. Because variations between expectations and reality cause uncertainty, Louis (1980) suggests that unrealistic expectations cause surprise after entry, which often creates a stressful and unsuccessful adaptation. Severe cases of surprise and maladjustment often result in a person exiting a group.

Group expectations. For groups, the anticipatory phase begins when individuals agree to form a group or when newcomers agree to join an established group (Rynes & Barber, 1990). In the latter case, established members anticipate the entry of new members and have expectations about them (Moreland & Levine, 1982). Groups that are more receptive to newcomers (e.g., form positive expectations about them) would be more likely to understand the changes that may occur in the group following the addition of new members. Whether individuals enter newly formed or established groups, members are expected to accept the group's goals, even though personal goals, at times, may supersede group goals in priority (Mackie & Goethals, 1987).

Although studies have detailed important aspects of the anticipatory socialization phase, few assess and relate the experiences of this phase with outcomes experienced by groups (Jablin, 1987). For example, established members may expect newcomers to remain silent on entering the new group and not be argumentative and refute their opinions. This example of a group expectation could subsequently affect communication in the group by suggesting who should speak most often and how (Bonito & Hollingshead, 1997). Similarly, it could affect socialization processes if newcomers are afraid to voice opinions.

The uncertainty of the anticipatory phase often can be reduced through formal group and organizational socialization practices. For example, Adelman and Frey (1997) reported that prospective residents at an AIDS residential facility received information packages, were interviewed by the staff, toured the house, met residents, and shared a meal with them. These audition practices (Sigman,

1985-1986) "help newcomers establish realistic, rather than inflated, expectations" (Adelman & Frey, 1997, p. 33). In newly formed groups, members who receive information about one another prior to the encounter phase experience less tension about being in the group because their uncertainty about members is reduced (Booth-Butterfield, Booth-Butterfield, & Koester, 1988).

Encounter Phase

Socialization practices constitute the learning process that officially begins in the encounter phase with full force (Reichers, 1987; Teboul, 1997). This phase is a period of indefinite length that involves members beginning to adjust, fit in, negotiate roles, and exhibit appropriate communicative behaviors. Encounter occurs when members compare expectations formed during the anticipatory socialization phase with the reality of group life (Van Maanen, 1976). Pre-affiliation perceptions and expectations are confirmed or disconfirmed, and inaccurate ones are reconstructed (Louis, 1980).

During the encounter phase, groups begin creating a culture, structure, and operating process as members establish norms and rules, some of which are about communication patterns. Scheerhorn and Geist (1997) define *norms* as the "recurrent patterns of behavior or thinking" (p. 92) that members come to accept as their way of being a group and doing group work, whereas *rules* are agreements about how to behave appropriately. Learning group norms and rules can be difficult for newcomers who enter large groups (Driskell et al., 1987), and, of course, in the case of new groups, members must create norms and rules. One reason why this process may be difficult is because group norms and rules can conflict with those individuals have used in prior groups.

Riggs and Knight (1994) found that newcomers' perceptions of group success or failure during the encounter phase affects the formation of their attitudes about group goals and member relationships. Newcomers begin

to compare how the new group differs from other groups with respect to tasks, relationships, processes, and activities, and whether the new group will succeed in meeting personal, as well as, group goals. Similarly, a group as a collective unit attempts to cope with the socializing of newcomers. Craig's (1996) investigation noted that even the timing of entering a task group as a solo newcomer made a difference, in that established members initially perceived and judged the newcomer's open-mindedness and contributions more positively than they did when several newcomers joined the group at the same time.

Goals and roles are two concepts that influence socialization during the encounter phase. Both individual and group goals and role expectations and behaviors are important topics for group discussion as members and the group strive to reduce uncertainty about each other and group outcomes. The following discussion illustrates the significance of these two concepts for understanding group socialization processes.

Goals. Gouran (1994) suggests that *goals* are what individuals and group members as a collective consider desired "end states" to achieve from joining/forming groups, engaging in group work, and establishing intragroup relationships. Individuals entering a group have personal goals for becoming members that may include attraction toward the group's goals (Sherif & Sherif, 1953). When the group's goals are attractive, newcomers engage in perceptual processes and communicative behaviors to determine the extent to which a group and its members can satisfy personal goals. For example, newcomers who seek job advancement may be more willing than other members who do not have that goal to take an active role in decision-making processes and task completion by contributing more time and effort to ensure that the group output is of the highest quality.

Groups are also confronted in the encounter phase by their task and relational goals. Rugs and Kaplan (1993) found that group task goals (e.g., quality decision making) facilitated information giving and sharing among members, whereas relational goals (e.g., mutual goodwill) facilitated discussion of acceptable behaviors and practices. Bales (1953) points out, however, that goals for maintaining relationships and performing tasks sometimes can be in conflict and that when this happens, groups confront equilibrium problems (in this volume, see Chapters 8 [Keyton] and 12 [Pavitt]).

Mackie and Goethals (1987) contend that, ideally, members and groups should strive for and achieve "goal isomorphism" (p. 145) by finding a balance between personal and group goals. Organizational socialization practices suggest that achieving such a balance leads to important outcomes, such as members' commitment. The strength of commitment depends on the valence of information-seeking and information-giving socialization tactics used by members and groups to reduce uncertainty about reaching goals (Allen & Meyer, 1990; Jones, 1986; Mignerey et al., 1995). In contrast, as Putnam and Poole (1987) point out, conflicts arise when the goals of individuals and groups are incompatible or cannot be balanced effectively. Thus, incompatible goals can affect socialization processes for both members and groups, especially when multiple group commitments force individuals to set priorities and make choices about continued membership.

Roles. One critical group activity is orienting members to their expected or negotiated roles (Benne & Sheats, 1948; Jones, 1983). The focus during the encounter phase is the complementary adjustment and accommodation between individual members and the group concerning desirable role behaviors and the appropriateness of each individual's choice (Katz & Kahn, 1978). Salazar (1996) characterizes this process as the positioning of group members in role space along group building/maintenance and task dimensions.

Members learn role behaviors as they monitor their new environments by observing situational cues and the communicative behaviors of others (Ashford & Cummings, 1983). Jablin (1985) explains that newcomers learn about role expectations through communication to and from established members who are associated with the task. In the case of newly formed groups, members rely on their beliefs about and history of enacting appropriate role behaviors in groups, and they are influenced by their motives for membership when competing with other members for role positions (Katz & Kahn, 1978; Zahrly & Tosi, 1989). Although the establishment of competence in role behaviors more than likely overlaps from the encounter to the assimilation phase that follows, role behaviors exhibited by group members during the encounter phase become patterned and expected over time. Consequently, when roles change, often as a result of adding new members, role strain occurs as members anticipate new roles and must learn how to behave in new ways (Moreland & Levine, 1984).

From a communication perspective, group members learn about or construct roles and role behavior by seeking information and feedback from others (Lester, 1987; Morrison, 1993a; Teboul, 1997). Feedback helps members not only to learn and evaluate role performance (Ashford, 1986; Ashford & Cummings, 1983), but also to feel supported in their roles by other group members (Meyers, 1998). Primary communication motives focus on alleviating tensions associated with being new (Moreland & Levine, 1982), getting acquainted (Rubin, 1990), and gaining acceptance by group members (Anderson & Martin, 1995; Booth-Butterfield et al., 1988; Schutz, 1966). In general, newcomers are motivated to reduce uncertainty about acceptable role behaviors and task-performance competencies (Lester, 1987; Morrison, 1993a; Salazar, 1996; Zahrly & Tosi, 1989).

Organizational research shows that newcomers respond to their roles differently on the basis of the socialization tactics used to shape the information they receive (Van Maanen & Schein, 1979). For example, Jones (1986) discovered that organizational newcomers socialized in more informal ways (e.g., through interpersonal interactions) adopted innovative orientations toward their roles, whereas those exposed to more formal procedures (e.g., group training) adopted maintenance role orientations that continued the established way of doing things.

Reichers (1987) suggests that the rate at which newcomers and groups move through the socialization process is a "function of proaction and interaction frequency on the part of newcomers and insiders" (p. 282). Morrison (1995) found that newcomers higher in information-seeking abilities were socialized more effectively into groups than those with lower abilities. Within an organizational context, the information that newcomers seek includes such topics as who are influential people outside the group who affect the group, organizational or group politics, and group history (Chao, O'Leary-Kelly, Wolf, Klein, & Gardner, 1994). They typically ask directly for technical and normative information from peers and leaders (Ashford, 1986; Comer, 1991; Morrison, 1993a, 1993b; Ostroff & Kozlowski, 1992) and often resort to overt or even indirect questioning of third parties (Meyers, 1998; Miller & Jablin, 1991). All such information is prioritized according to its usefulness (Morrison, 1995).

Assimilation Phase

Assimilation is a process of full integration into a group culture. A popular description of *culture* is the set of thoughts and customs that constitute a common interpretive framework for guiding members' experiences (Jablin, 1982; Levine & Moreland, 1991). Assimilation occurs when members are absorbed into a culture (Jablin, 1982) and establish a shared identity through symbolic interaction that builds group cohesion (Hess, 1993). In the light of Jablin's (1984) reasoning, assimilation occurs when newcomers become comfortable in a group or begin to communicate ideas and engage more assertively in behaviors affecting the development of group goals, tasks, procedures, and relationships. At the same time, assimilation means that established members communicate acceptance of newcomers, en-

tertain their ideas, and offer support. Thus, members engage in communicative practices that both influence and support one another as they create and recreate their group structures and perform such necessary functions as making decisions. Some research even indicates that newcomers have been socialized when evidence of changes in a group and its structure, including maintenance behaviors, is apparent (see Jablin, 1987).

In established groups, as previously explained, assimilation is no longer viewed as a linear, one-directional process in which newcomers must adapt to an existing group culture. McComb (1995) reasons that assimilation is achieved when established members and newcomers blend into a comfortable state of working together toward goals and tasks. The process of blending together does not always unfold smoothly, however, and both individuals and groups may need to re-initiate adaptation processes over the course of a group's life. Tension among members may also surface in response to new members, goals, tasks, and role behaviors. These changes may require members, either individually or collectively, to revisit the anticipatory and encounter phases previously experienced. Such apparent regressions can occur several times during a group's life span, with established members often initiating efforts to re-establish a good person and group fit (Smith & Berg, 1987).

Group culture and identification are two concepts that are helpful in understanding the assimilation phase of socialization. Both concepts share the idea that socialization is a process of mutual communicative influence among group members. The following discussion illustrates the significance of these two concepts for understanding group socialization.

Culture. In an organizational context, culture is a root metaphor describing what organizations are, not something they have (Smircich, 1983). This root metaphor helps explain socialization of newcomers into organizations, although it is difficult for researchers to identify and determine the effects of culture because of the variability of disciplinary perspectives about it (see Smircich & Calas, 1987). For example, Pacanowsky and O'Donnell-Trujillo (1982) propose a cultural perspective that seeks to answer questions concerning communicative activities (e.g., vocabulary) unique to an organization and how members make sense of their experiences within it. Framed within an interpretive approach to culture, the communication of organizational reality occurs through the words and symbols members use (Putnam, 1982). Similarly, ethnographic researchers describe how interactants use symbolic forms, such as stories, to interpret and make sense of organizations (e.g., Adelman & Frey, 1997; Brown, 1985; Trujillo, 1986, 1992).

A cultural approach to groups suggests that interdependent members create an entity like no other (e.g., assimilate) and make sense of what they do through participating in communicative behaviors unique to that group (Swogger, 1981). This approach suggests that culture is endemic in groups and permeates all phases and aspects of group life. In explaining group processes, Deal and Kennedy's (1982) dimensions of organizational culture are useful. These authors argue that *values* raise issues of right and wrong, *heroes* provide role models for behaviors, *rites* and *rituals* serve to acknowledge symbolic events and member accomplishments, and *communication networks* are essential in conveying to members information about the cultural characteristics of the environment.

According to Pacanowsky and O'Donnell-Trujillo (1982), organizational culture is learned by observing and participating in communicative behaviors; hence, it is essential that newcomers observe the behaviors and practices of group members. In new groups, socialization occurs as a result of communicative behaviors that create the beliefs, values, norms, roles, rules, and assumptions held by members as they uncover similarities and differences among themselves while negotiating the creation of a unique group culture (Feldman, 1981).

A cultural approach is particularly applicable to the assimilation phase of group socialization because the influence of group culture is probably felt and experienced most by newcomers who are trying to advance to full membership. Newcomers, in contrast to established members, are especially challenged to make sense of new group experiences. The concept of *sense making* is central to understanding culture (Louis, 1980; Trujillo, 1992). For example, it can be a motivating force behind uncertainty reduction strategies in which group members proactively engage in such behaviors as seeking information to learn about role performance (Meyers, 1998). Newcomers and established members, however, walk a fine line between adopting a group's culture and attempting to change it. Both become active agents in changing a group's culture while interacting with and adapting to it through the communicative behaviors unique to achieving group tasks and establishing member relations. The speed with which culture is learned or negotiated and accepted affects the time it takes for the assimilation of newcomers in groups, and vice versa (Moreland, 1985).

Identification. Studies of organizational identification offer another useful perspective on group socialization (see Bullis & Bach, 1989). According to Cheney (1983a), *identification* with a social collective (e.g., organization) occurs when members see their own values or interests coinciding with those of the collective. Identification is a powerful indicator that an individual begins to see the social collective and him- or herself conjoined. In Cheney's (1983b) terms, the "outer voice" of an organization and the individual's "inner voice" speak the same values, beliefs, and ideas and, thus, when the individual speaks, it is on behalf of both the self and the organization. Ferraris, Carveth, and Parrish-Sprowl (1993) add that identification results in feelings of membership, or "anchoring the self" (p. 344). Communication symbols or patterns that reflect "we-ness" on the part of group members, and, thereby, demonstrate that individual and group identity are conjoined, are strong evidence of successful socialization.

In the context of a two-way process, one issue concerns the extent to which individuals can change the values and beliefs of organizations, or, for purposes of this chapter, groups. Cheney and Tompkins (1987) see identification as both product and process. As individuals and the collective interact, a person's and the group's conceptualization of identity changes; identity, therefore, is created and recreated through interaction. This conception of identification is consistent with the view that members' communicative behaviors lead to changes on the part of both members and groups.

Exit Phase

Van Gennep (1908/1960) describes the exiting of individuals from groups or the leave-taking process as moving through phases of separation, transition, and incorporation. Individuals leave groups, search for other groups, and join new groups. An important consideration is that both individuals who leave a group and the remaining group members draw on prior experiences as influences affecting their reaction to each other. In effect, the exiting individual and the group engage in the socialization process as influenced by prior socialization experiences.

Some groups (e.g., families) may never disband, although they change as new members join and others leave. In some groups, disgruntled members leave or are forced to leave and the group continues; in others, the entire group disbands. Leaving a group can be initiated by individual members or by groups based on conditions that range from task completion to group dysfunction (Rose, 1989). Regardless of whether a leave-taking experience goes well or poorly, exiting groups often is traumatic for individuals and groups (Di Salvo, Nikkel, & Monroe, 1989).

In the exit phase, issues of interest focus on why members leave or groups disband, how endings take place, how communication

changes, and what is next for former members and/or remaining group members (Rose, 1989). Although group communication scholars acknowledge the important implications of the exit phase (see Sinclair-James & Stohl, 1997), they have largely neglected it (Keyton, 1993). The following discussion illustrates the importance of considering the leave-taking effects of the exit phase for both individuals and groups.

Individual leave-taking. According to Moreland and Levine (1982), the exit phase is complicated by the fact that individuals can psychologically leave before or during any phase of group development and become marginal members who display low commitment. During the formal exit phase, however, soon-to-be ex-members engage in reflection and evaluation of the group and member relationships they are leaving behind. They also form attitudes and impressions of the group experience to add to their library of experiences. Ebaugh (1988) suggests that as individuals leave the role of member behind, they search for post-group roles, often re-identifying with current or subsequent groups and accepting new role behaviors within them.

When leaving groups voluntarily, individuals can assist in the exit process by giving notice of leaving, working toward a smooth transition, and continuing some type of relationship with the group after exiting (Sinclair-James & Stohl, 1997). The importance of these behaviors is clear, for communication that happens during an individual's exit from a group affects how that individual acts in simultaneous or future groups (Keyton, 1993). When an individual has a satisfying group experience, including a good exit, that individual is more likely to be an active participant in other groups and may be more receptive to socialization processes.

Group leave-taking. For many groups (e.g., church, civic, school, sports, and organizational work groups), turnover is common. When there is turnover in a group, remaining members spend time dealing with relational issues that revolve around the loss of the member and, if a new member is added, how his or her replacement fits in (Kramer, 1993, 1994). Established members may sometimes resent those who left the group or may not understand the reasons for the exit. To prevent more members from leaving the group, a group must assess why members are leaving. One way of uncovering this information is to ask them (Sinclair-James & Stohl, 1997). Group members may also resent the fact that valuable time will have to be spent socializing new members (Kramer, 1993, 1994).

Some groups manage quite effectively the leaving of members and the welcoming of new members. The departure of a member, coupled with the addition of one or more new members, can breathe new life into a group (see Sinclair-James & Stohl, 1997). Leaving and entering processes, therefore, offer groups opportunities to define and redefine themselves. In effect, groups that excel at smooth transitions (i.e., deal well with exiting members and socializing new members) should be more effective at reaching their goals. In contrast, when an entire group disbands, all members experience the tensions produced by relinquishing group responsibilities, and they also confront relational issues, such as how to retain friendships with others from the group. Keyton (1993) suggests that when a group ends, members should devote a final meeting to evaluating the group experience and giving themselves a chance to say good-by.

Group Socialization Model: Groups

Although the model discussed above focused primarily on how individuals are socialized into groups, a dual perspective of socialization suggests that the process affects both individuals and groups. To explicate the effects of socialization at the group level, a socialization model for groups that is the corollary of the model for individual members is offered (see Figure 6.2). The model for groups implies that groups have permeable boundaries that permit outside influences to affect the socialization process. Furthermore, groups form and mature at variable rates in progressing through the five phases of beginning, anticipatory, encounter, assimilation, and ending. Although the phases are presented below in a linear manner, as with the model for individual members introduced earlier, it should be remembered that groups may go directly from the beginning phase to the assimilation phase and perhaps later regress to the anticipatory phase. Groups also vary in terms of the amount of time spent in each of the phases. Some groups, depending on the experience and expertise of its members, can move very rapidly through phases or perhaps skip some of the first three phases and move directly to the assimilation phase, where it is likely that the most serious and enduring task functions are accomplished before disbanding the group. The following brief discussion highlights the socialization phases for groups.

The *beginning* phase of group socialization occurs when the idea for group formation arises. Group goals and plans are formed by the person(s) responsible for creating a group. As one example, a senior executive decides that a team is needed to achieve a particular task and determines the number and type of group members who will be part of the team. The *anticipatory* phase involves selecting prospective members, planning potential group activities, and supplying pre-affiliation information to members. The *encounter* phase is the period when the group first meets and begins its work. Through members' interactions, the group begins to form a culture, define member roles, and establish task and relational objectives and procedures. In the *assimilation* phase, the group has clearly established a culture, and there is a sense among members as to how well the group is functioning (e.g., how quickly and efficiently the group is progressing toward its goals), what problems are to be solved, and the resources needed for both task work and relational maintenance. Changes in group goals, culture, or practices may be seen through the actions of influential group members. The *ending*

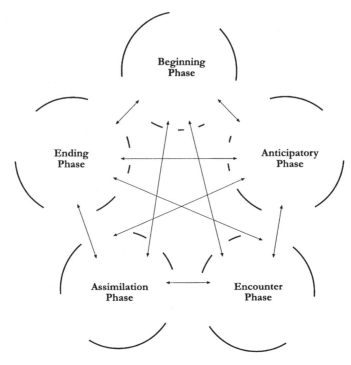

Figure 6.2. Group Socialization Model: Groups
NOTE: The model illustrates that each group moves through developmentally distinct socialization phases in a nonlinear cycle.

phase occurs when members recognize that a group has either accomplished its goals and no longer needs to meet or, for other reasons (e.g., time pressures), members discontinue meeting.

SETTING THE AGENDA FOR COMMUNICATION RESEARCH ON GROUP SOCIALIZATION

The communication-based phase models of group socialization introduced in this chapter represent frameworks from which to research socialization processes in groups. According to Barge and Frey (1997), the quality and success of group life experienced at both the individual and group levels depend on how various dialectical tensions are managed, especially those tied to goals, tasks, and relationships. The discussions in this chapter suggest that the quality and success of member and group life are, in part, determined by sociali-

zation processes, especially in terms of the management of tensions experienced over the course of a group's life span.

In essence, the models presented provide foundations for theory and research about the communication effects of socialization processes in groups. These models extend the scope of previous models of socialization, although researchers are encouraged to theorize about essential characteristics that are missing in each phase. There may also be other phases of individual and group development in addition to the ones identified in the models that can clarify how communication affects socialization. In terms of setting specific research agendas, researchers should consider complementary efforts in diverse disciplines and integrating group, organizational, and interpersonal communication research (see Crandall, 1978; Gouran, 1994). The following discussion identifies the primary needs in each of these three research areas.

Group Research

Researchers can draw on established theories as explanations of group socialization processes. For example, Structuration Theory explains the ways in which rules and resources are appropriated by group members to create and recreate group structures (in this volume, see chapters 1 [Gouran], 2 [Poole], and 7 [Hirokawa & Salazar]). The theory seems especially appropriate for understanding socialization processes, because, as discussed in this chapter, socialization processes are fundamentally concerned with how rules, resources, and structures are constructed and changed over the course of a group's existence.

The models presented also need to be fleshed out in important ways. For example, the model for individual members includes antecedent factors because such scholars as Gouran (1994), Frey (1997), Haslett and Ruebush (chapter 5, this volume), and Keyton and Frey (in press) have argued for their importance when explaining group communication processes. One way of expanding the model would be to consider the differences in resources that individuals bring to groups. For example, members differ in the knowledge, information, and communication skills they possess. Such resources as money and time also influence whether members join groups and how socialization unfolds. Lastly, the investigation of antecedent environmental factors might focus on how the facilitative and inhibitive structures that are in place affect newcomers and established members alike, such as those found in community and volunteer groups (see, respectively, Adelman & Frey, 1997; McComb, 1995).

Interesting questions that researchers might ask concern how communication and group socialization processes influence the practices that members (both new and established) engage in as they enter, adapt, change role behaviors, and exit groups, as well as how these processes and practices influence people's simultaneous and subsequent group experiences (Louis, 1980). By applying Uncertainty Reduction Theory and established group theories to investigate the characteristics found in each phase of the model for individual members, scholars can move beyond description of the socialization process to predictive models. In particular, researchers might investigate the predictive potential of members' communication traits during the encounter, assimilation, and exit phases for explaining effective or ineffective socialization (e.g., development of commitment to a group). They may also want to consider how socialization processes influence member satisfaction and/or other outcomes (Hess, 1993).

One criticism of group research is that researchers typically attend to positive outcomes and overlook negative ones. A significant research contribution would be to examine members' perceptions of ineffective communication (both verbal and nonverbal) during socialization processes. Another related research focus might be to understand how socialization processes contribute to negative impressions about groups, group work, or member relationships. Given that attitudes about group work are influential in affecting simultaneous and future group socialization processes (Falcione & Wilson, 1988), researchers need to determine the process by which such attitudes develop.

Organizational Research

Opportunities exist for collaborative efforts that apply what we know about organizational socialization processes to the context of groups, and vice versa, as the discussions in this chapter have shown. For example, organizational communication researchers have investigated the effects of socialization when newcomers replace senior group members (Kenny, Hallmark, Sullivan, & Kashy, 1993), and this focus may clarify how established members, especially those with seniority, react to newcomers in groups. Morrison (1993a, 1993b) also points out that many practices exist that influence socialization in organizations. For example, the mechanics of socialization may take the form of orientation programs (Ashforth & Saks, 1996; Reichers, Wanous, & Steele, 1994) and initiation practices (Hautaluoma, Enge, Mitchell, & Rittwager, 1991). These types of socialization practices seem worth investigating in the group context.

The material reviewed in this chapter also suggests a number of directions for future research on organizational socialization. Little attention has been given, for example, to conflict experienced by individuals over role performances in multiple groups and organizations. Studies of organizational socialization have also tended to focus on pre-entry and entry phases, but as the models presented here show, socialization processes occur over the course of a group's or organization's life span. Therefore, longitudinal studies of groups and organizations, which are employed less commonly than one-shot or short-term designs, are needed to study the entire socialization process (Bullis, 1993; Jablin, 1984).

Interpersonal Research

Group socialization research may also develop from the integration of interpersonal communication theories and principles. In this chapter, Uncertainty Reduction Theory proved useful in explaining group socialization processes. Although the implications and complexities surrounding the reduction of uncertainty about self and others' behaviors multiplies in groups, in comparison to dyadic interactions, Lester's (1987) work illustrates how uncertainty reduction is associated with effective organizational socialization. Group researchers can easily apply any one of the uncertainty reduction axioms advanced by Berger (1975) to the socialization of newcomers in established groups or members in newly formed groups.

Based on uncertainty reduction principles, the group socialization process could also be analyzed using discourse analysis, focusing on such forms as colloquialisms (Clair, 1996), memorable messages (Barge, Schlueter, & Hachtel, 1994; Stohl, 1986), and stories (Brown, 1985; Bullis, 1993). These foci seem especially appropriate for studying socialization processes, for these and other forms of discourse undoubtedly occur often and carry substantial weight in teaching new and established members about a particular group context.

CONCLUDING REMARKS

The models presented in this chapter lay foundations for conceptualizing how communication contributes to socialization processes in groups. These foundations provide unique opportunities to investigate how socialization processes affect group communication processes, practices, structures, and outcomes. Findings from such research undoubtedly will have value in terms of practical applications. They can help group members understand how socialization processes and practices influence the development of a high-quality group and how socialization experiences in one group are stored in their library of experiences and affect their behavior in other groups to which they do and will belong. This understanding, in turn, can assist members and groups in proactively creating a more meaningful socialization process, one that moves through the phases of adaptation and adjustment more effectively, and, thereby, strengthens chances for positive member experiences and effective group outcomes. Group educators and facilitators can use the models offered and the available and future research to create training modules in socialization practices and communicative behaviors that are designed to build members' competence in task/process skills and skills in building and maintaining meaningful member relationships. The study of communication and socialization in groups, thus, is important to scholars, practitioners, and group members alike.

REFERENCES

Adelman, M. B., & Frey, L. R. (1997). *The fragile community: Living together with AIDS.* Mahwah, NJ: Lawrence Erlbaum.

Allen, N. J., & Meyer, J. P. (1990). Organizational socialization tactics: A longitudinal analysis of links to newcomer's commitment and role orientation. *Academy
of Management Journal, 33,* 847-858.

Anderson, C. M., & Martin, M. M. (1995). The effects
of communication motives, interaction involvement,
and loneliness on satisfaction: A model of small
groups. *Small Group Research, 26,* 118-137.

Anderson, C. M., & Martin, M. M. (1999). How argumentativeness and verbal aggressiveness affect cohesion, consensus, and satisfaction in small groups.
Communication Reports, 12, 21-31.

Ashford, S. J. (1986). Feedback-seeking in individual
adaptation: A resource perspective. *Academy of Management Journal, 29,* 465-487.

Ashford, S. J., & Cummings, L. L. (1983). Feedback as an
individual resource: Personal strategies of creating
information. *Organization Behavior and Human Performance, 32,* 370-398.

Ashforth, B. E., & Saks, A. M. (1996). Socialization
tactics: Longitudinal effects on newcomer adjustment.
Academy of Management Journal, 39, 148-178.

Atkinson, J. K. (1965). Some general implications of
conceptual developments in the study of achievement-
oriented behavior. In M. R. Jones (Ed.), *Human motivation: A symposium* (pp. 3-29). Lincoln: University
of Nebraska Press.

Bales, R. F. (1953). The equilibrium problem in small
groups. In T. Parsons, R. F. Bales, & E. A. Shils (Eds.),
Working papers in the theory of action (pp. 111-161).
Glencoe, IL: Free Press.

Bales, R. F., & Strodtbeck, F. L. (1951). Phases in group
problem solving. *Journal of Abnormal and Social Psychology, 46,* 485-495.

Barge, J. K., & Frey, L. R. (1997). Life in a task group. In
L. R. Frey & J. K. Barge (Eds.), *Managing group life:
Communicating in decision-making groups* (pp. 29-
51). Boston: Houghton Mifflin.

Barge, J. K., Schlueter, D. W., & Hachtel, A. (1994,
November). *Memorable messages and newcomer socialization.* Paper presented at the annual meeting
of the Speech Communication Association, New
Orleans, LA.

Benne, K. D., & Sheats, P. (1948). Functional roles in
group members. *Journal of Social Issues, 4,* 41-49.

Berger, C. R. (1975). Proactive and retroactive attribution
processes in interpersonal communications. *Human
Communication Research, 2,* 33-50.

Berger, C. R. (1979). Beyond initial interaction: Uncertainty, understanding, and the development of interpersonal relationships. In H. Giles & R. St. Clair
(Eds.), *Language and social psychology* (pp. 122-144).
Baltimore, MD: University Park Press.

Berger, C. R. (1987). Communicating under uncertainty.
In M. E. Roloff & G. R. Miller (Eds.), *Interpersonal
processes: New directions in communication research*
(pp. 39-62). Newbury Park, CA: Sage.

Berger, C. R., & Calabrese, R. J. (1975). Some exploration in initial interaction and beyond: Toward a developmental theory of interpersonal communication.
Human Communication Research, 1, 99-112.

Bond, M. H., & Shiu, W. Y. (1997). The relationship
between a group's personality resources and the two
dimensions of its group process. *Small Group Research, 28,* 194-217.

Bonito, J. A., & Hollingshead, A. B. (1997). Participation
in small groups. In B. R. Burleson (Ed.), *Communication yearbook 20* (pp. 227-261). Thousand Oaks, CA:
Sage.

Booth-Butterfield, M., Booth-Butterfield, S., & Koester,
J. (1988). The function of uncertainty reduction in
alleviating primary tension in small groups. *Communication Research Reports, 5,* 146-153.

Bradley, P. H. (1980). Sex, competence, and opinion
deviation: An expectation states approach. *Communication Monographs, 47,* 101-110.

Brown, M. H. (1985). That reminds me of a story: Speech
action in organizational socialization. *Western Journal
of Speech Communication, 49,* 27-42.

Bullis, C. (1993). Organizational socialization research:
Enabling, constraining, and shifting perspectives.
Communication Monographs, 60, 10-17.

Bullis, C., & Bach, B. W. (1989). Socialization turning
points: An examination of change in organizational
identification. *Western Journal of Speech Communication, 53,* 273-293.

Caplow, T. (1964). *Principles of organization.* New York:
Harcourt, Brace & World.

Chao, G. T., O'Leary-Kelly, A. M., Wolf, S., Klein, H. J.,
& Gardner, P. D. (1994). Organizational socializa-
tion: Its content and consequences. *Journal of Applied
Psychology, 79,* 730-743.

Cheney, G. (1983a). On the various and changing meanings of organizational membership: A field study of
organization identification. *Communication Monographs, 50,* 342-362.

Cheney, G. (1983b). The rhetoric of identification and the
study of organizational communication. *Quarterly
Journal of Speech, 69,* 143-158.

Cheney, G., & Tompkins, P. (1987). Coming to terms with
organizational identification and commitment. *Central States Speech Journal, 38,* 1-15.

Cini, M. A., Moreland, R. L., & Levine, J. M. (1993).
Group staffing levels and responses to prospective and
new group members. *Journal of Personality and Social
Psychology, 65,* 723-734.

Cissna, K. N. (1984). Phases in group development: The
negative evidence. *Small Group Behavior, 15,* 3-32.

Clair, R. P. (1996). The political nature of the colloquial-
ism, "A real job": Implications for organizational socialization. *Communication Monographs, 63,* 249-
267.

Clatterbuck, G. W. (1979). Attributional confidence and
uncertainty in initial interactions. *Human Communication Research, 5,* 147-157.

Cohen, E. G. (1982). Expectation states and interracial
interaction in school settings. *Annual Review of Sociology, 8,* 209-235.

Cohen, E. G. (1984). The desegregated school: Problems
in status power and interethnic climate. In N. Miller
& M. B. Brewer (Eds.), *Groups in contact: The psy-*

chology of desegregation (pp. 77-96). Orlando, FL: Academic Press.

Colby, N., Hopf, T., & Ayres, J. (1993). Nice to meet you? Inter/intrapersonal perceptions of communication apprehension in initial interactions. *Communication Quarterly, 41,* 221-230.

Comer, D. (1991). Organizational newcomers' acquisition of information from peers. *Management Communication Quarterly, 5,* 64-89.

Craig, K. M. (1996). Are all newcomers judged similarly? Distinctiveness and time of entry in task-oriented groups. *Small Group Research, 27,* 383-397.

Crandall, R. (1978). The assimilation of newcomers into groups. *Small Group Behavior, 9,* 331-336.

Davies, M. F. (1994). Personality and social characteristics. In A. P. Hare, H. H. Blumberg, M. F. Davies, & M. V. Kent (Eds.), *Small group research: A handbook* (pp. 41-78). Norwood, NJ: Ablex.

Deal, T. E., & Kennedy, A. A. (1982). *Corporate cultures: The rites and rituals of corporate life.* Reading, MA: Addison-Wesley.

Di Salvo, V. S., Nikkel, E., & Monroe, C. (1989). Theory and practice: A field investigation and identification of group members' perceptions of problems facing natural work groups. *Small Group Behavior, 20,* 551-567.

Dion, K. K. (1985). Socialization in adulthood. In G. Lindzey & E. Aronson (Eds.), *Handbook of social psychology: Vol. 2. Special fields and applications* (pp. 123-147). New York: Random House.

Driskell, J. E., Hogan, R., & Salas, E. (1987). Personality and group performance. In C. Hendrick (Ed.), *Group processes and intergroup relations* (pp. 91-112). Newbury Park, CA: Sage.

Ebaugh, H.R.F. (1988). *Becoming an ex: The process of role exit.* Chicago: University of Chicago Press.

Etzioni, A. (1961). *A comparative analysis of complex organizations: On power, involvement, and their correlates.* New York: Free Press of Glencoe.

Falcione, R. L., & Wilson, C. E. (1988). Socialization process in organizations. In G. Goldhaber & G. Barnett (Eds.), *Handbook of organizational communication* (pp. 151-169). Norwood, NJ: Ablex.

Feldman, D. C. (1976). A contingency theory of socialization. *Administrative Science Quarterly, 21,* 433-452.

Feldman, D. C. (1981). The multiple socialization of organization members. *Academy of Management Review, 6,* 309-318.

Ferraris, C., Carveth, R., & Parrish-Sprowl, J. (1993). Interface precision benchworks: A case study in organizational identification. *Journal of Applied Communication Research, 21,* 343-357.

Frey, L. R. (1997). Individuals in groups. In L. R. Frey & J. K. Barge (Eds.), *Managing group life: Communicating in decision-making groups* (pp. 52-79). Boston: Houghton Mifflin.

Gouran, D. S. (1994). The future of small group communication research: Revitalization or continued good health? *Communication Studies, 45,* 29-39.

Gouran, D. S., & Fisher, B. A. (1984). The functions of human communication in the formation, maintenance, and performance of small groups. In C. C. Arnold & J. W. Bowers (Eds.), *Handbook of rhetorical and communication theory* (pp. 622-658). Boston: Allyn & Bacon.

Harris, L., & Cronen, V. E. (1979). A rules-based model for the analysis and evaluation of organizational communication. *Communication Quarterly, 27,* 12-28.

Hautaluoma, J. E., Enge, R. S., Mitchell, T. M., & Rittwager, F. J. (1991). Early socialization into a work group: Severity of initiations revisited. *Journal of Social Behavior and Personality, 6,* 725-748.

Hawkins, K., & Stewart, R. A. (1991). Effects of communication apprehension on perceptions of leadership and intragroup attraction in small task-oriented groups. *Southern Communication Journal, 57,* 1-10.

Heider, F. (1958). *The psychology of interpersonal relations.* New York: John Wiley.

Hess, J. A. (1993). Assimilating newcomers into an organization: A cultural perspective. *Journal of Applied Communication Research, 22,* 189-210.

Infante, D. A., & Rancer, A. S. (1982). A conceptualization and measure of argumentativeness. *Journal of Personality Assessment, 46,* 72-80.

Infante, D. A., & Rancer, A. S. (1996). Argumentativeness and verbal aggressiveness: A review of recent theory and research. In B. R. Burleson (Ed.), *Communication yearbook 19* (pp. 319-351). Thousand Oaks, CA: Sage.

Infante, D. A., & Wigley, C. J. (1986). Verbal aggressiveness: An interpersonal model and measure. *Communication Monographs, 53,* 61-69.

Jablin, F. M. (1982). Organizational communication: An assimilation approach. In M. E. Roloff & C. R. Berger (Eds.), *Social cognition and communication* (pp. 255-286). Beverly Hills, CA: Sage.

Jablin, F. M. (1984). Assimilating new members into organizations. In R. N. Bostrom (Ed.), *Communication yearbook 8* (pp. 594-624). Beverly Hills, CA: Sage.

Jablin, F. M. (1985). Task/work relationships: A life-span perspective. In M. L. Knapp & G. R. Miller (Eds.), *Handbook of interpersonal communication* (pp. 615-654). Beverly Hills, CA: Sage.

Jablin, F. M. (1987). Organizational entry, assimilation, and exit. In F. M. Jablin, L. L. Putnam, K. H. Roberts, & L. W. Porter (Eds.), *Handbook of organizational communication* (pp. 679-740). Newbury Park, CA: Sage.

Jones, G. R. (1983). Psychological orientation and the process of organizational socialization: An interactionist perspective. *Academy of Management Review, 8,* 464-474.

Jones, G. R. (1986). Socialization tactics, self-efficacy, and newcomers' adjustments to organizations. *Academy of Management Journal, 29,* 262-279.

Katz, D., & Kahn, R. L. (1978). *The social psychology of organizations* (2nd ed.). New York: John Wiley.

Kenny, D. A., Hallmark, B. W., Sullivan, P., & Kashy, D. A. (1993). The analysis of designs in which individuals are in more than one group. *British Journal of Social Psychology, 32,* 173-190.

Keyton, J. (1993). Group termination: Completing the study of group development. *Small Group Research, 24,* 84-100.

Keyton, J., & Frey, L. R. (in press). The effects of predispositions on group communication. In L. R. Frey (Ed.), *New directions in group communication.* Thousand Oaks, CA: Sage.

Keyton, J., Harmon, N., & Frey, L. R. (1996, November). *Grouphate: Implications for teaching group communication.* Paper presented at the annual meeting of the Speech Communication Association, San Diego, CA.

Kramer, M. W. (1993). Communication and uncertainty reduction during job transfers: Leaving and joining processes. *Communication Monographs, 60,* 178-198.

Kramer, M. W. (1994). Uncertainty reduction during job transitions: An exploratory study of the communication experiences of newcomers and transferees. *Management Communication Quarterly, 7,* 384-412.

Lacoursiere, R. B. (1980). *The life cycle of groups: Group developmental stage theory.* New York: Human Sciences Press.

Lester, R. E. (1987). Organizational culture, uncertainty reduction, and the socialization of new organizational members. In S. Thomas (Ed.), *Culture and communication: Methodology, behavior, artifacts, and institutions: Selected proceedings from the Fifth International Conference on Culture and Communication* (pp. 105-113). Norwood, NJ: Ablex.

Levine, J. M., & Moreland, R. L. (1991). Culture and socialization in work groups. In L. B. Resnick, J. M. Levine, & S. D. Teasley (Eds.), *Perspectives on socially shared cognition* (pp. 257-279). Washington, DC: American Psychological Association.

Louis, M. (1980). Surprise and sense making: What newcomers experience in entering unfamiliar organizational settings. *Administrative Science Quarterly, 25,* 226-251.

Mackie, D. M., & Goethals, G. R. (1987). Individual and group goals. In C. Hendrick (Ed.), *Group processes* (pp. 144-166). Newbury Park, CA: Sage.

Martin, M. M., & Anderson, C. M. (1998, April). *Interpersonal communication motives in small groups.* Paper presented at the annual meeting of the Eastern Communication Association, Saratoga Springs, NY.

McComb, M. (1995). Becoming a travelers aid volunteer: Communication in socialization and training. *Communication Studies, 45,* 297-316.

McCroskey, J. C. (1977). Oral communication apprehension: A summary of recent theory and research. *Human Communication Research, 4,* 75-96.

McCroskey, J. C., Hamilton, P. R., & Weiner, A. N. (1974). The effects of interaction behavior on source credibility, homophily, and interpersonal attraction. *Human Communication Research, 1,* 42-52.

McCroskey, J. C., & Richmond, V. P. (1990). Willingness to communicate: A cognitive view. *Journal of Social Behavior and Personality, 5,* 19-37.

McCroskey, J. C., & Richmond, V. P. (1992). Communication apprehension and small group communication. In R. S. Cathcart & L. A. Samovar (Eds.), *Small group communication: A reader* (6th ed., pp. 361-374). Dubuque, IA: Wm. C. Brown.

McGrath, J. E., & Gruenfeld, D. H. (1993). Toward a dynamic and systemic theory of groups: An integration of six temporally enriched perspectives. In M. M. Chemers & R. Aynam (Eds.), *Leadership theory and research: Perspectives and directions* (pp. 217-244). San Diego: Academic Press.

Mead, G. H. (1956). *The social psychology of George Herbert Mead* (A. Strauss, Ed.). Chicago: University of Chicago Press.

Meyers, S. A. (1998). GTAs as organizational newcomers: The association between supportive communication relationships and information seeking. *Western Journal of Communication, 62,* 54-73.

Mignerey, J. T., Rubin, R. B., & Gorden, W. I. (1995). Organizational entry: An investigation of newcomer communication behavior and uncertainty. *Communication Research, 22,* 54-85.

Miller, V. D., & Jablin, F. M. (1991). Information seeking during organizational entry: Influences, tactics, and a model of the process. *Academy of Management Review, 16,* 92-120.

Mobley, W. H., Griffeth, R. W., Hand, H. H., & Meglino, B. M. (1979). Review and conceptual analysis of the employee turnover process. *Psychological Bulletin, 86,* 493-522.

Moreland, R. L. (1985). Social categorization and the assimilation of "new" group members. *Journal of Personality and Social Psychology, 48,* 1173-1190.

Moreland, R. L., & Levine, J. M. (1982). Socialization in small groups: Temporal changes in individual-group relations. In L. Berkowitz (Ed.), *Advances in experimental social psychology* (Vol. 15, pp. 137-192). New York: Academic Press.

Moreland, R. L., & Levine, J. M. (1984). Role transitions in small groups. In V. L. Allen & E. VandeVliert (Eds.), *Role transitions: Explorations and explanations* (pp. 181-195). New York: Plenum.

Moreland, R. L., & Levine, J. M. (1988). Group dynamics over time: Development and socialization in small groups. In J. E. McGrath (Ed.), *The social psychology of time: New perspectives* (pp. 151-181). Newbury Park, CA: Sage.

Moreland, R. L., & Levine, J. M. (1989). Newcomers and oldtimers in small groups. In P. B. Paulus (Ed.), *Psychology of group influence* (2nd ed., pp. 143-186). Hillsdale, NJ: Lawrence Erlbaum.

Moreland, R., Levine, J., & Cini, M. (1993). Group socialization: The role of commitment. In M. A. Hogg & D. Abrams (Eds.), *Group motivation: Social psychological perspectives* (pp. 105-129). London: Harvester Wheatsheaf.

Morrison, E. W. (1993a). Longitudinal study of the effects of information seeking on newcomer socialization. *Journal of Applied Psychology, 78,* 173-183.

Morrison, E. W. (1993b). Newcomer information-seeking: Exploring types, modes, sources, and outcomes. *Academy of Management Journal, 36,* 557-589.

Morrison, E. W. (1995). Information usefulness and acquisition during organizational encounter. *Management Communication Quarterly, 9,* 131-155.

Ostroff, C., & Kozlowski, W. J. (1992). Organizational socialization as a learning process: The role of information acquisition. *Personnel Psychology, 45,* 42-65.

Pacanowsky, M. E., & O'Donnell-Trujillo, N. (1982). Communication and organizational cultures. *Western Journal of Speech Communication, 46,* 115-130.

Pepper, G. L. (1995). *Communicating in organizations: A cultural approach.* New York: McGraw-Hill.

Polzer, J. T., Kramer, R. M., & Neale, M. A. (1997). Positive illusions about oneself and one's group: Antecedents and consequences. *Small Group Research, 28,* 243-266.

Poole, M. S. (1990). Do we have any theories of group communication? *Communication Studies, 41,* 237-247.

Poole, M. S., & Baldwin, C. L. (1996). Developmental processes in group decision making. In R. Y. Hirokawa & M. S. Poole (Eds.), *Communication and group decision making* (2nd ed., pp. 215-241). Thousand Oaks, CA: Sage.

Putnam, L. L. (1982). Paradigms for organizational communication research: An overview and synthesis. *Western Journal of Speech Communication, 46,* 192-206.

Putnam, L. L., & Poole, M. S. (1987). Conflict and negotiation. In F. M. Jablin, L. L. Putnam, K. H. Roberts, & L. W. Porter (Eds.), *Handbook of organizational communication: An interdisciplinary perspective* (pp. 549-599). Newbury Park, CA: Sage.

Rancer, A. (1998). Argumentativeness. In J. C. McCroskey, J. A. Daly, M. M. Martin, & M. J. Beatty (Eds.), *Communication and personality: Trait perspectives* (pp. 149-170). Cresskill, NJ: Hampton.

Reichers, A. E. (1987). An interactionist perspective on newcomer socialization rates. *Academy of Management Review, 12,* 278-287.

Reichers, A., Wanous, J., & Steele, K. (1994). Design and implementation issues in socializing (and resocializing) employees. *Human Resource Planning, 17,* 17-25.

Riddle, B. L. (1994). Organizational communication, uncertainty reduction, and role-identity salience in the socialization of entering college students. *Dissertation Abstracts International, 56*(10A), 3793. (University Microfilms No. AAI96-04454)

Riggs, M. L., & Knight, P. A. (1994). The impact of perceived group success-failure on motivational beliefs and attitudes: A causal model. *Journal of Applied Psychology, 79,* 755-766.

Rose, S. R. (1989). Members leaving groups: Theoretical and practical considerations. *Small Group Behavior, 20,* 524-535.

Rothwell, J. D. (1998). *In mixed company: Small group communication.* Fort Worth, TX: Harcourt Brace.

Rubin, R. B. (1990). Communication competence. In G. M. Phillips & J. T. Wood (Eds.), *Speech Communication: Essays to commemorate the 75th anniversary of the Speech Communication Association* (pp. 104-129). Carbondale: Southern Illinois University Press.

Rubin, R. B., & Martin, M. M. (1998). Interpersonal communication motives. In J. C. McCroskey, J. A. Daly, M. M. Martin, & M. J. Beatty (Eds.), *Communication and personality: Trait perspectives* (pp. 287-308). Cresskill, NJ: Hampton.

Rubin, R. B., Perse, E. M., & Barbato, C. A. (1988). Conceptualization and measurement of interpersonal communication motives. *Human Communication Research, 14,* 602-628.

Rugs, D., & Kaplan, M. F. (1993). Effectiveness of informational and normative influences in group decision making depends on the group interactive goal. *British Journal of Social Psychology, 32,* 147-158.

Rynes, S. L., & Barber, A. E. (1990). Applicant attraction strategies: An organizational perspective. *Academy of Management Review, 15,* 286-310.

Salazar, A. J. (1996). An analysis of the development and evolution of roles in the small group. *Small Group Research, 27,* 475-503.

Scheerhorn, D., & Geist, P. (1997). Social dynamics in groups. In L. R. Frey & J. K. Barge (Eds.), *Managing group life: Communicating in decision-making groups* (pp. 81-103). Boston: Houghton Mifflin.

Schein, E. H. (1968). Organizational socialization and the profession of management. *Industrial Management Review, 9,* 1-16.

Schutz, W. C. (1966). *The interpersonal underworld.* Palo Alto, CA: Science and Behavior Books.

Sherif, M., & Sherif, C. W. (1953). *Groups in harmony and tension: An integration of studies on intergroup relations.* New York: Harper.

Sigman, S. J. (1985-1986). The applicability of the concept of recruitment to the communication study of a nursing home: An ethnographic case study. *International Journal of Aging and Human Development, 22,* 215-233.

Simmel, G. (1950). *The sociology of Georg Simmel* (K. H. Wolff, Trans.). New York: Free Press of Glencoe.

Sinclair-James, L., & Stohl, C. (1997). Group endings and new beginnings. In L. R. Frey & J. K. Barge (Eds.), *Managing group life: Communicating in decision-making groups* (pp. 308-334). Boston: Houghton Mifflin.

Smircich, L. (1983). Concepts of culture and organizational analysis. *Administrative Science Quarterly, 28,* 339-358.

Smircich, L., & Calas, M. B. (1987). Organizational culture: A critical assessment. In F. M. Jablin, L. L. Putnam, K. H. Roberts, & L. W. Porter (Eds.), *Handbook of organizational communication: An interdisciplinary perspective* (pp. 228-263). Newbury Park, CA: Sage.

Smith, K. K., & Berg, D. N. (1987). *Paradoxes of group life: Understanding conflict, paralysis and movement in group dynamics.* San Francisco: Jossey-Bass.

Sorensen, S. M. (1981, May). *Group-hate: A negative reaction to group work.* Paper presented at the annual meeting of the International Communication Association, Minneapolis, MN.

Stohl, C. (1986). The role of memorable messages in the process of organizational socialization. *Communication Quarterly, 34,* 231-249.

Stryker, S., & Statham, A. (1985). Symbolic interaction and role theory. In G. Lindzey & E. Aronson (Eds.), *Handbook of social psychology: Vol. 1. Theory and method* (pp. 311-378). New York: Random House.

Swogger, G., Jr. (1981). Human communication and group experiences. In J. E. Durkin (Ed.), *Living groups: Group psychotherapy and general system theory* (pp. 63-78). New York: Brunner/Mazel.

Teboul, JC. B. (1997). Scripting the organization: New hire learning during organizational encounter. *Communication Research Reports, 14,* 33-47.

Trujillo, N. (1986). Implications of interpretive approaches for organization communication research and practice. In L. Thayer (Ed.), *Organization—communication: Emerging perspectives: Vol. 2. Communication in organizations* (pp. 46-63). Norwood, NJ: Ablex.

Trujillo, N. (1992). Interpreting (the work and the talk of) baseball: Perspectives on ballpark culture. *Western Journal of Communication, 56,* 350-371.

Tuckman, B. W. (1965). Developmental sequence in small groups. *Psychological Bulletin, 63,* 384-399.

Tuckman, B. W., & Jensen, M. (1977). Stages of small-group development revisited. *Group and Organization Studies, 2,* 419-427.

Van Gennep, A. (1960). *The rites of passage* (M. B. Vizedom & G. L. Caffee, Trans.). Chicago: University of Chicago Press. (Original work published 1908)

Van Maanen, J. (1976). Breaking in: Socializing to work. In R. Dubin (Ed.), *Handbook of work, organization and society* (pp. 67-130). Chicago: Rand McNally.

Van Maanen, J. (1977). Experiencing organization: Notes on the meaning of careers and socialization. In J. Van Maanen (Ed.), *Organizational careers: Some new perspectives* (pp. 15-45). New York: John Wiley.

Van Maanen, J., & Schein, E. H. (1979). Toward a theory of organizational socialization. In B. M. Staw (Ed.), *Research in organizational behavior: An annual series of analytical essays and critical reviews* (Vol. 1, pp. 209-264). Greenwich, CT: JAI.

Wigley, C. J. (1998). Verbal aggression. In J. C. McCroskey, J. A. Daly, M. M. Martin, & M. J. Beatty (Eds.), *Communication and personality: Trait perspectives* (pp. 191-214). Cresskill, NJ: Hampton.

Yerby, J. (1975). Attitude, task, and sex composition as variables affecting female leadership in small problem-solving groups. *Speech Monographs, 42,* 160-168.

Zahrly, J., & Tosi, H. (1989). The differential effects of organizational induction process on early work role adjustment. *Journal of Organizational Behavior, 10,* 59-74.

PART III

Task and Relational Group Communication

7

Task-Group Communication and Decision-Making Performance

RANDY Y. HIROKAWA
University of Iowa

ABRAN J. SALAZAR
University of Rhode Island

Any simple problem can be made insoluble if enough meetings are held to discuss it.
—Mitchell's Law of Committees (author unknown)

Benjamin Franklin is credited with saying that nothing is certain in this world but death and taxes. Were he alive today, Franklin would certainly modify his statement to include participation in decision-making task groups, for working in groups is as prevalent in contemporary society as death and taxes. Consider, for example, that more than 80% of *Fortune* 500 companies in the United States rely on some form of group-based, decision-making system (Lawler & Mohrman, 1985). It is difficult to imagine a public facet of everyday life that is not influenced by the deliberations of decision-making task groups, for example, from government committees to courtroom juries to health care teams.

Given the importance of decision-making groups in everyday life, it is not surprising that the question of why some groups arrive at high-quality decisions whereas others do not has long been of interest to scholars from a variety of academic disciplines. Several decades of cross-disciplinary research indicate that group decision-making performance is attributable to a variety of influences, including informational resources (Kelley & Thibaut, 1969), group effort (Janis & Mann, 1977), critical thinking skills (Janis, 1982), and decision rules and logic (Davis, 1973; Senge, 1990).

Although group decision-making performance is affected by these and other influences, scholars have long suspected that the group interaction process is an important key to understanding and explaining why groups arrive at "good" or "bad" decisions. Indeed, interest in the relationship between group interaction and decision-making performance has a long and distinguished, if somewhat controversial, history. In his recent comprehensive review of the literature, Frey (1996) notes that although the study of group communication and decision making "did not begin in any substantial way until the 1950s . . . the seeds [of such interest] were planted in the first half of the 20th century" (p. 20). He identifies three early lines of research that had a significant impact on the contemporary study of the relationship between group communication and decision making: (a) work by social psychologists investigating the superiority of groups over individuals in terms of the speed and correctness of decision making (e.g., Barton, 1926; Marston, 1924; Ringelmann, 1913; Shaw, 1932; Watson, 1928), (b) pedagogical work by educators adapting Dewey's (1910, 1933) "reflective thinking" process as a model for democratic group problem solving and decision making (e.g., Baird, 1927; Elliot, 1927; McBurney & Hance, 1939; Sheffield, 1926; see Gouran, Chapter 1, this volume), and (c) research by sociologists and psychologists examining communication-related factors that contribute to effective group thinking and decision-making success (e.g., Carr, 1930; Chapple, 1940, 1942; Miller, 1939; Newsletter, 1937; Sanderson, 1938; Wrightstone, 1934).

Since the days of these early studies, scholars from a variety of academic fields have studied the effects of interaction on group performance (see reviews by Collins & Guetzkow, 1964; Frey, 1996; Hackman & Morris, 1975; Hare, 1976; McGrath, 1984). As a result, interaction has taken on unparalleled importance in the study of group decision-making effectiveness (Hirokawa, Salazar, Erbert, & Ice, 1996). In this chapter, we explore the relationship between group communication and decision-making performance in task groups. We start by examining some conceptual perspectives that position communication in unique ways vis-à-vis group decision making. These perspectives then serve as the basis for both a review of the research to date and an assessment of what needs to be accomplished in the future.

THEORETICAL PERSPECTIVES ON THE RELATIONSHIP BETWEEN GROUP COMMUNICATION AND DECISION-MAKING PERFORMANCE

Various explanatory perspectives have been advanced to account for the relationship between group communication and decision-making outcomes. These perspectives can be conceptually organized into three general views: (a) mediational, (b) functional, and (c) constitutive.

The Mediational Perspective

A long-standing view held by many scholars who study small groups is that the group interaction process serves as a medium through which the "true" determinants of group decision-making performance are able to exert influence. This perspective, thus, assumes that factors other than communication account for the performance of decision-making groups. This "mediational" view is reflected in the research literature in several different ways.

Some have claimed that group communication allows group members to acquire, distribute, and pool available knowledge/informational resources necessary for effective decision making. Leavitt (1951), for example, argues that communication facilitates effective group decision making to the extent that it results in the successful centralization of information in the hands of members who need it to help a group arrive at a high-quality decision. Similarly, Barnlund (1959) maintains that communication is most crucial for effective decision making when a group is characterized by an unequal distribution of vital knowledge/information among members. The opportunity for interaction enables informed individuals to communicate their knowledge to fellow group members (see Propp, Chapter 9, this volume, regarding collective information processing in groups).

Others have argued that communication allows group members to catch and remedy errors of individual judgment. Taylor and

Faust (1952) claim that the principal reason why groups generally outperform individual decision makers is because the discussion of ideas, suggestions, and rationales for preferred choices tends to expose individual members' informational, judgmental, and reasoning deficiencies that might go undetected if those individuals were making decisions on their own (see Propp, Chapter 9, this volume). Interaction provides the opportunity not only for group members to identify those errors, but also to remedy them before they can contribute to a regrettable decision. Janis (1982), for example, suggests that one of the main reasons John F. Kennedy's cabinet made better decisions during the Cuban Missile Crisis than during the Bay of Pigs fiasco was because Kennedy asked his brother Robert to play the role of a "devil's advocate" in key meetings during the missile crisis by arguing against whatever policy was forwarded. According to Janis, President Kennedy believed that the presence of a devil's advocate would ensure that all ideas received careful scrutiny for errors or flaws.

Each of the positions described above views communication as playing a mediating role in group decision making. The most comprehensive presentation of the mediational role of group interaction, however, is offered by Hackman (1990). Arguing that group decision-making effectiveness is the result of many independent factors, Hackman identified three main conditions that "enable" a group to make high-quality decisions: (a) exertion of sufficient *effort* to accomplish the task at an acceptable level of performance, (b) possession of adequate *knowledge and skill* relevant to the task at hand, and (c) utilization of task-performance *strategies* that are appropriate to the work and to the setting in which it is being performed. He calls these enabling conditions the "process criteria of effectiveness" (p. 9).

Hackman argues that several social and environmental conditions, in turn, influence a group's process criteria. These "supporting" factors include (a) a *group structure* that promotes competent work on the task, (b) an *environmental context* that supports and reinforces excellence, and (c) *expert coaching and process assistance.*

Within Hackman's theoretical framework, communication serves as the medium through which the process criteria of effectiveness, supporting factors, and, ultimately, group decision-making performance are linked. It is largely through communication that supporting factors influence how well the process criteria are satisfied. For example, a group facilitator or trainer who communicates information to group members provides them with some of the knowledge required to complete the task. Likewise, it is largely through communication that the process criteria are able to influence group decision-making and problem-solving performance. For instance, as noted earlier, interaction enables group members to pool and utilize the unique knowledge each member possesses, which helps them to make good decisions. In short, Hackman's Mediational Perspective views communication as a conduit that allows supporting factors to influence the process criteria of effectiveness and enables those criteria to ultimately influence group performance.

The Functional Perspective

In contrast to scholars who view communication as a passive and neutral medium that simply allows exogenous factors (like members' knowledge, skills, or effort) to affect group decision-making performance, several scholars suggest that interaction plays a much more active role (see, for example, Gouran & Hirokawa, 1983, 1996; Hirokawa & Scheerhorn, 1986; Janis, 1972, 1982, 1989; Janis & Mann, 1977). They argue that interaction is a *social tool* that group members use to perform or satisfy various prerequisites for effective decision making. Collectively, this perspective is referred to in the literature as the Functional Perspective.

One of the earliest functional perspectives was presented by Riecken (1958), who argued that interaction affects group decision performance by serving as the means by which persuasion among group members takes place. In this view, members use communication to persuade one another to accept their point of view. Shaw and Penrod (1964) made a similar point when they argued that the presence of knowledgeable members does not, in itself, lead to effective group decision making; members must, through interaction, successfully persuade others in the group to accept and use the information they contribute.

Perhaps the most detailed discussion of the Functional Perspective is presented by Gouran and Hirokawa (1983, 1986, 1996; see also Gouran, Hirokawa, Julian, & Leatham, 1993; Hirokawa & Scheerhorn, 1986; in this volume, see Chapters 1 [Gouran] and 2 [Poole]). Briefly, they argue that a group's final ("big") decision is the result of a series of ("small") subdecisions reached by members about four general questions that confront them:

1. Is there something about the present situation that requires a choice of some kind to be made?
2. What do we want to achieve or accomplish in deciding what to do?
3. What are the choices available to us?
4. What are the positive and negative aspects of each choice?

Gouran and Hirokawa suggest that the answers members arrive at collectively to these four questions form the social context within which a group's final decision is made and, as such, often serve as the justification or rationale for that decision.

Gouran and Hirokawa further posit that group interaction plays a key role in shaping the social context within which group decisions are made. That is, it is through interaction that members address and subsequently agree on the answers to these four crucial questions. Moreover, because that context serves as the basis for a group's decision, Gouran and Hirokawa maintain that the accuracy of a group's answers to these four questions is tied inextricably to the quality of the decision that emerges. They identify four specific ways that interaction can shape and influence the quality of a group's social con-

text and, in so doing, affect decision performance. Specifically, group interaction affects a group's (a) assessment of the problematic situation, (b) identification of goals and objectives, (c) identification of available choices, and (d) assessment of the positive and negative aspects of available choices.

The Constitutive Perspective

In contrast to the perceived role of communication in the Mediational and Functional Perspectives, other scholars have focused on its role in the constitution of group decisions. This Constitutive Perspective has been presented in the literature in two ways.

First, some scholars regard group decisions as "emerging texts or developing ideas" (Poole & Hirokawa, 1996, p. 8), in which communication is viewed as the process by which the form and content of those decisions are worked out. This "developmental" role of group communication is best reflected in the work of Poole and his associates (see, for example, Poole, 1981, 1983a, 1983b; Poole & Baldwin, 1996; Poole & Doelger, 1986; Poole & Roth, 1989a, 1989b; in this volume, see Chapters 1 [Gouran], 2 [Poole], 3 [Mabry], and 6 [Anderson, Riddle, & Martin]). Poole and Baldwin (1996) propose that group decisions emerge from and develop within "intertwining threads of [communicative] activity that evolve simultaneously and interweave in different patterns over time" (p. 222). They propose that these various strands of communicative activity contribute to the accumulation, elaboration, modification, and deletion of the ideas and premises that eventually shape the form and content of group decisions. By implication, then, Poole suggests that group decision-making performance can be accounted for by tracing a decision back through a group's interaction process to discover and understand how that choice ultimately was arrived at by the group.

The constitutive role of communication has also been presented in the literature using a "social constructionist" approach that views group decisions as social products emerging from and embedded in a "social milieu" (or "reality") that is both created and sustained through communication. Bormann's (1986, 1996) Symbolic Convergence Theory (SCT), as well as Poole, Seibold, and McPhee's (1985, 1986, 1996) adaptation of Giddens's (1979, 1984) Structuration Theory, offers clear examples of this second approach to explicating the constitutive role of group interaction (in this volume, see Chapters 1 [Gouran] and 2 [Poole]; see also Keyton, Chapter 8, this volume, regarding SCT as applied to the relational dimension of group life).

Bormann essentially argues that consensual group decisions emerge from the presence of *symbolic convergence,* defined as the overlapping of individuals' symbolic worlds; that is, the establishment of shared meanings among group members about important verbal and nonverbal signs and symbols. Bormann maintains that symbolic convergence is achieved through communication, specifically, communication that involves the sharing of stories. Storytelling helps other group members understand what a particular member means by, or how that member has interpreted, particular concepts, events, words, or phrases. Stories might describe a member's own or others' experiences, historical events, media events, or even imaginary events. Bormann calls those stories *fantasies* because they always refer to characters and events in some time and place other than the here and now.

The introduction of a fantasy, according to Bormann, offers others in a group the opportunity to join in the building of that fantasy, a process referred to as *fantasy chaining.* Fantasy chaining allows group members to

> jointly experience the same emotions, develop common heroes and villains, celebrate certain actions as laudable, and interpret some aspect of their common experience in the same way. Thus, they come to symbolic convergence about that part of their common experience. (Bormann, 1986, p. 226)

Bormann essentially argues that fantasy chaining in group interaction eventually re-

sults in symbolic convergence, which makes it possible for members to collectively agree on a decision. In short, a group's decision is a product of the shared rhetorical vision of its members. The way in which group members collectively "see" the world, therefore, significantly influences the choices they make. The theory would seem to suggest, then, that the quality of a group's shared vision—for example, its accuracy and thoroughness vis-à-vis the external world—ought to be related to the quality of the group's decision. Bormann cautions, however, that the relationship is not necessarily causal. Still, to the extent that members' beliefs, attitudes, values, and perceptions guide their choice making, SCT suggests that there is good reason to expect that the nature of a group's shared vision influences decision-making outcomes.

In presenting their adaptation of Giddens's (1979, 1984) Structuration Theory, Poole et al. (1985, 1986, 1996) argue that individual members draw on a group's rules and resources when they communicate and make decisions. *Rules* are statements about how things ought to be done; they describe and explain appropriate and expected communicative behavior in groups, as well as how members' communicative behavior should be interpreted. *Resources* are materials, knowledge, and skills that group members draw on to accomplish their task. Each group develops its own set of rules and resources, which together make up the group's *structures.* A group's structures are the "tools" members use to produce decisions.

An important concept in Structuration Theory is the *duality of structures,* in which structures exist in a reciprocal relationship with group members' interaction. For example, rules and resources influence group members' behavior; they are the means by which members choose among competing courses of action. At the same time, they are the product of interaction among members; through interaction, group members establish rules and utilize resources.

Although Structuration Theory was not developed to account for group decision-making performance per se, it nevertheless offers a clear statement of the constitutive nature of group interaction. Simply put, given that a group draws on its rules and resources to make decisions, which are themselves the determinants and products of interaction, the role of communication in group decision making involves facilitating the *creation and reinforcement of the social structures that give rise to decisions*. In short, the reciprocal relationship between structures and interaction can be viewed as a necessary prerequisite to group decision making.

RESEARCH ON COMMUNICATION AND GROUP DECISION-MAKING PERFORMANCE

Research examining the relationship between communication and group decision-making performance, to date, has been conducted primarily from either the Mediational or Functional Perspective; comparatively little research has adopted a Constitutive Perspective. In the remainder of this chapter, we review the extant literature to summarize what we have learned about the mediational, functional, and constitutive roles of group interaction, and, in so doing, note important gaps in our understanding of the relationship between communication and group decision-making performance.

We should also note here that group performance has been conceptualized by researchers in any of a number of ways. The performance outcomes studied most often by researchers focusing on group decision-making and problem-solving tasks include those that are assumed to result from general and/or particular aspects of group communication, including *consensus* (members' agreement with, or acceptance of, their group's choice), *satisfaction* (members' affective responses to their group's choice or the communication process used to arrive at a choice), *quality* (externally perceived evaluation of a group's choice), *accuracy* ("correctness" of a group's choice), and *speed* (amount of time needed to make a group choice, also referred

to as *efficiency*). Of these five outcomes, accuracy and quality have received the lion's share of attention by group communication scholars; hence, they are the focus of the following review.

Mediational Research

Recall that the Mediational Perspective treats communication as a medium through which the primary group determinants of performance exert their influence. Hence, for example, communication serves as a medium when it is the means for the acquisition, distribution, and pooling of information among group members. From this perspective, communication is primarily a medium for the influence of information on group performance when it enables members to catch and remedy errors in inferences made on the basis of the information with which the group works, employ effective strategies for testing inferences made on the basis of that information, and/or engage in substantive conflict for the purpose of analyzing that information. We now turn to those studies that treat communication primarily as a medium for the influence of information, as well as group members' effort, knowledge, and skill.

In examining the particular communicative acts associated with group decision-making accuracy, researchers have used a wide variety of observational coding schemes, with nearly as many different schemes as there have been investigations. In one of the first studies to examine this relationship, Lanzetta and Roby (1960) used a seven-category system that may be distilled to four aspects of group interaction, three of which implicate information distribution in groups: (a) total number of communicative behaviors produced, (b) total number of messages volunteering information, (c) total number of requests for information, and (d) the relative proportion of transmitted information.

Although Lanzetta and Roby focused on specific aspects of group interaction, their system is rather crude. While the categories implicate information, they were not theoretically grounded but, rather, represented an exploratory attempt to determine the nature of the relationship between communication and group decision accuracy. As such, the categories themselves were not theoretically or conceptually developed to apply to tasks in which accuracy is the standard by which group performance is determined; indeed, Lanzetta and Roby offered no theoretical rationale for why these particular categories should be related to the accuracy of group decisions.

A step in the right direction was Katzell, Miller, Rotter, and Venet's (1970) use of Bales's (1950) Interaction Process Analysis (IPA) categories. Because the IPA observational system consists of 12 categories (seems friendly, dramatizes, agrees, gives suggestion, gives opinion, gives information, asks for information, asks for opinion, asks for suggestion, disagrees, shows tension, and seems unfriendly; in this volume, see Chapters 8 [Keyton], 12 [Pavitt], and 17 [Socha]), it captures more fully the diversity of group interaction than does Lanzetta and Roby's system. Using IPA, however, to make assessments of the link between communication and group performance, such as accuracy of judgment, is questionable (see Hirokawa, 1982).

In their study, Lanzetta and Roby (1960) found (a) that the total number of communicative behaviors was unrelated to accuracy of group decision making and (b) an overall negative correlation between the frequency of occurrence of two categories of communicative behavior—"volunteered information" and "proportion of transmitted information" (relative to total information)—and decision accuracy. There was also an overall positive correlation between the "total number of requests for information" and decision accuracy. Perhaps most important, the measures of group interaction predicted task success (both time needed to make a decision and number of decision-making errors) *better* than measures of members' task-relevant knowledge or various task-training procedures (e.g., groups received practice time in applying principles or rules necessary for successful performance on the task of interest).

These findings are in line with those obtained by Katzell et al. (1970), whose study showed that effective groups demonstrated "faster rates of interaction," as well as more "agreement" and higher scores on "shows tension," and "tension release," than less effective groups; while less effective groups were characterized by more "giving of information," "asking for information," and "disagreements" than their more effective counterparts. The latter six categories are part of Bales's (1950) IPA system. The finding that information-related communication categories are inversely related to group decision accuracy is counterintuitive and underscores the need for theoretical development regarding the relationships among information, communication, and the accuracy of group decision-making performance.

In addition to studying categories of communicative utterances that deal with information, studies from a Mediational Perspective have examined the effects of different communication process procedures (see Sunwolf & Seibold, Chapter 15, this volume), as well as computer mediations (see Scott, Chapter 16, this volume), on group decision-making performance. Among the process procedures studied are the Nominal Group Technique (NGT) and the Delphi technique;[1] the computer mediations studied include various group decision support systems (GDSSs). The process procedures or computer mediations typically are compared to freely interacting (unstructured; hereafter, interacting) groups to determine which one better facilitates group decision-making performance (see Sunwolf & Seibold, Chapter 15, this volume, regarding structured versus naturally occurring/free group discussion).

One of the goals of these process procedures and computer mediations is to enhance the distribution and analysis of information in task groups. The exchange of information is affected by the strictures and organizational structure such processes impose on group communication, as well as the impact of such problems as group members' communication apprehension (i.e., members' fear of communicating; see Haslett & Ruebush, Chapter 5, this volume), evaluation apprehension (i.e., members' fear of having their positions/ ideas evaluated), and/or status differences (which may influence members' communication and/or evaluations made by others of that input; in this volume, see Chapters 5 [Haslett & Ruebush] and 10 [Ketrow]). For example, process procedures and computer mediations attempt to structure group discussion in such a way as to restrict conflict or focus it on the task and not on members and, thereby, reduce the effects of communication apprehension, evaluation apprehension, and status differences on group members' preferences, communicative behavior, and decision-making practices. By establishing processes and procedures that reduce the negative influences of group discussion itself, process procedures and computer mediations raise the probability of members exchanging more information, raising questions regarding faulty inferences, and applying their knowledge and skills more effectively, and exerting greater effort.

For studies using survival judgment tasks (such as Stranded in the Desert, NASA Moon Problem, and Lost at Sea, which are tasks that ask group members to arrive at a utility ranking of various items, identified in the task scenario, for ensuring their survival given certain adverse conditions in which they find themselves), findings are difficult to synthesize because of conflicting results. Three studies (Burleson, Levine, & Samter, 1984; Erffmeyer & Lane, 1984; Herbert & Yost, 1979) assessed the impact of various process procedures on performance for groups working on Hall and Watson's (1970) NASA Moon Problem. Comparing the performance of interacting groups with that of groups using the NGT, Burleson et al. (1984) found that interacting groups made the highest quality decisions. That finding is at odds with that of Herbert and Yost (1979), who determined that groups employing the NGT made higher quality decisions than those reaching consensus through unstructured interaction.

A further finding distinguishing these two studies is that of evidence of a *process gain* (group performance that exceeded that of the group's average member) in the interacting groups studied by Burleson and colleagues, whereas Herbert and Yost observed process gains for groups employing the NGT. In fact, Herbert and Yost found that interacting groups were more likely to experience a *process loss* (group performance level that was below that of the average member).

Adding more confusion to the picture, Erffmeyer and Lane (1984) compared four process procedures and found that Delphi groups produced the highest quality decisions, followed by groups using consensus, interacting, or NGT procedures. Consensus groups, however, achieved the highest level of member acceptance of the decisions. Reasons for the discrepant findings may be the different experimental guidelines used across studies, as well as modifications made in the original procedures given to the NGT and interacting groups.

Jarboe (1988) examined the effects of process procedures (reflective thinking and the NGT) on group interaction (as coded by observers using some of the categories of Bales's, 1950, IPA, as well as unique categories) and, in turn, the effects of the procedures and interaction on various group outputs, including quality of group solutions. She did not find an interaction effect between procedure and IPA interaction categories on decision quality, meaning that the effects of interaction on solution quality were not dependent on process procedure. She did, however, find main effects for the interaction categories of *ego-defensive communication* and *suggests solution* on solution quality.[2]

Salazar, Hirokawa, Propp, Julian, and Leatham (1994) investigated whether restricting the opportunity for members to engage in interaction affected the ability of groups to arrive at a numerical answer for reducing the number of majors in an academic department. Specifically, they compared the accuracy of interacting groups with those using a modified Delphi technique that prevented discussion.

Coders classified the communicative behaviors of the freely interacting groups according to a three-category observational system. Specifically, coders assessed the extent to which members engaged in communication that was (a) goal-directed, (b) focused on idea development, and (c) focused on evaluating ideas. Communication opportunity and the three interaction categories were examined for their relationship to group decision accuracy. The results showed that increased opportunity to communicate led to more accurate decisions, but the frequencies of occurrence of utterances falling into the three communication categories were not associated with groups' ability to arrive at correct decisions.

Focusing on process procedures as well, a systematic line of research has examined the effects of structured debate/conflict, such as that elicited by the procedures of Dialectical Inquiry (DI) and Devil's Advocacy (DA), on group decision-making performance (Schweiger & Sandberg, 1989; Schweiger, Sandberg, & Ragan, 1986; Schweiger, Sandberg, & Rechner, 1989; see also Cosier & Rechner, 1985; Priem & Price, 1991; Schwenk & Cosier, 1993; Schwenk & Valacich, 1994; in this volume, see Meyers & Brashers [Chapter 11] and Sunwolf & Seibold [Chapter 15]). Both DI and DA require group members to reach a decision and specify the assumptions made by them in reaching it. In DA, however, members critique the initial decision and the assumptions underlying it; the group then examines the critiques and submits another decision with new assumptions, and the new decision and its assumptions are once again critiqued. This cycle continues until the group proposes a decision that is acceptable to all members. In DI, the group critiques its initial decision and assumptions, and then proposes a new decision on the basis of assumptions that are opposite of those on which the initial decision was based. Members then discuss their assumptions and decisions until they reach agreement on a set of assumptions. Once those assumptions have been finalized, a new decision is made (see Meyers, 1997).

Variations of the above procedures (while still retaining the DA and DI labels) also have been used. Schweiger and his associates (Schweiger & Sandberg, 1989; Schweiger et al., 1986, 1989), for example, divided a group in half, with the first subgroup making a decision and providing the assumptions on which it was based, and the second subgroup either critiquing the original decision and its assumptions and providing a different decision with different assumptions or merely critiquing the original decision and its assumptions, depending on whether the group was assigned to the DA or DI condition. The subgroups then reassembled again as one group, and the full group was instructed to continue the process until consensus was reached.

DA and DI have been compared to each other, as well as to utilization of consensus or expert procedures for making decisions. Consensus (C) procedures entail free discussion by group members until a decision that is acceptable to all has been made. Expert (E) procedures entail consultants' providing informed advice on the decision to be made. Neither C nor E procedures, however, structure group conflict or debate, as do DA and DI.

Identifying which method results in the best group decisions is not easy in the light of the equivocal evidence (see Katzenstein, 1996). When compared to C, some studies have shown DA and DI procedures to be superior (Schweiger & Sandberg, 1989; Schweiger et al., 1986, 1989), whereas other studies have not (see Katzenstein, 1996). Schwenk and Valacich (1994) found evidence for the superiority of DA and DI over E, but Schwenk (1990), on the basis of a meta-analysis, concluded that the evidence is equivocal (see Katzenstein, 1996). The superiority of either DA, DI, C, or E may depend on the population being studied, whether a group's task is structured or unstructured, whether the intervention is implemented at the group or individual level, the measure employed in ascertaining the level of decision quality, and the expectations group members have about using these procedures (Priem & Price, 1991; see also Sambamurthy & Chin, 1994, regarding the effects of members' expectations on use of GDSSs). For example, if participants believe that one of the procedures elicits greater levels of disruptive conflict, that expectation may function as a self-fulfilling prophecy that negatively affects decision-making quality when members do make use of the procedure during group discussion. That effect may not be present when participants do not hold such expectations.

A handful of other studies have examined the effects on performance of other interaction-altering procedures in addition to DA and DI. For example, in an organizationally situated study, Eisenhardt (1989) found that groups using active conflict resolution strategies, which require an attempt to reach consensus on issues but has the person designated as the formal authority make the decision if the group stalls, were faster at making decisions than groups that used consensus strategies for handling conflict. Faster groups also achieved higher levels of group performance. Wall, Galanes, and Love (1987), focusing on conflict resolution in groups, also found that the use of *integrative conflict management styles*—characterized by all parties exhibiting cooperation in a problem-solving mode and "genuine information seeking or compromise" (p. 40)—was associated with higher quality decisions compared to the use of *distributive styles*—characterized by a winning and losing party, as well as verbal attempts to "elicit negative evidence, hostile questioning or badgering, voting (majority rule), railroading, or accommodation" (p. 40).

Studies examining the effects of communication modes on group decision-making quality have focused primarily on comparing computer-mediated (CM) and face-to-face (FtF) group discussion (e.g., Hiltz, Johnson, & Turoff, 1986). The results of such studies have been diverse, with the differences probably accounted for by varying experimental manipulations and operationalizations of the independent variables (e.g., different CM support systems) and task type. The conclusions of such investigations, consequently, are as equivocal as the research comparing DA, DI, C, and E process procedures. Some studies have revealed CM group discussions to result in higher quality decisions than FtF discussions, some report lower quality decisions, and still others have shown no difference (for a review of such studies, see McLeod, 1996; Scott, Chapter 16, this volume).

The studies just reviewed generally take it as a given that communication serves as a medium for the influence of the true determinants of group performance, such as members' knowledge, skill, and effort and the quality of information exchanged. Rarely, however, have communication process procedures, communication modes, and actual categories of communication been associated with members' knowledge, skill, and effort or the distribution and use of diverse information. Such an assessment is necessary to determine which communication process procedures, modes, or behaviors facilitate or impede these variables. This is a point we return to when discussing the directions that future research on the Mediational Perspective should take.

Functional Research

Empirical studies adopting the Functional Perspective typically have utilized a *comparison-contrast* method to determine whether group decision-making performance is associated with the enactment of particular functional communicative behaviors. Some investigators have employed the method of interaction analysis (see Poole, Keyton, & Frey, Chapter 4, this volume) to determine whether the frequency of microlevel types of function-oriented utterances demonstrated during group discussion discriminates between effective and ineffective group decision making (e.g., Graham, Papa, & McPherson, 1997; Hackman & Morris, 1975; Hirokawa, 1980, 1983, 1985; Katzell et al., 1970; Propp & Nelson, 1996). Other studies have distinguished effective from ineffective groups by utilizing macrolevel *global rating schemes* that ask coders to rate the extent to which an entire group discussion generally fulfilled certain functional prerequisites (e.g., Gouran, Brown, & Henry, 1978; Hirokawa, 1988; Hirokawa & Keyton, 1995; Hirokawa & Rost, 1992; see also Brilhart & Jochem, 1964, for an analysis of a globally implemented, function-oriented intervention).

A recent meta-analysis of empirical research examining the relationship between group communication and decision performance from a Functional Perspective revealed that group decision-making performance is most often related to group interaction concerned with the evaluation of *alternative choices* (Orlitzky & Hirokawa, 1997). Interestingly, some studies have found a strong positive correlation between group decision performance and members' assessment of positive qualities of alternative choices, but no corresponding correlation to the evaluation of negative qualities (e.g., Graham et al., 1997; Propp & Nelson, 1996). Other studies have found a strong positive correlation between group decision performance and the evaluation of negative qualities of alternative choices, but no corresponding correlation to the evaluation of positive qualities (e.g., Hirokawa, 1985, 1987). Still other research has found strong correlations between group decision performance and the evaluation of *both* positive and negative aspects of alternative choices (e.g., Hirokawa, 1985; Hirokawa & Rost, 1992).

Propp and Nelson (1996) account for the discrepant research findings by arguing that "a group can address either positive or negative consequences to improve decision performance. In other words, it may not be necessary to address both matters, as long as one is done well" (p. 42). Orlitzky and Hirokawa (1997) offer a different explanation, suggesting that the relationship between group decision performance and the evaluation of alternative choices is moderated by the *evaluation demand* of the task. More precisely, they argue that some tasks have a "positive bias," whereas others have a "negative bias." A *positive-biased task* is one in which the identification

of the positive qualities of alternative choices is more important for making a sound choice than the identification of their negative qualities. The selection of an award recipient is an example of a positive-biased task in that evaluation emphasis usually is placed on the accomplishments of each candidate; rarely, if ever, will a committee select an award recipient on the basis of his or her failures. In contrast, a *negative-biased task* is one in which the identification of the negative qualities of alternative choices is more important than the identification of their positive qualities in making a good decision. Pharmaceutical decisions made by the Food and Drug Administration (FDA) are a case in point. Although the effectiveness of a new drug (i.e., its positive quality) certainly is taken into account, the decision to approve its sale rests principally on the absence of harmful side effects associated with its use (i.e., its negative qualities). Orlitzky and Hirokawa (1997) maintain that there is likely to be a stronger relationship between group decision performance and the evaluation of positive qualities for positive-biased tasks and a stronger relationship between group decision performance and the evaluation of negative qualities for negative-biased tasks. We return to the issue of task demands later in the chapter.

Other important functional communicative behaviors found to be associated with high-quality group decision-making performance include *problem analysis* and *criteria establishment*. Across all tests of the Functional Perspective, problem analysis often has been found to have a stronger correlation to group decision performance (average correlation of .55) than criteria establishment (average correlation of .27). Although virtually every study has found a relationship between group decision-making performance and the establishment of criteria, however, not all studies have found such a relationship for problem analysis. This suggests that the relationship between group decision-making effectiveness and problem-analysis communicative behavior is moderated by task demands, whereas the relationship for criteria establishment is not.

Surprisingly, despite the purported value of brainstorming and other idea-generation techniques for improving group decision making (see Sunwolf & Seibold, Chapter 15, this volume), tests of the Functional Perspective across study conditions have found *choice generation* to be largely unrelated to group decision-making performance. Graham et al. (1997) suggest that the reason most studies have found this is twofold: (a) Groups often do not have to generate choices to make sound decisions because the range of plausible choices is dictated to them, and (b) there is no inherent relationship between the quantity and quality of choices considered by a group.

Instead of focusing solely on communicative function/group decision-making performance relationships, other researchers have attempted to uncover the *conditions* under which interaction might be significantly related to decision quality. Salazar (1995, 1996, 1997, 1998; Salazar et al., 1994), for example, identifies conditions under which interaction might make meaningful contributions to group decision-making quality. Salazar (1996) distinguished group decision-making situations on the basis on two characteristics: tractability (manageability) of the group task and the degree to which members possess similar knowledge/information regarding decision alternatives or prefer the same alternatives prior to discussion (prediscussion preferences; see Meyers & Brashers, Chapter 11, this volume). These two characteristics combine to indicate the degree of ambiguity faced by groups. Hence, for example, groups operating in situations in which the task is highly tractable (manageable) and their members share prediscussion preferences regarding decision alternatives, work in relatively unambiguous situations compared to those groups for which task tractability is low and members do not share prediscussion preferences.

Salazar's (1997) study found that homogeneity of group members' prediscussion preferences, in particular, had an impact on the production of utterances fulfilling the requi-

site functions of high-quality decision making. Groups composed of individuals whose members had similar prediscussion preferences tended to produce fewer communicative utterances fulfilling the functional requisites of successful decision making when compared to groups whose members held different prediscussion preferences. Furthermore, the data indicated a trend toward greater impact of communication on decision-making quality as the ambiguity associated with the decision-making situation increased—that is, as task intractability and heterogeneity of members' prediscussion preferences increased.

Constitutive Research

Of the three perspectives guiding group communication and decision-making performance research, the Constitutive Perspective has received relatively less attention from scholars. Research emanating from this perspective has emphasized how communication serves to create certain rhetorical visions in an audience, the framing of issues to an audience, and the reasons for why members tell stories (narratives) that lead to shared fantasies and group consciousness (see, for example, Bormann, Knutson, & Musolf, 1997; Cragan & Shields, 1992). Furthermore, in attempting to illuminate the social milieu in which groups work, Schwartzman (1989) examined how decisions were framed in light of meeting time limitations, group members' needs for power, and collective sense-making. In short, group decision-making research adopting a Constitutive Perspective seeks to understand the processes involved in the creation of the social environments in which groups work, and how those environments subsequently are related to group performance. Relatively little work emanating from this perspective, however, has focused on group performance. This is unfortunate, for this perspective clearly has the potential to increase understanding of the link between group communication and group decision making, and ultimately, why some groups perform better than others.

Some scholars have claimed that certain types of group fantasies or rhetorical visions may be linked to high-quality decision-making performance (Bormann, 1986, 1996; Hirokawa & Salazar, 1997). Cragan and Shields (1981), for example, distinguish among three types of rhetorical visions: pragmatic, social, and righteous. Pragmatic rhetorical visions are centered around practical and utilitarian goals, social rhetorical visions emphasize relationships and getting along with others, and righteous rhetorical visions emphasize overarching causes or issues and fighting the good fight. Clearly, depending on the nature of a group's task and group member relations, as well as the external audience that might be affected by the group's ultimate decision, one or the other of these rhetorical visions may facilitate effective group work, and, thus, performance.

In an applied study of Symbolic Convergence Theory, although one not focused on group communication per se, Cragan and Shields (1992) showed how restructuring organizational "sagas" helped improve organizational performance. Their study of an organization's desire to restructure its fantasies, stories, and rhetorical visions in a manner congruent with those of its customers and dealers showed that changes in the organization's sagas may have had an impact on subsequent increases in sales. The instructive findings of this study are the organization's efforts to build the environment in which it would make decisions and the emphasis it placed on how that environment would be perceived by stakeholders. Given the restructuring of its rhetorical vision and identity in the eyes of customers and dealers, the organization was able to make decisions that met with some success. Had the organization's rhetorical vision, or the view of that vision by customers and dealers, been perceived differently, the decisions, though they would have been the same, may have resulted in less-than-desired outcomes.

The same may perhaps be said of groups engaged in decision-making activity. That is, groups often structure the social reality in which they make decisions by telling stories, sharing fantasies, and building a rhetorical vision. Some of those rhetorical visions may be more conducive to high-quality group decision making than others. The identity a group creates for itself as its members tell stories, share fantasies, and, ultimately, build a rhetorical vision also may have a far-reaching impact on the success of group decisions that are destined to be implemented outside the group context, that is, in the group's environment.

Another line of research that has begun to focus on the constitutive nature of communication and its association with group decision-making and problem-solving performance revolves around the application of Structuration Theory. Recall that a structurational approach to group decision making attempts to determine how the "actions by members of social collectivities create the structures that enable and constrain future interaction" (Poole & DeSanctis, 1992, p. 5). As such, structurational research seeks to identify the ways in which group members create the conditions for interacting within the group and construct the reality within which decisions will be made. Key to understanding these enabling and constraining conditions are structures that comprise the rules and resources used/reinforced in group interaction.

Sambamurthy and Poole (1992; see also Sambamurthy, Poole, & Kelly, 1993) examined how group decision support systems influence group structures that, in turn, influence group decision making. Their study found that a group's ability to surface and resolve opposition (i.e., successfully managing substantive conflict) was influenced by the type of GDSS used. Hence, endogenous factors—in this case, type of GDSS—influence the construction of the social reality or social milieu in which groups carry out their work.

Other studies, although not explicitly tied to Structuration Theory, are nevertheless informative when examined from that theoretical view and, hence, a Constitutive Perspective. For example, a number of case studies focus on the processes by which various norms and rules (see Keyton, Chapter 8, this volume) become established, accepted, and repeatedly used in groups. Some of these norms and rules become a matter of habit for making decisions (they serve as a blueprint or backdrop against which decisions are made) and serve to promote or inhibit group decision-making performance. For example, group norms that emphasize cohesion and agreement (thus suppressing critical inquiry and analysis of issues and information; see Janis, 1982); use of rational as opposed to political decision-making strategies (Senge, 1990); clear, elevating goals and standards of performance (Larson & LaFasto, 1989); and cultural norms that specify customs and traditions to be used in decision-making (Salazar & Witte, 1996) partly form the social environment in which group decisions are made and affect decision-making performance accordingly. These rules and norms are constituted (given life), legitimated, and perpetuated (and, therefore, may be changed) through group members' communication with one another.

GROUP COMMUNICATION AND GROUP DECISION-MAKING PERFORMANCE THEORY AND RESEARCH: AN ASSESSMENT

In one of the most detailed studies of the relationship between group interaction and decision-making effectiveness, Hackman and Morris (1975) formed 108 groups and allowed them to spend 15 minutes on each of four intellective tasks. The procedures used in the study resulted in a total of 432 group discussions. Each group came up with written solutions to each of the tasks it discussed. Group performance was operationalized along six dimensions: action orientation, length, originality, quality of presentation, optimism, and issue involvement. Interaction was analyzed in terms of a 16-category coding system that focused on task-oriented interaction among group members. Despite all their efforts, the researchers found no consistent relationships between the group interaction variables and performance outcomes. They

concluded that the apparent complexity of this relationship makes it difficult to develop simple explanations.

The study of group communication and decision-making performance is well past its incipient stage. Over the years, this area of study has made great strides in dealing with the complexity of the group interaction/performance relationship identified by Hackman and Morris (1975). Many questions, however, still remain unanswered. In some ways, our view of this relationship is perhaps more complex than it was during the time of Hackman and Morris's research. In this section of the chapter, we attempt to deal with such complexity by identifying some of the questions still in need of answers, as well as proposing some answers or ways in which they might be answered. We frame this discussion against the background of Mediational, Functional, and Constitutive perspectives, focusing on issues that we believe should propel communication research on group performance into the 21st century.

Assessment of Mediational Perspective Research

Studies emanating from the Mediational Perspective, as explained above, focus primarily on how communication serves to mediate the "true" determinants of performance. Generally, the quality of a group's resources is one of the determinants and, specifically, the quality of the information with which groups work is one of the most important resources (see Propp, Chapter 9, this volume); however, examination of how information is treated, reformulated, refined, redefined, and otherwise used in making group decisions, aside from evaluative assessments (such as "ineffective groups drew erroneous conclusions from the information with which they had to work"), has suffered from a lack of systematic study in the communication discipline. The study of information distributions in groups recently has gained increased attention in the psychology discipline (see, for example, Stasser, 1992; Stasser & Titus, 1985, 1987), especially in the social psychology and organizational psychology subfields; that the communication discipline has not paid more attention to information is a curious development given that information sampling and use in group decision making are inherently communicative phenomena.

When group communication scholars have examined information, they often have treated it as an input that affects either group processes or outcomes. That is, groups are studied under the assumption that there are no changes in the amount of knowledge/information members hold prior to discussion. Thus, studies primarily attempt to predict decision-making outcomes on the basis of prediscussion knowledge/information; relatively little attention has been paid to how that shared information is changed during group discussion or how new information is acquired and treated in group discussion. Such analyses may yield greater predictive power than focusing solely on initial knowledge that group members possess.

Examining how information is treated in groups, including the factors that seem to facilitate and impede the exchange of information that is shared (as well as unshared knowledge) among group members, presumably would offer insight into the group communication/performance relationship. Hollingshead's (1996) research is instructive in this regard. She found that asking individuals in groups to rank order alternatives rather than seeking the best one improved the chances of all alternatives receiving scrutiny and, thus, increased the likelihood that information regarding all alternatives would be exchanged. Such procedures encourage group members to sample a greater diversity of information.

Relatedly, communication scholars would be wise to devote more attention to whether communication technology can be used to facilitate information exchange (see McLeod, 1996). An increasing number of studies are being conducted to assess the effects of computer mediation on group communication processes (see Scott, chapter 16, this volume). Although interaction analyses of computer-mediated group discussions (e.g., by using

Bales's IPA or Hirokawa's functional coding schemes) have been conducted, there has been little focus on whether CM groups are more likely to sample more pieces of information compared to FtF groups. Furthermore, we have no indication of how to go about improving information sampling during group discussion, whether it takes place in CM or FtF groups.

Another characteristic deserving attention is the examination of diversity (Maznevski, 1994; Wanous & Youtz, 1986) and how it affects group communication processes and performance. Diversity in a group may be assessed along many dimensions. Groups may contain, for example, individuals who hold diverse viewpoints and knowledge/information, come from diverse cultures and represent different ethnicities, and are of different sexes. The effects of such differences have been studied in a group context, especially as to how they affect group communication and decision-making performance (see Haslett & Ruebush, Chapter 5, this volume); however, theoretical development, especially as it concerns cultural/ethnic and information diversity, has been lacking. This is unfortunate because research clearly indicates that information diversity influences decision-making performance (see Stasser, 1992), as do cultural and ethnic diversity (see Maznevski, 1994). The exact processes by which they exert that influence, however, are unknown. Understanding various types of diversity and their short-term and long-term implications for members should lead to greater understanding of the mechanisms by which diversity influences group interaction and decision-making outcomes (see Gelatt, 1989; Jackson, May, & Whitney, 1995; Stacey, 1996).

Group communication theory and model development that may be classified as mediational should also focus on the particular communication processes taking place when group members use specific process procedures or modes of communication. When comparing the same formats on the same task (e.g., Burleson et al., 1984; Erffmeyer & Lane, 1984; Hegedus & Rasmussen, 1986), differences in group communication processes may account for discrepancies in the results of studies attributing superior performance to one process procedure or mode over another. More research examining how communication patterns and processes are affected by different communication procedures and modes needs to be conducted.

Although there are quite a few studies of how process procedures, such as the Delphi technique and the NGT, versus free discussion differentially affect group outcomes (see Sunwolf & Seibold, Chapter 15, this volume), few of these studies have actually determined how particular features of communication itself are affected by the imposition of these procedures on a group, and how any such changes in communication subsequently affect group outcomes. Katzenstein (1996), for example, argues for the need to examine the communication process in ascertaining the effects of DA and DI on group decision-making performance. This is something to which more attention should be paid by theorists and researchers interested in developing more comprehensive models of the relationship between group communication and outcomes from the Mediational Perspective.

Assessment of Functional Perspective Research

Although the examination of the functional nature of group interaction vis-à-vis decision-making performance has yielded some interesting findings, this perspective is not without its problems and critics. Several scholars have noted that inconsistency remains a problem in tests and applications of the perspective, particularly in natural group settings (see, for example, Graham et al., 1997; Propp & Nelson, 1996). Stohl and Holmes (1993) indict the functional perspective for operating within a "closed system" framework in which "decision quality is an objective characteristic or attribute that is apparent and measurable when the decision is produced. . . . Traditional short-term conceptualizations of decision quality have decontextualized the task, sepa-

rating it from its political and historical context" (pp. 606, 610). Scheerhorn, Geist, and Teboul (1994) note that the Functional Perspective accounts for group decision-making performance solely in terms of task-related functions and, as such, ignores a whole host of possible relational functions (see Keyton, Chapter 8, this volume, on the relational dimension of group life). Pavitt (1994) points out that the Functional Perspective has not fulfilled the theoretical commitments presupposed by a functional explanation because it has yet to establish direct causal links between group communication processes and the satisfaction of functional requirements (see also Pavitt, Chapter 12, this volume, regarding functional approaches to the study of group communication and leadership). In short, it is clear that research examining the functional nature of group interaction is far from complete.

Of all the criticisms leveled against research conducted from the Functional Perspective, the most irrefutable concerns its inconsistency. That is, although group decision performance has been found to be correlated with the enactment of a variety of functional communicative behaviors, the specific functions that correlate with group performance tend to vary from study to study. Although a number of methodological explanations have been offered to account for this inconsistency, the crux of the problem lies in the insensitivity to task differences in current explanations of the perspective. In short, there is good reason to believe that relationships between functional requirements and group decision performance are moderated by task variations. As noted earlier, for example, the evaluation demands of a task (e.g., whether it has a positive or negative bias) is likely to influence whether strong or weak correlations are discovered between group performance and the evaluation of the positive and negative qualities of alternative choices.

The first major challenge facing future researchers who adopt the Functional Perspective is, thus, to add a task-contingency component to the theory to make it more sensitive to task variations. Hirokawa and McLeod (1993) have begun to develop such an extension. Drawing on the developmental theory of group decision making, they argue that the functional requirements facing a group come from three sources: (a) objective task characteristics, (b) group task characteristics, and (c) group structural characteristics.

Objective task characteristics represent the inherent properties of a group's task that describe its very nature, independent of the knowledge and experience of the members working on it. Examples of such characteristics include *goal clarity*—the extent to which clearly defined goals exist at the outset of the decision process, *openness*—the number of preestablished decision options available to a group, and *decision impact*—whether the decision affects only the group or a wider constituency.

Group task characteristics consist of features of a group's task that depend on the group and the situation at hand, and, as such, are likely to vary from group to group. Examples of such characteristics include *novelty*—the degree to which a group has previous experience with the issues to be decided; *innovativeness*—the degree to which a group has to create a new solution, as opposed to adopting or adapting an existing one; and *urgency*—the degree of time pressure on a group to make a decision.

Group structural characteristics pertain to the nature of interpersonal relationships among group members, as well as the manner in which they work together. Examples of such characteristics include *cohesiveness*—whether members perceive a group as an entity and are attracted to it (see Keyton, Chapter 8, this volume); *power concentration*—the degree to which power is concentrated in one or a few members, as opposed to being shared among all members; *conflict history*—the degree to which group members previously have been involved in open clashes or conflict; and *size*—the number of members in a group.

Hirokawa and McLeod (1993) posit that the objective task, group task, and group structural characteristics present in a task situation determine the basic set of functional requirements that a group must overcome to successfully complete its task. For example, a group presented with an open task is faced with the challenge of generating and developing a range of optional choices to reach a final decision. If such a task is a novel one to group members, then they must also understand the task and the demands it places on them, as well as recognize the obstacles and barriers to successful task completion. Furthermore, if the group possesses a history of conflict among its members, members face the additional challenges of managing emotions and motivations to facilitate cooperative and coordinated actions and attitudes among conflicting individuals.

In sum, Hirokawa and McLeod view the relationship between functional communicative behaviors and group decision-making performance as being affected by a combination of task and social factors. These possibilities remain largely untested to date and, thus, represent one important avenue of expansion for the future development of the Functional Perspective.

Another crucial challenge facing advocates of the Functional Perspective concerns the presumed relationship between group interaction and the performance of functional requirements. One of the "first principles" of the Functional Perspective is that group communication is *instrumental*—that it is through symbolic behaviors and their accompanying meanings that group members meet functional requirements. In a thoughtful essay, however, Pavitt (1994) points out that the Functional Perspective currently is unable to establish clear and unambiguous linkages between the communicative behaviors of group members and the performance of functional requirements (see also Pavitt, Chapter 12, this volume). The problem, as Pavitt sees it, is that communicative behaviors can function at "multiple levels of abstraction"; hence, the same behavior can simultaneously perform more than one function at any given moment in time. Thus, a second major challenge facing proponents of the Functional Perspective is to describe, in clear and precise ways, what communicative behaviors and patterns of behaviors *necessarily lead* to the performance of functional requirements.

There are, of course, good theoretical reasons to believe that the performance of functional requirements is tied to the production of particular types and patterns of communicative behaviors. Poole (1983b) posits that the requisite structure of a task—the set of functional requirements generated by task contingencies—sets forth logical behavioral requirements for task completion. In other words, group members must engage in certain types of discussional activities to address the challenges generated by various contingency factors. For example, such interactional activities as "introducing ideas," "developing ideas," "critiquing ideas," "modifying ideas," and "integrating and synthesizing ideas" presumably are important and necessary for the resolution of functional requirements associated with "solution generation," "solution development," and "solution evaluation."

Unfortunately, the Functional Perspective is not sufficiently developed at this point in time to account for linkages between group interactional processes and the performance of functional requirements. Expanding the perspective in this way is essential because there is good reason to believe that simply producing specific communicative behaviors is neither a sufficient nor a necessary condition for the resolution of emergent functional requirements (Gouran & Hirokawa, 1983). What also appears important is the structuring or sequencing of behaviors; the satisfaction of emergent functional requirements is likely to depend not only on the proportion of particular interactional behaviors in a decision-making sequence but also on the order in which those behaviors appear in the sequence.

To date, the Functional Perspective has been concerned primarily with how well communication serves to ensure that functional requirements are satisfied. The implicit assumption underlying this perspective is that groups are inherently capable of fulfilling existing functional requirements. As those who have worked with "real-life" groups can attest, however, group decision making is an activity frequently performed under the influence of powerful social and environmental constraints that can and do interfere with members' ability to satisfy the essential requirements of the decision-making task. Unfortunately, although some proponents of the Functional Perspective have acknowledged that problems in the social and relational domains of a group can affect its ability to satisfy functional requirements (see, for example, Gouran & Hirokawa, 1986; Hirokawa & McLeod, 1993), they have not dealt with these constraints in any systematic way. This represents the third major challenge facing advocates of the Functional Perspective.

In his most recent book, *Crucial Decisions: Leadership in Policy Making and Crisis Management,* Janis (1989) advances a "constraints model" that provides a structure and typology for systematically exploring how the relationship between group communication and the performance of functional requirements is hindered by various constraints. In particular, he identifies cognitive, affiliative, and egocentric constraints.

Cognitive constraints come into play when the members of a decision-making group confront a task for which little information is available, time is sharply limited, and/or the matter to be resolved is beyond the "ordinary" level of complexity. According to Janis, the presence of cognitive constraints can cause a group to resort to standard operating procedures in making choices, rather than vigilantly performing the essential requirements of the task. For example, because of scheduling problems or unanticipated delays, the members of a health care team at a hospital must attend to patients in less time than they are usually allotted. In these "crisis" situations, team members often rely on "habits of mind"—conventional wisdom about what a problem is likely to be and what should be done about it—to reduce the amount of time they spend with each patient. In doing so, they attend to various functional requirements in a cursory manner, rather than the detailed, vigilant manner expected of them.

Affiliative constraints usually occur when relationships among group members are a dominant concern and members fear either deterioration in such relationships or undue influence from one or more individuals whose thinking is not in line with majority sentiments. For example, the development of close friendships among health care team members sometimes hinders those individuals from engaging in "tough-minded" questioning of each others' assessments and recommendations. In post-rotation interviews, they often admit that they deliberately refrained from "making an issue" of something because they wanted to preserve the camaraderie that had been fostered within the team. In short, the presence of "affiliative constraints" can hinder members' efforts to effectively address functional requirements during group interaction.

Egocentric constraints are likely to occur when at least one member of a group has a highly pronounced need for control or is otherwise driven by personal motivations. Such constraints are also most likely to emerge when a group member perceives him- or herself to be of higher status than other members of a group. In these instances, the individual may well attempt to "take over" the group by dominating the discussion and telling others what ought to be done and how they ought to do it. In short, the presence of a controlling member often results in the ineffective performance of functional requirements because the group addresses only those functions that the controlling member feels it is necessary for the group to address.

When any of these constraints becomes dominant, effective group decision making is likely to be undermined in significant ways. Understanding how these constraints affect the performance of functional requirements during group interaction beyond the type of anecdotal evidence we have provided, thus, represents a crucial step in the future development of the Functional Perspective.

Assessment of Constitutive Perspective Research

As we noted, research emanating from the Constitutive Perspective has been scarce to nonexistent. Much of the research about group decision making from this perspective has emphasized the role of group communication processes in the development of group identities, rhetorical visions, and, generally, the creation of the social environments in which groups operate. Little research has been conducted that links identities, rhetorical visions, and socially created environments to group performance.

The promise of the Constitutive Perspective for providing an understanding of the relationship between group communication processes and performance, however, is tremendous. In addition to examining the shared rhetorical visions that promote the establishment of effective group decisions, future research should also concentrate on determining the relationship between achieving symbolic convergence and group performance. For some groups, symbolic convergence may be a necessary ingredient for making a successful decision, whereas for other groups, it may not. For example, when working on a task that is very familiar to them, it may not be necessary for group members to engage in the processes necessary to achieve common understanding of the symbols (e.g., words and wordplay) associated with the task. Group members may need to go through such processes, however, when they work on an ambiguous task or in a turbulent environment. In an effort to achieve common interpretations of the task and the environment, group members may tell stories of similar tasks and environments in which they have worked previously. In this way, symbolic convergence is achieved and, possibly, group performance is enhanced.

In addition to the effects of the task, relationships among group members may also specify when symbolic convergence and a common group identity become important for making effective decisions. For example, groups composed of diverse individuals (say, along cultural lines) may be different in ways that make communication and the effective exchange of information difficult. Individuals in such groups may not share assumptions about the meanings of the evidence and information with which they have to make a decision, or may even differ in the approach or style they take to making decisions (see Haslett & Ruebush, Chapter 5, this volume). In such cases, the establishment of a common group identity and interpretation of important symbols probably would facilitate communication and decision making and, therefore, group effectiveness.

Future research from a Constitutive Perspective should also focus on constructing a typology of the rhetorical visions that typically are developed in the group setting. Such a typology would be useful for examining the types of groups and tasks for which these rhetorical vision types occur most frequently, and their relationship to decision-making performance.

The types of rules and resources (structures) that group members use in interaction also have received relatively little attention in the context of group performance. Of importance here, for example, is the examination of how certain structuring moves may serve to constrain group members' interactions in the future, which may limit the alternatives that may be considered in coming up with a decision. To the extent that consideration of alternatives becomes limited, the chances of making high-quality decisions would, most likely, be severely impaired.

Finally, more research needs to be done to identify and assess the impact of endogenous factors on the structures group members draw on in communicating with one another. For example, Poole and his colleagues, cited earlier, have launched a research program that focuses on how different variables influence the paths that groups follow in reaching a decision, and the impact of group decision support systems in shaping conflict patterns that occur in these groups. More research

clearly needs to focus on those factors that impinge from the outside on group interaction processes, and how those processes, in turn, influence group decision-making performance.

CONCLUSION

Reflecting on the research reviewed in this chapter, one might well ask, "What types of advice can communication scholars give to practitioners concerning how to improve the accuracy and quality of the decisions groups make, or help groups reach consensus?" The answer, sadly, is "Not much." We do not mean to imply that the research conducted over the past few years is not important or has failed to shed light on the link between communication and group outcomes. Quite the contrary: The impact and quality of the research has improved with each succeeding year. It appears, however, that the more we know about the relationship between communication and group outcomes, there is just as much, if not more, that we do not know. Of course, such is the nature of inquiry.

We have attempted in this chapter to orient the reader to the major approaches taken by scholars studying and practicing group communication and to specify some of the important findings about the relationship between group communication and group performance outcomes. The difficult part, of course, is making sense of the diversity of approaches and findings. Given that diversity, we described some issues on which scholars should focus in building integrative, as well as more comprehensive, theories and models. All the while, we have kept an eye on the practical side of this research, that is, how this research can be applied in the "real-world" setting to help groups cope with the significant issues and problems they confront every day. We believe that resolution of these issues will come from research about groups in a variety of settings and employing a variety of methods, for greater insight into the functioning of group work can come only from the juxtaposition of findings and conclusions drawn from research conducted in diverse settings and using diverse methods (see Bettenhausen, 1991). When steps are taken to fully satisfy such requirements, we surely will be in a better position to give good advice to those who work with and in groups.

NOTES

1. In NGT, a group follows a six-step procedure (see Pavitt & Curtis, 1994; see also Sunwolf & Seibold, Chapter 15, this volume). First, group members silently generate ideas and write them down. Second, a member, usually the leader, records each idea as each group member, in round-robin fashion, voices his or her ideas. Third, on each idea, members are invited to voice their thoughts and opinions; evaluative statements are kept to a minimum, while descriptive statements are sought. Fourth, members write down their ratings or rankings of the ideas so as to reduce the number that will be considered as a pool from which the group's final decision will come. After all members' ratings/rankings have been considered, the top 5 or 10 ideas are retained for further discussion. Fifth, members discuss their preliminary vote, examine the pool of remaining ideas, and raise questions they might have about any of the ideas in the pool. Finally, members rate or rank the ideas in the pool; the leader tabulates these ratings and writes them on paper or a chalkboard that all can see. The idea receiving the most favorable rating or ranking is the group's final choice.

In contrast, the Delphi technique consists of four steps. First, a "gatekeeper" prepares and distributes to group members a questionnaire that states the task and asks for solutions. Second, members write their solutions and send them back to the gatekeeper, who prepares a list of the solutions and sends it to group members, asking for arguments for and against each solution, as well as clarification of the solutions, if that is required; members also are asked to cast a preliminary vote on the solutions. Third, members return their written comments and votes to the gatekeeper, who distributes a questionnaire containing a summary of members' comments and the results of the preliminary vote; the gatekeeper also requests a final vote. Fourth, members submit their votes to the gatekeeper, who tabulates them; the solution receiving the most favorable vote is the group's chosen one. The number of iterations can vary with the Delphi technique, but some research suggests that the optimal number is three.

2. Jarboe's (1988) study examined the effects of communicative and noncommunicative variables on solution quality. Using these variables, three models were examined: (a) an input-output model examined the effects of noncommunicative variables on solution quality, (b) a process-output model examined the effects of communicative variables on solution quality, and (c) an input-process-output model examined the combined effects of communicative and noncommunicative variables on solution quality. In the present context, less *ego-defensive communication* was associated with higher quality solutions when the process-output model was examined but dropped out as a significant predictor and was replaced by *suggests solution* when the input-process-output model was examined.

REFERENCES

Baird, A. C. (1927). *Public discussion and debate*. Boston: Ginn.

Bales, R. F. (1950). *Interaction process analysis: A method for the study of small groups*. Cambridge, MA: Addison-Wesley.

Barnlund, D. C. (1959). A comparative study of individual, majority, and group judgment. *Journal of Abnormal and Social Psychology, 58*, 55-60.

Barton, W. A. (1926). The effect of group activity and individual effort in developing ability to solve problems in first year algebra. *Educational Administration and Supervision, 12*, 412-418.

Bettenhausen, K. L. (1991). Five years of groups research: What have we learned and what needs to be addressed. *Journal of Management, 17*, 345-381.

Bormann, E. G. (1986). Symbolic convergence theory and communication in group decision-making. In R. Y. Hirokawa & M. S. Poole (Eds.), *Communication and group decision-making* (pp. 219-236). Beverly Hills, CA: Sage.

Bormann, E.G. (1996). Symbolic convergence theory and communication in group decision making. In R. Y. Hirokawa & M. S. Poole (Eds.), *Communication and group decision making* (2nd ed., pp. 81-113). Thousand Oaks, CA: Sage.

Bormann, E. G., Knutson, R. L., & Musolf, K. (1997). Why do people share fantasies? An empirical investigation of a basis tenet of the symbolic convergence communication theory. *Communication Studies, 48*, 254-276.

Brilhart, J. K., & Jochem, L. M. (1964). Effects of different patterns on outcomes of problem solving discussion. *Journal of Applied Psychology, 48*, 175-179.

Burleson, B. R., Levine, B. J., & Samter, W. (1984). Decision-making procedure and decision quality. *Human Communication Research, 10*, 557-574.

Carr, L. J. (1930). Experimentation in face-to-face interaction. *Public American Sociological Society Papers, 24*, 174-176.

Chapple, E. D. (1940). Measuring human relations: An introduction to the study of interaction of individuals. *Genetic Psychology Monographs, 22*, 3-147.

Chapple, E. D. (1942). The measurement of interpersonal behavior. *Transactions of the New York Academy of Science, 4*, 222-233.

Collins, B. E., & Guetzkow, H. (1964). *A social psychology of group processes of decision-making*. New York: John Wiley.

Cosier, R. A., & Rechner, P. L. (1985). Inquiry method effects on performance in a simulated business environment. *Organizational Behavior and Human Decision Processes, 36*, 79-95.

Cragan, J. F., & Shields, D. C. (1981). *Applied communication research: A dramatistic approach.* Prospect Heights, IL: Waveland.

Cragan, J. F., & Shields, D. C. (1992). The use of symbolic convergence theory in corporate strategic planning: A case study. *Journal of Applied Communication Research, 20,* 199-218.

Davis, J. H. (1973). Group decision and social interaction: A theory of social decision schemes. *Psychological Review, 80,* 97-125.

Dewey, J. (1910). *How we think.* Boston: D. C. Heath.

Dewey, J. (1933). *How we think: A restatement of the relation of reflective thinking to the educative process* (2nd ed.). Boston: D. C. Heath.

Eisenhardt, K. M. (1989). Making fast strategic decisions in high-velocity environments. *Academy of Management Journal, 32,* 543-576.

Elliot, H. S. (1927). *The how and why of group discussion.* New York: Association Press.

Erffmeyer, R. C., & Lane, I. M. (1984). Quality and acceptance of an evaluative task: The effects of four group decision-making formats. *Group & Organization Studies, 9,* 509-529.

Frey, L. R. (1996). Remembering and "re-membering": A history of theory and research on communication and group decision making. In R. Y. Hirokawa & M. S. Poole (Eds.), *Communication and group decision making* (2nd ed., pp. 19-51). Thousand Oaks, CA: Sage.

Gelatt, H. B. (1989). Positive uncertainty: A new decision-making framework. *Journal of Counseling Psychology, 36,* 252-256.

Giddens, A. (1979). *Central problems in social theory: Action, structure, and contradiction in social analysis.* London: Macmillan.

Giddens, A. (1984). *The constitution of society: Outline of the theory of structuration.* Berkeley: University of California Press.

Gouran, D. S., Brown, C. R., & Henry, D. R. (1978). Behavioral correlates of perceptions of quality in decision-making discussions. *Communication Monographs, 45,* 51-63.

Gouran, D. S., & Hirokawa, R. Y. (1983). The role of communication in decision-making groups: A functional perspective. In M. S. Mander (Ed.), *Communications in transition: Issues and debates in current research* (pp. 168-185). New York: Praeger.

Gouran, D. S., & Hirokawa, R. Y. (1986). Counteractive functions of communication in effective group decision-making. In R. Y. Hirokawa & M. S. Poole (Eds.), *Communication and group decision-making* (pp. 81-90). Beverly Hills, CA: Sage.

Gouran, D. S., & Hirokawa, R. Y. (1996). Functional theory and communication in decision-making and problem solving-groups: An expanded view. In R. Y. Hirokawa & M. S. Poole (Eds.), *Communication and group decision making* (2nd ed., pp. 55-80). Thousand Oaks, CA: Sage.

Gouran, D. S., Hirokawa, R. Y., Julian, K. M., & Leatham, G. B. (1993). The evolution and current status of the functional perspective on communication and group decision-making and problem-solving groups. In S. A. Deetz (Ed.), *Communication yearbook 16* (pp. 573-600). Newbury Park, CA: Sage.

Graham, E. E., Papa, M. J., & McPherson, M. B. (1997). An applied test of the functional communication perspective of small group decision-making. *Southern Communication Journal, 62,* 269-279.

Hackman, J. R. (Ed.). (1990). *Groups that work (and those that don't): Creating conditions for effective teamwork.* San Francisco: Jossey-Bass.

Hackman, J. R., & Morris, C. G. (1975). Group tasks, group interaction process, and group performance effectiveness: A review and proposed integration. In L. Berkowitz (Ed.), *Advances in experimental social psychology* (Vol. 8, pp. 45-99). New York: Academic Press.

Hall, J., & Watson, W. H. (1970). The effects of a normative intervention on group decision making performance. *Human Relations, 23,* 299-317.

Hare, A. P. (1976). *Handbook of small group research* (2nd ed.). New York: Free Press.

Hegedus, D. M., & Rasmussen, R. V. (1986). Task effectiveness and interaction process of a modified nominal group technique in solving an evaluation problem. *Journal of Management, 12,* 545-560.

Herbert, T. T., & Yost, E. B. (1979). A comparison of decision quality under nominal and interacting consensus group formats: The case of the structured problem. *Decision Sciences, 10,* 358-370.

Hiltz, S. R., Johnson, K., & Turoff, M. (1986). Experiments in group decision making: Communication process and outcome in face-to-face versus computerized conferences. *Human Communication Research, 13,* 225-252.

Hirokawa, R. Y. (1980). *A function-oriented analysis of small group interaction within effective and ineffective decision-making groups: An exploratory investigation.* Unpublished doctoral dissertation, University of Washington, Seattle.

Hirokawa, R. Y. (1982). Group communication and problem-solving effectiveness I: A critical review of inconsistent findings. *Communication Quarterly, 30,* 134-141.

Hirokawa, R. Y. (1983). Group communication and problem-solving effectiveness II: An exploratory investigation of procedural functions. *Western Journal of Speech Communication, 47,* 59-74.

Hirokawa, R. Y. (1985). Discussion procedures and decision-making performance: A test of a functional perspective. *Human Communication Research, 12,* 203-224.

Hirokawa, R. Y. (1987). Why informed groups make faulty decisions: An investigation of possible interaction-based explanations. *Small Group Behavior, 18,* 3-29.

Hirokawa, R. Y. (1988). Group communication and decision-making performance: A continued test of the functional perspective. *Human Communication Research, 14,* 487-515.

Hirokawa, R. Y., & Keyton, J. (1995). Perceived facilitators and inhibitors of effectiveness in organizational work teams. *Management Communication Quarterly,* *8,* 424-446.

Hirokawa, R. Y., & McLeod, P. L. (1993, November). *Communication, decision development, and decision quality in small groups: An integration of two approaches.* Paper presented at the annual meeting of the Speech Communication Association, Miami Beach, FL.

Hirokawa, R. Y., & Rost, K. M. (1992). Effective group decision-making in organizations: A field test of vigilant interaction theory. *Management Communication Quarterly,* *5,* 267-288.

Hirokawa, R. Y., & Salazar, A. J. (1997). An integrated approach to communication and group decision making. In L. R. Frey & J. K. Barge (Eds.), *Managing group life: Communicating in decision-making groups* (pp. 156-181). Boston: Houghton Mifflin.

Hirokawa, R. Y., Salazar, A. J., Erbert, L., & Ice, R. J. (1996). Small group communication: Theory and research. In M. Salwen & D. Stacks (Eds.), *Integrated approaches to communication theory and research* (pp. 359-381). Hillsdale, NJ: Lawrence Erlbaum.

Hirokawa, R. Y., & Scheerhorn, D. R. (1986). Communication in faulty group decision-making. In R. Y. Hirokawa & M. S. Poole (Eds.), *Communication and group decision-making* (pp. 63-80). Beverly Hills, CA: Sage.

Hollingshead, A. B. (1996). The rank-order effect in group decision making. *Organizational Behavior and Human Decision Processes,* *68,* 181-193.

Jackson, S. E., May, K. E., & Whitney, K. (1995). Understanding the dynamics of diversity in decision-making teams. In R. A. Guzzo & E. Salas (Eds.), *Team effectiveness and decision-making in organizations* (pp. 204-261). San Francisco: Jossey-Bass.

Janis, I. L. (1972). *Victims of groupthink: Psychological studies of foreign policy decisions and fiascoes.* Boston: Houghton Mifflin.

Janis, I. L. (1982). *Groupthink: Psychological studies of policy decisions and fiascoes* (2nd ed.). Boston: Houghton Mifflin.

Janis, I. L. (1989). *Crucial decisions: Leadership in policy making and crisis management.* New York: Free Press.

Janis, I. L., & Mann, L. (1977). *Decision making: A psychological analysis of conflict, choice, and commitment.* New York: Free Press.

Jarboe, S. (1988). A comparison of input-output, process-output, and input-process-output models of small group problem-solving effectiveness. *Communication Monographs,* *55,* 121-142.

Katzell, R. A., Miller, C. E., Rotter, N. G., & Venet, T. G. (1970). Effects of leadership and other inputs on group process and outputs. *Journal of Social Psychology,* *80,* 157-169.

Katzenstein, G. (1996). The debate on structured debate: Toward a unified theory. *Organizational Behavior and Human Decision Processes,* *66,* 316-332.

Kelley, H. H., & Thibaut, J. W. (1969). Group problem solving. In G. Lindzey & E. Aronson (Eds.), *The handbook of social psychology: Vol. 4. Group psychology and phenomena of interaction* (2nd ed., pp. 1-101). Reading, MA: Addison-Wesley.

Lanzetta, J. T., & Roby, T. B. (1960). The relationship between certain group process variables and group problem-solving efficiency. *Journal of Social Psychology,* *52,* 135-148.

Larson, C. W., & LaFasto, F. M. J. (1989). *Teamwork: What must go right/what can go wrong.* Beverly Hills, CA: Sage.

Lawler, E., & Mohrman, S. (1985, January-February). Quality circles after the fad. *Harvard Business Review,* pp. 65-71.

Leavitt, H. J. (1951). Some effects of certain communication patterns on group performance. *Journal of Abnormal and Social Psychology,* *46,* 38-50.

Marston, W. M. (1924). Studies in testimony. *Journal of Criminal and Criminology,* *15,* 5-31.

Maznevski, M. L. (1994). Understanding our differences: Performance in decision-making groups with diverse members. *Human Relations,* *47,* 531-552.

McBurney, J. H., & Hance, K. G. (1939). *The principles and methods of discussion.* New York: Harper and Brothers.

McGrath, J. E. (1984). *Groups: Interaction and performance.* Englewood Cliffs, NJ: Prentice-Hall.

McLeod, P. L. (1996). New communication technologies for group decision making: Toward an integrative framework. In R. Y. Hirokawa & M. S. Poole (Eds.), *Communication and group decision making* (2nd ed., pp. 426-461). Thousand Oaks, CA: Sage.

Meyers, R. A. (1997). Social influence and group argumentation. In L. R. Frey & J. K. Barge (Eds.), *Managing group life: Communicating in decision-making groups* (pp. 183-201). Boston: Houghton Mifflin.

Miller, D. C. (1939). An experiment in the measurement of social interaction in group development. *American Sociological Review,* *4,* 241-251.

Newsletter, W. I. (1937). An experiment in the defining and measuring of group adjustment. *American Sociological Review,* *2,* 230-236.

Orlitzky, M. O., & Hirokawa, R. Y. (1997, November). *To err is human, to correct for is divine: A meta-analysis of research testing the functional theory of group decision-making effectiveness.* Paper presented at the annual meeting of the National Communication Association, Chicago.

Pavitt, C. (1994). Theoretical commitments presupposed by functional approaches to group discussion. *Small Group Research,* *25,* 520-541.

Pavitt, C., & Curtis, E. (1994). *Small group discussion: A theoretical approach* (2nd ed.). Scottsdale, AZ: Gorsuch Scarisbrick.

Poole, M. S. (1981). Decision development in small groups I: A comparison of two models. *Communication Monographs,* *48,* 1-24.

Poole, M. S. (1983a). Decision development in small groups II: A study of multiple sequences in decision making. *Communication Monographs,* *50,* 206-232.

Poole, M. S. (1983b). Decision development in small groups, III: A multiple sequence model of group decision development. *Communication Monographs,* *50,* 321-341.

Poole, M. S., & Baldwin, C. L. (1996). Developmental processes in group decision making. In R. Y. Hirokawa & M. S. Poole (Eds.), *Communication and group decision making* (2nd ed., pp. 215-241). Thousand Oaks, CA: Sage.

Poole, M. S., & DeSanctis, G. (1992). Microlevel structuration in computer-supported group decision making. *Human Communication Research, 19,* 5-49.

Poole, M. S., & Doelger, J. A. (1986). Developmental processes in group decision-making. In R. Y. Hirokawa & M. S. Poole (Eds.), *Communication and group decision-making* (pp. 35-61). Beverly Hills, CA: Sage.

Poole, M. S., & Hirokawa, R. Y. (1996). Introduction: Communication and group decision making. In R. Y. Hirokawa & M. S. Poole (Eds.), *Communication and group decision making* (2nd ed., pp. 3-18). Thousand Oaks, CA: Sage.

Poole, M. S., & Roth, J. (1989a). Decision development in small groups IV: A typology of group decision paths. *Human Communication Research, 15,* 323-356.

Poole, M. S., & Roth, J. (1989b). Decision development in small groups V: Test of a contingency model. *Human Communication Research, 15,* 549-589.

Poole, M. S., Seibold, D. R., & McPhee, R. D. (1985). Group decision-making as a structurational process. *Quarterly Journal of Speech, 71,* 74-102.

Poole, M. S., Seibold, D. R., & McPhee, R. D. (1986). A structurational approach to theory-building in group decision-making research. In R. Y. Hirokawa & M. S. Poole (Eds.), *Communication and group decision-making* (pp. 237-264). Beverly Hills, CA: Sage.

Poole, M. S., Seibold, D. R., & McPhee, R. D. (1996). The structuration of group decisions. In R. Y. Hirokawa & M. S. Poole (Eds.), *Communication and group decision making* (2nd ed., pp. 114-146). Thousand Oaks, CA: Sage.

Priem, R. L., & Price, K. H. (1991). Process and outcome expectations of the dialectical inquiry, devil's advocacy, and consensus techniques of strategic decision making. *Group & Organization Studies, 16,* 206-225.

Propp, K. M., & Nelson, D. (1996). Problem-solving performance in naturalistic groups: A test of the ecological validity of the functional perspective. *Communication Studies, 47,* 35-45.

Riecken, H. W. (1958). The effect of talkativeness on ability to influence group solutions to problems. *Sociometry, 21,* 309-321.

Ringelmann, M. (1913). Research on animate sources of power: The work of man. *Annales de l'Institut National Agronomique* (2e serie, tome XII), 1-40.

Salazar, A. J. (1995). Understanding the synergistic effects of communication in small groups: Making the most out of group member abilities. *Small Group Research, 26,* 169-199.

Salazar, A. J. (1996). Ambiguity and communication effects on small group decision-making performance. *Human Communication Research, 23,* 155-192.

Salazar, A. J. (1997). Communication effects on small group decision-making: Homogeneity and task as moderators of the communication-performance relationship. *Western Journal of Communication, 61,* 35-65.

Salazar, A. J. (1998). *Groups operating in complex environments: Learning, creativity and performance.* Unpublished manuscript, Texas A&M University, College Station.

Salazar, A. J., Hirokawa, R. Y., Propp, K. M., Julian, K. M., & Leatham, G. B. (1994). In search of true causes: Examination of the effect of group potential and group interaction on decision performance. *Human Communication Research, 20,* 529-559.

Salazar, A. J., & Witte, K. (1996). Communication and the decision-making process. In W. Donohue & D. Cai (Eds.), *Communicating and connecting: The functions of human communication* (pp. 277-304). Fort Worth, TX: Harcourt Brace.

Sambamurthy, V., & Chin, W. W. (1994). The effects of group attitudes toward alternative GDSS designs on the decision-making performance of computer supported groups. *Decision Sciences, 25,* 215-241.

Sambamurthy, V., & Poole, M. S. (1992). The effects of variations in capabilities of GDSS designs on management of cognitive conflict in groups. *Information Systems Research, 3,* 224-251.

Sambamurthy, V., Poole, M. S., & Kelly, J. (1993). The effects of variations in GDSS capabilities on decision making processes in groups. *Small Group Research, 24,* 523-546.

Sanderson, D. (1938). Group description. *Social Forces, 16,* 309-319.

Scheerhorn, D., Geist, P., & Teboul, JC. B. (1994). Beyond decision making in decision-making groups: Implications for the study of group communication. In L. R. Frey (Ed.), *Group communication in context: Studies of natural groups* (pp. 247-262). Hillsdale, NJ: Lawrence Erlbaum.

Schwartzman, H. B. (1989). *The meeting: Gatherings in organizations and communities.* New York: Plenum.

Schweiger, D. M., & Sandberg, W. R. (1989). The utilization of individual capabilities in group approaches to strategic decision-making. *Strategic Management Journal, 10,* 31-43.

Schweiger, D. M., Sandberg, W. R., & Ragan, J. W. (1986). Group approaches for improving strategic decision-making: A comparative analysis of dialectical inquiry, devil's advocacy, and consensus. *Academy of Management Journal, 29,* 51-71.

Schweiger, D. M., Sandberg, W. R., & Rechner, P. L. (1989). Experiential effects of dialectical inquiry, devil's advocacy, and consensus approaches to strategic decision-making. *Academy of Management Journal, 32,* 745-772.

Schwenk, C. R., & Cosier, R. A. (1993). Effects of consensus and devil's advocacy on strategic decision-making. *Journal of Applied Psychology, 23,* 126-139.

Schwenk, C., & Valacich, J. S. (1994). Effects of devil's advocacy and dialectical inquiry on individuals versus groups. *Organizational Behavior and Human Decision Processes, 59,* 210-222.

Senge, P. M. (1990). *The fifth discipline: The art and practice of the learning organization.* New York: Doubleday/Currency.

Shaw, M. E. (1932). Comparison of individuals and small groups in the rational solution of complex problems. *American Journal of Psychology, 44,* 491-504.

Shaw, M. E., & Penrod, W. T. (1964). Group effectiveness as a function of "legitimate" information. *Journal of Social Psychology, 62,* 241-246.

Sheffield, A. D. (1926). *Creative discussion: A statement of method for leaders and members of discussion groups and conferences* (3rd ed.). New York: American Press.

Stacey, R. D. (1996). *Complexity and creativity in organizations.* San Francisco: Berrett-Koehler.

Stasser, G. (1992). Pooling of unshared information during group discussions. In S. Worchel, W. Wood, & J. Simpson (Eds.), *Group process and productivity* (pp. 48-67). Newbury Park, CA: Sage.

Stasser, G., & Titus, W. (1985). Pooling of unshared information in group decision making: Biased information sampling during discussion. *Journal of Personality and Social Psychology, 48,* 1467-1478.

Stasser, G., & Titus, W. (1987). Effects of information load and percentage of shared information on the dissemination of unshared information during group discussion. *Journal of Personality and Social Psychology, 53,* 81-93.

Stohl, C., & Holmes, M. E. (1993). A functional perspective for bona fide groups. In S. A. Deetz (Ed.), *Communication yearbook 16* (pp. 601-614). Newbury Park, CA: Sage.

Taylor, D., & Faust, W. (1952). Twenty questions: Efficiency in problem solving as a function of size of group. *Journal of Experimental Psychology, 44,* 360-368.

Wall, V. D., Galanes, G. J., & Love, S. B. (1987). Small, task-oriented groups: Conflict, conflict management, satisfaction, and decision quality. *Small Group Research, 18,* 31-55.

Wanous, J. P., & Youtz, M. A. (1986). Solution diversity and the quality of group decisions. *Academy of Management Journal, 29,* 149-159.

Watson, G. B. (1928). Do groups think more efficiently than individuals? *Journal of Abnormal and Social Psychology, 23,* 328-336.

Wrightstone, J. W. (1934). An instrument for measuring group discussion and planning. *Journal of Educational Research, 27,* 641-650.

8

Relational Communication in Groups

JOANN KEYTON
The University of Memphis

Anyone who has a close set of friends or has felt the camaraderie that developed while working in a team in an organization has experienced the importance of the relational dimension of group life. This chapter focuses on relational messages in groups and relationships among group members by presenting seminal and representative research about relational messages, processes, and outcomes in groups. To date, there has been no attempt to organize or summarize this literature. Perhaps this is due to the difficulty of completing a comprehensive review of relevant literature, as much of the research on relationships in groups is embedded in task or decision-making group research (titles do not reference relational issues, nor are articles indexed with respect to them). The material reviewed here includes research by communication scholars and draws on the work of scholars from other disciplines (e.g., Management and Social Psychology) who address relational issues in groups, as well as research reflecting a wide variety of groups, from task-oriented groups (e.g., organizational teams) to relationship-oriented groups (e.g., social support groups).

The review is restricted to *interacting groups*. Although the term *relational commu-*

nication often is substituted for *interpersonal communication,* that substitution is not satisfactory in the group context, for the relational dynamics of groups, where multiple relationships must simultaneously be developed and managed, are more complex than those in dyads. Hence, although the interpersonal literature may inform the study of relational interaction in groups, it alone cannot explain the group context. Given these contextual distinctions, *relational communication in groups* refers to the verbal and nonverbal messages that create the social fabric of a group by promoting relationships between and among group members. It is the affective or expressive dimension of group communication, as opposed to the instrumental, or task-oriented, dimension (see Hirokawa & Salazar, Chapter 7, this volume). Thus, relational communication in groups encompasses both the structures and processes of a group's social reality—that is, "the connections, relations, and communication *among* members of the group" (Scheerhorn & Geist, 1997, p. 83).

Kelley and Thibaut (1954) argue that a group is a social context in which social influence occurs. Thus, messages can maintain or alter relationships among group members, as well as create the climate within which group members accomplish their tasks. All groups engage in relational communication, but they vary widely in the quantity and quality of their relational messages. With respect to quantity, family and social support groups, for example, favor relational over task communication (in this volume, see, respectively, Socha [Chapter 17] and Cline [Chapter 19]), whereas decision-making groups, such as organizational teams and work groups (see Greenbaum & Query, Chapter 20, this volume), favor task over relational messages. With respect to quality, both relationship-oriented and task-oriented groups can generate positive (e.g., supportive) and negative (e.g., hurtful) relational messages.

Apart from affecting a group's interaction environment, relational communication also affects individual group members. Relational messages help individuals identify where they fit within the network of intragroup relationships, the status and power other members attribute to them, and/or how well liked they are by other members. When group members communicate directly or indirectly about their relationships with one another, they provide cues about their own and other members' worth and identities that, ultimately, affect their self-esteem. Understanding the role of relational communication in groups, therefore, is important for group members and scholars alike.

POSITIONING THE RELATIONAL IN GROUP COMMUNICATION RESEARCH

As the first scholar to focus on relational issues in groups from a communication perspective, R. Morgan (1934) argued that students should be taught principles of cooperation to guide their interactions during group discussions. Early on, Benne and Sheats's (1948) functional role classification identified task roles as being distinct from group building, maintenance, and individual roles. Bales (1950) drew a similar distinction by classifying interaction as either task-related (that which

focuses on achieving a group's goal) or socioemotional (that which focuses on interpersonal relationships among group members) (in this volume, see Chapters 2 [Poole] and 12 [Pavitt]). Subsequently, he observed that the two dimensions are interdependent, in that failure to respond to socioemotional (or relational) demands eventually impedes a group's task performance. Later, Hare (1976) identified issues of control and affection as most representative of the socioemotional dimension of groups.

Although most group researchers focus on task-related messages, they readily acknowledge a relational component to messages generated within groups (see, for example, B. A. Fisher, 1979; Wheeless, Wheeless, & Dickson-Markman, 1982). Even when they are studied, however, relational messages are analyzed, for the most part, with respect to their impact on task messages or outcomes, rather than their impact on relationships among group members. Within such a framework, relational messages and relationships among members are seen as potentially facilitating, but more often as inhibiting, effective group performance (e.g., Collins & Guetzkow, 1964). Before turning to a review of the literature, I discuss why group researchers should be interested in relational communication and some possible reasons for the exclusion of relational issues in groups.

The focus of communication scholarship on groups, rooted initially in discussion (see Gouran, Chapter 1, this volume), now emphasizes decision-making tasks. In both streams of research, task issues are emphasized and relational issues are subordinated to them. Hirokawa and Gouran (1989), for example, discuss relational problems only with respect to how they impede group progress in performing decision-making tasks. Although scholars readily acknowledge the dual task/relational content of many messages, they have done little to explain how relationships among group members develop or how relational messages affect group processes or outcomes (such as group development and even decision making). Recently, however, some group communication scholars (see Frey, 1994a, 1994c, 1996; Gouran, 1994; Keyton, 1994; Meyers & Brashers, 1994) have argued that relationships among group members matter on many levels, including their role in establishing the climate within which group tasks are accomplished.

Other disciplines interested in the group context also have not privileged relationships in groups. Early researchers in Industrial and Organizational Psychology, for example, acknowledged, but then skirted, relational issues. A case in point are the Hawthorne studies (Roethlisberger & Dickson, 1946), a series of inquiries examining the effects of various environmental and social factors on worker performance that found that relational messages are powerful enough to shape on-the-job behavior. Even though the researchers acknowledged that "a social organization existed quite apart from the formal organization laid out on the organizational chart" and that work groups "provided an influential social context within which individuals acted" (Shea & Guzzo, 1987, p. 324), this research generally is regarded as studies of worker productivity, not relational issues in groups. Levine and Moreland's (1990) review of group research in Psychology demonstrates that although group social environments are considered important, group members' relationships with one another are not part of that consideration. Rather, the social environment of a group is said to consist of (a) intergroup relations, (b) the group's relationship to its larger organization, (c) the influence of other groups that share the group's members, and (d) influence by nongroup members. Consequently, little research has been conducted on members' relationships within groups.

Ironically, Shea and Guzzo (1987) complained that fellow management scholars concerned with the socioemotional consequences of group action (e.g., satisfaction) as elements of group effectiveness have ignored the relevance of these effects on that outcome. More recently, however, management scholars have embraced Hackman's (1990) position that one dimension of group effectiveness is the "degree to which the process of carrying out the work enhances the capability of members to work together interdependently in the future" (p. 6). The case studies in his edited collection suggest that this capability includes relational issues.

The focus on task rather than relational issues demonstrated across academic disciplines likely occurred, Seibold and Meyers (1988) explain, because

with few exceptions, "groups" have been operationalized as aggregates of fewer than six or seven teenage college students *who do not know each other well, have had little experience interacting together,* and are required or induced to collaborate—in artificial settings—on tasks that usually are contrived and/or have few valued consequences for the participants individually or collectively. (p. 8; italics added)

Operationalizing groups in this way severely limits opportunities for researchers to address relational issues, because relationships among group members are largely undeveloped as a result of how laboratory groups are created. With zero-history laboratory groups at the center of research, studying relational issues becomes difficult, if not impossible, for few, if any, substantive relational issues unfold within the constraints of that setting.

Another reason relational concerns have largely been ignored is that researchers too often focus on individual group members rather than on the group as a unit (Poole, 1990, 1994, 1998, also Chapter 2, this volume). Moreover, a number of scholars (e.g., Frey, 1994c, 1996; Meyers & Brashers, 1994; Wyatt, 1993) argue that relational issues in groups have been ignored because decision making reflects the domain of male (and, therefore, traditional research) interests, whereas relational issues reflect the domain of female interests. These scholars have called for group researchers to study more relationship-oriented groups, such as social support groups and women's groups. By broadening the term *group* to include groups of all types (see Propp & Kreps, 1994), researchers will widen their perspective from task groups to groups in which relational issues are primary.

Despite the general lack of attention to relationships and relational messages within groups, some researchers have started to recognize and explore their significance. The relatively recent move from the laboratory to natural group contexts, in particular, has helped researchers to pay more attention to relational issues. Cluck and Cline (1986), for example, proposed a series of questions regarding relational aspects of communication in self-help groups for the bereaved (see also Cline, Chapter 19, this volume). Edited collections (e.g., Frey, 1994b, 1995, in press; Guzzo & Salas, 1995; Hackman, 1990) vividly demonstrate the extent to which relational messages matter in a variety of group contexts. An exemplar of this research is Adelman and Frey's (1994, 1997) investigation of how relational communication (such as social support messages) mediates tensions between individuals and the collective group as community is created and sustained in an AIDS residential facility. Another example is Conquergood's (1994) study of how gang communication celebrates interconnectedness and strong attachments among members and, thereby, helps to create a home and a family for these marginalized members of society.

Three arguments support the position that relationships and relational messages need to be studied in the group context. First, many groups exist primarily to satisfy relational needs (e.g., families, friendship groups, and social support groups). Our society's reliance on groups to meet personal and relational needs has become so great that it is estimated that about 15 million U.S. Americans attend 500,000 support group meetings per week ("Unite and Conquer," 1990). These numbers, of course, do not account for those who play softball, soccer, and other team sports on a regular basis, nor do they include interactions of families, friends, religious groups, musical or performing groups, community/civic groups, and volunteer groups, among others. In each of these groups, relational issues are of central importance and most certainly affect whatever tasks are performed. Clearly, then, in the grand landscape of groups, relational issues are not always subordinate to task issues.

Second, even within primarily task-oriented groups, relational issues are related to task issues in crucial ways. Groups cannot accomplish their objectives or maintain their groupness solely through task-related communication. Inherent in group settings is the presence of other individuals with whom members must interact to accomplish a goal or perform a task. In doing so, members create or negate relationships with fellow group members. Gouran and Hirokawa (1996) provide support for this argument when they note that decision making can be constrained when relationships among group members "are a dominant concern and . . . [members] fear either deterioration in such relationships or undue influence from one or more individuals" (p. 61). Thus, relational interaction results in positive, negative, or indifferent feelings and/or attitudes on the part of members about their group, its tasks, and/or one's self. As Frey (1996) explains:

> Ignoring relational issues in [decision-making] groups ignores the historical context of groups which constitutes and continually is reconstituted by their communication practices and decision-making outcomes. This shared history, constructed socially over time through language, arguments, stories, and symbols, represents a "deep structure" that influences the "surface structure" of a group's interactional patterns and decision making. (p. 19)

This argument receives additional support from research suggesting that interpersonal problems and poor communication skills are cited most frequently by those who work in groups as reasons why groups are ineffective (Di Salvo, Nikkel, & Monroe, 1989). Thus, problems arising from the relational dimension of group life create as much, if not more, difficulty for group members than problems arising from task concerns.

It is also important for scholars to realize that decision-making groups do more than just make decisions. In a study of standing policy groups embedded in organizations (representing executive meetings and policy task forces in health organizations, tenants' groups, sales meetings, and departmental head meetings), Scheerhorn, Geist, and Teboul (1994) found the primary functions of these meetings to be (in order of frequency) information dissemination, decision making, coordination, motivation, and affiliation. Their data indicate that "decision making is merely one type of predominant activity within real decision-making groups" (p. 256). Hackman's (1990) collection of case studies reinforces the finding.

Third, the interdependence among group members calls attention to the significance of members' relationships. Relational interdependence (e.g., power relationships and role conflicts) is present also by virtue of group members' connections to others outside the group. Putnam and Stohl (1990, 1996) argue for a theoretical approach that "treats a group as a social system linked to its context, shaped by fluid boundaries, and altering its environment" (1996, p. 148). They call for the study of *bona fide groups,* which are intended as models or prototypes of an ideal group (in this volume, see Chapters 1 [Gouran] and 2 [Poole]). Bona fide groups have permeable and fluid boundaries, have ambiguous and shifting borders, and are interdependent with their contexts or environments. This perspective acknowledges that the members of any given group are also members of other groups and that group membership and boundaries can and do fluctuate. As a result, relationships among group members are altered by the presence or absence of relational or role conflict stemming from people's multiple memberships. Additionally, relationships among group members change when members leave or when newcomers enter a group (see Anderson, Riddle, & Martin, Chapter 6, this volume, regarding socialization practices in groups). Most important to the study of relationships and relational messages within groups, the

Bona Fide Group Perspective posits that the formation of group identity "centers on the degree to which members enact a sense of belongingness, loyalty, or commitment" to their group (Putnam & Stohl, 1996, p. 151).

As the discussion above reveals, few researchers have focused on how relational messages (a) are constructed, (b) function in group settings, (c) affect group tasks, and (d) influence relational outcomes. There are, however, good reasons for studying these processes and outcomes. Although there are few lines of clear, systematic research on relational communication in groups, and although the research that does exist has received uneven treatment, there is important information contained within existing studies that needs to be explicated both for the purpose of revealing what we currently know about relational communication in groups and for framing the agenda for future research in this area. Before turning to the existing research, I offer a framework for organizing this literature.

AN ORGANIZING FRAMEWORK FOR UNDERSTANDING RELATIONAL COMMUNICATION IN GROUPS

Figure 8.1 proposes a model for how *relational messages* function in groups and is used as an organizing device for the remainder of this chapter. The model identifies and organizes relational communication in groups in three ways. First, the model draws attention to the relational elements of all messages exchanged in groups (both messages that traditionally are viewed as relational and those viewed as task-oriented). Watzlawick, Beavin, and Jackson (1967) argue that content and relational information appears in all messages. The degree to which a message carries relational information varies on the basis of the message itself, as well as the verbal and nonverbal (see Ketrow, Chapter 10, this volume, regarding nonverbal communication in groups) style of the message sender. For example, when a group member takes the floor at the start of a meeting and shares her expectations for the meeting, she not only provides content

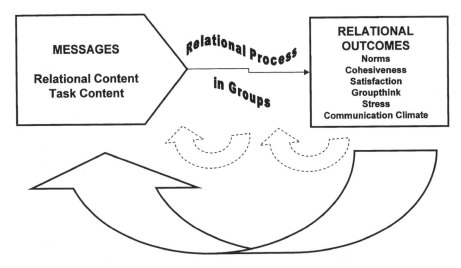

Figure 8.1. Relational Messages, Processes, and Outcomes in Groups

information that helps set the agenda but also provides relational messages that signify status, control, and dominance. Obviously, the relational impact of any message varies as a function of the dynamics of sender and receiver characteristics, sender-receiver relationships, and the group context.

Second, the model draws attention to the *relational processes* that occur as a result of communication in groups, such as group development, relationship development, and the development of shared meaning. Although much of the interpersonal literature could be extrapolated to the group context to help explain some of these relational processes, as mentioned previously, given the dynamics of multiple and simultaneous relationships occurring in groups, it is unclear whether this material can effectively explain relational processes in groups. Equally problematic, much of the research that appears to address relational processes in groups (in particular, research on norms) actually addresses the consequences of relational outcomes (e.g., what happens in groups as a result of norms being developed), rather than the role of relational processes in creating the outcomes (e.g., how norms are developed). It is this area of the model that holds the most promise for future research.

Third, the model draws attention to traditional, positively valenced *relational outcomes,* such as group norms, cohesiveness, and member satisfaction, as well as negatively valenced relational outcomes, such as groupthink and stress, that have been studied more recently. Thus, the model provides for a holistic understanding of how relational messages and processes affect relational outcomes in groups.

The model is cyclical in that relational outcomes affect subsequent task and relational messages, which, in turn, affect subsequent relational processes, and so forth. More important, the model is not intended to be a representation of group development over time in which relational outcomes occur only at the conclusion of a group's work. Rather, relational outcomes can be and are present throughout a group's history. Thus, the model can represent relational processes of a group that interacts for 1 hour, over many weeks, or even over many years.

In the next few sections, I examine research relevant to relational messages, processes, and outcomes in groups. Following this, I review research on relatively new topics that affect relational life in groups, including humor in groups, multicultural group issues, and the use of new technology. The chapter concludes with an evaluative summary of extant research and an agenda for future research on issues in groups.

RELATIONAL MESSAGES IN GROUPS

All messages in groups, as previously explained, contain some relational information (Watzlawick et al., 1967). Several approaches have been advanced to identify and account for the relational content of messages. Three of the most popular approaches used by group communication scholars are Interaction Process Analysis (IPA), the System for the Multiple Level Observation of Groups (SYMLOG), and the Interact System Model (ISM).

IPA and SYMLOG

Bales's (1950, 1953) Interaction Process Analysis is the seminal work in distinguishing between a group's task and relational (or socioemotional, as he called it) communicative functions (in this volume, see Chapters 2 [Poole], 12 [Pavitt], and 17 [Socha]). As a theory, as well as an observational system, IPA describes the type of messages forwarded and patterns of interactions in groups. According to Bales, each communicative act can be categorized into 1 of 12 mutually exclusive categories. Six categories describe group members' *socioemotional* communicative acts: shows solidarity/seems friendly, dramatizes/ releases tension, and agrees are acts that promote positive member relations; disagrees, shows tension, and shows antagonism/seems unfriendly are acts that promote negative member relations. Acts not coded into socioemotional categories are coded into one of six *task* categories: gives suggestion, gives opinion, gives orientation/information, asks for orientation/information, asks for opinion, and asks for suggestion.

According to Bales, group members strive to maintain equilibrium between task and relational efforts, which are in constant conflict. Too much attention to task concerns limits a group's attention to its relational issues, and vice versa. A group's emphasis on task or relational concerns, or its ability to maintain equilibrium between the two, should thus be evident in the talk that takes place in the group. Bales (1953) argued that groups need positive reinforcement (communicative acts of shows solidarity/seems friendly, dramatizes/ releases tension, and agrees) to offset negative reactions (communicative acts of disagree, shows tension, and shows antagonism/seems unfriendly). In fact, "a group needs positive reactions in excess of negative ones in order to get its tasks successfully completed" (McGrath, 1984, p. 151). A larger positive-to-negative ratio facilitates and regulates the flow of interaction among and affects the motivations of group members. Groups with a higher positive-to-negative ratio, therefore, should have greater member satisfaction (Bales, 1953).

Moving from external observations to participants' ratings, Bales and Cohen (1979) introduced SYMLOG, a second-generation theory and methodology drawn from IPA dimensions. Theoretically more complex than IPA, SYMLOG explains a group's relational field with respect to three dimensions. Using SYMLOG, group participants retrospectively rate themselves and each other member's interactions (another version allows observers to rate group members) according to 26 adjective phrases representing each possible pairing of three bipolar behavioral dimensions: *dominance/submissiveness, friendly/unfriendly,* and *instrumentally controlled/emotionally expressive.* Although one aspect of relational communication is distinguished from task communication on the instrumentally controlled/emotionally expressive dimension, relational information related to control and power issues is also referenced on the dominance/submissiveness dimension, and general affective attitudes are reflected on the friendly/unfriendly dimension.

The SYMLOG system is particularly good for revealing polarizations or tensions among group members on the three dimensions. As a result, SYMLOG can detect relational similarity or differences among group members. It also provides information about relationship development, as well as conflicts and tensions among group members and overall group development.

ISM

Rather than examining individual communicative acts like IPA does, B. A. Fisher and Hawes (1971) argued for the study of paired communicative acts from a General Systems Theory perspective in their Interact System Model (in this volume, see Chapters 2 [Poole], 3 [Mabry], and 12 [Pavitt]). An *interact* is the contiguous speaking act of one person followed by the act of another. B. A. Fisher (1971) first argued for and later demonstrated (1979) that communication consists of interdependent content and relationship dimensions. This finding directly contradicts Bales's (1950) earlier view that the two dimensions are distinct and tension producing. Interacts, therefore, are conceived along content *and* relationship dimensions, and the unique contribution of the ISM is that interacts can be classified in either or both content and relationship dimensions. Unfortunately, most studies have focused on the task dimension and ignored the relational dimension (e.g., see DeStephen, 1983; Ellis, 1979).

As an example of research on interacts in the group context, Ellis and McCallister (1980) studied relational control as "the moment-to-moment messages which express dominance, submissiveness, symmetry, and complementarity" (p. 37) (e.g., one-up or one-down messages). Relational control is an attempt to direct relationship definitions (Ellis, 1979) in that "messages have implications for how the interactants should define their relationship" (Ellis & McCallister, 1980, p. 37). Analyzing frequency and then patterns of coded verbal behavior, Ellis and McCallister found support for sex-type stereotypes in that sex-typed male groups used significantly more relational control messages than other groups (e.g., androgynous groups composed of members who have a balance of male and female characteristics). Lag sequential analysis demonstrated that control bids were met with subsequent control bids, thereby establishing competitive symmetry as the pattern of sex-typed male group members.

Hewes (1979) criticized interact-based research for eliminating the identification of the speakers, as well as their individual and relational attributes, and, thereby, decreasing the strength of interpretation. He also criticized ISM's use of sequence rather than length or clock time. He argued that clock time would provide a deeper understanding of relational development in groups because, for example, it provides some tangible index of members' dominance behavior. Finally, Hewes questioned the system's coding of contiguous pairs. He argued that this technique may describe dyadic interaction fairly well, but it fails to describe the complexity of group interaction, particularly when multiple members affect how the group conversation unfolds and changes over time. Despite these criticisms, ISM has potential for revealing relational dynamics; to date, however, studies have focused only on how relational control affects tasks like decision making, rather than investigating relational acts for their effects on group members' relationships.

Alternative Explorations of Relational Messages

Other explorations of relational messages are few. One notable exploration is a study by Cawyer and Smith-Dupre' (1995) of a social support group for people living with AIDS, family members, friends, lovers, and professional caregivers. They discovered at the microlevel a set of relationship messages not previously uncovered. Specifically, four types of messages generally fulfilling the function of providing support dominated this group's talk: communicating to heal, preparing for life changes, venting emotion, and changing society. Families and friendship groups are also likely to exchange these types of relational messages. Findings by Cawyer and Smith-Dupre' suggest that researchers' traditional reliance on studying decision-making and other task groups may be limiting discovery of other types of relational messages.

RELATIONAL PROCESSES IN GROUPS

Relational processes capture the dynamic capacity of group interaction and hold the greatest potential for revealing its relational intricacies. Several lines of theory and research can be classified under this component of the model. The first is the study of group development, which explores the stages through which groups progress over time. The second is relationship development in groups, that is, individuals' relationships with fellow group members, rather than the development of the group as a whole. The third deals with the development of shared meaning.

Group Development

There are many theories, perspectives, and studies of group development or maturation (in this volume, see Chapters 2 [Poole], 3 [Mabry], and 6 [Anderson et al.]), each of which shows varying levels of attention to relational processes in groups. Although most developmental models focus on how groups develop relative to decision making (see Poole & Baldwin, 1996), some of these models illuminate relational processes in groups. Models that focus solely on decision development or decision emergence in groups (e.g., B. A. Fisher, 1970) are excluded from this review.

Wheelan et al.'s (1994) review and synthesis of the group development literature shows that different approaches acknowledge that groups move through sequential stages or phases, although there is considerable disagreement about the number and order. Generally, group members focus attention initially on issues of *formation* (e.g., inclusion, identity, and role distinction). In the next general stage, members deal with *dependency issues* as revealed in power struggles, negative feelings, and competition among members. The third stage entails *resolution* of the conflicts generated in the previous stage. The fourth stage is almost exclusively one of *work* or *task inter-*action, and when the task is completed, groups move to a *termination* or *resolution* stage. Work contributing to this general pattern of group development, described in the following sections, includes IPA, Tuckman's theory of group development, Lacoursiere's Group Development Stage Theory, and the dialectical perspective.

IPA

Besides providing categories for identifying communicative functions, Bales (1950) also used IPA to study the phasic movements of groups in both single problem-solving sessions and in series of meetings over time. Bales described phases of group development on the basis of shifts in the relative rates demonstrated in the 12 categories of interaction. Three phases describe the instrumental or task orientation of a group: (a) *orientation,* or communication about the nature of the problem to be solved; (b) *evaluation,* or what to do and how to do it; and (c) *control,* or deciding what to do. Concentrating on these task activities, even when successful, produces relational strain among group members. Thus, a parallel cycle of three relational or socioemotional phases results: (a) *solidarity,* or agreement among members; (b) *tension reduction;* and (c) *group identification.* Throughout a group's development, Bales contends, members pursue a balance or equilibrium between task and socioemotional activity. Although most studies have focused on the task-orientation phases of ad hoc laboratory groups, "there seems to be a reasonable body of evidence supporting the proposed phase sequence" (McGrath, 1984, p. 153).

Tuckman's Theory of Group Development

Tuckman (1965) reviewed then-existing literature on therapy group development and identified four stages of development that cover group structure (patterns of interpersonal relationships) and task behavior (the nature of the work being done by a group).

The four stages of group structure are testing and dependence, intragroup conflict, development of group cohesion, and functional role-relatedness. These integrate with the four task stages of orientation and testing, emotional response to task demands, discussing oneself and other group members, and emergence of insight. The integrated stages are called *forming, storming, norming,* and *performing.* Later, a fifth stage, *adjourning,* was added (Tuckman & Jensen, 1977). Data supporting these stages was generated from studies of therapy, ad hoc laboratory, and training groups (Guzzo & Shea, 1992), which raises questions about the application of these stages to other types of groups, such as families and/or friendship groups.

Lacoursiere's Group Development Stage Theory

Lacoursiere's (1980) Group Development Stage Theory consists of five stages of psychological and social processes that blend into one another. Identifying both task and social-emotional characteristics of each stage, the positive and negative aspects of the latter are most relevant to this discussion. The first stage, *orientation,* reflects the positive expectations members have about participating in a group. At the same time, members may experience anxiety about their place, purpose, and goal in the group. This stage is followed by a *dissatisfaction* stage, during which group members discover that what they had hoped for and what actually is occurring do not coincide. Consequently, feelings of frustration and anger develop. The third stage, *resolution,* occurs as a transition from dissatisfaction to production. Discrepancies between expectations and actual experiences are narrowed, and new skills may be gained. Animosity among group members decreases, and group cohesion may start to develop. The fourth stage of *production* is characterized by members' positive feelings of being a part of a unique group experience. Members now work well together, which increases their task efficiency and effectiveness, although fatigue

may hamper group efforts. Finally, the *termination* stage takes place when members realize they have accomplished their task and start to deal with the impending dissolution of the group. Feelings of loss or sadness may surface simultaneously with feelings of enhanced self-esteem. Lacoursiere argues that these stages are part of the natural development of groups, and that all groups adhere to this developmental process, with some variations, of course.

Cissna (1984), on the basis of a review of group development studies, observes that although developmental changes, such as those identified by Lacoursiere, are broad enough to apply to most groups, not every group exhibits these stages of development. He notes that the generalizability of theories of group development is questionable given that they are based primarily on research on self-analytic or training groups. Cissna suggests that the following questions need to be addressed:

> What does and does not change about groups over time? How do different groups, and different types of groups, differ in their development? What external constraints and internal structures and processes are associated with what changes in group development? In what ways are the developments of different groups unique? (p. 28)

Answers to these questions are not, of course, limited to task groups. In fact, knowing if and how, for example, friendship groups differ from organizational teams in their development would be helpful in assisting reticent individuals to assimilate into different types of groups (in this volume, see Haslett & Ruebush, Chapter 5, regarding the effects of communication apprehension in groups, and Anderson et al., Chapter 6, regarding communication apprehension and group socialization processes). Knowing if and how relationship structures internal to a group facilitate and/or inhibit group development could provide substantial training or coaching benefits. Partial answers to these questions can be found in nonlinear approaches to group development, such as a dialectical explanation.

Dialectical Perspective

Although certainly not the first to promote the value of a dialectical perspective, K. K. Smith and Berg (1987) were the first to use it to provide an alternative explanation of group development. According to them, group members are particularly prone to viewing group interaction as "a struggle with opposites, especially the attempt to create meaning and coherence out of what seems to lack them" (p. 9). Starting from the premise that "group life is inherently paradoxical" (p. 11), Smith and Berg argue that group members inevitably experience conflict based on underlying emotional and psychological processes. These conflicts, or tensions, can be described as *paradoxes of belonging* (issues of identity, involvement, individuality, and boundaries), *engaging* (issues of disclosure, trust, intimacy, and regression), and *speaking* (issues of authority, dependency, creativity, and courage). As an example, family members experience many paradoxes of engagement. Children may trust their parents but also know that disclosing overly sensitive or controversial information, such as their drug and alcohol use, may, in effect, weaken the trust their parents have in them.

How members manage these tensions determines whether a group becomes stuck or develops. *Stuckness* refers to the "repetitive, often unconscious tensions that prevent a group from even doing the work of problem solving on scarce resources or compromising about conflicting needs" (K. K. Smith & Berg, 1987, p. 207). Alternatively, a group achieves *movement,* or the exploration of new ground, by immersing itself in, rather than removing itself from, the opposing forces. Thus, groups develop when members leave old patterns behind. As Smith and Berg explain, "Progress or development can be measured in terms of the group's ability to (1) define and understand the opposing forces active in the group and (2) find the links between them, the framework in which both are embedded" (p. 229).

Guzzo and Shea (1992) point out that Smith and Berg's perspective is in opposition to other frameworks suggesting that group development occurs when conflicts are resolved. Instead, according to a dialectical view of group development, change within a group is more indicative of other changes than it is of resolution. Guzzo and Shea note the similarities between this aspect of the dialectical view of group development and Bales's (1985; Bales & Cohen, 1979) more recent work, in which groups and individuals are presumed to move and develop along the three SYMLOG vectors that compose a group's field. The dialectical perspective also acknowledges the unique developmental needs of each group and assumes that group development does not happen uniformly or automatically.

Evidence that not all groups progress through linear stages of development can also be seen in Krueger's (1979) microscopic approach. Using Systems Information Processing Analysis (SIPA), which codes each utterance along four dimensions of information processing, Krueger found that approach-avoidance patterns were predominant. Although SIPA does not address relational issues specifically, the study supports Krueger's claim that "groups may develop through more stages than has been claimed in previous macromodels" (p. 322). This study raises important questions about the presumptions of models that propose linearly progressive group development.

Relationship Development in Groups

At least two theories provide perspective about how relationships develop among members in groups. Bion's Interaction Theory describes the emotional responses of group members that result in dependency, pairing, or fight-flight relationships, while Schutz's Fundamental Interpersonal Relationship Orientations (FIRO) hypothesizes that relationships in groups are created and sustained on the basis of members' expressed and desired needs for inclusion, affection, and control. Another area of research related to relationship development in groups is that of leadership emergence.

Bion's Interaction Theory

Although Bion was fundamentally concerned with group work/tasks, he recognized that members have emotional or relational reactions to task activities, especially when those activities do not go well. Bion's (1961) work on group development stemmed from his facilitation of therapy groups with neurotic patients and, later, with training groups (T-groups) at the National Training Laboratory in Bethel, Maine (in this volume, see Chapters 1 [Gouran] and 14 [Schultz]). Bion believed that groups had to progress through three emotional states: *dependency* (group members depend on a leader, someone external to the group, or preestablished procedures), *pairing* (members turn to one other member for support and intimacy), and *fight-flight* (members deal with conflict and threat by fighting or turning away from it). The three states describe stages of group development that are referenced by the relationships of group members (Rioch, 1970). Thus, the stage of development of a group is determined by the demonstrated relationships among group members.

Wheelan et al. (1994) empirically tested Bion's theory through content analysis of group discussions using the Group Development Observation System (Verdi & Wheelan, 1992; Wheelan & Verdi, 1992), a methodology grounded in the work of Bion (1961) and Stock and Thelen (1958). The focus of this observational system is on how relationships develop in a group. Of the seven coding categories it comprises, only one, *work statements,* is void of relational or social indicators. *Dependency statements* show an inclination to conform, follow, or receive direction from others, whereas *counterdependency statements* are those that assert independence from others. *Fight statements* capture conflict or struggle, whereas *flight statements* reference conflict avoidance. *Pairing statements* express positive affective feelings toward an-

other group member, and *counterpairing statements* express the avoidance of intimacy or connection. Wheelan and colleagues also classified these messages as reflecting the emotional themes of *acceptance, belonging, control,* and *feelings* and found that emotional themes dominated group conversations. Findings also revealed that groups mirror one another, or develop similarly, if they are part of the same larger system. Moreover, they also mirror the developmental patterns established by that larger system. Wheelan and colleagues concluded that there may be dimensions to a group's social world of which we are not aware, such as a collective unconscious or some type of social ecosystem.

Schutz's FIRO

FIRO (Schutz, 1958) describes three basic interpersonal needs that can influence people's communicative behavior in group settings (see Anderson et al., Chapter 6, this volume). *Inclusion* is the need to establish and maintain satisfactory relations with others, *control* is the need to establish and share power with others, and *affection* is the need to establish psychologically close relationships with others. Each of these needs varies with regard to the extent to which an individual expresses them and the extent to which he or she wants others to express them toward him or her. *Expressed needs* emphasize the group member as a sender, whereas *wanted needs* emphasize the member as a receiver. Although used more frequently in research to assess group composition, FIRO's premises of expressed and wanted needs can be extrapolated to examine ongoing group interaction.

FIRO provides a framework for analyzing the compatibility of relationships among group members and why certain types of relationships develop. Each member brings to a group setting a unique three-dimensional profile that is a mixture of expressed and wanted inclusion, control, and affection needs. The similarities of or differences in these needs among group members can be evaluated in terms of their compatibility. Not to be confused with liking, *compatibility* refers to how complementary group members are to one another. Relationally, ease, or compatibility, in communication occurs when there is a balance of group members who want to express a given need and members who want to receive it (see Frey, 1997). When members express and desire reciprocal levels of needs, they are more satisfied, and the group is more effective (Reddy & Byrnes, 1972), although the consistency of this conclusion has been challenged (Downs & Pickett, 1977). When incompatibility exists, group members need to spend substantial time resolving their relational differences. Thus, FIRO provides one explanation for why group communication climates can be positively or negatively valenced (Schutz, 1961). Recent research on needs reveals that relational needs of group members are related to their communicative abilities (for example, lonely group members are likely to be less responsive to others) and that members are more satisfied when their needs are met (e.g., Anderson & Martin, 1995).

Leadership Emergence

Although leadership is seen almost exclusively as a task-role function (see Pavitt, Chapter 12, this volume), it also can be viewed as a relationship one (or more) group member develops with other members. Theories of leadership emergence and transformational leadership examine relationship development specific to this group role. For example, using a rhetorical approach, Sharf (1978) examined the divisions and identifications that underlie struggles for leadership emergence in groups. She found that five steps occurred during these leadership struggles: (a) locating sources of division, (b) organizing hierarchy within the group, (c) identifying bonds of identification within the group, (d) inducing cooperation through rhetorical strategies, and (e) comparatively explaining and evaluating rhetorical attempts for their success at transcending divisions or engaging support. Fielding and Hogg (1997) have also explored how leadership emergence and support for the

leadership role develop through members' identification with leaders. Although focused narrowly on one type of group role, studies like these describe the development of leader-member relationships that often are fundamental to other relational issues in groups, such as group conflict and the development of a communication climate.

More recently, leadership has been examined as a function of relationship, rather than task, concerns. Bass (1985, 1990), citing the work of Burns (1978), conceives of a *transformational leader* as one who uses rhetorical skills to build a vision with which group members can identify. Transformational leaders do not rely solely on position power or use of organizational rewards; they create power and sustain relationships with group members through the use of dramatic and inspirational messages. Thus, group leadership, and other constructs traditionally explored from a task-oriented perspective, may find a new spirit when viewed from a relational perspective.

Development of Shared Meaning

Another type of relational process in groups is the development of shared meaning among members. Two theories that are especially helpful for explaining how group members create agreement, primarily through the use of stories, significant symbols, and rituals, are Symbolic Convergence Theory and Narrative Theory (see Cline's application of these theories to explain communication processes in social support groups, Chapter 19, this volume).

Symbolic Convergence Theory

Bormann's (1972, 1982, 1985, 1986, 1996) Symbolic Convergence Theory (SCT) describes and explains how group members come to share a common social reality (in this volume, see Chapters 1 [Gouran] and 2 [Poole]). Agreeing with Bales's (1950) account of how dramatizing communication—a message containing "one or more of the following: a pun or other wordplay, a double entendre, a figure of speech, an analogy, or an anecdote, allegory, fable, or narrative" (Bormann, 1996, p. 92)—helps create a common social reality for a group, Bormann (1972) notes that "when group members respond emotionally to the dramatic situation they publicly proclaim some commitment to an attitude" (p. 397). *Symbolic convergence,* the overlapping of group members' symbolic worlds, occurs when group members create and share *fantasies*—interpretations of events that meet members' emotional, psychological, and/or rhetorical needs. When group members' interpretations converge through interaction, a shared group consciousness emerges. This signals the transition from a collection of individuals to an identified group unit, and the transformation creates new relational dynamics for members' future interactions. The extent to which fantasies are shared, symbolic convergence occurs, and group consciousness is developed is, thus, a powerful indicator of the relational status of a group.

SCT consists of three parts (see Bormann, 1985, 1996). The first part concerns the discovery and arrangement of recurring forms of communication in a group. Patterns of communication developed and adhered to by members indicate the presence of a shared group consciousness. The second part of the theory describes and explains the dynamic capabilities of fantasies with respect to how a shared symbolic reality develops, is maintained, and/or declines. The third part explains why group members share fantasies. Of most promise to the study of relationships within groups is the notion that members share fantasy as a way of expressing common, but until then uncommunicated, concerns, particularly those related to group roles and member relationships.

SCT is a theory of relational processes in groups because when symbolic convergence occurs, it "creates a symbolic climate and culture that allow people to achieve empathic communication as well as a 'meeting of the minds' " (Bormann, 1996, p. 89). To achieve symbolic convergence, group members must share (a) enough symbolic ground to negoti-

ate the shared reality and (b) a common sentiment or emotional involvement with the symbols. For these types of sharing to occur, relationships must be of sufficient strength and quality to support emotional attachments among group members (Bormann, 1985).

Although SCT explains some important relational processes in groups, its application "in group research has focused primarily on explaining how group members come to make decisions and how they make sense of the decision-making process" (Propp & Kreps, 1994, pp. 7-8). One exception is Lesch's (1994) demonstration of how symbolic convergence achieved through the sharing of fantasy themes helps a group develop strategies for sustaining consciousness and membership in the presence of antagonistic forces. Her study of a coven of witches revealed several symbolic strategies—including keeping the group attractive, channeling energies toward surviving change, focusing on long-term survivability and stability, and bonding among members—that served to stabilize relational issues during periods of membership change. The theory, thus, has considerable potential for helping to understand how and why relational processes unfold in groups.

Narrative Theory

An often overlooked theory of how groups create and sustain shared meaning is W. R. Fisher's (1984) Narrative Theory. Fisher sees human beings essentially as storytellers, *homo narrans* who organize experiences into stories with plots, central characters, and action sequences. Group interaction, therefore, produces experiences from which people create stories and an audience to whom stories can be told; these stories, in turn, help create a shared reality and meaningful relationships among group members.

Hollihan and Riley (1987) used Narrative Theory to analyze Toughlove, a network of parental support groups designed to aid families with delinquent children. The degree to which the Toughlove story, a narrative that persuades parents to respond to child delinquency with discipline, became a repeatable and believable story for parents affected their acceptance of this interpretation of child rearing over other alternatives. Just as fantasies help group members create a shared reality from an SCT perspective, stories, within Narrative Theory, help collectively structure experiences for group members and, thus, serve as a foundation on which members form a common bond. Although storytelling and narrative perspectives have proved valuable for explaining phenomena in a wide variety of disciplines and fields of study, few scholars have employed them to study groups and group communication.

RELATIONAL OUTCOMES IN GROUPS

Traditionally, scholars have identified positive relational outcomes in groups, such as norms, cohesiveness, and member satisfaction. Relational outcomes can also be negative, however, as evidenced by groupthink, group stress, and group deviance. A third type of group relational outcome is communication climate, which spans the positive-negative continuum. The following sections describe each of these.

Positive Relational Outcomes in Groups

Norms

One of the first outcomes of group interaction often is the development of *group norms,* "recurrent patterns of behavior or thinking that come to be accepted in a group as the 'usual' way of doing things" (Scheerhorn & Geist, 1997, p. 92). Such expectations often become articulated as rules that are adopted by a group to regulate its members' behavior (Feldman, 1984). As the least visible, yet most powerful, form of social control that can be exerted in a group (Bettenhausen & Murnighan, 1985), norms shape members' beliefs, attitudes, and interactions. Most important, they provide clues about appropriate behaviors in group settings (Jackson, 1965). Although explicit, or formalized, norms also

can develop, it is the implicit, or informal, norms that most direct relational behavior in groups.

Norms emerge from relational interaction in groups and are a result of the psychological closeness and communicative linkages among members (Festinger, Schachter, & Back, 1968). With respect to their effect on group interaction, norms are "structural characteristics of groups that summarize and simplify group influence processes" (Hackman, 1992, p. 235). These powerful regulators of group members' behavior generally develop slowly, often implicitly, and typically unconsciously from social pressures exerted in group interaction.

Norms are more often researched as an outcome, rather than a process, variable. Feldman's (1984) review of the literature on norms identifies four ways they develop. First, norms can develop from explicit statements made by group leaders, especially about group survival or task success. Second, critical events in a group's history can establish a group precedent. For example, members may find that their interaction when faced with a pressing deadline is better than their more typical leisurely interaction. As a result, when the group is having difficulty coming to a decision, its members impose a 30-minute time limit on deliberations. Third, norms can develop simply from repetitive behavioral patterns that emerge in a group. This type of primacy effect is particularly strong for group seating arrangements (see Ketrow, Chapter 10, this volume) and meeting procedures (see Sunwolf & Seibold, Chapter 15, this volume). Finally, norms can be imported into groups from members' other group experiences (see Anderson et al., Chapter 6, this volume). This type of carryover norm assumes that expectations in different group situations will be the same. Research has not demonstrated which of these developmental processes results in the strongest group norms.

Although, on face value, norms appear to apply to all group members, member status within a group may affect their uniform application, which further emphasizes the relational nature of norms. High-status members may be exempt from norm expectations that other members are expected to follow. In general, however, when a member deviates from a group norm, the other members typically have one of three reactions (Hackman, 1992). First, they may try to correct the deviant member's behavior. Correction usually occurs outside the group and takes the form of advice, which generally is accepted by the deviant if he or she wants to maintain positive relationships with the other members. Second, if a deviant persists in nonnormative behavior, members may exert psychological and communicative pressure to form an in-group, and thereby distance themselves from the person, who now is "outside" the group (see Haslett & Ruebush, Chapter 5, this volume, regarding in-group/out-group perceptions). Outright rejection of a deviant is rare and usually occurs only when members believe that all other attempts to bring his or her behavior back in line with the group's norms have failed. At this point, the amount of communication with the deviant decreases substantially and effectively eliminates him or her from group discussions, along with eliminating opportunities to exert influence. As a result, realignment of group members' relationships occurs. Third, if a deviant presents a clear, credible alternative to the group norm and maintains that position over time, he or she sometimes can influence the group to accommodate him or her (see Meyers & Brashers, Chapter 11, this volume, for a discussion of minority influence). Thus, the degree to which group norms are effective in bringing a deviant back to a group's normative behavior depends on the clarity and persuasiveness of the relational messages exchanged between the deviant and other group members.

Cohesiveness

Cohesiveness, the degree to which members desire to remain in a group (Cartwright, 1968), is one of the outcome variables discussed most extensively in the group literature

(see Bettenhausen, 1991). Cohesiveness has been described as an attitude or feeling members have about their group, its task, or other members. Cohesiveness thus can be based on task or relational components, or both. This dual aspect of the cohesiveness construct requires specificity as to what makes a group attractive to an individual. For example, a person may join a group to practice a hobby (task) but continue to be a member long after that need is satisfied because he or she values the relationships developed within the group. Of course, the opposite can also be true in that when one's desire to be a group member is strong, he or she is more likely to be committed to the group and its task. Thus, depending on how cohesiveness is conceptualized and operationalized, it may or may not be a relational construct.

Thibaut and Kelley (1986) suggest that attraction to a group is based on the perceived rewards and costs an individual accrues as a result of membership. A person is more likely to be attracted to a group that offers rewards that outweigh any perceived membership costs. Thus, expecting to be a member of a tightly cohesive group is a reward; expecting to be a member of a group whose members are distant from one another is a perceived cost. Embedded in this position is the presumption that a person's attraction to a group is determined by needs and values, especially the expected value of the outcomes linked to membership as compared to other group membership opportunities.

Cartwright (1968) identified five major approaches to measuring group cohesiveness from members' perspective: interpersonal attraction among group members, evaluation of a group as a whole, closeness or identification with a group, expressed desire to remain a group member, and composite indices of the first four types of measurements. Drescher, Burlingame, and Fuhriman (1985) identified six means of measuring cohesiveness: physical or nonverbal indices, verbal style (emphasizing form over content), verbal content (topics or content of interaction), overt behavior (nonverbal behavior), covert behavior (subjective elements coded by expert raters, such as genuineness or empathy), and therapeutic intervention (assessment of techniques used by facilitators). The confusion that results from competing operationalizations of cohesion is compounded by the view that some types of cohesion are more important for certain types of groups (Stokes, 1983). For example, task cohesion is more important than relational cohesion for a short-term organizational team.

Methodological problems dominate the study of cohesiveness. As Evans and Jarvis (1980) explain:

> Cohesion is uniformly recognized as a group phenomenon, yet its measurement generally involves measuring the levels of attraction of individual group members and averaging them. . . . This method at least fails to take into account both variability in attraction among group members and the differential influence of group members. (p. 359)

Levine and Moreland (1990) identify three additional problems. First, cohesion has been studied as numerous concepts, including solidarity, morale, climate, and sense of community. Second, cohesion is a complex construct composed of a number of factors, yet it is often treated as being unidimensional. Third, confusion exists because cohesion can be a cause or an effect for something that happened in a group. Although these and other problems have been identified consistently (see Bednar & Kaul, 1978; Drescher et al., 1985; Evans & Jarvis, 1980; Mudrack, 1989), little advancement has occurred in the measurement of cohesion. These problems suggest that cohesion needs to be measured in more complex ways. Indeed, using multiple operationalizations of cohesion, Keyton and Springston (1990) found that a unification index (similarity of field positions) of group members' self-report ratings on the friendly/unfriendly and instrumentally controlled/emotionally expressive SYMLOG dimensions was a better predictor of cohesiveness than more traditional unidimensional questionnaire indices.

When examined as a process variable, as opposed to an outcome variable, cohesion can serve as an indicator of relational development within a group; that is, cohesiveness among group members is likely to change over time. Failure to consider this aspect of cohesion may, in part, be partially responsible for conflicting results obtained from different studies. Measuring cohesion at one point in time of a group's history as an outcome variable or consequence is different from treating it as a phenomenon that develops and changes over time through members' interactions.

Few studies have directly linked communication, and, in particular, relational messages, to the development or maintenance of group cohesion (see the review by Drescher et al., 1985). One reason, according to Weinberg (1979), is that cohesion emerged from the study of group dynamics in Social Psychology; therefore, its measurement was more often psychologically oriented, rather than communication based. To alleviate this deficiency, Weinberg developed the Group Cohesion Checklist based on the notion that a group's level of cohesion is directly related to members' usage of slang, or in-group speech. Thus, members' self-reports of these types of messages indicate their level of cooperation and maintenance.

Other studies examining communication and cohesiveness demonstrate that there is greater equality in participation in cohesive groups because members want to express their membership and identification with the group (Cartwright, 1968). Members who have the opportunity to share information and their feelings about the group's task and performance with other group members are more likely to have enhanced feelings of cooperation (Elias, Johnson, & Fortman, 1989). Alternatively, groups that promote task over relationship-building structures can inhibit or prevent cohesiveness from developing (Fuehrer & Keys, 1988). If too much structure is imposed on a group early in its history, members may become overly concerned with meeting structural requirements rather than building relationships with other group members. Group membership issues also affect the occurrence of cohesiveness, in that a group in which members complement one another's needs for interpersonal dominance (e.g., some members are high and others are low) is more likely to be cohesive than a group in which all members display high or low interpersonal dominance (Dyce & O'Connor, 1992).

Research also has demonstrated a dynamic relationship between group cohesiveness and task performance, such that the more cohesive a group is, the more likely it will perform more effectively (Evans & Dion, 1991; Mullen & Cooper, 1994). This relationship is often reciprocal (Greene, 1989), in that members of groups with high task cohesiveness put more energy into working with and for the group (Prapavessis & Carron, 1997). Members of cohesive groups are more likely to stick with the group throughout the duration of its task (Spink & Carron, 1994). This, in turn, creates more opportunities for norms to develop and be followed (Shaw, 1981). The relationship between cohesion and group performance is not straightforward, however; rather, it is substantially determined by the nature of the task (Gully, Devine, & Whitney, 1995; Langfred, 1998). When a group's task requires coordination, high levels of interaction, and joint performances from members, the cohesion-performance relationship is strong; however, when task interdependence is low, the relationship is much weaker. One could hypothesize that in the former condition, relational communication would be positive and strong, whereas relational communication in the latter case is negative and tenuous.

Finally, Evans and Jarvis (1980) recommend that researchers challenge the widely held assumption that cohesion consistently has positive effects. As they explain, "Too cohesive a group may cause members to be more concerned with the group itself than with the purpose for which the group exists" (p. 367). This issue has been studied as an aspect of groupthink (Janis, 1972), a relational outcome examined below.

Satisfaction

Initially contextualized in the interpersonal context (Hecht, 1978a, 1984), *satisfaction*, "commonly perceived of as the affect experienced when expectation-type standards are fulfilled" (Hecht, 1978b, p. 357), has been studied in both interpersonal and group contexts, but with few conclusive findings. Although certainly wide-ranging in terms of its potential application, in the group context, satisfaction often refers only to the positive feelings or attitudes group members have toward a group's decision (e.g., Green & Taber, 1980).

Hecht's (1978c) review of the literature on satisfaction identifies various and competing conceptualizations. First, satisfaction has been conceptualized as communication that gratifies such needs as achievement, affiliation, and dominance. A second approach is related to expectation fulfillment. Here, an individual develops a standard against which to compare outcomes. If the expectation is fulfilled, satisfaction occurs. From a third perspective, equivocality reduction, satisfaction occurs when uncertainty is reduced or eliminated at the same time that knowledge or control increases. From a fourth perspective, constraint-reinforcement, satisfaction is achieved when positive reinforcements are received as opposed to the constraints of punishment. A fifth perspective draws on Herzberg's (1970) two-factor theory, which utilizes a content-context dichotomy to discriminate between satisfaction and dissatisfaction, rather than assume that one is dissatisfied if satisfaction is absent.

To address the limited focus on communicative aspects of satisfaction, Hecht (1978c) offered the *discrimination-fulfillment approach* as an alternative. Conceptualized as an internal behavior, Hecht argues that communication satisfaction must be grounded in observable behavior, such as self-disclosure. Thus, the discrimination-fulfillment approach views communication satisfaction as an internal reinforcer following response behaviors to a stimulus. Within a group context, this means that each member develops standards by which to judge his or her interactive world; satisfaction, consequently, is "the reaction to encountering the world one has been conditioned to 'expect' " (Hecht, 1978c, p. 59). Such an approach grounds satisfaction in communicative behavior rather than viewing it solely as the fulfillment of mental states.

Heslin and Dunphy (1964) reviewed more than 450 studies of how member satisfaction has been articulated in the group literature. They found three primary dimensions of the construct. The first dimension, *status consensus,* conceptualizes satisfaction as consensus about the relative status of a group member, particularly a group's leader. Generally, when status consensus among members is high, member satisfaction is high, with the converse also being true. Moreover, members with high status are more likely to be active participators in a group. The second dimension, *perception of progress toward group goals,* refers to members' judgments of their group's progress rather than actual progress. Perceived progress toward group goals is associated with higher member satisfaction; conversely, failure to maintain goal progress reduces member satisfaction. The third dimension of group member satisfaction, *perceived freedom to participate,* relates to one's sense of opportunity to speak. Although all members may not have equal needs to participate, satisfaction depends on the view that one has the freedom to participate to the extent he or she wishes.

Considerable variability exists in how group member satisfaction is integrated with and explained by other variables. Group members' satisfaction may be influenced by their position of power in a group's communication network (Hrycenko & Minton, 1974), the quality of other group members' contributions (Gouran, 1973), the amount of conflict or how conflict is managed in a group (Wall, Galanes, & Love, 1987; Wall & Nolan, 1986, 1987), group decision outcomes (DeStephen & Hirokawa, 1988), maturity level or stage of group development (Krayer, 1988), their degree of participation (Cooper & Wood, 1974), and the proportion of group members who are unwilling to communicate (Burgoon, 1977). Thus, a variety of relational inputs, processes, and outcomes contribute to group members' levels of satisfaction.

Hecht's (1978b) review of the literature revealed many methodological problems in studying group satisfaction. For example, researchers frequently use a single item or a few items to measure the degree to which a participant is satisfied with a group experience. These one-item (see Gouran, 1973) or short group satisfaction measures, constructed by researchers for their own studies, virtually preclude any systematic pursuit of the construct. Another criticism stems from how dissatisfaction is viewed with respect to satisfaction. Traditionally, dissatisfaction is treated the same as zero satisfaction, but Hecht argues that these are not the same affect. Keyton (1991) provided evidence for this argument by distinguishing between behaviors that contributed to group members' satisfaction and dissatisfaction. For example, behaviors that increased satisfaction were global in nature, whereas dissatisfaction seemed to emanate from issues of equity and equality. She also found that satisfaction and dissatisfaction constructs could be distinguished by their universal or situational categories. For example, making suggestions to keep a group conversation on track was reported as contributing to members' satisfaction across a variety of group contexts; however, having a diversity of ideas was reported as contributing to members' satisfaction in some, but not other, group contexts. Finally, because satisfaction is studied almost exclusively as a dependent or outcome variable, little is known about it as a relational interactive process.

Negative Relational Outcomes in Groups

Just as interpersonal communication scholars have incorporated the negative or "dark side" of interpersonal communication and relationships (see Cupach & Spitzberg, 1994) into their research programs, so too should group researchers. Expanding the study of group deviants, norm breakers, and other aberrant group members and their behavior would enhance understanding of people's group experiences. As an example, Stohl and Schell (1991) vividly paint a portrait of a "farrago," a group member who acts as a catalyst for a group's dysfunction. Important to their conceptualization is the notion that a deviant does not act alone. Rather, a farrago is part of a dysfunctional group dynamic that "cannot be located within any one individual or a particular group meeting" (Stohl & Schell, 1991, p. 93). Thus, the dysfunction, and resulting deviance, is relational. As Stohl and Schell argue, a farrago (the dysfunction of both the individual and the group) "is developed and maintained in the continuing challenge and reinforcement of individuals' conceptions of the roles of others" (p. 96). Examples of negative relationship outcomes in groups include groupthink and group stress, both of which are discussed below.

Groupthink

One negative relational outcome of group interaction is *groupthink,* which Janis (1982) conceptualized as the tendency of highly cohesive groups to adopt faulty solutions when members fail to examine and analyze options critically. Most commonly associated with faulty group decision making, groupthink is most likely to arise when a group develops an extraordinarily high sense of cohesiveness, often as a reaction to pressures from the external environment. Contributing to this level of cohesiveness are language and interactional patterns that serve both to isolate the group from outsiders who possess critical information and to reduce members' attention to ethical and moral concerns. As a result, group members are not vigilant in their thinking, which can serve to narrow artificially what counts as an acceptable solution to a problem. Believing that the group has discovered the best solution, members develop feelings of invincibility and infallibility, which further insulate them from criticisms or new knowledge that could demonstrate that the group is wrong.

Janis (1982) argued that groupthink is likely to occur when three conditions are present. First, when group members overestimate their power and invulnerability, opportunities for questioning what they are doing or why are diminished. Under such circumstances, maintaining harmony or enhancing shared identity is perceived by members to be more important than considering information that may temporarily decrease group cohesiveness. Second, group members become closed-minded and reject information that is contrary to their preferred course of action. By insulating themselves from external influences and threats, members generate rationalizations that discount what they perceive to be potentially valuable information. Third, group members experience high pressure to conform because of strong leader-member relationships or because of the role the group plays relative to its environment. Pressure and stress are heightened when stakes are high or when the leader recommends a solution and members see no viable alternative. This pressure to conform induces self-censorship, which, in turn, causes members to believe that consensus exists in the group, even when it does not. In these cases, pleasing the leader becomes more important than considering the merits of discussion options. These conditions, which often result from the presence of affiliative constraints (Janis, 1989), create a working climate that rewards cohesiveness and conformity and punishes members for being different. Time pressures and high-risk or high-consequence decision making amplify these tendencies (Neck & Moorhead, 1995).

Janis and Mann (1977) specify some of the relational components of groupthink. When cohesiveness is high, group members are more psychologically dependent on one another and less willing to challenge ideas. Groupthink is also more likely to occur in groups in which members have a long and shared work history, are deeply embedded in their macro-organizational environments, and are insulated from the views of others. These conditions lead to full-blown groupthink. Not all these conditions need to exist, however, for groups to make faulty decisions or to develop groupthink problems; one or two of them may be sufficient.

The absence of disagreement (Courtright, 1978) or discounting of minority views (Alderton & Frey, 1983, 1986) may be primary contributors to groupthink. Groups that are too cohesive are less likely to allow discussion that criticizes the group, its activity, or the ideas its members generate. As a result, members develop premature concurrence, which shelters them from critical thinking. This type of interaction encourages members to believe that they have arrived at a unanimous decision and to terminate deliberations prematurely (Cline, 1994).

Recently, Mullen, Anthony, Salas, and Driskell (1994) challenged the presumed link between group cohesiveness and faulty decision making. Their meta-analysis revealed that only the interpersonal attraction component of cohesiveness (as opposed to the task attraction component) contributed to groupthink in the way that Janis first described. Other methodological approaches reveal different findings regarding groupthink. Cline's (1994) content analysis of President Richard Nixon's Watergate transcripts, for example, showed that "to the degree that members 'successfully' protect intergroup relationships, they are subject to self-deception regarding their vulnerabilities as a group" (p. 222). Thus, members create negative group consequences when the protection of member relationships results in self-entrapment.

Group Stress

There are various types of stress—psychological, cognitive, environmental, occupational, organizational, physiological, and social. Both Bales (1950; Bales & Cohen, 1979) and K. K. Smith and Berg (1987) have noted that stress creates tensions in relationships among group members, which eventually is revealed in their communication. Unfortunately, little research has documented the effects of stress in groups. B. B. Morgan and Bowers (1995) define teamwork stress as

"those stimuli or conditions that (1) directly affect the team members' ability to interact interdependently or (2) alter the team's interactive capacity for obtaining its desired objectives" (p. 267). In their review of the literature on stress, Morgan and Bowers acknowledge that internal factors, such as team size, composition, structure, and membership change, can create stress. In working with bona fide groups, a potential area of future research is to investigate the stress that occurs when group membership changes. Not only may the change process cause stress, as Morgan and Bowers suggest, but it seems likely that who the replacement or addition is, and how well the new member fits into the present group (see Anderson et al., Chapter 6, this volume), would also contribute to group stress.

Vachon's (1987) interviews of hospice workers, including physicians, nurses, social workers, clergy, volunteers, and others, demonstrate how stress is associated with work group relationships. Interviewees reported stress as being caused, in descending order, by communication problems within their work system, role ambiguity, and communication problems with team members and administrators. Interviewees also reported that some stress was attributable to lack of positive feedback from others in their work system. Others noted that their teams experienced high levels of internal conflict that often centered on issues of control. Thus, the lack of relationship or role congruency appears to stimulate the presence of group stress.

Group Communication Climate

The seminal perspective on *group communication climate*, the relative acceptance or rejection a member feels from group interactions, is that of Gibb (1961), who describes communication climates as being either defensive or supportive. A *defensive climate* exists "when an individual perceives threat or anticipates threat in the group" (p. 141). The use of defensive communication by one group member tends to create similar defensive reactions in others. The more defensive the communication in a group, the more likely it is that members will misperceive the motives, values, and emotions of other members. Conversely, a *supportive climate* reduces this type of defensive distortion through positive interaction and is also contagious. Gibb identified six categories of behaviors that contribute to the creation of a defensive climate—evaluation, control, strategy, neutrality, superiority, and certainty—and six categories that contribute to the creation of a supportive climate—description, problem orientation, spontaneity, empathy, equality, and provisionalism.

Recently, Broome and Fulbright (1995) generated a model of barriers to group problem solving and found that participants viewed both communication climate and various communicative behaviors as barriers to productive group work. Participants frequently mentioned dominance issues (in terms of power and in relationships), interpersonal conflict, and personal fears of criticism and reprisal as barriers to developing a positive, or supportive, group communication climate. The relational import of these barriers is explicit. They also mentioned other relational concerns, such as trust, respect, cohesiveness, and supportiveness. Listening was identified as a separate communication barrier, although how group members listen to one another is indicative of a group's communication climate (Gibb, 1961). Broome and Fulbright's analysis suggests that how well a group succeeds at solving problems is influenced by the relational nature of the group's communication climate.

Alternative Explorations of Relational Outcomes

The research focus on task, decision-making, and problem-solving groups may have biased the view of relational outcomes. An alternative way of viewing relational outcomes could be provided by studying groups in which relational development is the primary goal. For example, Wuthnow (1994) argues that social support groups exist to respond to some need in the lives of individuals or in the lives of

people they know and to give people a chance to talk about their problems or interests (see Cline, Chapter 19, this volume, on communication in social support groups). As a result, group outcomes shift from completing tasks to, for example, fighting addiction, providing words of encouragement or prayer, and meeting other such needs. Such outcomes as these are measured not at the group level but primarily at the individual level, where dealing with the concerns of daily life, emotions, and understanding one's identity are the desired results. These outcomes are less likely to occur in a group that cannot provide satisfying relationships and supportive relational communication for its members. Although primarily descriptive rather than explanatory, Wuthnow's survey data and short case studies reflect a growing trend in research on social support and other types of relationally oriented groups and how relational messages and opportunities to build relationships can serve as impetuses for group membership.

NEW DIRECTIONS IN RELATIONAL GROUP COMMUNICATION

Recently, scholars have started investigating new topics that contribute to understanding relational issues in groups. These include humor in groups, the impact of diversity on groups, the impact of group technology, and intimacy in groups.

Humor in Groups

The use of humor as a relational device in groups has received scant research attention. This is unfortunate because humor is an important source of information about relationships in groups and occurs frequently in work, social, and therapy groups, as well as in the groups of both children and adults. In one of the few studies to date, C. M. Smith and Powell (1988) found that group leaders who used self-disparaging humor were perceived to be more effective at relieving tension, better at encouraging member participation, and more willing to share opinions than leaders who used superior-targeted or subordinate-targeted disparaging humor. The findings are consistent with theories of facilitation suggesting that humor benefits the group process by promoting cohesiveness and reducing tension (see Block, Browning, & McGrath, 1983).

Two studies show that humor can fulfill important relational functions in groups. In a field study of operating room nurses, Denison and Sutton (1990) found that humor served two functions. First, it reduced tensions among surgical team members. Second, it provided variety when standard operating procedures were perceived as boring to surgical team members. Hierarchy among team members reinforced how and to what degree members laughed and joked. Nurses joked and laughed less than doctors, and doctors appeared to determine when humor could occur. Moreover, nurses initiating humor against doctors' wishes frequently were sanctioned. In another study, Vinton (1989) reported that humor served three relational-specific purposes in one work group. First, self-ridiculing jokes signaled to coworkers that one was willing to participate in a friendly, informal relationship. Second, teasing eased working relationships when members worked in cramped quarters. Third, bantering "helped lessen the status differentials that existed among the employees" (p. 164). Thus, for work groups, humor signified that informal relationships were being sought by members, helped to avoid work-induced stress, and lessened hierarchical effects.

Group Diversity

Much of the literature on group diversity focuses on how various types of group members work together on tasks (see Haslett & Ruebush, Chapter 5, this volume). Diversity research typically focuses on differences in values, beliefs, and work styles that are likely to result in differences in members' relational expectations. On the basis of participating in a long-term, culturally diverse work group, Bantz (1993) recommended that similar groups give some attention to building social cohesion, in addition to task cohesion, especially when cultural differences exist with respect to individualism versus collectivism orientations (see Hofstede, 1980).

Research on the effects of group diversity on relational issues in groups could perhaps provide new ways to facilitate the performance of task groups. A promising start in this direction is the Group Development Questionnaire (GDQ), which captures group members' perceptions about four stages of group development and is available in English, Japanese, and Spanish versions (Wheelan, Buzaglo, & Tsumura, 1998).

Group Technology

The use of computer technology (e.g., group decision support systems; see Scott, Chapter 16, this volume) can help groups achieve greater decision-making efficiency and effectiveness; however, technology can also overpower the relationship-building advantages groups develop from working face to face. Despite this potential problem, relational development can be accomplished through electronic channels, especially when group members expect to have long-term electronic interaction with one another (Walther, 1994; Walther & Burgoon, 1992). Taking time to develop electronic skills and social relationships is a key component in fostering group identity and rapport among electronically linked group members and can further increase the productivity groups accrue when using computer technology (Walther, 1997).

Intimacy in Groups

Only one study was located that investigated verbal intimacy, or the direct expression of feelings among group members. Studying therapy groups, Kavanaugh and Bollet (1983) identified 10 levels of verbal intimacy in groups, ranging from Level 1, no group-focused verbal interaction, to Level 10, direct expression of feeling about the group or group members. Level 1 interaction was characterized, in part, by two or more conversations going on in the group at the same time or long periods of silence. Level 10 interaction was characterized by "(1) here-and-now expression of feeling, (2) clear ownership of the feeling, and (3) use of a feeling-related word" (p. 47). Intimacy issues are central to relational messages, processes, and outcomes and should first be explored in groups that are primarily relationally oriented.

FUTURE RESEARCH DIRECTIONS

As this review of the extant literature suggests, there are many research challenges to those interested in studying relational aspects of groups. In the final section, I raise issues of context and recommend a theoretical perspective that can guide this research. The section ends with three specific conclusions.

Rethinking Group Context

Researchers need to rethink their interests in the groups they study. Too often, researchers rely on task or decision-making groups and ignore other groups that feature social engagement more prominently. For example, families seldom are considered by group researchers. In families, relational rather than task concerns are paramount, and "family communication brings the interrelationship among people to the forefront of inquiry" (Petronio & Braithwaite, 1993, p. 105; see Socha, Chapter 17, this volume). Families provide an important opportunity for studying stress in groups, as they often are havens of acceptance and support or can inflict emotional conflict and damage (Pearlin, 1982). Within this group context, researchers could examine how relational messages inhibit or facilitate stressful group interactions. Children's social groups also provide opportunities to examine how relational messages create expectations (and, perhaps, fear and anxieties) about group interaction. Researchers are beginning to suggest ways in which children's group relationships affect their acceptance and rejection of group interaction as adults (see, for example, Hart, Olsen,

Robinson, & Mandleco, 1997; Keyton, 1994; Socha, 1997; Socha & Socha, 1994).

Another important context to study is leaderless groups (see Counselman, 1991). Many self-help and support groups (e.g., Alcoholics Anonymous), as well as many friendship and social groups, are examples of leaderless groups. Few of these groups designate one member to serve in the formal role of leader. Sullivan's (1989) study of home parties (combined sales and socializing events held in private homes and attended almost exclusively by women) demonstrates the multifunctionality (e.g., learning about new products, visiting with friends, and developing new relationships) of such group events, which generally have been ignored by other scholars. In these and other group contexts, researchers may find that relational messages, processes, and outcomes are different from those demonstrated in decision-making task groups.

Need for Theoretical Perspectives

The study of relational dynamics in groups has been largely atheoretical. Even in those areas that have received a great deal of attention, such as cohesiveness, it is unlikely that researchers will develop a comprehensive theory in the near future. Some theoretical perspectives, however, do have potential to inform and guide communication research on relationships in groups. Structuration Theory, for example (in this volume, see Chapters 1 [Gouran], 2 [Poole], and 3 [Mabry]), provides researchers with rich theoretical ground for exploring relational messages, processes, and outcomes in groups. Although this theory has been employed primarily to explain group decision making, it has much potential for exploring relational issues, for it recognizes that groups possess and develop both a system (the social entity observable through patterns of relations) and a structure (rules and resources group members use to generate, sustain, and reproduce the system). Because of its focus on group interactional processes, Structuration Theory can provide insight into how groups provide opportunities for and then help maintain group member relationships, as well as how group norms, cohesiveness, member satisfaction, and communication climate are created and sustained. Structuration Theory, as Poole, Seibold, and McPhee (1996) contend, "provides a theory of group interaction commensurate with the complexities of the phenomenon" (p. 116). This or other theoretical perspectives (e.g., Self-Organizing Systems Theory; see Mabry, chapter 3, this volume) may help advance our knowledge of relational communication in groups.

Future Research Recommendations

Given the secondary consideration to relational issues in traditional group research, an approach grounded in the study of more relationally oriented groups may help researchers view relational communication in a new light. Thus, the first recommendation is to rethink the term *relational* in group communication. This is necessary because the constructs and methods traditionally associated with relational messages, processes, and outcomes were formed in response to the study of group task concerns. Studying relationally oriented groups would add to the current understanding of relationship development and relationship maintenance, and perhaps uncover additional relational issues. All groups, even decision-making task groups, involve relationships among group members, although the scope of relational elements could vary significantly based on group type. Thus, conceptualizing relational communication as the foundation, rather than as a subset, of group communication is one way to reframe the study of relational communication in groups. Currently, we must accept that our understanding of relational group communication is tentative and incomplete.

At the same time, although communication scholars studying task groups acknowledge the presence of relational messages, processes, and outcomes, their link to task outcomes is still not clear. Kaplan (1979) found that work group members who used high levels of maintenance expression (socioemotional content

verbally expressed in the group) were more satisfied but did not achieve greater task performance than groups whose members suppressed maintenance expression. To what degree this conclusion holds true for other types of task groups is not known. Thus, the second recommendation is to revisit the relational/task linkage in task groups once relational issues in groups have been reconceptualized, confirmed, and expanded. The relational/task linkage is particularly worthy of attention because so many relational issues seem to surface when bona fide groups are studied. For example, Glaser's (1994) field study of a troubled team reveals useful information about relationships in groups, despite the fact that she was called in to help the team accomplish its task. By raising relational issues and managing conflict without threatening relationships, and increasing the use of sincere mutual praise, support, and cooperation, team members were able to identify their roles and responsibilities more clearly and develop commitment to teamwork and innovation.

The third recommendation is to reorient the study of some traditional relational outcomes, particularly norms, cohesiveness, and satisfaction, so as to focus on them as processes. For example, although cohesiveness is often studied as a dependent variable, we lack a detailed understanding of how group cohesiveness forms, develops, and persists. Likewise, attention should be paid to developmental processes that lead to negative relationships. We need to know how group deviance develops, as well as ways in which stress is generated and dealt with by group members.

CONCLUSION

Group communication scholars have acknowledged the presence of relational messages and processes, but primarily insofar as they affect the task aspects of groups. Moreover, when scholars have had a relational focus, it has centered on positive aspects of group member relationships, and even then on only a few such aspects—specifically, symbol sharing, development of group cohesiveness, and group member satisfaction. Other positive relational consequences, such as trust or communication climate, have received less attention. There is, thus, much that we still need to discover about positive relational messages, processes, and outcomes in groups. In addition, negative relational messages, processes, and outcomes in groups (e.g., deviance and mistrust) have been virtually ignored. Focusing on this dark side of relational life in groups opens a wealth of questions to address. For example, why do some groups have such great difficulty developing positive relationships among group members? How do groups reject members, stigmatize them, or make them scapegoats for the rest of the group? To what extent can one member create and sustain stress for a group?

Researchers also often assume that group members' relationships are uniform and unvarying. It is more likely, however, that a member will form positive relationships with some members and antagonistic relationships with others. It is important, therefore, to assess how members construct their relational network within a group. Are group members trying to build positive and uniform relationships with all other members, or are some members selected because of an increased likelihood that they will provide support and positive feedback? Such a question encourages scholars, once again, to consider how subgroups develop and are maintained in group systems. Subgroup formation and other relational components of group interaction are expected to have strong influences on pressures to conform, provide pathways for influence, create opportunities for functional group roles to develop, and, yes, help groups accomplish tasks (of all kinds) with less stress and strain. Alternatively, it is just as important to know how task components of group interaction facilitate or inhibit the development of group members' relationships.

Although some studies on relational influence in groups have been conducted, Gouran (1994) argues that these studies "have revealed little concerning how the characteristics of interaction are affected by emergent or established relationships of the message producer and those to whom his or her comments are directed" (p. 34). He concludes that "relational factors presumably have an impact on what group members say. To ignore this is either to overestimate the importance of other determinants or to offer accounts of group interaction that are unnecessarily incomplete" (p. 34).

The most important challenge facing those who wish to study relational communication in groups is to examine how interaction creates, sustains, and changes the positive and negative relationships that develop among members. From my perspective, this challenge can best be addressed by longitudinal field and case studies. Relational messages, processes, and outcomes develop over time, and scholars must be "there" to see "these" happen. Many relational issues are likely to be out of the conscious attention of most group members unless relationships in the group are so negative that they require most of the group's energies, or so positive that members marvel at how well they get along. If group communication scholars broaden their conceptions of task and, thereby, allow for the study all types of groups, and if they adopt alternative methodologies, then the challenges identified here can more easily be addressed. I believe that these efforts will reveal that relational processes among group members are the foundation of the study of group communication.

REFERENCES

Adelman, M. B., & Frey, L. R. (1994). The pilgrim must embark: Creating and sustaining community in a residential facility for people with AIDS. In L. R. Frey (Ed.), *Group communication in context: Studies of natural groups* (pp. 3-22). Hillsdale, NJ: Lawrence Erlbaum.

Adelman, M. B., & Frey, L. R. (1997). *The fragile community: Living together with AIDS.* Mahwah, NJ: Lawrence Erlbaum.

Alderton, S. M., & Frey, L. R. (1983). Effects of arguments on group outcomes: The case of group polarization. *Central States Speech Journal, 34,* 88-95.

Alderton, S. M., & Frey, L. R. (1986). Argumentation in small group decision-making. In R. Y. Hirokawa & M. S. Poole (Eds.), *Communication and group decision-making* (pp. 157-174). Beverly Hills, CA: Sage.

Anderson, C. M., & Martin, M. M. (1995). The effects of communication motives, interaction involvement, and loneliness on satisfaction: A model of small groups. *Small Group Research, 26,* 118-137.

Bales, R. F. (1950). *Interaction process analysis: A method for the study of small groups.* Reading, MA: Addison-Wesley.

Bales, R. F. (1953). The equilibrium problem in small groups. In T. Parsons, R. F. Bales, & E. A. Shils (Eds.), *Working papers in the theory of action* (pp. 111-161). Glencoe, IL: Free Press.

Bales, R. F. (1985). The new field theory in social psychology. *International Journal of Small Group Research, 1,* 1-18.

Bales, R. F., & Cohen, S. P. (with Williamson, S. A.). (1979). *SYMLOG: A system for the multiple level observation of groups.* New York: Free Press.

Bantz, C. R. (1993). Cultural diversity and group cross-cultural team research. *Journal of Applied Communication Research, 21,* 1-20.

Bass, B. M. (1985). *Leadership and performance beyond expectations.* New York: Free Press.

Bass, B. M. (1990). *Bass & Stogdill's handbook of leadership: Theory, research, and managerial applications* (3rd ed.). New York: Free Press.

Bednar, R. L., & Kaul, T. J. (1978). Experiential group research: Current perspectives. In S. L. Garfield & A. E. Bergin (Eds.), *Handbook of psychotherapy and behavior change: An empirical analysis* (2nd ed., pp. 769-815). New York: Wiley.

Benne, K. D., & Sheats, P. (1948). Functional roles of group members. *Journal of Social Issues, 4,* 41-49.

Bettenhausen, K. L. (1991). Five years of groups research: What we have learned and what needs to be addressed. *Journal of Management, 17,* 345-381.

Bettenhausen, K., & Murnighan, J. K. (1985). The emergence of norms in competitive decision-making groups. *Administrative Science Quarterly, 30,* 350-372.

Bion, W. R. (1961). *Experiences in groups, and other papers.* New York: Basic Books.

Block, S., Browning, S., & McGrath, G. (1983). Humor in group psychotherapy. *British Journal of Medical Psychology, 56,* 89-97.

Bormann, E. G. (1972). Fantasy and rhetorical vision. The rhetorical criticism of social reality. *Quarterly Journal of Speech, 58,* 396-407.

Bormann, E. G. (1982). Colloquy I. Fantasy and rhetorical vision: Ten years later. *Quarterly Journal of Speech, 68,* 288-305.

Bormann, E. G. (1985). Symbolic convergence theory: A communication formulation. *Journal of Communication, 35*(4), 128-138.

Bormann, E. G. (1986). Symbolic convergence theory and communication in group decision-making. In R. Y. Hirokawa & M. S. Poole (Eds.), *Communication and group decision-making* (pp. 219-236). Beverly Hills, CA: Sage.

Bormann, E. G. (1996). Symbolic convergence theory and communication in group decision making. In R. Y. Hirokawa & M. S. Poole (Eds.), *Communication and*

group decision making (2nd ed., pp. 81-113). Thousand Oaks, CA: Sage.

Broome, B. J., & Fulbright, L. (1995). A multistage influence model of barriers to group problem solving: A participant-generated agenda for small group research. *Small Group Research, 26,* 25-55.

Burgoon, J. K. (1977). Unwillingness to communicate as a predictor of small group discussion behaviors and evaluations. *Central States Speech Journal, 28,* 122-133.

Burns, J. M. (1978). *Leadership.* New York: Harper & Row.

Cartwright, D. (1968). The nature of group cohesiveness. In D. Cartwright & A. Zander (Eds.), *Group dynamics: Research and theory* (3rd ed., pp. 91-109). New York: Harper & Row.

Cawyer, C. S., & Smith-Dupre', A. (1995). Communicating social support: Identifying supportive episodes in an HIV/AIDS support group. *Communication Quarterly, 43,* 243-258.

Cissna, K. N. (1984). Phases in group development: The negative evidence. *Small Group Behavior, 15,* 3-32.

Cline, R.J.W. (1994). Groupthink and the Watergate cover-up: The illusion of unanimity. In L. R. Frey (Ed.), *Group communication in context: Studies of natural groups* (pp. 199-223). Hillsdale, NJ: Lawrence Erlbaum.

Cluck, G. G., & Cline, R. J. (1986). The circle of others: Self-help groups for the bereaved. *Communication Quarterly, 34,* 306-325.

Collins, B. E., & Guetzkow, H. (1964). *A social psychology of group processes for decision-making.* New York: Wiley.

Conquergood, D. (1994). Homeboys and hoods: Gang communication and cultural space. In L. R. Frey (Ed.), *Group communication in context: Studies of natural groups* (pp. 23-55). Hillsdale, NJ: Lawrence Erlbaum.

Cooper, M. R., & Wood, M. T. (1974). Effectiveness of member participation and commitment in group decision making on influence, satisfaction, and decision riskiness. *Journal of Applied Psychology, 59,* 127-134.

Counselman, E. F. (1991). Leadership in a long-term leaderless women's group. *Small Group Research, 22,* 240-257.

Courtright, J. A. (1978). A laboratory investigation of groupthink. *Communication Monographs, 45,* 229-246.

Cupach, W. R., & Spitzberg, B. H. (Eds.). (1994). *The dark side of interpersonal communication.* Hillsdale, NJ: Lawrence Erlbaum.

Denison, D. R., & Sutton, R. I. (1990). Operating room nurses. In J. R. Hackman (Ed.), *Groups that work (and those that don't): Creating conditions for effective teamwork* (pp. 293-308). San Francisco: Jossey-Bass.

DeStephen, R. S. (1983). High and low consensus groups: A content and relational interaction analysis. *Small Group Behavior, 14,* 143-162.

DeStephen, R. S., & Hirokawa, R. Y. (1988). Small group consensus: Stability of group support of the decision, task process, and group relationships. *Small Group Behavior, 19,* 227-239.

Di Salvo, V. S., Nikkel, E., & Monroe, C. (1989). Theory and practice: A field investigation and identification of group members' perceptions of problems facing natural work groups. *Small Group Behavior, 20,* 551-567.

Downs, C. W., & Pickett, T. (1977). An analysis of the effects of nine leadership group compatibility contingencies upon productivity and member satisfaction. *Communication Monographs, 44,* 220-230.

Drescher, S., Burlingame, G., & Fuhriman, A. (1985). Cohesion: An odyssey in empirical understanding. *Small Group Behavior, 16,* 3-30.

Dyce, J., & O'Connor, B. P. (1992). Personality complementarity as a determinant of group cohesion in bar bands. *Small Group Research, 23,* 185-198.

Elias, F. G., Johnson, M. E., & Fortman, J. B. (1989). Task-focused self-disclosure: Effects on group cohesiveness, commitment to task, and productivity. *Small Group Behavior, 20,* 87-96.

Ellis, D. G. (1979). Relational control in two group systems. *Communication Monographs, 46,* 153-166.

Ellis, D. G., & McCallister, L. (1980). Relational control sequences in sex-typed and androgynous groups. *Western Journal of Speech Communication, 44,* 35-49.

Evans, C. R., & Dion, K. L. (1991). Group cohesion and performance: A meta-analysis. *Small Group Research, 22,* 175-186.

Evans, N. J., & Jarvis, P. A. (1980). Group cohesion: A review and reevaluation. *Small Group Behavior, 11,* 359-370.

Feldman, D. C. (1984). The development and enforcement of group norms. *Academy of Management Review, 9,* 47-53.

Festinger, L., Schachter, S., & Back, K. (1968). Operation of group standards. In D. Cartwright & A. Zander (Eds.), *Group dynamics: Research and theory* (3rd ed., pp. 152-164). New York: Harper & Row.

Fielding, K. S., & Hogg, M. A. (1997). Social identity, self-categorization, and leadership: A field study of small interactive groups. *Group Dynamics: Theory, Research, and Practice, 1,* 39-51.

Fisher, B. A. (1970). Decision emergence: Phases in group decision-making. *Speech Monographs, 37,* 53-66.

Fisher, B. A. (1971). Communication research and the task-oriented group. *Journal of Communication, 21,* 136-149.

Fisher, B. A. (1979). Content and relationship dimensions of communication in decision-making groups. *Communication Quarterly, 27,* 3-11.

Fisher, B. A., & Hawes, L. (1971). An Interact System Model: Generating a grounded theory of small groups. *Quarterly Journal of Speech, 57,* 444-453.

Fisher, W. R. (1984). Narration as a human communication paradigm: The case of public moral argument. *Communication Monographs, 51,* 1-22.

Frey, L. R. (1994a). The call of the field: Studying communication in natural groups. In L. R. Frey (Ed.), *Group communication in context: Studies of natural groups* (pp. ix-xiv). Hillsdale, NJ: Lawrence Erlbaum.

Frey, L. R. (Ed.). (1994b). *Group communication in context: Studies of natural groups.* Hillsdale, NJ: Lawrence Erlbaum.

Frey, L. R. (1994c). Introduction: Revitalizing the study of small group communication. *Communication Studies, 45,* 1-6.

Frey, L. R. (Ed.). (1995). *Innovations in group facilitation: Applications in natural settings.* Cresskill, NJ: Hampton.

Frey, L. R. (1996). Remembering and "re-membering": A history of theory and research on communication and group decision making. In R. Y. Hirokawa & M. S. Poole (Eds.), *Communication and group decision making* (2nd ed., pp. 19-51). Thousand Oaks, CA: Sage.

Frey, L. R. (1997). Individuals in groups. In L. R. Frey & J. K. Barge (Eds.), *Managing group life: Communicating in decision-making groups* (pp. 52-79). Boston: Houghton Mifflin.

Frey, L. R. (Ed.). (in press). *Group communication in context: Studies of bona fide groups* (2nd ed.). Mahwah, NJ: Lawrence Erlbaum.

Fuehrer, A., & Keys, C. (1988). Group development in self-help groups for college students. *Small Group Behavior, 19,* 325-341.

Gibb, J. R. (1961). Defensive communication. *Journal of Communication, 11,* 141-148.

Glaser, S. R. (1994). Teamwork and communication: A 3-year study of change. *Management Communication Quarterly, 7,* 282-296.

Gouran, D. S. (1973). Correlates of member satisfaction in group decision-making discussions. *Central States Speech Journal, 24,* 91-96.

Gouran, D. S. (1994). The future of small group communication research: Revitalization or continued good health? *Communication Studies, 45,* 29-39.

Gouran, D. S., & Hirokawa, R. Y. (1996). Functional theory and communication decision-making and problem-solving groups: An expanded view. In R. Y. Hirokawa & M. S. Poole (Eds.), *Communication and group decision making* (2nd ed., pp. 55-80). Thousand Oaks, CA: Sage.

Green, S. G., & Taber, T. D. (1980). The effects of three social decision schemes on decision group process. *Organizational Behavior and Human Performance, 25,* 97-106.

Greene, C. N. (1989). Cohesion and productivity in work groups. *Small Group Behavior, 20,* 70-86.

Gully, S. M., Devine, D. J., & Whitney, D. J. (1995). A meta-analysis of cohesion and performance: Effects of level of analysis and task interdependence. *Small Group Research, 26,* 497-520.

Guzzo, R. A., & Salas, E. (Eds.). (1995). *Team effectiveness and decision making in organizations* (pp. 9-45). San Francisco: Jossey-Bass.

Guzzo, R. A., & Shea, G. P. (1992). Group performance and intergroup relations in organizations. In M. D. Dunnette & L. M. Hough (Eds.), *Handbook of industrial and organizational psychology* (2nd ed., pp. 269-315). Palo Alto, CA: Consulting Psychologists Press.

Hackman, J. R. (Ed.). (1990). *Groups that work (and those that don't): Creating conditions for effective teamwork.* San Francisco: Jossey-Bass.

Hackman, J. R. (1992). Group influences on individuals in organizations. In M. D. Dunnette & L. M. Hough (Eds.), *Handbook of industrial and organizational psychology* (2nd ed., pp. 199-267). Palo Alto, CA: Consulting Psychologists Press.

Hare, A. P. (1976). *Handbook of small group research* (2nd ed.). New York: Free Press.

Hart, C. H., Olsen, S. F., Robinson, C. C., & Mandleco, B. L. (1997). The development of social and communicative competence in childhood: Review and a model of personal, familial, and extrafamilial processes. In B. R. Burleson (Ed.), *Communication yearbook 20* (pp. 305-373). Thousand Oaks, CA: Sage.

Hecht, M. L. (1978a). The conceptualization and measurement of interpersonal communication satisfaction. *Human Communication Research, 4,* 253-264.

Hecht, M. L. (1978b). Measures of communication satisfaction. *Human Communication Research, 4,* 350-368.

Hecht, M. L. (1978c). Toward a conceptualization of communication satisfaction. *Quarterly Journal of Speech, 64,* 47-62.

Hecht, M. L. (1984). Satisfying communication and relationship labels: Intimacy and length of relationship as perceptual frames of naturalistic conversations. *Western Journal of Speech Communication, 48,* 201-216.

Herzberg, F. (1970). The motivation-hygiene theory. In V. H. Broom & E. L. Deci (Eds.), *Management and motivation: Selected readings* (pp. 86-90). Baltimore: Penguin.

Heslin, R., & Dunphy, D. (1964). Three dimensions of member satisfaction in small groups. *Human Relations, 17,* 99-112.

Hewes, D. E. (1979). The sequential analysis of social interaction. *Quarterly Journal of Speech, 65,* 56-73.

Hirokawa, R. Y., & Gouran, D. S. (1989). Facilitation of group communication: A critique of prior research and an agenda for future research. *Management Communication Quarterly, 3,* 71-92.

Hofstede, G. (1980). *Culture's consequences: International differences in work-related values.* Beverly Hills, CA: Sage.

Hollihan, T. A., & Riley, P. (1987). The rhetorical power of a compelling story: A critique of a "Toughlove" parental support group. *Communication Quarterly, 35,* 13-25.

Hrycenko, I., & Minton, H. L. (1974). Internal-external control, power position, and satisfaction in task-oriented groups. *Journal of Personality and Social Psychology, 30,* 871-878.

Jackson, J. (1965). Social stratification, social norms, and roles. In I. D. Steiner & M. Fishbein (Eds.), *Current studies in social psychology* (pp. 301-309). New York: Holt, Rinehart & Winston.

Janis, I. L. (1972). *Victims of groupthink: A psychological study of foreign-policy decisions and fiascoes.* Boston: Houghton Mifflin.

Janis, I. L. (1982). *Groupthink: Psychological studies of policy decisions and fiascoes* (2nd ed.). Boston: Houghton Mifflin.

Janis, I. L. (1989). *Crucial decisions: Leadership in policy making and crisis management.* New York: Free Press.

Janis, I. L., & Mann, L. (1977). *Decision making: A psychological analysis of conflict, choice, and commitment.* New York: Free Press.

Kaplan, R. E. (1979). The utility of maintaining work relationships openly: An experimental study. *Journal of Applied Behavioral Science, 15,* 41-59.

Kavanaugh, R. R., Jr., & Bollet, R. M. (1983). Levels of verbal intimacy technique (LOVIT): An initial validation study of the measurement of verbal intimacy in groups. *Small Group Behavior, 14,* 35-49.

Kelley, H. H., & Thibaut, J. W. (1954). Experimental studies of group problem solving and process. In G. Lindzey (Ed.), *Handbook of social psychology* (Vol. 2, pp. 735-785). Reading, MA: Addison-Wesley.

Keyton, J. (1991). Evaluating individual group member satisfaction as a situational variable. *Small Group Research, 22,* 200-219.

Keyton, J. (1994). Going forward in group communication research may mean going back: Studying the groups of children. *Communication Studies, 45,* 40-51.

Keyton, J., & Springston, J. (1990). Redefining cohesiveness in groups. *Small Group Research, 21,* 234-254.

Krayer, K. J. (1988). Exploring group maturity in the classroom: Differences in behavioral, affective, and performance outcomes between mature and immature groups. *Small Group Behavior, 19,* 259-272.

Krueger, D. L. (1979). A stochastic analysis of communication development in self-analytic groups. *Human Communication Research, 5,* 314-324.

Lacoursiere, R. B. (1980). *The life cycle of groups: Group developmental stage theory.* New York: Human Sciences Press.

Langfred, C. W. (1998). Is group cohesiveness a double-edged sword? An investigation of the effects of cohesiveness on performance. *Small Group Research, 29,* 124-143.

Lesch, C. L. (1994). Observing theory in practice: Sustaining consciousness in a coven. In L. R. Frey (Ed.), *Group communication in context: Studies of natural groups* (pp. 57-82). Hillsdale, NJ: Lawrence Erlbaum.

Levine, J. M., & Moreland, R. L. (1990). Progress in small group research. In M. R. Rosenzweig & L. W. Porter (Eds.), *Annual review of psychology* (Vol. 41, pp. 585-634). Palo Alto, CA: Annual Reviews.

McGrath, J. E. (1984). *Groups: Interaction and performance.* Englewood Cliffs, NJ: Prentice Hall.

Meyers, R. A., & Brashers, D. E. (1994). Expanding the boundaries of small group communication research: Exploring a feminist perspective. *Communication Studies, 45,* 68-85.

Morgan, B. B., Jr., & Bowers, C. A. (1995). Teamwork stress: Implications for team decision making. In R. A. Guzzo & E. Salas (Eds.), *Team effectiveness and decision making in organizations* (pp. 262-290). San Francisco: Jossey-Bass.

Morgan, R. (1934). The technique of co-operation. *Quarterly Journal of Speech, 20,* 236-241.

Mudrack, P. E. (1989). Group cohesiveness and productivity: A closer look. *Human Relations, 42,* 771-785.

Mullen, B., Anthony, T., Salas, E., & Driskell, J. E. (1994). Group cohesiveness and quality of decision making: An integration of tests of the groupthink hypotheses. *Small Group Research, 25,* 189-204.

Mullen, B., & Cooper, C. (1994). The relation between group cohesiveness and performance: An integration. *Psychological Bulletin, 115,* 210-227.

Neck, C. P., & Moorhead, G. (1995). Groupthink remodeled: The importance of leadership, time pressure, and methodical decision-making procedures. *Human Relations, 48,* 537-557.

Pearlin, L. I. (1982). The social contexts of stress. In L. Goldberger & S. Breznitz (Eds.), *Handbook of stress: Theoretical and clinical aspects* (pp. 367-379). New York: Free Press.

Petronio, S., & Braithwaite, D. W. (1993). The contributions and challenges of family communication to the field of communication. *Journal of Applied Communication Research, 21,* 103-110.

Poole, M. S. (1990). Do we have any theories of group communication? *Communication Studies, 41,* 237-247.

Poole, M. S. (1994). Breaking the isolation of small group communication studies. *Communication Studies, 45,* 20-28.

Poole, M. S. (1998). The small group should be *the* fundamental unit of communication research. In J. S. Trent (Ed.), *Communication: Views from the helm for the 21st century* (pp. 94-97). Boston: Allyn & Bacon.

Poole, M. S., & Baldwin, C. L. (1996). Developmental processes in group decision making. In R. Y. Hirokawa & M. S. Poole (Eds.), *Communication and group decision making* (2nd ed., pp. 215-241). Thousand Oaks, CA: Sage.

Poole, M. S., Seibold, D. R., & McPhee, R. D. (1996). The structuration of group decisions. In R. Y. Hirokawa & M. S. Poole (Eds.), *Communication and group decision making* (2nd ed., pp. 114-146). Thousand Oaks, CA: Sage.

Prapavessis, H., & Carron, A. V. (1997). Cohesion and work output. *Small Group Research, 28,* 294-301.

Propp, K. M., & Kreps, G. L. (1994). A rose by any other name: The vitality of group communication research. *Communication Studies, 45,* 7-19.

Putnam, L. L., & Stohl, C. (1990). Bona fide groups: A reconceptualization of groups in context. *Communication Studies, 41,* 248-265.

Putnam, L. L., & Stohl, C. (1996). Bona fide groups: An alternative perspective for communication and small group decision making. In R. Y. Hirokawa & M. S. Poole (Eds.), *Communication and group decision making* (2nd ed., pp. 147-178). Thousand Oaks, CA: Sage.

Reddy, W. B., & Byrnes, A. (1972). Effects of interpersonal group composition on the problem-solving behavior of middle managers. *Journal of Applied Psychology, 56,* 516-517.

Rioch, M. J. (1970). The word of Wilfred Bion on groups. *Psychiatry, 33,* 56-66.

Roethlisberger, F. J., & Dickson, W. J. (1946). *Management and the worker: An account of a research program conducted by the Western Electric Company, Hawthorne Works, Chicago.* Cambridge, MA: Harvard University Press.

Scheerhorn, D., & Geist, P. (1997). Social dynamics in groups. In L. R. Frey & J. K. Barge (Eds.), *Managing group life: Communicating in decision-making groups* (pp. 81-103). Boston: Houghton Mifflin.

Scheerhorn, D., Geist, P., & Teboul, JC. B. (1994). Beyond decision making in decision-making groups: Implications for the study of group communication. In L. R. Frey (Ed.), *Group communication in context: Studies of natural groups* (pp. 247-262). Hillsdale, NJ: Lawrence Erlbaum.

Schutz, W. C. (1958). *FIRO: A three-dimensional theory of interpersonal behavior.* New York: Holt, Rinehart & Winston.

Schutz, W. C. (1961). On group composition. *Journal of Abnormal and Social Psychology, 62,* 275-281.

Seibold, D. R., & Meyers, R. A. (1988, June). *What has group research done for us lately? An expanded view of "group research," and prospects for the future.* Paper presented at the annual meeting of the International Communication Association, New Orleans, LA.

Sharf, B. F. (1978). A rhetorical analysis of leadership emergence in small groups. *Communication Monographs, 45,* 156-172.

Shaw, M. E. (1981). *Group dynamics: The psychology of small group behavior* (3rd ed.). New York: McGraw-Hill.

Shea, G. P., & Guzzo, R. A. (1987). Groups as human resources. In K. M. Rowland & G. R. Ferris (Eds.), *Research in personnel and human resources management* (pp. 323-356). Greenwich, CT: JAI.

Smith, C. M., & Powell, L. (1988). The use of disparaging humor by group leaders. *Southern Speech Communication Journal, 53,* 279-292.

Smith, K. K., & Berg, D. N. (1987). *Paradoxes of group life: Understanding conflict, paralysis, and movement in group dynamics.* San Francisco: Jossey-Bass.

Socha, T. J. (1997). Group communication across the life span. In L. R. Frey & J. K. Barge (Eds.), *Managing group life: Communicating in decision-making groups* (pp. 3-28). Boston: Houghton Mifflin.

Socha, T. J., & Socha, D. M. (1994). Children's task-group communication: Did we learn it all in kindergarten? In L. R. Frey (Ed.), *Group communication in context: Studies of natural groups* (pp. 227-246). Hillsdale, NJ: Lawrence Erlbaum.

Spink, K. S., & Carron, A. V. (1994). Group cohesion effects in exercise classes. *Small Group Research, 25,* 26-42.

Stock, D., & Thelen, H. A. (1958). *Emotional dynamics and group culture: Experimental studies of individual and group behavior.* New York: University Press.

Stohl, C., & Schell, S. E. (1991). A communication-based model of small-group dysfunction. *Management Communication Quarterly, 5,* 90-110.

Stokes, J. P. (1983). Components of group cohesion: Intermember attraction, instrumental value, and risk taking. *Small Group Behavior, 14,* 163-173.

Sullivan, S. J. (1989). Why do women do such womenly things? *Women's Studies in Communication, 12,* 66-89.

Thibaut, J. W., & Kelley, H. H. (1986). *The social psychology of groups* (2nd ed.). New Brunswick, NJ: Transaction Books.

Tuckman, B. W. (1965). Developmental sequence in small groups. *Psychological Bulletin, 63,* 384-399.

Tuckman, B. W., & Jensen, M.A.C. (1977). Stages of small-group development revisited. *Group & Organization Studies, 2,* 419-427.

Unite and conquer. (1990, February 5). *Newsweek,* pp. 50-55.

Vachon, M.L.S. (1987). Team stress in palliative/hospice care. *Hospice Journal, 3,* 75-103.

Verdi, A. F., & Wheelan, S. (1992). Developmental patterns in same-sex and mixed-sex groups. *Small Group Research, 23,* 356-378.

Vinton, K. L. (1989). Humor in the workplace: It is more than telling jokes. *Small Group Research, 20,* 151-166.

Wall, V. D., Jr., Galanes, G. J., & Love, S. B. (1987). Small, task-oriented groups: Conflict, conflict management, satisfaction, and decision quality. *Small Group Behavior, 18,* 31-55.

Wall, V. D., Jr., & Nolan, L. L. (1986). Perceptions of inequity, satisfaction, and conflict in task-oriented groups. *Human Relations, 39,* 1033-1052.

Wall, V. D., Jr., & Nolan, L. L. (1987). Small group conflict: A look at equity, satisfaction, and styles of conflict management. *Small Group Behavior, 18,* 188-211.

Walther, J. B. (1994). Anticipated ongoing interaction versus channel effects on relational communication in computer-mediated interaction. *Human Communication Research, 20,* 473-501.

Walther, J. B. (1997). Group and interpersonal effects in international computer-mediated collaboration. *Human Communication Research, 23,* 342-369.

Walther, J. B., & Burgoon, J. K. (1992). Relational communication in computer-mediated interaction. *Human Communication Research, 19,* 50-88.

Watzlawick, P., Beavin, J. H., & Jackson, D. D. (1967). *Pragmatics of human communication: A study of interactional patterns, pathologies, and paradoxes.* New York: Norton.

Weinberg, S. B. (1979). Measurement of communication aspects of group cohesion. *Journal of Applied Communication Research, 7,* 55-60.

Wheelan, S. A., Buzaglo, G., & Tsumura, E. (1998). Developing assessment tools for cross-cultural group research. *Small Group Research, 29,* 359-370.

Wheelan, S. A., McKeage, R. L., Verdi, A. F., Abraham, M., Krasick, C., & Johnston, F. (1994). Communication and developmental patterns in a system of interacting groups. In L. R. Frey (Ed.), *Group communication in context: Studies of natural groups* (pp. 153-180). Hillsdale, NJ: Lawrence Erlbaum.

Wheelan, S., & Verdi, A. F. (1992). Differences in male and female patterns of communication in groups: A methodological artifact? *Sex Roles, 27,* 1-15.

Wheeless, L. R., Wheeless, V. E., & Dickson-Markman, F. (1982). A research note: The relations among social and task perceptions in small groups. *Small Group Behavior, 13,* 373-384.

Wuthnow, R. (1994). *Sharing the journey: Support groups and America's new quest for community.* New York: Free Press.

Wyatt, N. (1993). Organizing and relating: Feminist critique of small group communication. In S. P. Brown & N. Wyatt (Eds.), *Transforming visions: Feminist critiques in communication studies* (pp. 51-86). Cresskill, NJ: Hampton.

PART IV

Group Communication Processes

9

Collective Information Processing in Groups

KATHLEEN M. PROPP
Northern Illinois University

All groups, regardless of their purpose, from task-oriented organizational work groups to relationally-oriented friendship groups, share a common exigency if they are to succeed: the need for members to share their individual knowledge with the group, and for the group as a collective unit to evaluate and use effectively its members' informational resources. It is through the sharing and processing of available information that group members are exposed to multiple perspectives, learn about one another, and influence one another in the process of attaining their goals, whatever they may be. Consequently, examining how information is shared, evaluated, and used is central to understanding task and relational dimensions of group life. Information processing can be used to explicate task processes in groups, in that information made available to members and how they use it are directly related to task performance. Information processing also can be used to explain relational processes, in that information affects group members' perceptions of one another and the relationships they form.

Although the dynamics of all groups can be informed by an investigation of information processing, perhaps nowhere is its role more

clear than in the making of decisions and solving of problems. In fact, the vast majority of research investigating information processing in groups examines its role in groups that perform these types of tasks. For that reason, this chapter focuses on information processing in problem-solving and decision-making groups.

More specifically, how information is collectively processed, and what facilitates or impedes this process, can explain why groups, at times, have been found to be superior to the average individual in terms of the quality and/or effectiveness of decisions made or actions taken. First, from a quantitative perspective, a group potentially has more information available to it than an individual, given that a group is composed of numerous members, each of whom brings his or her knowledge, experiences, and perspectives to the group context. As Thibaut and Kelley (1959) noted, groups have considerable ability "to gather and retain a wide range of information—an attribute most authorities would agree to be important for intelligent decision making" (p. 266). A second explanation is that a group may be more likely than an individual to recognize valid information (Lorge & Solomon,

225

1955) and reject erroneous information (Hirokawa & Pace, 1983). Consequently, by examining vigilantly the available information, a group may have not only a larger information base than an individual, but also a better one on which to base decisions. A third explanation is that a group is capable of processing more information than an individual (Laughlin, VanderStoep, & Hollingshead, 1991). This ability includes not only combining effectively the increased information available to a group but also identifying patterns that may not be recognized by an individual working alone and creating emergent solutions that no individual alone would have thought of prior to group discussion.

Although the explanations for the superiority of group performance over individual performance presented above have face validity, groups do not consistently manifest the noted qualities and often perform less well than individuals. Many factors may account for this outcome. The purpose of this chapter is to examine group decision making from a perspective that illuminates sources of success and failure in group performance: a collective information-processing perspective. More specifically, the chapter explores the role of communication in collective information processing, while taking into account the impact of characteristics of the knowledge/ information, group, and task environment.

To investigate differences in group performance from a collective information-processing perspective, I first establish the centrality of information in the performance of intellectual group tasks, such as solving problems and making judgments, inferences, and decisions. I then explore the roles of communication in the subprocesses of collective information processing. Next, I introduce a distillation model to illustrate the process of how a group develops its final collective information base from which a decision is made. Following this discussion, I incorporate noncommunicative factors in the model and indicate their influence on group discussion and collective information processing. Finally, I suggest directions for future research on collective information processing.

THE CENTRALITY OF INFORMATION TO GROUP PERFORMANCE

One clear theme connecting the explanations of the potential task superiority of groups over individuals discussed above is the assumed centrality of information to group problem solving and decision making. A brief examination of Dewey's (1910) rational thinking model, one of the most widely prescribed problem-solving models used by groups, either in whole or in some variation (in this volume, see Chapters 1 [Gouran], 7 [Hirokawa & Salazar], and 14 [Schultz]), illustrates how integral information is in each of its steps. In the first two steps, the recognition of difficulty and its location and definition (or statement of the problem), information makes group members aware of the difficulty and helps them to define the nature and characteristics of that problem. In the third step, the suggestion of possible solutions (or search for plausible alternatives), information is gathered about what potential solutions are available to the group. In the fourth step, development by reasoning of the hearing of suggestions (or the generation of criteria for evaluating alternative solutions), information determines what criteria should be used to evaluate potential solutions and the relative weighting of the selected criteria. Finally, in selection of the best solution, members use information gathered in the previous steps to analyze each viable solution and determine how well it satisfies the selected criteria; they then select a particular solution or determine whether additional alternatives may be necessary.

Information is so central to solving problems and making decisions that many scholars now recognize that group discussion in many instances may be viewed as "collective information-processing" interactions (see Hinsz, Vollrath, Nagao, & Davis, 1988). This has led many to adopt cognitive psychological approaches that focus on how members employ information available to them for the purpose of understanding why groups are sometimes superior to individuals in the performance of intellectual tasks (which represents process gains resulting from group interaction) and why they sometimes fail to live up to their potential (process losses).

A parsimonious definition of *information* is "knowledge communicated," where *knowledge* is the content and structure of a person's cognitive system. The cognitive system includes many types of data—facts, beliefs, attitudes, values, opinions, presumptions, memories, and so forth, that a person knows—as well as the organization of these data. The definition requires that for knowledge to become information, it must be communicated either verbally or nonverbally. That is, a person might *know* something, but to *inform,* he or she must communicate that knowledge in some manner. Communication, therefore, is central to understanding information because data are encoded (sending messages) and decoded (receiving messages). This perspective, thus, focuses attention on both the sender and receiver of information. Information is about sending data, but the relevance of those data in a given context are, of course, interpreted by the receiver, for "data gain meaning, they become information in the human sense, through interpretation" (Ritchie, 1991, p. 19). In exchanging information, interactants typically take into account the likely interpretations the other person(s) will make. Thus, the concept of information integrates both cognitive and communicative processes.[1]

Given this broad definition of information, *collective information processing* (CIP) may be defined as "the degree to which information, ideas, or cognitive processes are shared, and are being shared, among the group members and how this sharing of information affects both individual- and group-level outcomes" (Hinsz, Tindale, & Vollrath, 1997, p. 43). Underlying this definition are two assumptions about CIP: (a) Some level of shared or common knowledge must exist and is necessary for a group to operate, and (b) to share what group members do not have in common, they must exchange information. Interaction is the means by which common knowledge is discovered and unique knowledge may be shared with other members. Larson and Christensen (1993), thus, contend that cognitive processes, such as information acquisition/search, storage, and retrieval, occur not only at the individual level but also at the group level, and that these group-level cognitive processes, of which CIP is composed, are best studied by examining group discussion.

The definition of CIP also suggests that the way information is processed affects group outcomes, such as task performance. Consequently, understanding how group members use interaction to process information collectively is vital to understanding group performance (Hackman & Kaplan, 1974). Although the processing of information occurs initially at an individual cognitive level, in the group context, communication is the medium through which cognitions are shared and shaped by group members.

THE ROLE OF COMMUNICATION IN CIP

From a Functional Perspective on group communication (in this volume, see Chapters 1 [Gouran], 2 [Poole], and 7 [Hirokawa & Salazar]), forming an accurate information base (a collective pool of information) may be viewed as a requisite that affects the satisfaction of all other requirements of group problem-solving and decision-making tasks (Hirokawa & Scheerhorn, 1986). Put simply, a group must have accurate information to recognize and define a problem, identify potential solutions, establish criteria for evaluating solutions, evaluate the alternatives in the light of the criteria, and select the best one. Communication is the medium through which all these functions, including the establishment of a collective information base, are potentially satisfied in a group. Specifically, members' interaction may affect the development of a group's information base in two primary ways: It may be promotive or disruptive.

According to Gouran and Hirokawa (1983), *promotive* communication helps a group satisfy the requisites for successful decision making. In particular, communication can function in several promotive ways relative to the establishment of a valid, reliable, and adequate information base. First, it can serve to elicit all the available knowledge group members possess. Second, it can serve to facilitate the acceptance of what is deemed valid, relevant, and useful. Third, it can increase the probability of rejecting information lacking in these attributes. Fourth, it can help members see the need to gather new information or transform available information into an appropriate form that they can use to make effective decisions.

Communication, however, also can have a *disruptive* influence on the establishment of a group information base. Gouran and Hirokawa (1983) posit that communication has a disruptive influence when it prevents group members from satisfying any of the requisites for successful decision making. Communication can hamper the establishment of a valid, reliable, and useful information base in several ways. First, it may discourage members from contributing all the pertinent knowledge they possess. Second, it may convince members to accept information that is flawed or irrelevant. Third, it may lead members to reject information that is potentially valuable in reaching high-quality decisions.

A clearer picture of the specific role that communication plays in group performance may be gleaned by focusing on the major subprocesses of collective information processing and group decision making in which interaction plays a definite role: (a) information search, (b) information storage and retrieval, and (c) weighting and use of information. Although these subprocesses are interrelated and interdependent, for the purposes of discussion, I treat each separately.

Information Search

Einhorn and Hogarth (1981) suggest that the first major subprocess in individual or group decision making is information search. Searching for information includes the individual cognitive processes used to acquire information needed to make a decision; however, in CIP, information search also includes the manner in which group members collectively seek and communicate information. In this way, groups have the potential to use the collective knowledge of their members to achieve more informed decisions than their individual members searching alone (Stasser, 1988). The role of communication in this collective information search may be defined most straightforwardly as a neutral conduit through which the exchange of members' knowledge takes place. From this perspective, communication simply helps group members to create a larger pool of information on which to base decisions. Stasser (1988) suggests that this conduit role is especially important when members' collective knowledge favors one alternative (if it were to be shared), but the knowledge held by each individual biases him or her toward another alternative. Through the process of collective information search, members may begin to recognize that others have knowledge that can be added to their own to develop a clearer picture of the problem or issue being addressed, as well as solutions appropriate to solving it.

The characterization of communication as a neutral conduit used in the search for and dissemination of information provides a limited explanation of the role of communication in CIP. For a fuller understanding, one must not only look at the amount of potential information available to group members but also demonstrate under what conditions they will share their knowledge and utilize the information brought out during discussion. The answers suggest that communication may have a greater impact on CIP than the simple pooling of knowledge.

Information Storage and Retrieval

Storage and retrieval are related subprocesses found in most cognitive information-processing models and represent another instance in which communication plays a key role in CIP. *Storage* is the process by which information is entered into memory, whereas *retrieval* is the process by which those memories are accessed or recalled (Hinsz et al., 1997). These subprocesses are often combined in the study of group memory. It is important to note, however, that group memory performance involves not only the individual cognitive processes related to memory but also such social processes as collaboration regarding memory (Hinsz, 1990). It is this collective processing of individuals' and groups' memories that is of interest when examining the role of interaction in CIP, as communication is the means by which collective processing occurs.

In general, research on group memory has revealed that, when asked to recall information that they have been given, groups are superior to individuals across a variety of contexts (see Hartwick, Sheppard, & Davis, 1982). One possible explanation for the superiority of groups is that they have a larger pool of information available to them than do individuals because members can rely on one another's memory to construct the group's information base (Hinsz, 1990). In short, groups have multiple memories from which to draw, which increases the probability of the recall of specific items of information. For example, Vollrath, Sheppard, Hinsz, and Davis (1989) found that four-member groups made fewer *errors of omission* (failure to remember given information) than individuals when asked to recall and recognize information presented in a mock criminal trial. In this research, much like that on the subprocess of information search, the role of communication may be viewed as a neutral conduit through which memories are shared among fellow group members to reconstruct the given information base.

Research also has demonstrated, however, that the superiority of group over individual memory is based on more than the simple pooling of members' memories. Group memory is improved by members' correction of errors in information provided by fellow members. In such cases, communication has a promotive influence as the medium through which errors are found and corrected. Studies by Vollrath et al. (1989) and Hinsz (1990) support the view that groups are superior to individuals in correcting errors of memory. Although such studies suggest that error correction in collective memory processing is one factor contributing to superior group performance, most have failed, however, to look at actual group interaction.

To understand more fully the role of communication as a promotive influence in group memory, one must examine research that has focused directly on group interaction. The following studies provide indirect support of the role of communication in improving or correcting group members' memories. Although these studies examined general group decision-making tasks rather than tests of recognition or recall, the subprocesses of information storage and retrieval are implicit in their accomplishment. The primary difference is that group memory in a decision-making task incorporates individual group members' a priori experiences and knowledge, in addition to materials presented to the group.

In one study of group communication, Hirokawa and Pace (1983) analyzed interactional differences between effective and ineffective groups to determine what types of interaction distinguished performance. Two tasks that required recommendations for action were employed in this study: Half the groups received a plagiarism case, and the other half received a property damage case. Effectiveness was operationalized as the quality of the recommendation as evaluated by two sets of judges who had expertise and knowledge in each task context. Hirokawa and Pace found that members of effective groups carefully evaluated the validity of the contributions of their members, whereas members of ineffective groups tended to accept contributions without considering their validity. Similarly, Hirokawa (1987) determined that high-quality group decisions could be distinguished from low-quality decisions by the presence of second-guessing in the discussion. That is, the discussion characterizing high-quality decisions included retrospective questioning of choices and the challenging of questionable information that group members introduced. In a related study, Propp and Julian (1994) noted a positive relationship between utterances used by group members to stimulate the evaluation of information introduced by others and overall decision quality. These and other studies that focus on the role of interaction in group performance suggest that certain types of communication may be particularly effective in eliciting the careful examination of information and, hence, improving group memory, as well as group decision making.

Communication, however, is also a medium through which flawed thinking may be introduced into a group's information base and, therefore, may have an inhibitive influence on group memory. Hinsz (1990) identifies two types of flawed information that may become part of a group's memory: *errors of commission* (fabrications) and *errors of implication* (assumptions made from given information, but not actually present in the information).

Groups often fail to recognize these errors, with the result that the probability of a poor performance is increased. Aronsson and Nilholm (1990), for example, examined the recall and use of information in a simulation of lay judges' deliberations and discovered that communication had an inhibitive influence on group memory. During discussion, group members would often create spontaneous misrepresentations of the background material presented to them (errors of commission), and other members rarely corrected these misrepresentations (errors of omission). Moreover, they often accepted and treated these misrepresentations as "fact" in sub-

sequent interactions. Members also accepted and unknowingly re-disseminated background information that had been given to only one group member, rather than questioning whether the information had been part of the trial evidence provided to them.

The potentially inhibitive role of communication in group memory is further supported by research in which Hirokawa (1987) observed that decision-making groups often accepted poor information if they engaged in improbable fantasy chains (unrealistic hypothetical scenarios in which multiple group members participate) during group discussion. The communication of these extended and unrealistic stories created a sense of excitement and involvement that impeded group members from thinking critically about the information being presented and facilitated the acceptance of flawed information (errors of implication).

Weighting and Use of Information

A third subprocess in CIP involves how groups weight given items of information and, based on this weighting, decide how the information should be used in making decisions. Kaplan (1977) suggests that each piece of information has two properties: its scale value and weight. *Scale value* is the "quantitative position of the information on the judgment continuum" (p. 262). This property, thus, represents the valence of information with regard to the overall judgment being made. *Weight* is "the importance of that information for the judgment" (p. 263). Together, scale value and weight determine how a piece of information will be processed and what effect it will have on a group's final choice.

In CIP, the scale value and weight of information often are influenced by a group's discussion. Communication may change group members' perceptions of the valence of a given piece of information; it may also change the perceived importance of that information in making a decision and, hence, what information is actually used, as well as how it is used by members in reaching a decision.

By influencing how group members evaluate information, communication becomes a medium for social influence that may be promotive or disruptive (see Meyers & Brashers, Chapter 11, this volume, regarding social influence processes in groups). That is, members may be influenced by the group's discussion to change their evaluations of information, and this may facilitate the decision-making process or inhibit it. For example, a change in scale value occurs if a member convinces others in a group that a piece of information they think supports a certain alternative actually does not. Similarly, a change in weight occurs if a member convinces others that a piece of information is not as valuable or is more valuable than they originally thought.

Riecken (1958) posited that communication as a persuasive medium is important to group decision-making performance because it is the means by which members present and offer support for their preferences. In presenting one's preference, others may be convinced or persuaded to accept or reject a particular alternative. Persuasion of this type is closely related to the acceptance and rejection of information. By convincing other group members that one's preference is best, one member can change the group's scale value and weighting of available information. Information supporting the alternative becomes more salient and is utilized, whereas information not supporting the alternative may be repudiated or ignored. As Shaw and Penrod (1962) note, a person must convince others to accept and utilize information in making a collective decision; the presence of an item of information is not, ipso facto, sufficient. In short, information does not speak for itself.

Vinokur and Burnstein (1974) explored the persuasive influence of information in developing Persuasive Arguments Theory, a theory that posits that shifts occur in group members' preferences because not all persuasive arguments are known prior to discussion (see Meyers & Brashers, Chapter 11, this volume). They contend that the scale value and weight of information may be changed through group discussion in two ways: by the number of arguments presented and by their persuasiveness (based on their novelty). Hinsz and Davis (1984), in an experiment in which these two factors were manipulated independently, observed that both factors had a significant influence on the choices groups made.

Although these studies provide some evidence that discussion affects group outcomes, they did not focus directly on how communication influences the weighting and use of specific items of information. One study that did was conducted by Propp (1997), who examined the interactions of groups asked to provide recommendations in a child custody hearing. She discovered that how an item of information was evaluated in group discussion, based on the summed valence of group members' interaction, was a strong predictor of what specific items of evidence were used by groups to make decisions. That is, the collective evaluation of the given evidence influenced what items of information group members weighted heavily enough to use in reaching decisions. Another study that focused on the impact of communication on the weighting of information investigated whether members' evaluations of information become more uniform after group discussion (Wittenbaum & Stasser, 1998). Specifically, this study compared group members' evaluations of positions held by student body president candidates before and after discussion and found that the disparity in prediscussion evaluations decreased for positions that were discussed, but not for positions that were omitted from discussion. This study suggests that there is pressure toward uniformity of opinion about how information should be evaluated within groups, and that communication is the medium through which this influence is accomplished.

A DISTILLATION MODEL OF CIP

Although the amount and validity of individual group members' information clearly influences the decisions that groups make (Kelley & Thibaut, 1969), this information alone cannot explain why some groups reach higher quality decisions than others. Rather, it is the effort members put into the examination of available information that leads to a group's superior performance (see Janis, 1989; Janis & Mann, 1977). The role communication plays in that process, in terms of influencing the quality of collective information search, storage/retrieval, and weighting/use of information, is central yet equivocal. At times, communication serves a promotive function by helping group members to examine available information critically and use it effectively. At other times, it serves an inhibitive function in CIP by constraining members' ability to use informational resources effectively. To understand the relationship between CIP and group performance, one must be able to account not only for the role of communication but also for factors that mediate its influence. To do so, a model of collective information processing is presented: the Distillation Model of CIP (see Figure 9.1).

The Distillation Model of CIP illustrates how group discussion of information is mediated by characteristics of the knowledge/ information, group, and task environment. The model provides a way to summarize and organize the disparate findings on information use in groups reported from the fields of Communication, Psychology, Organizational Studies, and Sociology, while illustrating connections among the foci of these research areas under the rubric of CIP. The model also may serve as a heuristic device from which further analyses examining the linkages can proceed.

If one accepts the premise that group intellectual tasks, such as making decisions and solving problems, inherently involve CIP, it is clear that the quality of the final collective information base from which a group makes a decision is central to understanding group performance. If this information base is incomplete or contains flawed or irrelevant information, performance generally will suffer. Group members, therefore, must ascertain what information is available to them and then determine its value in making a choice or judgment. One can, therefore, conceptualize

effective CIP as a distillation process in which a group moves from a relatively large, collective knowledge base, the foundation of which is the knowledge possessed by each group member, to a refined information base from which irrelevant or invalid information is eliminated; appropriate weights are assigned to the remaining information, and a decision is made on the basis of that information.

The refinement of a final collective information base theoretically proceeds through four developmental stages: (a) *individual knowledge base*—knowledge that each member brings to the group concerning the task, (b) *group knowledge base*—collective knowledge available to a group as a whole, (c) *communicated information base*—information exchanged and shaped through group discussion, and (d) *final collective information base*—information accepted and utilized by a group to come to a decision. Although these stages are progressive, as in any process, the boundaries separating them in linear terms may be unclear, for the stages are interdependent and each stage has an impact on the other stages (e.g., see the discussion of group socialization phases in Anderson, Riddle, & Martin, Chapter 6, this volume). For purposes of discussion, each stage is examined separately to highlight principal factors that influence CIP at each stage; however, recognizing the interdependence of these developmental stages is central to understanding the extent to which CIP will be effective.

Individual Knowledge Base

As Figure 9.1 illustrates, in the first stage, each group member (A, B, C, and D, in this example) possesses his or her own knowledge base. In other words, each member brings to the task a knowledge base, some of which may or may not be shared with others in the group. The shape and size of this knowledge base varies from individual to individual on the basis of what he or she knows about the task at hand and past experiences in similar situations, as well as general knowledge and any information search the individual has con-

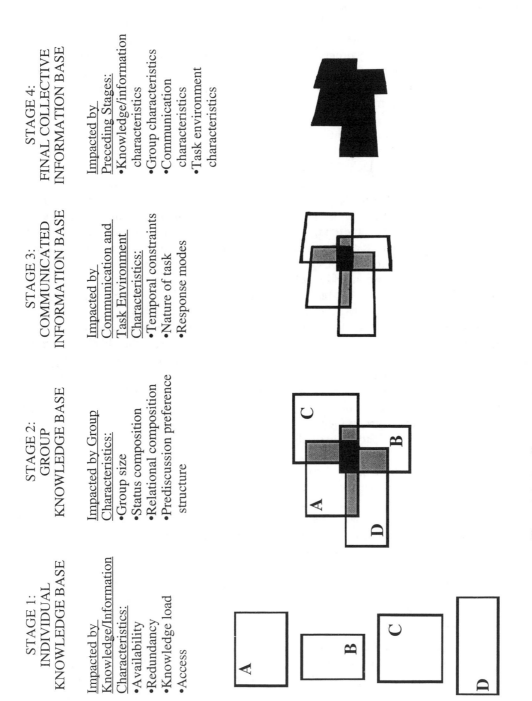

Figure 9.1. Distillation Model of Collective Information Processing

ducted prior to meeting with the group. An individual's knowledge base not only references what that person has to share with others but also influences his or her interpretation of information made available by others.

At this stage, characteristics of the knowledge possessed by each group member are factors that affect the ensuing stages of CIP. Individual members' knowledge sets the boundaries for what information potentially is available to a group, for a group cannot discuss or utilize information to which it does not have access. There also will be more or less redundancy in the pool of knowledge that members possess. If all members possess the same knowledge, they will be unable to inform one another in new ways. Possession of unique knowledge, therefore, is necessary for effective CIP. Similarly, the total amount of knowledge possessed by individuals creates the *knowledge load* of a group; that is, the sum total of individual members' knowledge sets the boundaries for the amount of information that potentially can be shared in group discussion. The size of the knowledge load may have an impact on CIP in that the larger the load, the more difficult it is to share and utilize fully the knowledge possessed by group members. In contrast, if the knowledge load is too small, group members may not possess enough knowledge to make a high-quality judgment or decision. Finally, whether an individual has access to his or her knowledge affects one's ability to remember and share that potential information with a group; that is, members might possess knowledge based on past experiences that is not readily at their disposal, thus hindering effective CIP.

Group Knowledge Base

In the second stage of the CIP Distillation Model, group members' individual knowledge bases are conceptually overlaid (as illustrated in Figure 9.1) to form the collective knowledge potentially available to a group. At this stage, the focus is on the group, not the individual, level. Rather than looking at what knowledge each individual brings to the process, one looks at the combined knowledge of group members.

At this stage, group-level characteristics of the knowledge possessed by a group as a collective unit are factors that may affect the ensuing stages of CIP. For example, the size of a group has an impact on the ensuing stages of information processing. As size increases, members find it more difficult to share all the information they individually possess. The status composition of a group may also affect whether members share information freely, as well as how members receive and evaluate information. Research demonstrates that in status-heterogeneous groups, higher status members are likely to contribute more to the discussion than lower status members (e.g., Smith-Lovin, Skvoretz, & Hudson, 1986), and the contributions of higher status members are more likely to be influential (e.g., Pugh & Wahrman, 1983).

The relational composition of a group is another characteristic that likely affects the later stages of CIP. For example, group members' familiarity with one another helps them determine what information they feel comfortable contributing and how others are apt to react to their contributions. Finally, the *prediscussion preference structure* of a group— whether there is consensus or conflict among individuals' preferences for a solution prior to group discussion—is another group-level characteristic that has an impact on the subsequent stages of CIP. Research shows that if members have drawn the same conclusion individually prior to group discussion (a consensus structure), they may perceive that they have similar knowledge and interpretations and, consequently, may perceive less need to inform each other; thus, information sharing is likely to be relatively low (Propp, 1997). In contrast, if members have drawn different conclusions based on their individual knowledge bases prior to group discussion (a conflict structure), information sharing and weighting become more important, because members must persuade others of the validity of their knowledge and interpretations. A group with initial conflicting preferences, therefore, usually establishes a larger communicated information base in the next stage.

Communicated Information Base

In the third stage of the CIP Distillation Model, the impact of group discussion becomes the central focus. The role of communication in collective information search, storage and retrieval, and weighting/use, therefore, must be taken into account at this stage. Knowledge held by group members but unknown to the others must be shared to have the potential of being utilized in the final collective information base. As explained earlier, discussion facilitates or inhibits group members' collective ability to recall information and provides the medium through which faulty memories are corrected or errors of commission and/or implication are introduced. Furthermore, discussion shapes the evaluation or weighting of information. Depending on the persuasiveness of members' arguments, members may reject some information as irrelevant or invalid, whereas other information may rise in importance and, thereby, change the initial preferences of group members.

As Figure 9.1 illustrates, characteristics of the knowledge bases possessed by individuals and groups in the first two stages have an impact on the qualities and amount of information communicated during the third stage. Thus, the communicated information base will resemble the individual and group knowledge bases, but it is unlikely that it will remain exactly the same. This is because group members choose what knowledge to share, and the ensuing discussion may, in turn, lead to alterations in interpretations of what is now information, which alters the information available to a group. Characteristics of the task environment also are important to the communicated information base, as they create the context for a group's discussion. For example, temporal constraints on the task may influence the amount and content of discussion by limiting the time allowed for sharing and evaluating information. The nature of the task also may influence a group's discussion by privileging certain types of information. For example, tasks that have a demonstrably correct answer privilege the use of facts as evidence, in contrast to tasks that involve making value judgments, in which appeals to social norms have an advantage (e.g., Kaplan, 1989). Similarly, the *response mode*—the type of analysis a group is asked to provide by an internal or external authority—has an effect on group discussion. For example, a group asked to evaluate all alternatives, such as the rank ordering of job candidates, is likely to display a more thorough information search and evaluation than a group asked to make a single choice, such as a jury's determination of a person's innocence or guilt.

Final Collective Information Base

The final stage in the CIP Distillation Model can be conceptualized as the output of the previous stages. At some point during the decision-making process, a group will render a choice or judgment. The information on which this decision is based is a result of the earlier stages of the CIP process. Given the nature of the individual members' knowledge, characteristics of the group, the role communication plays in collective information processing, and elements of the task environment, a group distills the knowledge and information available to members throughout the first three stages into a refined final collective information base that influences the decision made. In the light of the factors highlighted in the earlier stages of CIP, it is unlikely that all the members' knowledge will come to the group's attention. It is also possible that faulty information may have been introduced and/or the group may have been influenced to evaluate and use information in an inconsistent or incorrect manner. Each stage in CIP is, thus, potentially fraught with threats to the quality, as well as the quantity, of information possessed by a group and, consequently, a group's performance. Because the stages are interdependent, a processing problem in one stage can affect the collective information-processing performance of a group at subsequent stages and, ultimately, the quality of the decision reached. It is little wonder, then, that groups experience less frequently than expected the assembly bonuses that are hoped for when groups are used to perform intellectual tasks.

THE ROLE OF NONCOMMUNICATIVE FACTORS IN CIP

The model discussed above suggests that although communication is central to CIP, one also must account for the impact of noncommunicative factors that influence group discussion and how well members share, evaluate, and, ultimately, use information. A review of the extant literature suggests three general categories of noncommunicative factors that may mediate the role of communication in CIP: characteristics of the knowledge/information, the group, and the task environment.

Characteristics of Knowledge/Information

A large amount of research has focused on how characteristics of information given to a group can influence how it is processed. This line of research was initiated by Stasser and his colleagues (e.g., Stasser, Taylor, & Hanna, 1989; Stasser & Titus, 1985, 1987) and has led to the investigation of the effects of (a) the redundancy of the prediscussion distribution of knowledge, (b) the knowledge load and the level of common knowledge, and (c) access to information during discussion.

Prediscussion Knowledge Distribution

Because individual members often have only partial knowledge relevant to a task, a group often needs to piece together the knowledge possessed by its members to create a larger information base and a less individually oriented characterization of the situation. Stasser (1992b) suggests that the presumed benefit of working in groups depends on two conditions: (a) Members have some *unique*

knowledge they may share with the group, and (b) members *choose to share* their unique knowledge and, thereby, turn it into information. Stasser and Titus (1985), however, also note that although members often possess unique knowledge, the potential benefit of pooling that knowledge in group discussion may go unrealized because they often focus discussion on the *common* knowledge they possess rather than the unique knowledge each holds.

An information-sampling model has been posited as an explanation of how the level of redundancy for a given piece of information (common versus unique) influences whether it will be introduced into group discussion and used by members in making a decision (Stasser et al., 1989; Stasser & Titus, 1985, 1987). According to this model, the content of group discussion may be biased in two ways by the prediscussion distribution of knowledge. First, group discussion will be biased in favor of common knowledge, because the more members who possess a piece of knowledge, the greater the probability that it will be mentioned in discussion. Second, discussion will be biased in favor of the initial preferences of group members. In other words, members often advocate their initial preferences, and an initial consensus created by the prediscussion distribution of knowledge will decrease their perceived need to seek additional information and, thereby, lower the probability of discovering unique knowledge.

To examine the impact of the distribution of prediscussion knowledge on group decision making, Stasser and Titus (1985) gave groups a judgment task involving a political caucus meeting in which one of three candidates had to be selected on the basis of a mix of common and unique information made available to group members. The information provided to each group member simulated his or her individual knowledge of the topic prior to discussion. Information was selected and distributed in a manner that would severely bias members' initial preferences away from the "best" candidate (as determined by the balance of positive and negative items of information provided about each candidate). Members were given some different items of information, however, and if their unique knowledge was examined exhaustively, the group had the potential to discover the strongest candidate. As predicted, discussion enhanced rather than mitigated the initial bias of members; thus, few groups were successful in identifying the best candidate. Stasser and Titus concluded that groups required to reach a consensus often fail to combine unique knowledge resources effectively if their discussions are unstructured (see Sunwolf & Seibold, Chapter 15, this volume, regarding problems associated with naturally occurring, or unstructured, group discussion).

Reliance by group members on common knowledge and the failure to take into account unique knowledge have been confirmed in numerous studies (e.g., Gigone & Hastie, 1993, 1997; Larson, Christensen, Abbott, & Franz, 1996; Propp, 1997; Stasser, 1992a; Stasser et al., 1989; Stasser & Titus, 1985, 1987). Research testing the information-sampling model, thus, has provided significant evidence that the prediscussion distribution of knowledge affects what information group members share in discussion and use to make a decision.

Knowledge Load and Level of Common Knowledge

Stasser and Titus (1987) continued their examination of the distribution of prediscussion knowledge by expanding the information-sampling model created in their earlier study. They predicted that the tendency to rely on common knowledge would lessen under two conditions: (a) when the knowledge load is low (the sum total of individual members' knowledge available for discussion is small), and (b) when there is a low percentage of common knowledge among group members (most knowledge is unique prior to discussion). These two conditions represent additional characteristics of groups' knowledge/information that have a potential impact on CIP.

These additions to the information-sampling model are consistent with notions concerning groups' performance of *disjunctive tasks*. McGrath (1984) explains that, in a disjunctive task, "if one member of the group *does* the task, it is done for the group" (p. 57). For example, if one member has the answer to a math problem, the group has the answer; if one member can solve a riddle, the group can solve the riddle. Similarly, if a member informs the group of his or her knowledge, the knowledge becomes part of the group's collective information base. Based on this principle, common knowledge is more likely to be brought out in group discussion than unique knowledge because there are more individuals who have the potential to contribute it. If only one member of a group shares unique knowledge during group discussion, it becomes part of the collective information base. Consequently, if a proportionately large amount of unique knowledge is possessed by members, there is more chance that at least some of that knowledge will enter the discussion and become group information. The model, then, suggests that as the ratio of unique to common knowledge increases, the tendency to focus on common knowledge decreases. In addition, knowledge loads that are relatively low result in proportionately more information of any type being discussed. Hence, if the knowledge load is low, this should facilitate the exchange of unique information and, thereby, help group members to pool their prediscussion knowledge more effectively.

To test these assumptions, Stasser and Titus (1987) employed a 2 × 2 factorial experimental design that manipulated knowledge load (12 versus 24 items of evidence) and the percentage of knowledge that was shared initially by group members (33% versus 66% common). An analysis of what information members could recall after discussion showed that sizable amounts of unique knowledge were exchanged only when a low percentage of knowledge initially was held in common. Moreover, the low knowledge load/low percentage initially shared condition was the best combination of factors. Thus, both hypotheses received support, lending credence to the impact of knowledge load and percentage of common knowledge on CIP. These findings were replicated by Schittekatte (1996) and Schittekatte and Van Hiel (1996).

Access to Provided Information

A third characteristic of information affecting CIP is whether, during group discussion, members have access to information they have been provided prior to discussion. For example, in many states, jurors are not allowed to take notes at a trial and are not provided with complete access to court transcripts. Rather, they must request specific excerpts from the transcripts and, therefore, rely heavily on their memories when deliberating. When members do not have access to the information provided to them, what is retained by each member becomes knowledge that may or may not be shared with the group during discussion. Although group memory appears to be superior to individual memory, the line of research drawn from the information-sampling model has demonstrated that the collective memory for unique knowledge held by group members does not appear to be as good as that for common knowledge. Consequently, if only one juror remembers an item of evidence, there is less chance of this knowledge being shared with other jurors.

Working from the assumption that groups' ability to share unique knowledge is limited, Hollingshead (1996b) argued that giving access to a provided information base, such as court transcripts, should help group members to recall their knowledge and share this as information more thoroughly. Moreover, because unique knowledge is more likely to be forgotten by a group, access to provided information should have an especially strong impact on the retrieval of unique knowledge. In a study that predicted that access to an information sheet provided by the researcher would improve group memory, groups allowed to read from their information profiles throughout the discussion increased the amount of discussion of both common and unique information relative to groups that had access to their information sheets only prior to discussion and, therefore, had to rely on their members' memories of the information profiles. One interesting finding was that although groups increased their collective memory by having access to the information profiles, they were not more likely to discover the hidden profile created by the information distribution provided by the researchers. Hence, although access to information improved a group's collective memory by increasing the amount of pooled information, it did not have much influence on the weighting and use of that information.

Characteristics of the Group

Extant literature identifies a second category of noncommunicative factors that influence CIP involving variations in the composition of groups. These composition variations include (a) group size, (b) the status hierarchy of a group, (c) relationships in a group, and (d) the prediscussion preference structure of a group.

Group Size

The first characteristic of groups that has an impact on how knowledge is sampled and processed collectively as information is group size. Stasser et al. (1989) considered how group size affected the bias in information processing created by prediscussion knowledge distributions. The information-sampling model they used predicted that the advantage of common knowledge would increase as group size increased, presumably because of the higher number of individuals who have the potential to contribute an item of common knowledge to the discussion. The study employed the same political caucus simulation as earlier studies but this time involved both three- and six-person groups. Group discussions were recorded, and observers coded and tabulated the mention of any information that had come from the candidates' profiles provided to members prior to meeting together.

As predicted, all discussions contained the mention of significantly more items of information that had been common knowledge than unique; however, this tendency was greater for six-person groups than for three-person groups.

Status Hierarchy

A second characteristic of groups that influences CIP is the *status hierarchy* of a task-oriented group—the perceived prestige order of members vis-à-vis one another, which is initially determined by members' individual differences (Berger, Cohen, & Zelditch, 1973; Berger, Conner, & Fisek, 1974; Berger, Fisek, Norman, & Wagner, 1985; see Haslett & Ruebush, Chapter 5, this volume). Because little else is known about fellow group members initially, members use existing status characteristics—any available cues that can help to differentially evaluate a member's task competence—to construct a status hierarchy (Berger & Zelditch, 1977). These cues may be task-relevant or external to the particular task of the group. *Task-relevant cues* include the expertise or experience of group members with similar tasks, characteristics that logically might reflect their task competence. *External* or *diffuse cues* include perceived demographic differences, such as age, biological sex (as distinct from psychological gender), and race/ethnicity of an individual, if one assumes that these qualities are not related to the task at hand. Ridgeway and Berger (1986) argue that if members perceive differences in status (heterogeneous-status groups), the initial status hierarchy of a group is more likely to be legitimized than in groups in which no initial differences are perceived (homogeneous-status groups). In the latter case, the status structure develops during group discussion on the basis of such factors as members' task contributions and displayed abilities.

Perceived status hierarchies create performance expectations that group members hold for themselves and others, and these expectations influence members' behavior. Specifically, when members perceive that differences in status exist, higher status persons generally are expected to have more to contribute to the successful completion of the group's task than lower status persons. Consequently, these individuals are accorded more opportunities to participate, initiate more actions, receive more positive reactions, and exert more influence than those perceived as having lower status (see Meeker & Weitzel-O'Neill, 1977; Ridgeway & Berger, 1986).

The status hierarchy of a group may have an impact on CIP in several ways. First, because those who are perceived as higher in status have more opportunities to contribute, the probability of their knowledge being introduced as information into a group discussion is greater than that of those perceived as lower in status. Second, because higher status members receive more positive reactions to their contributions, the probability that their contributions will be weighted more heavily is greater than it is for other members. Finally, because higher status members are more influential, they are more likely to convince other members to accept their assessments and evaluations of the information that surfaces in a discussion and, thereby, what information a group ultimately uses in making decisions. To understand the impact of status characteristics on CIP more fully, the following sections explore the CIP effects of task-relevant and external cues separately.

Task-relevant status characteristics. Research on the relationship between status and group performance provides evidence that task-relevant status cues create performance expectations for group members that affect CIP. One approach of studies of this type is to compare the performance of homogeneous-status groups to heterogeneous-status groups by manipulating some form of members' expertise or experience. Performance differences between the two types of groups are then presumed to be a result of the status hierarchy created by the task-relevant cues. Other studies focus on within-group differences to ascertain whether higher status members behave differently from lower status members.

In an examination of the impact of task-relevant status cues on the dissemination of information, Wittenbaum (1998) manipulated task-relevant status by creating hetero-geneous-status groups composed of two "high-status" members with prior experience of working on a candidate-selection task and two "low-status" members with no such prior task experience. Wittenbaum hypothesized that although groups would demonstrate the information sampling bias observed in previous research (overreliance on knowledge that was held in common prior to discussion), high-status members, or those who had task-relevant experience, would exhibit less bias in the sharing of unique knowledge than low-status members. Several reasons were offered for the attenuated bias of high-status members: (a) Members with high performance expectations are more likely to take responsibility for remembering task-relevant knowledge, (b) these members are more likely to be asked to retrieve this knowledge during discussion because of their perceived expertise, and (c) in general, these members will be given more opportunities to speak, increasing the likelihood of sharing their unique knowledge. As expected, the results revealed that although groups did share more common than unique knowledge, high-status members were less likely to favor common knowledge than low-status members. It also was found that high-status individuals were more likely to repeat and advocate the use of unique information after it was brought out in discussion. Larson et al. (1996) found similar results when looking at the behavior of team leaders in groups of physicians diagnosing medical cases.

Wittenbaum and Stasser (1997) investigated why experienced group members display less bias in information sampling. Utilizing a recognition test, they noted that inexperienced members were better able to recognize experienced members' unique knowledge than experienced members were at recognizing inexperienced members' unique knowledge. They concluded that the attenuated bias

was not attributable to real or felt task competence but, instead, that the unique knowledge contributed as information to the group discussion by experienced members was ascribed greater importance by other members. This supports the notion that high-status group members are seen as more credible and, therefore, the information they share is weighted more heavily.

Hollingshead (1996a) studied the impact of status on group performance by examining what occurs when a low-status member possesses knowledge critical to the effective completion of a task. She operationalized status by manipulating student group composition based on year in school (presumed experience and/or knowledge) to create groups with freshman and senior members. Only one member was given the information necessary to adopt the correct alternative. Hollingshead found that if the member who was given the information was of relatively low status, it was less likely to surface in the information search; in addition, the person who possessed the unique, critical knowledge was not especially influential, and the group tended to make a poor decision.

External status characteristics. If task-relevant cues are not available, group members use external status cues to determine the status hierarchy. Although many external status characteristics—such as race, age, or socioeconomic class—may serve as cues used to create performance expectations in groups, sex, and its potential impact on CIP, has probably received the most attention (see Haslett & Ruebush, Chapter 5, this volume, regarding the impact of sex and gender as status characteristics in groups). An early study was Strodtbeck and Mann's (1956) examination of jury deliberations, which found that men were more likely than women to be active and to be identified by members as valuable to the group. The study also revealed that the contributions of men were more valued by both sexes than the contributions of women. In a more recent study, Pugh and Wahrman (1983) examined sex as an external status cue to explain influence behavior in mixed- and same-sex groups. When participants interacted with the opposite sex, males rejected influence attempts more than females; however, the rate of rejecting influence was approximately the same within same-sex groups.

Sex also has been linked to differential participation of men and women in group discussion. Smith-Lovin et al. (1986) manipulated the composition of experimental groups from all male to mixed to all female to determine whether sex represents a status characteristic. In same-sex groups, participation rates were roughly equivalent; in mixed-sex groups, the average male contribution increased and the average female contribution decreased. Lee (1993) obtained similar results in studying computer-based, cooperative learning groups (see Allen & Plax, Chapter 18, this volume, regarding communication in cooperative learning groups).

Differences in participation rates between heterogeneous-status groups (mixed-sex) and homogeneous-status groups (same-sex) provide clear evidence that external status characteristics have the potential to influence CIP. The higher participation rates of men in mixed-sex groups increases the probability that knowledge initially held by men will be contributed to the discussion, whereas the lower participation rates of women decreases the probability that their knowledge will be shared with a group. Hence, the information search of a mixed-sex group can be problematic because such groups run the risk of not incorporating all members' knowledge.

In research specifically examining information use, Propp (1995) discovered that group members were roughly twice as likely to use items of evidence introduced by men in making a group decision than those introduced by women. This occurred despite the fact that the amount of information introduced by men and woman was not significantly different. More important, Propp found an interaction effect in information usage between the sex of the information introducer and the prediscussion redundancy level of the knowledge possessed by group members. Specifically, the preferential treatment of information introduced by men was much stronger when the item of evidence was unique than when it was common to all members prior to group discussion. This finding suggests that the increased source credibility afforded to group members with high status has an especially strong effect on the weighting and use of unique information introduced into group discussion.

Relationships in Groups

A third characteristic of groups linked to CIP is the relational composition of a group. Research in this area has focused on whether group members are familiar with each other. Gruenfeld, Mannix, Williams, and Neale (1996), for example, tested the effect of this variable on the tendency for groups to rely heavily on common knowledge. They varied the composition of three-person groups from all individuals being familiar with each other, to two familiar individuals and one stranger, to all strangers. Gruenfeld and colleagues predicted that interpersonal knowledge of other members would reduce the tendency to rely on common knowledge in two ways: (a) Familiar members would be less likely to experience evaluation apprehension, and, therefore, would be less likely to suppress conflict or knowledge that may incite conflict; and (b) familiar members have increased knowledge of one another's interaction styles and skills and, therefore, would be less likely to experience process losses in the pooling of information.

The results indicated that groups of all strangers were most likely to identify the correct alternative when all members possessed the same knowledge, whereas groups of all-familiar members and two familiar/one unfamiliar members were most likely to identify the correct alternative when critical knowledge was possessed by one member prior to discussion. The investigators concluded that groups of strangers are more likely to aggregate their individual choices and adopt the preference of the majority. This allows groups of strangers to do well if knowledge is common to all members but hampers the discovery of hidden profiles if critical knowledge is possessed by only one group member. On the other hand, groups whose members are familiar with one another are more likely to pool their knowledge because they presumably are more comfortable disagreeing with one another. This helps them to achieve superior performance when critical knowledge is possessed by a particular group member.

Prediscussion Preference Structure

A final characteristic of groups that has an impact on CIP is the prediscussion preference structure of the group; that is, whether there is a consensus or conflict among individuals' preferences for a solution prior to group discussion. Ostensibly, this effect occurs because discussion is influenced by the prevailing opinions of group members. Studies supporting this contention suggest that group discussion will tend to favor the position initially favored by the majority of members (e.g., Bodenhausen & Lichtenstein, 1987; Hastie & Park, 1986; Hastie, Penrod, & Pennington, 1983; Pennington & Hastie, 1986, 1988; Schul & Burnstein, 1985). If members have an initial preference prior to discussion, they will selectively introduce and argue for pieces of information that support it. This tendency occurs because preference-consistent knowledge is more salient and more likely to be recalled during group discussion (Fishbein & Ajzen, 1975).

Burnstein and Vinokur (1977) suggest that each group member samples from a set of preexisting arguments and that the positive and negative balance of these arguments determines the member's relative position with respect to a preferred solution. Thus, members often hold positions determined by the balance of known arguments prior to group discussion, and the ensuing discussion will reflect the preponderance of support for these initial preferences (see Meyers & Brashers, Chapter 11, this volume). The result is that group discussion enhances prediscussion tendencies to favor a certain alternative. This

tendency influences not only what knowledge is shared but also how that information is weighted within group discussion. Groups that begin a discussion with preferences for certain alternatives weight information that supports members' initial preferences more heavily and are more likely to challenge information that supports another alternative.

The tendency for groups to focus on preference-consistent information is especially problematic if there is consensus among members regarding their prediscussion preferences. If members' prediscussion preferences are in conflict, Nemeth (1986) contends that the persistent presentation of minority views enhances the information processing of a group, even if it does not change the majority's prevailing choice (see Meyers & Brashers, Chapter 11, this volume, regarding majority/minority influence in groups). Nemeth suggests that groups exposed to minority views "are stimulated to attend to more aspects of the situation, they think in more divergent ways, and they are more likely to detect novel solutions or come to new decisions" (p. 25). Thus, a dissenting minority may influence CIP in a group, even if it is wrong or incapable of convincing the group to adopt its choice, by inducing more vigilant thought processes and reexamination of accepted premises.

Task Environment

A third category of noncommunicative variables affecting CIP consists of factors that affect the task environment. Several elements of the group decision-making context have been identified: (a) temporal constraints, (b) characteristics of the given task, and (c) the medium of communication used in the performance of the task.

Temporal Constraints

The amount of time a group has to complete an intellectual task has an effect on information processing. Restricted time may lead members to examine information less thoroughly and consider fewer decision alternatives. Karau and Kelly (1992) found that time limits were related inversely to th amount of focus on task completion in grou discussion. They suggested that under cond tions of time scarcity, groups are more like to "attend more readily to a restricted ran of features of the environment that seem m central to moving the task forward to t resolution" (p. 545). That is, discussion be focused narrowly on only what is nee to accomplish the given task, rather than how to perform optimally. In contrast, w a group is given too much time, member more likely to focus on nontask activity, as personal concerns and other issues unre-lated to the task, and this leads to less focus on task completion. Under optimal time condi-tions, a group has time to examine a relatively broad range of task-relevant features of the environment but not much time to spend on nontask activities; therefore, groups operating under optimal time conditions are more likely to focus on task performance or arriving at the highest quality outcome possible.

Temporal influence affects CIP because groups working under the condition of time scarcity cannot adequately search for mem-bers' knowledge and evaluate all the informa-tion made available during discussion. These groups are likely to consider a limited range of information that appears to their members to be the most relevant to completing the task; consequently, initial preferences have a great influence on group discussion. In contrast, groups given too much time run the risk of sharing information that is irrelevant to the task at hand and failing to focus on the infor-mation-processing needs of the group relevant to the task.

Characteristics of the Task

The type of task a group confronts is a second element of the task environment that appears to affect how a group processes infor-mation. Research in this area has focused on contrasting two types of influence that group members exert during discussion: normative and informational influence (Deutsch & Ger-

244 | Group Communication

commits plagiarism, are
tasks in that they ultimatel
prevailing values of a gr
Kaplan and Miller
the type of task gr
mode of influe
members. Spe
tive tasks w
informati
tional d
corr
si

from one anouncr
perceptions of reality. In this case, members' judgments are attributable to the information shared during group discussion. For example, a juror might share information about the cost of incarcerating a convicted murderer for life or the probability of the murderer's future release from prison, and this information may influence other jurors' judgments.

One factor that appears to determine the strength of informational influence in affect-ing a group's final choice is the type of task that members address. There are two primary types of tasks involving making choices that are located at the opposite ends of a contin-uum (Laughlin, 1980; Laughlin & Ellis, 1986; McGrath, 1984). *Intellective tasks* are those that presume there is an identifiable, correct answer, such as a math problem. The goal of groups when given an intellective task is to discover the "correct" answer (McGrath, 1984). *Decision-making tasks* are those that have no demonstrably correct answer; rather, they involve value judgments, and groups seek to decide what is "proper," "moral," or "effective" within given circumstances (Mc-Grath, 1984). In this type of task, the goal of groups is not to discover the "right" answer, but to find the answer that is supported by group consensus, the majority of its members, or whatever operating procedure guides the group decision-making process. For example, tasks involving questions of policy, such as the appropriate punishment for a student who

ecision-making
y are based on the
up's members.
(1987) predicted that
ups are given affects the
ce that operates on group
fically, discussions of intellec-
re predicted to be dominated by
nal influence because informa-
ata provide a means of establishing the
ctness of a solution. In contrast, discus-
ns of decision-making tasks were thought
to be dominated by normative influence, because appeals to social norms provide a means
to achieve consensus. The findings of Kaplan
and Miller's research, as well as other studies,
support these predictions by demonstrating
that groups are, in fact, likely to rely more
heavily on the use of information and evidence as arguments when they are solving
intellective tasks and to rely more heavily on
social norms when solving decision-making
tasks (e.g., Kaplan, 1989; Kaplan & Miller,
1987; Stasser & Stewart, 1992).

Billings and Scherer (1988) examined the
impact of a related aspect of the task, the
response modes required. Specifically, they
contrasted the response modes of judgment
versus choice. A *judgment response* requires
an explicit evaluation to be given of each
alternative under consideration. For example,
an admissions committee may be asked to rank
order graduate school applicants and provide
an explanation of why each applicant is acceptable or unacceptable. On the other hand,
a *choice response* requires that only one alternative be selected and the others rejected, such
as in the selection of a single graduate student
to be awarded a fellowship. In a review of
individual decision making, Billings and Scherer
argue that how a person is asked to respond
to a task is important to consider because it
may have an impact on his or her decision-
making processes. They found that requiring
an explicit judgment of each alternative increased the amount of information search and
led to the use of a more constant amount of
information and multidimensional processing
of that information as contrasts and compari-

sons between choices were made. They concluded that the response modes of choice
versus judgment have a strong and consistent
effect on how information is used in making
a decision.

Gigone and Hastie (1997) obtained similar
results in their examination of the impact of
judgment and choice response modes in group
decision making. They observed that judgment groups performed more thorough information searches and discussed more of the
available information than did choice groups.
Hollingshead (1996b) also demonstrated the
impact of response modes on CIP with groups
asked to rank order the alternatives versus
those that were asked only to make a single
choice.

Communication Medium

The third characteristic of the task environment that has been investigated is the communication medium through which CIP is
accomplished. The line of research related to
this factor has examined how new information technologies, such as electronic mail,
computer conferencing, and group decision
support systems (see Scott, Chapter 16, this
volume), in comparison to face-to-face discussion, may reduce the impact of status differences in decision-making groups. The assumption is that communication technologies have
the potential to lower awareness of social
differences and, hence, their impact on group
interaction.

Dubrovsky, Kiesler, and Sethna (1991) contrasted electronic mail and face-to-face discussion groups. They found that when groups
used e-mail, status inequalities were significantly reduced and members' participation
and influence were more nearly equal. The
explanation for these differences is that computer-mediated communication limits many
of the social context cues available in face-to-
face discussion (Sproull & Kiesler, 1986). This
allows people of low status to have less fear of
rejection and people of high status to have less
concern about maintaining their positions,

both of which facilitate more equal participation among group members.

Research by Weisband, Schneider, and Connolly (1995), however, calls into question the effectiveness of computer-mediated communication to alleviate the impact of status differences. In a series of studies, they reported that in both face-to-face and computer-mediated, anonymous conditions, high-status group members (MBA students) participated more and achieved disproportionate influence when contrasted with low-status members (undergraduate students). They concluded that, even in a context in which social cues were limited, when high-status group members were aware that a low-status person was in their group, they made assumptions about the identity of that person. This "labeling" was enough to influence the high-status members' behavior. Silver, Cohen, and Crutchfield (1994) also found that in groups interacting in a computer-mediated environment, high-status members dominated discussion by using significantly more words and initiating more ideas.

A second line of research examining the impact of computer-mediated versus face-to-face communication deals with the negative effects of communication technologies on CIP. Hollingshead (1996a) discerned that the use of a computer network did not diffuse the effects of status on the quality of group decisions. More important, computer-mediated communication actually "suppressed information exchange and reduced the influence of all group members, regardless of status" (p. 213). Hollingshead suggests that information suppression occurred because members suppressed the information and influence of members who were "information rich," rather than increasing the participation and involvement of low-status members in the discussion of information.

In a similar study, Hollingshead (1996b) examined a procedural manipulation designed to improve CIP, which involved asking groups to rank order the alternatives. Groups following this procedure were more likely to consider all the alternatives and exchange in-formation on less popular alternatives than were groups instructed to choose the best alternative, but this benefit was obtained only in face-to-face discussion. As in Hollingshead's previous study, computer-mediated groups suppressed information exchange and the decision procedure had no effect.

The findings on the impact of computer-mediated communication on status clearly are inconsistent. It is possible that under certain conditions, status differential may be alleviated by communication technologies, but the ability to generalize that effect is limited. Hollingshead, McGrath, and O'Connor (1993) examined several variables that may account for the inconsistencies in this literature. They acquired strong evidence concerning the mediating effects of experience with the technology and change in the group's membership, technology, or tasks, and only partial support for the impact of the type of task.

DIRECTIONS FOR FUTURE RESEARCH

The model presented above and literature reviewed provide the basis for many fruitful avenues for research on understanding group performance as related to episodes of CIP. First and foremost, it is important to focus on the connections among the developmental stages of the CIP Distillation Model. Most research to date concentrates on noncommunicative inputs and ties them to group outputs by inferring what happened during the communication process (thereby moving from Stage 2 to Stage 4). In other words, research has focused on how members' *knowledge* affects groups' choices while failing to examine how this knowledge is presented as *information* and weighted through group discussion. Even when information is examined, group discussion often has been studied in a simplistic manner, by coding for the mention of informational items. Research of this type cannot account for the transformation of knowledge that occurs as it becomes the final collective information base. The impact of individual and group knowledge on what happens in group discussion must be ascertained more clearly and completely. Similarly, although researchers have examined the relationship between group communication processes and outputs, many have failed to account for the inputs that potentially moderate group discussion (thus, focusing only on Stages 3 and 4). Future research should integrate inputs, communication processes, and outputs by focusing on how characteristics of the knowledge/information, group, and task environment affect how information is presented and, in turn, how this relates to the choices groups make. In other words, all four stages of the development of a final collective information base must be explored. For example, one might examine how unique knowledge possessed by a group member is presented as information to ascertain under what group and task conditions it is or is not utilized. Alternatively, one might examine how low-status group members use communication effectively to overcome biases associated with the processing of their input. To accomplish research of this type, coding schemes that can account for the form, as well as the content, of information must be developed and utilized. Put simply, we must study not only what knowledge is pooled, but also how that knowledge was presented and evaluated as information during group discussion. In this way, we can begin to ascertain how varying interpretations of information are negotiated and shaped through group discussion in the light of noncommunicative factors that have been found to influence the effectiveness of groups.

Future research should also examine the impact of CIP on a variety of group outcomes. The majority of research has focused on the correctness of a decision regarding intellective tasks or the quality of group decision making as determined by judgments of experts. Other outcomes, however, also are affected by CIP and may be of interest, such as group members' perceptions of the acceptability of decisions and members' satisfaction with the decision-making process, confidence that they have made the correct/best choice, and commitment to that choice. Gouran (1988) suggests that one measure of decision effectiveness that is generalizable across a variety of situations and tasks is the concept of "appropriateness." An *appropriate decision* is one that "represents the choice a group is obliged to make in light of its purpose, the requirements of the task, and what the analysis of information bearing on the available alternatives establishes as reasons for endorsing and rejecting each" (p. 257). The strength of this measure of a group's effectiveness is that it inextricably ties group products to group processes. The use of decision appropriateness may serve to further the study of CIP, in that for a decision to be deemed appropriate, one must account for how a group searches for and processes information in the light of the task requirements. Appropriateness, therefore, may be useful in integrating findings across a variety of group contexts by providing a common frame of reference from which conclusions can be drawn.

A related area for future research is the examination of groups that have made appropriate decisions to uncover what communication processes may facilitate CIP in the light of the impact of noncommunicative factors. In studies of noncommunicative factors that bias CIP, some groups do not fall prey to such biases. If noncommunicative variables that limit CIP are held constant, and some groups make appropriate decisions, this suggests that communication, at times, may have a counteractive influence and help groups to overcome the obstacles present in collective decision making. It is important to examine such decision-making groups to determine in what ways their members used communication and whether the findings can be generalized to inform possible intervention methods to improve group performance.

Moving from the laboratory into the field also is important for developing a more complete understanding of CIP. To date, almost all the research conducted have been experimental laboratory studies. Examining groups in a laboratory setting is useful, in that it allows researchers to control features of the knowledge/information, group, and task context to determine the effects of specific variables; however, members of natural, bona fide groups—those that have permeable boundaries, shifting borders, and are interdependent with their context (see Putnam & Stohl, 1990, 1994, 1996; in this volume, see Chapters 1 [Gouran] and 2 [Poole])—typically do not have the type of clearly defined, limited individual knowledge bases used in experimental designs, so the external validity of much of the laboratory research examining the impact of the characteristics of knowledge/information needs to be established. It is important to determine how groups process the knowledge members bring to the task—their beliefs, values, attitudes, and personal experiences, in addition to factual information. Examining bona fide groups necessitates operationalizing information in the broader sense advocated in this chapter, by incorporating members' assumptions, opinions, values, and so forth as forms of knowledge and potential information that are an inherent part of CIP, but that have been overlooked in most of the past research. Although this complicates the measurement of information and, hence, research designs, it is necessary for understanding more fully how groups process information in their natural settings.

The continuing examination of interventions that may improve information processing in bona fide groups is another area of valuable research (regarding group facilitation and intervention, in this volume, see Chapters 14 [Schultz], 15 [Sunwolf & Seibold], and 16 [Scott]). Much research has focused on improving collective information search through procedural manipulations, such as expert role assignment (Stasser, Stewart, & Wittenbaum, 1995; Stewart & Stasser, 1995), group decision support systems (Dennis, 1996), knowledge load and awareness of unique knowledge (Schittekatte, 1996), rank ordering of alternatives (Hollingshead, 1996b), and framing of the task (Stasser & Stewart, 1992). Although these studies provide potential methods to facilitate information exchange, little research

has been conducted to investigate potential remedies for errors in group memory and weighting of information. Because these subprocesses of CIP have also been shown to influence the final collective information bases of groups, it is important to determine what procedural manipulations or training will help groups to counteract or avoid the biases introduced in these processes.

Finally, it is important to extend CIP research beyond the examination of decision-making groups. Information processing is central to all types of groups, and many of these groups do not have the end goal of solving problems or making decisions. Members of family groups, social support groups, consciousness-raising groups, and friendship groups, to name just a few, all process information when they meet, yet little is known about the dynamics of CIP in these groups. For example, one could investigate the subprocesses of storage and retrieval in family groups to determine how collective memories are created and recalled and, in turn, the impact of these subprocesses on familial relationships (see Socha, Chapter 17, this volume, on communication in family groups). Alternatively, one might examine factors that suppress or facilitate information search in social support groups as the starting point to designing interventions that encourage the free and open exchange of members' knowledge, an important element of self-help treatment (see Cline, Chapter 19, this volume, on communication in social support/self-help groups).

CONCLUSION

Processing information is an overarching exigency of all groups. Quite simply, group members' knowledge must be shared to inform and influence other members. Whatever the desired outcome, be it an effective decision or stronger member relationships, successful group performance is determined, in large part, by members' ability to collectively process available knowledge and information. To understand group dynamics more fully, it is, therefore, imperative to continue to explore how communication facilitates or hinders the sharing of members' knowledge, the evaluation and weighting of shared information, and, finally, how this information ultimately is used by groups as they move toward their varied goals.

NOTE

1. It should be noted that the definition of information employed in this chapter is not used commonly in the literature reviewed on collective information processing. Typically, information is operationalized as items of evidence given to group members, and the distinction between knowledge as a cognitive form and information as a communicative form is not made. Rather, information is treated as analogous to knowledge. Drawing a distinction between knowledge group members possess and information shared with the group is useful, however, in delineating the stages of collective information processing, as it highlights the differences between what is initially known by members and how this may be transformed and shaped by group communication processes as it becomes the final collective information base from which a group decision is drawn. Therefore, for the purposes of this chapter, the differentiation between knowledge and information is utilized, even when the original work did not make such a distinction.

REFERENCES

Aronsson, K., & Nilholm, C. (1990). On memory and the collaborative construction and deconstruction of custody case arguments. *Human Communication Research, 17*, 289-314.

Berger, J., Cohen, B. P., & Zelditch, M. (1973). Status characteristics and social interaction. In R. J. Ofshe (Ed.), *Interpersonal behavior in small groups* (pp. 194-216). Englewood Cliffs, NJ: Prentice Hall.

Berger, J., Conner, T. L., & Fisek, M. H. (1974). *Expectation states theory: A theoretical research program.* Cambridge, MA: Winthrop.

Berger, J., Fisek, M. H., Norman, R. Z., & Wagner, D. G. (1985). The formation of reward expectation in status situations. In J. Berger & M. Zelditch (Eds.), *Status, rewards, and influence* (pp. 215-261). San Francisco: Jossey-Bass.

Berger, J., & Zelditch, M. (1977). Status characteristics and social interaction: The status organizing process. In J. Berger, M. H. Fisek, R. Z. Norman, & M. Zelditch (Eds.), *Status characteristics and social interaction: An expectation-states approach* (pp. 3-87). New York: Elsevier.

Billings, R. S., & Scherer, L. L. (1988). The effects of response mode and importance of decision-making strategies: Judgment versus choice. *Organizational Behavior and Human Decision Processes, 41*, 1-19.

Bodenhausen, G. V., & Lichtenstein, M. (1987). Social stereotypes and information-processing strategies: The impact of task complexity. *Journal of Personality and Social Psychology, 52*, 871-880.

Burnstein, E., & Vinokur, A. (1977). Persuasive argumentation and social comparison as determinants of attitude polarization. *Journal of Experimental Social Psychology, 9*, 315-332.

Dennis, A. R. (1996). Information exchange and use in small group decision making: You can lead a group to information, but you can't make it think. *Small Group Research, 27*, 532-550.

Deutsch, M., & Gerard, H. B. (1955). A study of normative and informational social influences upon individual judgment. *Journal of Abnormal and Social Psychology, 51*, 629-636.

Dewey, J. (1910). *How we think.* New York: D. C. Heath.

Dubrovsky, V. J., Kiesler, S., & Sethna, B. N. (1991). The equalization phenomenon: Status effects in computer-mediated and face-to-face decision making groups. *Human-Computer Interaction, 6*, 119-146.

Einhorn, H., & Hogarth, R. (1981). Behavioral decision theory: Processes of judgment and choice. *Annual Review of Psychology, 32*, 53-88.

Fishbein, M., & Ajzen, I. (1975). *Belief, attitude, intention and behavior: An introduction to theory and research.* Reading, MA: Addison-Wesley.

Gigone, D., & Hastie, R. (1993). The common knowledge effect: Information sharing and group judgment. *Journal of Personality and Social Psychology, 65*, 959-974.

Gigone, D., & Hastie, R. (1997). The impact of information on small group choice. *Journal of Personality and Social Psychology, 72*, 132-140.

Gouran, D. S. (1988). Group decision making: An approach to integrative research. In C. H. Tardy (Ed.), *A handbook for the study of human communication: Methods and instruments for observing, measuring, and assessing communication processes* (pp. 247-267). Norwood, NJ: Ablex.

Gouran, D. S., & Hirokawa, R. Y. (1983). The role of communication in decision-making groups: A functional perspective. In M. S. Mander (Ed.), *Communication in transition: Issues and debate in current research* (pp. 168-185). New York: Praeger.

Gruenfeld, D. H., Mannix, E. A., Williams, K. Y., & Neale, M. A. (1996). Group composition and decision making: How member familiarity and information distribution affect process and performance. *Organizational Behavior and Human Decision Processes, 67*, 1-15.

Hackman, J. R., & Kaplan, R. E. (1974). Interventions into group process: An approach to improving the effectiveness of groups. *Decision Sciences, 5*, 459-480.

Hartwick, J., Sheppard, B. H., & Davis, J. H. (1982). Group remembering: Research and implications. In R. A. Guzzo (Ed.), *Improving group decision making in organizations: Approaches from theory and practice* (pp. 41-72). San Diego, CA: Academic Press.

Hastie, R., & Park, B. (1986). The relationship between memory and judgment depends on whether the judgment task is memory-based or on-line. *Psychological Review, 93,* 258-268.

Hastie, R., Penrod, S. D., & Pennington, N. (1983). *Inside the jury.* Cambridge, MA: Harvard University Press.

Hinsz, V. B. (1990). Cognitive and consensus processes in group recognition memory performance. *Journal of Personality and Social Psychology, 59,* 705-718.

Hinsz, V. B., & Davis, J. H. (1984). Persuasive arguments theory, group polarization, and choice shifts. *Personality and Social Psychology Bulletin, 10,* 260-268.

Hinsz, V. B., Tindale, R. S., & Vollrath, D. A. (1997). The emerging conceptualization of groups as information processors. *Psychological Bulletin, 121,* 43-64.

Hinsz, V. B., Vollrath, D. A., Nagao, D. H., & Davis, J. H. (1988). Comparing the structure of individual and small group perceptions. *International Journal of Small Group Research, 4,* 159-168.

Hirokawa, R. Y. (1987). Why informed groups make faulty decisions: An investigation of possible interaction-based explanations. *Small Group Behavior, 18,* 3-29.

Hirokawa, R. Y., & Pace, R. (1983). A descriptive investigation of the possible communication-based reasons for effective and ineffective group decision making. *Communication Monographs, 50,* 363-379.

Hirokawa, R. Y., & Scheerhorn, D. R. (1986). Communication in faulty group decision-making. In R. Y. Hirokawa & M. S. Poole (Eds.), *Communication and group decision-making* (pp. 63-80). Beverly Hills, CA: Sage.

Hollingshead, A. B. (1996a). Information suppression and status persistence in group decision making: The effects of communication media. *Human Communication Research, 23,* 193-219.

Hollingshead, A. B. (1996b). The rank-order effect in group decision making. *Organizational Behavior and Human Decision Processes, 68,* 181-193.

Hollingshead, A. B., McGrath, J. E., & O'Connor, K. M. (1993). Group task performance and communication technology: A longitudinal study of computer-mediated versus face-to-face work groups. *Small Group Research, 24,* 307-333.

Janis, I. L. (1989). *Crucial decisions: Leadership in policymaking and crisis management.* New York: Free Press.

Janis, I. L., & Mann, L. (1977). *Decision making: A psychological analysis of conflict, choice, and commitment.* New York: Free Press.

Kaplan, M. F. (1977). Discussion polarization effects in a modified jury decision paradigm: Informational influences. *Sociometry, 40,* 262-271.

Kaplan, M. F. (1989). Task, situational, and personal determinants of influence processes in group decision making. In E. J. Lawler (Ed.), *Advances in group processes* (Vol. 6, pp. 87-105). Greenwich, CT: JAI.

Kaplan, M. F., & Miller, C. E. (1987). Group decision making and normative versus informational influence: Effects of type of issue and assigned decision rule. *Journal of Personality and Social Psychology, 53,* 306-313.

Karau, S. J., & Kelly, J. R. (1992). The effects of time scarcity and time abundance on group performance quality and interaction process. *Journal of Experimental Social Psychology, 28,* 542-571.

Kelley, H. H., & Thibaut, J. W. (1969). Group problem-solving. In G. Lindzey & E. Aronson (Eds.), *The handbook of social psychology: Vol. 4. Group psychology and phenomena of interaction* (2nd ed., pp. 1-101). Cambridge, MA: Addison-Wesley.

Larson, J. R., & Christensen, C. (1993). Groups as problem-solving units: Toward a new meaning of social cognition. *British Journal of Social Psychology, 32,* 5-30.

Larson, J. R., Christensen, C., Abbott, A. S., & Franz, T. M. (1996). Diagnosing groups: Charting the flow of information in medical decision-making teams. *Journal of Personality and Social Psychology, 71,* 315-330.

Laughlin, P. R. (1980). Social combination processes of cooperative problem-solving groups on verbal intellective tasks. In M. Fishbein (Ed.), *Progress in social psychology* (Vol. 1, pp. 127-155). Hillsdale, NJ: Lawrence Erlbaum.

Laughlin, P. R., & Ellis, A. L. (1986). Demonstrability and social combination processes on mathematical intellective tasks. *Journal of Experimental Psychology, 22,* 177-189.

Laughlin, P. R., VanderStoep, S. W., & Hollingshead, A. B. (1991). Collective versus individual induction: Recognition of truth, rejection of error, and collective information processing. *Journal of Personality and Social Psychology, 61,* 50-67.

Lee, M. (1993). Gender, group composition, and peer interaction in computer-based cooperative learning. *Journal of Educational Computing Research, 9,* 549-577.

Lorge, I., & Solomon, H. (1955). Two models of group behavior in the solutions of Eureka-type problems. *Psychometrika, 29,* 139-148.

McGrath, J. E. (1984). *Groups: Interaction and performance.* Englewood Cliffs, NJ: Prentice Hall.

Meeker, B. F., & Weitzel-O'Neill, P. A. (1977). Sex roles and interpersonal behavior in task-oriented groups. *American Sociological Review, 42,* 91-105.

Nemeth, C. J. (1986). Differential contributions of majority and minority influence. *Psychological Review, 93,* 23-32.

Pennington, N., & Hastie, R. (1986). Evidence evaluation in complex decision making. *Journal of Personality and Social Psychology, 51,* 242-258.

Pennington, N., & Hastie, R. (1988). Explanation-based decision making: Effects of memory structure on judgment. *Journal of Experimental Psychology, 14,* 521-533.

Propp, K. M. (1995). An experimental examination of biological sex as a status cue in decision-making groups and its influence on information utilization. *Small Group Research, 26,* 451-474.

Propp, K. M. (1997). Information utilization in small group decision making: A study of the evaluative interaction model. *Small Group Research, 28,* 424-453.

Propp, K. M., & Julian, K. M. (1994). Enhancing accurate information processing: An investigation of the role of verbal information probes in decision making. *Communication Reports, 7,* 145-152.

Pugh, M. D., & Wahrman, R. (1983). Neutralizing sexism in mixed-sex groups: Do women have to be better than men? *American Journal of Sociology, 88,* 746-762.

Putnam, L. L., & Stohl, C. (1990). Bona fide groups: A reconceptualization of groups in context. *Communication Studies, 41,* 248-265.

Putnam, L. L., & Stohl, C. (1994). Group communication in context: Implications for the study of bona fide groups. In L. R. Frey (Ed.), *Group communication in context: Studies of natural groups* (pp. 284-292). Hillsdale, NJ: Lawrence Erlbaum.

Putnam, L. L., & Stohl, C. (1996). Bona fide groups: An alternative perspective for communication and small group decision making. In R. Y. Hirokawa & M. S. Poole (Eds.), *Communication and group decision making* (2nd ed., pp. 147-178). Thousand Oaks, CA: Sage.

Ridgeway, C. L., & Berger, J. (1986). Expectations, legitimation, and dominance behavior in task groups. *American Sociological Review, 51,* 603-617.

Riecken, H. W. (1958). The effects of talkativeness on ability to influence group solutions to problems. *Sociometry, 21,* 309-321.

Ritchie, L. D. (1991). *Communication concepts 2: Information.* Newbury Park, CA: Sage.

Schittekatte, M. (1996). Facilitating information exchange in small decision-making groups. *European Journal of Social Psychology, 26,* 537-556.

Schittekatte, M., & Van Hiel, A. (1996). Effects of partially shared information and awareness of unshared information on information sampling. *Small Group Research, 27,* 431-449.

Schul, U., & Burnstein, E. (1985). When discounting fails: Conditions under which individuals use discredited information in making a judgment. *Journal of Personality and Social Psychology, 49,* 894-903.

Shaw, M. E., & Penrod, W. T. (1962). Does more information available to a group always improve group performance? *Sociometry, 25,* 377-390.

Silver, S. D., Cohen, B. P., & Crutchfield, J. H. (1994). Status differentiation and information exchange in face-to-face and computer-mediated idea generation. *Social Psychology Quarterly, 57,* 108-123.

Smith-Lovin, L., Skvoretz, J. V., & Hudson, C. G. (1986). Status and participation in six-person groups: A test of Skvoretz's comparative status model. *Social Forces, 64,* 992-1005.

Sproull, L., & Kiesler, S. (1986). Reducing social context cues: Electronic mail in organizational communication. *Management Science, 32,* 427-459.

Stasser, G. (1988). Computer simulation as a research tool: The DISCUSS model of group decision making. *Journal of Experimental Social Psychology, 24,* 393-422.

Stasser, G. (1992a). Information salience and the discovery of hidden profiles by decision making groups: A "thought experiment." *Organizational Behavior and Human Decision Processes, 52,* 156-181.

Stasser, G. (1992b). Pooling of unshared information during group discussion. In S. Worchel, W. Wood, & J. A. Simpson (Eds.), *Group process and productivity* (pp. 48-57). Newbury Park, CA: Sage.

Stasser, G., & Stewart, D. D. (1992). Discovery of hidden profiles by decision-making groups: Solving a problem versus making a judgment. *Journal of Personality and Social Psychology, 63,* 426-434.

Stasser, G., Stewart, D. D., & Wittenbaum, G. M. (1995). Expert roles and information exchange during discussion: The importance of knowing who knows what. *Journal of Experimental Social Psychology, 31,* 244-265.

Stasser, G., Taylor, L. A., & Hanna, C. (1989). Information sampling in structured and unstructured discussions of three- and six-person groups. *Journal of Personality and Social Psychology, 57,* 67-78.

Stasser, G., & Titus, W. (1985). Pooling of unshared information in group decision making: Biased information sampling during discussion. *Journal of Personality and Social Psychology, 48,* 1467-1478.

Stasser, G., & Titus, W. (1987). Effects of information load and percentage of shared information on the dissemination of unshared information during group discussion. *Journal of Personality and Social Psychology, 53,* 81-93.

Stewart, D. D., & Stasser, G. (1995). Expert role assignment and information sampling during collective recall and decision making. *Journal of Personality and Social Psychology, 69,* 619-628.

Strodtbeck, F. L., & Mann, R. D. (1956). Sex role differentiation in jury deliberations. *Sociometry, 19,* 3-11.

Thibaut, J. W., & Kelley, H. H. (1959). *The social psychology of groups.* New York: John Wiley.

Vinokur, A., & Burnstein, E. (1974). Effects of partially shared persuasive arguments on group-induced shifts: A group-problem-solving approach. *Journal of Personality and Social Psychology, 29,* 305-315.

Vollrath, D. A., Sheppard, B. H., Hinsz, V. B., & Davis, J. H. (1989). Memory performance by decision-making groups and individuals. *Organizational Behavior and Human Decision Processes, 43,* 289-300.

Weisband, S. P., Schneider, S. K., & Connolly, T. (1995). Computer-mediated communication and social information: Status salience and status differences. *Academy of Management Review, 38,* 1124-1151.

Wittenbaum, G. M. (1998). Information sampling in decision-making groups: The impact of members' task-relevant status. *Small Group Research, 29,* 57-84.

Wittenbaum, G. M., & Stasser, G. (1997, May). *The role of group member status in collective information sampling: Some psychological underpinnings.* Paper presented at the annual meeting of the Midwestern Psychological Association, Chicago.

Wittenbaum, G. M., & Stasser, G. (1998). The reevaluation of information during group discussion. *Group Processes & Intergroup Relations, 1,* 21-34.

10

Nonverbal Aspects of Group Communication

SANDRA M. KETROW
University of Rhode Island

Group communication theory, research, and practice have a long history of investigating the nature and effects of verbal aspects of messages. Examination of nonverbal cues (dynamic interactive behaviors, as well as contextual and environmental data) and their communicative functions in groups has been significantly less extensive, but no less important in illuminating group interactional processes and outcomes.

To understand communication in groups more fully requires further identification and integration of the role of nonverbal cues. In this chapter, I first examine the importance of nonverbal cues to understanding group interaction and then explore parameters for the study of these cues while explaining their types and functions. Second, I review relevant literature on nonverbal cues in the group context. Finally, I consider prospects for future research on nonverbal cues in groups.

SIGNIFICANCE AND OMISSION OF NONVERBAL CUES

Researchers concerned with nonverbal behavior claim that nonverbal aspects assume prominence over verbal elements as people assign meaning to messages (see Burgoon, 1980; Mehrabian, 1981). This appears to be particularly true for interpreting emotional and relational messages. In summarizing the importance of nonverbal aspects of messages on the basis of a review of research during the 1970s, Burgoon (1980) claims:

> The overwhelming conclusion has been that the nonverbal channels carry more information and are believed more than the verbal band, and that visual cues generally carry more weight than vocal ones. Beyond the face and voice—which have been studied most frequently—seating distance, body orientation, trunk lean, and eye contact have similarly been found to lead to more accurate judgments when compared to the verbal message alone. (p. 184)

Burgoon (1994) cites one series of studies which demonstrated that when verbal and nonverbal presentations were rated separately for their relative contribution to meaning, they were perceived as relatively equal in strength, but "when combined the nonverbal cues accounted for as much as 12.5 times as much variance in meaning as did the verbal statements" (p. 235). M. B. Walker and

251

Trimboli (1989) established in an experiment that the nonverbal channel, in contrast to the verbal, has primacy or dominance, particularly in conveying affective messages. These and other studies suggest that the examination of verbal messages without concomitant attention to the nonverbal stream is shortsighted at best and misleading at worst.

Much groundwork for the study of nonverbal aspects of messages in groups already exists in literature about contexts other than groups. Although the study of nonverbal cues in general has gathered steam since the 1970s, as Mabry (1989) noted in a statement that continues to be true 10 years later, "With the exception of proxemics, few elements of nonverbal behavior have been addressed systematically in studies of small group interaction" (p. 190). Major theories of group communication—such as Functional, Symbolic Convergence, and Structuration Theory (in this volume, see Chapters 1 [Gouran] and 2 [Poole])—traditionally have targeted verbal messages, either explicitly or implicitly. The paradigmatic emphasis on verbal messages has also held for pragmatic and pedagogical efforts in the field. Beebe, Barge, and McCormick (1994), for example, in their working measure of the "competent group communicator," provide explicit attention to verbal behavioral competencies in groups but none to nonverbal competencies. A revised measure on which they are working, however, explicitly stipulates careful attention to nonverbal aspects in assessing two areas of relational competencies—contributing to a supportive group climate and conflict management. As Beebe acknowledged, "We wholeheartedly agree that nonverbal communication is the key source in assessing group climate and plays a major role in the conflict management process" (personal communication, September 23, 1998).

This lack of attention to nonverbal behaviors is unfortunate because a substantial body of research examining nonverbal behavior and cues in groups exists, although it is true that there is little *systematic* research in this area. A few reviews of nonverbal communication

research *with a group thrust* recently have appeared (Andersen, 1992; Burgoon, 1992; Hare & Davies, 1994), but these essays mostly report research based on dyads and generalize the findings to the group context. This type of generalization is problematic because limited data exist to establish that findings from dyadic research have ecological validity for the group setting (see Keyton's, Chapter 8, this volume, discussion of this problem with respect to the study of relational communication in groups). The thrust of this chapter, therefore, is to review and assess *group-based* research. I should point out, however, that the extant research reviewed, like most of the research on group communication in general, is based on task rather than social groups.

NONVERBAL CUES AND COMMUNICATIVE FUNCTIONS

R. P. Harrison and Wiemann (1983) state that "for better or for worse, 'nonverbal communication' has become the familiar tag for nonword events of informational value" (p. 273). This general definition guides this review. I also use the terms *communication, cue, behavior,* and *message* somewhat synonymously, although they are distinct in certain respects. One other issue in defining nonverbal communication lies in distinguishing adequately between dynamic nonverbal behavior emitted by a person and more static stimuli or cues, such as proxemic distance among three group members or the width of a table separating them. This chapter lays the groundwork of a definition and taxonomy to guide the analysis of the nonverbal aspects of group interaction.

Nonverbal Codes and Properties

Two related taxonomies are useful for mapping an approach to the study of nonverbal communication in groups: (a) a set of types of nonverbal communicative cues and (b) a set of functions each cue or set of cues may serve. Descriptions of types of nonverbal cues map the territory of interest; these cues are some-

Table 10.1 Selected Descriptive Categories of Nonverbal Cues

Code	Set Description
From Burgoon, Buller, and Woodall (1996)	
Visual	Includes kinesics (bodily movements, including eyes) and physical appearance
Auditory	Includes vocalics (voice characteristics)
Contact	Includes haptics (touching) and proxemics (use of space)
Place	Includes environment (e.g., furnishings, color, and temperature) and artifacts
Time	Includes chronemics (interpersonal use of time)
From R. P. Harrison and Wiemann (1983, pp. 273-274)	
Performance	"Messages of the body, produced by the appearance or movement of the human body"
Artifactual "object"	"Produced by creating, arranging or displaying objects from personal dress to public monuments"
Spatio-temporal	"Messages of time and space"
Mediatory	"Media messages, such as art, music, special effects of visual or sound recording"

times intended to serve particular functions and often interpreted as doing so.

Although specific nonverbal grammars exist, such as Birdwhistell's (1970) detailed analysis of kinesic behavior, much of this chapter follows Burgoon, Buller, and Woodall's (1996) taxonomy of nonverbal cues (see Table 10.1). Their taxonomy is advantageous because it organizes such nonverbal cues into five sets, and it includes both dynamic and static nonverbal cues. Adding R. P. Harrison and Wiemann's (1983) mediatory nonverbal code allows for the inclusion of (or effects of) the use of media in task groups, especially when such groups utilize computerized group decision support systems or assemble via listservs, audio/videoconferencing systems, and the like (see Scott, Chapter 16, this volume, regarding communication technologies and group communication). This combined taxonomy provides a useful way to review the relevant research. For the most part, significant work on nonverbal cues in groups has been conducted in the following areas: (a) ki-

nesics (bodily movements), (b) proxemics (spatial usage) and group ecology (seating positions and furniture arrangements), (c) the conjunction of vocalics (vocal aspects) and chronemics (the use of time), and (d) physical appearance.

One problem in any review of research on nonverbal cues is that people tend to perceive them as a gestalt, rather than as singular cues (see Burgoon et al., 1996). Research on nonverbal communication, however, typically is conducted on singular cues; therefore, I review separately studies related to the four descriptive areas identified above: kinesics, proxemics and group ecology, vocalics and chronemics, and physical appearance.

Communicative Functions of Nonverbal Cues

In addition to understanding various types of nonverbal cues, knowing the functions such cues can serve in groups also is important. Concomitant examination of the functions of

Table 10.2 Functional Taxonomies of Nonverbal Cues

Code Type	Description or Example
From Ekman and Friesen (1969)	
Emblems	Nonverbal signs that replace verbal cues
Illustrators	Nonverbal cues that complement verbal meaning
Affect displays	Nonverbal cues that demonstrate emotions
Regulators	Nonverbal cues used to establish control
Adaptors	Nonverbal cues that display discomfort or show attachment toward another person
From Burgoon, Buller, and Woodall (1996)	
Message production, processing, and comprehension	Displays that aid in creating messages or understanding them, such as gesturing while speaking
Structuring interaction (including some features of the context)	Displays that exhibit control or privacy
Identification of self and others (e.g., of culture and gender), personality, and identity management	Displays or inferences of masculinity/femininity, gregariousness, etc.
Emotional expression and management	Displays of affect, such as approval, anger, or disagreement
Relational communication and management	Displays that aid in attributions of dominance, power, and intimacy
Managing conversations	Displays of turn-taking, topic management, and initiating and terminating interaction
Impression management	Displays of private behaviors, like crying, as well as public behaviors, like smiling
Social influence and facilitation (e.g., attractiveness and dynamism)	Displays, such as substantial eye contact or more facial expressiveness, that create credibility
Mixed messages and deception	Displays that include controlling eye contact, as well as agitated leg movement when lying

nonverbal cues allows for inferences regarding relationships among cues and their influence on various group processes and outcomes. Ekman and Friesen's (1969) classification of functions of kinesic behavior into emblems, illustrators, affect displays, regulators, and adaptors was seminal, but limited, because it only includes kinesics and a few social functions (see Table 10.2). More useful for organizing the literature on nonverbal behavior in groups is Burgoon et al.'s (1996) taxonomy of nine social functions that cut across all the nonverbal cues identified previously (see Table 10.2). The primary functions addressed in that literature thus far are (a) structuring interaction; (b) presenting and managing identity;

(c) communicating relationally, especially about negotiating dominance, power, and leadership; (d) communicating affect; and (e) managing conversations. These categories, of course, are not necessarily mutually distinct.

DESCRIPTIVE AND FUNCTIONAL ANALYSES OF NONVERBAL CUES IN GROUPS

Research on nonverbal communication exhibited during group interaction has targeted a few areas, primarily for the purpose of correlating nonverbal cues with their communicative functions. Much of this research has been designed to reveal how nonverbal behavior relates to social influence and similar relational functions (e.g., dominance or power). Most research has centered on the use of visual codes, including physical appearance characteristics (such as sex), and some on kinesics. There is also some literature on contact codes—specifically, proxemics, and combined auditory and chronemic codes—as well as group members' talkativeness or participation rates. Some studies have investigated single cues; others have examined multiple cues and codes. The following section, organized primarily by descriptive or structural nonverbal codes, reviews the central directions of such research, with an eye toward the social functions nonverbal cues serve.

Visual Codes and Group Communication

Kinesic Behavior in Groups

Four cue sets in the visual code of kinesics, or bodily movement, emerge as important to group research: gestures, posture, facial expressions, and eye behavior (some researchers categorize eye behavior separately, as *oculesics*). A fifth set of combined kinesic cues also has proven worth pursuing. Generally, these kinesic behaviors have been related to leader characteristics, leadership emergence, or member dominance in groups (see Pavitt, Chapter 12, this volume, regarding nonverbal behavior and group leadership). Other areas of interest include the effects of kinesic behavior on members' affective states or attitudes, as well as arousal.

Gestures. Gestures have been shown to be related to a number of group-relevant outcomes, especially perceptions of leadership. For example, research shows that "movement of extremities... [,] forward body leans, more emblem and illustrator gestures which are large and sweeping in nature, relaxed posture, and fewer adaptors" (Ketrow, 1992a, p. 7) are associated with leadership emergence or displays of leadership in groups (cf. Baird, 1977; Burgoon et al., 1996; Ellyson & Dovidio,

1985; Remland, 1984). Baird (1977), in a study of leadership emergence in groups, for instance, classified nonverbal behavior into four categories:

> dynamism, or the extent to which a participant moved his [or her] hands and arms; alertness, or the general activity of one's face and head during conversation; involvement, or the degree to which one's posture indicated an active interest in the discussion; and participation, or the frequency of a discussant's mouth movement, indicating verbal participation. (p. 355)

Independent raters, blind to leadership, recorded the occurrence of group members' nonverbal behaviors, and separate judges categorized them. Group members voted for the most influential member, and the person with the most votes was deemed the leader by the researcher. Baird found that only gesticulations of the shoulder and arms were significant predictors of who emerged as a group leader.

Curran and Loganbill (1983), in an experimental study, manipulated low and high levels of a set of nonverbal behaviors that included body lean, body stance, eye contact, and smiling, and measured their association with members' perceptions of the attractiveness of their appointed group leader. Members of 2- to 5-person groups, told to imagine themselves as meeting for the first time, watched together a videotape of a group leader presenting to them a description of the group, its activities, and its goals, and then rated the leader on a measure of attractiveness. Leaders with low levels of nonverbal displays did not maintain an open body stance, had little forward body lean, did not smile, and maintained eye contact with others only 30%-34% of the time. In contrast, leaders who exhibited high levels of nonverbal displays maintained an open stance 90%-98% of the time, engaged in forward body lean, established eye contact behavior, and averaged 3.5-4.5 smiles per group session.

The results ran counter to expectations, in that no differential effects were found between high and low levels of nonverbal behavioral displays with respect to participants' ratings of their group leader's attractiveness. Curran and Loganbill offered two possible explanations for the lack of significant findings for nonverbal behavior: (a) In initial stages of group development, members are highly anxious and inhibited in information intake and, therefore, pay limited attention to nonverbal behavior; and (b) nonverbal behaviors are more powerful if group members interact together in physical proximity rather than simply viewing a videotape.

The findings from Curran and Loganbill's (1983) research are consistent with Stein's (1975) earlier research, in which the value of the relative contribution of verbal and nonverbal communication varied with the type of group leadership hierarchy identified. Specifically, Stein reported that (a) "both verbal and nonverbal information contained cues of the coordination, harmony, and liking hierarchies" of their target groups; (b) nonverbal communication was less relevant to coordination than verbal communication; (c) "nonverbal cues seemed more important in perceiving liking than verbal cues"; and (d) "combined verbal and nonverbal information was important to perceiving harmony" (p. 131). In essence, these results supported his hypothesis that "both verbal and nonverbal behaviors in a group provide cues of the group members' leadership statuses independent of members' relative participation rates" (p. 131). The utility of Stein's work, however, is constrained by his failure when reporting the study to describe fully or operationalize nonverbal communication, and he seemed to assume that using video-only (no sound), full video-and-audio, filtered-speech, and text-only conditions would block adequately the verbal and nonverbal behaviors studied.

French and Stright (1991) extended Stein's work to leadership emergence in children's small groups. They asked naive raters who viewed videotapes of children's group interaction to rank each of the four members for leadership, and also had the children rank themselves. Observers' rankings of leadership were associated with amount of participation, but this did not match the leadership rankings made by the children, which were associated with "task-facilitative" behaviors. French and Stright explain this difference somewhat by speculating that the children ostensibly were operating at the second level of the developmental sequence of understanding leadership, in which "children highlight the ability of leaders to coordinate the group activity, mediate the demands of group members, encourage others, and promote positive relations" (p. 196), versus the first level, where leadership is viewed as authoritarian. Any nonverbal behaviors perceived as related to such leadership displays, therefore, are embedded in a general understanding of leadership.

Other studies have examined the relationship between kinesics and individual members' dominance or status in groups. Hold-Cavell and Borsutzky (1986), for instance, reported a positive relationship between use of gestures and status attributions in an investigation of preschool children playing in a group. They examined how gestures were associated with "attention rank," or what status each child held in the overall hierarchical structure within the group, as measured by how much attention a child demanded and received at different periods of time, by using either "gross body [sic] movements" or gestures and objects to seek attention. The researchers discovered significant main effects for "ostentatious body [sic] movements," as well as for "seeking attention with gestures," "seeking attention with objects," and engaging in both verbal and nonverbal (primarily via gestures) threats (pp. 48-50, 53). High-attention-ranking children made these movements more often than low-ranking children. It would be interesting to extend this line of work to see how adult group members gain attention via the use of gestures.

Facial expressions. Some research has investigated the use of kinesic cues to signal emotional expression, or affect, in groups. These cues primarily include facial expression and posture, but some studies have focused on gestures, as well as other nonverbal cues like touch. For example, the seminal construct of *immediacy,* defined as "the perceptual availability of persons to one another" (Mehrabian & Diamond, 1971, p. 282), is expressed, in part, via certain nonverbal cues, including smiling, forward leans, head nods, eye contact, and touching (Mehrabian, 1969, 1981; see also Andersen, 1985; Andersen & Andersen, 1984). Perceptual availability is directly related to how many of these nonverbal cues are possible to perceive. Proximity, or physical distance, influences the degree to which people can discern nonverbal cues. For example, certain features or movements of a person's face are not clearly visible beyond a certain distance. Hence, as Mehrabian (1981) concludes, "Closeness between a person and an object involves greater perceptual availability of that object to the person" (p. 14).

Nonverbal immediacy has been studied in the group context, although often researchers do not use that term. For example, Christensen (1995) linked teacher nonverbal immediacy behaviors to increased student participation in classroom situations. In a study concerning functional kinesic cues—facial expressions and emotional displays—Schuler and Peltzer (1978) reported that dyadic partners' decision making was more likely to be swayed by "friendly" nonverbal displays than by "unfriendly" nonverbal behavior. While a naive discussion participant debated the assigned issue with a confederate who acted in a friendly or unfriendly manner, in half the discussions, a third person was present who served as an observer for the group. Schuler and Peltzer operationalized nonverbal friendly behavioral cues as "frequent eye contact, friendly countenance (e.g., smiling if suitable), bodily orientation towards the partner sitting at the corner seat, and emotionally warm voice" and unfriendly nonverbal cues as "avoidance of eye contact, neutral or hostile countenance, bodily orientation rather away from partner or a reserved poise, and indifferent or aggressive voice" (pp. 117-118).

Exploring observers' evaluations of videotaped nonverbal affective reactions by group members to leaders during scripted discussion, Brown and Geis (1984) reported that nonverbal affective cues can reinforce members' perceptions of approval or disapproval. In their study, group members displayed nonverbal expressions of either approval or disapproval. Disapproval, for instance, was manipulated by the members showing

> fleeting facial expressions of doubt, sometimes shared in a glance with a partner. These cues were extremely subtle: a slight hardening of muscles around the mouth, an incipient knitting or raising of brows, a slight movement of the head or glance in the direction away from the leader and downward. (pp. 815-816)

One result was that leaders with legitimate authority (defined as support expressed by the group's supervisor) or with nonverbal peer approval were evaluated more favorably than leaders who had no legitimation or nonverbal peer approval. Men also received higher approval as leaders than equally competent women. The sex-evaluation bias was reversed, however, when the group supervisor personally backed the female leader and group members approved of the female leader. In short, affective support expressed nonverbally by group members (and with authority legitimation) increased a female leader's perceived competence as much as a male's.

Butler and Geis (1990) continued this program of research and discovered that although they offered the same suggestions and arguments, female group leaders elicited more negative nonverbal affective responses and fewer positive responses from both male and female subordinates than did male leaders. Butler and Geis believe that this differential effect constitutes evidence of the "concrete social mechanism" (p. 57) of stereotypic gender schemata.

Regarding other kinds of affective nonverbal displays, Firestien (1990; Firestien & McCowan, 1988) evaluated groups on the type of nonverbal and verbal communication in which members engaged and the quantity of ideas generated. Groups with members trained in creative production showed more nonverbal indications of humor (such as laughing and smiling), participated more, and produced more ideas than did members of untrained groups (see Sunwolf & Seibold, Chapter 15, this volume, regarding other differences between structured/trained and unstructured/free group discussions).

Scholars also have devoted attention to the relationships among perceived and behavioral dominance, facial expression, eye movement, and posture in groups. In one investigation of dominance and facial expressions during group discussion, Cashdan (1995) observed that for women, infrequent smiling related positively to hormonal correlates of dominance (androgen and estradiol). Weisfeld, Bloch, and Ivers (1984) found that in groups of adolescent girls, amount of eye contact and erect posture related to perceived dominance. Amount of eye contact correlated highly and positively with success in disputes (getting one's way), as well as being viewed as cheerful, attractive, and achievement oriented. Erect posture also correlated highly and positively with being perceived as achievement oriented, as well as many other attributes, including self-confidence, intelligence, leadership, sociability, popularity, and femininity.

Posture. Several studies point to a relationship between people's posture and their attitudes or affect displays in groups. Mehrabian's (1969, 1981; Mehrabian & Diamond, 1971) research on posture provides a baseline for how group members' posture and attitude displays are related. His research on dyads and groups demonstrated that certain kinds of posture are used to express greater or lesser displays of attitude or interest and positive or negative affect. Mehrabian and Diamond (1981) discovered that closer physical positions (averaging approximately 5 feet) and more direct body orientations ("directness" defined as "how many degrees one must turn to face another," whereby "a zero degree ori-

entation [face to face] is most direct" [p. 282]) by same-sex group members indicate greater immediacy, as well as that "immediacy [physical proximity] of seating is a correlate of the amount of conversation between strangers" (p. 288). Group members, particularly females, conversed more when oriented directly toward one another; large distances (up to 12 feet) were detrimental for participants tested as being more sensitive to rejection. The relationship between posture and social dominance, however, remains underexplored in groups, but certainly worth studying.

Mabry (1989) related patterns of group members' exhibited nonverbal kinesic cues to postulated group developmental patterns. In support of Mehrabian's (1969, 1981) notion that posture signifies one's attitude, Mabry discerned from two sensitivity groups (see Schultz, Chapter 14, this volume) that greater backward postural leans by members occurred in the first and last sessions and that face-to-face body orientation increased in the third session and then declined. He speculated that such postural shifts, in conjunction with eye behaviors observed, "seem consonant" with investigations indicating relatively high anxiety during early periods of the sequential development of sensitivity groups. Specifically, his results show a "striking pattern of high amounts of eye contact avoidance . . . that successively decline from session one" (p. 197). He further observed that direct eye contact increased among members as the sensitivity groups continued to meet. Mabry hypothesized that this tendency corresponds to group members' decreasing anxiety and rising "interpersonal involvement associated with increasing positive regard and affiliational desire" (pp. 198-199); however, he failed to test combinations of the nonverbal cues studied or the perceptions of coders or group members regarding the impact of any of these cues. Despite these problems, Mabry's study is heuristic for hypothesizing about the relationship between nonverbal behaviors and group development.

If Weisfeld et al.'s (1984) study is extended to adults, erect posture presumably would be associated with perceptions of members' dominance or social influence during group interaction. Standing posture versus sitting posture should also be related to group member dominance, according to Schwartz, Tesser, and Powell (1982), who noted that social dominance can be inferred from a person's vertical elevation, such as standing over another person or being taller than another. They tested the concept of "areal radiation," consisting of "three polarities in the space that surrounds the human body: right-left, anterior-posterior, and superior-inferior" (p. 114). Such meanings as "haughtiness, importance, intimacy, hostility, direction of action, superordination" (p. 114) and social dominance correlated to spatial areas that radiate from the body or, in other words, positions of the arms, body, and head, and to eye comfort, sitting and standing, and elevation.

Postural changes, particularly people's mirroring of another's posture, can also signify attitudes. LaFrance (1985) and LaFrance and Broadbent (1976), for example, found that an "us versus them" phenomenon appears in postural mirroring as a function of intergroup orientation. LaFrance required participants to first work in a dyad, then join another dyad to form a group (although they only anticipated interaction while visually assessing one another and listening to further instructions), and then rate one another for perceived cooperativeness. Dyads were given instructions to either cooperate, compete, or coact, or were given no instructions (control). Cooperating group members (whose scores were to be combined) mirrored posture more between groups than within groups, whereas competing group members (those vying for credit) showed the opposite pattern. That is, members instructed to cooperate not only mirrored posture more but also perceived others as being more cooperative, and vice versa for competing members.

One final study that is instructive for understanding how people's posture relates to various levels of engagement or involvement in group interaction was conducted by Doudin, Serpa, and deSousa-Sancho (1990),

who investigated how various body positions and postures signaled members' involvement or engagement in a family therapy group. The outcomes from this research seem consistent with Mehrabian's (1981) research on nonverbal immediacy, in that forward leans and movement toward other members were correlated with engagement or involvement as perceived by observers. Overall, this and the other studies reviewed show that one's posture is a powerful indicator of perceived and behavioral dominance, as well as attitudes or affect, toward other group members.

Eye behavior. Some researchers have examined the effects of group members' eye behavior on perceived status, dominance, and influence, as well as how it is used to express affect. In a program of study of group members' eye behavior and perceptions of dominance, Kalma (1991) observed—prior to the beginning of group interaction and after members' first glance toward others—that length of gaze not only was associated with attributions of dominance made by other members but also correlated positively with members' participation level (amount of talking) in a subsequent group discussion. Kalma (1992) subsequently reported results from three studies that showed that prolonged gaze regulates floor apportionment, or how group members distribute participation, for same-sex discussion triads. Prolonged gaze displays by a speaking member resulted in his or her yielding the floor, whereas the target of the gaze usually took control of the floor. Furthermore, status ratings taken after group discussion directly correlated to general degree of bodily activity, including looking behavior (Kalma, 1992). To counter the possible confounding effects of other nonverbal variables, Lamb (1986) also studied dominance behavior as demonstrated through initial eye gaze, as well as talking time and speaking order. When one person in a dyad had experience from a prior dyadic encounter earlier in the study, she or he was significantly more likely to speak first but would also tend to avert her or his gaze when initiating speech. Men, however, were much more likely than women to maintain eye gaze when initiating speech. Lamb thought that talk initiation, coupled with gaze aversion, probably illustrated a tendency to take the lead, while also putting the other at ease. In dyads where neither or both persons were experienced, nonverbal dominance behavior was equally probable. Although Lamb used dyads, he extrapolated the findings to group settings, suggesting that familiarity effects were evident in nonverbal behaviors exhibited by group members when taking the lead, dominating talking time, and gaining dominance by maintaining eye gaze, and that these behaviors could potentially affect a number of group outcomes.

Mabry (1989) reported that greater direct eye contact and face-to-face, or sociopetal, direct body orientation exhibited by group members corresponded to them being perceived as having greater "personal involvement associated with increasing positive regard and affiliational desire" (pp. 198-199). There were high amounts of eye contact avoidance that successively declined from the first session and a "commensurate increase in the amount of direct eye contact, also beginning after session one" (p. 197). Mabry believes that the developmental patterns noted for eye behavior in groups are consistent with previous research on visual behavior in other interactional settings.

Nonverbal cue combinations. Studies of combinations of kinesic cues have produced interesting results. In one study employing a combined nonverbal cues measure of arousal, Burgoon, LePoire, Beutler, and Engle (1993) reported that vocalic tension, nervous vocalizations, laughter, vocal expressiveness, and random kinesic movement by members of psychotherapy groups were associated with higher measurements of their arousal.

Member dominance and influence are the most popular outcome foci in research on the effects of nonverbal cue combinations in groups. Rosa and Mazur (1979), for example, observed that those who spoke first in zero-history group discussions were perceived af-

terward by other members as being of higher status, although greater eye glances ultimately appeared to account for attributions of higher status. They concluded that when a group is composed of strangers, "they very quickly make use of whatever limited status cues are immediately at hand, even such subtle signs as eye contact and speaking order" (p. 30).

In a more recent investigation of the effects of nonverbal cue combinations on perceptions of group member dominance, Ridgeway (1987) noted that a female confederate in triads was most influential when she displayed "high-level" nonverbal task cues (defined as presenting ideas with sustained eye gaze, rapid verbal response, and rapid rate of speech, as well as a "confident" tone), but not more influential when she displayed dominance, submissiveness, or low-level nonverbal task cues. Valid manipulations resulted in a dominant confederate displaying "significantly louder, firmer, angrier voice tone, a sterner facial expression, and more intrusive gestures" (p. 688). This dominant confederate also had an erect posture, similar to the high-level nonverbal task cues target, but was less relaxed with posture, had more forward leaning, and had more direct eye contact than the submissive target. Dominant and high-level nonverbal task cues confederates were perceived to give about the same amount of eye contact while speaking, but the dominant member differed in eye-contact quality, specifically, staring with lowered brows. Ridgeway concluded that the "association between nonverbal behavior and influence in task groups is indeed due to task cues, rather than true dominance behavior" (p. 692) and that pure dominance cues are not enough to win desired influence.

Leadership often is equated with dominance or influence, and it too has received attention with respect to the enactment and measurement of multiple nonverbal behaviors. For example, Gitter, Black, and Walkley (1976) noted a high magnitude effect of nonverbal communication on attributions of the extent to which a person fulfilled the leadership role. They operationalized "strong versus weak" nonverbal communication by instructing an actor to deliver a message, first simulating a "leader," and then a "follower," by varying "voice, gesture, facial contortion, etc." (p. 1117). Although they failed to carefully delimit nonverbal cue combinations, the manipulation was successful in that confederates exhibiting these respective sets of nonverbal cues were perceived by participants who viewed their filmed presentations as leaders or followers.

Nonverbal displays also have been found to be associated with perceptions of dominance in groups of children or adolescents in addition to adult groups. Children have been found to use aggressive posture and "tone of voice" to establish dominance over other children in groups, and occasionally use threatening gestures or physical force, including clenched fists or jutting chins, as well as bumping, elbowing, shoving, or pinching, to get other children to behave as the aggressor wishes (Hatch, 1987). Observational indices have been used in conjunction with participants' ratings to determine that a specific boy in adolescent male groups was perceived as dominant or subordinate (Savin-Williams, 1977). These observational indices typically code verbal dominance behavior, but some reference nonverbal reactions as well. This occurs, for instance, in a verbal command when one person tells another to shut up, and that person becomes silent and casts his eyes downward, refuses to comply, or ignores the boy giving the command and turns away.

Social influence of leaders or dominating individuals also has been linked to the expression of nonverbal cues of involvement, as well as dominance. Blanck and Rosenthal (1992), for example, investigated the influence on jury verdicts of trial judges' nonverbal microbehaviors (eye contact with the jury, smiles, head nods or shaking the head, significant hand movements, forward leans toward jury, significant changes in posture, body position or body movements, and self-touching) when instructing the jury. Although the coders worked from videotapes of the judges, the data were taken from real trials. Aside from

the strength of the trial evidence presented, either negative or positive nonverbal reactions by judges to evidence where juries attribute bias or prejudice resulted in reversals of conviction on appeal.

Badzinski and Pettus (1994) extended this research by assessing the relationship of judges' nonverbal involvement to trial outcomes. Although they failed to conceptually define nonverbal involvement, their intent seems aligned with Edinger and Patterson's (1983) definition of nonverbal involvement, which is similar to, but more extensive than, nonverbal immediacy or intimacy, including the behaviors of "(a) interpersonal distance, (b) gaze, (c) touch, (d) body orientation, (e) lean, (f) facial expressiveness, (g) talking duration, (h) interruptions, (i) postural openness, (j) gestures of a relational nature, (k) head nods, and (l) paralinguistic cues such as volume, speech rate, and intonation" (p. 31). Badzinski and Pettus operationalized low nonverbal involvement as

> having the judges lean back with a rocking motion and avoid visual contact with the defendant. The judge's arms were either crossed or close to the body, and he or she engaged in frequent object adaptors such as pen tapping and paper shuffling. (p. 313)

High nonverbal involvement was operationalized as "having the judge lean forward and orient body and head toward the defendant with arms open. He or she looked intently at the defendant and nodded frequently in response to the defendant's remarks" (p. 313).

Badzinski and Pettus uncovered support for the main effect of nonverbal involvement, in that high-involved judges were perceived as more credible than low-involved judges. The researchers inferred that jurors regard high involvement by judges very positively, although this main effect apparently was influenced by judges' sex. Specifically, female judges were not perceived similarly negatively for low- and high-level exhibitions of nonverbal involvement, but male judges were perceived as more credible and attractive if they signaled high involvement (but not negatively for low involvement). Female jurors perceived male and female judges similarly, but male jurors rated male judges higher than females regardless of nonverbal involvement levels. Furthermore, high-involved judges were seen as more attractive and attentive than low-involved judges, although there was less of an effect for sex than for perceptions of credibility. Male jurors attributed less credibility to female than male judges. These findings are consistent with Butler and Geis's (1990) conclusions concerning differential ratings of male and female leaders by group members based on the leader's expression of affective behavior.

In sum, the same types of nonverbal cue combinations (e.g., prolonged gaze, limited response latency, rapid speech, and so forth) exhibiting involvement that have been shown to be related to perceptions of partners' persuasiveness and influence in dyads (see Ketrow, 1992a, 1992b) also seem to apply to perceptions of members' dominance and social influence in groups. Other, more restricted cue combinations or singular nonverbal cues also seem to influence group members' perceptions of someone's involvement, leadership, attractiveness, and likability, as well as perceptions of intragroup harmony, and even gains in coordination with others.

Physical Appearance and Artifacts in Group Interaction

The nature and effects of group members' personal nonverbal characteristics, especially physical appearance and artifacts, has been a fruitful area of research. These characteristics, along with members' psychological characteristics and in conjunction with group size, constitute an important part of the composition of any particular group. Studies of group composition have been concerned primarily with various process and outcome effects resulting from members' homogeneity (similarity) versus heterogeneity (diversity) (see Haslett & Ruebush, Chapter 5, this volume).

A sizable body of research exists regarding the effects in groups of people's physical appearance characteristics other than artifacts and perceived attractiveness. Presumably, *physical appearance* cues, such as biological sex (often misconstrued as gender, which is a psychological expectation or enactment of particular sex roles and may be constructed as much from kinesic cues as from biological appearance), race or ethnicity (judged on the basis of physiognomy and skin, hair color and texture, eye color, and so forth), body shape (or somatotype), and other body characteristics (e.g., height or able-bodiedness), affect group members' initial reactions to one another. Perceptions of physical characteristics, along with so-called "adornment features," or *artifacts,* such as clothing, jewelry and other accessories, and cosmetics, influence whether a person interacts at all with another and, if so, the nature of that interaction. The following sections explore such static nonverbal appearance cues as age, physical size, sex, gender, race, and culture as precursors to and mediators of group interaction.

Age, physical size, and sex/gender. Shaw (1981) offers brief syntheses regarding the effects of people's age and physical size on some limited phenomena in groups, such as conformity behavior. He also provides one of the earliest reviews on the effects of sex and race on group interactional behaviors.

Many scholars employ age as a discrete contextual variable. Evidence on the role of age perceptions in regard to group outcomes has not been well integrated, with a few exceptions. A search uncovered only one study relevant to age as a nonverbal characteristic for adults in groups. In that quasi-experimental study, Baker and Eaton (1992) reported that "seniority [in an organization] is a more significant factor than chronological age in influencing an individual's value to the group" (p. 337). This finding, however, should be interpreted within the limitations of their experimental method, which had undergraduate students rank hypothetical male employees of respective ages of 30 years, "40s," and 60 years. Thus, the study offers speculative data about age effects based on young adults' perceptions.

The paucity of research on age as a physical nonverbal cue that might affect group interaction and outcomes is evident. Unlike the growing body of research on sex/gender and race as diffuse status characteristics (see below; see also Haslett & Ruebush, Chapter 5, this volume), few scholars studying the group context have employed age as a potentially important physical appearance cue.

With regard to the effects of members' physical size on group outcomes, the research is also limited. Height, for example, has been found to correlate slightly to perceived group leadership (Shaw, 1981). A handful of studies of dyadic interactions have also reported relationships between obesity and various outcomes, including children maintaining greater physical distance from chubby children (Lerner, Karabenick, & Meisels, 1975; Lerner, Venning, & Knapp, 1975), overweight individuals having difficulty in gaining entrance to college (DeJong & Kleck, 1986), people preferring to work with normal-weight versus obese persons (Jasper & Klassen, 1990), and general derogation and stigmatization on the basis of being overweight (Cahnman, 1968; Horvath, 1981). Effects of people's disabilities have received limited attention but show similar patterns of negative bias (Kleck & DeJong, 1983).

The impact of biological sex in groups seems to have been explored more thoroughly than other physical characteristic variables. Early research revealed differences in group interaction and outcomes attributable to having male or female leaders, as well as male or female members. Later research provides more sophisticated assessment of the effects of sex but tends either to be inconclusive or to contradict earlier research.

Reviews of relevant research by Baird (1976) and Shaw (1981) revealed inconsistent findings regarding the effects of members' sex on group interaction and/or outcomes. For instance, Shaw reported that mixed-sex groups perform less efficiently than same-sex groups; however, this relationship appears to be affected by the type of task being performed. Davies (1994a) and Wood (1987) provide limited evidence of performance differences between mixed- and same-sex groups, but, again, this relationship appears to be affected by task type and, additionally, by members' interactional style. In particular, Wood found that males performed better than females at both the individual and group levels when a high amount of task-oriented activity was required, but that women's interactional styles (e.g., "positive social behavior," such as agreeing and acting friendly" [p. 54], behaviors that have large nonverbal components) facilitated group performance when tasks required a high degree of social activity.

Other researchers also have considered how a person's sex affects group members' perceptions of another's competence or argumentative skill (Bradley, 1980; Ketrow, 1983), how members' satisfaction depends on the gender of their group leader (Alderton & Jurma, 1980), and how members' sex affects evaluations of group leaders. The results, however, are equivocal, with only some studies finding sex differences. Contradictory evidence may result from the problem of studying biological sex rather than gender. Older studies that focused only on sex, for example, showed that males emerged more consistently than females as leaders of groups, despite equivalence in type of communication exhibited, or, at least, that males and females were valued differentially as group leaders (e.g., Eagley, 1970; Golub & Canty, 1982; Graves & Powell, 1982; Hoffman & Maier, 1982; Jago & Vroom, 1982; see also Pavitt, Chapter 12, this volume).

Some later studies, however, indicate that group leaders emerge as a result of particular types of verbal and/or nonverbal communicative behavior in which they engage, such as talkativeness or "high-task" cues (Ridgeway, 1987), rather than on the basis of sex. Offermann's (1986) study, for example, found that when there were many more rather than fewer nonverbal cues from which to judge, there were no statistically significant differences in performance and leadership evaluations of men and women. Offermann did concede, however, that the probability of continued success was seen by members as being lower for groups with female leaders than for those with male leaders, apparently because of the reduced status and competence attributed to women. Offermann's findings are supported by several other studies, including those by Butler and Geis (1990) and Goktepe and Schneier (1988).

In Bradley's (1980) study, women who demonstrated task-related competence by providing opinions that were "deviant" from other group members and arguing from evidence effectively neutralized stereotypical sex-biased evaluations. Similarly, a female functioning as a competent procedural specialist in a group in Ketrow's (1983) study was evaluated more favorably on dimensions of procedural, analytical, and socioemotional performance than two males performing similarly in groups. Hawkins (1995) extended this research further, reporting that regardless of biological sex *or* gender, engaging in task-relevant communication predicted group leadership emergence. Kolb (1997), however, found that although sex did not predict leadership emergence in groups, there was a significant relationship between possessing masculinity characteristics and leadership emergence. Some research, then, suggests that biological sex may not play as significant a role in groups as previously thought, but gender orientation might.

Bradley (1980) posited that sex serves as an external status characteristic, and Halberstadt and Saitta (1987) also suggested that gender functions as "a categorizing strategy and as a diffuse status characteristic" (p. 257). Based on sex as a physical characteristic, women typically are accorded lower status and, therefore, attributed lower presumed competence than men. Propp (1995) investigated sex as a nonverbal indicator of status on the use of information in group decision making, and reported that when males introduced information, it was twice as likely to be used by the group as when offered by females, particularly if that knowledge was held uniquely by only the males in a mixed-sex group (see Propp, Chapter 9, this volume, on collective information processing in groups).

Porter, Geis, and Jennings-Walstead (1983) reported that group members use situational cues, including head-of-table seating position, in addition to sex, to assign leadership status. Crocker and McGraw (1984) found that when a group had a lone female, she was not as likely to be perceived as a group leader as one of the males, but a lone male in a group was likely to be perceived as a leader. This is consistent with Kanter's (1977) findings concerning "token" females or those of races or ethnicities different from the dominant type. Kanter indicated that when sex, race, or ethnicity was "skewed" in a group, such that there was a larger number of one type than another, the numerically dominant types controlled the group and determined its culture (e.g., language, tasks, and patterns). Consequently, the few minority members are called "tokens" because they cannot achieve enough power to make any difference.

A number of studies indicate that "followers'" perceptions are affected by the sex of a group leader, although, as has been pointed out, recent research indicates that sex may not be a very powerful explanatory variable. In short, sex is associated with the emergence of leaders in groups and can result in differences in males' and females' perceived competence in groups, with a bias toward males being perceived more as leaders and contributing more to task completion. Canary and Emmers-Sommer (1997) maintain that research findings of sex differences in general are problematic and depend on whether one looks at perceptions and expectations or at actual behaviors. For example, they cite Burgoon and Dillman's (1995) research on dyadic immediacy behaviors. When men engaged in high-immediacy cues of "close proximity, touch, and eye contact," they were perceived as being "more *powerful* than women," whereas the same nonverbal cues for women resulted in perceptions of greater *equality, similarity,* and *trustworthiness* than men" (Canary &

Emmers-Sommer, 1997, p. 95). Moreover, meta-analyses of interactional differences between males and females reveal quite small effect sizes. Still, J. A. Hall's (1984) extensive review of research mostly on dyads, albeit now 15 years old but certainly relevant to the study of nonverbal behavior in groups, indicates that nonverbal communication "qualifies as one area in which sex differences remain robust" (Canary & Emmers-Sommer, 1997, p. 9). Clearly, more research needs to be conducted about the effects of sex and gender in groups, and the way any such effects may change over time.

Race, ethnicity, and culture. Findings that challenge common assumptions about interactional and outcome patterns made on the basis of studies of predominantly White, middle-class U.S. Americans are largely the product of studies of the effects of race in dyadic situations. During the 1960s, many studies appeared, no doubt because of the waxing interest in civil rights. A group focus currently is emerging as interest in diversity increases.

Distinctions among race, ethnicity, and culture are not drawn finely in the literature reviewed but should be made. *Race* generally is considered a "genetically transmitted physical characteristic" (Houghton Mifflin, 1993, p. 1125), but as a perceived nonverbal cue, it may be mediated by other appearance cues, including kinesic ones, that derive from culture. *Ethnicity* is the background or character associated with a shared and "distinctive racial, national, religious, linguistic, or cultural heritage" (Houghton Mifflin, 1993, p. 471). *Culture* consists of socially transmitted beliefs, values, behavioral patterns, and the "products of human work and thought [e.g., art]" (Houghton Mifflin, 1993, p. 337). The point should be made that race, as a static nonverbal cue, and ethnicity or culture, more often dynamic kinesic and proxemic cues but sometimes conveyed by artifacts, often interact. Ethnicity and culture often carry particular ways of interacting nonverbally as part and parcel of a shared and distinctive heritage.

Shaw (1981) indicated that available research from the 1960s and early 1970s showed that race affected the way members interacted in groups. On the basis of that research, he concluded that "the racial composition of the group clearly influences the feelings and behaviors of group members" (p. 227). One specific finding he reported was that, in group situations, "blacks also tend to talk to whites more than to other blacks" (p. 226). Shaw's conclusion, although dated, has received support in later research on group interactional patterns (Davies, 1994a; Johnson & Johnson, 1985; Schofield & Sagar, 1977). Katz (1970), for example, reported that in heterogeneous groups, Whites participated more than Blacks and were perceived by both to have more task ability and exert more influence.

More recent research indicates additional co-cultural effects from racial composition that emerge in groups. Research on performance outcomes associated with racial composition of groups indicates that when a task requires limited group interaction, racial composition has no detectable effect (see Haslett & Ruebush, Chapter 5, this volume, regarding the effects of group composition on group processes and outcomes). When a task requires members to interact and coordinate their activities, however, all-Black or all-White groups perform more effectively than racially heterogeneous groups, although heterogeneous groups may be more beneficial to Blacks. Overall, racially integrated (versus homogeneous) groups containing both African Americans and Caucasians appear to improve "the performance and attitudes of blacks without adversely affecting the performance and attitudes of whites" (Davies, 1994a, p. 74; see also Ruhe & Eatman, 1977). Regarding attitudes related to racial perceptions in groups, quite a few studies have investigated methods to improve race relations in groups, primarily by having racially heterogeneous members engage in cooperative behavior, which promotes greater attraction among members (Davies, 1994a; also see Johnson & Johnson, 1982, 1985; Johnson, Johnson, & Maruyama,

1983). This effect is particularly true when group members help one another.

A number of studies expand beyond African Americans and Caucasians to investigate nonverbal cues associated with other races, as well as to use race or ethnicity itself as a nonverbal cue. Consistent with Aiello and Jones's (1971) finding that middle-class White children in dyads stand farther apart than lower-class Black or Puerto Rican children, Moore and Porter (1988) noted a difference between Hispanic and White female group leaders in their use of space. Specifically, Hispanics used less space and interacted with others at closer distances than Whites. Kelsey (1998) investigated the impact of racial differences between Caucasian and Chinese males in " 'power-and-prestige' hierarchies" for task groups on "individual participation rates, influence on the group's decision, evaluation of contributions, and overall rating of performance" (pp. 603-604). The groups consisted of either one "token" Chinese among three Caucasians or, conversely, a token Caucasian among three Chinese, and Kelsey controlled for fluency of language and socioeconomic status. Individuals rated one another, after working on a joint task, on level of participation, influence, and leadership. Independent observers also rated each member on these characteristics. Kelsey found that Chinese tokens had the lowest participation and influence ratings, whereas Caucasian tokens had the highest ratings; judges rated a Caucasian in all groups as the "person who had the highest participation rate and influence level and who showed the most leadership qualities" (p. 620). Conversely, Craig and Rand (1998) found that whether or not they were solo, African Americans were more likely than Whites to be perceived as group leaders following group interaction on an idea-generation task. Thus, the evidence of bias for majority race does not seem to hold up across all studies, suggesting that race as a diffuse nonverbal status characteristic should be explored more thoroughly.

Using a broader cross section of members of different races, Walfoort and Watters (1996) report a preliminary case study revealing dramatic differences in nonverbal interactional styles and patterns among all-Caucasian U.S. American, Hispanic, African American, and Japanese task groups. Of the four groups, Japanese men were most restrained in nonverbal expressiveness, followed by Caucasians. African Americans were louder and more vocally active, laughed more often, were more active in trunk movement, and were more expressive with gestures, while Hispanic group members were the most expressive with respect to pitch and changes in volume and the most kinesically active in getting up and walking around as they gesticulated with expansive movements. Cox, Lobel, and McLeod (1991) also contrasted group task behaviors related to differences in cultural norms for four ethnic groups (U.S. Anglos and Blacks, as well as Asian Americans and Hispanics). They confirmed the hypothesis that "groups composed of people from collectivist cultural traditions [Asians] displayed more cooperative behavior than those from individualistic cultural traditions [Anglo Americans]" (p. 827).

Kanter's (1977) token member perspective that "skewed" sex, race, or ethnicity in a group allows the dominants to set the interactional patterns and group culture and hold power over outcomes has been tested by other researchers. For example, when ethnic representation in a group was low, Cox et al.'s (1991) group members conformed to majority norms. In particular, Hispanics acted more competitively when there were few of them in a group. Using multicultural groups composed of participants from diverse ethnic origins, including European Canadians, Black Canadians, Asians, and Indians, Kirchmeyer (1993) and Kirchmeyer and Cohen (1992) found that the contribution level of minority members was significantly less than that of majority members. Furthermore, minorities evaluated themselves much lower on a measure of communication competence.

As with gender, race serves as a diffuse status characteristic in the absence of other cues (Adams, 1980, 1983; Lockheed & Hall,

1976). There are also interaction effects between sex and race. For example, Black females tend to be perceived as being more similar to White males in respect to activity and assertiveness (Adams, 1980, 1983; Davies, 1994a), and non-Caucasian females tend to be submissive in interaction (e.g., allow themselves to be interrupted more and initiate less). Adams (1980, 1983) assessed the combined effects of sex and race on dominance behavior, positing that sex-role stereotypes differ for Whites and Blacks. She found that White males and Black females tended to initiate more verbal acts and assume positions of more influence than Black males, followed by White females (see also Davies, 1994a; Lockheed & Hall, 1976).

As Walfoort and Watters (1996) and Davies (1994a) contend, outcomes from research that treat sex and race as separate variables may be suspect. These physical characteristics intersect and must, therefore, be considered together. With the growing increase of diversity in organizations and institutions, understanding the effects of racial and cultural differences is critical to working and socializing effectively in groups (see Haslett & Ruebush, Chapter 5, this volume).

Artifacts. Artifacts, unfortunately, have been virtually ignored by group researchers. An exception is Ketrow (1994), who noted that most of the males in mixed-sex task groups in four different organizations either came to meetings without suit jackets or removed them at the beginning of meetings; females, however, generally did not alter their attire and, for the most part, appeared more fully attired or "packaged." This difference in attire seemed to be related indirectly to the relative status of males and females. Most of the men interrupted the women in the group, or were often deferred to by the women, with the exception of one female facilitator, who was a managing editor and thus outranked all others. Differences in attire (artifacts) also might affect or reflect social influence in groups, but little evidence about these matters is available.

Overall, although physical characteristics are static cues, in that they do not change much, if at all, during group interaction (Ketrow, 1992a), the available research suggests that they affect group interaction. More systematic investigation of the effects of sex/gender, race, ethnicity, culture, and other nonverbal appearance cues on group interaction and outcomes would certainly be valuable.

Place, Contact, and Time Codes Affecting Groups

Place Codes

The heart of investigation for proxemics (and occasionally the rest of the group's environment) is often classified as *group ecology,* defined as "the study of seating positions and furniture arrangement" (Andersen, 1992, p. 283; see also Sommer, 1969). Among all areas in the nonverbal domain, place codes, known as *proxemics* (use of space) or *environmental cues* (such as furnishings and room temperature), probably have received the most sustained scrutiny by group researchers.

Burgoon (1992) explicates group ecology by relying on E. T. Hall's (1966/1982) proxemics model for organizing physical space, which consists of three types of space: fixed feature, semi-fixed feature, and informal. Fixed-feature space (like the walls and doors of a room) and semi-fixed-feature space (movable parts of an environment, such as chairs) tend to be considered static variables and are studied as "ways in which architecture, interior design, [and] furniture arrangement . . . influence spacing behavior" (Burgoon, 1992, p. 289). A third type of personal space is informal space, which is "how we orient toward and distance ourselves from other members of the group" (Burgoon, 1992, p. 288).

Perhaps the static nature of these variables and the relative ease of their measurement may explain why group ecology has garnered so much attention. Similar to work in other areas of nonverbal communication, the study of proxemics in groups overlaps somewhat with other place subcodes, such as the physical environment, and, to a certain extent, with group size. It is thus also linked to density, crowding, and territoriality. One reason for the overlap of proxemics with group size is that the physical space available to group members depends on the total size of the space available, that is, *density:* The more people relative to a space of given dimensions, the more dense it is. Whereas density is a measure of available physical space, a related construct, *crowding,* is a negative psychological variable based on individuals' personal space preferences and the size of the space available. A final relevant consideration is that of *mental, or virtual, space,* which typically applies to group members who are connected by technology. Generally, the sharing of physical space contains an accompanying, but unstated, assumption among group members of shared mental space as well. Virtual groups, however, may need to have their members' mental space parameters measured. As technology links more and more individuals in groups, as well as linking groups within and among organizations, exploration of this frontier has begun to occur (see Scott, Chapter 16, this volume, regarding research on communication technology and group communication).

Although the subcode of proxemics has received notable attention, the subcode of contact, or touch, has been largely ignored. A search uncovered only a handful of studies pertaining to the use of touch in groups, and these are explained below.

Finally, *chronemics,* or use of time, has been examined only insofar as floor dominance—conceptualized as talkativeness or vocal productivity—is defined as a chronemic cue. Talkativeness is often treated as a verbal cue, and sometimes as a vocalic or auditory cue, but it is better treated as a time-use cue. As the review below shows, other time elements, such as punctuality and duration, have received only limited attention in research on dyads and virtually none in research on groups.

Group ecology. Some researchers have focused on how people's use of personal space is related to such group processes/outcomes as

leadership. Andersen (1992) and Burgoon (1992), in their reviews of prior research, speculate about the findings with respect to (a) linkages between or among status, power, and leadership to proxemic privilege and interactional patterns (such as proximity and eye contact); (b) seating arrangements and members' participation; (c) centrality of seating position and directions of group interaction; and (d) members' preferences for seating arrangement and task in relation to liking, attraction, involvement, arousal, and comfort. The following discussion outlines some of the major findings.

Centrality of seating position, the most central location in a group's physical arrangement, allows for greater member participation, dominance, influence, and initiation, and positively influences attributions of leadership. Those exhibiting dominance and control tend to take the most central seating positions and also maintain greater physical distances from others (see, for example, Davies, 1994b; Hiers & Heckel, 1977; Strodtbeck & Hook, 1961). Several studies (Lecuyer, 1976; Strodtbeck & Hook, 1961; Sommer, 1969) indicate that leaders take the perceived end positions of either rectangular or circular tables, and conversely, that individuals seated at the ends are perceived as leaders. Granstrom (1986) found support for these observations in a study of communication patterns between leaders and followers in informal groups of teenagers, with perceived leaders dominating the physical and psychological space in these groups. Baker (1984) reported that when two persons were seated on one side of a rectangular table, with three persons on the other side, one of the two was more likely to emerge as the leader, at least as identified by group members. In four groups observed in organizations, Ketrow (1994) determined that the persons identified by observers and members of each group as most influential (not including the facilitator) took a central seating position, usually at the opposing end of the table from the facilitator.

In an interesting study, albeit of dyads, the twin concepts of centrality and visibility were applied by Schwartz et al. (1982) to examine how persons' use of space is related to perceived dominance. As part of the earlier-noted construct of areal radiation, three spatial-use cues were found to be related to perceived dominance: lateral opposition, precedence, and vertical placement. Specifically, a group member to one's right, or right-handed placement (lateral opposition), was most likely to be perceived as dominant. Second, using figures showing a person as being either in front of or behind another to signify precedence, someone perceived as being physically "first" or "before" another was viewed as having precedence and, therefore, greater dominance. Third, social dominance aligned in opposite ways, low and high, respectively, with two types of vertical placement: a vertically inferior seated person and a vertically superior elevated person. Physical elevation tended to be equated with dominance, and sublimation with subordination, but this perception depended on the amount of energy required to maintain that position. Usually an elevated person was rated as dominant regardless of whether the lower figure sat or stood, but when the elevated person sat and the lower one stood, dominance ratings were about equal. Moreover, related to the three cues, rest or physical inactivity correlated negatively with power, especially when "displacement of the body mass is commonly used to exhibit deference" (Schwartz et al., 1982, p. 115). The lower one's status or power, therefore, the more energy must be expended while in the presence of another person of greater status or power. Schwartz and colleagues' more complex conceptualization of the use of space is, in contrast to previous conceptualizations, an intriguing one, but it has not been tested in a group setting.

Proxemic behavior may relate to aspects of leadership emergence that involve influencing group interaction. Shaw (1981) notes that "there are consequences of spatial arrangements which are not so obvious" (p. 133), such as the impact of seating arrangements on group interaction, as demonstrated by the "Steinzor effect." The Steinzor effect occurs in face-to-face group discussions in which members direct more comments to persons seated across the table and facing them than to those in adjacent seating positions (Steinzor, 1950), particularly in the presence of strong directive leaders (Hearn, 1957). In one of the few studies of the redistribution of space and seating assignments relative to group members' status, Suzuki (1986) observed that, in a later meeting, members reseated themselves from their initial chosen arrangement according to status and perceived territory.

A couple of researchers have reported that members of all-female groups generally interact at closer distances than members of mixed-sex or all-male groups (e.g., Patterson & Schaeffer, 1977; Pedersen, 1977). Pedersen (1977) observed that when women approached a group from behind or groups facing away, they maintained smaller personal physical distance than men. Mehrabian and Diamond (1971) further observed that women, as well as men with affiliative tendencies, selected closer seating positions in groups, and that more conversation occurred between those seated closer and those oriented in a physically more direct manner to each other (see also Giesen & McClaren, 1976). Some cultural variables also influence space use. Moore and Porter (1988), in a study of 6th-grade females working in groups on a cooperative task, noted that Hispanic females used less vertical and horizontal space than did Anglo females and were less likely to intrude physically on or interrupt other group members.

The effects of seating arrangement have been explained in terms of the regulation of privacy among group members. Davies (1994b) argued that "members' seating choices may therefore indicate their desired level of privacy" (p. 27). Greater or lesser verbal participation rates and visibility, or visual accessibility, are associated with particular seating locations and, hence, to more or less social stimulation and contact (Koneya, 1977). Visibility and sociopetal spaces, those that "tend to bring people together" (E. T. Hall, 1966/1982, p. 108, citing a series of studies in the 1950s on space usage in hospitals; see also Mehrabian, 1981), are associated with socioemotional group outcomes, such as greater social interaction and friendship choices (Davies, 1994b; Greenberg, 1976; Michelini, Passalacqua, & Cusimano, 1976).

Group members' preferences for personal space can be explained by a number of theoretical perspectives. Burgoon and her associates (e.g., Burgoon, 1978; Burgoon & Aho, 1982, Burgoon, Dillman, & Stern, 1993; Burgoon, Stern, & Dillman, 1995), in a program of research on space usage in dyads, have conceptualized and tested Interpersonal Proxemics Violations Theory. According to this theory, there is a perceived level of appropriate intimacy desired between interactants, and nonverbal cues can be used to identify the degree of intimacy. If an interaction is perceived as overly intimate, interactants typically compensate to regulate the deviation. Another theory, Argyle and Dean's (1965) Intimacy Equilibrium Theory, stipulates that in any interaction there are "various 'approach' forces [that] pull people together (such as the need for affiliation or contact) and 'avoidance' forces that push people apart (such as fear of social embarrassment or rejection)" (Davies, 1994b, p. 21). Another explanatory model, Patterson's (1976, 1982) Arousal-Labeling Theory, predicts reciprocal, as well as compensatory, changes based on intimacy level. Specifically, "changes in intimacy level produce changes in nonspecific *arousal* . . . that accentuates existing feelings" (Davies, 1994b, p. 21). Reciprocity or compensation depends on the valence of the feeling produced, as well as its intensity, and these bases of interaction are variable. For example, when a group member is aroused negatively, she or he may compensate to reduce anxiety or discomfort by moving a chair farther away from other members.

As is the case with other cognitive-psychological "balance" theories, these theories argue that individuals are motivated to reach a state of equilibrium that is comfortable. Several studies help explain how individuals reciprocate or compensate nonverbally and/or verbally to one another during interaction to achieve equilibrium. Burgoon and colleagues (Burgoon, Dillman, et al., 1993, 1995) summarize these: An equilibrium model may be pertinent only to a small set of immediacy behaviors, such as those "related to physical comfort (proximity, lean, orientation, gaze)" (Burgoon et al., 1995, p. 104), and reciprocity of increased, as well as decreased, exhibitions of nonverbal cues related to involvement (e.g., decreases in gaze were reciprocated) prevails in all violation conditions, including between highly rewarding interactants who are perceived positively (e.g., liking and approval), and in situations of high and low involvement.

Patterson's model, in particular, helps explain Ryen and Kahn's (1975) research finding that orientations of intergroup cooperation or competition result in different seating preference effects following winning or losing, particularly given affective arousal related to wins or losses. Following intergroup cooperation, participants sat nearer to both in-group and out-group members but preferred their own group members (regarding in-groups/out-groups, in this volume, see Chapters 5 [Haslett & Ruebush] and 11 [Meyers & Brashers]). Following intergroup competition with no feedback on win-loss outcomes, members sat near their in-group members and relatively far away from out-group members. When such win-loss competition was followed by feedback, winning group members tried to sit relatively close to the losers, but the losers tried to sit farther away from the winners. More theory testing and development in group settings certainly is needed.

Density and crowding. Some research shows effects resulting from density and crowding. Davies (1994b) differentiated functional or social density (variations in the number of people in a given space who directly affect a person's feelings or behavior) from spatial density (variations in the amount of space available to a given number of people). As he noted, "High density may be a necessary but not a sufficient condition for crowding to occur" (p. 29).

Crowding has been shown to affect people's arousal and comfort levels. On public beaches, less space per person is claimed among larger than smaller groups (Edney & Jordan-Edney, 1974). Males are more likely to feel somewhat constrained or crowded than are females when placed in the same spatial arrangement, and will claim more territory than females. Groups that stay at a beach longer also claim more territory, but groups of friends claim less space at the beach than groups of strangers (Davies, 1994b; Edney & Grundmann, 1979; Edney & Jordan-Edney, 1974; H. W. Smith, 1981).

In another context, male groups in smaller, as opposed to larger, rooms have been found to be more competitive, gave more severe sentences to defendants in mock trials, and evaluated themselves less positively; in contrast, female groups in larger, rather than smaller, rooms were more competitive, rated themselves less positively, and gave more severe sentences in mock trials (Shaw, 1981). Valacich, George, Nunamaker, and Vogel (1994), studying group interaction facilitated by technology, manipulated group size and whether members were in the same room or separate offices (distributed) to determine the effect on group idea generation. The researchers believe that the nonsignificant size by proximity interaction effect was due partially to the task, which affected idea generation more than did space. The notion that group members in a room together generate more ideas than dispersed members seems related to the general construct of the facilitating effect of the presence of others (see Zajonc's, 1965, review; see also Kent, 1994).

With regard to other types of tasks, a study by Seta, Paulus, and Schkade (1976) of four coacting group members in a cooperative condition showed that they performed better on a simple memory task than dyads, but the result was just the reverse in a competitive condition. In a second experiment, close seating (members spaced 2 feet apart) resulted in better group performance on a maze-solution task under a condition of cooperation, but less proximity (members spaced 5 feet apart) resulted in improved performance on the same type of task in a competitive condition.

In a qualitative study, Ketrow (1993) observed that one 12-step group of Alcoholics Anonymous (AA) split into two smaller groups when the density reached a level that apparently exceeded tolerance for crowdedness (among other reasons raised for the split). The effect of this split was debated in the larger group, which had more people who had been members of this AA group longer. Continued attempts to assimilate the smaller group from its separate space into a larger group were made, unsuccessfully. Not many task groups could break into smaller groups in that fashion and survive, nor would explicit attention be paid by group members, or, perhaps, by researchers, to the nonverbal cue of crowdedness as an important causal factor for such a decision, or as it affects the quality of interaction for each new subgroup.

Group size, composition, and interaction. The nonverbal cue of group size has been related to member proximity and participation. Early research on the effects of group size, however, did not take into account the variables of sex, race, and ethnic characteristics.

Group size has been related to group idea generation and consensus development. Valacich et al. (1994) reported that larger technology-mediated groups (e.g., 9, 12, and 18 members) generated more unique and higher quality ideas than smaller groups (e.g., 3, 4, and 6 members). Mullen's (1991) meta-analysis examined the effects of relative group size on the salience of in-group and out-group construction of the majority and minority. The analysis indicated that "proportionate group sizes [of in-group and out-group] are a better predictor of the effect of the group on the individual than the mere size of the in-group, or of the out-group, or of the total group" (p. 299) on various social behaviors, including conformity, prosocial behavior, social loafing, and participation in classroom discussions. For example, the results of 67 hypothesis tests revealed that majority members consistently underestimated, and minority members over-estimated, their group's consensus. His results are consistent with Kanter's (1977) work on token group members cited earlier. Further-more, Mullen cited studies revealing the ten-dency for one group member to account for most of the increases in verbal participation in direct relation to increased group size, and that this increased participation and, thus, centrality of focus accounted for perceptions of that person as an emergent leader. Lit-tlepage and Silbiger (1992) found support for the well-known tendency toward uneven and skewed participation in moderately sized and larger groups. They also found that the ability of the group to recognize expertise of individ-ual members increased with group size.

Studying group composition, some re-searchers have investigated ratios of men to women, such as indicated earlier for sex and "token" women (e.g., Kanter, 1977), as well as for racial and ethnic composition. Most of the research related to physical visual non-verbal cues reviewed earlier has demonstrated patterns of effects for these cues on group processes and outcomes.

Virtual group space and technology. Early research on computer-mediated communica-tion (CMC) suggested that CMC is deperson-alizing because of the absence of nonverbal cues. Several researchers have found, how-ever, that nonverbal cues are created in the absence of typical visual, auditory, or tactile cues—for example, the proliferation of "emo-ticons," symbols that stand for emotional cues, like :), which is a smile (face symbol turned sideways), or the use of "emoting" cues, like <<Shrug>>, embedded in text comments. Short, Williams, and Christie (1976) posit that social presence, representing a continuum of quantity of physical, psycho-logical, and nonverbal cues available to inter-actants, is central to how individuals process interaction. *Social presence* is defined as the "degree to which a communication medium is perceived to be socio-emotionally similar to a face-to-face conversation. The quality . . .

indicates the degree to which an individual feels that a communication partner is actually present during their exchange" (Rogers, 1986, p. 52). Rogers points out that "communica-tion media high in social presence are those in which nonverbal as well as verbal communi-cation occurs" (p. 52). Low social presence generally is unsatisfying and leaves people in some situations, such as those involving con-flict, unable to resolve differences effectively or meet their goals. Researchers agree that face-to-face (FtF) meetings are preferred over distributed meetings, especially when politi-cally or interpersonally complex issues are involved (Farmer & Hyatt, 1994; Kiesler & Sproull, 1992; McGrath, 1984; Short et al., 1976), because "restricted modalities of com-munication may attenuate social context cues, such as body language and facial expressions, required for such tasks" (Farmer & Hyatt, 1994, p. 332).

A couple of studies have tested whether social presence predominates in group mem-bers' interaction and affects related outcomes. Although he did not identify his study as investigating this construct, Stein (1975) com-pared four conditions ranging across the spec-trum of social presence: full video plus sound, video with filtered speech (sound with only certain frequencies retained), video/no sound, and text (script)/no sound. The results showed that "both verbal and nonverbal behaviors in small groups provide cues of the group mem-bers' emergent leadership statuses inde-pendent of their relative participation rates" (p. 132). The best accuracy of evaluations by participants in judging a target group's leader-ship hierarchies were obtained in the condi-tion with full information, which included all nonverbal cues. As a clearer test of social presence, Farmer and Hyatt (1994) investi-gated the fit of three communication modes to group performance and strategy, comparing FtF, audio/telephone conferencing, and screensharing combined with audioconfer-encing groups (screensharing "allows distrib-uted computer-supported meeting partici-pants to view each others' terminal display screens and use and manipulate graphical and textual information on each others' computers while all participants watch," p. 338). Not surprisingly, the audioconferencing groups performed more poorly on the task than the other two group types. One interpretation of this result offered by the researchers is that as task complexity increases, the fit between task and media deteriorates "because communication channels are no longer adequate" (p. 361), but they also argue that a corresponding increase in social complexities is exacerbated by the limits of these media.

One area that is relatively underexplored is how room and personal-space metaphors might function as spatial models for conversations in virtual computer spaces, especially for those involving computer-supported group work. A couple of recent studies shed light on this issue. Some of the same interactional processes and outcomes for FtF groups seem to apply to virtual groups. Finholt and Sproull (1990) demonstrated through an analysis of electronic mail of 96 company employees that "some groups behaved like real social groups, despite the fact that they shared no physical space, their members were invisible, and their interaction was asynchronous" (p. 41). Walther and Burgoon (1992) uncovered support for the view that CMC group members experience relational communication similar to FtF group members (see also Scott, Chapter 16, this volume).

The conceptualization of a mental or virtual interactional space seems best related to an analog of vocalic (auditory) cues related to talkativeness, or participation. Research on use of technology to support task-group interaction indicates that participation evens out more compared to FtF interaction, and those who tend to be silent in FtF contexts are more active. In contrast to CMC groups, Mullen's (1991) meta-analysis shows that as FtF group size increases, dominance of participation by one (or a few) members increases as well. Rao (1995), investigating the effects of feedback allowed by comparing telephone (audio) and computer conferencing technologies on group

members' comprehension and satisfaction, found that the greater feedback provided by teleconferencing was related to greater comprehension and speaker satisfaction, but not listener satisfaction. There were no differences in comprehension, listener satisfaction, or speaker satisfaction across technologies, and Rao suggests that these functions of nonverbal signals can be mapped systematically across technologies.

Contact Codes

Touch, also called *haptics,* has been shown in research on individuals and dyads to be crucial to physical and mental health, the development of intimacy (relationships), and perceptions of warmth, liking, affiliation, and social support (Burgoon et al., 1996). Initiation of touch also influences perceptions of dominance or status in dyads (Major & Heslin, 1982), as well as compliance with requests (Burgoon et al., 1996; Hare & Davies, 1994; Kleinke, 1977; Paulsell & Goldman, 1984; Willis & Hamm, 1980). An extensive search, however, yielded only a handful of studies examining touch in groups; the findings, sketchy though they are, seem similar to those for dyads.

D. N. Walker (1975) identified patterns of touch for group members related to building affiliation and expressing caring (social support). Touches on hands, shoulders, and arms, and—when interactants were seated—on the knee were perceived positively by the person being touched. Despite minimal description of the kind of supportive touch given, Lovrin (1995) indicated that eight 8-year-old girls who had been orphaned by AIDS and who were in group therapy demonstrated extreme sensitivity to one another and engaged in caring nonverbal behavior, including touch, as a way of expressing support. Touching occurred generally following painful self-disclosure and prior to speech, and usually in conjunction with the supporters' moving their chairs closer and leaning toward the discloser.

Time Codes (Chronemics)

Time-related variables of talkativeness and initiation of talk generally are classified as vocalic (see next section), but these might be classified more appropriately as timing (punctuation of sequences) and duration (floor dominance). *Talkativeness* (also referred to as speaking time, participation rate, productivity, or floor dominance) is cited as a primary causal variable that explains much of the variance in perceptions of group leadership or member influence. There is a robust relationship between floor dominance and perception of power in groups (Dovidio, Brown, Heltman, Ellyson, & Keating, 1988; Littlepage & Silbiger, 1992), despite covariation effects that might be attributed to a group member's task competence, such as "informedness" or greater task familiarity, or social roles. *Initiation of talk* is not examined directly as a major independent variable in these studies, but some evidence supports the view that such initiation of sequences is a timing phenomenon that contributes to perceptions of leadership and/or influence (Ketrow, 1991b, 1994; Rosa & Mazur, 1979).

Only one study has examined the effects of *response latency* (the length of time for one interactant to respond when another pauses or gives over a turn) on members' participation in groups (Willard & Strodtbeck, 1972). Similar to the findings from many other studies, shorter latencies and greater participation were related to perceptions of group leadership emergence.

Auditory Codes

Auditory codes include all the features of the voice, including fundamental frequency (perceived volume), rate of speech, pitch, fluency, perceived voice quality (e.g., nasality), and vocal expressiveness (inflection or variety) (Burgoon et al., 1996; Ketrow, 1992b). Response latencies, convergence of volume, rate, inflection, and interruptions have received attention in research on dyads, but only limited focus in research on groups.

Research on dyads and individuals reveals that initiating comments, low response latency in conversation, verbal fluency, speaking at a fairly rapid rate, using a "confident" vocal tone, and greater vocal expressiveness and variety (see Burgoon et al., 1996; Ridgeway, 1987) are signs of status, competence, credibility, persuasiveness, and high task-orientation (Ketrow, 1992b). These results have been corroborated in group situations studied by Scherer (1979). Andersen (1999) speculates that these vocalic behaviors, coupled with the greater frequency and longer duration of turns for higher status group members, may be the means by which people regain the floor and talk even more.

Talkativeness is fairly well established as an important variable in studies of social influence, including leadership emergence, in groups (e.g., Morris & Hackman, 1960; Ng, Bell, & Brooke, 1993; Regula & Julian, 1973; Riecken, 1958; Rosa & Mazur, 1979; Scherer, 1979; Sorrentino & Boutellier, 1975; Stang, 1973; Stein, 1975; Stein & Heller, 1979; Zdep, 1969). Scherer (1979) claims that the research evidence shows that "participation seems to be the single most important predictor of perceived influence or perceived leadership in small group discussions" (p. 106; see also Andersen, 1999). More recently, Butler and Geis (1990) noted that male and female leaders were judged by their group members not to differ in eye contact, gaze direction, body, or body posture, although there was a $p < .05$ difference in body movement, with greater movement for male than for female leaders. Even though female leaders talked more than males, group members gave males higher rates of positive affect per minute of talking; that is, "the more male leaders talked, the more pleased responses they received" (p. 56) from group members.

One other vocal variable that has received attention is interruption behavior. Studies on dyads and, in more limited reports, groups have not found interruptions to be related to dominance perceptions or to common stereotypes related to interruptions (e.g., the belief that men interrupt women more) (Dindia,

1987). Hare and Davies (1994), however, claim that more confident persons and those unafraid of negative evaluation interrupt more. In addition, because men often possess these characteristics, they interrupt women more often in group situations. Research on dyads also indicates that people of higher status and power (typically men) interrupt more often, but an interaction with sex does not seem to have been tested in groups. Ng et al. (1993) found that turns acquired in mixed-sex groups through interruptions were associated with higher influence rankings by members, and that these interruption turns were better predictors of influence than non-interruption turns (i.e., overall talkativeness or aggregate turns). From a cross-cultural perspective, Scherer (1979) found differences for the number of interruptions between German and U.S. males in simulated juries. For U.S. male jurors, the number of interruptions correlated positively with perceived influence, but for German jurors, it was negatively correlated. German males also spoke at a higher level of pitch than did U.S. males, and perceptions of greater task ability were attributed to the deeper pitch of U.S. men. Greater pitch range (more expressive voice and varying intonation contours with a greater range) and loudness, however, tended to be associated with more influence. These results are consistent with differences noted for men and women in exhibited vocalic cues.

Convergence, the movement to match another's vocal or verbal patterns, has a robust body of research in the dyadic context. In dyads, women tend to converge to male vocalic patterns (Mulac, Studley, Wiemann, & Bradac, 1982). The tendency of regional dialectal speakers to increase their rates, for example, to converge more closely with those speaking at faster speeds, and other such accommodation patterns are well reported in the literature on dyads (see Ketrow, 1992b). No research tests of convergence or accommodation have been performed in mixed-sex groups, although Cox et al. (1991) noted that minorities tend to accommodate, or converge, to the dominant patterns in multicultural groups. This nonverbal behavior also bears further examination.

DIRECTIONS FOR RESEARCH

The literature reviewed above demonstrates that much of the territory in the nonverbal realm of group communication has been at least initially mapped; however, much remains unknown about nonverbal aspects of interaction in groups. Although inferences may be and have been drawn to the group context from research on individuals and dyads, the study of nonverbal communication in groups demands far more attention than it has received.

Several content areas hold promise for future research on nonverbal group communication. The following discussion is organized partly around some of the functional nonverbal cue areas identified earlier in the chapter. The privileging of a functional perspective runs somewhat counter to the tenor of the preceding review of the literature, which was organized primarily with respect to structural patterns, such as kinesics and proxemics, and with the functions embedded therein. Using select functions implied by the descriptive or structural cues areas as an organizing pattern, however, creates a more useful framework than does the descriptive or structural cues considered alone. Only using structural cues, such as gestures, facial expressions, and posture, limits scholars to describing their frequency or patterns of occurrence (or absence), or how differences occur under particular conditions. In contrast, using functional cue sets allows scholars to take these same descriptions and explain, for example, what a shift in physical distance as related to sex might signify. Some descriptive cues, of course, demand further attention by group researchers, and these are identified within the parameters of relevant functions. Accordingly, at least four functional areas appear to be heuristic: relational communication, emotional communication, identity management and impression formation, and interaction management. After addressing these four areas, I consider the need for context-sensitive research and some of the methodological issues that need to be resolved.

Functional Nonverbal Areas Needing Research

Relational Communication

One fruitful avenue for research concerns how relational meanings are communicated nonverbally in groups. In particular, such relational elements as liking, attraction, and involvement generally are considered to be expressed nonverbally (see Burgoon et al., 1996; Mehrabian, 1981), as well as sometimes verbally, and should have an impact on group processes and outcomes (see Keyton, Chapter 8, this volume, regarding relational communication in groups). For example, physical attributes may be measured with regard to the extent to which they evince attraction; affiliation and involvement may be established by particular nonverbal immediacy cues, including smiling, forward leans, and head nods. The impact of greater expression of immediacy or postural mirroring on group outcomes might be greater concordance, coordination, or cohesiveness; in instances in which fewer of these nonverbal cues are present, or absent, relevant outcomes may be lesser agreement among group members or lower member satisfaction and commitment. The extant literature also demonstrates that influence, dominance, and control, as indicated by nonverbal behavior, seem related to perceptions of member status, power, and leadership. Programmatic investigation of unexplored or underexplored nonverbal cues associated with relational communication in groups, thus, is a promising avenue for research.

Emotional Communication

Emotional or affective communication undoubtedly is expressed via nonverbal behavior and potentially has important effects on group processes and outcomes. For example, comfort and arousal levels are exhibited by such nonverbal cues as relative rigidity or relaxation, posture, seating or standing positions, body orientations, and neutrality or expressiveness of facial affect expressions, among others. These behaviors, in turn, may signal various stages of group development, as Mabry (1989) has suggested, as well as other processes, and potentially may lead to particular outcomes. B. L. Smith (1993), for example, found that problem-solving groups in which members displayed significant nonverbal (and verbal) behavior discounting others (e.g., facial expressions of disgust, like rolling one's eyes) produced significantly fewer ideas and showed significantly lower emotional responses than did control groups in which no discounting occurred. Such nonverbal behaviors may have important effects on such phenomena as group cohesiveness, conflict management in groups, or even message acceptance by members.

There is fairly solid evidence concerning seating behavior as an important dimension of spatial ecology; however, we need more rigorous testing of how other variables, such as sex/gender, race, ethnicity, and culture, might affect seating arrangements and, subsequently, such matters as members' arousal or involvement. Because of the limited evidence that exists concerning people's emotional life in groups, the study of emotional communication is a very rich area for those interested in nonverbal communication in groups.

Identity Management and Impression Formation

Group members possess physical characteristics and exhibit kinesic displays that establish a perceptual schema of identity for those who interact with them and, thus, affect how impressions are formed and managed. Regardless of whether individuals are conscious of their own or others' physical attributes, such as age or race, the research reviewed in this chapter illustrates that group members' sex/gender, racial, ethnic, and cultural characteristics affect how various nonverbal cues are exhibited and may influence several interactional processes and outcomes. Dominance, for example, may be expressed differently nonverbally depending on one's sex/gender or cultural origin, and members may react differently to group leaders as a result of these nonverbal behavioral markers.

One question that needs to be answered is what nonverbal cues relate to identity presentation and management in groups and in what combinations they are most predictive of performance in task groups. One specific direction for identity presentation and management is to explore how appearance and kinesic cues relate to sex/gender, race/ethnicity, or age in relation to social influence, versus the discounting of such physical characteristics or kinesic cues. We need to know more about how these and other diffuse status cues can be offset by other nonverbal (or verbal) behaviors. Limited evidence indicates that people attribute different qualities, such as wisdom or status, based on age, as well as sex/gender. Kinesic cues signifying gender (not sex, necessarily) have been neither well established nor examined in terms of how they influence group interactional processes and outcomes.

Surprisingly, no research has explored physical attractiveness per se as a variable influencing group outcomes. As a dependent variable, Curran and Loganbill (1983) claim that it is a key feature associated with group members' ability to influence other members, and this is particularly true for group leaders. Members' ratings of a leader's attractiveness (both physical and social), however, have been reported to be unaffected by displays of nonverbal behaviors (Curran & Loganbill, 1983). No research was found that examined the relative attractiveness of group members. Key questions about perceived attractiveness as a component of identity presentation and management center on how it influences group processes and outcomes. To illustrate, a member perceived as attractive may receive more nonverbal attention cues than others, which ultimately could lead to greater perceived influence.

Although deceptive and mixed messages usually are considered to serve a separate function from impression presentation and management, research on dyads points to how certain nonverbal presentations are more or less believable (Andersen, 1999; Burgoon et al., 1996). Furthermore, the act of presenting a lie, and the nonverbal cues that this entails, or giving contradictory verbal and nonverbal cues is indicative that an individual intends to present a particular kind of identity.

Judgments of others' identities usually require an ability to discern the nonverbal cues being presented. Such judgment relates to identity presentation and management in that individuals wish or intend to be perceived in particular ways. One area requiring accurate decoding, as just mentioned, is that of deception (as well as encoding by the liar). When a group member deliberately lies, whether spontaneously or in a planned way, only evidence derived from dyads exists to suggest whether group members may accurately present or discern deceptive nonverbal cues. For example, Keating and Heltman (1994) found that children and adults who were leaders deceived differently with nonverbal cues and that (as might be expected) adults were better at deceiving. Research on nonverbal encoding and decoding ability in dyads generally indicates that females have more ability than males (Ambady, Hallahan, & Rosenthal, 1995; Burgoon et al., 1996), but the differences appear to depend on such factors as whether a previous relationship among interactants is present. Ambady et al. (1995) reported that zero-acquaintance members in groups were not as accurate in judging such personality traits as expressiveness and sociability as those who had developed a history of working together. Additionally, the more accurate judges "tended to be less sociable and performed better on tests of [nonverbal] decoding accuracy" (p. 519). Other factors, like anxiety or communication apprehension, also have been shown in dyads to decrease ability to accurately decode nonverbal cues (Schroeder & Ketrow, 1997). More information is required about how nonverbal cues are used to manage identity and form impressions, especially regarding decoding and encoding accuracy for group members.

Interaction Management

Nonverbal cues serving to manage interaction are certainly important to study. Such cues, for example, are used to express dominance and subordination of, as well as cooperation and competition with, others during interaction. Interaction management and group decisional outcomes may be linked by such nonverbal cues as who initiates discussion, who interrupts and controls the floor, or how members are nonverbally recognized or reacted to via facial and other kinesic indicators of affect. For example, in dyads, eye contact and backchannel responses (vocalic or kinesic responses, such as "Uh, huh," coupled with head nodding, intended to indicate interest, understanding, or turn continuation) differ depending on one's sex/gender, race, or ethnic origin (see Burgoon et al., 1996). "Yeah, yeah" from a female as a male dominates the floor in a meeting may mean to her that she is listening and following his discourse, and may be intended to prompt him to continue; however, he may interpret this backchanneling cue as indicating acceptance of his ideas. Such confusion in the meaning and function of this and other cues might lead to later problems in reaching agreement and affect each member's level of satisfaction or dissatisfaction with the interaction, as well as with the other members of a group.

Process patterns in groups also are affected by nonverbal behaviors. It might be the case that gaze aversion and some other postural cues or shifts accompany group member exhibitions of silence and may be part of the process that results in groupthink (Janis, 1972, 1982) or the so-called "Abilene effect" (Harvey, 1974), an implicit acquiescence to a group norm or action to which members actually object. For example, increasing group pressure to conform is applied to opinion deviates (see Keyton, chapter 8, this volume), but how that occurs nonverbally is not well understood. One could speculate that, kinesi-

cally, members' eyes, faces, and bodies orient toward a deviant and that they engage in more forward leans, along with an increased tempo of exchange. Limited research is also available on the practice of silence by group members. General silences by all members are related to process phases in therapy groups (Lewis, 1977), but more investigation is needed regarding what silence indicates and how it functions in other types of groups.

Chronemic cues also contribute to the management of interaction in groups. Frequently, group members complain about those who dominate (usually behind the dominator's back) and meetings that run overly long or do not get to important agenda items because too much time was spent on something less consequential. Chronemic variables of punctuality (arriving at group meetings or events "on time" versus late or early arrivals), length of discussions (total meeting length, whether social or task group), and timing (such as delay of response or response latencies) should be examined for their influence on group processes and outcomes.

Limited attention has been paid to how norms and expectations concerning seating, or how shifts in group composition (such as via the loss of members or assimilation of new members), affect seating choices, territoriality, and space/proxemics, as well as how norms about such nonverbal behavior integrate with ongoing verbal interaction or are related to various group outcomes. Arrow and McGrath (1993) investigated how groups lose and assimilate, or simply rotate, members, but neglected to develop propositions relative to such nonverbal cues as proxemics and territory or interruptions. What happens when members are seated in chairs that swivel or are of an unequal plane, or when one member turns her or his back on another member? Is that seen as a slight, an indication of nonreceptivity or nonacceptance of the other, or as the completion of a task or interaction? (Note that although the shunned member may be silenced, which is part of interaction management, consider that these actions also may be part of identity management.) We may assume that group members typically are seated, but consider the effects of a facilitator who stands. Another agenda item for future research, then, is closer examination of interaction management processes with respect to seating arrangements and preferences.

Some related correlates and effects of vocalics are well known, as well as what occurs when vocalics cross over to chronemics; faster rate, greater talkativeness, and initiation are tied to perceptions of member influence and dominance. Little is known, however, about the tempo of a group's interactions, the duration of responses, response latencies, silences, and turn-taking. More evidence is needed concerning how floor dominance, including interruptions or talkativeness, may promote or inhibit perceived or actual group progress. If one member interrupts or is more vocally productive than other members, it is possible that she or he may be perceived as competitive and not contributing effectiveness to the group. Other nonverbal or verbal cues may offset such a perception. Descriptive studies are needed to map out this area.

If there is a psychological construct of mental space and territory analogous to actual usage or preference for physical personal space, territory, and density/crowdedness, no one seems to have related the observable to the imagined or indicated how such a perception as mental crowdedness (an overly dense nimbus) relates to actual group performance. Instructive is Benford, Bullock, Cook, and Harvey's (1993) spatial model, based on two key concepts: focus, representing the subspace in which an individual focuses her or his attention, and nimbus, "a subspace within which a person projects their [sic] presence" (p. 217). Such issues are increasingly relevant as reliance on technology grows, and because research shows that members of computer-mediated groups approximate in many ways FtF groups in their relational development and interaction. For example, how does asynchronicity in CMC groups compare to the kind of synchronous turn-taking and response latencies present in FtF groups? Other studies comparing FtF with CMC groups indicate

that reliance on social presence is critical for any group, particularly for resolving conflict or larger complex issues in groups (Rogers, 1986; Short et al., 1976; E. Williams, 1977; F. Williams, 1987; F. Williams & Rice, 1983). Thus, conceptualization of a mental nonverbal space, the study of the impact of technology on inferences about members' relationships, and more research on interaction patterns of CMC are imperative.

Context-Sensitive Research

The context within which group members interact has a potentially significant impact on the expression and interpretation of their nonverbal behavior. At the macrolevel, the context can be differentiated with regard to task versus social groups (in this volume, see, respectively, Hirokawa & Salazar [Chapter 7] and Keyton [Chapter 8]). Within the task-group context, which has been the central focus of the literature reviewed in this chapter, a number of specific contexts have not been studied but deserve consideration because of the potential important effects associated with nonverbal behaviors. For example, if a mission team is unaware that high density (and, thus, we suppose, high crowdedness levels) relates to ineffective decisions because of its effects on intensifying members' arousal levels, members may not take necessary steps to compensate. Several studies identify the neglect of and the need for psychological research concerning space labs and for proposed space-station projects (see A. A. Harrison, Clearwater, & McKay, 1989; Nicholas, 1989; Stewart, 1988; Taylor, 1989). Military and federal agencies also presumably would be interested in this research, as it applies to such confined group contexts as submarines, tanks, battleships, and aircraft carriers, as well as isolated research posts, such as Arctic stations and astronomical, biological, and geological observatories.

The investigation of nonverbal cues in social groups is also significant and may reveal processes and outcomes different from those of task groups. Many social groups could be examined, including gangs; "street-corner" groups, such as the ones that still "hang" in locations like Providence, Rhode Island's predominantly Italian Federal Hill; groups in pubs, such as those found in Ireland, Great Britain, and Scotland, or in local bars in the United States; 12-step or other social support/self-help groups; and athletic teams, including Little League and other types of "play" groups.

Researchers need to know, in particular, whether the same nonverbal cues or patterns that correlate with such perceptions as that of social influence or affiliation in task groups are obtained as well in social groups. For example, nonverbal relational communication and its effects undoubtedly differ for therapeutic or social support groups vis-à-vis task groups; displays of nonverbal anger, for example, may be detrimental to the work of a task group but beneficial to that of a social support group (see Cline, Chapter 19, this volume, on communication in social support/self-help groups).

Absent from the extant research, and relevant to different group contexts, has been any real attention to haptics, which has been demonstrated in research on individuals and dyads to have powerful effects on people's intellectual development and physical and emotional health, as well as the development of relationships. Touch is one of the more salient indicators of affect and social support, as well as dominance and control. We need to know the effect of touching people in groups (or lack thereof). Norms in many task groups seem to preclude touching, but social support and other relationally oriented groups have different standards and expectations. For example, a hug often is acceptable for men on the playing field in sports, but not in the workplace. The area of haptics and its relevant social functions in groups needs at least descriptive study.

Methodological Issues

Attention must be given to some important methodological issues that affect research on nonverbal communication in groups, because the group context poses some serious challenges to those who wish to study nonverbal behavior. First, some nonverbal features and effects are endemic to the group context, and researchers need to identify these. Once this objective has been reached, a significant barrier remains: the complex nature of nonverbal behavior in groups, not to mention the complexity of the group context itself. The study of nonverbal behaviors, like that of verbal behaviors, in dyads is much easier than examining nonverbal behaviors in a group because of the sheer number of people involved. An example is that of seating arrangements and their relationship to emergent leadership (see Pavitt, Chapter 12, this volume).

A second related methodological issue is the assumption that nonverbal cues are processed as a gestalt, a synergistic effect of the combination of many nonverbal cues, which presents several challenges. Deconstructing a gestalt is formidable. One must identify which of the myriad cues are salient and what impact individual cues or combinations of cues have in contrast to the aggregate effect of all the cues taken together. For example, does eye contact (or lack thereof) plus smiling outweigh forward leans and head nodding in demonstrating message receptiveness? Mabry (1989) provided good descriptions of nonverbal cue frequencies but failed to note how the group members studied were seated in relation to one another. For example, how would the nonverbal cues of *arms on lap, palms up* or *arms on lap, palms down* have been measured or altered in occurrence if these individuals were seated at a table or in a circle with no barriers? Some guidance on this point may be derived from nonverbal studies of dyads, especially those by Burgoon (1978) and her colleagues (Burgoon & Aho, 1982; Burgoon, Dillman, et al., 1993; Burgoon et al., 1995) on expectancy violation in conversational distance; others employing an immediacy construct (e.g., Ketrow, 1991a); cues related to relational messages (Burgoon, Buller, Hale, & deTurck, 1984); and Mabry's (1989) examination of nonverbal aspects of group development (although he did not examine either combinations of cues or sequences of occurrence). Some of these studies utilize complex designs that attempt to test for the gestalt effect of nonverbal cues in groups. Observing or sampling the nonverbal cues of one person in a group may be similarly fruitless to observing only one nonverbal cue, because individuals in groups coact. Thus, all group members must be observed as a gestalt as well.

In making decisions about which particular nonverbal cues or combinations to study, it may be helpful, as I have argued in this chapter, to assume a functional approach. Such an approach suggests the need for descriptive attempts to catalog appropriate nonverbal cues and combinations and the various functions they typically serve. Consider one illustration of conversation management in groups via nonverbal cues. Topic change or topic exhaustion may be signaled less by sentence and word shifts than by such nonverbal cues as restlessness (high activity level of random movement and posture, such as fidgeting), fewer involvement cues (such as leaning away from the group), or inattentiveness (signaled, for example, by less eye contact).

Third, in terms of experimental studies that manipulate variables and observe the effects, complex nonverbal combinations are difficult to manipulate, such as the many nonverbal cues that signal immediacy versus singular cues of direct eye contact or smiling only. Investigators also need to conduct co-verbal studies of concomitant language and nonverbal aspects in groups because of the evidence cited earlier indicating nonverbal channel dominance and differences (e.g., Walker & Trimboli, 1989). Commonly, nonverbal cues aid in making sense of verbal statements, but more crucially, they provide the material for inferences about emotions and relationships that may not be apparent in the verbal statements alone.

A fourth methodological issue has to do with valence, that is, whether one combines more positive or "immediate" nonverbal cues (or negative ones, such as frowns and looking away) in terms of linear combinations or whether one should simply subtract the posi-

tive from the more negatively perceived cues. That is, there may be a synergistic effect resulting from the combination of nonverbal cues. Perceived valence (positive or negative) and relative weights of nonverbal cues are also probably influential. A methodological issue related to valence is that of the presence or absence of nonverbal cues. A fair amount of eye contact versus no eye contact leads to very different interpretations by observers or participants.

One more methodological problem is related to the possibility that one cue or different combinations may be interpreted in several ways and, thereby, contribute to multi-functionality. The question, therefore, is whether and, if so, how all the nonverbal cues of interest in a particular study should be combined into an aggregate. A related concern with the validity of functional interpretations also is raised.

A sixth issue is the internal and external validity of findings extrapolated from dyads to groups. Some dyadic-level findings do not translate well to the group context. An example involving eye contact illustrates this point. Eye contact in dyads has been shown to be related to perceptions of a person's attentiveness, but in groups, one can give but fleeting eye contact to all other members at a given point in time, or one member rolling her or his eyes cannot be seen by all other members (or perhaps even by the target of her or his disdain). We also need to consider whether the patterns found to be exhibited by children or adolescents are similar to those of adults. Some research reported in this chapter indicates that children manifest nonverbal cues related to perceptions of leadership differently than do adults, particularly in terms of children discounting participation rates for perceived leadership (French & Stright, 1991). Research on dyads indicates as well that children process nonverbal cues differently than do older persons (Burgoon et al., 1996).

A seventh issue related to the context within which research takes place, as well as the group context itself, is the traditional reliance on laboratory groups. Although such work is valuable and should continue, researchers would be wise to heed Putnam and Stohl's (1990, 1994, 1996) observation that ecological validity in group research demands testing ideas in bona fide groups—those that have permeable boundaries, have shifting borders, and are interdependent with their contexts. Ketrow (1994), Walfoort and Watters (1996), and others have shown that nonverbal behavior in bona fide groups is not divorced from the context within which it is embedded. Norms of interrupting, for example, differed radically among four bona fide teams that Ketrow (1994) observed; individuals who interrupted and gained the floor in two teams were those with higher power or status positions in their organization. Walfoort and Watters (1996) found that cultural affiliation, such as being Puerto Rican or Japanese, created differences in group interactional patterns and task achievement. These case studies suggest that more research is needed to determine whether processes and outcomes observed in laboratory groups are indeed valid in bona fide groups.

Finally, examinations of changes in nonverbal cues over time also are needed. Mabry (1989) attempted to account for such changes by using longitudinal sampling and taking segments across the life span of the groups observed. One-shot sampling might be easier, but it would be preferable to engage in segmented longitudinal or continuous sampling.

CONCLUSION

This review has reaffirmed the fruitfulness of research begun decades ago on nonverbal messages in groups. Researchers, however, have barely scratched the surface of this fertile area. Several vital areas hold promise for future research, including how nonverbal aspects are associated with relational communication, emotional communication, identity management and impression formation, and interaction management processes and outcomes in groups. Researchers also need to be more sensitive to context, as well as to a number of methodological issues. An expanded understanding of group communication processes and outcomes also demands that research investigate *both* verbal and nonverbal messages as crucial components. The material reviewed herein should contribute to that end.

REFERENCES

Adams, K. A. (1980). Who has the final word? Sex, race, and dominance behavior. *Journal of Personality and Social Psychology, 38,* 1-8.

Adams, K. A. (1983). Aspects of social context as determinants of Black women's resistance to challenges. *Journal of Social Issues, 39,* 69-78.

Aiello, J. R., & Jones, S. E. (1971). Field study of the proxemic behavior of young school children in three subcultural groups. *Journal of Personality and Social Psychology, 19,* 351-356.

Alderton, S. M., & Jurma, W. E. (1980). Genderless/gender-related task leader communication and group satisfaction: A test of two hypotheses. *Southern Speech Communication Journal, 46,* 48-60.

Ambady, N., Hallahan, M., & Rosenthal, R. (1995). On judging and being judged accurately in zero-acquaintance situations. *Journal of Personality and Social Psychology, 69,* 518-529.

Andersen, P. A. (1985). Nonverbal immediacy in interpersonal communication. In A. W. Siegman & S. Feldstein (Eds.), *Multichannel integrations of nonverbal behavior* (pp. 1-36). Hillsdale, NJ: Lawrence Erlbaum.

Andersen, P. A. (1992). Nonverbal communication in the small group. In R. S. Cathcart & L. A. Samovar (Eds.), *Small group communication: A reader* (6th ed., pp. 272-286). Dubuque, IA: Wm. C. Brown.

Andersen, P. A. (1999). *Nonverbal communication.* Mountain, View, CA: Mayfield.

Andersen, P. A., & Andersen, J. F. (1984). The exchange of nonverbal immediacy: A critical review of dyadic models. *Journal of Nonverbal Behavior, 8,* 327-349.

Argyle, M., & Dean, J. (1965). Eye-contact, distance, and affiliation. *Sociometry, 28,* 289-304.

Arrow, H., & McGrath, J. E. (1993). Membership matters: How member change and continuity affect small group structure, process, and performance. *Small Group Research, 24,* 334-361.

Badzinski, D. M., & Pettus, A. B. (1994). Nonverbal involvement and sex: Effects on jury decision making. *Journal of Applied Communication Research, 22,* 309-321.

Baird, J. E., Jr. (1976). Sex differences in group communication: A review of relevant research. *Quarterly Journal of Speech, 62,* 179-192.

Baird, J. E., Jr. (1977). Some nonverbal elements of leadership emergence. *Southern Speech Communication Journal, 42,* 352-361.

Baker, P. M. (1984). Seeing is behaving: Visibility and participation in small groups. *Environment and Behavior, 16,* 159-184.

Baker, P. M., & Eaton, G. G. (1992). Seniority and age as causes of dominance in social groups: Macaques and men. *Small Group Research, 23,* 322-343.

Beebe, S., Barge, J. K., & McCormick, K. (1994, July). *The competent group communicator.* Paper presented at the Speech Communication Association Summer Conference on Performance Assessment of Speech Communication, Alexandria, VA.

Benford, S., Bullock, A., Cook, N., & Harvey, P. (1993). From rooms to cyberspace: Models of interaction in large virtual computer spaces. *Interacting With Computers, 5,* 217-237.

Birdwhistell, R. L. (1970). *Kinesics and context: Essays on body motion communication.* Philadelphia: University of Pennsylvania Press.

Blanck, P. D., & Rosenthal, R. (1992). Nonverbal behavior in the courtroom. In R. S. Feldman (Ed.), *Applications of nonverbal behavioral theories and research* (pp. 89-115). Hillsdale, NJ: Lawrence Erlbaum.

Bradley, P. H. (1980). Sex, competence, and opinion deviation: An expectation states approach. *Communication Monographs, 47,* 101-110.

Brown, V., & Geis, F. L. (1984). Turning lead into gold: Evaluations of men and women leaders and the alchemy of social consensus. *Journal of Personality and Social Psychology, 46,* 811-824.

Burgoon, J. K. (1978). A communication model of personal space violations: Explication and an initial test. *Human Communication Research, 4,* 129-142.

Burgoon, J. K. (1980). Nonverbal communication research in the 1970s: An overview. In D. Nimmo (Ed.), *Communication yearbook 4* (pp. 179-197). New Brunswick, NJ: Transaction Books.

Burgoon, J. K. (1992). Spatial relationships in small groups. In R. S. Cathcart & L. A. Samovar (Eds.), *Small group communication: A reader* (6th ed., pp. 287-300), Dubuque, IA: Wm. C. Brown.

Burgoon, J. K. (1994). Nonverbal signals. In M. L. Knapp & G. R. Miller (Eds.), *Handbook of interpersonal communication* (2nd ed., pp. 229-285). Thousand Oaks, CA: Sage.

Burgoon, J. K., & Aho, L. (1982). Three field experiments on the effects of violations of conversational distance. *Communication Monographs, 49,* 71-88.

Burgoon, J. K., Buller, D. B., Hale, J. L., & deTurck, M. A. (1984). Relational messages associated with nonverbal behaviors. *Human Communication Research, 10,* 351-378.

Burgoon, J. K., Buller, D. B., & Woodall, D. (1996). *Nonverbal communication: The unspoken dialogue* (2nd ed.). New York: McGraw-Hill.

Burgoon, J. K., & Dillman, L. (1995). Gender, immediacy, and nonverbal communication. In P. J. Kalbfleisch & M. J. Cody (Eds.), *Gender, power, and communication in human relationships* (pp. 63-81). Hillsdale, NJ: Lawrence Erlbaum.

Burgoon, J. K., Dillman, L., & Stern, L. A. (1993). Adaptation in dyadic interaction: Defining and operationalizing patterns of reciprocity and compensation. *Communication Theory, 3,* 295-316.

Burgoon, J. K., LePoire, B. A., Beutler, L. E., & Engle, D. (1993). Nonverbal indices of arousal in group psychotherapy. *Psychotherapy, 30,* 635-645.

Burgoon, J. K., Stern, L. A., & Dillman, L. (1995). *Interpersonal adaptation: Dyadic interaction patterns.* Cambridge, UK: Cambridge University Press.

Butler, D., & Geis, F. L. (1990). Nonverbal affect responses to male and female leaders: Implications for leadership evaluations. *Journal of Personality and Social Psychology, 58,* 48-59.

Cahnman, W. J. (1968). The stigma of obesity. *Sociological Quarterly, 9,* 283-299.

Canary, D. J., & Emmers-Sommer, T. M. (1997). *Sex and gender differences in personal relationships.* New York: Guilford.

Cashdan, E. (1995). Hormones, sex, and status in women. *Hormones and Behavior, 29,* 354-366.

Christensen, L. J. (1995, November). *Classroom situations which lead to student participation.* Paper presented at the annual meeting of the Speech Communication Association, San Antonio, TX.

Cox, T. H., Lobel, S. A., & McLeod, P. L. (1991). Effects of ethnic group cultural differences on cooperative and competitive behavior on a group task. *Academy of Management Journal, 34,* 827-847.

Craig, K. M., & Rand, K. A. (1998). The perceptually "privileged" group member: Consequences of solo status African Americans and Whites in task groups. *Small Group Research, 29,* 339-358.

Crocker, J., & McGraw, K. M. (1984). What's good for the goose is not good for the gander: Solo status as an obstacle to occupational achievement for males and females. *American Behavioral Scientist, 27,* 357-369.

Curran, J., & Loganbill, C. R. (1983). Factors affecting the attractiveness of a group leader. *Journal of College Student Personnel, 24,* 350-355.

Davies, M. F. (1994a). Personality and social characteristics. In A. P. Hare, H. H. Blumberg, M. F. Davies, & M. V. Kent (Eds.), *Small group research: A handbook* (pp. 41-78). Norwood, NJ: Ablex.

Davies, M. F. (1994b). The physical situation. In A. P. Hare, H. H. Blumberg, M. F. Davies, & M. V. Kent (Eds.), *Small group research: A handbook* (pp. 11-39). Norwood, NJ: Ablex.

DeJong, W., & Kleck, R. E. (1986). The social psychological effects of overweight. In C. P. Herman, M. P. Zanna, & E. T. Higgins (Eds.), *Physical appearance stigma and social behavior: The Ontario Symposium* (Vol. 3, pp. 65-86). Hillsdale, NJ: Lawrence Erlbaum.

Dindia, K. (1987). The effects of sex of subject and sex of partner on interruptions. *Human Communication Research, 13,* 345-371.

Doudin, P. A., Serpa, S. R., & deSousa-Sancho, A. C. (1990). Formations corporelles d'un groupe au cours d'une seance de therapie familiale: Analyses structurale et statistique [Body positions of a group during a family therapy session: Structural and statistical analyses]. *Schweizerische Zeitschrift fur Psychologie, 49,* 108-122.

Dovidio, J. F., Brown, C. E., Heltman, K., Ellyson, S. L., & Keating, C. F. (1988). Power displays between women and men in discussions of gender-linked tasks: A multichannel study. *Journal of Personality and Social Psychology, 55,* 580-587.

Eagley, A. H. (1970). Leadership style and role differentiation as determinants of group effectiveness. *Journal of Personality, 38,* 509-524.

Edinger, J. A., & Patterson, M. L. (1983). Nonverbal involvement and social control. *Psychological Bulletin, 93,* 30-56.

Edney, J. J., & Grundmann, M. J. (1979). Friendship, group size, and boundary size: Small group spaces. *Small Group Behavior, 10,* 124-135.

Edney, J. J., & Jordan-Edney, N. L. (1974). Territorial spacing on a beach. *Sociometry, 37,* 92-104.

Ekman, P., & Friesen, W. V. (1969). The repertoire of nonverbal behavior: Categories, origins, usage and coding. *Semiotica, 1,* 49-98.

Ellyson, S. L., & Dovidio, J. F. (1985). Power, dominance, and nonverbal behavior: Basic concepts and issues. In S. L. Ellyson & J. F. Dovidio (Eds.), *Power, dominance, and nonverbal behavior* (pp. 1-28). New York: Springer-Verlag.

Farmer, S. M., & Hyatt, C. W. (1994). Effects of task language demands and task complexity on computer-mediated work groups. *Small Group Research, 25,* 331-366.

Finholt, T., & Sproull, L. S. (1990). Electronic groups at work. *Organizational Science, 1,* 41-64.

Firestien, R. L. (1990). Effects of creative problem solving training on communication behaviors in small groups. *Small Group Research, 21,* 507-521.

Firestien, R. L., & McCowan, R. J. (1988). Creative problem solving and communication behavior in small groups. *Creativity Research Journal, 1,* 106-114.

French, D. C., & Stright, A. L. (1991). Emergent leadership in children's small groups. *Small Group Research, 22,* 187-199.

Giesen, M., & McClaren, H. A. (1976). Discussion, distance, and sex: Changes in impressions and attraction during small group interaction. *Sociometry, 39,* 60-70.

Gitter, A. G., Black, H., & Walkley, J. (1976). Nonverbal communication and the judgment of leadership. *Psychological Reports, 39,* 1117-1118.

Goktepe, J. R., & Schneier, C. E. (1988). Sex and gender effects in evaluating emergent leaders in small groups. *Sex Roles, 19,* 29-36.

Golub, S., & Canty, E. M. (1982). Sex-role expectations and the assumption of leadership by college students. *Journal of Social Psychology, 54,* 153-154.

Granstrom, K. (1986). Interactional dynamics between teenage leaders and followers in the classroom. *Journal of Social Psychology, 24,* 335-341.

Graves, L. M., & Powell, G. N. (1982). Sex differences in implicit theories of leadership: An initial investigation. *Psychological Reports, 50,* 689-690.

Greenberg, J. (1976). The role of seating position in group interaction: A review, with applications for group trainers. *Group & Organization Studies, 1,* 310-327.

Halberstadt, A. G., & Saitta, M. B. (1987). Gender, nonverbal behavior, and perceived dominance: A test of the theory. *Journal of Personality and Social Psychology, 53,* 257-272.

Hall, E. T. (1982). *The hidden dimension.* New York: Anchor Books. (Original work published 1966)

Hall, J. A. (1984). *Nonverbal sex differences: Communication accuracy and expressive style.* Baltimore: Johns Hopkins University Press.

Hare, A. P., & Davies, M. F. (1994). Social interaction. In A. P. Hare, H. H. Blumberg, M. F. Davies, & M. V. Kent (Eds.), *Small group research: A handbook* (pp. 169-193). Norwood, NJ: Ablex.

Harrison, A. A., Clearwater, Y. A., & McKay, C. P. (1989). The human experience in Antarctica: Applications to life in space. *Behavioral Science, 34,* 253-271.

Harrison, R. P., & Wiemann, J. P. (1983). The nonverbal domain: Implications for theory, research and practice. In J. M. Wiemann & R. P. Harrison (Eds.), *Nonverbal interaction* (pp. 271-285). Beverly Hills, CA: Sage.

Harvey, J. B. (1974). The Abilene paradox: The management of agreement. *Organizational Dynamics, 3,* 63-80.

Hatch, J. A. (1987). Status and social power in a kindergarten peer group. *Elementary School Journal, 88,* 79-92.

Hawkins, K. W. (1995). Effects of gender and communication content on leadership emergence in small task-oriented groups. *Small Group Research, 26,* 234-249.

Hearn, G. (1957). Leadership and the spatial factor in small groups. *Journal of Abnormal and Social Psychology, 54,* 269-272.

Hiers, J. M., & Heckel, R. V. (1977). Seating choice, leadership, and locus of control. *Journal of Social Psychology, 103,* 313-314.

Hoffman, R., & Maier, N.R.F. (1970). Sex differences, sex composition, and group problem-solving. *Journal of Abnormal and Social Psychology, 63,* 453-456.

Hold-Cavell, B. C., & Borsutzky, D. (1986). Strategies to obtain high regard: Longitudinal study of a group of preschool children. *Ethology and Sociobiology, 7,* 39-56.

Horvath, T. (1981). Physical attractiveness: The influence of selected torso parameters. *Archives of Sexual Behavior, 10,* 21-24.

Houghton Mifflin Company. (1993). *The American heritage college dictionary* (3rd ed.). Boston: Author.

Jago, A. G., & Vroom, V. H. (1982). Sex differences in the incidence and evaluation of participative leadership behavior. *Journal of Applied Psychology, 67,* 776-783.

Janis, I. L. (1972). *Victims of groupthink: A psychological study of foreign-policy decisions and fiascoes.* Boston: Houghton Mifflin.

Janis, I. L. (1982). *Groupthink: Psychological studies of policy decision and fiascoes* (2nd ed.). Boston: Houghton Mifflin.

Jasper, C. R., & Klassen, M. L. (1990). Stereotypical beliefs about appearance: Implications for retailing and consumer issues. *Perceptual and Motor Skills, 71,* 519-528.

Johnson, D. W., & Johnson, R. T. (1982). Effects of cooperative, competitive, and individualistic learning experiences on cross-ethnic interaction and friendships. *Journal of Social Psychology, 118,* 47-58.

Johnson, D. W., & Johnson, R. T. (1985). Relationships between Black and White students in intergroup cooperation and competition. *Journal of Social Psychology, 125,* 421-428.

Johnson, D. W., Johnson, R. T., & Maruyama, G. M. (1983). Interdependence and interpersonal attraction among heterogeneous and homogeneous individuals: A theoretical formulation and a meta-analysis of the research. *Review of Educational Research, 53,* 5-54.

Kalma, A. (1991). Hierarchisation and dominance assessment at first glance. *European Journal of Social Psychology, 21,* 165-181.

Kalma, A. (1992). Gazing in triads: A powerful signal in floor apportionment. *British Journal of Social Psychology, 31,* 21-39.

Kanter, R. M. (1977). Some effects of proportions on group life: Skewed sex ratios and responses to token women. *American Journal of Sociology, 82,* 465-490.

Katz, I. (1970). Experimental studies of Negro-White relationships. *Advances in Experimental Social Psychology, 5,* 71-117.

Keating, C. F., & Heltman, K. R. (1994). Dominance and deception in children and adults: Are leaders the best misleaders? *Personality and Social Psychology, 20,* 312-321.

Kelsey, B. L. (1998). The dynamics of multicultural groups: Ethnicity as a determinant of leadership. *Small Group Research, 29,* 602-623.

Kent, M. V. (1994). The presence of others. In A. P. Hare, H. H. Blumberg, M. F. Davies, & M. V. Kent (Eds.), *Small group research: A handbook* (pp. 81-105). Norwood, NJ: Ablex.

Ketrow, S. M. (1983, April). *Role specialization as a strategy for female leadership.* Paper presented at the annual meeting of the Southern Speech Communication Association, Orlando, FL.

Ketrow, S. M. (1991a). Nonverbal communication and customer satisfaction in computer-assisted transactions. *Management Communication Quarterly, 5,* 192-219.

Ketrow, S. M. (1991b). Role specialization and perceptions of leadership. *Small Group Research, 22,* 492-514.

Ketrow, S. M. (1992a, November). *Nonverbal correlates of leadership and organizational outcomes.* Paper presented at the annual meeting of the Speech Communication Association, Chicago.

Ketrow, S. M. (1992b). Vocal attributes of a telemarketer and persuasiveness: A review. *Journal of Direct Marketing, 4,* 7-21.

Ketrow, S. M. (1993). *Participation and disclosure in a twelve-step Alcoholics Anonymous group.* Unpublished manuscript, University of Rhode Island, Kingston.

Ketrow, S. M. (1994). *Argumentation in bona-fide groups.* Unpublished manuscript, University of Rhode Island, Kingston.

Kiesler, S., & Sproull, L. (1992). Group decision making and communication technology. *Organizational Behavior and Human Decision Process, 52,* 96-123.

Kirchmeyer, C. (1993). Multicultural task groups: An account of the low contribution level of minorities. *Small Group Research, 24,* 127-148.

Kirchmeyer, C., & Cohen, A. (1992). Multicultural groups: Their performance and reactions with constructive conflict. *Group and Organization Management, 17,* 153-170.

Kleck, R. E., & DeJong, W. (1983). Physical disability, physical attractiveness, and social outcomes in children's small groups. *Rehabilitation Psychology, 28,* 78-91.

Kleinke, C. L. (1977). Compliance to requests made by gazing and touching experimenters in field settings. *Journal of Experimental Social Psychology, 101,* 218-223.

Kolb, J. A. (1997). Are we still stereotyping leadership? A look at gender and other predictors of leader emergence. *Small Group Research, 28,* 370-393.

Koneya, M. (1977). Privacy regulation in small and large groups. *Group & Organization Studies, 2,* 324-335.

LaFrance, M. (1985). Postural mirroring and intergroup relations. *Personality and Social Psychology Bulletin, 11,* 207-217.

LaFrance, M., & Broadbent, M. (1976). Group rapport: Posture sharing as a nonverbal indicator. *Group & Organization Studies, 1,* 328-333.

Lamb, T. A. (1986). The familiarity effect in small group hierarchy research. *Journal of Social Psychology, 126,* 51-56.

Lecuyer, R. (1976). Social organization and spatial organization. *Human Relations, 29,* 1045-1060.

Lerner, R. M., Karabenick, S. A., & Meisels, M. (1975). Effects of age and sex on the development of personal space schemata toward body build. *Journal of Genetic Psychology, 127,* 91-101.

Lerner, R. M., Venning, J., & Knapp, J. R. (1975). Age and sex effects on personal space schemata toward body build in late childhood. *Developmental Psychology, 11,* 855-856.

Lewis, B. F. (1977). Group silences. *Small Group Behavior, 8,* 109-120.

Littlepage, G. E., & Silbiger, H. (1992). Recognition of expertise in decision-making groups: Effects of group size and participation patterns. *Small Group Research, 23,* 344-355.

Lockheed, M. E., & Hall, K. P. (1976). Conceptualizing sex as a status characteristic: Applications to leadership training strategies. *Journal of Social Issues, 32,* 111-124.

Lovrin, M. (1995). Interpersonal support among 8-year-old girls who have lost their parents or siblings to AIDS. *Archives of Psychiatric Nursing, 9,* 92-98.

Mabry, E. A. (1989). Developmental aspects of nonverbal behavior in small group settings. *Small Group Behavior, 20,* 190-202.

Maier, N.R.F. (1970). Male versus female discussion leaders. *Personnel Psychology, 23,* 455-471.

Major, B., & Heslin, R. (1982). Perceptions of cross-sex and same-sex nonreciprocal touch: It is better to give than receive. *Journal of Nonverbal Behavior, 6,* 148-162.

McGrath, J. E. (1984). *Groups: Interaction and performance.* Englewood Cliffs, NJ: Prentice Hall.

Mehrabian, A. (1969). Some referents and measures of nonverbal behavior. *Behavior Research Methods and Instrumentation, 1,* 203-207.

Mehrabian, A. (1981). *Silent messages: Implicit communication of emotions and attitudes* (2nd ed.). Belmont, CA: Wadsworth.

Mehrabian, A., & Diamond, S. G. (1971). Seating arrangement and conversation. *Sociometry, 34,* 281-289.

Michelini, R. L., Passalacqua, R., & Cusimano, J. (1976). Effects of seating arrangement on group participation. *Journal of Social Psychology, 99,* 179-186.

Moore, H. A., & Porter, N. K. (1988). Leadership and nonverbal behaviors of Hispanic females across school equity environments. *Journal of Women Quarterly, 12,* 147-163.

Morris, C. G., & Hackman, J. R. (1960). Behavioral correlates of perceived leadership. *Journal of Personality and Social Psychology, 13,* 350-361.

Mulac, A., Studley, L. B., Wiemann, J. M., & Bradac, J. J. (1982). Male and female gaze in same-sex and mixed-sex dyads. *Human Communication Research, 13,* 323-343.

Mullen, B. (1991). Group composition, salience, and cognitive representations: The phenomenology of being in a group. *Journal of Experimental Social Psychology, 27,* 297-323.

Ng, S. K., Bell, D., & Brooke, M. (1993). Gaining turns and achieving high influence ranking in small conversational groups. *British Journal of Social Psychology, 32,* 265-275.

Nicholas, J. M. (1989). Interpersonal and group-behavior skills training for crews on space stations. *Aviation, Space, and Environmental Medicine, 60,* 603-608.

Offermann, L. R. (1986). Visibility and evaluation of female and male leaders. *Sex Roles, 14,* 533-543.

Patterson, M. L. (1976). An arousal model of interpersonal intimacy. *Psychological Review, 83,* 235-245.

Patterson, M. L. (1982). A sequential functional model of nonverbal exchange. *Psychological Review, 89,* 231-249.

Patterson, M. L., & Schaeffer, R. E. (1977). Effects of size and sex composition on interaction distance, participation, and satisfaction in small groups. *Small Group Behavior, 8,* 433-442.

Paulsell, S., & Goldman, M. (1984). The effect of touching different body areas on prosocial behavior. *Journal of Social Psychology, 122,* 269-273.

Pedersen, D. M. (1977). Factors affecting personal space toward a group. *Perceptual and Motor Skills, 45,* 735-743.

Porter, N., Geis, F. L., & Jennings-Walstead, J. (1983). Are women invisible as leaders? *Sex Roles, 9,* 1035-1049.

Propp, K. M. (1995). An experimental examination of biological sex as a status cue in decision-making groups and its influence on information use. *Small Group Research, 26,* 451-474.

Putnam, L. L., & Stohl, C. (1990). Bona fide groups: A reconceptualization of groups in context. *Communication Studies, 41,* 248-265.

Putnam, L. L., & Stohl, C. (1994). Group communication in context: Implications for the study of bona fide groups. In L. R. Frey (Ed.), *Group communication in context: Studies of natural groups* (pp. 284-292). Hillsdale, NJ: Lawrence Erlbaum.

Putnam, L. L., & Stohl, C. (1996). Bona fide groups: An alternative perspective for communication and small group decision making. In R. Y. Hirokawa & M. S. Poole (Eds.), *Communication and group decision making* (2nd ed., pp. 147-178). Thousand Oaks, CA: Sage.

Rao, V. S. (1995). Effects of teleconferencing technologies: An exploration of comprehension, feedback, satisfaction and role-related differences. *Group Decision and Negotiation, 4,* 251-272.

Regula, R. C., & Julian, J. W. (1973). The impact of quality and frequency of task contribution on perceived ability. *Journal of Social Psychology, 89,* 115-122.

Remland, M. S. (1984). Leadership impressions and nonverbal communication in a superior-subordinate interaction. *Communication Quarterly, 32,* 41-48.

Ridgeway, C. L. (1987). Nonverbal behavior, dominance, and the basis of status in task groups. *American Sociological Review, 52,* 683-694.

Riecken, H. W. (1958). The effect of talkativeness on ability to influence group solutions of problems. *Sociometry, 21,* 309-321.

Rogers, E. M. (1986). *Communication technology: The new media in society.* New York: Free Press.

Rosa, E., & Mazur, A. (1979). Incipient status in small groups. *Social Forces, 58,* 18-37.

Ruhe, J. A., & Eatman, J. (1977). Effects of racial composition on small work groups. *Small Group Behavior, 8,* 479-486.

Ryen, A. H., & Kahn, A. (1975). Effects of intergroup orientation on group attitudes and proxemic behavior. *Journal of Personality and Social Psychology, 31,* 302-310.

Savin-Williams, R. C. (1977). Dominance in a human adolescent group. *Animal Behavior, 25,* 400-406.

Scherer, K. R. (1979). Voice and speech correlates of perceived social influence in simulated juries. In H. Giles & R. N. St. Clair (Eds.), *Language and social psychology* (pp. 88-120). Baltimore: University Park Press.

Schofield, J. W., & Sagar, H. A. (1977). Peer interaction patterns in an integrated middle school. *Sociometry, 40,* 130-138.

Schroeder, J., & Ketrow, S. M. (1997). Social anxiety and performance in an interpersonal perception task. *Psychological Bulletin, 81,* 991-996.

Schuler, H., & Peltzer, U. (1978). Friendly versus unfriendly nonverbal behavior: The effects on partner's decision-making preferences. In H. Brandstätter, J. H. Davis, & H. Schuler (Eds.), *Dynamics of group decisions* (pp. 113-131). Beverly Hills, CA: Sage.

Schwartz, B., Tesser, A., & Powell, E. (1982). Dominance cues in nonverbal behavior. *Social Psychology Quarterly, 45,* 114-120.

Seta, J. J., Paulus, P. B., & Schkade, J. K. (1976). Effects of group size and proximity under cooperative and competitive conditions. *Journal of Personality and Social Psychology, 34,* 47-53.

Shaw, M. E. (1981). *Group dynamics: The psychology of small group behavior* (3rd ed.). New York: McGraw-Hill.

Short, J. E., Williams, E., & Christie, B. (1976). *The social psychology of telecommunications.* New York: John Wiley.

Smith, B. L. (1993). Interpersonal behaviors that damage the productivity of creative problem-solving groups. *Journal of Creative Behavior, 27,* 171-187.

Smith, H. W. (1981). Territorial spacing on a beach revisited: A cross-national exploration. *Social Psychology Quarterly, 44,* 132-137.

Sommer, R. (1969). *Personal space: The behavioral basis of design.* Englewood Cliffs, NJ: Prentice Hall.

Sorrentino, R. M., & Boutellier, R. G. (1975). The effect of quantity and quality of verbal interaction on ratings of leadership ability. *Journal of Experimental Social Psychology, 11,* 403-411.

Stang, D. G. (1973). Effect of interaction rate on ratings of leadership and liking. *Journal of Personality and Social Psychology, 27,* 405-408.

Stein, R. T. (1975). Identifying emergent leaders from verbal and nonverbal communications. *Journal of Personality and Social Psychology, 32,* 125-135.

Stein, R. T., & Heller, T. (1979). An empirical analysis of the correlations between leadership status and participation rates reported in the literature. *Journal of Personality and Social Psychology, 37,* 1993-2002.

Steinzor, B. (1950). The spatial factor in face-to-face discussion groups. *Journal of Abnormal and Social Psychology, 45,* 552-555.

Stewart, R. A. (1988). Habitability and behavioral issues of space flight. *Small Group Behavior, 19,* 434-451.

Strodtbeck, F. L., & Hook, L. H. (1961). The social dimensions of a 12-man jury table. *Sociometry, 24,* 397-415.

Suzuki, Y. (1986). A study in seat-taking in meeting situations: Territorial maintenance and status in group. *Japanese Journal of Psychology, 57,* 83-86.

Taylor, A. J. (1989). Behavioural science and outer space research. *Aviation, Space, and Environmental Medicine, 60,* 815-816.

Valacich, J. S., George, J. F., Nunamaker, J. F., Jr., & Vogel, D. R. (1994). Physical proximity effects on computer-mediated group idea generation. *Small Group Research, 25,* 83-104.

Walfoort, S., & Watters, K. (1996, November). *Comparative small group culture analysis of communication issues.* Paper presented at the annual meeting of the Speech Communication Association, San Diego, CA.

Walker, D. N. (1975). A dyadic interaction model for nonverbal touching behavior in encounter groups. *Small Group Behavior, 6,* 308-324.

Walker, M. B., & Trimboli, A. (1989). Communicating affect: The role of verbal and nonverbal content. *Journal of Language and Social Psychology, 8,* 229-248.

Walther, J. B., & Burgoon, J. K. (1992). Relational communication in computer-mediated interaction. *Human Communication Research, 19,* 50-88.

Weisfeld, G. E., Bloch, S. A., & Ivers, J. W. (1984). Possible determinants of social dominance among adolescent girls. *Journal of Genetic Psychology, 144,* 115-129.

Willard, D., & Strodtbeck, F. L. (1972). Latency of verbal response and participation in small groups. *Sociometry, 35,* 161-175.

Williams, E. (1977). Experimental comparison of face-to-face and mediated communications: A review. *Psychological Bulletin, 61,* 963-976.

Williams, F. (1987). *Technology and communication behavior.* Belmont, CA: Wadsworth.

Williams, F., & Rice, R. E. (1983). Communication research and the new media technologies. In R. N. Bostrom (Ed.), *Communication yearbook 7* (pp. 200-224). Beverly Hills, CA: Sage.

Willis, F. N., & Hamm, H. K. (1980). The use of interpersonal touch in securing compliance. *Journal of Nonverbal Behavior, 5,* 49-55.

Wood, W. (1987). Meta-analytic review of sex differences in group performance. *Psychological Bulletin, 102,* 53-71.

Zajonc, R. B. (1965). Social facilitation. *Science, 149,* 269-274.

Zdep, S. M. (1969). Intragroup reinforcement and its effects on leadership behavior. *Organizational Behavior and Human Performance, 4,* 284-298.

11

Influence Processes in Group Interaction

RENÉE A. MEYERS
University of Wisconsin–Milwaukee

DALE E. BRASHERS
University of Illinois Urbana–Champaign

More than 40 years ago, Asch (1951, 1956) discovered how readily group members can be influenced by fellow confederates who supply wrong answers to obvious questions. These studies, and others like them on cohesiveness (Back, 1951) and social comparison (Festinger, 1950, 1954), provided the foundation for much theorizing about, and numerous investigations of, influence processes in small groups. More recently, the study of group influence has broadened to include a variety of contexts, including juries (Badzinski & Pettus; 1994; Barge, Schlueter, & Pritchard, 1989), health care groups (Adelman & Frey, 1994, 1997; Berteotti & Seibold, 1994; Frey, Adelman, & Query, 1996; Frey, Query, Flint, & Adelman, 1998), political groups (Ball, 1994; Barge & Keyton, 1994; Brock & Howell, 1994), computer-mediated groups (Brashers, Adkins, & Meyers, 1994; Brashers, Adkins, Meyers, & Mittleman, 1995), and organizational work groups (Barker, Melville, & Pacanowsky, 1993; Barker & Tompkins, 1994), among others. Recent reviews of group research in

management (Bettenhausen, 1991), psychology (Levine & Moreland, 1990), and communication (Cragan & Wright, 1990) all point to the prominence of group influence as an important topic of study.

Our reading of past research in this domain suggests some shared defining characteristics that serve as boundary conditions for the review presented in this chapter. First, most investigations have been conducted on *decision-making* groups, a focus characteristic of much research on group communication (see Frey, 1994a, 1996; Scheerhorn, Geist, & Teboul, 1994; Sykes, 1990). Second, researchers have conceived of social influence as a *verbal* activity. Although some scholars in this domain have not actually studied influence as verbal communication (e.g., they have focused on cognitive processes or written arguments), they typically have conceived of it in that way. Nonverbal communication is also certainly important to the influence process (see Ketrow, Chapter 10, this volume); however, it plays a lesser role in this review. Third, group researchers have studied influence from

Message Levels

Message Production Sites	Valence	Argument	Conflict Communication Strategies
Individual	Cell 1 Social Comparison Theory (SCT)	Cell 4 Persuasive Arguments Theory (PAT)	Cell 7 Conflict Styles
Subgroup	Cell 2 Distributed Valence Model (DVM) Majority/Minority Influence	Cell 5 Tag-team Argument Structured Argument: Devil's Advocacy Dialectical Inquiry	Cell 8 Coalitions
Group/intergroup	Cell 3 Group Valence Model (GVM)	Cell 6 Conversational Argument	Cell 9 Bargaining/Negotiation In-group/Out-group

Figure 11.1. Organizing Framework for Studying Group Influence

three *source production sites:* individual influence, subgroup influence, and group/intergroup influence. For example, social psychological research has focused most often on influence at the individual level, research on majority/minority influence has been concerned with the role of the subgroup, and research on bargaining and negotiation has concentrated on groups seeking to influence other groups. Finally, scholars have viewed the primary goal of social influence as *instrumental*—inducing or persuading another to comply with one's suggestions, proposals, or recommendations (see Seibold, Cantrill, & Meyers, 1994). Although other types of goals, such as relational and identity goals (see R. A. Clark, 1984; R. A. Clark & Delia, 1979; Tracy, 1984; Tracy & Moran, 1983), are considered important to influence processes in groups, their specific role has been investigated less often.

In the first part of this chapter, we use these four defining characteristics to frame a review of relevant research on group influence processes. Because we cannot review all the scholarship on group influence here, we examine some of the most prominent theories, models,

and research programs. We recognize that, in making such choices, we exclude many important and deserving investigative endeavors; nevertheless, we believe this review highlights some of the most influential scholarship concerning conceptions of, and research on, group influence. In the second part of this chapter, we move from a historical focus to future directions in group influence research. We provide an overview of some recent developments in the study of group influence and speculate on potentially fruitful avenues for continued research in this domain.

AN ORGANIZING FRAMEWORK FOR STUDYING GROUP INFLUENCE

Drawing on the four defining characteristics of group influence research outlined above, we propose an organizing grid (see Figure 11.1). On the surface, this figure categorizes research on group influence primarily according to its message level and message source production, but it is actually undergirded by all four of the characteristics of group influence mentioned previously. First, most of the research on influence we review has been conducted on decision-making groups versus relationally oriented groups (such as support groups, friendship groups, and families). Because influence is an important part of all groups, however, not just those making decisions (see Frey, 1994b, 1995, in press, for some studies of influence in nondecision-making groups), we discuss influence processes in these other types of groups in the final part of the chapter.

Second, influence typically is conceived as a verbal activity that is manifested on three message levels (see Poole, Seibold, & McPhee, 1985; Seibold, Poole, & McPhee, 1980). *Valence,* the most basic level of verbal influence messages, indicates the degree of positive or negative sentiment for or against a preferred option. Valence statements reflect group members' preferences (e.g., "I think option B is our best bet"). *Argument,* a second-level verbal influence message, adds depth to valenced messages by offering reasons for, or evidence against, a preferred option. These arguments supply rational substantiation for group members' personal valenced leanings, involving attempts to move the group toward convergence on a final preferred choice (e.g., "Option B is the best choice because it is most cost-effective"). *Conflict communication strategies,* the most complex message type, are accumulations of valenced messages, arguments, and other influence tactics (e.g., threats, personal attacks, and promises, among other tactics) that result in broader, more encompassing persuasive endeavors, such as conflict, coalition formation, bargaining, and negotiation.

Third, the framework is based on the assumption that influence is generated at one of the three production sites identified previously: the individual, subgroup, or group/intergroup site. Finally, we are concerned primarily with group influence that has as its primary goal *instrumental* ends. The decision to limit discussion to instrumental goals stems from two premises. First, a primary focus on decision-making groups in this domain makes attention to instrumental or task goals central. Second, little research to date has systematically addressed the role of other types of goals in influence attempts.

In the next section, we review exemplars of group influence theory and research for each cell of the grid and evaluate them for their contribution to our collective knowledge about influence processes in groups. It is important to keep in mind that these cells are not mutually exclusive and that cross-linkages between and among cells do occur. For example, majority/minority influence has been investigated at both the valence and, more recently, argument message levels. Similarly, bargaining tactics might occur between or among subgroups or groups. Moreover, in most cases, the pattern of results across rows and columns tends to be complementary (rather than contradictory), which further suggests the interdependent nature of these message levels and production sites.

OVERVIEW OF THEORIES, MODELS, AND RESEARCH PROGRAMS

Cell 1: Valence Message Level, Individual Production

One of the most extensively tested theories of social influence conceived at the valence message level/individual production site is Social Comparison Theory (SCT) (see Baron & Roper, 1976; Goethals & Zanna, 1979; Myers, 1982; Myers, Bruggink, Kersting, & Schlosser, 1980; Sanders & Baron, 1977). The theory was designed to explain polarization (i.e., the tendency for a group to select a more extreme solution after interacting than the average group members' prediscussion preference). Proponents of SCT assert that prior to group discussion, individuals guess where others might stand on an issue (members' valences) and then choose an initial decision that reflects their perceptions of that group position. The main function of group discussion is to allow members to reveal their valences toward the decision choices so that comparisons can be made among members. It is during the comparison process that social influence occurs, and the result is that some members may change their opinions.

Although this theory conceives of influence as an output of members' valenced opinion statements, researchers typically do not study actual communication. Instead, individual group members estimate other members' responses prior to discussion, or they receive information about others' prediscussion preferences or the group norm (the average or median of individuals' preferences) and then make their final decision choice (see Propp, Chapter 9, this volume).

Although there is much scholarly debate over whether information about others' choices alone is sufficient to produce influence (e.g., see Sanders & Baron, 1977; Vinokur, 1971), Social Comparison Theory persists. In most current theorizing, SCT is paired with another theory, typically Persuasive Arguments Theory (PAT; see below), or is subsumed within a more general theory, such as Social Identity Theory, which explains social influence in terms of the processes whereby informational content (see PAT) becomes socially validated (see SCT) (see Mackie & Cooper, 1984; Turner, 1985; Turner & Oakes, 1986). As Latane and Liu (1996) recently noted, however, both social comparison processes and persuasive argumentation probably play a role in the influence process:

> For many aspects of our lives, social comparison may be more influential than conversation, and it does not take much discussion with the other people in a classical music hall to realize that our Bermuda shorts are out of place. For cognitively elaborated attitudes, however, influence may depend on persuasive arguments delivered through conversation. (p. 30)

Cell 2: Valence Message Level, Subgroup Production

In this cell, two prominent research streams are reviewed as exemplars of social influence processes produced at the subgroup site via valenced messages. The first is the Distributed Valence Model (DVM), and the second deals with majority/minority influence. The DVM (McPhee, Poole, & Seibold, 1982) is a predictive model in which each group member's valenced comments for each decision option are noted as being either positive or negative. Using majority rule (or some other subgroup combinatorial rule), the option favored by the largest subgroup is the predicted group choice.

Tests of this model have shown it to be a fairly accurate predictor of group choice. In an investigation of 10 four-person groups whose task was to decide on a topic of study, McPhee et al. (1982) found that the DVM accounted for 74.4% of the variance in groups' choices. Most recently, Meyers and Brashers (1998) utilized two versions of the DVM to investigate message-outcome links. They found that one version, the DV Rank Sum Model (a model in which ties between options are broken using a rank-sum method; see McPhee et al., 1982), accurately predicted 91.1% of the group choices. A second version, the DV Majority Model (the traditional model without broken ties), accurately predicted 88.9% of the group choices.

The predictive power of the DVM, however, recently has been questioned by Hoffman and Kleinman (1994), who concluded that it generally was inferior to an alternative model they advanced (the Group Valence Model reviewed below). In a subsequent response, McPhee (1994) strongly defended the efficacy and power of the DVM to predict group outcomes accurately from the valence of subgroup members' discussion comments. In particular, because this model utilizes majority rule as its primary combinatorial rule, research findings stemming from it support the large body of research on the influential role of the majority in group decision-making contexts.

Majority/Minority Influence

The second exemplar chosen to represent Cell 2 (valence message level, subgroup production) is majority/minority influence research. Early research on majority influence (e.g., Asch, 1951, 1956) indicated that individuals can be pressured to conform to an obvious incorrect answer when confronted by a majority. More recent research shows that the majority in a group generally exerts more influence than minority subgroups (Davis, 1973; Nemeth & Wachtler, 1983; Zaleska, 1976), and that its strategies of influence can include social pressure, ridicule, and even derision (Nemeth & Wachtler, 1983). Some researchers have suggested that the result of such majority influence is the movement of group members toward convergence (rather than internalization), and this occurs only at the manifest or surface level (Moscovici & Lage, 1976; Nemeth, 1986). That is, individuals who "give in" or converge with other group members secretly maintain their own positions once a group discussion is terminated.

A number of researchers have advanced explanations of how majority influence works in group discussion. Moscovici, Lage, and Naffrechoux (1969) were among the earliest researchers to suggest that the cause of majority influence was not the sheer number of majority members or the social pressure they exerted per se, but the consistency of the valence of their comments. In a later study, Moscovici and Faucheux (1972) found that when majority members were inconsistent in presenting their proposals, they were less likely to influence minority members. Research on the DVM (described previously) supports these findings. Specifically, McPhee et al. (1982) found that if a majority of group members express "clear favor for an option, it tends to be adopted" (p. 272).

Although majority influence appears to have considerable impact on group deliberation and outcomes, minority subgroups also can exert influence under various conditions (see Alvaro & Crano, 1997; Brewer & Crano, 1994; Crano, 1994; Crano & Hannula-Bral, 1994; Kruglanski & Mackie, 1990; Levine & Russo, 1987; Mugny & Perez, 1991; Perez & Mugny, 1990; Wood, Lundgren, Ouellette, Busceme, & Blackstone, 1994). As with majority influence, one important determinant of minority subgroup success is consistency in valenced comments (Moscovici et al., 1969; Nemeth & Wachtler, 1974; Wood et al., 1994; see Haslett & Ruebush, Chapter 5, this volume). Although most researchers have not considered consistency as an interaction-based variable (instead, operationalizing it as a series of repetitive statements produced by a confederate in a noninteractive group context), findings from this program of research provide glimpses into how consistency might function in actual group influence attempts. Moscovici and Lage (1976), for example, found that a minority that maintained a position influenced majority group members at both the surface (compliance) and private (internalized) decision levels, but an inconsistent minority had little chance of exerting any influence. Nemeth (1982; see also Nemeth & Staw, 1989) points out that early in group deliberation, minority subgroup members are likely to encounter resistance, even outright derision, from the majority. If the minority subgroup persists and consistently maintains its valence toward a decision choice, however, while resisting influence attempts from the majority, members of the majority may begin to show doubt in their position and/or even may convert to the minority viewpoint.

The effects of minority subgroup consistency, however, may be closely tied to the quality of their persuasive appeals. Garlick and Mongeau (1993) suggest that a minority subgroup will have even greater impact if its members produce arguments of high quality (as identified by a group of 72 raters using a semantic differential scale on measures of effectiveness, reasonableness, and persuasiveness), as well as remain behaviorally consistent. They indicate that "although behavioral consistency may lead to perceptions of confidence and commitment to a position, the quality of the minority's arguments may potentially determine how behavioral consistency is evaluated" (p. 303).

Besides consistency and quality, another determinant of minority influence that has received attention is the relative size of the minority and majority (Stasser, Kerr, & Davis, 1989; see Haslett & Ruebush, Chapter 5, this volume). Empirical research in which the size of a minority varies while holding the majority constant suggests that a single-member minority is less influential than a minority of two or three (Arbuthnot & Wagner, 1982; Moscovici & Lage, 1976; Mugny & Papastamou, 1980; Nemeth, Wachtler, & Endicott, 1977). More recently, R. D. Clark and Maass (1990) showed that as the size of the majority increased (from 4 to 8 to 12), minority influence declined. They concluded that

> our results strongly suggest that the 2:4 ratio between minority and majority frequently recorded in the minority influence literature may actually represent an optimal ratio for minority influence to occur. Whereas higher minority to majority ratios may be unsuccessful in enhancing minority influence (Nemeth et al., 1977), a decrease in the minority to majority ratio may be detrimental. (pp. 115-116)

Another determinant of minority influence success, although research on this topic is limited, is the group's response to minority comments. Alderton and Frey (1983, 1986) report that favorable reactions to minority positions (those that encourage the examination of the positions) are associated with less group polarization, whereas unfavorable reactions (those that immediately negate the minority position) are associated with increased polarization. Similarly, R. D. Clark (1990), using a set of hypothetical written vignettes and arguments, found that research participants perceived minority arguments as more influential when a number of majority members deserted and supported the minority viewpoint. In addition, if minority members responded successfully to majority arguments by refuting them, the minority was more likely to be influential. This final set of studies is important because social influence is viewed as an interactive process rather than a one-way forwarding of comments and, thus, provides

a more complex and richer picture of the minority influence process.

In addition to investigations of the determinants of minority/majority influence, other researchers have focused on the influence-outcome relationship. For example, minority influence has been associated with higher quality group decisions (Nemeth, 1986; Nemeth, Mosier, & Chiles, 1992; Peterson & Nemeth, 1996). Nemeth (1986) found that those exposed to a minority viewpoint exhibit more divergent thought processes (e.g., consider more potential solutions) than those exposed to the majority view (see also Legrenzi, Butera, Mugny, & Perez, 1991; Smith, Tindale, & Dugoni, 1996). Similarly, participants exposed to a minority viewpoint are more likely to find correct, novel, and creative solutions than those exposed only to the majority view (Mucchi-Faina, Maass, & Volpato, 1991; Nemeth, 1986; Nemeth & Wachtler, 1983; Van Dyne & Saavedra, 1996; Wood et al., 1994). When minority members are successful in influencing group opinion, they are more likely to cause all group members to think about the complexity of the issue as a whole and, thereby, examine more potential solutions, rather than concentrating only on a few (DeDrue & DeVries, 1993; Trost, Maass, & Kenrick, 1992). Exposure to minority views also leads to more private acceptance (internalization) of ideas by all group members (Maass & Clark, 1984; Moscovici, 1980; Mugny, 1982; Nemeth, 1986), as well as more accurate recall of information (Nemeth, Mayseless, Sherman, & Brown, 1990).

Although the evidence demonstrates the value of minority influence to group decision making, most of the research shows that the majority subgroup typically is the victor in such group decision-making situations. Research on mock juries, for example, reveals that the side the majority favors before group discussion becomes the verdict about 90% of the time (Davis, 1973; Nemeth, 1986). This does not mean that minority influence should be discounted: If a minority presents its valenced comments in a consistent and confident manner, the majority size is not overwhelming, and the other members' responses are favorable, it also can influence the final group choice.

Cell 3: Valence Message Level, Group/Intergroup Production

The Group Valence Model (GVM), developed by Hoffman and colleagues (Hoffman, 1979, 1994; Hoffman & Kleinman, 1994) is an excellent example of influence conducted at the valence message level and produced by the entire group. The GVM, like the DVM, focuses on the evaluative dimension (the valence) of members' comments during group discussion. Unlike the DVM, which takes each individual's preferences into account, the GVM views valence as a group property. That is, it predicts final group outcomes from the total number of comments (positive and negative) offered in relation to a given decision proposal, independent of the participants providing the comments.

Hoffman (1979) noted that in about 85% of the decision-making groups he studied, the GVM accurately predicted the final group choice. In more recent tests, Hoffman and Kleinman (1994) suggest that the GVM is generally superior to the DVM in predictive power. Meyers and Brashers (1998), however, found no significant differences between the predictive accuracy of these two models. In fact, in those cases in which a small subgroup offered many positive comments for one option, and the larger majority favored a different option but offered fewer overall comments, the GVM was found to predict the final group decision choice less well than a DV Rank Sum model. In such cases, it appears that groups choose the alternative favored by the majority of *members* rather than the majority of *comments*. Still, in Meyers and Brashers's study, it appeared that, at least in some groups, a minority subgroup that was more vocal than the majority was able to move the group closer to its solution (even though the group did not choose the exact proposal advocated by the minority), which provides indirect support for the predictions of the GVM as well.

To date, both the GVM and the DVM have been shown to be accurate predictors of group decisions. Only in those cases in which the minority is more vocal than the majority does the GVM sometimes fail to predict as accurately as the DV Rank Sum model. Continued research on the impact of valenced statements on group decision outcomes clearly is warranted, because understanding more fully the power of valence alone to influence groups and group members, as well as its impact when coupled with argumentative and/or conflict communication strategies, will provide a much more complete picture of the complexities of the group influence process.

Cell 4: Argument Message Level, Individual Production

One of the best-known theories of influence, one that fits within this cell, is Persuasive Arguments Theory (PAT). According to this theory, arguments are group members' reasons for a position generated during the process of making their private decision choice prior to group discussion (Vinokur & Burnstein, 1974). PAT scholars assume that there exists in any social community a standard set of socially derived and culturally specific arguments for any given decision option and that each individual possesses some of or all these arguments. As a result of ignorance or lack of recollection, however, the same arguments may not be equally available to all participants in a particular group decision-making situation (Burnstein, 1982). PAT scholars predict that novel arguments (e.g., arguments that were not considered by group members prior to discussion and that are stimulated by, or created in, group discussion) provide the impetus for members to reconsider their initial decision choices (Burnstein, 1982). As members become convinced of the merits of the novel arguments, they alter their opinions in the direction of the alternative supported by those arguments (Burnstein, Vinokur, & Pichevin, 1974).

In the past decade, researchers have advocated combining PAT and Social Comparison

Theory into a single theory of group influence. After conducting a meta-analysis of 21 studies of group polarization investigating PAT and SCT explanations, Isenberg (1986) suggested that "investigators develop theories that account for the interaction between SCT and PAT and that address the factors that moderate the emergence of one or the other form of influence" (p. 1149). Social Identity Theory, which assumes that participants' perceptions of group membership direct and control their interaction attempts (see Mackie, 1986; see also Seibold, Meyers, & Sunwolf, 1996, for a more complete explanation of this theory), and Dynamic Social Impact Theory (see explanation later in this chapter; see also Latane, 1996a, 1996b, 1996c, 1997) represent two steps in that direction.

Although PAT essentially is noninteractional in nature, because researchers study arguments individuals generate *prior* to entering group discussion, it continues to be viewed as a viable explanation of group influence by many social psychologists. From a communication perspective, however, there is evidence that interaction-based models (see Meyers, 1989a, 1989b) that incorporate communication as a central element in the influence process may represent more accurate descriptors and predictors of group influence.

Cell 5: Argument Message Level, Subgroup Production

In this cell, two exemplars of social influence constructed at the argument message level and subgroup production site are reviewed: tag-team argument and structured argument forms (in this case, dialectical inquiry and devil's advocacy). Tag-team argument is a topically coherent set of claims, evidence, warrants, justifications, and agreements that is co-constructed in group interaction by two or more members (see Brashers & Meyers, 1989; Canary, Brossmann, & Seibold, 1987; Meyers, Seibold, & Brashers, 1991; Seibold, McPhee, Poole, Tanita, & Canary, 1981). In short, subgroup members supply evidence for others' claims or offer

premises for others' conclusions, and, thereby, provide a complete argument of claim and evidence. In addition, Brashers and Meyers (1989) found that tag-team arguments are maintained by means of consistent support for a decision option and repetitive agreement among tag-team members. They concluded that agreement can "serve to connect members' arguments, provide coherence between team members' arguments, and establish a unified, comprehensible line of reasoning" (p. 546). Although research on tag-team argument is still in its infancy, results suggest that this form of argument both promotes cohesion among subgroup members and persuades opposing factions. This form of argument is, therefore, persuasive because it "presents a unified view of what supporters consider reasonable" (Canary et al., 1987, p. 33).

Both dialectical inquiry and devil's advocacy are forms of structured argument between two opposing subgroups within the same group (see Meyers, 1997; Schweiger, Sandberg, & Ragan, 1986). Typically, the structure for this form of argument is imposed on the group by an outside facilitator in an effort to improve the group's decision-making abilities. In dialectical inquiry, advocates of one decision proposal and proponents of an alternative plan debate the different assumptions that underlie their plans until they reach consensual agreement on a set of assumptions, and, ultimately, a final decision plan. Devil's advocacy is essentially a three-step process that involves having one subgroup develop and advocate a proposal, the other subgroup analyze and criticize it, and both subgroups work to revise it. This process can then be repeated with the other subgroup. Thus, instead of having each subgroup develop a separate plan simultaneously (as is done in dialectical inquiry), each subgroup takes a turn developing and revising a single proposal (see Meyers, 1997; in this volume, see Hirokawa & Salazar [Chapter 7] and Sunwolf & Seibold [Chapter 15]).

Research on the effectiveness of these two types of structured argument indicates that they are both useful for identifying members' assumptions and evaluating critical knowledge in group decision-making situations (see Cosier, 1981; Schweiger, Sandberg, & Rechner, 1989). When testing against consensus decision making, Schweiger et al. (1986) found that "both dialectical inquiry and devil's advocacy were more effective than consensus in generating high quality recommendations and underlying assumptions" (p. 66), but that consensus "may be more functional than either dialectical inquiry or devil's advocacy for preserving harmony within the group" (p. 67). Schwenk and Cosier (1993) similarly concluded that although these types of structured argument may be helpful in moving a group toward a high-quality decision, they can damage group morale because subgroup members may become hostile toward each other in the process. Some form of team building, therefore, may be necessary to restore cohesiveness and morale in a group after it has engaged in structured argument.

Cell 6: Argument Message Level, Group/Intergroup Production

For this cell, we overview the research program on conversational argument in groups. This research has roots in Structuration Theory (Giddens, 1984; in this volume, see Chapters 1 [Gouran] and 2 [Poole]) and has been carried on in both the group and interpersonal arenas (see Brossmann & Canary, 1990; Canary et al., 1987; Canary, Brossmann, Brossmann, & Weger, 1995; Canary, Ratledge, & Seibold, 1982; Canary, Weger, & Stafford, 1991; Meyers & Brashers, 1995, 1998; Meyers, Brashers, Winston, & Grob, 1997; Meyers et al., 1991; Seibold, Canary, & Ratledge, 1983; Seibold et al., 1981). To date, the research has produced important findings about the structure and character of argument in groups. For example, Canary et al. (1987) identified four broad categories of argument structures in decision-making groups: simple arguments (one, and only one, point is developed), compound arguments (extending an

aspect of support for a point, embedding an argument within another, or using two parallel argument forms), eroded arguments (undeveloped arguments resulting from interruption or discontinuation), and convergent arguments (jointly created by two or more people). In addition, Meyers et al. (1991) provided an initial picture of the distribution of argument acts in 45 decision-making group discussions, finding that argument "was characterized primarily and almost exclusively by Assertions, Elaborations, and Agreement" (p. 60).

Most recently, because coder reliabilities needed enhancing, Meyers and Brashers (1995) developed a multistage method for coding group argument that improved reliability among coders. In addition, they outlined a model of group argument that coherently draws together past theoretical and empirical work from the conversational argument research domain (Meyers & Brashers, 1998). In tests of this model, they found that three of the four argument message types (claims, reasoning statements, and agreements) were accurate predictors of final group decision outcomes. Disagreement-relevant intrusions (perhaps because of the lack of disagreement found in many groups' decision-making discussions) were less accurate predictors of decision outcomes. Meyers and Brashers (1998) conclude that these argument statements have force because they serve higher-level functions in group decision-making interactions. In short, these statements have impact not only because they are valenced toward a given decision proposal but also because they generate interactional argument that stimulates more complex reasoning and/or helps to forge agreement among group members.

Thus far, we have looked at social influence as valence and as argument. In the next section, we turn our attention to broader and more complex communication strategies, specifically, those generated in, and by, conflict in groups. Social influence is inherent in conflict because interdependent group members (or groups) perceive competing goals or competing means to a goal (Folger, Poole, & Stutman, 1997; Hocker & Wilmot, 1985; Putnam & Poole, 1987), and they wish, or need, to resolve those differences. In the next section, we review some of the communication strategies produced at the individual, subgroup, and group/intergroup sites of social influence production.

Cell 7: Conflict Communication Strategy Level, Individual Production

At the individual level, conflict communication strategies are enacted as particular conflict management styles. Styles have been viewed as traits of individuals (Witteman, 1991), participants' enactments (Lindskold & Han, 1988), communicative behaviors (Wall, Galanes, & Love, 1987), and self-reports of conflict management preferences (Witteman, 1991). Across these studies, researchers have labeled conflict management styles as accommodating, avoiding, collaborating, competing, and compromising (Thomas & Kilmann, 1974); solution-oriented, controlling, and nonconfrontational (Putnam & Wilson, 1982); integrative (i.e., cooperative) versus distributive (i.e., competitive) (Sillars, Coletti, Parry, & Rogers, 1982); and accommodative versus exploitive (Vinacke, Mogy, Powers, Langan, & Beck, 1974). Nicotera (1997) argues that various methods of classifying conflict management styles are based on two dimensions: "the extent to which an individual emphasizes (1) his or her own goals and interests and (2) the goals and interests of the other person" (p. 115; see also Nicotera, 1993, 1994; Thomas & Kilmann, 1974).

Research has shown that there are individual and situational correlates of conflict management styles. Shockley-Zalabak and Morely (1984), for example, determined that persons with high scores on communication apprehension in dyadic encounters, in comparison to those with low scores, were more likely to use accommodating or avoiding styles and less likely to use competing, collaborating, or compromising styles. Baxter and Shepard (1978) discovered that masculine and androgynous individuals (those with both masculine and feminine characteristics) were more likely to approve of competitive styles than those who were feminine. With regard to situational correlates, Wall and Nolan (1987) reported that conflicts among group members about people in the group (i.e., relational conflicts) were managed most often by an avoidant communication style, whereas conflicts about the group's task were managed by an integrative style. Gero (1985) studied group consensus versus majority decision styles and discerned that participants in groups using a consensus style were more likely than participants in groups utilizing a majority style to characterize their interactions as "friendlier, more agreeable, and more cooperative" (p. 496).

Researchers also have linked conflict management styles to group outcomes. Group members report being more satisfied under conditions of integrative rather than avoidant conflict management styles (e.g., Wall & Galanes, 1986; Wall & Nolan, 1987). Witteman (1991) discovered that members' satisfaction with the communication in their group, decision-making activity, and the group's leader were positively associated with a solution-oriented style, negatively associated with a nonconfrontational style, and not related to a controlling (e.g., forcing) style. In a meta-analysis of 122 studies, D. W. Johnson, Maruyama, Johnson, Nelson, and Skon (1981) observed that cooperative styles were more effective (e.g., in promoting achievement and productivity) than competitive or individualistic styles (see also Blumberg, 1994). Moreover, Wall et al. (1987) established that an integrative conflict management style was associated with higher quality group decisions than was a distributive style. Finally, Lindskold and Han (1988) learned that having a conciliatory (i.e., accommodative) member in an otherwise tough (i.e., competitive) group did little to change the overall competitive climate of the group.

Cell 8: Conflict Communication Strategy Level, Subgroup Production

Conflict communication strategies at the subgroup level are reflected in intragroup conflict practices. Research on majority and minority influence (reviewed previously) and coalitions (e.g., Chertkoff & Esser, 1977; Putnam, 1986) has demonstrated that group members perceive the forming and maintaining of subgroups to be a powerful communicative influence strategy within groups in conflict.

As Brashers and Meyers (1989) note, research has shown that coalitions form when individuals with few resources (Chaney & Vinacke, 1960; W. A. Gamson, 1961), little power (W. A. Gamson, 1964; Willis, 1962), or a need to increase bargaining leverage (Chertkoff & Esser, 1977; Komorita & Chertkoff, 1973; Komorita & Kravitz, 1979) "seek alignment with other members in an effort to increase their share of expected payoffs" (p. 543). Segal (1979) observes that coalitions form in response to group members' perceptions that one of them has inordinate power in the group. Often, group members in that study were willing to sacrifice their own gain to defeat the person perceived to be the "top dog," perhaps because of a sense of "commonality" that exists among members relatively low in power. Similarly, ambiguity about the distribution of power and resources might lead to coalition formation. Mannix and White (1992) discovered that coalitions were more likely to form when a group lacked an established distribution rule for resources, even when coalition formation was detrimental to the group. Finally, others have suggested that coalitions may form on the basis of the popularity of a group member and the reciprocation of attraction among group members (Norton, 1979), when there emerges a "rhetoric of identification" (e.g., when subgroup members identify more with the subgroup than with the group) (Gresson, 1978), when communication among group members is restricted, or when conflict management styles are accommodative (Vinacke et al., 1974).

Although coalitions can serve a facilitative function for subgroup influence attempts, they also may be detrimental to the overall health of a group. Vitz and Kite (1970) found that groups high in internal subgroup conflict were more likely to engage in risky behavior than were groups low in internal conflict, resulting in them being more vulnerable to threats from outside groups. Coalitions also can decrease communication among group members. In a study of triads, Buchli and Pearce (1975) noted that "the formation of a coalition, as we expected, does reduce communication accessibility between members of the coalition and the excluded person" (p. 219). Members of coalitions might reduce communication with other group members because they view them as deviants (Pendell, 1990).

Thus, coalitions form when subgroups perceive the need to influence other subgroups. Coalitions can facilitate subgroup influence attempts but may harm the overall health of the group if communication is reduced or the group's attention to external threats is diverted. Coalitions, however, may not last forever in groups. Ellis and Fisher (1975) argue that competing coalitions begin to disintegrate when "members of both coalitions realize they must come to some common ground of agreement" (p. 209).

Cell 9: Conflict Communication Strategy Level, Group/Intergroup Production

This cell includes research on group conflict communication strategies utilized in intergroup conflicts, such as bargaining and negotiation and in-group/out-group differentiation. Studies of conflict between groups have focused on intraorganizational groups (e.g., Pfeffer & Salancik, 1977; Putnam & Jones, 1982a, 1982b; Putnam, Van Hoeven, & Bullis, 1991; Salancik & Pfeffer, 1978), as well as conflicts between societal groups, such as conflicts between AIDS activist groups and government agencies (e.g., Brashers & Jackson, 1991; Fabj & Sobnosky, 1993, 1995). Intergroup conflicts involve group members working together to confront or challenge an opposing group; individuals may be designated by groups to act as their representatives in bargaining and negotiation contexts (Putnam & Jones, 1982a).

Bargaining and Negotiation

Communication research has focused on the patterns of interaction that evolve during bargaining and negotiation interactions. Bargaining and negotiation, according to Putnam et al. (1991), is "a process in which two or more parties who hold incompatible goals engage in a give-and-take process to reach a mutually acceptable solution" (p. 86). According to Putnam and Jones (1982b), the bargaining and negotiation process "differs from group problem solving in the types of messages used and in the evolution of bargaining stages, and . . . communication patterns distinguish between the initial and latter stages of bargaining" (p. 262).

In the communication discipline, bargaining and negotiation has been studied as a form of argument (see Donohue, Diez, & Stahle, 1983; Keough, 1987, 1989; Putnam & Geist, 1985; Putnam, Wilson, Waltman, & Turner, 1986; Walker, 1988). On the basis of a study of bargaining between a teachers' union and a school district, Putnam et al. (1986) maintain that parties in negotiation interactions create arguments in which they "exchange, defend, and modify proposals and counterproposals as ways of developing a mutually acceptable solution" (p. 63). Moreover, Putnam and Geist (1985) found that arguments in bargaining and negotiation were constructed more often with analogy, cause, and hypothetical examples than with "hard facts" or "data" (p. 243).

Researchers also have used fantasy theme analysis, which analyzes the communicative act of creating/sharing a "fantasy," defined as the "creative and imaginative shared interpretation of events that fulfills a group's psychological or rhetorical need to make sense of their experience and to anticipate their future" (Bormann & Bormann, 1992, p. 110;

see also Bormann, 1985, 1996; Poole, Chapter 2, this volume). Putnam et al. (1991) found that different bargaining rites and rituals characterized negotiations in two school districts. In one district, "negotiators engaged in the collective development of a legal document, complete with written proposals, ongoing deliberations at the table, and judgments of precedent cases" (p. 98). In the other district, "bargaining rituals . . . resembled shuttle diplomacy between two top secret teams who sent ambassadors to work behind closed doors" (p. 98). Different "fantasy themes," defined as concrete narratives about events (see Bormann & Bormann, 1992), also were evident in the districts: "Fantasy themes in District 1 focused on third parties, professional negotiators, and opponents while in District 2 fantasy themes centered on past negotiators and historical scenes" (Putnam et al., 1991, p. 98). Putnam et al. speculate that these differences may be due, in part, to divergence on the symbolic meaning of bargaining because of the multiple goals that negotiation can meet (e.g., reducing conflict, facilitating communication, enhancing solidarity, and balancing power). Finally, on the basis of their study of bargaining scenarios, in which one individual represented management and another represented labor, Putnam and Jones (1982a) concluded that confrontational management of intergroup conflict can lead to "attack-defend" sequences that can "escalate to a lose-lose situation" (p. 191).

In-Group/Out-Group Differentiation

Another line of research on intergroup conflict has focused on communication strategies that increase or decrease in-group/out-group differentiation (e.g., B. M. Johnson, 1975; Pittam & Gallois, 1997). In-group/out-group differentiation occurs when individuals use social categories (e.g., gender or race) to distinguish members of their own category (in-group) from members of another category (out-group) (Wilder, 1986; see also Haslett & Ruebush, Chapter 5, this volume). One strategy for managing in-group/out-group conflict is to minimize real or perceived resource differences between the groups. For example, Brashers and Jackson (1991) argue that the AIDS Coalition to Unleash Power (ACT UP) confronted government and medical scientific groups about drug-testing procedures by educating themselves in the areas of expertise of those groups. They note that "ACT UP did not simply 'beat' the medical establishment by coercing retreat from technical values; rather they changed its practices and its presumptions about the generation of knowledge" (p. 287).

Another strategy might involve the verbal and nonverbal communication style choices made by group members. Communication Accommodation Theory (see Giles, Coupland, & Coupland, 1991; Giles, Mulac, Bradac, & Johnson, 1987) posits that individuals use converging or diverging communication styles to decrease or increase differentiation, respectively, between themselves and members of other groups. Converging communication styles are characteristic of speakers who desire "social approval" or want a "high level of communication efficiency" (Giles et al., 1987, pp. 36-37). Diverging communication styles, in contrast, characterize speakers who want to "communicate a contrastive self-image" or desire to "dissociate personally from the recipients or the recipients' definition of the situation" (p. 37).

In situations in which in-group/out-group differentiation is a strategy of group members, increasing communication between groups may decrease in-group/out-group tensions. Bornstein, Rapoport, Terpel, and Katz (1989) concluded that restricting communication to within-group discussion increased in-group/out-group bias, whereas between-group discussion blurred that distinction, leading members of the groups in which between-group discussion was allowed to remain more committed to between-group agreements. Alternatively, others have argued that in-group/out-group differences can be framed as advantages. For example, Thalhofer's (1993) research shows that intergroup conflict can be reduced through "niche differentiation," a form of nonevaluative differentiation in which the roles of different "groups are equally valued in terms of their contributions to the intergroup environment" (p. 30).

In summary, we reviewed research that exemplifies communication conflict strategies at each of the three sites of source production (individual, subgroup, and group/intergroup). Research on conflict management styles has focused mainly on what styles group members use and under what conditions they employ those styles in group interactions. Research on coalitions has shown that coalitions are created and maintained as a mechanism for influencing group members in a variety of situations, including those in which there are power or resource inequities, ambiguous resource distribution rules, or particular attractive forces between subgroups. Finally, when groups are in conflict with other groups, they may use bargaining and negotiation or attempt to increase or decrease in-group/out-group differentiation as communicative strategies to manage conflicts.

FUTURE DIRECTIONS IN RESEARCH ON GROUP INFLUENCE

In this final section of the chapter, we speculate on what the future holds for scholars working in this research domain. First, we discuss future directions for researchers studying influence as valenced messages and identify new avenues of investigation for the Group Valence and Distributed Valence models and for majority/minority research. Second, we suggest some new directions for research on argumentation in groups. Finally, we consider potentially fruitful avenues for research on group conflict communication strategies.

Valenced Messages as Influence

GV and DV Models

The debate over the superiority of the GV and DV models for predicting group decision outcomes continues (Hoffman, 1994; McPhee, 1994), but past investigations suggest that both models are accurate predictors. It is usually only in those circumstances in which a majority provides few positively valenced statements for a preferred option, a more vocal minority offers a great number of statements for its favored option, and the group opts for the proposal favored by the majority that the DVM is a better predictor than the GVM. Such situations probably occur rarely (see McPhee et al., 1982; Meyers & Brashers, 1998).

It is time to accept both models as accurate predictors and begin using them to investigate other questions. For example, researchers might move beyond valenced statements to predict outcomes from group arguments or conflict communication strategies. Recently, Meyers and Brashers (1998) investigated the group argument-outcome link using these models as predictor mechanisms and determined that arguments had force above and beyond their valenced quality. Although all statements used to predict outcomes in this investigation were valenced, some statements predicted better than others. Claims, convergence-seeking statements, and reason-giving statements were especially accurate predictors, suggesting that it is more than just the valence of messages that influences group members' choices: The use of evidence, reasoning, and agreement make some statements more persuasive than others.

Using these models to study conflict communication strategies could also prove to be fruitful. By investigating the predictive ability of all three message levels (valence, argument, and conflict communication strategies), researchers might better understand how they function together to affect a group's decision choice. For example, it is important to determine whether influence is merely a function of the number of valenced statements (whether by the whole group, as advocated by the GVM, or distributed by subgroup, as proposed by the DVM), or whether it is a more complex process involving argumentative elements (e.g., evidence, backing, and justifica-

tions) and strategic moves (e.g., creating coalitions, teams, or bargaining/negotiation tactics). We also do not know whether these layers of messages function hierarchically in group discussion to influence outcomes (e.g., members begin with valenced statements, and as group discussion progresses and/or the influence process becomes more difficult, members move to argumentative strategies and eventually conflict communication strategies), or whether valence, argument, and conflict communication strategies are interwoven cumulatively throughout a group's interaction so that the subgroup that presents the most influential "package" of strategies supporting its decision choice will be most persuasive.

In addition, researchers need to investigate more complex versions of the DV and GV models. For example, in past investigations, statements were coded as being either "for" or "against" a given proposal, thereby creating a dichotomous variable. Meyers and Brashers (1998) incorporated continuous variables (relative strength of support or nonsupport) into these models to account for the strength of conviction for a proposal (operationalized as the proportion of supportive members or arguments), as well as the relative strength of the decision outcomes. Using these proportional measures allowed for finer statistical distinctions in assessing the predictive capacity of the models.

Using proportional measures may open several new avenues for future research. For example, such a revised model seems necessary to predict better when a minority will be successful in its communicative influence attempts. Previous research suggests that the size of both the majority and the minority may alter influence outcomes. It seems likely, therefore, that in a group of five members, if the proportion is two minority members to three majority members in favor of a proposal, the minority subgroup has a better chance of influencing the final group decision than if the proportion is one minority member to four majority members. By that same logic, two minority members in a group of five should be more influential than two minority members in a group of nine.

Similarly, in those situations in which the proportion of statements or arguments is obviously skewed toward one proposal, we might predict that proposal more accurately as the group's choice. In situations in which the proportion of arguments is balanced more equally between two proposals, we might predict a choice that is a more middle-of-the-road compromise solution (if such a solution is possible). Hence, using proportional measures, whether on valenced statements, arguments, or conflict communication strategies, will allow for finer distinctions in assessing the predictive accuracy of the GV and DV models and should, thereby, increase our knowledge about the communication-outcome link in groups.

Majority/Minority Influence Research

Perhaps one of the most important contributions scholars can make to the body of research on majority/minority influence is to integrate knowledge about group *communication* with past noninteractional efforts in this domain (see Alderton & Frey, 1983, 1986; Garlick, 1993; Garlick & Mongeau, 1992, 1993; Meyers, Brashers, & Jerzak, 1998, for initial steps in that direction). Investigations of actual communication differences (or similarities) between minority and majority subgroups in group discussion clearly is needed. Recently, Gebhardt and Meyers (1994) investigated consistency—a noninteraction-based variable defined as repetition of a statement by a confederate to a set of research participants—from a communication perspective by studying the consistency of members' messages produced in actual group discussions. Results from an analysis of 16 groups revealed that subgroups whose members were *communicatively* consistent (i.e., consistently offered statements in support of a decision proposal throughout discussion, voiced consistent agreement for the preferred decision proposal, and actively refuted statements that favored the alternative proposal)

did, indeed, have a greater chance of affecting the group outcome.

It also would be of value to begin to study argumentative and conflict communication strategy differences between majority and minority subgroups (see Meyers & Brashers, 1998, for initial steps in this direction). Perhaps it is not their consistency, confidence, or size that makes subgroups influential, but, instead, the quality of the arguments they present or their abilities to form influential coalitions through interaction. Social psychologists Levine and Thompson (1996) suggest that research that attends to majority and minority *interaction* "might increase understanding of how groups deal with conflict" (p. 767).

Another promising avenue for future research derives from Latane's (1981, 1996a, 1996c; Latane & Nida, 1980; Latane & Wolf, 1981) work on Social Impact Theory. According to this theory, majority and minority views are seen as potential outcomes of a single process mediated by a common set of variables—strength, immediacy (physical or perceptual closeness), and number of individuals in the subgroup (Latane & Wolf, 1981). Latane and Bourgeois (1996) recently suggested that as individuals interact (mostly with those in closest physical or perceptual proximity to them), they self-organize. Group members cluster into subgroups around issues (especially if the initial minority constitutes about one third of the members), and this clustering can "force groups to preserve a continuing diversity of opinion" (p. 42). Latane and Bourgeois suggest that self-organizing is one theoretical explanation for the continued existence, and sometimes success, of minority subgroups in group interaction. Minority subgroups sometimes are able to influence the majority because their ideas are more fresh, elegant, realistic, or demonstrably correct than those of the majority (Latane & Wolf, 1981).

Finally, we might import models of influence based on individual information-processing capacities to explain the differential impact of majority and minority subgroups (see Propp, Chapter 9, this volume, regarding collective information processing in groups). One model that might prove especially helpful in this endeavor is the Elaboration Likelihood Model (ELM) (see Hale, Lemieux, & Mongeau, 1995; O'Keefe, 1990; Petty & Cacioppo, 1986a, 1986b), which posits that "receivers tend toward one of two paths to attitude change, the central route or the peripheral route" (Hamilton, Hunter, & Boster, 1993, p. 50). In the central route, receivers are motivated to think about the issue or argument under consideration, whereas in the peripheral route, attitude change results from non-issue-relevant concerns (see Petty & Cacioppo, 1981).

It may be that group members process information from majority and minority subgroups in these differential ways, which, in turn, results in private or public acceptance of a position. In majority influence situations, because of normative pressure to conform, group members may respond to the influence attempt rather than the problem being addressed and thus accept majority arguments with only peripheral consideration. Conversely, in minority influence situations, without the same type of pressure to conform, group members may be more motivated to focus on the validity of the minority position, and, thereby, systematically process and privately consider the merits of the arguments (Moscovici, 1980). Dual-process models (e.g., the ELM model), therefore, may help "explain the paradox of people moving publicly toward the majority and privately toward the minority when simultaneously exposed to majority and minority influence" (Peterson & Nemeth, 1996, p. 15). Exploring more fully the merits of this model (and other models) for explaining differential influence by majority and minority subgroups seems a worthwhile endeavor.

Argument as Influence

Although much work remains to be done on identifying the structures, forms, and content of arguments in groups, as well as under-

standing more fully how argument affects both decisional and relational group processes and outcomes (see Gouran, 1990; Jarboe, 1988; Meyers & Brashers, 1998, for research that examines the influence-outcome link), one particularly useful move for future research is to explore forms of group argument that do not necessarily fit into the current "normative" models. To date, most definitions of group argument have been conceived within traditional frameworks grounded in rationality and reasonableness (see Ketrow, Meyers, & Schultz, 1998; Meyers & Brashers, in press). Three general assumptions of such a model are that argument is (a) rational, (b) directed toward convergence, and (c) a civil, decorous activity. Although these assumptions may well hold for argument in most conventional decision-making groups, they may not apply to argument that occurs in many other groups.

We can think of some controversies in which the arguments expressed by group members would not seem to meet any of these three assumptions. We all know families, for example, in which arguments between or among siblings are lifelong battles that never reach convergence, and/or where arguing is anything but civil (see Socha, Chapter 17, this volume, for research on family communication). We probably all have had friends with whom we "agree to disagree" about particular topics. Many support group discussions are characterized more by emotional than rational argument, and/or argument that does not move the group toward convergence (see Cline, Chapter 19, this volume, for research on communication in support groups).

On a larger scale, some activist groups, such as ACT UP, argue their cases using nontraditional forms (e.g., by flaunting sexuality and using taboo phrases) (Brashers & Jackson, 1991; Fabj & Sobnosky, 1993, 1995). For example, members of ACT UP infiltrated the 1988 Republican National Convention by posing as participants and then unfurled banners to promote their cause (J. Gamson, 1989). In addition, members of ACT UP often are verbally aggressive during public demonstrations and commit acts of civil disobedience (e.g., "die-ins" in which activists lie in the street, form funeral processions that march down busy streets and block traffic, and blow whistles on the floor of the New York Stock Exchange to halt trading) that result in arrest and sentencing. Similarly, anti-abortion groups argue their case by picketing abortion clinics, displaying bumper stickers, shouting derogatory names to women who cross picket lines, and distributing explicit videotapes of aborted fetuses.

The strategies and tactics of these and other groups do not appear, on the surface, to fit the traditional definition of argument as rational, are largely not directed toward consensus on a given issue, and very often are uncivil and defamatory. Hence, if we are to explain these forms of group influence, it is important that we move beyond the traditional model of argument toward a broader, more inclusive view that considers an array of argument structures, forms, strategies, and content.

Conflict Communication Strategies as Influence

Another important area for research is examination of how conflict management styles are manifested in communicative behavior. To date, there are few clear theoretical connections between conflict management styles as abstract constructions and communicative behaviors as concrete implementations of those styles, in general or in groups. There no doubt are numerous dimensions on which concrete messages vary (see O'Keefe, 1987), beyond such gross distinctions as "affective" (relational) versus "substantive" (task-oriented) conflict messages. For example, Bell (1983) found that group communication in conflict situations exhibited simpler syntax and greater vocabulary redundancy than in nonconflict situations, which might result from increased cognitive load or the perceived need for understanding. A communication analysis of conflict management styles might also lead to a more complete assessment of the communication climate of a group (see Pace, 1990, for a discussion of competitive versus cooperative climates in group conflict).

Continued investigation of the use of cooperative or competitive conflict communication management strategies also is needed. After reviewing contradictory research findings about whether group members respond cooperatively or competitively under conditions of scarce resources, Kramer (1990) proposed that members respond competitively because of large group size or group differentiation (i.e., the development of subgroups), whereas members who respond cooperatively may do so because of ease of intragroup communication, structural solutions (e.g., electing a leader), procedural solutions (e.g., negotiation), voluntary restraint, rewards for cooperation, or high levels of group identification. In addition, Chertkoff and Mesch (1997) propose that a primary mechanism underlying the success of cooperation or competition is the reward system under which a group operates (e.g., group versus individual distribution), which can lead to communicative blocking or helping behaviors. Research that tests all these predictions is needed.

With the advent of new technologies for group communication and decision making (see Scott, Chapter 16, this volume), research that examines how the introduction of technology might affect the conflict communication strategies of a group is needed. Recent research indicates that some communication strategies in groups may be altered by new communication media (see, for example, Brashers et al., 1994; Brashers et al., 1995; Poole, Holmes, & DeSanctis, 1991).

Finally, at the group/intergroup level, researchers need to continue researching the impact of conflict on relational processes in groups (see Keyton, Chapter 8, this volume). As various scholars have argued, conflict may be healthy for a system (e.g., see Ruben, 1978); for instance, groups may need conflict to be successful at mixed-motive tasks (O'Connor, Gruenfeld, & McGrath, 1993). Conflict also may cause deterioration of a group system, however, particularly if conflict management strategies encourage subgroup division or escalation or maintenance of the conflict rather than its resolution.

One recommendation for future researchers in all these areas is to branch out by investigating influence processes in nondecision-making groups. There are many types of groups in which influence is not aimed at affecting decisions. Influence in some groups may center around inculcating values (e.g., cults, church groups, religious education groups, and families). In other groups, influence may be focused on increasing learning (e.g., study groups, book clubs, educational groups, and classrooms) (see Allen & Plax, Chapter 18, this volume, regarding group communication in the formal educational context). Still other groups may seek to influence social behaviors (e.g., support groups, friendship groups, and peer groups). An interesting line of investigation would be to determine whether influence occurs similarly or differently in these types of groups as compared to decision-making groups. Certainly, this is an area ripe for study.

Finally, researchers in this domain must take seriously Hewes's (1986, 1996) assertion that communication may not influence decision-making outcomes at all. Hewes argues that communicative influence must be viewed as sequentially structured and asserts that there is no evidence that communication has an impact on outputs independent of input factors (see Pavitt, Chapter 12, this volume, for a more complete discussion). Hewes has been instrumental in prodding group communication researchers to examine more carefully their beliefs about the influence-outcome relationship, and to consider the roles of input and process factors on outcomes (see Hirokawa, Erbert, & Hurst, 1996; Jarboe, 1988; Salazar, 1996, for some examples of researchers who have begun to explore those factors). Continued research linking influence processes to group outcomes clearly is needed (see Gouran, 1990; Jarboe, 1988; Meyers & Brashers, 1998).

CONCLUSION

In this chapter, we provided an overview of prominent theories, models, and research programs concerning influence processes in groups. Our review suggests an area rich in intellectual history that is supported by a cadre of dedicated scholars (from many disciplines) who continue to conduct research on influence processes in groups. As we have attempted to indicate, the future holds many opportunities for such interested researchers. Scholars from the communication discipline are especially well situated to make important inroads into unlocking some of the secrets of the interaction-influence relationship if the investigation of communicative behavior remains central to research endeavors. By doing so, we can hope to understand and explain more fully the important role interaction plays in the creation, development, and impact of the influence process on a variety of group processes and outcomes in the many types of groups in which people participate.

REFERENCES

Adelman, M. B., & Frey, L. R. (1994). The pilgrim must embark: Creating and sustaining community in a residential facility for people with AIDS. In L. R. Frey (Ed.), *Group communication in context: Studies of natural groups* (pp. 3-22). Hillsdale, NJ: Lawrence Erlbaum.

Adelman, M. B., & Frey, L. R. (1997). *The fragile community: Living together with AIDS.* Mahwah, NJ: Lawrence Erlbaum.

Alderton, S. M., & Frey, L. R. (1983). Effects of reactions to arguments on group outcome: The case of group polarization. *Central States Speech Journal, 34,* 88-95.

Alderton, S. M., & Frey, L. R. (1986). Argumentation in small group decision-making. In R. Y. Hirokawa & M. S. Poole (Eds.), *Communication and group decision-making* (pp. 157-173). Beverly Hills, CA: Sage.

Alvaro, E. M., & Crano, W. D. (1997). Cognitive responses to minority- or majority-based communications: Factors that underlie minority influence. *British Journal of Social Psychology, 35,* 105-121.

Arbuthnot, J., & Wagner, M. (1982). Minority influence: Effects of size, conversion, and sex. *Journal of Psychology, 111,* 285-295.

Asch, S. E. (1951). Effects of group pressure upon the modification and distortion of judgments. In H. S. Guetzkow (Ed.), *Groups, leadership and men: Re-*

search in human relations (pp. 177-190). Pittsburgh, PA: Carnegie Press.

Asch, S. E. (1956). Studies of independence and submission to group pressure I: On minority of one against a unanimous majority. *Psychological Monographs, 70*(10, Whole No. 417).

Back, K. W. (1951). Influence through social communication. *Journal of Abnormal and Social Psychology, 46,* 9-23.

Badzinski, D. M., & Pettus, A. B. (1994). Nonverbal involvement and sex: Effects on jury decision making. *Journal of Applied Communication Research, 22,* 309-321.

Ball, M. A. (1994). Vacillating about Vietnam: Secrecy, duplicity, and confusion in the communication of President Kennedy and his advisors. In L. R. Frey (Ed.), *Group communication in context: Studies of natural groups* (pp. 181-198). Hillsdale, NJ: Lawrence Erlbaum.

Barge, J. K., & Keyton, J. (1994). Contextualizing power and social influence in groups. In L. R. Frey (Ed.), *Group communication in context: Studies of natural groups* (pp. 85-106). Hillsdale, NJ: Lawrence Erlbaum.

Barge, J. K., Schlueter, D. W., & Pritchard, A. (1989). The effects of nonverbal communication and gender on impression formation in opening statements. *Southern Communication Journal, 54,* 330-349.

Barker, J. R., Melville, C. W., & Pacanowsky, M. E. (1993). Self-directed teams at XEL: Changes in communication practices during a program of cultural transformation. *Journal of Applied Communication Research, 21,* 297-312.

Barker, J. R., & Tompkins, P. K. (1994). Identification in the self-managing organization: Characteristics of target and tenure. *Human Communication Research, 21,* 223-240.

Baron, R. S., & Roper, G. (1976). Reaffirmation of social comparison views of choice shifts: Averaging and extremity effects in an autokinetic situation. *Journal of Personality and Social Psychology, 33,* 521-530.

Baxter, L. A., & Shepard, T. L. (1978). Sex-role identity, sex of other, and affective relationship as determinants of interpersonal conflict-management styles. *Sex Roles, 4,* 813-825.

Bell, M. A. (1983). A research note: The relationship of conflict and linguistic diversity in small groups. *Central States Speech Journal, 34,* 128-133.

Berteotti, C. R., & Seibold, D. R. (1994). Coordination and role-definition problems in health-care teams: A hospice case study. In L. R. Frey (Ed.), *Group communication in context: Studies of natural groups* (pp. 107-131). Hillsdale, NJ: Lawrence Erlbaum.

Bettenhausen, K. L. (1991). Five years of groups research: What we have learned and what needs to be addressed. *Journal of Management, 17,* 345-381.

Blumberg, H. H. (1994). Cooperation, competition, and conflict resolution. In A. P. Hare, H. H. Blumberg, M. F. Davies, & V. Kent (Eds.), *Small group research: A handbook* (pp. 213-236). Norwood, NJ: Ablex.

Bormann, E. G. (1985). Symbolic convergence theory: A communication formulation. *Journal of Communication, 35*(4), 128-138.

Bormann, E. G. (1996). Symbolic convergence theory and communication in group decision making. In R. Y. Hirokawa & M. S. Poole (Eds.), *Communication and group decision making* (2nd ed., pp. 81-113). Thousand Oaks, CA: Sage.

Bormann, E. G., & Bormann, N. C. (1992). *Effective small group communication* (5th ed.). Edina, MN: Burgess International.

Bornstein, G., Rapoport, A., Terpel, L., & Katz, T. (1989). Within- and between-group communication in intergroup competition for public goods. *Journal of Experimental Social Psychology, 25,* 422-436.

Brashers, D. E., Adkins, M., & Meyers, R. A. (1994). Argumentation and computer-mediated decision making. In L. R. Frey (Ed.), *Group communication in context: Studies of natural groups* (pp. 263-282). Hillsdale, NJ: Lawrence Erlbaum.

Brashers, D. E., Adkins, M., Meyers, R. A., & Mittleman, D. (1995). The facilitation of argumentation in computer-mediated group decision-making interactions. In F. H. van Eemeren, R. Grootendorst, J. A. Blair, & C. A. Williard (Eds.), *Special fields and cases: Proceedings of the Third International Conference on Argumentation* (pp. 606-621). Amsterdam, The Netherlands: Sic Sat.

Brashers, D. E., & Jackson, S. (1991). "Politically-savvy sick people": Public penetration of the technical sphere. In D. W. Parson (Ed.), *Argument in controversy: Proceedings of the Seventh Speech Communication Association/American Forensic Association Conference on Argumentation* (pp. 284-288). Annandale, VA: Speech Communication Association.

Brashers, D. E., & Meyers, R. A. (1989). Tag-team argument and group decision-making: A preliminary investigation. In B. E. Gronbeck (Ed.), *Spheres of argument: Proceedings of the Sixth Speech Communication Association/American Forensics Association Conference on Argumentation* (pp. 542-550). Annandale, VA: Speech Communication Association.

Brewer, M. B., & Crano, W. D. (1994). *Social psychology.* St. Paul, MN: West.

Brock, B. L., & Howell, S. (1994). Leadership in the evolution of a community-based political action group. In L. R. Frey (Ed.), *Group communication in context: Studies of natural groups* (pp. 135-152). Hillsdale, NJ: Lawrence Erlbaum.

Brossmann, B. G., & Canary, D. J. (1990). An observational analysis of argument structures: The case of *Nightline. Argumentation, 4,* 199-212.

Buchli, R. D., & Pearce, W. B. (1975). Coalition and communication. *Human Communication Research, 1,* 213-221.

Burnstein, E. (1982). Persuasion as argument processing. In H. Brandstätter, J. H. Davis, & G. Stocker-Kreichgauer (Eds.), *Group decision making* (pp. 103-124). New York: Academic Press.

Burnstein, E., Vinokur, A., & Pichevin, M. F. (1974). What do differences between own, admired, and attributed choices have to do with group induced shifts in choice? *Journal of Experimental Social Psychology, 10,* 428-443.

Canary, D. J., Brossmann, B. G., & Seibold, D. R. (1987). Argument structures in decision-making groups. *Southern Speech Communication Journal, 53,* 18-37.

Canary, D. J., Brossmann, J. E., Brossmann, B. G., & Weger, H., Jr. (1995). Toward a theory of minimally rational argument: Analyses of episode-specific effects of argument structures. *Communication Monographs, 62,* 185-212.

Canary, D. J., Ratledge, N. T., & Seibold, D. R. (1982, November). *Argument and group decision-making: Development of a coding scheme.* Paper presented at the annual meeting of the Speech Communication Association, Louisville, KY.

Canary, D. J., Weger, J., Jr., & Stafford, L. (1991). Couples' argument sequences and their associations with relational characteristics. *Western Journal of Speech Communication, 55,* 159-179.

Chaney, M. V., & Vinacke, W. E. (1960). Achievement and nurturance in triads varying in power distribution. *Journal of Personality and Social Psychology, 35,* 237-249.

Chertkoff, J. M., & Esser, J. K. (1977). A test of three theories of coalition formation when agreements can be short term or long term. *Journal of Personality and Social Psychology, 60,* 237-249.

Chertkoff, J. M., & Mesch, D. J. (1997). Performance under different reward systems: A reconceptualization of the cooperative-competitive-individualistic literature. In E. J. Lawler (Ed.), *Advances in group processes* (Vol. 14, pp. 1-27). Greenwich, CT: JAI.

Clark, R. A. (1984). *Persuasive messages.* New York: Harper & Row.

Clark, R. A., & Delia, J. G. (1979). Topoi and rhetorical competence. *Quarterly Journal of Speech, 65,* 187-206.

Clark, R. D., III. (1990). Minority influence: The role of argument refutation of the majority position and social support for the minority position. *European Journal of Social Psychology, 20,* 489-497.

Clark, R. D., III, & Maass, A. (1990). The effects of majority size on minority influence. *European Journal of Social Psychology, 20,* 99-117.

Cosier, R. A. (1981). Dialectical inquiry in strategic planning: A case of premature acceptance? *Academy of Management Review, 6,* 643-648.

Cragan, J. F., & Wright, D. W. (1990). Small group communication research of the 1980s: A synthesis and critique. *Communication Studies, 41,* 212-236.

Crano, W. D. (1994). Context, comparison, and change: Methodological and theoretical contributions to a theory of minority (and majority) influence. In S. Moscovici, A. Mucchi-Faina, & A. Maass (Eds.), *Minority influence* (pp. 17-46). Chicago: Nelson-Hall.

Crano, W. D., & Hannula-Bral, K. A. (1994). Context/categorization model of social influence: Minority and majority influence in the formation of a novel

response form. *Journal of Experimental Social Psychology, 30,* 247-276.

Davis, J. H. (1973). Group decision and social interaction: A theory of social decision schemes. *Psychological Review, 80,* 97-125.

DeDrue, C.K.W., & DeVries, N. K. (1993). Numerical support, information processing, and attitude change. *European Journal of Social Psychology, 23,* 647-662.

Donohue, W. A., Diez, M. E., & Stahle, R. B. (1983). New directions in negotiation research. In R. N. Bostrom (Ed.), *Communication yearbook 7* (pp. 249-279). Beverly Hills, CA: Sage.

Ellis, D. G., & Fisher, B. A. (1975). Phases of conflict in small group development: A Markov analysis. *Human Communication Research, 1,* 195-212.

Fabj, V., & Sobnosky, M. J. (1993). Responses from the street: ACT UP and community organizing against AIDS. In S. C. Ratzan (Ed.), *AIDS: Effective health communication for the 90's* (pp. 91-109). Washington, DC: Taylor & Francis.

Fabj, V., & Sobnosky, M. J. (1995). AIDS activism and the rejuvenation of the public sphere. *Argumentation and Advocacy, 31,* 163-184.

Festinger, L. (1950). A theory of social comparison processes. *Human Relations, 7,* 117-140.

Festinger, L. (1954). Informal social communication. *Psychological Review, 57,* 271-282.

Folger, J. P., Poole, M. S., & Stutman, R. K. (1997). *Working through conflict: Strategies for relationships, groups, and organizations* (3rd ed.). New York: HarperCollins.

Frey, L. R. (Ed.). (1994a). *Group communication in context: Studies of natural groups.* Hillsdale, NJ: Lawrence Erlbaum.

Frey, L. R. (1994b). The naturalistic paradigm: Studying small groups in the postmodern era. *Small Group Research, 25,* 551-577.

Frey, L. R. (Ed.). (1995). *Innovations in group facilitation: Applications in natural settings.* Cresskill, NJ: Hampton.

Frey, L. R. (1996). Remembering and "re-membering": A history of theory and research on communication and group decision making. In R. Y. Hirokawa & M. S. Poole (Eds.), *Communication and group decision making* (2nd ed., pp. 19-51). Thousand Oaks, CA: Sage.

Frey, L. R. (Ed.). (in press). *Group communication in context: Studies of bona fide groups* (2nd ed.). Mahwah, NJ: Lawrence Erlbaum.

Frey, L. R., Adelman, M. B., & Query, J. L., Jr. (1996). Communication practices in the social construction of health in an AIDS residence. *Journal of Health Psychology, 1,* 383-397.

Frey, L. R., Query, J. L., Jr., Flint, L. J., & Adelman, M. B. (1998). Living together with AIDS: Social support processes in a residential facility. In V. J. Derlega & A. P. Barbee (Eds.), *HIV and social interaction* (pp. 129-146). Thousand Oaks, CA: Sage.

Gamson, J. (1989). Silence, death, and the invisible enemy: AIDS activism and social movement "newness." *Social Problems, 36,* 351-365.

Gamson, W. A. (1961). A theory of coalition formation. *American Sociological Review, 26,* 373-382.

Gamson, W. A. (1964). Experimental studies in coalition formation. In L. Berkowitz (Ed.), *Advances in experimental social psychology* (Vol. 1, pp. 81-110). New York: Academic Press.

Garlick, R. (1993). Single, double, and triple minorities and the evaluations of persuasive arguments. *Communication Studies, 44,* 273-284.

Garlick, R., & Mongeau, P. A. (1992). Majority/minority size and the evaluations of persuasive arguments. *Communication Research Reports, 9,* 43-53.

Garlick, R., & Mongeau, P. A. (1993). Argument quality and group member status as determinants of attitudinal minority influence. *Western Journal of Speech Communication, 57,* 289-308.

Gebhardt, L. J., & Meyers, R. A. (1994). Subgroup influence in decision-making groups: Examining consistency from a communication perspective. *Small Group Research, 26,* 147-168.

Gero, A. (1985). Conflict avoidance in consensual decision processes. *Small Group Behavior, 16,* 487-499.

Giddens, A. (1984). *The constitution of society: Outline of the theory of structuration.* Berkeley: University of California Press.

Giles, H., Coupland, J., & Coupland, N. (1991). *Contexts of accommodation: Developments in applied sociolinguistics.* Cambridge, UK: Cambridge University Press.

Giles, H., Mulac, A., Bradac, J. J., & Johnson, P. (1987). Speech accommodation theory: The next decade and beyond. In M. McLaughlin (Ed.), *Communication yearbook 10* (pp. 13-48). Newbury Park, CA: Sage.

Goethals, G. R., & Zanna, M. P. (1979). The role of social comparison in choice shifts. *Journal of Personality and Social Psychology, 37,* 1469-1476.

Gouran, D. S. (1990). Exploiting the predictive potential of structuration theory. In J. A. Anderson (Ed.), *Communication yearbook 13* (pp. 313-322). Newbury Park, CA: Sage.

Gresson, A. D. (1978). Phenomenology and the rhetoric of identification: A neglected dimension of coalition communication inquiry. *Communication Quarterly, 26,* 14-23.

Hale, J., Lemieux, R., & Mongeau, P. (1995). Cognitive processing of fear arousing message content. *Communication Research, 22,* 459-474.

Hamilton, M. A., Hunter, J. E., & Boster, F. J. (1993). The Elaboration Likelihood Model as a theory of attitude formation: A mathematical analysis. *Communication Theory, 3,* 50-65.

Hewes, D. E. (1986). A socio-egocentric model of group decision-making. In R. Y. Hirokawa & M. S. Poole (Eds.), *Communication and group decision-making* (pp. 265-291). Beverly Hills, CA: Sage.

Hewes, D. E. (1996). Small group communication may not influence decision making: An amplification of socio-egocentric theory. In R. Y. Hirokawa & M. S. Poole (Eds.), *Communication and group decision making* (2nd ed., pp. 179-212). Thousand Oaks, CA: Sage.

Hirokawa, R. Y., Erbert, L., & Hurst, A. (1996). Communication and group decision-making effectiveness. In R. Y. Hirokawa & M. S. Poole (Eds.), *Communication and group decision making* (2nd ed., pp. 269-300). Thousand Oaks, CA: Sage.

Hocker, J. L., & Wilmot, W. W. (1985). *Interpersonal conflict* (2nd ed.). Dubuque, IA: Wm. C. Brown.

Hoffman, L. R. (Ed.). (1979). *The group problem solving process: Studies of a valence model.* New York: Praeger.

Hoffman, L. R. (1994). Reply to McPhee. *Human Communication Research, 21,* 64-66.

Hoffman, L. R., & Kleinman, G. B. (1994). Individual and group in group problem solving: The Valence Model redressed. *Human Communication Research, 21,* 36-59.

Isenberg, D. J. (1986). Group polarization: A critical review and meta-analysis. *Journal of Personality and Social Psychology, 50,* 1141-1151.

Jarboe, S. (1988). A comparison of input-process, process-output, and input-process-output models of small group problem-solving effectiveness. *Communication Monographs, 55,* 121-142.

Johnson, B. M. (1975). Images of the enemy in intergroup conflict. *Central States Speech Journal, 26,* 84-92.

Johnson, D. W., Maruyama, G., Johnson, R., Nelson, D., & Skon, L. (1981). Effects of cooperative, competitive, and individualistic goal structures on achievement: A meta-analysis. *Psychological Bulletin, 89,* 47-62.

Keough, C. M. (1987). The nature and function of argument in organizational bargaining research. *Southern Speech Communication Journal, 53,* 1-17.

Keough, C. M. (1989). Strategic conduct analysis of contract negotiations: Application of a structurational coding scheme. In B. E. Gronbeck (Ed.), *Spheres of argument: Proceedings of the Sixth Speech Communication Association/American Forensics Association Conference on Argumentation* (pp. 569-575). Annandale, VA: Speech Communication Association.

Ketrow, S. M., Meyers, R. A., & Schultz, B. (1998). Processes and outcomes related to nonrational argument in societal groups. In J. F. Klumpp (Ed.), *Argument in a time of change: Proceedings of the Tenth National Communication Association/American Forensics Association Conference on Argumentation* (pp. 103-109). Annandale, VA: Speech Communication Association.

Komorita, S. S., & Chertkoff, J. M. (1973). A bargaining theory of coalition formation. *Psychological Review, 80,* 149-162.

Komorita, S. S., & Kravitz, D. A. (1979). The effects of alternatives in bargaining. *Journal of Experimental Social Psychology, 15,* 145-157.

Kramer, R. M. (1990). The effects of resource scarcity on group conflict and cooperation. In E. J. Lawler (Ed.), *Advances in group processes: Theory and research* (Vol. 7, pp. 151-177). Greenwich, CT: JAI.

Kruglanski, A. W., & Mackie, D. M. (1990). Majority and minority influence: A judgmental process analysis. In W. Stroebe & M. Hewstone (Eds.), *European review of social psychology* (Vol. 1, pp. 229-261). Chichester, UK: Wiley.

Latane, B. (1981). Psychology of social impact. *American Psychologist, 36,* 343-356.

Latane, B. (1996a). Dynamic social impact: The creation of culture by communication. *Journal of Communication, 46*(4), 13-25.

Latane, B. (1996b). Dynamic social impact: Robust predictions from simple theory. In R. Hegselmann, U. Mueller, & K. G. Troitzsch (Eds.), *Modelling and simulation in the social sciences from the philosophy of science point of view* (pp. 287-310). Dordrecht, The Netherlands: Kluwer Theory & Decision Library.

Latane, B. (1996c). Strength from weakness: The fate of opinion minorities in spatially distributed groups. In E. Witte & J. H. Davis (Eds.), *Understanding group behavior: Consensual action by small groups* (pp. 193-220). Hillsdale, NJ: Lawrence Erlbaum.

Latane, B. (1997). Dynamic social impact: The societal consequences of human interaction. In C. McGarty & S. A. Haslam (Eds.), *The message of social psychology: Perspectives on mind in society* (pp. 200-221). Cambridge, MA: Blackwell.

Latane, B., & Bourgeois, M. J. (1996). Experimental evidence for Dynamic Social Impact: The emergence of subcultures in electronic groups. *Journal of Communication, 46*(4), 35-47.

Latane, B., & Liu, J. H. (1996). The intersubjective geometry of social space. *Journal of Communication, 46*(4), 26-34.

Latane, B., & Nida, S. (1980). Social impact theory and group influence: A social engineering perspective. In P. B. Paulus (Ed.), *Psychology of group influence* (pp. 3-34). Hillsdale, NJ: Lawrence Erlbaum.

Latane, B., & Wolf, S. (1981). The social impact of majorities and minorities. *Psychological Review, 88,* 438-453.

Legrenzi, P., Butera, F., Mugny, G., & Perez, J. (1991). Majority and minority influence in inductive reasoning: A preliminary study. *European Journal of Social Psychology, 21,* 239-248.

Levine, J. M., & Moreland, R. L. (1990). Progress in small group research. In M. R. Rosenzweig & L. W. Porter (Eds.), *Annual review of psychology* (Vol. 41, pp. 585-634). Palo Alto, CA: Annual Reviews.

Levine, J. M., & Russo, E. M. (1987). Majority and minority influence. In C. Hendrick (Ed.), *Group processes: Review of personality and social psychology* (Vol. 8, pp. 13-54). Newbury Park, CA: Sage.

Levine, J. M., & Thompson, L. (1996). Conflict in groups. In E. T. Higgins & A. W. Kruglanski (Eds.), *Social psychology: Handbook of basic principles* (pp. 745-776). New York: Guilford.

Lindskold, S., & Han, G. (1988). Group resistance to influence by a conciliatory member. *Small Group Behavior, 19,* 19-34.

Maass, A., & Clark, R. D., III. (1984). Hidden impact of minorities: Fifteen years of minority influence. *Psychological Bulletin, 95,* 428-450.

Mackie, D. M. (1986). Social identification effects in group polarization. *Journal of Personality and Social Psychology, 50,* 720-728.

Mackie, D. M., & Cooper, J. (1984). Group polarization: The effects of group membership. *Journal of Personality and Social Psychology, 46,* 575-585.

Mannix, E. A., & White, S. B. (1992). The effect of distributive uncertainty on coalition formation in organizations. *Organizational Behavior and Human Decision Processes, 51,* 198-219.

McPhee, R. D. (1994). Response to Hoffman and Kleinman. *Human Communication Research, 21,* 60-63.

McPhee, R. D., Poole, M. S., & Seibold, D. R. (1982). The valence model unveiled: Critique and alternative formulation. In M. Burgoon (Ed.), *Communication yearbook 5* (pp. 259-278). New Brunswick, NJ: Transaction Books.

Meyers, R. A. (1989a). Persuasive Arguments Theory: A test of assumptions. *Human Communication Research, 15,* 357-381.

Meyers, R. A. (1989b). Testing Persuasive Argument Theory's predictor model: Alternative interactional accounts of group argument and influence. *Communication Monographs, 56,* 112-132.

Meyers, R. A. (1997). Social influence and group argumentation. In L. R. Frey & J. K. Barge (Eds.), *Managing group life: Communicating in decision-making groups* (pp. 183-201). Boston: Houghton Mifflin.

Meyers, R. A., & Brashers, D. E. (1995). Multi-stage versus single-stage coding of small group argument: A preliminary comparative assessment. In S. Jackson (Ed.), *Argumentation and values: Proceedings of the Ninth Speech Communication Association/American Forensics Association Conference on Argumentation* (pp. 93-100). Annandale, VA: Speech Communication Association.

Meyers, R. A., & Brashers, D. E. (1998). Argument in group decision-making: Explicating a process model and investigating the argument-outcome link. *Communication Monographs, 65,* 261-281.

Meyers, R. A., & Brashers, D. E. (in press). Rethinking traditional approaches to argument in groups. In L. R. Frey (Ed.), *New directions in group communication.* Thousand Oaks, CA: Sage.

Meyers, R. A., Brashers, D. E., & Jerzak, J. (1998, November). *Majority/minority influence: Identifying argumentative patterns and predicting argument-outcome links.* Paper presented at the annual meeting of the National Communication Association, New York City.

Meyers, R. A., Brashers, D. E., Winston, L., & Grob, L. (1997). Sex differences and group argument: A theoretical framework and empirical investigation. *Communication Studies, 48,* 19-41.

Meyers, R. A., Seibold, D. R., & Brashers, D. E. (1991). Argument in initial group decision-making discussions: Refinement of a coding scheme and a descriptive quantitative analysis. *Western Journal of Speech Communication, 55,* 47-68.

Moscovici, S. (1980). Toward a theory of conversion behavior. In L. Berkowitz (Ed.), *Advances in experimental social psychology* (Vol. 13, pp. 209-239). New York: Academic Press.

Moscovici, S., & Faucheux, C. (1972). Social influence, conformity bias, and the study of active minorities. In L. Berkowitz (Ed.), *Advances in experimental social psychology* (Vol. 6, pp. 149-202). New York: Academic Press.

Moscovici, S., & Lage, E. (1976). Studies in social influence III: Majority versus minority influence in a group. *European Journal of Social Psychology, 6,* 149-174.

Moscovici, S., Lage, E., & Naffrechoux, M. (1969). Influence of a consistent minority on the responses of a majority in a color perception task. *Sociometry, 32,* 365-380.

Mucchi-Faina, A., Maass, C., & Volpato, C. (1990). Social influence: The role of originality. *European Journal of Social Psychology, 21,* 183-198.

Mugny, G. (1982). *The power of minorities.* New York: Academic Press.

Mugny, G., & Papastamou, S. (1980). When rigidity does not fail: Individualization and psychologization as resistances to the diffusion of minority innovations. *European Journal of Social Psychology, 10,* 43-62.

Mugny, G., & Perez, J. A. (1991). *The social psychology of minority influence.* Cambridge, UK: Cambridge University Press.

Myers, D. G. (1982). Polarizing effects of social interaction. In H. Brandstätter, J. H. Davis, & G. Stocker-Kreichgauer (Eds.), *Group decision making* (pp. 125-161). New York: Academic Press.

Myers, D. G., Bruggink, J. B., Kersting, R. C., & Schlosser, B. (1980). Does learning others' opinions change one's opinions? *Personality and Social Psychology Bulletin, 6,* 253-260.

Nemeth, C. (1982). Stability of faction position and influence. In G. H. Brandstätter, J. H. Davis, & G. Stocker-Kreichgauer (Eds.), *Group decision making* (pp. 185-213). New York: Academic Press.

Nemeth, C. (1986). Differential contributions of majority and minority influence. *Psychological Review, 93,* 23-32.

Nemeth, C. J., Mayseless, O., Sherman, J., & Brown, Y. (1990). Exposure to dissent and recall of information. *Journal of Personality and Social Psychology, 58,* 429-437.

Nemeth, C. J., Mosier, K., & Chiles, C. (1992). When convergent thought improves performance: Majority versus minority influence. *Personality and Social Psychology Bulletin, 18,* 139-144.

Nemeth, C., & Staw, C. J. (1989). The tradeoffs of social control and innovation in groups and organizations. In L. Berkowitz (Ed.), *Advances in experimental social psychology* (Vol. 22, pp. 175-210). New York: Academic Press.

Nemeth, C., & Wachtler, J. (1974). Creating the perceptions of consistency and confidence: A necessary condition for minority influence. *Sociometry, 37,* 529-540.

Nemeth, C., & Wachtler, J. (1983). Creative problem solving as a result of majority vs. minority influence. *European Journal of Social Psychology, 13,* 45-55.

Nemeth, C., Wachtler, J., & Endicott, J. (1977). Increasing the size of the minority: Some gains and some losses. *European Journal of Psychology, 7,* 15-27.

Nicotera, A. M. (1993). Beyond two dimensions: A grounded theory model of conflict-handling behavior. *Management Communication Quarterly, 6,* 282-306.

Nicotera, A. M. (1994). The use of multiple approaches to conflict: A study of sequences. *Human Communication Research, 20,* 592-621.

Nicotera, A. M. (1997). Managing conflict communication in groups. In L. R. Frey & J. K. Barge (Eds.), *Managing group life: Communication in decision-making groups* (pp. 104-130). Boston: Houghton Mifflin.

Norton, R. W. (1979). Identifying coalitions: Generating units of analysis. *Small Group Behavior, 10,* 343-354.

O'Connor, K. M., Gruenfeld, D. H., & McGrath, J. E. (1993). The experience and effects of conflict in continuing work groups. *Small Group Research, 24,* 362-382.

O'Keefe, D. J. (1987, November). *Message description.* Paper presented at the annual meeting of the Speech Communication Association, Boston.

O'Keefe, D. J. (1990). *Persuasion: Theory and research.* Newbury Park, CA: Sage.

Pace, R. C. (1990). Personalized and depersonalized conflict in small group discussions: An examination of differentiation. *Small Group Research, 21,* 79-96.

Pendell, S. D. (1990). Deviance and conflict in small group decision making: An exploratory study. *Small Group Research, 21,* 393-403.

Perez, J., & Mugny, G. (1990). Minority influence: Manifest discrimination and latent influence. In D. Abrams & M. Hogg (Eds.), *Social identity theory: Constructive and critical advances* (pp. 101-120). London: Harvester Wheatsheaf.

Peterson, R. S., & Nemeth, C. J. (1996). Focus versus flexibility: Majority and minority influence can both improve performance. *Personality and Social Psychology Bulletin, 22,* 14-23.

Petty, R. E., & Cacioppo, J. T. (1981). *Attitudes and persuasion: Classic and contemporary approaches.* Dubuque, IA: Wm. C. Brown.

Petty, R. E., & Cacioppo, J. T. (1986a). *Communication and persuasion: Central and peripheral routes to attitude change.* New York: Springer-Verlag.

Petty, R. E., & Cacioppo, J. T. (1986b). The elaboration likelihood model of persuasion. In L. Berkowitz (Ed.), *Advances in experimental social psychology* (Vol. 19, pp. 123-205). New York: Academic Press.

Pfeffer, J., & Salancik, G. R. (1977). Administrator effectiveness: The effects of advocacy and information on resource allocations. *Human Relations, 30,* 641-656.

Pittam, J., & Gallois, C. (1997). Language strategies in the attribution of blame for HIV and AIDS. *Communication Monographs, 64,* 201-218.

Poole, M. S., Holmes, M., & DeSanctis, G. (1991). Conflict management in a computer-supported meeting environment. *Management Science, 37,* 926-953.

Poole, M. S., Seibold, D. R., & McPhee, R. D. (1985). Group decision-making as a structurational process. *Quarterly Journal of Speech, 71,* 74-102.

Putnam, L. L. (1986). Conflict in group decision-making. In R. Y. Hirokawa & M. S. Poole (Eds.), *Communication and group decision-making* (pp. 135-155). Beverly Hills, CA: Sage.

Putnam, L. L., & Geist, P. (1985). Argument in bargaining: An analysis of the reasoning process. *Southern Speech Communication Journal, 50,* 225-245.

Putnam, L. L., & Jones, T. S. (1982a). Reciprocity in negotiations: An analysis of bargaining interaction. *Communication Monographs, 49,* 171-191.

Putnam, L. L., & Jones, T. S. (1982b). The role of communication in bargaining. *Human Communication Research, 8,* 262-280.

Putnam, L. L., & Poole, M. S. (1987). Conflict and negotiation. In F. M. Jablin, L. L. Putnam, K. H. Roberts, & L. W. Porter (Eds.), *Handbook of organizational communication* (pp. 549-599). Newbury Park, CA: Sage.

Putnam, L. L., Van Hoeven, S. A., & Bullis, C. A. (1991). The role of rituals and fantasy themes in teachers' bargaining. *Western Journal of Speech Communication, 55,* 85-103.

Putnam, L. L., & Wilson, C. E. (1982). Communicative strategies in organizational conflicts: Reliability and validity of a measurement scale. In M. Burgoon (Ed.), *Communication yearbook 6* (pp. 629-652). Beverly Hills, CA: Sage.

Putnam, L. L., Wilson, S., Waltman, M. S., & Turner, D. (1986). The evolution of case arguments in teachers' bargaining. *Journal of the American Forensic Association, 23,* 63-81.

Ruben, B. D. (1978). Communication and conflict: A systems-theoretic perspective. *Quarterly Journal of Speech, 64,* 202-210.

Salancik, G. R., & Pfeffer, J. (1978). Uncertainty, secrecy, and the choice of similar others. *Social Psychology, 41,* 246-255.

Salazar, A. J. (1996). Ambiguity and communication effects on small group decision-making performance. *Human Communication Research, 23,* 155-192.

Sanders, G. S., & Baron, R. S. (1977). Is social comparison irrelevant for reducing choice shifts? *Journal of Experimental Social Psychology, 13,* 303-314.

Scheerhorn, D., Geist, P., & Teboul, J. C. B. (1994). Beyond decision making in decision-making groups: Implications for the study of group communication. In L. R. Frey (Ed.), *Group communication in context: Studies of natural groups* (pp. 247-262). Hillsdale, NJ: Lawrence Erlbaum.

Schweiger, D. M., Sandberg, W. R., & Ragan, J. W. (1986). Group approaches for improving strategic decision-making: A comparative analysis of dialectical inquiry, devil's advocacy, and consensus. *Academy of Management Journal, 29,* 51-71.

Schweiger, D. M., Sandberg, W. R., & Rechner, P. L. (1989). Experiential effects of dialectical inquiry, devil's advocacy, and consensus approaches to strate-gic decision making. *Academy of Management Journal, 32,* 745-772.

Schwenk, C. R., & Cosier, R. A. (1993). Effects of consensus and devil's advocacy on strategic decision-making. *Journal of Applied Social Psychology, 23,* 126-139.

Segal, J. (1979). Coalition formation in tetrads: A critical test of four theories. *Journal of Psychology, 103,* 209-219.

Seibold, D. R., Canary, D. J., & Ratledge, N. T. (1983, November). *Argument and group decision-making: Interim report on a structurational research program.* Paper presented at the meeting of the Speech Communication Association, Washington, DC.

Seibold, D. R., Cantrill, J. G., & Meyers, R. A. (1994). Communication and interpersonal influence. In M. L. Knapp & G. R. Miller (Eds.), *Handbook of interpersonal communication* (2nd ed., pp. 542-588). Thousand Oaks, CA: Sage.

Seibold, D. R., McPhee, R. D., Poole, M. S., Tanita, N. E., & Canary, D. (1981). Argument, group influence, and decision outcomes. In G. Ziegelmueller & J. Rhodes (Eds.), *Dimensions of argument: Proceedings of the Second Summer Speech Communication Association/American Forensics Association Conference on Argumentation* (pp. 663-692). Annandale, VA: Speech Communication Association.

Seibold, D. R., Meyers, R. A., & Sunwolf. (1996). Communication and influence in group decision making. In R. Y. Hirokawa & M. S. Poole (Eds.), *Communication and group decision making* (2nd ed., pp. 242-268). Thousand Oaks, CA: Sage.

Seibold, D. R., Poole, M. S., & McPhee, R. D. (1980, April). *New prospects for research in small group communication.* Paper presented at the annual meeting of the Central States Speech Association, Chicago.

Shockley-Zalabak, P. S., & Morley, D. D. (1984). An exploratory study of relationships between preferences for conflict styles and communication apprehension. *Journal of Language and Social Psychology, 3,* 213-218.

Sillars, A. L., Coletti, S. F., Parry, D., & Rogers, M. A. (1982). Coding verbal conflict tactics: Nonverbal and perceptual correlates of the "avoidance-distributive-integrative" distinction. *Human Communication Research, 9,* 83-95.

Smith, C. M., Tindale, R. S., & Dugoni, B. L. (1996). Minority and majority influence in freely interacting groups: Qualitative versus quantitative differences. *British Journal of Social Psychology, 35,* 137-149.

Stasser, G., Kerr, N. L., & Davis, J. H. (1989). Influence processes and consensus models in decision-making groups. In P. B. Paulus (Ed.), *Psychology of group influence* (2nd ed., pp. 279-326). Hillsdale, NJ: Lawrence Erlbaum.

Sykes, R. E. (1990). Imagining what we might study if we really studied small groups from a speech perspective. *Communication Studies, 41,* 200-211.

Thalhofer, N. N. (1993). Intergroup differentiation and reduction of intergroup conflict. *Small Group Research, 24,* 28-43.

Thomas, K. W., & Kilmann, R. H. (1974). *Thomas-Kilmann conflict MODE instrument*. Tuxedo, NY: Xicom.

Tracy, K. (1984). The effect of multiple goals on conversational relevance and topic shift. *Communication Monographs, 51*, 274-287.

Tracy, K., & Moran, J. P. (1983). Conversational relevance in multiple-goal settings. In R. T. Craig & K. Tracy (Eds.), *Conversational coherence: Form, structure, and strategy* (pp. 116-135). Beverly Hills, CA: Sage.

Trost, M. R., Maass, A., & Kenrick, D. (1992). Minority influence: Ego involvement alters cognitive processes and reverses private acceptance. *Journal of Experimental Social Psychology, 28*, 234-254.

Turner, J. C. (1985). Social categorization and the self-concept: A social cognitive theory of group behavior. In E. J. Lawler (Ed.), *Advances in group processes: Theory and research* (Vol. 2, pp. 77-122). Greenwich, CT: JAI.

Turner, J. C., & Oakes, P. J. (1986). The significance of the social identity concept for social psychology with reference to individualism, interactionism, and social influence. *British Journal of Social Psychology, 25*, 237-252.

Van Dyne, L., & Saavedra, R. (1996). A naturalistic minority influence experiment: Effects of divergent thinking, conflict and originality in work-groups. *British Journal of Social Psychology, 35*, 151-167.

Vinacke, W. E., Mogy, R., Powers, W., Langan, C., & Beck, R. (1974). Accommodative strategy and communication in a three person matrix game. *Journal of Personality and Social Psychology, 29*, 509-525.

Vinokur, A. (1971). Review and theoretical analysis of the effects of group processes upon individual and group decisions involving risk. *Psychological Bulletin, 76*, 231-250.

Vinokur, A., & Burnstein, E. (1974). Effects of partially shared persuasive arguments on group induced shifts: A group problem-solving approach. *Journal of Personality and Social Psychology, 19*, 305-315.

Vitz, P. C., & Kite, W. R. (1970). Factors affecting conflict and negotiation within an alliance. *Journal of Experimental Social Psychology, 6*, 233-247.

Walker, G. (1988). Bacharach and Lawler's theory of argument in bargaining: A critique. *Journal of the American Forensic Association, 24*, 218-232.

Wall, V. D., & Galanes, G. J. (1986). The SYMLOG dimensions and small group conflict. *Central States Speech Journal, 37*, 61-78.

Wall, V. D., Galanes, G. J., & Love, S. B. (1987). Small, task-oriented groups: Conflict, conflict management, satisfaction, and decision quality. *Small Group Behavior, 18*, 31-55.

Wall, V. D., & Nolan, L. L. (1987). Small group conflict: A look at equity, satisfaction, and styles of conflict management. *Small Group Behavior, 18*, 188-211.

Wilder, D. A. (1986). Social categorization: Implications for creation and reduction of intergroup conflict. In L. Berkowitz (Ed.), *Advances in experimental social psychology* (Vol. 19, pp. 291-355). New York: Academic Press.

Willis, R. H. (1962). Coalitions in the tetrad. *Sociometry, 25*, 358-376.

Witteman, H. (1991). Group member satisfaction: A conflict-related account. *Small Group Research, 22*, 24-58.

Wood, W., Lundgren, S., Ouellette, J. A., Busceme, S., & Blackstone, T. (1994). Minority influence: A meta-analytic review of social influence processes. *Psychological Bulletin, 115*, 323-345.

Zaleska, M. (1976). Majority influence on group choices among bets. *Journal of Personality and Social Psychology, 33*, 8-17.

12

Theorizing About the Group Communication-Leadership Relationship

Input-Process-Output and Functional Models

CHARLES PAVITT
University of Delaware

The literature on group leadership is staggering. Extrapolating from the number of citations in Bass (1990), I would estimate that close to 8,000 relevant studies have been published. In the light of this massive research effort and the reasonable notion that the performance of group leadership is instantiated in communication, it should be no surprise that scholars and educators have treated this area as an integral part of group communication pedagogy. Group communication textbooks generally contain significant portions devoted to leadership (for some recent examples, see Ellis & Fisher, 1994; Frey & Barge, 1997; Pavitt & Curtis, 1994), and communication curricula include relevant discussion in courses on groups and often entire courses on leadership alone.

Despite this attention, it is my contention that communication is not central to many of the classic theories about leadership. Even more to the point, communication scholars and educators seemingly have not recognized that absence. The textbook discussions cited above, including my own, indiscriminately mix discussion of communication- and non-communication-based approaches to the study of leadership, without recognizing the distinction. An example helps to make the point. If the textbook presentations cited above are representative, then a consensus exists in the communication field that there have been five major approaches to leadership.

The first of these, the *trait approach,* distinguishes leaders from followers on the basis of a set of personal characteristics, such as intelligence, initiative, and dominance. Although there is no formal "theory" of leadership traits, standard treatments link traits directly with leader emergence or group performance, while ignoring communication (Stogdill, 1948).

The second, the *style approach,* asserts that leaders' manner of leading groups determines their success. The classic distinction among democratic, autocratic, and laissez-faire leadership styles was based on Lewin's (1951) field theory, and although these leadership styles are often operationalized in communicative terms, communication is not a critical concept in the theory.[1]

The third, the *emergent approach,* explores the process by which initially leaderless groups evolve a leadership structure. Communication is an integral part of that process and is treated as such by relevant researchers.

The fourth, the *contingency approach,* examines the impact of multiple factors—including leader and group member characteristics, leadership style, and task—on leader performance. Traditionally, contingency theories have disregarded communication, although, as I mention at the end of this chapter, this is beginning to change.

The fifth, the *functional approach,* addresses the instrumental role that leadership behaviors play in task accomplishment and group survival. Most of, if not all, these behaviors are communicative.

Any serious discussion of leadership must include all these approaches, and group communication pedagogy would be seriously incomplete if any were neglected. We should recognize, however, that only the emergent and functional approaches are fundamentally communication-based. Thus, when noncommunication-based approaches are included in chapters on leadership *as a communicative process* (as in Barge, 1997) or in a book on small group *discussion* (as in Pavitt & Curtis, 1994) with no comment on their fundamental differences from communication-based approaches, it invites confusion concerning what function, if any, communication plays in group leadership dynamics.

One reason communication- and noncommunication-based approaches to leadership have been so intermixed may be that not enough attention has been paid to the *explanatory forms* that communication-based theories of any phenomenon can take. The primary goal of this chapter is to apply these explanatory forms to theorizing about the relationship between communication and group leadership. To the extent that I am successful in meeting this goal, the result will serve both as a catalog of the *content* that past work in this area has included and future work might include and as a guide for how this content can be *formulated* into communication-based theory.

I emphasize two explanatory forms that are particularly relevant to group communication: the input-process-output and functional models. In the following sections, I discuss these forms before turning to the specific issue of group leadership.

TWO EXPLANATORY FORMS FOR COMMUNICATION THEORY

The Input-Process-Output Model

The input-process-output (hereafter "I-P-O") model reflects a causal process notion of communication. In a causal process model, certain objects are "generative mechanisms"; in other words, by their very nature, they are capable of affecting other objects. Some scholars have described this presumption as sufficient for a causal explanation (e.g., Bhaskar, 1978; Harre & Madden, 1975), leading them to concentrate on examples of causal processes in which cause and effect are directly associated. Causes are often linked only indirectly with their effects, however, and an explanation of these linkages requires more than an understanding of relevant generative mechanisms. In these cases, a more complete account requires description of any intermediaries that serve as conduits for the transfer of force from cause to effect (Salmon, 1984). In addition, a complete causal explanation would include the impact of any generative mechanisms and intervening conduits that serve to "counteract" the main causal linkages (Humphreys, 1988).

An I-P-O model of group communication describes a causal process by which the manipulation of generative mechanisms affects the amount or content of group discussion that acts as an intervening conduit and, in turn, affects outcomes thought to be conceptually subsequent to group discussion. Although analysts have explicated the I-P-O model only relatively recently (Hackman & Morris, 1975), it has been implicit in explanations of group discussion since the beginning of speech communication scholarship. An early example was the assumption that the adoption of formal decision-making procedures (e.g., reflective thinking) enhances the quality of group decisions through structuring a group's communication (McBurney & Hance, 1939; see Sunwolf & Seibold, Chapter 15, this volume). Since that time, many I-P-O group models have been proposed both outside (e.g., Karau & Kelly, 1992; Lorge & Solomon, 1955; Steiner, 1966) and inside (e.g., Hewes, 1986; Poole & DeSanctis, 1992; Salazar, 1996) the communication discipline.

In group research, I-P-O models have been used almost exclusively for the study of group decision making; however, they are just as relevant to many other aspects of group behavior, including leadership. I-P-O models can be applied to leadership in two ways. First, one can attempt to account for leadership as an output by asking the question of how a person comes to be viewed as performing a leadership role in a group. Second, one can attempt to account for the effects of leadership as an input by focusing on how a person in a leadership role can affect group communication and subsequent performance. I describe work relevant to both applications later in this chapter.

The Functional Model

Whereas causal explanations are attempted answers to the question, "How did such-and-such come about?," functional explanations (best described in Wright, 1976) are attempted answers to the question, "What is the purpose of such-and-such?" A functional explanation attempts to account for the presence of an attribute or action in terms of its role in the operation of some process or in maintaining the well-being of some entity. To borrow Trusted's (1987) example, grasshoppers are green because it helps them hide in the grass and evade predators. Functional explanations operate under what Hempel (1965) called a "hypothesis of self-regulation"; that is, the continued operation of the relevant system (in the example, the grasshopper's survival) is

predicated on it developing appropriate characteristics (its color). A complete functional explanation includes as its basis some underlying principle, such as natural selection (as in the grasshopper example) or human design, that governs the functional relationship under examination. A complete functional explanation also includes factors that both contribute to and counteract system functioning, although counteracting factors do not qualify as functions.[2] To finish the example, if children are particularly fascinated by green insects, their actions (e.g., capturing them) might counteract the advantages of grasshoppers' color.

Most communication theories that provide a functional explanation have adopted a particular type, "structural-functionalism," as a framework for delineating the necessary parts of a functional theory about social systems. Following from Fontes and Guardalabene (1976), this framework consists of:

1. the parts of the system,
2. the goals of the system,
3. the "functions" (behaviors) that keep the system moving toward its goals, and
4. the "structures," or attributes, of the system that perform these functions.

The theorist then fills in the framework with content relevant to the particular type of social system under examination. A general structural-functionalist approach to the functioning of a group would look something like this:

1. Groups consist of people involved in interdependent activities.
2. Groups have a set of goals.
3a. To reach these goals, the performance of certain functions is necessary. In general, these functions are instantiated through communicative acts.
3b. Certain other types of communicative acts serve as counteracting factors that make goal achievement less likely.
4. Social structures must develop within groups to ensure that the necessary

functions are performed and that counteracting factors are overcome. These social structures are called "roles."

The differences among theorists proposing functional explanations of group behavior can be found in the specific goals, functions, counteracting factors, and roles believed to be most critical. Later, I consider a few important examples as applied to group leadership.

Contrasts Between the Models

I-P-O and functional approaches to communication theory must be contrasted in much the same way as an epistemological relativist, such as Kuhn (1962), would contrast differing paradigms. One hallmark of relativism is the assertion that scientific concepts have different meanings when used in different paradigms. Although the concept "communication" has the same referent, verbal and nonverbal behavior, in both I-P-O and functional models, the sense of the term differs fundamentally. In an I-P-O model, communication serves as a conduit allowing for the impact of causal generative mechanisms on output. Communication is, thus, a passive medium. In a functional model, communication plays a more active role by allowing for one type of output rather than another. Because of this difference in interpretation, it would be theoretically incoherent to attempt to integrate I-P-O and functional models, or to "reduce" one to the other.

Similarly, the two models differ in their interpretation of the concept "group leadership." Thus, a discussion of the definition of "group leadership" must await the context provided by each model. In the following sections, I turn to those models and discuss, in turn, functional theorizing about the impact of group leadership roles and causal theorizing about the emergence and consequences of group leaders.

FUNCTIONAL THEORIZING ABOUT GROUP LEADERSHIP: STRUCTURAL-FUNCTIONALISM

In structural-functional theorizing, the concept "group leadership" refers to those functions that are instrumental in guiding a group to its goals, and a "leader" is a group member who regularly performs at least some of these functions. Thus, any group member can lead, irrespective of assigned position or the perceptions of other group members. Relevant theorists, however, differ on their conceptualization of group leadership functions, as the following discussion shows.

Bales

Bales probably is best known for his (1950) Interaction Process Analysis (IPA) scheme for coding group discussion and his positing, based on research findings using IPA, of a "linear phase model" of group development (see Keyton, Chapter 8, this volume). Most relevant to the present concerns is some lesser-known work best described in Bales (1953), in which a classic example of structural-functional theorizing is proposed.

According to Bales, groups have two major goals: survival (maintenance) and task performance. Maintenance requires group cohesion and necessitates the enactment of communicative acts performing "positive socioemotional" functions, such as stating agreement, releasing tension, and showing solidarity with other group members. Task performance requires constructive conflict and necessitates communicative acts performing task-oriented functions, such as giving and asking for information, opinions, and suggestions. The problem, in Bales's view, is that an inherent contradiction exists between group maintenance and task-performance goals. Conflict, even when constructive, leads to tension that can damage cohesiveness and threaten group maintenance, but too much attention to cohesion stifles constructive conflict and threatens task-performance quality. In addition, communicative acts counteracting group maintenance ("negative socioemotional" functions), such as disagreements, displays of tension, and antagonism among members, can further damage group cohesion and maintenance.

Bales specifically designed IPA to explore how groups attempt to manage the maintenance/task-performance contradiction. Research results with groups performing mostly artificial tasks implied that "healthy" groups achieve an equilibrium between the demands of task and maintenance through the use of several communicative tactics. For example, after a period of task work, group members defuse the resulting tension with some positive socioemotional talk and then return to the task when the tension dissipates. When negative socioemotional talk occurs, tension is released in stages, first through some task discussion (for example, by giving opinions about a disputed policy), followed by positive socioemotional talk. In total, discussion in "healthy" groups contains several times as much positive socioemotional as negative socioemotional talk and about twice as much task as maintenance talk (see Bales, 1953, for relevant data).

To ensure that equilibrium is sustained and the dual goals of task performance and maintenance are achieved, a structure of group leadership roles must evolve. It follows that two major group leadership roles are critical: task and maintenance leadership. Bales concentrated on the individuals who were judged by other group members to be the highest performer of each type of leadership. In his studies, the most frequent talker tended to be the most highly respected but most disliked member of the group; since Bales, that member has often been labeled the "task leader." The second-most frequent talker was less respected than the first but often was the most liked member of the group; that member has often been labeled the "maintenance leader."

A careful examination of the findings from Bales's studies, however, casts some doubt on those labels. First, Bales failed to examine through content coding whether members judged as occupying those roles actually performed a plurality of the associated behaviors.

Second, participants' ratings implied a further distinction between two different types of "task" leaders: the "best-idea" person (hereafter referred to as the "substantive leader") and the person who gave the most "guidance" (the "procedural leader"). The same person was seen as fulfilling both roles about half the time; when different people were chosen, the person considered to be the overall "group leader" was more likely to be the procedural, rather than the substantive, leader (Bales & Slater, 1955).

What is clear from the data is that as groups progressed from their first to later meetings, participants' ratings of all three of these roles tended to become more differentiated among members. Bales believed this to be an inevitable consequence of the maintenance/task-performance contradiction: Task leaders cause tension and become disliked, so a different person eventually comes to specialize in tension reduction (maintenance). Studies of groups performing more real-life tasks than those used in Bales's studies (e.g., Turk's, 1961, study of groups of nursing students discussing nursing-oriented issues), however, show that members tend to like their emergent task leader. The extreme role differentiation found by Bales thus appears to be an artifact of task artificiality.

Unlike the distinction between task and maintenance *leaders,* the distinction between task and maintenance leadership *functions,* as well as the further division of task functions into substantive and procedural, appears sound. The validity of the task/maintenance function distinction, however, has been subject to a feminist critique by Wyatt (1993). Two implications of Wyatt's discussion are worth noting. First, the distinction is most applicable to group decision-making contexts and is problematic in circumstances in which task work *is* maintenance, such as therapy, consciousness-raising, and support groups (see Cline, Chapter 19, this volume). Second, because utterances can simultaneously perform both task and maintenance functions, the unequivocal distinction between the two made in content-analytic coding schemes (e.g., IPA) may misrepresent the interactional significance of many utterances. For example, stating agreement is considered to be a maintenance function by Bales, but other content analysts consider it to be a task function (Fisher, 1974; Poole & Roth, 1989; Scheidel & Crowell, 1964); clearly, in group discussion, it can concurrently serve both functions.

Benne and Sheats

Although Benne and Sheats's (1948) essay listing functional roles that group members can perform during discussion predated Bales's relevant published work and can be considered the foundational statement of the functional approach to group discussion, it is examined here to compare it with Bales's position. Contrasting their view with the then-prevalent tendency to concentrate on the position of a single "group leader" (e.g., early researchers adopting the trait approach; see Stogdill, 1948), Benne and Sheats advanced a perspective of group leadership as a set of functions that helps groups perform satisfactorily; members share in leading groups to the extent that they perform these functions. Examples of task roles include both substantive (such as initiator, opinion giver, and elaborator) and procedural (such as coordinator, orienter, and procedural technician); examples of maintenance roles include encourager, harmonizer, and compromiser. In addition, Benne and Sheats identified a set of "individual" roles, such as aggressor, dominator, and recognition seeker, as counteracting factors that need to be overcome. All these roles are defined in terms of explicit behavioral functions.

Benne and Sheats's approach is based on nonsystematic observations of groups and is purely descriptive and atheoretical. It can be assumed that they view task and maintenance roles as critical for group performance, although there is no discussion of which functional roles are most critical, how the roles interrelate, or any explanatory mechanism analogous to Bales's equilibrium model. Benne and Sheats do state that groups in dif-

ferent stages of their task work probably require members to fulfill different roles. For instance, there is more of a need for an "evaluator-critic" when members evaluate solutions than when they analyze their task. Although it is never stated, there is perhaps a presumption in Benne and Sheats's thinking that the more members enact task and maintenance roles, and the less they perform individual roles, the more successful a group will be. Other functional theorists, however, would dispute this presumption. I have already discussed Bales's position that the sequence and proportion of task and maintenance activities is more important than the amount. Rauch and Behling (1984) argued that too much task leadership can lead to negative outcomes when a group's task is clearly structured and understood by members, whereas too much maintenance leadership can be dissatisfying to members when it is perceived as redundant and an obstruction to progress on a group's task.

Beyond Task and Maintenance Leadership Functions

Many other inventories of group leadership functions have been published (for an especially well-developed example, see Luthans & Lockwood, 1984). Of particular note are attempts to move beyond the venerable task/maintenance distinction. Schutz (1961), for example, proposed that groups have three critical functional areas: the "conflict-free" sphere (task), interpersonal relations, and "outer reality," or adaptation of the group to its external environment. The latter functional area includes regulating the optimal amount of interaction with, control over, and intimacy with other groups. Ancona and Caldwell (1988) developed a list of these "external" functions under the activity categories of "scout" (bringing information into a group), "ambassador" (exporting information out of a group), "sentry" (controlling the entry of information into a group), and "guard" (controlling the export of information out of a group). Ancona and Caldwell described groups as attempting to negotiate an equilibrium between the needs for interaction with and protection from the environment. Given this view, perhaps a theory analogous to Bales's may be devised from this work that can account for the performance of external functions.

Criticisms of Functional Approaches to Group Leadership

I (see Pavitt, 1994) previously presented two criticisms of functional approaches to group discussion that are relevant to group leadership as well. I will mention them in passing, referring the reader to the original discussion for the details, and propose a third criticism. First, a list of functions does not a theory make. Its empirical flaws notwithstanding, Bales's account of group equilibrium represents sound functional theorizing and provides a feasible explanatory principle for group communication and leadership phenomena. Most other accounts do little more than list some proposed functions, with minimal theoretical justification. For example, although Ancona and Caldwell make a convincing argument for going beyond the task/maintenance distinction, this distinction, with all its implications, follows neatly from Equilibrium Theory in a way that their external functions, at least at the present time, do not. The greatest challenge facing functional approaches to group leadership, therefore, is the advancement of theory that encompasses all the critical functional dimensions and behaviors theorists have proposed.

Second, there is inherent ambiguity in the concept of "function" predicated on the issue of abstraction level; that is, any communicative act can be described functionally at varying levels of abstraction. For example, the utterance, "The second proposal has been adopted by some corporations," simultaneously gives information (Bales) and elaborates (Benne and Sheats). Elaboration, however, is more abstract than giving information, because one gives information "in order to" elaborate (or, said another way, elaborates "by means of" giving information), rather than the

other way around. Because the functions proposed by Bales and by Benne and Sheats are on different conceptual levels, it is entirely possible for the empirical relationship of each with group outcomes to differ. If that is the case, then Bales's finding that outcomes are related to the sequence and proportion of functions and Benne and Sheats's suggestion that functions are linked to outcomes by sheer amount (perhaps curvilinearly, if Rauch and Behling, 1984, are correct) are not contradictory. Any researcher attempting to relate the performance of leadership functions with group task and maintenance outcomes, therefore, must consider the level of abstraction of any proposed set of leadership functions, to see which are and are not potentially in conflict. An empirical examination of the relationships among function sets on differing levels of abstraction would be most welcome (see Hirokawa, 1994).

A third criticism from the standpoint of communication scholarship is the danger that group leadership functions will be described without a detailed consideration of the communicative correlates of these functions. Bales's work escapes this criticism because it focuses specifically on the function of communicative acts. Benne and Sheats's original work has been developed to encompass communication by Jones and the Friends Peace Committee and Life Center of Philadelphia (see Pavitt & Curtis, 1994). The same, however, is not true for Ancona and Caldwell's work, and there is no evidence as yet that external functions are instantiated through communicative acts that cannot be classified as either task or maintenance. Research on the communicative correlates of external functions, therefore, would be valuable.

CAUSAL THEORIZING ABOUT GROUP LEADERSHIP: I-P-O MODELS

Group Leadership as Output: The Emergent Approach

In the emergent approach, "group leadership" is a perceptual judgment made by members of a group about one another. Simply put, a group member is a "leader" if other group members judge her or him as one. A great deal is known about the process by which these judgments are made. Given that an I-P-O model of group leadership emergence presumes that group communication is linked with these judgments, I begin with a discussion of the process-output linkage. To complete an I-P-O model, I continue with a description of various input factors associated with group communication.

The Process-Output Linkage

The emergent approach to group leadership stems from the notion that communication is the most important factor in determining which member of a group that lacks a firm, preexisting status structure will come to be perceived by the members as the group's leader. The empirical support for this position is strong. Meta-analyses relating the sheer amount of verbal participation in a group with judgments of task leadership have found correlations in the range of .50 to .70 (Mullen, Salas, & Driskell, 1989; Stein & Heller, 1983). Noncorrelational studies imply the same tendency; for example, Bales and Slater (1955) and Kirscht, Lodahl, and Haire (1959) found the perceived leader to be the most frequent contributor in 50% and 64% of their respective task groups.

What has been unclear is whether the content of discussion, rather than the sheer amount, affects emergent group leadership. Several studies report that the proportion of different types of content has the same relationship with perceived group leadership as total talk time (e.g., Kirscht et al., 1959; Morris & Hackman, 1969; Pavitt, Whitchurch, McClurg, & Petersen, 1995). For example, Lonetto and Williams (1974) detected no significant differences between perceived leaders' and other group members' proportional use of IPA categories. These results imply that emergent leaders might not say anything substantially different from other group members, but just more of the same thing.

Despite finding no general differences in content between emergent leaders and other group members, however, Morris and Hackman (1969) and Crockett (1955) report some content differences between high participators who were and were not viewed as leaders. For example, in Crockett's study, verbally active leaders performed proportionally more "problem-proposing" and "information-seeking" acts, and proportionally less "elaborating" acts, than verbally active nonleaders. As already noted, the second-most frequent talker in Bales's (1953) groups tended to be judged by other members as low on task leadership. Furthermore, although talk time and a composite measure of the IPA "attempted answers" categories correlated almost identically with perceived group leadership in Kirscht and colleagues' (1959) data, talk time and attempted answers correlated only .39 with each other. This finding contradicts the notion that emergent leaders simply say more of the same things that other group members say. Finally, Hawkins (1995) found perceived leadership to be strongly associated with group members' participation relevant to Hirokawa's (1982) critical discussion functions (e.g., "problem analysis" and "evaluation" of positive qualities; in this volume, see Poole [Chapter 2] and Hirokawa & Salazar [Chapter 7]) and unrelated to discussion irrelevant to those functions.

Some of the best evidence that discussion content matters in group leadership emergence over and above mere talk time comes from studies employing qualitative methods. Geier's (1967; see also Fisher, 1974) observations of and interviews with members about the emergence of leaders in their group revealed a two-stage model in which amount of discussion first distinguished candidates for perceived leadership from noncandidates, and content later distinguished successful from failed candidates. Building on that work, Sharf (1978) hypothesized that successful candidates would be those members who are most able to articulate a "rhetorical vision," a shared symbolic social reality with which all members could identify, thereby laying a foundation for a consensual group image of how to respond to task and maintenance difficulties. On the basis of audiotapes of two groups discussing their class projects, Sharf was able to describe the rhetorical visions offered by various rivals for group leadership, although the amount of data was insufficient to contrast successful and unsuccessful contenders.

There is also research evidence suggesting that engaging in procedural functions is particularly associated with emergent group leadership. Frey (1989) found perceived leaders and nonleaders to be distinguished more by number of procedurally-relevant than policy-relevant communicative acts. In the Bales and Slater (1955) study mentioned previously, the member rated as highest on "guiding the discussion" was chosen as the task leader 78.6% of the time. Ketrow (1991) formed three-person groups whose members were trained to specialize, respectively, in maintenance, substantive, and procedural communication; observers of videotapes of these groups' discussions most often judged the procedural specialist to be the group's leader. Baker's (1990) qualitative observations and interviews revealed that a concern with procedure (such as giving direction) rather than substantive task functions (such as initiating and developing proposals) was associated with emergent group leadership. Also relevant are a series of studies by Schultz (1974, 1978, 1980, 1982) in which emergent group leadership was associated with group members' postdiscussional judgments of one another's procedurally relevant attributes (e.g., formulates goals, summarizes, and gives direction) but not substantively relevant attributes (e.g., being informative, imaginative, and precise). Judgments of behaviors after the fact, however, are too tainted by preconceptions to be entirely trustworthy (Shweder & D'Andrade, 1980). Schultz's findings, therefore, need to be verified through content coding of interaction to determine whether emergent leaders' and nonleaders' behaviors actually differed as group member judgments implied.

Two factors distinguish between the studies in which discussion content was and was not

found to affect group leadership evaluations. Most studies that imply that discussion content is inconsequential used zero-history laboratory groups performing "artificial" tasks whose outcomes had no real consequence for the participants (e.g., Kirscht et al., 1959; Lonetto & Williams, 1974; Morris & Hackman, 1969). In contrast, studies revealing discussion content effects have tended to employ standing groups performing "real" tasks with consequential outcomes (e.g., Baker, 1990; Crockett, 1955; Frey, 1989; Geier, 1967; Hawkins, 1995; Sharf, 1978). In addition, the groups in Bales and Slater's (1955) study, although performing artificial tasks, were *not* zero-history. In a reanalysis of Pavitt et al.'s (1995) data, Pavitt, Whitchurch, Siple, and Petersen (1997) found discussion content to be related to leadership emergence for standing groups performing a real task but not for zero-history groups performing an artificial task. This suggests that past findings of no effects for discussion content probably are methodological artifacts. Future research needs to disambiguate whether group history or task consequentiality is the specific critical variable distinguishing circumstances in which verbal content does and does not affect group leader emergence.

As this review makes clear, much research has been performed relating verbal behavior to group leadership emergence. In contrast, there has been little work on nonverbal behavior and emergent group leadership (see Ketrow, Chapter 10, this volume, for a review of research on nonverbal communication in groups). Baird (1976), for example, found that the quantity of various nonverbal behaviors performed by group members, particularly gesturing and vertical head movements, correlated with leader emergence. Stogdill's (1948) classic review of trait-relevant leadership research included studies that found speech fluency to be associated with group members' perceptions of leaders. Clearly, more research regarding the relationship between nonverbal behavior and group leadership emergence is needed before a definitive conclusion can be drawn.

The Input-Process Linkage

The material reviewed above leads to the tentative conclusion that group members' communicative activity is related to leadership emergence, especially if verbal content is task relevant and, in particular, procedural in nature. The next step in developing an I-P-O model of group leadership emergence is to describe input factors that have been associated with the amount and type of communication enacted by group members. The following set of factors, though far from complete, has been the focus of significant research study (the interested reader should also consult a review complementary to the present effort by Bonito and Hollingshead, 1997).

Seating position. Studies show that people sitting at the ends of a rectangular table tend to be more talkative than those sitting at other positions (Hare & Bales, 1963; Strodtbeck & Hook, 1961) and are judged consistently by observers as their group's leader (Davenport, Brooker, & Munro, 1971; Pellegrini, 1971). The tendency for talk turns to alternate across a table when a group does not have a dominant member (Hearn, 1957; Steinzor, 1950) results in leaders tending to emerge from the least-populated side of the table, where group members have proportionally more talk time (Howells & Becker, 1962).

Individual predispositions. Several individual difference variables have been associated with amount and content of participation in group discussion (see Haslett & Ruebush, chapter 5, this volume, regarding the effects of individual differences on group communication). In particular, several personality traits have undergone examination. Burgoon (1977), for example, found the trait measure of "unwillingness to communicate" to be inversely related to talk time and amount of information seeking and giving in group discussion. Cronshaw and Ellis (1991) reported that high self-monitors—those who are characteristically attentive to their behavior and

adapt to the requirements of social situations (Snyder, 1979)—were more likely to perform task leadership behaviors than low self-monitors. Garland and Beard (1979), however, had shown earlier that self-monitoring effects hold only for women when groups perform certain types of tasks, such as idea generation through brainstorming. Frey (1989) described associations between some of the communicator styles proposed by Norton (1978, 1983; e.g., contentious/argumentative, attentive, and friendly) and the amount of different types of argumentative acts forwarded during group discussion. Hare and Bales (1963), not surprisingly, discovered an association between a trait measure of talkativeness and talk time by individuals in groups. They also found that group members high on an anxiety measure tended to shy away from the ends of a table and, thereby, shield themselves from any expectation that they would dominate discussion. Finally, self-confidence has been associated with attempts to influence other group members (French & Snyder, 1959).

The most ambitious attempt to associate individual predispositions with group communication was by Bales (1970). Bales proposed that both personality and group behavior could be classified on a three-dimensional scheme: Up/Down (dominance versus submission), Positive/Negative (social concern versus lack of concern), and Forward/Backward (conventionality versus radicalism). Bales measured these dimensions through questionnaires gauging impressions of group members made by observers or the members themselves. More relevant to the issue, this dimensional scheme can be used to infer relationships between personality measurements and behavioral tendencies as measured by IPA. For example, people rated as Up tended to be high on Cattell's Adventurous, Thurstone's Active, and the Minnesota Multiphasic Personality Inventory's (MMPI) Dominant trait measures and engaged in relatively little of the "gives information" IPA function during group discussion, whereas people rated as Positive were high on the MMPI Intellectual Suppressor measure and on the "shows solidarity/seems friendly" and "asks for opinion" IPA functions. (See Bales, 1970, chapter 6 and Appendix 1, for a complete discussion and references to the measures cited.)

Reinforcement. There is sufficient evidence to conclude that rewarding people for speaking increases their subsequent amount of communication, whereas punishing them results in decreases. Several relevant studies have used standard operant-conditioning methods, such as green lights as rewards and red lights for punishments (e.g., Aiken, 1965a; Bavelas, Hastorf, Gross, & Kite, 1965; Oakes, Droge, & August, 1960). Aiken (1965b) found that rewards increased discussion across all of Bales's IPA categories but punishments lowered discussion in only about half of them. In somewhat more realistic research, similar effects have occurred as a consequence of confederates' positively or negatively scripted responses to research participants (Levinger, 1959; Pepinsky, Hemphill, & Shevitz, 1958). Mortensen's (1966) study of student groups revealed that members who had received messages categorized as "recognition" and "support" increased their leadership-relevant communicative acts over time, whereas those not receiving these messages decreased their leadership acts.

Assigned leadership. Surprisingly, research has *not* supported the notion that assigned leaders actually perform the type of leadership-oriented communicative acts discussed in this chapter (Carter, Haythorn, Shriver, & Lanzetta, 1951; Mortensen, 1966). Instead, members with knowledge relevant to a group's task are most likely to perform the communicative acts associated with leadership (Hemphill, 1961; Marak, 1964).

Gender. Gender often has been associated with amount and type of participation in groups, but one must interpret these findings very carefully. Several researchers have found evidence that the content of women's talk tends to be *proportionally* higher in mainte-

nance and lower in task functions than men's (Eskilson & Wiley, 1976; Piliavin & Martin, 1978), and relevant reviews of the literature (Anderson & Blanchard, 1982; Eagly & Johnson, 1990) support this finding. One should not, however, conclude that this translates into a difference in sheer *amount* of communication. Some studies show that men talk more than women in mixed-gender groups (e.g., Strodtbeck, James, & Hawkins, 1957; Strodtbeck & Mann, 1956), although Anderson and Blanchard (1982), in a review of 10 relevant studies, found no differences in talk time. If we can presume that men do talk more than women in mixed-gender groups, there is some evidence that this preponderance is in the task dimension and that men and women perform an equal number of maintenance functions (Nemeth, Endicott, & Wachtler, 1976). Finally, Porter and Geis (1981) observed that women sitting at the head of a table in mixed-gender groups were *not* consistently judged as their group's leader, in contrast to men who were judged as being the group's leader.

Toward an Explanation of the Linkages

In summary, a number of input factors are associated with amount and type of communication in groups, which, in turn, relate to group leadership emergence. To complete the theoretical account requires the addition of an explanation based on relevant generative mechanisms. The review above suggests some possibilities for explaining the input-process relationship. First, as described earlier, some individual predispositions lead to variations in the amount of talk exhibited by group members. Second, factors such as relevant knowledge may lead some group members to believe that they are *entitled* to a high proportion of the floor. Third, the tendency for reinforcement to increase member participation may be mediated through heightened self-confidence, and higher self-confidence, in turn, may contribute to knowledgeable people's relative talkativeness. Fourth, high-status people tend to gravitate to the head of a table

(Strodtbeck & Hook, 1961), where they speak more.

With respect to the process-output linkage, two cognitive mechanisms are clearly relevant. First, a wealth of research has shown that drawing attention to a person leads to that person being attributed responsibility for her or his actions (Taylor & Fiske, 1975). Phillips and Lord (1981), for example, used various camera angles to demonstrate that visual salience increases observers' attributions of responsibility for group actions to the visually salient person. Bales (1970) noted that talkative group members draw attention to themselves through their domination of the floor; the same effect is likely involved in the leadership emergence of non–verbally active members (Baird, 1976). Sitting at the head of a table places those persons in the most visually salient position, which would explain the positive judgments of their leadership (Bass & Klubeck, 1952; Strodtbeck & Hook, 1961). In the operant-conditioning reinforcement studies described earlier, the identity of the reinforced member was obvious to all, and her or his emergent leadership (Aiken, 1965a; Bavelas et al., 1965) may be partly a result of such increased salience.

Second, there is clear evidence that observers' preconceptions about the attributes of an object have a powerful effect on their judgments about that object (see Shweder & D'Andrade, 1980). People have "implicit theories" about the attributes of prototypic leaders (Pavitt & Sackaroff, 1990); perceived attributes of group members are compared to these implicit theories, and members are considered leaders to the extent that the two match (Calder, 1977; Lord & Maher, 1991; Pavitt et al., 1995). If a group member, for example, believes that the "ideal leader" is someone who "states the group's procedure" and "encourages member participation," that person would judge other members' leadership as being high to the extent that they exhibit those behaviors. Evidence from questionnaire studies suggests that even "imaginary" leaders (e.g., someone described as "the head of a manufacturing company in the cen-

ter of the country") are rated in the context of such preconceptions (Eden & Leviatan, 1975; Rush, Thomas, & Lord, 1977; Weiss & Adler, 1981). Even seating position effects are attributable, in part, to the belief that certain chairs are prototypically associated with group leadership.

Finally, it is important to stress that gender differences may be descriptive of relevant communicative phenomena but do not provide an explanation for those phenomena. What is needed are relevant generative mechanisms underlying gender-linked effects. For example, consistent with findings by French and Snyder (1959), Instone, Major, and Bunker (1983) determined that self-confidence differences accounted for gender effects on the number of "influence" messages forwarded during group discussion (see Meyers & Brashers, Chapter 11, this volume, on social influence processes in groups). In addition, implicit-theory-based gender-role expectations likely interact with actual interactional differences in determining the tendency for men to emerge as task leaders and women as maintenance leaders (Eagly & Karau, 1991) and were used by Porter and Geis (1981) to account for their finding that a woman at the head of a table, in contrast to a man, is not likely to be judged as the leader of her mixed-gender group.

In summary, the finding that amount and type of discussion exhibited by members is associated with group leadership emergence can be expanded into an I-P-O model by including input factors that affect that discussion, along with satisfactory generative mechanisms. This expanded emergent approach is not, however, the only I-P-O model relevant to group leadership. What follows is a discussion of two others: the charismatic and mediational approaches.

Leadership as Input: The Charismatic Approach

Seemingly ignored throughout the early history of leadership research have been cases in which leaders have inspired followers to extraordinary levels of performance. The recent recognition of such events has led to an interest in "charismatic leadership" (see Bryman, 1992; Conger, 1989). The charismatic approach shares with the emergent approach the conception of "leadership" as a judgment made by others (in this case, followers). Although most organizational leaders are assigned rather than emergent, the attribution of "charisma" to a leader is a perceptual process, and the impact of a charismatic leader on followers is a consequence of that perception.

The notion of a leader as a charismatic figure who inspires unusual dedication from followers stems from scholarship in political science and religious studies. Its adoption into group and organizational theory, however, has been problematic. Much relevant research consists of case studies of both well-known (e.g., Lee Iacocca of Chrysler, Steven Jobs of Apple, and Mary Kay Ash of Mary Kay Cosmetics) and lesser-known figures that report the tactics that led to their immediate success. Missing is the fact that, in most of these cases, success was short-lived. Furthermore, although self-report research of subordinates shows correlations as high as .80 between charismatic leadership and *perceived* performance, correlations between charismatic leadership and *objective* performance measures are in the order of .30. The inflated self-report data probably result from the tendency for people to attribute more responsibility for both success and failure to leadership than to other, equally plausible factors, such as task difficulty (Meindl & Ehrlich, 1987; Meindl, Ehrlich, & Dukerich, 1985). This implies that group members react to success by attributing it to the characteristics they believe successful leaders "ought" to have (see Bryman, 1992).

Despite these research problems, charismatic leadership presents a new group leadership "style" worthy of serious consideration, and despite differences in details, a consensual I-P-O model of its impact can be synthesized from such scholars as Bass (1985), Bryman (1992), Conger (1989), and House (1977). Accordingly, charismatic leaders tend to have

a set of relevant predispositions (high need for power, great self-confidence, willingness to take risks, and strong conviction in their beliefs), sufficient relevant experience, and an abstract but easily understood "vision" of what their group or organization ought to stand for (e.g., Job's quest to improve education through bringing computers to the masses). They tend to display a number of behaviors characteristic of the value system underlying their vision, such as maintaining a prodigious work schedule and demonstrating their own personal success. Most notably, charismatic leaders are able to communicate effectively the content of their vision, as well as confidence in their followers' abilities to attain it, by using emotional, metaphorical, and picturesque language and animated vocal and gestural displays. (For hypothesized message content differences between charismatic and noncharismatic leaders, see Shamir, House, & Arthur, 1993.) When such communication is successful, the result in followers is unusual confidence in and loyalty to the leader, strong identification with their group and the leader's vision, high motivation and commitment, and increased self-confidence. Such results are forthcoming, however, only when the situation is particularly stressful and uncertain, group members are creative and dedicated, and the leader has sufficient autonomy to see her or his vision through to completion. Furthermore, other predispositions serve as counteracting factors that limit a charismatic leader's long-term effectiveness. Charismatic leaders tend to be cognitively simple, and, as a consequence, inflexible, autocratic, and self-serving, with little tolerance for disagreement. In the long run, their relationships with both superiors and subordinates often deteriorate and become dysfunctional (see Bass, 1985; Bryman, 1992; Conger, 1989; House, 1977).

Welcome additions to the evidence concerning charismatic leadership and communication are some recent experimental studies. Howell and Frost (1989) operationalized the distinctions among task, maintenance, and charismatic leadership "styles" through a manipulation of the communication to research participants by a confederate "leader" describing an executive, decision-making simulation task. As an example of part of this manipulation, a confederate "task leader" told participants to follow the task instructions using a "moderate" tone of voice and "neutral" facial expressions, a "maintenance leader" told them to relax while working using a "warm" tone of voice and "friendly" facial expressions, and a "charismatic leader" expressed confidence in their ability using a "captivating" tone of voice and "animated" facial expressions. The charismatic style resulted in better overall task performance and participant satisfaction, as well as a higher capability to overcome low-performance norms (manipulated through the behavior of confederate "coworkers"), than either of the other two styles. Howell and Frost's manipulation, however, confounded verbal content with nonverbal and paralinguistic style; in disambiguating these, Kirkpatrick and Locke (1996) found that the content of a charismatic leader's communication affected performance through the intervention of group members' performance goals and self-efficacy. Both studies employed individual tasks in multiple-person settings, and the examination of actual group tasks would be a natural extension of this work.

The generative mechanisms relevant to charismatic leadership are similar to those applicable to the emergent leadership approach. As described above, leader behavior, on the input side, is partly a function of predisposition. On the output side, the legitimization of charismatic leaders seems to depend on unusual, attention-grabbing behavioral (e.g., prodigious work schedule) and communicative tactics and results in predictable salience effects for leaders and their messages. As Conger (1989) proposed, followers may then develop a particularly strong and positive impression of such leaders (e.g., as confident, visionary, trustworthy, and expert), which may, in turn, increase followers' self-confidence, motivation, and compliance. In those cases in which charismatic leaders

eventually fail, these declines may be a partial result of changes in followers' impressions of them (e.g., to being stubborn, dictatorial, and back-stabbing). Further study of this process during the entire "life cycle" of charismatic leadership effects would be valuable.

Leadership as Input: The Mediational Approach

Although the "mediational approach" to group leadership originally was proposed by organizational theorist Weick (1978), communication theorists have taken the lead in developing it. Fisher (1986) was responsible for importing the notion into communication scholarship, and Barge (1996; see also Barge & Hirokawa, 1989) has begun the work of formalizing its tenets. As in the functional model, "group leadership" is seen as a set of behaviors aiding group goal attainment, and a "group leader" is a person who regularly performs these behaviors. I have, however, placed the mediational approach under the I-P-O umbrella as a result of the proposal by both Fisher and Barge that individual difference factors affect the performance of these behaviors.

The mediational approach is based on the idea that decision-making groups are faced with a potentially overwhelming number of options for interpreting the task-relevant information at their disposal (see Propp, Chapter 9, this volume, for an overview of information processing in decision-making groups). The basic function of leadership, therefore, is to devise a set of procedures for limiting the number of plausible interpretations and, as a consequence, the number of feasible courses of action, to a cognitively manageable level. Leadership as a medium for informational simplification is instantiated through communication; hence, in this approach, a leader's communication intervenes between various input variables and leadership effectiveness as an output.

Mediational leadership theorists thus far have focused on delineating relevant input variables that affect a leader's ability to structure the group discussion process. Fisher (1986) suggested that cognitive complexity and communicative adaptability on the part of a leader are critical for allowing her or him to respond well to situational constraints. Although in general agreement with Fisher, Barge (1996) has begun delineating a more specific contingency approach. Barge listed a series of competencies, including the ability to direct a group's procedure and maintain positive relationships among group members, necessary for a leader to manage both the flux of information available and the interaction among group members. The extent to which these competencies need to be enacted in any particular circumstance, according to Barge, depends on such factors as task complexity, group climate, role clarity, and a group's interdependence with its environment. Although this line of research is promising, what remains unclear about the mediational perspective of group leadership is the specific role of communication in the I-P-O linkage and what generative mechanisms, other than leader attributes, are needed for an adequate explanation.

Criticisms of the I-P-O Model

There have been two major challenges to the I-P-O model. The first was contained in Fisher and Hawes's (1971) argument for the Interact Systems Model (ISM) of a group as communicative process (in this volume, see Chapters 2 [Poole], 3 [Mabry], and 8 [Keyton]) as an alternative to the traditional Human Systems Model (HSM) of a group as a collection of people (see Poole, Chapter 2, this volume). Whereas the HSM directs attention to the relationships among "traditional" input and output variables, such as cohesiveness, power, and leadership, the ISM limits inquiry into group discussion process and those input variables that directly affect that process. Fisher and Hawes's claim that "the dependent variable is always the process of small group development" (p. 453) seemingly disqualifies the study of the process-output relationship and implies a rejection of the I-P-O model.

Although the majority of research articles on groups published in communication journals during the 1970s were ISM-oriented, by the end of the decade, the presumptions on which the ISM was based were the target of several major criticisms. I limit the discussion to just one, made most explicitly by Becker (1980): that group communication research was no longer addressing its traditional concern with improvement in group practice. About this time, ISM-based research largely disappeared. Although it is difficult to say exactly why, it is clear that researchers returned to the traditional concern with output, approached both through I-P-O (most explicitly in Hewes, 1986; Jarboe, 1988) and functional (Gouran, 1981; Hirokawa, 1982) alternatives.

There is one implication of the ISM model that has not received the attention it deserves from theorists and researchers: that communicative processes must be studied in terms of the sequential structure of utterances. This implication was taken up by Hewes (1986) in the second major challenge to the I-P-O model. Hewes argued that communication, by its very nature, must be approached as sequential structure. Sequential structure means that each utterance responds to an utterance that occurred beforehand in the discussion, and if this is not the case, then it is difficult to conceive of the discussants as *communicating* with one another. The only research discussed in this chapter that considers communicative process as sequential structure is Bales's (1953) analysis of the conditional probabilities among the 12 IPA categories for consecutive utterances when made by the same member and by different group members. The issue of sequential structure in leadership communicative acts cries out for both theory and research from both causal and functional perspectives.

Hewes's (1986) essay offered a second criticism of I-P-O research: that there have been no unambiguous empirical demonstrations that communicative process is related to output variables independent of the impact of relevant input variables on that output. Without such a demonstration, there is no evidence that communication is a generative mechanism in its own right; thus, it can be ignored in favor of more parsimonious input-output models. In a later reprise, Hewes (1996) explicitly noted that if the communicative process cannot be shown to be a generative mechanism, then it plays no explanatory role in group communication theory.

I agree with much, but not all, of Hewes's second criticism. It is true that there have been no unambiguous empirical demonstrations of the causal efficacy of communicative process. Furthermore, such a demonstration should not be expected, because communication is *not* a causal agent; as described earlier, it is a conduit for transferring causal force from input to output. This does not, however, cause any problems for I-P-O models. I-P-O models, *by their very nature,* treat communicative process as a conduit that allows for the effects of input on output. Any research demonstration that process variables account for more variance in output variables than do input variables means, within the context of I-P-O models, either that communicative process variables have been measured more reliably than input variables or that there are other relevant input variables that have been overlooked by the researcher. Nevertheless, this does not mean that communication scholars should ignore process variables. As discussed earlier, a complete explanation of a causal process requires an examination of enabling intermediaries along with generative mechanisms.

Hewes's essays have had a salutary impact on research on group decision making in leading scholars to make more defensible claims about process-output relationships and to consider explicitly the relative impact of inputs and processes on outputs (Hirokawa, 1988; Jarboe, 1988; Salazar, 1996). Because none of these studies has examined the sequential structure of group communication, however, none provides any evidence that group members were, in actuality, *speaking with one another;* thus, Hewes's challenge remains unanswered.

Neither Hewes's essay nor responses to it have had any impact on group leadership theory as of yet. In fact, group leadership may be an area in which the presumptions underlying Hewes's claims can undergo examination. As this chapter has shown, there is strong evidence that amount of communication is strongly associated with group leadership emergence when that communication is task relevant. One can presume that an emergent leader's utterances are in general responses to other members' previous utterances and, thereby, maintain a coherent group discussion. What if this were not the case? Would, for example, a group's most talkative member still emerge as a perceived leader if her or his input, even if task relevant, was not normally in response to other members, through, for example, constant abrupt topic changes? If research showed this to be the case, Hewes's argument might be disconfirmed.

CONCLUSION

In this chapter, I discussed four approaches to group leadership: the functional, emergent, charismatic, and mediational. These represent only a small fraction of the entire literature on group leadership theory and research; however, they are a very special fraction, because they take on two of the explanatory forms of communication-based theory. The vast majority of traditional and recent theories about leadership do not take on these forms; they attempt to explain and predict leadership effectiveness as a consequence of such factors as follower characteristics, situational constraints, and possible leadership styles (for a good review, see Yukl, 1981). Even in the context of leadership style, the concept of "communication" appears only rarely in these theories, and when it does, the treatment is insufficiently developed. In addition, many well-known leadership theories do not address groups as a particular concern. More broadly, the theoretical interests of the majority of organizational leadership scholars and those who work from a group communication perspective have been widely divergent. For most organizational theorists, leadership is synonymous with the day-to-day management of subordinates; for group communication theorists, leadership is a behavioral pattern enacted in or a perceptual judgment that emerges through group discussion.

This is not to suggest that noncommunication-based approaches are unamenable to transformation. As the review of the emergent leadership approach makes clear, communication-oriented personal characteristics fit comfortably and possibly can serve as generative mechanisms in I-P-O theories. The most promising avenue for infusing noncommunication-based theorizing with a communication basis, however, is through a redefinition of "leadership style" into communication terminology. Several organizational leadership theories include leadership style as a factor in explaining followers' job performance and/or satisfaction, and conceivably can be transformed into I-P-O models with a reorientation of "style" performing the intervening role. Here, I consider four classic organizational leadership theories that could undergo this reconceptualization.

In his *Contingency Theory* relating situational and leader characteristics, Fiedler (1978) proposed the existence of a trait called "LPC" (an acronym for "least preferred co-worker"), which I interpret along "cognitive complexity" lines as leaders' ability to distinguish between the task and social needs of their followers. "High-LPC" leaders can make that distinction and tend to have a socially oriented style, whereas "low-LPC" leaders cannot and tend toward a task-oriented style. The task style seems to be the more successful of the two in situations where leaders' ability to predict and control outcomes is either low (because floundering groups need direction) or high (probably because such task-oriented leaders give successful groups the autonomy they want), whereas the social style is more successful in intermediate situations (because such groups need encouragement). Leadership style thus mediates between the inputs of task and situation and the output of group performance.

Whereas Fiedler's theory implies that leadership style is a consequence of predisposition, Vroom and Yetton's (1973) *Normative Model* posits that leadership style is a consequence of choice. That choice is selected from options including autocratic, consultative (in which leaders make decisions after discussing the problem with followers), participative (in which leaders make decisions along with followers), and delegative (in which leaders ask followers to make decisions), and should be based on such factors as the importance of the decision, the amount of task-relevant information possessed by leaders and followers, and the degree to which followers accept an autocratic decision, among others. These factors would be input variables linked through leadership style, with task performance and follower satisfaction as outputs.

Hersey and Blanchard's (1969) *Situational Theory* also implies that leadership style is a result of choice. In this case, leaders must estimate followers' willingness and capability to take responsibility, and adopt task or social styles accordingly. This view differs from Bales's, for example, in the claim that these two styles are not mutually exclusive; some circumstances require leaders to perform both. Analogously to Fiedler, Hersey and Blanchard believe that a task orientation is most helpful when followers need direction, whereas a maintenance orientation is called for when followers understand the task but need encouragement. Neither style is needed when followers can work independently; leaders delegate work and leave followers alone. Hence, leadership style mediates between followers' motivations and capabilities and task performance.

House and Dessler's (1974) *Path-Goal Theory* includes the notion that a leader, through choice of style, can affect followers' expectations about the consequence of their work and, in turn, their performance and satisfaction. Style choices include supportive, directive, participative, and achievement oriented. Inputs that determine the impact of style choice on output include followers' predispositions and abilities, as well as various task factors.

Not one of these four classic leadership theories includes a serious discussion of the communication correlates of leadership style, although there have been a few attempts to determine these correlates. In their experiments mentioned above, Howell and Frost (1989) and Kirkpatrick and Locke (1996) operationalized task, maintenance, and charismatic leadership styles in communicative terms. Groupthink researchers have done the same for autocratic and participative styles (Flowers, 1977; Leana, 1985; Peterson, 1997), but these efforts lack systematization. More recent work by management theorists has made some inroads in this respect (Hersey, Blanchard, & Johnson, 1996; Yukl, 1981). One early effort from the communication literature is Sargent and Miller's (1971) attempt to distinguish autocratic and democratic leadership styles with respect to IPA categories. They found, for example, autocratic leaders to be proportionally higher in the IPA "attempted answers" categories, as well as proportionally lower in the "questions" categories, than democratic leaders. The search for communication correlates of leadership style deserves far more attention than it has thus far received.

Finally, it is natural to wish for integrations of causal and functional thinking into "complete" communication-based theories of group leadership. It is true that causal and functional theories can, in principle, be integrated (Trusted, 1987); however, this impulse must be guarded against, because in practice, the two perspectives imply different and opposing conceptions of communication. In causal theories, communication serves as a conduit that allows for the impact of causal generative mechanisms on output, whereas in functional theories, communication plays a more active role by allowing for one type of output rather than another. This is not to say that "informal" connections between complementary theories of each type cannot be made. One obvious example is the association between Bales's earlier (1953) functional approach, relating

task and maintenance achievement with relevant communicative functions, and his later (1970) causal work, linking individual predispositions with tendencies to perform these functions. Other fruitful linkages between causal and functional theories of communication and group leadership surely are possible.

NOTES

1. According to Lewin (1951), a group exists within a "life-space" that represents the current relationship between the group and various goals (locations in the life-space). A group's leader is capable of moving the group in its life-space either toward or away from these goals. A democratic leader attempts to move the group toward its goals, an autocratic leader attempts to move the group toward the leader's goals, and a laissez-faire leader makes no attempt to move the group.

2. I have stated (Pavitt, 1994) that counteracting factors cannot be considered "functions" and, as a consequence, ought not be part of a functional explanation. I now consider the latter half of that claim to be wrong. This issue has significance for attempts at functional explanations of group decision making in which negative influences have been considered (Gouran, 1981).

REFERENCES

Aiken, E. G. (1965a). Changes in interpersonal descriptions accompanying the operant conditioning of verbal frequency in groups. *Journal of Verbal Learning and Verbal Behavior, 4,* 243-247.

Aiken, E. G. (1965b). Interaction process analysis changes accompanying operant conditioning of verbal frequency in small groups. *Perceptual and Motor Skills, 21,* 52-54.

Ancona, D. G., & Caldwell, D. F. (1988). Beyond task and maintenance: Defining external functions in groups. *Group & Organization Studies, 13,* 468-494.

Anderson, L. R., & Blanchard, P. N. (1982). Sex differences in task and social-emotional behavior. *Basic and Applied Social Psychology, 3,* 109-139.

Baird, J. E., Jr. (1976). Some nonverbal elements of leadership emergence. *Southern Speech Communication Journal, 42,* 352-361.

Baker, D. C. (1990). A qualitative and quantitative analysis of verbal style and the elimination of potential leaders in small groups. *Communication Quarterly, 38,* 13-26.

Bales, R. F. (1950). *Interaction process analysis: A method for the study of small groups.* Cambridge, MA: Addison-Wesley.

Bales, R. F. (1953). The equilibrium problem in small groups. In T. Parsons, R. F. Bales, & E. A. Shils (Eds.), *Working papers in the theory of action* (pp. 111-161). Glencoe, IL: Free Press.

Bales, R. F. (1970). *Personality and interpersonal behavior.* New York: Holt, Rinehart & Winston.

Bales, R. F., & Slater, P. E. (1955). Role differentiation in small decision-making groups. In T. Parsons & R. F. Bales (Eds.), *Family, socialization and interaction process* (pp. 259-306). Glencoe, IL: Free Press.

Barge, J. K. (1996). Leadership skills and the dialectics of leadership in group decision making. In R. Y. Hirokawa & M. S. Poole (Eds.), *Communication and group decision making* (2nd ed., pp. 301-342). Thousand Oaks, CA: Sage.

Barge, J. K. (1997). Leadership as communication. In L. R. Frey & J. K. Barge (Eds.), *Managing group life: Communicating in decision-making groups* (pp. 202-233). Boston: Houghton Mifflin.

Barge, J. K., & Hirokawa, R. Y. (1989). Toward a communication competency model of group leadership. *Small Group Behavior, 20,* 167-189.

Bass, B. M. (1985). *Leadership and performance beyond expectations.* New York: Free Press.

Bass, B. M. (1990). *Bass and Stogdill's handbook of leadership: Theory, research, and managerial applications* (3rd ed.). New York: Free Press.

Bass, B. M., & Klubeck, S. (1952). Effects of seating arrangements on leaderless group discussion. *Journal of Abnormal and Social Psychology, 47,* 724-727.

Bavelas, A., Hastorf, A. H., Gross, A. E., & Kite, W. M. (1965). Experiments on the alteration of group structure. *Journal of Experimental Social Psychology, 1,* 55-70.

Becker, S. L. (1980). Directions for small group research for the 1980s. *Central States Speech Journal, 31,* 221-224.

Benne, K. D., & Sheats, P. (1948). Functional roles of group members. *Journal of Social Issues, 4*(2), 41-49.

Bhaskar, R. (1978). *A realist theory of science* (2nd ed.). Atlantic Highlands, NJ: Humanities Press.

Bonito, J. A., & Hollingshead, A. B. (1997). Participation in small groups. In B. R. Burleson (Ed.), *Communication yearbook 20* (pp. 227-261). Thousand Oaks, CA: Sage.

Bryman, A. (1992). *Charisma and leadership in organizations.* London: Sage.

Burgoon, J. K. (1977). Unwillingness to communicate as a predictor of small group discussion behaviors and evaluations. *Central States Speech Journal, 28,* 122-133.

Calder, B. J. (1977). An attribution theory of leadership. In B. M. Staw & G. R. Salancik (Eds.), *New directions in organizational behavior* (pp. 179-204). Chicago: St. Clair Press.

Carter, L., Haythorn, W., Shriver, B., & Lanzetta, J. (1951). The behavior of leaders and other group members. *Journal of Abnormal and Social Psychology, 46,* 589-595.

Conger, J. A. (1989). *The charismatic leader: Behind the mystique of exceptional leadership.* San Francisco: Jossey-Bass.

Crockett, W. H. (1955). Emergent leadership in small, decision-making groups. *Journal of Abnormal and Social Psychology, 51,* 378-383.

Cronshaw, S. F., & Ellis, R. J. (1991). A process investigation of self-monitoring and leader emergence. *Small Group Research, 22,* 403-420.

Davenport, W. G., Brooker, G., & Munro, N. (1971). Factors in social perception: Seating position. *Perceptual and Motor Skills, 33,* 747-752.

Eagly, A. H., & Johnson, B. T. (1990). Gender and leadership style: A meta-analysis. *Psychological Bulletin, 108,* 233-256.

Eagly, A. H., & Karau, S. J. (1991). Gender and the emergence of leaders: A meta-analysis. *Journal of Personality and Social Psychology, 60,* 685-710.

Eden, D., & Leviatan, U. (1975). Implicit leadership theory as a determinant of the factor structure underlying supervisor behavior scales. *Journal of Applied Psychology, 60,* 736-741.

Ellis, D. G., & Fisher, A. B. (1994). *Small group decision making: Communication and the group process* (4th ed.). New York: McGraw-Hill.

Eskilson, A., & Wiley, M. G. (1976). Sex composition and leadership in small groups. *Sociometry, 39,* 183-194.

Fiedler, F. E. (1978). The contingency model and the dynamics of the leadership process. In L. Berkowitz (Ed.), *Advances in experimental social psychology* (Vol. 11, pp. 59-112). New York: Academic Press.

Fisher, B. A. (1974). *Small group decision making: Communication and the group process.* New York: McGraw-Hill.

Fisher, B. A. (1986). Leadership: When does the difference make a difference? In R. Y. Hirokawa & M. S. Poole (Eds.), *Communication and group decision-making* (pp. 197-215). Beverly Hills, CA: Sage.

Fisher, B. A., & Hawes, L. C. (1971). An interact system model: Generating a grounded theory of small groups. *Quarterly Journal of Speech, 57,* 444-453.

Flowers, M. L. (1977). A laboratory test of some implications of Janis's groupthink hypothesis. *Journal of Personality and Social Psychology, 35,* 888-896.

Fontes, N., & Guardalabene, N. (1976). Structural-functionalism: An introduction to the literature. *Human Communication Research, 2,* 299-310.

French, J. P., Jr., & Snyder, R. (1959). Leadership and interpersonal power. In D. Cartwright (Ed.), *Studies in social power* (pp. 118-149). Ann Arbor: University of Michigan, Research Center for Group Dynamics, Institute for Social Research.

Frey, L. R. (1989). Exploring the input-throughput-output relationship in small groups: Communicative predispositions, argumentation and leadership. *World Communication, 18*(2), 43-70.

Frey, L. R., & Barge, J. K. (Eds.). (1997). *Managing group life: Communicating in decision-making groups.* Boston: Houghton Mifflin.

Garland, H., & Beard, J. F. (1979). Relationship between self-monitoring and leader emergence across two task situations. *Journal of Applied Psychology, 64,* 403-420.

Geier, J. G. (1967). A trait approach to the study of leadership in small groups. *Journal of Communication, 17,* 316-323.

Gouran, D. S. (1981). Unanswered questions in research on communication in the small group: A challenge for the 1980s. *Communication, 10,* 17-31.

Hackman, J. R., & Morris, C. G. (1975). Group tasks, group interaction process, and group performance effectiveness: A review and proposed integration. In L. Berkowitz (Ed.), *Advances in experimental social psychology* (Vol. 8, pp. 45-99). New York: Academic Press.

Hare, A. P., & Bales, R. F. (1963). Seating position and small group interaction. *Sociometry, 26,* 480-486.

Harre, R., & Madden, E. H. (1975). *Causal powers: A theory of natural necessity.* Totowa, NJ: Rowman & Littlefield.

Hawkins, K. W. (1995). Effects of gender and communication content on leadership emergence in small task-oriented groups. *Small Group Research, 26,* 234-249.

Hearn, G. (1957). Leadership and the spatial factor in small groups. *Journal of Abnormal and Social Psychology, 54,* 269-272.

Hempel, C. G. (1965). *Aspects of scientific explanation and other essays in the philosophy of science.* New York: Free Press.

Hemphill, J. K. (1961). Why people attempt to lead. In L. Petrullo & B. M. Bass (Eds.), *Leadership and interpersonal behavior* (pp. 201-215). New York: Holt, Rinehart & Winston.

Hersey, P., & Blanchard, K. H. (1969). Life cycle theory of leadership. *Training and Development Journal, 23*(5), 26-34.

Hersey, P., Blanchard, K. H., & Johnson, D. E. (1996). *Management of organizational behavior* (7th ed.). Upper Saddle River, NJ: Prentice Hall.

Hewes, D. E. (1986). A socio-egocentric model of group decision-making. In R. Y. Hirokawa & M. S. Poole (Eds.), *Communication and group decision-making* (pp. 265-291). Beverly Hills, CA: Sage.

Hewes, D. E. (1996). Small group communication may not influence decision making: An amplification of socio-egocentric theory. In R. Y. Hirokawa & M. S. Poole (Eds.), *Communication and group decision making* (2nd ed., pp. 179-212). Thousand Oaks, CA: Sage.

Hirokawa, R. Y. (1982). Group communication and problem-solving effectiveness: A critical review of inconsistent findings. *Communication Quarterly, 30,* 134-141.

Hirokawa, R. Y. (1988). Group communication and decision-making performance: A continued test of the functional perspective. *Human Communication Research, 14,* 487-515.

Hirokawa, R. Y. (1994). Functional approaches to the study of group discussion: Even good notions have their problems. *Small Group Research, 25,* 542-550.

House, R. J. (1977). A 1976 theory of charismatic leadership. In J. G. Hunt & L. L. Larson (Eds.), *Leadership: The cutting edge: A symposium held at Southern Illinois University, Carbondale, October 27-28, 1976* (pp. 189-207). Carbondale: Southern Illinois University Press.

House, R. J., & Dessler, G. (1974). The path goal theory of leadership: Some post hoc and a priori tests. In J. Hunt & L. Larson (Eds.), *Contingency approaches to leadership: A symposium held at Southern Illinois University, Carbondale, May 17-18, 1973* (pp. 29-55). Carbondale: Southern Illinois University Press.

Howell, J. M., & Frost, P. J. (1989). A laboratory study of charismatic leadership. *Organizational Behavior and Human Decision Processes, 43,* 243-269.

Howells, L. T., & Becker, S. W. (1962). Seating arrangement and leadership emergence. *Journal of Abnormal and Social Psychology, 64,* 148-150.

Humphreys, P. W. (1988). Scientific explanation: The causes, some of the causes, and nothing but the causes. In P. Kitcher & W. C. Salmon (Eds.), *Minnesota studies in the philosophy of science: Vol. 13. Scientific explanation, space, and time* (pp. 283-306). Minneapolis: University of Minnesota Press.

Instone, D., Major, B., & Bunker, B. B. (1983). Gender, self-confidence, and social influence strategies: An organizational simulation. *Journal of Personality and Social Psychology, 44,* 322-333.

Jarboe, S. (1988). A comparison of input-process, process-output, and input-process-output models of small group problem-solving effectiveness. *Communication Monographs, 55,* 121-142.

Karau, S. J., & Kelly, J. R. (1992). The effects of time scarcity and time abundance on group performance quality and interaction process. *Journal of Experimental Social Psychology, 28,* 542-571.

Ketrow, S. M. (1991). Communication role specializations and perceptions of leadership. *Small Group Research, 22,* 492-514.

Kirkpatrick, S. A., & Locke, E. A. (1996). Direct and indirect effects of three core charismatic leadership components on performance and attitudes. *Journal of Applied Psychology, 81,* 36-51.

Kirscht, J. D., Lodahl, T. M., & Haire, M. (1959). Some factors in the selection of leaders by members of small groups. *Journal of Abnormal and Social Psychology, 58,* 406-408.

Kuhn, T. S. (1962). *The structure of scientific revolutions.* Chicago: University of Chicago Press.

Leana, C. R. (1985). A partial test of Janis's groupthink model: Effects of group cohesiveness and leader behavior on defective decision making. *Journal of Management, 11,* 5-17.

Levinger, G. (1959). The development of perceptions and behavior in newly formed social power relationships. In D. Cartwright (Ed.), *Studies in social power* (pp. 83-98). Ann Arbor: University of Michigan, Research Center for Group Dynamics, Institute for Social Research.

Lewin, K. (1951). *Field theory in social science: Selected theoretical papers* (D. Cartwright, Ed.). New York: Harper & Row.

Lonetto, R., & Williams, D. (1974). Personality, behavioural and output variables in a small group task situation: An examination of consensual leader and non-leader differences. *Canadian Journal of Behavioural Science, 6,* 59-74.

Lord, R. G., & Maher, K. J. (1991). *Leadership and information processing: Linking perceptions and performance.* Boston: Unwin Hyman.

Lorge, L., & Solomon, H. (1955). Two models of group behavior in the solution of eureka-type problems. *Psychometrika, 20,* 139-148.

Luthans, F., & Lockwood, D. L. (1984). Toward an observation system for measuring leader behavior in natural settings. In J. G. Hunt, D.-M. Hosking, C. A. Schriesheim, & R. Stewart (Eds.), *Leaders and managers: International perspectives on managerial behavior and leadership* (pp. 117-141). New York: Pergamon.

Marak, G. E. (1964). The evolution of leadership structure. *Sociometry, 27,* 174-182.

McBurney, J. H., & Hance, K. G. (1939). *The principles and methods of discussion.* New York: Harper and Brothers.

Meindl, J. R., & Ehrlich, S. B. (1987). The romance of leadership and the evaluation of organizational performance. *Academy of Management Journal, 30,* 91-106.

Meindl, J. R., Ehrlich, S. B., & Dukerich, J. M. (1985). The romance of leadership. *Administrative Science Quarterly, 30,* 78-102.

Morris, C. G., & Hackman, J. R. (1969). Behavioral correlates of perceived leadership. *Journal of Personality and Social Psychology, 13,* 350-361.

Mortensen, C. D. (1966). Should the discussion group have an assigned leader? *Speech Teacher, 15,* 34-41.

Mullen, B., Salas, E., & Driskell, J. E. (1989). Salience, motivation, and artifact as contributions to the relation between participation rate and leadership. *Journal of Experimental Social Psychology, 25,* 545-559.

Nemeth, C., Endicott, J., & Wachtler, J. (1976). From the '50s to the '70s: Women in jury deliberations. *Sociometry, 39,* 293-304.

Norton, R. W. (1978). Foundations of a communicator style construct. *Human Communication Research, 4,* 99-112.

Norton, R. W. (1983). *Communicator style.* Beverly Hills, CA: Sage.

Oakes, W. F., Droge, A. E., & August, B. (1960). Reinforcement effects on participation in group discussion. *Psychological Reports, 7,* 503-514.

Pavitt, C. (1994). Theoretical commitments presupposed by functional approaches to group discussion. *Small Group Research, 25,* 520-541.

Pavitt, C., & Curtis, E. (1994). *Small group discussion: A theoretical approach* (2nd ed.). Scottsdale, AZ: Gorsuch Scarisbrick.

Pavitt, C., & Sackaroff, P. (1990). Implicit theories of leadership and judgments of leadership among group members. *Small Group Research, 21,* 374-392.

Pavitt, C., Whitchurch, G. G., McClurg, H., & Petersen, N. (1995). Melding the objective and subjective sides of leadership: Communication and social judgments in decision-making groups. *Communication Monographs, 62,* 243-264.

Pavitt, C., Whitchurch, G. G., Siple, H., & Petersen, N. (1997). Communication and emergent group leadership: Does content count? *Communication Research Reports, 14,* 470-480.

Pellegrini, R. J. (1971). Some effects of seating position on social perception. *Psychological Reports, 28,* 887-893.

Pepinsky, P. N., Hemphill, J. K., & Shevitz, R. N. (1958). Attempts to lead, group productivity and morale under conditions of acceptance and rejection. *Journal of Abnormal and Social Psychology, 57,* 47-54.

Peterson, R. S. (1997). A directive leadership style can be both virtue and vice: Evidence from elite and experimental groups. *Journal of Personality and Social Psychology, 72,* 1107-1121.

Phillips, J. S., & Lord, R. G. (1981). Causal attributions and perceptions of leadership. *Organizational Behavior and Human Performance, 28,* 143-163.

Piliavin, J. A., & Martin, R. R. (1978). The effects of the sex composition of groups on style of social interaction. *Sex Roles, 4,* 281-296.

Poole, M. S., & DeSanctis, G. (1992). Microlevel structuration in computer-supported group decision making. *Human Communication Research, 19,* 5-49.

Poole, M. S., & Roth, J. (1989). Decision development in small groups IV: A typology of group decision paths. *Human Communication Research, 15,* 323-356.

Porter, N., & Geis, F. (1981). Women and nonverbal leadership cues: When seeing is not believing. In C. Mayo & N. M. Henley (Eds.), *Gender and nonverbal behavior* (pp. 39-61). New York: Springer-Verlag.

Rauch, C. F., Jr., & Behling, O. (1984). Functionalism: Basis for an alternative approach to the study of leadership. In J. G. Hunt, D.-M. Hosking, C. A. Schriesheim, & R. Stewart (Eds.), *Leaders and managers: International perspectives on managerial behavior and leadership* (pp. 45-62). New York: Pergamon.

Rush, M. C., Thomas, J. C., & Lord, R. G. (1977). Implicit leadership theory: A potential threat to the internal validity of leader behavior questionnaires. *Organizational Behavior and Human Performance, 20,* 93-110.

Salazar, A. J. (1996). Ambiguity and communication effects on small group decision-making performance. *Human Communication Research, 23,* 155-192.

Salmon, W. C. (1984). *Scientific explanation and the causal structure of the world.* Princeton, NJ: Princeton University Press.

Sargent, J. F., & Miller, G. R. (1971). Some differences in certain communication behaviors of autocratic and democratic leaders. *Journal of Communication, 21,* 233-252.

Scheidel, T. M., & Crowell, L. (1964). Idea development in small discussion groups. *Quarterly Journal of Speech, 50,* 140-145.

Schultz, B. (1974). Characteristics of emergent leaders of continuing problem-solving groups. *Journal of Psychology, 88,* 167-173.

Schultz, B. (1978). Predicting emergent leaders: An exploratory study of the salience of communicative functions. *Small Group Behavior, 9,* 109-114.

Schultz, B. (1980). Communicative correlates of perceived leaders. *Small Group Behavior, 11,* 175-191.

Schultz, B. (1982). Argumentativeness: Its effects in group decision-making and its role in leadership perception. *Communication Quarterly, 30,* 368-375.

Schutz, W. C. (1961). The ego, FIRO theory and the leader as completer. In L. Petrullo & B. M. Bass (Eds.), *Leadership and interpersonal behavior* (pp. 48-65). New York: Holt, Rinehart & Winston.

Shamir, B., House, R. J., & Arthur, M. B. (1993). The motivational effects of charismatic leadership: A self-concept based theory. *Organization Science, 4,* 577-594.

Sharf, B. F. (1978). A rhetorical analysis of leadership emergence in small groups. *Communication Monographs, 45,* 156-172.

Shweder, R. A., & D'Andrade, R. G. (1980). The systematic distortion hypothesis. In R. G. D'Andrade (Ed.), *Fallible judgment in behavioral research* (pp. 37-58). San Francisco: Jossey-Bass.

Snyder, M. (1979). Self-monitoring processes. In L. Berkowitz (Ed.), *Advances in experimental social psychology* (Vol. 12, pp. 85-128). Orlando: Academic Press.

Stein, R. T., & Heller, T. (1983). The relationship of participation rates to leadership status: A meta-analysis. In H. H. Blumberg, A. P. Hare, V. Kent, & M. Davies (Eds.), *Small groups and social interaction* (Vol. 1, pp. 401-406). Chichester, UK: John Wiley & Sons.

Steiner, I. D. (1966). Models for inferring relationships between group size and potential group productivity. *Behavioral Science, 11,* 273-283.

Steinzor, B. (1950). The spatial factor in face to face discussion groups. *Journal of Abnormal and Social Psychology, 45,* 552-555.

Stogdill, R. M. (1948). Personal factors associated with leadership: A survey of the literature. *Journal of Psychology, 25,* 35-71.

Strodtbeck, F. L., & Hook, L. H. (1961). The social dimension of a 12-man jury table. *Sociometry, 24,* 397-415.

Strodtbeck, F. L., James, R. M., & Hawkins, C. (1957). Social status in jury deliberations. *American Sociological Review, 22,* 713-719.

Strodtbeck, F. L., & Mann, R. D. (1956). Sex role differentiation in jury deliberations. *Sociometry, 19,* 3-11.

Taylor, S. E., & Fiske, S. T. (1975). Point of view and perceptions of causality. *Journal of Personality and Social Psychology, 32,* 439-445.

Trusted, J. (1987). *Inquiry and understanding: An introduction to explanation in the physical and human sciences.* London: Macmillan.

Turk, H. (1961). Instrumental and expressive ratings reconsidered. *Sociometry, 24,* 76-81.

Vroom, V. H., & Yetton, P. (1973). *Leadership and decision making.* Pittsburgh, PA: University of Pittsburgh Press.

Weick, K. E. (1978). The spines of leaders. In M. McCall, Jr., & M. M. Lombardo (Eds.), *Leadership: Where else can we go?* (pp. 37-61). Durham, NC: Duke University Press.

Weiss, H. M., & Adler, S. (1981). Cognitive complexity and the structure of implicit leadership theories. *Journal of Applied Psychology, 66,* 69-78.

Wright, L. (1976). *Teleological explanations: An etiological analysis of goals and functions.* Berkeley: University of California Press.

Wyatt, N. (1993). Organizing and relating: Feminist critique of small group communication. In S. P. Bowen & N. Wyatt (Eds.), *Transforming visions: Feminist critiques in communication studies* (pp. 51-86). Cresskill, NJ: Hampton.

Yukl, G. A. (1981). *Leadership in organizations.* Englewood Cliffs, NJ: Prentice Hall.

13

Group Communication and Creativity Processes

SUSAN JARBOE
Juniata College

ay wisdom suggests that creativity is a quasi-magical characteristic of an individual: "For a long time it was believed that creativity was inherited or a 'God-given' phenomenon; you either had it or you didn't" (Thompson, 1991, p. 43). The popular image is that of a poet, painter, or musician with a muse the rest of us do not encounter. In the realm of science, we think of genius rather than magic; the Ben Franklins or Thomas Edisons are special, unique individuals who have traits or characteristics others do not. The creative accomplishments of these individuals are a source of mystery and wonder. Even when the process of achievement is articulated, it remains inaccessible to the understanding of everyday persons (Isaksen & Murdock, 1993).

In the later half of the 20th century, creativity became the object of research by psychologists, educators, and social scientists, who undertook the systematic study of this complex human phenomenon. More recently, creativity has become of interest to members of other professions, including scholars of business and management, executives and managers in a variety of enterprises, and organizational consultants and trainers, all wishing

to enhance the creative potential of individuals, groups, and organizations. In fact, it appears that the study of creativity was the emerging discipline of the 1990s (see Amabile, 1996; Isaksen, 1987; Isaksen & Murdock, 1993; Isaksen, Murdock, Firestien, & Treffinger, 1993a, 1993b; Kuhn, 1993; Runco, 1994c).

Some of this upsurge of interest in creativity is economic in origin; specifically, it is aimed at improving the competitiveness of U.S. companies in global markets (see Berger, 1987; Carr, 1994; Grossman, 1982; Mansfield, 1989; Peters, 1990; Reich, 1987; Rosenberg, 1990). Given the rapid pace of contemporary corporate life, organizations need to keep abreast of change (Isaksen & Murdock, 1993) and be adaptable (Basadur, 1993). In addition, the shift from an industrial to an information society means that U.S. employees have different expectations for work activity, among them professional development and an increased role in making decisions (Burnside, Amabile, & Gryskiewicz, 1988; Miller, 1987). Emerging simultaneously has been the notion that it is human nature to be creative and that creativity is an essential component of any self-improvement routine (Carr, 1994; Miller,

1987; Ward, Finke, & Smith, 1995) and for self-actualization (Isaksen & Murdock, 1993). Finally, there is an awareness that contemporary organizations have a responsibility to address the array of complex problems facing society today, problems that require imaginative solutions (see Barrett, 1998; Burnside et al., 1988; Carr, 1994; Johnson & Hackman, 1995).

Although creative activity often is portrayed as the lonely artist painting a picture in a garret or the reclusive scientist constructing an invention in a cellar, many of today's creative endeavors occur in group settings. Groups and teamwork are now recognized as essential to organizational growth and development (D. R. Anderson, 1990; Blanchard, 1987; Hyde, 1986; Reich, 1987), whether they are short-term "virtual" teams or long-term "professional" teams (Vance & Deacon, 1995). Focus groups, constructed primarily for the purpose of generating ideas rather than making decisions, are used widely in applied contexts (see Bortree, 1986; Kreps, 1995; Seymour, McQuarrie, & McIntyre, 1987), especially those involving product marketing (Buggie, Scheuing, & Vaccaro, 1990; Cramp, 1995; Kane, 1987). Quality circles, which identify and resolve work-related problems (Greene, 1986; see Schultz, Chapter 14, this volume), are trained in both logical and creative strategies and are believed to improve the effectiveness of a variety of organizations, such as health care (Burda, 1990), school systems (Wilson, 1990), government (Harris, 1990; Larson, 1989), or various businesses (Brossard, 1990; Denton, 1990; Landes, 1990; Whyte, 1989). They also may contribute to employee satisfaction and morale (Buch & Spangler, 1990; Clark & McGee, 1988; Eisman, 1990; Elizur, 1990; Sklarow, 1989).

Inquiries into the nature of creativity permeate many fields of interest and vary in degree of abstraction, from psychoanalytic notions of fear in the psychology journals to practical nuts-and-bolts prescriptions for promoting creativity in trade magazines. Such diversity may tempt communication scholars to jump on the "creativity bandwagon"; indeed, some already have. Such a leap, however, should not be undertaken lightly. Hence, the central question addressed in this chapter is whether group communication research should include creativity as part of its scholarly enterprise and, if so, to what extent. To answer that question, first I acquaint the reader with the way creativity is conceptualized and defined in three contexts: within individuals, groups, and organizations. I then assess the potential disciplinary links between issues pertinent to Group Communication and Creativity, as well as several methodological considerations crucial for an effective interface. Finally, I explore the capability and motivation of group communication scholars to tackle theory and research on creativity and group communication.

ORIENTATIONS TO CREATIVITY

There is some agreement, yet little consensus, regarding the concept of creativity. Ten years ago, Ackoff and Vergara (1988) reported that there were well more than 100 definitions in the literature. Ochse (1990) wryly commented that creativity "refers to a variety of phenomena that have very little in common besides the words used when referring to them—and any discrepancies in conclusions of studies on creativity should therefore not be surprising" (p. 3). Dominant perspectives on creativity emerge from three intellectual traditions: traits and thinking styles of individuals (Cognitive Psychology), communication processes and procedures in groups (Social Psychology, as well as Communication), and products and production in organizations (Organizational Behavior).

The Creative Individual

Group communication scholars need to understand creativity at the individual level of analysis for three reasons. First, individual creativity can contribute to group composition effects. Groups are not homogeneous; they consist of aggregates of unique individuals who may respond variously to external and internal stimuli. Second, models of group behavior, both descriptive and prescriptive, are, to some degree, based on theories of individual behavior, and the quality of this fit with respect to creativity should be reviewed. Finally, assuming creativity is a discipline (see Isaksen & Murdock, 1993, for ontological, epistemological, and axiological criteria for creativity as a discipline) and that it is worthwhile to study creative processes in groups, it behooves group communication scholars to understand the origins and evolution of this discipline.

Psychological Investigations

Psychologists' interest in creativity usually is traced to Guilford's (1950) address to the American Psychological Association, in which he called for systematic study of creativity. This led psychologists to attempt to identify the traits and abilities of creative individuals and then to correlate those factors with such characteristics as personality, intelligence, cognition, and motivation (Ochse, 1990; Runco, 1991).

Bachtold (1982) reviewed research on personality and creativity conducted on individuals engaged in a variety of creative pursuits and posited a set of core characteristics of creative people: active, energetic, impulsive, spontaneous, uninhibited, sensitive, autonomous, independent, individualistic, and unconventional. Kao (1991) also summarized characteristics of the creative person culled from previous syntheses: openness to experience; seeing things in unusual ways; curiosity; accepting and reconciling apparent opposites; tolerance of ambiguity; independence in judgment, thought, and action; needing and assuming autonomy; self-reliance; not being subject to group standards and control; willingness to take calculated risks; persistence; sensitivity to problems; fluency; flexibility; originality; responsiveness to feelings; openness to unconscious phenomena; motivation; freedom from fear of failure; the ability to concentrate; thinking in images; and selectivity.

Psychologists have also sought to discern mental processes that underlie creativity, which, to some extent, are indicators of intelligence. This is relevant to group communication and performance because, according to Ochse (1990), "A team of people may develop good products by building upon one another's ideas; but each idea comes from within the mind of one person" (pp. 171-172). Furthermore, de Bono (1992) claims, "It is essential to understand the type of information system operating in the brain in order to understand creativity and to design simple, usable creative tools" (p. 185).

At present, there are two major classes of cognitive theories relevant to creativity. *Divergent production theories* explore factors that potentially structure the intellect (Guilford, 1967). For example, Guilford's (1967) model, summarized well by Scheidel and Crowell (1979), is a good example of a divergent production theory: Fluency is "the ability to produce many similar ideas," flexibility is "the ability to change to other categories of ideas than the usual ones," originality is "the ability to produce responses that are statistically rare," and elaboration is "the ability to fill out details" (pp. 165-166). *Associative theories* focus on the number and arrangement of cognitive elements; ideas can be associated on the basis of similarity, serendipity, contiguity (Mednick, 1963), or remote domains (Mednick, 1962). Weisberg (1993) pointed out that analogic transfer, one type of association based on reasoning by analogy, requires information storage, retention, and retrieval, as well as mental problem representation. In short, "Creativity requires the combination and reorganization of extant categories to generate new ideas or problem-solutions" (Mumford, Reiter-Palmon, & Redmond, 1994, p. 6).

Creative thinking is often contrasted to logical thinking. Simon (1987) clarified the terminology associated with types of thinking, as applied to decision making:

> Sometimes the term rational (or logical) is applied to decision making that is consciously

analytic, the term nonrational to decision making that is intuitive and judgmental, and the term irrational to decision making and behavior that responds to the emotions or that deviates from action chosen rationally. (p. 57)

Tubbs (1992), using the popular "right-brain/left-brain" dichotomy, tied rational (logical) decision making to the left brain and irrational (intuitive) to the right brain, but as Simon (1987) admonished, "It is the differences in behavior, and not the differences in the hemispheres, that are important. Reference to the two hemispheres is a red herring that can only impede our understanding of intuitive, 'nonlogical' thought" (p. 59). As for irrational emotions, Runco (1994b) hypothesized that "it is easy to view affective processes as alogical, but it is probably more reasonable to view them as having their own logic" (p. 115).

Isaksen (1988a) differentiates creative thinking from critical thinking; creative thinking is the process "in which one makes and communicates meaningful new connections by devising unusual new possibilities," whereas critical thinking is the process "in which one analyzes and develops mechanisms to compare and contrast ideas; improve and refine concepts; screen, select, and support alternatives; and make judgments and effect decisions" (p. 140). These different processes are often labeled *divergent* and *convergent* thinking, respectively (see Albrecht, 1987; Baer, 1993; Rawlinson, 1981; Runco, 1991; Scheidel, 1986; Whitfield, 1975).

Creative thinking has been correlated with various personality traits. In a study of information-processing styles, McCrae (1987) concluded that divergent thinking was consistently associated with openness to experience, but not with neuroticism, extroversion, agreeableness, or conscientiousness. Divergent thinking and openness also correlated with items composing a scale that measures creative personality. Bachtold (1982) found that styles of divergent thinking varied with temperament: In comparison to those who scored low, high scorers on verbal elaboration were more

emotional, high scorers on figural elaboration were more active, and high scorers on verbal flexibility and originality were less sociable.

The relationship between indicants of individuals' creativity and their communicative behavior has received limited attention. In a study of 256 professionals from research and development institutions, Keller and Holland (1978) explored relationships among innovativeness, personality, and communication role. Innovative/technological communication was predicted by a high innovative orientation and a low need for clarity, typical characteristics of creative individuals. Comadena (1984), in a study of brainstorming groups (which encourage the creation of ideas within a nonjudgmental group environment; see Osborn, 1957; Sunwolf & Seibold, Chapter 15, this volume), discovered that individuals higher in idea production (one sign of creativity) had less communication apprehension and a greater tolerance for ambiguity than those who were lower in idea production.

Whatever individuals' capabilities might be, creative performance cannot occur in a vacuum; it requires general knowledge for associative creativity, as well as expertise in an area relevant to the situation at hand for divergence. As Feldhusen (1993) explains:

The creative problem solver has a large, fluent, conceptually well-organized knowledge base on which he or she draws selectively to create a new schema or synthesis which solves the problem. The creative individual is a relative expert in a domain who can analyze problems effectively, perceive deficiencies, and envision the outcomes of potential solutions or designs. (p. 46)

Self-Imposed Constraints on Creativity

Even if people are not geniuses, one cannot help but wonder why people do not function at their creative maximum when circumstances allow; as Becker (1994) asks, "There is no way that we can avoid or stop creating—is there?" (p. 172). There are, however, barriers within individuals that prevent them from manifesting their creativity, whether or not they are in a group setting. Jones (1993) sorted these individual-level barriers into four categories: (a) strategic, which refers to preferred styles of problem solving and tolerance for uncertainty; (b) values, including attitudes and flexibility of their application; (c) perceptual, which involves physical acuity and awareness of one's environment; and (d) self-image, which is related to the readiness to use resources and assert oneself. Within each category are constraints that could affect people's behavior in groups.

Fear of set breaking. From the earliest years, even in cultures that privilege individualism, like the United States (see Haslett & Ruebush, Chapter 5, this volume), compliance with social rules is valued, and rule violation is punished. When individuals have an opportunity to think outside the parameters of these rules, a negative affective response to the process can be triggered, a reaction Schuldberg (1994) calls "horror." For example, the simple chaos produced by brainstorming can be disturbing to the orderly mind; taken to an extreme, unruly groups degenerate into gangs, crowds, or mobs. Facilitators who have seen uneasiness in group participants during a "Who Should Be Saved?" exercise, as they prioritize fictitious persons with regard to whose life should be saved (for instance, by a heart transplant or refuge in a lifeboat), are seeing shades of shame at violating a taboo. Similar discomfort can arise when using "antirules," such as reverse brainstorming, where group members contemplate what would make a problem worse (see Sunwolf & Seibold, Chapter 15, this volume). Related to this fear of set breaking is a sense of blasphemy: If an individual is creative, he or she has acquired or assumed some "God-like" characteristics that are not appropriate for mere mortals (Becker, 1994). Dealing with one's fear of set breaking and the social pressures that lead people to not go beyond the rules is, thus, a prerequisite for becoming a creative individual. As Hare (1992) concluded:

In sum, the creative person is essentially a nonconformist with the capacity to pursue nonconforming and creative ideas in the face of societal pressures to see things as others have seen them and leave things as others have found them. (p. 157)

Fear of rejection. Throughout time, people have associated creativity with madness (Isaksen & Murdock, 1993). Kirton (1989) observed that innovators may be isolated because of their unconventionality, whereas adaptors find it easier to work with others. Hence, when performing any activities associated with creative endeavors, one runs the risk of being perceived of as mad and rejected for being so. As Isaksen (1988b) explains:

This myth asserts that creativity is based on the psychological processes of neurosis or psychosis, that it is a function of a troubled mind. According to this myth, creativity is something to be avoided like any other form of pathology or sickness. (p. 148)

Certainly, anecdotal evidence abounds with famous inventors, poets, artists, and musicians who had some sort of mental quirk, if not actual dysfunction. There is also some indication that creativity is associated with bipolar mood disorder (Bowden, 1994; Richards, 1994). Even colloquial forms of criticism unconsciously reflect the belief that creativity is associated with madness; a wild idea can be met with "That's crazy" or "You're nuts." Thus, creative expression may be self-censored for fear of being rebuffed or stereotyped as "odd" (Basadur, 1994; V. Johnson, 1993; Miller, 1987; Schuldberg, 1994).

Lack of motivation. Although people may have creative talents or abilities, these are not necessarily on tap when needed. In fact, what sparks the creative process in an individual, "genius" or not, is a source of speculation and research in both Cognitive Psychology and Organizational Behavior, because motivation, interest, and effort are viewed as essential for creative activity (Hurst, Rush, & White,

1989; Kao, 1991; Rawlinson, 1981; Vance & Deacon, 1995).

Runco (1994b) hypothesized that some sort of tension must occur to trigger creative responses. *Reactive creativity* is associated with a negative stimulus—a problem to be solved or a gap to be bridged. The motivation is one of necessity (the "mother of invention") or frustration (Barrett, 1998; Heinzen, 1994), which produces a negative set of responses, such as desperation, anxiety, and overly rigid or simple cognitions. Ochse (1990) explains the connection of stress or tension to creative activity: "I do not propose that stress plays a facilitating role in actual creative performance: I suggest that it motivates the creator-to-be to develop skills and excel" (p. 176). *Proactive creativity,* in contrast, is based on perceptions of opportunity, tension reduction, and abundant resources, which arouse pleasure and divergent thought. Whatever the stimulus, many are unwilling to attempt new things because of fear they might fail (Whitfield, 1975) or a lack of confidence in their own creativity (Miller, 1987; Rawlinson, 1981); they thus lack the motivation to try.

In research on rewards and motivation, Amabile, Hennessey, and Grossman (1986) found that contracting to do an activity for a reward had a negative effect on creativity, but no reward or a noncontracted reward did not deter creativity; furthermore, "this support appears to be strong and generalizable across different subject populations, reward types, reward presentations, and creativity tasks" (p. 14). This finding runs counter to the usual guideline of rewarding performance. Isen, Daubman, and Nowicki (1987), for example, found that providing positive affect improved performance on two tasks requiring creativity.

Motivation drives effort, which is essential because creative activity is hard work, or "99% perspiration" (Gamache & Kuhn, 1989; Rawlinson, 1981). As Ochse (1990) intoned:

> Those who require that creativity implies excellence, and assess it in terms of the capacity to produce something of original cultural value . . . are likely to find that creative ability is no spontaneous emergence of inherent qualities; no special intellectual process; no gift—but a hard-earned prize. (p. 260)

Inadequate cognitive heuristics. Some patterns of thought in particular repress creative thinking: the assumption of one right answer, not challenging the obvious, and evaluating too quickly (Basadur, 1994; Rawlinson, 1981). Overreliance on prototypes, recency effects (Schuldberg, 1994), and too much faith in past experience (Basadur, 1994) also stifle creativity. One remedy is not only to "train out" those biases but also to design new cognitive heuristics. For example, Ward et al. (1995) proposed the "new materials" heuristic: "Consider not just how those materials could be used to do the same things better, but also what new things might be done with those materials" (p. 127). They also suggested casting the problem at the most abstract level at the start of problem solving, and, when using analogic reasoning, choosing analogies for their relevance, prior success, and abstraction.

Reluctance to play. The activities that support creative performance are sometimes seen as frivolous (Isaksen & Murdock, 1993), and such attitudes can inhibit creative activity. If adults suffer from the "loss of the power of childlike inquiry" (Basadur, 1994, p. 255), then returning to some sort of innocent state is a way to free minds from values or patterns of thought that are so habitual that people are unaware of them (V. Johnson, 1993). People may be reluctant to do so for several reasons, including fear of looking foolish (Whitfield, 1975). Others may see it as inappropriate for their status in life; many are imbued with a Western cultural value of "Life is real, life is earnest" and, therefore, as adults, they "put away childish things." Such persons will need a legitimizing norm that "play is okay." One recommendation is for institutions to provide a place for play, such as a "creative corner" (Michalko, 1994) that might have beanbags and modeling clay. A "humor room" (V. Johnson, 1993) could contain cartoons, rubber chickens, and clown costumes. Running down the hall or making paper airplanes might also release one from unwritten rules (Byers, 1992). Those who find these suggestions outrageous might settle for work breaks that include physical activity (Vance & Deacon, 1995), interaction, meditation, or learning.

Summary

Defining creativity at the individual level of analysis depends on the context, in this case, individuals as members of groups and teams. In summarizing the thinking of psychoanalysts, humanistic psychologists, and psychometricians (who focus on the unconscious, natural, or genetic origins of creativity in individuals) and of associationists, Gestalt psychologists, and information-processing theorists (who maintain that creativity is a property of thought processes that can be developed and improved through training and structured experiences), Ackoff and Vergara (1988) conclude:

> We have defined creativity in problem solving and planning as the ability of a subject in a choice situation to modify self-imposed constraints so as to enable him or her to select courses of action or produce outcomes that he or she would not otherwise select or produce and that are more efficient or valuable than any he or she would otherwise have chosen. (p. 87)

The Creative Group

It is apparent that individuals vary considerably in creative capacity. What happens when they work in groups is a central concern of organizational theorists and practitioners, because creative work, as a result of its complexity, frequently is a team endeavor (Clark, 1989-1990; Sethia, 1993). As Mensch (1993) explains:

> Teamwork is an essential ingredient for successful innovation and transformation. Time and time again studies of successful innovation have emphasized the need for and importance of close cooperation among members of multifunctional groups . . . [even though teamwork] may sometimes also lead to shared misperceptions, agreement on unsuitable goals, or wrong ways. (p. 262).

With the group as the unit of analysis, orientations to creativity have become more sophisticated over time. Weick's (1979) simple conception of group creativity reveals the influence of associative cognition; he described the creativity process as putting old things into new combinations and new things into old ones. Sethia (1993), in contrast, emphasizes divergence, seeing creativity as "the ability of individuals or groups to generate on a sustained basis significantly original ideas or solutions to problems" (p. 385). The processes that contribute (or not) to this capacity are outlined by Hare (1992), who adapted Taylor's (1975) categories of individual creativity to group discussion: *Expressive* creativity is "work that is personally need-oriented and unrelated to group work or providing background facts"; *technical* creativity is "work that is maintaining and routine in character"; *inventive* creativity is "suggesting alternative ways for solving a problem or clarifying already established plans"; *innovative* creativity is "active problem solving by introducing unusual points of view"; and *emergentive* creativity is "work that is highly insightful and integrative. It often interprets what has been going on in the group and brings together in a meaningful way a series of experiences" (Hare, 1992, p. 39). Finally, Baer (1993) differentiated creative activity in terms of time: *real-time* spontaneous performance with no chance of revision, such as conversations or emergencies, versus *multistage* performances that allow time for evaluating and revising solutions.

Given the emphasis on teamwork, the applied and trade literature is replete with models, methods, techniques, exercises, activities, and tips for improving group effectiveness through creative activity (e.g., D. R. Anderson, 1990; Barrett, 1998; Couger, 1990; J. Gordon & Zemke, 1986; V. Johnson,

1993; Michalko, 1994; Thompson, 1991). At the macrolevel, there are models for creative problem solving and decision making; at the microlevel, there are divergent strategies to generate ideas. A number of group-level barriers also must be overcome.

Models of Creative Group Problem Solving and Decision Making

One of the major trends in group creativity is a focus on the process by which a group approaches a task, problem, or issue; the focus is on those factors that increase the likelihood of a creative outcome. To that end, scholars have attempted to design procedures to handle various kinds of tasks for various kinds of goals under various kinds of circumstances (see Sunwolf & Seibold's review of research on formal group process procedures, Chapter 15, this volume). Just as rational models for group discussion originated from Dewey's (1910) model of individual reflective thinking (in this volume, see Chapters 1 [Gouran], 7 [Hirokawa & Salazar], and 9 [Propp]), so are creative models based on Wallas's (1926) four-stage model of individual creative thinking: preparation, incubation, illumination, and verification. Nonrational, or creative, decision making is intuitive, in that the individual can seldom articulate the process, but it is logical in the sense that the decisions are made on the basis of experience and knowledge ("preparation"). The illumination phase, where creative ideas arise, often occurs after an incubation period—"a break from a problem that results in an insight experience" (Ward et al., 1995, p. 114). Ward and colleagues distinguish intuition from insight in the following way:

> Intuition and insight are similar in that you are not consciously aware of the mental steps leading to either one; they are experiences that seem to erupt suddenly into your mind without forewarning. The two differ, however, in that insight is considered to be the production of a relatively full-blown idea,

whereas intuition is better regarded as a lead or a hunch. (p. 115)

Modifying Wallas's (1926) model, Rawlinson (1981) added the concept of effort, and Kao (1991) attached interest and exploitation of ideas. Hurst et al. (1989) had seven requirements in their model: imagination, motivation, planning, action, evaluation, satisfaction, and realization. Kuhn (1988) saw an advantage to having two incubation phases to capitalize on the possibility of both intuition and insight: problem recognition and "naive" incubation/gestation, information/knowledge search and detailed preparation, "knowledgeable" incubation/gestation, alternative solution formulation, alternative solution evaluation, choice of solution implementation, and feedback and reassessment.

Isaksen's (1988b) six-step model of creative problem solving has both a divergent and a convergent component in every phase, a concept also supported by Basadur (1994). The first three phases center on problem sensitivity (mess finding, data finding, and problem finding), and the last three phases focus on new challenges (idea finding, solution finding, and acceptance finding). Mumford et al. (1994) stressed associative thinking in their eight-step agenda: problem construction, information encoding, category search, specification of best-fitting categories, combination and reorganization of best-fitting categories, idea evaluation, implementation, and monitoring.

The focus on finding problems in addition to solving them is important. Ochse (1990) believes that "the most crucial aspect of creative problem-solving is *finding* the problem, and that sensitivity to problems is a notable characteristic of creative people. Indeed, problem finding has been described as a creative process in itself" (p. 187). Feldhusen's (1993) 11-step model emphasized problem formulation in its first five phases: (a) sensing that a problem exists, (b) formulating questions to clarify it, (c) determining its causes, (d) identifying its relevant aspects, (e) determining its specific nature, (f) clarifying the goal or desired solution, (g) judging if more information is needed to solve the problem, (h) redefining or creating a new use of a familiar object or concept, (i) seeing implications of a possible action, (j) selecting the best or most unusual solution among several possible solutions, and (k) sensing what follows the problem solution.

Models of creative group problem solving balance and integrate rational, irrational, and nonrational behavior (see Jarboe, 1996). The logical behavior associated with information gathering, defining the problem, and evaluation of solutions is the rational component (see Hirokawa & Salazar, Chapter 7, this volume). Such phases as illumination and insight are nonrational, whereas incubation and the hilarity (Mattimore, 1994) associated with creativity are irrational. There is some evidence that this tripartite blend of behavior is beneficial, as groups trained in a method similar to Kao's (1991) approach, introduced earlier, had a more effective process (Firestien, 1990) and groups using a creative problem-solving method similar to Isaksen's (1988b) model, explained above, yielded positive effects after training, as well as 2 weeks later (Basadur, Graen, & Green, 1982). Rickards (1993), however, cautioned:

> Creative problem solving does not "solve" complex problems, but makes them more manageable. The product is primarily committed actions for making progress. As their problems are complex, creative problem solving will not produce complete resolution, and will be evaluated by the managers as having failed. (p. 168)

Strategies for Divergent Thinking

Because so much creative activity relies on having a pool of ideas, coming up with those ideas is an important part of the creative process. *Ideation* can be defined as "idea generation without evaluation" (Basadur, 1994, p. 237). Ideation strategies not only are being used by practitioners in applied settings but also are being refined, tested, and evaluated in laboratory and field research (see Jarboe,

1996; Sunwolf & Seibold, Chapter 15, this volume). Most influential has been Osborn's (1957) classic divergent strategy of brainstorming. One line of research investigates barriers to brainstorming success. Some blocks are, of course, at the individual level; Jablin, Seibold, and Sorenson (1977) found that highly apprehensive communicators produced less on a brainstorming task than those low in this trait. Social loafing (the tendency to let others carry the load) decreased when group members thought their contributions could be directly attributed to them, as well as compared to others' responses (Harkins & Jackson, 1985). Other potential obstacles to brainstorming effectiveness include evaluation apprehension (Diehl & Stroebe, 1987) and time pressure (Kelly & Karau, 1993). There also may be a tendency to relax prematurely. Basadur and Thompson (1986), for example, tested the brainstorming principle of "extended effort" (i.e., getting as many ideas as possible and not stopping after the first few) and found that the most preferred ideas came in the latter two-thirds of the idea list, which indicates the desirability of extended effort.

A popular phrase, presently satirized in television commercials, is "thinking out of the box" (Vance & Deacon, 1995), or what de Bono (1967) called *lateral thinking*. One strategy is *reframing,* which breaks a mind-set by placing the problem in a different frame of reference (see Watzlawick, Beavin, & Jackson, 1974). A strategy that utilizes associative reasoning is the *random-word technique* (de Bono, 1992). While a group addresses a problem area, a word is chosen randomly from a list of random words (which is changed frequently). Associations between the random word and the problem area are then explored. Another divergent approach, *mindboggling,* takes brainstorming to an extreme as participants are deliberatively provocative. It is "a deliberate attempt to blow our minds out of the box. Wilder than brainstorming, mindboggling is thinking out of the box like nobody's business. . . . It should be a wide open madhouse" (Vance & Deacon, 1995, p. 164). De Bono (1992) describes a mental operation, *movement,* that utilizes divergent cognition: "Movement is based on the word to: what does this flow to, what does this lead to?" (p. 191). This type of thinking is in contrast to analytical or judgmental thinking that defines what something is or is not. The *lotus blossom technique* (Tatsuno, 1990) is similar in a visual way: A central theme is written in the center of a drawing of a lotus flower, and then group members produce related ideas ("petals") that can become the centers of other blossoms. *Visual group confrontation* (Geschka, 1993) begins with an irrational phase in which five or so pictures accompanied by music are provided to promote relaxation, which is followed by a work phase where a different set of pictures is provided to confront the problem. Other idea-generation devices include *synectics* (W. Gordon, 1961), which combines ideas from disparate domains, and *excursion* (Gryskiewicz, 1987), which uses scenarios to stimulate ideas.

Brainstorming has written versions, such as *brainwriting* (Geschka, Schaude, & Schlicksupp, 1975), in which members write down ideas and exchange their papers to spur more thought. With *freewriting* (Offitzer, 1993), members connect their ideas on paper instead of just listing them. In a *trigger session* (Rickards, 1974), members brainstorm off one another's lists. *Card exchange* (Geschka, 1993) uses associative reasoning; cards with one idea per card can be shuffled and sorted into categories or *clusters* (Offitzer, 1993) or *storyboards* (Maturi, 1993).

The Nominal Group Technique (NGT; Delbecq, Van de Ven, & Gustafson, 1975) is another popular method that has spawned research on ideation strategies. The phases of the NGT are (a) silent, independent idea generation; (b) round-robin listing of ideas; (c) serial discussion for clarification without criticism or debate; (d) individual ranking or rating of ideas; (e) discussion to clarify the vote; and (f) a final vote. Groups using the NGT have been found to produce better quality decisions than those generated by conventionally interacting (hereafter, interacting) groups on a ranking task (Nemiroff, Pasmore,

& Ford, 1976). Groups using the NGT and the *Delphi technique* (which uses a series of written questionnaires to arrive at a decision; see Delbecq et al., 1975) produced more ideas, and the NGT groups produced more unique ideas, when compared to interacting groups (Van de Ven & Delbecq, 1974), but a similar study revealed no differences between interacting groups and NGT groups in terms of the number of ideas generated, the number of unique ideas, or the quality of responses (Green, 1975). In a comparison of interacting, consensus, NGT, and Delphi groups, Delphi groups had the highest quality decisions and NGT groups had the lowest (Erffmeyer & Lane, 1984).

Whether the NGT is an appropriate procedure depends on the nature of a group's task. With a structured problem, the NGT has been shown to be superior compared to consensus in decision quality (Herbert & Yost, 1979). In an applied study of implementation attempts comparing the NGT and "structured discussion" (essentially, the reflective thinking model), groups using the NGT were more effective on simple tasks, groups using structured discussion were best on moderately complex tasks, and there was no difference on complex tasks; in addition, NGT groups yielded higher rates of implementation (White, Dittrich, & Lang, 1980). On a personnel task, groups using *problem-centered leadership,* which relies on a leader's ability to facilitate the group problem-solving process (Maier, 1952), were more effective, as measured by an index of quality and acceptance, than were groups using the NGT or the Delphi technique (Miner, 1979).

In terms of satisfaction, results have been mixed. Groups using the NGT have been found to be more satisfied than interacting and Delphi groups (Van de Ven & Delbecq, 1974), but groups employing consensus were more satisfied with their performance and decisions than NGT or interacting groups (Nemiroff et al., 1976). Group members trained in brainstorming and the NGT reported more satisfaction and saw their group process and communication as more effective than did members of untrained groups (Kramer, Kuo, & Dailey, 1997).

It should be noted that the rules for the NGT are evolving. In one study, use of written cards during the verbal input phase to provide anonymity increased participants' satisfaction (Fox, 1989). When individual work, unstructured discussion, and social facilitation were substituted for the round-robin recording and polling phases, NGT participants had more task-related discussion and were more satisfied (Hegedus & Rasmussen, 1986). Structured pauses, one form of incubation, and a discussion phase that goes beyond mere clarification are believed to increase the flexibility of the NGT in handling unstructured problems and increasing members' acceptance of decisions (Bartunek & Murnighan, 1984).

Group-Level Barriers

With all the techniques discussed above for addressing problems and generating ideas (as well as analytical, critical, rational, and logical methods of debate, discussion, and evaluation, which are not addressed herein), one would think that groups would be able to maximize their creative performance, but just as individuals have constraints on manifesting creativity, so, too, do groups. Some individual-level constraints operate more powerfully on people in the group setting, and the group provides its own pressures as well. The most dominant problems are examined below.

Conformity to group norms. Similar to the fear of set breaking, conformity to the norms and customs of a particular group can suppress creativity (Basadur, 1994; Blake & Mouton, 1987; Rawlinson, 1981; Schuldberg, 1994; Whitfield, 1975). Based on the Kirton Adaptation-Innovation Inventory (Kirton, 1976), which measures the degree to which an individual is likely to adapt or innovate, high innovators within an organizational context tend to be unconventional, whereas high adaptors tend to conform to the prevailing norms (Kirton, 1989). This lack of ego

strength may be exacerbated in a climate that is punishing. Increased feedback and attention from leaders could spur group members to risk nonconformity.

New group norms are often necessary to encourage creativity (N. Anderson, Hardy, & West, 1992). For example, de Bono (1992) advocates the norm of the "green hat": A call for "green hat thinking" is a call for new ideas. Blake and Mouton (1987) suggest tackling problematic norms directly, with group members identifying the problem, gathering facts and data to show that a norm is counterproductive, providing opportunities to vent feelings and emotions, codifying agreements made, following up to support changes in norms, and having this change effort mesh with other group and organizational change efforts.

Unwillingness to collaborate. Vance and Deacon (1995) hypothesized that everyone has a "phantom team"—the sum of experiences, good and bad, with groups and teams—that affects one's predisposition to work in groups (see Anderson, Martin, & Riddle, Chapter 6, this volume, regarding the effects of people's "library of experiences" in groups). This is not specific only to creative endeavors, of course. Common complaints center on problems with procedure (e.g., nothing gets done, meetings take too much time, or the process is disorganized), participation (e.g., some do not do their share, no one listens, or conflicts are not resolved), and leadership (e.g., no leader, dominant leader, struggles for leadership, or leader takes all the credit). The result can be fear of confrontation (Miller, 1987), aggression (Schuldberg, 1994), lack of trust in others (Basadur, 1994), and disrespect, even for those who are acknowledged experts in domains other than one's own (Talbot, 1993).

To change these attitudes, members should have rewarding experiences that occur in a group; after all, one cannot just "autocratically order all group members to participate and to insist that they enjoy it" (Isaksen, 1988b, p. 155). One strategy is to address these concerns head-on. A *powwow* (Vance & Deacon, 1995), for example, is a moderately structured icebreaker that has the goal of promoting open, friendly, and pleasant social interaction so as to lay groundwork for later task work. *Skills and interest inventories* can generate interest in fellow members, and a *data dump* allows team members to express whatever thoughts and feelings they have about the project, no matter how negative. In the case of a team that is markedly ineffective, Kirton (1989) notes that changing leaders will not work because it leads to resentment; he suggests that the group designate a mediator who becomes an informal leader and liaison with any external authorities.

Differences in members' interaction styles. The behavior of colleagues can inhibit one's creative activity (Talbot, 1993). Conformists (adaptors) may be reluctant to collaborate with nonconformists (innovators) because they feel intimidated by more aggressive social styles. As Kirton (1989) explains:

> Innovators are generally seen by adaptors as being abrasive and insensitive . . . because the innovator attacks the adaptor's theories and assumptions, explicitly when he feels that the adaptor needs a push . . . implicitly when he shows a disregard for the rules, conventions, standards of behaviour. . . . What is even more upsetting for the adaptor is the fact that the innovator does not even seem to be aware of the havoc he is causing. (pp. 56-57)

Furnishing positive mutual experiences through creative training or problem-solving sessions can give group members an actual demonstration of their ability to work together. A trained facilitator, a neutral agent who can foster collaboration and manage interaction, is essential for attempts at enlightenment to be successful (see Schultz's overview of group diagnosis and intervention, Chapter 14, this volume). It might be helpful for group members to understand the interplay between the task (see Hirokawa & Salazar, Chapter 7, this volume) and social

(see Keyton, Chapter 8, this volume) dimensions as groups go through various developmental phases (in this volume, see Chapters 2 [Poole], 3 [Mabry], 6 [Anderson et al.], and 8 [Keyton]). If the problem is so serious that members avoid communicating (unwillingness to collaborate), new norms about group communication (such as asking for feedback; see Michalko, 1994) and meetings (their purpose and structure; see Michalko, 1994; Vance & Deacon, 1995) may become necessary because so many ways to enhance creativity involve uninhibited communication.

Mistrust of creative people within the group. Not every group will have a genius, but it is not uncommon for members to vary in their creative potential and manifestations thereof. Just as adaptors (conformists) find innovators (nonconformists) irksome, Kirton (1989) avers that innovators can be equally disappointed with conformists:

> Innovators tend to see adaptors as stuffy and unenterprising, wedded to systems, rules and norms which, however useful, are too restricting for their [the innovators'] liking. Innovators seem to overlook how much of the smooth running of the system around them depends on good adaptiveness, but seem acutely aware of the less acceptable face of efficient bureaucracy. (p. 57)

Keller's (1986) research, however, demonstrates the need for both adaptors and innovators in project groups, as "innovative members enhance a project's quality rather than its performance in terms of budget and schedule" (p. 724).

To be creative, people need time and liberation from petty rules; therefore, group leaders and members should recognize individual creativity, encourage freedom of expression, and defend creatively performing people from attacks by others (Rooks, 1987). Ochse (1990) simultaneously cautions and encourages "prima donnas": "Creators are not relieved of their responsibility of being knowledgeable, skilled and adaptive to prevailing needs. Great minds are indeed disciplined—but they are not confined" (p. 179). In contrast, rather than promoting a creative star, Becker (1994) urges giving "more credit and encouragement to being a 'supportive' team player" (p. 168). The perceived tension between creative individuals and the collective group structure, however, may not be necessary. As Barrett (1998) explains:

It was once believed that individualism and teamwork were as incompatible as oil and water, and that having anything done by a team was a surefire way to douse the flames of creativity, performance, and enterprise. It's now recognized that individual stars can help a business team perform better, while a good team can bring out the best in its individual stars. (p. 67)

Whatever their level of creative proficiency, group members need to realize that there is an array of important innovative roles that support creative activity in groups. Although each theorist labels the roles differently, their concepts are similar: energizers or shapers (Belbin, 1993; Miller, 1987); sponsors, who play a support role (Miller, 1987); inventors or plants, who are originators of ideas (Belbin, 1993; Miller, 1987); project managers or co-ordinators (Belbin, 1993; Miller, 1997); coaches, who help less experienced people (Miller, 1987); gatekeepers or liaisons (Belbin, 1993; Miller, 1987); internal monitors (Belbin, 1993; Miller, 1987); task specialists, implementers, and completer-finishers, who seem to do the work (Belbin, 1993); and facilitators (Belbin, 1993; Miller, 1987). Michalko (1994) suggests that people change places for periods of time, both to foster creativity and to understand one another's situation. McCrimmon (1995), however, cautions that roles, even innovative ones, can lock people in behavioral boxes, paradoxically one of the very barriers to creativity such roles try to prevent.

Summary

To be creative, groups need to learn problem-solving and ideation techniques and overcome individual-level and group-level barriers to creative performance. Intervention and training are frequently the means by which such changes are accomplished, often within the context of large organizations.

The Creative Organization

Because groups do not function in isolation, but as parts of larger social systems (see Putnam & Stohl, 1990, 1996; in this volume, see Gouran [Chapter 1] and Poole [Chapter 2]), the relationship between a group and its milieu is an important influence on group creativity (Kao, 1991; Talbot, 1993). The clearest example of this is with regard to groups in organizations. Basadur (1993) argues that organizations reap several economic benefits when creativity is encouraged: efficiency, adaptability (improved goods and services), flexibility, lower turnover, and less absenteeism. There are also personnel outcomes: cognitive development, such as strategic thinking, rational decision making, and leadership skills; and affective outcomes, such as motivation, commitment, job enrichment and satisfaction, trust, self-confidence, and willingness to take initiative.

In the applied and trade literatures on organizations, writers often distinguish *creativity* from *innovation*. As Whitfield (1975) explains, "Creativity applied to the product of mental activity may be defined in terms of unexpectedly appropriate combinations or associations of ideas," whereas innovation is "the development of a creative idea into a finished article" (p. 9). Albrecht (1987) states that "innovation is the process of transforming creativity into profit" (p. 15). Creativity is "novel associations (new ideas) that are useful," whereas innovation is "the successful implementation of new useful ideas" (Burnside et al., 1988, p. 170). As Van Gundy (1987) complained, however, "The terms 'creativity' and 'innovation' often are used interchangeably, thus making comparative distinctions difficult. Publications that do make a distinction frequently lack agreement on how to define creativity and innovation" (p. 358). Generally speaking, in applied contexts, the hallmark of creativity is a set of unusual or new ideas that are not necessarily "good." For a creative idea to be "good," it has be put into effective practice, at which time it becomes an "innovative" idea. Creativity, therefore, is a necessary and important means to an end, but it is not an end in itself.

As with groups, conceptions of creativity in organizations have evolved. Perhaps the most significant evolution has been the understanding that creativity is a process. As Basadur (1994) recognizes, "Creativity in organizations can be conceptualized as a continuous and circular finding and solving of new and old problems, and an implementing of new solutions for the betterment of the organization and its members" (p. 257).

System Impacts

Just as individuals and groups can hinder group creativity, systemic influences can thwart or support a group's creative efforts. Vance and Deacon (1995) unpacked a basic irony concerning management in organizations: "The concept of organization and free-flowing creativity might sound mutually exclusive, but they're not. The highest creativity occurs in well-organized environments. . . . Confused people are not creative people" (Vance & Deacon, 1995, p. 119). As Burnside et al. (1988) explain:

> The creativity of ideas produced within the organization is largely a function of the internal environment and its effect on stimulating or obstructing the creativity of employees. The organization's innovativeness is related to the structures and policies that affect its ability to implement creative ideas and turn them into innovative products or services. (p. 170)

Of the myriad internal forces that can affect creative activity, the ones that impinge the most on groups are climate and culture, leadership (specifically, leaders' conflicts of interest), and the organization's stage of development or maturation.

Climate and culture. Although lack of intrinsic motivation depresses the arousal of creativity, a person's "intrinsic motivation can be influenced not only by his [or her] own initial spark of interest in the task, but also by everything in the organization which might lead that initial interest to sputter away or to burn even more brightly" (Hill & Amabile, 1993, p. 425). Maxon (1988) claims that an organizational climate that promotes innovation depends on five factors: structures, rewards, objectives, removing fears, and training for innovation. Along these lines, Burningham and West (1995) found that innovative groups (judged to be so by organizational members external to the groups) had high scores on vision, task orientation, participative safety, and support for innovation. Hill and Amabile (1993), summarizing a decade of research, say that creativity drops when there is an expectation of evaluation, people are being watched (surveillance), rewards are contracted for (not a bonus), there is competition for prizes, and there are restricted choices on goal paths.

Koberg and Chusmir (1987) studied individual differences in three organizational cultures: bureaucratic, innovative, and supportive. Those with a high need for power had more job satisfaction in bureaucratic cultures, those with a high need for achievement were more satisfied in innovative cultures, and those with high need for affiliation were more satisfied in supportive cultures. Surprisingly, bureaucratic culture (one purpose of which is to slow the rate of change) was positively correlated with creativity, although the researchers argue that this finding may be a function of the specific departments sampled. There was no significant link between supportive culture and creativity; Koberg and Chusmir suggest that a supportive culture might have rigid social norms of group cohesiveness and relationship orientation that could discourage task orientation and nonconformity, along the lines of Janis's (1972) groupthink hypothesis (where members' striving for unanimity overrides their motivation to realistically appraise alternative courses of action; see Keyton, Chapter 8, this volume).

Leaders' conflicts of interest. Because management and administrators of an organization have the power to stifle or encourage group creativity (Glassman, 1989; Kearns, 1988), "creative leadership" is a major theme in the applied literature. Not only do group leaders have to cope with members' socially learned desire "to please" (Miller, 1987), but leaders themselves also have psychological barriers that often prevent creativity and change from occurring, such as fear of failure (Gamache & Gagliano, 1988), lack of confidence (Talbot, 1993), loss of face, or hurt pride (F. G. Anderson, 1988). A manager's resistance may be stronger if he or she is an adaptor who is responsible for innovators. Badawy (1987) cleverly depicted 12 ways a manager can kill creativity: drag your feet; say "yes," but do not do it; wait for a full analysis; do not follow up; call many meetings; put the idea into channels; boost the cost estimates; wait for market surveys; stick to protocol; worry about the budget; lack a sense of urgency; and if a good idea isn't yours, don't push it. Talbot (1993) would add these: provide the solution, override the team decision, play people off against each other, be undecided, take the credit for the team, and withhold information.

In contrast, if leaders wish to induce and support creativity in the groups and teams for which they are responsible, Kanter (1988) advocates "kaleidoscopic" thinking, or shaking people up and out of traditional assumptions; communicating visions; being persistent; building coalitions; using teamwork; and sharing the credit. Munitz (1988) advises "rewarding instincts counter to one's own" and being open to feedback "when others suggest 'far out' ideas about leadership style"

(pp. 491-492). Perhaps the most important element is to ensure effective communication within the group (Basadur, 1987).

Even when leaders are not professionally or personally threatened by creative people or their activities, a conflict between managerial and developmental roles can arise. Several authors agree that the role of "creativity enhancer" should not fall to the manager of a work group, who can "overmanage" the process (Basadur, 1987). Miller (1987) has stated that a major barrier to effective meetings, be they for generating ideas or for making decisions, is that the person with the most investment in the outcome usually is the one who leads the discussion (i.e., the manager). He identifies five problems that occur when managers lead their own meetings:

> They block participation by talking two to three times too much . . . they find it hard to be nonjudgmental . . . they focus on content and ignore process . . . they find it hard to share decision-making power (or participants find it hard to take it when offered) . . . [and] staff end up with less buy-in, responsibility, and personal development. (p. 139)

Miller encourages a clear separation of the person with authority who can call a meeting from the person in charge of conducting the meeting. Similarly, Albrecht (1987) contends that one requirement for the creative strategy process is "a trained facilitator who can guide the overall process while the executives concentrate on the issues at hand" (p. 181). Research tends to support this requirement. Offner, Kramer, and Winter (1996) found that interacting groups with facilitators produced more ideas that those without facilitators and about the same number of ideas as nominal groups (those in which members work independently and do not interact).

Organizational maturation. Because organizations evolve and change over time, there may be points in their life cycle where creativity is more or less likely to occur. Albrecht (1987) contends that creativity dies a normal death in most organizations because of their natural evolution. One of the first forces is growth: things slow down, internal groups compete more, there may be malorganization, and members may feel a loss of identification with their organization. Organizational success also can sometimes kill creativity because there may be less motivation to take risks and a tendency to neglect other or newer opportunities: "The commitment to performance, perfection, and efficiency is a stand against innovation" (Albrecht, 1987, p. 19). Too much knowledge of a field causes tunnel vision, or the "it can't be done" syndrome (Basadur, 1994). Even when a change effort has begun, given today's trend toward "musical chairs management" (Gamache & Kuhn, 1989), it is difficult to continue the process. Finally, conservatism accelerates in times of economic distress. When threats to survival loom on the horizon, organizations are less likely to risk being creative. As Vance and Deacon (1995) cogently put it:

> Organizational development used to be a term that stood for developing people. Over the years, the term has come to stand for layoffs and outbound counseling. . . . Cutting staff size and training programs as the first alternative to bad financial news is a dead giveaway that the leader probably didn't understand the value of people to begin with. (p. 177)

Intervention for Change

Although there is a high level of creativity appropriately designated as "genius," there is also latent creative talent in everyone, and this potential can be enhanced (see Isaksen & Murdock, 1993; Mattimore, 1994; Ward et al., 1995; Weisberg, 1993). Kao (1991), however, hints that attempts to manipulate creativity in groups may not be universally supported: "To speak of 'managing creativity' may sound paradoxical or even frivolous; the search for creativity has often been linked to magic, the demonic, or the divine. How could such a process be *managed*?" (p. 19).

Of the several kinds of organizational interventions, training is essential for group members because of inadequacies in individuals' attitudes and thinking skills (Basadur, 1994). As Howard (1987) explains:

> In creativity tests on individuals of all ages, creativity scores invariably drop about 90% between ages five and seven, and by age forty an individual is only about 2% as creative as he was at age five. The hope of creativity research is that what is trained out can be trained back in. (p. 3)

Without digressing into the theory and practice of industrial training programs in creativity (see, for example, Feldhusen, 1993; Gamache & Gagliano, 1988; Gamache & Kuhn, 1989; Grossman, 1982; Hequet, 1992; Isaksen, 1983; C. E. Johnson & Hackman, 1995; Talbot, 1993), one critical objective of these programs is to dispel myths and assumptions about creativity and creative people (Rickards, 1993). Apprehension about the unruly behavior of others can be ameliorated by an understanding of the creative process itself: that construction of the new often requires destruction of the old. Similarly, an individual's experience with creative activities can be structured so that sensations of fear or loss are balanced by the energy and playfulness that mark the lighter side of creativity. Basadur, Graen, and Scandura (1986) found that the attitudes of manufacturing engineers toward divergent thinking in solving problems became more positive after training. This effect was more consistent with intact work groups than with individuals.

Other training objectives include raising awareness about the role of creativity in modern organizations, illustrating how an organization can be enhanced by creative activity, and providing basic skills related to creativity (Rickards, 1993). Treffinger, Isaksen, and Dorval (1994) prescribed a three-stage process for learning creative problem solving. First, participants must learn and use such basic thinking tools as brainstorming, analogies, and inferences. They should then learn and practice systematic problem solving through case studies, simulations, role playing, and the like. Finally, they are ready to address real challenges and work on real problems. As a result of such training, participants experience an increase in self-esteem and self-confidence (Talbot, 1993).

For groups and teams, process interventions might include the use of meeting-management, team-building, conflict-management, or problem-solving techniques (Bookman, 1988; see Sunwolf & Seibold, Chapter 15, this volume). Because learning is hard to measure, Talbot (1993) advocates follow-up sessions to assess and reinforce changes emanating from training. An accompanying structural intervention can also reinforce learning, such as de Bono's (1992) *creative hit list,* a formal list of issues that require creative treatment (no more than half of which may be problems) and is printed in in-house publications, posted on bulletin boards, and copied on postcards for people to keep in their pockets.

Training, or any other kind of intervention, does not, of course, come with a guarantee. Leaders want what Gamache and Gagliano (1988) identified as two classic conflicting management demands: outstanding short-term performance utilizing creative, open-minded thinking versus new ideas that have little or no risk, require little or no change, need little or no resource allocation, allow quick implementation, and yield a big profit. This "myth of the magic idea" (Gamache & Kuhn, 1989) engenders unrealistic expectations about what interventions designed to promote creativity can and cannot do. Broome and Fulbright (1995) offer the following caveat:

> The best efforts of the most talented and well-trained facilitator can be ineffective in the face of planning shortfalls, methodology deficiencies, differences in cultural expectations, inadequate group composition, organizational culture limitations, resource constraints, communication barriers, climate concerns, and attitude problems. (p. 45)

Thus, training requires an organization-wide commitment, because for meaningful payoffs, there must be a "critical mass" of people who share the appropriate perspective and relevant skills. Furthermore, other kinds of interventions may be necessary to change organizational culture and leadership. These commitments entail a serious investment of money and time off-line. Senior executives and organizational leaders must seriously consider Carr's (1994) question: "Building a new kind of organization, one that maintains its frame flexibility, encourages diversity, and deals openly with conflict—is it really worth all this just for an organization to be creative?" (p. 161).

SETTING THE AGENDA FOR THE STUDY OF GROUP COMMUNICATION AND CREATIVITY

The desire to increase creativity has permeated all levels of human systems. Enabling the creative energy of individuals to surface, designing and facilitating groups to be creative, and, at the organization level, ensuring quality leadership and a climate conducive to creativity form both a research and a practical agenda. Although many may want quick-fix remedies for the types of barriers to creativity identified previously, scholars recognize that the long-term effectiveness of creativity-enhancement programs requires the systematic study of creativity and innovation processes. It is through theoretical developments that the ultimate payoffs for scholars, practitioners, and, ultimately, group members will occur. Thus, the agenda should not be so much the discovery of immediately applicable techniques as an understanding of the processes of creativity and innovation. Accordingly, group communication inquiries should focus on creative group communication as it functions simultaneously as a result of input conditions, creative or not, and a precursor of group outcomes; in other words, it should aim to determine whether and how creative group communication processes make a difference (see Jarboe, 1996). To that end, some preliminary issues need to be addressed.

First, group communication scholars must develop effective operational definitions of creativity. Clearly, the word defies simple explanation. As this review has shown, it can refer to a trait, skill, process, or product, and all those denotations could be employed usefully in group communication research. Such diversity, however, precludes effective theory construction, a problem that Isaksen and Murdock (1993) deplore:

> It appears that most individuals who attempt to assess creativity have based their work on entirely different or, at times, unspecified, theoretical and definitional approaches. Instead of having a high degree of convergence on assessment methodologies, there is an array which varies in theoretical grounding as well as in the quality of technique. (p. 18)

To avoid being sidetracked into a scholarly debate about *the* definition of a creative group, communication scholars should, at the very least, clarify definitions of such adjectives as "expressive" or "spontaneous," typically used in referencing creativity, so that the degree of convergence across investigations can be specified. In many cases, it would be preferable not to use the word "creativity" at all, but, rather, to adhere to specific factors, such as ideation, flexibility, analogic thinking, and so forth, that have more consensual understanding in their referents.

Second, scholars need to prioritize group communication research needs within the domain of creative activity. For example, a study of human resource professionals identified the following major barriers to communication in creative group problem solving: the impact of context, structures for group work, cultural diversity, climate (including power and the potential for reprisal), and how individuals' attitudes are influenced by group factors (Broome & Fulbright, 1995). In terms of priorities for the study of group communication and creativity, the following lines of investigation might prove fruitful. These are followed by a discussion of some methodological issues that need to be considered.

Potential Lines of Inquiry

Individual Differences and Group Composition

Some time ago, Valentine and Fisher (1974) expressed the need to assess group members' creativity, adaptiveness, or innovation and then study their interaction in groups so as to identify the communicative manifestations of innovative and noninnovative people, and the resultant impact on group reasoning, creativity, and decision effectiveness, as well as participant satisfaction. When composition cannot be a manipulated variable, as when studying most natural groups, relevant individual characteristics should still be assessed as potential covariates or to provide baseline data when some sort of training in creativity is part of the research agenda.

Abilities and attitudes. Clearly, the creative abilities of group members are a dominant theme in the literature on creativity. The challenge, according to Kirton and de Ciantis (1989), is to "create the right balance and foster tolerance amongst team members who may have very different cognitive styles" (p. 95). Graham and Dillon (1974) found that groups constructed on the basis of individual brainstorming ability were more effective when composed of highly creative members. Nemeth and Kwan (1987) hypothesized that exposure to majority viewpoints leads to convergent thinking in a group and that exposure to minority viewpoints leads to divergent thinking. Participants exposed to minority viewpoints outperformed others on an anagram task because they used all possible strategies to solve the problem; that is, they thought divergently (see Meyers & Brashers, Chapter 11, this volume, regarding research on majority/minority influence in groups). Whitfield (1975) suggested assessing potential members for a creative group task on their attitudes toward problems and on three kinds of thinking ability: creative, analytical, and judicial. Hurst et al. (1989) advocated that top management groups consist of a mix of Jungian cognitive styles or types: intuitives, feelers, thinkers, and sensors (see Haslett & Ruebush, Chapter 5, this volume, regarding the effects of these cognitive styles on individuals and group processes and outcomes).

Another individual difference that potentially affects group creativity is members' attitudes toward the group task, creativity itself, creative members, and creative techniques used in group discussion. For example, Comadena (1984) discovered that participants who produced the most ideas during brainstorming saw the task as more attractive than did those lower in idea production. Because negative attitudes foster obstacles to creativity, prediscussion dispositions should be considered as possible covariates (see Anderson et al., Chapter 6, this volume, regarding the effects of individuals' characteristics, including attitudes and personality predispositions, on group socialization processes).

Creativity as a Communication Process

Making people aware of communication and assessing the effects of such awareness are clearly within the arena of group communication scholarship. As applied to group creativity, Baer (1993) observed, "Knowing when to apply divergent-thinking skill is at least as important as the degree to which one has the skill available" (p. 17). Along this line, Basadur (1994) identified several communication problems that affect creativity: group members often are unable to communicate clearly and simply, they fail to define terms, they assume others know what is meant, they are unaware of process issues, they talk about solutions before the problem, there is poor leadership of meetings, other important group communicative activities do not occur, and there is no debriefing (reflection on the strengths and limitations of the groups' interaction process). Although all these problems merit attention, two areas are particularly relevant to enhancing creative group communication: communication strategies and problem-solving agendas.

Communication strategies. A review of the various techniques for enhancing creativity shows communication rules for the group as a whole or for various roles within it as a common component. Some of these rules, such as Osborn's (1957) rules for brainstorming, have been refined and tested in both laboratory and applied settings. For example, Vance and Deacon (1995) reject the traditional "no criticism" rule. They suggest that negative reactions should not be self-censored, but instead brought up, listed, and tabled (not discussed at that time). De Bono (1992) criticizes that rule for another reason: "Many approaches to creative thinking talk about delaying, suspending, or deferring judgment. . . . Telling someone not to use judgment does not tell that person what to do" (p. 191).

As another example, elaboration is a sign of divergence, and one way to increase elaboration is through the brainstorming rule of encouraging "piggybacking." Unfortunately, we do not have any sense of how often that actually happens in proportion to manifestations of other creative communication processes, such as making lists and explication. Are "piggybacked" ideas more likely to become innovative ones, compared to ideas developed in other ways? Does "piggybacking" occur immediately after an idea is presented, or later in the group process? Does this timing make any difference?

Although the ideation processes described in this review constitute a valuable component of creative activity, it may be that group communication scholars spend too much time on ideation and not enough on associative devices, such as analogies, metaphors, images, and scenarios. As de Bono (1992) asserts:

The brain is not designed to be creative. The traditional notion that it is enough to release inhibitions is inadequate. Releasing inhibitions will produce a mild sort of creativity. To produce serious creativity, we have to go further and to use methods which are not natural. The traditional process of brainstorming is a little better than nothing, but it is far too weak. (p. 173)

Comparing, contrasting, and combining divergent and associative ideation processes would represent a significant advance in applied group communication research while contributing to theoretical developments in the study of problem-solving thought and behavior.

Problem-solving agendas. At present, the various theories and models of creativity previously outlined are supported by little substantive research but, instead, have been derived from rational models of group problem solving or phase theories of group development and adapted by using psychological perspectives, intuition, experience, and common sense. One obvious priority should be to compare creative models to rational models of problem-solving effectiveness in straightforward tests of various procedures.

An alternative is to adopt a functional view of creativity that focuses not on the steps themselves, but on their utility (see Chapters 1 [Gouran], 2 [Poole], and 7 [Hirokawa & Salazar] regarding Functional Theory as applied to the study of group communication). Models of creative problem solving have additional functions and phases—silence, incubation, and quiet reflection on one's own, for example—designed to arouse interest and increase motivation. For instance, does a period of incubation promote inspiration? Weisberg (1993), assessing relevant research, questioned the value of an incubation phase, saying that it has not been adequately or systematically tested and that the research that does exist, such as Olton's (1979) and Olton and Johnson's (1976) work, has revealed that groups with an incubation period perform no better than groups without one. In addition, Weisberg questioned the supposition that illuminations occur during periods of low cortical arousal (the "sleep on it" idea). In an empirical study, however, a variety of artists reported the value of distancing and time in the creative process (Cawelti, Rappaport, & Wood, 1992).

One crucial creative problem-solving phase is identifying problems and sorting the trivial ones from those that are important. "*Finding* new and useful *problems* to solve is a separate and more important stage of the creative process than finding useful *solutions* to already identified problems" (Basadur, 1994, p. 238). Problems that appear unassailable, as well as problems that cross organizational functions and department lines, often are avoided. This phase is also important because the set of operations associated with effective problem construction provides a plan for problem-solving activities and, thereby, contributes to the originality and quality of the resulting solutions. Whether an extensive information search is advantageous in this phase is open to dispute; Holder (1988) maintains that it is required to develop a vision, whereas Scharf (1990) claims that assessing what presently exists is not necessary (see Propp, Chapter 9, this volume, regarding collective information processing in groups). Furthermore, problem identification can be motivational because of self-determined goals (Mumford et al., 1994). For example, Runco and Okuda (1988) discovered that more divergent thinking occurred in adolescents when participants discovered problems than when problems were presented to them.

Comparing logical behaviors (use of evidence, inference, logic, and reasoning) and creative communicative ones (list making, description, explication, and elaboration) also is of interest. An understanding of the interplay of these components within group discussion phases could reveal how creative and critical thinking are balanced, or need to be balanced, over the course of group problem-solving or decision-making interactions. For example, Basadur (1994) maintains that ratios of ideation to evaluation should vary over the stages of the process: more ideation in problem finding, an equal ratio in problem solving, and more evaluation in solution implementation. Understanding the conditions under which such equilibrium is possible or desirable would forward the conceptual development and application of problem-solving communication processes, as well as contribute to more general theory construction in the study of group communication.

The Social Dimension

Although the primary purpose of enhancing creativity in groups is to improve the quality of task outcomes, the social dimension of groups must also be conducive to creative behavior or else task performance will suffer (Keller, 1986). Cohesion and conflict, either actual or perceived, are two major social processes that interface with task effectiveness insofar as creativity is concerned (Hare, 1982). There has to be enough cohesion for trust, or else participants will not participate freely, but not so much cohesion that the pressure to conform outweighs creative or critical thinking; this is a delicate balance.

Given that creative and innovative persons are not uniformly welcomed in groups and organizations, attitudes toward and perceptions of such individuals would be a valuable postinteraction outcome measure (see, for example, Alderton, 1980; Bradley, 1980), which is easily accomplished by adapting self-report measures of participant satisfaction, a common output variable in group communication research (see Keyton, Chapter 8, this volume). If individuals' prediscussion attitudes were also assessed, the attitudinal impact of group communication might be uncovered. At the very least, however, participants' satisfaction with a group and its processes should remain a standard outcome measure.

Interventions for training, problem solving, or conflict management often are conducted by a group facilitator, who uses, avoids, and promotes specific communicative behaviors. In addition to examining professional facilitators in context, training individuals to facilitate groups as part of a manipulation would increase process awareness and empower members (see Schultz, Chapter 14, this volume). Reactions to the facilitator, as well as to perceived and actual group effectiveness,

would be an important component of this research. As Mensch (1993) argues, "True progress in diagnosis and resolution of conflicts cannot be made unless the participants themselves use diagnostic tools and become self-aware of their own situation" (p. 263).

New Technologies

Whether creativity can be enhanced by new technologies, such as group decision support systems, is another important direction for research (see Scott, Chapter 16, this volume, regarding research on communication technology and group communication). Kiesler (1988) thought that communication channels—in particular, computer communication technologies—can contribute to the development of creative environments. Some divergent processes, such as ideation, are well suited to such a medium. For instance, Valacich, Dennis, and Nunamaker (1992) found that nine-person groups generated more and better ideas than three-person groups using a computer-mediated ideation system, but that members of the smaller groups made fewer critical remarks and were more satisfied. Technology also can affect the social environment: The inhibiting effects of status differences, for example, can be ameliorated by the anonymity of group computer-communication technologies (Cooper, Gallupe, Pollard, & Cadsby, 1998; Herschel & Andrews, 1993; Jessup, Connolly, & Galegher, 1990). Roy, Gauvin, and Limayem (1996) found that continuous display feedback during electronically mediated brainstorming increased social matching (how group members, be they high or low performers, adapt their contributions to be similar to others) and that feedback at the end of interaction increased the number of unique ideas.

One can also easily manipulate particular variables using new technologies. For example, Connolly (1990) tested the effects of supportive and critical feedback by using anonymous confederates. Sosik, Avolio, and Kahai (1998) used anonymous and specified leaders to examine the effects of two leadership styles:

(a) transactional, where goal setting and statements were emphasized; and (b) transformational, where intellectual stimulation and consideration for individuals were stressed (see Pavitt, Chapter 12, this volume, on group communication and leadership).

On the other hand, Broome and Chen (1992) claim that present tools are ill-equipped for the study of creative group problem solving: "If computer-assisted methods are to be used responsibly in working with complex issues, they cannot be based on the traditional rational model of human thinking. . . . Computer assistance, then, must support the group's creative search process" (p. 225). Such assistance is on the way in the form of knowledge acquisition, problem representation, and solution heuristics (Williams, Deighan, & Kotnour, 1992).

Methodological Considerations

In any research endeavor, there are difficulties with conducting appropriate and worthwhile research. The challenges inherent in the study of creativity and innovation are not specific to this arena alone; many of the same difficulties also arise in psychological, social-psychological, and group communication research. Although research strategies should not drive research questions, methodological dilemmas can limit the type of questions that can be studied well. These include the measurement of relevant phenomena, including the individual, the creative outcome, and process effectiveness; tasks, or the focus of the creative endeavor; and the design of research.

Measurement of Relevant Phenomena

The individual. Establishing the baseline level of creativity in individuals is important to practitioners, who want to use those persons' talents effectively, and to trainers, who want to develop their skills. It is also valuable to researchers who wish to explore the impact of creative individuals on various group communication processes and outcomes. Whether

this can be done reliably is open to question. Early tests assessed thinking in the abstract, such as the Minnesota Tests of Creative Thinking (Torrance, 1962), the Remote Association Test (Mednick, 1962), and the Human Information Processing Survey (Torrance, Taggart, & Taggart, 1984). Tests developed later were more contextually sensitive. For example, to assess individual predispositions to creativity, Basadur and Finkbeiner (1985) developed a Preference for Ideation instrument that measures attitudes toward creativity that can affect creative performance, such as a tendency to be premature in critically evaluating ideas, the degree to which new ideas are valued, and the belief that creative thinking is bizarre. A similar measure is the Jones Inventory of Barriers to Effective Problem-Solving (JIB; Jones, 1993). Scales to measure innovativeness are the Innovativeness Scale (Hurt, Joseph, & Cook, 1977), the Innovation subscale of the Jackson Personality Inventory (Jackson, 1976), the Kirton Adaptation-Innovation Inventory (Kirton, 1976), and the Open-Processing Scale (Leavitt & Walton, 1975). Goldsmith (1986) concluded that these four scales measure "related but not identical constructs, just as the theories they represent define innovativeness differently. Whether any of the four scales measures a distinct construct called 'innovativeness' is still open to doubt" (p. 87). Although a valid, reliable, numerical measure of creativity would be enormously convenient for researchers, unfortunately, "when scores on creativity tests are compared with *other ratings of creativity* the correlations are also generally low. . . . There is usually an almost zero correlation between scores on these tests and various criteria of creativity in adult creators" (Ochse, 1990, p. 205). Finally, an increasing challenge to all instrumentation in this field is the necessity for cross-cultural validation (Rickards, 1993).

The creative outcome. How to evaluate the quality of the group product is a problem for all research on groups (see Gouran, 1990), but it is particularly salient for assessing creative outcomes. In applied contexts, creativity is measured by whether a chosen idea can be implemented, but that does not differentiate the trivial from the profound. Firestien (1993) noted that there can be a difference between critical acclaim and commercial success. Luckenbach (1987) suggested "Big C" and "little c" to distinguish between levels of creativity: "creativity with a little c for innovative but not very impactful problem solving; creativity with a capital C for the big breakthrough innovation" (p. 80). Both Taylor (1975) and Baer (1993) describe the ultimate in creativity, a paradigm shift, which could be assessed only with historical hindsight.

When examining the impact of ideation techniques, outcome measures often include quantity of ideas (e.g., Firestien, 1990; Jarboe, 1988) and uniqueness of ideas (e.g., Comadena, 1984; Jarboe, 1988; Roy et al., 1996). Ward et al. (1995) defined a "creative product" in terms of its appropriateness (a workable solution to some relevant problem) and its novelty or newness. Newness in and of itself is not important, however; Ward et al. state that only if a novel idea begets a useful invention, a valid discovery, should it count as creative, and furthermore, "the way in which creative ideas resemble old ideas are just as important as the ways they differ" (p. 10).

Just as with the measurement of creative individuals, scholars have pursued a numerical way to measure creative outcomes. For example, Besemer and O'Quin (1993) designed the Creative Product Semantic Scale as a generic instrument for judging important features of creative products: novelty (original, surprising, and germinal), practicality (valuable, logical, and useful), and value (organic, elegant, complex, understandable, and well crafted). This is an advance over global or single-item measures, for, as Firestien (1993) argues, evaluation of creative products should not be reduced to a single number.

What Amabile (1983b) observed many years ago may still be true today:

Although some . . . suggest that it is possible to articulate criteria of creativity that are clearly stated and readily translated into as-

sessment, the hope of delineating clear objective criteria is still to be met. Indeed, it can be argued that objective ultimate criteria for identifying products as creative will never be articulated. (p. 359)

Expanding on his point of view, Amabile (1996) advocated consensus of appropriate persons for measuring the quality of the products, outcomes, or responses judged as creative. Who is an appropriate judge, however, may not be immediately clear. Those who produce ideas or who supervise those who do may not be objective critics. Various domains may have their own experts who may be reasonably objective but not completely free of bias (Runco, 1994a). Criteria also change over time (Ochse, 1990). Finally, creative outcomes are not value-free; as Gamache and Kuhn (1989) claim, "The ultimate decision should have a large component of intuition—'gut feel'—in it" (p. 119).

Process effectiveness. Whether it is functioning as a product of the creative input conditions and/or as a precursor to the creative outputs, communicative behavior must be assessed. There are challenges inherent in any approach to examining human communication, including the diversity of researchers' theoretical orientations and choosing who is to conduct the observation. Assessments by participants themselves also present difficulties: Completion of surveys, viewing tapes, or interviews with the researcher take time; the assessment may interfere with the process if administered at various points during groups' discussions, either within or across meetings; and, as ever, the findings may be influenced by a social desirability bias (Kacen & Rozovski, 1998).

The major quandary is to assess whether a group process is, indeed, creative. Some have given up the attempt. For example, Amabile (1996) concluded, "Given the current state of psychological theory and research methodology, a definition based on process is not feasible" (p. 33); thus, "the identification of a thought process or subprocess as creative must finally depend upon the fruit of that process" (p. 33). As Kuhn (1988) explains, "Activities may seem creative up front based on intent but uncreative with hindsight based on results. Those who engage in creative activities have the burden of proof that their unestablished way is better than the established way" (p. xviii).

This point of view, however, is not universal. Weisberg (1993) asks:

Should the designation of a product as creative depend on whether it is successful and/or positively evaluated by others in the field? . . . Even if a novel product of goal-directed activity fails to accomplish the task for which it was made—that is, even if it is unsuccessful— it should still in my view be called creative, because from a cognitive perspective, success and failure are equivalent. (pp. 244-245)

This distinction between product and process is important for building communication theory. That is, should we deem the process effective if groups follow the rules, but their outputs are not judged creative? This is similar to the group intervention perspective that Block (1981) affirms: One can have a flawless consultation even if the group or organization does nothing as a result of one's efforts.

Just how much consensus can be obtained among various observers is a research question in itself. For example, Reagan and Rohrbaugh (1990) describe four competing perspectives on evaluating decision-process effectiveness, each derived from a particular values framework: rational, political, consensual, and empirical. They designed an evaluation instrument to measure process effectiveness and assessed its workability across different kinds of groups with three types of raters: facilitators, participants, and observers. Kacen and Rozovski (1998) assessed ratings among support group participants, direct observers, and indirect observers who watched a videotape of the group's interactions. On 11 outcome measures, including innovation, differences surfaced only for a measure of self-discovery.

The creative process also can be evaluated by experts who specialize in facilitation, although it may still be difficult to get consensus on the meaning of events. For instance:

One surefire way to know that your brainstorming session is "happening" is when you, the facilitator, begin to hear the participants throw out quips, jests, japes, and jokes that are rife with sexual innuendo. . . . It's a signal that the formal has yielded to the informal, that repression has given way to spontaneity, that fear has been replaced by fun . . . that posturing has been superseded by honesty. (Mattimore, 1994, p. 167)

Whether this perception of climate would be shared by members of both sexes is questionable, because behaviors perceived as informal by one social group can be interpreted as harassment by another. Furthermore, sexual innuendo is often a tentative step to sexual overture, which, though not inherently bad, is an egocentric behavior in the group context.

Using expert judges or participants to make global assessments of creative processes does not necessarily uncover the actual communicative behaviors that lead to particular creative functions being fulfilled. Decisions must also be made about the unit of analysis, such as thought units, speaking turns, lines of reasoning, or fantasy chains, that could help answer the research questions under study (see Poole, Keyton, & Frey, Chapter 4, this volume, on group communication methodology). It is necessary to identify and classify these behaviors, which is a highly complex process, if theory and intervention are to be improved. A critique of the many coding schemes that have been used in communication research is not appropriate here, but it seems that a system would have to be designed that could address logical and creative processes simultaneously. For example, Burningham and West (1995) classify group discussion interactions into six categories: task support, personal support and safety, participation, innovating, appraising, and resistance.

Once units of observation are obtained and coded, another challenge is interpreting raw data to identify processual patterns; that is, to place chronological communication events into conceptual tracks (such as people, ideas, transactions, context, and outcomes) to identify cycles and breakpoints (Van de Ven, 1988). This sophisticated treatment of communicative phenomena reflects the notion of process, or change over time, inherent in both communication and innovation. In fact, Van de Ven (1988) maintains that the study of innovation is the study of change itself, not a particularly easy phenomenon to address.

Tasks

A common criticism of group communication research has been the nature of the discussion stimulus, which is often an unrealistic or inappropriate task imposed by researchers on laboratory groups. This difficulty is avoided with natural groups, but without a common task typology (see McGrath, 1984; Shaw, 1981), it is difficult to sort out task effects on processes and outcomes (see Hirokawa & Salazar, Chapter 7, this volume, regarding task effects on group communication). As Ochse (1990) warns, "Any arguments as to the sequence and duration of stages in problem solving is, however, likely to be sterile, as problems vary across many dimensions" (p. 197).

Although creative problem solving requires an early phase of identifying the problem (Mumford & Gustafson, 1988), some decision-making research begins at the decision phase, with decision alternatives provided to the group. In such cases, generation of those alternatives is not the question under study, as it is in ideation tasks (e.g., "Unusual uses for a brick"). Furthermore, tasks often are selected that have clear measures of outcome quality so that it can be determined which group made the best decision. The study of creativity, however, necessitates the use of other types of tasks. Creative tasks are unstructured, nonalgorithmic (where the path to the solution is not clear; see Amabile, 1983a), and the measure of quality is consensual. Many decision-making and ideational tasks therefore are not appropriate for the study of creativity, which would benefit from increased use of real-world problems (Runco, 1994a).

Despite the problems noted, some sense of divergence could be analyzed. For example, the appropriate decision in many of the "survival" exercises (where people rank order items used to survive such traumatic events as crash-landing on the moon) relies on finding innovative uses for a common object, such as the lens of a flashlight being used as a reflector, or its case being used as a scoop. Burningham and West (1995), in addition to the quantity of new ideas, evaluated the newness of ideas, as well as their significance and effectiveness. Kelly and Karau (1993) assessed the number of categories of ideas to determine the presence of a "focus effect" (where groups pursue one line of thought to the exclusion of others), as well as originality and feasibility of ideas. Assessing or even promoting these kinds of interactions through training might illuminate the processes by which group outcomes are developed.

Whatever task is used should suit the competence of group members. Applied contexts have specific decision rules that are an obvious function of the task, such as quality control and marketing, and group members are well aware of them. In laboratory settings, however, the task may have to be chosen to fit the sample. Three dimensions of creative performance are critical: *domain-relevant* includes factual knowledge, technical skills, and any special talents required by the domain; *creativity-relevant* includes appropriate cognitive style, implicit or explicit knowledge of heuristics for generating creative ideas, and work style; and *task motivation* refers to attitudes toward the task and perceptions of one's own motivation for undertaking the task (Amabile, 1983b). To manipulate or control these dimensions might require extensive pretesting of group discussion stimuli. There are also ethical considerations in selecting a task. Although negative stimuli or stress, such as an emergency, can arouse creative responses, "few would regard the suggestion that discomfort plays a role in the development of creative ability as useful for promoting creativity" (Ochse, 1990, p. 175).

Research Designs

Lewin (1988) criticizes several research strategies used to examine creative and innovative processes. On classic hypothesis-testing strategies, he concludes, "Given the present state of knowledge, hypotheses testing will not prove fruitful. This literature has had scant influence in research on creativity and innovation" (pp. 137-138). He believes that the major value of empirical research is to generate new hypotheses, primarily through integrative meta-analytic techniques. Longitudinal field studies follow processes of innovation from beginning to end (Van de Ven, 1988), whereas real-time clinical research cases (Parker, 1982) have a shorter-term investment. Yin (1994) advocates replicated case research, studying the same question across organizations, to enhance the generalizability of conclusions. Action research is based on an intervention in an organization, where "innovation or creativity events can be engineered in such a way as to reveal useful case information for theory building or validation" (Lewin, 1988, p. 140). Research in applied settings is complicated by the need to balance not always compatible considerations. Researchers must accommodate their clients because the useful and appropriate outcome of any intervention is determined by the problem situation, but clients must be willing to allow the intervention to be structured in a way that lends itself to a research study.

Laboratory studies, in which variables are manipulated or controlled, also can play an important role, as long as the task is well designed (Weisberg, 1993). For research related to educating groups about creativity and creative communication, using college student samples is particularly efficient because training in techniques and strategies can be readily and ethically incorporated into a course syllabus, which streamlines the research project, enables the researcher to have control, and gives students the benefit of recent advances in theory (see Jarboe, 1988; Jarboe & Witteman, 1996).

CONCLUSION: THE CHALLENGE

The purpose of this chapter was to determine whether systematically incorporating creativity into group communication research would be beneficial for theory, research, and practice. Despite conceptual confusion regarding the creativity construct and scattershot research, understanding creative inputs, processes, and outputs is essential for understanding how groups can increase their effectiveness and attention to creativity can enhance theory construction in group communication. Perhaps the most surprising, yet obvious, conclusion is that the communication discipline is uniquely placed to make a contribution that no other discipline can: to assess the communicative manifestations of purposefully creative interaction in groups. Creativity, as an emerging discipline, is presently dominated by an uneasy and unspoken alliance between Cognitive Psychology and Organizational Behavior. Group communication scholarship is, for the most part, relatively unnoticed, perhaps because its focus has been narrow, with attention placed almost exclusively on ideation.

Perhaps not everyone sees the group as a meaningful context for examining creativity. For example, Hill and Amabile's (1993) model of organizational innovation does not distinguish individual from group activity; they are at the same level of analysis. McCrimmon (1995) recently cautioned that teamwork is not a panacea for every managerial conundrum. Similarly, in arguing that creative genius includes the habit of working alone, Ochse (1990) added, "The suggestion that creative activity is facilitated by solitude is not, however, kindly taken by modern workers in the field: the current tendency is to attempt to promote creativity through group interaction" (p. 171). Carr (1994) posed a provocative question:

Why are teams so popular these days, so popular in fact that many writers identify them as *the* way to manage an organization? One answer: They're a fad, promising higher quality and quantity and lower cycle time to companies starving for all three. (p. 131)

In contrast, other scholars see the value of a group perspective. As Van Gundy (1987) posits:

Most innovation research treats an entire organization as the unit of analysis. However, given the complex nature and size of modern organizations, it is likely that the innovation process occurs simultaneously within many different subsystems of the same organization and involves many different innovations. By making organizational subsystems the unit of analysis many of the inconsistent results in the literature may be explained. (p. 374)

The group is the arena in which individual creativity is shared through communication and where the assembly affect occurs through communication to produce creative outcomes. The group, with its communication process, is the mediating link between an individual's psychological processes and an organization's culture. For group communication scholarship to be acknowledged as a meaningful contributor to research on creativity requires moving beyond issues related merely to divergent thinking and ideation strategies.

The reason group communication scholars have not broadly and systematically addressed creativity in the past may be, in large part, the sources of research questions. First, there is no driving force to study creativity, as there is with people who work in applied settings or work with those who do, who have a considerable investment in the enhancement of creativity and innovation; presently, their very survival is perceived to depend on it. Furthermore, there is unity among practitioners, even those with disparate interests, to challenge threats to organizational effectiveness and to maximize opportunities to enhance it. Academicians, in contrast, often function as inde-

pendent entrepreneurs; unity of perspective, much less teamwork, is not required for individual achievement. We are free to follow our own pursuits and survive by our own individual wits. Although this permits the individual creativity of intelligent scholars (geniuses?), it retards the compilation of a body of knowledge necessary for theoretical maturation or, in other words, innovative communication theory.

Why creative problem solving as a specific activity has not been studied more in group communication research might be explained in the discipline's roots in rhetoric and logic. Although the "irrational" side of human behavior, addressed in such areas as emotional appeals in attitude change or various aspects of social cognition, is also part of our heritage, group communication theory and research have drawn more heavily from the traditions of discussion and debate, which emphasize evidence, logical reasoning, and linear argument (see Frey, 1996; Gouran, Chapter 1, this volume, on the history of group communication theory and research). The resulting attention to rational problem solving and decision making is valuable, but it is also incomplete for describing intelligent groups. Simon (1987), writing about scholarly perceptions of nonrational decision making, could have been describing communication scholars as well:

Those whose goal is to improve management-decision processes, have felt less comfortable with it. It appears to vindicate snap judgments and to cast doubt on the relevance of management-science tools, which almost all involve deliberation and calculation in decision making. (p. 58)

In fact, the emphasis on logic and reason may be a veneer of "civilization" that we are attempting to overlay on groups that, after all, consist of very human beings. The creative impulses of individuals are constrained from their earliest years, to their own disadvantage, as well as to the detriment of the groups to which they belong. We must be wary of unwittingly contributing to that repression by neglecting the role of nonrational and irrational processes in intelligent group problem solving and decision making.

Finally, as individual scholars and human beings, we are subject to the same kinds of forces and attitudes that are barriers to creative performance. Studying communicative behavior, beyond gross judgments of performance, is potentially unrewarding work: After all, communication data are difficult to collect, complicated to analyze, and professionally inefficient in the light of how scholarly productivity often is measured (i.e., number of publications per annum). Ironically, as Isaksen and Murdock (1993) point out:

> Another source of resistance to the study of creativity is the belief that creativity involves only fun, enjoyment, and merrymaking. Therefore, creativity cannot involve anything of substance or hard work. Certainly nothing resembling scientific inquiry could be applied to such a subject. (p. 27)

Furthermore, the odds are that some of us are adaptors and some of us are innovators, and we probably know which we are. Creativity is chaotic, messy, and discomfiting, whereas rationality is controllable, ordered, and reassuring. It might be comfortable to think that rational, logical discussion is all that is necessary for effective group performance, but that is an unrealistic and potentially dangerous hope. To acknowledge the role of nonrational behavior in the groups we study implies acknowledgment of our own nonrationality as well. This is a psychological hurdle for many reared in the academic tradition, and, of course, the organizations in which we work are not especially noted for their climates of innovation.

Poole (1990), pondering the status of group communication theories, wrote:

> Where small group communication research falls short is in inspiration. We have not intrigued, puzzled, or spoken to most people's condition. I fear we have overemphasized technique and propositional soundness at the expense of creativity. Creativity and a certain

element of playfulness are just as important as sound theory construction. (p. 246)

De Bono (1992) states our choices frankly: "Now we can sit around under trees waiting for apples to fall on our heads, or we can deliberately shake the tree" (p. 188). Perhaps the greatest payoff from the study of communication and creativity will be liberating ourselves from our own psychological, disciplinary, and communicative constraints.

REFERENCES

Ackoff, R. L., & Vergara, E. (1988). Creativity in problem solving and planning. In R. L. Kuhn (Ed.), *Handbook for creative and innovative managers* (pp. 77-89). New York: McGraw-Hill.

Albrecht, K. (with Albrecht, S.). (1987). *The creative corporation*. Homewood, IL: Dow Jones-Irwin.

Alderton, S. M. (1980). Attributions of responsibility for socially deviant behavior in decision-making discussions as a function of situation and locus of control of attributer. *Central States Speech Journal, 31*, 117-127.

Amabile, T. M. (1983a). *The social psychology of creativity*. New York: Springer-Verlag.

Amabile, T. M. (1983b). The social psychology of creativity: A componential conceptualization. *Journal of Personality and Social Psychology, 45*, 357-376.

Amabile, T. M. (1996). *Creativity in context: Update to the social psychology of creativity*. Boulder, CO: Westview.

Amabile, T. M., Hennessey, B. A., & Grossman, B. S. (1986). Social influences on creativity: The effects of contracted-for reward. *Journal of Personality and Social Psychology, 50*, 14-23.

Anderson, D. R. (1990, September). Increased productivity via group decision making. *Supervision*, pp. 6-10.

Anderson, F. G. (1988, September). Interdepartmental autonomy in large corporations. *Supervision*, pp. 14-18.

Anderson, N., Hardy, G., & West, M. (1992). Management team innovation. *Management Decision, 30*, 17-21.

Bachtold, L. M. (1982). Divergent thinking and temperamental traits. *Psychological Reports, 51*, 419-422.

Badawy, M. K. (1987). How to prevent creativity mismanagement. In A. D. Timpe (Ed.), *Creativity: The art and science of business management* (pp. 176-188). New York: Facts on File.

Baer, J. (1993). *Creativity and divergent thinking: A task-specific approach*. Hillsdale, NJ: Lawrence Erlbaum.

Barrett, D. (1998). *The paradox process: Creative business solutions where you least expect to find them*. New York: Amacom.

Bartunek, J. M., & Murnighan, J. K. (1984). The nominal group technique: Expanding the basic procedure and underlying assumptions. *Group & Organization Studies, 9,* 417-432.

Basadur, M. (1987). Needed research in creativity for business and industrial applications. In S. G. Isaksen (Ed.), *Frontiers of creativity research: Beyond the basics* (pp. 390-416). New York: Bearly.

Basadur, M. (1993). Impacts and outcomes of creativity in organizational settings. In S. G. Isaksen, M. C. Murdock, R. L. Firestien, & D. J. Treffinger (Eds.), *Nurturing and developing creativity: The emergence of a discipline* (pp. 278-313). Norwood, NJ: Ablex.

Basadur, M. (1994). Managing the creative process in organizations. In M. A. Runco (Ed.), *Problem finding, problem solving, and creativity* (pp. 237-268). Norwood, NJ: Ablex.

Basadur, M., & Finkbeiner, C. T. (1985). Measuring preference for ideation in creative problem-solving training. *Journal of Applied Behavioral Science, 21,* 37-49.

Basadur, M., Graen, G. B., & Green, S. G. (1982). Training in creative problem solving: Effects on ideation and problem finding and solving in an industrial research organization. *Organizational Behavior and Human Performance, 30,* 41-70.

Basadur, M., Graen, G. B., & Scandura, T. A. (1986). Training effects on attitudes toward divergent thinking among manufacturing engineers. *Journal of Applied Psychology, 71,* 612-617.

Basadur, M., & Thompson, R. (1986). Usefulness of the ideation principle of extended effort in real world professional and managerial creative problem solving. *Journal of Creative Behavior, 20,* 23-34.

Becker, G. M. (1994). Making it or finding it. In M. P. Shaw & M. A. Runco (Eds.), *Creativity and affect* (pp. 168-180). Norwood, NJ: Ablex.

Belbin, R. M. (1993). *Team roles at work.* Oxford, UK: Butterworth-Heinemann.

Berger, M. (1987, October). Japan's energetic new search for creativity. *International Management,* pp. 71-77.

Besemer, S. P., & O'Quin, K. (1993). Assessing creative products: Progress and evaluation. In S. G. Isaksen, M. C. Murdock, R. L. Firestien, & D. J. Treffinger (Eds.), *Nurturing and developing creativity: The emergence of a discipline* (pp. 331-349). Norwood, NJ: Ablex.

Blake, R. R., & Mouton, J. S. (1987). Don't let group norms stifle creativity. In A. D. Timpe (Ed.), *Creativity: The art and science of business management* (pp. 124-131). New York: Facts on File.

Blanchard, K. (1987, June). Meetings that work. *Today's Office,* pp. 9-11.

Block, P. (1981). *Flawless consulting: A guide to getting your expertise used.* San Diego: University Associates.

Bookman, R. (1988). Rousing the creative spirit. *Training and Development Journal, 42,* 67-71.

Bortree, W. H. (1986, November). Focus groups reduce innovation risks. *Bank Marketing,* pp. 18-24.

Bowden, C. L. (1994). Bipolar disorder and creativity. In M. P. Shaw & M. A. Runco (Eds.), *Creativity and affect* (pp. 73-86). Norwood, NJ: Ablex.

Bradley, P. H. (1980). Sex, competence, and opinion deviation: An expectation states approach. *Communication Monographs, 47,* 101-110.

Broome, B. J., & Chen, M. (1992). Guidelines for computer-assisted problem solving: Meeting the challenges of complex issues. *Small Group Research, 23,* 216-236.

Broome, B. J., & Fulbright, L. (1995). A multistage influence model of barriers to group problem solving: A participant-generated agenda for small group research. *Small Group Research, 26,* 25-55.

Brossard, M. (1990). Workers' objectives in quality improvement. *Employee Relations, 12,* 11-16.

Buch, K., & Spangler, R. (1990). The effects of quality circles on performance and promotions. *Human Relations, 43,* 573-582.

Buggie, F. D., Scheuing, E. E., & Vaccaro, V. L. (1990, Fall). An innovative approach to new product development. *Review of Business,* pp. 27-32, 46.

Burda, D. (1990, November 12). Hospital teams find solutions, savings through quality management. *Modern Healthcare,* p. 44.

Burningham, C., & West, M. A. (1995). Individual, climate and group interaction processes as predictors of work team innovation. *Small Group Research, 26,* 106-117.

Burnside, R. M., Amabile, T. M., & Gryskiewicz, S. S. (1988). Assessing organizational climates for creativity and innovation. In Y. Ijiri & R. L. Kuhn (Eds.), *New directions in creative and innovative management: Bridging theory and practice* (pp. 169-185). Cambridge, MA: Ballinger.

Byers, M. M. (1992, January). Cultivating creativity. *Association Management,* pp. 35-37.

Carr, C. (1994). *The competitive power of constant creativity.* New York: Amacom.

Cawelti, S., Rappaport, A., & Wood, B. (1992). Modeling artistic creativity: An empirical study. *Journal of Creative Behavior, 26,* 83-94.

Clark, I. D. (1989-1990). Encouraging innovation in a government department. *Optimum, 20,* 60-73.

Clark, S. G., & McGee, W. (1988). Evaluation: A method of transition. *Journal for Quality and Participation, 11,* 50-54.

Comadena, M. E. (1984). Brainstorming groups: Ambiguity tolerance, communication apprehension, task attraction, and individual productivity. *Small Group Behavior, 15,* 251-264.

Connolly, T. (1990). Effects of anonymity and evaluative tone on idea generation in computer mediated groups. *Management Science, 36,* 689-703.

Cooper, W. H., Gallupe, R. B., Pollard, S., & Cadsby, J. (1998). Some liberating effects of anonymous electronic brainstorming. *Small Group Research, 29,* 147-178.

Couger, J. D. (1990, October 29). Creativity in information systems. *Computerworld,* pp. 123-124.

Cramp, B. (1995, September 21). The art of bonding. *Marketing,* pp. 32-36.

de Bono, E. (1967). *New think: The use of lateral thinking in the generation of new ideas.* New York: Basic Books.

de Bono, E. (1992). *Sur/petition: Creating value monopolies when everyone else is merely competing.* New York: HarperBusiness.

Delbecq, A. L., Van de Ven, A. H., & Gustafson, D. H. (1975). *Group techniques for program planning: A guide to nominal group and Delphi processes.* Glenview, IL: Scott, Foresman.

Denton, D. K. (1990, August). Customer-focused management. *HR Magazine,* pp. 62-63, 66-67.

Dewey, J. (1910). *How we think.* Boston: D. C. Heath.

Diehl, M., & Stroebe, W. (1987). Productivity loss in brainstorming groups: Toward the solution of a riddle. *Journal of Personality and Social Psychology, 53,* 497-509.

Eisman, R. (1990, May). How hospitals heal morale. *Incentive,* pp. 99-106.

Elizur, D. (1990). Quality circles and quality of work life. *International Journal of Manpower, 11,* 3-7.

Erffmeyer, R. C., & Lane, I. M. (1984). Quality and acceptance of an evaluative task: The effects of four group decision-making formats. *Group & Organization Studies, 9,* 509-529.

Feldhusen, J. F. (1993). A conception of creative thinking and creativity training. In S. G. Isaksen, M. C. Murdock, R. L. Firestien, & D. J. Treffinger (Eds.), *Nurturing and developing creativity: The emergence of a discipline* (pp. 31-50). Norwood, NJ: Ablex.

Firestien, R. L. (1990). Effects of creative problem-solving training on communication behaviors in small groups. *Small Group Research, 21,* 507-521.

Firestien, R. L. (1993). The power of product. In S. G. Isaksen, M. C. Murdock, R. L. Firestien, & D. J. Treffinger (Eds.), *Nurturing and developing creativity: The emergence of a discipline* (pp. 261-277). Norwood, NJ: Ablex.

Fox, W. M. (1989). The improved nominal group technique. *Journal of Management Development, 8,* 20-27.

Frey, L. R. (1996). Remembering and "re-membering": A history of theory and research on communication and group decision making. In R. Y. Hirokawa & M. S. Poole (Eds.), *Communication and group decision making* (2nd ed., pp. 19-51). Thousand Oaks, CA: Sage.

Gamache, R. D., & Gagliano, C. C. (1988). Toolbox for practical creativity. In R. L. Kuhn (Ed.), *Handbook for creative and innovative managers* (pp. 101-112). New York: McGraw-Hill.

Gamache, R. D., & Kuhn, R. L. (1989). *The creativity infusion: How managers can start and sustain creativity and innovation.* New York: Harper & Row.

Geschka, H. (1993). The development and assessment of creative thinking techniques: A German perspective. In S. G. Isaksen, M. C. Murdock, R. L. Firestien, & D. J. Treffinger (Eds.), *Nurturing and developing creativity: The emergence of a discipline* (pp. 215-236). Norwood, NJ: Ablex.

Geschka, H., Schaude, G. R., & Schlicksupp, H. (1975). Modern techniques for solving problems. In M. M. Baldwin (Ed.), *Portraits of complexity: Applications of systems methodologies to societal problems* (pp. 1-7). Columbus, OH: Battelle Memorial Institute.

Glassman, E. (1989, April). Creative problem solving: Your role as leader. *Supervisory Management,* pp. 37-42.

Goldsmith, R. E. (1986). Convergent validity of four innovativeness scales. *Educational and Psychological Measurement, 46,* 81-87.

Gordon, J., & Zemke, R. (1986). Making them more creative. *Training, 23,* 30-45.

Gordon, W.J.J. (1961). *Synectics: The development of creative capacity.* New York: Harper & Row.

Gouran, D. S. (1990). Evaluating group outcomes. In G. M. Phillips (Ed.), *Teaching how to work in groups* (pp. 175-196). Norwood, NJ: Ablex.

Graham, D. K., & Dillon, P. C. (1974). Creative supergroups: Group performance as a function of individual performance on brainstorming tasks. *Journal of Social Psychology, 93,* 101-105.

Green, T. B. (1975). An empirical analysis of nominal and interacting groups. *Academy of Management Journal, 18,* 63-73.

Greene, R. J. (1986). Applying the creative process to circles. *Quality Circles Journal, 9,* 25-30.

Grossman, S. R. (1982). Training creativity and creative problem-solving. *Training and Development Journal, 36,* 62-68.

Gryskiewicz, S. S. (1987). Predictable creativity. In S. G. Isaksen (Ed.), *Frontiers of creativity research: Beyond the basics* (pp. 305-313). New York: Bearly.

Guilford, J. P. (1950). Creativity. *American Psychologist, 5,* 444-454.

Guilford, J. P. (1967). *The nature of human intelligence.* New York: McGraw-Hill.

Hare, A. P. (1982). *Creativity in small groups.* Beverly Hills, CA: Sage.

Hare, A. P. (1992). *Groups, teams, and social interaction: Theories and applications.* New York: Praeger.

Harkins, S. G., & Jackson, J. M. (1985). The role of evaluation in eliminating social loafing. *Personality and Social Psychology Bulletin, 11,* 457-465.

Harris, R. H., Jr. (1990). Five roads to excellence. *Journal for Quality and Participation, 13,* 54-58.

Hegedus, D. M., & Rasmussen, R. V. (1986). Task effectiveness and interaction process of a modified nominal group technique in solving an evaluation problem. *Journal of Management, 12,* 545-560.

Heinzen, T. E. (1994). Situational affect: Proactive and reactive creativity. In M. P. Shaw & M. A. Runco (Eds.), *Creativity and affect* (pp. 127-146). Norwood, NJ: Ablex.

Hequet, M. (1992). Creativity training gets creative. *Training, 29,* 41-46.

Herbert, T. T., & Yost, E. B. (1979). A comparison of decision quality under nominal and interacting consensus group formats: The case of the structured problem. *Decision Sciences, 10,* 358-370.

Herschel, R. T., & Andrews, P. H. (1993). Empowering employees in group work. *Information Strategy: The Executive's Journal, 9*(Spring), 36-42.

Hill, K. G., & Amabile, T. M. (1993). A social psychological perspective on creativity: Intrinsic motivation and creativity in the classroom and workplace. In S. G.

Isaksen, M. C. Murdock, R. L. Firestien, & D. J. Treffinger (Eds.), *Understanding and recognizing creativity: The emergence of a discipline* (pp. 400-453). Norwood, NJ: Ablex.

Holder, R. J. (1988). Visioning: An energizing tool. *Journal for Quality and Participation, 11,* 18-22.

Howard, N. (1987). Business probe: The creative spark. In A. D. Timpe (Ed.), *Creativity: The art and science of business management* (pp. 3-11). New York: Facts on File.

Hurst, D. K., Rush, J. C., & White, R. E. (1989). Top management teams and organizational renewal. *Strategic Management Journal, 10,* 87-105.

Hurt, H. T., Joseph, K., & Cook, C. D. (1977). Scales for the measurement of innovativeness. *Human Communication Research, 4,* 58-65.

Hyde, W. D. (1986, December). How small groups can solve problems and reduce costs. *Industrial Engineering,* pp. 42-49.

Isaksen, S. G. (1983). Toward a model for the facilitation of creative problem solving. *Journal of Creative Behavior, 17,* 18-31.

Isaksen, S. G. (Ed.). (1987). *Frontiers of creativity research: Beyond the basics.* New York: Bearly.

Isaksen, S. G. (1988a). Human factors for innovative problem solving. In R. L. Kuhn (Ed.), *Handbook for creative and innovative managers* (pp. 139-146). New York: McGraw-Hill.

Isaksen, S. G. (1988b). Innovative problem solving in groups. In Y. Ijiri & R. L. Kuhn (Eds.), *New directions in creative and innovative management: Bridging theory and practice* (pp. 145-168). Cambridge, MA: Ballinger.

Isaksen, S. G., & Murdock, M. C. (1993). The emergence of a discipline: Issues and approaches to the study of creativity. In S. G. Isaksen, M. C. Murdock, R. L. Firestien, & D. J. Treffinger (Eds.), *Understanding and recognizing creativity: The emergence of a discipline* (pp. 13-47). Norwood, NJ: Ablex.

Isaksen, S. G., Murdock, M. C., Firestien, R. L., & Treffinger, D. J. (Eds.). (1993a). *Nurturing and developing creativity: The emergence of a discipline.* Norwood, NJ: Ablex.

Isaksen, S. G., Murdock, M. C., Firestien, R. L., & Treffinger, D. J. (Eds.). (1993b). *Understanding and recognizing creativity: The emergence of a discipline.* Norwood, NJ: Ablex.

Isen, A. M., Daubman, K. A., & Nowicki, G. P. (1987). Positive affect facilitates creative problem solving. *Journal of Personality and Social Psychology, 52,* 1122-1131.

Jablin, F. M., Seibold, D. R., & Sorenson, R. L. (1977). Potential inhibitory effects of group participation on brainstorming performance. *Central States Speech Journal, 28,* 113-121.

Jackson, D. N. (1976). *Jackson Personality Inventory manual.* Goshen, NY: Research Psychologists Press.

Janis, I. L. (1972). *Victims of groupthink: A psychological study of foreign-policy decisions and fiascoes.* Boston: Houghton Mifflin.

Jarboe, S. (1988). A comparison of input-output, process-output, and input-process-output models of small group problem-solving effectiveness. *Communication Monographs, 55,* 121-142.

Jarboe, S. (1996). Procedures for enhancing group decision making. In R. Y. Hirokawa & M. S. Poole (Eds.), *Communication and group decision making* (2nd ed., pp. 345-383). Thousand Oaks, CA: Sage.

Jarboe, S., & Witteman, H. (1996). Intra-group conflict management in task-oriented groups: The influence of problem source and problem analysis. *Small Group Research, 27,* 316-338.

Jessup, L. M., Connolly, T., & Galegher, J. (1990). The effects of anonymity on GDSS group process with an idea-generating task. *MIS Quarterly, 14,* 313-321.

Johnson, C. E., & Hackman, M. Z. (1995). *Creative communication: Principles & applications.* Prospect Heights, IL: Waveland.

Johnson, V. (1993, September). Problem solving. *Successful Meetings,* pp. 228-231.

Jones, L. (1993). Barriers to creativity and their relationship to individual, group, and organizational behavior. In S. G. Isaksen, M. C. Murdock, R. L. Firestien, & D. J. Treffinger (Eds.), *Nurturing and developing creativity: The emergence of a discipline* (pp. 133-154). Norwood, NJ: Ablex.

Kacen, L., & Rozovski, U. (1998). Assessing group processes: A comparison among group participants', direct observers', and indirect observers' assessment. *Small Group Research, 29,* 179-211.

Kane, C. L. (1987). How to increase the odds for successful brand extension. *Journal of Product Innovation Management, 4,* 199-203.

Kanter, R. M. (1988). Change-master skills: What it takes to be creative. In R. L. Kuhn (Ed.), *Handbook for creative and innovative managers* (pp. 91-99). New York: McGraw-Hill.

Kao, J. J. (1991). *Managing creativity.* Englewood Cliffs, NJ: Prentice Hall.

Kearns, D. T. (1988). Changing a corporate culture: Leadership through quality. In R. L. Kuhn (Ed.), *Handbook for creative and innovative managers* (pp. 243-253). New York: McGraw-Hill.

Keller, R. T. (1986). Predictors of the performance of project groups in R&D organizations. *Academy of Management Journal, 29,* 715-726.

Keller, R. T., & Holland, W. E. (1978). Individual characteristics of innovativeness and communication in research and development organizations. *Journal of Applied Psychology, 63,* 759-762.

Kelly, J. R., & Karau, S. J. (1993). Entrainment of creativity in small groups. *Small Group Research, 24,* 179-198.

Kiesler, S. (1988). Technology and the development of creative environments. In Y. Ijiri & R. L. Kuhn (Eds.), *New directions in creative and innovative management: Bridging theory and practice* (pp. 89-102). Cambridge, MA: Ballinger.

Kirton, M. J. (1976). Adaptors and innovators: A description and measure. *Journal of Applied Psychology, 61,* 622-629.

Kirton, M. J. (1989). Adaptors and innovators at work. In M. J. Kirton (Ed.), *Adaptors and innovators: Styles of creativity and problem-solving* (pp. 56-78). New York: Routledge.

Kirton, M. J., & de Ciantis, S. (1989). Cognitive style in organizational climate. In M. J. Kirton (Ed.), *Adaptors and innovators: Styles of creativity and problem-solving* (pp. 79-96). New York: Routledge.

Koberg, C. S., & Chusmir, L. H. (1987). Organizational culture relationships with creativity and other job-related variables. *Journal of Business Research, 15,* 397-409.

Kramer, M. W., Kuo, C. L., & Dailey, J. C. (1997). The impact of brainstorming techniques on subsequent group processes: Beyond generating ideas. *Small Group Research, 28,* 218-242.

Kreps, G. L. (1995). Using focus group discussions to promote organizational reflexivity: Two applied communication field studies. In L. R. Frey (Ed.), *Innovations in group facilitation: Applications in natural settings* (pp. 177-199). Cresskill, NJ: Hampton.

Kuhn, R. L. (Ed.). (1988). *Handbook for creative and innovative managers.* New York: McGraw-Hill.

Kuhn, R. L. (Ed.). (1993). *Generating creativity and innovation in large bureaucracies.* Westport, CT: Quorum.

Landes, J. (1990, October 15). The 90s will be the decade of the customer. *National Underwriter,* p. 10.

Larson, J. S. (1989). Employee participation in federal management. *Public Personnel Management, 18,* 404-414.

Leavitt, C., & Walton, J. R. (1975). Development of a scale for innovativeness. In M. J. Schlinger (Ed.), *Advances in consumer research* (pp. 545-554). Ann Arbor, MI: Association for Consumer Research.

Lewin, A. Y. (1988). Research on creative and innovative management. In Y. Ijiri & R. L. Kuhn (Eds.), *New directions in creative and innovative management: Bridging theory and practice* (pp. 131-143). Cambridge, MA: Ballinger.

Luckenbach, T. A. (1987). Encouraging "little C" and "big C" creativity. In A. D. Timpe (Ed.), *Creativity: The art and science of business management* (pp. 80-82). New York: Facts on File.

Maier, N.R.F. (1952). *Principles of human relations, applications to management.* New York: Wiley.

Mansfield, E. (1989, March/April). Technological creativity: Japan and the United States. *Business Horizons,* pp. 48-53.

Mattimore, B. W. (1994). *99% inspiration: Tips, tales and techniques for liberating your business creativity.* New York: Amacom.

Maturi, R. J. (1993, July 19). Disney's legacy lives. *Industry Week,* pp. 50-52.

Maxon, J. (1988). Creating new ideas. *Management Decision, 26,* 40-43.

McCrae, R. R. (1987). Creativity, divergent thinking, and openness to experience. *Journal of Personality and Social Psychology, 52,* 1258-1265.

McCrimmon, M. (1995). Teams without roles: Empowering teams for greater creativity. *Journal of Management Development, 14,* 35-41.

McGrath, J. E. (1984). *Groups: Interaction and performance.* Englewood Cliffs, NJ: Prentice-Hall.

Mednick, S. A. (1962). The associative basis of the creative process. *Psychological Review, 69,* 220-232.

Mednick, S. A. (1963). The associative basis of the creative process. In M. T. Mednick & S. A. Mednick (Eds.), *Research in personality* (pp. 583-596). New York: Holt, Rinehart & Winston.

Mensch, G. O. (1993). A managerial tool for diagnosing structural readiness for breakthrough innovations in large bureaucracies (technocracies). In R. L. Kuhn (Ed.), *Generating creativity and innovation in large bureaucracies* (pp. 257-281). Westport, CT: Quorum.

Michalko, M. (1994). Bright ideas. *Training & Development, 48,* 44-47.

Miller, W. C. (1987). *The creative edge: Fostering innovation where you work.* Reading, MA: Addison-Wesley.

Miner, F. C., Jr. (1979). A comparative analysis of three diverse group decision making approaches. *Academy of Management Journal, 22,* 81-93.

Mumford, M. D., & Gustafson, S. B. (1988). Creativity syndrome: Integration, application, and innovation. *Psychological Bulletin, 103,* 27-43.

Mumford, M. D., Reiter-Palmon, R., & Redmond, M. R. (1994). Problem construction and cognition: Applying problem representations in ill-defined domains. In M. A. Runco (Ed.), *Problem finding, problem solving, and creativity* (pp. 3-39). Norwood, NJ: Ablex.

Munitz, B. (1988). Creative management demands creative leadership. In R. L. Kuhn (Ed.), *Handbook for creative and innovative managers* (pp. 487-493). New York: McGraw-Hill.

Nemeth, C. J., & Kwan, J. L. (1987). Minority influence, divergent thinking, and detection of correct solutions. *Journal of Applied Social Psychology, 17,* 788-799.

Nemiroff, P. M., Pasmore, W. A., & Ford, D. L., Jr. (1976). The effects of two normative structural interventions on established and *ad hoc* groups: Implications for improving decision making effectiveness. *Decision Sciences, 7,* 841-855.

Ochse, R. E. (1990). *Before the gates of excellence: The determinants of creative genius.* Cambridge, UK: Cambridge University Press.

Offitzer, K. (1993, February). How to battle burn-out. *Successful Meetings,* pp. 141-144.

Offner, A. K., Kramer, T. J., & Winter, J. P. (1996). The effects of facilitation, recording, and pauses on group brainstorming. *Small Group Research, 27,* 283-298.

Olton, R. M. (1979). Experimental studies of incubation: Searching for the elusive. *Journal of Creative Behavior, 13,* 9-22.

Olton, R. M., & Johnson, D. M. (1976). Mechanisms of incubation in creative problem solving. *American Journal of Psychology, 89,* 617-630.

Osborn, A. F. (1957). *Applied imagination: Principles and procedures of creative problem-solving.* New York: Scribner.

Parker, R. C. (1982). *The management of innovation.* New York: John Wiley and Sons.

Peters, T. (1990). Get innovative or get dead (part 1). *California Management Review, 33,* 9-26.

Poole, M. S. (1990). Do we have any theories of group communication? *Communication Studies, 41,* 237-247.

Putnam, L. L., & Stohl, C. (1990). Bona fide groups: A reconceptualization of groups in context. *Communication Studies, 41,* 248-265.

Putnam, L. L., & Stohl, C. (1996). Bona fide groups: An alternative perspective for communication and small group decision making. In R. Y. Hirokawa & M. S. Poole (Eds.), *Communication and group decision making* (2nd ed., pp. 147-178). Thousand Oaks, CA: Sage.

Rawlinson, J. G. (1981). *Creative thinking and brainstorming.* New York: John Wiley.

Reagan, P., & Rohrbaugh, J. (1990). Group decision process effectiveness: A competing values approach. *Group & Organization Studies, 15,* 20-43.

Reich, R. B. (1987). Entrepreneurship reconsidered: The team as hero. *Harvard Business Review, 65,* 77-83.

Richards, R. (1994). Creativity and bipolar mood swings: Why the association? In M. P. Shaw & M. A. Runco (Eds.), *Creativity and affect* (pp. 45-72). Norwood, NJ: Ablex.

Rickards, T. (1974). *Problem-solving through creative analysis.* New York: Wiley & Sons.

Rickards, T. (1993). Creativity from a business school perspective: Past, present, and future. In S. G. Isaksen, M. C. Murdock, R. L. Firestien, & D. J. Treffinger (Eds.), *Nurturing and developing creativity: The emergence of a discipline* (pp. 155-176). Norwood, NJ: Ablex.

Rooks, R. (1987). Creativity and conformity: Finding the balance. In A. D. Timpe (Ed.), *Creativity: The art and science of business management* (pp. 148-151). New York: Facts on File.

Rosenberg, D. (1990). Where did the passion go? *International Journal of Manpower, 11,* 20-22.

Roy, M. C., Gauvin, S., & Limayem, M. (1996). Electronic group brainstorming: The role of feedback on productivity. *Small Group Research, 27,* 215-247.

Runco, M. A. (1991). *Divergent thinking.* Norwood, NJ: Ablex.

Runco, M. A. (1994a). Conclusions concerning problem finding, problem solving, and creativity. In M. A. Runco (Ed.), *Problem finding, problem solving, and creativity* (pp. 271-290). Norwood, NJ: Ablex.

Runco, M. A. (1994b). Creativity and its discontents. In M. P. Shaw & M. A. Runco (Eds.), *Creativity and affect* (pp. 102-126). Norwood, NJ: Ablex.

Runco, M. A. (Ed.). (1994c). *Problem finding, problem solving, and creativity.* Norwood, NJ: Ablex.

Runco, M. A., & Okuda, S. M. (1988). Problem discovery, divergent thinking, and the creative process. *Journal of Youth and Adolescence, 17,* 211-220.

Scharf, A. (1990). Seven guides to breakthrough thinking. *Journal of Management Consulting, 6,* 37-39.

Scheidel, T. M. (1986). Divergent and convergent thinking in group decision-making. In R. Y. Hirokawa & M. S. Poole (Eds.), *Communication and group decision-making* (pp. 113-130). Beverly Hills, CA: Sage.

Scheidel, T. M., & Crowell, L. (1979). *Discussing and deciding: A desk book for group leaders and members.* New York: Macmillan.

Schuldberg, D. (1994). Giddiness and horror in the creative process. In M. P. Shaw & M. A. Runco (Eds.), *Creativity and affect* (pp. 87-101). Norwood, NJ: Ablex.

Sethia, N. K. (1993). Leadership for creativity in organizations: A prototypical case of leading multidisciplinary teams of professionals. In R. L. Kuhn (Ed.), *Generating creativity and innovation in large bureaucracies* (pp. 385-391). Westport, CT: Quorum.

Seymour, D. T., McQuarrie, E. F., & McIntyre, S. H. (1987). Focus groups and the development of new products by technologically driven companies: A comment. *Journal of Product Innovation Management, 4,* 50-60.

Shaw, M. E. (1981). *Group dynamics: The psychology of small group behavior* (3rd ed.). New York: McGraw-Hill.

Simon, H. A. (1987). Making management decisions: The role of intuition and emotion. *Academy of Management Executive, 1,* 57-64.

Sklarow, G. (1989, July 17). Zero defects: Old theme—new twist. *Industry Week,* pp. 35-38.

Sosik, J. J., Avolio, B. J., & Kahai, S. S. (1998). Inspiring group creativity: Comparing anonymous and identified electronic brainstorming. *Small Group Research, 29,* 3-31.

Talbot, R. J. (1993). Creativity in the organizational context: Implications for training. In S. G. Isaksen, M. C. Murdock, R. L. Firestien, & D. J. Treffinger (Eds.), *Nurturing and developing creativity: The emergence of a discipline* (pp. 177-214). Norwood, NJ: Ablex.

Tatsuno, S. M. (1990). Creating breakthroughs the Japanese way. *Research and Development, 32,* 336-142.

Taylor, I. A. (1975). An emerging view of creative actions. In I. A. Taylor & J. W. Getzels (Eds.), *Perspectives in creativity* (pp. 297-324). Chicago: Aldine.

Thompson, T. N. (1991). Dialectics, communication, and exercises for creativity. *Journal of Creative Behavior, 25,* 43-51.

Torrance, E. P. (1962). *Guiding creative talent.* Englewood Cliffs, NJ: Prentice Hall.

Torrance, E. P., Taggart, B., & Taggart, W. (1984). *Human information processing survey.* Bensenville, IL: Scholastic Testing Service.

Treffinger, D. J., Isaksen, S. G., & Dorval, K. B. (1994). Creative problem solving: An overview. In M. A. Runco (Ed.), *Problem finding, problem solving, and creativity* (pp. 223-236). Norwood, NJ: Ablex.

Tubbs, S. L. (1992). *A systems approach to small group interaction* (4th ed.). New York: McGraw-Hill.

Valacich, J. S., Dennis, A. R., & Nunamaker, J. F., Jr. (1992). Group size and anonymity effects on computer-mediated idea generation. *Small Group Research, 23,* 49-73.

Valentine, K. B., & Fisher, B. A. (1974). An interaction analysis of verbal innovative deviance in small groups. *Speech Monographs, 41,* 413-420.

Van de Ven, A. H. (1988). Requirements for studying innovation processes. In Y. Ijiri & R. L. Kuhn (Eds.), *New directions in creative and innovative management: Bridging theory and practice* (pp. 187-199). Cambridge, MA: Ballinger.

Van de Ven, A. H., & Delbecq, A. L. (1974). The effectiveness of nominal, Delphi, and interacting decision making group processes. *Academy of Management Journal, 17,* 605-621.

Van Gundy, A. (1987). Organizational creativity and innovation. In S. G. Isaksen (Ed.), *Frontiers of creativity research: Beyond the basics* (pp. 358-379). New York: Bearly.

Vance, M., & Deacon, D. (1995). *Think out of the box.* Franklin Lakes, NJ: Career Press.

Wallas, G. (1926). *The art of thought.* New York: Harcourt, Brace.

Ward, T. B., Finke, R. A., & Smith, S. M. (1995). *Creativity and the mind: Discovering the genius within.* New York: Plenum.

Watzlawick, P., Beavin, J., & Jackson, D. (1974). *Change: Principles of problem formation and problem resolution.* New York: W. W. Norton.

Weick, K. (1979). *The social psychology of organizing* (2nd ed.). Reading, MA: Addison-Wesley.

Weisberg, R. W. (1993). *Creativity: Beyond the myth of genius.* New York: W. H. Freeman.

White, S. E., Dittrich, J. E., & Lang, J. R. (1980). The effects of group decision-making process and problem-situation complexity on implementation attempts. *Administrative Science Quarterly, 25,* 428-440.

Whitfield, P. R. (1975). *Creativity in industry.* Baltimore: Penguin.

Whyte, G. (1989, June). Dakotah: A world class act. *Bobbin,* pp. 130-133.

Williams, K. E., Deighan, J., & Kotnour, T. (1992). Knowledge acquisition for group problem solving. *Computers & Industrial Engineering, 23,* 459-462.

Wilson, J. (1990). Investing in our future: Quality and participation for students and school staff. *Journal for Quality and Participation, 13,* 78-81.

Yin, R. K. (1994). *Case study research: Design and methods* (2nd ed.). Thousand Oaks, CA: Sage.

PART V

Group Communication Facilitation

14

Improving Group Communication Performance

An Overview of Diagnosis and Intervention

BEATRICE G. SCHULTZ
University of Rhode Island

A fundamental question for those who study, facilitate, and work in groups is how to improve a group's effectiveness with respect to interactions and outcomes. As the chapters in this volume show, scholars have conducted thousands of studies examining such variables as group goals and tasks, member characteristics, conformity and deviance, leadership, conflict, cohesion, and group problem solving and decision making. Despite this ever-increasing volume of research studies, many scholars lament the fact that group members often fail to apply the basic knowledge provided by such studies in their deliberations (see Cragan & Wright, 1990; Hirokawa, 1987; Janis, 1982; Levine & Moreland, 1990; Poole, 1991).

Clearly, much more remains to be done if we are to understand both how groups function and the processes that enhance group functioning. If members are to improve the internal dynamics of the groups in which they participate, and especially the processes used to solve problems and make decisions, then researchers and practitioners will need to consider more fully how to assist members in acquiring a basic knowledge of group dynamics and an understanding of the particular communicative acts likely to have the greatest impact on what group members say and do—and even more, how to apply this knowledge to the myriad situations that members encounter.

In that light, this chapter offers perspectives for evaluating and changing group behavior. The discussions of theories, research, and intervention strategies are designed to illustrate processes and methods that can help group members achieve more satisfying and productive experiences. The focus of the chapter is on group intervention at the macrolevel (see Sunwolf & Seibold, Chapter 15, this volume, for more specific group facilitation procedures). The focus here is on theories and methods that can be useful in changing ineffective group processes to more effective ones and on examining the obstacles that stand in the way of this accomplishment.

The chapter addresses changing the performance of groups from two process perspectives: (a) a *diagnostic process*—how specifically chosen individuals (facilitators, consultants, or group members) can observe group behavior and evaluate a group's strengths and deficiencies, and (b) an *intervention process*—how facilitators, consultants, or group members with insight into effective group processes can suggest potential remedies for altering the internal dynamics of a group. The chapter begins with a brief history and description of the group intervention process, focusing on findings and conclusions about interventions acquired from experiential practice and training. The assumption behind this perspective is that although theoretical claims and results from experimental research provide insight and understanding into group behavior, they do not lead necessarily to the skilled behaviors that produce effective group functioning. Explanations and suggestions derived from observation and actual practice often are more able to specify the actions group members should undertake to produce desired outcomes (see Bunker, 1992). The two processes, however, are interdependent: Practice without a theoretical base would be too dependent on intuition or rules of thumb, and theoretical explanations not accompanied by directions for specific actions are likely to be too difficult for group members to put into practice.

The chapter also explains how the processes of observation and providing feedback can be used to evaluate important group components, such as interactional patterns and decision-making outcomes. The final sections conclude with suggestions for future research and illustrate some of the typical obstacles group members encounter and some remedies for surmounting them.

ORIGINS OF GROUP INTERVENTION

The need to be able to do something, to intervene, in a group and change existing patterns is a concern shared by many theorists and practitioners (e.g., Argyris, 1970; Bennis, Benne, & Chin, 1969; Bradford, Gibb, & Benne, 1964; Frey, 1995a, 1995b; Gouran, 1994). Indeed, the study of intervention in groups has a long history. Beginning in the first half of the 20th century and spurred by such cultural forces during the 1920s, 1930s, and 1940s as labor-management tensions stemming from the Great Depression, the need for effective leadership to fight fascist-democratic

wars, and deeply embedded conflict arising from racial inequality in the United States, to name a few, many social and behavioral scientists sought ways to change such inhumane social and political conditions. The study of groups became a central part of this effort because public discussion was perceived as one effective approach for dealing with these issues (Alderfer, 1992; see Frey, 1996; Gouran, Chapter 1, this volume).

Scholars proclaimed the value of group discussion as both an educational tool and a method for social and political reform. The art of group discussion was equated with building democratic values. To this end, books, such as Baird's (1928) *Public Discussion and Debate*, described how to conduct and participate in group discussions. Public meetings became a focal place for people to engage in discussions leading to decisions. Moreover, researchers found that as people engaged in group discussion, they were better able to address issues of fact, could make decisions more quickly, and were more likely to make decisions that were superior to what an individual working alone could make. The data from these early studies consistently showed that following group discussion, judgments tended to be both more accurate and acceptable (see, for example, Jenness, 1932, and Timmons, 1939; for a review of the early history of group discussion, see Dickens & Hefferman, 1949; Frey, 1996; Gouran, 1985; Hare, 1973; Timmons, 1941).

The impetus for using discussion methods to improve the problem-solving and decision-making ability of individuals and groups came largely from the work of philosopher John Dewey (in this volume, see Chapters 1 [Gouran], 7 [Hirokawa & Salazar], 9 [Propp], and 18 [Allen & Plax]). Dewey (1910) identified a process he called *reflective thinking* that included a series of five sequential steps reflecting a systematic, rational approach to solving problems:

(1) a felt difficulty, (2) its location and definition, (3) suggestions of possible solutions, (4) development by reasoning of the bearing of suggestions, and (5) further observation

and experiment leading to its acceptance or rejection; that is, the conclusion of belief or disbelief. (p. 72)

The influence of Dewey's reflective thinking process is evident in the variety of group discussion, problem-solving, and decision-making procedures recommended by current scholars (see Sunwolf & Seibold, Chapter 15, this volume). What we learned from Dewey, and from those who subsequently adapted his work to the group context, is that attention to the requirements of a rational approach to problem solving has a positive effect on a group's ability to deal with issues and is more likely to yield high-quality solutions (see Gouran & Hirokawa, 1986; Hirokawa & Salazar, Chapter 7, this volume; Jarboe, 1988; Maier & Maier, 1957; Pavitt, 1993; Poole, Chapter 2, this volume). Although studies of task groups indicate that a careful consideration of discussion, problem-solving, and decision-making procedures should produce higher quality solutions and decisions, however, many studies show that groups often do not follow these procedures or achieve their intended results. Groups also do not necessarily solve problems more effectively by using a *rational model* (see Braybrooke & Lindblom, 1970; Gouran, 1991; Hirokawa, 1985; Jarboe, 1996; Schultz & Ketrow, 1996; Zey, 1992).

The proposition that the use of rational problem-solving and decision-making procedures leads to better group outcomes has been tested in a variety of circumstances, and no specific rational model has been found to be consistently better than any other. Indeed, as Janis and Mann (1977) observe, members who take rational approaches to group decision making may be in a minority. Rational models are time-consuming and complex, and group members may not have the necessary information available to use them effectively. There are many reasons why such approaches do not produce higher quality group solutions; for example, individuals who dominate or who have diverse agendas, conflicting interests, lack of commitment, fear of conflict,

or the need to protect their self-image, among other characteristics, can undercut the advantages offered by prescribed procedures. Although the discussion process that results from following these prescribed procedures is supposed to lead to better group decisions, the characteristics and behaviors of members and their interpersonal relations in a group also influence group performance (in this volume, see Chapters 5 [Haslett & Ruebush], 6 [Anderson, Riddle, & Martin], and 8 [Keyton]). As Gouran (1991) explains, the odds of having a climate in which rational choice is possible are increased only when there are participants who deliberately make an effort to create it. Such conflicting data about the effectiveness of rational models for improving group discussion and performance point to the need for further identification of the types of interventions that could produce more positive results.

During the same period that group discussion methods were being hailed as an antidote to noncritical thinking, scholars from cognate disciplines were also evaluating the potential for various group processes to change adverse social and political conditions (see Gouran, Chapter 1, this volume). They conducted controlled laboratory and field studies to explore the social processes produced by small groups. This scientific approach to understanding group phenomena began in the late 1930s and early 1940s with such foci as the effects of autocratic, democratic, and laissez-faire leadership styles on group performance (Lewin, Lippitt, & White, 1939; see Pavitt's review of group communication-leadership theory and research, Chapter 12, this volume). Lewin and colleagues found that when boys enrolled in an after-school club were led by an authoritarian leader (who was completely in charge of all activities), they produced the most of any of the groups when the leader was present but displayed little initiative if the leader left the room. Under a laissez-faire leader (who gave direction only if asked), they produced very little and experienced a great deal of frustration. Only under the guidance of a democratic leader (who sought input from club members about which activities to undertake and how to work on them) did participants display interest in the task and produce, regardless of whether the leader was present. The study thus showed how a leader's communicative style affects group performance and suggested that a leader's effectiveness and subsequent group performance can be improved by training that fits the needs of a group. It also revealed the potential for an intervention that provides positive reinforcement while a group is in progress, either by directing the leader to increase his or her participation rate or by directing his or her activity to some content area (Hare, 1976).

Lewin and his associates continued to study groups in both laboratory and field settings. These inquiries indicated that a science of group processes was possible. This perspective led researchers to study not only task processes in groups but also the interpersonal or maintenance processes occurring in groups (see Keyton, Chapter 8, this volume). Beginning in the 1930s and 1940s, and continuing into the 1950s, researchers in several academic disciplines, especially in Social Psychology and Sociology, began to study groups—such as families, therapy and counseling groups, minority groups, and groups in formal organizations—as social systems (see Mabry, Chapter 3, this volume, on groups as systems). They were interested in the forms groups take, their fundamental relational and task processes, and the consequences of those processes. Researchers analyzed variables and processes that encouraged group members to take risks, become leaders, and resist forces leading to conformity for the sake of conformity. They also sought ways to help members learn more about themselves and others as they interacted in groups (see Asch, 1951, 1955; Lewin et al., 1939; Sherif, 1936).

An example of the type of work produced during this period was an experiment by Sherif (1936) that showed the influence of a group on the judgments of individuals. Sherif asked members of a group to judge how far a dot of light had moved, when, in reality, the light had not moved at all (the so-called autokinetic effect). Their responses reflected a convergence to a group norm, that is, an expressed agreement with the majority's responses, even though the response was incorrect.

Another example showing the power of a group to influence members was an experiment by Asch (1951), who focused on the conditions promoting conformity to or independence from group standards. Participants were asked to match one of three lines to a projected single black line. All judgments were expressed orally. One participant in each group was naive; all others were coached to answer on preselected critical trials in a way that was seemingly incongruous with the apparent match. Naive participants conformed one third of the time to the erroneous judgments expressed by the majority.

An important finding of both the Sherif and Asch experiments is the demonstration of a general tendency to conform to group norms. Even if this pressure is informal, it appears to be sufficiently potent to lead some individuals to express a judgment differing from the one they hold privately (Hare, 1976). Both experiments, consequently, showed possibilities for intervening in groups. If group members appear to be constrained by established norms or the pressure of majority influence, a facilitator, consultant, or group member could intervene, pointing out how these studies illustrate the potential power of group norms and the willingness of some members to conform to majority pressure, even when they know they should not. Such an intervention might lead group members to act differently than they would have without this knowledge.

Beginning in the 1950s, the focus of group research on task processes and social relations shifted to the microlevel analysis of communicative acts and interactional processes, usually within tightly controlled laboratory contexts (see Gouran, Chapter 1, this volume). Bales's (1950) Interaction Process Analysis (IPA) marked a turning point in the study of group process, for it provided a detailed observational scheme for coding group members' communicative behaviors so that they could be recorded, isolated, and interpreted (in this volume, see Chapters 8 [Keyton], 12 [Pavitt], and 17 [Socha]). By categorizing members' behaviors into discrete categories, IPA allows an observer to interpret whether participants' comments are helpful or disruptive to a group and whether they are balanced across task and social dimensions. Based on his research, Bales even developed a set of general norms for task groups about what percentage of communicative acts should characterize each category of the coding scheme. The information gleaned from the coding scheme, therefore, can be used to estimate the effectiveness of a group, as well as individual members' performance, and to change those patterns that hinder effective performance. Bales's work subsequently led to the development of many observational coding schemes for understanding the internal dynamics of groups (see Ellis & Fisher, 1994; Hare, Blumberg, Davies, & Kent, 1994; Keyton, 1997), a methodology that continues to be used by many researchers today.

EXPERIENTIAL METHODS FOR CHANGING GROUPS

During the same period that experimental and observational studies were being conducted, other groups and organizations were focusing on specific methods for training participants to become more effective group members. Various approaches were used to increase both people's understanding of group dynamics and their sensitivity to the effects of their behavior, and that of others, in a group. Such organizations as the National Training Laboratories and the Tavistock Institute offered training programs in which people were taught interpersonal communication and group process skills for achieving more effective group behavior. A number of universities also used a laboratory approach to evaluate variables, such as leadership skills and member participation patterns, that affected group performance. The concept of training to improve performance was also adopted by many industrial organizations, which sought ways to increase productivity and participant satisfaction through such formats as quality circles and project teams. Each of these is discussed below.

National Training Laboratory T-Groups

The National Training Laboratories (NTL) in Bethel, Maine, pursued a process of experiential training for effecting changes in group members' interactions and the internal dynamics of groups. NTL training was based on an assumption that changing people's "natural" ways of behaving to more consciously chosen acts would significantly improve the quality of both group processes and outcomes. The primary focus of this training, therefore, was on the personal learning of the individual within a group context. The objective was increased interpersonal communication competence in the many groups in which people participate, whether on the job, in the community, or in the family. The theory underlying NTL training was that one learns how to learn from experience, such as by participating in a group and observing and evaluating one's behavior and trying new behaviors and seeing their effects. In this way, one learns some new behavioral skills (Bennis et al., 1969). In particular, NTL utilized a unique type of group, called a "laboratory group," to help people learn about and change their behavior in groups and stressed the role of feedback in the learning and change process.

Laboratory Groups

Many of the early NTL experiments with intervention were accomplished in *laboratory groups*. Begun as a project by Lewin in 1946, the laboratory group experience was designed to encourage individuals to experiment with more effective ways of learning and new ways of behaving (Schein & Bennis, 1965). These laboratory group experiences were conducted in what were called "T-groups" (training groups), in a process also called "sensitivity training," which became one of the methods used most widely in interpersonal and group communication skills training.

The primary goal of T-groups was to help individuals to understand group dynamics through participation in a group that had as its purpose the development and examination of itself. A second goal was to help members learn about how they, as individuals, interact in groups and to be able to recognize and change ineffective behavioral patterns (see Wheelan, 1994). In such a setting, it was believed that participants could develop effective interpersonal communication skills that could be applied in their workplaces, as well as in many other groups in which they participate.

T-groups had no formal leaders, preset agendas, or rules by which to operate, although each group did have in common a trainer who intervened in the group discussion as appropriate. The trainer (more typically, cotrainers) was not a member of the group per se, but was, nevertheless, considered essential to the learning process. A trainer's primary role was to encourage participants to share their observations of the group and to develop their own rules of operation. The leadership style was nondirective, focusing primarily on processes occurring in the group, especially the issues and dilemmas that members needed to resolve, such as how they wanted to spend their time and how they dealt with power and influence. Leadership thus could create a climate that fostered maximum learning.

To offset the tendency to operate in learned, ritualistic ways, participants had to establish new types of group structures. Because T-groups had no preset structures, members had to create their own goals, develop norms, and determine their approach to leadership. As Bradford et al. (1964) reported in their analysis of laboratory training groups, this was not an easy task; although these groups worked initially without a definite structure, members soon tried to create one to manage the anxiety they felt in working in such an ambiguous context. This process provided the trainer, as well as participants, with opportunities to observe the contrasting needs and styles of group members. Some partici-

pants discovered that they had unrealistic attitudes toward other members, and others acknowledged their stereotyping of special kinds or classes of people. Some recognized that they had problems with authority figures, while others realized they were prone to avoid conflict. T-groups thus encouraged participants to identify their typical patterns of group behavior, especially their unproductive interactional patterns, and to seek remedies. Practitioners involved in this type of training defined their task as "reeducation." Reeducation was distinctly different from indoctrination; it was neither manipulation nor persuasion, implying instead a deliberative, planned change in which people became aware of how and what to change (see Benne & Birnbaum, 1960).

The Role of Feedback

An important component of NTL training was the emphasis on *feedback,* the direct commenting on a person's behavior by another. Influenced by the work of Lewin (1947, 1951), feedback became the foundation of T-group training. Lewin had argued that the study of group behavior required examining how individuals see and construct reality. He stressed, therefore, that individuals should examine and discuss with other members their group experiences and, thereby, learn directly about the effects of their behavior on other members as individuals and on the group as a whole. The assumption was that group processes would improve as individuals learned about themselves from data provided by other group members and undertook conscious changes in their behavior. Additionally, T-groups provided a safe environment in which individuals could be aided by supportive feedback statements made by others in the group. The belief was that when a person acquired information about his or her actions by either confirmation or disconfirmation from other group members within a supportive environment, the person would understand him- or herself more fully. As Norbert Weiner, an early communication theorist, aptly put it, "I never know what I said until I hear the response to it" (quoted in Schein & Bennis, 1965, p. 41).

Another goal of providing feedback was to enable T-group participants to go through a process of unlearning or "unfreezing" before new learning or "refreezing" could be initiated (Lewin, 1947). Learning to unfreeze meant "switching cognitive gears," that is, altering entrenched cognitive maps as a way to reduce automatic thinking (Friedman & Lipshitz, 1992). An important outcome of this process was individuals', as well as the group's, awareness of, and sensitivity to, reactions in themselves and others. It enabled people to see situations differently and to become aware of how they select, interpret, and act on information and, thereby, question the assumptive beliefs and values underlying their typical, patterned actions (Friedman & Lipshitz, 1992). The process encouraged learning from the consequences of one's actions through attention to and disclosure of one's own and others' emotions. It also helped group members to develop insights about the linkages among personal values, goals, and the requirements of the situation, how to diagnose obstacles, and how to overcome these barriers so as to achieve common goals (Friedman & Lipshitz, 1992).

Tavistock Institute Training

Although use of T-groups probably was the method of interpersonal and group skills training used most extensively from the 1950s through the 1970s, with thousands of people participating in programs offered by NTL, other organizations also were concerned with improving interpersonal and group interaction. The Tavistock Institute in London, for example, initiated a different type of training from that of NTL, one based on the psychoanalytical work of Bion (1961) but still using groups as the medium for learning.

Working within the basic distinction between task and socioemotional dimensions of group life (in this volume, see Chapters 7 [Hirokawa & Salazar], 8 [Keyton], and 12 [Pavitt]), Bion presumed that as group mem-

bers worked together, one or more of three emotional states would keep them from engaging in productive work: (a) fight or flight, (b) pairing, and (c) dependency (see Keyton, Chapter 8, this volume). The terms "fight" and "flight" refer, respectively, to the ways in which a group tries to preserve itself by attacking or avoiding things it finds threatening (Bormann, 1990). When members *fight*, they respond negatively to whatever idea or action is proposed; when they are in *flight*, they flee a group physically and/or psychologically. *Pairing* refers to a situation in which a member tries to form a coalition with one other member based on compatible needs for the purpose of creating a new idea. *Dependency* involves relying on someone else (e.g., a strong leader) to relieve members of having to find ways of solving problems and making decisions themselves (Thibaut & Kelley, 1959). Groups that mature do not let these emotional responses (oriented toward fantasy) interfere with the task needs of the group. Bion believed that by becoming aware of these emotional responses, group members could maximize the possibility of working together effectively (see Bormann, 1990).

Tavistock methods involved diagnosing the group as a single unit and treating it as a patient for whom interventions (strong medicine) sometimes were required. Although advocates of this method took a psychoanalytical approach to understanding groups and organizational systems, their primary focus was on interpreting and improving the interpersonal sensitivity of individuals. For example, if a group member expressed opposition to a leader, the Tavistock approach focused on searching for a general rule to explain why that individual expressed such opposition and why such an attack was necessary at that developmental point in the group's work. In contrast, the NTL method, which emphasized group learning, would focus on what lessons the group could learn from this situation that could be applied to other situations (Hare, 1976).

The Tavistock method of learning about individuals in groups from a Freudian psychoanalytic perspective was adopted and expanded in the 1960s by the Rice Institute of Washington, D.C. Using a format of study conferences and workshops, small and large groups were observed and analyzed in ways analogous to a psychotherapy session. Whether a group displayed extreme independence or overdependence on an authority figure, or alternated between fighting authority and fleeing from it, the emphasis was on encouraging group members to discover how they can best solve problems (see Bormann, 1990; Rice, 1965; Wheelan, 1994).

Even though the Tavistock system did not take firm root in the United States, the particular orientation of enhancing individuals' abilities through the medium of group experience did find a place in California in the early 1950s. Carl Rogers and Abraham Maslow, for example, promoted a humanistic psychology that focused on the possibilities of human change, a view that led to the encounter group movement of the 1960s and 1970s and an independent movement centered at Esalen (Big Sur, California) that emphasized personal improvement through group work (Hare, 1976).

Effects of Experiential Training

A reasonable body of evidence indicates that after participation in T-groups, sensitivity training, Tavistock groups, and/or encounter groups, people report an immediate gain in positive personal behavior, such as greater sensitivity, more expressiveness, and more comfort with self (Miles, 1971). Strong and Claiborn (1982) also concluded from a review of comparative social-psychological perspectives that the activity of examining tasks, goals, norms, and cohesiveness in T-groups had very high potential for promoting long-lasting change. There has not been sufficient or systematic evaluation, however, of the long-term gains of such training after participants return to their "normal" group life. As noted by Shaw (1981), problems with evaluating the effectiveness of experiential groups are both theoretical and practical. Theoreti-

cally, it is hard to generalize about the experiences participants have in these groups and the desirable outcomes from those experiences (Schein & Bennis, 1965). A wide range of outcomes is expected, such as changes in attitudes, motivation, sensitivity to the feelings of others, and understanding of group dynamics. Measuring the relationship between the methods used in experiential groups and expected outcomes is problematic when both the methods and outcomes are difficult to define conceptually and, therefore, operationally.

A second problem is that most of the reported changes in individuals after participating in these groups come from self-report instruments. The most common procedure is to ask participants about their reactions to the group experience after it has occurred. Even when participants are assessed before and after the group experience, the results are not necessarily attributable to the group experience. Some personality factors may account for or interact with the group experience; for example, some research shows that sensitivity training is particularly effective for helping those with authoritarian personalities become less authoritarian (Shaw, 1981). Other studies concerning personality change, however, are not so strongly supportive of the proposition that experiential group experiences are affected by or alter participants' personalities (Kaplan, 1979).

Although the results of experiential training are mixed and the long-term effectiveness is contestable (see, for example, Aronson, 1980; Bednar & Kaul, 1979; Kaplan, 1979; Shaw, 1981), and although the teaching of these techniques has declined in recent years, advocates of interpersonal skills and human relations training in laboratory groups support it as an important method for bringing about positive change in people (Forsyth, 1983). Perhaps most important, from the perspective of scholarship on groups, Bormann (1990) observed that the effects of such work on the study of groups, particularly group communication, are readily apparent. T-group theory and research contributed substantially to the development of general theories of group communication. Bormann believes that group communication theory and practice (such as his own Symbolic Convergence Theory; see Bormann, 1986, 1996; in this volume, see Chapters 1 [Gouran], 2 [Poole], 7 [Hirokawa & Salazar], and 8 [Keyton]) represents a combination of the results of empirical research on T-groups and some of the values and practices of the human relations movement.

Training in University Laboratories

A number of scholars working at universities—Case Western; University of California, Los Angeles; Boston University; Yale; and the University of Michigan, among others—also were interested in group training but focused their efforts on scientifically evaluating the effects of specific types of training. Researchers utilized numerous methods— including case studies, observations, self-reports, and experimental studies—to examine the validity of various research questions and hypotheses (see Cragan & Wright, 1990; Janis, 1982; Levine & Moreland, 1990; Maier, 1963; Maier & Maier, 1957). For example, Hall and Williams (1970) found that when group members received specific training in procedures that improve problem solving, they became more adept at handling new problem-solving group tasks. An important research finding from the work of Blake and Mouton (1962, 1964) showed that group members intent on changing themselves could do so with the use of instruments designed to give them feedback. Even the use of such self-administered instruments as checklists and rating scales gave participants an increased understanding of personal and group issues; through this feedback, they learned which behaviors to change.

Contemporary researchers continue to examine the effects of specific forms of training on group members (see Sunwolf & Seibold's review of research on process procedures, Chapter 15, this volume). For example, Basadur, Graen, and Green (1982) and Firestien (1990) found that after training in creative problem solving, individuals demonstrated improvement in finding and solving problems (see Jarboe, Chapter 13, this volume, on creativity and group communication). Friedman and Lipshitz (1992) reported that group members undergoing training in creative problem solving, in comparison to group members who did not receive such training, exhibited more positive communication, including participating more, generating more ideas, and criticizing other members' ideas less. Finally, Stone and O'Gorman (1991) found that training group members in how to assess the meaning of each other's actions by seeking more information influenced other helping behaviors, such as reciprocity in providing information.

Project Teams and Quality Circles

Although laboratory training programs that teach theory and develop intervention skills have largely disappeared from university campuses, there has been a general resurgence of interest in groups. In many organizations today, working in groups is the primary means by which the tasks of the organization get done (see Greenbaum & Query, Chapter 20, this volume, for a review of communication in organizational work groups). For example, organizations frequently use project teams to solve problems or pursue new ideas, because group decision making is believed to be more productive than traditional, individual decision making. The objective is to enable people to work together more effectively as a way to improve organizational performance and increase members' satisfaction with and commitment to the organization.

Some organizations have implemented such innovations as quality circles to transform their organizations (Scholtes, Joiner, & Streibel, 1988). *Quality circles* (originally known as quality control circles) emerged in Japan after World War II as a group discussion method for improving previously poorly made industrial products (Napier & Gershenfeld, 1989). In the United States, quality circles were introduced in 1974, primarily in industrial settings, to improve the quality of products as well as to introduce innovations; in more recent years, they increasingly are being used with nonproduction workers who also engage in work innovations. Members of quality circles typically are volunteers from an organization who engage in group discussion about such issues as translating organizational goals into practice or suggesting changes in ineffective work rules. Organizational leaders anticipate that workers' participation in these group discussions will lead to their greater perceived involvement in organizational planning, and both leaders and workers expect to see improved quality, production, and working conditions resulting from these discussions (Dean, 1985; Royal & Golden, 1981).

Quality circles have yielded mixed results with respect to their effectiveness (Ferris & Wagner, 1985). When they work, changing the culture of an organization and the way organizational members communicate (see Stohl, 1986, 1987; Stohl & Jennings, 1988), it is because certain factors are present: sufficient training of participants, access to good information, measurable goals, and groups created from intact work teams (Larson & LaFasto, 1989). Perhaps the most important factor is training in relevant skills. For example, Bettenhausen (1991) discovered that training quality circle members in the principles of Transactional Analysis Theory (awareness of and sensitivity to types of responses—adult-, parent-, or childlike, for example) prior to implementing the program improved communication. In particular, such training helped participants learn to listen to and pay attention to one another's problems. Mitchell (1986) also noted that team members significantly improved their intragroup relations after an intervention based on Alignment Theory, a perspective that stresses the process of disclosing individual frames of reference.

What also emerged from research studies and practice, however, was that project teams and quality circles were not working as well as they should, not only because members lacked sufficient skills in group processes but also because of differences in members' attitudes (Marks, 1986). Workers in the United States, compared to those in Japan, for example, are more likely to have an individualistic orientation and lack an appropriate perspective for how to work in teams. In many organizations, middle managers, who typically are not trained in team-building skills, often are reluctant to accept ideas from subordinates (Napier & Gershenfeld, 1989). Although training of participants in quality circles appears to be important, especially for the impact such groups have on their organizational lives (such as intragroup and intergroup communication and job advancement), research shows that participants do not change their fundamental attitudes about their organization, job challenges, and personal responsibility (see Marks, Mirvis, Grady, & Hackett, 1985). The research data indicate that not only should team members be trained for quality circles to work effectively but also that it may be just as important to train the entire organization.

Equally important from a research and facilitation perspective is the finding that teamwork can aid the solving of problems only when team members are trained to do so. The positive benefits of training occur when there is an understanding among members that successful group performance comes from developing and exchanging ideas, identifying and accepting compatible goals, solving problems as a group, and acknowledging that rewards belong to the group as a whole (see Turner, 1982; Vanderslice, Rice, & Julian, 1987). When team members are encouraged to help one another test ideas, receive feedback, and understand the impact of their communicative behavior and interpersonal interactions on the ability to perform effectively as a team, then they are applying the wisdom provided by group researchers. Appropriate training, therefore, is an important factor in any decision to use groups and teams.

IMPROVING GROUP COMMUNICATION PERFORMANCE

The challenge for applied researchers and those interested in facilitating and improving group processes is to provide data that lead group members to understand how groups work and how to make them work better. Although literally thousands of studies have explored group processes and have produced a substantial body of knowledge about the characteristics of effective group performance, members generally are unable to translate research findings into practical prescriptions for creating effective groups. Discovering, articulating, and enacting the means for achieving group performance effectiveness thus continue to be desirable foci for researchers, practitioners, and group members alike.

Improving group performance, to date, can be examined from two interdependent perspectives: (a) evidence from theory and research studies that offer *explanatory theories* for improving group interaction, such as explanations about how member composition, participation patterns, problem-solving efforts, and decision-making skills affect the achievement of group goals and members' satisfaction with that achievement; and (b) experiential knowledge acquired from trainers, consultants, and group members through observation, feedback, and analysis in the form of *practical theories* that offer specific recommendations for improving group performance. Both perspectives are essential for providing significant data, diagnoses, and directions for improved performance.

Applicable Knowledge From Research Studies

Studies during the past 40 years have resulted in a substantial body of knowledge about group characteristics, processes, and structures that distinguish effective from ineffective groups. For example, researchers have studied such factors as whether a group's task is of high or low ambiguity and how this affects the ways that group members solicit information to reach a decision (see Hirokawa & Salazar, Chapter 7, this volume, regarding task group communication and decision-making performance), whether a group's resources are employed effectively to analyze

information (see Propp, Chapter 9, this volume), whether homogeneous versus heterogeneous composition of a group affects the consideration of alternative or contrary explanations (see Haslett & Ruebush, Chapter 5, this volume), whether consensus is reached too quickly to allow for the consideration of unintended consequences (see Salazar, 1995), and whether unexamined role expectations lead to incapacitating role conflicts and poor performance (see Salazar, 1995).

With all the information available from these studies, the question is why group members fall prey to stereotypical problems. Why, for example, are so many groups seemingly unable to use the resources brought to them by their members in the most productive way? As Steiner (1972) has noted, "The adequacy of the resources available to an individual or group determines its potential productivity; the appropriateness of its processes determines how well its actual productivity approximates its potential productivity" (p. 9). Thus, an important question is under what conditions groups are likely to experience a process loss or process gain. The following is a brief overview of some research findings that have significant implications for effective group performance, findings that undoubtedly would be profitable for group members to know. These findings also have important implications for group facilitation; if group members are to acquire the necessary knowledge and skills, they must be willing to evaluate their own processes or to invite a consultant or trainer to provide evaluative assistance and offer possible remedies for overcoming process losses.

First, there is no single blueprint for how a group should work through a problem to a decision or solution. To the contrary, groups are more likely to go through a series of phases in what Poole and Baldwin (1996) represent as a *multiple sequence model;* that is, groups do not necessarily solve problems in a sequential order, but, instead, take many paths to reach their goal (Scheidel & Crowell, 1964; in this volume, see Chapters 2 [Poole] and 3 [Mabry]). Rather than assuming that as group members work through a problem they will take each step in order, the findings from research offer a different conclusion: Thinking through a problem means movement, back and forth, among issues and possible solutions (Schein, 1969). Knowing that groups continually repeat several phases is important because it informs members that they should not expect a group to develop in a linear fashion; instead, they should accept that the group will discuss, argue, and reconsider many of the same issues time and again before a problem can be resolved and a decision reached (Wheelan, 1994; Wheelan & McKeage, 1993).

Second, many studies point to the likelihood of higher quality decisions emerging if a group analyzes a problem in depth, generates options for solution, and evaluates the potential consequences of the proposed solutions (Brilhart & Jochem, 1964; Larson, 1969; Maier & Maier, 1957). Janis's (1982) view is that this form of *vigilance* leads to rational choices and that a group's identification of alternatives and their likely consequences affects the quality of both the discussion process and the group decision (see Hirokawa & Salazar, Chapter 7, this volume). Paradoxically, some research indicates that groups seldom engage in appropriate interactional behavior likely to be of value for enhancing their problem-solving effectiveness (see Gouran & Hirokawa, 1986; Hirokawa & Rost, 1992). In a study examining naturally occurring group vigilance, Hirokawa (1987) suggested that group members should not wait for high-quality interactions or outcomes to arrive by chance. This implies the need for interventions that have practical value for improving group performance and remedying the deficiencies group members encounter.

Another implication from the extant research is that more than adhering to procedural or rational models is involved in producing high-quality group decisions. As Gouran (1994) explains, particular interventions may be critical for responding to digressions, process disruptions, and other inadequacies in task performance: "Of particular value would be the explorations of the ways in which group members come to understand the extent to which they have satisfied the requirements of their tasks" (p. 36). Thus, when group members learn to recognize inadequacies and ways to surmount them, they are more likely to use processes that lead to high-quality outcomes.

Third, research studies suggest that if groups are to improve their performance, then consideration should be given to the composition of the group, as well as to the complexity of the task. For example, if a group is highly homogeneous, if members share the same information, and if the task is familiar, easily structured, and low in ambiguity, then consensus can be reached fairly easily, although it may not lead necessarily to an effective decision. In contrast, if a group's task is unfamiliar or difficult, not easily structured, and highly ambiguous, the likely reaction by members is to try to reduce the ambiguity by asking questions and seeking information (Salazar, 1995). With increasing uncertainty, there is greater motivation to engage in systematic analysis; if there is little or no uncertainty, then there is less impetus for members to engage in serious questioning of the group's assumptions and decisions. One implication of this research is the advantage of composing a group that reflects diversity in members' knowledge, resources, and predispositions, so that conditions of uncertainty can emerge to enhance the discussion of issues (see Haslett & Ruebush, Chapter 5, this volume, regarding the effects of group composition).

Fourth, and related closely to the linkage among the predispositions of group members, conditions of uncertainty, and the motivation to seek more information, is the relationship between conflict communication and effective problem-solving and decision-making group performance. A clash of ideas can lead members to scrutinize and test ideas more so than if the clash had not occurred. As Janis (1982) observed in his work on *groupthink* (a condition in which unanimity and conformity are overvalued and dissent equated with disloyalty; see Keyton, Chapter 8, this volume), when group members consciously avoid conflicts over ideas, they impair their consideration of important information and alternative solutions. Fisher (1970a), in his research on group development, reported that successful decision-making groups almost invariably go through a conflict phase in which ideas are proposed and discussed, some are accepted, others are modified, and still others are rejected.

When people are in conflict over ideas, they participate in a communication process in which the expression of divergent ideas is more likely to lead to genuine consensus, in contrast to that emanating from group pressure for conformity. The difficulty for groups is in identifying the positive use of conflict because of members' inclination to smooth over disagreements, change the subject, tell one another not to argue, or use humor to escape (Herman, 1983; Schultz, 1982). The research, however, clearly underscores the desirability of group members' perceiving the value of conflict. Also necessary are interventions to encourage members to express divergent viewpoints as a way to sort out good from bad proposals, relevant from nonessential data, and substantive from incidental or frivolous suggestions (see Meyers & Brashers, Chapter 11, this volume, on social influence processes in groups).

Fifth, researchers have come to realize the extent to which forces both within and outside groups contribute to process losses or gains within groups' problem-solving and decision-making activities. To illustrate this point, Gouran and Hirokawa (1986) compare a small group to a vehicle traveling along a path. The vehicle begins at some initial state and progresses along a path toward its destination—a desired or intended goal—unless, of course, such internal factors as the engine malfunctioning or such external factors as a severe snowstorm or unexpected road construction interfere with the goal. Similarly, as a group moves along its path, the nature of members' interactions within the group affects whether the group reaches its goal (Salazar, 1995). Other factors also influence the decision process; there are not only physical constraints (e.g., time available) but also

such psychological constraints as the influence of the expectations of the leader or other members of the group, as well as members' reference groups (any past, current, or admired group that significantly shapes the way a person feels and thinks; Kelley, 1952; Napier & Gershenfeld, 1989; see Anderson et al., Chapter 6, this volume, on group socialization processes). The more relevant a group is to an individual, the more likely it is that it will serve as a frame of reference to him or her.

Sixth, according to Gouran and Hirokawa (1983, 1986; see also Gouran, 1997), two types of obstacles can adversely affect a group's performance. *Relational obstacles* arise from attacks on group members' personalities or character; they also may stem from tangential statements that prevent members from discussing the actual task, interruptions at inappropriate times, and jokes or other diversions. *Task obstacles* represent statements of disapproval without sufficient analysis of proposed goals and solutions or may include requests for members' opinions rather than assessments based on the information a group has, appeals for repeated evaluations of an alternative discussed previously, or bringing forth at the end of a deliberation an alternative not shared earlier. Equally disruptive are such reminders as "We're running out of time, let's just finish it up" and similar types of comments that often lead a group to premature consensus. Facilitative influence, in contrast, consists of statements that help resolve disagreements, encourage critical examination of ideas, are responsive to the contributions of others, and are accompanied by reasons for the viewpoint expressed, regardless of whether the statement is one of agreement or disagreement. When a group falters because of negative influences and members wish to move the group back on track, they are obliged to consider countermeasures, or what Gouran (1992) calls *counteractive influence*. For example, if members are being pressured to go along with the opinion of a high-status member, a counteractive measure on the part of a member or consultant could refer the group to the customary practices established by members, such as "The norms of this group make it possible for every individual to discuss and influence the group. We need to continue our discussion so that we can reach a consensus that reflects the views of the entire group." If there is an emotional outburst, then one can ask for reasons why a member disagrees so vehemently, an intervention that can change a potentially volatile situation into a more constructive one (see Putnam & Geist, 1985; Schultz, Ketrow, & Urban, 1995).

Although existing literature does not provide conclusive answers to the initial question raised as to why some groups succeed so well in using the abilities and resources of their members whereas others apparently fail to do so, the findings from research offer group members basic knowledge about effective group functioning. From a practical perspective, it would seem useful to impart such information when a group first begins to work. From a research perspective, the question is whether providing the findings from Communication and other types of research on groups to members will lead to more effective group performance. One suspects that it would, given that from the very beginning of its operation, a group "is in the grip of powerful initial structures that will affect all future development" (Wheelan, 1994, p. 33). In this sense, it may take a consultant, trainer, or, more likely, a competent group member to observe group interactions and provide feedback to members and, thereby, offer the help needed to develop a more effective group process.

Applicable Knowledge From Practitioners

According to Lewin (1947), one of the more significant methods for changing group behavior is to observe what is going on in a group and then provide feedback to participants. Whether a group uses a trainer or an observer to offer feedback or relies on a member's feedback based on observational measures or information derived from members' self-reports, the common goal is to assist group members in becoming more effective in

their interactions and in achieving their individual and group goals. The emphasis on observation and feedback, the basic components of T-group training, encompasses the methods practitioners generally use in trying to improve group performance. To engage in this process successfully requires practitioners to use four special skills:

observation—discovering what is happening in a group,
feedback and evaluation—interpreting the strengths and weaknesses of group processes and outcomes,
diagnosing—determining what changes would help a group become more effective, and
training—helping group members to practice new behaviors (Dyer, 1984).

A major responsibility of a person who intervenes in groups is to determine which interventions encourage members to engage in self-examination and assume mutual responsibility for effective interaction and group performance. Intervening in a group means encouraging group members to (a) talk about and explore the reasons for their current performance, (b) set their own goals for improved performance, (c) try out and practice new ways of behaving, and (d) engage in feedback sessions that analyze the effectiveness of the new behaviors (Dyer, 1984).

Observing Group Processes

A major tool for determining when and how to intervene in a group is to observe the processes that occur in that group. Schein (1987), for example, sees the observational process as the key to "setting the agenda" for an intervention. As a group discusses its task, the consultant observes the interaction and notes how members interact, their roles and patterns of communication, the power issues among members, the conflict-management techniques employed, evidence of leadership and followership, and the general climate in the group.

The rationale for observation is that by watching and recording group behaviors, interactions, and events, a consultant can discover the strengths and weaknesses that characterize a group. A consultant (or members of a group), at this stage, is interested in observing such factors as (a) who talks to whom and with what effect; (b) how themes and topics are developed, argued for, and accepted or rejected; and (c) the nature and effects of other relevant variables, such as goal achievement, the distribution of power and influence, and the interaction of individuals and subgroups.

Schein (1987) recommends the use of a clinical descriptive method, in which direct (overt) observation allows a consultant to observe the social system over a period of time and collect information through a variety of means (e.g., verbal and nonverbal interaction, paper-and-pencil instruments, interviews, and self-reports). In addition to such general methods of observation, there are several specific observational procedures for coding group communication that can be used effectively to provide feedback to some groups, such as Bales's (1950) IPA (Interaction Process Analysis) and Bales and Cohen's (1980) SYMLOG (System for the Multiple Level Observation of Groups (see Keyton, 1997, and Chapter 8, this volume; Wheelan, 1994).

Providing Feedback and Evaluation

After a period of observation, the consultant gives the group feedback and an organizing principle (e.g., a theory, model, or axiom) by which members can begin to distinguish between their typical and optimal behavior. The consultant asks many questions designed to elicit nondefensive, conceptual responses from group members (Schein, 1987). These questions direct members' attention to the process level by asking, for example, "What is happening to us now?", "How are we seeing, feeling, and acting with respect to this shared information?", and "How do we want to see, feel, and act?" Sometimes, consultants use videotape or audiotape to record group interaction and then play it back to members to allow them to see and evaluate the behaviors in which they engaged. The consultant may also conduct one-on-one feedback sessions with individual members if this is needed. The emphasis of these sessions, however, typically is not on the individual member but rather on the behaviors that affect groups (DeWine, 1994). Friedman and Lipshitz (1992) contend that members will become more cognizant of the actions that take a group along an ineffective path if they are confronted about how they act in groups and the ways in which they resist learning new behaviors.

One of the objectives in providing feedback to group members is to let them know how they are performing with respect to their task and intragroup relationships and whether improvements can be made in these areas. The few studies that have examined process interventions (e.g., studies of feedback) support the view that knowledge of how a group is doing, coupled with the setting of challenging goals, produces improvements in group performance (Nadler, 1979). A study by Leathers (1972), for example, indicates that the quality of feedback influences the quality of the outcome in problem-solving groups. Other researchers report little difference following process improvements, although they acknowledge that much anecdotal evidence exists to support the claim that process feedback affects performance positively (see Kernaghen & Cooke, 1990; McCleod, Liker, & Lobel, 1992).

A review by Nadler (1979) showed that most experimental studies of feedback have occurred with respect to task groups, and although feedback has been found to have a positive effect on task accomplishment, few studies have examined its effects on interpersonal behavior in such groups. Still, Bormann (1990) believes that feedback helps build relationships among group members and improves member satisfaction. He asserts that honest feedback, expressed in terms of feelings from one member to another, followed by a realistic attempt to change, is basic to the relational dynamics of groups.

Kaplan (1979) finds two sources, both experimental artifacts, for the failure of some studies to find a significant relationship between process interventions and group task performance. Experiments that fail to show such relationships suffer either an ecological validity problem—because most groups participating in laboratory studies are given simple tasks that do not create many process problems—or an experimental design problem—such as the failure to isolate process interventions as independent variables. McCleod et al. (1992) suggest that to overcome these problems, other measures should be used to validate the effects of feedback, such as providing groups with measurable standards of interpersonal group processes, measuring their processes against these standards, and providing feedback about actual changes in performance. They also point out that none of the studies reporting little or no change in group performance indicates whether actual changes in group processes following interventions were observed, and that this needs to be incorporated into future research.

Studies using videotape to deliver feedback to task groups have found actual changes in members' behaviors (Walter, 1975; Walter & Miles, 1972). Walter's (1975) study presented feedback in two ways: For one group, he videotaped sessions and provided feedback analyzing group processes; in a second group, he showed a videotape of a group modeling appropriate behaviors. The second intervention method was more effective for changing group behavior, although only the effect on group task performance was evaluated in this study.

The most supportive data for the benefits of providing process feedback come from studies examining the effect of task feedback on work motivation. Klein (1989) observed that when individuals receive timely, specific results about their previous performance and set goals for subsequent performance, significant changes result. Hackman (1987) confirms that feedback has a positive effect on such outcomes as group cohesion and member satisfaction, and that it contributes to individual growth and well-being. These studies support what practitioners assert is an important evaluation process for change: If people are given standards of interpersonal processes relevant to task conditions, they set goals relevant to those standards.

Diagnosing Group Problems and Recommending Changes

Once salient issues have been identified through observation and feedback processes, a consultant's role is to assist (coach) group members in understanding the strengths and weaknesses of their group and to work with them to identify alternatives for problematic behavior. The ability to change how members interact depends fundamentally on diagnosing recurring patterns of behavior that affect the group and suggesting new ways of behaving. Dyer (1972, 1977) defines a diagnostic intervention as somewhere between opinion-giving and developing a theory or insight about what is keeping a group from performing at a satisfactory level. The diagnostic intervention is exploratory, a hypothesizing type of comment designed to get members to enter into a process of diagnosing their group's problems.

After group members are given information about some of the problems they are experiencing—such as a lack of a supportive climate, inadequate cohesiveness, or dysfunctional communication patterns that interfere with goal attainment—then what is supposed to happen? Practitioners argue that knowing that a problem exists sometimes helps a group to identify some ways of treating it, although identification of a problem may not necessarily be sufficient for knowing how to solve it (Argyris & Schon, 1978; Stone & O'Gorman, 1991). Feedback presumably leads members to a conscious awareness of their group's processes, but a planned change requires that a consultant (or members) suggest what has to be changed and how the changes can be implemented (Benne & Birnbaum, 1960; Schoonover & Dalziel, 1996).

Many of the barriers to change are embedded in a group's culture. Within any group, one can experience some of the following elements that affect people's willingness to change: role expectations; identity; the influence of tradition, status, biases, and stereotypical reactions; and leadership and power struggles. As members learn about their behavior, they can question or suggest hypotheses concerning the group's communication processes and the various procedures they use (Dyer, 1972). If members are willing to critically examine their group's communication processes, they can determine whether they have shared their experiences, information, and opinions in ways that affect, either positively or negatively, the quality of their group's discussions, and whether the way they communicate leads to goal achievement and member satisfaction. (For an explanation of numerous ways to diagnose and evaluate group processes, as well as instruments and exercises designed to provide group members with insight into effective and dysfunctional group performance, see Keyton, 1997; Napier & Gershenfeld, 1989; Pfeiffer & Jones, 1974-1979; Schultz, 1996; Wheelan, 1994).

Practicing New Skills

If groups are to change ineffective processes to more facilitative ones, then the academic and experiential literatures offer valuable theoretical and practical advice. In addition, members need opportunities, including realistic simulations, for practicing new behaviors with which they wish to become competent (DeWine, 1994). Following are a few illustrative examples of interventions that group members can undertake on their own or with the help of a consultant or trainer. They illustrate a fundamental principle of intervention: It must be based on observation and feedback about what has been observed, suggest reasons for the problematic behavior observed, indicate possible remedies to surmount the obstacles, and provide opportunities for practicing and assessing the effectiveness of new behaviors.

Metadiscussion. The concept of a "metadiscussion" is derived from the work of Lewin (1947, 1951), who believed that members should analyze their group experiences and discuss with other members the effects of their behavior on the group as a whole. *Metadiscussion* is an intervention process designed to confront barriers that prevent groups from achieving effective performance by focusing on the deficiencies members perceive to be thwarting the group's work, including task and interpersonal obstacles, while ruling discussions of members' personalities to be out of bounds. Group members' responsibility is to discuss possible changes for improving their working relationships, the processes used in making decisions, and the factors that contribute to member satisfaction with the group's outcomes. For metadiscussion to succeed, a group has to establish a climate that encourages open discussion. A basic tenet is that everyone should be able to express, without fear, satisfaction or dissatisfaction with one's own goals and/or the goals of the group (Bennis et al., 1969).

A focus on group processes through metadiscussion entails exploring what is happening in the group in the "here and now." Thus, it is concerned with how group members exchange messages and respond to ideas as they occur. As an illustration, a group member could state in a part of a session devoted to metadiscussion, "I was curious as to whether the group is aware that only two people have talked so far about this issue. Shouldn't we hear from more members?" Whatever problems members bring forth as they engage in metadiscussion, they need to ask what seems to contribute to the situation. Despite the difficulties arising from the sharing of criticism during metadiscussion, group members can overcome many of the barriers to change by discussing them openly, becoming more aware of their own behavior, planning regular assessment sessions, and employing practice sessions (see Bradford et al., 1964).

A reminder role. There are many intervention techniques designed to encourage group members to adopt facilitative roles (see Benne & Sheats's, 1948, classic list of such roles). For example, "devil's advocacy" and "dialectical inquiry" have been used widely as techniques for improving group argumentation and decision making (in this volume, see Chapters 7 [Hirokawa & Salazar], 11 [Meyers & Brashers], and 15 [Sunwolf & Seibold]). As a structured technique, *devil's advocacy* divides a group into two subgroups. One subgroup develops and advocates a plan, the other subgroup critiques it, and both subgroups work to revise the plan (see Meyers, 1997). *Dialectical inquiry*, in contrast, involves structured debate between two opposing subgroups with different plans. The two subgroups debate the different assumptions underlying their plans until they reach agreement, then work together to develop a final recommendation. Schweiger, Sandberg, and Ragan (1986), in a study comparing devil's advocacy with dialectical inquiry and consensus methods for improving group decision making, reported that both devil's advocacy and dialectical inquiry generally were more effective than consensus (in which participants were encouraged to state their assumptions and recommendations and then freely discuss them until they reach a final decision), but that groups were less satisfied with devil's advocacy and dialectical inquiry than with consensus.

The *reminder role*, in contrast, is conceptualized as a way to impose a rational structure on group members, but one that does not interrupt ongoing group interaction. The person occupying the reminder role serves as a catalyst to a group, a type of "process observer" or "intervenor" who is willing to ask for a reconsideration of issues or express a concern about the rush to decision by group members. One of the deficiencies identified in decision-making groups, as explained previously, is the tendency of members to succumb to pressures for conformity and unanimity. Members under the influence of a majority position differing from their own sometimes feel compelled to sacrifice independence of judgment, even when they know that the majority is in error or that the agreed-upon decision is not defensible (Gouran, 1982). There is evidence, however, that although groups with established norms may be resentful of those members who do not adhere to group norms, they will sometimes be thankful that one of their members held out in the interest of assisting the group in making the best choice (Fisher, 1970b; Harnack, 1963).

The role of a reminder can be undertaken by any group member. It is a role that reflects more closely Janis's (1982) concept of vigilance, which, as explained previously, implies continuously attending to group processes by asking critical questions about them. A reminder can influence a group's decision processes by being an effective process observer and, if the group accepts such a role, a reminder may be able to influence the group's dynamics. For example, Schultz et al. (1995), in a study evaluating the effect of a reminder role on group decision processes and outcomes, discovered that groups trained in problem-solving processes made higher quality decisions than untrained groups (as judged by students in an advanced course on group decision making who were trained to evaluate the quality of decisions presented in the policy recommendations of each group), but that groups with nonleader reminders produced policy recommendations judged to be of significantly higher quality than either trained or leader-reminder groups. Because members do not typically engage in these functions, this study suggests that intervening to have an individual perform reminder functions can enhance group decision-making effectiveness.

The non-participating member. A frequent complaint of group members is that not everyone seems to be working for the good of the group. Latane and Harkins (1979) introduced the term *social loafing* to describe this phenomenon in a study revealing that some group members tend to do less than they would if they were working alone. The perception of inequity in individual effort can create internal conflict in groups and sometimes lowers morale. The question is what type of intervention will help a member of a group who seems unwilling (or perhaps unable) to do his or her share.

A number of studies have identified the circumstances in which social loafing appears, as well as remedies to deal with it (see Viega, 1991; Williams, Harkins, & Latane, 1981; see also Sunwolf & Seibold, Chapter 15, this volume). Probably the most effective means is for other members to refer to the norms of the group, one of which is that each individual has a responsibility for contributing to the fulfillment of the group's task. A discussion of the research concerning equity in effort and the acceptance of equity among members at the start of a group can assist in minimizing social loafing.

A second approach is to discuss the problem openly and ask for suggestions for how to deal with it. Harkins and Szmanski (1989) report that group evaluations of individual members' contributions could be used effectively if a group acknowledges and supports a standard against which individual members can measure themselves. Thus, emphasizing that the prosperity of a group depends on the perception that all members are performing equitably tends to offset social loafing.

CONCLUSION

Two important ways of facilitating groups have been identified in this chapter. One rests on the assumption that an understanding of the theoretical bases and research studies of group communication and problem solving/decision making gives people important information for improving the performance of the groups in which they participate. By being familiar with theory and research that explain how groups become effective, participants gain insight into the essential and effective components of group interaction. A second approach emphasizes that examining group processes through formal observation, feedback, diagnosis, and practicing of new skills allows members to identify problematic actions and change their behavior. With awareness and training, members can markedly reduce the deficiencies frequently evidenced in group interaction.

The knowledge gained from theoretical explanations, research findings, and experiential wisdom offers group members opportunities and methods to become more competent and fulfill their individual and group objectives. When members understand what is happening in a group at any given moment, they can facilitate the group's progress by establishing attainable goals, constructing effective norms, and encouraging open communication and, thereby, strengthen a group's ability to meet the needs of both the task and the members.

Understanding effective group communication performance, however, requires future studies that can document the importance of both perspectives stressed in this chapter. For example, there is a need to test empirically various interventions for confronting such typical obstacles as member dominance, digressions from task issues, interpersonal disruptions, and other inadequacies in group interactions. The questions one must ask before attempting to intervene are how to intervene and, even more important, when to intervene. Determining the how and when of intervention is a function of what is taking place in a group. For the person who intervenes, whether as a trainer, consultant, or group member, this means discovering what types of feedback and suggestions will be effective in changing existing patterns and, at the same time, encouraging members to participate in the process. Equally important is discovering how to induce members to accept such processes as questioning assumptions and using various forms of effective argumentation as necessary tools for competent group decision making. Another important contribution would be to demonstrate how interactions can be both analytical and argumentative yet respectful of the views of others, or how working cooperatively to reach a decision is often likely to be more productive than competitive practices for promoting high-quality decisions and a more cohesive and satisfying group experience. Additional research is needed to document the conditions that make one group more effective than another. Perhaps by exploring such matters as the effects on group process of group members' commitment to a quality solution, the changes in group processes when members are given basic knowledge about effective group functions, or whether self-report instruments, observational coding schemes, or feedback provided by a consultant is more likely to enhance group effectiveness, we can acquire more practical information for preparing individuals to participate effectively in groups.

There also is a need to discover people's subjective reactions to group intervention processes. Researchers rarely ask participants about their emotional reactions to interventions designed to reduce or eliminate ineffective practices. Natural groups may also resist adopting suggested procedures for improving performance if these are offered without sufficient explanation and consultation. Even then, some recent theorizing from a dialectical/paradoxical perspective raises serious questions about the willingness of group members to accept facilitation from a third party or even from a fellow group member. Frey (1995b) and Stohl (1995a, 1995b) argue that the group facilitation process is filled with design and implementation paradoxes. For example, a group that is having problems making decisions may resist incorporating into its processes intervention techniques designed to help groups make decisions. That resistance can be seen as negative (e.g., the group is fighting the suggestions of a consultant) or as a healthy sign that members are becoming more capable of making decisions as a group by resisting facilitation efforts imposed by an external agent. A central dilemma, then, for any person who wishes to intervene in a group—whether as an external agent or as an internal member—is how to be responsive to members' needs, goals, and cultural values, and yet be able to suggest and help apply potentially effective group intervention techniques that members may resist as unnatural and unnecessary. Only when scholars and practitioners take into account theoretical issues, research findings, and experiential learn-ings will a fuller understanding of the multiple influences among individuals, groups, and organizations and the promises and benefits of group facilitation and intervention be understood and realized.

REFERENCES

Alderfer, C. P. (1992). Editor's introduction: Contemporary issues in professional work with groups. *Journal of Applied Behavioral Science, 28,* 9-14.

Argyris, C. (1970). *Intervention theory and method: A behavioral science view.* Reading, MA: Addison-Wesley.

Argyris, C., & Schon, D. A. (1978). *Organizational learning: A theory of action perspective.* Reading, MA: Addison-Wesley.

Aronson, E. (1980). *The social animal* (3rd ed.). San Francisco: W. H. Freeman.

Asch, S. E. (1951). Effects of group pressure upon the modification and distortion of judgments. In H. Guetzkow (Ed.), *Groups, leadership, and men: Research in human relations* (pp. 170-190). Pittsburgh, PA: Carnegie Press.

Asch, S. E. (1955). Opinions and social pressure. *Scientific American, 193*(5), 31-35.

Baird, A. C. (1928). *Public discussion and debate.* Boston: Ginn.

Bales, R. F. (1950). *Interaction process analysis: A method for the study of small groups.* Cambridge, MA: Addison-Wesley.

Bales, R. F., & Cohen, S. P. (with Williamson, S. A.). (1980). *SYMLOG: A system for the multiple level observation of groups.* New York: Free Press.

Basadur, M., Graen, G. B., & Green, S. G. (1982). Training in creative problem-solving: Effects on ideation, problem finding, and problem solving in an industrial research organization. *Organizational Behavior and Human Performance, 36,* 41-70.

Bednar, R. L., & Kaul, T. (1979). Experiential group research: What never happened. *Journal of Applied Behavioral Science, 15,* 311-319.

Benne, K. D., & Birnbaum, M. (1960). Change does not have to be haphazard. *School Review, 68,* 283-293.

Benne, K. D., & Sheats, F. (1948). Functional roles of group members. *Journal of Social Issues, 4,* 41-49.

Bennis, W. G., Benne, K. D., & Chin, R. (Eds.). (1969). *The planning of change: Readings in the applied behavioral sciences* (2nd ed.). New York: Holt, Rinehart & Winston.

Bettenhausen, K. L. (1991). Five years of group research: What have we learned and what needs to be addressed. *Journal of Management, 17,* 345-381.

Bion, W. R. (1961). *Experiences in groups, and other papers.* New York: Basic Books.

Blake, R. R., & Mouton, J. S. (1962). The instrumented training laboratory. In I. Weschler & E. Schein (Eds.), *Issues in human relations training* (pp. 61-67). Washington, DC: National Training Laboratories.

Blake, R. R., & Mouton, J. S. (1964). *The managerial grid: Key orientations for achieving production through people*. Houston, TX: Gulf.

Bormann, E. G. (1986). Symbolic convergence theory and communication in group decision-making. In R. Y. Hirokawa & M. S. Poole (Eds.), *Communication and group decision-making* (pp. 219-236). Beverly Hills, CA: Sage.

Bormann, E. G. (1990). *Small group communication: Theory and practice* (3rd ed.). New York: Harper & Row.

Bormann, E. G. (1996). Symbolic convergence theory and communication in group decision making. In R. Y. Hirokawa & M. S. Poole (Eds.), *Communication and group decision making* (2nd ed., pp. 81-113). Thousand Oaks, CA: Sage.

Bradford, L. P., Gibb, J. R., & Benne, K. D. (Eds.). (1964). *T-group theory and laboratory method: Innovation in re-education*. New York: Wiley.

Braybrooke, D., & Lindblom, C. E. (1970). *A strategy of decision: Policy evaluation as a social process*. New York: Free Press.

Brilhart, J. K., & Jochem, L. M. (1964). Effects of different patterns on outcomes of problem-solving discussions. *Journal of Applied Psychology, 48*, 175-179.

Bunker, B. B. (1992). From theory to practice: A review of recent books on small groups. *Journal of Applied Behavioral Science, 28*, 137-155.

Cragan, J. F., & Wright, D. W. (1990). Small group communication research of the 1980s: A synthesis and critique. *Communication Studies, 41*, 212-236.

Dean, J. W. (1985). The decision to participate in quality circles. *Journal of Applied Behavioral Science, 21*, 317-327.

Dewey, J. (1910). *How we think*. Boston: D. C. Heath.

DeWine, S. (1994). *The consultant's craft: Improving organizational communication*. New York: St. Martin's.

Dickens, M., & Hefferman, M. (1949). Experimental research in group discussion. *Quarterly Journal of Speech, 35*, 23-29.

Dyer, W. G. (1972). *The sensitive manipulator* (Rev. ed.). Provo, UT: Brigham Young University Press.

Dyer, W. G. (1977). *Team building: Issues and alternatives*. Reading, MA: Addison-Wesley.

Dyer, W. G. (1984). *Strategies for managing change*. Reading, MA: Addison-Wesley.

Ellis, D. G., & Fisher, B. A. (1994). *Small group decision making: Communication and the group process* (4th ed.). New York: McGraw-Hill.

Ferris, G. R., & Wagner J. A., III. (1985). Quality circles in the United States: A conceptual re-evaluation. *Journal of Applied Behavioral Science, 21*, 155-167.

Firestien, R. (1990). Effects of creative problem solving training on communication behaviors in small groups. *Small Group Research, 21*, 507-521.

Fisher, B. A. (1970a). Decision emergence: Phases in group decision making. *Speech Monographs, 37*, 53-66.

Fisher, B. A. (1970b). The process of decision modification in small discussion groups. *Journal of Communication, 20*, 51-64.

Forsyth, D. E. (1983). *An introduction to group dynamics*. Monterey, CA: Brooks/Cole.

Frey, L. R. (1995a). Applied communication research on group facilitation in natural settings. In L. R. Frey (Ed.), *Innovations in group facilitation: Applications in natural settings* (pp. 1-24). Cresskill, NJ: Hampton.

Frey, L. R. (1995b). Magical elixir or what the top tells the middle to do to the bottom?: The paradoxes and promises of facilitating work teams for promoting organizational change and development. In R. Cesaria & P. Shockley-Zalabak (Eds.), *Organization means communication: Making the organizational concept relevant to practice* (pp. 173-188). Rome: Servizio Italiano Publicazioni Internazionali.

Frey, L. R. (1996). Remembering and "re-membering": A history of theory and research in communication and group decision making. In R. Y. Hirokawa & M. S. Poole (Eds.), *Communication and group decision making* (2nd ed., pp. 19-51). Thousand Oaks, CA: Sage.

Friedman, V. J., & Lipshitz, R. (1992). Teaching people to shift cognitive gears: Overcoming resistance on the road to model II. *Journal of Applied Behavioral Science, 28*, 118-136.

Gouran, D. S. (1982). *Making decisions in groups: Choices and consequences*. Glenview, IL: Scott, Foresman.

Gouran, D. S. (1985). The paradigm of unfulfilled promise: A critical examination of the history of research on small groups in Speech Communication. In T. W. Benson (Ed.), *Speech Communication in the 20th century* (pp. 90-108, 386-392). Carbondale: Southern Illinois University Press.

Gouran, D. S. (1991). Rational approaches to decision-making and problem-solving discussion. *Quarterly Journal of Speech, 77*, 343-358.

Gouran, D. S. (1992). Principles of counteractive influence in decision-making and problem-solving groups. In R. S. Cathcart & L. A. Samovar (Eds.), *Small group communication: A reader* (6th ed., pp. 221-235). Dubuque, IA: Wm. C. Brown.

Gouran, D. S. (1994). The future of small group communication research: Revitalization or continued good health? *Communication Studies, 45*, 29-39.

Gouran, D. S. (1997). Effective versus ineffective group decision making. In L. R. Frey & J. K. Barge (Eds.), *Managing group life: Communicating in decision-making groups* (pp. 133-155). Boston: Houghton Mifflin.

Gouran, D. S., & Hirokawa, R. Y. (1983). The role of communication in decision-making groups: A functional perspective. In M. S. Mander (Ed.), *Communications in transition: Issues and debate in current research* (pp. 168-185). New York: Praeger.

Gouran, D. S., & Hirokawa, R. Y. (1986). Counteractive functions of communication in effective group decision-making. In R. Y. Hirokawa & M. S. Poole (Eds.), *Communication and group decision-making* (pp. 81-90). Beverly Hills, CA: Sage.

Hackman, J. R. (1987). The design of work teams. In J. W. Lorsch (Ed.), *Handbook of organizational behavior* (pp. 315-342). Englewood Cliffs, NJ: Prentice Hall.

Hall, J., & Williams, M. S. (1970). Group dynamics training and improved decision making. *Journal of Applied Behavioral Science, 6,* 39-68.

Hare, A. P. (1973). Theories of group development and categories for interaction analysis. *Small Group Behavior, 4,* 259-304.

Hare, A. P. (1976). *Handbook of small group research* (2nd ed.). New York: Free Press.

Hare, A. P., Blumberg, H. M., Davies, M. F., & Kent, M. V. (1994). *Small group research: A handbook.* Norwood, NJ: Ablex.

Harkins, S. G., & Szmanski, K. (1989). Social loafing and group evaluation. *Journal of Personality and Social Psychology, 56,* 934-941.

Harnack, V. R. (1963). A study of the effect of an organized minority upon a discussion group. *Journal of Communication, 13,* 12-24.

Herman, R. (1983). Intervening in groups: A repertoire and language of group skills for self-directed learning in decision-making groups. *Small Group Behavior, 14,* 445-464.

Hirokawa, R. Y. (1985). Discussion procedures and decision-making performance: A test of the functional perspective. *Human Communication Research, 12,* 203-224.

Hirokawa, R. Y. (1987). Why informed groups make faulty decisions: An investigation of possible interaction-based explanations. *Small Group Behavior, 18,* 3-29.

Hirokawa, R. Y., & Rost, K. M. (1992). Effective group decision making in organizations: Field test of the vigilant interaction theory. *Management Communication Quarterly, 5,* 267-288.

Janis, I. L. (1982). *Groupthink: Psychological studies of policy decisions and fiascoes* (2nd ed.). Boston: Houghton Mifflin.

Janis, I. L., & Mann, L. (1977). *Decision-making: A psychological analysis of conflict, choice, and commitment.* New York: Free Press.

Jarboe, S. (1988). A comparison of input-output, process-output, and input-process-output models of small group problem-solving effectiveness. *Communication Monographs, 55,* 121-142.

Jarboe, S. (1996). Procedures for enhancing group decision making. In R. Y. Hirokawa & M. S. Poole (Eds.), *Communication and group decision making* (2nd ed., pp. 345-383). Thousand Oaks, CA: Sage.

Jenness, A. (1932). The role of discussion in changing opinion regarding a matter of fact. *Journal of Abnormal and Social Psychology, 27,* 279-296.

Kaplan, R. E. (1979). The conspicuous absence of evidence that process consultation enhances task performance. *Journal of Applied Behavioral Science, 15,* 346-360.

Kelley, H. H. (1952). Two functions of reference groups. In G. E. Swanson, T. M. Newcomb, & E. L. Hartley (Eds.), *Readings in social psychology* (pp. 410-414). New York: Holt, Rinehart & Winston.

Kernaghen, J. A., & Cooke, R. A. (1990). Teamwork in planning innovative projects: Improving group performance by rational and interpersonal interventions in group process. *IEEC Transactions on Engineering Management, 87,* 109-116.

Keyton, J. (1997). Coding communication in decision-making groups. In L. R. Frey & J. K. Barge (Eds.), *Managing group life: Communicating in decision-making groups* (pp. 236-269). Boston: Houghton Mifflin.

Klein, H. J. (1989). An integrated control theory model of work motivation. *Academy of Management Review, 14,* 150-172.

Larson, C. E. (1969). Forms of analysis and small group problem-solving. *Speech Monographs, 36,* 452-455.

Larson, C. E., & LaFasto, F.M.J. (1989). *Teamwork: What must go right/what can go wrong.* Newbury Park, CA: Sage.

Latane, B. K., & Harkins, S. (1979). Many hands make light the work: The causes and consequences of social loafing. *Journal of Personality and Social Psychology, 37,* 822-832.

Leathers, D. (1972). Quality of group communication as a determinant of group product. *Speech Monographs, 39,* 166-173.

Levine, J. M., & Moreland, R. L. (1990). Progress in small group research. *Annual Review of Psychology, 41,* 525-634.

Lewin, K. (1946). Action research and minority problems. *Journal of Social Issues, 2,* 34-46.

Lewin, K. (1947). Frontiers in group dynamics. *Human Relations, 1,* 1-20.

Lewin, K. (1951). *Field theory in social science: Selected theoretical papers* (D. Cartwright, Ed.). New York: Harper & Row.

Lewin, K., Lippitt, R., & White, R. (1939). Patterns of aggressive behavior in experimentally created social climates. *Journal of Social Psychology, 10,* 271-299.

Maier, N.R.F. (1963). *Problem-solving discussions and conferences: Leadership methods and skills.* New York: McGraw-Hill.

Maier, N.R.F., & Maier, R. A. (1957). An experimental test of the effects of "developmental" vs. "free" discussion on the quality of group discussion. *Journal of Applied Psychology, 41,* 320-323.

Marks, M. L. (1986, March). The question of quality circles. *Psychology Today,* pp. 36-46.

Marks, M. L., Mirvis, P. H., Grady, F., & Hackett, E. J. (1985). Employee participation in a quality circle program: Impact on quality of work life, productivity, and absenteeism. *Journal of Applied Psychology, 71,* 61-69.

McCleod, P. L., Liker, J. K., & Lobel, S. A. (1992). Process feedback in task groups: An application of goal setting. *Journal of Applied Behavioral Science, 28,* 15-41.

Meyers, R. A. (1997). Social influence and group argumentation. In L. R. Frey & J. K. Barge (Eds.), *Managing group life: Communicating in decision-making groups* (pp. 183-201). Boston: Houghton Mifflin.

Miles, M. B. (1971). *Learning to work in groups: A program guide for educational leaders.* New York: Teachers College Press.

Mitchell, R. R. (1986). Team building by disclosure of internal frames of reference. *Journal of Applied Behavioral Science, 21,* 15-28.

Nadler, D. A. (1979). The effects of feedback on task group behavior: A review of the experimental research. *Organizational Behavior and Human Performance, 23,* 309-338.

Napier, R. W., & Gershenfeld, M. K. (1989). *Groups: Theory and experience* (4th ed.). Boston: Houghton Mifflin.

Pavitt, C. (1993). What (little) we know about formal group discussion procedures: A review of relevant research. *Small Group Research, 24,* 217-235.

Pfeiffer, J. W., & Jones, J. E. (Eds.). (1974-1979). *A handbook of structured experiences for human relations training* (Vols. 1-6). La Jolla, CA: University Associates.

Poole, M. S. (1991). Procedures for managing meetings: Social and technological innovations. In R. A. Swanson & B. O. Knapp (Eds.), *Innovative meeting management* (pp. 53-110). Austin, TX: 3M Meeting Management Institute.

Poole, M. S., & Baldwin, C. L. (1996). Developmental process in group decision-making. In R. Y. Hirokawa & M. S. Poole (Eds.), *Communication and group decision making* (2nd ed., pp. 215-241). Thousand Oaks, CA: Sage.

Putnam, L. L., & Geist, P. (1985). Argument in bargaining: An analysis of the reasoning process. *Southern Speech Communication Journal, 50,* 225-245.

Rice, A. K. (1965). *Learning for leadership: Interpersonal and intergroup relationships.* London: Tavistock.

Royal, E., & Golden, S. (1981). Attitude similarity and attraction to an employee group. *Psychological Reports, 48,* 251-254.

Salazar, A. J. (1995). Understanding the synergistic effects of communication in small groups: Making the most out of group member abilities. *Small Group Research, 26,* 169-199.

Scheidel, T. M., & Crowell, L. (1964). Idea development in small discussion groups. *Quarterly Journal of Speech, 50,* 140-145.

Schein, E. H. (1969). *Process consultation: Vol. 1. Its role in organizational development.* Reading, MA: Addison-Wesley.

Schein, E. H. (1987). *Process consultation: Vol. 2. Lessons for managers and consultants.* Reading, MA: Addison-Wesley.

Schein, E. H., & Bennis, W. G. (1965). *Personal and organizational change through group methods: The laboratory approach.* New York: Wiley.

Scholtes, P. R., Joiner, B., & Streibel, B. (1988). (Eds.). *The team handbook: How to use teams to improve quality* (2nd ed.). Madison, WI: Joiner.

Schoonover, S. C., & Dalziel, M. M. (1996). Developing leadership for change. In R. S. Cathcart, L. A. Samovar, & L. D. Herman (Eds.), *Small group communication: Theory and practice* (7th ed., pp. 394-403). Dubuque, IA: Brown & Benchmark.

Schultz, B. (1982). Argumentativeness: Its effect in group decision making and its role in leadership perception. *Communication Quarterly, 30,* 368-375.

Schultz, B. G. (1996). *Communicating in the small group: Theory and practice* (2nd ed.). New York: HarperCollins.

Schultz, B., & Ketrow, S. M. (1996). Improving decision quality in the small group: The role of the reminder. In R. S. Cathcart, L. A. Samovar, & L. D. Herman (Eds.), *Small group communication: Theory and practice* (7th ed., pp. 404-410). Dubuque, IA: Brown & Benchmark.

Schultz, B., Ketrow, S. M., & Urban, D. M. (1995). Improving decision quality in the small group: The role of the reminder. *Small Group Research, 26,* 521-541.

Schweiger, D. M., Sandberg, W. R., & Ragan, J. W. (1986). Group approaches for improving strategic decision making: A comparative analysis of dialectical inquiry, devil's advocacy, and consensus. *Academy of Management Journal, 28,* 51-71.

Shaw, M. E. (1981). *Group dynamics: The psychology of small group behavior* (3rd ed.). New York: McGraw-Hill.

Sherif, M. (1936). *The psychology of social norms.* New York: Harper.

Steiner, I. D. (1972). *Group process and productivity.* New York: Academic Press.

Stohl, C. (1986). Quality circles and changing patterns of communication. In M. L. McLaughlin (Ed.), *Communication yearbook 9* (pp. 511-531). Beverly Hills, CA: Sage.

Stohl, C. (1987). Bridging the parallel organization: A study of quality circle effectiveness. In M. L. McLaughlin (Ed.), *Communication yearbook 10* (pp. 416-429). Beverly Hills, CA: Sage.

Stohl, C. (1995a). Facilitating bona fide groups: Practice and paradox. In L. R. Frey (Ed.), *Innovations in group facilitation: Applications in natural settings* (pp. 325-332). Cresskill, NJ: Hampton.

Stohl, C. (1995b). Paradoxes of participation. In R. Cesaria & P. Shockley-Zalabak (Eds.), *Organization means communication: Making the organizational communication concept relevant to practice* (pp. 199-215). Rome: Servizio Italiano Publicazioni Internazionali.

Stohl, C., & Jennings, K. (1988). Volunteerism and voice in quality circles. *Western Journal of Speech Communication, 52,* 238-251.

Stone, N. J., & O'Gorman, M. (1991). Trained helping behaviors and group performance. *Psychological Reports, 68,* 1291-1299.

Strong, S. R., & Claiborn, C. D. (1982). *Change through interaction: Social psychological processes of counseling and psychotherapy.* New York: Wiley.

Thibaut, J. W., & Kelley, H. H. (1959). *The social psychology of groups.* New York: John Wiley.

Timmons, W. M. (1939). *Decisions and attitudes as outcomes of the discussion of a social problem* (Contributions to Education, No. 777). New York: Bureau of Publications, Teachers College, Columbia University.

Timmons, W. M. (1941). Discussion, debating, and research. *Quarterly Journal of Speech, 27,* 415-421.

Turner, J. C. (1982). Towards a cognitive redefinition of the social group. In H. Tajfel (Ed.), *Social identity and intergroup relations* (pp. 15-40). Cambridge, UK: Cambridge University Press.

Vanderslice, V. J., Rice, R. W., & Julian, J. W. (1987). The effects of participation in decision making on worker satisfaction and productivity: An organizational stimulation. *Journal of Applied Social Psychology, 17,* 158-170.

Viega, J. F. (1991). The frequency of self-limiting behavior in groups: A measure and an explanation. *Human Relations, 44,* 877-895.

Walter, G. A. (1975). Effects of videotape feedback and modeling on the behaviors of group members. *Human Relations, 28,* 121-138.

Walter, G. A., & Miles, R. E. (1972). Essential elements for improving task-group membership behaviors. *Proceedings of the American Psychological Association, 7,* 461-462.

Wheelan, S. A. (1994). *Group processes: A development perspective.* Boston: Allyn & Bacon.

Wheelan, S. A., & McKeage, R. (1993). Developmental patterns in small and large groups. *Small Group Research, 24,* 60-83.

Williams, K., Harkins, S., & Latane, B. (1981). Identifiability as a deterrent to social loafing: Two cheering experiments. *Journal of Personality and Social Psychology, 40,* 303-311.

Zey, M. (1992). Criticisms of rational choice models. In M. Zey (Ed.), *Decision making: Alternatives to rational choice models* (pp. 9-31). Newbury Park, CA: Sage.

15

The Impact of Formal Procedures on Group Processes, Members, and Task Outcomes

SUNWOLF
Santa Clara University

DAVID R. SEIBOLD
University of California, Santa Barbara

When the group dynamics movement was born in the late 1930s (see Gouran, Chapter 1, this volume), group discussion researchers endorsed beliefs in the *collective* strength of people and the value of cooperative interaction (Phillips & Wood, 1984). Since the early research of McBurney and Hance (1939), itself an adaptation of Dewey's (1910) reflective thinking model, ample evidence suggests that formal discussion and problem-solving procedures help groups perform better (see Poole, 1991). For example, higher quality decisions are produced by techniques that encourage group members to analyze a problem, establish solution criteria, and identify and evaluate alternative choices (Hirokawa, 1985; Hirokawa, Erbert, & Hurst, 1996). While noting that formal procedures may increase the time needed for group discussion, Pavitt (1993) concludes that in the majority of studies, many procedures are shown to be advantageous.

At the same time, *which* procedure(s) should be used, and under *what* circumstances, remains unclear (Jarboe, 1996). Pavitt and Curtis (1994), for example, conclude that there are no studies that offer insights into when the reflective thinking technique is helpful, and that only studies involving the Nominal Group Technique remain the exception to the dearth of research concerning *when* groups should use particular procedures. Some groups may even be *hurt* by the use of these techniques (Pavitt, 1993; see also Hewes, 1996).

Research on the effects of formal techniques to enhance group problem solving and decision making spans the disciplines of Communication, Social Psychology, Sociology, Organizational Studies, and Business Management. The range of procedures examined includes those designed to manage conflict, build consensus, structure meetings, make decisions, solve problems, produce ideas, evaluate risks, and build teams. In this chapter, we examine more than 50 years of research crossing most of these disciplines, and we attempt to synthesize claims concerning the effects of members' use of formal procedures on group processes, individual group members, and task outcomes. These formal procedures have been referred to by a variety of terms: discussion, problem solving, and decision making are the ones used most frequently. We refer to them here as "process" procedures, which highlights the effects of these procedures on communication processes in groups and offers the further advantage of a broad term that encompasses all three descriptive categories of techniques. Toward those ends, we first examine the limitations of group discussions in which process procedures are not utilized, and then propose a model that provides a functional framework for organizing the findings of previous research. We conclude the chapter with suggestions for enhancing the vitality of research on formal group procedures.

DIFFICULTIES WITH NATURALLY OCCURRING (FREE) GROUP DISCUSSION

The range of prescriptive procedures developed with the goal of making groups more effective reflects, in part, the difficulties inherent in group work. The perceived need for formal process procedures presumes that something is wrong with free discussion in groups (see Pavitt, 1993). At the outset, we acknowledge that groups often are effective without using formal procedures, although a substantial body of research demonstrates potential problems when groups do not use them. We focus on those problems here.

"Naturally occurring" and "free" group discussion frequently are used interchangeably in the literature, and we use them here to refer to the *communication processes of task groups that have not been required or encouraged to use formal group process techniques,* nor do they do so on their own. Although any group naturally will engage in some structur-

ing and restructuring of its discussion, naturally occurring or free group discussion occurs when formal structures have not been suggested or imposed on either the group or its individual members, from either outside or within the group.

Free discussion has been found to affect group processes negatively in myriad interconnected ways (see Dunnette, Campbell, & Jaastad, 1963). Groups with no formal process structures may not use their time effectively, consuming either more or less time than is needed for successful task completion. Premature idea evaluation has been observed (Collaros & Anderson, 1969), because group members engaged in free discussion often feel they must find solutions quickly (Poole, 1991). Scheidel and Crowell (1964) reported a tendency for free group discussion to consist of sequences of individual proposals each evaluated and then dropped in favor of the next proposal; the demands of reflective thinking, in which all proposals are made before any are discussed, appear unnatural (Pavitt, 1993). Real time may be distorted as members perceive the time available to them to be shorter than it actually is (see Holsti, 1971; Langer, Wapner, & Werner, 1961). Without the use of process procedures, groups become solution-oriented prematurely (Shure, Rogers, Larsen, & Tassone, 1962), tend to go straight to the choice phase while disregarding careful analysis of the problem (Maier, 1970), neglect planning (Shure et al., 1962), or select the first available solution (Hall & Watson, 1970). Under time pressure, members sacrifice individual thinking, look for shortcuts, and ignore issues that should be considered to ensure a high-quality decision (Maier, 1970). Planning is rare in free-discussion groups (Hackman & Kaplan, 1974; Shure et al., 1962), and members find it difficult to identify distinct subtasks or even to determine when a task has been completed (Poole, 1991).

The unmanaged presence of other people may result in social pressures, conformity, or discussion loafing. Unstructured communication in groups has been shown to trigger conformity pressures (Torrance, 1957), domination by a minority of members (Chung & Ferris, 1971), and unexpressed ideas by some members (Collaros & Anderson, 1969). Conformity pressures on members who disagree with the majority can stifle expression of opposing views and prevent full exploration of problems (Schacter, 1968), low-status members may be pressured to surrender opinions (Torrance, 1957), and social pressure within a group may lead to silent disagreement (Maier, 1967). Unfortunately, group majorities frequently have the power to determine the final outcome in free-discussion formats (MacCoun & Kerr, 1988), which can lead to inappropriate and ineffective solutions and alienated members. "Social loafing," or cognitive loafing, may occur, whereby individuals may reduce effort when working in a group compared to the amount exerted when working alone (Rogelberg, Barnes-Farrell, & Lowe, 1992; Valacich & Schwenk, 1995a, 1995b; Weldon & Mustari, 1988; see also Schultz, Chapter 14, this volume). Members often assume that their individual contributions are unnecessary because others have made or can be expected to make the needed communication contributions. "Free riders," those who obtain benefits from being in a group but do not bear a proportional share of the costs, commonly are observed in unstructured group discussions, and they seem to appear more frequently as group size increases (Albanese & Van Fleet, 1985). A further result of the free-rider effect is the "sucker" effect, as group members see a capable other who is free riding and reduce their own efforts (Kerr, 1983). Much of the research on social loafing, however, has involved low-effort tasks, such as brainstorming, in which free riding may not be a significant performance inhibitor (see the observations of Diehl & Stroebe, 1987).

Furthermore, conflict may go unmanaged in naturally occurring group discussions. Conflicts among members are difficult for most groups and can contribute to group polarization, the creation of bad feelings among members, and even the disintegration of a group (Poole, 1991). Groups may become trapped in escalating conflict spirals or, alternatively, in cycles of conflict avoidance (Folger & Poole, 1994; Folger, Poole, & Stutman, 1993; Poole, 1991). In addition, criticism of members' ideas leads to inhibition, self-censorship, reduced creativity, and potential conflict. Conflict also may emerge as a function of status, with high-ranking members taking a greater proportion of turns and, consequently, having more opportunities to influence outcomes (Ng, Bell, & Brooke, 1993), and frequently having greater influence than other group members (Poole, 1991). When influential members dominate a discussion, other members may become reluctant to contribute their ideas (Janis, 1972, 1989; Janis & Mann, 1977). These and other related dynamics may lead women and persons of color, in particular, to experience feelings of exclusion in the communication processes of demographically diverse groups; such effects include low-quality instrumental exchanges, self-censorship, and withdrawal (Elsass & Graves, 1997).

Under conditions of free discussion, when self-censorship occurs—as a result of group conflict, criticism of members, or pressures to conform—judgments may not be expressed; information may not be shared (Collaros & Anderson, 1969), especially relevant non-common knowledge (Stasser, 1992; Stasser & Titus, 1985; see Propp, Chapter 9, this volume, on collective information processing in groups); and dominant leaders may sap members' individual initiative (Poole, 1991). Paradoxically, although many members' ideas are stifled in unregulated discussion, individual members' needs still may dominate group goals. Too much independence in a group may shatter group cohesion and encourage members to privilege individual needs over group goals (Deutsch, 1973). In free discussion, members often experience difficulty balancing both task (see Hirokawa & Salazar, Chapter 7, this volume) and social needs (see Keyton, Chapter 8, this volume), and they may feel unable to contribute wholeheartedly to the content of a decision discussion while working on group relationships (Hewes, 1986). Group members thus may adopt the first available solution to avoid the social tensions associated with disagreement (Hall & Watson, 1970) and thereby experience such negative outcomes as false consensus or groupthink.

In groups that do not use formal process procedures, members often experience difficulty in both listening to and retaining relevant information offered by other members. Unable to pay full attention to multiple alternatives simultaneously, members focusing on one aspect may not listen attentively to other ideas (Hewes, 1986; Poole, 1991). For example, Brenner (1973) reported that people who spoke in free-discussion meetings were unable to recall the remarks of the person who spoke just before them.

A solution to the aforementioned difficulties and dilemmas has been the creation of specific discussion, decision-making, and problem-solving techniques. Such prescriptions and procedures are designed to improve group discussion processes. This is not to imply that the use of formal procedures eradicates all the problems that potentially plague free discussion. Research on the inhibiting effects of formal process procedures will be explored later in the chapter. These formats, however, offer groups various models of structuring techniques, processes designed to lessen social pressure, decrease social loafing, equalize participation, promote nonjudgmental idea generation, or facilitate knowledge extraction and information exchange, among many other functions. The assumption is that group communication will be enhanced and more effective group decisions and solutions will result.

A FRAMEWORK FOR RESEARCH ON FORMAL PROCESS PROCEDURES

Relevant Constructs

Decision making and *problem solving* are terms that have been described in broad and contradictory ways, resulting in some confusion (for multistage process definitions, see Poole, 1991; Ross, 1989; Zander, 1982; for specific distinctions between decision-making

and problem-solving processes, see Gouran, 1997). For the purpose of this review, *group problem solving* refers to the communication processes in which group members engage when their task is to overcome some unsatisfactory situation or obstacle to achieving a goal, whereas *group decision making* refers to the communication processes in which group members engage when their task is to make a choice among several alternatives. As a result, whereas group problem solving necessarily involves components of decision making because choices are made to accomplish the overarching task of solving the problem under consideration, group decision making may occur independently of problem-solving processes.

A variety of terms have been employed to refer to formal procedures. Pavitt (1993) defines a *formal discussion procedure* as "an ordered sequence of steps for decision-making groups to follow in their discussions" (p. 217), whereas Poole (1991) defines *meeting procedures* as "sets of rules or guidelines which specify how a group should organize its process to achieve a particular goal" (p. 55). Jarboe (1996) delineates three levels of problem-solving procedures: *problem-solving models* are procedures designed to tackle the overall difficulty facing a group, operating at a macrolevel by providing a cognitive framework to take the group from the start of a problem to the finish when it is solved (such as Dewey's, 1910, reflective thinking; Scheidel & Crowell's, 1979, problem management sequence; or Delbecq & Van de Ven's, 1971, program planning model); *problem-solving devices* are procedures that operate at the microlevel and assist groups in achieving subgoals (such as quality circles, cognitive maps, synectics, or brainstorming); and *problem-solving strategies* are the practical manifestations of problem-solving models and devices that are adopted or adapted by a group (i.e., the enactment of a model or device by a particular group). This chapter offers an inclusive approach to the categorization of group procedures, and so defines a *formal group process procedure* as any *imported or created structure enacted by a task group specifically for the purpose of enhancing discussion, problem solving, or decision making.* (It should be noted that although groups create and recreate such structures and, thereby, generate unique applied versions of formal process procedures, the studies reviewed here do not attempt to investigate group-created or revised procedures. This chapter covers investigations of *imported* structures, those introduced to a group through the prior training or experiences of one or more group members.)

Focus of Prior Reviews

Previous reviews of literature by Communication scholars on the impact of formal techniques on group discussion, problem solving, and decision making generally have focused on the *types* of procedures employed and their characteristics (e.g., Jarboe, 1996; Pavitt & Curtis, 1994; Poole, 1991; Seibold & Krikorian, 1997). Jarboe (1996) categorized formal procedures at both the macrolevel (rational models, creative models, and planning models) and microlevel (identifying goals and prioritizing problems, analyzing problems, setting decision criteria, generating ideas, designing and evaluating solutions, applying decision-making schemes, and implementing and evaluating solutions). Pavitt and Curtis (1994) analyzed research on formal procedures by examining the order of steps in such procedures, their overall effectiveness in improving group decision quality observed across situations, and members' reactions to their use. Poole's (1991) typology incorporated five dimensions for comparing and evaluating meeting procedures: (a) scope (extent to which a procedure applies to specific tasks or is general in purpose), (b) restrictiveness (extent to which a procedure limits group activity), (c) comprehensiveness (extent to which the rules of a procedure are specific or general), (d) group control (degree to which an expert is needed to run a procedure), and (e) member involvement (number of cooperating members needed to use a procedure). Jensen and Chilberg (1991) identified six cri-

teria for choosing a procedure: task focus, time cost, conflict potential, social needs, promotion of cohesion, and pressure to conform. These previous discussions, consequently, move from types of procedures, to a review of relevant research, to criteria for comparing and evaluating procedures.

In this review, we introduce an alternative way of conceptualizing procedures based on the group process *functions* they serve within a group. Formal procedures affect any or all of four functions: (a) providing structure (structuring), (b) facilitating analysis (analyzing), (c) encouraging creativity (creating), or (d) managing conflict and developing agreement (agreeing) (see Table 15.1). *Structuring procedures* outline the order and manner in which communication occurs during group meetings; *analyzing procedures* help members evaluate, question, investigate, and rank ideas; *creating procedures* are used to generate new ideas; and *agreeing procedures* are used to indicate individual members' preferences, manage conflict, and reach a group decision.

PROPOSED MODEL

We offer a synthetic model, the Function Impact Model, that organizes areas of previous research bearing on formal group process procedures. The model provides a conceptual framework for summarizing what research reveals about how these procedures affect group processes, individual members, and task outcomes (see Figure 15.1). The model also reflects the dynamic, cyclical process of solving problems or making decisions in groups and contrasts natural discussion with discussion aided by a formal procedure. Specifically, the model suggests that the characteristics of the task, the group, and the individual members affect any group discussion, which proceeds either free from or guided by formal procedures and, ultimately, results in enhancing and/or inhibitive effects on the task, group, and members.

The Function Impact Model suggests that formal procedures affect the four separate but interrelated functions in task groups (structur-

Table 15.1 Group Process Procedures Categorized by Function

Procedures That Help Groups Structure	Procedures That Help Groups Analyze	Procedures That Help Groups Create	Procedures That Help Groups Agree
Robert's Rules of Order A particular written authoritative guide used to conduct meetings by parliamentary procedure	**Reflective Thinking** Six preconstructed questions (What is the problem? What are its causes? What are the solution criteria? What are possible solutions? What is the best solution? and What is the method of implementation?) are answered by a group using this rational decision process	**Brainstorming** Designed to generate ideas and promote creativity by reducing premature evaluation, using a facilitator to enforce four rules (no criticism, quantity is wanted, the wilder the ideas the better, and piggybacking on other ideas is encouraged)	**Voting Procedure** Methods of indicating individual members' preferences: simultaneous (raised hands, vocal), sequential (round-robin), secret ballot (written), or open (vocal)
Parliamentary Procedure A rigid structure for meetings of large groups that uses a formal leader and provides for the introduction of administrative issues, old and new business, and voting on motions made by members	**Devil's Advocacy** One member critiques a group's plan, raising questions about its assumptions and consequences but not offering a counterplan	**Reverse Brainstorming** Using the same rules as brainstorming, group members generate ideas or solutions that would make the problem worse, and after generating a list, consider implications of doing the opposite	**Decision Rule** A group achieves decisions through a predetermined level of support (e.g., two-thirds majority, simple majority, decision by authority, minority decision, consensus, or unanimity), often rejecting minority viewpoints and using competitive, partisan communication
Agenda A written document that identifies issues to be considered during a meeting, outlines the order in which they will be discussed, classifies items according to the type of treatment they require, and specifies the amount of time allotted to each issue	**Delphi Method** A group of experts works independently in rounds, where individual ideas are listed, reported to all, and individually ranked, followed by reconsideration of rankings	**Idea Writing** Four-step prediscussion procedure for exploring the meaning of generated ideas in writing: divide into subgroups, each member writes ideas to a stimulus question, forms are shared for other members' written reactions, and each member reads reactions to his or her initial response, followed by discussion	**Weighting System** Allows a group to evaluate its ideas against a set of criteria by recognizing that some factors may be more important than others; numerical weights are assigned to selected criteria, and potential solutions are rated on how well they satisfy each criterion so that overall scores can be obtained
Standard Agenda Performance An agenda format that inserts a PERT-like implementation plan into a standard agenda, with relevant events evaluated as they are implemented	**Dialectical Inquiry** Two subgroups each develop a plan, then both groups meet together to debate those plans, reach consensus on the most important issues, and develop a single course of action	**Consensus Mapping** Uses individual idea cards from group members that are sorted into various classifications to build a solution model	**Straw Poll** Nonbinding voting method designed to encourage members to indicate preliminary preferences while feeling free to change their positions after group discussion
Discussion Formats Formats that allow task groups to interact with outsiders to gather information and ideas, including symposium (series of speeches), panel (audience may direct comments to group members), colloquy (experts questioned from selected members of the audience), forum (any audience member may interact with group), roundtable, and charette (intense series of meetings with those affected by decision)	**Nominal Group Technique** Members work individually and simultaneously, using a facilitator, to privately list advantages and disadvantages of a decision or plan, publicly list results, and privately rank listed items, followed by public report of average scores	**Lateral Thinking Approach** A nonsequential method of discussion that is generative, encourages topic change for the sake of moving ideas and discussion, does not require correctness at any stage, welcomes chance intrusions, and uses variable categories, labels, and classifications	**Consensus Rules** Noncompetitive method of reaching a group decision in which all members eventually agree to agree, notwithstanding individual preferences, utilizing six rules for the discussion—avoid arguing for favorite proposals, avoid using against-them statements, avoid agreeing just to avoid conflict, reject specific decision rules, view differences as helpful, and view initial agreements as premature and suspect
	Flowchart Graphical representation of a step-by-step process outlining basic underlying structures and using an agreed-on symbol system (rectangles, lines, circles, and arrows)	**Buzz Groups** Members are divided into smaller groups for brief periods during a meeting to generate ideas on the same issue that subsequently are analyzed by the entire group	**Problem-Centered Leadership** A method of consensus building that relies on a skilled leader who acts as a facilitator for the entire problem-solving process, encouraging a group toward agreement

Procedures That Help Groups Structure	Procedures That Help Groups Analyze	Procedures That Help Groups Create	Procedures That Help Groups Agree
	Multiattribute Decision Analysis Aids a group in finding the most efficient series of questions to distinguish an object from a class of objects, by asking what sequence of questions yields the most efficient outcome	**Morphological Analysis** Encourages new ideas by breaking a problem into its major parts, listing all possible topics under each heading, and then randomly combining these topics to generate new solutions by forcing together elements that seem unrelated	**Negotiation** A group attempts to accommodate competing goals of its members through a series of trade-offs, using competitive, partisan communication
	Problem Census Used at the beginning of a meeting to guide discussion, the procedure polls members to introduce, list, and rank problems for consideration at that or future meetings	**Role Storming** Each group member is asked to assume the role of a person who may be affected by or affect the problem, then brainstorm the problem from that person's point of view in a group session	
	Single-Question Format A group is asked to focus on the one thing it wishes to accomplish, and then subquestions are generated that must be answered before the group can answer the single question formulated	**Ideals Method** Combines solution generation with solution implementation by having a group generate ideas about the function of proposed solutions, then gather information, design the system, and evaluate its effectiveness	
	Fishbone Diagram A graphical technique used to uncover possible causes and effects of process problems, using a process of elimination to help a group focus on actual significant issues	**Synectics** Uses diverse-membership groups, with a leader guiding discussion through flexible stages: explanation of problem by expert, initial suggestions proposed, dream solutions generated, questions asked by leader to stimulate new thinking, and an attempted force-fit of generated creative ideas to the problem	
	6M Analysis Using a worksheet, group members examine a problem's causes from six points of view: manpower, machinery, methods, materials, money, and minutes	**BrainWriting** Group members generate ideas silently and in writing on index cards, with each member writing down one idea per card and passing it on to stimulate new ideas for the next member, as all members write down on a separate card any new ideas suggested	
	Cognitive Map An alternative to linear outline formats for organizing information in a graphic form, so that relationships can be viewed in a visual, holistic pattern; main points appear in the center and related ideas branch outward, with less important ideas at the edge; arrows and geometric shapes indicate links among ideas	**Object Stimulation** Designed to present a different perspective on a problem, using unrelated stimuli objects with no apparent relation to the problem; a list of objects unrelated to the problem is generated, one object is selected and described in detail, and each description is used as a stimulus to generate ideas; all ideas are written down, and rounds are repeated for other objects	
	Journalist's 6 Questions Helps group quickly structure how a problem is defined by asking six specific questions: Who? What? When? Where? Why? and How?	**Excursion** Uses imaginative scenarios to stimulate ideas and encourage groups members to think in contextual terms and to adopt "what if" ideation generation	

(continued)

Table 15.1 Group Process Procedures Categorized by Function (*Continued*)

Procedures That Help Groups Structure	Procedures That Help Groups Analyze	Procedures That Help Groups Create	Procedures That Help Groups Agree
	Pareto Analysis Using graphical diagrams, charts frequencies and percentages of problem categories at different points in time for the purpose of measuring change and identifying trends	**Visioning** Idea generation in which group members are guided in focusing their energy on the desired end state, imagining specific details, the effects, and how it would function	
	Ideal-Solution Format A group answers questions, one at a time, to analyze a problem: what is the nature of the problem, the ideal solution from the point of view of all involved, conditions that could be changed to achieve a solution, and the solution that best approximates the ideal	**Collective Notebook** Idea-generation method in which members do not meet face-to-face but instead generate ideas over an extended period of time; a notebook with the problem statement is given to each member, who writes down one idea every day for a month, with a co-ordinator summarizing ideas	
	Is/Is Not Analysis A group uses a chart of questions to ensure focus on actual problems: What is/is not the area with the problem? What are/are not the symptoms of the problem? When is/is not the problem observed? Where does/does not the problem occur? and Who is/is not affected by the problem?	**Lotus Blossom** A diagram method that functions as a visual brain-storm, in which each member is given a problem written in the center, and thinks of related ideas that are written in surrounding circles, generating new ideas to the original problem until the diagram is complete	
	Force-Field Analysis A group formulates a statement of its goal, then analyzes each goal by noting what driving forces make it likely to be achieved and what restraining forces make it unlikely to be achieved, and then addresses how to increase or decrease these forces	**Semantic Intuition** Reverses the normal creative procedure by first creating a name, then producing an idea based on it; groups generate two sets of words related to major problem elements, combine two words from each set, use the combination to generate an idea, and repeat	
	Stepladder Technique Regulates involvement by structuring the sequential entry of members and their ideas about a problem into a core group, beginning by having two members work on the problem, after which another member joins, presents a solution, and discussion occurs, followed by another member joining in the same manner	**Creative Problem Solving** Contains some components of rational problem solving (data gathering, problem definition, solution generation and evaluation) but differs in motivating members' efforts, allowing for incubation phases where task work ceases, designating specific imagin-ation phases, and giving attention to social dimen-sions of a group	
	Risk Procedure Designed to avoid premature implementation of decisions; members are asked individually to identify major risks involved with adopting the preferred solution, and the collective list is then considered by the group		

402

Program Evaluation and Review Technique (PERT)

A group develops a chart to structure which member should do what tasks at specified periods of time relevant to accomplishing a proposed plan

Incrementalism

Designed to avoid the complexities of traditional problem analysis and incur less risk by exploring solutions that represent small changes from the status quo, using small steps that can accumulate into meaningful change; a group lists only alternatives that differ incrementally from the status quo, looks for the proposal that has the best immediate consequences without considering long-range goals, and chooses the best alternative by voting

Multidimensional Scaling

A method of comparing solutions against preset criteria with numerical ratings; top-ranked items are rated numerically on specific criteria (i.e., desirability and importance) and then sorted into similar groupings

Mixed Scanning

An incremental decision-making method that breaks a solution down into small steps that are implemented sequentially, with the least expensive and most reversible changes at the beginning, and incorporating a review procedure to identify problems as the solution progresses

Focus Groups

A method of gathering information in which reactions to an issue or proposed solution are gathered from representative groups of people who would be affected by the proposed decision or change

Interpretive Structural Modeling

A method of identifying relationships among specific items that define an issue or problem, used after a group has generated ideas to impose order on the complexity of the items; relevant items are related in paired comparisons (e.g., will lead to, is less important than, and should be cut before)

Expert Approach

Outside expert consultants are brought in as resources to a group to provide advice and recommendations

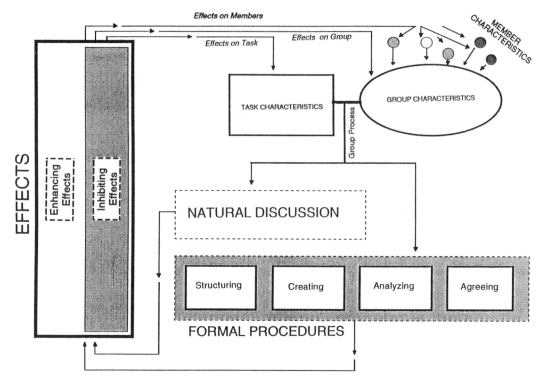

Figure 15.1. Effects of Natural Discussion or Formal Techniques on Group Decision Making

ing, creating, analyzing, and agreeing) while also acknowledging the role of member, group, and task characteristics in the communication process. Prior research has examined the effectiveness of procedures on a variety of outcomes by focusing on

- characteristics of individual group *members*, including tolerance for ambiguity (Comadena, 1984), enhanced commitment to group decisions (Erffmeyer & Lane, 1984), creativity (Graham & Dillon, 1974), thinking ability (Pyron, 1964; Pyron & Sharp, 1963; Sharp & Milliken, 1964), communication apprehension (Jablin, Seibold, & Sorenson, 1977; Jablin, Sorenson, & Seibold, 1978), status (Jablin et al., 1978), and other individual difference variables, such as gender (McLeod, Lobel, & Cox, 1996; see overview of research in Shaw, 1981);

- characteristics of the *group,* such as group climate (Bowers & Hausser, 1977), group-procedure fit (Poole, 1991), and cooperative, competitive, or mixed-motive groups (Thompson, Mannix, & Bazerman, 1988); or
- characteristics of *task outcomes,* including more accurate predictions (Cosier, 1978), increased success of strategic decisions (Dean & Sharfman, 1996), decreased number of deadlocked juries (Kerr & MacCoun, 1985), and higher quality decisions (Maier & Maier, 1957), as well as more ideas and more unique ideas (Van de Ven & Delbecq, 1974).

In addition to representing the interrelationships among member, group, and task characteristics, and delineating specific functions of formal procedures, the model illuminates both the facilitative and inhibitive effects that can be associated with natural discussion and procedure-aided group problem solving. A dynamic process results, as positive and negative outcomes and experiences further affect group members, the group, and the group's present and future tasks.

REVIEW OF RESEARCH

The research reviewed below is organized in terms of the Function Impact Model depicted in Figure 15.1. We first discuss the types of procedures investigated. We then attend to antecedent conditions to group decision making or problem solving that affect other components of the model. Third, we analyze the specific functions affected by the procedures. Finally, we review the effects of these procedures on group members, the group, and/or the task itself. We organize this review through a chronological summary of 33 representative studies conducted between 1957 and 1997 and, thereby, indicate the historical development of research on group procedures (see Table 15.2). Each included study is reviewed with respect to (a) the procedure(s) investigated, (b) any theoretical perspective guiding the research, (c) the number and type of participants, (d) the size of the groups studied, (e) the length of time allowed for the task, (f) the nature of the task, (g) the dependent variables measured, and (h) general findings. (One boundary condition is that the literature investigating the effects of technology as a facilitation procedure, such as group decision support systems and other computer-augmented decision aids, is beyond the scope of this review; for a review of the impact of technology on group communication, see Scott, Chapter 16, this volume.)

Procedures Investigated

Table 15.2 summarizes studies of devil's advocacy (9 studies), consensus (9), brainstorming (5), dialectical inquiry (5), Nominal Group Technique (NGT; 4), reflective thinking (2), Delphi technique (2), polling (2), and pooling (2). The following procedures are reported in only one study: stepladder; leader-

delayed opinions; reminder; force-field analysis; vigilant interaction processes; creative problem solving; ideal-solution, single-question, and staticized procedures; and agenda. This total of 33 studies contrasts sharply with the 56 prescriptive process procedures described in Table 15.1, which categorizes each technique by the primary group process function affected by its use. Clearly, a large number of the techniques created for use by groups remain understudied. Furthermore, structuring (5 procedures) and agreeing (7) functions have fewer formal procedures available to draw on than the functions of analyzing (26) and creating (18), even taking into consideration the argument that some techniques, such as NGT, are multi-functional.

Antecedent Conditions

As depicted in Figure 15.1, individual member characteristics, group characteristics, and task characteristics are important antecedents to the group processes that result from the use of formal procedures. Specific antecedent conditions investigated have included group climate (Bowers & Hausser, 1977); group-procedure fit (Poole, 1991); task-procedure fit (Nutt, 1984; Thompson et al., 1988); the importance of member training, experience, or practice (Basadur, Graen, & Green, 1982; Dillon, Graham, & Aidells, 1972; Hirokawa & Rost, 1992; Pavitt, 1993; for an excellent summary, see Poole, 1991); the importance of leader training (Green, 1975; Miner, 1979); the role of procedural champion (Bryson & Roerig, 1989; Poole, 1991); members' motivation (Poole, 1991; Thompson et al, 1988); and the degree to which the task decision mattered to participants (White, Dittrich, & Lang, 1980).

Process Functions: Structuring, Analyzing, Creating, and Agreeing

Synthesis of findings to date requires a cautionary note about the limitations of the designs from which such findings were derived: student participants, single-meeting formats, truncated time to make a decision, and small group size all limit potential applications of results. The majority of these studies were conducted on zero-history student groups; the few investigations of "real-world" groups offer scant descriptions of group history or prior members' experiences with formal procedures or task groups, both of which may affect members' use of or reaction to using process techniques. In addition, "real-world" groups are faced with "real" problems, rather than artificially constructed tasks that may result in lower motivation levels, decreased saliency for participants, and changes in ways members use the formal procedures (see Dillon et al., 1972, who found that group members had difficulty adhering to rules of brainstorming on problems they cared about). Of the 33 studies reviewed in Table 15.2, 88% were conducted using student participants, with only 12% involving participants from natural groups; only one study observed more than one meeting; and more than 50% of the groups were allowed to meet for 30 minutes or less. Although group size has not been examined in connection with the efficiency of using formal techniques, the majority of studies (82%) are based on applications to groups of six or fewer members, which may not reflect the probably larger membership of the majority of "real-world" problem-solving and decision-making groups. Despite these limitations, guided specifically by the predominant function of the procedure, the following synopses appear to be warranted.

Providing Structure

Procedures that help groups structure the topics, order, and manner of their discussions have been largely ignored by researchers. One way that groups structure discussions is by using agendas, which set out the order in which issues will be raised, discussed, or voted on (Seibold, 1992; Seibold & Krikorian, 1997). When agendas are followed strictly, issues are considered individually and are not reintroduced once the next topic has started (Thompson et al., 1988).

Plott and Levine (1978) found that agendas tended to produce decisions that they were designed to influence; listing items for discussion produced decisions about them. This research, however, did not measure other variables of interest, such as length of time for discussion, member satisfaction, or decision quality and quantity. Research on the interaction of agendas and decision rules by Thompson et al. (1988) found that three-person-group negotiations that followed an explicit agenda and used a majority decision rule demonstrated a more unequal distribution of individual members' resources and were more likely to rely on two-person coalitions than groups that used no agenda with majority rule, an explicit agenda with unanimity rule, or no agenda with unanimity rule. They concluded that specific issue agendas, which allowed negotiators to tally win/loss results for each issue, were less effective for small negotiating groups than problem-solving agendas.

The effects on individual, group, or task outcomes of such structuring techniques as Robert's Rules of Order, parliamentary procedure, or specific discussion formats (e.g., symposium, colloquy, or forum) remain to be investigated. Research has indicated, however, that formal structures may produce different types of communication in group discussion. Putnam (1979), measuring preference for procedure and order in groups, found that high-preference-for-procedural-order groups generated more communication characterized by summaries, goal-related statements, and procedural clarifications, whereas low-preference-for-procedural-order groups produced more communication characterized by vacillating between task and socioemotional issues, switching topics, and introducing interruptions. Her research has not yet been extended to explanations for the observed ineffectiveness of many formal procedures. Some researchers argue that groups function best when they operate under structures, such as agendas, that set boundaries, timing, and order for discussions (Phillips, 1970; Thompson et al., 1988), though the specific effects of these structures have been underinvestigated.

Procedures[a] and Study	Theoretical Perspectives	Participants/Discussion Time	Task	Dependent Variables	Findings
Brainstorming (Kramer, Kuo, & Dailey, 1997)	Structuration Theory	200 undergraduates (five-member groups) Time:[b] 10 min to brainstorm, unlimited discussion thereafter	Developing program for high school students visiting a university	Decision quality (effective-feasible-creative-interesting) and member satisfaction	No difference in decision quality of untrained, brainstorming, and nominal groups. Brainstorming and nominal group members more satisfied and felt that communication and group processes were more effective than untrained group members.
Brainstorming (McLeod, Lobel, & Cox, 1996)		135 paid graduates and undergraduates (three- to five-member groups) Time: 15 min	Generating ideas to get more tourists to visit the United States	Idea quality (effective-feasible) and members' attraction to group	Ideas produced by ethnically diverse groups more effective and feasible. Homogeneous group members reported marginally more attraction to their groups than ethnically diverse groups.
Brainstorming (Offner, Kramer, & Winter, 1996)		180 undergraduates (four-member groups) Time: 20 min	Improving campus security	Number of ideas generated	Interacting groups with a facilitator outperformed groups without, and did as well as nominal groups. Flip chart and use of pauses during discussion did not increase the number of ideas.
Devil's advocacy (DA), pooling, and consensus (Plous, 1995)		Undergraduates: 85-97-92-100 (4 experiments) (three- to four-member groups) Time: 10 min	Estimating intervals and confidence levels in item list	Number of items correct; confidence levels of members in group's performance	Only pooling technique yielded well-calibrated interval estimates. DA and groups using other debiasing procedures did not outperform individuals working alone. All members overestimated their group performance by a greater margin than their individual or pooled performance.
Reminder, reflective thinking, force-field analysis (Schultz, Ketrow, & Urban, 1995)		262 undergraduates (five- to seven-member groups) Time: unlimited	Recommending policies and solutions for unwed pregnant teens	Problem definition, number of alternatives, appropriate remedies, reasons	Groups trained in decision processes produced higher quality decisions. Groups that completed requisite functions outperformed other groups. Non-leader-reminder groups produced higher quality decisions than leader-reminder groups.
Emotional vs. objective devil's advocacy (DA) (Valacich & Schwenk, 1995a)		255 undergraduates (five-member groups) Time: 15 min + 10 min, if needed	Assigning sales territory to two salespeople	Quality of solution (potential sales)	Individuals and computer groups developed and considered more solution alternatives, although face-to-face groups reached consensus in fewest voting rounds. Objective DA treatment produced higher quality decisions than emotional DA.
Devil's advocacy (DA), dialectical inquiry (DI), expert (Valacich & Schwenk, 1995b)		220 undergraduates (five-member groups) Time: 15 min + 10 min, if needed	Assigning sales territory to two salespeople	Quality of solution (potential sales) and member satisfaction (with solution and decision process)	DA groups developed and considered more alternative solutions, selected higher quality recommendation than DI or expert. Computer groups more satisfied with process, and developed and considered more solution alternatives than face-to-face groups, but required more voting rounds for agreement. No differences between computer and face-to-face groups in members' satisfaction with the decision.
Devil's advocacy (DA), dialectical inquiry (DI), individuals vs. groups (Schwenk & Valacich, 1994)		250 undergraduates (five-member groups) Time: 15 min	Assigning sales territory to two salespeople	Quality of solution (potential sales)	DA led to superior performance when individuals and groups combined. DA benefited individuals more than DI; groups made effective use of either technique. DA groups discussed more innovative alternatives.

(Continued)

Table 15.2 Representative Studies of Formal Group Process Procedures (Continued)

Procedures[a] and Study	Theoretical Perspectives	Participants/Discussion Time	Task	Dependent Variables	Findings
Consensus (C), devil's advocacy (DA) (Murrell, Stewart, & Engel, 1993)		101 graduate students (four- to five-member groups) Time: 20 min	Selecting new manager; three task structures (additive, disjunctive, and conjunctive)	Decision accuracy, decision quality, group atmosphere	For decision accuracy, C more effective with additive task, DA more effective with disjunctive; both effective with conjunctive. For decision quality, C best for additive, DA best on disjunctive; equal on conjunctive. Members felt better about group and decision with C, even when performance was down.
Consensus (C), devil's advocacy (DA) (Schwenk & Cosier, 1993)		152 undergraduates (four-member groups) Time: not reported	Strategizing to either acquire a company or develop new products	Number and quality of assumptions and recommendations, critical evaluation, member satisfaction	Number and quality of assumptions did not differ by decision technique. Groups with higher consensus about objectives gave more assumptions and were of higher quality than lower levels of consensus. DA had higher levels of critical evaluation, but members had less desire to work with group in future. DA increased commitment of high-C members to decision, but not low-C members.
Vigilant Interaction Processes (Hirokawa & Rost, 1992)	Vigilant Interaction Theory	Nine groups of utility company employees (five-to six-member groups) Time: unlimited	Organizing series of activities to help employees reduce cardiovascular risk factors	Quality of decision and number of utterances about task, criteria, positive and negative evaluation	More high-quality decisions if (a) members produced more facilitative and less inhibitive utterances about problem/task analysis, (b) absence of efforts to inhibit criteria development, (c) effective evaluation of positive qualities of choices, and (d) utterances promoting group's efforts to identify negative qualities of choices.
Stepladder (Rogelberg, Barnes-Farrell, & Lowe, 1992)		120 undergraduates (four-member groups) Time: 35-45 min	Solving winter survival exercise	Quality of decision, quality of best individual member's decision	Stepladder produced higher quality decisions and group decisions surpassed the quality of their best individual members' decisions 56% of time compared to 13% for conventional groups.
Leader delayed-opinion, leader outset-opinion (Anderson & Balzer, 1991)		Undergraduates + 19 graduates (four 22-member groups) Time: 20 min	Solving residence hall life problems	Number of alternatives, feasibility, and likelihood of adoption	Groups with leaders who delayed stating their opinions generated more alternative solutions to the problems, which were rated more feasible and more likely to be adopted. Discussion time longer under leader-delayed opinion.
Dialectical inquiry (DI), devil's advocacy (DA), and consensus (C) (Priem & Price, 1991)		172 graduates and undergraduates (imaginary four-member groups) Time: 30 min	Providing imaginary recommendations (unspecified)	Amount of conflict, decision confidence, and postdecision group affect	No differences on cognitive conflict. Confidence highest on C, lower with either DI or DA. Members expected higher harmony to result using C, moderate during DI, lower during DA. Higher affect expected in DI than DA, more positive feelings expected in D than DA.
Creative problem solving (CPS) (Firestien, 1990)		200 undergraduates (five-member groups) Time: 5 min	Getting groups to stay at a resort hotel	Amount of participation, criticism, support, humor, number of ideas	CPS-trained groups participated more, criticized ideas less, supported ideas more, exhibited more humor, and produced more ideas than untrained groups.
Straw poll (polling sequence and timing) (Davis, Kameda, Parks, Stasson, & Zimmerman, 1989)	Social Decision Scheme	780 undergraduates (six-member groups) Time: 1 hr	Rendering a verdict in mock criminal trial	Change in individual's vote from pre- to postdiscussion	Influence of sequential or simultaneous polling was significant at the individual level, but not at the level of group consensus.

Procedures[a] and Study	Theoretical Perspectives	Participants/Discussion Time	Task	Dependent Variables	Findings
Dialectical inquiry (DI), devil's advocacy (DA), and consensus (C) (Schweiger, Sandberg, & Rechner, 1989)		120 middle- and upper-middle-level managers (four-member groups) Time: unlimited	Solving two strategic management dilemmas	Performance quality, members' reactions, time required	Groups using DI and DA made higher quality decisions (better assumptions and recommendations, higher critical reevaluation) than C; no difference between DA and DI. C groups had higher member acceptance of decision and shorter meetings. Experience improved performance.
Dialectical inquiry (DI), devil's advocacy (DA), and consensus (C) (Schweiger, Sandberg, & Ragan, 1986)		120 graduate students (four-member groups) Time: unlimited	Analyzing and solving problems facing company	Assumptions (number, validity, importance), member acceptance and satisfaction	Both DI and DA led to higher quality recommendations and assumptions than C. DI was more effective than DA on quality of assumptions. Members of C groups expressed more satisfaction and desire to continue to work with group and greater acceptance of group decision.
Reflective thinking, ideal-solution, single question, and natural discussion (Hirokawa, 1985)	Functional	162 undergraduates (three-member groups) Time: 1 hr	Deciding on appropriate form of discipline (for plagiarizing)	Task functions (understanding, identifying alternatives, assessing consequences)	Regardless of discussion format, satisfaction of two or more conditions produced higher quality decisions. Ability to understand choice and assess negative consequences had greater impact than ability to identify alternatives and assess positive consequences.
Polling (secret polling, open polling) (Kerr & MacCoun, 1985)	Social Decision Scheme	612 undergraduates (3-, 6-, or 12-person juries) Time: 10 min	Rendering a verdict in mock criminal trial	Verdict or hung jury, length of time to verdict	When cases were close, hung jury was less likely with public polling in 3-person groups; in 6- and 12-person groups, open polling increased likelihood of hung jury. No effect of polling on time to reach verdict, except in 6-person clear-case, where secret-poll juries took longer.
Nominal, interacting, and staticized groups (Burleson, Levine, & Samter, 1984)		120 undergraduates (four-member groups) Time: 25 min	Solving NASA Moon Survival Problem and Island Problem	Quality of group and individual decisions	Interacting groups produced better decisions than nominal or staticized groups. Consensual decisions of interacting groups were better than the pooled decisions of groups, but not better than the decisions of the best individuals (partial assembly-effect bonus).
Majority vs. minority influence (Nemeth & Wachtler, 1983)		162 male undergraduates (six-member groups) Time: not reported	Finding all comparison figures in which a standard figure was/was not embedded	Judgment (novel-correct), members' moods, members' perceptions of confederates	Members exposed to a minority made novel and correct judgments not suggested by the minority. Majority effective in gaining following, forcing members to choose between majority's position or remain independent, but not in seeking novel solutions. Members felt more awkward, embarrassed, fearful, and frustrated in majority-influence condition.
Creative problem solving (Basadur, Graen, & Green, 1982)		32 engineering employees (16-member groups) Time: no group discussion	Engaging in a series of diverse tasks during intensive training	Preference for and practice of ideation, performance in problem finding and problem solving	2 weeks after training, members showed greater preference for ideation in problem solving, but not in problem finding; greater practice of ideation in problem finding/solving and problem-finding performance, but not in problem-solving performance.
Brainstorming (Jablin, 1981)		104 undergraduates (four-member groups) Time: 15 min	Proposing steps to attract more European tourists to the United States	Perceived status of members, number of ideas	Nominal brainstorming groups produced more ideas than interacting groups.
Brainstorming (Philipsen, Mulac, & Dietrich, 1979)		48 undergraduates (four-member groups) Time: 12 min	Generating ideas to solve a human relations dilemma	Number of ideas generated, number of good ideas	Interacting groups generated fewer total ideas and good ideas than nominal groups. In written condition (as opposed to verbal), no difference between nominal and interacting groups.

Table 15.2 Representative Studies of Formal Group Process Procedures (Continued)

Procedures[a] and Study	Theoretical Perspectives	Participants/Discussion Time	Task	Dependent Variables	Findings
Nominal Group Technique (NGT), Delphi, and Problem-Centered Leadership (PCL) (Miner, 1979)		240 undergraduates (four-member groups) Time: 30-min training, unlimited discussion	Assigning workers to positions	Decision quality (effectiveness), employee acceptance	PCL showed greater solution effectiveness (20% higher than NGT or Delphi). PCL had highest mean acceptance by members.
Agenda (Plott & Levine, 1978)	Mathematical Decision Rule Approach	261 paid undergraduates (21-person groups) Time: not reported	Choosing alternative alphabet letters	Appropriateness of outcome	Agendas tended to produce the decisions they were designed to influence.
Consensus (Gouran & Geonetta, 1977)		75 undergraduates (five-member groups) Time: 30 min	Discussing social issues	Agreement with group's conclusion (consensus or nonconsensus groups); frequency of statements	Statements developing themes were followed more frequently by similar statements and comments of understanding; offers of information followed more frequently by requests for information. Limited support for the consensual outcome of a decision-making discussion being functionally related to structure of communication. Groups not employing consensus demonstrated communication characterized by randomness in responses to various statements of other members.
Nominal Group Technique (NGT), natural discussion, trained leadership (Green, 1975)		70 undergraduates (five-member groups) Time: 50 min	Solving problems students noticed in course	Number of items, number of unique responses, quality of responses	No difference in quantity and quality for any groups. Natural discussion groups with permissive leaders had the most unique responses.
Consensus (C) and natural discussion (Nemiroff & King, 1975)		216 undergraduate (four-member groups) Time: 40 min	Solving NASA Moon Survival Problem	Decision quality, utilization of resources, assembly effect, time used	C groups produced higher quality decisions, utilized average and best resources more fully, and achieved assembly-effect bonus more often. C groups used 50% more time on task than natural discussion groups.
Nominal Group Technique (NGT), Delphi, natural discussion (Van de Ven & Delbecq, 1974)		420 undergraduates (seven-member groups) Time: unlimited over many meetings	Defining job description (dorm counselor)	Quantity of ideas, group satisfaction	NGT and Delphi found equally effective, and both more effective than natural discussion. NGT produced twice as many ideas as natural groups. NGT generated more unique ideas than Delphi. NGT members showed greater satisfaction than Delphi; no difference in satisfaction between Delphi and natural discussion groups.
Natural discussion vs. trained consensus (Hall & Watson, 1970)		148 managers (four- to six-member groups) Time: unlimited	Solving NASA Moon Survival Problem	Correctness of decision, use of resources, creativity, amount of synergism	Instructed groups produced superior decisions and more creative decisions, and 75% surpassed performance of most proficient member. No difference in use of available resources.
Natural discussion vs. developmental model (Maier & Maier, 1957)		194 undergraduates (four- to five-member groups) Time: unlimited (usually 30 min)	Deciding whether employee should accept new job	Quality of decision (correctness), ratio of unanimous to split decisions	Twice as many groups using developmental model reached the correct decision as the natural discussion groups; natural discussion had slightly higher frequency of unanimous decisions.

a. Procedures = independent variables.

b. Time = Length of time given to groups for discussion.

410

Encouraging Creativity

In direct contrast to agendas, which lead groups to consider issues independently of other issues, are procedures that allow for simultaneous discussion of issues and the unconstrained generation of ideas. Seven of the studies specifically investigated procedures that help groups create and generate ideas, although of the 18 procedures discussed in the literature and summarized in Table 15.1, only brainstorming and creative problem solving have received attention (see also Jarboe, Chapter 13, this volume, on group communication and creativity processes).

Brainstorming (in which a group's goal is to generate the maximum number of creative solutions to specific problems) became popular after being introduced by Osborn (1957), who argued that the average person could generate about twice as many ideas when working in a group than when working alone. Subsequent studies consistently indicate that Osborn overstated the benefits of brainstorming, for they show that nominal groups (those in which members work independently and do not interact) outproduce brainstorming groups (Jablin, 1981; Jablin et al., 1977; Mullen, Johnson, & Salas, 1991; see the review of prior research by Paulus, Dzindolet, Poletes, & Camacho, 1993). Interacting brainstorming groups repeatedly generate fewer total ideas, as well as fewer quality ideas, than nominal groups (Jablin et al., 1977; Philipsen, Mulac, & Dietrich, 1979). The inferior performance of interacting brainstorming groups has been attributed to premature evaluation of ideas, social loafing, or free riding (Diehl & Stroebe, 1987), as well as being the result of different levels of communication apprehension among members (Jablin et al., 1977). Dunnette et al. (1963) argued that some members were inhibited simply by the presence of other group members. Interacting groups with a facilitator appear to outperform groups without a facilitator when they both use brainstorming techniques, but nevertheless perform similarly to nominal groups (Offner, Kramer, & Winter, 1996). One interesting finding, however, is that electronic brainstorming groups may be more productive in terms of generating ideas than nonelectronic groups (Gallupe, Bastianutti, & Cooper, 1991). Paulus et al. (1993) conclude that the popularity of group brainstorming may derive from its *perceived* productivity, finding in a survey that most individuals believed they would generate more ideas in groups than alone, and, in a second experiment, that individuals tend to take credit for a disproportionate amount of the brainstorming activity in groups.

Two specific findings from the extant literature merit further study. First, brainstorming techniques may have impact at the *individual* level, and second, ethnic *diversity* may enhance the productivity of brainstorming groups. With regard to the first point, Kramer, Kuo, and Dailey (1997) found no differences in decision quality among untrained (group members were told simply to reach a decision), brainstorming (members were instructed in brainstorming principles with a practice session), and nominal groups (members were instructed in the use of the NGT and given a practice session). Effects on individual members were noted, in that brainstorming group members reported greater satisfaction than members of untrained groups, but no more satisfaction than individuals performing alone. With regard to the second point, McLeod et al. (1996) found that ideas produced by ethnically diverse brainstorming groups were both more effective and more feasible than those produced by homogeneous brainstorming groups, even though members of homogeneous groups reported marginally more attraction to their group.

Brainstorming is only one piece of the process of creative problem solving. Training in more complete stages of creative problem solving that involves finding new, useful problems to solve, or involves implementing solutions, in addition to simply generating solutions, has been underinvestigated (Basadur et al., 1982). Creative problem-solving techniques appear to make a difference, as members of groups trained in these techniques participate more, criticize ideas less, and produce more ideas than members of untrained groups (Firestien, 1990). Basadur et al. (1982) tested groups trained in creative problem solving at both 2-week and 4-week intervals and found that residual effects may continue after the initial training, including greater use of ideation in problem *finding* and greater preference for ideation in problem *solving*. It is interesting that although trained members indicated a greater preference for ideation, no greater use of ideation in actual problem-solving performance was evidenced.

Some investigations focusing on the analysis function of problem-solving groups have uncovered results about the effects of techniques on the creative process. More unique ideas are associated with groups' use of the NGT than with the Delphi method (Van de Ven & Delbecq, 1974), more novel judgments arise when groups are structured with exposure to a minority judgment compared to structures that exposure the group to a majority judgment (Nemeth & Wachtler, 1983; see Meyers & Brashers, Chapter 11, this volume, regarding group majority/minority research), members discussed more innovative alternatives using devil's advocacy and dialectical inquiry (Schwenk & Valacich, 1994), and interacting groups with permissive leaders produced more unique responses than nominal groups or groups with authoritarian leaders (Green, 1975).

Facilitating Analysis

From the early study by Maier and Maier (1957) on the correctness of decisions in free-discussion versus developmentally trained groups, to recent studies on the correctness of decisions using devil's advocacy, pooling, or consensus procedures (Plous, 1995), the most prevalent group process function investigated has been the assessment of how group members analyze problems. Researchers repeatedly study group decision-making analysis by attempting to measure the effectiveness of decisions produced by the analysis process.

Procedures leading to superior group decisions are consensus (compared to natural discussion, Hall & Watson, 1970; compared to free-discussion groups, Nemiroff & King, 1975; compared to devil's advocacy for an additive task, Murrell, Stewart, & Engel, 1993), the NGT (compared to free discussion, Van de Ven & Delbecq, 1974), problem-centered leadership (compared to the NGT and the Delphi method, Miner, 1979), continually interacting groups (compared to nominal groups with no interaction or staticized groups, with discussion preceding individual rankings that were then averaged, Burleson, Levine, & Samter, 1984), dialectical inquiry (compared to consensus and devil's advocacy, Schweiger, Sandberg, & Ragan, 1986; Schweiger, Sandberg, & Rechner, 1989), devil's advocacy (better on disjunctive tasks than consensus, Murrell et al., 1993; objective devil's advocacy produced higher quality decisions than emotional devil's advocacy, which used strong challenges and a negative tone, Schweiger et al., 1986; Schwenk & Valacich, 1994; Valacich & Schwenk, 1995b; compared to dialectical inquiry, Valacich & Schwenk, 1995a), leader-delayed opinion (compared to leader-outset opinion, Anderson & Balzer, 1991), stepladder (compared to conventional groups that were informed that members could derive a group solution any way they wanted, Rogelberg et al., 1992), reminder (non-leader-reminders more effective than leader-reminders, Schultz, Ketrow, & Urban, 1995), reflective thinking, and force-field analysis (trained outperformed untrained groups when they completed the requisite functions, Schultz et al., 1995).

Some analysis procedures have been compared repeatedly with one another (e.g., devil's advocacy, in which one subgroup or member critiques a proposal by a second subgroup, and dialectical inquiry, in which two subgroups negotiate between two different proposals; in this volume, see Chapters 7 [Hirokawa & Salazar] and 11 [Meyers & Brashers]). Analysis procedures, however, have undergone limited comparisons to procedures that help groups structure, create, or agree, and many procedures that affect analysis have not been cross-compared (e.g., problem-centered leadership has not been compared with leader-delayed/leader-outset opinion, nor has devil's advocacy been compared to the reflective thinking technique).

Managing Conflict and Developing Agreement

A substantial body of research has shown that a certain amount of conflict can be healthy and functional in groups and may increase members' involvement level (Pavitt & Curtis, 1994), promote cohesiveness (Nicotera, 1995), improve decision making (e.g., Janis & Mann, 1977; Schwenk, 1988), and generate creative problem solving (Nicotera, 1997). Cosier and Schwenk (1990) suggest that fostering disagreement in a structured setting may lead to better group decisions. Successful management of group conflict can lead to increased member satisfaction (Schwenk & Cosier, 1993; Schweiger et al., 1986).

A fundamental question regarding the structuring of group discussion, problem solving, and decision making is *how* conflict should be structured. For example, is it most effective to encourage a strong and emotional critique, or does a vigorous challenge insert a negative emotional tone into the group climate that distracts members from their task of reaching a high-quality decision? Valacich and Schwenk (1995b) raised the question of whether milder, more objective forms of critique might be more effective than those given in negative, emotional tones. They found that to produce the highest solution quality, questioning statements made by a group member acting in the role of devil's advocate should be objective (which they operationalized as mild critique that pointed to the possibility of alternative solutions).

In addition to methods of structuring group conflict, methods that allow groups to measure conflict have been studied. Voting procedures are methods that achieve group decisions through some predetermined criterion of support (e.g., simple majority or two-thirds majority). Unless the decision rule is unanimity, voting procedures do not require unanimous acceptance of decisions; the primary objective of this method is resolution and closure, superseding concerns for harmony or equal representation of points of view (Wood, 1984). Polling procedures assist members in determining the extent of agreement present during group discussion, but they continue to be a little-investigated tool in group research. Public polling (raising hands or voting verbally) in juries appears to diminish the likelihood of deadlock in 3-person groups, whereas in 6- and 12-person groups, open polling increases the likelihood of a hung jury (Kerr & MacCoun, 1985). Sequential polling (going around a circle with each person voting in turn), as compared to simultaneous polling (raising hands all at once), also changes individual members' votes from their prepolling preferences (Davis, Kameda, Parks, Stasson, & Zimmerman, 1989).

Some studies have emphasized the results of polling procedures rather than the process of using polling during group discussion and have focused on the emergence of unanimity from initially conflicting individual opinions. Investigating leader-led free discussion (in which the designated leader poses the problem and then conducts a permissive discussion) versus leader-led developmental discussion (in which the leader breaks the problem into parts to ensure systematic coverage of each phase), Maier and Maier (1957) determined that free-discussion groups had a slightly higher frequency of unanimous decisions. Consensus procedures have been studied widely, but generally research has focused on the manner in which these procedures help groups analyze, rather than resolve, conflict. For example, studies that compare the benefits of consensus to devil's advocacy with regard to the number of correct answers on a judgment task investigate the analysis function, rather than the agreeing function afforded by the procedure. Nemiroff and King (1975) found that consensus-trained groups took longer to complete a task than free-discussion groups, but a shorter time than groups that used dialectical inquiry or devil's advocacy. Members of consensus groups, moreover, experienced greater satisfaction and desire to continue working together (Schweiger et al., 1986) and better feelings about their group (Murrell et al. 1993), as well as greater acceptance of group decisions (Murrell et al., 1993; Schweiger et al., 1986; Schweiger et al., 1989). Polling procedures and the timing of their use may have inhibiting effects on group discussion as members see majority factions emerge. When a smaller subgroup tried to influence the group decision, Nemeth and Wachtler (1983) observed that, compared to minority-influence conditions, group members in majority-influence conditions reported feeling more awkward, embarrassed, fearful, and frustrated.

A consensus decision is one that all members have a part in shaping and that all find at least minimally acceptable as a means of accomplishing some mutual goal (Wood, 1984). Inherent in consensus procedures are the assumptions that group discussion should be cooperative and that agreement is possible. Consensus appears to have a positive reputation for potential users: Group members report greater expectations for harmony to result from consensus discussions (Priem & Price, 1991). The level of consensus achieved in a group may be a significant factor in generating commitment to a decision, as demonstrated by Schwenk and Cosier (1993), who reported members' increased commitment to decisions made in high-consensus groups but not in low-consensus groups. In that same study, groups with higher consensus about objectives made higher quality decisions than groups with lower levels. Finally, communication in consensus groups using certain procedures shows less conflict and more agreement. For example, Gouran and Geonetta (1977) noted in consensus groups that statements developing themes were followed more frequently by similar statements and comments of understanding.

Enhancing and Inhibiting Effects of Procedures on Members, Groups, and Tasks

The majority of studies reports enhanced outcomes with the use of formal procedures, but a few studies show no effects for the tested procedures, or inhibiting effects, which are explored in the following subsections.

Enhancing Effects

The effectiveness of formal procedures has been reported at the group, individual member, and task outcome levels. Although this review is concerned with research investigating the behavior of *groups,* and although there are a number of conceptual problems in drawing inferences about group-level outcomes from studies of individual performance (see Davis, 1982; Davis et al., 1989), such inferences can be drawn (Davis et al., 1989). We organize the effects observed from the various studies into effects on individual members, the group itself, and the task.

Individual member effects. Enhancing effects on individual group members using formal techniques have included changes in members' satisfaction, commitment to group decisions, memory and use of relevant information during meetings, participation, responsiveness to comments of other members, reduction in anxiety, exhibition of humor, and changes in individual decision preferences. Member satisfaction with both group communication processes and decisions made has been shown (Valacich & Schwenk, 1995a). Findings also show increased commitment of members to group decisions. For example, devil's advocacy resulted in decision commitment by members in groups with high consensus concerning group objectives compared to low-consensus groups (Schwenk & Cosier, 1993), and members of problem-centered leadership groups had the highest mean acceptance of decisions (Miner, 1979). A "priming effect" of agendas has been found on the likelihood that members will both remember and use relevant information during meetings

(Higgins, 1989; Wyer & Srull, 1981). Group members' communication has been found to be less nearly random and more responsive to comments of other group members in consensus than in nonconsensus groups (Gouran & Geonetta, 1977), and a reduction in individual member anxiety can occur with devil's advocacy (Valacich & Schwenk, 1995b). Group members trained in creative problem solving participated more, criticized ideas less, supported ideas more, and exhibited more humor than members of untrained groups (Firestien, 1990). Changes in individual verdict preferences have been observed, such that a simultaneous voting procedure changed members' decisions little or not at all, whereas individual members' votes did change if the polling procedure was sequential (Davis, Stasson, Ono, & Zimmerman, 1988), with critical third- and fourth-position not-guilty sayers preceded by guilty sayers changing votes significantly more often (Davis et al., 1989; Davis et al., 1988). An added bonus to individual members is the finding that members of interacting groups make better individual decisions subsequent to interaction than members of staticized or nominal groups (Burleson et al., 1984); structuring group discussion may not only improve the quality of decisions made by groups but also benefit individuals in their personal decision making. Some procedures thus appear to have significant enhancing effects on individual group members, although a particular procedure may be good for some people and bad for others, as with members high in preference for procedural order or communication apprehension (Pavitt, 1993; see Jablin's, 1981, finding that people high in communication apprehension gain a greater advantage from using certain brainstorming procedures than do people low in communication apprehension).

Group effects. Groups emerge as more attractive and garner increased loyalty from members as a result of using some formal procedures, as well as develop a more effective ability to subdivide tasks and avoid deadlock. Members using consensus felt better about their groups compared to devil's advocacy groups, even when group performance was lower (Murrell et al., 1993), and experienced a higher desire to continue working with that group (Schweiger et al., 1986). Consensus groups achieved the "assembly-effect bonus" (consensual decisions reached in groups were better than the average of the individual members' decisions) more often than those using free discussion (Nemiroff & King, 1975). It should be noted that because research indicates that members of homogeneous groups are more attracted to their groups than those in ethnically diverse groups (McLeod et al., 1996), the particular membership composition of groups using formal techniques may be contributing to the attraction/loyalty effects observed. Groups as a whole were felt to have used a more effective communication process by members of brainstorming and nominal groups than by members of untrained groups (Kramer et al., 1997). Procedures may help groups delimit subtasks, increase group motivation, and foster useful self-criticism (Poole, 1991). Deadlock was less likely with public polling procedures in 3-person groups, and less likely with secret ballots in 6- and 12-person groups (Kerr & MacCoun, 1985).

Task effects. Although the *quality* of group decisions has been a frequently measured outcome of studies on formal procedures, researchers have operationalized "quality" in a variety of ways (e.g., decision quality as "effective, feasible, creative, or interesting," Kramer et al., 1997; as "potential sales," Valacich & Schwenk, 1995b; or as "effectiveness of decisions," Miner, 1979). As a result, it is difficult to compare or cumulate studies that report "higher quality" results.

With this caution in mind, higher quality decisions have been detected in groups utilizing process procedures. For example, stepladder groups produced higher quality decisions and surpassed the quality of their best member 56% of the time compared to 13% in free-discussion groups (Rogelberg et al., 1992). Valacich and Schwenk (1995a) reported that objective devil's advocacy groups produced higher quality decisions than emotional devil's advocacy groups. More generally, devil's advocacy groups developed more alternative solutions and selected higher quality recommendations than dialectical inquiry or expert groups (Valacich & Schwenk, 1995a). If a group is not cohesive, or if a problem faced is particularly volatile, procedures that minimize conflict might be preferred, such as Hall's consensus rules (Hall & Watson, 1970; also see Nemiroff, Pasmore, & Ford, 1976; Pavitt, 1993). Other findings include more ideas produced in facilitated groups than groups without facilitation (Offner et al., 1996), use of the NGT producing twice as many ideas as free discussion (Van de Ven, 1974), and nonleader reminders producing higher quality decisions than leader-reminder groups (Schultz et al., 1995).

More accurate decisions also result when using particular procedures. For example, consensus has been found to be more effective with an additive task, whereas devil's advocacy was more effective with a disjunctive task (Murrell et al., 1993). Twice as many groups using a developmental model (a leader-directed discussion agenda) reached the correct decision in a judgment task in comparison with free-discussion groups (Maier & Maier, 1957). Private, in contrast to public, polling increased the rate of hung juries (Kerr & MacCoun, 1985). Face-to-face meetings proved to be less effective than computer-mediated meetings in producing quality decisions and member satisfaction with the decision-making process (Valacich & Schwenk, 1995a, 1995b), though more communication and more supportive messages may be exchanged in face-to-face groups (Valacich & Schwenk, 1995a). Comparing computer-mediated and face-to-face devil's advocacy conditions, Valacich and Schwenk (1995b) found that groups with mild-toned criticisms of proposed plans produced higher quality decisions than groups in which strong negative criticism was encouraged, with the observed difference being greater in the face-to-face groups.

Increased *quantity* of solutions occurs as well in groups utilizing selected procedures.

For example, leader delayed-opinion groups generated more alternative solutions to problems, which were also rated as more feasible and more likely to be adopted, compared to conditions in which leaders stated their opinions immediately after the presentation of the problem (Anderson & Balzer, 1991). More ideas also were produced by nominal brainstorming groups than by interacting groups (Jablin, 1981; Philipsen et al., 1979).

Finally, some procedures appear to institute higher levels of task closure (or a sense of achievement of task), as group members reported feeling the greatest lack of closure in interacting meetings as compared to those using the Delphi technique or nominal procedures (Van de Ven, 1974). Of course, the benefits accruing from using formal group process procedures are not generalizable to all tasks because *communication* in groups is affected by task type. For example, interaction among members appears to foster high-quality group decisions when the task facing the group is relatively complex, requires a considerable amount of information processing, raises value questions, or requires a multiple-stage approach (Burleson et al., 1984; Hackman & Morris, 1975; Sorenson, 1971). Some procedures are designed for organizing entire meetings where proposals are clearly differentiated and sides are cleanly defined (e.g., Robert's Rules of Order), whereas others are best used for coordinating extensive debates with multiple viewpoints (e.g., Delphi method) or for idea development and evaluation (e.g., NGT) (see Nutt's, 1984, classification of procedures by specific task).

Inhibiting Effects

Some studies report inhibiting effects with the use of formal procedures, resulting in negative outcomes, or "dark side" effects (see Poole, 1991). For example, Burleson et al. (1984) reported a partial assembly effect, where consensual decisions of interacting groups were not better than the decisions of the best individuals.

Researchers acknowledge that some procedures slow groups down; indeed, procedures are intended to slow groups down somewhat. Some studies have shown discussion time to be longer under delayed-leader opinion groups (Anderson & Balzer, 1991; Bryson & Roerig, 1989), with consensus groups using 50% more time on their task than free-discussion groups (Nemiroff & King, 1975), objective computer-mediated devil's advocacy formats taking more time than emotional face-to-face conditions (Valacich & Schwenk, 1995b), and Delphi groups taking twice as long as no-procedure groups in task completion (Nemiroff & King, 1975). Unanimous decision rule procedures have been found to lead to increased time to reach agreement (Castore & Murnighan, 1978) and greater probability of group impasses (Hastie, Penrod, & Pennington, 1983).

Other inhibiting effects from the use of formal procedures have included groupthink, grouphate, blocking, boredom, frustration, unexpressed ideas, mistaken estimation of group performance, blocking of ideas, dysfunctional conflict, and unequal participation. Cohesive, highly structured groups may have a proclivity to sap members' individual initiative, creativity, and willingness to criticize, resulting in inappropriate premature solutions (Janis, 1972). Members of devil's advocacy groups not only had less desire to work with their groups in the future (Schwenk & Cosier, 1993) but also reported feeling more awkward, embarrassed, fearful, and frustrated using procedures that fostered majority-influence conditions, in which a majority of members attempted to change the decision of other members (Nemeth & Wachtler, 1983). Groups using devil's advocacy, pooling, or consensus procedures overestimated their group performance (Plous, 1995). Studies of brainstorming procedures have often reported negative member evaluations and satisfaction levels (Dunnette et al., 1963; Mullen et al., 1991), and brainstorming prescriptions did not overcome the blocking of new ideas by individual members (Diehl & Stroebe, 1987). Emotional devil's advocacy (negative criticism

or carping) has been found to stifle group decision outcomes in face-to-face groups, promote a higher incidence of critical evaluative comments, and introduce dysfunctional conflict as members become committed to and argue for one alternative (Valacich & Schwenk, 1995b). Van de Ven (1974) reported that equality of participation increased in nominal groups compared to free-discussion or Delphi groups, as did a perceived sense of closure, accomplishment, and interest in future phases of problem solving.

Explanations for Observed Effects

Although studies often report important differences in effects on members, groups, and tasks with the use of formal techniques, these findings themselves do not explain why such differences exist. Researchers who have offered useful explanations for their reported findings have postulated the effectiveness of formal procedure utilization to be the result of (a) improved substantive group discussion, (b) changes in group discussion processes, (c) improved individual performance, (d) enhanced group climate, (e) appropriate interpretation of task by members, or (f) inhibited reactions to the presence of other group members. We treat each of these in turn.

Improved Group Discussion

Research shows that procedures affect whether or not group members discuss relevant choices, point out potential negative consequences, offer criticisms of ideas and proposals, engage in delayed-leader opinion-giving, and stimulate the expression of a wide range of ideas. First, the quality of a group decision appears to be associated with the performance of certain analytic functions (see Gouran & Hirokawa, 1983; Hirokawa, 1982, 1983a, 1983b, 1988; Hirokawa & Pace, 1983; Hirokawa & Scheerhorn, 1986; in this volume, see Chapters 1 [Gouran], 2 [Poole], and 7 [Hirokawa & Salazar]). Hirokawa (1985) discerned that group decision-making performance depends on members' abilities to understand the choice-making situation and assess the negative consequences of alternative choices; groups satisfying these functions produced higher quality decisions than groups not satisfying them. These results imply that the effectiveness of a formal process technique may depend on its ability to improve group discussion through structured analysis. Second, the feeling of becoming submerged in a group and losing awareness of one's own individuality (deindividuation) may account for lessened evaluation apprehension and increased incidence of critical evaluative comments among individual group members in carping (strong, negative criticism) devil's advocacy conditions (Valacich & Schwenk, 1995b). Third, procedures that require formal leaders to delay stating their opinions until later in the discussion may produce higher quality alternatives because members make more efficient use of their collective pool of knowledge (Anderson & Balzer, 1991). Finally, Poole (1991) suggests that such procedures as synectics operate to jar members out of their mental "ruts" and permit the free flow of ideas or associations that do not occur when members feel natural social inhibitions.

Changes in Group Discussion Processes

In addition to improving the substantive discussion of specific ideas and opinions, formal procedures may affect the manner in which group discussion occurs. It has been suggested that some procedures invoke different communication *processes* and cognitive processing within groups. For example, Valacich and Schwenk (1995a) note that the sharp critical comments of an emotional devil's advocate in group discussion seemed to encourage other members to become committed to one particular alternative, argue for it, and argue against other alternatives. They further suggest that anonymity may have caused computer-mediated groups to mimic the carping devil's advocacy and, in effect, turn the session into a shouting match among proponents of alternative solutions. Changes in cognitive processes of members during discussion has

been noted and attributed to formal procedures. Various studies have revealed that using *problem-solving functions* and adapting them to the situation is more important than adhering to suggested steps of a specific procedure (Hirokawa, 1985), and that enhancing the *quality of thought* of group members affects various outcomes (see the overview by Jarboe, 1996, and studies by Priem & Price, 1991, and Schwenk & Cosier, 1993).

Improved Individual Performance

Formal procedures, by providing rules accessible to all members of the group, enable a group to harness individual thinking in a sensible structure by coordinating members' thinking, setting objective ground rules, eliminating member participation differences or premature idea criticism, and increasing members' sense of personal involvement. Examining the effects of training in creative problem solving, Basadur et al. (1982) were confronted with anomalous results: Training led to no preference for ideation in problem finding, yet practice and performance in problem finding showed improvement in results. They suggest that it may be the case that participants can be made to *enact* problem finding (behavior) and yet still not *like* problem finding (attitude). Increased commitment of individuals to group decisions may result from procedures that equalize participation, because research indicates that participation in making a decision increases commitment to it (Poole, 1991); procedures with rules that increase group involvement help to level the playing field. Increased member participation may result from a reduction in uncertainty, as procedures help members understand the situation and gain a sense of control (Poole, 1991). Hewes (1996) argues that turn-taking management devices, for example, regulate the flow of communication while providing the opportunity for members to state their evaluations of the task and, thereby, enhance their sense of involvement.

Enhanced Group Climate

Unmanaged conflicts threaten a climate of cooperation in groups by polarizing positions and creating the potential for bad feelings to develop. Escalating conflict spirals, or equally dangerous cycles of conflict avoidance, are avoided by procedures that help groups directly confront existing disagreements (Poole, 1991). Straw polls, for example, allow disagreements to emerge, but members are free to indicate the tentative nature of their initial votes. The use of a devil's advocate who does not necessarily personally agree with the counterarguments offered prevents premature attachment to a faulty decision. A climate of accessible, shared leadership may result from procedures that require leaders to refrain from favoring a particular alternative at the outset of a discussion and may set the pattern for a noncritical atmosphere during group discussion. Anderson and Balzer (1991) suggest that the withholding of leader opinion early in a discussion may allow group members to "piggyback" on early group ideas as well as suggest completely different alternatives without fear of criticism. Cartwright and Zander (1968) argue that when members are aware of leadership functions, through exposure to alternative procedures for running meetings, they tend to help with these functions (see also Poole, 1991).

Appropriate Interpretation of Task

Some groups experience difficulties when members are not clear about their group's goals. Inappropriate solutions and wasted efforts may result when group members focus their efforts on misperceived tasks. As discussed above, research indicates that dialectical inquiry and expert groups are not as effective as devil's advocacy groups in generating large numbers of solutions. Group members in both expert and dialectical inquiry treatments, for example, may view their task as one of choosing between in-hand solutions rather than generating more solutions, whereas devil's advocacy groups may feel a greater

need to develop a viable solution (Valacich & Schwenk, 1995a). Although "real-world" groups may not benefit from procedures, such as the fishbone diagram or is/is not analysis, that help avoid work on misperceived tasks, research has been lacking on these procedures. Furthermore, it is not always clear from reported studies that participants perceived the task correctly (e.g., improving the quality of decision or increasing the number of ideas generated).

Inhibited Reactions to the Presence of Other Group Members

The inferior performance of interacting brainstorming groups to individuals performing alone may be attributable to the effort of members to make a good impression on one another, the withholding of ideas, or self-censoring (Gallupe et al., 1991; Paulus et al., 1993). Although criticism of ideas may inhibit contributions, the group experience itself may lead some members to produce fewer ideas or ideas of diminished quality as a result of social loafing or free riding. Albanese and Van Fleet (1985) discovered a free-riding tendency in groups related to group size, such that it increases as size increases. Postulated that members compare the benefits of contributing to the group's task versus free riding and tend more to choose the latter as the size of the group increases. Albanese and Van Fleet suggested that the basic strategy for countering the free-riding tendency may be to provide formal group structures that link the individual member's incentive system to the group's success. As group size increases, individuals focus on the group's generation of ideas and exert less than full individual effort (see Diehl & Stroebe, 1987).

Diehl and Stroebe conclude that, although many factors play a role, the major inhibitory factor is productivity blocking (member behavior that disrupts or interrupts the idea of another member), which results when individuals have to contend with other members generating ideas at the same time as they are attempting to generate their own. Despite the demonstrable problems associated with group brainstorming, the technique remains a popular tool, which may be the result of individual member illusion of group productivity engendered by the technique. Paulus et al. (1993) surveyed *expected* performance in group brainstorming and discovered that most individuals believed they would generate more ideas in groups than they would alone.

LIMITATIONS AND SUGGESTIONS FOR RESEARCH ON GROUP PROCEDURES

The literature on the effects of formal procedures on discussion, problem-solving, and decision-making groups suffers in a variety of areas: (a) atheoretical approaches to research questions, (b) difficulties with methodological design, (c) unaccounted-for normative and affective factors in the decision processes, (d) tendencies to focus on outcomes to the exclusion of processes, (e) absence of synthetic models for the effects observed, (f) failure to investigate the effect of experience with techniques, and (g) omission of cultural and diversity variables. We examine these in detail.

Atheoretical Approaches to Research Questions

The vast majority of the studies summarized in Table 15.2 could be characterized as "variable analytic" rather than theory driven, resulting in findings that do not confirm, challenge, or extend extant theories of group decision making (in this volume, see Chapters 1 [Gouran], 2 [Poole], and 7 [Hirokawa & Salazar]). Only six of the studies contained theoretical underpinnings (Social Decision Scheme Model, Functional Theory, Vigilant Interaction Theory, Structuration Theory, and Mathematical Decision Rule Approach). The Social Decision Scheme Model was used to create a thought experiment, particularly to extrapolate group outcomes from individual results, to test the effects of polling sequence and timing (Davis et al., 1989; Kerr & MacCoun, 1985). Plott and Levine (1978), who

investigated the manner in which a group's decision may be affected by controlling only the agenda, offered a mathematical approach to procedural influence on group decisions that created a "stochastic" group member, influenced by an economic decision-rule approach, but departed from the traditional decision-theoretic mode of analysis by treating individuals as random variables over decision rules. Hirokawa's (1985) work tested Functional Theory, as well as Vigilant Interaction Theory (Hirokawa & Rost, 1992). Most recently, Structuration Theory has been imported into an investigation of the differences in decision quality of untrained, brainstorming, and nominal groups (applying Structuration Theory to noncomputer-augmented groups versus procedures in face-to-face settings, Kramer et al., 1997). Poole and colleagues (Poole & DeSanctis, 1992; Poole, DeSanctis, Kirsch, & Jackson, 1995) have used Adaptive Structuration Theory to study how groups appropriate the formal procedures (e.g., ranking, brainstorming, and polling) embedded in group decision support system (GDSS) software.

There are, however, other theoretical approaches to group communication that could guide research on formal group procedures. Currently unexplored matters include:

1. *Field Theory*'s argument that the common life-space created by a group is sustained by group cohesion, which enhances group decision making, providing potential insights into which variables should be taken into account in selecting procedures to help groups structure, analyze, create, or agree;

2. *Interaction Theory*'s concern with differences between consensus and nonconsensus groups (see, for example, Gouran's, 1969, finding that consensus groups were characterized by more orientation statements than nonconsensus groups), which has the potential to offer useful explanations concerning which procedures that helped groups agree should be applied in certain contexts;

3. *Symbolic Convergence Theory*'s position that the integration by group members of shared fantasy themes into a unified rhetorical vision gives them a correspondingly broader view, which would be useful for explaining which procedures generate member support for decisions, as well as which procedures that help groups create ideas offer the most effective ways to enhance the generation of ideas (see Bormann, 1972, 1982, 1986, 1996);

4. *Persuasive Arguments Theory*'s explanation of the process of social influence in decision-making groups, which holds that members shift opinions as a result of persuasive arguments favoring the direction of that shift (see Alderton & Frey, 1986; Meyers & Brashers, Chapter 11, this volume; Seibold, Meyers, & Sunwolf, 1996), which could explain the manner in which procedures that help groups agree function to influence individual members' opinion shifts; and

5. The *Bona Fide Groups Perspective*'s emphasis, among other things, on examining the relationship between group context and decision-making processes (Putnam & Stohl, 1990, 1996), which might be applied to investigate the external variables that affect the success of using specific formal techniques in task groups.

These and other theories available to guide research on formal group process procedures (see Poole, Chapter 2, this volume) offer robust explanatory power for understanding the effectiveness of these techniques.

Difficulties With Methodological Design

Notwithstanding the valuable knowledge gleaned from the previous research, there remain certain methodological problems that need to be solved. First, the research designs employed to study formal procedures often are oversimplifications, with some incorporating low-effort, nonconsequential tasks in which many "real-world" group processes fail to develop. For example, most investigations have limited the number of available ways for a group to approach a problem, such as specifying the use of only dialectical inquiry or devil's advocacy (Valacich & Schwenk, 1995a), as opposed to offering any of the variety of other structuring procedures that are available to approach the task. Second, some studies did not control for groups' failure to follow procedures, as with groups that were given a planning period but neglected to use it properly (Hackman & Kaplan, 1974). Third, some studies did not plan for members' resistance to procedures, such as the finding that more than 50% of user groups did not follow procedures faithfully (Poole & DeSanctis, 1990; see Poole, 1991). Fourth, some designs insufficiently allowed for an investigation of the *mechanisms* by which process techniques might work, for example, the "black box" basis for training managers in creativity techniques (Basadur et al., 1982), in which training was provided "just to see what happens," without attempting preliminarily to discover what relevant attitudes or behaviors might be involved.

Furthermore, threats to the external validity of studies through ecological design errors persist in research on group procedures, including the consistent use of student participants, lack of training, artificial motivation of members, nonconsequential tasks, and limited time with minimal interaction conditions (see Table 15.2). The costly requirements of "real-world" replication (e.g., complex tasks with consequential outcomes), which demands significant time and effort by participants, create serious obstacles to routine empirical verification of inferences drawn from more limited laboratory studies. One consequence seems to have been the practice of having students engage in truncated task discussions (5- to 20-minute discussions appearing commonly) and simulations. When student groups perform nonconsequential tasks and truncated discussions, the criticism of developed plans, for example, involves milder statements than the strong criticisms offered in "real-world" task groups (Schwenk & Cosier, 1980; Valacich & Schwenk, 1995b).

The overwhelming majority of studies have relied on undergraduate college students (29 of the 33 studies); some have involved participants from business-oriented groups (i.e., engineers, Basadur et al., 1982; managers, Hall & Watson, 1970; utility company employees, Hirokawa & Rost, 1992; and middle- and upper-middle-level managers, Schweiger et al., 1989). Although the involvement of student participants undoubtedly reflects the difficulty of gaining access to "real-world" discussion, problem-solving, and decision-making groups, as well as the inherent problems of conducting field work, the extension of findings from student-participants to concerns faced by ongoing natural groups is correspondingly limited. *Replicated* observations with nonstudent groups have been neglected.

Studies also have varied in terms of *decision saliency* for group members (see Pavitt's, 1993, summary of studies on this dimension). In a longitudinal field investigation of 24 companies, Dean and Sharfman (1996) studied situations where the decision would affect members. Most studies have utilized simulated business problems, such as the recommended assigning of employees to jobs (Miner, 1979), selecting managers (Murrell et al., 1993), managing strategic management dilemmas (Schweiger et al., 1989), making company acquisitions (Schwenk & Cosier, 1993), or assigning sales territory (Schwenk & Valacich, 1994; Valacich & Schwenk, 1995a). Others have involved the NASA Moon Survival Problem (Burleson et al., 1984; Hall & Watson, 1970; Nemiroff & King, 1975), mock trial jury deliberations (Davis et al., 1989; Kerr & MacCoun, 1985), student-relevant issues—such as what to do about plagiarizing (Hirokawa, 1985), developing a program for high school students visiting a university (Kramer et al., 1997), offering ideas to improve campus security (Offner et al., 1996), and advising unwed pregnant teens (Schultz et al., 1995)—and even artificial abstractions, such as comparing figures (Nemeth & Wachtler, 1983) and choosing

alphabet letters (Plott & Levine, 1978). The degree to which the tasks are salient to the lives of group members may affect their motivation to participate, as well as the ease with which they are willing to either surrender divergent viewpoints or influence other members to surrender their viewpoints. Saliency of the task and its outcomes to participating members must be considered alongside traditionally studied outcome variables, such as member satisfaction, time required to reach a decision, number of ideas generated, or ability to reach consensus.

Problem solving and decision making are multiphased activities in which outcomes can be assessed in numerous ways, though some variables appear to be understudied relative to the use of formal procedures. Dependent variables that have been well studied include the quality of decisions made, quantity of ideas, correctness of decision, and member satisfaction (see Table 15.2). Variables that have received some attention include use of resources (Hall & Watson, 1970; Nemiroff & King, 1975), acceptance of members' decisions (Schweiger et al., 1986), change in individual members' votes (Davis et al., 1989), members' confidence in the decision (Priem & Price, 1991), members' participation (Firestien, 1990), individual members' mood (Nemeth & Wachtler, 1983; Priem & Price, 1991), group atmosphere (Murrell et al., 1993), perceived status of members (Jablin, 1981), length of time to decision (Kerr & MacCoun, 1985; Nemiroff & King, 1975; Schweiger et al., 1989), novelty of judgment (Nemeth & Wachtler, 1983), criticism or support for ideas (Firestien, 1990), achievement of task functions (Hirokawa, 1985), number and validity of assumptions made by a group (Schweiger et al., 1986), and reasons offered for solutions (Schultz et al., 1995).

Although communication during group decision making has been understudied, some researchers have preserved and analyzed the group process of decision making itself, by recording and transcribing all of a group's communication and noting solution clarifications, supportive and critical remarks, and questions (see Valacich & Schwenk, 1995a, 1995b). The collection of participant narratives concerning firsthand subjective group discussion and problem-solving and decision-making experiences, as well as the utilization of ethnographic methods, offers new methodological avenues that avoid some of the limitations of laboratory studies and field experiments.

In summary, research on group procedures suffers from a number of significant methodological concerns. It should be noted, however, that these concerns are consistent with the observations described and decried by Frey (1996) in a review of the history of group communication and decision-making research. He found that most studies assessed student, zero-history laboratory groups meeting only once to solve researcher-created (often artificial) tasks (see also Cragan & Wright, 1990; Frey, 1994b; Scheerhorn, Geist, & Teboul, 1994; Sykes, 1990). This history illuminates the underinvestigation of some constructs, such as *group history*, despite ample evidence that group members orient their talk to the discourse that preceded it (see Bonito & Hollingshead, 1997, as well as Arrow & McGrath's, 1993, investigation of the effects of member change and continuity on group structure, process, and performance). Other constructs that remain largely unexplored are the effects of *embeddedness* in larger institutional contexts (Bushe & Johnson's, 1989, study of contextual variables affecting task group outcomes in organizations accounted for 41% of the variance in task accomplishment), the impact of changing *attendance* (Arrow & McGrath, 1993), *membership changes* (see Arrow & McGrath, 1993, who found that for certain tasks, groups with a guest member or spontaneous membership changes performed better than groups with stable membership and demonstrated higher cohesiveness), and *group size*, which is an important factor in the distribution of participation (Bonito & Hollingshead, 1997).

A focus on natural group issues with discussion procedures suggests another avenue for research: examination of the effects of *time*, addressing how the use of formal procedures changes over the course of several meetings. To what degree are these procedures *recreated* by members as they become more familiar with their use, as they address a multiplicity of tasks, and as leadership and membership changes? Any of, or all, these factors (history, embeddedness, attendance, membership changes, group size, and time) may interact with formal procedures to affect group communication and task outcomes.

To enhance the vitality of research on group process procedures, we encourage researchers to find ways to embrace a *participant-centered agenda* to inform the design of their studies. A connected, cooperative, and collaborative approach to research with "real-world" participants can expand knowledge, while at the same time privileging the voices and experiences of the people whose lives are most likely to be affected by the use or nonuse of these procedures.

Unaccounted-for Normative and Affective Factors in Decision Processes

Zero-history groups operating under severe task time constraints (e.g., 15 minutes) have little chance to develop group norms regarding their communication processes or the structured procedures they are being asked to utilize. Contractor and Seibold (1993), for example, used computer simulations designed to measure how groups appropriate and use a group decision support system (GDSS), which combines communication, computer, and decision technologies to facilitate group work. They observed that it took a considerable numbers of trials using the GDSS before interactional patterns and appropriation norms stabilized. Nor has research on formal techniques taken into account the finding that the nature of member participation changes as a function of how experts and novices learn to collaborate on a task (Clark & Schaefer, 1989; Isaacs & Clark, 1987).

Members of time-starved task groups may also direct little, if any, effort toward the social dimension of the group (see Keyton, Chapter

8, this volume), particularly if the group meets only once and will not be reconstructed. The social dimension is crucial in "real-world" groups. Understanding changes as members become more familiar, not only with each other over time but also with their assigned task and the formal procedure being used, has been neglected. Scheerhorn et al.'s (1994) study of natural decision-making groups (board of trustees, management council, finance department, sales teams, hospital task force, and departmental hotel chain meeting) speculated that groups develop norms regarding preferred communicative episodes and the amount of time to be spent on each type. Truncated discussion times in laboratory studies may also obscure the "real-world" phenomenon of "impasse." When artificial groups are instructed to reach a decision in 30 minutes, for example, more agreement may be observed than might occur when group members make complex decisions that will have some effect on them. In the "real world," decisional impasses are more frequent, and research should find a way to reflect that possibility (Thompson et al., 1988).

Tendencies to Focus on Outcome

Although Hirokawa's (1985) Functional Theory and Hirokawa and Rost's (1992) applied study of Vigilant Interaction Theory are clearly process oriented in that they investigate the content of group decision-making processes, most research testing formal procedures has been overwhelmingly outcome oriented. Most often, a single decision process is assessed by noting the outcomes that occur, and the study is influenced by two widely accepted tautologies (that good decisions are good and bad decisions are bad) that ignore the fundamental questions of whether ineffective discussion processes may result in good outcomes and whether quantitatively measured poor outcomes may result in enhancing effects on group processes. In investigating group decision process effectiveness, Reagan and Rohrbaugh (1990) argued that research

designs that assess the effectiveness of a particular form of decision process on the basis of outcome data do not take into account the possibility that unreasonable group processes may be linked over time with a windfall. Outcome-focused research marginalizes the role of communication in the emergence of decisions and results in a dearth of information about *how* groups enact, modify, and recreate the specific procedures they use.

Because practical constraints limit the scope of any research study, the findings may offer little insight or definitive knowledge into the entire process of problem solving. Studies of group brainstorming, for example, typically investigate how members generate alternative solutions to problems but stop short of how they subsequently evaluate the solutions generated. Frey's (1994a, 1994b) call for group communication researchers to employ the Naturalistic Paradigm and Putnam and Stohl's (1990, 1996) call for investigations of *bona fide groups* (in this volume, see Chapters 1 [Gouran] and 2 [Poole]) underscore the need to examine the contextualized boundaries of formal process techniques.

Absence of Synthetic Models to Explain Effects

The general failure of researchers studying formal procedures to offer conceptual frameworks to explain the effects predicted or observed has left gaps in (a) organizing the findings of various studies, (b) relating observations of one study to the previous literature, and (c) providing unified themes to guide future investigations of procedural effects. A model proposed by Bonito and Hollingshead (1997) to organize the literature on participation in groups is an example of the power such a model can provide in enhancing understanding of what is known and what remains to be known about group processes. Their two-dimensional model illuminates the role of antecedent conditions (group/member/task characteristics, technology, and time) that precede participation opportunities in groups and the consequences of participation (on those who hear it, the group decision, and subsequent acts by members), which suggests the dynamic nature by which multiple effects provide a feedback loop into future antecedent conditions. Similarly, the model of perspectives concerning the effectiveness of decision processes offered by Reagan and Rohrbaugh (1990) uses a competing values approach that emphasizes potentially conflicting demands on the group decision-making process. The unique contribution of this model is that it provides a conceptual framework within which four perspectives can be juxtaposed against one another, as well as against the values most salient to each perspective. In a similar vein, the Function Impact Model proposed in this chapter is offered as but one means of interpreting (and investigating) the potential impacts of formal procedures on discussion, problem-solving, and decision-making processes and outcomes.

Another useful model that generates potential explanations for observed group problem-solving processes is Broome and Fulbright's (1995) multistage influence model of barriers to group problem solving (utilizing the point of view of organizational participants). Broome and Fulbright focus attention on questions about the effects of cultural diversity on group participation, communication barriers to full participation, resource constraints on effective decision results, and the influence of organizational culture.

Failure to Investigate the Effect of Experience With Techniques

Past studies have focused predominantly on single meetings of groups. As a consequence, researchers have not investigated sufficiently what effects increased familiarity and experience with particular techniques might have on variables of interest (e.g., decreased time in meetings, increased productivity, members' increased acceptance of decision, and members' satisfaction with group decision). What little research does exist points to the need to take experience into account. Schweiger et al. (1989), for example, investigating dialectical inquiry, devil's advocacy, and consensus procedures, noted that experience with each technique improved group performance.

Omission of Cultural and Diversity Variables

Only a few studies have investigated the relationship between members' cultural backgrounds and preference for formal techniques in task groups, even though diversity of membership has become increasingly salient in "real-world" group contexts, especially in groups in organizations (see Haslett & Ruebush, Chapter 5, this volume). Kirchmeyer (1993) attempted to account for the "low" contribution levels of minorities (defined in the dominant culture's terms) in multicultural task groups, and Kirchmeyer and Cohen (1992), who examined the effects of constructive conflict on culturally diverse task groups, found that members of ethnic minorities contributed considerably less to decisions than nonminorities. A theoretical model of the dynamics underlying the experiences of women and people of color in demographically diverse task groups is offered by Elsass and Graves (1997), who suggest that diversity-related processes may differentially affect individuals' task behaviors. Researchers have tacitly assumed that use of formal process procedures in groups should minimize individual differences by enabling and coordinating members' contributions through the requirements of each technique. Explicit tests of that assumption are much needed, especially with demographically diverse groups (see Perez, Hosch, Ponder, & Trejo's, 1993, study of the effects of defendants' and jurors' ethnicity on jury decision making).

In addition to ethnic, as well as gender, differences, diversity of membership may include divergent levels of commitment and types of goals. Most prescriptive procedures for improving the quality of group processes are designed for either cooperative or competitive groups, but not for mixed-motive groups. Thompson et al. (1988) have suggested that groups involved in negotiation tasks, for example, have members with diverse resources, as well as diverse motivations, that need to be taken into account in prescribing the use of formal discussion procedures. Diversity effects in task groups may enhance, alter, or override the demonstrated effects of formal process procedures, as reviewed earlier in this chapter.

CONCLUSION

Few aspects of organizational life have been criticized more than group meetings (see Seibold, 1979). As a tool, the group meeting has been broadly maligned, yet the work that moves our social, economic, governmental, health care, and legal organizations is largely accomplished in decision-making and problem-solving groups that set agendas, adopt goals, address problems, and choose among alternative solutions. It is vital for the well-being of society that this group work be performed effectively and successfully. Group decisions are increasingly consequential, governing what things are done or not done, what directions are pursued or ignored, and whose voice is heard or dismissed. In a growing society where the individual's voice may be lost, group work is fundamentally concerned with the use and exercise of applied power, and research concerning the process of solving problems and agreeing on decisions provides a window to the enactment of that power.

Table 15.1 reflects the rich variety of prescriptive techniques for task groups that already have been developed and points to the promise of new directions in the creation of systematic programs of applied research that inform group practitioners about how they can choose, use, adapt, and recreate these procedures. What distinguishes empirical scholarship on formal group process procedures is its inherent capacity to improve the vast world of human problem solving and decision making and, thereby, improve the quality of the lives of people in communities everywhere.

REFERENCES

Albanese, R., & Van Fleet, D. D. (1985). Rational behavior in groups: The free-riding tendency. *Academy of Management Review, 10,* 244-255.

Alderton, S. M., & Frey, L. R. (1986). Argumentation in small group decision-making. In R. Y. Hirokawa & M. S. Poole (Eds.), *Communication and group decision-making* (pp. 157-174). Beverly Hills, CA: Sage.

Anderson, L. E., & Balzer, W. K. (1991). The effects of timing of leaders' opinions on problem-solving groups: A field experiment. *Group & Organization Studies, 16,* 86-101.

Arrow, H., & McGrath, J. E. (1993). Membership matters: How member change and continuity affect small group structure, process, and performance. *Small Group Research, 24,* 334-361.

Basadur, M., Graen, G. B., & Green, S. G. (1982). Training in creative problem solving: Effects on ideation and problem finding and solving in an industrial research organization. *Organizational Behavior and Human Performance, 30,* 41-70.

Bonito, J. A., & Hollingshead, A. B. (1997). Participation in small groups. In B. R. Burleson (Ed.), *Communication yearbook 20* (pp. 227-261). Thousand Oaks, CA: Sage.

Bormann, E. G. (1972). Fantasy and rhetorical vision: The rhetorical criticism of social reality. *Quarterly Journal of Speech, 58,* 396-407.

Bormann, E. G. (1982). Colloquy I. Fantasy and rhetorical vision: Ten years later. *Quarterly Journal of Speech, 58,* 396-407.

Bormann, E. G. (1986). Symbolic convergence theory and communication in group decision-making. In R. Y. Hirokawa & M. S. Poole (Eds.), *Communication and group decision-making* (pp. 219-236). Beverly Hills, CA: Sage.

Bormann, E. G. (1996). Symbolic convergence theory and communication in group decision making. In R. Y. Hirokawa & M. S. Poole (Eds.), *Communication and group decision making* (2nd ed., pp. 81-113). Thousand Oaks, CA: Sage.

Bowers, D. G., & Hausser, D. L. (1977). Work group types and intervention effects in organizational development. *Administrative Science Quarterly, 22,* 76-96.

Brenner, M. (1973). The next-in-line effect. *Journal of Verbal Learning and Verbal Behavior, 12,* 320-323.

Broome, B. J., & Fulbright, L. (1995). A multistage influence model of barriers to group problem solving: A participant-generated agenda for small group research. *Small Group Research, 26,* 25-55.

Bryson, J., & Roerig, W. D. (1989). Mobilizing innovation efforts: The case of governmental strategic planning. In A. H. Van de Ven, H. L. Angle, & M. S. Poole (Eds.), *Research on the management of innovation: The Minnesota studies* (pp. 583-610). Cambridge, MA: Ballinger.

Burleson, B. R., Levine, B. J., & Samter, W. (1984). Decision-making procedure and decision quality. *Human Communication Research, 10,* 557-574.

Bushe, G. R., & Johnson, A. L. (1989). Contextual and internal variables affecting task group outcomes in organizations. *Group & Organization Studies, 14,* 462-482.

Cartwright, D., & Zander, A. (1968). Leadership and performance of group functions: Introduction. In D. Cartwright & A. Zander (Eds.), *Group dynamics: Research and theory* (3rd ed., pp. 301-318). New York: Harper & Row.

Castore, C. H., & Murnighan, J. K. (1978). Determinants of support for group decisions. *Organizational Behavior and Human Performance, 22,* 75-92.

Chung, K. H., & Ferris, M. J. (1971). An inquiry of the nominal group process. *Academy of Management Journal, 14,* 520-524.

Clark, H. H., & Schaefer, E. F. (1989). Contributing to discourse. *Cognitive Science, 13,* 259-294.

Collaros, P. A., & Anderson, L. R. (1969). The effect of perceived expertness upon creativity of members of brainstorming groups. *Journal of Applied Psychology, 53,* 159-163.

Comadena, M. E. (1984). Brainstorming groups: Ambiguity tolerance, communication apprehension, task attraction, and individual productivity. *Small Group Behavior, 15,* 251-264.

Contractor, N. S., & Seibold, D. R. (1993). Theoretical frameworks for the study of structuring processes in group decision support systems: Adaptive structuration theory and self-organizing systems theory. *Human Communication Research, 19,* 528-563.

Cosier, R. A. (1978). The effects of three potential aids for making strategic decisions on predictive accuracy. *Organizational Behavior and Human Performance, 22,* 295-306.

Cosier, R. A., & Schwenk, C. R. (1990). Agreement and thinking alike: Ingredients for poor decisions. *Academy of Management Executive, 4,* 69-74.

Cragan, J. F., & Wright, D. W. (1990). Small group communication research of the 1980s: A synthesis and critique. *Communication Studies, 41,* 212-236.

Davis, J. H. (1982). Social interaction as a combinatorial process in group decision. In H. Braatter, J. H. Davis, & G. Stocker-Kreichgauer (Eds.), *Group decision making* (pp. 17-58). London: Academic Press.

Davis, J. H., Kameda, T., Parks, C., Stasson, M., & Zimmerman, S. (1989). Some social mechanics of group decision making: The distribution of opinion, polling sequence, and implications for consensus. *Journal of Personality and Social Psychology, 57,* 1000-1012.

Davis, J. H., Stasson, M., Ono, K., & Zimmerman, S. (1988). Effects of straw polls on group decision making: Sequential voting pattern, timing, and local majorities. *Journal of Personality and Social Psychology, 55,* 918-926.

Dean, J. W., Jr., & Sharfman, M. P. (1996). Does decision process matter? A study of strategic decision-making effectiveness. *Academy of Management Journal, 39,* 368-396.

Delbecq, A. L., & Van de Ven, A. H. (1971). A group process model for problem identification and program planning. *Journal of Applied Behavioral Science, 7,* 466-491.

Deutsch, M. (1973). *The resolution of conflict.* New Haven, CT: Yale University Press.

Dewey, J. (1910). *How we think.* Boston: D. C. Heath.

Diehl, M., & Stroebe, W. (1987). Productivity loss in brainstorming groups: Toward the solution of a riddle. *Journal of Personality and Social Psychology, 53,* 497-509.

Dillon, P. C., Graham, W. K., & Aidells, A. L. (1972). Brainstorming on a "hot" problem: Effects of training and practice on individual and group performance. *Journal of Applied Psychology, 56,* 487-490.

Dunnette, M. D., Campbell, J., & Jaastad, R. (1963). The effect of group participation on brainstorming effectiveness for two industrial samples. *Journal of Applied Psychology, 47,* 30-37.

Elsass, P. M., & Graves, L. M. (1997). Demographic diversity in decision-making groups: The experiences of women and people of color. *Academy of Management Review, 22,* 964-973.

Erffmeyer, R. C., & Lane, I. M. (1984). Quality and acceptance of an evaluative task: The effects of four group decision-making formats. *Group & Organization Studies, 9,* 509-529.

Firestien, R. L. (1990). Effects of creative problem-solving training on communication behaviors in small groups. *Small Group Research, 21,* 507-521.

Folger, J. P., & Poole, M. S. (1984). *Working through conflict.* Glenview, IL: Scott, Foresman.

Folger, J. P., Poole, M. S., & Stutman, R. (1993). *Working through conflict: A communication perspective* (2nd ed.). Glenview, IL: Scott, Foresman.

Frey, L. R. (1994a). The call of the field: Studying communication in natural groups. In L. R. Frey (Ed.), *Group communication in context: Studies of natural groups* (pp. ix-xiv). Hillsdale, NJ: Lawrence Erlbaum.

Frey, L. R. (1994b). The naturalistic paradigm: Studying small groups in the postmodern era. *Small Group Research, 25,* 551-557.

Frey, L. R. (1996). Remembering and "re-membering": A history of theory and research on communication and group decision making. In R. Y. Hirokawa & M. S. Poole (Eds.), *Communication and group decision making* (2nd ed., pp. 19-51). Thousand Oaks, CA: Sage.

Gallupe, R. B., Bastianutti, L. M., & Cooper, W. H. (1991). Unblocking brainstorms. *Journal of Applied Psychology, 76,* 137-142.

Gouran, D. S. (1969). Variables related to consensus in group discussions of questions of policy. *Speech Monographs, 37,* 217-218.

Gouran, D. S. (1997). Effective versus ineffective group decision making. In L. R. Frey & J. K. Barge (Eds.), *Managing group life: Communicating in decision-making groups* (pp. 133-155). Boston: Houghton Mifflin.

Gouran, D. S., & Geonetta, S. C. (1977). Patterns of interaction in decision-making groups at varying distances from consensus. *Small Group Behavior, 8,* 511-524.

Gouran, D. S., & Hirokawa, R. Y. (1983). The role of communication in decision-making groups: A functional perspective. In M. S. Mander (Ed.), *Communications in transition: Issues and debate in current research* (pp. 168-185). New York: Praeger.

Graham, W. K., & Dillon, P. C. (1974). Creative supergroups: Group performance as a function of individual performance on brainstorming tasks. *Journal of Social Psychology, 93,* 101-105.

Green, T. B. (1975). An empirical analysis of nominal and interacting groups. *Academy of Management Journal, 18,* 63-70.

Hackman, J. R., & Kaplan, R. E. (1974). Interventions into group process: An approach to improving the effectiveness of groups. *Decision Processes, 5,* 459-480.

Hackman, J. R., & Morris, C. G. (1975). Group tasks, group interaction process, and group performance effectiveness: A review and proposed integration. In L. Berkowitz (Ed.), *Advances in experimental social psychology* (Vol. 8, pp. 45-99). New York: Academic Press.

Hall, J., & Watson, W. H. (1970). The effects of a normative intervention on group decision making performance. *Human Relations, 23,* 299-317.

Hastie, R., Penrod, S., & Pennington, N. (1983). *Inside the jury.* Cambridge, MA: Harvard University Press.

Hewes, D. E. (1986). A socio-egocentric model of group decision-making. In R. Y. Hirokawa & M. S. Poole (Eds.), *Communication and group decision-making* (pp. 265-291). Beverly Hills, CA: Sage.

Hewes, D. E. (1996). Small group communication may not influence decision-making: An amplification of socio-egocentric theory. In R. Y. Hirokawa & M. S. Poole (Eds.), *Communication and group decision making* (2nd ed., pp. 179-212). Thousand Oaks, CA: Sage.

Higgins, E. T. (1989). Knowledge accessibility and activation: Subjectivity and suffering from unconscious sources. In J. S. Uleman & J. A. Bargh (Eds.), *Unintended thought* (pp. 75-123). New York: Guilford.

Hirokawa, R. Y. (1982). Group communication and problem-solving effectiveness, I: A critical review of inconsistent findings. *Communication Quarterly, 30,* 134-141.

Hirokawa, R. Y. (1983a). Group communication and problem-solving effectiveness: An investigation of group phases. *Human Communication Research, 9,* 291-305.

Hirokawa, R. Y. (1983b). Group communication and problem-solving effectiveness, II: An exploratory investigation of procedural functions. *Western Journal of Speech Communication, 47,* 59-74.

Hirokawa, R. Y. (1985). Discussion procedures and decision-making performance: A test of the functional perspective. *Human Communication Research, 12,* 203-224.

Hirokawa, R. Y. (1988). Group communication and decision-making performance: A continued test of the functional perspective. *Human Communication Research, 14,* 487-515.

Hirokawa, R. Y., Erbert, L., & Hurst, A. (1996). Communication and group decision-making effectiveness. In R. Y. Hirokawa & M. S. Poole (Eds.), *Communication*

and group decision making (2nd ed., pp. 269-300). Thousand Oaks, CA: Sage.

Hirokawa, R. Y., & Pace, R. (1983). A descriptive investigation of the possible communication-based reasons for effective and ineffective group decision-making. *Communication Monographs, 50,* 363-379.

Hirokawa, R. Y., & Rost, K. M. (1992). Effective group decision making in organizations: Field test of the vigilant interaction theory. *Management Communication Quarterly, 5,* 267-288.

Hirokawa, R. Y., & Scheerhorn, D. R. (1986). Communication in faulty group decision-making. In R. Y. Hirokawa & M. S. Poole (Eds.), *Communication and group decision-making* (pp. 63-80). Beverly Hills, CA: Sage.

Holsti, O. (1971). Crises, stress, and decision-making. *International Social Science Journal, 23,* 53-67.

Isaacs, E. A., & Clark, H. H. (1987). References in conversation between experts and novices. *Journal of Experimental Psychology: General, 116,* 26-37.

Jablin, F. M. (1981). Cultivating imagination: Factors that enhance and inhibit creativity in brainstorming groups. *Human Communication Research, 7,* 245-258.

Jablin, F. M., Seibold, D. R., & Sorenson, R. L. (1977). Potential inhibitory effects of group participation on brainstorming performance. *Central States Speech Journal, 28,* 113-121.

Jablin, F. M., Sorenson, R. L., & Seibold, D. R. (1978). Interpersonal perception and group brainstorming performance. *Communication Quarterly, 26,* 36-44.

Janis, I. L. (1972). *Victims of groupthink: Psychological studies of foreign policy decisions and fiascoes.* Boston: Houghton Mifflin.

Janis, I. L. (1989). *Crucial decisions: Leadership in policymaking and crisis management.* New York: Free Press.

Janis, I. L., & Mann, I. (1977). *Decision-making: A psychological analysis of conflict, choice, and commitment.* New York: Free Press.

Jarboe, S. (1996). Procedures for enhancing group decision making. In R. Y. Hirokawa & M. S. Poole (Eds.), *Communication and group decision making* (2nd ed., pp. 345-383). Thousand Oaks, CA: Sage.

Jensen, A. D., & Chilberg, J. C. (1991). *Small group communication: Theory and application.* Belmont, CA: Wadsworth.

Kerr, N. L. (1983). Motivation losses in small groups: A social dilemma analysis. *Journal of Personality and Social Psychology, 45,* 819-828.

Kerr, N. L., & MacCoun, R. J. (1985). The effects of jury size and polling method on the process and product of jury deliberations. *Journal of Personality and Social Psychology, 48,* 349-363.

Kirchmeyer, C. (1993). Multicultural task groups: An account of the low contribution levels of minorities. *Small Group Research, 24,* 127-148.

Kirchmeyer, C., & Cohen, A. (1992). Multicultural groups: Their performance and reactions with constructive conflict. *Group & Organizational Management, 17,* 153-170.

Kramer, M. W., Kuo, C. L., & Dailey, J. C. (1997). The impact of brainstorming techniques on subsequent group processes: Beyond generating ideas. *Small Group Research, 28,* 218-242.

Langer, J., Wapner, S., & Werner, H. (1961). The effects of danger upon the experience of time. *American Journal of Psychology, 74,* 94-97.

MacCoun, R., & Kerr, N. L. (1988). Asymmetric influence in mock jury deliberations: Jurors' bias for leniency. *Journal of Personality and Social Psychology, 54,* 21-33.

Maier, N.R.F. (1967). Assets and liabilities in group problem solving: The need for an integrative function. *Psychological Review, 74,* 239-249.

Maier, N.R.F. (1970). *Problem solving and creativity in individuals and groups.* Belmont, CA: Brooks/Cole.

Maier, N.R.F., & Maier, R. A. (1957). An experimental test of the effects of "development" vs. "free" discussions on the quality of group decisions. *Journal of Applied Psychology, 41,* 320-323.

McBurney, J. H., & Hance, K. G. (1939). *The principles and methods of discussion.* New York: Harper.

McLeod, P. L., Lobel, S. A., & Cox, T. H., Jr. (1996). Ethnic diversity and creativity in small groups. *Small Group Research, 27,* 248-264.

Miner, F. C., Jr. (1979). A comparative analysis of three diverse group decision making approaches. *Academy of Management Journal, 22,* 81-93.

Mullen, B., Johnson, C., & Salas, E. (1991). Productivity loss in brainstorming groups: A meta-analytic integration. *Basic and Applied Social Psychology, 12,* 3-23.

Murrell, A. J., Stewart, A. C., & Engel, B. T. (1993). Consensus versus devil's advocacy: The influence of decision process and task structure on strategic decision making. *Journal of Business Communication, 30,* 399-414.

Nemeth, C., & Wachtler, J. (1983). Creative problem solving as a result of majority vs. minority influence. *European Journal of Social Psychology, 13,* 45-55.

Nemiroff, P. M., & King, D. C. (1975). Group decision-making performance as influenced by consensus and self-orientation. *Human Relations, 28,* 1-21.

Nemiroff, P. M., Pasmore, W. A., & Ford, D. L., Jr. (1976). The effects of two normative structural interventions on established and ad hoc groups: Implications for improving decision making effectiveness. *Decision Sciences, 7,* 841-855.

Ng, S. H., Bell, D., & Brooke, M. (1993). Gaining turns and achieving high influence ranking in small conversational groups. *British Journal of Social Psychology, 32,* 265-275.

Nicotera, A. M. (Ed.). (1995). *Communication and conflict: Communicative processes.* Albany: State University of New York Press.

Nicotera, A. M. (1997). Managing conflict communication in groups. In L. R. Frey & J. K. Barge (Eds.), *Managing group life: Communicating in decision-making groups* (pp. 104-130). Boston: Houghton Mifflin.

Nutt, P. (1984). *Planning methods: For health and related organizations.* New York: Wiley.

Offner, A. K., Kramer, T. J., & Winter, J. P. (1996). The effects of facilitation, recording, and pauses on group brainstorming. *Small Group Research, 27,* 283-298.

Osborn, A. F. (1957). *Applied imagination: Principles and procedures of creative problem-solving.* New York: Scribner.

Paulus, P. B., Dzindolet, M. T., Poletes, G., & Camacho, L. M. (1993). Perception of performance in group brainstorming: The illusion of group productivity. *Personality and Social Psychology Bulletin, 19,* 78-89.

Pavitt, C. (1993). What (little) we know about formal group discussion procedures: A review of relevant research. *Small Group Research, 24,* 217-235.

Pavitt, C., & Curtis, E. (1994). *Small group discussion: A theoretical approach* (2nd ed.). Scottsdale, AZ: Gorsuch Scarisbrick.

Perez, D. A., Hosch, H. M., Ponder, B., & Trejo, G. C. (1993). Ethnicity of defendants and jurors as influences on jury decisions. *Journal of Applied Social Psychology, 23,* 1249-1262.

Philipsen, G., Mulac, A., & Dietrich, D. (1979). The effects of social interaction in group idea generation. *Communication Monographs, 46,* 119-125.

Phillips, G. M. (1970). PERT as a logical adjunct to the discussion process. In R. S. Cathcart & L. A. Samovar (Eds.), *Small group communication* (pp. 166-176). Dubuque, IA: Wm. C. Brown.

Phillips, G. M., & Wood, J. T. (Eds.). (1984). *Emergent issues in human decision making.* Carbondale: Southern Illinois University Press.

Plott, C. R., & Levine, M. E. (1978). A model of agenda influence on committee decisions. *American Economic Review, 68,* 146-160.

Plous, S. (1995). A comparison of strategies for reducing interval overconfidence in group judgments. *Journal of Applied Psychology, 80,* 443-454.

Poole, M. S. (1991). Procedures for managing meetings: Social and technological innovation. In R. A. Swanson & B. O. Knapp (Eds.), *Innovative meeting management* (pp. 53-109). Austin, TX: 3M Meeting Management Institute.

Poole, M. S., & DeSanctis, G. (1990). Understanding the use of group decision support systems: The theory of adaptive structuration. In C. Steinfield & J. Fulk (Eds.), *Organizations and new information technology* (pp. 175-195). Newbury Park, CA: Sage.

Poole, M. S., & DeSanctis, G. (1992). Microlevel structuration in computer-supported group decision-making. *Human Communication Research, 19,* 5-49.

Poole, M. S., DeSanctis, G., Kirsch, L., & Jackson, M. (1995). Group decision support systems as facilitators of quality team efforts. In L. R. Frey (Ed.), *Innovations in group facilitation: Applications in natural settings* (pp. 299-323). Cresskill, NJ: Hampton.

Priem, R. L., & Price, K. H. (1991). Process and outcome expectations for the dialectical inquiry, devil's advocacy, and consensus techniques of strategic decision making. *Group & Organization Studies, 16,* 206-225.

Putnam, L. L. (1979). Preference for procedural order in task-oriented small groups. *Communication Monographs, 46,* 193-218.

Putnam, L. L., & Stohl, C. (1990). Bona fide groups: A reconceptualization of groups in context. *Communication Studies, 41,* 248-265.

Putnam, L. L., & Stohl, C. (1996). Bona fide groups: An alternative perspective for communication and small group decision making. In R. Y. Hirokawa & M. S. Poole (Eds.), *Communication and group decision making* (2nd ed., pp. 147-178). Thousand Oaks, CA: Sage.

Pyron, H. C. (1964). An experimental study of the role of reflective thinking in business and professional conferences and discussions. *Speech Monographs, 31,* 157-161.

Pyron, H. C., & Sharp, H., Jr. (1963). A quantitative study of reflective thinking and performance in problem-solving discussion. *Journal of Communication, 21,* 46-53.

Reagan, P., & Rohrbaugh, J. (1990). Group decision process effectiveness: A competing values approach. *Group & Organization Studies, 15,* 20-43.

Rogelberg, S. G., Barnes-Farrell, J. L., & Lowe, C. A. (1992). The stepladder technique: An alternative group structure facilitating effective group decision making. *Journal of Applied Psychology, 77,* 730-737.

Ross, R. S. (1989). *Small groups in organizational settings.* Englewood Cliffs, NJ: Prentice Hall.

Schacter, S. (1968). Deviation, rejection, and communication. In D. Cartwright & A. Zander (Eds.), *Group dynamics: Theory and research* (3rd ed., pp. 165-181). Beverly Hills, CA: Sage.

Scheerhorn, D., Geist, P., & Teboul, JC. B. (1994). Beyond decision making in decision-making groups: Implications for the study of group communication. In L. R. Frey (Ed.), *Group communication in context: Studies of natural groups* (pp. 247-262). Hillsdale, NJ: Lawrence Erlbaum.

Scheidel, T. M., & Crowell, L. (1964). Idea development in small discussion groups. *Quarterly Journal of Speech, 50,* 104-145.

Scheidel, T. M., & Crowell, L. (1979). *Discussing and deciding: A deskbook for group leaders and members.* New York: Macmillan.

Schultz, B., Ketrow, S. M., & Urban, D. M. (1995). Improving decision quality in the small group: The role of the reminder. *Small Group Research, 26,* 521-541.

Schweiger, D. M., Sandberg, W. R., & Ragan, J. W. (1986). Group approaches for improving strategic decision making: A comparative analysis of dialectical inquiry, devil's advocacy, and consensus. *Academy of Management Journal, 29,* 51-71.

Schweiger, D. M., Sandberg, W. R., & Rechner, P. L. (1989). Experiential effects of dialectical inquiry, devil's advocacy, and consensus approaches to strategic decision-making. *Academy of Management Journal, 32,* 745-772.

Schwenk, C. R. (1988). Effects of devil's advocacy on escalating commitment. *Human Relations, 41,* 769-782.

Schwenk, C. R., & Cosier, R. A. (1980). Effects of the expert, devil's advocate, and dialectical inquiry methods on prediction performance. *Organizational Behavior and Human Performance, 26,* 409-424.

Schwenk, C. R., & Cosier, R. A. (1993). Effects of consensus and devil's advocacy on strategic decision-making. *Journal of Applied Social Psychology, 23,* 126-139.

Schwenk, C., & Valacich, J. S. (1994). Effects of devil's advocacy and dialectical inquiry on individuals versus groups. *Organizational Behavior and Human Decision Processes, 59,* 210-222.

Seibold, D. R. (1979). Making meetings more successful: Plans, formats, and procedures for group problem solving. *Journal of Business Communication, 16,* 3-20.

Seibold, D. R. (1992). Making meetings more successful: Plans, formats, and procedures for group problem solving. In R. S. Cathcart & L. A. Samovar (Eds.), *Small group communication: A reader* (6th ed., pp. 178-191). Dubuque, IA: Wm. C. Brown.

Seibold, D. R., & Krikorian, D. H. (1997). Planning and facilitating group meetings. In L. R. Frey & J. K. Barge (Eds.), *Managing group life: Communicating in decision-making groups* (pp. 270-305). Boston: Houghton Mifflin.

Seibold, D. R., Meyers, R. A., & Sunwolf. (1996). Communication and influence in group decision making. In R. Y. Hirokawa & M. S. Poole (Eds.), *Communication and group decision making* (2nd ed., pp. 242-268). Thousand Oaks, CA: Sage.

Sharp, H., Jr., & Milliken, J. (1964). The reflective thinking ability and the product of problem-solving discussion. *Speech Monographs, 31,* 124-127.

Shaw, M. E. (1981). *Group dynamics: The psychology of small group behavior* (3rd ed.). New York: McGraw-Hill.

Shure, G. H., Rogers, M. S., Larsen, I. M., & Tassone, J. (1962). Group planning and task effectiveness. *Sociometry, 25,* 263-282.

Sorenson, J. R. (1971). Task demands, group interaction, and group performance. *Sociometry, 34,* 483-495.

Stasser, G. (1992). Information salience and the discovery of hidden profiles by decision making groups: A "thought experiment." *Organizational Behavior and Human Decision Processes, 52,* 156-181.

Stasser, G., & Titus, W. (1985). Pooling of unshared information in group decision making: Biased information sampling during discussion. *Journal of Personality and Social Psychology, 48,* 1467-1478.

Sykes, R. E. (1990). Imagining what we might study if we really studied small groups from a speech perspective. *Communication Studies, 41,* 200-211.

Thompson, L. L., Mannix, E. A., & Bazerman, M. H. (1988). Group negotiation: Effects of decision rule, agenda, and aspiration. *Journal of Personality and Social Psychology, 54,* 86-95.

Torrance, E. P. (1957). Group decision making and disagreement. *Social Forces, 35,* 314-318.

Valacich, J. S., & Schwenk, C. (1995a). Devil's advocacy and dialectical inquiry effects on face-to-face and computer-mediated group decision making. *Organi-*

zational Behavior and Human Decision Processes, 63, 158-173.

Valacich, J. S., & Schwenk, C. (1995b). Structuring conflict in individual, face-to-face, and computer-mediated group decision making: Carping versus objective devil's advocacy. Decision Sciences, 26, 369-392.

Van de Ven, A. (1974). Group decision-making effectiveness. Kent, OH: Kent State University Center for Business and Economic Research Press.

Van de Ven, A. H., & Delbecq, A. L. (1974). The effectiveness of nominal, Delphi, and interacting group decision making processes. Academy of Management Journal, 17, 605-621.

Weldon, E., & Mustari, E. L. (1988). Felt dispensability in groups of coactors: The effects of shared responsibility and explicit anonymity on cognitive effort. Organizational Behavior and Human Decision Processes, 41, 330-351.

White, S. E., Dittrich, J. E., & Lang, J. R. (1980). The effects of group decision-making process and problem-situation complexity on implementation attempts. Administrative Science Quarterly, 25, 428-440.

Wood, J. T. (1984). Alternative methods of group decision-making: A comparative examination of consensus, negotiation, and voting. In G. M. Phillips & J. T. Wood (Eds.), Emergent issues in human decision making (pp. 3-18). Carbondale: Southern Illinois University Press.

Wyer, R. S., Jr., & Srull, T. K. (1981). Category accessibility: Some theoretical and empirical issues concerning the processing of social stimulus information. In E. T. Higgins, C. P. Herman, & M. P. Zanna (Eds.), Social cognition: The Ontario symposium (Vol. 1, pp. 161-197). Hillsdale, NJ: Lawrence Erlbaum.

Zander, A. (1982). Making groups effective. San Francisco: Jossey-Bass.

16

Communication Technology and Group Communication

CRAIG R. SCOTT
The University of Texas at Austin

A variety of societal influences in recent years have encouraged an increased reliance on groups and teams in several diverse contexts. Most notably, various programs in organizations—such as business process re-engineering and other efforts directed at dispersed decision-making authority, reduced cycle times, improved global competitiveness, and increased flexibility—regularly involve an emphasis on teams (Coleman, 1995; Creighton & Adams, 1998). As Larson and LaFasto (1989) conclude, the growing complexity of problems in organizations and society demands collaborative efforts.

A variety of intervention techniques and discussion/decision-making/problem-solving procedures have emerged over the years to enhance group processes and outcomes (in this volume, see Chapters 14 [Schultz] and 15 [Sunwolf & Seibold]). Among these and other facilitation efforts designed to assist groups, it is perhaps the use of advanced electronic and digital technologies—especially those supporting communication and collaboration—that is

most strongly affecting this emphasis on teams in organizations and other contexts. Even though some of the technologies capable of supporting groups have been around for more than 20 years, only recently have societal conditions and technological developments created an environment conducive to the rapid development of such tools (see Coleman, 1995). Although technology growth, in general, is astounding (e.g., Lipnack & Stamps, 1997, estimate personal computer sales of $100 million annually by the year 2000), the increasing interest in technologies to support groups is equally impressive. If recent predictions were correct, organizations involved with computer-based technology to support groups constituted a $5.5-10 billion worldwide industry by the end of 1998 (Coleman, 1995; Khoshafian & Buckiewicz, 1995). As Grudin and Poltrock (1997) argue, the growth of the World Wide Web (WWW), the Internet, and the widespread use of groupware programs, such as Lotus Notes, are key indicators of our readiness for technologies that support

AUTHOR'S NOTE: I wish to thank the Austin Technology Incubator for its continued support of my research on group communication technologies.

groups. Already, group support technologies have been used by several million people and are a key resource in more than 1,500 organizations today (Briggs, Nunamaker, & Sprague, 1998; Nunamaker, 1997), and application of these technologies should extend well into the next millennium (Simon & Marion, 1996).

With the current usage and predicted growth in technologies to support groups, one would expect to see a fair amount of research in this area. Indeed, the multidisciplinary field known as Computer-Supported Collaborative (sometimes Cooperative) Work (CSCW) has emerged to explore issues related to technology and teamwork. Although work in this area has grown steadily since its beginnings in the mid-1980s (Khoshafian & Buckiewicz, 1995), Briggs et al. (1998) contend that this research area is still much closer to its beginning than to its end.

Despite the fact that these systems supporting groups are primarily *communication* technologies (Grudin & Poltrock, 1997) and that many of the "1,001 research questions" that remain in this area (see Briggs et al., 1998) seem well suited to examination from a communication perspective, relatively little scholarship on these systems has emerged from the Communication field. Orlikowski (1993) observes that the more collaborative features of group technologies have scarcely been researched, and others note that research efforts in this area should be directed toward a better understanding of groups (Grudin & Poltrock, 1997; Khoshafian & Buckiewicz, 1995) and communication (Khoshafian & Buckiewicz, 1995; O'Dwyer, Giser, & Lovett, 1997; O'Malley, 1995), as opposed to just technology. Clearly, there has been interest in group communication technologies (GCTs) in Communication, pioneered by the efforts of Marshall Scott Poole and his colleagues (e.g., Poole & DeSanctis, 1990, 1992; Poole, DeSanctis, Kirsch, & Jackson, 1995; Poole & Holmes, 1995). Relative to other disciplines, however, research on CSCW in Communication remains underrepresented. Additionally, Eom's (1998) recent citation analysis of the

literature in the Decision Support field demonstrates the general inattention other scholars have paid to even the existing work in Communication.

In the light of both the growing interest in technologies to support groups/teams and the need for stronger communication perspectives on this subject, this chapter reviews recent research on a wide range of communication technologies used to facilitate group interaction. I begin this effort by proposing a key organizing framework and some relevant terminology to provide an appropriate focus for this chapter. Having done that, I next review recent GCT research in two key contexts: laboratory research groups and organizational work teams. The chapter closes with a few conclusions concerning issues across these contexts, as well as suggestions for further work in this area.

FRAMEWORKS AND TERMINOLOGY

Sense-Making Frameworks

There has been no shortage of frameworks and theories for categorizing and making sense of the work relevant to GCTs. Most schemes focus on the technologies themselves, and the most common frameworks differentiate these technologies along spatial (e.g., users meeting in the same room versus different rooms) and temporal (e.g., users working at the same time versus different times) dimensions. Although the labels vary, and several extensions have been offered (e.g., Creighton & Adams, 1998; Finn & Lane, 1998; McGrath & Hollingshead, 1994), the focus on space and time remains. Several function-based categories also have emerged (e.g., Blundell, 1997; Coleman, 1997c; Grudin & Poltrock, 1997), as have analytic schemes focused more specifically on differences among technologies (e.g., Collins-Jarvis & Fulk, 1993), groups of technologies (e.g., McGrath & Hollingshead, 1994), or specific features of single technologies (e.g., Seibold, Heller, & Contractor, 1994). Each of these frameworks provides a valuable way of beginning to make sense of these technologies. Even more valuable are theories of technology use, such as Adaptive Structuration Theory (DeSanctis & Poole, 1994; Poole & DeSanctis, 1990, 1992) and Self-Organizing Systems Theory (Contractor & Seibold, 1993) (in this volume, see Chapters 2 [Poole] and 3 [Mabry]), as well as various others (e.g., social influence, social presence, media richness, dual capacity, and uses and gratifications) that actually provide explanations for the processes by which technological and other variables influence one another.

Despite the value of such theories to explain the processes underlying the relationships between variables, they are not as well suited for initially organizing findings in a large body of literature. Instead, a general systemic approach that focuses on outcomes and group processes that the technologies (and other inputs) support is best suited for the type of review undertaken in this chapter (see Mabry, Chapter 3, this volume, for an overview of Systems Theory). There are at least three recent input-process-output models that help describe communication technology as it relates to group communication. First, Dennis, George, Jessup, Nunamaker, and Vogel (1988; see also Martz, Vogel, & Nunamaker, 1992), offer a model focused specifically on electronic meetings. Their framework emphasizes four types of inputs (work group issues, task concerns, external context, and technology) as they affect meeting processes and various outcomes. Second, Mennecke, Hoffer, and Wynne (1992) build on Dennis et al.'s (1988) work with a developmental model centered on the technology-supported group meeting that describes inputs (task, member, group, and meeting characteristics), processes (facilitation, technological support, structural factors, and sociotechnical issues), outcomes (group performance and development, as well as individual perceptions), extra-meeting socialization (e.g., member interactions between a series of formal meetings), and feedback from current to subsequent meetings (which they describe as group learning). Third, McGrath and

Hollingshead (1994) propose a framework that consists of four broad sets of variables: (a) input factors (including technology, but also member attributes, group attributes, tasks/projects/purposes, and contextual factors), (b) organizing concepts (metaphors that treat a group as an information-processing system, a consensus-generating system, or a vehicle for motivating/regulating behavior), (c) process variables (participation, information-processing effectiveness, consensus generating, and normative regulation), and (d) outcome factors (such as task performance/effectiveness, user satisfaction, and member relations).

By focusing on the technology-supported group meeting, incorporating various processes related to it, and paying attention to feedback and group development over time, a combination of these frameworks provides a more useful systemic model that can be applied to a wide range of situations in which GCTs are utilized. I call this synthesized framework the *meeting-process model*. Collectively, the model features four sets of inputs (context, group/member characteristics, task characteristics, and technology), meeting processes, outcomes, and feedback. Before applying this model to research on GCTs, let me offer a few comments about each part of the framework.

The Meeting-Process Model

Context Input

The following section of this volume (Part VI: Group Communication Contexts and Applications) focuses on several specific contexts of group interaction: family (Socha, Chapter 17), education (Allen & Plax, Chapter 18), social support/self-help (Cline, Chapter 19), and organizations (Greenbaum & Query, Chapter 20). Despite calls to study bona fide groups—those that have permeable boundaries, have shifting borders, and are interdependent with their context (see Putnam & Stohl, 1990, 1994, 1996)—and move scholarly efforts into field settings (e.g., Frey, 1994a, 1994b; in this volume, see Chapters 1 [Gouran] and 2 [Poole]), another important and time-honored context in which we have studied (and will likely continue to study) interacting groups is the research laboratory. For purposes of this chapter, I examine two comparable contexts in which most of the GCT work has been done: the research laboratory and the organization. Unfortunately, this means omitting some very interesting work in the areas of education[1] and social support.[2] Notable differences in goals (see Kolodner & Guzdial, 1996) and relevant outcomes in these areas, however, preclude a detailed analysis of these contexts.

Group/Member Characteristics Input

Although numerous group/member characteristics are potentially relevant, three topics deserving special mention here are group size, proximity of members, and member status. Historically, size has been a defining feature of groups; a small group, for example, is small enough so that members can get to know one another personally and have a say in group matters (see Socha, 1997). Communication technologies, however, may support interaction and opportunities for mutual influence among markedly larger numbers of members (making group size of special importance here). Second, communication technologies have redefined interacting groups by largely eliminating the requirement that members be spatially and temporally copresent; "virtual" teams may include members who send/receive messages at different times from different physical locations. Finally, member status (based on gender, position of authority, expertise, and other characteristics, perceptions, or qualifications) is not always as apparent when mediated as it is in face-to-face situations (because of reduced cues and social presence, as well as anonymity in some cases), which makes this variable of special relevance to groups using technology.

Task Characteristics Input

The nature of a group's work has long been considered an important part of group interaction. Indeed, several studies point to task differences as being particularly powerful in explaining outcomes in using GCTs (e.g., Benbasat & Lim, 1993; Farmer & Hyatt, 1994). Most pertinent to this chapter is McGrath's (1984) decision typology, which classifies tasks into four general quadrants: generate (including creativity and planning tasks), choose (including intellective and decision-making tasks; see Propp, Chapter 9, this volume), negotiate, and execute.

Meeting Processes

Whether for a so-called virtual team (Lipnack & Stamps, 1997) or something more traditional, the meeting represents an important "coming together" of group members, be it for an informal project meeting, a formal strategy session, or some type of research experiment. Because meetings usually involve an occasion for increased interaction among group members, they increasingly are being aided with various technologies that support communication. Notably, these technologies have sometimes created new facilitation roles (e.g., technographer or technology facilitator), reemphasized the need for rarely used roles (e.g., formal process facilitator), or altered traditional leadership roles among group members in managing these meetings. Other meeting-process interventions (e.g., devil's advocacy, dialectical inquiry, and specific team-building strategies; see Sunwolf & Seibold, Chapter 15, this volume, for a comprehensive review of such interventions) may also take on special meaning in the context of an electronic group meeting. Thus, facilitation, leadership, and other meeting-process interventions receive attention in this chapter.[3]

Outcomes

The outcomes of relevance with GCTs are largely the same as those associated with group communication in general. This chapter reviews four broad categories of outcomes (suggested by the work informing the meeting-process model) directly relevant to the laboratory and organizational contexts in which groups employ communication technologies. These include task/decision performance (quantity and quality of output, as well as consensus about and commitment to a task/decision), efficiency (minimal expenditure of resources, especially in terms of time, needed to complete a task or meeting), member satisfaction (with process and outcome, as well as with the group and its members), and communication (participation, influence, information exchange, and specific message types). Although other outcomes, such as conflict and members' commitment to the group and/or the discussion, have received some attention in this literature, these four categories clearly represent the primary research outcomes. These outcomes, especially performance and efficiency, have been assessed through both self-reports of users' perceptions and more objective, observable means.

Feedback

Perhaps the least theorized about (not to mention least researched) aspect of the meeting-process model concerns feedback and group learning over time. Although there are theories of group decision development (e.g., Fisher, 1970; Poole, 1983a, 1983b; Poole & Roth, 1989) and general group development related to time (see McGrath, 1991; McGrath, Arrow, Gruenfeld, Hollingshead, & O'Connor, 1993; Mennecke et al., 1992) (in this volume, see Chapters 1 [Gouran], 2 [Poole], 3 [Mabry], and 6 [Anderson, Riddle, & Martin]), only Mennecke and colleagues' model emphasizes the effects of feedback from one meeting to the next. Calls for longitudinal studies to assess changes over time have been numerous, but actual research of this nature has been the exception. As the process-oriented model clearly shows, however, outcomes from one meeting feed into another via the ongoing process of group communication; thus, this chapter pays attention to issues of feedback from one meeting to the next and group development over time in the context of GCT usage by noting the extent to which research does and does not consider such issues.

Technology

As the title of this chapter indicates, the most central and unique part of the model is the technology input. The emphasis on technology, however, should not be mistaken for technological determinism; in fact, by first highlighting the various parts of the meeting-process model and drawing attention to various other issues that must be considered along with technology, I mean to avoid such criticism. Nevertheless, given the difficulty in addressing all influences simultaneously, the chapter highlights technology as it ultimately relates to various outcomes. To begin carving out the space (virtual and otherwise) relevant to this review of GCTs, it is first necessary to define more clearly such terms as *technology, communication technology,* and *group communication technology* (see Table 16.1 for these and several other relevant definitions).

Technology and Communication Technology

If technology is conceived in a broad sense as apparatuses and techniques that help accomplish something, we can imagine a sizable list of technologies relevant to groups (e.g., a gavel, a flipchart, a meeting agenda, or the brainstorming technique). The most common conceptualization of technology, however, is the apparatus variety (a device, tool, or machine). Furthermore, as we conjure images of technologies at the close of the 20th century, we are certain to focus on the microcomputer and the variety of peripheral technologies related to it. Of course, these machines were designed as computational—not *communication*—technologies, and even today, only a portion of what various computer technologies do concerns human-human interaction. Even when we consider the computer technologies that are of relevance to communication, many of them serve only an enabling function (e.g., networks and client/server

Table 16.1 Key Terms

Term (and acronym)	Definition (and examples)
Technology	Any apparatus (device, tool, or machine) or technique (process) used to help accomplish a task (e.g., gavel or brainstorming technique)
Communication technology (CT)	Any apparatus (device, tool, or machine) or technique (process) used to help accomplish exchange of messages (e.g., pencil or the Internet)
End-user communication technology and enabling communication technology	End-user communication technologies are those directly employed by people to accomplish message exchange (e.g., telephone handset or electronic mail interface), as opposed to enabling communication technologies that provide the largely invisible infrastructure that may carry a message from one end user to another (e.g., intranet or satellite)
New communication technology (NCT)	Electronic, and usually digital, communication technologies that provide greater interactivity and control than the mass media (e.g., desktop videoconferencing or computer-based messaging)
Group communication technology (GCT)	Any communication technology used by a group/team, but especially those technologies designed with group use in mind (e.g., group decision support system [GDSS] or audioconferencing system)
Computer-supported collaborative work (CSCW)	A broad movement and interdisciplinary field concerned with how groups of people use computing technology in their work
Groupware (or teamware or meetingware)	Umbrella term for the technologies used in computer-supported collaborative work to provide communication, collaboration, and coordination (e.g., Lotus Notes)
Electronic meeting system (EMS)	A specific type of groupware providing support for mediated group meetings (e.g., videoconferencing or group support systems [GSS])
Group decision support system (GDSS) and group support system (GSS)	A specific type of electronic meeting system that combines communication, decision, and computer technologies to assist teams in problem solving (GDSS) or varied group activities (GSS; e.g., GroupSystems or VisionQuest)
Face-to-face (FtF)	A problematic label for traditional, person(s)-to-person(s), nonelectronically mediated interaction that usually serves as a point of comparison for technology-supported interaction

technology; see Simon & Marion, 1996) that makes them invisible to the typical user. Thus, an appropriate focus for this chapter is on what are called *end-user communication technologies,* or those directly employed by people to promote communicative exchanges.

With this focus on end-user communication technologies, we must still remember that technologies to help people interact with others have existed for quite some time (e.g., smoke signals, drums, printing presses, and pencils). Later additions include the telephone, the telegraph, and mass communication media. Today, the "new" media (Rice & Bair, 1984) take advantage of electronics and the digital age to provide interactants with an increasing variety of options, including computer-based messaging, data conferencing, audioconferencing, videoconferencing, and various advanced phone capabilities. As Lipnack and Stamps (1997) observe, the new media have not generally replaced those previously in existence; rather, they have added to the communication technology menu. It is these relatively new electronic, and usually digital, communication technologies used increasingly by people in organizations and other settings today that constitute the focus of this chapter.

Group Communication Technology (GCT)

Having defined new communication technologies for purposes of this chapter, I can now examine GCTs. Historically, in organizations in North America, most technologies have been concerned primarily with enhancing individual productivity (e.g., word processing) or enterprise-wide efforts and have ignored the needs of small and large groups (Coleman, 1995; Grudin, 1994; Grudin & Poltrock, 1997). Recent years, however, have seen a dramatic shift in attention, as various stakeholders have begun to emphasize technologies to support teamwork. The terms used to describe this new focus on groups and teams, and the general categories of technologies to support it, are numerous: computer-

supported collaborative work (CSCW), groupware, teamware, meetingware, electronic meeting systems (EMSs), group decision support systems (GDSSs), group support systems (GSSs), computer-mediated communication systems (CMCSs), collaborative computing, collaborative support systems, work-group computing, and multiuser applications (see Table 16.1).

Although there is no consensus on the matter, it is most useful to think of CSCW as a broad movement or interdisciplinary field "concerned with bringing computing technology face-to-face with groups of people as they work together" (Bock & Marca, 1997, p. 501). Relatedly, *groupware* (or the more trendy "teamware" or "meetingware") is the umbrella term for technologies that support CSCW (Bock & Marca, 1997; Coleman, 1997c; Khoshafian & Buckiewicz, 1995), whether that be in meetings or elsewhere (for detailed discussion, see Lloyd, 1994). Groupware comes in many forms (Coleman, 1997c), but only some of them support communication.[4] Those that do include e-mail, desktop videoconferencing, meeting room videoconferencing, audioconferencing and other phone capabilities, shared documents and whiteboards, GDSSs/GSSs, and computer conferencing (CC); less often included are electronic bulletin boards, desktop publishing, listserves, group authoring software, voice/speech applications, and some forms of virtual reality (see Blundell, 1997; Coleman, 1997a, 1997c; Grudin, 1994; Grudin & Poltrock, 1997; Khoshafian & Buckiewicz, 1995; Neuwirth & Wojahn, 1996; Sinclair & Hale, 1997).

The type of groupware perhaps most relevant to this chapter is EMSs. Although some explanations suggest otherwise (see Dennis et al., 1988; Khoshafian & Buckiewicz, 1995), it is best to consider EMSs as a specific type of groupware directed toward providing support for mediated group meetings (including videoconferencing, whiteboards, CC, and audioconferencing). GDSSs, or the more inclusive GSSs (for those systems that support more than decision making), are a specific type of EMS that provides text-based communication and several forms of decision support designed especially for groups.

In a sense, a communication technology is a GCT if it is used by a group, regardless of intent (I have simply highlighted the most obvious examples here). Of course, the technology input in the meeting-process model is concerned with more than just the specific GCT used. Also of interest are specific features of technologies (e.g., anonymity, language, and interface options) that may influence group meetings and their outcomes. One of the additional features receiving research attention is the support provided by Level 1 (basic communication features, such as display screens and message exchange) and Level 2 (previous level plus decision-modeling tools and agendas) systems (see Sambamurthy, Poole, & Kelly, 1993). Relatedly, GCT functionality may vary along several dimensions, including dispersion of group members (dispersed across two or more sites versus proximately located in the same room), duration of decision-making project (one-time meeting versus ongoing series of meetings), and meeting temporality (synchronous meetings with members contributing at the same time versus asynchronous meetings with members contributing at different times). Finally, various GCTs may be compared to one another, contrasted with traditional nonelectronic forms of interaction, or used in various combinations. Describing specific technologies, features, and dimensions—as well as various comparisons and combinations of them—allows for a richer analysis of GCTs in use.

REVIEW OF RECENT GCT STUDIES

Having described the meeting-process model and narrowed in on the still rather wide domain of GCTs, I now review the literature on the use of laboratory research groups and organizational work teams. This review includes studies from a wide range of disciplines that have been published in the past 5 years. There are two primary reasons for this restriction. First, several relevant reviews of this

body of literature were conducted approximately 5 years ago (Benbasat & Lim, 1993; Collins-Jarvis & Fulk, 1993; McGrath & Hollingshead, 1994); to review that literature again would be redundant. These earlier reviews do provide an important point of comparison for the later studies reviewed here (see the discussion later in this chapter). Second, space limitations preclude a more exhaustive review (especially considering the large number of studies published in this growing area in just the past 5 years).

To characterize the specific work on GCTs in both the laboratory and organizational contexts, I first use the elements of the meeting-process model to provide a general description of this research. Second, I review findings related to the four sets of outcomes mentioned earlier. Throughout, I concentrate on comparisons between GCTs and what is most conveniently called *face-to-face* (FtF) forms of interaction.[5] I also discuss comparisons based on variations in the features of a single technology or variations across two or more technologies.

Descriptive Characteristics Based on the Meeting-Process Model

Context

The laboratory context encompasses scholarship involving student groups assembled for purposes of an investigatory study (or with very limited history together in a course). It is not surprising that of the 81 laboratory studies reviewed here (in several cases a single article reports several unique studies), all but 6 were experiments. The others used the classroom as a laboratory and employed more of a case study methodology.

The organizational context encompasses scholarship focusing on teams composed of organizational members working on job- or role-related tasks. In nearly all instances, these are ongoing teams of individuals who interact with one another with some degree of regularity (see Greenbaum & Query, Chapter 20, this volume, for a review of research on communication in organizational work groups). Of the 50 organizational studies reviewed here, only 4 used an experimental approach. Almost half the research employed what the authors described as a case or field study methodology, which involved the use of multiple methods and detailed analysis at one or more sites or at multiple points in time. Of the remaining studies, questionnaires were mailed to participants in five instances, administered immediately after a meeting in three situations, and used along with a diary (one study) or interviews (one study). Three studies used interviews exclusively to gather data, and one other combined interviews with content analysis. Two studies utilized meeting participants' debriefing comments as the data source. Six additional pieces reported summaries of relevant case study results, even though they were not actually write-ups of the cases themselves.

Group/Member Characteristics

Among the laboratory studies, 60 made use of groups of five or less, with the modal size being three members (*n* = 19). The two largest groups examined had just more than 40 members (Aiken, Sloan, Paolillo, & Motiwalla, 1997) and just more than 20 members (Reinig, Briggs, & Nunamaker, 1998). The remainder had 4 to 14 members each. The size of the teams in the organizational studies varied, but the majority fell into the 10-20 range; thus, the organizational teams are on average larger than the laboratory groups.

Sixty-two of the laboratory studies involved undergraduates from a wide range of majors, 9 used MBA or other graduate students, and another 10 employed a mix of graduate and undergraduate students. The organizational context in which the work teams were embedded included mostly for-profit businesses, but also government and military organizations, public utilities, and several private and public educational institutions. The vast majority of studies in both contexts were conducted in the United States; however, at least four laboratory studies involved international students, and one dealt specifically with groups in another country (Petrovic & Krickl, 1994). Furthermore, the organizational research reported here included teams from Japan, Australia, New Zealand, Canada, Israel, and across Europe.

To characterize the organizational groups in terms of nationality is a bit misleading, because several were virtual teams composed of members from multiple countries. In fact, seven studies focused on how synchronous, asynchronous, or some combination of technologies were used to support teams dispersed across organizations or organizational sites. Nine more studies concentrated on team members who were dispersed more locally in their organization (using predominantly asynchronous technologies for support). Among the laboratory groups, only 5 studies entailed asynchronous interaction among dispersed participants; 12 studies involved synchronous interaction among dispersed participants (not including studies in which interacting members were spread out at different places in the same room). In both contexts, the majority of studies focused on nonvirtual teams using various technologies to support their interactions.

Several of the laboratory studies specifically examined member or group characteristics, such as gender (Herschel, Cooper, Smith, & Arrington, 1994; Robichaux, 1994), status/influence (Hollingshead, 1996a; Scott & Easton, 1996; Weisband, Schneider, & Connolly, 1995), logical and numerical group size (Mennecke, 1997; Valacich, George, Nunamaker, & Vogel, 1994; Valacich, Wheeler, Mennecke, & Wachter, 1995), preferences for procedural order (Wheeler, Mennecke, & Scudder, 1993), high and low coordination/collaboration (Horton & Biolsi, 1994; Knoll & Jarvenpaa, 1998), nationality (Aiken, Hwang, De Magalhaes, & Martin, 1993; Aiken, Kim, Hwang, & Lu, 1995; Daily, Whatley, Ash, & Steiner, 1996; El-Shinnawy & Vinze, 1997), future anticipation of group interaction (Walther, 1994, 1997), group versus individual salience (Walther, 1997), and majority/minority opinions (Dennis, Hilmer, & Taylor, 1998). Other laboratory studies reported on differences between groups using the same technology in very different ways (Poole & Holmes, 1995; Scalia & Sackmary, 1996). Generally, the organizational studies were not as likely to entail explicit comparisons based on group/member characteristics; however, there were some comparisons based on team performance (Poole et al., 1995), group cooperativeness (Zack & McKenney, 1995), high and low experience as facilitators (Niederman, Beise, & Beranek, 1996), occupational differences of team members (Saunders, Robey, & Vavarek, 1994), and team types (Gowan & Downs, 1994; Yates, Orlikowski, & Okamura, 1995). Group roles were also examined within GSS meetings in organizations (Zigurs & Kozar, 1994).

Task Characteristics

Tasks in the laboratory context included a number of tasks involving hidden profiles, case analysis, strategic planning, ethics/values scenarios, and various brainstorming activities; thus, the tasks tend to be about choosing and generating—and, to a lesser extent, negotiating—as defined by McGrath's (1984) typology. Task type appears to have been manipulated as a specific variable in less than 10 of these laboratory studies. These particular studies compared some variation of choosing and generating tasks (see Sia, Tan, & Wei, 1996, 1997; Strauss, 1997; Strauss & McGrath, 1994), whereas others examined differences in task complexity level (Carey & Kacmar, 1997; Farmer & Hyatt, 1994) and structure (Kahai, Sosik, & Avolio, 1997; Ocker, Hiltz, Turoff, & Fjermestad, 1996). Furthermore, even though most studies allowed for as much time as needed to complete the task, more than a dozen articles reported using timed tasks. One study looked specifically at decision making under time pressure (Smith & Hayne, 1997). Conversely, none of the organizational studies compared task type. The types of teams involved, however, gives some feel for the diversity of the tasks in this context: inspection, strategic planning, administrative, quality, process improvement, customer support, auditing, software development, special task force, policing, management, budget, sales, focus/assessment, leadership, and various other project groups.

Technologies

In both contexts, more than half the studies made use of GSSs (GroupSystems, VisionQuest, SAMM, SAGE, GroupForum, and OptionLink were each mentioned in at least three laboratory studies, but GroupSystems was the most common in both contexts). More than a dozen laboratory studies also reported using some form of CC, with Vax Notes the most mentioned by name. The remainder of the laboratory studies examined e-mail, phone, audioconferencing, videoconferencing, screen-sharing programs, or some type of Web-based software. Five organizational studies involved groups using Lotus Notes, another five focused on some type of videoconferencing, four reported on CC, another four described the use of e-mail, and one used an intranet Web-based system. The remaining six organizational studies concerned groups using a combination of the above and other technologies.

More than half the studies in each context compared the technology of interest to FtF interaction; however, the comparison was only by implication in most of the organizational studies (i.e., actual FtF comparison groups were used only in the laboratory context). Comparisons across different technologies were rare in both contexts. Although only 3 organizational studies examined groups using variations of a single technology, 27 of the laboratory groups were examined on their use of different features of a single technology (e.g., anonymity, interface, language, and support level).

Meeting Processes

Meeting-process issues related to electronic meetings emerged in only a few forms.

Several laboratory studies directly examined variations in the facilitation of electronic meetings (Anson, Bostrom, & Wynne, 1995; Wheeler & Valacich, 1996) or the facilitator's ability to create a certain meeting climate in the technology-supported teams (Shepherd, Briggs, Reinig, Yen, & Nunamaker, 1996; Wheeler et al., 1993). Two laboratory studies considered the impact of leadership style in electronic meetings (Kahai et al., 1997; Sosik, Avolio, & Kahai, 1998) and two additional studies investigated the effect of using devil's advocacy and dialectical inquiry techniques with technology-supported groups (Valacich & Schwenk, 1995a, 1995b). One laboratory study compared structured and unstructured decision processes (Mennecke, 1997) using an EMS. In the organizational context, two experimental studies explored process issues. Bamber, Watson, and Hill (1996) examined agenda structure as it affected GSS and non-GSS teams, and McClernon and Swanson (1995) looked at the effect of team-building interventions in GDSS and non-GDSS meetings (for additional discussion of interventions with groups/teams, in this volume, see Chapters 14 [Schultz] and 15 [Sunwolf & Seibold]).

Feedback and Time

Issues of feedback (e.g., from one meeting to the next) and time emerged in several ways in these studies but were rarely examined in either context. Nearly all the organizational groups and at least 11 of the laboratory groups reviewed here had both some past experience working together as well as expectations of future interactions. Several studies included repeated-measures experimental designs or extended sampling periods; nevertheless, only a few laboratory experiments (see Alavi, Wheeler, & Valacich, 1995; Chidambaram, 1996; Contractor, Seibold, & Heller, 1996; Daily et al., 1996; Galegher & Kraut, 1994: Knoll & Jarvenpaa, 1998; Sosik, Avolio, & Kahai, 1997; Storck & Sproull, 1995) and even fewer organizational studies (see Fish, Kraut, Root, & Rice, 1993; McClernon & Swanson, 1995; Zack, 1993, 1994; Zack &

McKenney, 1995) actually measured and reported findings reflecting technology use at multiple points in time. Even these generally fail to capture developmental issues, group learning over time, or feedback from one meeting to the next.

Outcomes Related to Group Performance

Table 16.2 lists the findings for both laboratory and organizational groups on group performance, meeting efficiency, and member satisfaction. For each, the findings are divided into categories where GCT teams are superior to FtF teams, FtF teams are superior to GCT teams, GCT and FtF teams show no difference, and studies of variations in GCTs. I describe here only some of the key findings in each context.

GCTs > FtF

Several laboratory studies reported that GCTs improved some aspect of group performance as compared to FtF groups. Hightower, Sayeed, Warkentin, and McHaney (1998), for example, found that groups using a synchronous CC system performed better on a business case. GSS-supported groups proposed more solutions (Valacich & Schwenk, 1995a) and considered more alternatives in another business case (Valacich & Schwenk, 1995a, 1995b). On a brainstorming task, EMS groups outperformed FtF groups for both unique and high-quality contributions (Valacich, Paranka, George, & Nunamaker, 1993). Gallupe, Cooper, Grise, and Bastianutti (1994) also reported higher performance for electronic brainstorming groups in two different experiments. Daily et al. (1996), moreover, reported that GDSS groups produced more ideas on several timed campus-problem tasks. Chidambaram and Jones (1993) indicated that EMS-supported groups not only used a higher quality decision process but also generated more solutions than their FtF counterparts. Under time pressure, decision quality was greater for GSS groups (Smith & Hayne, 1997), and under conditions of a majority/

Table 16.2 Summary of GCT Research Findings Related to Group Performance, Meeting Efficiency, and Member Satisfaction

	Group Performance		Meeting Efficiency		Member Satisfaction	
	Laboratory	*Organizational*	*Laboratory*	*Organizational*	*Laboratory*	*Organizational*
Group communication technologies > face-to-face	Alavi (1994) Chidambaram and Jones (1993) Daily, Whatley, Ash, and Steiner (1996) Dennis, Hilmer, and Taylor (1998) Easton, Eickelmann, and Flatley (1994) Gallupe, Cooper, Grise, and Bastianutti (1994) Hightower, Sayeed, Warkentin, and McHaney (1998) Ocker, Hiltz, Turoff, and Fjermestad (1996) Olaniran (1994) Petrovic and Krickl (1994) Smith and Hayne (1997) Valacich, Paranka, George, and Nunamaker (1993) Valacich and Schwenk (1995a) Valacich and Schwenk (1995b)	Bamber, Watson, and Hill (1996) Bikson (1996) Campbell (1997) Ciborra (1996) Coleman (1997a) Creighton and Adams (1998) de Vreede (1998) Di Pietro (1995) Dishman and Ayres (1996) Failla (1996) Kock and McQueen (1997) McClernon and Swanson (1995) Nunamaker, Briggs, and Mittleman (1995) Nunamaker, Briggs, Romano, and Mittleman (1997) Orlikowski (1996) Romm and Pliskin (1998) Sheffield and Gallupe (1994) Spuck, Prater, and Palumbo (1995) Turoff, Hiltz, Bahgat, and Rana (1993) Van Genuchten, Cornelissen, and Van Dijk (1998) Venkatesh, Leo, Kuzawinski, and Diamond (1996) Williams and Wilson (1997)	Condon and Cech (1996) Karan, Kerr, Murthy, and Vinze (1996)	Bikson (1996) Boutte, Jones, Hendricks, and Rodger (1996) Ciborra (1996) Coleman (1997a) Creighton and Adams (1998) Di Pietro (1995) Dishman and Ayres (1996) Jackson, Aiken, Vanjani, and Hasan (1995) Kline and Gardiner (1997) Kock and McQueen (1997) Nunamaker, Briggs, and Mittleman (1995) Nunamaker, Briggs, Romano, and Mittleman (1997) Pollard (1996) Sheffield and Gallupe (1994) Turoff, Hiltz, Bahgat, and Rana (1993) Van Genuchten, Cornelissen, and Van Dijk (1998) Venkatesh, Leo, Kuzawinski, and Diamond (1996) Williams and Wilson (1997) Zack and McKenney (1995)	Alavi (1994) Chidambaram (1996) Gundersen, Davis, and Davis (1995) Olaniran (1996) Scalia and Sackmary (1996) Valacich and Schwenk (1995a) Valacich, Paranka, George, and Nunamaker (1993)	Boutte, Jones, Hendricks, and Rodger (1996) Ciborra (1996) de Vreede (1998) Liou and Nunamaker (1993) Lou and Scammell (1996) Nunamaker, Briggs, and Mittleman (1995) Orlikowski (1996) Palmer (1998) Romm and Pliskin (1998) Sheffield and Gallupe (1994) Turoff, Hiltz, Bahgat, and Rana (1993) Van Genuchten, Cornelissen, and Van Dijk (1998) Venkatesh, Leo, Kuzawinski, and Diamond (1996)

(continued)

Table 16.2 Summary of GCT Research Findings Related to Group Performance, Meeting Efficiency, and Member Satisfaction (Continued)

	Group Performance		Meeting Efficiency		Member Satisfaction	
	Laboratory	Organizational	Laboratory	Organizational	Laboratory	Organizational
Face-to-face > group communication technologies	Carey and Kacmar (1997) El-Shinnawy and Vinze (1997) Farmer and Hyatt (1994) Galegher and Kraut (1994) Olaniran (1994) Olaniran (1996) Petrovic and Krickl (1994) Radford, Morganstern, McMickle, and Lehr (1994) Strauss and McGrath (1994)	Bikson (1996) Campbell (1997) Ciborra (1996) Ciborra and Suetens (1996) Fish, Kraut, Root, and Rice (1993) Kline and Gardiner (1997) Kock and McQueen (1997) McClernon and Swanson (1995) Pollard (1996)	Carey and Kacmar (1997) Dennis, Hilmer, and Taylor (1998) Dennis (1996) Farmer and Hyatt (1994) Galegher and Kraut (1994) Gundersen, Davis, and Davis (1995) Hightower, Sayeed, Warkentin, and McHaney (1998) Hollingshead (1996a) Hollingshead (1996b) Knoll and Jarvenpa (1998) Olaniran (1994) Petrovic and Krickl (1994) Radford, Morganstern, McMickle, and Lehr (1994) Smith and Hayne (1997) Valacich and Schwenk (1995a) Valacich and Schwenk (1995b)	Ciborra and Patriotta (1996) Kock and McQueen (1997)	Carey and Kacmar (1997) Galegher and Kraut (1994) Olaniran (1996) Scalia and Sackmary (1996) Storck and Sproull (1995) Strauss (1997) Walther (1994) Warkentin, Sayeed, and Hightower (1997)	Ciborra (1996) Ciborra and Patriotta (1996) Fish, Kraut, Root, and Rice (1993) Liou and Nunamaker (1993) Orlikowski (1993)

	Group Performance		Meeting Efficiency		Member Satisfaction	
	Laboratory	Organizational	Laboratory	Organizational	Laboratory	Organizational
Group communication technologies = face-to-face	Alavi, Wheeler, and Valacich (1995) Anson, Bostrom, and Wynne (1995) Carey and Kacmar (1997) Chidambaram and Jones (1993) Daily, Whatley, Ash, and Steiner (1996) Dennis (1996) Farmer and Hyatt (1994) Galegher and Kraut (1994) Gundersen, Davis, and Davis (1995) Harmon, Schneer, and Hoffman (1995) Hollingshead (1996a) Lim and Benbasat (1997) Massey and Clapper (1995) Ocker, Hiltz, Turoff, and Fjermestad (1996) Storck and Sproull (1995) Strauss and McGrath (1994) Valacich, Paranka, George, and Nunamaker (1993) Valacich and Schwenk (1995a)	Bamber, Watson, and Hill (1996) Campbell (1997) Lou and Scammell (1996)	Radford, Morganstern, McMickle, and Lehr (1994)	Bamber, Watson, and Hill (1996) Campbell (1997) Kline and Gardiner (1997) Lou and Scammell (1996)	Alavi, Wheeler, and Valacich (1995) Anson, Bostrom, and Wynne (1995) Dennis (1996) Easton, Eickelmann, and Flatley (1994) Karan, Kerr, Murthy, and Vinze (1996) Olaniran (1996) Petrovic and Krickl (1994) Strauss and McGrath (1994) Valacich, Paranka, George, and Nunamaker (1993) Valacich and Schwenk (1995a)	Kline and Gardiner (1997) McClernon and Swanson (1995)

(continued)

Table 16.2 Summary of GCT Research Findings Related to Group Performance, Meeting Efficiency, and Member Satisfaction (*Continued*)

	Group Performance		Meeting Efficiency		Member Satisfaction	
	Laboratory	*Organizational*	*Laboratory*	*Organizational*	*Laboratory*	*Organizational*
Variations in group communication technologies	Aiken, Sloan, Paolillo, and Motiwalla (1997) Gallupe, Cooper, Grise, and Bastianutti (1994) Karan, Kerr, Murthy, and Vinze (1996) Olaniran (1995) Roy, Gauvin, and Limayem (1996) Sambamurthy and Chin (1994) Sambamurthy, Poole, and Kelly (1993) Shepherd, Briggs, Reinig, Yen, and Nunamaker (1996) Sia, Tan, and Wei (1996) Sosik, Avolio, and Kahai (1998) Toth (1996) Valacich, George, Nunamaker, and Vogel (1994) Wheeler, Mennecke, and Scudder (1993)	Bikson (1996) Dorando, Stratis, O'Donnell, and O'Donnell (1993) Niederman, Beise, and Beranek (1996) Satzinger and Olfman (1995)	Ahern and Durrington (1995) Toth (1996)	Aiken, Sloan, Paolillo, and Motiwalla (1997) Niederman, Beise, and Beranek (1996)	Aiken, Hwang, De Magalhaes, and Martin (1993) Aiken, Kim, Hwang, and Lu (1995) Aiken, Sloan, Paolillo, and Motiwalla (1997) Galegher and Kraut (1994) Olaniran (1995) Sambamurthy and Chin (1994) Sambamurthy, Poole, and Kelly (1993) Wheeler, Mennecke, and Scudder (1993)	Aiken, Sloan, Paolillo, and Motiwalla (1997) Niederman, Beise, and Beranek (1996)

minority opinion split, GSS groups made better decisions (Dennis et al., 1998).

In general, the studies of organizational groups yielded stronger perceptions of performance with GCTs than without them. Bikson's (1996) study of GroupSystems at the World Bank, for example, revealed that 97% of users felt objectives were fully or partially met and another 91% indicated the GSS contributed to achieving objectives; furthermore, users reported that the anonymity of the system allowed for higher quality contributions and actually improved the intellectual products of the organization. Studies of teams using a GDSS at Marriott's Group Decision Center (Coleman, 1997a; Di Pietro, 1995) revealed 30,000 quality ideas in a 9-month period, savings of $1 million in person hours, more ideas and more implementable ideas than in traditional meetings, more creativity because of the anonymity provided by the system, and more democratic decision making. Looking at videoconference meetings in the Australian federal government, 38% of Campbell's (1997) survey respondents reported a decrease in absenteeism, approximately 55% noted a decrease in business trips and travel costs, 60% mentioned shorter meetings, and 46% perceived increased structure in meetings. Turoff, Hiltz, Bahgat, and Rana's (1993) review of distributed GSSs suggested improved decision quality in setting standards, improved continuity across meetings, and greater accuracy in zero-based budgeting. Sheffield and Gallupe's (1994) studies of teams of New Zealand industry leaders using GroupSystems revealed overall effectiveness and meeting outcomes scores of 6.22 and 6.24, respectively, on a 7-point scale. Van Genuchten, Cornelissen, and Van Dijk's (1998) case studies of inspection teams using a computer-based GSS revealed markedly more effective detection of defects and fairly strong ratings by participants for the system.

FtF > GCTs

Several of the laboratory studies revealed that FtF groups displayed higher task/decision performance, especially when considering decision quality. Specifically, Petrovic and Krickl (1994) and Olaniran (1994) observed that FtF groups generated higher quality ideas. Similarly, Galegher and Kraut (1994) noted that perceived quality in two business cases was significantly greater in the FtF condition as compared to both a CC and CC + phone arrangement. Radford, Morganstern, McMickle, and Lehr (1994) also reported lower decision quality by synchronous CC groups as compared to FtF, audioconferencing, and videoconferencing groups working on the NASA moon survival task. Farmer and Hyatt (1994) discovered that audioconferencing groups made poorer decisions than FtF groups or screen-sharing groups. Several other laboratory studies suggest that FtF groups outperformed technology-supported groups, at least for certain types of tasks (Carey & Kacmar, 1997; El-Shinnawy & Vinze, 1997; Olaniran, 1996; Strauss & McGrath, 1994).

Some organizational studies of groups have also supported the view that traditional FtF meetings result in better performance than technology-supported teams, or that there are serious drawbacks to using GCTs. Kock and McQueen (1997), in a field study of seven process-improvement teams using an asynchronous e-mail conferencing system, found that 50% of participants indicated no change or even decreased performance as compared to FtF interactions. Ciborra and Suetens's (1996) case study of Lotus Notes to support internationally dispersed teams revealed that users rarely used the technology or perceived any benefit from it. Kline and Gardiner's (1997) interviews with teleconferencing and e-mail users in Canada indicated that many felt the technologies were more costly than anticipated, were less effective than FtF, and generally did not live up to expectations. Fish et al.'s (1993) exploration of video links to support more informal communication revealed that the technology was not as well suited to solving problems, was less useful for carrying out work tasks, and was worse at maintaining relationships as compared to FtF. McClernon and Swanson (1995) also noted that a team-building intervention without GDSS support resulted in better quality of group process (which they label as an alternate way of assessing group performance when outcomes are not readily available) as perceived by users than was found in the intervention with GDSS support.

$GCTs = FtF$

A large number of findings related to the performance of laboratory groups indicated no consistent differences between GCT and FtF groups. The most common finding here concerned decision quality. Carey and Kacmar (1997), Chidambaram and Jones (1993), Daily et al. (1996), Dennis (1996), Harmon, Schneer, and Hoffman (1995), Hollingshead (1996a), Lim and Benbasat (1997), Strauss and McGrath (1994), and Valacich and Schwenk (1995a) all found no effect on decision quality between EMS-supported groups and FtF groups. Similarly, Ocker et al. (1996) reported no difference in the written quality of a task report between FtF and CC groups. As for other performance measures, Massey and Clapper (1995) detected no difference in the number of nonredundant ideas between GSS and non-GSS groups on a brainstorming task. Anson et al. (1995) observed no performance differences between GSS and non-GSS groups in a strategy design and implementation task. Gundersen, Davis, and Davis (1995) reported no difference in members' confidence or commitment to the decisions for a choosing task. Screen-sharing technology groups and FtF groups exhibited no detectable difference in performance on two concept-learning tasks (Farmer & Hyatt, 1994). Relatedly, Valacich et al. (1993) uncovered no performance differences between audioconferencing and FtF teams engaged in a brainstorming task. Performance in two business cases showed no differences among FtF, CC, and CC + phone conditions (Galegher & Kraut, 1994).

Among the studies of organizational groups suggesting no performance differences between GCT and FtF teams, Campbell (1997) reported that only 26% of users responding to a survey felt GSS meetings were more effective; another 67% said there was no change in the level of consensus reached in electronic meetings. Lou and Scamell (1996) found that Lotus Notes users' assigned ratings on a measure of increased quality of work were only at the middle of a 5-point scale. Bamber et al. (1996) also detected no difference between GSS and FtF conditions in terms of group consensus.

GCT Variations

Several variations in a single technology or across different technologies seemed to result in performance differences among the laboratory studies. Less restrictive EMS environments (based on facilitation, training, and system-based activities) had higher decision quality than more restrictive EMS environments (Wheeler et al., 1993). Sia et al. (1996) found that use of a common (public) screen, as opposed to individual ones, on a GSS resulted in higher commitment to decisions and greater consensus change during decision-making (but not intellective) tasks. Two studies revealed that the more advanced communication and decision-making features of a Level 2 GDSS resulted in better performance than more basic Level 1 systems (Sambamurthy & Chin, 1994; Sambamurthy et al., 1993). Distributed GSS groups outperformed more proximate GSS groups on brainstorming tasks for both number of unique ideas and the quality of those ideas (Valacich et al., 1994). Additionally, anonymous groups demonstrated better brainstorming performance than identified groups when using an EMS in one instance (Sosik et al., 1998); however, another study showed no difference between anonymous/identified conditions on choice shift (Karan, Kerr, Murthy, & Vinze, 1996). When anonymity, parallel input, and brainstorming memory were removed from a GSS, electronic groups performed more poorly than nonelectronic groups (Gallupe et al., 1994). Aiken et al. (1997) briefly described three brainstorming studies in which the pool-writing method produced more comments than the gallery-writing method, but without any differences in the quality of those comments.

Several studies of organizational groups also focused on variations in technology as related to performance. Dorando, Stratis, O'Donnell, and O'Donnell (1993) conducted one of the few studies to compare GDSS-only and GDSS + FtF interaction. In their study, GDSS + FtF groups produced more original solutions, but both the depth and uniqueness of evaluation were better for GDSS-only groups. Bikson (1996) concluded that the best GSS sessions are half FtF and half technology based. Satzinger and Olfman's (1995) survey of professionals' technology needs to support groups suggested that group-based software tools (similar to GDSS) were perceived as more useful between meetings than during dispersed electronic or FtF meetings. Finally, Niederman et al.'s (1996) interviews with GSS facilitators revealed that meeting outcomes and measurable results are key issues in GSS meetings, even though linking goodness of outcomes to a particular process was perceived by the facilitators to be difficult. Respondents also believed that, as facilitators, they could help improve meeting outcomes, such as performance, when using GSS technology.

Outcomes Related to Meeting Efficiency

GCTs > FtF

Only two studies of laboratory groups suggested improved efficiency of meetings with GCTs as compared to FtF interactions, and one of these was a study of dyads. Condon and Cech (1996) found that two-person teams using synchronous CC took less time and went through fewer decision sequences than FtF dyads. Karan et al. (1996) also found that GDSS groups took slightly less time to reach consensus than FtF groups on an unstructured auditing task.

Conversely, a large number of research findings on organizational groups pointed to improved efficiency when using GCTs. Bikson's (1996) study at the World Bank, for instance, showed 50% greater efficiency in meetings, with one unit using a single electronic meeting to accomplish what would usually take 6 days. Turoff et al. (1993), in a summary of CC systems, documented how the technology allowed for faster processes in setting standards and less time needed to do zero-based budgeting. Boutte, Jones, Hendricks, and Rodger (1996) described how Ciba Geigy reduced new product development time and travel time with videoconference support. Kock and McQueen's (1997) study of asynchronous groupware used by process-improvement teams revealed 93% less time spent in group meetings and an overall decrease in the amount of time the group was in existence. Venkatesh, Leo, Kuzawinski, and Diamond's (1996) study of 40 computer-aided quality-improvement teams at Xerox revealed that cycle time in one project diminished from 48 to 4 days (saving millions of dollars) and that in another project it was reduced 30-50%, unscheduled production interruptions dropped 75%, and meeting efficiency in teams improved 50%. A control team at Silicon Graphics using a GCT accomplished in 30 minutes what previously required 20 hours (Creighton & Adams, 1998).

FtF > GCTs

The majority of the studies of laboratory groups indicated that GCT-supported groups are not as efficient as FtF groups. Knoll and Jarvenpaa (1998), for example, reported an increase in the amount of time groups using e-mail required to complete tasks. Petrovic and Krickl (1994) also reported that EMS meetings lasted longer. Several researchers have noted that computer-supported groups simply took longer to reach a decision than did noncomputer-supported groups (Carey & Kacmar, 1997; Dennis, 1996; Gundersen et al., 1995; Hightower et al., 1998; Hollingshead, 1996a, 1996b; Olaniran, 1994; Smith & Hayne, 1997; Valacich & Schwenk, 1995a, 1995b). Additionally, Dennis et al. (1998)

found that GSS groups took longer to complete a problem-solving task when members received similar levels of information (but actually reported no difference in time to reach a decision when only some group members received most of the information). Galegher and Kraut (1994) noted that FtF groups were more efficient than two different computer-mediated groups in that their planning phase peaked sooner, they were less likely to report needing additional planning, and they needed less time to communicate (especially toward the end of the task). Farmer and Hyatt (1994) observed that audioconferencing and screen-sharing groups both made fewer decisions per minute. Radford et al. (1994) also reported less efficiency for CC groups.

Despite the many claims for improved efficiency with GCTs, some studies of organizational groups have indicated that FtF meetings are more efficient. Ciborra and Patriotta (1996), for instance, found that the use of Lotus Notes by Unilever project teams actually slowed decision making; however, they contend that the preexisting organizational culture and structure had more to do with this outcome than did the technology. Kock and McQueen (1997) noted that, not surprisingly, a new asynchronous e-mail system increased the lag time it took each group member to contribute.

GCTs = FtF

Only one laboratory study showed no difference between electronic and FtF conditions for meeting efficiency. Radford et al. (1994) observed that groups using audioconferencing or audio/videoconferencing were just as efficient as FtF groups on the NASA moon survival task. Among the organizational research on groups, Campbell's (1997) study of videoconferencing systems uncovered little change in the amount of time needed to make decisions. Bamber et al. (1996), in their experiment with senior auditors, found that anonymous GSS groups actually took slightly, but not significantly, longer to make decisions than did FtF teams. Lou and Scamell's (1996)

survey of users' acceptance of Lotus Notes revealed fairly neutral responses when members were asked if the technology increased the efficiency of their work. Kline and Gardiner (1997) reported that teleconferencing and e-mail users felt the technology did not reduce response time in dealing with problems.

GCT Variations

Two studies of laboratory groups reported variations in technology related to meeting efficiency. First, Toth (1996) noted that graphical feedback added to Internet relay chat did not change discussion duration as compared to the computer condition without that feedback. Second, Ahern and Durrington (1995) reported that anonymous GSS groups spent longer per visit than identified GSS groups on four problem-solving tasks.

Only two studies of organizational groups have considered variations in technology as they relate to meeting efficiency. In one, Aiken et al. (1997) noted in an analysis of several stakeholder groups using an EMS that gallery-writing forms of electronic brainstorming took less meeting time than did pool-writing methods. In the other, Niederman et al.'s (1996) survey of GSS facilitators clearly pointed to the perceived importance of efficient use of time in electronic meetings and the belief that meeting facilitation helps to achieve that efficiency.

Outcomes Related to Member Satisfaction

GCTs > FtF

Several studies of laboratory groups have indicated that members of technology-supported groups experienced greater satisfaction than members of FtF groups. For example, in a study by Chidambaram (1996), GSS-support correlated positively to members' satisfaction with outcomes, but only after a few meetings on the GSS. As for satisfaction with group process, Valacich and Schwenk (1995a) noted that GSS members reported higher satisfaction. Looking at two different types of satisfaction with group processes, Valacich et al. (1993) discovered that GSS members were more satisfied with the precision of the process than were non-GSS members and that distributed team members using either a GDSS or an audioconferencing system were more satisfied with the accuracy of the process. Although not a direct comparison with FtF, 66% of respondents reported being extremely or very satisfied with the outcome, and 56% were extremely or very satisfied with the process in a study using a synchronous CC system (Scalia & Sackmary, 1996).

Several studies of organizational groups also reported increased member satisfaction associated with using GCTs. Palmer's (1998) survey of virtual team members in government and the private sector revealed generally positive attitudes toward information technology in general—linking that technology to success. Nunamaker, Briggs, and Mittleman (1995) reported improved member satisfaction as a result of using an EMS at Boeing and IBM, whereas Turoff et al. (1993) documented increased process satisfaction for members of a zero-based budgeting team using CC. Liou and Nunamaker's (1993) case study of GroupSystems use by a help services group in a manufacturing company revealed that users' liking of the system was a result of speed, thoroughness, quantity of information, timeliness of feedback, and the memory the system created. In a case study of EMS use in the investigations office of a police department, de Vreede (1998) gathered data showing a 4.4 satisfaction rating with the session (on a 5-point scale) and general enjoyment of collaborating in this way. Van Genuchten et al. (1998) reported somewhat lower, but still positive, general satisfaction scores for members of various inspection teams using a GSS (3.71-3.80 on a 5-point scale). Lou and Scamell (1996) also reported process-satisfaction scores between 3 and 4 on a 5-point scale in their survey of Lotus Notes users.

FtF > GCTs

A number of studies of laboratory groups suggested higher satisfaction outcomes for members of FtF, as compared to GCT, teams. Warkentin, Sayeed, and Hightower (1997) found that FtF group members were more cohesive, more satisfied with the process, and more satisfied with the outcome than were group members using a Web-based, asynchronous CC system. Similarly, Strauss (1997) reported that FtF groups were more cohesive and their members more satisfied on judgment tasks than were groups and their members using a synchronous CC system. Carey and Kacmar (1997) also reported higher general satisfaction for members of FtF groups as compared to those using a CC system. Galegher and Kraut (1994) observed that not only were FtF group members more satisfied overall with the communication than were group members in two different computer-supported conditions, but FtF members also perceived the process to be fairer, easier, and of higher quality.

Only a handful of studies of organizational groups have found GCTs, as compared to FtF, to be less satisfying to users. Notably, Ciborra and Patriotta's (1996) study of Lotus Notes revealed that users were dissatisfied because they felt the information on the system was too open and not private enough; furthermore, users perceived Lotus Notes to reinforce centralization, even though organizational leaders felt it made things more democratic. In a study by Fish et al. (1993), participants using videoconferencing for informal communication generally did not like it: 40% of users indicated they did not like one of the major features of the technology, and most felt that the technology was simply unsatisfactory for group work. Liou and Nunamaker (1993) noted that factors leading to dissatisfaction included the burnout, tedious consolidation of items, and heavy structure imposed by most GSSs. Other causes of dissatisfaction with GCTs were lack of needed bandwidth to handle the volume of information flowing between group members

(Ciborra, 1996) and lack of time for adequate training (Orlikowski, 1993).

GCTs = FtF

Several studies of laboratory groups have reported no differences between GCT and FtF conditions with respect to member satisfaction outcomes. Petrovic and Krickl (1994), for example, detected no difference between EMS and traditional (with a moderator) meetings for either process satisfaction or attitude toward technology/moderator. Karan et al. (1996) also observed no difference in process satisfaction between GDSS and FtF members. Looking at two different measures of process satisfaction, Valacich et al. (1993) were unable to discern any difference between members of electronic and nonelectronic groups in satisfaction with the accuracy of the process or between distributed and proximate group members in satisfaction with the precision of the process. Another study showed no difference in satisfaction with the solution between GSS and non-GSS group members (Valacich & Schwenk, 1995a). Alavi et al.'s (1995) study of videoconferencing conditions also revealed no differences from FtF groups for process or outcome satisfaction. Strauss and McGrath (1994) reported several findings related to member satisfaction and noted little difference between members of FtF and synchronous CC groups for idea-generation tasks.

Only two studies of organizational groups suggested evidence of comparable satisfaction levels (based on measures of group cohesiveness) for GCT and FtF team members. McClernon and Swanson (1995) noted that group cohesiveness was perceived as similar in GDSS and FtF groups. Additionally, interviews with teleconferencing and e-mail users revealed that the anticipated increases in levels of group cohesiveness over FtF meetings were never reached (Kline & Gardiner, 1997).

GCT Variations

Several studies of laboratory groups have looked at technology variations as related to group member satisfaction. For example, two studies uncovered evidence of better attitudes and satisfaction for group members working with Level 2, as opposed to Level 1, GDSSs (Sambamurthy & Chin, 1994; Sambamurthy et al., 1993). Aiken et al. (1997) reported two experiments revealing that participants were more satisfied with gallery-writing styles than pool-writing methods of electronic brainstorming. Surprisingly, Wheeler et al. (1993) found that GDSS users in a more restrictive setting were more satisfied with the process and the outcome than were users in less restrictive environments. Two studies of GDSS use by Aiken et al. indicated no difference in satisfaction levels between English and Malaysian users (Aiken et al., 1993) or between users of English and Korean language interfaces (Aiken et al., 1995); however, the small sample sizes ($n = 19$ and 12, respectively) would have made any differences difficult to detect. With regard to different technologies, CC alone actually resulted in greater perceived ease of usage and more overall satisfaction than a CC + phone condition among group members analyzing business cases (Galegher & Kraut, 1994).

Although very few studies of organizational groups have examined variations in technology related to member satisfaction, Aiken et al. (1997) observed greater satisfaction with gallery-writing, as opposed to pool-writing, forms of electronic brainstorming. Niederman et al.'s (1996) survey of GSS facilitators also yielded evidence suggesting that outcome and process satisfaction were important concerns, but they were not mentioned by as many facilitators as expected.

Outcomes Related to Communication

This set of outcomes includes four communication variables: participation, influence, information exchange, and specific message types. Table 16.3 summarizes findings for this set of outcome variables.

GCTs > FtF

Among the studies of laboratory groups, two studies of EMS-supported groups revealed greater participation by members (Gallupe et al., 1994; Petrovic & Krickl, 1994). Furthermore, Strauss (1997) reported that members of CC groups participated more equally. Several studies of organizational groups support the claim that GCTs generally increase members' participation in meetings as compared to FtF, or induce generally higher levels of participation (Bikson, 1996; Sheffield & Gallupe, 1994; Slater & Anderson, 1994; Venkatesh et al., 1996; Williams & Wilson, 1997). Boutte et al. (1996) also reported increased attendance at meetings supported with EMSs. Other studies have produced evidence of more equal participation among members in GSS meetings (McClernon & Swanson, 1995; Niederman et al., 1996).

Among the studies of influence in laboratory groups, only Dennis et al. (1998) reported that members of GSS groups exerted more normative influence than did members of FtF groups. Similarly, only a few studies of organizational groups have suggested that GCTs result in increased influence as compared to FtF. Kock and McQueen (1997) observed that an asynchronous CC system suppressed the organizational hierarchy and, thereby, gave GCT users greater influence. Similarly, Pollard (1996) found that the anonymity in EMSs reduced positional bias and helped to reduce status perceptions. Williams and Wilson (1997) noticed in their interviews with groupware users a perceived increase in opportunities to influence, although users also perceived very little reduction in power distance.

With regard to information exchange, Strauss's (1997) laboratory study indicated that synchronous CC groups had more efficient exchange of information, even though they were not necessarily more effective at task performance. Dennis (1996; Dennis et al., 1998) also reported that more information was exchanged with a GSS than without it. Several studies of organizational groups

also showed that information exchange was better with GCTs than without them. Bikson (1996), for example, reported better exchange (and greater credibility) of information in electronic meetings. Positive evaluations for information exchange were also given by other GSS users (Sheffield & Gallupe, 1994). Williams and Wilson (1997) produced evidence of greater access to information with groupware, and Dennis, Tyran, Vogel, and Nunamaker (1997) concluded that the task structure and process support provided by GSSs have a positive impact on the production, identification, and integration of information.

Among research on laboratory groups reporting specific message types, electronic group interaction displayed more requests for information and action, orienting of suggestions with requests for information, suggestions with incorporated orientations, and metalanguage than in FtF groups (Condon & Cech, 1996). Strauss (1997) also observed that synchronous CC groups, in contrast with FtF groups, were characterized by more supportive communication in intellective tasks (but not other task types), but also a higher proportion of disagreements across tasks. In comparison to FtF groups, computer-supported groups also forwarded more critical arguments (Valacich & Schwenk, 1995a). Massey and Clapper (1995) report that group members using a GDSS with anonymous input showed more comfort suggesting ideas, discussing sensitive issues, and expressing strong (and even negative) feelings toward other group members without worrying about what they thought. Finally, Williams and Wilson (1997) was the only study of an organizational team reporting superior messages with GCTs, as opposed to FtF; specifically, they noted better written arguments with a GSS.

FtF > GCTs

Most of the studies of laboratory groups revealed that FtF group members participated more than did members of technology-supported groups. Among the CC studies reporting more total statements/words/messages in

Table 16.3 Summary of GCT Findings Related to Communication Outcomes

		Participation	Influence	Information Exchange	Specific Message Type
Group communication technologies > face-to-face	Laboratory	Gallupe, Cooper, Grise, and Bastianutti (1994) Petrovic and Krickl (1994) Strauss (1997)	Dennis, Hilmer, and Taylor (1998)	Dennis (1996) Dennis, Hilmer, and Taylor (1998) Strauss (1997)	Condon and Cech (1996) Massey and Clapper (1995) Strauss (1997) Valacich and Schwenk (1995a)
	Organizational	Bikson (1996) Boutte, Jones, Hendricks, and Rodger (1996) McClernon and Swanson (1995) Niederman, Beise, and Beranek (1996) Sheffield and Gallupe (1994) Slater and Anderson (1994) Venkatesh, Leo, Kuzawinski, and Diamond (1996) Williams and Wilson (1997)	Kock and McQueen (1997) Pollard (1996) Williams and Wilson (1997)	Bikson (1996) Dennis, Tyran, Vogel, and Nunamaker (1997) Sheffield and Gallupe (1994) Williams and Wilson (1997)	Williams and Wilson (1997)
Face-to-face > group communication technologies	Laboratory	Hightower, Sayeed, Warkentin, and McHaney (1998) Hollingshead (1996a) Olaniran (1996) Strauss (1997) Valacich and Schwenk (1995a) Valacich and Schwenk (1995b) Weisband, Schneider, and Connolly (1995)	Hollingshead (1996a)	Dennis (1996) Dennis, Hilmer, and Taylor (1998) Hightower and Sayeed (1996) Hightower, Sayeed, Warkentin, and McHaney (1998) Hollingshead (1996b)	Condon and Cech (1996) Hollingshead (1996a) Valacich and Schwenk (1995a)
	Organizational	Campbell (1997) Ciborra and Patriotta (1996) Ciborra and Suetens (1996) Kock and McQueen (1997) Orlikowski (1993) Pollard (1996) Turoff, Hiltz, Bahgat, and Rana (1993)	McClernon and Swanson (1995)	Pollard (1996) Spuck, Prater, and Palumbo (1995) Turoff, Hiltz, Bahgat, and Rana (1993) Williams and Wilson (1997)	Campbell (1997) Fish, Kraut, Root, and Rice (1993) Spuck, Prater, and Palumbo (1995)

		Participation	Influence	Information Exchange	Specific Message Type
Group communication technologies = face-to-face	Laboratory	Strauss (1997) Weisband, Schneider, and Connolly (1995)	Contractor, Seibold, and Heller (1996) Harmon, Schneer, and Hoffman (1995) Scott and Easton (1996) Weisband, Schneider, and Connolly (1995)	Warkentin, Sayeed, and Hightower (1997)	Reinig, Briggs, and Nunamaker (1998) Strauss (1997)
	Organizational		Campbell (1997) Saunders, Robey, and Vavarek (1994)	Fish, Kraut, Root, and Rice (1993)	Di Pietro (1995)
Variations in group communication technologies	Laboratory	Ahern and Durrington (1995) Everett and Ahern (1994) Roy, Gauvin, and Limayem (1996) Toth (1996) Weisband, Schneider, and Connolly (1995)	Sia, Tan, and Wei (1996) Sia, Tan, and Wei (1997) Toth (1996)		Ahern and Durrington (1995) Sambamurthy, Poole, and Kelly (1993) Toth (1996)
	Organizational	Ciborra and Patriotta (1996) Dorando, Stratis, O'Donnell, and O'Donnell (1993) Lou and Scammell (1996) Palmer (1998)			Di Pietro (1995) Dorando, Stratis, O'Donnell, and O'Donnell (1993) Hayne and Rice (1997) Hinds and Kiesler (1995)

FtF groups are Hightower et al. (1998), Hollingshead (1996a), Olaniran (1996), Strauss (1997), and Weisband et al. (1995). With anonymous GSS input, Valacich and Schwenk (1995a, 1995b) also detected greater participation by FtF team members.

Similarly, a number of studies of organizational groups have suggested that GCTs result in reduced levels of participation as compared to FtF (Ciborra & Patriotta, 1996; Ciborra & Suetens, 1996; Kock & McQueen, 1997; Orlikowski, 1993). In a survey of videoconference users, Campbell (1997) noted that 53% of respondents saw a decrease in the ease of participation, 56% felt meeting interaction decreased, and 52% noted a decrease in opportunities to express opinions as compared to FtF meetings. In their review of CC studies, Turoff et al. (1993) observed one case in which users perceived that fewer people participated more (in contrast with FtF meetings). Pollard (1996), moreover, argued that EMS users did not participate as much because they were more concise in their typing.

Among the studies of influence in laboratory groups, Hollingshead (1996a) observed that the member with the most information needed for a task was rated as more influential in FtF groups than in CC groups. Additionally, at least one study of an organizational group showed more nearly equal influence in FtF, as opposed to GCT, interactions. Specifically, a team-building intervention without GDSS support resulted in greater equality of influence among members than when the GDSS was included (McClernon & Swanson, 1995).

Most studies of laboratory groups uncovered evidence of more effective information exchange in FtF, compared to GCT, meetings (Hightower & Sayeed, 1996; Hightower et al., 1998; Hollingshead, 1996b). Dennis (1996; Dennis et al., 1998) reported that even though more information was exchanged with GSSs, members exhibited less thinking about it, use of it, and learning of previously unknown information. Those same two studies also indicated that the information exchanged was perceived as less credible in GSS as opposed to non-GSS meetings. The research on information exchange in organizational groups has shown that information overload may also be more of a problem with GCTs than in FtF meetings (Pollard, 1996; Spuck, Prater, & Palumbo, 1995; Williams & Wilson, 1997; see Propp, Chapter 9, this volume, regarding knowledge/information load in collective information processing in groups). Relatedly, Turoff et al. (1993) found that although some GCT teams experienced increased load, others used the technology to decrease load.

Among the studies examining specific message types in laboratory groups, Condon and Cech (1996) noted that FtF conditions, in contrast to electronic ones, contained more elaborations, repeats, and discourse markers in a mutual planning task. Valacich and Schwenk (1995a) determined that FtF group discussions had more supportive arguments, solution clarifications, and questions about the problem. Another study revealed that CC groups made fewer indirect references to critical information (Hollingshead, 1996a). Several studies of organizational groups also indicated declines in certain types of GCT, as opposed to FtF, messages. In groups using videoconferencing systems, Campbell (1997) reported that 65% of survey respondents perceived decreases in informal communication, 63% experienced decreases in nontask talk, and 70% reported decreases in social conversations relative to traditional meetings. Spuck et al.'s (1995) study concluded that talk is brief and not well substantiated on a GSS. Fish et al. (1993) ascertained that the random autocruise function of the videoconferencing system they studied was not as well suited for informal messages as was FtF.

GCTs = FtF

Among the studies focusing on participation in laboratory groups, Strauss (1997) observed that synchronous CC and FtF group members commented equally in meetings that had an intellectual task. Relatedly, Weisband et al. (1995) discovered that FtF and CC groups exhibited similarly high levels of participation inequality. None of the studies of organizational groups found participation to be equal in these two conditions.

Several findings from the laboratory groups seemed to be consistent with the status persistence view on influence, which argues that high status/influence members remain so even in technology-supported groups that might be designed to equalize influence. For instance, Weisband et al. (1995) conducted two separate experiments in which computer-mediated groups were less egalitarian than FtF groups in terms of members' influence. Similarly, Scott and Easton (1996) found that even though members' influence levels were perceived to be more equal during a GDSS meeting than immediately prior to such a meeting, the usually high- and low-influence members (in FtF meetings) were still viewed as such during the GDSS meetings. Additionally, Contractor et al. (1996) noted that members of anonymous and identified GDSS groups were less likely to influence one another than were FtF group members early in a series of meetings; by a third meeting, however, there were no differences (which suggests that over time, influence becomes increasingly like that found in FtF situations). Relatedly, Harmon et al. (1995) noted that established group structures (such as influence and status) carry over into audioconferencing meetings.

Two studies of organizational groups also suggested very little difference between FtF and GCT teams when it comes to factors related to influence. Not even 40% of respondents in Campbell's (1997) survey of videoconference users believed the technology resulted in increased visibility and/or a higher personal profile in the organization. Saunders et al.'s (1994) study of CC identified several differences in influence as related to occupation, specifically in terms of who initiated and received information (which suggests a reinforcement of more traditional FtF group communication structures).

As for information exchange, Warkentin et al. (1997) observed no difference in their laboratory study of the effectiveness of information exchanged among members of Web-based CC groups and FtF groups; however, the dramatic differences in time spent with each medium (25 minutes in FtF meetings versus weeks of CC meetings) is a potential confound. Among the research on information exchange with organizational groups showing no difference between FtF and GCT teams, Fish et al. (1993) noted that the cruiser videoconferencing system was as good as FtF for routine information exchanges.

Among the studies of specific message types in laboratory groups, Strauss (1997) reported that FtF and synchronous CC groups exhibited no difference in frequency of personal attacks on members. Exploring the on-line attacks of a person, known as "flaming," Reinig et al. (1998) classified only 5 of 1,692 GSS comments as flaming and another 31 as "buffoonery." Di Pietro's (1995) study of an organizational group also noted there were almost no rude comments on the GDSS system, despite its allowance for anonymity.

GCT Variations

A handful of laboratory studies have looked at how variations in technology affected participation. For example, a constant public screen during electronic brainstorming tended to equalize participation of group members more so than other display options (Roy, Gauvin, & Limayem, 1996). Two studies by Ahern (Ahern & Durrington, 1995; Everett & Ahern, 1994) also showed anonymous group members to be more participative and to write more words per message than those in non-anonymous conditions in a computer-supported group; however, Weisband et al. (1995) detected no difference in participation between members of identified and anonymous CC groups. Toth (1996) found no differences in total messages when comparing Internet relay chat with and without graphic feedback about group opinions.

A few studies of organizational groups have also investigated how variations in technology relate to members' participation. Palmer (1998) found that virtual teams within government made greater use of e-mail, fax, and groupware, whereas virtual teams in the private sector tended to utilize fax and intranets. Ciborra and Patriotta (1996) found that project teams utilized other communication technologies to avoid using Lotus Notes and to target information more specifically to various others. Dorando et al. (1993) observed that GDSS groups whose members also engaged in oral communication had more total comments than groups using the GDSS only. In another study, Lotus Notes users' self-reported participation was more than twice as great as computer-monitored participation levels (Lou & Scamell, 1996).

Only a few studies of laboratory groups have considered relationships between variations in technology and members' influence. Sia et al. (1996) noted that GSS groups using individual screens had more influence equality among members than did groups with a common/public screen. In another study, Sia et al. (1997) noted that GSS groups using an icon-based interface had more influence attempts and that there was a greater inequality of influence among members in the text-based GSS groups. Finally, first-advocacy effects were stronger in groups using Internet relay chat with graphic feedback, as opposed to the chat condition alone (Toth, 1996). None of the research on organizational groups has directly considered variations in technology as related to members' influence. Furthermore, there was no research in either the laboratory or organizational context that directly reported on how variations in technology relate to information exchange in groups.

Finally, relatively few studies of laboratory groups have examined variations in technology as they relate to specific message types. In a study by Sambamurthy et al. (1993), groups using a Level 1 GDSS contributed more solution elaboration statements, but those using a Level 2 system offered more insightful orientation comments. A text-based GSS elicited more general group comments, whereas an icon-based system resulted in more interpersonal comments (Ahern & Durrington, 1995). Other studies have examined normative and persuasive messages in various types of computer-mediated groups (see Toth, 1996).

Several studies of organizational groups have also focused on variations in technology as related to specific message types. Relevant here is research by Dorando et al. (1993), which revealed that Bellcore GDSS groups using technology and FtF communication in their meetings produced more supportive comments than did those groups using the GDSS only. Additionally, several researchers have noted the benefits and drawbacks of anonymous messages in technology-supported meetings (Jackson, Aiken, Vanjani, & Hasan, 1995; Nunamaker et al., 1995; Pollard, 1996; Slater & Anderson, 1994; Spuck et al., 1995; Turoff et al., 1993; Venkatesh et al., 1996), but only two studies dealt with the accuracy of source attributions for anonymous messages (Di Pietro, 1995; Hayne & Rice, 1997). Both found that anonymous messages are not very accurately connected to their sources by EMS users.

CONCLUSIONS AND FUTURE DIRECTIONS

Reviewing the research in this area is one thing; making sense of it is another. In an effort to do at least some of the latter, I begin this section by drawing some conclusions pertaining to the recent GCT research reviewed here. I then compare and contrast those findings to three literature reviews that leave off where this one begins. Drawing on those conclusions and comparisons, as well as some of my own observations of key trends in this area, I offer several directions for future research on GCTs.

Conclusions About
Recent GCT Research

As one can gather from this review, recent research has not resolved past criticisms concerning mixed and inconclusive findings (for a recent critique, see Seibold et al., 1994). Furthermore, the findings as presented here do not readily account for what are important differences in the scope and quality of the studies reviewed (i.e., several of the studies, especially in the organizational context, lack the methodological rigor and efforts at objectivity found in the laboratory context, and many of the laboratory studies lack the external validity of the organizational studies). Even with those cautions in mind, we can begin to see a few patterns in these studies.

Group Performance

Research in both contexts suggests that GSSs can lead to improved group performance, especially as measured quantitatively. For example, of the 14 laboratory studies reporting that GCT-supported teams outperformed FtF teams, 11 pertained to GSSs, and 9 of those relied entirely or in part on quantitative measures of performance. Many of these involved brainstorming tasks, for which the parallel input and the structure of the GSS allowed for greater productivity. There was also substantial evidence from studies of organizational groups that GSSs improved group performance, but here the performance improvements were for both quantity and quality. Part of the explanation for these differences lies in the somewhat different ways in which quality was assessed in the two contexts.

In both bodies of literature, the studies reporting that GCT teams performed worse than or equal to FtF groups were those where a variety of technologies, but especially audioconferencing and CC, were used. For example, in the laboratory research, five studies indicated that FtF teams had better performance quality, and nine studies showed no difference. Interestingly, 10 of those 14 stud-

ies finding as good or better performance for FtF teams compared audioconferencing or CC groups to FtF groups. Clearly, not all GCTs provide the same level of support, and some (such as CC and audioconferencing) may result in poorer performance when compared to FtF groups.

In the laboratory context, task effects emerged (especially when FtF groups had higher performance), and several variations in technology (Level 2 GSSs, anonymity, display of ideas on a common screen, and social comparison in electronic brainstorming) generally improved group performance. Although detailed discussion of task effects is beyond the scope of this chapter (see Benbasat & Lim, 1993; Farmer & Hyatt, 1994), the findings for the technology variations suggest that it may be specific features of a technology (e.g., communication support, decision-making tools, and anonymous input)—not just the technology itself—that facilitate improvement in group performance. In the organizational context, the studies reporting better performance for GCT teams relied mostly on in-depth case study and other qualitative methods, whereas those findings that technology-supported teams performed no better or even worse than FtF teams emerged almost exclusively from questionnaires, interviews, and/or experiments. The research methodology matters, in that the case/field studies generally revealed big-picture perceptions about the role of the technology in the organization, whereas some of the other methods isolated more specific instances of technology use.

Meeting Efficiency

The findings with respect to meeting efficiency varied markedly across the two contexts. Nearly all the laboratory studies revealed that GCT groups took more time to complete tasks than did FtF groups. The findings from the two studies showing greater efficiency when using GCTs may be accounted for by the fact that one used only two-person groups (which many scholars would not even classify as a group) and the other employed groups with a fair amount of history (which is rare in this context). In general, these laboratory studies were one-shot experiments involving one relatively short meeting; thus, it is not surprising that GCT teams, usually interacting on these systems for the first time, take longer than FtF groups using a more familiar method.

With the organizational teams, the majority of the evidence points to greater meeting efficiency when using GCTs as compared to groups without that support. In contrast to the laboratory studies, many of these assessments were of longer projects with multiple group meetings, which may have allowed for such efficiencies to emerge. Additionally, the studies of organizational groups tended to have a broader notion of meeting efficiency that went beyond time savings (e.g., person-hours and travel costs saved). The studies indicating decreased efficiency (or no difference) were more likely to make comparisons to Lotus Notes, some form of teleconferencing, or e-mail (the lone GSS study fitting here was experimental in nature and, thus, qualitatively different from most GSS research in this context). Again, the specific GCT being used may also affect relative meeting efficiency given each technology's unique features and capabilities.

Member Satisfaction

Research in these two contexts showed mixed findings about the effects of technology on group member satisfaction. GSS group members were equally as satisfied as, or more so than, FtF group members in both contexts. In fact, studies reporting less member satisfaction with GCTs generally did not compare GSSs to FtF. For example, approximately three fourths of the studies reporting greater satisfaction in FtF, as opposed to GCT, teams involved various types of CC. Similarly, the studies of organizational groups suggesting that FtF team members are more satisfied tended to be case studies of technologies other than GSSs. The laboratory studies reporting greater member satisfaction, especially pro-

cess satisfaction, in technology-supported groups usually involved GSSs (even though some studies showed no differences in members' satisfaction with processes or outcomes between GSS and FtF teams). The greater sophistication and features of many GSSs that led to improved group performance may also have helped to increase member satisfaction; however, certain GSS features may contribute more than others to member satisfaction. Laboratory studies, for example, revealed that Level 2 GSSs were associated with more process and outcome satisfaction than were Level 1 systems.

The studies of organizational work teams showed generally greater member satisfaction over an even wider range of technologies. The somewhat higher member satisfaction in the organizational context can be attributed, in part, to the greater long-term investment that these users may have in the various technologies. Greater consideration of the technologies initially and, perhaps, more regular usage likely contributed to stronger feelings of satisfaction among these users. It is also possible that the sometimes rather sizable investments that organizations make in these technologies may leave employees with the view that they cannot afford not to be satisfied given the commitments they and their organization have already made to the GCT—what one might refer to as a "sunk-cost" mentality.

Communication

There were several similarities and differences in the various communication outcomes when comparing these two contexts. First, the laboratory studies revealed that CC group members participated less; similarly, the studies of organizational groups showed evidence of lower or equal member participation rates (compared to FtF) for groups using non-GSS technologies. Research in both contexts also yielded evidence of higher member participation rates in groups using GSSs. The parallel input of most GSSs, which is sometimes seen as one of the primary advantages of such systems, may well contribute to greater member participation. Furthermore, anonymity was among the important influences on member participation in laboratory groups; however, timing issues (e.g., project phase or time of day) and assessment method (e.g., computer-monitored versus self-reported estimate) were important influences on people's participation in organizational groups. The emergence of these different issues in the two contexts, therefore, is partly an artifact of the methods used. Anonymity was rarely even considered in studies of organizational groups, project phase was largely irrelevant to the one-shot laboratory meetings, and comparisons across multiple assessments of the same variable were extremely rare.

Second, the findings concerning influence were difficult to compare across the two contexts, not only because they were mixed but also because of the lack of studies of influence among organizational work teams using GSSs. Nevertheless, evidence supporting the status-persistence view and effects for technology interface emerged in the laboratory context. Thus, it may well be that influence patterns from FtF group interaction are carried over, at least partially, into GSS meetings so that status effects and differential influence are still quite possible even with systems designed to minimize them.

Third, the findings for information exchange were contradictory, with studies of laboratory groups indicating that GCTs are not as good as FtF and studies of organizational groups indicating that GCTs are better than FtF (but may also cause information overload problems). Again, the largely one-shot experimental nature of the studies conducted in the laboratory may hinder information exchange, especially as compared to the extended observations and meetings that characterized several of the studies of organizational groups.

Finally, research in both contexts revealed several different variations in specific message types between GCT and FtF groups. The exact pattern of the differences, however, is unclear and in need of further study. Additionally, both contexts showed a general lack of flam-

ing comments in technology-supported teams, which runs counter to early predictions of disinhibited behavior on computer-mediated communication systems.

Comparisons to Previous Reviews of Research

Because the research reported here covers only approximately the past 5 years, it is important to consider how these findings compare and contrast to earlier reviews. Three fairly comprehensive reviews published in 1993 and 1994 provide appropriate points of comparison (especially because two of the three come from the field of Communication).

The most extensive of the earlier reviews is McGrath and Hollingshead's (1994) text on groups and technology, which reported findings from 51 empirical studies, most of which were conducted in the laboratory context. Several of their criticisms of this research still ring true: not much comparison of various electronic technologies, not much research on the effects of task dimensions on technology use, not enough on different time/space combinations, and not enough longitudinal research. As for particular findings, the research cited in this chapter is consistent with that reviewed by McGrath and Hollingshead, in that both reviews showed better quantitative group performance (especially for GSSs), positive effects for anonymity and group size on quantitative measures of performance for technology-assisted groups, less efficiency, and less participation. Additionally, both reviews reported mixed findings for group decision quality and member satisfaction with process and outcome, important impacts of task type on performance, and varied message types exchanged in FtF versus technology-supported groups.

The major differences in the review presented in this chapter are fewer, and mixed, findings for member equality of participation, lower member satisfaction with non-GSS technologies, and lower decision quality—especially for groups using non-GSS technologies. The findings for equality of participation are not unlike those related to equality of influence (status persistence), which has noted the carryover of traditional group norms and structures into EMSs. Additionally, as users' technology savvy begins to raise their expectations about these GCTs, some of the less advanced GCTs are very likely to be perceived as less satisfying and less able to contribute to high-quality group decisions.

A second review is Benbasat and Lim's (1993) meta-analysis of 31 GSS experimental studies from 1970 to 1992. In comparison, the current review suggests three observations. First, whereas Benbasat and Lim found that GSSs resulted in greater group decision quality (at least for low-complexity tasks), the cumulative findings from the laboratory research in this chapter suggest that GSSs have a stronger influence on quantitative, as opposed to qualitative, aspects of group performance. Second, findings supporting status persistence in this chapter are consistent with Benbasat and Lim's conclusion that GSS members still defer to members of higher status. Third, both reviews indicated that more complex Level 2 (as opposed to Level 1) GSSs result in improved group performance and member satisfaction. Although the differences in findings related to performance quality are somewhat more difficult to explain, the other two findings are consistent with earlier comments about carryover from FtF group experiences and how more sophisticated technologies can create higher member satisfaction and group performance (partly because of the increased coordination they make possible).

Finally, Collins-Jarvis and Fulk's (1993) review of outcomes (decision quality, group efficiency, and member satisfaction) associated with electronic meeting systems (teleconferencing, GDSS, and CC) provides several points of comparison to the research on laboratory and organizational groups reviewed in this chapter. As for group performance quality, they found that CC and GDSS groups produced decisions of quality at least equal to, if not higher than, their FtF counterparts, yet this was more characteristic of the field studies they reviewed than the laboratory

studies. The current review supports the conclusion that performance quality is higher for GSS groups in the organizational context. The findings for the laboratory context, however, are somewhat less positive. Additionally, the two reviews are consistent in noting that task variations seem to make a difference in group performance outcomes. As for efficiency (i.e., time to make a decision), Collins-Jarvis and Fulk concluded that GDSS-supported organizational groups were more efficient than non-GDSS groups, which is consistent with the findings presented in this chapter. They reported mixed findings for laboratory groups, but the current review shows stronger evidence that GDSS/GSS laboratory groups are less efficient than FtF groups. The finding in this chapter that all GCTs were less efficient than FtF is consistent with Collins-Jarvis and Fulk's conclusions concerning CC but suggests less efficiency for teleconferencing than they reported. Shorter projects and timed laboratory tasks (as opposed to estimates of how long FtF methods would have taken) both help explain why FtF and technology-supported teams might differ in efficiency measured as time to reach a decision; however, the discrepancy between the two reviews is less clear.

As for member satisfaction, the two reviews generally point to the conclusion that GDSS group members are at least as satisfied as, if not more so than, those in FtF groups, and that members of organizational groups are relatively more satisfied than teams studied in the laboratory context. Additionally, studies in both reviews suggest that members of CC groups especially may be less satisfied than FtF group members. Again, this may have much to do with the features and capabilities of the technology in light of the expectations and needs of the users.

Suggestions for Future Work

It is not my intent to leave the reader with another summary of this literature that offers the discouraging conclusion that there is a mix of uninterpretable findings that demand reconciliation of differences before research in this area can proceed. In fact, the comparisons across these research contexts and in relation to previous research reveal several points of compatibility (as well as some obvious differences). Rather than focus on past concerns, the somewhat foreseeable technological advancements and the markedly less predictable social usage practices for GCTs provide a number of exciting opportunities. With that in mind, let me briefly comment on three key trends important to future work in this area, followed by several considerations for communication scholars.

Key Trends

An important trend is the increasing availability of GCTs, facilitated by more Web-based systems, greater use of the Internet (and, ultimately, Internet II), and enhanced portability of equipment. Several Web-based GSSs (e.g., Facilitate.com and Soft Bicycle) already exist, and several of the major vendors of EMSs (e.g., GroupSystems and MeetingWorks) have Web versions of their products available. The Internet also promises improved CC, desktop videoconferencing, audioconferencing, and shared documents. It is possible that Web-based and Internet-supported GCTs may look and feel very different from most of the GCTs of the 1990s; thus, the outcomes associated with such communication technologies may have to be reexamined. Others have predicted that the World Wide Web will not make groupware obsolete (Clark, Downing, & Coleman, 1997; Karacapilidis & Pappis, 1997), which may mean that an expanding variety of GCTs will be available for use and study. Even more important with regard to availability will be the increased ease (resulting from portability and falling prices) with which many groups can use GCTs. It is not difficult to theorize why increased availability may mean increased opportunities for repeated use, less personal and group investment in the technology, and more instances of adoption/rejection/reinvention— any one of which could drastically affect research outcomes.

A second, related, trend is the continuing convergence of these technologies (see Baldwin, McVoy, & Steinfield, 1996). Marshak (1994), for example, predicted that this convergence will be so complete and that groupware will become so ingrained in the way we work that it will be transparent and ubiquitous to users. Although few of the studies reviewed here considered combinations of technologies (much less combinations involving traditional FtF interaction), it seems clear that group work increasingly may be supported by communication technologies that provide live videoconferencing, text-based document sharing, audio connections, anonymous voting, and shared whiteboards. One need not look much beyond Microsoft's NetMeeting to see several of these combinations; it is interesting that the structured group meeting features (e.g., agendas, anonymity, and polling) seem to be some of the last pieces in this convergence. Given the findings presented here that GSS groups generally were superior to groups supported by other technologies on most outcomes, GSS technologies should be an important part of this convergence. Thus, future research will need to consider increased convergence of various technology and channel combinations (including FtF) and what that means for group communication theory, research, and practice. This convergence will also make available multiple channels on a single technology, which provides further challenges to scholars conducting research in this area.

A final trend concerns distributed and dispersed (virtual) groups. In one sense, it seems odd to label any group "virtual," because it is just as "real" as any other group (and the consequences of its actions may, in many cases, be even more important). If we are indeed going to see increasing needs for collaboration between individuals in different times and places, there is also a need for more sophisticated research to explore this phenomenon. Clearly, not enough emphasis has been placed on what it means to be dispersed in this sense. One of the exciting efforts related to dispersed groups is the creation of more realistic virtual meeting environments (e.g., large video panels that display views of the participants as though they were all seated around a table), better on-line facilitation, and even more possibilities for human-machine communication through the use of virtual reality (see Nunamaker, 1997).

Directions for Communication Research

There is no shortage of recent advice on future research directions in this area (see Briggs et al., 1998; Nunamaker, 1997), but let me suggest four key considerations specifically for communication scholars interested in groups. First, as communication researchers, we are well positioned to explore specific communication issues associated with GCTs. I have reviewed several findings related to member participation, influence, information exchange, and several specific message types here, and those should continue to receive attention. Additionally, the nature of many GCTs makes anonymity and partial anonymity an important communication variable deserving further attention. Although most GDSSs include or allow for anonymous input of ideas and votes, a sense of anonymity also is created in any mediated environment, especially if people are working together in a text-based environment without much time to become acquainted. In short, anonymous versus nonanonymous idea contribution has been examined as an input variable with these technologies, but we should also be examining processes and outcomes related to anonymity (e.g., perceived anonymity of self and other, as well as ability to identify others' comments) and the nature of anonymous messages (e.g., persuasiveness and credibility; see Anonymous, 1998).

Another communication issue deserving further attention is feedback (which is true of group communication research in general; in this volume, see Chapters 14 [Schultz] and 20 [Greenbaum & Query]). Although some GSSs have been used to support feedback processes in quality improvement (Aiken, Hasan, & Vanjani, 1996) and in control self-assessment

(Friedberg et al., 1997), there has been very little research on how GCTs can be used to solicit and provide feedback. Explorations of how GCTs influence the timeliness, specificity, frequency, sensitivity, and other dimensions of feedback may provide useful information on the viability of these systems for providing groups and group members with valuable feedback.

A second direction is reflected in the call to think more processually and longitudinally about this research area (see George & Jessup, 1997). The least theorized and least researched portion of the meeting-process model in this review is the notion of feedback from one meeting to the next. The fact is, however, that many teams use GCTs for more than a single meeting. They are involved in projects with multiple meetings that may include a variety of technologies to support their interactions during and between those formal meetings. Furthermore, many of those teams will also engage in FtF interactions during and between meetings. All these interactions potentially feed into subsequent group meetings and alter the meeting process. Only by looking at groups and their projects more processually and studying them at multiple points in time can we begin to develop a fuller picture of group communication (and the technologies used to support it). As an example, several students and I have been examining how repeated usage of GSSs affects members' anonymity, influence, and participation over time. We have labeled this project the "virtual honeymoon" to highlight the changing nature of group technology use over time (see Scott, Garrett, Timmerman, & Quinn, 1997).

In addition to longitudinal research, let me issue the standard call for use of multiple measures and methodologies. Case studies conducted via questionnaires, observations, interviews, and textual analysis provide very rich ways to explore GCTs and their effects. Clearly, several of the studies of organizational groups reviewed here have taken advantage of these methods; however, I stop well short of declaring that we should quit doing laboratory studies because they do not always match conditions found in organizational settings. At least until GCTs become more integrated with existing desktop technologies, even field sites where these technologies are used may resemble a laboratory (e.g., special computerized decision rooms and videoconference facilities). Laboratory studies may tell us a great deal about the dynamics of groups using technologies, especially in instances where field settings are not accessible, direct comparisons between important conditions are not readily available, combinations and variations in communication technologies have not reached a critical level of use in organizations, or we simply do not know where to begin inquiry into this regularly changing area of research. Additionally, many of the laboratory-based studies in this research are stronger methodologically, at least with regard to internal validity. This not only suggests caution in interpreting some of the less rigorous studies of organizational teams but also demands that research on groups in this setting be more systematic and methodologically sound. Whenever possibly, of course, laboratory studies must also make adjustments to improve generalizability when that is a goal. The use of larger project teams, groups with both a history and an anticipated future, and realistic tasks on which those groups would naturally be working can make findings from this research more comparable to the organizational teams most likely to use GCTs. Scholarship that can combine the control and explicit conditions for comparison found in laboratory groups with the complex set of issues that characterize work teams in organizational settings promises to yield the most useful data.

Finally, future efforts must go beyond the limitations of the framework employed here. Although the meeting-process model is useful for organizing variables and categorizing relationships, it does not provide any explanation of the processes by which these variables influence one another. Social influence, structurational, and other theories that provide communicative accounts for how these different constructs influence one another are necessary if we are to move beyond simple causal rela-

tions to process-based explanations. For example, in writing this review I was occasionally reminded by the findings (only some of which are presented here) that not all groups use technology in the same ways, nor do they always use them in expected ways. Furthermore, not all individual group members necessarily use the same technology similarly or in ways that are consistent with the spirit of the system. As proponents of Adaptive Structuration Theory (DeSanctis & Poole, 1994; Poole & DeSanctis, 1990, 1992) and sociotechnical views about technology point out, we should not necessarily expect those similarities within or across groups, nor should we expect all usage practices to be consistent with the intended use of the technology. Thus, we need such theories to help explain not only how groups use technologies, but also the complex processes that relate the parts of the meeting-process model to one another.

CONCLUSION

Amid the regularly changing face of technology today, it is safe to say that various electronic and digital technologies to support communication will be used increasingly by groups in the future. As a means of understanding our current knowledge of research about group communication technologies, this chapter reviewed 131 data-based studies, published in the past 5 years, of GCT usage by teams in laboratory and organizational contexts. Using a synthesis of previous research frameworks labeled the meeting-process model, this chapter characterized the research in each context, compared GCT teams to FtF teams, contrasted findings across the two research contexts, and established parallels to earlier reviews of research on this topic. The meeting-process model also reminds us that outcomes depend as much or more on issues of context, group member characteristics, task features, and meeting processes as they do the technology itself. That is good news for communication scholars, because it makes explicit the fact that if one wants to understand this exciting new area of GCTs, one must also understand a great deal about communication processes in groups and meetings. Fortunately, that will continue to be an area in which we remain experts.

NOTES

1. The field of Education continues to be a context in which computers and other technologies have found great application. Although much of this involves using the computer to simply present information to individual students (making it neither group-based nor especially interactive), GCTs increasingly are being utilized under the rubric of computer-supported collaborative learning and distance learning. Although much of the published work in this area reports mainly "lessons learned," there are several more research-oriented studies on the subject in recent years (see Derycke & Vieville, 1994; Money, 1996; Neuwirth & Wojahn, 1996; Ross, 1996; Schwartz, 1995; Sietz & Bodendorf, 1994; Wegerif, 1996).

2. The use of GCTs in the context of social support seems to be an especially important topic. Several recent studies have examined telephone and computer-based social support (Galinsky, Schopler, & Abell, 1997; Mickelson, 1997; Schoch & White, 1997; Weinberg, Schmale, Uken, & Wessel, 1996). Additionally, research into a variety of on-line communities has expanded traditional notions of "group" and provides yet another related context where GCTs are used to provide a type of social support (see Aycock & Buchignani, 1995; Baym, 1997; Curtis, 1997; Korenman & Wyatt, 1996; Snyder & Kurtze, 1996; Turkle, 1997).

3. Meeting processes can mean several things, including the communicative behaviors and patterns that occur during the meeting. Additionally, Adaptive Structuration Theory (DeSanctis & Poole, 1994; Poole & DeSanctis, 1990, 1992) has helped scholars focus on how users appropriate technological (and other) structures during a meeting. For my purposes, however, I treat meeting processes as the range of interventions and procedures directly tied to how a meeting itself is accomplished and, thus, distinguish it from inputs and subsequent outcomes.

4. As Grudin and Poltrock (1997) have argued, some groupware is more appropriate for collaboration (shared whiteboards) or coordination (calendars and group schedulers) than for communication, even though all three overlap. Among the current commercial groupware products supporting communication are IBM's Lotus Notes, Novell's GroupWise, Team Ware's TeamWARE, and Hewlett-Packard's communication and collaboration tools; conferencing systems like Majordomo, Cold Fusion, Netmanage, Netscape's CoolTalk, and White Pine's CU-See Me; Xerox's LiveWorks; Microsoft's Exchange and Outlook; Netscape's Collabra Share; Attachmate's OpenMind; Digital's TeamLinks Office; Mesa's Conference +; Oracle's InterOffice; SoftArc's FirstClass; and Uniplex's onGO Office (see Coleman, 1997b; Sinclair & Hale, 1997; Technology Forecast, 1997). Group author-

ing software products include Quilt, PREP, and GROVE (Khoshafian & Buckiewicz, 1995).

5. FtF is used broadly to describe traditional, person-to-person, nonelectronically mediated interaction. The term is problematic in that group members can also use technologies to support their communication when they are physically colocated (e.g., a GDSS room); thus, some have used the term to describe whether group members are colocated or dispersed. The more common technique adopted here is to use FtF as a point of comparison against any mediated communication. I should also note that many researchers use the term *verbal* in contrasting FtF to some form of technology; however, this is a misnomer in that all forms of text-based interaction (which is most groupware at this time) are essentially verbal (i.e., written). *Oral* would be a more appropriate contrasting term, but it too is problematic for technologies that also involve an oral component (e.g., audioconferencing). Thus, FtF is used throughout this chapter as the point of comparison for mediated group interactions.

REFERENCES

Ahern, T. C., & Durrington, V. (1995). Effects of anonymity and group saliency on participation and interaction in a computer-mediated small-group discussion. *Journal of Research on Computing in Education, 28,* 133-147.

Aiken, M., Hasan, B., & Vanjani, M. (1996). Total quality management: A GDSS approach. *Information Systems Management, 13,* 73-75.

Aiken, M., Hwang, C., De Magalhaes, R., & Martin, J. (1993). A comparison of Malaysian and American groups using a group decision support system. *Journal of Information Science, 19,* 489-491.

Aiken, M., Kim, D., Hwang, C., & Lu, L. (1995). A Korean group decision support system. *Information & Management, 28,* 303-310.

Aiken, M., Sloan, H., Paolillo, J., & Motiwalla, L. (1997). The use of two electronic idea generation techniques in strategy planning meetings. *Journal of Business Communication, 34,* 370-382.

Alavi, M. (1994). Computer-mediated collaborative learning: An empirical evaluation. *MIS Quarterly, 18,* 159-174.

Alavi, M., Wheeler, B. C., & Valacich, J. S. (1995). Using IT to reengineer business education: An exploratory investigation of collaborative telelearning. *MIS Quarterly, 19,* 293-312.

Anonymous. (1998). To reveal or not to reveal: A theoretical model of anonymous communication. *Communication Theory, 8,* 381-407.

Anson, R., Bostrom, R., & Wynne, B. (1995). An experiment assessing group support system and facilitator effects on meeting outcomes. *Management Science, 41,* 189-208.

Aycock, A., & Buchignani, N. (1995). The E-mail murders: Reflections on "dead" letters. In S. G. Jones (Ed.), *Cybersociety: Computer-mediated communica-*

tion and community (pp. 184-231). Thousand Oaks, CA: Sage.

Baldwin, T. F., McVoy, D. S., & Steinfield, C. (1996). Convergence: Integrating media, information, & communication. Thousand Oaks, CA: Sage.

Bamber, E. M., Watson, R. T., & Hill, M. C. (1996). The effects of group support system technology on audit group decision making. Auditing: A Journal of Practice and Theory, 15, 122-134.

Baym, N. K. (1997). Interpreting soap operas and creating community: Inside an electronic fan culture. In S. Kiesler (Ed.), Cultures of the Internet (pp. 103-120). Mahwah, NJ: Lawrence Erlbaum.

Benbasat, I., & Lim, L. (1993). The effects of group, task, context, and technology variables on the usefulness of group support systems: A meta-analysis of experimental studies. Small Group Research, 24, 430-462.

Bikson, T. K. (1996). Groupware at the World Bank. In C. U. Ciborra (Ed.), Groupware and teamwork: Invisible aid or technical hindrance? (pp. 145-183). Chichester, UK: John Wiley & Sons.

Blundell, D. (1997). Collaborative presentation technologies: Meetings, presentations, and collaboration. In D. Coleman (Ed.), Groupware: Collaborative strategies for corporate LANs and intranets (pp. 269-320). Upper Saddle River, NJ: Prentice Hall.

Bock, G. E., & Marca, D. A. (1997). Designing groupware: A management primer. In D. Coleman (Ed.), Groupware: Collaborative strategies for corporate LANs and intranets (pp. 501-529). Upper Saddle River, NJ: Prentice Hall.

Boutte, F. D., Jones, E. C., Hendricks, B., & Rodger, G. J. (1996). Group dynamics of video conferencing. Hydrocarbon Processing, 75, 139-143.

Briggs, R. O., Nunamaker, J. F., Jr., & Sprague, R. H., Jr. (1998). 1001 unanswered research questions in GSS. Journal of Management Information Systems, 14, 3-21.

Campbell, J. (1997). The impact of videoconference meetings on the pattern and structure of organisational communication. Singapore Management Review, 19, 77-93.

Carey, J. M., & Kacmar, C. J. (1997). The impact of communication mode and task complexity on small group performance and member satisfaction. Computers in Human Behavior, 13, 23-49.

Chidambaram, L. (1996). Relational development in computer-supported groups. MIS Quarterly, 20, 143-163.

Chidambaram, L., & Jones, B. (1993). Impact of communication medium and computer support on group perceptions and performance: A comparison of face-to-face and dispersed meetings. MIS Quarterly, 17, 465-492.

Ciborra, C. U. (1996). Mission critical: Challenges for groupware in a pharmaceutical company. In C. U. Ciborra (Ed.), Groupware and teamwork: Invisible aid or technical hindrance? (pp. 91-120). Chichester, UK: John Wiley & Sons.

Ciborra, C. U., & Patriotta, G. (1996). Groupware and teamwork in new product development: The case of

a consumer goods multinational. In C. U. Ciborra (Ed.), Groupware and teamwork: Invisible aid or technical hindrance? (pp. 121-142). Chichester, UK: John Wiley & Sons.

Ciborra, C. U., & Suetens, N. T. (1996). Groupware for an emerging virtual organization. In C. U. Ciborra (Ed.), Groupware and teamwork: Invisible aid or technical hindrance? (pp. 185-209). Chichester, UK: John Wiley & Sons.

Clark, A. S., Downing, C. E., & Coleman, D. (1997). Groupware at Big Six consulting firms: How successful was it? In D. Coleman (Ed.), Groupware: Collaborative strategies for corporate LANs and intranets (pp. 533-561). Upper Saddle River, NJ: Prentice Hall.

Coleman, D. (1995). Groupware: Technology and applications. In D. Coleman & R. Khanna (Eds.), Groupware: Technology and applications (pp. 3-41). Upper Saddle River, NJ: Prentice Hall.

Coleman, D. (1997a). Electronic meetings as today's presentations. In D. Coleman (Ed.), Groupware: Collaborative strategies for corporate LANs and intranets (pp. 183-191). Upper Saddle River, NJ: Prentice Hall.

Coleman, D. (Ed.). (1997b). Groupware: Collaborative strategies for corporate LANs and intranets. Upper Saddle River, NJ: Prentice Hall.

Coleman, D. (1997c). Groupware—the changing environment. In D. Coleman (Ed.), Groupware: Collaborative strategies for corporate LANs and intranets (pp. 1-38). Upper Saddle River, NJ: Prentice Hall.

Collins-Jarvis, L., & Fulk, J. (1993, November). Decision outcomes in face-to-face and electronically-mediated group meetings: A 1993 research review. Paper presented at the annual meeting of the Speech Communication Association, Miami, FL.

Condon, S. L., & Cech, C. G. (1996). Functional comparison of face-to-face and computer-mediated decision making interactions. In S. C. Herring (Ed.), Computer-mediated communication: Linguistic, social and cross-cultural perspectives (pp. 65-80). Amsterdam: John Benjamins.

Contractor, N. S., & Seibold, D. R. (1993). Theoretical frameworks for the study of structuring processes in group decision support systems: Adaptive structuration theory and self-organizing systems theory. Human Communication Research, 19, 528-563.

Contractor, N., Seibold, D. R., & Heller, M. A. (1996). Interactional influence in the structuring of media use in groups: Influence in members' perceptions of group decision support system use. Human Communication Research, 22, 451-481.

Creighton, J. L., & Adams, J.W.R. (1998). CyberMeeting: How to link people and technology in your organization. New York: Amacom.

Curtis, P. (1997). Mudding: Social phenomena in text-based virtual realities. In S. Kiesler (Ed.), Cultures of the Internet (pp. 121-142). Mahwah, NJ: Lawrence Erlbaum.

Daily, B., Whatley, A., Ash, S. R., & Steiner, R. L. (1996). The effects of a group decision support system on culturally diverse and culturally homogeneous group decision making. *Information & Management, 30,* 281-289.

de Vreede, G. (1998). Collaborative business engineering with animated electronic meetings. *Journal of Management Information Systems, 14,* 141-164.

Dennis, A. R. (1996). Information exchange and use in group decision making: You can lead a group to information, but you can't make it think. *MIS Quarterly, 20,* 433-457.

Dennis, A. R., George, J. F., Jessup, L. M., Nunamaker, J. F., Jr., & Vogel, D. R. (1988). Information technology to support electronic meetings. *MIS Quarterly, 12,* 591-624.

Dennis, A. R., Hilmer, K. M., & Taylor, N. J. (1998). Information exchange and use in GSS and verbal group decision making: Effects of minority influence. *Journal of Management Information Systems, 14,* 61-88.

Dennis, A. R., Tyran, C. K., Vogel, D. R., & Nunamaker, J. F., Jr. (1997). Group support systems for strategic planning. *Journal of Management Information Systems, 14,* 155-184.

Derycke, A. C., & Vieville, C. (1994). Real-time multimedia conferencing system and collaborative learning. In M. F. Verdejo & S. A. Cerri (Eds.), *Collaborative dialogue technologies in distance learning* (pp. 236-257). Berlin: Springer-Verlag.

DeSanctis, G., & Poole, M. S. (1994). Capturing the complexity in advanced technology use: Adaptive structuration theory. *Organization Science, 5,* 121-147.

Di Pietro, C. (1995). Meetingware and organizational effectiveness. In D. Coleman & R. Khanna (Eds.), *Groupware: Technology and applications* (pp. 434-473). Upper Saddle River, NJ: Prentice Hall.

Dishman, P., & Aytes, K. (1996). Exploring group support systems in sales management applications. *Journal of Personal Selling & Sales Management, 16,* 65-77.

Dorando, S., Stratis, G., O'Donnell, L., & O'Donnell, B. T., Sr. (1993). Observations on performance of GDSS-mediated groups in a business environment. *Office Systems Research Journal, 12*(1), 13-20.

Easton, A. C., Eickelmann, N. S., & Flatley, M. E. (1994). Effects of an electronic meeting system group writing tool on the quality of written documents. *Journal of Business Communication, 31,* 27-40.

El-Shinnawy, M., & Vinze, A. S. (1997). Technology, culture and persuasiveness: A study of choice-shifts in group settings. *International Journal of Human-Computer Studies, 47,* 473-496.

Eom, S. B. (1998). Relationships between the decision support system subspecialties and reference disciplines: An empirical investigation. *European Journal of Operational Research, 104,* 31-45.

Everett, D. R., & Ahern, T. C. (1994). Computer-mediated communication as a teaching tool: A case study. *Journal of Research on Computing in Education, 26,* 336-357.

Failla, A. (1996). Technologies for co-ordination in a software factory. In C. U. Ciborra (Ed.), *Groupware and teamwork: Invisible aid or technical hindrance?* (pp. 61-88). Chichester, UK: John Wiley & Sons.

Farmer, S. M., & Hyatt, C. W. (1994). Effects of task language demands and task complexity on computer-mediated work groups. *Small Group Research, 25,* 331-366.

Finn, T. A., & Lane, D. R. (1998, July). *A conceptual framework for organizing communication and information systems.* Paper presented at the annual meeting of the International Communication Association, Jerusalem, Israel.

Fish, R. S., Kraut, R. E., Root, R. W., & Rice, R. E. (1993). Video as a technology for informal communication. *Communications of the ACM, 36,* 48-61.

Fisher, B. A. (1970). Decision emergence: Phases in group decision-making. *Communication Monographs, 37,* 53-66.

Frey, L. R. (1994a). The call of the field: Studying communication in natural groups. In L. R. Frey (Ed.), *Group communication in context: Studies of natural groups* (pp. ix-xiv). Hillsdale, NJ: Lawrence Erlbaum.

Frey, L. R. (1994b). The naturalistic paradigm: Studying small groups in the postmodern era. *Small Group Research, 25,* 551-577.

Friedberg, A. H., Pianin, R. T., Cheung, L. S., Coleman, J. M., Hollander, J. A., & Woodruff, P. L. (1997). Tools for control self-assessment. *Information Systems Audit and Control Journal, 1,* 24-28.

Galegher, J., & Kraut, R. E. (1994). Computer-mediated communication for intellectual teamwork: An experiment in group writing. *Information Systems Research, 5,* 110-138.

Galinsky, M. J., Schopler, J. H., & Abell, M. D. (1997). Connecting group members through telephone and computer groups. *Health & Social Work, 22,* 181-188.

Gallupe, R. B., Cooper, W. H., Grise, M., & Bastianutti, L. M. (1994). Blocking electronic brainstorms. *Journal of Applied Psychology, 79,* 77-86.

George, J. F., & Jessup, L. M. (1997). Groups over time: What are we really studying? *International Journal of Human-Computer Studies, 47,* 497-511.

Gowan, J. A., Jr., & Downs, J. M. (1994). Video conferencing human-machine interface: A field study. *Information & Management, 27,* 341-356.

Grudin, J. (1994). Groupware and social dynamics: Eight challenges for developers. *Communications of the ACM, 37,* 92-105.

Grudin, J., & Poltrock, S. E. (1997). Computer-supported cooperative work and groupware. In M. V. Zelkowitz (Ed.), *Advances in computers* (pp. 269-320). San Diego: Academic Press.

Gundersen, D. E., Davis, D. L., & Davis, D. F. (1995). Can DSS technology improve group decision performance for end users? An experimental study. *Journal of End User Computing, 7*(2), 3-10.

Harmon, J., Schneer, J. A., & Hoffman, L. R. (1995). Electronic meetings and established decision groups: Audioconferencing effects on performance and structural stability. *Organizational Behavior and Human Decision Processes, 61,* 138-147.

Hayne, S. C., & Rice, R. E. (1997). Attribution accuracy when using anonymity in group support systems. *International Journal of Human-Computer Studies, 47,* 429-452.

Herschel, R. T., Cooper, T. R., Smith, L. F., & Arrington, L. (1994). Exploring numerical proportions in a unique context: The group support systems meeting environment. *Sex Roles, 31,* 99-123.

Hightower, R., & Sayeed, L. (1996). Effects of communication mode and prediscussion information distribution characteristics on information exchange in groups. *Information Systems Research, 7,* 451-465.

Hightower, R. T., Sayeed, L., Warkentin, M. E., & McHaney, R. (1998). Information exchange in virtual work groups. In M. Igbaria & M. Tan (Eds.), *The virtual workplace* (pp. 199-216). Hershey, PA: Idea Group.

Hinds, P., & Kiesler, S. (1995). Communication across boundaries: Work, structure, and use of communication technologies in a large organization. *Organization Science, 6,* 373-393.

Hollingshead, A. B. (1996a). Information suppression and status persistence in group decision making: The effects of communication media. *Human Communication Research, 23,* 193-219.

Hollingshead, A. B. (1996b). The rank-order effect in group decision making. *Organizational Behavior and Human Decision Processes, 68,* 181-193.

Horton, M., & Biolsi, K. (1994). Coordination challenges in a computer-supported meeting environment. *Journal of Management Information Systems, 10,* 7-24.

Jackson, N. F., Aiken, M. W., Vanjani, M. B., & Hasan, B. S. (1995). Support group decisions via computer systems. *Quality Progress, 28,* 75-78.

Kahai, S. S., Sosik, J. J., & Avolio, B. J. (1997). Effects of leadership style and problem structure on work group process and outcomes in an electronic meeting system environment. *Personnel Psychology, 50,* 121-146.

Karacapilidis, N. I., & Pappis, C. P. (1997). A framework for group decision support systems: Combining AI tools and OR techniques. *European Journal of Operational Research, 103,* 373-388.

Karan, V., Kerr, D. S., Murthy, U. S., & Vinze, A. S. (1996). Information technology support for collaborative decision making in auditing: An experimental investigation. *Decision Support Systems, 16,* 181-194.

Khoshafian, S., & Buckiewicz, M. (1995). *Introduction to groupware, workflow, and workgroup computing.* New York: John Wiley & Sons.

Kline, T.J.B., & Gardiner, H. (1997). The successful adoption of groupware: Perceptions of the users. *Human Systems Management, 16,* 301-306.

Knoll, K., & Jarvenpaa, S. L. (1998). Working together in global virtual teams. In M. Igbaria & M. Tan (Eds.), *The virtual workplace* (pp. 2-23). Hershey, PA: Idea Group.

Kock, N., & McQueen, R. (1997). A field study of the effects of asynchronous groupware support on process improvement groups. *Journal of Information Technology, 12,* 245-259.

Kolodner, J., & Guzdial, M. (1996). Effects with and of CSCL: Tracking learning in a new paradigm. In T. Koschmann (Ed.), *CSCL: Theory and practice of an emergent paradigm* (pp. 307-320). Mahwah, NJ: Lawrence Erlbaum.

Korenman, J., & Wyatt, N. (1996). Group dynamics in an E-mail forum. In S. C. Herring (Ed.), *Computer-mediated communication: Linguistic, social and cross-cultural perspectives* (pp. 225-242). Amsterdam: John Benjamins.

Larson, C. E., & LaFasto, F. M. (1989). *Teamwork: What must go right/what can go wrong.* Newbury Park, CA: Sage.

Lim, L., & Benbasat, I. (1997). The debiasing role of group support systems: An experimental investigation of the representative bias. *International Journal of Human-Computer Studies, 47,* 453-471.

Liou, Y. I., & Nunamaker, J. F., Jr. (1993). An investigation into knowledge acquisition using a group decision support system. *Information & Management, 24,* 121-132.

Lipnack, J., & Stamps, J. (1997). *Virtual teams: Reaching across space, time, and organizations with technology.* New York: John Wiley & Sons.

Lloyd, P. (Ed.). (1994). *Groupware in the 21st century: Computer supported cooperative working toward the millennium.* Westport, CT: Praeger.

Lou, H., & Scamell, R. W. (1996). Acceptance of groupware: The relationships among use, satisfaction, and outcomes. *Journal of Organizational Computing and Electronic Commerce, 6,* 173-190.

Marshak, D. S. (1994). The disappearance of groupware. In P. Lloyd (Ed.), *Groupware in the 21st century: Computer supported cooperative working toward the millennium* (pp. 24-28). Westport, CT: Praeger.

Martz, W. B., Jr., Vogel, D. R., & Nunamaker, J. F., Jr. (1992). Electronic meeting systems: Results from the field. *Decision Support Systems, 8,* 141-158.

Massey, A. P., & Clapper, D. L. (1995). Element finding: The impact of a group support system on a crucial phase of sense making. *Journal of Management Information Systems, 11,* 149-176.

McClernon, T. R., & Swanson, R. A. (1995). Team building: An experimental investigation of the effects of computer-based and facilitator-based interventions on work groups. *Human Resource Development Quarterly, 6,* 39-58.

McGrath, J. E. (1984). *Groups: Interaction and performance.* Englewood Cliffs, NJ: Prentice Hall.

McGrath, J. E. (1991). Time, interaction, and performance (TIP): A theory of groups. *Small Group Research, 22,* 147-174.

McGrath, J. E., Arrow, H., Gruenfeld, D. H., Hollingshead, A. B., & O'Connor, K. M. (1993). Groups, tasks, and technology: The effects of experience and change. *Small Group Research, 24,* 406-420.

McGrath, J. E., & Hollingshead, A. B. (1994). *Groups interacting with technology.* Thousand Oaks, CA: Sage.

Mennecke, B. E. (1997). Using group support systems to discover hidden profiles: An examination of the influence of group size and meeting structures on information sharing and decision quality. *International Journal of Human-Computer Studies, 47*, 387-405.

Mennecke, B. E., Hoffer, J. A., & Wynne, B. E. (1992). The implications of group development and history for group support system theory and practice. *Small Group Research, 23*, 524-572.

Mickelson, K. D. (1997). Seeking social support: Parents in electronic support groups. In S. Kiesler (Ed.), *Cultures of the Internet* (pp. 157-178). Mahwah, NJ: Lawrence Erlbaum.

Money, W. H. (1996). Applying group support systems to classroom settings: A social cognitive learning theory explanation. *Journal of Management Information Systems, 12*, 65-80.

Neuwirth, C. M., & Wojahn, P. G. (1996). Learning to write: Computer support for a cooperative process. In T. Koschmann (Ed.), *CSCL: Theory and practice of an emergent paradigm* (pp. 147-170). Mahwah, NJ: Lawrence Erlbaum.

Niederman, F., Beise, C. M., & Beranek, P. M. (1996). Issues and concerns about computer-supported meetings: The facilitator's perspective. *MIS Quarterly, 20*, 1-22.

Nunamaker, J. F., Jr. (1997). Future research in group support systems: Needs, some questions and possible directions. *International Journal of Human-Computer Studies, 47*, 357-385.

Nunamaker, J. F., Briggs, R. O., & Mittleman, D. D. (1995). Electronic meeting systems: Ten years of lessons learned. In D. Coleman & R. Khanna (Eds.), *Groupware: Technology and applications* (pp. 146-193). Upper Saddle River, NJ: Prentice Hall.

Nunamaker, J. F., Jr., Briggs, R. O., Romano, N. C., Jr., & Mittleman, D. (1997). The virtual office workspace: GroupSystems web and case studies. In D. Coleman (Ed.), *Groupware: Collaborative strategies for corporate LANs and intranets* (pp. 231-253). Upper Saddle River, NJ: Prentice Hall.

Ocker, R., Hiltz, S. R., Turoff, M., & Fjermestad, J. (1996). The effects of distributed group support and process structuring on software requirements development teams: Results on creativity and quality. *Journal of Management Information Systems, 12*, 127-153.

O'Dwyer, G., Giser, A., & Lovett, E. (1997). Groupware & reengineering: The human side of change. In D. Coleman (Ed.), *Groupware: Collaborative strategies for corporate LANs and intranets* (pp. 565-595). Upper Saddle River, NJ: Prentice Hall.

Olaniran, B. A. (1994). Group performance in computer-mediated and face-to-face communication media. *Management Communication Quarterly, 7*, 256-281.

Olaniran, B. A. (1995). Perceived communication outcomes in computer-mediated communication: An analysis of three systems among new users. *Information Processing & Management, 31*, 525-541.

Olaniran, B. A. (1996). A model of group satisfaction in computer-mediated communication and face-to-face meetings. *Behaviour & Information Technology, 15*, 24-36.

O'Malley, C. (1995). Designing computer support for collaborative learning. In C. O'Malley (Ed.), *Computer supported collaborative learning* (pp. 283-297). Berlin: Springer-Verlag.

Orlikowski, W. J. (1993). Learning from Notes: Organizational issues in groupware implementation. *The Information Society, 9*, 237-250.

Orlikowski, W. J. (1996). Evolving with Notes: Organizational change around groupware technology. In C. U. Ciborra (Ed.), *Groupware and teamwork: Invisible aid or technical hindrance?* (pp. 23-59). Chichester, UK: John Wiley & Sons.

Palmer, J. W. (1998). The use of information technology in virtual organizations. In M. Igbaria & M. Tan (Eds.), *The virtual workplace* (pp. 71-85). Hershey, PA: Idea Group.

Petrovic, O., & Krickl, O. (1994). Traditionally-moderated versus computer supported brainstorming: A comparative study. *Information & Management, 27*, 233-243.

Pollard, C. E. (1996). Electronic meeting systems: Specifications, potential, and acquisition strategies. *Journal of Systems Management, 47*, 22-28.

Poole, M. S. (1983a). Decision development in small groups II: A study of multiple sequences in decision making. *Communication Monographs, 50*, 206-232.

Poole, M. S. (1983b). Decision development in small groups, III: A multiple sequence theory of group decision development. *Communication Monographs, 50*, 321-341.

Poole, M. S., & DeSanctis, G. (1990). Understanding the use of group decision support systems: The theory of adaptive structuration. In J. Fulk & C. Steinfield (Eds.), *Organizations and communication technology* (pp. 175-195). Newbury Park, CA: Sage.

Poole, M. S., & DeSanctis, G. (1992). Microlevel structuration in computer-supported group decision making. *Human Communication Research, 19*, 5-49.

Poole, M. S., DeSanctis, G., Kirsch, L., & Jackson, M. (1995). Group decision support systems as facilitators of quality team efforts. In L. R. Frey (Ed.), *Innovations in group facilitation: Applications in natural settings* (pp. 299-321). Cresskill, NJ: Hampton.

Poole, M. S., & Holmes, M. E. (1995). Decision development in computer-assisted group decision making. *Human Communication Research, 22*, 90-127.

Poole, M. S., & Roth, J. (1989). Decision development in small groups IV: A typology of decision paths. *Human Communication Research, 15*, 323-356.

Putnam, L. L., & Stohl, C. (1990). Bona fide groups: A reconceptualization of groups in context. *Communication Studies, 41*, 248-265.

Putnam, L. L., & Stohl, C. (1994). Group communication in context: Implications for the study of bona fide groups. In L. R. Frey (Ed.), *Group communication in context: Studies of natural groups* (pp. 284-292). Hillsdale, NJ: Lawrence Erlbaum.

Putnam, L. L., & Stohl, C. (1996). Bona fide groups: An alternative perspective for communication and small group decision making. In R. Y. Hirokawa & M. S.

Poole (Eds.), *Communication and group decision making* (2nd ed., pp. 147-178). Thousand Oaks, CA: Sage.

Radford, G. P., Morganstern, B. F., McMickle, C. W., & Lehr, J. K. (1994). The impact of four conferencing formats on the efficiency and quality of small group decision making in a laboratory experiment setting. *Telematics and Information, 11,* 97-109.

Reinig, B. A., Briggs, R. O., & Nunamaker, J. F., Jr. (1998). Flaming in the electronic classroom. *Journal of Management Information Systems, 14,* 45-59.

Rice, R. E., & Bair, J. H. (1984). New organizational media and productivity. In R. E. Rice & Associates (Eds.), *The new media: Communication, research and technology* (pp. 198-215). Beverly Hills, CA: Sage.

Robichaux, B. P. (1994). Sex and beliefs about computer-based information systems: An examination of group support systems. *Omega International Journal of Management Science, 22,* 381-389.

Romm, C. T., & Pliskin, N. (1998). Group development in the virtual workplace: The story of a strike. In M. Igbaria & M. Tan (Eds.), *The virtual workplace* (pp. 368-388). Hershey, PA: Idea Group.

Ross, J. A. (1996). The influence of computer communication skills on participation in a computer conferencing course. *Journal of Educational Computing Research, 15,* 37-52.

Roy, M. C., Gauvin, S., & Limayem, M. (1996). Electronic group brainstorming: The role of feedback on productivity. *Small Group Research, 27,* 215-247.

Sambamurthy, V., & Chin, W. W. (1994). The effects of group attitudes toward alternative GDSS designs on the decision-making performance of computer-supported groups. *Decision Sciences, 25,* 215-241.

Sambamurthy, V., Poole, M. S., & Kelly, J. (1993). The effects of variations in GDSS capabilities on decision-making processes in groups. *Small Group Research, 24,* 523-546.

Satzinger, J. W., & Olfman, L. (1995). Computer support for group work: Perceptions of the usefulness of support scenarios and end-user tools. *Journal of Management Information Systems, 11,* 115-148.

Saunders, C. S., Robey, D., & Vavarek, K. A. (1994). The persistence of status differentials in computer conferencing. *Human Communication Research, 20,* 443-472.

Scalia, L. M., & Sackmary, B. (1996). Groupware and computer-supported cooperative work in the college classroom. *Business Communication Quarterly, 59,* 98-110.

Schoch, N. A., & White, M. D. (1997). A study of the communication patterns of participants in consumer health electronic discussion groups. *Journal of the American Society for Information Science Proceedings, 34,* 280-292.

Schwartz, H. (1995). Cross-cultural team teaching: Electronic mail for literary analysis. In E. Boschmann (Ed.), *The electronic classroom: A handbook for education in the electronic environment* (pp. 173-179). Medford, NJ: Learned Information.

Scott, C. R., & Easton, A. (1996). Examining equality of influence in group decision-making system interaction. *Small Group Research, 27,* 360-382.

Scott, C. R., Garrett, D. M., Timmerman, C. E., & Quinn, L. (1997, May). *When the honeymoon is virtually over: Declining benefits associated with repeated usage of a computerized group decision support system.* Paper presented at the annual meeting of the International Communication Association, Montreal, Canada.

Seibold, D. R., Heller, M. A., & Contractor, N. S. (1994). Group decision support systems (GDSS): Review, taxonomy, and research agenda. In B. Kovacic (Ed.), *New approaches to organizational communication* (pp. 143-168). Albany: State University of New York Press.

Sheffield, J., & Gallupe, R. B. (1994). Using electronic meeting technology to support economic policy development in New Zealand: Short-term results. *Journal of Management Information Systems, 10,* 97-116.

Shepherd, M. M., Briggs, R. O., Reinig, B. A., Yen, J., & Nunamaker, J. F., Jr. (1996). Invoking social comparison to improve electronic brainstorming: Beyond anonymity. *Journal of Management Information Systems, 12,* 155-170.

Sia, C., Tan, B.C.Y., & Wei, K. (1996). Exploring the effects of some display and task factors on GSS user groups. *Information & Management, 30,* 35-41.

Sia, C., Tan, B.C.Y., & Wei, K. (1997). Effects of GSS interface and task type on group interaction: An empirical study. *Decision Support Systems, 19,* 289-299.

Sietz, R., & Bodendorf, F. (1994). Innovative support technologies for tele- and team-work at universities. In M. F. Verdejo & S. A. Cerri (Eds.), *Collaborative dialogue technologies in distance learning* (pp. 97-108). Berlin: Springer-Verlag.

Simon, A. R., & Marion, W. (1996). *Workgroup computing: Workflow, groupware, and messaging.* New York: McGraw-Hill.

Sinclair, J. T., & Hale, D. B. (1997). *Intranets vs. Lotus Notes.* Boston: AP Professional.

Slater, J. S., & Anderson, E. (1994). Communication convergence in electronically supported discussions: An adaptation of Kincaid's convergence model. *Telematics and Informatics, 11,* 111-125.

Smith, C.A.P., & Hayne, S. C. (1997). Decision making under time pressure: An investigation of decision speed and decision quality of computer-supported groups. *Management Communication Quarterly, 11,* 97-126.

Snyder, H., & Kurtze, D. (1996). Chaotic behavior in computer mediated network communication. *Information Processing & Management, 32,* 555-562.

Socha, T. J. (1997). Group communication across the life span. In L. R. Frey & J. K. Barge (Eds.), *Managing group life: Communicating in decision-making groups* (pp. 3-28). Boston: Houghton Mifflin.

Sosik, J. J., Avolio, B. J., & Kahai, S. S. (1997). Effects of leadership style and anonymity on group potency and effectiveness in a group decision support system environment. *Journal of Applied Psychology, 82,* 89-103.

Sosik, J. J., Avolio, B. J., & Kahai, S. S. (1998). Inspiring group creativity: Comparing anonymous and identified electronic brainstorming. *Small Group Research,* 29, 3-31.

Spuck, D. W., Prater, D. L., & Palumbo, D. B. (1995). Using electronic meeting system support in the design of the graduate core curriculum. *Educational Technology Research & Development,* 43, 71-80.

Storck, J., & Sproull, L. (1995). Through a glass darkly: What do people learn in videoconferences? *Human Communication Research,* 22, 197-219.

Strauss, S. G. (1997). Technology, group process, and group outcomes: Testing the connections in computer-mediated and face-to-face groups. *Human-Computer Interactions,* 12, 227-266.

Strauss, S. G., & McGrath, J. E. (1994). Does the medium matter? The interaction of task type and technology on group performance and member reactions. *Journal of Applied Psychology,* 79, 87-97.

Technology forecast. (1997). Menlo Park, CA: Price Waterhouse.

Toth, J. (1996). The effects of combining interactive graphics and text in computer-mediated small group decision-making. In D. L. Day & D. K. Kovacs (Eds.), *Computers, communication and mental models* (pp. 74-88). London: Taylor & Francis.

Turkle, S. (1997). Constructions and reconstructions of self in virtual reality: Playing in the MUDs. In S. Kiesler (Ed.), *Cultures of the Internet* (pp. 143-155). Mahwah, NJ: Lawrence Erlbaum.

Turoff, M., Hiltz, S. R., Bahgat, A.N.F., & Rana, A. R. (1993). Distributed group support systems. *MIS Quarterly,* 17, 399-417.

Valacich, J. S., George, J. F., Nunamaker, J. F., Jr., & Vogel, D. R. (1994). Physical proximity effects on computer-mediated group idea generation. *Small Group Research,* 25, 83-104.

Valacich, J. S., Paranka, D., George, J. F., & Nunamaker, J. F., Jr. (1993). Communication concurrency and the new media: A new dimension for media richness. *Communication Research,* 20, 249-276.

Valacich, J. S., & Schwenk, C. (1995a). Devil's advocacy and dialectical inquiry effects on face-to-face and computer-mediated group decision making. *Organizational Behavior and Human Decision Processes,* 63, 158-173.

Valacich, J. S., & Schwenk, C. (1995b). Structuring conflict in individual, face-to-face, and computer-mediated group decision making: Carping versus objective devil's advocacy. *Decision Sciences,* 26, 369-393.

Valacich, J. S., Wheeler, B. C., Mennecke, B. E., & Wachter, R. (1995). The effects of numerical and logical group size on computer-mediated idea generation. *Organizational Behavior and Human Decision Processes,* 62, 318-329.

Van Genuchten, M., Cornelissen, W., & Van Dijk, C. (1998). Supporting inspections with an electronic meeting system. *Journal of Management Information Systems,* 14, 165-178.

Venkatesh, M., Leo, R. J., Kuzawinski, K. M., & Diamond, L. P. (1996). A microcomputer-aided support environment for Xerox quality improvement teams: A case study. *Journal of Organizational Computing and Electronic Commerce,* 6, 131-159.

Walther, J. B. (1994). Anticipated ongoing interaction versus channel effects on relational communication in computer-mediated interaction. *Human Communication Research,* 20, 473-501.

Walther, J. B. (1997). Group and interpersonal effects in international computer-mediated collaboration. *Human Communication Research,* 23, 342-369.

Warkentin, M. E., Sayeed, L., & Hightower, R. (1997). Virtual teams versus face-to-face teams: An exploratory study of a Web-based conference system. *Decision Sciences,* 28, 975-995.

Wegerif, R. (1996). Collaborative learning and directive software. *Journal of Computer Assisted Learning,* 12, 22-32.

Weinberg, N., Schmale, J., Uken, J., & Wessel, K. (1996). Online help: Cancer patients participate in a computer-mediated support group. *Health & Social Work,* 21, 24-29.

Weisband, S. P., Schneider, S. K., & Connolly, T. (1995). Computer-mediated communication and social information: Status salience and status differences. *Academy of Management Journal,* 38, 1124-1151.

Wheeler, B. C., Mennecke, B. E., & Scudder, J. N. (1993). Restrictive group support systems as a source of process structure for high and low procedural order groups. *Small Group Research,* 24, 504-522.

Wheeler, B. C., & Valacich, J. S. (1996). Facilitation, GSS, and training as sources of process restrictiveness and guidance for structured group decision making: An empirical assessment. *Information Systems Research,* 7, 429-450.

Williams, S. R., & Wilson, R. L. (1997). Group support systems, power, and influence in an organization: A field study. *Decision Sciences,* 28, 911-937.

Yates, J., Orlikowski, W. J., & Okamura, K. (1995). Constituting genre repertoires: Deliberate and emergent patterns of electronic media use. *Academy of Management Journal* (Best Paper Proceedings), 353-357.

Zack, M. H. (1993). Interactivity and communication mode: Choice in ongoing management groups. *Information Systems Research,* 4, 207-239.

Zack, M. H. (1994). Electronic messaging and communication effectiveness in an ongoing work group. *Information & Management,* 26, 231-241.

Zack, M. H., & McKenney, J. L. (1995). Social context and interaction in ongoing computer-supported management groups. *Organization Science,* 6, 394-422.

Zigurs, I., & Kozar, K. A. (1994). An exploratory study of roles in computer-supported groups. *MIS Quarterly,* 18, 277-297.

PART VI

Group Communication Contexts and Applications

17

Communication in Family Units

Studying the First "Group"

THOMAS J. SOCHA
Old Dominion University

Recent calls to widen the lens on group communication (e.g., Frey, 1988, 1994d; Putnam & Stohl, 1990) have focused on the need to "move away from studying isolated, zero-history laboratory groups and to strive for real-world significance by studying groups embedded in natural contexts" (Stohl & Putnam, 1994, p. 285). In response, a number of scholars have offered conceptual, theoretical, and methodological insights into how this might best be achieved (e.g., Frey, 1994a, 1994c, 1995a; Putnam, 1994; Putnam & Stohl, 1996; Stohl & Putnam, 1994), and a number of case studies of natural groups have appeared in the group communication literature (Frey, 1994b, 1995b, in press). These efforts have already called attention to groups that were ignored previously, such as children's groups (Keyton, 1994; Socha & Socha, 1994), gangs (Conquergood, 1994), and women's groups (Meyers & Brashers, 1994). Clearly, a wider lens offers a more panoramic view of group communication to account for the expansive array of groups across the life span. This is a far more complex, and interesting, picture of group communication than snapshots of zero-history student groups communicating in laboratories.

The thrust to expand the range of groups studied has also led scholars to focus on what is clearly the most significant first "group" for us all—the family. Unfortunately, for a variety of reasons to be explored later in this chapter, group communication researchers and family communication researchers have interacted little since the late 1970s. Consequently, what we know about communication in "groups" continues to be largely disconnected from what we know about communication in "families." There are good reasons, however, to reopen what I hope will be a mutually beneficial dialogue between communication researchers who study groups and families.

First, efforts to broaden the range of groups studied should include family units if a comprehensive understanding of groups is to be realized. The cross-fertilization that will occur as a result of the increased range and more comprehensive understanding can potentially benefit both fields of study. According to sociologist R. H. Turner (1970):

Since a great deal of study has been devoted to . . . small groups, both stable and transitory, within and outside . . . organizations, it would be wasteful to overlook such generalizations as a ready source for principles that might apply to the family. (p. 9)

The converse is also worth considering: that studies of families can be a ready source of principles that might apply to other types of groups. In particular, principles about group communication learned in families, the first group, might form a foundation for principles that govern people's behavior in other groups.

Second, considerable overlap exists between the concepts of "family" and "group." According to Walters (1982), "some groups (e.g., communes, cohabitants, roommates) share characteristics common to families . . . [such as] a long history . . . intimate experiences, behavior that is motivated by mutual benevolence, and problem-solving processes that are similar . . . to families" (p. 842). In addition, both terms refer to interdependent, interacting units that today represent increasingly diverse memberships and a wide variety of forms. According to Handel (1992), "the concept of families takes on many forms, including single-parent, bi-nuclear, blended, two-parent lesbian, two-parent gay. The increased variety of forms constitutes a continuing rationale for studying whole families, whatever their form" (p. 17). There are also striking similarities between Putnam and Stohl's (1990) characteristics of "bona fide groups"—such as stable, but permeable, boundaries and shifting borders (in this volume, see Chapters 1 [Gouran] and 2 [Poole])—and Afrocentric conceptualizations of the "family" as an extended network of kin and nonkin demarcated by permeable, symbolic boundaries (Hill et al., 1993). Most important, both research areas share a common unit of analysis: a collective unit in addition to dyads and individuals contained within it. According to Stafford and Dainton (1995), however, family communication researchers have focused more heavily on family members' relationships (primarily married couples) than on whole family units (see also Aust, 1998; Fitzpatrick & Badzinski, 1985; Handel, 1992). Stafford and Dainton argue that to understand family relationships more fully,

more attention needs to be given to understanding how family members' relationships are affected by the context of the whole family unit, as well as how they are influenced by units outside the family. Focusing on the group as a collective entity, of course, is a strength of group communication research, and family communication scholars can learn from this work. In turn, the focus on relationships in families may inform the work of group communication scholars.

Finally, the family of origin is the first and typically the longest lasting group in a person's life. Thus, what goes on inside a child's family of origin, for example, not only should affect that child's behavior in groups outside the family during childhood, and vice versa (see, for example, Socha & Socha, 1994), but also may affect participation in groups later across his or her life span (see Anderson, Riddle, & Martin, Chapter 6, this volume, regarding the impact of group experiences on individuals' subsequent participation in groups). Because membership in a person's family of origin, as well as his or her current family (in whatever form that may take), extends across the life span, what goes on in family units should affect participation in all groups across the life span, and vice versa (see Socha, 1997). Indeed, individuals are simultaneously members of families *and* many groups outside the family. Thus, calls for examination of more diverse forms of families are mirrored by calls for studies of more diverse groups.

In the hope of rekindling dialogue between those who study group communication and those who study family communication, I first review (a) early sociological and psychological research that applied group methods to whole family units, (b) past conceptual and theoretical approaches to communication in whole family units, and (c) various measures employed to study whole families and the interactions that take place therein. These reviews culminate in a summary of insights gained from family research that are applicable to other types of groups and a recommendation for an integrative, life-span developmental approach to the study of groups that regards the family as our first "group."

EARLY APPROACHES TO THE FAMILY AS A GROUP

Historically, sociologists who study the family (e.g., Hess & Handel, 1959; Parsons & Bales, 1955) regarded the nuclear family as a special kind of primary group. Drawing on Cooley (1955), Litwak and Szelenyi (1969) described the qualities of primary groups as frequent face-to-face interaction, permanence, high affectivity, non-instrumentality (i.e., members set and manage their own agenda as opposed to managing an agenda set by others), and diffuseness (i.e., characterized by members engaging in diverse, interchangeable functions and roles). Other examples of primary groups are extended kin, neighborhood groups, and friendship peer groups.

During the 1960s, some sociologists employed what I label a "one-approach-fits-all-groups" strategy and used the same types of measurement instruments to study both task groups in laboratories and families. Given space limitations and the intended audience for this chapter, I focus in particular on a few early sociological studies that used Bales's (1950) Interaction Process Analysis (IPA) to study family units. IPA has been one of the most widely used measures of group process and is still in use today (in this volume, see Chapters 3 [Mabry], 8 [Keyton], and 12 [Pavitt]). It was also a very popular (albeit, as will be shown, unsuccessful) tool in early studies of family interaction.

IPA is designed to permit study of communicative acts (any verbal or nonverbal message that an observer can understand; see Keyton, 1997) and does so by categorizing them into 12 categories that reflect six task and six socioemotional (positive and negative) behaviors. IPA's task message categories are asks for information/orientation, gives information/orientation, asks for opinions, gives opinions, asks for suggestions, and gives suggestions. IPA's positive and negative socioemotional categories are agrees, disagrees, dramatizes/

shows tension release, shows tension, seems friendly/shows solidarity, and seems unfriendly/shows antagonism (Bales, 1950). Later, based on extensive research on groups, Bales (1970) developed some general norms for how often a given message category should occur in a successful task group. For example, messages classified as "giving information/orientation" should appear 20.7%-31.2% of the time.

Cheek (1964a, 1964b, 1965a, 1965b) conducted a series of IPA studies on interaction in three-person families that contained a normal or schizophrenic child. The results indicated that fathers of normal and schizophrenic children differed little during discussion with their child. Mothers of schizophrenic children, however, tended to be withdrawn and cold in these interactions (as indicated by the overall low frequency of messages and the use of few socioemotional messages). Finally, normal children expressed more negative socioemotional behavior (i.e., more disagreements) than schizophrenic children.

Winter and Ferreira (1967) conducted a study to test whether IPA could differentiate among four types of family triads: those triads having a normal child (nonclinical), an emotionally maladjusted child, a schizophrenic child, and a delinquent child. Across the four types of family units, members disagreed and experienced more conflict than was the case in the ad hoc groups Bales (1950) studied. Schizophrenic family units, which typically display extreme verbal communication patterns (e.g., in emotional displays), differed, in particular, from normal family units (e.g., they showed more tension and disagreement). Only minor differences (or no differences at all) were found between and among the other types of units, including cases in which large differences were expected (e.g., between emotionally maladjusted and normal families). Winter and Ferreira (1967) concluded by asking, "What knowledge have we gained . . . by applying the IPA to . . . groups of families?" and then answering, "Unfortunately, very little" (p. 169). They further argued that given difficulties in coding reliability experienced in their study and other studies of families (i.e., a 33% disagreement rate between and among coders), "IPA in its present form is not suited for work with families" (p. 170).

Although Winter and Ferreira (1967) raised serious concerns about using IPA to study nuclear families, they did find some interesting characteristics of families. Specifically,

> families seemed to reflect similarity of behavior, not complementary behavior. In addition . . . one might also mention subtle patterns of nonverbal and verbal communication within a family, and the immensely rich contextual *historical* background against which a remark by one family member is judged by the others. (p. 171, italics added)

Indeed, they concluded that the nuclear family is a "special" group in which it "may always be more difficult to measure interaction . . . than in problem-solving groups of college students" (p. 171). In contrast to most task groups, whether in the laboratory or in natural settings, families interact over many years and in diverse types of episodes. Thus, although families and groups share some elements, as explained previously, early IPA studies (flaws and all) did reveal that families did not behave like ad hoc task groups. As Bochner (1976) concluded on the basis of a review of past studies of nuclear families using IPA, as well as other group approaches:

> Empirical studies of families seldom produce results which are consistent with empirical studies of ad hoc groups. Perhaps ad hoc groups *never reach* the state of structural permanence so characteristic of families. If so, it may prove advantageous to compare families to groups which are more similar structurally, such as prolonged encounter groups, or to abandon this line of research entirely. (p. 384, italics added)

Most family communication researchers heeded the advice of Bochner and others and moved away from using approaches grounded in ad hoc group communication research traditions and developed theories, research approaches, and methods more suited to studying the unique qualities of family units. These early efforts, however, tended to rely on interpersonal communication theories and methods that emphasized dyads, particularly marital partners. This emphasis was due, in part, to the soaring divorce rates in the United States, difficulties in gaining access to families, and methodological challenges inherent in studying entire family units.

THE NEED FOR AN INTEGRATIVE APPROACH

The abbreviated, narrow slice of the history of the one-approach-fits-all-groups strategy presented above shows that early family researchers *did* see connections between families and other types of groups. More recently, Walters (1982) argued that "knowing which qualities are inherent to families and which are more likely to be found in other groups . . . would be useful" (p. 848). Both group researchers and family researchers eventually lost sight of these connections, in part because of (a) early empirical research using zero-history, task-group methods that showed groups and families to be different, (b) early family communication research that emphasized interpersonal communication and de-emphasized group communication theories and methods, and (c) group communication research that focused narrowly and almost exclusively on zero-history task groups (and, thereby, excluded such groups as families).

It is time to reconsider the connections between families and other types of groups. In particular, there is a need for a conceptual framework of group communication that emphasizes the interconnectedness between and among all groups and recognizes the primacy and uniqueness of the family unit as the initial context where group communication is experienced and where group communication skills are first learned.

A potential conceptual framework to accomplish this goal emerges from the important concern in group communication theory and research with how groups develop (in this volume, see Chapters 2 [Poole], 3 [Mabry], and 6 [Anderson et al.]). For example, Winter and Ferreira's (1967) use of the term "historical" and Bochner's (1976) use of "never reach" emphasize the fact that all groups *develop* over time. One of the major critiques of laboratory group research is that it is difficult, if not impossible, to generalize the results from such studies to natural groups (such as families), and one reason for this is not simply that these are different contexts of group communication, but rather that studies often compare different group communication contexts at different times in the groups' development. In addition, one-shot case studies conducted in the laboratory or field cannot account for developmental changes experienced in groups over time. It is also important to acknowledge that group experiences occur in the context of the life course of developing individuals (see Socha, 1997). Thus, developmentally speaking, communication in early adult groups (e.g., ages 18-30) will not only reflect the needs and tensions individuals experience in early adulthood but also will be affected by individual members who are at vastly different stages of development with respect to group communication skills.

One useful perspective for accounting for change and growth in groups and group members is a life-span developmental framework. This perspective has informed family communication research, as well as research in interpersonal and organizational communication, and recently has been applied to the study of group communication (Frey & Barge, 1997). Coupled with the concept of the bona fide group (Putnam & Stohl, 1990), this approach potentially can lead to a fuller understanding of group communication. Key among the many questions raised by this approach is this: If group communication, like all communication, is developmental, then where does the process of learning about group communication begin? Before addressing this question and articulating what this perspective entails for the study of group and family communication, I review past conceptual and theoretical work about communication in whole family units.

COMMUNICATION IN WHOLE FAMILIES

There have been numerous reviews of family communication theories and research studies (e.g., Aust, 1998; Bochner & Eisenberg, 1987; Fitzpatrick & Badzinski, 1985, 1994; Fitzpatrick & Ritchie, 1993; Vangelisti, 1993), as well as extensive reviews written by scholars in allied fields that either directly or indirectly concern family communication (e.g., Boss, Doherty, LaRossa, Schumm, & Steinmetz, 1993; Burr, Hill, Reiss, & Nye, 1979; Handel & Whitchurch, 1994). These reviews uniformly point out the lack of studies examining communication in entire family systems and explicitly call for such work. According to Fitzpatrick and Badzinski (1985), who echo Riskin and Faunce (1972), "the least studied family unit was the family unit itself" (p. 717). Indeed, as noted previously, family communication research (both inside and outside the Communication discipline) has focused primarily on dyadic relationships (e.g., marriage) or triads (for an exception, see Reiss, 1981).

To avoid ground that has been well covered by others, but still provide an organized glimpse at some of the past conceptual and theoretical work about communication in whole families, I use Fitzpatrick and Ritchie's (1993) "family research metaphors" to organize a review of selected family communication theoretical perspectives. Given space limits, I include only prominent theoretical perspectives covered in family communication textbooks (see Arliss, 1993; Beebe & Masterson, 1986; Galvin & Brommel, 1996; Noller & Fitzpatrick, 1993; Pearson, 1989; L. Turner & West, 1998; Yerby, Buerkel-Rothfuss, & Bochner, 1990). Where relevant, I also point out commonalities between family and group communication theories. I then highlight some of the specific topics studied in family communication by means of a review of methods and measurement instruments. Finally, I conclude this section with a brief distillation of findings from family communication research that can be applied to the study of group communication.

CONCEPTUAL AND THEORETICAL APPROACHES

Fitzpatrick and Ritchie (1993) argued that adopting the "family as small group" metaphor (e.g., see Strodtbeck, 1954; Walters, 1982) meant applying assumptions about "groups" to the study of families. Historically, they explained, "this metaphor focuses attention on task accomplishment and role performance. Like all small groups, families are said to have common goals or objectives without which the group would not exist" (p. 573).

Adopting the family-as-small-group metaphor also meant accepting assumptions about "communication" when studying families. One initial imported notion was that "communication functions to exchange information required for successful task accomplishment and role performance" (Fitzpatrick & Ritchie, 1993, p. 573). This information-based conceptualization (associated primarily with the structural-functional approach discussed below) was later rejected by family communication scholars as being too narrow, because it overemphasized cognitive and behavioral aspects of family communication and left out relational functions. Fitzpatrick and Ritchie's two theoretical perspectives of communication relevant to the family-as-a-small-group metaphor are the Structural-Functional Perspective and Role Theory.

Early family sociologists (e.g., Parsons, 1959; Parsons & Bales, 1955) busied themselves with the task of identifying the principles that led to different kinds of linkages between and among family members and how these systems of linkages—more specifically, structures—facilitated or inhibited accomplishing such societal functions as socializing the young. Topics (common in reviews of the Structural-Functional Perspective as applied to families, such as Adams, 1980) included marriage arrangements, types of marriages, household arrangements, residential clustering and location, systems of descent, authority (including status and decision-making patterns), and types of families.

Noller and Fitzpatrick (1993), however, criticized the Structural-Functional Perspective for having too narrow of a view of communication (i.e., overemphasizing information management) and ignoring "companionship, intimacy, or love" (p. 39). Today, family communication scholars view the perspective as outdated, but some still use it as a springboard to discuss more expanded views of family that do emphasize communication. One such expansion pertains to roles and family communication.

Every family communication textbook published to date covers family roles as a process where "each individual seeks and negotiates . . . a place in the social system" (Kantor & Lehr, 1975, p. 179). L. H. Turner and West (1998), for example, discuss role taking, role evaluation, role messages, role allocation, role expectations, role performance, role conflict, role models, gender roles, and gender-role socialization. Galvin and Brommel (1996) review the McMaster (University) model of family functioning (see Epstein, Bishop, & Baldwin, 1982), which describes five essential functions that underlie family roles: (a) adult sexual fulfillment and gender modeling for children, (b) nurturing and emotional support, (c) individual development, (d) kinship maintenance and family management, and (e) providing basic resources.

Although some roles may be unique to family groups, such as those enacted by children, there are obvious commonalities between roles in families and other types of groups. These commonalities can be seen in lists of group roles, such as the classic one by Benne and Sheats (1948; see Pavitt, Chapter 12, this volume). One particularly striking similarity related to roles is found between Lewin and colleagues' autocratic, democratic, and laissez-faire "leadership" styles (e.g., Lewin, Lippit, & White, 1939) and Baumrind's (1971, 1991) authoritarian, authoritative, and permissive "parenting" styles. Given the similarities in treatments of roles in family and group communication research, it would seem fruitful to study how individuals navigate multiple roles in their multiple groups across the life span.

According to Fitzpatrick and Ritchie (1993), three additional metaphors underscore past family communication research: family as a private mini-culture, family as a resource exchange system, and family as a set of relationships. I review the mini-culture metaphor in some detail as it pertains most to groups, and I refer readers to Fitzpatrick and Ritchie's discussion of the family as a social exchange system and family as a set of relationships, as these metaphors pertain more to interpersonal communication.

According to Fitzpatrick and Ritchie (1993), the metaphor of "family as a private mini-culture" emphasizes concepts that typically are found in studies of communication and culture, such as values, rules, and rituals. Families create their own unique culture and personal symbol system (e.g., some family stories have meaning only to family members). Theories that I discuss under this metaphor are Systems Theory, in particular Kantor and Lehr's (1975) model of family types; Rules Theory; theories of family stories; developmental theories; and dialectical approaches.

Whitchurch and Constantine (1993) reviewed the systems approach (in this volume, see Chapters 1 [Gouran], 2 [Poole], and 3 [Mabry]) to families and family communication, and much of their review will be familiar to group scholars. As previously noted, there have been few, if any, systemic studies of families, in part because of methodological difficulties summarized by Broderick (1993): reliance on linear explanations of family functions (in the face of circular causality), the lack of longitudinal studies (most studies stressed the early years and failed to examine development), and restriction of the focus to the coresident family (only people living in the same house) and, thereby, excluding interfaces between the family and external systems (such as schools and health care facilities), as well as individuals outside the family. I consider these problems in a subsequent section.

Kantor and Lehr (1975) developed a model of family types that depicts family systems engaging in the task of distance-regulation, or negotiating closeness. According to them, this is the primary task of a family system. Families use resources (labeled "access dimensions") of time, space, and energy to achieve goals (labeled "target dimensions") of power (i.e., autonomy and freedom), meaning (i.e., family identity), and affect (i.e., cohesion).

Kantor and Lehr (1975) combined access and target dimensions to derive three types of families: closed, open, and random. *Closed families* are ones in which members interact among themselves in fixed spaces (e.g., rooms with designated purposes), adhere to regular time schedules (e.g., fixed times for meals and recreation), and expend energy in consistent ways. In contrast, in *open families,* members interact in movable, variable spaces with outsiders admitted, have more flexible time constraints, and expend energy as needed to meet challenges as they arise. *Random families* are those for which space, time, and energy dimensions are irregular and chaotic (e.g., members sleeping late in various rooms and eating early at times, late at other times).

A rules theoretical perspective also appears in virtually every family communication textbook. Typically, these texts define communication rules, identify types of rules (such as implicit, explicit, and meta-rule; see Laing, 1971), and discuss family rule development, family rule management, and how rules are affected by culture. These discussions of family communication rules are very similar to group textbook discussions about group communication rules insofar as both families and nonfamily groups develop rules that help create supportive relations, a positive climate, and task accomplishment, as well as rules that work against these goals (see also Satir, 1988).

Theories of family stories, or narratives, also are relevant to the family-as-mini-culture metaphor. Family Narrative Theory is linked to the theoretical perspectives of Symbolic Interactionism and Social Constructionism, which seek to understand families by examining members' individual understandings and shared realities that are created and sustained between and among family members through their communication. In general, family stories, like all stories, can be analyzed by looking at content (e.g., type of story, such as birthing), story features (e.g., dramatic elements, family themes, and family metaphors), story functions (e.g., family identity construction), and performance (e.g., speaker qualities and rate).

A life-span perspective is particularly helpful for understanding family stories, for, as L. H. Turner and West (1998) explain, "family stories function differently at different times in the family's life cycle, and in doing so, often provide help for the family during a specific developmental period" (p. 209). Family Narrative Theory has a clear counterpart in group communication with Bormann's (1986) Symbolic Convergence Theory, which also emphasizes group storytelling (in this volume, see Chapters 1 [Gouran], 2 [Poole], and 8 [Keyton]).

Unlike studies of groups that typically examine input from all group members, past studies of the family-as-mini-culture do not include all family members (for an exception, see Ritchie & Fitzpatrick, 1990). Many family researchers gather data only from adult members and couples, but then draw conclusions about the entire family unit. One important exception to this is Reiss (1981), who had family members work alone to solve a problem, then work together as a family, and then work again as individuals. This approach allowed for assessment of the contribution of the family unit to solving problems and making decisions over and above that of individual members, as well as the determination of differences in family problem-solving and decision-making styles. Three dimensions were found to characterize these family styles: *configuration* (a family's contribution to the meaning of the problem), *coordination* (similarity of members and their willingness to develop conjoint solutions to problems), and *closure* (the willingness of the family to not rush to a premature solution). An information-processing model underlies Reiss's approach (see Propp, Chapter 9, this volume, regarding collective information processing in groups). Reiss was especially interested in describing how families use information in response to "crises"; that is, how they restructure their rule system, or "family paradigm" (Reiss, 1981), to meet new demands on the system.

Finally, developmental approaches and, most recently, dialectical approaches appear in theorizing about family communication. Models of the family life cycle, for example, are commonplace in family theorizing (e.g., Carter & McGoldrick, 1989). These models describe the unique sets of circumstances that confront families at various stages in the family life span (e.g., early marriage). Although stage models are open to criticism (e.g., not defining stages precisely and viewing development as linear instead of nonlinear; in this volume, see Chapters 2 [Poole], 3 [Mabry], and 6 [Anderson et al.]), they explicitly acknowledge development and are a mainstay of family communication research. Parallels have begun to emerge between developmental approaches to family communication and developmental approaches to groups (Lacoursiere, 1980) and group communication (Frey & Barge, 1997).

The most recent theoretical addition is Family Dialectical Theory. The resulting work has identified and examined prominent dialectical tensions occurring in the context of family life, such as autonomy-connection, openness-protection, and novelty-predictability (see Baxter, 1988). This is similar to dialectical work relating to other types of groups besides families (see, for example, Adelman & Frey, 1994, 1997; Frey, 1999; Smith & Berg, 1987).

Within this mix of conceptual and theoretical approaches, family researchers have studied various topics. I review some of this work below within the context of methodological approaches, not only to acquaint those outside family communication with some of these topics but also to provide a glimpse at past efforts that have grappled with some important methodological issues that confront scholars who seek to study entire families.

METHODOLOGICAL APPROACHES

Because groups and families share a number of common features, it is not surprising to find similarities in approaches to measuring these features in group and family research. Of course, there are also unique aspects of family units, as well as unique measurements, such as a scale that assesses family communication about sex (Warren, 1995).

Before reviewing examples of various selected measures, I consider some general problems in measuring family units that mirror some of the problems confronting those who study groups. According to Ransom, Fisher, Phillips, Kokes, and Weiss (1990), researchers interested in families have sometimes gathered data from individuals in families and then used this information to draw family-level conclusions. To help avoid conceptual slippage, they propose a classification scheme consisting of three categories of data. Category I consists of "data representing family [group] characteristics" (p. 52). Data may be collected about individual family members (e.g., the employment of a parent), family dyads (e.g., the number of years a husband and wife have been married), and/or the entire nuclear family (e.g., size and stage of life cycle), as well as extended family (e.g., size or network density). Reporting various family demographics is an example of Category I data.

In group communication research, Category I data are used to identify and describe the type of group studied. For example, the case studies reported in Frey (1994b, 1995a) define types of groups on the basis of Category I data (e.g., Conquergood's, 1994, study of street gangs). Category I data are important in establishing baseline comparisons that can be used to differentiate between and among types of group systems.

Category II represents "data generated by individual [family members] outside face-to-face family situations" (Ransom et al., 1990, p. 53). Data can be acquired by etic (outsiders' viewpoints) or emic (insiders' viewpoints) procedures and be about a family member, a family dyad, a nuclear family, or an extended family. Category II data can remain uncombined (i.e., individual family members' reports), be combined (e.g., family members' scores are summed or averaged to construct a

conjoint index), or be contrasted (e.g., difference scores between or among family members are used to construct a conjoint index). Mathematically combining family members' scores to derive a composite index that represents the family group remains theoretically, not to mention statistically, problematic. Data collected from individuals and combined for purposes of dyadic or group-level analyses may result in a distorted index. A good example of Category II data is Rubin's (1976, 1994) analyses of interviews with blue-collar parents and children, in which she determined how they managed issues of race, class, and gender within their families and identified common themes across families.

Category III refers to "data generated during family interaction . . . [which] can reflect individual, dyadic, or group processes" (Ransom et al. 1990, p. 55). The focus of such data can be on an individual family member's behavior during family interaction, a family dyad, the entire nuclear family, or the extended family. The data can be observed as they occur in their natural environment (e.g., in a family's home; see Henry, 1971), or "provided," that is, obtained via observing family interaction during simulations (e.g., a family decision-making simulation; see Reiss, 1981). Henry (1971), for example, described interaction in the homes of families where a mentally ill member had returned after being institutionalized. He did this to illuminate reasons why many such patients return to institutions (rather than remain at home).

There are hundreds of coding schemes and rating scales that allow for the acquisition of Category II and III data about families (for a catalog, see Touliatos, Perlmutter, & Straus, 1990). I have chosen to highlight examples of measures that (a) allow for collection of Category II and III data about the family as a unit, (b) relate to topics studied by group and family communication scholars, and (c) may be "new" to group communication researchers. I include well-known measures as well as relatively obscure ones; hence, the list serves heuristic as well as summative purposes (see Table 17.1). The topics that the measures are

Table 17.1 A Selected List of Measurement Instruments That Assess Various Dimensions of Family Units

Dimension	Instrument	Citation
Conflict	Structural Family Interaction Scale	Perosa, Hansen, and Perosa (1981)
	Inventories of Conflict (Marital, etc.)	Olson (1983)
	Family Interaction Coding Scheme	Patterson (1982)
	Child Abuse Potential Inventory	Milner (1989)
	Family Interaction Coding Scheme	Reid (1986)
Environment	Home Observation for Measurement of the Environment	Bradley and Caldwell (1977)
	Home Observation Assessment Method	Steinglass (1979)
Family images	Self-Report Family Inventory	Beavers, Hampson, and Hulgus (1985)
	Family Photo Assessment Process	Blinn (1988)
	Kvebaek Family Sculpture Technique	Cromwell, Fournier, and Kvebaek (1980)
	Family Attachment Style	Bartholomew and Horowitz (1991)
Interaction	Global Coding Scheme	Bell and Bell (1984)
	Clinical Rating Scales for the Circumplex Model of Marital and Family Systems	Olson et al. (1985)
	Family Alliances Coding Scheme	Gilbert and Christensen (1988)
	Marital and Parental Subsystem Interaction Over Time	Belsky, Youngblade, Rovine, and Volling (1991)
	Event History Analysis	Griffin (1993)
	Pattern Interaction Card Sort	Reiss (1971)
	Questionnaire on Planning Behaviors	Beard and Firebaugh (1978)
	Family Interaction Coding Scheme	Hannum and Mayer (1984)
Networks	Interconnectedness of Social Networks Index	Udry and Hall (1965)
	Personal Network Inventory	Oliveri and Reiss (1981)
	Boundary Ambiguity Scale	Boss and Greenberg (1984)
Policies and routines	Family Policy Inventory	Pershing (1979)
	Family Routines Inventory	Boyce, Jensen, James, and Peacock (1983)
	Family Celebrations Index	McCubbin and Thompson (1987)

designed to assess typically appear in family communication texts (and, in many cases, group communication texts). The list does not include family therapy measures but, instead, focuses on those measures applicable to non-clinical families. Some of the measures, however, such as the Kvebaek Family Sculpture Technique (Cromwell, Fournier, & Kvebaek, 1980), originally were developed for clinical purposes but with modifications could be adapted for general research purposes. The

validity of these measures and how widely they have been used varies considerably (the sources cited for each measure provide further details about these matters).

Conflict

Although conflict affects the entire family, family communication researchers have studied conflict mostly at the dyadic level (see Noller, Feeney, Peterson, & Sheehan, 1995).

A few researchers have developed group-level indices and/or examined group-level conflict processes. For example, Perosa, Hansen, and Perosa's (1981) Structured Family Interaction Scale, designed to measure, among other things, conflict avoidance, conflict resolution, conflict expression without resolution, and triangulation (i.e., avoiding direct interaction by using a third party), allows for the acquisition of Category II data and family scores. Olson's (1983) various inventories of marital, parent-child, and parent-adolescent conflict allow for both Category II and III data at the dyadic level by gathering self-reports about conflict, as well as by coding dyadic interaction. These inventories could be modified for studying entire families. Patterson's (1982) Family Interaction Coding Scheme yields Category III data about "coercive" or conflictful family processes, with the goal of identifying interactional styles of homes with problem children. Observers use 29 criteria to code family interactions in real time (minimum of 70 minutes) when all family members are present at home, but they focus on one family member at a time (selected in random order). Finally, a couple of schemes consider the problem of interaction in abusive families. Milner's (1989) Child Abuse Potential Inventory is a 160-item questionnaire that assesses a parent's potential for committing physical abuse. Reid's (1986) Family Interaction Coding Scheme categorizes family members' behavior at 6-second intervals using 29 behavioral categories to assess differences in the sequences of behaviors of abusive and nonabusive families.

Environment

The concept of *family home environment* refers to the total, global impact that family members, home space, and home objects have on family members. Bradley and Caldwell (1977), for example, focused on the impact of family home environment on infants, preschool, and elementary school-aged children by using an observational coding scheme, the Home Observation for Measurement of the Environment, yielding Category II and III data. Items assess family members' behaviors (e.g., parental responses to verbal behaviors), as well as objects in the home (e.g., the number of books children own). A similar measure developed by Steinglass (1979), the Home Observation Assessment Method, focuses more heavily on a family's use of space (e.g., particular locations in a home and time spent in those places), as well as their interaction in a given space.

Family Images

The family image measures included in Table 17.1 yield Category II data about a given family's perceptions and attitudes toward itself and its members. Some of the measures are conventional, such as the Self-Report Family Inventory (Beavers, Hampson, & Hulgus, 1985), which assesses members' perceptions of their family using a battery of scales; others are unconventional. For example, Blinn's (1988) Family Photo Assessment Process involves obtaining family members' ratings of family photos to assess family cohesiveness, expressiveness, conflict, independence, achievement, intellectualism, activity level, moral/religious emphasis, outdoor orientation, and temporal orientation. The Kvebaek Family Sculpture Technique (Cromwell et al., 1980) involves family members moving wooden sculptures of people representing members of their family on a grid to assess degree of family cohesiveness. Both these measures have potential application in group communication research, particularly given that a certain amount of cohesiveness is a desired outcome of group interaction (see Keyton, Chapter 8, this volume). In some situations, such as children's groups, one cannot always use paper-and-pencil measures to assess cohesiveness (or other outcomes), and these unconventional techniques make such assessments possible. It should be noted, however, that Kvebaek's technique (and others like it) was designed for clinical and/or therapeutic purposes. Thus, the technique may require modification and refinement for use as a research tool in studying group communication because of the potential negative impact that information obtained from the technique might pose, for example, to group stability if shared with group members. Finally, the Family Attachment Style instrument (Bartholomew & Horowitz, 1991) emphasizes that members' attachment to their family varies (i.e., some form secure attachments, whereas others form anxious-ambivalent attachments).

Interaction

Most of the instruments in Table 17.1 designed to measure family interaction enable the collection of Category III data (alone or in combination with Category II data), either in response to observing the completion of artificial tasks by family members or from their natural interaction. Some of these coding schemes/rating scales offer a wide lens through which to view family interaction (e.g., Bell & Bell, 1984; Olson et al., 1985); others, such as the Family Alliances Coding Scheme (Gilbert & Christensen, 1988), have a narrower lens through which to view, in this particular case, positive, negative, and neutral messages between and among family alliances (coalitions). Other schemes/scales assess subsystem interaction (Belsky, Youngblade, Rovine, & Volling, 1991), significant family episodes over time (Griffin, 1993), and the role of family interaction in solving problems (Reiss, 1971) and planning (Beard & Firebaugh, 1978). One of these instruments, Clinical Rating Scales for the Circumplex Model of Marital and Family Systems (Olson et al., 1985), is a theoretically grounded approach used to examine family cohesion and adaptability. It is a widely cited model of family system interaction (see Olson, 1986).

Some of the categories in these observational coding schemes, such as those in Hannum and Mayer's (1984) Family Interaction Coding Scheme, are similar to the categories in Bales's (1950) IPA, such as agreement and disagreement. In the light of past research, reviewed previously, that argued that families and groups are different (e.g., families have more negative interactions than other types of groups), a comparative examination of coding schemes used to study interaction in a wide variety of groups is needed to identify commonalities, as well as differences, in the types of messages used in groups and families.

Networks

The earliest research examining family networks is Bott's (1971) study in England of the impact that family networks have on the distribution of domestic labor (e.g., the impact of friends' marital habits on one's own marriage). Since then, studies have focused on the impact of social networks on marital-role segregation (Udry & Hall, 1965), developing romantic relationships (e.g., Parks, Stan, & Eggert, 1983), and boundaries between families and the outside world (Boss & Greenberg, 1984). One well-developed network approach is the Personal Network Inventory (Oliveri & Reiss, 1981), which uses a questionnaire to construct and describe qualities of a family's network (e.g., size, density, help received, and positive sentiment). Oliveri and Reiss were especially interested in network stability and the interconnections of friendship and family networks.

The Boundary Ambiguity Scale (Boss & Greenberg, 1984) measures family members' perceptions of who is and who is not part of a given family system and the nature of their involvement. For example, a father may be technically present (i.e., resides in the home), but because he is underinvolved (e.g., emotionally and/or in day-to-day activities), he is considered functionally absent (see Buerkel-Rothfuss, Fink, & Buerkel, 1995). Such a measure has potential utility in the study of group communication, especially in the light of Putnam and Stohl's (1990) Bona Fide Groups Perspective, for assessing the perceptions of who is "really" in a group and who is on the margins.

Policies and Routines

There is a clear connection between the policies and routines scales included in Table 17.1

and research from a Structuration Theory perspective (see Poole, Seibold, & McPhee, 1986, 1996; in this volume, see Chapters 1 [Gouran], 2 [Poole], and 3 [Mabry]) that examines how rules and resources create and recreate group structures. The Family Policy Inventory (Pershing, 1979), for example, describes family policies as perceived by its members, as well as identifies areas in which members' understandings of policies differ. Many task groups in business have a range of policies, and the extent to which such policies are shared and valued would seem to be an important aspect of group functioning (for research on communication in organizational work groups, see Greenbaum & Query, Chapter 20, this volume).

Everyday routines are understudied in family communication, but the Family Routines Inventory (Boyce, Jensen, James, & Peacock, 1983) identifies routines involving two or more family members and assesses their significance to family members. Routines are important in families, especially those with young children, where they provide structure for children to navigate the day (such as morning routines and homework routines).

Finally, two communication routines that are understudied in families and groups but are, nevertheless, important (some might say vital) are celebration and play. The Family Celebrations Index (McCubbin & Thompson, 1987) is a self-report measure that identifies what holidays families celebrate and how they celebrate them. There is little doubt that families and groups engage in play activity and that this is beneficial; however, in many coding schemes—such as Bales's (1950) IPA category of dramatizing/shows tension release—play, celebration, and just plain "having fun" are often viewed as detracting problem-solving and decision-making groups from the task at hand. Future research needs to examine more closely what makes communicating in families and groups "fun" for members; for example, what makes them smile or laugh, and how families and groups balance the play-work dialectic. For a long time, the fields of family and group communication have examined the serious side of families and groups; it is time we learned about the playful side as well!

LEARNING ABOUT "GROUPS" FROM "FAMILIES"

What can be learned about group communication from what has been discovered in family communication research? Given the lack of studies of entire families, this is a difficult question to answer. Drawing on what is known from Communication studies that do examine entire families and the results of studies in Family Therapy (an area not covered in this review but one on which family communication scholars have often drawn), I offer four ideas that might begin to reconnect what we know about families with what we know about groups and move toward an integrated, developmental approach to group communication.

First, communication patterns learned in the family of origin persist across generations (see Cohler & Greenbaum, 1981; Kramer, 1985). For better or worse, what is learned in the family of origin serves as a foundation for what goes on in future families, and, by extension, for communication in groups outside the family. Thus, the domain of group communication research should include not only the life span of any particular group (the most common approach) but also individuals' participation in groups over the entire human life span, starting with the family as the first "group."

Second, family members, especially children, are exposed to functional and dysfunctional ways of communicating, and this exposure potentially has significant implications for how they manage their interactions in their family as well as other groups (see Hall, 1991). For example, one communication pattern appearing in troubled families (i.e., those who seek therapy) is triangulation, which refers to "a situation in which a third person serves as a go-between for two other family members, thus sparing those two family members from interacting directly" (Yerby et al., 1990, p. 173). In particular, "Many times a child will take on symptoms such as bed-wetting or temper tantrums or drug use as a way to focus the family away from [troubles with] the marital relationship" (Yerby et al., 1990, p. 175). Given the negative effects of triangulation on family members (e.g., disconnecting them from each other), it would seem reasonable to examine this process and its effects on individual members in other types of groups that are experiencing problems. Thus, in addition to studying functional ways of communicating in groups, group communication scholars should also focus on dysfunctional ways.

Third, troubled families display particular qualities, such as an inability to balance flexibility and stability (Haley, 1976; Steier, Stanton, & Todd, 1982). According to Steier et al. (1982), troubled families adhere to familiar patterns of relating when situations call for new ways of relating, such as during their children's adolescence period; they also might not develop consistency in patterns of relating and become chaotic. As in the study of families, it is important that scholars studying other types of groups seek to identify the qualities of troubled groups, possibly including inability to manage the flexibility-stability dialectic, as well as understand the effects these troubled groups have on individual members. This should also include studying how both a group and its individual members cope with the stress created by these tensions. This work might also examine members' participation in dysfunctional models of family and how that exposure might affect participation in groups outside the family (see Hall, 1991).

Fourth, "the nature of [a family's] boundary says much about family functioning" (Yerby et al., 1990, p. 76), including how families manage authority and the autonomy-interdependence dialectic. A moderate degree of openness to the outside world, including the family of origin, neighborhood, and so forth, is linked to healthy family functioning (Haley, 1976). For example, if a family's boundaries are rigid, members may keep to themselves and ignore or screen out information inconsistent with their family's values, as

well as monitor what information leaves the family. This point underscores the need for permeable boundaries of families—indeed, all groups—and further justifies the study of groups from the Bona Fide Groups perspective (Stohl & Putnam, 1994).

TOWARD AN INTEGRATIVE APPROACH TO GROUP COMMUNICATION ACROSS THE LIFE SPAN

In this chapter, I have argued that the "family" should be regarded as our first and longest "group" in a lifetime of being involved in "groups." There is no doubt that the "family" is a unique type of group; however, conceptualizing the family as unique and different from all other groups, which has tended to happen in the past, not only masks commonalities among these groups but also disconnects the family group from developmental processes of learning how to communicate in groups. Like all communication, we *learn* how to communicate in groups. It is simply a fact that many of our "communication firsts" take place in the family group. The family, therefore, plays a significant role not only in how people learn to communicate using language (Yingling, 1995) and in relationships (Dixson, 1995), but also in how they learn to communicate in groups.

A life-span developmental approach to group communication (see Frey, 1999; Frey & Barge, 1997; Socha, 1997) places the family as the first of many interlinked groups over the course of a person's lifetime. Such a perspective opens up new and important avenues for joint family and group communication explorations. For example, Dixson's (1995) work on the impact that parent-child communication has on children's cognitive models of relationships could profitably be extended to groups. Dixson states that relationships (and one could substitute "groups") "occur both in the minds of [members] as . . . well as between [members]" (p. 43). In particular, families "influence children's models [of groups], . . . that is, beliefs and expectations about [groups]"

(p. 47). Finally, "children's subsequent [participation in groups] may alter children's models of [groups acquired from the family]" (p. 47). Studying children's models of family units and examining how these models are used, refined, or abandoned in children's early interaction in other types of groups (e.g., play groups, classroom groups, and scouts), as well as how models of interaction in nonfamily groups are then bought back to the family and used, refined, or abandoned, is an important future joint venture for group and family communication scholars and practitioners alike.

Another joint venture could be to conduct systematic studies of clusters of groups at various stages over the course of the human life span. For example, comparative studies of how adolescents communicate in their different groups would begin to construct a more detailed picture of the complexities of how adolescents use communication to navigate among and within groups.

Finally, many of the approaches and measures used to study communication in family units (and groups) included in this review are certainly not without flaws. Cooperation is needed between family and group communication researchers both to improve existing approaches and to develop new, innovative approaches to describing, assessing, and analyzing communication in families and other types of groups. One suggestion might be to hold preconferences sponsored by the Family Communication Division and the newly formed Group Communication Division of the National Communication Association on studying communication in families and groups.

There is much to be gained for the study of group communication, family communication, and the Communication field at large by reopening a dialogue between group and family communication scholars. I am confident that this conversation will result not only in a better understanding of communication in our first "group" but also in a better understanding of communication in the entire "family" of "groups" across the life span.

REFERENCES

Adams, B. (1980). *The family: A sociological interpretation* (3rd ed.). Boston: Houghton Mifflin.
Adelman, M. B., & Frey, L. R. (1994). The pilgrim must embark: Creating and sustaining community in a residential facility for people with AIDS. In L. R. Frey (Ed.), *Group communication in context: Studies of natural groups* (pp. 3-22). Hillsdale, NJ: Lawrence Erlbaum.
Adelman, M. B., & Frey, L. R. (1997). *The fragile community: Living together with AIDS.* Mahwah, NJ: Lawrence Erlbaum.
Arliss, L. P. (1993). *Contemporary family communication: Messages and meanings.* New York: St. Martin's.
Aust, P. J. (1998, February). *A modern assessment of family communication: Revisiting Bochner's small group frontier.* Paper presented at the annual meeting of the Western Speech Communication Association, Denver, CO.
Bales, R. F. (1950). *Interaction process analysis: A method for the study of small groups.* Cambridge, MA: Addison-Wesley.
Bales, R. F. (1970). *Personality and interpersonal behavior.* New York: Holt, Rinehart & Winston.
Bartholomew, K., & Horowitz, L. (1991). Attachment styles among young adults: A test of a four category model. *Journal of Personality and Social Psychology, 61,* 226-244.
Baumrind, D. (1971). Current patterns of parental authority. *Developmental Psychology Monographs, 4*(1), 1-102.
Baumrind, D. (1991). Parenting styles and adolescent development. In R. Learner, A. C. Petersen, & J. Brooks-Gunn (Eds.), *Encyclopedia of adolescence* (Vol. 2, pp. 746-758). New York: Garland.
Baxter, L. (1988). A dialectical perspective on communication strategies in relationship development. In S. Duck (Ed.), *Handbook of personal relationships: Theory, research, and interventions* (pp. 257-273). New York: Wiley.
Beard, D., & Firebaugh, F. M. (1978). Morphostatic and morphogenic planning behaviors in families: Development of a measurement instrument. *Home Economics Research Journal, 6,* 192-205.
Beavers, W. R., Hampson, R. B., & Hulgus, Y. F. (1985). The Beavers' systems approach to family assessment. *Family Process, 24,* 398-405.
Beebe, S. A., & Masterson, J. T. (1986). *Family talk: Interpersonal communication in the family.* New York: Random House.
Bell, D. C., & Bell, L. G. (1984). *Family research project progress report.* Minneapolis: University of Minnesota. (ERIC Document Reproduction Service No. ED 248 420)
Belsky, J., Youngblade, L., Rovine, M., & Volling, B. (1991). Patterns of change and parent-child interaction. *Journal of Marriage and the Family, 53,* 487-498.
Benne, K. D., & Sheats, P. (1948). Functional roles of group members. *Journal of Social Issues, 4,* 41-49.

Blinn, L. (1988). The family photo assessment process (FPAP): A method for validating cross-cultural comparisons of family social identities. *Journal of Comparative Family Studies, 19*, 17-35.

Bochner, A. P. (1976). Conceptual frontiers in the study of families: An introduction to the literature. *Human Communication Research, 2*, 381-397.

Bochner, A. P., & Eisenberg, E. M. (1987). Family process: Systems perspectives. In C. R. Berger & S. H. Chaffee (Eds.), *Handbook of communication science* (pp. 540-563). Beverly Hills, CA: Sage.

Bormann, E. G. (1986). Symbolic convergence theory and communication in group decision-making. In R. Y. Hirokawa & M. S. Poole (Eds.), *Communication and group decision-making* (pp. 219-236). Beverly Hills, CA: Sage.

Boss, P. G., Doherty, W. J., LaRossa, R., Schumm, W. R., & Steinmetz, S. K. (Eds.). (1993). *Sourcebook of family theories and methods: A contextual approach.* New York: Plenum.

Boss, P., & Greenberg, J. (1984). Family boundary ambiguity: A new variable in family stress theory. *Family Process, 23*, 535-546.

Bott, E. (1971). *Family and social networks: Rules, norms, and external relationships in ordinary urban families* (2nd ed.). London: Tavistock.

Boyce, W. T., Jensen, E. W., James, S. A., & Peacock, J. L. (1983). The family routines inventory: Theoretical origins. *Social Science and Medicine, 17*, 193-200.

Bradley, R., & Caldwell, B. (1977). Home observation for measurement of the environment: A validation study of screening efficiency. *American Journal of Mental Deficiency, 81*, 417-420.

Broderick, C. B. (1993). *Understanding family processes: Basics of family systems theory.* Newbury Park, CA: Sage.

Buerkel-Rothfuss, N., Fink, D., & Buerkel, R. (1995). Communication in the father-child dyad: The intergenerational transmission process. In T. J. Socha & G. H. Stamp (Eds.), *Parents, children and communication: Frontiers of theory and research* (pp. 63-85). Mahwah, NJ: Lawrence Erlbaum.

Burr, W. R., Hill, R., Reiss, I. L., & Nye, F. I. (Eds.). (1979). *Contemporary theories about the family.* New York: Free Press.

Carter, B., & McGoldrick, M. (Eds.). (1989). *The changing family life cycle: A framework for family therapy* (2nd ed.). Boston: Allyn & Bacon.

Cheek, F. E. (1964a). The schizophrenic mother in word and deed. *Family Process, 3*, 155-177.

Cheek, F. E. (1964b). A serendipitous finding: Sex roles and schizophrenia. *Journal of Abnormal Social Psychology, 69*, 392-400.

Cheek, F. E. (1965a). Family interaction patterns and convalescent adjustment of the schizophrenic. *Archives of General Psychiatry, 13*, 138-147.

Cheek, F. E. (1965b). The father of the schizophrenic. *Archives of General Psychiatry, 13*, 336-345.

Cohler, B. J., & Greenbaum, H. U. (with Robbins, D. M.). (1981). *Mothers, grandmothers, and daughters: Personality and child-care in three-generation families.* New York: Wiley.

Conquergood, D. (1994). Homeboys and hoods: Gang communication and cultural space. In L. R. Frey (Ed.), *Group communication in context: Studies of natural groups* (pp. 23-55). Hillsdale, NJ: Lawrence Erlbaum.

Cooley, C. H. (1955). Primary groups. In P. A. Hare, E. F. Borgatta, & R. F. Bales (Eds.), *Small groups: Studies in social interaction* (pp. 175-203). New York: Knopf.

Cromwell, R., Fournier, D., & Kvebaek, D. (1980). *The Kvebaek Family Sculpture Technique: A diagnostic and research tool in family therapy.* Jonesboro, TN: Pilgrimage.

Dixson, M. D. (1995). Models and perspectives of parent-child communication. In T. J. Socha & G. H. Stamp (Eds.), *Parents, children and communication: Frontiers of theory and research* (pp. 43-61). Mahwah, NJ: Lawrence Erlbaum.

Epstein, N. B., Bishop, D. S., & Baldwin, L. M. (1982). McMaster model of family functioning. In F. Walsh (Ed.), *Normal family processes* (pp. 115-141). New York: Guilford.

Fitzpatrick, M. A., & Badzinski, D. M. (1985). All in the family: Interpersonal communication in kin relationships. In M. L. Knapp & G. R. Miller (Eds.), *Handbook of interpersonal communication* (pp. 687-736). Beverly Hills, CA: Sage.

Fitzpatrick, M. A., & Badzinski, D. M. (1994). All in the family: Interpersonal communication in kin relationships. In M. L. Knapp & G. R. Miller (Eds.), *Handbook of interpersonal communication* (2nd ed., pp. 726-771). Thousand Oaks, CA: Sage.

Fitzpatrick, M. A., & Ritchie, L. D. (1993). Communication theory and the family. In P. G. Boss, W. J. Doherty, R. LaRossa, W. R. Schumm, & S. K. Steinmetz (Eds.), *Sourcebook of family theories and methods: A contextual approach* (pp. 565-589). New York: Plenum.

Frey, L. R. (1988, November). *Meeting the challenges posed during the 70s: A critical review of small group communication research during the 80s.* Paper presented at the annual meeting of the Speech Communication Association, New Orleans, LA.

Frey, L. R. (1994a). Call and response: The challenge of conducting research on communication in natural groups. In L. R. Frey (Ed.), *Group communication in context: Studies of natural groups* (pp. 293-304). Hillsdale, NJ: Lawrence Erlbaum.

Frey, L. R. (Ed.). (1994b). *Group communication in context: Studies of natural groups.* Hillsdale, NJ: Lawrence Erlbaum.

Frey, L. R. (1994c). Introduction: Revitalizing the study of small group communication. *Communication Studies, 45*, 1-6.

Frey, L. R. (1994d). The naturalistic paradigm: Studying small groups in the postmodern era. *Small Group Research, 25*, 551-577.

Frey, L. R. (1995a). Applied communication research on group facilitation in natural settings. In L. R. Frey (Ed.), *Innovations in group facilitation: Applications in natural settings* (pp. 1-23). Cresskill, NJ: Hampton.

Frey, L. R. (Ed.). (1995b). *Innovations in group facilitation: Applications in natural settings.* Cresskill, NJ: Hampton.

Frey, L. R. (1999). Teaching small group communication. In A. L. Vangelisti, J. A. Daly, & G. W. Friedrich (Eds.), *Teaching communication: Theory, research, and methods* (2nd ed., pp. 99-113). Mahwah, NJ: Lawrence Erlbaum.

Frey, L. R. (Ed.). (in press). *Group communication in context: Studies of bona fide groups* (2nd ed.). Mahwah, NJ: Lawrence Erlbaum.

Frey, L. R., & Barge, J. K. (Eds.). (1997). *Managing group life: Communicating in decision-making groups.* Boston: Houghton Mifflin.

Galvin, K. M., & Brommel, B. J. (1996). *Family communication: Cohesion and change* (4th ed.). New York: HarperCollins.

Gilbert, R., & Christensen, A. (1988). The assessment of family alliances. In R. J. Prinz (Ed.), *Advances in behavior assessment of children and families* (Vol. 4, pp. 221-254). Greenwich, CT: JAI.

Griffin, W. A. (1993). Event history analysis of marital and family interaction: A practical introduction. *Journal of Family Psychology, 6,* 211-229.

Haley, J. (1976). *Problem-solving therapy.* New York: Grune & Stratton.

Hall, F. (1991). Dysfunctional managers: The next human resource challenge. *Organizational Dynamics, 20,* 48-57.

Handel, G. (1992). The qualitative tradition in family research. In J. F. Gilgun, K. Daly, & G. Handel (Eds.), *Qualitative methods in family research* (pp. 12-21). Newbury Park, CA: Sage.

Handel, G., & Whitchurch, G. G. (Eds.). (1994). *The psychosocial interior of the family* (4th ed.). Hawthorne, NY: Aldine de Gruyter.

Hannum, J. W., & Mayer, J. M. (1984). Validation of two family assessment approaches. *Journal of Marriage and the Family, 46,* 741-748.

Henry, J. (1971). *Pathways to madness.* New York: Random House.

Hess, R. D., & Handel, G. (1959). *Family worlds: A psychosocial approach to family life.* Chicago: University of Chicago Press.

Hill, R. B., Billingsley, A., Engram, E., Malson, M., Rubin, R. H., Stask, C. B., Stewart, J. B., & Teele, J. E. (1993). *Research on the African-American family: A holistic perspective.* Westport, CT: Auburn House.

Kantor, D., & Lehr, W. (1975). *Inside the family.* San Francisco: Jossey-Bass.

Keyton, J. (1994). Going forward in group communication research may mean going back: Studying the groups of children. *Communication Studies, 45,* 40-51.

Keyton, J. (1997). Coding communication in decision-making groups. In L. R. Frey & J. K. Barge (Eds.), *Managing group life: Communicating in decision-making groups* (pp. 236-269). Boston: Houghton Mifflin.

Kramer, J. R. (1985). *Family interfaces: Transgenerational patterns.* New York: Brunner/Mazel.

Lacoursiere, R. (1980). *The life cycle of groups: Group developmental stage theory.* New York: Human Sciences Press.

Laing, R. D. (1971). *The politics of the family and other essays.* New York: Pantheon.

Lewin, K., Lippit, R., & White, R. (1939). Patterns of aggressive behavior in experimentally created social climates. *Journal of Science Psychology, 10,* 271-299.

Litwak, E., & Szelenyi, I. (1969). Primary group structures and their functions: Kin, neighbors, and friends. *American Sociological Review, 34,* 465-481.

McCubbin, H. I., & Thompson, A. I. (1987). FCELEBI: Family celebrations index. In H. I. McCubbin & A. I. Thompson (Eds.), *Family assessment inventories for research and practice* (pp. 169-172). Madison: University of Wisconsin Press.

Meyers, R. A., & Brashers, J. K. (1994). Expanding the boundaries of small group communication research: Exploring a feminist perspective. *Communication Studies, 45,* 68-85.

Milner, J. S. (1989). Applications and limitations of the child abuse potential inventory. *Early Child Development and Care, 42,* 85-97.

Noller, P., Feeney, J., Peterson, C., & Sheehan, G. (1995). Learning conflict patterns in the family: Links between marital, parental, and sibling relationships. In T. J. Socha & G. H. Stamp (Eds.), *Parents, children, and communication: Frontiers of theory and research* (pp. 273-298). Mahwah, NJ: Lawrence Erlbaum.

Noller, P., & Fitzpatrick, M. A. (1993). *Communication in family relationships.* Englewood Cliffs, NJ: Prentice Hall.

Oliveri, M. E., & Reiss, D. (1981). The structure of families' ties to their kin: The shaping role of social constructions. *Journal of Marriage and the Family, 43,* 391-407.

Olson, D.H.L. (1983). *Inventories of premarital, marital, parent-child, and parent-adolescent conflict.* St. Paul: University of Minnesota, Department of Family Social Science.

Olson, D.H.L. (1986). Circumplex Model VII: Validation studies and FACES III. *Family Process, 25,* 337-351.

Olson, D.H.L., McCubbin, H. I., Barnes, H., Larsen, A., Muxem, M., & Wilson, M. (1985). *Family inventories: Inventories used in a national survey of families across the family life cycle.* St. Paul: University of Minnesota, Department of Family Social Science.

Parks, M. R., Stan, C. M., & Eggert, L. L. (1983). Romantic involvement and social network involvement. *Social Psychology Quarterly, 46,* 116-131.

Parsons, T. (1959). The social structure of the family. In R. N. Anshen (Ed.), *The family: Its function and destiny* (Rev. ed., pp. 241-274). New York: Harper.

Parsons, T., & Bales, R. F. (1955). *Family socialization and interaction process.* Glencoe, IL: Free Press.

Patterson, G. R. (1982). *A social learning approach: Vol. 3. Coercive family process.* Eugene, OR: Castalia.

Pearson, J. C. (1989). *Communication in the family: Seeking satisfaction in changing times.* New York: Harper & Row.

Perosa, L., Hansen, J., & Perosa, S. (1981). Development of the structured family interaction scale. *Family Therapy, 8,* 77-90.

Pershing, B. (1979). Family policies: A component of management in the home and family setting. *Journal of Marriage and the Family, 41,* 573-581.

Poole, M. S., Seibold, D. R., & McPhee, R. D. (1986). A structurational approach to theory-building in group decision-making research. In R. Y. Hirokawa & M. S. Poole (Eds.), *Communication and group decision-making* (pp. 237-264). Beverly Hills, CA: Sage.

Poole, M. S., Seibold, D. R., & McPhee, R. D. (1996). The structuration of group decisions. In R. Y. Hirokawa & M. S. Poole (Eds.), *Communication and group decision making* (2nd ed., pp. 114-146). Thousand Oaks, CA: Sage.

Putnam, L. L. (1994). Revitalizing small group communication: Lessons learned from a bona fide group perspective. *Communication Studies, 45,* 97-102.

Putnam, L. L., & Stohl, C. (1990). Bona fide groups: A reconceptualization of groups in context. *Communication Studies, 41,* 248-265.

Putnam, L. L., & Stohl, C. (1996). Bona fide groups: An alternative perspective for communication in small group decision making. In R. Y. Hirokawa & M. S. Poole (Eds.), *Communication and group decision making* (2nd ed., pp. 146-178). Thousand Oaks, CA: Sage.

Ransom, D. C., Fisher, L., Phillips, S., Kokes, R., & Weiss, R. (1990). The logic of measurement in family research. In T. W. Draper & A. C. Marcos (Eds.), *Family variables: Conceptualization, measurement, and use* (pp. 48-63). Newbury Park, CA: Sage.

Reid, J. B. (1986). Social interaction patterns in families of abused and nonabused children. In C. Zahn-Waxler, E. M. Cummings, & R. Iannotti (Eds.), *Altruism and aggression: Biological and social origins* (pp. 238-257). Cambridge, UK: Cambridge University Press.

Reiss, D. (1971). Varieties of consensual experience III: Contrast between families of normals, delinquents, and schizophrenics. *Journal of Nervous and Mental Disease, 146,* 384-403.

Reiss, D. (1981). *The family's construction of reality.* Cambridge, MA: Harvard University Press.

Riskin, J., & Faunce, E. E. (1972). An evaluation review of family interaction research. *Family Process, 11,* 365-455.

Ritchie, L. D., & Fitzpatrick, M. A. (1990). Family communication patterns: Measuring intrapersonal perceptions of interpersonal relationships. *Communication Research, 17,* 523-545.

Rubin, L. B. (1976). *Worlds of pain: Life in the working-class family.* New York: Basic Books.

Rubin, L. B. (1994). *Families on the fault line: America's working class speaks about the family, the economy, race, and ethnicity.* New York: HarperCollins.

Satir, V. (1988). *The new peoplemaking.* Mountain View, CA: Science & Behavior Books.

Smith, K. K., & Berg, D. N. (1987). *Paradoxes of group life: Understanding conflict, paralysis, and movement in group dynamics.* San Francisco: Jossey-Bass.

Socha, T. J. (1997). Group communication across the life span. In L. R. Frey & J. K. Barge (Eds.), *Managing group life: Communicating in decision making groups* (pp. 3-28). Boston: Houghton Mifflin.

Socha, T. J., & Socha, D. M. (1994). Children's task-group communication: Did we learn it all in kindergarten? In L. R. Frey (Ed.), *Group communication in context: Studies of natural groups* (pp. 227-246). Mahwah, NJ: Lawrence Erlbaum.

Stafford, L., & Dainton, M. (1995). Parent-child communication within the family system. In T. J. Socha & G. H. Stamp (Eds.), *Parents, children, and communication: Frontiers of theory and research* (pp. 3-21). Mahwah, NJ: Lawrence Erlbaum.

Steier, F., Stanton, M., & Todd, T. C. (1982). Patterns of turn-taking and alliance formation in family communication. *Journal of Communication, 32*(4), 148-160.

Steinglass, P. (1979). The Home Observation Assessment Method (HOAM): Real-time naturalistic observation of families in their homes. *Family Process, 18,* 337-354.

Stohl, C., & Putnam, L. L. (1994). Group communication in context: Implications for the study of bona fide groups. In L. R. Frey (Ed.), *Group communication in context: Studies of natural groups* (pp. 285-292). Mahwah, NJ: Lawrence Erlbaum.

Strodtbeck, F. L. (1954). The family as three-person group. *American Sociological Review, 19,* 23-29.

Touliatos, J., Perlmutter, B. F., & Straus, M. A. (Eds.). (1990). *Handbook of family measurement techniques.* Newbury Park, CA: Sage.

Turner, L. H., & West, R. (1998). *Perspectives on family communication.* Mountain View, CA: Mayfield.

Turner, R. H. (1970). *Family interaction.* New York: Wiley.

Udry, J. R., & Hall, M. (1965). Marital role segregation and social networks in middle-aged couples. *Journal of Marriage and the Family, 27,* 392-395.

Vangelisti, A. L. (1993). Communication in the family: The influence of time, relational prototypes, and irrationality. *Communication Monographs, 60,* 42-54.

Walters, L. H. (1982). Are families different from other groups? *Journal of Marriage and the Family, 44,* 841-850.

Warren, C. (1995). Parent-child communication about sex. In T. J. Socha & G. H. Stamp (Eds.), *Parents, children and communication: Frontiers of theory and research* (pp. 173-201). Mahwah, NJ: Lawrence Erlbaum.

Whitchurch, G. G., & Constantine, L. L. (1993). Systems theory. In P. G. Boss, W. J. Doherty, R. LaRossa, W. R. Schumm, & S. K. Steinmetz (Eds.), *Sourcebook of family theories and methods: A contextual approach* (pp. 325-352). New York: Plenum.

Winter, W. D., & Ferreira, A. J. (1967). Interaction process analysis of family decision-making. *Family Process, 6,* 155-172.

Yerby, J., Buerkel-Rothfuss, N., & Bochner, A. (1990). *Understanding family communication* (2nd ed.). Scottsdale, AZ: Gorsuch Scarisbrick.

Yingling, J. (1995). The first relationship: Infant-parent communication. In T. J. Socha & G. H. Stamp (Eds.), *Parents, children and communication: Frontiers of theory and research* (pp. 23-41). Mahwah, NJ: Lawrence Erlbaum.

18

Group Communication in the Formal Educational Context

TERRE H. ALLEN
TIMOTHY G. PLAX
California State University, Long Beach

Participation in small groups is an integral part of the educational experience in the United States. For nearly three decades, scholars in education have examined the effects of group instruction on such outcomes as academic achievement (D. W. Johnson, Maruyama, Johnson, Nelson, & Skon, 1981), social status (Slavin, 1980), group cohesion (Aaronson, Blaney, Stephan, Sikes, & Smapp, 1978), friendship patterns (Slavin, 1979), race relations (Hansell & Slavin, 1981), and student self-esteem (R. T. Johnson & Johnson, 1983; Madden & Slavin, 1983a; Oickle, 1980). Noteworthy, and illustrative of the substantive nature of this area, is the comprehensive body of research regarding instructional practices comparing the effects of individualistic, competitive, and cooperative (small group) learning on achievement outcomes (D. W. Johnson et al., 1981; Slavin, 1983a, 1983b). In spite of the inherent value of this area, however, group communication scholars have virtually ignored the wealth of empirical findings contained in the educational literature about the use of groups in instructional practices.

This chapter attempts to remedy that neglect by providing a review, synthesis, and evaluation of research on groups in the educational context, with a restrictive, yet key, focus on the formal educational setting. Specifically, this chapter provides a historical overview and reviews (a) definitional issues related to groups in the classroom, (b) research about the structure of groups in the classroom, (c) theoretical issues relevant to communication and group research in the educational context, and (d) research addressing the learning outcomes of group versus individualized instruction. Included is an examination of the comparative philosophies and theories that have influenced scholarship in this area, as well as a number of the shortcomings of the literature. The chapter concludes with a discussion of directions for future investigations.

GROUPS IN THE EDUCATIONAL CONTEXT

Groups in the educational context include groups of students, groups of teachers (e.g., team-teaching groups), and mixtures of both. The expression *educational context* is defined, most appropriately, in terms of traditional and/or nontraditional (e.g., employee training, alcohol and drug education programs, and play and activity groups) forms of education. Because the literature regarding educational contexts encompasses such a broad range of topics, we have chosen to limit the scope of this chapter in two ways. First, where possible, we center our review and synthesis on the formal educational context from elementary school instruction through graduate education. The age range of student participants in the research reviewed is 7-25 years. Framing the chapter in this way casts this review within a life-span or developmental perspective (see Socha, 1997; Socha & Socha, 1994).

Second, we limit the review to the role of groups in the formal classroom. For that reason, such groups as team-teaching groups, social groups, play/activity groups, extracurricular groups, and gangs do not fall within the scope of this review. Similar to adult task groups, student learning groups are directed toward end products, operationalized in the educational context as student achievement or other learning outcomes. The general focus of this chapter, then, is on research regarding the role of group work used as an instructional method in the classroom to affect student achievement or cognitive and affective learning. The primary purpose is to identify the structural and interactional components of groups that provide a basis for understanding communicative patterns and behaviors in the classroom that affect student achievement (see Figure 18.1 for a framework for structuring the group communication research on students K-graduate school for the years 1970-1998).

HISTORICAL UNDERPINNINGS OF GROUP RESEARCH IN THE EDUCATIONAL CONTEXT

Early Research in Group Communication

In a review of research on groups, Hill (1982) notes that the research exploring cooperative learning groups was inspired by early studies of group performance. She points to the late 1800s as the period of initial investigation into group behavior. Research concerning group versus individual performance began with Tripplett's (1897) study of pacemaking and competition in bicycle racing. According to Cartwright and Zander (1968), research during the period from 1889 to 1905 identified the central ideas that have driven investigations of group processes for almost a century. Scholars in the late 1800s and early 1900s focused on two issues: (a) whether groups perform better than individuals, and (b) the types of problems best solved in groups. Also significant in defining the contemporary study of groups was the period from 1920 to 1940, during which investigators were guided by two basic questions: (a) What kinds of problems are solved best by individuals working alone, side by side, or in groups?; and (b) What influences individuals, in the face of group pressure, to conform to norms? Similarly, education scholars during this period sought to determine whether individuals' educational performance was enhanced by group processes.

Changes in Public Education

Important to both the study and use of groups in the educational context was a significant change in thinking about instructional practices in U.S. education. According to Rippa (1992), the formative period in U.S. education (1803-1882) was guided by the Emersonian conception of individualism. Essentially, Emerson believed that respect for the individual was the secret of education. The

Level 1: Educational Context	Level 2A: Grouping Method	Level 2B: Teacher Roles	Level 2C: Group Outcomes	Level 3: Other Variables
Phase 1: Elementary education (Grades K-2, ages 5-7)	Ability grouping Intensive instruction grouping	Teacher as group leader • Assigns turns • Accounting signals • Pattern turns	Cognitive learning outcomes Affective learning outcomes	Sex/gender Subject matter Group size
Phase 2: Upper elementary school (Grades 3-5, ages 8-11)	Cooperative learning grouping Collaborative learning grouping	Teacher as facilitator • Stimulates participation • Keeps group moving		Group structure Instructional practices
Phase 3: Middle school (Grades 6-9, ages 12-15)				Physical handicap
Phase 4: High school (Grades 10-12, ages 15-18)		Teacher as provider of group structure • Defines group goals • Defines individual acountability • Provides rewards		Emotional handicap Intellectual handicap
Phase 5: College/university (Grades 13-17, ages 19-22)				
Phase 6: Graduate education (Grades 18-22, ages 22-26)				

Figure 18.1. Group Communication Research on Students in K-Graduate School, 1970-1998

Emersonian view, therefore, did not advocate group work in the classroom; instead, students learned best by working individually.

Dewey (1899, 1916), on the other hand, advocated a different view. He was highly critical of teacher-dominated classrooms that privileged the instruction of individuals. He believed that nonparticipative, teacher-governed instructional practices were narrow and alienated children from learning. He advocated, instead, a "new" system in which learning was self-motivated, enjoyable, and child-centered, and, perhaps most important, emphasized the development of *social* skills and behavior. Dewey, therefore, encouraged active student learning through direct experience and participation with others. He also advocated the conception of a teacher as a group leader who affects, but does not completely determine, students' motivation, participation, and learning. Dewey's thinking, thus, changed the focus from individualized learning to group learning and laid the foundation for the development of contemporary principles and methods of classroom organization and instruction.

CONTEMPORARY STUDIES OF GROUPS IN EDUCATIONAL CONTEXTS

Contemporary research on groups in the educational context can be traced to the essential elements of Dewey's philosophy of public education, in particular, the teacher as group leader, the encouragement of cooperation among students, and the promotion of student motivation. Many of the principles and methods of instruction developed during the 20th century have involved students working in small groups. Keyton (1994) maintains, however, that children's groups often are overlooked as a context for the study of group communication. Moreover, although interpersonal processes, group processes, and effective communication have been identified by education scholars as the defining components of group instructional practices, scholars have not defined what constitutes effective interpersonal or group communication (see D. W. Johnson & Johnson, 1975). To study groups in the educational context, one must examine the structural and interactional components of such groups.

Groups in the Classroom

A variety of terms are used to describe the structural and interactional components of contemporary educational classrooms. Two basic structural elements of classrooms are whole-class instruction versus part-class instruction (Sharan, Hertz-Lazarowitz, & Ackerman, 1980). Traditionally, students are taught in a whole-class format, and the teacher's role is that of leader/facilitator of communication in the classroom. Part-class instruction, in contrast, requires that teachers assign students to work in small groups in the classroom, and the specific structural features of the classroom vary according to teacher and student interactional dynamics. During part-class instruction, teachers may take the central role of leader/facilitator or groups of students may work interdependently, without the direct supervision of the teacher.

The basic process components of contemporary classrooms can be characterized in terms of teachers' and students' communicative behavior and patterns of interaction in the classroom. Teachers may serve as the primary communicator, or students may communicate among themselves. Guided by Dewey's philosophy, contemporary research in education has focused on students communicating with other students in whole-class and part-class instruction. The term *collaborative learning* refers to a broad range of classroom activities, such as group discussions, whole-class discussions, interactive computer sessions, and peer tutoring, in which students interact with one another (Bruffee, 1993). Collaborative learning is a type of active learning, as distinguished from the more traditional model of student as passive learner. Collaborative learning, however, takes place in both whole-class and part-class structures, and teachers may play either a central or peripheral role as the communication facilitator.

To underscore the importance of *communication* to the dynamics of small groups in the educational context, it is necessary to detail the structural and interactional components that provide the bases for defining groups in this context. A review of the literature reveals that there are at least two elements of the structural components of groups (or part-class instruction) in the educational context that have specific relevance to communication in the classroom: grouping methods and incentive structures.

Grouping Methods

Teachers utilize at least four methods of grouping students in achieving part-class instruction: ability grouping, intensive instruction grouping, cooperative learning grouping, and collaborative learning grouping. Each of these methods constitutes a distinct type and differs from the others according to group processes, communicative patterns, group member roles, teacher roles, and learning outcomes.

Ability grouping involves teachers dividing a class on the basis of academic criteria so that they can instruct a more homogeneous group of students (Cohen, 1986). *Intensive instruction grouping* involves students working in groups directly with a teacher in an effort to provide more individualized instruction in a specific academic domain (e.g., computer instruction groups). The primary difference between ability groups and intensive instruction groups is the criteria used for selecting students for group membership. In intensive instruction groups, members are assigned not on the basis of academic criteria but rather according to some other teacher-imposed rules designed to meet instructional needs. *Cooperative learning grouping* occurs when teachers assign students to work together in a group to the degree that they can participate in a task, without direct and immediate supervision of the teacher (Cohen, 1986). Cooperative learning groups exist under conditions in which there is a task-oriented exchange among classroom peers, with pupils cooperating in order to earn recognition, grades, and/or other rewards (Slavin, 1989-1990). *Collaborative learning grouping* occurs when teachers assign students to work together in a group without direct or immediate supervision of the teacher. Collaborative groups are used as units for promoting peer tutoring and pupil rehearsal of learning materials planned and provided by the teacher. The primary factor that distinguishes cooperative learning grouping from collaborative learning grouping is the incentive structures related to group versus individual rewards.

Incentive Structures

According to D. W. Johnson et al. (1981), there are three incentive structures related to reward-based learning that exist in educational contexts: individualistic, competitive, and cooperative. An *individualistic incentive structure* rewards students on the basis of the quality of their work independent of the work of other students. A *competitive incentive structure* provides maximum rewards to some students and minimum rewards to other students. A *cooperative incentive structure* rewards students in direct proportion to the quality performance of their student work group. In the classroom context, the reward distribution provides a specific type of structure that motivates students to behave individualistically, competitively, or cooperatively.

D. W. Johnson and Johnson (1975) distinguished incentive structures on the basis of how each goal structure promotes different patterns of interaction among students. They identified 11 interpersonal behaviors that distinguish cooperative, competitive, and individualistic incentive structures: (a) interaction among students, (b) mutual liking, (c) effective communication, (d) trust, (e) acceptance and support, (f) utilization of personal resources, (g) helping and sharing, (h) emotional involvement, (i) coordination of effort, (j) division of labor, and (k) divergent and risk-taking thinking. D. W. Johnson and Johnson (1975) characterized cooperative incentive structures by a high degree of each interpersonal behavior, competitive incentive structures by a low degree, and individualistic incentive structures by the lack of interaction among students.

Incentive structures clearly influence interactional dynamics and communicative behavior in the classroom. Students' and teachers' communication motives and behaviors required for cooperative incentive structures are qualitatively and quantitatively different from those required for competitive and individualistic incentive structures. Furthermore, collaborative and cooperative groups require interpersonal and group communicative behaviors that ability and intensive instruction groups do not. The structural and interactional components of cooperative learning groups, as well as their impact on learning outcomes, provide a great deal of information regarding group communication in the educational context. The unique properties of co-operative learning groups, in terms of structural and interactional dynamics, therefore, require further clarification and examination.

Distinguishing Cooperative Learning Groups From Other Types of Learning Groups

We previously defined four types of grouping methods that are common in classroom settings: ability grouping, intensive instruction grouping, collaborative learning grouping, and cooperative learning grouping. Research findings on ability and intensive instruction groups parallel findings on instructional practices for whole-class instruction. For instance, Hammersley (1974) found that student participation in these groups was restricted to occasional inserts into the stream of a teacher's presentation. In contrast, collaborative and cooperative learning groups are different from whole-class instruction or ability and intensive learning groups because students in these groups operate as interdependent learners (Cohen, 1986).

Research regarding ability and intensive instruction groups has focused on how teachers stimulate participation (Hammersley, 1974), handle turn allocation (McDermott, 1976), maintain the attention of group members (Gump, 1967), and encourage content flow within group interaction (Doyle, 1986). For example, Eder (1982a) compared the communicative patterns of high-ability groups and low-ability groups. He discovered that participation was minimal in low-ability groups and that when members did participate, their comments were likely to be irrelevant to the topic. Furthermore, teachers instructing low-ability groups were more likely to interrupt reading turns (Allington, 1980), orient to listeners during turns (Eder, 1982b), and allow members to interrupt during the group session (Eder, 1982b).

D. W. Johnson, Johnson, Holubec, and Roy (1984) identified four elements of cooperative learning groups that differentiate them from other types of learning groups: (a) face-to-face interaction, (b) cooperative incentive structure, (c) individual accountability, and (d) interpersonal and small group skills. Cooperative learning groups usually include four to five students working together to achieve some common goal. Individual accountability is conceptualized and operationalized as students demonstrating that they have individually mastered the material, and the group members' combined level of learning is then used as a measure of group learning. Interpersonal and group skills are the students' means for working together and achieving group goals.

Communicative patterns in each type of group depend on group processes, members' roles, and the role of the teacher. Communicative patterns, the teacher's roles, and students' roles in groups and intensive instruction groups are similar to communicative patterns, the teacher's roles, and students' roles in whole-class instruction. For instance, communication in ability and intensive learning groups requires that the teacher exercise direct supervision over students, group members communicate mainly with the teacher, and the teacher serve as group leader or facilitator. In contrast, collaborative and cooperative learning groups require the teacher to delegate authority and supervise indirectly; consequently, communication is mainly among group members, and students communicate primarily with one another about their task. *Only* the cooperative learning group, by definition, has a cooperative incentive structure. In such groups, learning outcomes and/or rewards are directly proportional to the quality of the work done by the students as a group. Students are individually accountable for their own work, but also are rewarded for their contributions to others' learning. In comparison, members of collaborative learning groups are individually accountable for their own learning, but there is no extrinsic reward structure for contributions to others' learning.

Besides interdependence of members and lack of direct teacher participation in the group, the *combination* of two elements distinguishes cooperative learning groups from other types of classroom groups: *group incentive structure* and *individual accountability.* Slavin (1987) observed that groups of elementary students working together in the classroom, without individual accountability and group rewards, were not likely to achieve any cognitive or affective benefits. Newman and Thompson (1987) concluded that groups of secondary school students did not achieve cognitive learning outcomes unless they had cooperative incentive structures, individual accountability, and competition with other groups. Clearly, incentive structures are critical for defining the structural and interactional dynamics of groups in the classroom; therefore, it is necessary to clarify further the theoretical issues regarding incentive structures and the role that they play in learning outcomes.

Theoretical Issues in Cooperative Learning

Education scholars have sought to determine whether cooperative learning practices are more likely to enhance student achievement than traditional, whole-class instructional practices. Guided by classic studies in group dynamics, education researchers have advanced two major types of theories to explain and predict the outcomes of cooperative learning groups: motivational and cognitive theories. *Motivational theories* focus primarily on the effects of reward or incentive structures under which students in cooperative learning groups operate. In contrast, *cognitive theories* focus primarily on the effects of working together versus working alone.

Motivational theories. Deutsch (1949) provided the theoretical bases for defining incentive structures in the classroom context. He identified three goal structures that education scholars have used to conceptualize and operationalize incentive structures in the classroom: (a) *cooperative goals*—each individual's goal-oriented efforts contribute to others' goal attainment, (b) *competitive goals*—each individual's goal-oriented efforts frustrate

others' goal attainment, and (c) *individualistic goals*—each individual's goal-oriented efforts have no consequences for others' goal attainment.

Motivational theorists view incentive structures as the central issue in understanding how instructional practices affect learning outcomes. In fact, over the past 30 years, a tremendous amount of research has focused on incentive structures, and scholars continue to debate the merits of cooperative learning versus competitive and individualistic learning. Three primary questions regarding incentive structures have surfaced:

- Which incentive structure enhances student performance?
- Which incentive structure is most effective for various types of learning? (see Bloom, 1976)
- Which incentive structure is appropriate for learning and skill acquisition in various academic disciplines?

Cognitive theories. Whereas motivational theories lead educators to focus on incentive structures, cognitive theories enable them to predict whether or not groups will achieve a goal. Slavin (1990) identified two types of cognitive theories in cooperative learning research: developmental and cognitive elaboration theories. Developmental theorists, such as Piaget (1926), believe that certain types of knowledge—for example, language, morality, and symbol systems (such as math and reading)—can be learned only in interactions with others. Working under the umbrella of Piaget's developmental perspective, a number of education scholars have tested the role of interaction among students on learning tasks and achievement (e.g., Damon, 1984; Murray, 1982; Wadsworth, 1984). Taken as a whole, these studies indicate that interaction among students improves their mastery of concepts and creates proacademic norms.

Cognitive elaboration theories are concerned with mental architecture (i.e. cognitive structuring) and less with social interaction. Research in cognitive psychology has revealed that if information is to be retained in memory, the learner must engage in some sort of cognitive restructuring, or elaboration, of the material (Wittrock, 1978). Research on cooperative learning has focused on the role of student-student interaction in enabling this cognitive restructuring or elaboration process. Devin-Sheehan, Feldman, and Allen (1976), for instance, found that peer tutoring was an effective means of cognitive restructuring, resulting in achievement benefits for both tutors and tutees.

Melothe and Deering (1994) compared the two theoretical models of motivation and cognitive elaboration with regard to task talk in cooperative learning groups. They established two conditions of cooperation: One group was structured according to a cooperation-as-motivation model (the reward condition), and the other was structured according to a cognitive elaboration model (the strategic condition). The reward condition involved a cooperative activity of studying together as a stimulus designed to motivate learners. The strategic condition involved guided activities that forced learners to reflect on and analyze their learning (a type of cognitive elaboration). The results indicated that the strategic condition yielded more explanations, task-related questions, and talk about the academic topic in comparison to the reward condition.

Melothe and Deering (1994) note that motivational theories address whether groups perform certain tasks better than individuals, developmental theories question the role of social interaction in learning, and cognitive elaboration theories detail the role of student/student interaction in restructuring or elaboration. These researchers affirmed that the rewards associated with cooperation produce effective interdependence among teammates, whereas cognitive elaboration promotes deep processing of information, concepts, and meanings. These two theories thus provide the bases for structuring cooperative and collaborative learning groups in the classroom, and scholars have identified a number of different methods teachers use to achieve the benefits of cooperative incentive motivation and cognitive elaboration.

Cooperative and Collaborative Learning Methods

Cooperative Learning Methods

Since the 1970s, education scholars have researched the applications of cooperative learning groups in the classroom. Newman and Thompson (1987), on the basis of an exhaustive review of the relevant literature, identified five cooperative learning methods commonly employed in elementary and secondary classrooms. These five methods, based on Newman and Thompson's characterization, involve groups of four to six students, with interdependence among group members, such that individual success requires some degree of group success and vice versa (that is, individual accountability and cooperative incentive structures). Elements that distinguish these five methods are whether there is intergroup competition, amount of teacher involvement in the group activity, and the amount of student autonomy.

The method of Student Team-Achievement Divisions (STAD) (Slavin, 1978a) assigns students to four-member teams that are mixed in terms of students' performance level, sex, and ethnicity. The teacher presents a lesson, and then students work in their teams to ensure that all members have mastered the lesson. Each student takes an examination on the lesson. Students' scores, based on the degree of individual improvement over previous scores, contribute to a team score, and teams with high scores are rewarded (e.g., tokens, prizes, and/or recognition in the school newsletter). There are two variations of STAD that apply specifically to teaching reading: Team-Assisted Individualization (TAI) and Cooperative Integrated Reading and Comprehension (CIRC) instruction.

Teams-Games-Tournaments (TGT) (DeVries & Slavin, 1978) utilizes the same structure as STAD, but instead of an examination at the end of the lesson, students engage in a tournament and compete with members of other teams. In TGT, teammates prepare for the tournament by studying worksheets together and explaining problems to one another. Instead of taking individual examinations, students compete as a team with classmates of similar achievement from other teams. Students earn points for their team on the basis of their relative success against competitors, and teams with high scores are rewarded.

Jigsaw (Aaronson et al., 1978) involves students working in six-member teams. Each member is assigned, by the teacher, a specific section of academic material and asked to become an "expert" on that section. Next, "experts" from different teams meet in groups to discuss their sections. Members then return to their own groups and take turns teaching their sections. Students take examinations individually, and team members' scores are combined to form a team score. The team scores are announced in a class or school newsletter.

Group Investigation (GI) (Sharan & Sharan, 1976) is a method in which the entire class is organized into small groups using cooperative inquiry, group discussion, and cooperative planning to complete assigned projects. Each group presents its project to the entire class. There is no intergroup competition; each group receives its own evaluation from the teacher.

Learning Together (LT) (D. W. Johnson & Johnson, 1975) involves students working in groups to produce a single project. One unique aspect of LT is the attention that goes into training teachers to facilitate the philosophy of LT, which includes positive interdependence, face-to-face interaction, individual accountability, social skills, and group processing. Student outcomes are assessed by a combination of individual performance and the overall performance of the group. Rewards include teacher praise, tokens, and privileges. Again, there is no intergroup competition.

Some scholars suggest that group communication skills are a necessary component of cooperative learning and that teachers must spend as much time instructing students on social and communication skills as they do on academic content (see Clarke, Wideman, & Eadie, 1990; D. W. Johnson, Johnson, & Holubec, 1994). According to Clarke et al. (1990), there are two categories of skills necessary for effective cooperative group activities: task and working relationship. These skills represent the typical breakdown in the group communication literature (in this volume, see Chapters 7 [Hirokawa & Salazar] and 8 [Keyton]). Task communication skills enable group members to complete the assigned academic work and include asking questions, asking for clarification, checking for others' understanding, elaborating on others' ideas, following directions, getting the group back to work, listening actively, sharing information and ideas, and summarizing for understanding. Working relationship communication skills help members build and sustain the group's disposition and ability to work together. They include acknowledging contributions, checking for agreement, disagreeing in an agreeable way, encouraging others, expressing support, inviting others to talk, keeping things calm, mediating, responding to ideas, sharing feelings, and showing appreciation for others' contributions.

Vermette (1998) argues that most scholarship in the area of cooperative learning identifies the five methods detailed above as the *only* methods that attempt to implement the theoretical and operational aspects of cooperative learning. Despite the inherent value of cooperative learning in increasing students' cognitive and affective learning, teachers and other practitioners often find these methods cumbersome because of the amount of work required to coordinate classroom activities. Furthermore, teachers are not likely to have the training necessary to teach the types of interpersonal and group communication skills required for successful participation in cooperative leaning groups.

Collaborative Group Methods

Teachers and other practitioners have begun to utilize collaborative group methods that eliminate the cooperative incentive structure and focus attention strictly on peer-directed interaction intended to engage students in cognitive elaboration. Webb, Troper, and Fall (1995) define collaborative learning groups as peer-directed small groups in which students engage in verbal interactions that involve both giving and receiving explanations. Variations of collaborative instructional methods are used in a wide variety of academic disciplines. For example, collaborative computer activities include a combination of individual, dyadic, and group work (see Chernick, 1990).

Vermette (1998) identified three methods that focus mainly on collaboration as opposed to cooperation: Dansereau's Dyads, Kagan's Structural Approach, and Cohen's Complex Instruction. First, O'Donnell, Dansereau, Hall, and Rocklin (1987) developed a dyadic learning strategy, called Dansereau's Dyads, that has been implemented on the college level and involves same-sex college students working as partners to read, summarize, understand, and quiz one another. Second, Kagan's (1992) Structural Approach was developed from the hypothesis that different instructional outcomes require different interaction structures. Kagan detailed a series of in-class strategies that are content-free ways to organize instruction involving student-to-student interaction, such as Numbered-Heads-Together and Think-Pair-Share. Third, Cohen (1994) developed a collaborative approach, called Complex Instruction, based on status issues in heterogeneously constructed teams. This approach emphasizes the teacher's role in grouping students into heterogeneous teams and communicating to students the importance of interdependence and collaboration as they relate to "real-world" experiences.

Collaborative learning methods vary according to academic domain, which prohibits our providing an exhaustive list of all the types of collaborative methods that have been described in the relevant literature. In general, collaborative learning methods focus on peer interaction as a means of enhancing cognitive elaboration. There is no inherent cooperative incentive structure, and group-level outcomes rarely are considered. Cooperative learning research, on the other hand, has focused more on the cooperative incentive structure, individual accountability, and group-level outcomes. The following section provides a review and synthesis of research regarding cognitive and affective learning outcomes of cooperative, individual, and competitive learning and provides a review of the limited research on collaborative group learning. We organize the review of literature according to phases of learning or grade level, consistent with the research in this area. It is important to note that few studies have investigated the role of cooperative learning in kindergarten, first, or second grade. In general, 5- to 7-year-olds are not viewed as developmentally ready to respond to incentive structures or to be able to engage in cognitive elaboration.

Outcomes of Cooperative and Collaborative Learning Groups

The plethora of research regarding learning outcomes focuses on cooperative, as opposed to collaborative, learning. The research regarding collaborative learning outcomes is limited to a few studies of elementary school and college student participants. Studies of whole-class instruction versus cooperative learning groups focus on students' achievement outcomes in terms of both cognitive and affective learning. Whole-class instructional practices generally serve as a control condition, whereas types of cooperative learning structures serve as experimental conditions. Identical learning materials are given to control and experimental groups. Once the material has been discussed thoroughly either by the teacher or by the group members, identical tests are given to the whole-class (control) learning group and the cooperative (experimental) learning groups. Cognitive learning is operationalized as test scores on the content of the material covered in an academic unit, and *effect size* is used as a measure of the impact of cooperative learning on student achievement. Glass, McGaw, and Smith (1981) define effect size as the proportion of a standard deviation by which an experimental group exceeds a control group and generally consider an index of +2.5 to be educationally meaningful.

Cognitive Learning Outcomes of Cooperative Learning

Lower elementary grades. Studies of 3rd, 4th, and 5th graders engaged in whole-class instruction versus STAD, TGT, TAI, LT, and Jigsaw cooperative learning groups indicate that students in cooperative learning groups engage in more cognitive learning of the content material than when the material is presented in a whole-class format. Studies have investigated such effects across a wide variety of subject domains, including language arts (DeVries & Mescon, 1975; DeVries, Mescon, & Shackman, 1975b; Gonzales, 1981; Slavin, 1980), reading comprehension (Gonzales, 1981; Stevens, Slavin, Farnish, & Madden, 1988), spelling (Kagan, Zahn, Widaman, Schwarzwald, & Tyrell, 1985; Stevens, Madden, Slavin, & Farnish, 1987; Tomblin & Davis, 1985; Van Oudenhoven, Van Berkum, & Swen-Koopmans, 1987; Van Oudenhoven, Wiersma, & Van Yperen, 1987), math (Gonzales, 1981; L. C. Johnson, 1985; Madden & Slavin, 1983b; Mason & Good, 1993; Robertson, 1982; Slavin & Karweit, 1981; Slavin, Leavey, & Madden, 1984; Webb & Farivar, 1994), verbal analogies (DeVries, Mescon, & Shackman, 1975a), and computer program performance (Chernick, 1990).

Upper elementary grades. Studies comparing whole-class instruction to cooperative learning groups in the 6th, 7th, and 8th grades have concentrated mainly on language arts and math. Investigations utilizing STAD structure in 7th- and 8th-grade language arts showed significant effect sizes, demonstrating greater cognitive learning gains in cooperative learning groups over whole-class instruction (Slavin, 1977a; Slavin & Oickle, 1981). Similarly, DeVries, Lucasse, and Shackman (1980) reported significant effect sizes for 7th- and 8th-grade language arts instruction utilizing TGT structures in comparison to whole-class instruction. Sharan et al. (1984) noted a significant effect size for cognitive learning in GI and STAD learning structures in 7th-grade English and literature instruction. They also found significant effect sizes for 7th graders in STAD groups in English as a second language and English literature over 7th graders in whole-class instruction. Edwards, DeVries, and Snyder (1972) reported a significant effect size for 7th-grade math instruction in TGT groups over whole-class instruction when all students were taught by the same teacher.

Other investigations focusing on 7th- and 8th-grade cooperative learning have revealed significant effect sizes for LT, STAD, TGT, and Jigsaw groups as compared to whole-class instruction in science (Okebukola, 1985, 1986a). Rich, Amir, and Slavin (1986) found a significant effect size for LT groups over whole-class instruction in 7th-grade history. Sharan et al. (1984) reported significant effect sizes for GI and STAD group instruction over whole-class instruction in 7th-grade ESL and literature classes. Sharan and Shachar (1988) found significant effect sizes for Jigsaw and GI group instruction over whole-class instruction in 8th-grade geography and history classes.

High school. Investigations of cooperative learning in grades 9 through 12 focus mainly on science and math instruction; a few investigations have examined cooperative learning in the humanities. For example, DeVries, Edwards, and Wells (1974) found a significant effect size for 10th, 11th, and 12th graders in TGT groups compared to whole-class instruction in U.S. history. In general, studies of 9th-, 10th-, and 11th-grade math instruction tend to favor cooperative learning over whole-class instruction. For example, in comparison to whole-class instruction, Slavin and Karweit (1984) uncovered a significant effect size in

9th-grade general math for STAD; Sherman and Thomas (1986) found the same for 10th-grade general math for STAD groups; and Artzt (1983) detected significant effect sizes for LT instruction in 9th-, 10th-, and 11th-grade math classes.

Studies of cooperative learning in high school science have yielded mixed results. Humphreys, Johnson, and Johnson (1982) reported a significant effect size favoring LT groups as compared to competitive learning and whole-class instruction for 9th-grade physical science. In contrast, Lazarowitz, Baird, Hertz-Lazarowitz, and Jenkins (1985) observed no significant differences between Jigsaw groups and whole classes in 10th-, 11th-, and 12th-grade biology. Moreover, Sherman and Zimmerman (1986) indicated that the significant effect size in their study favored whole-class instruction over GI groups in 10th-grade biology. Sherman and Zimmerman, however, utilized a relatively small sample of 46 students, and the duration of instruction was only 7 weeks.

In one of the most extensive high school studies to date, Okebukola (1984) examined data for more than 700 students in one of three learning conditions in 9th-grade biology classes: LT cooperative learning groups, competitive individualized instruction, and whole-class instruction. The results showed a significant effect size favoring LT over whole-class instruction, but competitive individualized instruction produced more favorable learning outcomes than LT. Okebukola (1986b) sought to extend previous investigations by comparing LT cooperative learning to competitive learning as mediated by student learning style preferences (cooperative versus competitive). Learning style preference significantly influenced learning outcomes, such that students who preferred cooperative learning to competitive learning demonstrated significantly greater achievement in cooperative learning groups.

College-level instruction. College-level instruction does not parallel that of elementary, junior high, or high school in terms of co-operative learning structures. Although education researchers have demonstrated the importance of cooperative learning in academic achievement, at the college level, there are many drawbacks to implementing such group work. Fraser, Diener, Beaman, and Kelem (1977) contend that college instructors are reluctant to utilize cooperative learning techniques because they require different types of coordination and organization of course material than techniques utilized routinely by college instructors in their lectures. Furthermore, they found that for most college instructors, one or more of these added "costs" serves as a deterrent to using cooperative learning activities. The majority of group instructional methods used in the college classroom, therefore, are collaborative rather than cooperative group activities.

Louth, McAllister, and McAllister (1990) compared individualistic, collaborative, and cooperative methods of instruction in college freshman-level writing classes. The control group members had no interaction with other students on writing assignments, the collaborative groups read and responded to one another's writing assignments, and the cooperative group produced a team-writing assignment. The results revealed no significant differences across the three groups on the posttest assessments of writing ability. An examination of the pretest scores, however, indicated that the control group had significantly higher pretest writing abilities. A secondary analysis indicated that writing growth occurred in both collaborative and cooperative conditions, but not in the individualistic condition.

Consensus and controversy regarding cognitive learning outcomes in cooperative learning groups. D. W. Johnson et al. (1981) utilized a meta-analytic approach to investigate the effects of cooperative, competitive, and individualistic goal structures on student achievement. The meta-analysis included studies across all grade levels, including college, and examined the effects of the three goal structures on cognitive and affective learning.

Their results showed that of the 122 studies compared according to three meta-analytic procedures (voting, effect size, and z score), cooperative learning was considerably more effective than competitive or individualistic learning in terms of promoting student achievement and productivity. No significant difference emerged between competitive and individualistic goal structures for student achievement or productivity.

Although the majority of the research demonstrates the effectiveness of cooperative learning structures over individualistic or competitive learning structures, there are concerns regarding the effects of cooperative goal structures on students' cognitive learning in high school and college-level instruction. Newman and Thompson (1987) challenge the assumption of the effectiveness of cooperative learning in Grades 10 through 12, given that relatively few studies have been conducted in those grades. Similarly, Davidson (1985) questions the role of group goals and individual accountability in cooperative learning at the college level, because the results from the relatively few studies conducted at that level are not consistent with the findings from elementary, middle, or junior high school.

A second point of controversy concerns the role of cooperative group work in higher-order conceptual learning. Most studies comparing cooperative, competitive, and individualistic goal structures have focused on learning basic skills in mathematics, language arts, and reading. Davidson (1985) concludes that the effects of cooperative learning are limited to learning computational skills, simple concepts, and simple application problems and that relatively few studies examine the effects of cooperative structures on higher-order conceptual learning. Slavin (1989) notes, however, that in areas other than cognitive learning, there is broader consensus regarding the effects of cooperative group structures. In particular, there is consensus among scholars that cooperative learning methods have positive effects on a wide array of affective outcomes.

Affective Learning Outcomes of Cooperative Learning

Research regarding the effects of cooperative learning instruction compared to whole-class instruction has considered cooperative learning as a means of enhancing the quality of interpersonal relationships among students as well as enhancing students' self-esteem (Slavin, 1991). Given that cooperative learning represents an active, rather than a passive, form of learning, and because interdependence of group members is a key function of this type of learning, education scholars theorize that cooperative learning should have positive effects on social, motivational, and attitudinal outcomes. In particular, they have investigated the effects of cooperative learning on students' (a) liking of the class, (b) interpersonal attraction, (c) self-esteem, (d) locus of control, (e) intergroup relations, and (f) acceptance of mainstreamed students.

Liking of the class. A number of the studies reviewed previously included pretest and posttest questionnaires designed to measure liking of the class, the school, and the subject matter. In general, investigators hypothesize that students in cooperative learning groups would develop significantly greater liking of class, subject matter, and school than students engaged in whole-class learning. A number of studies revealed that students in cooperative learning groups did report greater liking of the class (DeVries et al., 1974; Edwards & DeVries, 1972, 1974; Humphreys et al., 1982; D. W. Johnson, Johnson, Johnson, & Anderson, 1976; Lazarowitz, Baird, Bowlden, & Hertz-Lazarowitz, 1982; Slavin & Karweit, 1981; Slavin et al., 1984; Wheeler & Ryan, 1973). Ethnicity, however, appears to be a moderating variable in liking of the class; for example, Blaney, Stephan, Rosenfield, Aronson, and Sikes (1977) found, in comparing Jigsaw groups to individualistic learning, that Euro-American and African American students reported greater liking of the class in the cooperative condition, whereas Mexican

American students reported greater liking in the control condition.

Interpersonal attraction and friendship patterns. Several investigators have theorized that cooperative learning methods should produce increased interpersonal attraction among classmates, operationally defined as students' reports of liking classmates and feeling liked by classmates (Blaney et al., 1977; Cooper, Johnson, Johnson, & Wilderson, 1980; DeVries & Edwards, 1973; D. W. Johnson & Johnson, 1981b; Oickle, 1980; Slavin, 1977c, 1978b; Slavin & Karweit, 1981; Slavin et al., 1984). These scholars theorize that the increased contact gained from working in cooperative learning groups should produce perceived similarity among group members, because students engage in pleasant activities together and work toward common goals; this perceived similarity, in turn, should increase interpersonal attraction among group members. In general, the research does show that when students learn to cooperate, they also learn to like one another. The effects of cooperative group activities on interpersonal attraction are particularly strong in junior high and high school settings (see Slavin, 1978b).

Other investigations have defined interpersonal attraction as mutual concern, group cohesiveness, and number of friendships. For example, DeVries and Edwards (1973) observed significant gains for mutual concern in TGT groups compared to their whole-class counterparts, but there was no significant difference between the experimental and control groups on measures of cohesiveness or number of friends named. Slavin (1977c) found that, in classrooms of emotionally disturbed adolescents, students in TGT groups indicated a significantly greater increase in friends following the learning session than did students in the control group.

A number of studies have defined interpersonal attraction in terms of friendship patterns (Cooper et al., 1980; D. W. Johnson & Johnson, 1981b; D. W. Johnson et al., 1976; Slavin & Karweit, 1981; Slavin et al., 1984). In general, these studies demonstrated that in

cooperative learning groups, students named more people as "friends" than students in control groups. Slavin and Karweit (1981) also asked students to list those with whom they would not like to work with in the future, and students in cooperative learning groups listed fewer students than did their counterparts in control groups.

Slavin et al. (1984) utilized teachers' perceptions of their students' friendship patterns in TAI groups and control classes. They asked teachers to rate the number of friends the students had, appraise the extent to which students were rejected by others, and evaluate students' use of negative peer behaviors, such as fighting with other students and picking on other students. The results from two separate experiments indicated that teachers rated students in TAI groups as forming more friendships than students in control groups. The first study also yielded significant results for less negative peer behavior in TAI groups; however, the second study did not show significant differences among the groups.

Student self-esteem. Slavin (1990) posited that one of the most critical affective outcomes of cooperative learning groups is the degree to which such groups increase students' beliefs that they are valuable and important individuals—that is, their self-esteem. Several studies have utilized versions of Coopersmith's (1967) Self-Esteem Inventory, a multidimensional scale adapted for use in education that includes such dimensions as general, social, and academic self-esteem (e.g., Allen & Van Sickle, 1984; Blaney et al., 1977; DeVries et al., 1980; Geffner, 1978; R. T. Johnson & Johnson, 1983; D. W. Johnson, Johnson, & Scott, 1978; Lazarowitz et al., 1982; Madden & Slavin, 1983a; Slavin & Karweit, 1981; Slavin et al., 1984). In general, studies have not revealed consistent findings related to these dimensions of self-esteem.

Research findings are not consistent in terms of self-esteem, with one notable exception in the research on Jigsaw groups, which have shown positive effects in increasing students' self-esteem (Blaney et al., 1977;

Geffner, 1978; Lazarowitz et al., 1982). Scholars believe that because students are assigned the role of an "expert" in a particular area in these groups, and the group depends on their expertise, they will likely experience increases in self-esteem compared to their counterparts in whole-class instruction.

Locus of control. According to Slavin (1990), cooperative incentive structures provide a context that allows students to attribute their success to their own behavior, rather than to luck or some other external source. He posited that because cooperative learning is measured by individual gains along with group gains, and because students contribute to one another's learning, they should view themselves as responsible for the gains achieved. He also argued that because internal locus of control (the attribution of responsibility to one's self) has been shown to be the personality variable that is related most consistently to high academic performance, researchers must explore the role of cooperative learning groups in increasing students' attributions about their responsibility for their own academic success.

Studies across a variety of cooperative group methods have shown that internal locus of control is positively influenced by cooperative learning structures. Slavin (1978b), for example, found that students in STAD groups, compared to those in control groups, reported that the group learning activity increased their attributions of ownership of learning outcomes. DeVries et al. (1974) noted that students in TGT learning groups were more likely to report that they felt their learning outcomes were due to their own performance than were students in the control group. Gonzales (1979) reported similar results for students in Jigsaw groups, as did D. W. Johnson et al. (1978) for students in LT groups.

Intergroup relations. A great deal of research has focused on the role of cooperative learning in promoting intergroup relations. Slavin (1990) criticized traditional education for not providing conditions conducive to interaction among students of different ethnic groups. He argued that cooperative learning structures provide an ideal solution by offering students opportunities to interact with students from different ethnic backgrounds.

Results from various studies have confirmed that cooperative learning groups enhance intergroup relations. Slavin (1977b, 1979) determined that students in STAD groups reported more cross-racial friendships than students in a control group after a 12-week instructional period. Similarly, Slavin and Oickle (1981) found that STAD group members reported more White/Black friendships, and Sharan et al. (1984) observed that students in STAD groups, compared to those in control groups, had more positive attitudes toward Middle Eastern and European Jews in Israeli classrooms. Kagan et al. (1985) found that both STAD and TGT group structures appeared to reverse a trend toward ethnic polarization among Anglo, Hispanic, and African American students.

Similar results apply to other types of cooperative groups. DeVries, Edwards, and Slavin (1978), as well as Oishi, Slavin, and Madden (1983), observed that students in TGT groups were more likely to increase friendships outside their racial group than were students in a control group. Gonzales (1979) reported that Anglo and Asian American students in Jigsaw groups demonstrated more positive attitudes toward Mexican American students than did their counterparts in control groups. Cooper et al. (1980) and D. W. Johnson and Johnson (1981a) also noted that students in LT groups engaged in more cross-cultural interaction than students in individualized instruction.

Sharan et al. (1984) investigated more than 700 students' cooperative behavioral patterns in same-ethnic and cross-ethnic cooperative (GI and STAD), competitive, and individualistic learning structures. They divided cooperative behavior into verbal and nonverbal categories. Their results indicate that students in cooperative learning groups are more likely to engage in verbal and nonverbal cooperative behaviors with cross-ethnic peers. Teachers in the investigation also reported that the cooperative behaviors among students in GI and STAD groups extended to contexts outside the classroom. Hansell and Slavin (1981), investigating the degree of reported closeness in cross-ethnic friendships, asked more than 400 7th graders in STAD groups and control classrooms, "Who are your best friends in the class?" Students in STAD groups were significantly more likely to indicate reciprocated, close relationships among cross-ethnic peers.

Acceptance of mainstreamed students. Scholars have been interested in the role of cooperative learning in increasing students' acceptance of academically mainstreamed students, and they have employed the same types of procedures used to investigate intergroup relations. For instance, students are asked, "Who are your friends in the class?" and "Whom do you NOT want to work with on a class project?" Investigators have attempted to identify reported friendships with mainstreamed students and to identify students who are rejected by their peers. Results from these studies have yielded somewhat mixed results regarding acceptance of mainstreamed students.

Cooper et al.'s (1980) investigation revealed significantly more friendships between academically and emotionally handicapped students in LT cooperative learning groups than in control groups. D. W. Johnson and Johnson (1981b) also found that students in LT groups reported accepting more cross-handicapped work partners. Some investigations of the influence of cooperative groups on acceptance of mainstreamed students, however, have not yielded significant findings (e.g., Armstrong, Johnson, & Balow, 1981; R. T. Johnson & Johnson, 1983; Madden & Slavin, 1983a).

Slavin (1977c) investigated the influence of TGT groups on acceptance of middle-school emotionally disturbed students of normal intelligence. Emotionally disturbed, mainstreamed students in TGT groups were more likely to be listed as "friends" by their classmates and more likely to be selected as work

partners than their counterparts in control classes. Janke (1978) replicated this study in a high school population and obtained similar results. Janke also found that the teachers identified emotionally disturbed high school students in TGT groups as exhibiting fewer disruptive behaviors and greater attendance rates than their counterparts in control groups.

In summary, cooperative learning groups provide a context for promoting interdependence and peer communication in the classroom, as well as a context for students to develop relationships with students whom they might not normally select as friendship partners. As such, cooperative learning groups can promote prosocial norms by enabling students to increase their self-esteem, improve interracial relations, and accept mainstreamed students. Education scholars agree that the majority of affective outcomes are directly attributable to the cooperative incentive structure. Cooperative incentive structures include group goals and individual accountability that, in turn, motivate students to develop relationships with peers and take one another's learning seriously. Furthermore, studies of cooperative learning have demonstrated equal success in achieving cognitive and affective outcomes in urban, rural, and suburban schools, as well as with students of different ethnic backgrounds. Rather than having teachers exert power in the classroom to increase student learning, cooperative learning groups empower students and motivate them to take an active role in their own learning achievements and to contribute actively to their peers' learning achievements.

Collaborative Group Process and Learning Outcomes

Research on collaborative learning groups focuses more on student-related activities than on measures of learning outcomes. Essentially, there are two reasons why learning outcomes are not the central focus of this research. First, collaborative learning activities lack the requirements of the cooperative incentive structure, in that there is a lack of accountability to the group (e.g., the students' learning outcome is not a part of group-defined learning), and there are no group-level outcome measures (students' scores are not grouped together as part of a reward structure). This is important because education scholars view incentive structure as the central issue in understanding how instructional practices affect learning outcomes. Collaborative learning groups do not have well-defined incentive structures; that is, the structure of collaborative learning (engaging in peer interaction, but no individual accountability to the group and no group-level outcome or rewards) allows students to engage in the group activities with cooperative, competitive, or individualistic goals in mind. Assessment of the role of incentive structure on learning outcomes, therefore, is minimal.

The second reason why learning outcomes are of limited concern in studies of collaborative learning groups is that the central theoretical focus has been on the impact of peer interaction on cognitive elaboration, and the link to learning is indirect. Cognitive elaboration is linked to learning, and collaborative learning groups provide an opportunity for students to engage in cognitive elaboration. Essentially, research on collaborative groups focuses on the constructivists' view of learning, in which learners actively construct new understandings (see Vygotsky, 1978). Constructive activities involve oral communicative activities that students use to accomplish cognitive elaboration; they include stating the topic, paraphrasing the learning material, referring to personal knowledge, generating questions, creating analogies, and answering questions. These activities have been linked to learning outcomes when students are working alone in the classroom (e.g., Chan, Burtis, Scardamalia, & Bereiter, 1992; Coleman, 1992; Dansereau, 1988; King, 1990). Recently, research has examined the degree to which students engage in constructive activities in collaborative learning groups (see Webb, 1992, 1993), and it has found that it depends on pre-activity group communication training (see Webb et al., 1995).

Empirical results on the relationship between collaborative learning groups and learning outcomes in elementary and junior high school are inconsistent (see Webb, 1989; Webb et al., 1995). In fact, Webb's (1989) review of the literature revealed only five studies that reported significant cognitive learning outcomes for collaborative learning groups. The majority of studies of cognitive learning outcomes were conducted in elementary schools; there is a lack of research regarding collaborative learning groups and learning outcomes at the high school level.

Collaborative learning outcomes of college-level instruction have received some attention. Research demonstrates that the use of collaborative groups in large lecture classes has significant effects on student achievement. For example, studies of the effectiveness of peer-monitoring programs based on collaborative tutoring (Bronfenbrenner, 1979; Fraser et al., 1977; Hamblin, Buckholdt, Ferritor, Kozloff, & Blackwell, 1971; Hamblin, Hathaway, & Wodarski, 1971) indicate that in large lecture classes (100 or more students), peer-monitoring, in which students attend a specifically assigned peer discussion group on a weekly basis, produces better learning outcomes (defined by test scores) than students attending lectures only. The methods employed for peer-training include pairing students within discussion groups and preparing students to motivate one another.

Dobos (1996), in a study that focused primarily on affective outcomes of collaborative learning, examined the effects of college students' communication expectations and communication apprehension on intrinsic rewards in collaborative learning groups. She found that students with above-average presession expectations and below-average apprehension reported above-average expectation fulfillment and satisfaction. Likewise, students with below-average presession expectations and above-average apprehension reported below-average expectation fulfillment and satisfaction. Dobos concluded that emergent motivation, conceptualized as intrinsic rewards that emanate from individuals' experience with a task activity, influences how students respond to collaborative learning activities and the satisfaction they associate with the collaborative learning experience.

CONCLUDING COMMENTS

To say that the research on small group activities in the formal instructional context is substantial is to understate the magnitude of scale of this heavily investigated and historically anchored area. Our review and synthesis provides an in-depth overview of this very important area of educational inquiry. Recall that we began by noting that communication scholars have virtually neglected this literature, and we set as part of our task in this chapter to remedy this neglect by probing deep into the relevant educational literature and, where possible, highlighting parallels to group processes examined in communication research.

The research reviewed in this chapter revealed that there are two types of group structures employed in the formal instructional context. Each type functions to facilitate student learning in different ways.

- In *cooperative learning groups,* incentive structures are combined with opportunities for cognitive elaboration. In this way, the incentive structure provides the motivation for learning and group interaction provides the means for engaging in cognitive elaboration. Research reviewed in this chapter supports a developmental interpretation of the learning that occurs in cooperative learning groups, such that students build relationships with other students while engaging in a variety of learning modalities. In this way, critical thinking, relationship, and team-building skills are enhanced through the numerous in-class group experiences that occur developmentally over the life of one's formal education. Dewey's (1899, 1916) philosophy argues that these skills are transferable to aspects of one's life that extend beyond the classroom.

- Although not as effective as cooperative learning groups, *collaborative learning groups* focus on group interaction as the means for engaging in cognitive elaboration. In these groups, cooperative incentive structures do not exist. Comparing the two types of learning groups suggests that cooperative groups are a more instructionally sound approach to affecting learning outcomes in the classroom. In fact, collaborative learning groups contribute to a more passive environment, which can inhibit on-task performance and, consequently, can curtail student learning.

Group communication is central to motivation and cognitive elaboration. For cooperative incentive structures to promote motivation, interpersonal processes are required to foster cooperation among group members. In other words, group members must provide one another with opportunities for helping and sharing, acceptance and support, coordination of effort, and divergent and risk-taking thinking. Moreover, for cognitive elaboration to take place, members must engage in oral communicative behaviors, such as stating the topic, paraphrasing the learning material, referring to personal knowledge, raising questions, and creating analogies.

Heuristically speaking, future research should be directed toward (a) explaining the central role of communicative exchanges among student participants and between instructors and students during cooperative and collaborative learning activities, and (b) explicating the effects of such exchanges on both cognitive and affective learning outcomes. Projects designed to address the relationships among communicative processes and learning outcomes in cooperative and collaborative learning activities could be tested within the framework of either motivational or cognitive elaboration models.

Examples of more specific questions that follow from the broader research concerns include the following:

What types of message influence strategies are employed by teachers during cooperative and collaborative group activities that are associated with increases in learning outcomes?

Which teacher message strategies actually affect student learning outcomes during the cognitive elaboration process?

What types of message influence strategies do students employ with one another during cooperative and collaborative group activities?

How does the exchange of messages among students affect the cognitive elaboration process in terms of actual learning outcomes?

Which student influence messages mediate the learning that occurs during cognitive elaboration?

Are the message strategies employed by teachers and students in cooperative learning groups different from those employed during other types of student groupings or in whole-class instruction?

Are students more or less likely to resist teachers' attempts to influence them in cooperative learning groups versus ability groups or whole-class instruction?

Finally, it is very important to investigate how cooperative and collaborative instructional practices influence the development and stability of attitudes toward group work in general. Answering each of these questions will give researchers, educators, and trainers greater insight into the dynamics of group processes in the educational setting.

It is important that this chapter end with the reminder that participation in groups continues to be an integral part of the educational experience in the United States. Students participate in group activities in the classroom, on the playground, and in a variety of extracurricular organizations, such as Boy Scouts and Girl Scouts, little league sports, and dance. Of these, the type that has been studied the most is the classroom group. Although initial experiences with groups begin in the family (see

Socha, Chapter 17, this volume), most formalized education about group processes occurs in the classroom. We cannot, therefore, underestimate the impact of classroom group activities on group experiences outside the formal educational context. Moving beyond the scope of this chapter, then, numerous compelling questions remain regarding the influence of participation in classroom groups on participation in other types of group experiences throughout one's life.

REFERENCES

Aaronson, E., Blaney, N., Stephan, C., Sikes, J., & Smapp, M. (1978). *The jigsaw classroom.* Beverly Hills, CA: Sage.

Allen, W. H., & Van Sickle, R. L. (1984). Learning teams and low achievers. *Social Education, 48,* 60-64.

Allington, D. L. (1980). Teacher interruption behaviors during primary-grade oral reading. *Journal of Educational Psychology, 71,* 371-377.

Armstrong, L. M., Johnson, D. W., & Balow, B. (1981). Effects of cooperative vs. individualistic learning experiences on interpersonal attraction between learning-disabled and normal-progress elementary school students. *Contemporary Educational Psychology, 6,* 102-109.

Artzt, A. F. (1983). *The comparative effects of the student-team method of instruction and the traditional teacher-centered method of instruction upon student achievement, attitude, and social interaction in high school mathematics courses.* Unpublished doctoral dissertation, New York University.

Blaney, N. T., Stephan, C., Rosenfield, D., Aronson, E., & Sikes, J. (1977). Interdependence in the classroom: A field study. *Journal of Educational Psychology, 69,* 121-128.

Bloom, B. S. (1976). *Human characteristics and school learning: Experiments by nature and design.* New York: McGraw-Hill.

Bronfenbrenner, U. (1979). *The ecology of human development.* Cambridge, MA: Harvard University Press.

Bruffee, K. A. (1993). *Collaborative learning: Higher education, interdependence, and the authority of knowledge.* Baltimore: Johns Hopkins University Press.

Cartwright, D., & Zander, A. (Eds.). (1968). *Group dynamics: Research and theory* (3rd ed.). New York: Harper & Row.

Chan, C.K.K., Burtis, P. J., Scardamalia, M., & Bereiter, C. (1992). Constructive activity in learning from text. *American Educational Research Journal, 29,* 97-118.

Chernick, R. S. (1990). Effects of interdependent, coactive, and individualized work conditions on pupils' educational computer program performance. *Journal of Educational Psychology, 82,* 691-695.

Clarke, J., Wideman, R., & Eadie, S. (1990). *Together we learn.* Englewood Cliffs, NJ: Prentice Hall.

Cohen, E. (1986). *Designing groupwork: Strategies for the heterogeneous classroom.* New York: Teachers College Press.

Cohen, E. (1994). *Designing groupwork: Strategies for the heterogeneous classroom* (2nd ed.). New York: Teachers College Press.

Coleman, E. B. (1992). *Facilitating conceptual understanding in science: A collaborative explanation-based approach.* Unpublished doctoral dissertation, University of Toronto, Canada.

Cooper, L., Johnson, D., Johnson, R., & Wilderson, F. (1980). Effects of cooperative, competitive, and individualistic experiences on interpersonal attraction among heterogeneous peers. *Journal of Social Psychology, 111,* 243-252.

Coopersmith, S. (1967). *The antecedents of self-esteem.* San Francisco: W. H. Freeman.

Damon, W. (1984). Peer education: The untapped potential. *Journal of Applied Developmental Psychology, 5,* 331-343.

Dansereau, D. F. (1988). Cooperative learning strategies. In C. E. Weinstein, E. T. Goetz, & P. A. Alexander (Eds.), *Learning and study strategies: Issues in assessment, instruction, evaluation* (pp. 102-103). New York: Academic Press.

Davidson, N. (1985). Small-group learning and teaching in mathematics: A selective review of the research. In R. E. Slavin, S. Sharan, S. Kagan, R. Hertz-Lazarowitz, C. Webb, & R. Schmuck (Eds.), *Learning to cooperate, cooperating to learn* (pp. 211-230). New York: Plenum.

Deutsch, M. (1949). A theory of cooperation and competition. *Human Relations, 2,* 129-152.

Devin-Sheehan, L., Feldman, R., & Allen, V. (1976). Research on children tutoring children: A critical review. *Review of Educational Research, 46,* 355-285.

DeVries, D. L., & Edwards, K. J. (1973). Learning games and student teams: Their effects on classroom processes. *American Educational Research Journal, 10,* 307-318.

DeVries, D. L., Edwards, K. J., & Slavin, R. E. (1978). Biracial learning teams and race relations in the classroom: Four field experiments on Teams-Games-Tournament. *Journal of Educational Psychology, 70,* 356-362.

DeVries, D. L., Edwards, K. J., & Wells, E. H. (1974). *Teams-Games-Tournament in the social studies classroom: Effects of academic achievement, student attitudes, cognitive beliefs, and classroom climate* (Report No. 173). Baltimore: Johns Hopkins University Press.

DeVries, D. L., Lucasse, P. R., & Shackman, S. L. (1980). *Small group vs. individualized instruction: A field test of relative effectiveness* (Report No. 293). Baltimore: Johns Hopkins University Press.

DeVries, D. L., & Mescon, I. T. (1975). *Teams-Games-Tournament: An effective task and reward structure in the elementary grades* (Report No. 189). Baltimore: Johns Hopkins University Press.

DeVries, D. L., Mescon, I. T., & Shackman, S. L. (1975a). *Teams-Games-Tournaments effects on reading skills in elementary grades* (Report No. 200). Baltimore: Johns Hopkins University Press.

DeVries, D. L., Mescon, I. T., & Shackman, S. L. (1975b). *Teams-Games-Tournaments in the elementary classroom: A replica tion* (Report No. 190). Baltimore: Johns Hopkins University Press.

DeVries, D. L., & Slavin, R. E. (1978). Teams-Games-Tournament (TGT): Review of ten classroom experiments. *Journal of Research and Development in Education, 12,* 28-38.

Dewey, J. (1899). *Psychology as philosophic method.* Berkeley, CA: University Chronicle.

Dewey, J. (1916). *Democracy and education: An introduction to the philosophy of education.* New York: Macmillan.

Dobos, J. A. (1996). Collaborative learning: Effects of student expectations and communication apprehension on student motivation. *Communication Education, 45,* 118-134.

Doyle, W. (1986). Classroom organization and management. In M. C. Wittrock (Ed.), *Handbook of research on teaching* (3rd ed., pp. 392-431). New York: Macmillan.

Eder, D. (1982a). Differences in communicative styles across ability groups. In L. C. Wildinson (Ed.), *Communicating in classrooms* (pp. 245-264). New York: Academic Press.

Eder, D. (1982b). The impact of management and turn allocation activities on student performance. *Discourse Processes, 5,* 147-159.

Edwards, K. J., & DeVries, D. L. (1972). *Learning games and student teams: Their effects on student attitudes and achievement* (Report No. 147). Baltimore: Johns Hopkins University Press.

Edwards, K. J., & DeVries, D. L. (1974). *The effects of Teams-Games-Tournament and two structural variations on classroom processes, student attitudes, and student achievement* (Report No. 172). Baltimore: Johns Hopkins University Press.

Edwards, K. J., DeVries, D. L., & Snyder, J. P. (1972). Games and teams: A winning combination. *Simulation & Games, 3,* 247-269.

Fraser, S. C., Diener, E., Beaman, A. L., & Kelem, R. T. (1977). Two, three, or four heads are better than one: Modifications of college performance by peer monitoring. *Journal of Educational Psychology, 69,* 101-108.

Geffner, R. (1978). *The effects of interdependent learning on self-esteem, interethnic relations, and intra-ethnic attitudes of elementary school children: A field experiment.* Unpublished doctoral dissertation, University of California, Santa Cruz.

Glass, G. V, McGaw, B., & Smith, M. L. (1981). *Meta-analysis in social research.* Beverly Hills, CA: Sage.

Gonzales, A. (1979, August). *Classroom cooperation and ethnic balance.* Paper presented at the annual meeting of the American Psychological Association, New York.

Gonzales, A. (1981). *An approach to interdependent/ cooperative bilingual education and measures related to social motives.* Unpublished manuscript, California State University, Fresno.

Gump, P. V. (1967). *The classroom behavior setting: Its nature and relation to student behavior* (Final report). Washington, DC: U.S. Office of Education, Bureau of Research. (ERIC Document Reproduction Service No. ED 015 515)

Hamblin, R. L., Buckholdt, D., Ferritor, D., Kozloff, M., & Blackwell, L. (1971). *The humanization process: A social behavioral analysis of children's problems.* New York: Wiley-Interscience.

Hamblin, R. L., Hathaway, C., & Wodarski, J. S. (1971). Group contingencies in peer tutoring and accelerating academic achievement. In E. Ramp & B. Hopkins (Eds.), *A new direction for education: Behavior analysis* (pp. 41-53). Lawrence: University of Kansas, Department of Human Development.

Hammersley, M. (1974). The organization of pupil participation. *Sociological Review, 22,* 355-368.

Hansell, S., & Slavin, R. E. (1981). Cooperative learning and the structure of interracial friendships. *Sociology of Education, 54,* 98-106.

Hill, G. W. (1982). Group versus individual performance: Are n + 1 heads better than one? *Psychological Bulletin, 91,* 517-539.

Humphreys, B., Johnson, R., & Johnson, D. W. (1982). Effects of cooperative, competitive, and individualistic learning on students' achievement in science class. *Journal of Research in Science Teaching, 19,* 351-356.

Janke, R. (1978, April). *The Teams-Games-Tournament method and the behavioral adjustment and academic achievement of emotionally impaired adolescents.* Paper presented at the annual meeting of the American Educational Research Association, Toronto, Canada.

Johnson, D. W., & Johnson, R. T. (1975). *Learning together and alone: Cooperation, competition, and individualization.* Englewood Cliffs, NJ: Prentice Hall.

Johnson, D. W., & Johnson, R. T. (1981a). Effects of cooperative and individualistic learning experiences on interethnic interaction. *Journal of Educational Psychology, 73,* 444-449.

Johnson, D. W., & Johnson, R. T. (1981b). The integration of the handicapped into regular classrooms: Effects of cooperative and individualistic instruction. *Contemporary Educational Psychology, 6,* 344-355.

Johnson, D. W., Johnson, R. T., & Holubec, E. J. (1994). *The nuts and bolts of cooperative learning.* Edina, MN: Interaction.

Johnson, D. W., Johnson, R. T., Holubec, E. J., & Roy, P. (1984). *Circles of learning: Cooperation in the classroom.* Alexandria, VA: Association for Supervision and Curriculum Development.

Johnson, D. W., Johnson, R. T., Johnson, J., & Anderson, D. (1976). The effects of cooperative vs. individualized instruction on student prosocial behavior, attitudes toward learning, and achievement. *Journal of Educational Psychology, 68,* 446-452.

Johnson, D. W., Johnson, R. T., & Scott, L. (1978). The effects of cooperative and individualized instruction on student attitudes and achievement. *Journal of Social Psychology, 104,* 207-216.

Johnson, D. W., Maruyama, G., Johnson, R., Nelson, D., & Skon, L. (1981). Effects of cooperative, competitive, and individualistic goal structures on achievement: A meta-analysis. *Psychological Bulletin, 89,* 47-62.

Johnson, L. C. (1985). *The effects of the groups of four cooperative learning models on student problem-solving achievement in mathematics.* Unpublished doctoral dissertation, University of Houston.

Johnson, R. T., & Johnson, D. W. (1983). Effects of cooperative, competitive, and individualistic learning experiences on social development. *Exceptional Children, 49,* 323-329.

Kagan, S. (1992). *Cooperative learning resources for teachers.* Riverside: University of California Press.

Kagan, S., Zahan, G. L., Widaman, K. F., Schwarzwald, J., & Tyrell, G. (1985). Classroom structural bias: Impact of cooperative and competitive classroom structures on cooperative and competitive individuals and groups. In R. E. Slavin, S. Kagan, R. Hertz-Lazarowitz, C. Webb, & R. Schmuck (Eds.), *Learning to cooperate, cooperating to learn* (pp. 230-265). New York: Plenum.

Keyton, J. (1994). Going forward in group communication research may mean going back: Studying the groups of children. *Communication Studies, 45,* 40-51.

King, A. (1990). Enhancing peer interaction and learning in the classroom through reciprocal questioning. *American Educational Research Journal, 27,* 664-687.

Lazarowitz, R., Baird, H., Bowlden, V., & Hertz-Lazarowitz, R. (1982). *Academic achievements, learning environment, and self-esteem of high school students in biology taught in cooperative-investigative small groups.* Unpublished manuscript, The Technion, Haifa, Israel.

Lazarowitz, R., Baird, J. H., Hertz-Lazarowitz, R., & Jenkins, J. (1985). The effects of modified Jigsaw on achievement, classroom social climate, and self-esteem in high school science classes. In R. E. Slavin, S. Sharan, S. Kagan, R. Hertz-Lazarowitz, C. Webb, & R. Schmuck (Eds.), *Learning to cooperate, cooperating to learn* (pp. 266-290). New York: Plenum.

Louth, R., McAllister, C. E., & McAllister, H. A. (1990). The effects of collaborative writing techniques on freshman writing and attitudes. *Journal of Experimental Education, 61,* 215-224.

Madden, N. A., & Slavin, R. E. (1983a). The effects of cooperative learning on the social acceptance of mainstreamed academically handicapped students. *Journal of Special Education, 17,* 171-182.

Madden, N. A., & Slavin, R. E. (1983b). Mainstreaming students with mild academic handicaps: Academic and social outcomes. *Review of Educational Research, 53,* 519-569.

Mason, D. A., & Good, T. L. (1993). Effects of two-group and whole-class teaching on regrouped elementary students' mathematics achievement. *American Educational Research Journal, 30,* 328-360.

McDermott, R. P. (1976). *Kids make sense: An ethnographic account of the interactional management of success and failure in one first-grade classroom.* Unpublished doctoral dissertation, Stanford University, Stanford, CA.

Melothe, M. S., & Deering, P. D. (1994). Task talk and task awareness under different cooperative learning conditions. *American Educational Research Journal, 31,* 138-165.

Murray, F. B. (1982). Teaching through social conflict. *Contemporary Educational Psychology, 7,* 257-271.

Newman, F. M., & Thompson, J. (1987). *Effects of cooperative learning on achievement in secondary schools: A summary of research.* Madison: University of Wisconsin, National Center on Effective Secondary Schools.

O'Donnell, A. M., Dansereau, D. F., Hall, R. H., & Rocklin, T. R. (1987). Cognitive, affective, and metacognitive outcomes of scripted cooperative learning. *Journal of Educational Psychology, 79,* 421-437.

Oickle, E. (1980). *A comparison of individual and team learning.* Unpublished doctoral dissertation, University of Maryland, Baltimore.

Oishi, S., Slavin, R. E., & Madden, N. A. (1983, April). *Effects of student teams and individualized instruction on cross-race and cross-sex friendships.* Paper presented at the annual meeting of the American Educational Research Association, Montreal, Canada.

Okebukola, P. A. (1984). In search of a more effective interaction pattern in biology laboratories. *Journal of Biological Education, 18,* 305-308.

Okebukola, P. A. (1985). The relative effectiveness of cooperativeness and competitive interaction techniques in strengthening students' performance in science class. *Science Education, 69,* 501-509.

Okebukola, P. A. (1986a). Impact of extended cooperative and competitive relationships on the performance of students in science. *Human Relations, 39,* 673-682.

Okebukola, P. A. (1986b). The influence of preferred learning styles on cooperative learning in science. *Science Education, 70,* 509-517.

Piaget, J. (1926). *The language and thought of the child.* New York: Harcourt Brace.

Rich, Y., Amir, Y., & Slavin, R. E. (1986). *Instructional strategies for improving children's across-ethnic relations.* Ramat Gan, Israel: Institute for the Advancement of Social Integration in Schools.

Rippa, S. A. (1992). *Education in a free society: An American history* (7th ed.). New York: Longman.

Robertson, L. (1982). *Integrated goal structuring in the elementary school: Cognitive growth in mathematics.* Unpublished doctoral dissertation, Rutgers University, New Brunswick, NJ.

Sharan, S., Hertz-Lazarowitz, R., & Ackerman, Z. (1980). Academic achievement of elementary school children in small group vs. whole class instruction. *Journal of Experimental Education, 48,* 125-129.

Sharan, S., Kussell, P., Hertz-Lazarowitz, R., Bejarano, Y., Raviv, S., & Sharan, Y. (1984). *Cooperative learning in the classroom: Research in desegregated schools.* Hillsdale, NJ: Lawrence Erlbaum.

Sharan, S., & Shachar, H. (1988). *Language and learning in the cooperative classroom.* New York: Springer-Verlag.

Sharan, S., & Sharan, Y. (1976). *Small-group teaching.* Englewood Cliffs, NJ: Educational Technology.

Sherman, L. W., & Thomas, M. (1986). Mathematics achievement in cooperative versus individualistic goal-structured high school classrooms. *Journal of Educational Research, 79,* 169-172.

Sherman, L. W., & Zimmerman, D. (1986, November). *Cooperative versus competitive reward-structured secondary science classroom achievement.* Paper presented at the annual meeting of the School Science and Mathematics Association, Lexington, KY.

Slavin, R. E. (1977a). Classroom reward structure: An analytic and practical review. *Review of Educational Research, 47,* 633-650.

Slavin, R. E. (1977b). A student team approach to teaching adolescents with special emotional and behavioral needs. *Psychology in the Schools, 14,* 77-84.

Slavin, R. E. (1977c). *Student team learning techniques: Narrowing the achievement gap between the races* (Report No. 228). Baltimore: Johns Hopkins University Press.

Slavin, R. E. (1978a). Student teams and achievement divisions. *Journal of Research and Development in Education, 12,* 39-49.

Slavin, R. E. (1978b). Student teams and comparison among equals: Effects on academic performance and student attitudes. *Journal of Educational Psychology, 70,* 532-538.

Slavin, R. E. (1979). Effects of biracial learning teams on cross-racial friendships. *Journal of Educational Psychology, 71,* 381-387.

Slavin, R. E. (1980). Cooperative learning. *Review of Educational Research, 50,* 315-342.

Slavin, R. E. (1983a). *Cooperative learning.* New York: Longman.

Slavin, R. E. (1983b). When does cooperative learning increase student achievement? *Psychological Bulletin, 94,* 429-445.

Slavin, R. E. (1987). Ability grouping and student achievement: A best-evidence synthesis. *Review of Educational Research, 57,* 293-336.

Slavin, R. E. (1989). Cooperative learning and student achievement. In R. E. Slavin (Ed.), *School and classroom organization* (pp. 45-57). Hillsdale, NJ: Lawrence Erlbaum.

Slavin, R. E. (1989-1990). Research on cooperative learning: Consensus and controversy. *Educational Leadership, 58,* 52-54.

Slavin, R. E. (1990). *Cooperative learning: Theory, research, and practice.* Boston: Allyn & Bacon.

Slavin, R. E. (1991). Synthesis of research on cooperative learning. *Educational Leadership, 48,* 82-89.

Slavin, R. E., & Karweit, N. (1981). Cognitive and affective outcomes of an intensive student team learning experience. *Journal of Experimental Education, 50,* 29-35.

Slavin, R. E., & Karweit, N. (1984). Mastery learning and student teams: A factorial experiment in urban general mathematics classes. *American Educational Research Journal, 21,* 725-726.

Slavin, R. E., Leavey, M., & Madden, N. A. (1984). Combining cooperative learning and individualized instruction: Effects on student mathematics achievement, attitudes, and behaviors. *Elementary School Journal, 84,* 409-422.

Slavin, R. E., & Oickle, E. (1981). Effects of cooperative learning teams on student achievement and race relations: Treatment by race interaction. *Sociology of Education, 54,* 174-180.

Socha, T. J. (1997). Group communication across the life span. In L. R. Frey & J. K. Barge (Eds.), *Managing group life: Communicating in decision-making groups* (pp. 3-28). Boston: Houghton Mifflin.

Socha, T. J., & Socha, D. M. (1994). Children's task-group communication: Did we learn it all in kindergarten? In L. R. Frey (Ed.), *Group communication in context: Studies of natural groups* (pp. 227-247). Hillsdale, NJ: Lawrence Erlbaum.

Stevens, R. J., Madden, N. A., Slavin, R. E., & Farnish, A. M. (1987). Cooperative integrated reading and composition: Two field experiments. *Reading Research Quarterly, 22,* 433-454.

Stevens, R. J., Slavin, R. E., Farnish, A. M., & Madden, N. A. (1988, April). *Effects of cooperative learning and direct instruction in reading comprehension strategies on main idea identification.* Paper presented at the annual meeting of the American Educational Research Association, New Orleans, LA.

Tomblin, E. A., & Davis, B. R. (1985). *Technical report of the evaluation of the race/human relations program: A study of cooperative learning environment strategies.* San Diego: San Diego Public Schools.

Tripplett, N. (1897). The dynamogenic factors in pacemaking and competition. *American Journal of Psychology, 9,* 507-533.

Van Oudenhoven, J. P., Van Berkum, G., & Swen-Koopmans, T. (1987). Effect of cooperation and shared feedback on spelling achievement. *Journal of Educational Psychology, 79,* 92-124.

Van Oudenhoven, J. P., Wiersma, B., & Van Yperen, N. (1987). Effects of cooperation and feedback by fellow pupils on spelling achievement. *European Journal of Psychology of Education, 2,* 83-91.

Vermette, P. J. (1998). *Making cooperative learning work: Student teams in K-12 classrooms.* Upper Saddle River, NJ: Prentice Hall.

Vygotsky, L. S. (1978). *Mind in society: The development of higher psychological processes.* Cambridge, MA: Harvard University Press.

Wadsworth, B. J. (1984). *Piaget's theory of cognitive and affective development* (3rd ed.). New York: Longman.

Webb, N. M. (1989). Peer interaction and learning in small groups. *International Journal of Educational Research, 12,* 21-40.

Webb, N. M. (1992). Testing a theoretical model of student interaction and learning in small groups. In R. Hertz-Lazarowitz & N. Miller (Eds.), *Interaction in cooperative groups: The theoretical anatomy of group learning* (pp. 102-119). Cambridge, UK: Cambridge University Press.

Webb, N. M. (1993). Collaborative group versus individual assessment in mathematics: Processes and outcomes. *Educational Assessment, 1,* 131-152.

Webb, N. M., & Farivar, S. (1994). Promoting helping behaviors in cooperative small groups in middle school mathematics. *American Education Research Journal, 31,* 369-395.

Webb, N. M., Troper, J. D., & Fall, R. (1995). Constructive activity and learning in collaborative small groups. *Journal of Educational Psychology, 87,* 406-423.

Wheeler, R., & Ryan, F. L. (1973). Effects of cooperative and competitive classroom environments on the attitudes and achievement of elementary school students engaged in social studies inquiry activities. *Journal of Educational Psychology, 65,* 402-407.

Wittrock, M. C. (1978). The cognitive movement in instruction. *Educational Psychologist, 13,* 15-29.

19

Communication in Social Support Groups

REBECCA J. WELCH CLINE
University of Florida

The duty of helping one's self in the highest sense involves the helping of one's neighbours.
—Smiles (1866, p. iii)

Evidence indicates a burgeoning growth of social support groups as Americans search for a sense of community bounded not by streets and villages, but rather by shared experiences, symbols, and worldviews. Wuthnow (1994) declared the growth of social support groups so strong as to constitute a "small-group movement" that arguably redefines the concept of "community" (p. 2). *Social support* or *self-help groups* are small groups formed for the specific purpose of providing mutual aid among members who share a common dilemma. This chapter (a) chronicles the transformation from reliance on geographic neighborhoods to social support groups, (b) explores the nature of social support groups, (c) analyzes communication processes that are at the heart of social support groups, (d) assesses social support group outcomes, and (e) outlines the limits of extant research and suggests directions for future work.

SELF-HELP GROUPS AS ALTER COMMUNITIES

Because of their proliferation during the past 25 years, self-help groups tend to be seen as a recent innovation. Although attributes of contemporary society have contributed to their explosive growth, self-help groups have a lengthy history.

History and Growth of Self-Help Groups

Katz and Bender (1976a, 1976b) provide the most extensive documentation of the history of self-help groups and their development, tracing them from before the Middle Ages to the 20th century. Forerunners of today's self-help groups emerged initially to meet survival needs, then later because of the inadequacies of alternative services (e.g., church and state) to address the unmet needs of the poor, the underprivileged, and the powerless. These forerunners include the tribes of preliterate societies, trade guilds of the Middle Ages, and England's 19th-century mutual aid "Friendly Societies" that provided help for the poor (Katz & Bender, 1976b). The prelude to present-day self-help groups was the initiation of Alcoholics Anonymous (AA) in 1935 (see Lieberman & Snowden, 1993). Although social scientists were slow to recognize the existence and significance of modern-day self-help groups, by 1978, President Carter's Mental Health Commission proposed self-help as "a major health intervention."

Estimates of the magnitude of participation in self-help groups vary widely but are uniformly high (e.g., Jacobs & Goodman, 1989; Kurtz, 1997). From a nationally representative survey, Wuthnow (1994) reports that 40% of adults in the United States (about 75 million people) participate in an organized "small group that meets regularly and provides . . . support for its members" (p. 4), and that more than three million such groups exist; however, he includes Sunday school classes and Bible study groups, groups typically not included by other scholars studying self-help groups. Even so, about two thirds of Wuthnow's respondents who felt a need for "deep emotional support" reported their need being "met fully" by participation in these groups. Moreover, 52% and 26%, respectively, indicated that the terms "support group" and "self-help group" applied to their current group. Thus, Wuthnow estimates that 8 to 10 million adults in the United States participate in a total of at least a half-million self-help groups.

In reporting the history of self-help groups, Katz and Bender (1976a) mistakenly believed that the phenomenon had "reached a crescendo" in the 1960s (p. 277). Robinson and Henry (1977), however, refer to the 1970s as "the self-help decade" (p. 7). In the 1990s, the growth of self-help groups in the United States may not have peaked. Observers predict that self-help groups will become "standard practice" by the year 2000 (Tyler, 1980, p. 20), if

not *the* major method of care (Prochaska & Norcross, 1982).

Reasons for the Growth of Social Support Groups

Several societal changes account for the explosive growth of social support groups (see, for example, Gartner & Riessman, 1977; Katz & Bender, 1976a; Riessman & Carroll, 1995). These changes are rooted in changing social and health care structures and processes.

Losses of Traditional Sources of Social Support

Traditionally, the geographic community, including the extended family, provided social support to its members. Although that support often required adherence to the norms of a highly homogeneous community, within those confines, community members "could count on strong communal support" (Shaffer & Anundsen, 1993, p. 6). Industrialization and the growth of technology radically changed the geographic landscape and yielded parallel losses in familial and community social support. In turn, people turned increasingly to professional sources (e.g., psychologists), but with substantial dissatisfaction. Social support groups emerged to provide an alternative sense of community (Wuthnow, 1994).

The failure of family and friends. Increased geographic mobility changed family and neighborhood structures and disrupted social continuity (Cluck & Cline, 1986). The urbanized and commuting lifestyle of the late 20th century replaced community with anonymity and social bonding with fragmentation (Wuthnow, 1994). Many people stigmatized by their dilemma found their families guilty of such stigmatization (Cluck & Cline, 1986; Daniolos, 1994; Wright, 1997). For example, people with AIDS (Daniolos, 1994) and the bereaved (Cluck & Cline, 1986) commonly report being misunderstood, judged negatively, and re-jected by their own families. Alcoholics com-plain that no one really understands or cares about them and find themselves "bucking a hostile world" (Bales, 1944, p. 274; see also Wright, 1997). People who are stigmatized often encounter difficult conversational topics when interacting with those who are nonstig-matized, resulting in other people avoiding them (e.g., Sullivan & Reardon, 1986), invali-dating their significance, or inappropriately joking about them, and ultimately resulting in their isolation (Wright, 1998). As the informal support of family and friends broke down, people looked for alternative sources of sup-port. It is not surprising, then, that the meta-phor of "family" recurs to describe connec-tions among social support group members (see Adelman & Frey, 1997; Daniolos, 1994).

The failure of professionals. As traditional communities disappeared, people increasingly turned to professionals for support. In turn, institutions became increasingly complex and overburdened, and were criticized for being unresponsive, depersonalizing, and dehuman-izing. Professional caregiving is often criti-cized for framing dilemmas as defects in the individual (Cluck & Cline, 1986) and for imploring providers to maintain a social dis-tance that creates a cold and analytic climate (Kutscher, 1970). McKnight (1995) argues that reliance on "professionalism" functions to destroy "community competence" (p. xi). He contends that professional social services are disabling when all needs are labeled defi-ciencies, professional expertise replaces per-sonal experience, professional opinion dis-places social support, and professional-client relationships disable natural community-building tendencies.

Changing Health Care Needs

Medical advances yielded greater longevity, a growing population with chronic illness, and a wider range of constituencies. Needs out-stripped available services for millions of peo-ple with more than 30 million hypertensive, 11 million emotionally depressed, 10 million addicted to alcohol, 6 million addicted to other drugs, 54 million infected with STDs, and more than 1 million infected with HIV in the United States (Riessman & Carroll, 1995). Increased demands coincided with massive changes in a health care system overwrought with needs for cost containment.

The Acceptability of Alternative Help

Changes in social structure made reliance on "distant" sources of social support (e.g., relative strangers) increasingly acceptable. The media contributed to that acceptance with dramatic, documentary, and talk-show portrayals of self-help groups. Several charac-teristics of self-help groups also attracted members (see, for example, Cluck & Cline, 1986; Powell, 1987): lack of fees, the "person-alness" of a peer context (e.g., Mullan, 1992), access to professionals in supportive roles (e.g., Robinson & Henry, 1977), continuity of support, and care for neglected dilemmas and populations viewed as untreatable (e.g., Wasserman & Danforth, 1988).

Recognition of Diverse Dilemmas

The diversity of predicaments addressed by self-help groups continues to grow. Scholars concede that creating an elegant typology is futile (see Katz & Bender, 1976a, 1976b; Riessman & Carroll, 1995). The typology most often cited recognizes issues as diverse as (a) handling behavioral problems, (b) manag-ing common stressful situations, (c) coping with stigma and discrimination, and (d) pro-moting self-actualization and growth (Levy, 1976). Specific issues are as varied as alcohol-ism, HIV/AIDS, ostomy, child abuse, single parenting, bereavement, runaway children, hearing impairment, recovery from heart at-tacks, coping with abortion, unemployment, parenting as a grandparent, and impotence.

THE NATURE OF
SOCIAL SUPPORT GROUPS

Scholars agree on several defining characteristics of social support groups. Logically, understanding the nature of social support groups requires attention to "social support."

Defining Social Support Groups

Efforts to differentiate between "social support" and "self-help" groups (e.g., Gottlieb, 1988) invariably produce contradictions. Thus, most scholars use these terms interchangeably (as is done in this chapter). Although analysts recognize that groups occurring naturally in everyday family and friendship contexts offer social support, the term *social support group* describes a more formally organized phenomenon.

Defining Characteristics

Defining social support groups begins by distinguishing them from traditional group psychotherapy. In fact, accounts of support groups often imply criticism of the professionalism found in psychotherapy groups (Klass, 1982). Scholars distinguish group psychotherapy from social support groups in several ways. *Psychotherapy groups* are characterized by (a) institutional affiliation, fees, appointments, and records; (b) a clinical environment; (c) a high degree of structure; (d) preset agendas for changing behavior; (e) status differentiation between professionals and clients; (f) unilateral self-disclosure by clients and social support from professionals; and (g) therapists as authorities (see Dean, 1970-1971; Gartner & Riessman, 1977).

Katz and Bender (1976b) offered the definition of self-help groups cited most often:

Self-help groups are voluntary, small group structures for mutual aid and the accomplishment of a special purpose. They are usually formed by peers who have come together for mutual assistance in satisfying a common need, overcoming a common handicap or life-disrupting problem or bringing about social and/or personal change. (p. 9)

A review of the larger array of definitions (e.g., Gartner & Riessman, 1977; Gottlieb, 1988; Kurtz, 1997; Levy, 1976; Silverman & Cooperband, 1975) reveals six commonly identified characteristics: (a) a shared dilemma, (b) provision and receipt of support, (c) the search for common solutions, (d) informal interaction, (e) a nonhierarchical structure, and (f) voluntary membership.

Concepts and Benefits of Social Support

Understanding social support is necessary to understanding social support groups. The nature and functions of social support are similar, regardless of whether social support occurs in naturally developed (e.g., family and friends) or more formally organized social support groups.

Defining Social Support

Multiple components constitute social support (see Cutrona & Russell, 1990). Social support addresses interpersonal needs for relational (e.g., emotional support, attachment, belongingness, and network support), confirmational (e.g., reassurance of worth, esteem support, and affirmation), and instrumental (e.g., tangible aid, material support, and information) care.

Interpersonal needs for care intensify under stress. Cutrona and Russell (1990) define stress as "a relationship between the person and the environment in which the individual perceives that something of personal value is at stake and judges that his or her resources are taxed or overwhelmed by the situation" (p. 324). Thus, stress, and the resulting need for social support, is a function of a person's *perception* of his or her ability to respond to a threat.

Communication approaches to conceptualizing social support stem from the premise that psychological well-being and social adjustment depend on a person's belief in his or her ability to predict and control experiences (Brenders, 1987). Albrecht and Adelman (1987b) unified the literature by theoretically linking the perceptual and communicative dimensions of social support. They defined *social support* as "verbal and nonverbal communication between recipients and providers that reduces uncertainty about the situation, the self, the other, or the relationship, and functions to enhance a perception of personal control in one's life experience" (p. 19). Thus, social support is manifest in communication processes. Ford, Babrow, and Stohl (1996) clarify that social support is more a matter of managing than reducing uncertainty. Their perspective recognizes both the destructive potential of certainty and the constructive potential of uncertainty. Consequently, they define *supportive communication* as that which "functions to facilitate adaptive uncertainty management" (p. 191). Supportive messages function to manage uncertainty by changing an individual's perspective on cause-effect contingencies, facilitating skill acquisition, offering tangible assistance, conveying relational support, and confirming his or her experiences and feelings (Albrecht & Adelman, 1987b).

Social Support and Health

Formal study of the health consequences of social support began with the recognition that social relationships are linked to susceptibility to disease (Cassel, 1976); they can buffer against pathology, accelerate recovery from illness, and enhance compliance with treatment regimens (Sarason, Sarason, & Pierce, 1990). Illness and other crises produce uncertainty by creating ambiguity, adding complexity, enhancing needs for information, and promoting unpredictability (Mischel, 1988). These factors contribute to a person's perception of limited resources for action. The senses of helplessness and hopelessness engendered serve as an impetus for seeking communica-

tion to help manage that perception (Albrecht & Adelman, 1987b).

A review of early research on the health consequences of social support yielded "uniformly positive" results (S. Cohen & Syme, 1985, p. 20). Analysts later identified weaknesses in early research and discovered potentially negative health consequences of social support (e.g., Albrecht & Adelman, 1987a; DiMatteo & Hays, 1981). For example, social support may disrupt family equilibrium, result in caregiver burnout, interfere with patient compliance, and promote dependence by those receiving support (Albrecht & Adelman, 1987a). Most critics concede, however, that social support likely has some causal relationship with health status.

Evidence indicates that social support is associated with recovery from and coping with serious illness and injury (DiMatteo & Hays, 1981). Social support has been linked with favorable symptom change (e.g., with asthma, migraine headaches, and hypertension), enhanced recovery (e.g., from a stroke), adaptive responses to the diagnosis of terminal illness (e.g., resulting in greater longevity, better interpersonal relationships, and better emotional adjustment), and greater compliance with medical regimens (DiMatteo & Hays, 1981). Health-facilitating social support may come from sources as diverse as family (e.g., Eggert, 1987), friends (e.g., Adelman, Parks, & Albrecht, 1987b), and work and professional relationships (Ray, 1987). Although most research focuses on "strong ties" (primary relationships), support from "weak ties" (nonprimary relationships, for example, with bartenders and hairdressers) also yields health benefits (Adelman, Parks, & Albrecht, 1987a). Thus, interacting with a group of relative strangers who share a dilemma has the potential to be socially supportive.

COMMUNICATION PROCESSES IN SOCIAL SUPPORT GROUPS

Communication processes lie at the heart of social support groups. In studying those processes, scholars have focused on the macro-level to the near exclusion of the microlevel. At the macrolevel, analysts have explored the relationship between group communication processes and group ideology. Substantial attention to middle-ground concepts has emphasized the role of group communication climate and leadership, and very little research has focused on microlevel communication processes, that is, actual dialogue, specific messages, and their effects.

The Role of Ideology in Social Support Groups

Whether explicit or implicit, ideologies function to create a sense of community where members share a similar worldview. Although community traditionally is associated with geographic boundaries, contemporary concepts of community focus on shared meanings and emotional connections (A. P. Cohen, 1985) as the basis for what Hunter (1974) calls a "symbolic community." From this perspective, a community may be viewed as a symbolic social system in which people are connected by shared beliefs, values, and communicative practices (see Adelman & Frey, 1997). Thus, social support groups can be seen as "fixed communities of beliefs" (Antze, 1976, p. 325) whose ideologies provide members with a map for understanding and addressing life's problems and finding effective solutions (Shaffer & Galinsky, 1989).

Social support group ideologies can be classified in terms of the concept of *locus of control*, the dominant perceived source of control of outcomes. An *external locus of control* reflects the perception that outcomes are determined by forces outside the self and independent of one's own actions (e.g., luck, fate, and/or powerful others), whereas an *internal locus of control* indicates that outcomes are contingent on one's own behavior (Rotter, 1966). Some social support groups advocate an external locus of control, whereas others advocate an internal locus of control, as a worldview for

understanding members' problems and their solutions.

Although social support groups tend to place either an external or an internal locus of control ideology in the foreground, the alternative lurks in the background. Thus, at the same time that groups with an external ideology advocate external powers as central to coping, the individual plays a pivotal role in surrendering to that ideology. Similarly, although groups with an internal ideology emphasize self-responsibility, they acknowledge the role of the group in helping members (Klass, 1982). The worldview in the foreground dominates in influencing a group's communication processes.

The Ideology of Surrendering Control

Social support groups espousing surrender of control to external sources (typically, a higher being) prescribe explicit beliefs and rituals (Antze, 1976; Gartner & Riessman, 1977). Alcoholics Anonymous represents the most widespread of social support groups advocating an external orientation, accounting for more than 1.3 million members in the United States (Kurtz, 1997). AA's ideology is explicated in a 12-step program that has been adopted by a host of look-alike "anonymous groups" (e.g., Gamblers Anonymous, Cocaine Anonymous, and groups for smokers, debtors, delinquents, and families of prisoners).

Alcoholics Anonymous advocates that the best way to remain sober is to target one's energy *away from self* by helping others remain sober (Shaffer & Galinsky, 1989). AA proffers that some individuals are physiologically incapable of drinking moderately, a problem over which they have little control. AA's external orientation is apparent in its key tenet that "the member has to *admit his/her powerlessness* before recovery is possible" (Mäkelä et al., 1996, p. 117). The 12 steps direct members to believe in a higher power, turn their lives over to God, and promulgate AA's externally oriented message.

AA relies on an oral tradition, as well as written documents, to promulgate its ideology (Mäkëla et al., 1996). Meetings center on reviewing and reinforcing the 12 steps. The structure, rules, rituals, and slogans impose an external orientation in a format that generally is the same across meetings and chapters. The main part of meetings consists of highly rule-governed talking in turn in a "nonconversational" style (i.e., speakers do not reply to previous remarks).

Twelve-step programs are not the exclusive proprietors of an external orientation. Antze (1976) describes Recovery, Inc. and Synanon groups in external terms. Recovery, Inc., a group for people with mental illness, takes a medicalized view (i.e., external experts diagnose the problem). Synanon, a group for drug addicts, imposes external control via explicit rules for everyday behavior, as well as an "attack therapy" process that places control with the group. In summary, externally oriented social support groups direct members to discard much of their sense of personal control in order to enact personal change.

The Ideology of Self-Responsibility

In contrast to AA and similar groups, the majority of remaining social support groups subscribe to an internally oriented ideology. They reinforce values of personal responsibility and personal control. The tenets of internally oriented groups echo humanistic philosophy (e.g., Rogers, 1961): the potential for individuals to help themselves, particularly when afforded a facilitating environment (i.e., the group's social support), the inherent value of individuals' experiences and feelings, and the value of freedom to choose.

Internally oriented social support groups advocate self-reliance as the basis for coping and change. "Answers" are sought from one's self rather than from others, and experiential knowledge is valued over knowledge from other sources. Internally oriented groups profess that the route to growth and healing is awareness of feelings and experiences, which provides a basis for self-direction. Thus, inter-

nally oriented groups attempt to provide members with a facilitating climate in which self-direction can emerge, rather than offering external structure, direction, or advice. For example, The Compassionate Friends, a social support group for people coping with the death of a child, explicitly identifies the principles of "maintaining freedom of belief and action" (Klass, 1988, p. 116) as central to coping with grief. Those principles are reflected in such statements as, "We understand that each parent must find his or her own way through grief" and "We never suggest that there is a correct way to grieve or that there is a preferred solution to the emotional and spiritual dilemmas raised by the death of our children" (p. 116).

Klass (1982) observed that the philosophy of The Compassionate Friends is articulated more implicitly than explicitly. That philosophy, however, is communicated implicitly via group conversational patterns. Unlike 12-step groups, Compassionate Friends does not require members to speak. Typical meetings are characterized by open-ended conversations that focus on members expressing feelings and reporting similar experiences. The content of communication often is highly emotional; crying is common. One commonly expressed feeling is anger toward others (outside the group) who are unhelpful or fail to understand the bereaved parent's feelings. Members encourage one another to express their feelings; that encouragement is based on the belief that feelings cannot be avoided. Thus, the tears, expression of rage, and confrontation are "considered curative, not dysfunctional" (p. 315). Members' feelings are accepted both implicitly and explicitly; they are reassured that their experience is normal, shared, and necessary to healing.

Both Antze (1976) and Humphreys (1996) attribute members' recovery in both externally and internally oriented social support groups to their altered or reinforced worldviews. A new social reality emerges from the communication that occurs in these groups (Ford, 1989). Whether group activities function to frame or reframe an individual's perspective as external or internal, communication processes in social support groups function to reinforce an ideology that becomes the members' worldview.

The Middle Ground: Typical Group Communication Processes

Two middle-ground communication concepts recur in typical accounts of social support groups: a supportive communication climate and transactional leadership via the dual roles of helpee and helper.

Communication Climate

Descriptions of communication processes in social support groups echo Gibb's (1961) notion of a "supportive climate" (i.e., empathy, spontaneity, and egalitarianism) and Rogers's (1961) portrayal of a "helping relationship" (e.g., empathy, acceptance, and genuineness). Typical accounts describe communication in social support groups as mutually understanding, supportive, and empathic; accepting of divergent views; and genuine, open, and expressive (e.g., Balk, Tyson-Rawson, & Colletti-Wetzel, 1993; Kurtz, 1990). Levy (1976) contends that these communication processes constitute the *curative factors* in social support groups.

A supportive climate is believed to promote personal disclosure that is therapeutic in itself (e.g., Droge, Arntson, & Norton, 1986; Katz, 1993). Groups with members as diverse as parents of cult members (Halperin, 1987), people with affective disorders (Karp, 1992), and coronary heart disease patients (Hildingh, Fridlund, & Segesten, 1995) report self-disclosure and the expression of feelings to be significant facilitative processes. Furthermore, open discussion leads to greater information exchange.

The above description is representative of the literature in general; however, group communication patterns clearly diverge on the basis of ideology. Some of the characteristics of groups described above (i.e., supportive communication) are identified as typical of

AA and other 12-step externally oriented groups (e.g., Berenson, 1990), as well as internally oriented groups. Although the *same* communication processes are described, the functions of those processes may *differ*. For example, although 12-step programs encourage members to share personal experience, that sharing appears to be directed more toward validating the group's program (e.g., testimony consistent with the 12 steps) than toward confirming members' experiences as inherently valid and valuable (as is characteristic of internally oriented groups). In contrast, internally oriented groups focus on providing a facilitative climate as the mechanism for change, as well as viewing it as inherently valuable. Katz (1993) argues that the potential of social support groups lies in their ability to meet members' needs for personal security and belongingness by creating a climate in which members can express feelings and examine experiences. In internally oriented groups, identifying with one another's feelings creates an insider perspective that functions to enhance members' sense of personal control by consensual validation of experiences and meanings (Gottlieb, 1988).

The communication climate of externally oriented groups often differs sharply from a supportive climate. Dean's (1970-1971) description of Recovery, Inc. emphasizes the attending physician's authority (most members are under a physician's care) and members' loss of control and responsibility (see also Antze, 1976). Although Dean characterizes the climate as supportive, in fact, members' feelings are devalued as they compete to win the group's approval, thereby creating a climate that is subtly strategic and evaluative, characteristics of a defensive climate (see Gibb, 1961).

Similarly, Antze's (1976) description of Synanon depicts an explicitly external ideology with correspondingly high structure. Members engage in two forms of interaction characterized by rigid rules. "The Floor" refers to everyday interaction, in or outside a group's meetings, and "the Game" refers to a form of "attack therapy" (p. 338). When engaged in "The Floor," the group seeks perfectionism, mandates correcting others' behavior, disregards individuals' feelings, and posits the highest value as following rules. During "the Game," the "Heart of Synanon," members express feelings in the form of "dumping" (as in "dumping garbage" or "discharging a toxic or dangerous substance") (Antze, 1976, p. 339). In practice, "the Game" provokes an individual via verbal attack, anything short of physical violence, until he or she is reduced to tears or explodes with anger. The goal is to break down everyday concealment of the self that might keep that member from participating in the group. Thus, interaction in Synanon groups reflects control, superiority, and strategy, characteristics indicative of a defensive rather than a supportive climate (Gibb, 1961). In this fashion, the group maintains external control over its members.

Finally, whereas internally oriented groups consistently advocate and promote supportive climates, externally oriented groups tend to exhibit structural features that may discourage or interfere with providing emotional support by replacing the expression of emotion with rituals, rules, and information giving. Thus, supportive climates and associated processes are more typically characteristic of internally oriented rather than externally oriented social support groups.

Leadership in Social Support Groups

The nature of leadership in social support groups varies. Most groups do not designate a leader, relying instead on naturally emerging leadership that reflects the helper principle. Some groups have an added layer of leadership provided by facilitators, often professionals.

The helper principle. A central concept of social support groups is that individuals help themselves both by accepting and by offering help (see, for example, Franko, 1987). Riessman (1965) first identified the shift in roles from helpee to helper as "the helper-therapy principle." The principle encompasses a complex process of cognitive reframing during which rookie helpers become veterans (Mullan, 1992; see Anderson, Riddle, & Martin, chapter 6, this volume, regarding group socialization processes by which newcomers become veterans).

While being helped, group members benefit from personalized learning, social approval in a supportive communication climate, and observing others struggling with similar problems (Gartner & Riessman, 1977). Disclosures by more senior members result in identification and reduced isolation for newer members (Mullan, 1992). As members make the transition from helpee to helper, retelling their stories validates their experiences and reminds them, as well as other members, of their progress (Shaffer & Galinsky, 1989). Experienced members function as facilitators as well as role models (Balk et al., 1993). Their role transformation accents the shift from uncertainty to personal control. Leadership evolves naturally through helper-helpee relationships, rather than via designated leaders (particularly in internally oriented groups). In general, personal experience is valued over professional training, yet professionals, as well as experienced group members, may play the role of facilitator.

The role of professionals. Many social support groups rely on professionals in some capacity. A relatively symbiotic relationship has grown recently between social support groups and the health care system. Often, as members recognize the need to deal with complex psychological problems, they become more open to including health professionals in some capacity. In turn, social support groups become more integrated with the health care system (Katz, 1992).

The primary responsibility of a facilitator in a social support group lies in promoting the communication processes associated with the group's ideology. When the facilitator is a professional, informal tasks include mediating tensions and conflicts, maintaining appropriate boundaries, helping to create a safe environment, and diverting uncontrolled negative affect (Halperin, 1987), skills that require an understanding of group processes (Kurtz, 1990).

Microlevel Communication Processes

Little research attends to the interactional processes cast as central to social support groups. Burleson, Albrecht, Goldsmith, and Sarason (1994) lament that only limited research in the larger arena of social support examines "specific features of the messages through which people attempt to express different forms of social support" (p. xviii). As they point out, not all such communicative efforts are equally successful; the intent to be supportive often does not function as support. The potential for social support attempts to be ineffective or even counterproductive points to the need for research that describes, analyzes, and explains the effects of various microlevel communicative behaviors.

Few investigations of social support groups focus on group dialogue and members' messages. Taken as a whole, these investigations clarify the self-reflexive relationship between communication and the construction of community. By focusing on interaction, scholars illuminate how communication functions to create and sustain a sense of community via a worldview that binds members together. Investigators also pinpoint how a community's ideology may influence the very nature of the group's messages.

Communication Creates Community

Communication is integral to creating community, regardless of geographic boundaries. Research conducted on social support groups in residential, traditional, and computer-mediated contexts illustrates the role of communication in creating symbolic community.

Members of social support groups in residential settings have both immediate and ongoing physical proximity to each other. Adelman and Frey (1997) analyzed the supportive communication occurring in an AIDS residential community. Their study clarifies how a symbolic community emerges within a context where a physical community structure exists. Through a variety of communicative practices, members achieve "*symbolic convergence*, the sharing of a common social reality" (p. 41) and sustain a shared identity that creates community (see Bormann, 1986). For example, members share a vision of the residence as a "community where people live, not die, with AIDS" (Adelman & Frey, 1997, p. 41). The researchers also found storytelling to be a significant process for establishing community. The storytelling process, focused in this context both on successful coping and on the realities of living with illness, yields collective interpretations that help create shared norms, values, and goals.

Daniolos (1994) also analyzed the dialogue of a formal AIDS support group within a residential setting. Daniolos clarified how group themes, such as "themes of abandonment, loss of health and independence, and lack of control and great uncertainty" (p. 138), helped members to identify with one another and permitted a sense of "family" to emerge. In this case, symbolic convergence, readily seen in the form of group cohesion, emerged via the dual processes of members establishing commonality of experience while contrasting themselves with "outsiders" (including caregivers, often spoken of as intrusive and invasive).

Although residential support groups are atypical of social support groups, the processes for creating a symbolic community within them appear similar to those in traditional support group settings. For example, Cawyer and Smith-Dupre' (1995), in observing a traditional social support group for people with AIDS, family members, friends, lovers, and professional caregivers, also found storytelling to be a significant group format. In this group, storytelling functioned to establish commonality of experience and emotions and to promote relationship development, the bases for developing a symbolic community. Likewise, Cawyer and Smith-Dupre' observed in this traditional support group the insider-outsider phenomenon noted by Daniolos in a residential support group. Cawyer and Smith-Dupre' noted that members' "us and them" attitudes regarding support group members versus friends and family helped to cement the members into a symbolic community.

Establishing the cohesion necessary to develop a symbolic community is particularly difficult in AIDS groups because of members' shortened lives, the unpredictable course of the disease, and stigma (Tunnell, 1991). Daniolos (1994) noted that a "secure, non-judgmental, and accepting" communication climate was central to "promoting a sense of chosen 'family' " (p. 149). Similarly, Cawyer and Smith-Dupre' (1995) observed that characteristics of a supportive climate (i.e., self-disclosure, empathy, and spontaneous expression of emotions) dominated the talk of the AIDS support group they investigated. These observations suggest, again, the role that shared ideology plays in the interactional processes of social support groups.

In contrast to residential and traditional groups, computer-mediated social support groups lack both a physical structure and physical proximity among members. In the absence of physical proximity, on-line participants provide support exclusively via messages to create what Rheingold (1993) calls a "virtual community." An investigation by Braithwaite, Waldron, and Finn (1999) of a computer-mediated support group illustrates the centrality of communication to creating a support community. Braithwaite and colleagues coded the messages posted on a support network for people with disabilities and found that emotional (40%) and informational (32%) support behaviors dominated the messages, and that esteem support (18%) also occurred frequently. It is not surprising, given the lack of physical proximity, that network (7%) and tangible support (3%) occurred infrequently.

Ideology Influences Communication

Earlier in this chapter, I established the general significance of ideology in distinguish-

ing how social support groups function. Here, I focus directly on how ideology influences, both explicitly and implicitly, the content and processes of communication in social support groups.

Explicit influences. Ideology can influence communication explicitly by establishing themes and content that function to espouse a worldview and through storytelling that reinforces that worldview. Wright's (1997) analysis of interaction during AA meetings casts the therapeutic value of AA as occurring via a "process of reinterpreting life events through the group's world view" (p. 94). Wright discovered that the emergent interaction categories (e.g., sobriety contingent on daily changes in life and service as part of ongoing recovery) contained "shared ideology action/interaction strategies that guide the member through the various stages of the AA recovery process" (p. 99).

Similarly, Rasmussen and Capaldi (1990) clarified the processes by which AA's ideology is maintained via interaction. Using a narrative approach, they identified themes emerging in members' impromptu testimony that center around the myth of rebirth. AA members tell both the drinking story, or the degeneration process, and the sobriety story, in which the individual is transformed or reborn. Rasmussen and Capaldi contend that the contrasting themes facilitate self-acceptance dialectically by emphasizing the union of the old and new selves while reaffirming their differences and, at the same time, reinforce the importance of AA to the sobriety process.

Implicit influence. Findings from a narrative analysis by Vanderford, Arrington, and Grant (1998) illustrate how an implicit external ideology can influence communication processes in social support groups. The researchers studied parallel social support groups for men with prostate cancer and their wives ("Man to Man" and "Side by Side") and found interaction in both groups to be almost devoid of emotional content and support. This is not surprising in the light of the arguments made in this chapter regarding the devaluing of emotional expression in externally oriented social support groups. Even the lack of emotional support in the Man to Man group (which might be partially explained by gender, given that men tend to offer support more often through action than by expressing feelings; Tannen, 1990) probably is best explained by the group's external orientation. The dominance of a biomedical orientation is evident in the group's structure and content. Joint meetings begin with a lecture by a medically oriented speaker and a question-and-answer session, followed by separate meetings for men and women. The men's meetings, facilitated by a physician, invariably are dominated by information sharing. The women's meetings are similarly devoid of emotional expression. The facilitator sets the stage for an external orientation; her agenda focuses on her now-dead husband who founded these self-help groups. In a ritualistic fashion, she tells his story to open each meeting. Someone always asks about her own cancer survivorship, and she responds by disregarding her own suffering. Her story of his story functions to "glorify action and triumph over fear and disease" (Vanderford et al., 1988, p. 19) and to establish the norm of avoiding topics of vulnerability and self-interest. Following the facilitator's lead, the members define their role externally as a helper to their husbands rather than participating to "help themselves." The implicit rule of "husband-as-topic" results. The women also adhere rigidly to the rule that they must "get around the circle" in their 1-hour session; members who talk too long are prodded to move on. Thus, the group's communication processes mirror the group's implicit external ideology, one that discourages a focus on self.

In summary, although limited in number, analyses focusing on interaction in social support groups clarify relationships between macrolevel ideology and microlevel communication processes. Interaction analyses appear to be viable and valuable methods for unveiling important but elusive relationships between ideology and communicative behaviors.

THE VALUE OF SOCIAL SUPPORT GROUPS

Consistent with the larger body of literature on social support (e.g., Albrecht & Adelman, 1987a), social support groups no doubt influence members in negative as well as positive ways. Potential negative influences include relying on simplistic and authoritarian belief systems, fostering dependence, promoting learned helplessness, blaming victims, lowering self-esteem, rejecting useful expertise, reinforcing sick roles, and sanctioning destructive interaction (e.g., Albrecht & Adelman, 1987a; Albrecht, Burleson, & Goldsmith, 1994; Gartner & Riessman, 1977; Powell, 1987). Empirical evidence regarding the outcomes of social support groups, however, generally supports their efficacy.

Drawing conclusions about the efficacy of social support groups is tenuous because of the difficulty of implementing carefully controlled studies. The literature abounds with hearsay and self-serving testimony, yet the conclusion about these groups that "many people have been helped by them seems beyond dispute" (Katz & Bender, 1976b, p. 235). Extant evidence is of two major types: (a) pre-post and post hoc data reporting "effects" of participating in social support groups (much of which relies on self-reports), and (b) studies comparing the efficacy of self-help groups with other interventions and control conditions. (What constitutes a "control group," however, often amounts to members of the general population without the problem, or to people facing the same dilemma who have not availed themselves of social support groups.)

An Array of Outcomes

Empirical research has investigated a wide array of outcome variables. These range from changes in affect and cognition to changes in behavior.

Affective and Cognitive Outcomes

Advocates of social support groups describe a facilitative process that members' affective and cognitive reports confirm. Members report feeling validated (Fiske, Davis, & Horrocks, 1995) and better understood and less isolated (Potasznik & Nelson, 1984) as a result of participation. Generally, members feel both helped (e.g., Jason, 1985) and satisfied (e.g., Gottlieb, 1988; Kaye, Neary, Peters, & Feingold, 1992).

Mental health and attitudinal benefits reported by members include reduced neurotic distress (e.g., Galanter, 1988), increased hope (e.g., Wilson & Soule, 1981), reduced depression and loneliness (e.g., Redburn & Juretich, 1989), greater self-esteem (e.g., Kurtz, 1990), increased comfort in care-taking roles (e.g., Medvene & Krauss, 1989), and improved problem-solving ability (Hunka, O'Toole, & O'Toole, 1985).

Comparison- and control-group studies also show benefits for social support group members in the form of higher self-esteem (Hinrichsen, Revenson, & Shinn, 1985), a more internal health locus of control (perceived control over health outcomes), greater satisfaction with available social support (Barlow, Macey, & Struthers, 1993), greater responsibility-taking for drug misuse (Nurco, Primm, Lerner, & Stephenson, 1995), increased optimism and less preoccupation with losses (Vachon, Lyall, Rogers, Freedman-Letofsky, & Freeman, 1980), better adjustment (Gordon, Kapostins, & Gordon, 1965), and improved life satisfaction (Lieberman & Gourash, 1979).

Some studies, however, show that the benefits of social support groups are no greater than for other interventions. For example, both a cognitive behavioral approach and social support groups for depressed HIV-infected people (Kelly, Murphy, Bahr, & Kalichman, 1993) and depressed cancer patients (Evans & Connis, 1995) reduced depression, hostility, and somatization. The cancer patients who were associated with social support groups, however, showed more posi-

tive changes at a 6-month follow-up than did those experiencing the cognitive behavioral approach (Evans & Connis, 1995). Similarly, for widows, "confidant groups," consciousness-raising groups (Barrett, 1978), individual psychotherapy (Marmar, Horowitz, Weiss, & Wilner, 1988), and social support groups were equally effective in influencing self-esteem, grief, anxiety, and depression. Given their relatively lower cost, the fact that social support groups compare well with alternative treatments suggests their value.

Relatively little evidence points to negative outcomes associated with participation in social support groups. In one study, depressed postpartum mothers experienced decreases in self-confidence (Fleming, Klein, & Corter, 1992); in another, people with genital herpes became less able to cope and decreased depression less than those in a comparison group (Manne, Sandler, & Zautra, 1986).

Communication and Relational Outcomes

Proponents of social support groups argue that members learn communication skills through modeling and practice that carry over to other contexts. Members report improved communication with health professionals), with spouses (e.g., Gordon et al., 1965; Lieberman & Gourash, 1979; Wilson & Soule, 1981), in social networks (e.g., Vachon et al., 1980), and in the workplace (e.g., Weiner & Caldwell, 1983-1984).

Findings are not uniformly positive, however. For example, sexually abusive males in a communication training program, in conjunction with a social support group, became more confident about using appropriate communicative behavior than did those in social support groups alone (Wollert, 1988). Another study revealed that neither bereaved parents who participated in social support groups nor those in individual psychotherapy experienced improved relational functioning (Videka-Sherman & Lieberman, 1985).

Health Behaviors, Recovery, and Other Goal-Related Behaviors

The ultimate goal of most social support groups is behavioral and/or functional change. Numerous studies conclude, on the basis of members' reports, that such changes occur. Stronger empirical evidence from comparison- and control-group studies indicates that people with an array of diseases and disorders experience improved health and physiological function as a result of social support group participation. Similar evidence indicates that self-help groups promote health and wellness behaviors. (Table 19.1 summarizes health behavioral and functional changes associated with participating in social support groups.) The findings, however, are not unanimous. For example, marijuana-dependent adults in a social support group significantly reduced marijuana use, but no more so than those in a cognitive behavioral relapse prevention group treatment (Stephens, Roffman, & Simpson 1994). Similarly, senior citizens in a health promotion group did not improve their health behaviors compared to a control group (Lieberman & Gourash, 1979).

SETTING THE RESEARCH AGENDA

Despite some caveats, substantial evidence affirms the potential of social support groups to facilitate uncertainty management that results in health-benefiting outcomes. Furthermore, the literature suggests that communication is the primary means by which community is created and sustained in social support groups. Thus, it seems clear that communication research on social support groups has much explanatory and pragmatic potential. A better understanding of directions for future research on communication in these groups begins with an examination of limitations in the extant literature.

Limitations in the Literature

The assumed effectiveness of social support groups has influenced both the dominant research question and the research paradigm. The dominant implicit research hypothesis in the extant literature is this: "Social support groups are effective." The almost exclusive focus on outcomes has yielded a wealth of anecdotal and case study assessments while neglecting basic systematic description, theory development, and theory-driven research. That focus also has oriented researchers toward a "black box" or "input-output" model that neglects potentially potent group process areas, such as the nature of group interaction associated with particular inputs and/or outcomes. In turn, critics have tended to judge the literature via a hypothetico-deductive approach that relies on the criteria associated with experimental and quasi-experimental designs, while ignoring alternative explanatory paradigms.

The Absence of Theory

Assuming that social support groups are effective in facilitating constructive change among members, the question of how they function to effect change remains open. The few attempts to place social support groups into a larger theoretical framework have focused on the individual as the unit of analysis, with an emphasis on psychological rather than social phenomena. The larger body of social support literature provides the general framework that social support functions to facilitate uncertainty management and, thereby, to enhance an individual's perceived control. Communication is theorized as central to those outcomes, yet how support groups facilitate uncertainty management remains unclear. The few scholars who have proposed alternative theoretical frameworks focus on *individual* rather than *group* change. They offer a series of change mechanisms to explain social support group functioning (e.g., altruism, catharsis, imitative behavior, empowerment, interpersonal learning, identification, and self-understanding) (Kurtz, 1997), yet a unified group framework is absent.

Although few studies have been based on theory, some scholars have discussed an array

Table 19.1 Health Behavior and Functional Change Associated With Social Support Group Participation

Change	Members	Source
Case study self-reports		
Greater abstinence	Alcoholics	Kurtz (1990)
Reduced abuse	Abusive parents	Kurtz (1990)
Eating foods previously avoided; fewer dental visits	Denture wearers	Fiske, Davis, and Horrocks (1995)
Fewer symptoms, less use of professional services, fewer and shorter hospitalizations, less taking of medication	Psychiatric patients	Galanter (1988), Kurtz (1988)
Comparison and control group studies		
Compliance with exercise programs	Ankylosing spondylitis patients	Barlow, Macey, and Struthers (1993)
Improvement in joint tenderness	Rheumatoid arthritis patients	Shearn and Fireman (1985)
Fewer and shorter hospitalizations	Mental patients	Edmunson, Bedell, Archer, and Gordon (1982)
Increased longevity	Metastasized breast cancer patients	Spiegel (1993)
Greater abstinence	Smokers	Gruder, Mermelstein, Kirkendol, and Hedeker (1993)
Reduced substance abuse	Alcohol and cocaine users	McKay, Alterman, McLellan, and Snider (1994)
Less use of alcohol and psychotropic drugs	Widows	Lieberman and Videka-Sherman (1986)
Greater weight control	Obese people	Perri, McAdoo, McAllister, Lauer, and Yancy (1986)
Improved cardiovascular function, greater weight loss, less percentage body fat, less chronic tension, lower blood pressure	Obese people	Clifford, Tan, and Gorsuch (1991)
Greater contact with infants	Mothers of premature babies	Minde, Shosenberg, Marton, Thompson, Ripley, & Burns (1980)
Reduced risky sexual behavior	Depressed HIV patients	Kelly, Murphy, Bahr, and Kalichman (1993)
More exercise, practice of safe sex	Persons with AIDS in a residential facility	Frey, Query, Flint, and Adelman (1998)
Fewer symptoms	Adults undergoing bracing or surgery for scoliosis	Hinrichsen, Revenson, and Shinn (1985)
Healthier children, 4-6 years later	New mothers	Gordon, Kapostins, and Gordon (1965)

of theories, post hoc, to explain findings. These include Social Exchange Theory, Social Comparison Theory, and theories focusing on socialization processes, social networks, and behavioral conditioning (see, for example, Powell, 1987; Wills, 1985). Typically, however, these discussions frame outcomes in social support groups in terms of personal processes, such as self-transformation (e.g., Silverman, 1992); few address how social support *groups* figure into that process.

In summary, the body of knowledge regarding social support groups is limited by the general failure of researchers to conduct theory-based research. In particular, scholars have ignored group- and process-oriented theory.

Threats to the Validity of Research

From the perspective of controlled experimental investigation, social support groups are viewed as treatments that cause outcomes. Using traditional criteria for evaluating experiments, some analysts deem this body of research rampant with limitations, to the point of being "primitive" (Riordan & Beggs, 1987, p. 428) and drawing conclusions warned as being "hazardous" (Levy, 1976, p. 315). Numerous critics identify an array of validity problems in social support group research (e.g., Jacobs & Goodman, 1989; Kurtz, 1990; Maton, 1993; Meissen & Warren, 1993), while others warn about the limitations of relying on experimental procedures.

Typical criticisms. Design, measurement, and sampling problems abound in the literature. Most researchers assume that simple association with a support group constitutes an experimental treatment; however, members vary considerably in length of participation (from a single meeting to years of multiple weekly meetings) and degree of involvement (from merely attending meetings to taking active leadership roles). Specifying the type of participation is important because some research indicates initial negative effects of social support group participation, followed by long-term improvement (Jacobs & Goodman,

1989). Other research shows a higher degree of involvement to be associated with greater benefits (e.g., Kaye et al., 1992; Kurtz, 1990). Together, these studies raise the question of what constitutes an experimental treatment within the context of social support group research.

Measurement-based criticisms of the literature include heavy reliance on anecdotal evidence, retrospective self-reports, and single-item measures. The diversity of variables measured, in conjunction with little sustained focus, adds to the difficulty of synthesizing outcomes-based research.

Sampling issues result from group members being self-selected and representing a relatively homogeneous population (typically White, middle-class, educated females) (Chesler, Barbarin, & Lebo-Stein, 1984). People who join social support groups likely value talk as a means for addressing problems, for example, women (Tannen, 1990). They may be particularly motivated or desperate, or have beliefs or personalities that play a role in their decision to join a group. Studies also are criticized both for small samples and for oversampling long-term members. High attrition rates are common in social support groups (Shaw, Cronan, & Christie, 1994); thus, sampling outcomes for long-term members likely skews results (Lieberman & Bond, 1979). In 1990, almost half of AA's new members stopped attending within 3 months (Luke, Roberts, & Rappaport, 1993), an index of the potential for sampling bias. Furthermore, what constitutes a representative sample of support *groups* is unclear when attempting to synthesize outcomes.

The limits of experimental research. Conducting carefully controlled evaluations of social support groups is difficult. Support groups operate in highly varied contexts. Culling group effects is complicated by the fact that members tend to use other interventions concurrently. Support groups also usually do not keep their own records. They tend to be open ended and protective of members' privacy and, therefore, are reluctant to be studied. Voluntary affiliation is argued to be both attractive to members and responsible for positive outcomes (Meissen & Warren, 1993). Perhaps more problematic from a traditional research perspective, standard experimental designs that rely on random assignment to interventions likely alter the nature of the membership, compromise the natural group processes, and jeopardize their potential helpfulness.

Directions for Future Research

Limitations evidenced in previous research provide road signs for future research, including the need for theory development and addressing support groups as a social phenomenon. Moreover, from a communication perspective, in which both social support and other small groups are understood as communication phenomena, communication research offers much explanatory potential.

Putting the "Group" Into Social Support Group Research

Despite the fact that social support *groups* are the phenomenon at issue, extant experimental research has not examined the group as the unit of analysis. Although a growing body of literature addresses evidence that groups provide "help," little attention has been paid to the "group" and its communication, the ostensible helping process.

Future research needs to focus on the social character of support groups by addressing concepts assumed important in the literature but not systematically observed, including cohesiveness, communication climate, members' role definitions and shifts from helpee to helper, and leadership emergence, maintenance, and contention. Not only have group communication and other process variables been ignored, but so too have group structural properties that may influence group processes and outcomes, such as size, composition, diversity, organizational structure, and stability of membership (Maton, 1993).

Putting "Communication" Into Social Support Group Research

Ironically, a literature that attributes the benefits of social support groups to their interactive nature is characterized by research that has systematically excluded investigation of communication processes. Although members report that self-disclosure, empathy, and listening are characteristic of social support group interactions, research has neglected those, as well as other, communication processes. Identifying the specific group communication processes that lead to constructive outcomes remains a task for future research.

Communication theory offers some alternative and potentially profitable frameworks for research on social support groups. Personal control theories—specifically, Uncertainty Reduction Theory (see Albrecht & Adelman, 1987b) and Problematic Integration Theory (see Ford et al., 1996)—can account for the benefits of social support groups in terms of uncertainty management that enhances individuals' perceived control. Group interaction is posited to provide the basis for cognitive reframing, skill acquisition, tangible assistance, and relational support. Although personal control theories may be extrapolated to explain the power of social support groups, such as the internal-external locus of control framework developed in this chapter, few scholars have made this extension and little research has built on it (for exceptions, see Arntson & Droge, 1987; Droge et al., 1986).

Among the most promising theories for investigating social support groups are those rooted in symbolic interactionism. These theories take the perspective that "meaning is created and sustained by interaction in the social group" (Littlejohn, 1996, p. 159). Through interaction emerge the structural features of groups (e.g., roles, norms, rules, and status hierarchy), which, in turn, help to define the group as community. Among these promising theories are Narrative Theory, Symbolic Convergence Theory, the dialectical approach, and Interactional Theory.

Both Narrative and Symbolic Convergence Theory emphasize the role of stories and scripts of actors in producing meaning and, ultimately, in creating reality. Narrative Theory (see Fisher, 1987) focuses on the process of storytelling as an important means by which reality, or a worldview, emerges to unify and coordinate human activity. Both Narrative and Symbolic Convergence Theory (see Bormann, 1986, 1996) help to clarify how members of social support groups come to share the themes, visions, values, and meanings that constitute group ideology, which, in turn, provides the foundation for the emergence of connection and community. Although limited in quantity, both narrative research (e.g., Rasmussen & Capaldi, 1990; Vanderford et al., 1998) and theme analyses rooted in Symbolic Convergence Theory (e.g., Ford, 1989) indicate the promise of these theories for explaining social support groups from a communication perspective.

A dialectical approach to investigating social support groups may be particularly helpful for integrating apparent contradictions in the literature (see Adelman & Frey, 1997). This perspective focuses on the on-going changing tensions in social support groups and how participants manage those tensions through communicative practices. A dialectical perspective might clarify the interdependence between internal and external orientations in social support groups. In fact, the very nature of support groups appears to be a dialectic: respecting diversity while sustaining a unified community. Understanding how social support groups yield both positive and negative outcomes simultaneously likely relates to the dialectical nature of these groups (see Adelman & Frey, 1997).

Finally, although not previously applied to social support groups, Interactional Theory (Watzlawick, Beavin, & Jackson, 1967), which stresses the transactional nature of communication, offers a framework for investigating relationships among messages, their functions, and the development of relationships within social systems. Interactional Theory could guide investigation into social support groups as systems (see Mabry, Chapter 3, this volume), focusing on the relational, as well as content, meanings of messages (see Keyton, Chapter 8, this volume), and how those messages sustain the group as a community-system.

Expanding the Social Support Group Movement

Because social support groups have proliferated as a grassroots movement, scholars have given little consideration to increasing their use. If they are, indeed, effective, as the literature suggests, then policymakers ought to be interested in expanding their use beyond their current application to homogeneous populations, particularly to people who often are disenfranchised by traditional human services (e.g., minorities, the elderly, and low socioeconomic populations). Although the evidence is limited, it tends to support the position that social support groups render substantial aid to specific disenfranchised populations. For example, evidence indicates that the elderly are particularly at risk for deficits in social support (Tremethick, 1997) and that social support groups can bolster the support systems of the elderly in general. The same applies to other marginalized subgroups, such as older gay people (Slusher, Mayer, & Dunkle, 1996). Other research indicates that social support groups for cancer patients provide emotional assistance, especially for minorities, who more often report that such groups help with continuing treatment (Guidry, Aday, Zhang, & Winn, 1997). The potential for social support groups to address the needs of expanded populations (i.e., especially beyond those of middle-class Whites) should be explored.

Social Support in Cyberspace

Scholars have paid scant attention to social support groups that do not occur face-to-face (e.g., telephone, radio broadcast, and computer-mediated groups) (see Jason, 1985). Rheingold (1993) contends that electronically created symbolic communities, or virtual communities, may do "just about everything that people do in real life" (p. 1), including sharing support. Their capacity for "many to many" contact creates the means to "bind isolated individuals into a community" (p. 13).

Although little is known about the effectiveness of computer-mediated support groups, several advantages relative to face-to-face encounters appear obvious. For example, computer-mediated social support groups may offer around-the-clock availability, faster response, and reduction of physical differences that often induce relational distance among people (e.g., gender, age, ethnicity, and disability) because of the absence of visual and aural cues (see Scott, Chapter 16, this volume). At the same time, the opportunity to think about what to say may encourage participation by reticent or less confident people. In addition, computer-mediated social support groups allow participation by people who live in remote areas, are too sick to leave their homes, or wish to maintain anonymity.

Garton and Wellman (1995), although focusing on task-oriented groups, summarize characteristics of electronically mediated groups that may make them more or less effective than face-to-face groups. Those characteristics include status equalization, reduced nonverbal cues, lowered inhibitions regarding message content and language, and enhanced difficulty in achieving consensus. Ironically, the anonymity and distance associated with computer-mediated groups may actually make them safer environments for creative (nonconforming) efforts at being supportive (e.g., sharing poetry and using self-deprecating humor) (Braithwaite et al., 1999) as well as negative self-disclosures (e.g., a murder confession; "Man Confesses," 1998).

Limited findings indicate that on-line support groups function in important ways that are similar to face-to-face groups. For example, bulletin board "groups" have been shown to "extend the community" of hemophiliac members through messages that focus on relationship development and network solidarity while providing information, organizing

political action, enhancing psychological and physical well-being, and potentially lowering health care costs (Scheerhorn, Warisse, & McNeilis, 1995). In addition, research has shown that people with disabilities, participating in an on-line group, can gain emotional and informational support while understandably providing limited network and tangible assistance (Braithwaite et al., 1999). Given the potential of computer-mediated groups to meet otherwise unmet needs at a relatively low cost, more research needs to investigate their advantages and disadvantages relative to other sources of social support.

CONCLUSION

A phenomenon upheld as a "major trend" and emerging as "standard practice" at the close of the 20th century has yet to be taken seriously by researchers for what it is: a small group communication phenomenon. The processes presumed to make social support and self-help groups significant health-promoting vehicles, their communication processes, and the "community" or "neighborly" characteristics that mark a group rather than a collection of individuals all cry out for the attention of communication scholars.

REFERENCES

Adelman, M. B., & Frey, L. R. (1997). *The fragile community: Living together with AIDS.* Mahwah, NJ: Lawrence Erlbaum.
Adelman, M. B., Parks, M. R., & Albrecht, T. L. (1987a). Beyond close relationships: Support in weak ties. In T. L. Albrecht, M. B. Adelman, & Associates (Eds.), *Communicating social support* (pp. 126-147). Newbury Park, CA: Sage.
Adelman, M. B., Parks, M. R., & Albrecht, T. L. (1987b). Supporting friends in need. In T. L. Albrecht, M. B. Adelman, & Associates (Eds.), *Communicating social support* (pp. 105-125). Newbury Park, CA: Sage.
Albrecht, T. L., & Adelman, M. B. (1987a). Dilemmas of social support. In T. L. Albrecht, M. B. Adelman, & Associates (Eds.), *Communicating social support* (pp. 240-254). Newbury Park, CA: Sage.
Albrecht, T. L., & Adelman, M. B. (1987b). Rethinking the relationship between communication and social support: An introduction. In T. L. Albrecht, M. B. Adelman, & Associates (Eds.), *Communicating social support* (pp. 13-39). Newbury Park, CA: Sage.

Albrecht, T. L., Burleson, B. R., & Goldsmith, D. (1994). Supportive communication. In M. L. Knapp & G. R. Miller (Eds.), *Handbook of interpersonal communication* (2nd ed., pp. 419-449). Thousand Oaks, CA: Sage.

Antze, P. (1976). The role of ideologies in peer psychotherapy organizations: Some theoretical considerations and three case studies. *Journal of Applied Behavioral Science, 12*, 323-346.

Arntson, P., & Droge, D. (1987). Social support in self-help groups: The role of communication in enabling perceptions of control. In T. L. Albrecht, M. B. Adelman, & Associates (Eds.), *Communicating social support* (pp. 148-171). Newbury Park, CA: Sage.

Bales, R. F. (1944). The therapeutic role of Alcoholics Anonymous as seen by a sociologist. *Quarterly Journal of Studies in Alcohol, 5*, 267-278.

Balk, D. E., Tyson-Rawson, K., & Colletti-Wetzel, J. (1993). Social support as an intervention with bereaved college students. *Death Studies, 17*, 427-450.

Barlow, J. H., Macey, S. J., & Struthers, G. R. (1993). Health locus of control, self-help and treatment adherence in relation to ankylosing spondylitis patients. *Patient Education & Counseling, 20*, 153-166.

Barrett, C. J. (1978). Effectiveness of widows' groups in facilitating change. *Journal of Consulting & Clinical Psychology, 46*, 20-31.

Berenson, D. (1990). A systemic view of spirituality: God and Twelve Step programs as resources in family therapy. *Journal of Strategic & Systemic Therapies, 9*, 59-70.

Bormann, E. G. (1986). Symbolic convergence theory and communication in group decision-making, In L. L. Putnam & M. E. Pacanowsky (Eds.), *Communication and organizations: An interpretive approach* (pp. 219-236). Beverly Hills, CA: Sage.

Bormann, E. G. (1996). Symbolic convergence theory and communication in group decision making. In R. Y. Hirokawa & M. S. Poole (Eds.), *Communication and group decision making* (2nd ed., pp. 81-113). Thousand Oaks, CA: Sage.

Braithwaite, D. O., Waldron, V. R., & Finn, J. (1999). Communication of social support in computer-mediated groups for people with disabilities. *Health Communication.*

Brenders, D. A. (1987). Perceived control: Foundations and directions for communication research. In M. L. McLaughlin (Ed.), *Communication yearbook 10* (pp. 86-116). Newbury Park, CA: Sage.

Burleson, B. R., Albrecht, T. L., Goldsmith, D. J., & Sarason, I. G. (1994). Introduction: The communication of social support. In B. R. Burleson, T. L. Albrecht, & I. G. Sarason (Eds.), *Communication of social support: Messages, interactions, relationships, and community* (pp. xi-xxx). Thousand Oaks, CA: Sage.

Cassel, J. (1976). The contribution of the social environment to host resistance. *American Journal of Epidemiology, 104*, 107-123.

Cawyer, C. S., & Smith Dupre', A. (1995). Communicating social support: Identifying supportive episodes in an HIV/AIDS support group. *Communication Quarterly, 43*, 243-258.

Chesler, M. A., Barbarin, O. A., & Lebo-Stein, J. (1984). Patterns of participation in a self-help group for parents of children with cancer. *Journal of Psychosocial Oncology, 2*(3-4), 41-64.

Clifford, P. A., Tan, S.-Y., & Gorsuch, R. L. (1991). Efficacy in a self-directed behavioral health change program: Weight, body composition, cardiovascular fitness, blood pressure, health risk, and psychosocial medicating variables. *Journal of Behavioral Medicine, 14*, 303-323.

Cluck, G. G., & Cline, R. J. (1986). The circle of others: Self-help groups for the bereaved. *Communication Quarterly, 34*, 306-325.

Cohen, A. P. (1985). *The symbolic construction of community.* London: Routledge.

Cohen, S., & Syme, S. L. (1985). Issues in the study and application of social support. In S. Cohen & S. L. Syme (Eds.), *Social support and health* (pp. 3-22). Orlando, FL: Academic Press.

Cutrona, C. E., & Russell, D. W. (1990). Type of social support and specific stress: Toward a theory of optimal matching. In B. R. Sarason, I. G. Sarason, & G. R. Pierce (Eds.), *Social support: An interactional view* (pp. 319-366). New York: John Wiley & Sons.

Daniolos, P. T. (1994). House calls: A support group for individuals with AIDS in a residential setting. *International Journal of Group Psychotherapy, 44*, 133-152.

Dean, S. R. (1970-1971). Self-help group psychotherapy: Mental patients rediscover will power. *International Journal of Social Psychiatry, 17*, 72-78.

DiMatteo, M. R., & Hays, R. (1981). Social support and serious illness. In B. H. Gottlieb (Ed.), *Social networks and social support* (pp. 117-148). Beverly Hills, CA: Sage.

Droge, D., Arntson, P., & Norton, R. (1986). The social support function in epilepsy self-help groups. *Small Group Behavior, 17*, 139-163.

Edmunson, E., Bedell, J. R., Archer, R. P., & Gordon, R. E. (1982). Integrating skill building and peer support: The early intervention and community network development projects. In R. Slotnick & A. M. Jeger (Eds.), *Community mental health and behavioral-ecology: A handbook of theory, research and practice* (pp. 127-139). New York: Plenum.

Eggert, L. L. (1987). Support in family ties: Stress, coping, and adaptation. In T. L. Albrecht, M. B. Adelman, & Associates (Eds.), *Communicating social support* (pp. 80-104). Newbury Park, CA: Sage.

Evans, R. L., & Connis, R. T. (1995). Comparison of brief group therapies for depressed cancer patients receiving radiation treatment. *Public Health Reports, 110*, 306-311.

Fisher, W. R. (1987). *Human communication as narration: Toward a philosophy of reason, value, and action.* Columbia: University of South Carolina Press.

Fiske, J., Davis, D. M., & Horrocks, P. (1995). A self-help group for complete denture wearers. *British Dental Journal, 178*, 18-22.

Fleming, A. S., Klein, E., & Corter, C. (1992). The effects of a social support group on depression, maternal attitudes and behavior in new mothers. *Journal of Child Psychology and Psychiatry and Allied Disciplines, 33,* 685-698.

Ford, L. A. (1989). Fetching good out of evil in AA: A Bormannean fantasy theme analysis of The Big Book of Alcoholics Anonymous. *Communication Quarterly, 37,* 1-15.

Ford, L. A., Babrow, A. S., & Stohl, C. (1996). Social support messages and the management of uncertainty in the experience of breast cancer: An application of problematic integration theory. *Communication Monographs, 63,* 189-207.

Franko, D. L. (1987). Anorexia nervosa and bulimia: A self-help group. *Small Group Behavior, 18,* 398-407.

Frey, L. R., Query, J. L., Jr., Flint, L. J., & Adelman, M. B. (1998). Living together with AIDS: Social support processes in a residential facility. In V. J. Derlega & A. P. Barbee (Eds.), *HIV and social interaction* (pp. 129-146). Thousand Oaks, CA: Sage.

Galanter, M. (1988). Zealous self-help groups as adjuncts to psychiatric treatment: A study of Recovery, Inc. *American Journal of Psychiatry, 145,* 1248-1253.

Gartner, A., & Riessman, F. (1977). *Self-help in the human services.* San Francisco: Jossey-Bass.

Garton, L., & Wellman, B. (1995). Social impacts of electronic mail in organizations: A review of the research literature. In B. R. Burleson (Ed.), *Communication yearbook 18* (pp. 434-453). Thousand Oaks, CA: Sage.

Gibb, J. (1961). Defensive and supportive climates. *Journal of Communication, 11,* 141-148.

Gordon, R. D., Kapostins, E. E., & Gordon, K. K. (1965). Factors in postpartum emotional adjustment. *Obstetrical Gynecology, 25,* 156-166.

Gottlieb, B. H. (1988). Marshaling social support: The state of the art in research and practice. In B. H. Gottlieb (Ed.), *Marshaling social support: Format, processes, and effects* (pp. 11-51). Newbury Park, CA: Sage.

Gruder, C. L., Mermelstein, R. J., Kirkendol, S., & Hedeker, D. (1993). Effects of social support and relapse prevention training as adjuncts to a televised smoking-cessation intervention. *Journal of Consulting & Clinical Psychology, 61,* 113-120.

Guidry, J. J., Aday, L. A., Zhang, D., & Winn, R. J. (1997). The role of informal and formal social support networks for patients with cancer. *Cancer Practice, 5,* 241-246.

Halperin, D. (1987). The self-help group: The mental health professional's role. *Group, 11,* 47-53.

Hildingh, C., Fridlund, B., & Segesten, K. (1995). Social support in self-help groups, as experienced by persons having coronary heart disease and their next of kin. *International Journal of Nursing Studies, 32,* 224-232.

Hinrichsen, G., Revenson, T., & Shinn, M. (1985). Does self-help help? An empirical investigation of scoliosis peer support groups. *Journal of Social Issues, 41,* 65-87.

Humphreys, K. (1996). World view change in Adult Children of Alcoholics/Al-Anon self-help groups: Restructuring the alcoholic family. *International Journal of Group Psychotherapy, 46,* 255-263.

Hunka, C. D., O'Toole, A. W., & O'Toole, R. (1985). Self-help therapy in Parents Anonymous. *Journal of Psychosocial Nursing & Mental Health Services, 23,* 24-32.

Hunter, A. (1974). *Symbolic communities: The persistence and change of Chicago's communities.* Chicago: University of Chicago.

Jacobs, M. K., & Goodman, G. (1989). Psychology and self-help groups: Predictions on a partnership. *American Psychologist, 44,* 536-545.

Jason, L. A. (1985). Using the media to foster self-help groups. *Professional Psychology: Research and Practice, 16,* 455-464.

Karp, D. A. (1992). Illness ambiguity and the search for meaning: A case study of a self-help group for affective disorders. *Journal of Contemporary Ethnography, 21,* 139-170.

Katz, A. H. (1992). Professional/self-help group relationships: General issues. In A. H. Katz, H. I. Hedrick, D. H. Isenberg, L. M. Thompson, T. Goodrich, & A. H. Kutscher (Eds.), *Self-help: Concepts and applications* (pp. 56-60). Philadelphia: Charles Press.

Katz, A. H. (1993). *Self-help in America: A social movement perspective.* New York: Twayne.

Katz, A. H., & Bender, E. I. (1976a). Self-help groups in Western society: History and prospects. *Journal of Applied Behavioral Science, 12,* 265-282.

Katz, A. H., & Bender, E. I. (1976b). *The strength in us: Self-help groups in the modern world.* New York: New Viewpoints.

Kaye, L. W., Neary, V. A., Peters, R., & Feingold, D. (1992). *Self-help support groups for older women: Towards a national model of rebuilding elder networks* (Final report). Bryn Mawr, PA: Bryn Mawr College, Graduate School of Social Work & Social Research.

Kelly, J. A., Murphy, D. A., Bahr, G. R., & Kalichman, S. C. (1993). Outcome of cognitive-behavioral and support group brief therapies for depressed, HIV-infected persons. *American Journal of Psychiatry, 150,* 1679-1686.

Klass, D. (1982). Self-help groups for the bereaved: Theory, theology, and practice. *Journal of Religion and Health, 21,* 307-324.

Klass, D. (1988). *Parental grief: Solace and resolution.* New York: Springer.

Kurtz, L. F. (1988). Mutual aid for affective disorders: The Manic and Depressive Association. *American Journal of Orthopsychiatry, 58,* 152-155.

Kurtz, L. F. (1990). The self-help movement: Review of the past decade of research. *Social Work With Groups, 13*(3), 101-115.

Kurtz, L. F. (1997). *Self-help and support groups: A handbook for practitioners.* Thousand Oaks, CA: Sage.

Kutscher, A. (1970). Practical aspects of bereavement. In B. Schoenberg, A. C. Carr, D. Peretz, & A. H. Kutscher (Eds.), *Loss and grief: Psychological manage-*

ment in medical practice (pp. 280-297). New York: Columbia University Press.

Levy, L. H. (1976). Self-help groups: Types and psychological processes. *Journal of Applied Behavioral Science, 12*, 310-322.

Lieberman, M. A., & Bond, G. R. (1979). Problems in studying outcomes. In M. A. Lieberman, L. D. Borman, & Associates (Eds.), *Self-help groups for coping with crisis: Origins, members, and impact* (pp. 323-340). San Francisco: Jossey-Bass.

Lieberman, M. A., & Gourash, N. (1979). Effects of change groups on the elderly. In M. A. Lieberman, L. D. Borman, & Associates (Eds.), *Self-help groups for coping with crisis: Origins, members, and impact* (pp. 387-405). San Francisco: Jossey-Bass.

Lieberman, M. A., & Snowden, L. R. (1993). Problems in assessing prevalence and membership characteristics of self-help group participants. *Journal of Applied Behavioral Science, 29*, 166-180.

Lieberman, M. A., & Videka-Sherman, L. (1986). The impact of self-help groups on the mental health of widows and widowers. *American Journal of Orthopsychiatry, 56*, 435-449.

Littlejohn, S. W. (1996). *Theories of human communication* (5th ed.). Belmont, CA: Wadsworth.

Luke, D. A., Roberts, L., & Rappaport, J. (1993). Individual, group context, and individual-group fit predictors of self-help group attendance. *Journal of Applied Behavioral Science, 29*, 216-238.

Mäkëla, K., Arminen, I., Bloomfield, K., Eisenbach-Stangl, I., Bergmark, K. H., Kurube, N., Mariolini, N., Ólafsdóttir, H., Peterson, J. H., Phillips, M., Rehm, J., Room, R., Rosenqvist, P., Rosovsky, H., Stenius, K., Swiatkiewicz, G., Woronowicz, B., & Zielinski, A. (1996). *Alcoholics Anonymous as a mutual-help movement: A study in eight societies.* Madison: University of Wisconsin Press.

Man confesses murder on Internet. (1998, May 1). *The Gainesville Sun*, p. A2.

Manne, S., Sandler, I., & Zautra, A. (1986). Coping and adjustment to genital herpes: The effects of time and social support. *Journal of Behavioral Medicine, 9*, 163-177.

Marmar, C. R., Horowitz, M. J., Weiss, D. S., & Wilner, N. R. (1988). A controlled trial of brief psychotherapy and mutual-help group treatment of conjugal bereavement. *American Journal of Psychiatry, 145*, 203-209.

Maton, K. I. (1993). Moving beyond the individual level of analysis in mutual help group research: An ecological paradigm. *Journal of Applied Behavioral Science, 29*, 272-286.

McKay, J. R., Alterman, A. I., McLellan, A. T., & Snider, E. C. (1994). Treatment goals, continuity of care, and outcome in a day hospital substance abuse rehabilitation program. *American Journal of Psychiatry, 151*, 254-259.

McKnight, J. (1995). *The careless society: Community and its counterfeits.* New York: BasicBooks.

Medvene, L. J., & Krauss, D. H. (1989). Causal attributions and parent-child relationships in a self-help

group for families of the mentally ill. *Journal of Applied Social Psychology, 19*, 1413-1430.

Meissen, G. J., & Warren, M. L. (1993). The self-help clearinghouse: A new development in action research for community psychology. *Journal of Applied Behavioral Science, 29*, 446-463.

Minde, K., Shosenberg, N., Marton, P., Thompson, J., Ripley, J., & Burns, S. (1980). Self-help groups in a premature nursery: A controlled valuation. *Journal of Pediatrics, 96*, 933-940.

Mischel, M. H. (1988). Uncertainty in illness. *Image: Journal of Nursing Research, 20*, 225-232.

Mullan, F. (1992). Rewriting the social contract in health. In A. H. Katz, H. I. Hedrick, D. H. Isenberg, L. M. Thompson, T. Goodrich, & A. H. Kutscher (Eds.), *Self-help: Concepts and applications* (pp. 61-67). Philadelphia: Charles Press.

Nurco, D. N., Primm, B. J., Lerner, M., & Stephenson, P. (1995). Changes in locus-of-control attitudes about drug misuse in a self-help group in a methadone maintenance clinic. *International Journal of the Addictions, 30*, 765-778.

Perri, M. G., McAdoo, W. G., McAllister, D. A., Lauer, J. B., & Yancey, D. Z. (1986). Enhancing the efficacy of behavior therapy for obesity: Effects of aerobic exercise and a multicomponent maintenance program. *Journal of Consulting and Clinical Psychology, 54*, 670-675.

Potasznik, H., & Nelson, G. (1984). Stress and social support: The burden experienced by the family of a mentally ill person. *American Journal of Community Psychology, 12*, 589-607.

Powell, T. J. (1987). *Self-help organizations and professional practice.* Silver Spring, MD: National Association of Social Workers.

Prochaska, J. D., & Norcross, J. C. (1982). The future of psychotherapy: A Delphi poll. *Professional Psychology, 13*, 620-627.

Rasmussen, K., & Capaldi, C. (1990). The narratives of Alcoholics Anonymous: Dialectical "good reasons." In R. Trapp & J. Schuetz (Eds.), *Perspectives on argumentation: Essays in honor of Wayne Brockriede* (pp. 243-257). Prospect Heights, IL: Waveland.

Ray, E. B. (1987). Supportive relationships and occupational stress in the workplace. In T. L. Albrecht, M. B. Adelman, & Associates (Eds.), *Communicating social support* (pp. 172-191). Newbury Park, CA: Sage.

Redburn, D. E., & Juretich, M. (1989). Some considerations for using widowed self-help group leaders. *Gerontology & Geriatrics Education, 9*, 89-98.

Rheingold, H. (1993). *The virtual community: Homesteading on the electronic frontier.* Reading, MA: Addison-Wesley.

Riessman, F. (1965). The "helper" therapy principle. *Social Work, 10*(2), 27-32.

Riessman, F., & Carroll, D. (1995). *Redefining self-help: Policy and practice.* San Francisco, CA: Jossey-Bass.

Riordan, R. J., & Beggs, M. S. (1987). Counselors and self-help groups. *Journal of Counseling and Development, 65*, 427-429.

Robinson, D., & Henry, S. (1977). *Self-help and health: Mutual aid for modern problems.* London: Martin Robertson.

Rogers, C. R. (1961). *On becoming a person: A therapist's view of psychotherapy.* Boston: Houghton Mifflin.

Rotter, J. B. (1966). Generalized expectancies for internal versus external control of reinforcement. *Psychological Monographs, 80*(Whole No. 609).

Sarason, B. R., Sarason, I. G., & Pierce, G. R. (1990). Traditional views of social support and practical implications of defining and assessing social support. In B. R. Sarason, I. G. Sarason, & G. R. Pierce (Eds.), *Social support: An interactional view* (pp. 9-25). New York: John Wiley & Sons.

Scheerhorn, D., Warisse, J., & McNeilis, K. S. (1995). Computer-based telecommunication among an illness-related community: Design, delivery, early use, and functions of HIGHnet. *Health Communication, 7,* 301-325.

Shaffer, C. R., & Anundsen, K. (1993). *Creating community anywhere: Finding support and connection in a fragmented world.* New York: Putnam.

Shaffer, J.B.P., & Galinsky, M. D. (1989). *Models of group therapy* (2nd ed.). Englewood Cliffs, NJ: Prentice Hall.

Shaw, W. S., Cronan, T. A., & Christie, M. D. (1994). Predictors of attrition in health intervention research among older subjects with osteoarthritis. *Health Psychology, 13,* 421-431.

Shearn, M. A., & Fireman, B. H. (1985). Stress management and mutual support groups in rheumatoid arthritis. *American Journal of Medicine, 78*(5), 23-27.

Silverman, P. R. (1992). Critical aspects of the self-help experience. In A. H. Katz, H. I. Hedrick, D. H. Isenberg, L. M. Thompson, T. Goodrich, & A. H. Kutscher (Eds.), *Self-help: Concepts and applications* (pp. 76-89). Philadelphia: Charles Press.

Silverman, P. R., & Cooperband, A. (1975). On widowhood: Mutual help and the elderly widow. *Journal of Geriatric Psychiatry, 8*(1), 9-27.

Slusher, M. P., Mayer, C. J., & Dunkle, R. E. (1996). Gays and Lesbians Older and Wiser (GLOW): A support group for older gay people. *Gerontologist, 36,* 118-123.

Smiles, S. (1866). *Self-help: With illustrations of character, conduct, and perseverance* (2nd ed.). London: Murray.

Spiegel, D. (1993). *Living beyond limits: New hope and help for facing life-threatening illness.* New York: New York Times Books.

Stephens, R. S., Roffman, R. A., & Simpson, E. E. (1994). Treating adult marijuana dependence: A test of the relapse prevention model. *Journal of Consulting & Clinical Psychology, 62,* 92-99.

Sullivan, C. F., & Reardon, K. K. (1986). Social support satisfaction and health locus of control: Discriminators of breast cancer patients' style of coping. In M. L. McLaughlin (Ed.), *Communication yearbook 9* (pp. 707-722). Beverly Hills, CA: Sage.

Tannen, D. (1990). *You just don't understand: Women and men in conversation.* New York: William Morrow.

Tremethick, M. J. (1997). Thriving, not just surviving: The importance of social support among the elderly. *Journal of Psychosocial Nursing and Mental Health Services, 35*(9), 27-31.

Tunnell, G. (1991). Complications in group psychotherapy with AIDS patients. *International Journal of Group Psychotherapy, 41,* 481-498.

Tyler, L. E. (1980). The next twenty years. *The Counseling Psychologist, 8,* 19-21.

Vachon, M. L., Lyall, W. A., Rogers, J., Freedman-Letofsky, K., & Freeman, S. J. (1980). A controlled study of self-help intervention for widows. *American Journal of Psychiatry, 137,* 1380-1384.

Vanderford, L., Arrington, M. I., & Grant, C. H. (1998, April). *Man to Man and Side by Side, they cope with prostate cancer: Self-help and social support.* Paper presented at the Kentucky Conference on Health Communication, Lexington.

Videka-Sherman, L., & Lieberman, M. (1985). The effects of self-help and psychotherapy intervention on child loss: The limits of recovery. *American Journal of Orthopsychiatry, 55,* 70-82.

Wasserman, H., & Danforth, H. E. (1988). *The human bond: Support groups and mutual aid.* New York: Springer.

Watzlawick, P., Beavin, J. H., & Jackson, D. D. (1967). *Pragmatics of human communication: A study of interactional patterns, pathologies, and paradoxes.* New York: W. W. Norton.

Weiner, M. F., & Caldwell, T. (1983-1984). The process and impact of an ICU nurse support group. *International Journal of Psychiatry in Medicine, 13,* 63-80.

Wills, T. A. (1985). Supportive functions of interpersonal relationships. In S. Cohen & S. L. Syme (Eds.), *Social support and health* (pp. 61-82). Orlando, FL: Academic Press.

Wilson, A. L., & Soule, D. J. (1981). The role of a self-help group in working with parents of a stillborn baby. *Death Education, 5,* 175-186.

Wollert, R. (1988). An evaluation of a communications training program within a self-help group for sexually abusive families. *Community Mental Health Journal, 24,* 229-235.

Wright, K. B. (1997). Shared ideology in Alcoholics Anonymous: A grounded theory approach. *Journal of Health Communication, 2,* 83-99.

Wright, K. B. (1998, February). *The communication of social support in self-help groups.* Paper presented at the annual meeting of the Western Communication Association, Denver, CO.

Wuthnow, R. (1994). *Sharing the journey: Support groups and America's new quest for community.* New York: Free Press.

20

Communication in Organizational Work Groups

A Review and Analysis of Natural Work Group Studies

HOWARD H. GREENBAUM
Hofstra University

JIM L. QUERY, JR.
Loyola University Chicago

The importance of working in groups in organizations has never been more clear than it is at present. Taylor and Bowers (1972) vividly described the fundamental role of groups as the basic building block of organizations (see also Hackman & Walton, 1986). A large amount of both the running of daily operations and the planning of substantial organizational change is now initiated and carried out at the group or team level (Beckhard, 1969), especially in those organizations seeking to follow a participative model (Ancona, 1990). Organizational decision making, thus, has increasingly shifted from a single executive to committees, task forces, and teams charged with identifying problems, proposing solutions, and implementing policies. Within such a work environment, "A new job skill is being required of employees from line workers to executives, the ability to work cooperatively and productively in teams" (Glaser, 1994, p. 282).

Although many scholars have recognized the increasing prevalence and importance of organizational work groups (e.g., Bettenhausen, 1991; Gist, Locke, & Taylor, 1987; Greenbaum, Kaplan, & Metlay, 1988; Guzzo & Dickson, 1996; Putnam & Stohl, 1996), several "thorny" issues hinder our understanding of these seemingly vital organizational units. Perhaps the most significant problem is the lack of unifying theoretical frameworks for synthesizing the research that already has accumulated. McGrath's (1984) succinct criticism, directed at group research in general, certainly applies to research on organizational work groups: "We have become much better at gathering evidence about groups than at building good theory to help us understand it" (p. xiii). The result, according to McGrath and Altman (1966), is clear:

> Though we have a very high volume of research activity, we have not had a rapid

growth of a body of knowledge, because we are not gaining empirical evidence in a form which permits us to integrate it cumulatively with prior evidence. (p. 68)

The call for the synthesis and integration of accumulated knowledge was the impetus for this chapter. In this chapter, we present a unifying theoretical framework for understanding the research literature on communication in organizational work groups. We define an *organizational work group* as three or more persons who perceive themselves to be a work group, interact somewhat regularly together over time, and are embedded within a network of interlocking tasks, roles, and relationships that often include interacting with other work groups or individuals within and/or outside the organization (see Jablin & Sussman, 1983; McGrath, 1984).

We have three purposes for this chapter. The first is to present a general conceptual framework that provides a useful system for organizing research findings on organizational work groups. The framework proposed is fundamentally an organizing tool and, thus, should be clearly differentiated from full or mid-range substantive theory, as exemplified by Homans's (1950) theory of dynamic interrelationships of internal and external group variables, Hackman and Morris's (1975) theoretical five-dimensional framework illustrating the effects of input and process variables on group effectiveness, and McGrath's (1964, 1984) input, process, output theory of group behavior that sets the stage for testing the level of concordance of data elements relative to individual variables and variable relationships (see McGrath & Altman, 1966).

The second purpose is to use this framework or classification system to organize and analyze recent research on communication in natural organizational work groups. Finally, our third purpose is to employ the findings from this analysis to propose directions for future research on communication in organizational work groups.

A CLASSIFYING SYSTEM FOR STUDYING ORGANIZATIONAL WORK GROUP VARIABLES

The Nature of Classification Systems

Classification is the general process of grouping entities on the basis of their degree of similarity. Classification systems may be unidimensional (items classified with respect to one factor) or multidimensional (items classified with respect to multiple factors). A *typology* or *taxonomy* is a particular type of classification that provides a conceptual, multidimensional composite that typically is characterized by labels or names for the various cells (Bailey, 1994). The term taxonomy is used primarily in the biological sciences (e.g., to classify zoological or botanical species), whereas typology is used primarily in the social sciences (e.g., to classify the types of communication media employed in a survey of organizations). The classification system presented in this chapter is a typology. We first present a conceptual, multidimensional classification scheme consisting of cells or categories and then identify empirical examples (i.e., organizational group variables) relative to each of the cells.

Previous Group Behavior Classification Systems

There have been only a few attempts to articulate classification schemes for organizing the findings from research on small groups. The most notable ones are those developed by McGrath and Altman (1966), Rice (1978), and Bass (1982). We review each below.

McGrath and Altman (1966) developed a classification system consisting of 31 variable classes, which they derived from a sample of 250 studies of groups published between 1950 and 1962. Their initial approach to analyzing variables and relationships among them within any given research study consisted of classifying each research variable into six analytic categories, the totality of which was considered to be an operational definition of that variable. They found, however, that only three categories were sufficient for explaining research studies about groups: (a) object of judgment (member, group, or environment), (b) source of data (member, group, or environment), and (c) mode or type of characteristic being judged (state/condition or action/process). The 31 variable classes formed from the analysis of variables in 250 research studies were divided in terms of inputs (variables present prior to group interaction), processes (members' or group interaction), and outputs (outcomes); hence, they reflect the classification scheme of Systems Theory (see Mabry, Chapter 3, this volume).

Rice (1978) subsequently applied McGrath and Altman's (1966) classification scheme to the research literature on Fiedler's (1967) Least Preferred Co-Worker (LPC) Scale. Rice employed 11 categories to analyze relevant variables investigated in 66 randomly selected LPC studies. Five of these categories were adapted from McGrath and Altman, and six additional dimensions were developed specifically for evaluating LPC theory and research. The categories advanced by McGrath and Altman, as partially explained above, consisted of object of judgment, source of data, mode being judged, nature of the judgment task (evaluative or descriptive), and viewpoint of source (objective or subjective). The six LPC dimensions, together with formal definitions and examples, are found in earlier work by Rice (1975). This approach enabled Rice to develop a classification table of 19 variable classes to categorize the variables studied in previous LPC research. Two examples of the variable classes were "LPC person's judgments about states of other group members" and "actions of LPC person described and evaluated by others."

Rice reported that the classification scheme proved useful for organizing and evaluating the state of the existing literature on LPC theory and research. He concluded that researchers should consider using formal classification approaches to evaluate bodies of literature when developing theory.

A further utilization of McGrath and Altman's (1966) classification system is the substantive theory and model advanced by Bass (1982). Using five state/condition variable classes (members' abilities, biographical characteristics, and positions in the team, along with properties of the group and conditions imposed on the group) and two action/process variable classes (interaction processes and measures of performance) drawn from McGrath and Altman's 31-category system, Bass formulated a theory of team productivity. He then validated it by categorizing relevant empirical studies published during the time period of 1950-1980.

To our knowledge, no one has continued the valuable work initiated by McGrath and Altman (1966), Rice (1978), and Bass (1982) to classify, explain, and evaluate research conducted on organizational work groups, especially with respect to studying the role of communication in such groups. One purpose of this chapter is to remove that deficiency.

Group Variables Classification System: An Organizing Framework

The Group Variables Classification System (GVCS) was first developed by Greenbaum et al. (1988) as an assessment tool for judging the utility of 16 evaluation programs concerned with the performance of quality circles in organizations, a group method that involves employees engaging in a discussion about how to improve their organization (see Schultz, Chapter 14, this volume). The effectiveness of these quality circle evaluation programs was gauged by first determining the variables examined by a specific evaluation program, then classifying them in terms of input, process, output, and feedback (evaluations of input, process, and output variables), and finally concluding as to area of concentration and area of brief treatment or omission. Later, Kaplan and Greenbaum

Table 20.1 The Group Variables Classification System: Identification of Variable Classes[a] for the Classification of Specific Variables[b]

Variable Types	System Stages			
	Input →	Process →	Output →	Feedback →
Task variables	TI	TP	TO	TF
Member variables	MI	MP	MO	MF
Structure variables	SI	SP	SO	SF
Environment variables	EI	EP	EO	EF

NOTE: The abbreviations within the table stand for the column and row; for example, the upper left-hand entry, TI, stands for the row (Task variables, T) and column (Input, I).

a. A variable class consists of all specific variables that meet the two-dimensional data requirements of a particular variable type and a particular system stage. For example, TI, the abbreviation for Task Input, is a predesigned variable class intended to hold Task variables of the Input system stage.

b. "Specific variable" refers to the nomenclature of the actual variables employed in a research study (e.g., group cohesion).

(1991) and Greenbaum, Kaplan, and Damiano (1991) employed the GVCS to determine the central focus and areas of omission of widely used group behavior measurement instruments. Subsequently, they recognized that the system resembled McGrath's (1964) framework and could be used as a tool for organizing knowledge across studies of group dynamics and organizations.

There are three basic elements of the GVCS: (a) *system stages*—four stages of Input, Process, Output, and Feedback; (b) *group variable types*—four types within each system stage consisting of Task (i.e., characteristics linked directly to work goals, such as job difficulty and production methods), Member (i.e., attributes individuals bring to a group, such as communication competence), Structure (e.g., general group characteristics, such as group size, and social relations, such as conflict) and Environment (i.e., characteristics of other groups in the organization or external to it that can influence the group at hand, such as top management and government regulatory agencies); and (c) *variable classes*—16 classes of variables formed by the matrix of system stages and group variable types (see Tables 20.1 and 20.2).

System Stages

The arrows in Table 20.1 that connect input, process, output, and feedback variables indicate system-stage relationships, which can be thought of as system dynamics. Specifically, working from a Systems Perspective, input variables (such as members' communication style and group size) influence process variables (such as members' participation and conflict), which, in turn, influence output variables (such as member satisfaction and group productivity), and feedback variables assess the efficiency and effectiveness of the input, process, and/or output system stages (see Jarboe, 1988, regarding the tenets of input-process-output models; in this volume, see Chapters 3 [Mabry] and 12 [Pavitt]). Table 20.2 provides more detailed information about each of the four system stages by presenting the variable classes for each stage along with abbreviated definitions and illustrative variables.

Preceding the development of the GVCS, Gist et al. (1987) employed a systems-based model of group interaction to explain and evaluate empirical studies focusing on group effectiveness. In their model, inputs consisted

Table 20.2 Variable Classes, Definitions, and Illustrations of the Group Variables Classification System

Class	Definition	Illustrative Variables
Input		
Task input	Task requirements and characteristics	Task difficulty, time constraints
Member input	Member traits	Knowledge, personality, competencies
Structure input	Group conditions and status of intragroup relations	Group size, composition, cohesion
Environment input	External forces affecting group	Company policies, customer needs
Process		
Task process	Actions transforming resources	Strategies for task completion, decision-making methods
Member process	Activities of individual members	Participation, effort expended
Structure process	Interaction among group members	Communication, conflict, teamwork
Environment process	Interaction with other groups	Intergroup communication, government agency investigation
Output		
Task output	Group products	Number of ideas generated, quality of decisions
Member output	Change in members' skills or attitudes	Skills development, satisfaction, morale shift
Structure output	Group development	Change in norms, cohesiveness
Environment output	Group's influence on other groups	Change in perceived group status within an organization, development of a consumer user manual
Feedback		
Task feedback	Assessment of task input, process, output	Cost study, product quality report
Member feedback	Assessment of member input, process, output	Annual appraisal, identification of training needs
Structure feedback	Assessment of structure input, process, output	Teamwork survey
Environment feedback	Assessment of environment input, process, output	Management awards, customer comments

of group structure, group strategies, leadership, and reward allocations; processes included influence, group development, and group decision making; and outcomes included group performance, quality of work life, and members' capability of working independently in the future. No provision, however, was made for feedback as a system stage, as is done in the GVCS.

Variable Classes

The GVCS requires that each specific variable of a research study be analyzed to determine the system stage and variable type it represents. This analysis permits derivation of the variable class to which that particular variable belongs. All specific research variables are assigned to one of the 16 variable classes, and all relationships between specific variables within a given research study are reframed to reflect relationships between variable classes. For example, a finding from a research study that intergroup communication influences group productivity would call for the classification of the independent variable (intergroup communication) as Environment Process and the classification of the dependent variable (group productivity) as Task Output; the relationship is abbreviated as EP-TO. This procedure, consequently, can facilitate a review of research on groups by compressing hundreds of specific variables into the 16 variable classes.

As indicated in Table 20.2, the four Input variable classes consist of properties of the task, member(s), structure, and environment that exist prior to the occurrence of group activity. Illustrative variables include task difficulty (Task Input), members' competencies (Member Input), group composition (Structure Input), and company policies (Environment Input). The four Process variable classes consist of activities employed for the purpose of achieving task, member, structure, or environment goals. Illustrative variables include decision-making methods (Task Process), effort expended by members (Member Process), group conflict (Structure Process), and intergroup communication (Environment Process). The four Output variable classes consist of outcomes resulting primarily from input-process linkages. Illustrative variables include decision quality (Task Output), member satisfaction (Member Output), group cohesiveness (Structure Output), and the perceived status of the group by external others (Environment Output). Finally, the four Feedback classes consist of variables representing evaluations of one or more aspects of the Input, Process, or Output stages. Illustrative variables include product quality reports (Task Feedback), annual appraisal of members (Member Feedback), post–group meeting evaluations (Structure Feedback), and special management recognition of the group (Environment Feedback).

Variable-Class Relationships

The literature examining organizational group behavior provides the following three bases for classifying relationships among variable classes. First, *specific-variable relationships* show how a research variable, such as "intergroup communication," is related to another specific research variable, such as "group productivity," in an independent-dependent variable relationship, in this case as "intergroup communication influences group productivity." In state-of-the-art literature reviews, this kind of relationship generally is classified under the heading of the independent variable, in this case, intergroup communication (see Bettenhausen, 1991; Levine & Moreland, 1990).

Second, *system-stage relationships* show how variables in a research study are related in terms of Input, Process, Output, and Feedback system stages. These system dynamics suggest that input variables influence process variables, which influence output variables, which, in turn, provide the basis for various types of feedback affecting input, process, and output variables (see Table 20.1). With this approach, a study of the effects of intergroup communication on group productivity is identified as Process-Output research.

Third, *variable-class relationships* illustrate relationships between variable classes, such as Task Input and Task Output. As noted previously, once variables have been assigned to the predefined classes, resulting relationships can then be drawn between the variable classes (see Bass, 1982; Greenbaum & Kaplan, 1997; McGrath, 1964; McGrath & Altman, 1966). A research study of the effects of intergroup communication on group performance, therefore, is an Environment Process-Task Output study, or EP-TO. Discussion of the study would take place under the heading of Environment Process, the variable class containing the independent variable of intergroup communication, or under the heading of the variable-class relationship investigated in the study (i.e.,

Environment Process-Task Output; see Bass, 1982).

Eight system-stage relationships and 128 variable-class relationships can be drawn from the 16-cell GVCS. The eight system-stage relationships consist of I-P, I-O, I-F, P-O, P-F, F-I, F-P, and F-O. Each system-stage relationship has a potential of 16 variable-class relationships. For example, in the I-O system-stage relationship, Task Output is influenced by Task Input (TI-TO), Member Input (MI-TO), Structure Input (SI-TO), and Environment Input (EI-TO). Each of the Output categories, or classes of variables (Task, Member, Structure, and Environment), then, can be involved in four Input-Output relationships, one relationship with each of the Input classes. Therefore, there are 16 possibilities in the I-O system-stage relationships. For the eight system-stage relationships, there are 128 potential variable-class relationships.

In the next section, we use this conceptual framework as the basis for a multiyear analysis of research about communication in natural work groups. We then employ the findings from this analysis to set directions for future communication research on natural work groups.

A GVCS ANALYSIS OF NATURAL WORK GROUP ARTICLES WITH COMMUNICATION VARIABLES, 1993–1995

We present in this section research on communication in natural organizational work groups published in journals from 1993 to 1995 and indicate research findings in terms of topical areas (e.g., decision making/problem solving) and GVCS variable classes and system-stage relationships. This approach includes identification of the communication variables in this body of research, which facilitates an evaluation of the state of the literature along with the identification of areas that may deserve more or less attention from researchers, as well as providing an initial basis for judging

the merits of the GVCS as an explanatory research tool.

Consistent with these goals, we first indicate the policy guidelines for the literature surveyed. Second, we explain the application of the methodology, including data sources and methods for collecting and processing them. Third, we present the findings, both in general topical and GVCS classification format, for the identified group studies dealing with communication variables.

Policy Guidelines for the Survey of Literature

Time Period Covered

We designated the 3-year span of 1993-1995 as the publication period of interest. At the project's inception, the 1995 data were from the last complete year for which published journal information was available on the PsychLit and ERIC computerized databases. We chose a 3-year period because it was comparable to time periods utilized in recent state-of-the-art reviews (e.g., Bettenhausen, 1991, Levine & Moreland, 1990).

Type of Study Selected

The organizational work group was the central unit of interest and, thus, literature involving other types of groups (e.g., therapy groups, social support groups, and juries) was excluded from consideration. Because of the extensive number of articles on organization work groups in general, we concentrated on field studies and field experiments (i.e., those that focused on work groups operating in the natural environment of an organization), of which there were 83. This choice was strongly influenced by the widespread call across disciplinary lines for more externally valid research about groups. For instance, Shaw (1981) argued that it would be helpful to compare results from laboratory studies with those obtained from field-based studies. Cragan and Wright (1990) concluded that "there is a great need for research that takes existing small group communication theory and demonstrates its utility to small group problems in applied (natural) settings" (p. 228). Frey (1994c) issued a similar and cogent observation: "Only by studying groups in their natural environment can researchers produce contextually sensitive insights" (p. 556; see also Frey 1994a, 1994b, 1995). Finally, drawing from earlier reviews by Poole (1990) and Sykes (1990), Propp and Nelson (1996) concluded that "most critics today agree that if small group communication research is to have real-world significance, it must be based on the study of natural groups" (p. 35).

Journals Reviewed

Various library databases, such as PsychLit and ERIC, were searched to locate relevant articles, and when the information furnished from the article abstract did not provide sufficient data, we had recourse to the actual journal containing the particular article. Almost 90 journals provided relevant articles that represented work in most of the social sciences.

Use of Article Abstracts

Because of the extensive nature of this investigation, covering all the social sciences, our general procedure was to utilize article abstracts to the extent possible. The original article was consulted only when one or more of the following occurred:

1. The abstract did not clearly indicate the specific research variables studied,
2. Unusual terminology appeared in the abstract and was not fully defined therein,
3. Relationships between variables were not stated in understandable terms, or
4. The abstract was not at the beginning of the article.

Approximately 10% of the selected research studies required the acquisition of the full article for one of these reasons.

The use of abstracts to review literature has proven valuable in other contexts. For example, Scheerhorn, Geist, and Teboul (1994) used *Communication Abstracts* to document the types of communicative episodes studied in the group communication research literature. Hare (1976) used a somewhat similar strategy to examine group research indexed in *Psychological Abstracts* from 1927 to 1974 and *Sociological Abstracts* from 1953 to 1974.

Methodology Applied to the 1993–1995 Selected Studies

Once the studies of natural work groups were selected, procedures for accomplishing the project entailed analyzing each study, establishing intercoder reliability for the GVCS coding of variables and relationships contained therein, and identifying the studies evidencing communication research. Each of these steps is explained below.

Analysis of Individual Research Studies

Each of the studies was analyzed to derive the following information: (a) author(s), publication year, bibliographical reference, and article abstract; (b) the central topic studied (e.g., leadership); (c) names of independent, dependent, and moderating (i.e., a variable that influences an independent-dependent relationship) variables specific to the research; (d) the GVCS variable class for each of the variables; and (e) GVCS variable-class relationships. Thus, for a specific variable, such as group members' communication style, the variable class generally would be Member Input (MI). This determination required the designation of two dimensions: system stage (Input, Process, Output, or Feedback) and variable type (Task, Member, Structure, or Environment). Coders then ascertained the variable-class relationships between variables. For example, the effects of members' communication style on group effectiveness was categorized as Member Input-Task Output, or simply MI-TO.

Establishment of Intercoder Reliability

Working independently, each of the authors analyzed the 83 natural work group studies for the specific research variables, the particular variable class for each research variable, and the relationship of that variable class to other variable classes in the particular study. Across the 83 studies, each of the investigators made a total of 341 decisions for each of the three areas of specific variable identification, GVCS variable class, and GVCS relationships of variable classes. This process yielded a total of 1,023 decisions per coder. Across the three areas, the coders agreed 97.1%, 98.2%, and 98.5% of the time, based on Holsti's (1969) intercoder reliability formula. Wimmer and Dominick (1994), addressing the issue of an acceptable level of intercoder reliability, note that "as a rule of thumb, most published content analyses typically report a minimum reliability coefficient of about 90% when using Holsti's formula" (p. 180). Hence, we considered reliability to be sufficiently high to warrant continuation.

Identification of Studies About Communication in Work Groups

Our basic strategy for isolating the research on communication in organizational work groups from the larger sample of 83 studies was to determine whether any variables in each article could be construed as communication based, that is, as focusing on some aspect of message behavior. This analysis yielded 55 studies of communication in natural work groups (see Appendix). Although few of the articles included the word "communication" in the title, part of or all the article's content was considered to be about communication in natural work groups.

FINDINGS OF THE SURVEY AND GVCS APPLICATION

The findings of this investigation of studies of communication in natural work groups are presented in six sections. The first few sections focus on the research settings of the general articles on work groups, frequency of topics, and research functions of the communication variables studied. The remaining sections address the findings with respect to system-stages and system-stage variable types, the 16 variable classes, and system-stage variable relationships within topical areas.

Research Settings of Articles on Work Groups

The investigation of the literature covering the 3-year period resulted in the selection of 311 articles from 88 journals relevant to the subject of organizational work group behavior. The relative frequencies of the different research settings were as follows: 47% laboratory experiments, 27% field studies and field experiments, 20% theoretical studies, 3% meta-analytic studies, and 3% studies about measurement issues. These figures show that the laboratory experiment was by far the most prevalent type, with about 1.8 such studies for each natural work group study (i.e., field experiments/studies). It is noteworthy that 74% of the published studies were empirical, with about two thirds of those being laboratory experiments and one third being field experiments/studies.

Frequency of Topics in Studies of Natural Work Groups With Communication Variables

Table 20.3 presents the 13 topics researched in the 55 studies of communication in natural groups. The topics are listed in order of highest frequency: leadership (10), decision making/problem solving (9), communication and communication media (7), feedback (6), participation (6), meetings/group interaction (5), conflict management (4), training (4), intergroup communication (3), communication technology (3), voting systems (3), creativity/innovativeness (3), and equity (2). Total topics numbered 65 (10 articles included two communication topics; for example, article 49 appears under intergroup

Table 20.3 Natural Organizational Work Group Literature, 1993-1995: Group Communication Topics, Frequencies, and Bibliographic References

Communication Topics	Frequencies	Bibliographic References
Leadership	10	02, 07, 11, 17, 24, 26, 27, 32, 35, 44
Decision making/problem solving	9	03, 10, 20, 26, 36, 37, 40, 41, 45
Communication/communication media	7	14, 19, 27, 29, 40, 44, 47
Feedback	6	01, 12, 13, 22, 28, 46
Participation	6	15, 18, 33, 48, 49, 55
Meetings/group interaction	5	05, 34, 43, 51, 53
Conflict management	4	20, 21, 31, 50
Training	4	06, 30, 39, 42
Intergroup communication	3	16, 38, 49
Communication technology	3	09, 25, 54
Voting systems (including consensus)	3	13, 23, 34
Creativity/innovativeness	3	04, 08, 52
Equity (fairness and bias)	2	12, 31
Total number of topics	65	

NOTE: The full bibliographical reference for each article appears in the Appendix, which is indexed numerically and alphabetically. Certain articles included in the above table contained more than one topic; hence, the total number of topics is more than the number of articles.

communication and again under participation). In addition to listing the topics, Table 20.3 identifies the bibliographic reference numbers that relate to each, so that for the topic of intergroup communication, for instance, with a frequency of 3 articles, the appropriate references are 16, 38, and 49 (see Appendix).

Research Functions of Communication Variables

The 55 articles revealed 97 specific variables related to communicative behavior. Each of the variables was examined for its function in the particular study with respect to whether it was independent, dependent, or moderating. This was important for differentiating studies that concentrated on the influence of communication on other variables (i.e., communication as an independent variable) from those concerned with variables affecting a given communication variable (i.e., communication as a dependent variable) and those

examining the effect of a communication variable on an independent-dependent variable relationship (i.e., communication as a moderating variable). For all 13 topic areas, communication was an independent variable 50% of the time, a dependent variable 37% of the time, and a moderating variable 13% of the time (see Table 20.4).

These overall figures for all studies held to a great extent when examining each of the 13 individual topic areas. Some differences, however, did emerge. Specifically, intergroup communication was employed solely as an independent variable; 5 of the 13 topic areas (conflict management, training, intergroup communication, voting systems, and creativity) did not study communication as a moderating variable; and four of the topic areas (communication/communication media, meetings/group interaction, participation, and training) ran counter to the general averages by having the communication variable functioning as a dependent variable more frequently than as an independent variable.

Table 20.4 Research Functions of Communication Variables by Variable Type and System Stage

Variable Type	Research Function	System Stages				
		Input	Process	Output	Feedback	Total
Task	IV	2	4	0	3	9
	DV	0	3	8	0	11
	MV	0	1	0	2	3
Member	IV	4	2	0	2	8
	DV	0	3	4	1	8
	MV	2	3	0	0	5
Structure	IV	18	6	0	3	27
	DV	0	10	6	1	17
	MV	1	3	0	0	4
Environment	IV	4	0	0	0	4
	DV	0	0	0	0	0
	MV	0	1	0	0	1
Total	IV	28	12	0	8	48 (49.5%)
	DV	0	16	18	2	36 (37.1%)
	MV	3	8	0	2	13 (13.4%)
Total number of research variables		31	36	18	12	97 (100.0%)

NOTE: IV = independent variable, DV = dependent variable, and MV = moderating variable.

System Stages and System-Stage Variable Types

Table 20.5 indicates the system stages (Input, Process, Output, and Feedback) and system-stage variable types (Task, Member, Structure, and Environment) represented by the 97 communication variables in the 55 natural group research studies. First, with respect to the four system stages, 32% of the variables were classified as Input, 37% as Process, 19% as Output, and 12% as Feedback. Thirty-six of the communication variables were Process variables, indicators of behaviors or actions; 31 were Input variables and 18 were Output variables, both indicative of states or conditions; and 12 were Feedback variables, those that evaluated Input, Process, or Output variables.

Second, in respect to system-stage variable types, 23.7% of all variables were classified as Task, 21.6% as Member, 49.5% as Structure, and 5.2% as Environment. The Structure variable type accounted for almost 50% of all communication variables; Task and Member variable types had 24% and 22% of all variables; and Environment variables had the lowest level of frequency, with just 5% of all variables.

As a result of the large percentage of communication-related variables classified as

Table 20.5 System Stages, Variable Types, and Variable Classes of Communication Variables in 1993-1995 Natural Organizational Work Group Research Studies

Variable Types	System Stages				
	Input	Process	Output	Feedback	Totals
Task	2	8	8	5	23 (23.7%)
Member	6	8	4	3	21 (21.6%)
Structure	19	19	6	4	48 (49.5%)
Environment	4	1	0	0	5 (5.2%)
Totals	31	36	18	12	97
Percentage	32.0	37.1	18.6	12.4	100.0%

Structure (49.5%), that subcategory of system-stages was further investigated. We found that this subcategory could be usefully analyzed in terms of Organizational Structure (e.g., leadership and group policies), Social Structure (e.g., group interpersonal relations, conflict, and cooperation), and Physical Structure (group size, group composition, group space, and facilities). On that basis, Organizational Structure accounted for 26.8%, Social Structure for 18.6%, and Physical Structure for 4.1% of the communication variables.

Examination of individual topic areas indicated that the above-noted popularity of the Structure variable type was true of most topic areas, with the exception of participation, training, and intergroup communication. The least popular variable type, Environment, was absent from 11 of the 13 topic areas. The two areas credited with Environment research were training and intergroup communication.

Popularity of the 16 Variable Classes

Examination of Table 20.5 permits further breakdowns in terms of the 16 GVCS variable classes. Structure Process and Structure Input, each with 19 variables (19.6%), were the most popular variable classes. The least popular variable classes, those with less than 5% of all communication variables, included Member Feedback, 3 variables (3.1%); Member Output, 4 variables (4.1%); Structure Feedback,

4 variables (4.1%); Task Input, 2 variables (2.1%); and all the Environment variable classes of Environment Input, 4 variables (4.7%), Environment Process, 1 variable (1%), and Environment Output and Environment Feedback, each with no communication variables.

In the intermediate range of variable-class activity, defined as greater than 5% of communication variables and less than the 19.6% level of the two leading classes, were the following six variable classes: Member Process, Task Process, and Task Output, each with 8 variables (8.2%); Member Input and Structure Output, each with 6 variables (6.2%); and Task Feedback, with 5 variables (5.2%).

In summary, the two most active variable classes of Structure Process and Structure Input, accounting for 12.5% of the GVCS model variable classes, had almost 40% of the communication variables; the six intermediate activity variable classes, accounting for 37.5% of the GVCS model variable classes, encompassed 42%; and the eight least active variable classes, accounting for 50% of the GVCS model variable classes, had only 18% of the communication variables.

System-Stage Relationships Within Topic Areas

Table 20.6 presents a system-stage analysis of the 55 work group studies under review.

(continued)

Table 20.6 System-Stage Relationships of Communication Variables in 1993–1995 Natural Work Group Research Studies

			Relationships & Article Reference Numbers					
Topic	Number of Articles	Number of Relationships	Input-Process	Input-Output	Input-Feedback	Process-Output	Process-Feedback	Feedback-Output
Leadership	10	15	11 27	02 07 11 17 24 27 32 35 44	27	11 24 26		
Decision making/problem solving	9	12	41	10 36 37 40 41 45		03 10 20 26 45		
Communication/communication media	7	11	19 27	14 27 29 40 44	27	14 29 47		
Feedback	6	9		12 46		22	28	
Participation	6	9	48 55	18 33 48 49		15 18 55		
Meetings/interaction	5	7	51	34 43 53		34 53		05

Table 20.6 System-Stage Relationships of Communication Variables in 1993–1995 Natural Work Group Research Studies (Continued)

Topic	Number of Articles	Number of Relationships	Relationships & Article Reference Numbers					
			Input-Process	Input-Output	Input-Feedback	Process-Output	Process-Feedback	Feedback-Output
Conflict management	4	6	31	21 31		20 50 31		
Training	4	6	06 30	39 42		42 30		
Intergroup communication	3	5	38 16	38 49		16		
Communication technology	3	7		09 25 54		09 25 54		25
Voting types	3	4		34		23 34		13
Creativity	3	6		04[a] 04 08 52		04 52		
Equity	2	3	31	12				12
Totals	65	100	14	44	2	30	1	9
Percentage		100	14	44	2	30	1	9

NOTE: The reference numbers in this table correspond to numbers in the Appendix to this chapter, where complete bibliographical information for each of the 55 research studies under review is listed.

a. This article was coded as having two distinct I-O relationships.

Results are shown under the 13 communication topic headings previously discussed. The following results were found for the 100 total relationships observed: 44% Input-Output, 30% Process-Output, 14% Input-Process, 9% Feedback-Output, 2% Input-Feedback, and 1% Process-Feedback. Within the 13 topic areas, it generally was the case that Input-Output studies were equal to or greater than the total of Input-Process and Process-Output studies, and Input-Process research was less than Process-Output investigations. This survey also uncovered no studies of the influence of Feedback on Input or Process variables.

IMPLICATIONS, CRITIQUE, AND FUTURE DIRECTIONS

That organizational work groups would attain a pervasive and powerful position throughout U.S. society was forecast more than 40 years ago by Whyte (1956) and is widely evidenced today. What Whyte did not foresee, however, were the various and often disparate paths that the study and understanding of organizational work groups would take across the disciplinary fields of Group Dynamics, Organizational Studies, and Group Communication. To untangle some of the conceptual underbrush, we have described the nature of such groups, explicated key perspectives that guide research on these groups, and advanced a model to help synthesize some of the findings from various lines of disciplinary scholarship. We now interpret the findings, identify key implications, critique our study, and suggest directions for future research.

Interpretations and Implications of Research Findings

Research Settings

Despite the previously identified calls for more externally valid group research, our findings indicated that laboratory studies of organizational work groups still outnumber field studies and field experiments at a 1.8 to 1 ratio. Furthermore, among the original pool of 311 studies, 74% were empirical, with two thirds of these being laboratory experiments and one third being field studies. Although these figures are somewhat disconcerting in terms of responding to the need for increased generalizability, they do show a marked improvement from the much larger laboratory-to-field study ratio reported in McGrath and Altman's (1966; see p. 51)[1] review of the literature.

Several explanations could account for this increase in field research. For instance, it could be that investigators have realized that tightly controlled research designs conducted in the laboratory are often not the most effective for understanding the fluid and often apparently seamless nature of "real-life" groups (especially those in organizations; see Clegg & Hardy, 1996), the rich variety of natural organizational work groups (see Cohen & Bailey, 1997), and the spiraling use of new communication channels and technologies, such as videoconferencing and the Internet, by such groups (see Shulman, 1996; see also Scott, Chapter 16, this volume). It is also possible that a growing number of investigators, intent on helping organizational decision makers address complex and pressing problems, are opting for social action-oriented, field-based research. This type of research facilitates building rich contextual theories that subsequently can inform problem-specific interventions.

Research Topics

As noted previously, 55 of the 83 natural work group studies were deemed to be communication based. This level of activity is somewhat encouraging, as it suggests a recognition of the importance of examining message behavior across disciplinary lines of inquiry to better understand the nature of groups. Scholars may, thus, be recognizing that communication is a central process that helps members of organizational work groups to organize, interpret reality, coalesce, and avoid entropy (see Kreps, 1980; Weick, 1969, 1979). Stohl and Redding (1987) summarized the importance of communication in the organizational context succinctly: "It is an axiom that organizations cannot exist without communication" (p. 451).

The findings also reveal that across a variety of organizational settings—military, manufacturing, and law enforcement, as well as research and development organizations—there appears to be some consensus on the five most important communication topics to study (constituting 58% of the identified topics): leadership, decision making/problem solving, communication/communication media, feedback, and participation. Some of these, such as leadership, decision making/ problem solving, and communication, are classic variables that historically have interested group communication scholars; others, such as feedback and perhaps participation, reflect variables that play particularly important roles in work groups embedded within organizations; and still others, such as communication media, may reflect the interface of contemporary, general group communication interests and the specific interest in the organizational context where such media are most likely to be used.

On closer scrutiny, however, there is a troubling side to this body of research. As noted earlier, only a few of the 55 articles included the word "communication" in the title. More alarming is that few of these studies privileged communication as the central process of work group creation, maintenance, and termination. For example, key group outcomes, such as the occurrence of groupthink/risky shifts or the development of group cohesion, were most often evaluated in terms of individual psychological and/or societally-based origins, and not with respect to being outcomes that result from communication processes. Perhaps, too, the glossing over of the role of communication in groups could be due to the marked focus on outcomes per se, as opposed to focusing specifically on group interaction. As Davis (1986) lamented, "The overwhelming research interest in group-level outcomes (perhaps not too surprising, given that the research target is indeed the task-oriented

group) has overshadowed or at least deflected attention from interaction processes" (p. 10). Pavitt (Chapter 12, this volume) describes a similar pattern in the study of communication and group leadership.

At this juncture, it is tempting to suggest that scholars in other disciplines, such as Psychology and Sociology, and lines of inquiry, such as Group Dynamics and Organizational Studies, concentrate on communication as a common focal point. Such a response would be a disservice to these academic fields and, ultimately, key publics. As the nature of organizations, and the groups within them, continue to change and develop, accompanying levels of equivocality and flux can best be managed and understood when organizational work groups are examined from a variety of intellectual perspectives. It also would be naive to suggest that a coming together would be beneficial if only communication were the primary focus.

What, then, should occur? Skilled and apprentice navigators—scholars, practitioners, and students—should seek the important common markers along the paths traveled by work groups and the central processes that unify them. Communication scholars, in particular, must be ready and able to articulate what it is that we do, as well as apply our perspective of focusing on message behavior to the study of organizational work groups. Such a process should help to demonstrate how communication research can better inform theory building and testing in other disciplines, as well as how it is distinct from, yet compatible with, research conducted in other academic fields.

Research Functions of Communication Variables

Across the 13 topic areas, communication was an independent variable 50% of the time, a dependent variable 37% of the time, and a moderating variable 13% of the time. It is not surprising that communication has been operationalized so frequently as an independent variable. As Jarboe reports, "Process-output models look at communication as the major independent variable(s)" (1988, p. 121). This approach positions communication as occupying a prominent role as a variable that makes a difference in these groups. As Jarboe aptly argues, however, on closer examination, process-output models may pose some problems, especially with regard to controlling for demand characteristics that can cloud the evaluation of the impact of process variables on outputs, especially in cross-sectional studies. For example, when communication efficacy (a process variable) is operationalized as an independent variable, there is conflicting evidence concerning its positive influence on the quality of group outputs (see Hirokawa, 1990). Thus, high levels of communication efficacy can potentially contribute to a variety of group outcomes, but they offer no guarantee of effective group performance. Although this is true for groups in general, it is especially the case for organizational work groups, which are influenced by myriad other factors, such as organizational goals, resources, and culture. Hence, the positioning of certain types of communication processes in the independent variable role will not always translate into favorable, demonstrable outcomes.

In the light of the interdisciplinary study of organizational work groups, it is also not especially remarkable that communication frequently has been operationalized as a dependent variable. For example, Lee and Jablin (1995) examined the impact of the interaction situation—routine, deteriorating, or escalating—on group maintenance communicative behaviors. This type of approach, classified in the GVCS as Structure Input-Structure Process (SI-SP), tends to be somewhat consistent with a mechanistic view of communication (see Fisher, 1978) that assesses the impact of situations on communication processes in terms of their enabling and blocking characteristics; subsequent interventions then seek to maximize the enablers and eradicate the blockers. Not all SI-SP studies, however, operationalize communication as a mechanistic dependent variable. For example, Sias and Jablin (1995), examining relationships among

differential manager-employee relations, employees' perceptions of the fairness of their managers, and coworker communication, found that differential treatment of employees by managers influenced the communication engaged in among coworkers. The researchers concluded that employees' perceptions are often socially constructed by work group members through discourse. This study, thus, focused on communication in organizational work groups from an interpretive-symbolic perspective (see Krone, Jablin, & Putnam, 1987).

By pinpointing the philosophical approach underlying the operationalization of communication as a dependent variable, it also may be possible to ascertain the extent to which a study reflects either a "container metaphor" of a group, in which only internal group processes are of concern, or the Bona Fide Groups Perspective, which emphasizes the permeability of group boundaries and the interactive effects of the external environment on internal processes in groups and vice versa (see Putnam & Stohl, 1990, 1994, 1996; in this volume, see Chapters 1 [Gouran] and 2 [Poole]). Communication plays a dominant role in this view in helping group members to continually "define their boundaries and negotiate relationships with their context" (Putnam & Stohl, 1996, p. 149). In general, studies adopting a mechanistic view are in concert with the container metaphor; studies employing an interpretive-symbolic approach are congruent with the Bona Fide Groups Perspective.

Other researchers have cast communicative behavior in the role of a moderating variable, one that influences an independent-dependent variable relationship. For example, Innami (1994) examined the role of group communication as an independent variable (classified as SP) on the dependent variable of quality of group decisions (classified as TO; see also Keller, 1994) while also studying the influence of two moderating variables, members' reasoning orientation (classified as MP) and attitudinal positions on organizational issues (classified as MP). The results showed that the quality of group decisions increased to the extent that members exchanged facts and reasons (reasoning orientation) and decreased to the extent that members did not change their positions (positional orientation). Although the use of communication as a moderating variable across all the studies was only 13%, it suggests a positive pattern in which researchers are seeking to better tease out the multidimensional and dispersed effects of communication relative to an array of group input, process, and output variables. As research designs continue to evolve to better address the many facets of group interaction, it is reasonable to expect that studies viewing communication processes as a moderating variable will increase.

System Stages, Variables Type, and System-Stage Relationships

The findings indicated that the system stage studied the most was Process, which contained 37% of the 97 communication variables. In particular, such process variables as "interaction among group members" and "activities of individual members" were investigated significantly more than chance alone would predict. Closely following this level of activity were the communication variables residing within the Input stage (32%). This finding is consistent with the large number of previous studies that have employed Input-Output models (see Jarboe, 1988). Investigators thus appear to be continuing to examine "how significant input variables (typically psychological or situational constraints) affect group communication and outcomes" (Frey, 1996, p. 29). One example from the studies reviewed in this chapter is that of Jehn (1995), who examined the extent to which task-related and relationship-related intragroup conflicts (TI and SI, respectively) affected group performance (TO), as influenced by three moderating variables of task type, group interdependence, and conflict norms. By studying various moderator variables, this study positioned communication not only as an independent variable but also as a moderating variable. Such studies may help to identify variables worthy of investigation that ultimately lead to better explanatory power for understanding the effects of various inputs on outcomes (i.e., Input-Output models) by also gauging the effects of other inputs on the processes that those original inputs subsequently become (i.e., Input-Process models).

The results for the system stages of Output (19%) and Feedback (12%) show that a small, yet promising, shift has begun that supplants a prior pattern of emphasizing outputs as the be-all and end-all of group communication. One explanation for such movement is that researchers, particularly with respect to studying feedback variables, may be starting to embrace and examine the reflexive nature of outputs on group communication. As Poole and Hirokawa (1996) explain, "Most process theorists would argue that there is a recursive relationship such that outcomes 'loop back' to influence group processes and some exogenous variables" (p. 15). As more researchers extend their work to include feedback as a significant component of I-P-O models of group communication, thereby creating I-P-O-F models, the gap between the number of output and feedback variables studied can be expected to narrow and, ultimately, the study of feedback variables in organizational work groups may approach that of outputs. At its present level, however, the feedback category remains underdeveloped given the number of studies devoted to it (see Scott, Chapter 16, this volume, regarding the need to focus more on feedback processes in the study of computer-mediated groups). This is a perplexing finding in the light of the crucial role of feedback for groups embedded within organizational structures, for such groups report to someone else and typically receive feedback concerning their performance.

Regarding variable types, approximately 50% of all communication variables were classified as Structure. Subdividing the category showed that Organizational Structure (e.g., group leadership and group policies) was first with 27% of the articles; Task was second, with 24%; Member was third, with 22%; Social Structure (e.g., group interpersonal relations and group cliques) was fourth, with approximately 19%; Environment was fifth, with 5%; and Physical Structure (e.g., group size and composition) was sixth, with 4%. Organizational Structure, Task, and Member research thus accounted for almost three quarters of all research on communication in natural organizational work groups. This level of activity probably reflects, to some extent, the influence of organizational decision makers, who often permit researchers access if they explore ways to improve group communication processes deemed important by top management (i.e., Organizational Structure), which may perhaps lead researchers to focus less on exemplars of group message behavior (i.e., Social Structure). This finding also reflects the long-standing research practice in both the communication discipline and cognate fields of concentrating on the task dimension of groups and discounting, to some extent, the social dimension of group life (see Keyton, Chapter 8, this volume). More attention undoubtedly should be given to understanding the social structure of groups.

Examining individual topic areas, the least popular research variable type, Environment, was present in only 2 of the 13 topic areas—training and intergroup communication. This finding suggests a need for communication scholars to take more seriously the Bona Fide Groups Perspective by making intergroup communication and other forms of communicative boundary spanning, as well as the effects of environmental variables on internal group processes, primary foci of research.

With respect to the 100 system-stage relationships found in the 55 communication articles, 44% were Input-Output relationships, 30% were Process-Output, 14% were Input-Process, 9% were Feedback-Output, 2% were Input-Feedback, and 1% were Process-Feedback; no relationships were found for Feedback-Input or Feedback-Process. In terms of the 13 topic areas, Input-Output

studies were the predominant type of investigation; Input-Process investigations occurred only half as frequently. In certain topic areas, there was no Input-Process research (communication technology, voting systems, and creativity), and Process-Output research was missing for the topics of intergroup communication and equity. Finally, although there were nine Feedback-Output relationships studied, no studies investigated Feedback-Input or Feedback-Process relationships.

These findings raise several issues. Perhaps the most troubling, in terms of accumulating knowledge, is that the frequency distribution, with its highly uneven levels, indicates that there is little replication of findings across studies examining system-stage relationships. On the basis of their review of the literature, McGrath and Altman (1966) arrived at a similar observation, concluding that there was

> relatively little replication in the use of variables across studies and in tests of specific relationships. . . . Nearly one third of the variable classes used in the sample of approximately 250 studies appeared in only a single study of the sample, and nearly two thirds [of the variable classes] appeared in seven or fewer studies. (p. 68)

The findings from our study reveal that this lack of replication occurs not just for particular variables and variable types, but also for certain types of system-stage relationships and especially for particular types of topics.

Popularity of Variable Classes

When the 97 communication variables were categorized in terms of the 16 GVCS variable classes, two clear findings emerged. First, almost 40% of the total communication variables resided in the Structure variable classes, a large representation relative to the other variable classes. Second, six variable classes were not well represented and accounted for only 18% of the total communication variables. The least popular variable classes were Environment Input, Environment Process, and Environment Output, as well as the three Feedback variable classes (Member, Structure, and Environment). Especially disturbing was the absence of any communication variables for the Environment Output and Feedback variable classes. Such a paucity of research examining message behavior in these areas may suggest a continuing reluctance to jettison the container metaphor of organizational work groups, and thereby overlooking the inextricable relationship between important communication variables, such as intergroup communication (EP) and post–group meeting critiques (SF), and variables classified under the variable type of Environment (Input, Process, Output, Feedback) and the system stage of Feedback (Task, Member, Structure, Environment).

Critique and Directions for Future Research

Limitations of the Study

There are at least four limitations on the explanatory power of the present study. The first and second limitations concern the number of studies selected and the exclusion of published book chapters focusing on communication in natural organizational work groups. At first glance, the 55 studies selected may appear as lacking in terms of representativeness, especially when compared to larger samples with non-communication-based parameters, such as the one drawn by McGrath and Altman (1966). Such a claim should be tempered, however, as the studies in our sample were drawn from 83 studies originally culled from 311 studies in almost 90 journals. A related concern is that book chapters were excluded from the analysis. This concern has merit: Explanatory power undoubtedly was reduced by focusing solely on journal articles.

The third issue of concern is the reductionistic and variable-analytic nature of our analysis. Critics (e.g., Bormann, 1970; Frey, 1994c) have indicted this tradition in general (see

Poole, Chapter 2, this volume). We suggest, however, that although some depth of explanation may have been sacrificed, this is the manner in which the bulk of group research is, in fact, framed and conducted. For this type of research, the GVCS provides a way of synthesizing studies across the I-P-O-F system stages and, thereby, helps identify the current state of the literature and the gaps that need to be filled. The GVCS is presently limited, however, in its ability to analyze qualitative studies of communication in organizational work groups, especially because the majority of such research does not employ independent and dependent variables per se. We would suggest that it might be of value to close this analytical gap by collecting narratives from group members as they traverse the I-P-O-F system-stages. The collected stories could then help identify values, characters, and recurring messages that contribute to individual and group decision making across a wide array of organizational contexts (see Query & Kreps, 1993; Vanderford, Smith, & Harris, 1992).

The fourth issue that affects the level of generalizability of the findings is the focus on studies that examine relationships between only two variables. In its present form, the GVCS is not yet fully capable of treating complex, multivariate studies that examine organizational work groups, a formidable limitation with which other scholars have grappled (e.g., McGrath, 1984; McGrath & Altman, 1966). In those instances where the selected studies involved multiple variables across the Input-Process-Output system stages, we identified the variable types, variable classes, and the relationships among them. In many cases, this resulted in a relatively simple I-O relationship consisting of an independent and a dependent variable, whereas in other cases, the analysis resulted in two or more relationships that included both an I-P and a P-O relationship, each with independent and dependent variables. In a small number of cases, the research study was analyzed as incorporating moderating variables, and a slightly more complex coding procedure was employed. For instance, Hirokawa and Keyton (1995) examined two independent variables (group members' skill/knowledge and motivation), one dependent variable (task-completion effectiveness), and four moderating variables (competent leadership, organizational assistance, adequate information resources, and compatible work schedules). The independent and dependent variables were designated as MI-TO, and the moderating variables were coded as the GVCS relationships of SI-(MI-TO), EI-(MI-TO), EI-(MI-TO), and TI-(MI-TO), respectively. Hence, we attempted to categorize a multivariate relationship that went beyond simple two-variable relationships. Future refinement of the GVCS should address the evaluation of more complex, multivariate research designs.

Future Research

To promote integration of the extant literature, an important strategy is to observe, measure, and understand the message behavior of natural organizational work groups across the I-P-O-F system stages. In concert with such an approach, several questions emerge that might guide future research:

- What recurring messages and underlying themes, if any, characterize work groups as they move through I-P-O-F system stages, and what are their relationships to the previously identified 13 topic areas?
- Having established a baseline for these messages and underlying themes, in what ways do work group members' narratives change to accommodate environmental conditions, such as member turnover, redefinition of a group's mission, and high levels of uncertainty where previously there was little?
- How does an ongoing and periodic evaluation program as feedback influence work group messages across the I-P-O system-stages?

- If the 1997-1999 literature were compared to the 1993-1995 survey, would the results be the same?
- What trends can be discerned from studying the literature over time regarding Feedback system-stage and Environment variable-type studies?
- For a specific topic area (e.g., leadership), what additional insight may be obtained by examining studies involving the system stages of Input-Process, Process-Output, and Process-Feedback, compared to a similar assessment of Input-Output studies?

Informed responses to these and other questions will be forthcoming if the literature on organizational work groups, in general, and their communicative behavior, in particular, is continually analyzed and processed according to some unifying model, such as the GVCS.

Other courses of action seem appropriate as well to further help unify the various studies on natural organizational work groups. For instance, if a major institution were to house the GVCS, act as a clearinghouse, and make the model available in an on-line environment, the increased access could significantly facilitate theory building and testing, as well as the replication of studies and the analyses of them, across disciplinary lines. Scholarly chapters, currently excluded from this analysis, also could be incorporated. Suggestions from key publics for streamlining the terminology and further improving the model could be collected, evaluated, and acted on. The results of new additions to the database and subsequent GVCS processing could then be updated and widely disseminated on a periodic basis to reach a large, global audience. The technology exists for this expansion, as evidenced, for example, by the Physician-Database Query (PDQ) on-line information system housed by the National Cancer Institute (see Kreps, Roderer, & Query, 1986). The PDQ, used extensively by Cancer Information Service personnel, is updated every 3 months and appears in a two-screen format. Both screens present information about clinical trials, treatment regimens, names of oncologists conducting clinical research, and other related information. The "sides" of the presentation screen differ, however, as they target laypersons and medical personnel (primarily physicians). For the former audience, terminology that the average person can understand is used; for the latter audience, terminology that presumes a medical education is featured. Readability levels of both presentation modes are assessed periodically by a group of experts (see Kreps et al., 1986). The same strategies certainly could be applied to the GVCS.

CONCLUSION

As the new millennium draws near, organizational work groups will continue to evolve and undergo previously unanticipated changes. Although several factors will influence their daily activities and ultimate success, such as members' increased technological expertise, ability to avoid groupthink, and the successful management of conflict, one central feature will continue to be the primary process shaping this form of group life—communication. Poole and Hirokawa's (1996) explanation of the significance of communication in group life certainly applies to organizational work groups: "The catalyst for such social chemistry is communication. It is the medium for the coordination and control of group activities, member socialization, group integration, and conflict management, among other functions" (p. 3).

The challenge for those who seek to study communication in groups, including organizational work groups, is clear: We must accumulate, replicate, and synthesize knowledge within theoretical frameworks and explanatory models to better explain, understand, and, ultimately, predict group interaction. This chapter is one step in that direction.

NOTE

1. In concert with Redding's (1970) position, we collapsed field experimental studies into the laboratory studies' category since "considerably tight controls" were present (McGrath & Altman, 1966, p. 51).

APPENDIX

Natural Work Group Research Studies With Group Communication Variables, 1993-1995

01 Alkemade, N. D., Bissecker, R. J., & Steensma, H. O. (1994). Increasing task performance by objective feedback. *Gedrag An Organisatie, 7,* 65-70.

02 Basu, R., & Green, S. G. (1995). Subordinate performance, leader-subordinate compatibility, and exchange quality in leader-member dyads: A field study. *Journal of Applied Social Psychology, 25,* 77-92.

03 Broome, B. J., & Fulbright, L. (1995). A multistage influence model of barriers to group problem solving: A participant-generated agenda for small group research. *Small Group Research, 26,* 25-55.

04 Burningham, C., & West, M. A. (1995). Individual, climate, and group interaction processes as predictors of work team innovation. *Small Group Research, 26,* 106-117.

05 Clawson, V. R., Bostrom, R. P., & Anson, R. (1993). The role of the facilitator in computer-supported meetings. *Small Group Research, 24,* 547-565.

06 Cooley, E. (1994). Training an interdisciplinary team in communication and decision-making skills. *Small Group Research, 25,* 5-25.

07 Feyerherm, A. E. (1994). Leadership in collaboration: A longitudinal study of two interorganizational rule-making groups. *Leadership Quarterly, 5,* 253-270.

08 Fontenot, N. A. (1993). Effects of training in creativity and creative problem finding upon business people. *Journal of Social Psychology, 133,* 11-22.

09 Fulk, J. (1993). Social construction of communication technology. *Academy of Management Journal, 36,* 921-950.

10 Gastil, J. (1993). Identifying obstacles to small group democracy. *Small Group Research, 24,* 5-27.

11 George, J. M. (1995). Leader positive mood and group performance: The case of customer service. *Journal of Applied Social Psychology, 25,* 778-794.

12 Goltz, S. M. (1993). Dynamics of leaders' and subordinates' performance-related discussions following monitoring by leaders in group meetings. *Leadership Quarterly, 4,* 173-187.

13 Gowan, J. A., & McNichols, C. W. (1993). The effects of alternative forms of knowledge representation on decision-making consensus. *International Journal of Man-Machine Studies, 38,* 489-507.

14 Haythornwaite, C., Wellman, B., & Mantei, M. (1995). Work relationships and media use: A social network analysis. *Group Decision and Negotiation, 4,* 193-211.

15 Hellman, C. M. (1994). Participation in decision making and committee members' intent to remain. *Psychological Reports, 74*, 490.

16 Hewstone, M., Carpenter, J., & Franklyn-Stokes, A. (1994). Intergroup contact between professional groups: Two evaluation studies. *Journal of Community and Applied Social Psychology, 4*, 347-363.

17 Hirokawa, R. Y., & Keyton, J. (1995). Perceived facilitators and inhibitors of effectiveness in organizational work teams. *Management Communication Quarterly, 8*, 424-446.

18 Hodson, R., Creighton, S., Jamison, C. S., & Riebel, S. (1994). Loyalty to whom? Workplace participation and development of consent. *Human Relations, 47*, 895-909.

19 Ibarra, H. (1995). Race, opportunity, and diversity of social circles in managerial networks. *Academy of Management Journal, 38*, 673-703.

20 Innami, I. (1994). The quality of group decisions, group verbal behavior, and intervention. *Organizational Behavior and Human Decision Processes, 60*, 409-430.

21 Jehn, K. A. (1995). A multimethod examination of the benefits and detriments of intragroup conflict. *Administrative Science Quarterly, 40*, 256-282.

22 Jones, S. D., Buerkle, M., Hall, A., Rupp, L., & Matt, G. (1993). Work group performance measurement and feedback: An integrated comprehensive system for a manufacturing department. *Group & Organization Management, 18*, 269-291.

23 Jones, B. (1994). A comparison of consensus and voting in public decision making. *Negotiation Journal, 10*, 161-171.

24 Keller, T., & Dansereau, F. (1995). Leadership and empowerment: A social exchange perspective. *Human Relations, 48*, 127-137.

25 Keller, R. T. (1994). Technology-information processing fit and the performance of R&D project groups: A test of contingency theory. *Academy of Management Journal, 37*, 167-179.

26 Korsgaard, M. A., Schweiger, D. M., & Sapienza, H. J. (1995). Building commitment, attachment, and trust in strategic decision-making teams: The role of procedural justice. *Academy of Management Journal, 38*, 60-84.

27 Kramer, M. W. (1995). A longitudinal study of superior-subordinate communication during job transfers. *Human Communication Research, 22*, 39-64.

28 Landau, J. (1995). The relationship of race and gender to managers' ratings of promotion potential. *Journal of Organizational Behavior, 16*, 391-400.

29 Lee, J., & Jablin, F. M. (1995). Maintenance communication in superior-subordinate work relationships. *Human Communication Research, 22*, 220-257.

30 Leedom, D. K., & Simon, R. (1995). Improving team coordination: A case for behavior-based training. *Military Psychology, 7*, 109-122.

31 Leon, G. R., Kafner, R., Hoffman, R. G., & Dupre, L. (1994). Group processes and task effectiveness in a Soviet-American expedition team. *Environment and Behavior, 26*, 149-165.

32 Mael, F. A., & Alderks, C. E. (1993). Leadership team cohesion and subordinate work unit morale and performance. *Military Psychology, 5*, 141-158.

33 Marshall, A. A., & Stohl, C. (1993). Being "in the know" in a participative management system. *Management Communication Quarterly, 6*, 372-404.

34 Murrell, A. J., Stewart, A. C., & Engel, B. T. (1993). Consensus versus devil's advocacy: The influence of decision process and task structure on strategic decision making. *Journal of Business Communication, 30*, 399-414.

35 Orpen, C., & Hall, C. (1994). Testing the "substitutes" model of managerial leadership: An examination of moderators of the relationships between leader reward and punishment behaviors and employee job satisfaction. *Studia Psychologica, 36*, 65-68.

36 Pacanowsky, M. (1995). Team tools for wicked problems. *Organizational Dynamics, 23*, 36-51.

37 Parker, L. E., & Price, R. H. (1994). Empowered managers and empowered workers: The effects of managerial support and managerial perceived control on workers' sense of control over decision making. *Human Relations, 47*, 911-928.

38 Perrott, S. B., & Taylor, D. M. (1994). Ethnocentrism and authoritarianism in the police: Challenging stereotypes and reconceptualizing ingroup identification. *Journal of Applied Social Psychology, 24*, 1640-1664.

39 Ray, R. G., Hines, J., & Wilcox, D. (1994). Training internal facilitators. *Training and Development, 48*, 45-48.

40 Reynolds, M. (1994). Decision-making using computer conferencing: A case study. *Behaviour and Information Technology, 13*, 239-252.

41 Robertson, P. J., & Kwong, S. S. (1994). Decision making in school-based management leadership councils: The impact of council membership diversity. *Urban Review, 26*, 41-54.

42 Rothstein, A. S. (1993). Group maturity in a teacher centre policy board. *Journal of Educational Administration, 31*, 39-58.

43 Seers, A., Petty, N. M., & Cashman, J. F. (1995). Team-member exchange under team and traditional management: A naturally occurring quasi-experiment. *Group & Organization Management, 20*, 18-38.

44 Sias, P. M., & Jablin, F. M. (1995). Differential and superior-subordinate relations, perceptions of fairness, and coworker communication. *Human Communication Research, 22*, 5-38.

45 Smith, P. B., Peterson, M. F., & Misumi, J. (1994). Event management and work team effectiveness in Japan, Britain, and USA. *Journal of Occupational and Organizational Psychology, 67*, 33-43.

46 Smither, J. W., Wohlers, A. J., & London, M. (1995). A field study of reactions to normative versus individualized upward feedback. *Group & Organization Management, 20*, 61-89.

47 Storck, J., & Sproull, L. (1995). Through a glass darkly: What do people learn in videoconferences? *Human Communication Research, 22*, 197-219.

48 Tang, T. L. P., Tollison, P. S., & Whiteside, H. D. (1993). Differences between active and inactive quality circles in attendance and performance. *Public Personnel Management, 22*, 579-590.

49 Van Aken, E. M., Monetta, D. J., & Sink, D. S. (1994). Affinity groups: The missing link in employee involvement. *Organizational Dynamics, 22*, 38-54.

50 Van de Vliert, E., Euwema, M. C., & Huismans, S. E. (1995). Managing conflict with a subordinate or a superior: Effectiveness of conglomerated behavior. *Journal of Applied Psychology, 80*, 271-281.

51 Volkema, R. J., & Niederman, F. (1995). Organizational meetings: Formats and information requirements. *Small Group Research, 26*, 3-24.

52 Weaver, W. T. (1993). Anatomy of a creative problem solving meeting. *Journal of Creative Behavior, 27*, 236-269.

53 Welsh, T. M., Miller, L. K., & Altus, D. E. (1994). Programming for survival: A meeting system that survives 8 years later. *Journal of Applied Behavioral Analysis, 27*, 423-433.

54 Williams, T. A. (1994). Information technology and self managing work groups. *Behaviour and Information Technology, 13*, 268-276.

55 Zamanou, S., & Glaser, S. R. (1994). Moving toward participation and involvement: Managing and measuring organizational culture. *Group & Organization Management, 19*, 475-502.

REFERENCES

Ancona, D. G. (1990). Outward bound: Strategies for team survival in an organization. *Academy of Management Journal, 33*, 334-365.

Bailey, K. D. (1994). *Typologies and taxonomies: An introduction to classification techniques.* Thousand Oaks, CA: Sage.

Bass, B. M. (1982). Individual capability, team performance, and team productivity. In M. D. Dunnette & E. A. Fleishman (Eds.), *Human performance and productivity: Vol. 1. Human capability assessment* (pp. 179-232). Hillsdale, NJ: Lawrence Erlbaum.

Beckhard, R. (1969). *Organization development: Strategies and models.* Reading, MA: Addison-Wesley.

Bettenhausen, K. L. (1991). Five years of groups research: What we have learned and what needs to be addressed. *Journal of Management, 17*, 345-381.

Bormann, E. G. (1970). The paradox and promise of small group research. *Speech Monographs, 37*, 211-217.

Clegg, S. R., & Hardy, C. (1996). Introduction: Organizations, organization, and organizing. In S. R. Clegg, C. Hardy, & W. R. Nord (Eds.), *Handbook of organization studies* (pp. 1-28). Thousand Oaks, CA: Sage.

Cohen, S. G., & Bailey, D. E. (1997). What makes teams work: Group effectiveness research from the shop floor to the executive suite. *Journal of Management, 23*, 239-290.

Cragan, J. F., & Wright, D. W. (1990). Small group communication research of the 1980s: A synthesis and critique. *Communication Studies, 41*, 212-236.

Davis, J. H. (1986). Foreword. In R. Y. Hirokawa & M. S. Poole (Eds.), *Communication and group decision-making* (pp. 7-12). Beverly Hills, CA: Sage.

Fiedler, F. E. (1967). *A theory of leadership effectiveness.* New York: McGraw-Hill.

Fisher, B. A. (1978). *Perspectives on human communication.* New York: Macmillan.

Frey, L. R. (1994a). The call of the field: Studying communication in natural groups. In L. R. Frey (Ed.), *Group communication in context: Studies of natural groups* (pp. ix-xiv). Hillsdale, NJ: Lawrence Erlbaum.

Frey, L. R. (Ed.). (1994b). *Group communication in context: Studies of natural groups.* Hillsdale, NJ: Lawrence Erlbaum.

Frey, L. R. (1994c). The naturalistic paradigm: Studying small groups in the postmodern era. *Small Group Research, 25*, 551-577.

Frey, L. R. (1995). Applied communication research on group facilitation in natural settings. In L. R. Frey (Ed.), *Innovations in group facilitation: Applications in natural settings* (pp. 1-23). Cresskill, NJ: Hampton.

Frey, L. R. (1996). Remembering and "re-membering": A history of theory and research on communication and group decision making. In R. Y. Hirokawa & M. S. Poole (Eds.), *Communication and group decision making* (2nd ed., pp. 19-51). Thousand Oaks, CA: Sage.

Gist, M. E., Locke, E. A., & Taylor, M. S. (1987). Organizational behavior: Group structure, process and effectiveness. *Journal of Management, 13*, 237-257.

Glaser, S. R. (1994). Teamwork and communication: A 3-year case study of change. *Management Communication Quarterly, 7*, 282-296.

Greenbaum, H. H., & Kaplan, I. T. (1997, August). *A classification system for organizational group variables and their relationship.* Paper presented at the annual meeting of the Academy of Management, Boston.

Greenbaum, H. H., Kaplan, I. T., & Damiano, R. (1991). Organizational group measurement instruments: An integrated survey. *Management Communication Quarterly, 5*, 126-148.

Greenbaum, H. H., Kaplan, I. T., & Metlay, W. (1988). Evaluation of problem-solving groups: The case of quality circle programs. *Group & Organization Studies, 13*, 133-147.

Guzzo, R. A., & Dickson, M. W. (1996). Teams in organizations: Recent research on performance and effectiveness. *Annual Review of Psychology, 47*, 307-338.

Hackman, J. R., & Morris, C. G. (1975). Group tasks, group interaction process, and group performance effectiveness: A review and proposed integration. In L. Berkowitz (Ed.), *Advances in experimental social psychology* (Vol. 8, pp. 45-99). New York: Academic Press.

Hackman, J. R., & Walton, R. E. (1986). Leading groups in organizations. In P. S. Goodman & Associates

(Eds.), *Designing effective work groups* (pp. 72-119). San Francisco: Jossey-Bass.

Hare, A. P. (1976). *Handbook of small group research* (2nd ed.). New York: Free Press.

Hirokawa, R. Y. (1990). The role of communication in group decision-making efficacy: A task-contingency perspective. *Small Group Research, 21,* 190-204.

Hirokawa, R. Y., & Keyton, J. (1995). Perceived facilitators and inhibitors of effectiveness in organizational work teams. *Management Communication Quarterly, 8,* 424-446.

Holsti, O. R. (1969). *Content analysis for the social sciences and humanities.* Reading, MA: Addison-Wesley.

Homans, G. C. (1950). *The human group.* New York: Harcourt, Brace & World.

Innami, I. (1994). The quality of group decisions, group verbal behavior, and intervention. *Organizational Behavior and Human Decision Processes, 60,* 409-430.

Jablin, F. M., & Sussman, L. (1983). Organizational group communication: A review of the literature and model of the process. In H. H. Greenbaum, R. L. Falcione, & S. A. Hellweg (Eds.), *Organizational communication: Abstracts, analysis and overview* (Vol. 8, pp. 11-41). Beverly Hills, CA: Sage.

Jarboe, S. (1988). A comparison of input-output, process-output, and input-process-output models of small group problem-solving effectiveness. *Communication Monographs, 55,* 121-142.

Jehn, K. A. (1995). A multimethod examination of the benefits and detriments of intragroup conflict. *Administrative Science Quarterly, 40,* 256-282.

Kaplan, I. T., & Greenbaum, H. H. (1991). A diagnostic model for OD interventions. *Public Administration Quarterly, 14,* 519-532.

Keller, R. T. (1994). Technology-information processing fit and the performance of R&D project groups: A test of contingency theory. *Academy of Management Journal, 37,* 167-179.

Kreps, G. L. (1980). A field experimental test and revaluation of Weick's model of organizing. In D. Nimmo (Ed.), *Communication yearbook 4* (pp. 389-398). New Brunswick, NJ: Transaction Books.

Kreps, G. L., Roderer, N., & Query, J. L., Jr. (1986, August). *Description of the process of creating and updating PDQ files* (In-house report). Bethesda, MD: National Cancer Institute.

Krone, K. J., Jablin, F. M., & Putnam, L. L. (1987). Communication theory and organizational communication: Multiple perspectives. In F. M. Jablin, L. L. Putnam, K. H. Roberts, & L. W. Porter (Eds.), *Handbook of organizational communication: An interdisciplinary perspective* (pp. 18-40). Newbury Park, CA: Sage.

Lee, J., & Jablin, F. M. (1995). Maintenance communication in superior-subordinate work relationships. *Human Communication Research, 22,* 220-257.

Levine, J. M., & Moreland, R. L. (1990). Progress in small group research. *Annual review of psychology, 41,* 585-634.

McGrath, J. E. (1964). *Social psychology: A brief introduction.* New York: Holt, Rinehart & Winston.

McGrath, J. E. (1984). *Groups: Interaction and performance.* Englewood Cliffs, NJ: Prentice Hall.

McGrath, J. E., & Altman, I. (1966). *Small group research: A synthesis and critique of the field.* New York: Holt, Rinehart & Winston.

Poole, M. S. (1990). Do we have any theories of group communication? *Communication Studies, 41,* 237-247.

Poole, M. S., & Hirokawa, R. Y. (1996). Introduction: Communication and group decision making. In R. Y. Hirokawa & M. S. Poole (Eds.), *Communication and group decision making* (2nd ed., pp. 3-18). Thousand Oaks, CA: Sage.

Propp, K. M., & Nelson, D. (1996). Problem-solving performance in naturalistic groups: A test of the ecological validity of the functional perspective. *Communication Studies, 47,* 35-45.

Putnam, L. L., & Stohl, C. (1990). Bona fide groups: A reconceptualization of groups in context. *Communication Studies, 41,* 248-265.

Putnam, L. L., & Stohl, C. (1994). Group communication in context: Implications for the study of bona fide groups. In L. R. Frey (Ed.), *Group communication in context: Studies of natural groups* (pp. 284-292). Hillsdale, NJ: Lawrence Erlbaum.

Putnam, L. L., & Stohl, C. (1996). Bona fide groups: An alternative perspective for communication and small group decision making. In R. Y. Hirokawa & M. S. Poole (Eds.), *Communication and group decision making* (2nd ed., pp. 147-178). Thousand Oaks, CA: Sage.

Query, J. L., Jr., & Kreps, G. L. (1993). Using the critical incident method to evaluate and enhance organizational effectiveness. In S. L. Fish & G. L. Kreps (Eds.), *Qualitative research: Applications in organizational communication* (pp. 63-77). Cresskill, NJ: Hampton.

Redding, W. C. (1970). Research setting: Field studies. In P. Emmert & W. Brooks (Eds.), *Methods of research in communication* (pp. 105-159). Boston, MA: Houghton Mifflin.

Rice, R. W. (1975). *The esteem for least preferred coworker (LPC) score: What does it measure?* Unpublished doctoral dissertation, University of Utah, Salt Lake City.

Rice, R. W. (1978). Formal classification of research information: Empirical test of the McGrath-Altman approach and an illustrative case. *American Psychologist, 33,* 249-264.

Scheerhorn, D., Geist, P., & Teboul, JC. B. (1994). Beyond decision making in decision-making groups: Implications for the study of group communication. In L. R. Frey (Ed.), *Group communication in context: Studies of natural groups* (pp. 247-262). Hillsdale, NJ: Lawrence Erlbaum.

Shaw, M. E. (1981). *Group dynamics: The psychology of small group behavior* (3rd ed.). New York: McGraw-Hill.

Shulman, A. D. (1996). Putting group information technology in its place: Communication and good work group performance. In S. R. Clegg, C. Hardy, &

W. R. Nord (Eds.), *Handbook of organization studies* (pp. 357-374). Thousand Oaks, CA: Sage.

Sias, P. M., & Jablin, F. M. (1995). Differential and superior-subordinate relations, perceptions of fairness, and coworker communication. *Human Communication Research, 22,* 5-38.

Stohl, C., & Redding, W. C. (1987). Messages and message exchange processes. In F. M. Jablin, L. L. Putnam, K. H. Roberts, & L. W. Porter (Eds.), *Handbook of organizational communication: An interdisciplinary perspective* (pp. 451-502). Newbury Park, CA: Sage.

Sykes, R. E. (1990). Imagining what we might study if we really studied small groups from a speech perspective. *Communication Studies, 41,* 200-211.

Taylor, J. C., & Bowers, D. G. (1972). *Survey of organizations: A machine-scored standardized questionnaire instrument.* Ann Arbor: University of Michigan Press.

Vanderford, M. L., Smith, D. H., & Harris, W. S. (1992). Value identification in narrative discourse: Evaluation of an HIV education demonstration project. *Journal of Applied Communication Research, 2,* 123-160.

Weick, K. E. (1969). *The social psychology of organizing.* Reading, MA: Addison-Wesley.

Weick, K. E. (1979). *The social psychology of organizing* (2nd ed.). Reading, MA: Addison-Wesley.

Whyte, W. H. (1956). *The organization man.* Garden City, NY: Doubleday.

Wimmer, R. D., & Dominick, J. R. (1994). *Mass media research: An introduction* (4th ed.). Belmont, CA: Wadsworth.

Author Index

Subject Index

About the Editor

Lawrence R. Frey (Ph.D., University of Kansas, 1979) is Professor and Chair of the Department of Communication at The University of Memphis. His research is designed to demonstrate the applied value of research to "real-life" groups and encourage the use of naturalistic research methods. He is the author or editor of six books, two special journal issues, and more than 40 book chapters and journal articles. His coauthored text (with Mara Adelman) titled *The Fragile Community: Living Together With AIDS* received the 1998 National Jesuit Book Award from Alpha Sigma Nu and the 1998 Distinguished Book Award from the National Communication Association's (NCA) Applied Communication Division; his edited text *Group Communication in Context: Studies of Natural Groups* received the 1995 Gerald R. Miller Book Award from the NCA's Interpersonal and Group Interaction Division and the 1994 Distinguished Book Award from the Applied Communication Division. He has served as an associate editor on 11 editorial boards and as a consulting reviewer for many other journals. He is Past President of the Central States Communication Association and recipient of the Outstanding Young Teacher Award from that organization.

About the Associate Editors

Dennis S. Gouran (Ph.D., University of Iowa, 1968) is Professor of Speech Communication and Labor Studies and Industrial Relations at The Pennsylvania State University. The author of nearly 100 books, book chapters, and journal articles dealing with communication in decision-making groups, Professor Gouran has achieved recognition for his contributions to scholarly inquiry in being named a National Communication Association Distinguished Scholar and recipient of The Pennsylvania State University Faculty Scholar's Medal for the Social and Behavioral Sciences. A former president of both the Central States Communication Association and the National Communication Association, he also has served as editor of the *Central States Speech Journal* and *Communication Monographs*. In 1993, he received the National Communication Association's Distinguished Service Award.

Marshall Scott Poole (Ph.D., University of Wisconsin, 1980) is Professor of Speech-Communication at Texas A&M University. He has conducted research and published extensively on the topics of group and organizational communication, computer-mediated communication systems, conflict management, and organizational innovation. He has coauthored or edited four books, including *Communication and Group Decision Making* (two editions), *Working Through Conflict* (three editions), and *Research on the Management of Innovation*. He has published in a number of journals, including *Management Science, MIS Quarterly, Human Communication Research, Academy of Management Review,* and *Communication Monographs*. He is currently Senior Editor of *Information Systems Research and Organization Science*.

About the Contributors

Terre H. Allen (Ph.D., Louisiana State University, 1990) is Associate Professor of Speech Communication at California State University, Long Beach, where she regularly teaches small group communication at the undergraduate and graduate levels. Her research interests include investigations of how individuals use knowledge structures when engaging in interpersonal, small group, and classroom contexts. She has contributed to such journals as *Human Communication Research, Communication Education, Communication Research Reports,* and *Communication Research.* She also has served as an associate editor for *Women's Studies in Communication* and *The Speech Communication Teacher.*

Carolyn M. Anderson (Ph.D., Kent State University, 1992) is Associate Professor in The School of Communication, The University of Akron. She primarily teaches and researches small groups, health communication, and organizational communication. She has studied or taught in China, Cuba, and Poland. Her articles have appeared in regional, national, and international journals. Numerous convention papers have earned top paper awards. Prior to receiving her doctorate, she worked in business for many years as a member of work teams, a project leader, and an entrepreneur. She provides service to the community as a public speaker, consultant, and organizational trainer.

Dale E. Brashers (Ph.D., University of Arizona, 1994) is Assistant Professor in the Department of Speech Communication at the University of Illinois at Urbana-Champaign. His research interests include research methodology as well as decision making in group and health communication contexts. His work on these topics has been published in *Human Communication Research, Communication Monographs, Western Journal of Communication, Communication Studies, Southern Communication Journal, Communication Quarterly, AIDS Care,* and *Journal of the Association of Nurses in AIDS Care.* His recent work includes a project designed to develop an intervention to assist persons living with AIDS to better manage the uncertainty associated with their illness.

Rebecca J. Welch Cline (Ph.D., The Pennsylvania State University, 1975) is Associate Professor of Health Communication in the Department of Health Science Education, University of Florida, Gainesville, where she teaches and conducts research in interpersonal, small group, and health communication. Her recent research focuses on interpersonal communication and HIV/AIDS, including HIV prevention, communication with people with HIV disease, and gender issues associated with communicating about HIV/AIDS. Her research has appeared in *Communication Monographs, Human Communication Research, Journal of Applied Communication Research, Journal of Personal and Social Relationships, Communication Yearbook 7, AIDS & Public Policy, Journal of American College Health,* and other publications.

Howard H. Greenbaum (Ph.D., Columbia University, 1952) is Distinguished Professor Emeritus of Business at Hofstra University in Hempstead, New York. Earlier, he was a senior executive for an industrial organization and served on the financial resource staff of the National Bureau of Economic Research. His research on communication audits and work-group measurement methods and evaluation has appeared in the *Academy of Management Journal, Group & Organization Studies, Journal of Business Communication, Journal of Applied Communication Research,* and *Management Communication Quarterly.* In 1994, he served as an Associate Editor of the text *Communication Research Measures: A Sourcebook.* He has served as Chair and Secretary of the Organizational Communication divisions of the Academy of Management and the International Communication Association, respectively.

Beth Bonniwell Haslett (Ph.D., University of Minnesota, 1971) is a Professor in the Department of Communication at the University of Delaware. Her teaching and research interests include developmental communication, organizational communication, leadership, and diversity and gender issues in communication. In 1992, she published *The Organizational Woman: Power and Paradox,* with F. L. Geis and M. R. Carter. She has published two other books and numerous articles on organizational and developmental communication.

Randy Y. Hirokawa (Ph.D., University of Washington, 1980) is Professor and Chair of the Department of Communication Studies at the University of Iowa. His research interests include communication and group decision-making effectiveness, as well as interdisciplinary health care team education and training. He is the author of more than 60 articles and book chapters as well as coeditor of the text *Communication and Group Decision Making* (two editions). He is the former editor of *Communication Studies* and has served, or is serving, on the editorial boards of *Communication Monographs, Communication Studies, Organizational Science,* and *Small Group Research.*

Susan Jarboe (Ph.D., University of Wisconsin, 1986) designs organizational environments conducive to enhanced group intelligence, specializing in discussion procedures for maximum group problem-solving effectiveness. Her research assesses communicative behavior as a consequence of input conditions and as a precursor of group outcomes. Her work has appeared in *Communication Monographs, Small Group Research,* and *Journal of Applied Communication Research.* She also consults with private industry and donates her facilitation expertise to local community and nonprofit groups. Having taught at several universities around the country, she is presently a Visiting Assistant Professor at Juniata College in Pennsylvania.

Sandra M. Ketrow (Ph.D., Indiana University, 1982) is a Professor in the Department of Communication Studies at the University of Rhode Island. Her research focuses on group processes and outcomes as well as nonverbal communication. She is also interested in argumentation in group deliberations, particularly with respect to social and family groups. With more than 20 years of academic experience, she also has more than 10 years of experience in the private sector in marketing, advertising, publishing, and public television. She has consulted with AT&T as well as several hospitals and other public and private agencies regarding nonverbal messages and image.

Joann Keyton (Ph.D., The Ohio State University, 1987) is Associate Professor in the Department of Communication at The University of Memphis. Her primary teaching responsibilities are communication research methods, communication theory, group communication, and organizational communication at both undergraduate and graduate levels. Fifteen of her publications and convention papers on group communication, organizational communication, and sexual harassment have won honors. Her text *Group Communication: Process and Analysis* was published recently. Currently, she is a member of the editorial review boards of *Journal of Applied Communication Research, Southern Communication Journal,* and *Small Group Research.*

Edward A. Mabry (Ph.D., Bowling Green State University, 1972) is Associate Professor in the Department of Communication at the University of Wisconsin–Milwaukee.

Matthew M. Martin (Ph.D., Kent State University, 1992) is Associate Professor in the Communication Studies Department at West Virginia University, Morgantown. He teaches a wide variety of communication courses, with a special emphasis on family and small group communication. His research interests focus on communication trait research, communication competence, and scale development. He has presented numerous papers at international, national, regional, and local conventions and has coedited or coauthored three book chapters. His contributions to the community include statewide seminar teaching.

Renée A. Meyers (Ph.D., University of Illinois, 1987) is Associate Professor in the Department of Communication at the University of Wisconsin–Milwaukee. Her research interests include group decision making and argument, as well as the role of communication in cooperative learning groups. Her articles have

appeared in *Human Communication Research, Communication Monographs, Western Journal of Communication, Communication Studies, Southern Communication Journal, Small Group Research,* and *Communication Yearbook,* among other publications. She serves on the editorial boards of several communication journals.

Charles Pavitt (Ph.D., University of Wisconsin, 1983) is Associate Professor in the Department of Communication at the University of Delaware. His research interests lie in two areas: face-to-face communication in formal settings and the impact of the philosophy of science on communication theory. He writes a column published in two homebrewing club newsletters and for the past 6 years has performed at various times with Gamelan Lake of the Silver Bear in Newark, Delaware, and the Gamelan Institute of Washington at the Indonesian Embassy in Washington, D.C.

Timothy G. Plax (Ph.D., University of Southern California, 1974) is Professor of Speech Communication at California State University, Long Beach. He has done extensive research in the areas of persuasion, group communication, and organizational communication, but he is best known for his programmatic research in instructional communication. He has contributed to such journals as *Human Communication Research, Communication Monographs, Communication Education,* and *Communication Research Reports.* He also has served as an internal executive consultant for the Rockwell International Corporation. With more than 25 years as a communication researcher, he has extensive experience with groups in the corporate and instructional arenas.

Kathleen M. Propp (Ph.D., University of Iowa, 1991) is Associate Professor in the Department of Communication at Northern Illinois University, DeKalb. Her teaching and research interests include small group communication, communication theory, and conflict management, with a primary emphasis on the cognitive and communication processes that affect decision-making efficacy. Her recent lines of research have examined groups' use of information and how disparate interpretations of evidence are negotiated in decision-making processes, as well as how noncommunicative factors influence this process. Her work has appeared in *Human Communication Research, Small Group Research, Communication Studies, Communication Reports,* and the *Journal of Communication Studies.*

Jim L. Query, Jr. (Ph.D., Ohio University, 1990) is Associate Professor in the Department of Communication at Loyola University Chicago. He was president of the Alzheimer's Association of Tulsa, Oklahoma, from 1991 to 1994. In addition to being a summer research fellow and consultant with the National Cancer Institute, he has worked and taught at the Indiana University School of Nursing, the Ohio University College of Osteopathic Medicine and School of Interpersonal Communication, and the University of Tulsa. The bulk of his research examines the communication of social support during major life events, such as retirement, caregiving during Alzheimer's, and living with AIDS. He has published four journal articles, four chapters in scholarly books, three textbook chapters, and two book reviews. He has served on a number of editorial boards, including those of *American Behavioral Scientist, Health Communication,* and the *Journal of Health Communication.* He also has held several professional offices in the International Communication Association and the National Communication Association.

Bruce L. Riddle (Ph.D., Kent State University, 1994) is a Visiting Assistant Professor in the Department of Communication Studies at Kent State University. His teaching and research background is in organizational, small group, and interpersonal communication, with special emphasis on socialization processes. He has presented numerous convention papers, published in communication and related journals, and taught a team-building

seminar in Russia. Prior to earning his doctorate, he worked in higher education for more than 25 years in top managerial positions. He is active in the community as a tutor, trainer, and consultant.

Jenn Ruebush (M.A., University of Delaware, 1998) received her bachelor's degree from the University of New Mexico and her master's degree from the University of Delaware. Her area of specialization for the master's degree was organizational communication. She is especially interested in organizational processes in volunteer agencies and hopes to work in that sector.

Abran J. Salazar (Ph.D., University of Iowa, 1991) is Associate Professor in the Department of Communication Studies at the University of Rhode Island. He has published journal articles and book chapters on the relationship between group communication and decision-making performance, group roles, and social support and health. In addition to his attempts to understand the role of informal groups in promoting well-being, his current interests lie in applying the sciences of complexity toward acquiring a better understanding of the role of group communication processes in promoting creativity and learning.

Beatrice G. Schultz (Ph.D., University of Michigan, 1969) is Professor Emerita in the Department of Communication Studies at the University of Rhode Island. She has spent much of the past 30 years conducting research on leadership and the dynamics of group decision-making effectiveness. Her research interests cover various areas of group performance, with a special interest in facilitating group problem solving and decision making.

Craig R. Scott (Ph.D., Arizona State University, 1994) is Assistant Professor in the Department of Speech Communication at The University of Texas at Austin. His research related to group communication technologies has been published in *Small Group Research,*

Communication Education, Communication Quarterly, Communication Reports, and *Communication Theory.* His work on group communication technologies has received top paper awards from both the Group Communication Division of the National Communication Association and the Technology Division of the International Communication Association. He has introduced a variety of group communication technologies into the small group communication course at UT-Austin, where he teaches both a graduate seminar and an undergraduate course on new communication technologies in the workplace.

David R. Seibold (Ph.D., Michigan State University, 1975) is Professor and Chair of the Department of Communication at the University of California, Santa Barbara. Author of nearly 100 publications on group communication, organizational change, and interpersonal influence, he has received numerous research and teaching awards. He currently is Editor of the *Journal of Applied Communication Research* and serves on the boards of many other journals. He has served as Chair of the Interpersonal and Small Group Interaction Division of the National Communication Association and is the current Chair of the Organizational Communication Division of the International Communication Association. He also works closely with many business, government, and health organizations. Whenever possible, he gets away to bicycle, and he has cycled extensively in North America, Europe, and Asia.

Thomas J. Socha (Ph.D., University of Iowa, 1988) is Associate Professor of Communication, Old Dominion University, Norfolk, Virginia. His research examines parent-child communication, family communication and race, and children's communication. His publications include two coedited books, book chapters, and articles in these topic areas. He currently is Vice-Chair of the National Communication Association's Family Communication Division and Chair of the Southern States Communication Association's Interpersonal Communication Division. He has appeared in local and regional media and been quoted in newspapers and magazine stories, including one that appeared in *TV Guide.* He recently was awarded the designation "University Professor" for being among the best teachers at Old Dominion University, an honor that includes additional university funding for his professional activities. He will hold the title for 4 years. He recently became the Founding Editor of the *Journal of Family Communication.*

Sunwolf (Ph.D., University of California, Santa Barbara, 1998; J.D., University of Denver College of Law, 1976) is Assistant Professor of Communication at Santa Clara University. A former trial attorney, she serves on the faculties of the National Criminal Defense College, Mercer Law School, and the Institute for Criminal Advocacy, California Western School of Law. Her research interests focus on courtroom persuasion, jury deliberations, creative group processes, and social influence in group decision making. She is also a professional storyteller, with corresponding research investigating the pedagogical and persuasive effects of oral storytelling and narrative. Her research has appeared in *Communication Monographs* and *The Howard Journal of Communications.*